THE VIRGIN ENCYCLOPEDIA OF

FIFTIES MUSIC

THIRD EDITION

COMPILED AND
EDITED BY

COLIN LARKIN

In Association with
MUZE UK Ltd

Dedicated to Kelly and her chips and egg

First published in Great Britain in 2002 by
Virgin Books Ltd
Thames Wharf Studios
Rainville Road
London W6 9HA

A catalogue record for this book is available
from the British Library.

ISBN 1 85227 937 0

muze

Written, edited and produced by
MUZE UK Ltd
All editorial enquiries and complaints
should be sent to:
Suite 16, Arcade Chambers, 28 High Street,
Brentwood, Essex, CM14 4AH.
www.muze.com

Editor-In-Chief: Colin Larkin
Assistant Editor: Nic Oliver
Production Editor: Susan Pipe
Typographic Design: Roger Kohn
Design Assistant: Aku Young
Very special thanks to Trev Huxley, Paul Zullo
and Tom Goldsworthy of Muze Inc., and to
KT Forster and Carolyn Thorne of Virgin Books.

Typeset by Roving Kind Studio
Printed and bound in Great Britain by
Mackays of Chatham plc, Chatham, Kent

INTRODUCTION

THE FABULOUS FIFTIES. Were they? Or were we swept along with the tidal wave of optimism now that war had truly ended. The music of the day was attempting to be cosmopolitan. In the USA, pop lived side by side with R&B. The cheese in the middle of the sandwich was rock 'n' roll, and it tasted like nothing on earth. Grand theft was made from Fats Domino and Dinah Washington, and sparkling white crooners attempted rock 'n' roll. Few would argue that Elvis Presley and Jerry Lee Lewis did a pretty fine job. Others stayed with their own roots, which were firmly welded to the great American songbook. Forty years later we are still basking in the genius of Ella Fitzgerald and Frank Sinatra. Their output of classic songs on albums of the fifties is untouchable. Thank goodness Ella and Frankie gave a titanic-wide berth to rock 'n' roll and stayed with what they knew.

I was fortunate in having the best of both worlds. I spent a lot of the period between 1950-1956 living on a travelling fairground. My parents badly needed work and most weekends and public holidays were spent listening to music, and at night sleeping on the top floor of a converted double-decker bus that doubled as a tyre store. While they worked, I would wander from noon to midnight through a technicolour Wurlitzer juke-box of image, and sound. All rides had their own turntable and boxes of 78s, together with a heavenly sounding, ripped Tannoy speaker. Each ride played its own music, and as you wandered, loud, distorted Little Richard or Lloyd Price would give way to a passive Doris Day, who would become Jo Stafford a few yards later. Imagine turning a radio dial and finding just about every station playing a fantastic song simultaneously. The fairground was just like that, only in colour and with the smell of fried onions and candy floss.

The fairground certainly taught me to love and appreciate most pop, R&B and rock 'n' roll. When I returned home to the quiet calm of my older brother's bedroom, I would be fed a diet of Frankie, Ella, *Oklahoma* and *Carousel*. Few would argue that the glut of cover versions of American pop hits in the early fifties were mainly poor imitations. Denmark Street publishers sought out unremarkable UK crooners to 'get a cover' of the American hit. In the UK charts between May and June 1955 were three 'Cherry Pink And Apple Blossom White', three 'Stranger In Paradise' and three 'Unchained Melody'. Those cigar-puffing charlatans could have killed the industry stone-dead had it continued. They didn't, and the fifties' apprentices became the sixties' master-craftsmen. For now, just wallow and fantasize about pink Vauxhall Crestas, Mecca Ballrooms, white suits with two-inch turn-ups, Sinatra hats, Alma Cogan frocks and real nylon stockings with fine point heels. Nostalgia is just not what it used to be.

The choice of entries for this book will satisfy most people. There will be a few complaining that so and so is left out. The decade represents what I think is this artist's most popular decade. Certainly Duke Ellington, Frank Sinatra and others had massive success outside this decade. Ultimately it is the flavour of the fifties I am trying to conjure up. You will find the companion books *Stage & Film Musicals* and the *Sixties* will cover all the others. *The Virgin Encyclopedia Of Fifties Music* is one of a major series of books taken from the multi-volume *Encyclopedia Of Popular Music*. Other titles already available are:

The Virgin Encyclopedia Of Sixties Music
The Virgin Encyclopedia Of Seventies Music
The Virgin Encyclopedia Of Eighties Music
The Virgin Encyclopedia Of Nineties Music
The Virgin Encyclopedia Of Jazz
The Virgin Concise Encyclopedia Of Popular Music
The Virgin Encyclopedia Of Stage & Film Musicals
The Virgin Encyclopedia Of Indie & New Wave
The Virgin Encyclopedia Of The Blues
The Virgin Encyclopedia Of Country Music
The Virgin Encyclopedia Of R&B And Soul
The Virgin Encyclopedia Of Heavy Rock
The Virgin Encyclopedia Of Dance Music
The Virgin Encyclopedia Of Reggae

ENTRY STYLE

All albums, EPs (extended play 45s), newspapers, magazines, television programmes, films and stage musicals are referred to in italics. All song titles appear in single quotes. We spell rock 'n' roll like this. There are two main reasons for spelling rock 'n' roll with 'n' as opposed to 'n'. First, historical precedent: when the term was first coined in the 50s, the popular spelling was 'n'. Second, the 'n' is not simply an abbreviation of 'and' (in which case 'n' would apply) but as a phonetic representation of n as a sound. The ' ', therefore, serve as inverted commas rather than as apostrophes. The further reading section at the end of each entry has been expanded to give the reader a much wider choice of available books. These are not necessarily recommended titles but we have attempted to leave out any publication that has little or no merit.

We have also started to add videos at the end of the entries, but have decided not to list DVDs, simply because there is not enough time. Again, this is an area that is expanding faster than we can easily cope with, but there are many items in the videography and the filmography. Release dates in keeping with albums attempt to show the release date in the country of origin. We have also tried to include both US and UK titles in the case of a title change.

DATES OF BIRTH

Occasionally we hear from an artist or manager asking us to change the date of birth, usually upwards, to make the artist younger. We have to reluctantly comply with this unless we have sighted birth registration details. We are constantly seeking accurate birth data, and confirmed corrections would be gratefully received.

DISCOGRAPHY

In attempting to put the record label with albums I am very aware that most labels listed are either from the USA or the UK. These will continue to be our prime sources. We have attempted to list the label (and country) where the release was first issued. Because of the continuing CD revolution and the constant repackaging we have listed the most recent reissues. What we have not done is to list the latest label. That would be too much of a task. Once again please refer to the web site www.muze.com for both US and UK labels and catalogue numbers as well as track listings. This book is not meant to be a discographical tool; we are more concerned with the artist's music and career. For the majority of artists in this work, complete discographies have been compiled. However, on occasion, the discography section at the end of an entry is incomplete. This is not due to lack of effort on our behalf but simply to the fact that some artists, have had such extensive careers that it is impossible to go back over numerous decades of files. From our experience, most record companies do not retain this detailed information. The aim of the discography is to allow the reader to investigate further the work of a particular artist. We have included, where possible, the regular albums together with the first year of release date in the known country of origin, which is generally in the USA or the UK. In many cases the delay in releasing the record in another country can be years. Some Latin, African, Caribbean and other Third World recordings have been assigned approximate release dates as the labels often do not carry any release date. We do not list bootlegs but one or two may have accidentally crept in.

In the case of recordings made before the general availability of the LP (album), approximately 1950, we have aimed to inform the reader of the date of recordings and the year of release. Since the advent of the compact disc in 1982, and its subsequent popularity, the reissue market has expanded enormously. There are outstanding reissue programmes going ahead, usually with bonus tracks or alternative takes. Companies such as Collectables and Rhino in the USA and Ace and Castle in the UK are just two labels putting two-on-one, a fantastic bonus taking advantage of the CD over short-timed vinyl albums from the 50s and 60s. Our MUZE online database contains every CD release since day one.

ALBUM RATINGS

Due to many requests from librarians and readers we continue to rate all albums. All new releases are reviewed either by myself or by our team of contributors. We also take into serious consideration the review ratings of the leading music journals and critics' opinions.

Our system is slightly different to most 5 Star ratings in that we rate according to the artist in question's work. Therefore, a 4 Star album from Ella Fitzgerald may have the overall edge over a 4 Star album by Dennis Lotis. Sorry Den.

Our ratings are carefully made, and consequently you will find we are very sparing with 5 Star and 1 Star albums.

★★★★★

Outstanding in every way.
A classic and therefore strongly recommended. No comprehensive record collection should be without this album.

★★★★

Excellent.
A high standard album from this artist and therefore highly recommended.

★★★

Good.
By the artist's usual standards and therefore recommended.

★★

Disappointing.
Flawed or lacking in some way.

★

Poor. An album to avoid unless you are a completist.

PLAGIARISM

In maintaining the largest text database of popular music in the world, we are naturally protective of its content. We license to approved licensees only. It is both flattering and irritating to see our work reproduced without credit. Time and time again over the past few years I have read a newspaper obituary, knowing that I wrote that line or phrase. Secondly, it has come to our notice that other companies attempting to produce their own rock or pop encyclopedias use our material as a core. Flattering this might also be, but highly illegal. We have been making sure over the past two years that the publishers of these maverick music guides will be stopped once and for all for plagiarizing work that has taken us a lifetime to assemble. Having spent many hours with our lawyers taking action, I do know a bit about copyright law. Be careful and mostly, be warned, we usually know who you are. Our text appears on hundreds of websites, mostly unofficial ones. Once again, thanks for the compliment but make sure that you always credit and acknowledge us as your source (copyright MUZE UK or Encyclopedia Of Popular Music), otherwise we will have to shut you down.

CHART POSITIONS & RECORD SALES

The aim of this book is not to document chart positions and record sales. Many are discussed in passing but are ultimately left to the main books available. The reference books we have used were those formerly edited by Gambaccini, Rice and Rice, but now we use the new bible *The Complete Book Of The British Charts, Singles And Albums*, edited by Brown, Kutner and Warwick for the UK. Joel Whitburn's (*Top Pop Singles*, *Top Pop Albums*, *Country Singles*, *R&B Singles* and *Pop Memories*) for the USA are published by Record Research and are absolutely indispensable. Our chart information from 1952 to 1960 was originally taken from the *New Musical Express* and from 1960 to 1968 were gleaned from the *Record Retailer*. While we have adhered to the BMRB in the main we feel that the *New Musical Express* and the recently departed *Melody Maker* charts were accepted more than the dreary *Record Retailer*, as the latter published its chart before the weekly sales were recorded. If we were to have stuck religiously to the *Record Retailer*, then the Beatles would have only had one record entering the chart at number 1. And cor blimey, we can't have that! It is generally known that most of their records reached number 1 on the week of release in the UK, and this was reflected in the main weekly music papers. This aberration fortunately does not occur in the USA, thanks to the longevity and accuracy of *Billboard* and Joel Whitburn's efforts. We now use the UK chart published by *Music Week*.

For the USA, when we refer to a gold disc for singles it signifies sales of 1,000,000 copies pre-1989 and 500,000 thereafter. The RIAA (Record Industry Association Of America) made this change in 1989, and *Billboard* followed suit. Similarly, when platinum awards were introduced, they initially signified sales of 2,000,000 copies and post-1989 of 1,000,000. For albums from 1958 to 1974, the term gold refers to LPs that sold $1 million worth of units at manufacturers' wholesale prices. Recognizing that due to rising prices the number of units necessary to gain gold status was dropping, the RIAA as of 1 January 1975 added the further proviso that to be gold an LP had to have sold at least 500,000 copies. A platinum LP has to have sold 1,000,000 copies. In the UK the BPI determines – singles: platinum 600,000 units, gold 400,000 and silver 200,000. For albums: platinum 300,000, gold 100,000, silver 60,000. For the recent introduction of CD box sets, a 4-CD box has to sell 250,000 copies to go platinum, although this does not apply to two-disc sets at the present time.

CRITICAL OPINION

The aim was always to strike a balance between being highly opinionated and bland, with a sprinkle of humour. We have attempted to express the generally accepted opinion and have not set out to be controversial (except in some cases where we hope our entries on certain lesser-known artists will lead to a reappraisal of their work).

ACKNOWLEDGEMENTS

Always first and foremost, Johnny Rogan, who continues to be a fair critic and a good friend. He was the first person to hear of my proposal for the original Encyclopedia and agreed to be involved. His great attention to detail shaped the original editorial style-sheet, and he was instrumental in approaching some early contributors. Additionally there is always at the end of a phone the free advice of Pete Frame, Peter Doggett, Johnny Black and Fred Dellar. And if I fancy a weepy chat about how great Brian Wilson or Dylan is, Stuart Batsford is top of the list. Chris Charlesworth is a most agreeable and experienced Bayko builder. Continuing praise for the efforts of Pete 'the hound' Bassett and his Quite Great company, Anita, Louise and Dave. And thanks to my late Dad for getting me hooked in this business by buying me a magic transistor radio, the Fidelity reel-to-reel and the red Dansette.

Appreciation again and again to production editor Susan Pipe; efficient, trustworthy and loyal as ever, a rare thing in this day and age. Similarly invaluable is my non-stop chattering assistant editor Nic Oliver. Michael Kaye continues as our database/software developer, his determination to fix bugs is admirable.

Our contributors are further reduced in number, as we now update and amend all our existing text and write most of the new stuff. Our team over the past year has included: Jim Allen, Ian Bell, Dominic Chadwick, Tony Clayton-Lea, Jurgen Funk, Dave Gil de Rubio, Karen Glossop, David Hemingway, Joel McIver, Jake Kennedy, Sam Hendricks, Ben Hogwood, Ed Houghton, Mark Keresman, Siobhan Long, Dan Nosworthy, Alex Ogg, Jon Staines, Richard Wilson. Alongside, Spencer Leigh, Hugh T. Wilson and Salsri Nyah, continue to supply their specialist knowledge. The 'very necessary' Bruce Crowther continues to produce anything we throw at him, providing it is jazz. And to Carl Newsum and Dennis of Slipped Disc II in Chelmsford. Support your local independent record shop.

Past contributors' work may still appear in this volume, so just in case, I acknowledge with thanks once again: Simon Adams, David Ades, Mike Atherton, Gavin Badderley, Alan Balfour, Michael Barnett, John Bauldie, Johnny Black, Chris Blackford, Pamela Boniface, Keith Briggs, Michael Ian Burgess, Paul M. Brown, Tony Burke, John Child, Linton Chiswick, Rick Christian, Alan Clayson, Paul Cross, Norman Darwen, Roy Davenport, Peter Doggett, Kevin Eden, John Eley, Lars Fahlin, Tim Footman, John Fordham, Per Gardin, Ian Garlinge, Mike Gavin, Andy Hamilton, Mark Hodkinson, Brian Hogg, Mike Hughes, Arthur Jackson, Mark Jones, Max Jones, Simon Jones, Ian Kenyon, Dave Laing, Steve Lake, Paul Lewis, Graham Lock, John Martland, Bernd Matheja, Chris May, Dave McAleer, David McDonald, York Membery, Toru Mitsui, Greg Moffitt, Michael Newman, Pete Nickols, Lyndon Noon, Zbigniew Nowara, James Nye, Ken Orton, Ian Peel, Dave Penny, Alan Plater, Barry Ralph, John Reed, Emma Rees, Jamie Renton, Lionel

Robinson, Johnny Rogan, Alan Rowett, Dave Sissons, Neil Slaven, Chris Smith, Steve Smith, Mitch Solomons, Christopher Spencer, Mike Stephenson, Sam Sutherland, Jeff Tamarkin, Ray Templeton, Christen Thomsen, Liz Thompson, Gerard Tierney, John Tobler, Adrian T'Vell, Pete Wadeson, Frank Warren, Ben Watson, Pete Watson, Simon Williams, Val Wilmer, Dave Wilson and Barry Witherden. Others that have been missed are either through my own sloppy error or deliberate intention.

Record Company Press Offices. These invaluable people are often bombarded with my requests for biogs and review copies. A few actually respond, and those that do are very important to us. It always amazes me how some major record companies completely ignore our numerous requests and others of similar stature are right on the button. Thanks this time especially to Matt Wheeler and Rich Dawes at Polydor, Alan Robinson, Dorothy Howe and Matt Sweeting at Sanctuary, Erik James, Florence Halfon, Rick Conrad and Carlos Anaia at Warners, Dave Clark at Quite Great, Sue and Dave Williams at Frontier Promotions, Tones Sansom and Vanessa Cotton at Triad Publicity, Joe Foster, Andrew Lauder at Evangeline, Bob, Neil Scaplehorn at Ace, Murray Chalmers, Chris Latham and the team at Parlophone/Capitol, Mike Gott at BGO, Tim Wright and Ian McNay at Cherry Red/RPM, Mick Houghton at Brassneck, Zoe Stafford at RCA, Shane O'Neill at Universal, Ted Cummings at MCA, Jonathan Gill at Demon, Paul at Big Moon, Mal Smith at Delta, Darren Crisp at Crisp Productions, Richard Wootten and Pat Tynan at Koch International.

To the few friends who you can trust, colleagues and family who play no direct part in producing these books but make my life more tolerable: Nils von Veh, Fred Nelson, Stuart Batsford, Danny Sperling, Bob Harris, Johnnie Walker, Kathleen Dougherty, Chris Braham, David Gould, Roger Kohn, Roy Sheridan, Kip Trevor, Alan Lynch, John Burton, David Larkin, Sabra Larkin, Kay and Kevin, Sally Decibelle and the four long lost London cousins, Danny, Peter, Michael and John.

To all our colleagues in the USA at Muze Inc., and MUZE UK, who oil the smooth running of our UK unit. And especially, but in no order whatsoever to Gary Geller, Scott Lehr, Ra Ra Ra Raisa Howe, Catherine Hamilton, Justin Sedgmond, Ian Bell, Karien de Witt, Jennifer Rose, Bernadette Elliott, Paul Parrierra (and the Raiders), Jim Allen, Terry Vinyard, Mark Keresman, Phil Antman, Bill Schmitt, Jeanne Petras, Stephanie Jones, Ed Moore, Mike Lupitkin, Michael Kennedy, Mike Doustan, Tom Goldsworthy and of course Marc 'party hard' Miller, Paul 'the faster we go' Zullo and Trev 'Brooklyn fitness club' Huxley. Finally, love to Kelly and the tins, Goldie, Dan and Tom, who have had very little to do with this one.

Colin Larkin,
February 2002

ACE, JOHNNY

b. John Marshall Alexander Jnr., 9 June 1929, Memphis, Tennessee, USA, d. 24 December 1954, Houston, Texas, USA. Ace began his professional career as an R&B singer in 1949, playing piano in a band that eventually evolved into the Beale Streeters, which included at various times B.B. King, Bobby Bland, Rosco Gordon and Earl Forest. The Beale Streeters established a considerable reputation and toured Tennessee and the surrounding states, giving Ace the experience to develop into an outstanding blues ballad singer. In 1952, he was signed by Duke Records and secured a number 1 R&B hit with his debut, 'My Song' (a hit for Aretha Franklin in 1968). The languid song, sung with Ace's distinctive blues-flavoured smoothness and a touch of sadness in his voice, determined his direction for seven subsequent hits in the USA, notably 'Cross My Heart' (number 3 R&B 1953), 'The Clock' (number 1 R&B 1953) 'Saving My Love For You' (number 2 R&B 1953), 'Please Forgive Me' (number 6 R&B 1954), and 'Never Let Me Go' (number 9 R&B 1954). Ace, by committing suicide playing Russian Roulette backstage at a concert at Houston's City Auditorium on Christmas Eve 1954, made his death his claim to fame, unfairly obscuring the fine music of his legacy. He had two posthumous hits, 'Pledging My Love' (number 1 R&B 1955) and 'Anymore' (number 7 R&B 1955); the former was Ace's only mainstream success, reaching number 17 on *Billboard's* national pop chart. Duke Records released a 10-inch and 12-inch album, and both became perennial sellers.
● ALBUMS: *The Johnny Ace Memorial Album* 10-inch album (Duke 1955) ★★★, *The Johnny Ace Memorial Album* 12-inch album (Duke 1957) ★★★.
● FURTHER READING: *The Late Great Johnny Ace And The Transition From R&B To Rock 'N' Roll*, James M. Salem.

ADAMS, CLIFF

b. 21 August 1923, Southwark, London, England, d. 22 October 2001, England. As a boy, Adams was a chorister at St Mary le Bow in East London, but yearned to become involved in popular music. After studying the piano and organ, he played in dance bands before joining the Royal Air Force in World War II, spending three years in Africa In the late 40s he arranged for several name bands, including Stanley Black and Ted Heath, and in 1949 formed the Stargazers. They became one of the top UK vocal groups of the 50s on radio and records, their hits including the novelties, 'Close The Door (They're Coming In The Window)' and 'Twenty Tiny Fingers', plus two UK chart-toppers,

'Broken Wings' and 'I See The Moon'. In 1954 Adams formed the Show Band Singers group for Cyril Stapleton's BBC Show Band, which backed vocalists including Frank Sinatra, Eartha Kitt and Frankie Laine. This led to *Sing Something Simple*, a half-hour programme of 'songs simply sung for lovers', featuring the Singers, piano accordionist Jack Emblow's Quartet, and a piano solo by Adams. It made its debut as a 'six-week stand-in' on the BBC Light Programme on 3 July 1959, and celebrated its 35th Anniversary with a special programme on BBC Radio 2 in August 1994. Four years later, Adams received a Gold Badge Award from BASCA (British Academy of Songwriters Composers and Authors) his 'special or lasting contribution' to Britain's entertainment industry. Adams also composed music, and his work for television commercials included Murraymints ('Too-good-to-hurry mints'), Smash ('For Mash – Get Smash') and Fry's Turkish Delight. He had a UK Top 40 hit in 1960 with his 'Lonely Man Theme', which was used in the memorable 'You're never alone with a Strand' cigarette commercial. In 1976 he composed the music for the West End musical *Liza Of Lambeth*, an adaptation of Somerset Maugham's novel, which featured a book and lyrics by William Rushton and Bernie Stringler.
● ALBUMS: *Sing Something Simple* i (Pye 1960) ★★★, *Sing Something Simple* ii (Pye 1962) ★★★, *Sing Something Simple '76* (Warwick 1976) ★★★, *Something Old, Something New* (One-Up 1977) ★★★, *100th Sing Something Simple* (BBC 1979) ★★★, *Songs To Remember* (Ronco 1983) ★★★, *Sing Something Silver* (BBC 1984) ★★★, *Sing Something Disney* (BBC 1985) ★★★, *Sing Something Country* (Pickwick 1990) ★★, *Sing Something Simple The Sinatra Way* (MFP 1991) ★★★, *Sing Something Simple To Victory* (MFP 1995) ★★★.
● COMPILATIONS: *Sing Something Simple: 100 Golden Greats* (Ronco 1983) ★★★, *All The Very Best Of Sing Something Simple* (Pickwick 1995) ★★★.

ADDERLEY, CANNONBALL

b. Julian Edwin Adderley, 15 September 1928, Tampa, Florida, USA, d. 8 August 1975, Gary, Indiana, USA. Cannonball Adderley was one of the great saxophonists of his generation. His fiery, blues-soaked interpretations of Charlie Parker's alto legacy brought jazz to many people hitherto untouched by it. In the 60s he launched a new genre, soul jazz, whose popularity has survived undiminished into the new millennium.
Cannonball was derived from 'Cannibal', a nickname earned at high school on account of his prodigious appetite. He studied brass and reed instruments there between 1944 and 1948. Until 1956 he was band director at Dillerd High School, Lauderdale, Florida, as well as leader of his own jazz quartet. While serving in the forces he became director of the 36th Army Band, an ensemble that included his younger brother Nat Adderley on trumpet. Persuaded to go to New York by legendary alto saxophonist and R&B singer Eddie 'Cleanhead' Vinson, Cannonball created a

sensation at the Café Bohemia, playing alongside bassist Oscar Pettiford. In 1958 he signed to Riverside Records and over the next six years released a series of albums, many of them recorded live, that laid the foundations of the soul-jazz genre. As well as his brother Nat, Adderley's first group featured a superb rhythm section in Sam Jones and Louis Hayes, supplemented by pianist Bobby Timmons, who also wrote the group's first hit, 'This Here'.

From 1957-59 Adderley was part of the classic Miles Davis Quintet, an astonishing group of individuals that also included John Coltrane (tenor), Bill Evans or Red Garland (piano), Paul Chambers (bass) and Philly Joe Jones (drums). As well as playing on the celebrated *Kind Of Blue*, Cannonball recorded his own album, the magnificent *Somethin' Else*, for Blue Note Records – Davis guested on the recording, a rare honour. After leaving Davis, Cannonball re-formed his own band, with Nat still on cornet. In 1961 Yusef Lateef joined on tenor saxophone and stayed for two productive years. This band nurtured the talents of electric pianists Joe Zawinul, and then George Duke. It was Zawinul's 'Mercy, Mercy, Mercy', recorded live at the Club Delisa in Chicago, that provided Adderley with his next major hit, reaching number 11 in the US charts in February 1967. The title was indicative of the band's fondness for gospel-orientated, black consciousness themes. Their last hit was 'Country Preacher', again a Zawinul composition, which peaked in early 1970 (number 29 in the R&B charts). Straight jazz never again enjoyed such mass appeal.

When asked about his inspirations, Adderley cited the swing alto saxophonist Benny Carter and, of course, Charlie Parker – but his understanding of blues distortion also enabled him to apply the *avant garde* lessons of John Coltrane and Ornette Coleman. His alto saxophone had a special immediacy, a welcome reminder of the blues at the heart of bebop, an element that jazz rock – the bastard offspring of soul jazz – too often suppressed.

● ALBUMS: *Presenting Cannonball* (Savoy 1955) ★★★, *Julian 'Cannonball' Adderley* (EmArcy 1955) ★★★, *Julian 'Cannonball' Adderley And Strings* (EmArcy 1956) ★★, *In The Land Of Hi-Fi* (EmArcy 1956) ★★★, *Sophisticated Swing* (EmArcy 1957) ★★★★, *Cannonball's Sharpshooters* (EmArcy 1958) ★★★, *Jump For Joy* (EmArcy 1958) ★★★, *Portrait Of Cannonball* (Riverside 1958) ★★★, *Somethin' Else* (Blue Note 1958) ★★★★★, *Things Are Gettin' Better* (Riverside 1958) ★★★★, *The Cannonball Adderley Quintet In San Francisco* (Riverside 1959) ★★★, *Cannonball Adderley Quintet In Chicago* (Mercury 1959) ★★★, *Cannonball Takes Charge* (Riverside 1959) ★★, *Cannonball Adderley Quintet At The Lighthouse* (Riverside 1960) ★★★, *Them Dirty Blues* (Riverside 1960) ★★★, *What Is This Thing Called Soul?* (Pablo 1960) ★★★★, *The Lush Side Of Cannonball Adderley* (Mercury 1961) ★★★, *African Waltz* (Riverside 1961) ★★★, *Cannonball Enroute* (Mercury 1961) ★★★, *Cannonball Adderley And The Poll-Winners* (Riverside 1961)

★★★, *Cannonball Adderley Quintet Plus* (Riverside 1961) ★★★, with Ray Brown *Ray Brown With The All Star Big Band Featuring Cannonball Adderley* reissued as *Two For The Blues* (Verve 1962) ★★★★, with Nancy Wilson *Nancy Wilson/Cannonball Adderley* (Capitol 1962) ★★★★, with Bill Evans *Know What I Mean?* (Riverside 1962) ★★★★, *The Cannonball Adderley Sextet In New York* (Riverside 1962) ★★, *Cannonball's Bossa Nova* (Riverside 1963) ★★, *Jazz Workshop Revisited* (Riverside 1963) ★★, *Nippon Soul* (Riverside 1964) ★★★, with John Coltrane *Cannonball And Coltrane* (Limelight 1964) ★★★, *Domination* (Capitol 1965) ★★, *Fiddler On The Roof* (Capitol 1965) ★★, with Ernie Andrews *Live Session* (Capitol 1965) ★★★, *Cannonball Adderley Live* (Capitol 1965) ★★★, with Nat Adderley *Them Adderley's* (Limelight 1966) ★★★, *Great Love Themes* (Capitol 1966) ★★, *Why Am I Treated So Bad?* (Capitol 1966) ★★★★, *Mercy, Mercy, Mercy! Live At "The Club"* (Capitol 1967) ★★★★, *74 Miles Away/Walk Tall* (Capitol 1967) ★★, *Cannonball In Europe* (Riverside 1967) ★★★, *Accent On Africa* (Capitol 1968) ★★★, *Cannonball In Person* (Capitol 1969) ★★★, *Planet Earth* (Riverside 1969) ★★, *Country Preacher* (Capitol 1970) ★★★, *The Price You Got To Pay To Be Free* (Capitol 1970) ★★, *The Black Messiah* (Capitol 1972) ★★★, *Inside Straight* (Fantasy 1973) ★★, *Pyramid* (Fantasy 1974) ★★★, *Big Man* (Fantasy 1975) ★★, *Phenix* (Fantasy 1975) ★★, *Lovers* (Fantasy 1976) ★★★, *Spontaneous Combustion* 1955 recording (Savoy 1976) ★★★, *In Japan* (Blue Note 1990) ★★★, *Radio Nights* (Virgin 1991) ★★, *Cannonball Adderley And His Quintet* 1969 recording (RTE 1994) ★★★.

● COMPILATIONS: *Cannonball's Greatest Hits* (Riverside 1962) ★★★★, *The Best Of Cannonball Adderley* (Riverside 1968) ★★★★, *Cannonball Adderley Collection Volumes 1 – 7* (Landmark 1988) ★★★, *Best Of Cannonball Adderley The Capitol Years* (Capitol 1991) ★★★, *Quintet Plus* (Ace 1992) ★★★, *Greatest Hits* (CEMA 1992) ★★★, *Portrait Of Cannonball* (Ace 1993) ★★★, *Jazz Profile* (Blue Note 1997) ★★★★, *Greatest Hits: The Riverside Years* (Milestone 1998) ★★★★, *This Here* 1955-1959 recordings (Giants Of Jazz 1998) ★★★, *Cannonball Adderley Meets Miles Davis* (Giants Of Jazz 1998) ★★★, *Work Song* 1960-1969 recordings (Giants Of Jazz 1998) ★★★, as the Adderley Brothers *The Summer Of '55* (Savoy 2000) ★★★★, *Cannonball Adderley's Finest Hour* (Verve 2001) ★★★.

● FURTHER READING: *Dis Here*, Chris Sherman.

ADDINSELL, RICHARD

b. Richard Stewart Addinsell, 13 January 1904, Oxford, England, d. 14 November 1977, Chelsea, London, England. A leading composer for the theatre and feature films, Addinsell read law at Hertford College, Oxford, but was more interested in music and the theatre. He studied briefly at the Royal College of Music, and then in Berlin and Vienna. During the late 20s he began to contribute music to revues and shows such as *Little Miss Danger*, *R.S.V.P.*, *The Charlot Show* and *Adam's Opera*. In 1931 he supplied the music for the

incidental songs in *The Good Companions* (from J.B. Priestley's novel), and, for some 30 years, continued to write for the theatre, often in collaboration with the entertainer Joyce Grenfell. He provided material for several shows in which she appeared, such as *Tuppence Coloured* (1947), *Penny Plain* (1951), *Joyce Grenfell Requests The Pleasure* (1954) and *Joyce Grenfell – A Miscellany* (1957). It was for his film work, however, that Addinsell is probably best remembered. From 1936 through to the early 60s, he wrote the music for some of the best UK films, particularly those of the 'stiff upper lip' variety, so prevalent around the time of World War II. His scores included *The Amateur Gentleman* (1936), *Dark Journey, Farewell Again, South Riding, Fire Over England, Vessel Of Wrath, Goodbye, Mr. Chips, The Lion Has Wings, Contraband, Men Of The Lightships, Gaslight, Dangerous Moonlight, Love On The Dole, The Siege Of Tobruk, Blithe Spirit, Diary For Timothy, The Passionate Friends, The Black Rose, Scrooge, Encore, Tom Brown's Schooldays, Sea Devils, Beau Brummell, The Prince And The Showgirl, The Admirable Crichton, A Tale Of Two Cities, Loss Of Innocence, The Greengage Summer, The Waltz Of The Toreadors, The Roman Spring Of Mrs. Stone* and *Life At The Top* (1965). The score of *Dangerous Moonlight* (1941) contained Addinsell's most well-known composition, 'The Warsaw Concerto', played on the soundtrack by pianist Louis Kentner with the London Symphony Orchestra. The piece became enormously popular, and was a hit for saxophonist Freddy Martin and his Orchestra in the USA. More than 10 years after his death, Addinsell's music was heard again at a London theatre when the revue *Re: Joyce!* (1988), 'A celebration of the work of Joyce Grenfell' starring Maureen Lipman with Denis King, opened in the West End. It has since returned on two occasions, and a televised version was shown at Christmas 1991. In 1995 several of his attractive themes and melodies were released on CD, played by the BBC Concert Orchestra.
● COMPILATIONS: *British Light Music-Richard Addinsell* (Marco Polo 1994) ★★★.

ADLER, LARRY

b. Lawrence Cecil Adler, 10 February 1914, Baltimore, Maryland, USA, d. 6 August 2001, London, England. Adler preferred to be described simply as a 'mouth organist' – yet he was arguably the most accomplished and celebrated exponent of the instrument there has ever been. Of Russian heritage, his orthodox Judaism gave him the opportunity to train in religious music, and he became a cantor at the age of 10. He sang, and learned to play the piano and mouth organ by ear from listening to phonograph records, and could not actually read music until 1941. After being expelled from the Peabody Conservatory of Music for playing 'Yes, We Have No Bananas' instead of the scheduled classical piece, he won the Maryland harmonica championship in 1927. Shortly afterwards, he ran away to New York and joined one of the Paramount units, playing in movie theatres between features. He was also presented as a 'ragged urchin' ('just in from the street, folks!') in vaudeville, and in Lew Leslie's revue, *Clowns In Clover* (1928). He also served as Eddie Cantor's stooge for a time, and accompanied Fred Astaire in Florenz Ziegfeld's *Smiles*.

His lifelong admiration and appreciation of George Gershwin began when he was introduced to the composer by Paul Whiteman, and his interpretations of Gershwin's works, especially *Porgy And Bess* and 'Rhapsody In Blue' (on which Adler was sometimes accompanied by a piano-roll made by Gershwin himself), are definitive. (Many years later in 1981, Adler's haunting version of Gershwin's 'Summertime' played a significant role in the success of the enormously popular UK ice dancers Torvill and Dean.) In 1934, after further speciality roles on stage in *Flying Colors* and on film in Paramount's *Many Happy Returns*, in which he was backed by Duke Ellington's Orchestra, Adler was spotted at New York's Palace Theatre by the English producer Charles B. Cochran, who engaged him for the London revue *Streamline*. Shortly after the show opened, sales of mouth organs in the UK increased by several thousand per cent, and fan clubs proliferated. Adler played the top nightclubs, and the 1937 revue *Tune Inn* was built around him. After marrying top model Eileen Walser, he toured South Africa and Australia before returning to the USA in 1939, where he gained national recognition in the classical field when he appeared as a soloist with the Chicago Women's Symphony Orchestra.

During the 40s, Adler appeared at Carnegie Hall with the dancer Paul Draper, and toured with him extensively in the USA, Africa and the Middle East, entertaining troops, and insisting on a non-segregation policy between whites and blacks at concerts. Adler also entertained in the South Pacific with artists such as Carol Landis, Martha Tilton and comedian Jack Benny, and worked consistently for the war effort and the Allied forces. He was 'on duty' again in 1951 during the Korean conflict. By then, as a high-profile liberal, he had been included on McCarthy's 'communist' blacklist, and moved to live and work in England, only for the 'red spectre' to follow him even there. In 1954, he was forced by the Rank film organization to give up his billing rights on US prints of the classic comedy film *Genevieve*, for which he had written the gentle but highly distinctive score. The music was duly nominated for an Academy Award, and an embarrassed Rank could only offer orchestra conductor Muir Mathieson's name as composer. Fortunately for them it did not win the Oscar – voters preferred Dimitri Tiomkin's music for *The High And The Mighty* – and Adler had to wait until 1986 for the Academy's official recognition of his work. In 1952, Adler performed at a Royal Albert Hall Promenade Concert, when he was 'forced' to encore Ralph Vaughan Williams' 'Romance For Mouth Organ, Piano And Strings', a piece that had been written especially for him. In the 50s, although domiciled in the UK, Adler made frequent, although often difficult, trips to the USA and worked in many other countries of the world with major symphony orchestras. In 1963 as a soloist at the Edinburgh Festival, Adler gave the first performance of 'Lullaby Time', a string quartet written by George Gershwin in 1921, and presented to Adler by Ira Gershwin. That piece, and several other unpublished works by composers such as Cole Porter, Harold Arlen and Richard Rodgers, were included on the late 60s recording *Discovery*.

Adler's own most familiar composition is the music for *Genevieve*, but he also composed the music for other movies, including *The Hellions*, *King And Country*, *A High Wind In Jamaica* and *The Great Chase*. His work for television programmes and plays included *Midnight Men*, along with concert pieces such as 'Theme And Variations'. Composers who wrote specially commissioned pieces for him included Malcolm Arnold, Darius Milhaud, Arthur Benjamin, Gordon Jacobs, and others. In 1965 Adler was back at the Edinburgh Festival with his one-man show, *Hand To Mouth*, and in 1967 and 1973, gave his services to Israel in aid of those affected by the Six Day and Yom Kippur wars. In 1988, as busy as ever, he appeared at New York's Ballroom club with Harold Nicholas, one half of the legendary dance team the Nicholas Brothers. To many, the engagement brought back memories of Adler's tours in the 40s with his friend, tap-dancer Paul Draper. As usual on these occasions, Adler skilfully blended classical selections with a 'honky-tonk jazz' approach to numbers written by the great popular songwriters of the past. The following year he performed in concert at London's Royal Albert Hall, marking his 75th birthday, accompanied by pianist John Ogden, and the Wren Orchestra conducted by Stanley Black.

During the early 90s he played regularly at the Pizza on the Park, sometimes accompanied by 'The Hot Club Of London', and recalled numbers forever associated with him, such as Ravel's 'Bolero'. After Adler guested on Sting's 1993 release, *Ten Summoners Tales*, the rock singer returned the compliment and appeared on Adler's 80th birthday celebration, *The Glory Of Gershwin*. They were joined by other stars from the rock world such as Meat Loaf, Kate Bush, Peter Gabriel and Sinéad O'Connor. The media interest generated by this project – the album just failed to reach the top of the UK album chart, although it gained Adler a place in *The Guinness Book Of Records* – led to him making sell-out appearances at venues such as the Jazz Café and the Café Royal. He also embarked on *A Living Legend – The Final Tour* late in 1994, and encored with appearances in Japan, Australia and New Zealand two years later. In 1998, he presented the BBC Radio 2 series *Larry Adler's Century*, which he laced with fascinating anecdotes. In the year 2001 the composer Sir John Tavener was commissioned to write a piece especially for Adler, and the cabaret space at the Pizza On The Park was re-named Larry's Room as a tribute to this great artist. The same August, Adler died in London's St.

Thomas hospital after a long battle with cancer.

In a remarkable career as a musician, journalist, and author, Larry Adler seemed to have met and worked with almost everyone who was anyone in showbusiness, politics, and many other walks of life. A tennis fanatic, he once played in a doubles match with Charlie Chaplin, Greta Garbo, and Salvador Dali, and he was always prepared to talk about it. In fact, his great charm was that he was prepared to talk about anything to anybody.

● ALBUMS: *Discovery* (RCA Victor 1968) ★★★★, *Harmonica* (Phase 4 1979) ★★★, *Plays Gershwin, Porter, Kern, Rodgers, Arlen And Gould* (RCA 1985) ★★★★, *Live At The Ballroom* (Newport 1986) ★★★, *Works For Harmonica And Orchestra* (Accordion 1987) ★★★, *The Mouth Organ Virtuoso* (EMI 1994) ★★★.

● COMPILATIONS: *Golden Age Of Larry Adler* (Golden Age 1986) ★★★, *Larry Adler In Concert* (EMI 1991) ★★★, *Maestro Of The Mouth Organ* (ASV 1995) ★★★★, *The Best Of Larry Adler* (MFP 1996) ★★★★.

● FURTHER READING: *How I Play*, Larry Adler. *Jokes And How To Tell Them*, Larry Adler. *It Ain't Necessarily So: An Autobiography*, Larry Adler. *Me And My Big Mouth*, Larry Adler.

● FILMS: *Operator 13* aka *Spy 13* (1934), *Many Happy Returns* (1934), *The Singing Marine* (1937), *Calling All Stars* (1937), *Sidewalks Of London* aka *St Martin's Lane* (1938), *Music For Millions* (1944), *Three Daring Daughters* aka *The Birds And The Bees* (1948).

AINSWORTH, ALYN

b. 24 August 1924, Bolton, Lancashire, England, d. 4 October 1990, London, England. A highly respected musical director and arranger for records, television and the West End stage, Ainsworth studied guitar from the age of seven, left school at 14 to join Herman Darewski's Orchestra as a boy soprano, and sang at the London Palladium. When his voice broke, he returned to Bolton and became an assistant golf professional, playing guitar in his own band, the Falcons, while also studying musical arranging. In the late 40s he worked as a staff arranger for Oscar Rabin, and then Geraldo, one of the top UK dance bands.

In 1951 he began to arrange for the newly formed BBC Northern Variety Orchestra, and, when its conductor, Vilem Tausky, moved to the Northern Symphony Orchestra, Ainsworth was offered the job of resident conductor with the NVO. In December 1952, BBC Television launched *The Good Old Days* from the City Variety Theatre in Leeds – this music-hall show ran for over 30 years – and Ainsworth and the Northern Variety Orchestra provided the appropriate musical setting. Economics, it is said, obliged the BBC to prune the orchestra, removing all the members of the string section, bar one, and renaming it the Northern Dance Orchestra. With the help of musicians such as trumpeter Syd Lawrence, Ainsworth welded the NDO into one of the finest units of its kind in the world. Based in Manchester for a decade, Ainsworth and the NDO appeared on numerous radio and television programmes, accompanying singers such as Frankie Vaughan, Ronnie Hilton and David Whitfield. Together with singer Sheila Buxton and laid-back announcer Roger Moffat, they had their own highly acclaimed late-night UK television show, *Make Way For Music*.

In 1961 Ainsworth moved from Manchester to London to serve as musical director for the imported American musical *Bye Bye Birdie*, which starred Chita Rivera and UK rock 'n' roller Marty Wilde. Between 1958 and 1965, the Alyn Ainsworth Orchestra also recorded a number of orchestral pieces for George Martin. During the 60s Ainsworth became a leading conductor and arranger for West End shows such as *Gentlemen Prefer Blondes*, *Hello, Dolly!*, *A Funny Thing Happened On The Way To The Forum*, *She Loves Me* and *Sweet Charity*. He also orchestrated Leslie Bricusse and Anthony Newley's *The Roar Of The Greasepaint – The Smell Of The Crowd*. The 60s also saw the start of his long and successful collaboration with singer Shirley Bassey, during which time he acted as her musical director for many cabaret seasons in the UK and abroad. Back home in Britain, Ainsworth's television credits included Val Parnell's *Sunday Night At The London Palladium*, *International Cabaret From The Talk Of The Town*, *The David Nixon Show*, *Dee Time*, *The Cannon And Ball Show*, *Search For A Star*, *Night Of Hundred Stars*, *The BAFTA Awards*, *Live From Her Majesty's*, *Bruce's Big Night Out*, more than 10 *Royal Command Performances*, and many 'specials' featuring artists such as Cilla Black, Russ Abbott, Stanley Baxter, Vera Lynn and Lulu. He also composed the theme music for several of the shows. His other compositions included 'Bedtime For Drums', 'Italian Sunset', 'Mi Amor', 'Pete's Party' and 'If I Were A Buddy Rich Man'. Ainsworth was also associated with the Brotherhood Of Man, and conducted for them at the Eurovision Song Contest which they won in 1976 with 'Save Your Kisses For Me'. He also worked with many visiting Americans, including Johnny Mathis, Neil Sedaka, and Barry Manilow. Ainsworth also collaborated with the Beverley Sisters on their recording of 'Triplets', among others, and was engaged for a time to one of the twins, Teddie. His own records included a rare excursion into rock 'n' roll with '18th Century Rock', credited to 'Alyn Ainsworth with The Rock-A-Fellas', and the more typically smooth *Themes And Dreams* and *True Love*.

The ultimate professional, Ainsworth would often conduct the first house of one West End show, and the second house of another, after rehearsing for television during the day. He was capable of producing his best work under extreme pressure, while also motivating others, and was the man on whom producers could rely for the big occasion.

● ALBUMS: *Themes And Dreams* (Pickwick 1982) ★★★, *True Love* (Hallmark 1982) ★★★.

ALBERT, EDDIE

b. Edward Albert Heimberger, 22 April 1908, Rock Island, Illinois, USA. A singer and actor in theatre and films, with a range that extends from 'amiable, best friend' parts, through to overbearing, thoroughly nasty character roles. Albert began his career as a singer, and worked in theatres and on radio with the Threesome, and then teamed with Grace Bradt to form the Honeymooners – Grace and Eddie. He made his Broadway debut at the Empire Theatre in the play *O Evening Star* (1935), which was followed by *Brother Rat* (1936) and *Room Service* (1937). A year later, he played Antipholus of Syracuse and introduced 'This Can't Be Love' in *The Boys From Syracuse*. During World War II, Albert served as a lieutenant in the US Navy, and it was 1949 before he returned to the Broadway musical theatre in *Miss Liberty* (1949), in which he sang the appealing 'Let's Take An Old-Fashioned Walk'. Nine years later he took over from David Wayne in *Say, Darling*, and then succeeded Robert Preston as Professor Harold Hill in *The Music Man*, in January 1960. In between, he continued to perform in serious plays on Broadway and in regional theatre. He also carved out an impressive career in films, which total more than 70 to date. These have included several musicals such as *On Your Toes* (1939), *Hit Parade Of 1947*, *Meet Me After The Show* (1951) and *The Girl Rush* (1955). In the 50s he had two particularly good roles, firstly in *Oklahoma!* (1955), in which he played pedlar-man Ali Hakim, and then in *The Joker Is Wild* (1957), where, as the accompanist of comedian Joe E. Lewis (played by Frank Sinatra), he was outstanding. Albert has been seen on the screen in dramatic roles in films such as *Brother Rat* (1938), *Four Wives* (1939), *Smash Up* (1947), *Carrie* (1952), *Roman Holiday* (1953), *I'll Cry Tomorrow* (1955), *Attack!* (1956), *The Teahouse Of The August Moon* (1956), *The Roots Of Heaven* (1958), *Orders To Kill* (1958), *The Longest Day* (1962), *Captain Newman MD* (1963), *The Heartbreak Kid* (1972) and *The Longest Yard* (1974), continuing into the 90s. His extensive television credits include many films and series, including *Leave It To Larry* (1952), *Green Acres* (1965-70), *Switch* (1975-76) and *The Chocolate Soldier* (1984). In the 50s Albert appeared in a television adaptation of *A Connecticut Yankee*, and had a sophisticated nightclub act with his wife Margo. Their son, Edward Albert, is a film and television actor.

● ALBUMS: *Eddie Albert* (Columbia) ★★★, *One God* (Kapp 1954) ★★★, *Eddie Albert And Margo* (Kapp 1956) ★★★★, *September Song* (Kapp 1957) ★★★.

ALBERY, DONALD

b. Donald Arthur Rolleston Albery, 19 June 1914, London, England, d. 14 September 1988, Monte Carlo. A producer and theatre-owner, Albery came from a family steeped in theatrical history – his paternal grandfather was the playwright James Albery, and his father was Sir Bronson Albery, who founded what became the Society of West End Theatres. Donald Albery was educated in Switzerland before serving as general manager of Sadlers Wells Ballet from 1941-45. He started out as a producer in 1953, and throughout the 50s and

60s presented or co-presented several notable plays, such as *The Living Room*, *Waiting For Godot*, *A Taste Of Honey* and *Who's Afraid Of Virginia Woolf?* His first musical production was *Grab Me A Gondola* in 1956, and this was followed by a mixture of smash hits and minor flops, which included *Zuleika* (1957), *Irma La Douce* (1958), *Make Me An Offer* (1959), *Fings Ain't Wot They Used T'Be* (1960), *Oliver!* (1960), *The Art Of Living* (1960), *Not To Worry* (1962), *Blitz!* (1962), *Fiorello!* (1962), *Oliver!* (New York 1963), *Instant Marriage* (1964), *Jorrocks* (1966), *Oliver!* (London revival 1967), *Man Of La Mancha* (1968), *Mandrake* (1970) and *Popkiss* (1972). Albery also enjoyed a long-runner with the revue *Beyond The Fringe* in 1961. In 1962 he took over the Wyndham Group of London theatres from his father, consisting of Wyndham's, the New (later re christened the Albery) and the Criterion; Albery later also acquired the Piccadilly Theatre. Albery was knighted in 1977, and sold his Group to Associated Newspapers a year later, when he retired. His son Ian took over as manager.
● FURTHER READING: *All On Stage: Charles Wyndham And The Alberys*, W. Trewin.

ALDRICH, RONNIE

b. 15 February 1916, Erith, Kent, England, d. 30 September 1993. As a gifted young pianist Aldrich undertook extensive studies, including a period at the Guildhall School of Music in London. Later, he worked with the Folkestone Municipal Orchestra before his career was interrupted by World War II. During the war he played piano and arranged for the RAF Dance Orchestra, remaining with the band after the war when, as the Squadronaires, it became one of the most popular of UK big bands. Aldrich led the band during the 50s, continuing until its dissolution in 1964. Subsequently, he was employed as a musical director for Thames Television, and also played piano and directed specially formed orchestras for record dates and radio performances.
● ALBUMS: *All Time Hits Of Jazz* (Ace Of Clubs 1960) ★★★, *Melody And Percussion For Two Pianos* (1961) ★★★★, *Ronnie Aldrich And His Two Pianos* (1961) ★★★, *Love Story* (1971) ★★★, *For The One You Love* (Decca 1980) ★★★, *One Fine Day* (Decca 1981) ★★★, *Night Birds* (MFP 1982) ★★★, *Tender Love ... Tender Moments* (Contour 1982) ★★★, *The Unforgettable Sound Of Ronnie Aldrich And His 2 Pianos* (Decca 1984) ★★★★, *Sea Dreams* (MFP 1984) ★★★, *Silver Bells* (Audio Fidelity 1984) ★★★, *28 Great Piano Classics* (Horatio Nelson 1985) ★★★, *Soft And Wicked* (Jasmine 1985) ★★★, *The Aldrich Feeling* (Decca 1986) ★★★, *All-Time Piano Hits* (Decca 1986) ★★★, *Focus On Ronnie Aldrich* (Decca 1986) ★★★, *For All Seasons* (MFP 1987) ★★★, *Two Pianos In Hollywood* (London 1988) ★★★, *An Hour Of Ronnie Aldrich* (Hour Of Pleasure/EMI 1988) ★★★.

ALTON, ROBERT

b. Robert Alton Hart, 28 January 1897, Bennington, Vermont, USA, d. 12 June 1957, Hollywood, California, USA. A particularly innovative and stylish choreographer for the musical stage and Hollywood, Alton appeared on Broadway as a dancer in *Take It From Me* (1919) and *Greenwich Village Follies* (1924) before staging the dance scenes for comedian Joe Cook's last Broadway musical, *Hold Your Horses* (1933). Thereafter, during the rest of the 30s through to the early 50s, he choreographed a mixture of revues and musical comedies, among which were some of the biggest hits of the day. They included *Ziegfeld Follies* (1934), *Life Begins At 8:40* (1934), *Anything Goes* (1934), *Thumbs Up!* (1934), *Parade* (1935), *Ziegfeld Follies* (1936), *Hooray For What!* (1937), *Between The Devil* (1937), *You Never Know* (1938), *Leave It To Me!* (1938), *One For The Money* (1939), *The Streets Of Paris* (1939), *Too Many Girls* (1939), *Du Barry Was A Lady* (1939), *Two For The Show* (1940), *Panama Hattie* (1940), *Higher And Higher* (1940), *Pal Joey* (1940), *Sons O' Fun* (1941), *By Jupiter* (1942), *Count Me In* (1942), *Ziegfeld Follies* (1943), *Laffing Room Only* (1944), *Hazel Flagg* (1953) and *Me And Juliet* (1953). Alton also served as both choreographer and director on *Early To Bed* (1943), the 1952 Broadhurst Theatre revival of *Pal Joey* (with David Alexander), and *The Vamp* (1955).
In parallel with his stage work, Alton created some classic dance scenes in a number of highly successful and fondly remembered movie musicals, such as *You'll Never Get Rich* (1941, the 'Wedding Cake Walk' sequence), *The Harvey Girls* (1946, the Oscar-winning 'On The Atchison, Topeka, And The Santa Fe'), *Ziegfeld Follies* (1946, 'This Heart Of Mine'), *Good News* (1947, with Charles Walters, 'Varsity Drag'), *Easter Parade* (1948, 'The Girl On The Magazine Cover', 'Shaking The Blues Away', 'A Couple Of Swells'), *The Pirate* (1948, with Gene Kelly, 'Be A Clown'), *Annie Get Your Gun* (1950, 'I'm An Indian Too'), *Show Boat* (1951, 'I Might Fall Back On You', 'Life Upon The Wicked Stage'), and many more. His other film credits, mostly for MGM, included *Strike Me Pink* (1936), *Bathing Beauty* (1944, with Jack Donohue), *Till The Clouds Roll By* (1946), *Words And Music* (1948, with Kelly), *The Barkleys Of Broadway* (1949), *In The Good Old Summertime* (1949), *Pagan Love Song* (1950, also directed), *The Belle Of New York* (1952), *I Love Melvin* (1953), *Call Me Madam* (1953), *White Christmas* (1954), *There's No Business Like Show Business* (1955) and *The Girl Rush* (1955). In many cases, stars such as Gene Kelly and Fred Astaire would stage one or more of the numbers in their own movies, and there were other occasions when additional choreographers were called in to work alongside Alton, such as on *There's No Business Like Show Business*, when all Marilyn Monroe's dance routines were created by Jack Cole. In a varied and distinguished career, Allen also directed *Merton Of The Movies* (1947), the second film remake of Harry Leon Wilson's endearing novel, which starred Red Skelton, Virginia O'Brien, Alan Mowbray, Gloria Grahame and Leon Ames.

AMES BROTHERS

This family group from Malden, Massachusetts,

USA, was consistently popular from the late 40s through the 50s. Brothers Joe Urick (b. 3 May 1924), Gene Urick (b. 13 February 1925), Vic Urick (b. 20 May 1926, d. 23 January 1978, Nashville, Tennessee, USA) and Ed Urick (b. 9 July 1927, Malden, Massachusetts, USA) started singing together in high school and won several amateur contests in their home town. They first sang professionally in Boston, and later in clubs and theatres in New York, Chicago and Hollywood. After recording 'A Tree In A Meadow' with Monica Lewis, for the independent Signature label, they signed for Coral Records, later switching to RCA-Victor Records. After minor successes with 'You, You, You Are The One' and 'Cruising Down The River', they hit number 1 in 1950 with the novelty 'Rag Mop'/'Sentimental Me' (a million-seller). During the 50s they were extremely popular in stage shows and on US television, with their skilful blend of comedy and an uncomplicated singing style on bouncy numbers and ballads.

They also had four more million-selling records: 'Undecided' (backed by Les Brown and his orchestra), 'You You You', 'The Naughty Lady Of Shady Lane' and 'Melodie D'Amour'. Their other US Top 20 hits were 'Can Anyone Explain? (No, No, No!)', 'Music! Music! Music!', 'Stars Are The Windows Of Heaven', 'Oh Babe!', 'Wang Wang Blues', 'I Wanna Love You', 'Auf Wiederseh'n Sweetheart', 'String Along', 'My Favorite Song', 'The Man With The Banjo', 'My Bonnie Lassie', 'It Only Hurts For A Little While', 'Tammy', 'A Very Precious Love' and 'Pussy Cat'. Around the late 50s the group disbanded, but Ed Ames continued as a solo act, appearing frequently on US television. He also had hit singles in 1967 with 'My Cup Runneth Over' and 'Who Will Answer?', plus several 60s US chart albums.

● ALBUMS: *Sing A Song Of Christmas* (Coral 1950) ★★, *In The Evening By The Moonlight* (Coral 1951) ★★★★, *Sentimental Me* (Coral 1951) ★★★, *Hoop-De-Hoo* (Coral 1951) ★★★, *Sweet Leilani* (Coral 1951) ★★★, *Favorite Spirituals* (Coral 1952) ★★★, *Home On The Range* (Coral 1952) ★★★, *Merry Christmas 1952* (Coral 1952) ★★★, *Favorite Songs* (Coral 1954) ★★★★, *It Must Be True* (RCA Victor 1954) ★★★, *Ames Brothers Concert* (Coral 1956) ★★, *Love's Old Sweet Song* (Coral 1956) ★★★, *Exactly Like You* (RCA Victor 1956) ★★★, *Four Brothers* (RCA Victor 1956) ★★★★, *The Ames Brothers With Hugo Winterhalter* (RCA Victor 1956) ★★, *Sounds Of Christmas Harmony* (Coral 1957) ★★★, *Love Serenade* (Coral 1957) ★★★★, *Sweet Seventeen* (RCA Victor 1957) ★★★, *There'll Always Be A Christmas* (RCA Victor 1957) ★★★, *Destination Moon* (RCA Victor 1958) ★★★, *Smoochin' Time* (RCA Victor 1958) ★★★, *Words & Music With The Ames Brothers* (RCA Victor 1959) ★★★★, *Ames Brothers Sing Famous Hits Of Famous Quartets* (RCA Victor 1959) ★★★, *Sing The Best In Country* (RCA Victor 1959) ★★, *Sing The Best Of The Bands* (RCA Victor 1960) ★★★, *The Blend And The Beat* (RCA Victor 1960) ★★★, *Hello Amigos* (RCA Victor 1960) ★★★, *Sweet & Swing* (RCA Victor 1960) ★★★, *Knees Up!* (RCA Victor 1963) ★★★.

● COMPILATIONS: *The Best Of The Ames Brothers* (RCA Victor 1958) ★★★★, *Our Golden Favorites* (Coral 1960) ★★★★, *The Very Best Of The Ames Brothers* (Taragon 1998) ★★★★.

ANDREWS SISTERS

Female vocal group comprising sisters LaVerne (b. 6 July 1911, Mound, nr. Minneapolis, Minnesota, USA, d. 8 May 1967, Brentwood, California, USA), Maxene (b. 3 January 1916, Mound, nr. Minneapolis, Minnesota, USA, d. 21 October 1995, Boston, Massachusetts, USA) and Patty Andrews (b. 16 February 1918, Mound, nr. Minneapolis, Minnesota, USA), lead singer and soloist. In the early 30s the sisters appeared in vaudeville and toured with the Larry Rich band before joining Leon Belasco at New York's Hotel Edison in 1937. With their new manager Lou Levy (b. 3 December 1910, Brooklyn, New York City, New York, USA, d. October 1995), who later married Maxene, they signed for Decca Records and almost immediately had a massive hit in 1938 with 'Bei Mir Bist Du Schoen', a Yiddish song from 1933, with a new lyric by Saul Chaplin and Sammy Cahn. This was followed by the novelty 'Hold Tight, Hold Tight', and 'Roll Out The Barrel', an Americanized version of the old Czechoslovakian melody, 'The Beer Barrel Polka', which became one of World War II's smash hits and helped them to become the most popular female vocal group of the war years.

They went to Hollywood in 1940 to appear in *Argentine Nights* with the Ritz Brothers, and featured in several movies starring comedians Abbott and Costello, including *Buck Privates*, in which they sang 'Boogie Woogie Bugle Boy'. In *Hollywood Canteen*, Warner's 1944 star-studded morale booster, the sisters sang 'Don't Fence Me In', later a chart-topper with Bing Crosby. Their fruitful career-long collaboration with Crosby also included 'Pistol Packin' Mama', 'Is You Is, Or Is You Ain't My Baby?', 'Ac-Cent-Tchu-Ate The Positive', 'The Three Caballeros', 'Along The Navajo Trail', 'Jingle Bells' and 'Sparrow In The Tree Top'. They also recorded with several other artists such as Les Paul ('Rumors Are Flying'), Burl Ives ('Blue Tail Fly'), Danny Kaye ('Civilisation' and 'The Woody Woodpecker Song'), Carmen Miranda ('Cuanto La Gusta'), Guy Lombardo ('Christmas Island') and country singer Ernest Tubbs ('I'm Biting My Fingernails And Thinking Of You'). The sisters own unaided hits, accompanied mainly by the Vic Schoen Orchestra, were a mixture of novelty, commercial boogie-woogie, calypso, jazzy numbers and heartfelt ballads. Following that first Yiddish hit in 1938, they were consistently in the charts with records such as 'Says My Heart', 'Say Si Si', 'Beat Me, Daddy, Eight To The Bar', 'I, Yi, Yi, Yi, Yi (I Like You Very Much)', 'I'll Be With You In Apple Blossom Time', 'Three Little Sisters', 'Strip Polka', 'Straighten Up And Fly Right' and 'Underneath The Arches'/'You Call Everybody Darling', which was recorded in the UK and accompanied by the Billy Ternent Orchestra.

In 1949 Patti Andrews topped the US chart with her solo record, 'I Can Dream, Can't I?'/'I Wanna

Be Loved', and in 1953 she left the group to go solo. The sisters still worked together occasionally until LaVerne's death in 1967. At their peak for just over a decade, their immediately identifiable close harmony sound, coupled with a swinging, vigorous delivery, eventually gained them world record sales in excess of 60 million, making them perhaps the most successful and popular female group ever. Bette Midler's frenetic revival of 'Boogie Woogie Bugle Boy' in 1973 revived some interest in their records, and in 1974 Patti and Maxene were reunited for *Over Here!*, a Broadway musical with a World War II setting that ran for over a year. In the early 80s Maxene underwent heart surgery, but in 1985 she was able to record her first solo album, *Maxene: An Andrews Sister*, a mixture of new material and some of the group's old hits. In 1991, four years before her death, she made her 'in-person' debut as a solo artist, in aid of charity, at the Beaux Arts Ball in Brighton, England. Patti continues to work, touring the UK in 1990 on a wave of wartime nostalgia with the current Glenn Miller Orchestra.

● ALBUMS: *Merry Christmas* 10-inch album (Decca 1950) ★★★, *Christmas Greetings* 10-inch album (Decca 1950) ★★★, *Tropical Songs* 10-inch album (Decca 1950) ★★★, *The Andrews Sisters* 10-inch album (Decca 1950) ★★★★, *Club 15* 10-inch album (Decca 1950) ★★★, *Berlin Songs* 10-inch album (Decca 1950) ★★, *Christmas Cheer* 10-inch album (Decca 1950) ★★★, *Mr Music* film soundtrack (Decca 1951) ★★★, *I Love To Tell The Story* 10-inch album (Decca 1951) ★★★, *Country Style* 10-inch album (Decca 1952) ★★, *My Isle Of Golden Dreams* 10-inch album (Decca 1952) ★★★, *Sing Sing Sing* 10-inch album (Decca 1953) ★★★, *Curtain Call* (Decca 1956) ★★★, *Jingle Bells* (Decca 1956) ★★★, *By Popular Demand* (Decca 1957) ★★★, *The Andrew Sisters In Hi-Fi* (Capitol 1957) ★★★★, *Fresh And Fancy Free* (Capitol 1957) ★★★★, *Dancing Twenties* (Capitol 1958) ★★★, *The Andrews Sisters Present* (Dot 1963) ★★★, *The Andrews Sisters Go Hawaiian* (Dot 1965) ★★.
Solo: Maxene Andrews *Maxene: An Andrews Sister* (DRG 1985) ★★★.

● COMPILATIONS: *Great Golden Hits* (Dot 1962) ★★★, *Great Country Hits* (Dot 1964) ★★★, *The Best Of The Andrews Sisters* (MCA 1973) ★★★★, *Beat Me Daddy Eight To The Bar* (MFP/EMI 1982) ★★★★, *Jumpin' Jive* (MCA 1986) ★★★★, *16 Golden Classics* (Timeless 1987) ★★★★, *Hold Tight – It's The Andrews Sisters* (Dance Band Days/Prism 1987) ★★★★, *Rarities* (MCA 1988) ★★★, *Christmas With The Andrews Sisters* (Pickwick 1988) ★★★, *Says My Heart* (Happy Days 1989) ★★★, *50th Anniversary Collection, Volume One* (MCA 1990) ★★★★, *50th Anniversary Collection, Volume Two* (MCA 1990) ★★★, *Capitol Collectors Series* (Capitol 1991) ★★★, *Their All-Time Greatest Hits* (MCA 1994) ★★★★, *Their Complete Recordings Together* (MCA 1996) ★★★, with Bing Crosby *The Essential Collection* (Half Moon 1998) ★★★, *Greatest Hits: The 60th Anniversary Collection* (MCA 1998) ★★★★, *The Best Of The Andrews Sisters: The Millennium Collection* (MCA 2000) ★★★★.

● FILMS: *Argentine Nights* (1940), *In The Navy* (1941), *Hold That Ghost* (1941), *Buck Privates* (1941), *What's Cooking?* (1942), *Private Buckaroo* (1942), *Give Out, Sisters* (1942), *How's About It?* (1943), *Always A Bridesmaid* (1943), *Swingtime Johnny* (1943), *Moonlight And Cactus* (1944), *Follow The Boys* (1944), *Hollywood Canteen* (1944), *Her Lucky Night* (1945), *Road To Rio* (1947), *Melody Time* (1948), *The Phynx* Patti cameo (1970), *The Gong Show Movie* Patti cameo (1980).

ANKA, PAUL

b. 30 July 1941, Ottawa, Ontario, Canada. A prolific songwriter and child prodigy, Anka was one of the major teen-idols of the 50s. He burst onto the scene in 1957 with the self-written 'Diana', an intense ballad describing the frustration and unrequited love of a young teenager for a slightly older female. With its distinctive rhythm pattern, the song was powerfully evocative and stayed at the top of the UK charts for a lengthy nine weeks, as well as reaching number 1 in the USA. It sold a reported 10 million copies worldwide. Anka followed it with a series of hits such as 'You Are My Destiny', 'Put Your Head On My Shoulder' and 'Puppy Love'. Adolescent worries and the desire to be taken seriously by condescending parents were familiar themes in those songs and contributed greatly to his success. As the 50s drew to a close, he wisely moved away from teen ballads and planned for a long-term future as a songwriter and cabaret artist. His moving 'It Doesn't Matter Anymore' was a posthumous UK number 1 for Buddy Holly in 1959. By this time Anka had begun an acting career, appearing in *Let's Rock* and *Girls Town*, the latter of which included the huge US hit 'Lonely Boy'.
During the 60s the former teen star was a regular at New York's Copacabana and Los Angeles' Coconut Grove, and was much in demand on the nightclub circuit. Additionally, he attempted a serious acting career, making an appearance in *The Longest Day* (for which he also composed the title song). For much of the decade, however, he was earning large sums of money appearing at Las Vegas hotels. The success of Donny Osmond, meanwhile, who took 'Puppy Love' to the top in Britain, kept Anka's early material alive for a new generation. Songwriting success continued, most notably with Frank Sinatra's reading of his lyric to 'My Way' and Tom Jones's million-selling 'She's A Lady'. In the 70s, Anka himself returned to number 1 in the USA courtesy of a risqué duet with his protégé Odia Coates, with the song '(You're) Having My Baby'. A spree of hits followed, punctuated by regular supper-club appearances. As late as 1983, the former 50s teen star was back in the charts with 'Hold Me Till The Mornin' Comes'. He continued to play lucrative seasons in Las Vegas and Atlantic City, and toured Europe in 1992 for the first time in 25 years. The following year he threatened to sue Dulux, a UK paint manufacturer, when their television commercial portrayed a sheepdog apparently singing a parody of 'My Way'. In 1996 he released

his first album aimed at the Latin market, with some of his greatest hits sung in Spanish and duets with artists including Celine Dion, Julio Iglesias and Jose Luis Rodriguez.

● ALBUMS: *Paul Anka* (ABC 1958) ★★★, *My Heart Sings* (ABC 1959) ★★★, *Paul Anka Swings For Young Lovers* (ABC 1960) ★★★★, *Anka At The Copa* (ABC 1960) ★★★, *It's Christmas Everywhere* (ABC 1960) ★★★, *Strictly Instrumental* (ABC 1961) ★★, *Diana* (ABC 1962) ★★★★, *Young, Alive And In Love!* (RCA Victor 1962) ★★★★, *Let's Sit This One Out!* (RCA Victor 1962) ★★★, *Our Man Around The World* (RCA Victor 1963) ★★★, *Songs I Wished I'd Written* (RCA Victor 1963) ★★, *Excitement On Park Avenue* (RCA Victor 1964) ★★★, *Strictly Nashville* (RCA Victor 1966) ★★, *Paul Anka Alive* (RCA Victor 1967) ★★, *Goodnight My Love* (RCA Victor 1969) ★★★, *Life Goes On* (RCA Victor 1969) ★★★, *Paul Anka* (Buddah 1971) ★★, *Jubilation* (Buddah 1972) ★★, *Anka* (United Artists 1974) ★★★, *Feelings* (United Artists 1975) ★★★, *The Painter* (United Artists 1976) ★★★, *The Music Man* (United Artists 1977) ★★★, *Listen To Your Heart* (RCA 1978) ★★, *Both Sides Of Love* (RCA 1981) ★★★, *Walk A Fine Line* (Columbia 1983) ★★★, *Italiano* (Crescent 1987) ★★★, *Amigos* (Globo/Sony 1996) ★★★, *A Body Of Work* (Epic 1999) ★★.

● COMPILATIONS: *Paul Anka Sings His Big 15* (ABC 1960) ★★★★, *Paul Anka Sings His Big 15, Volume 2* (ABC 1961) ★★★, *Paul Anka Sings His Big 15, Volume 3* (ABC 1961) ★★, *Paul Anka's 21 Golden Hits* (RCA 1963) ★★★, *Paul Anka Gold* (Sire 1974) ★★★★, *Times Of Your Life* (United Artists 1975) ★★★, *Paul Anka At His Best* (United Artists 1979) ★★★★, *The Original Hits Of Paul Anka* (Columbia 1987) ★★★, *30th Anniversary Collection* (Rhino 1989) ★★★, *The Ultimate Collection* (Capitol 1992) ★★★★, *The Best Of United Artists Years* (Capitol 1996) ★★★★, *The Very Best Of Paul Anka* (RCA 2000) ★★★★.

● FILMS: *Let's Rock* aka *Keep It Cool* (1958), *Girls Town* aka *The Innocent And The Damned* (1959), *The Private Life Of Adam And Eve* (1961), *Look In Any Window* (1961), *The Longest Day* (1962), *Lonely Boy* (1962), *Iskelmäprinssi* (1990), *Captain Ron* (1992), *Ordinary Magic* aka *Ganesh* (1993), *Mr. Payback: An Interactive Movie* (1995), *Mad Dog Time* (1996), *3000 Miles To Graceland* (2001).

ANTHONY, RAY

b. Raymond Antonini, 20 January 1922, Bentleyville, Pennsylvania, USA. After playing in local bands in Cleveland, Anthony spent brief spells in the trumpet sections of the Al Donahue, Glenn Miller and Jimmy Dorsey orchestras. Following a four-year period in the US Navy, where he led a services orchestra, Anthony formed his own band in 1946 and signed with Capitol Records. The band became one of the top attractions of the 50s, touring colleges and universities, producing hit singles such as 'At Last', 'Harbour Lights', the television themes from *Dragnet* and *Peter Gunn*, plus novelty dance numbers such as 'The Bunny Hop' and 'I Can't Tell A Waltz From A Tango'. From the start, the band

had always had a Millerish reed sound, so when the Miller 'revival' happened they participated more successfully than most. Anthony appeared with his band in two movies, Fred Astaire's *Daddy Long Legs* and *This Could Be The Night*. He appeared on his own in the Jayne Mansfield/Tom Ewell rock 'n' roll spoof *The Girl Can't Help It*, and in an eerie piece of Hollywood casting, featured as the saxophone-playing Jimmy Dorsey in the Red Nichols biopic *The Five Pennies*.

In the 60s, with a limited market for 16-piece bands, Anthony formed the Bookend Review, with a female vocal duo and a small band, playing clubs and lounges throughout the USA. In 1976, after eight years with Ranwood Records, he began releasing material on his own Aero Space label. He revived the Ray Anthony Orchestra during the 80s, and remains active in preserving big-band music for schools and radio stations.

● ALBUMS: include *Ray Anthony's Orchestra* (Capitol 1953) ★★★★, *Sweet And Lovely* (Capitol 1953) ★★★★, *House Party* (Capitol 1953) ★★★★, *I Remember Glenn Miller* (Capitol 1954) ★★★★, *Arthur Murray Swing Foxtrots* (Capitol 1955) ★★★, *Golden Horn* (Capitol 1955) ★★★★, *Jam Session At The Tower* (Capitol 1956) ★★★, *Dream Dancing* (Capitol 1956) ★★★★, *Star Dancing* (Capitol 1957) ★★★, *Young Ideas* (Capitol 1957) ★★★★, *The Dream Girl* (Capitol 1958) ★★★★, *Dances in Love* (Capitol 1958) ★★★, *Dancing Over The Waves* (Capitol 1959) ★★★, *Anthony Plays Allen* (Capitol 1959) ★★★, *Sound Spectacular* (Capitol 1960) ★★★, *Worried Mind* (Capitol 1962) ★★★★, *Lo Mucho Te Quiero* (Ranwood 1968) ★★★, *Love Is For The Two Of Us* (Ranwood 1968) ★★★, *Arthur Murray Dance Party* (Aero Space) ★★★, *Tribute* (Aero Space) ★★★, *Dancing Alone Together: Torch Songs For Lovers* (Aero Space) ★★★, *A Trip Through 50 Years Of Music* (Aero Space) ★★★, *Dream Dancing In Hawaii* (Aero Space) ★★★, *Swing Back To The 40's* (Aero Space 1991) ★★★, *In The Miller Mood* (Aero Space 1992) ★★★, *In The Miller Mood, Vol. II* (Aero Space 1995) ★★★, *Dream Dancing II* (Aero Space 1995) ★★★, *Dream Dancing Christmas* (Aero Space 1995) ★★★, *Party Dancing* (Aero Space 1996) ★★★, *Boogie, Blues And Ballads* (Aero Space 1997) ★★★, *Dream Dancing In The Latin Mood* (Aero Space 1998) ★★★, *Swing Club* (Aero Space 1999) ★★★★, *Dream Dancing III: In The Romantic Mood* (Aero Space 2000) ★★★, *Dream Dancing IV: In The Mellow Mood* (Aero Space 2001) ★★★.

ARMSTRONG, LILLIAN

b. Lillian Hardin, 3 February 1898, Memphis, Tennessee, USA, d. 27 August 1971, Chicago, Illinois, USA. A classically trained pianist, Hardin worked extensively in Chicago in the 20s, becoming highly popular both as a solo performer and also playing with the bands of Sugar Johnny, Freddie Keppard and Joe 'King' Oliver. It was while she was with Oliver that she met and married the band's newest recruit, Louis Armstrong. Aware of her new husband's massive talent, and being hugely ambitious for him, she persuaded Louis to start his own band, and was herself a crucial presence in his classic Hot Five and Hot Seven groups. Personality clashes later made their marriage untenable and they were divorced.

Lillian Armstrong's subsequent career found her leading bands for club work and on numerous radio and recording dates. From the 50s onwards she worked mostly as a solo pianist and singer, usually in Chicago, although she sometimes played at festivals in the USA and Europe, where she also appeared in clubs. An occasional composer, one of her songs, 'Just For A Thrill', was recorded in the 50s by Ray Charles. She died in 1971 while taking part in a memorial concert for Louis, who had died a few weeks earlier.
● ALBUMS: *Satchmo And Me* (Riverside 1956) ★★★, *Lil Hardin Armstrong And Her Orchestra* (Riverside 1962) ★★★.

ARMSTRONG, LOUIS

b. 4 August 1901, New Orleans, Louisiana, USA, d. 6 July 1971, New York City, New York, USA. It is impossible to overstate Louis 'Satchmo' Armstrong's importance in jazz. He was one of the most influential artists in the music's history. He was also more than just a jazz musician, he was an enormously popular entertainer (a facet upon which some critics frowned) and although other black jazz men and women would eventually be welcomed in the upper echelons of white society, Armstrong was one of the first. He certainly found his way into millions of hearts otherwise closed to his kind. Had Armstrong been born white and privileged, his achievement would have been extraordinary; that he was born black and in desperately deprived circumstances makes his success almost miraculous. Armstrong achieved this astonishing breakthrough largely by the sheer force of his personality.

Louis Armstrong was born and raised in and around the notorious Storyville district of New Orleans. His exact date of birth only became known in the 90s, although for many years he claimed it to be 4 July 1900, a date which was both patriotic and easy to remember and, as some chroniclers have suggested, might have exempted him from army service. Run-down apartment buildings, many of them converted to occasional use as brothels, honky-tonks, dance halls and even churches, were his surroundings as he grew up with his mother and younger sister (his father having abandoned the family at the time of Louis's birth). His childhood combined being free to run the streets with obligations towards his family, who needed him to earn money. His formal education was severely restricted but he was a bright child and swiftly accumulated the kind of wisdom needed for survival; long before the term existed, Louis Armstrong was 'streetwise'. From the first he learned how to hustle for money and it was a lesson he never forgot. Even late in life, when he was rich and famous, he would still regard his career as a 'hustle'. As a child, apart from regular work, among the means he had of earning money was singing at street corners in a semi-formal group.

Armstrong's life underwent a dramatic change when, still in his early teens, he was sent to the Colored Waifs Home. The popularly supposed reason for this incarceration, encouraged by Armstrong's assisted autobiography, was that, in a fit of youthful exuberance he had celebrated New Year's Eve (either 1912 or 1913) by firing off a borrowed pistol in the street. Whatever the reason, the period he spent in the home changed his life. Given the opportunity to play in the home's band, first as a singer, then as a percussionist, then a bugler and finally as a cornetist, Armstrong found his métier. From the first, he displayed a remarkable affinity for music, and quickly achieved an enviable level of competence not only at playing the cornet but also in understanding harmony. Released from the home after a couple of years, it was some time before Armstrong could afford to buy an instrument of his own, but he continued to advance his playing ability, borrowing a cornet whenever he could and playing with any band that would hire him. He was, of course, some years away from earning his living through music but took playing jobs in order to supplement earnings from manual work, mainly delivering coal with a horse and cart.

Through his late teens, Armstrong played in many of the countless bands that made their home in New Orleans (not all of which could be thought of as jazz groups), gradually working his way upwards until he was in demand for engagements with some of the city's best bands. The fact that Armstrong's introduction to music came through the home's band is significant in that he was inducted into a musical tradition different from that which was currently developing into the newly emergent style known as jazz. The Waif's Home band played formal brass band music that placed certain demands upon musicians, not least of which were precision and an ornate bravura style. When Armstrong put this concept of music to work with the ideals of jazz, it resulted in a much more flamboyant and personalized musical form than the ensemble playing of the new New Orleans jazz bands. Not surprisingly, this precocious young cornet player attracted the attention of the city's jazz masters, one of whom, Joe 'King' Oliver, was sufficiently impressed to become his musical coach and occasional employer. By the time that Armstrong came under Oliver's wing, around 1917, the older man was generally regarded as the best cornetist in New Orleans and few challenged his position as 'the King'.

Already displaying signs of great ambition, Armstrong knew that he needed the kind of advancement and kudos King Oliver could offer, even though Oliver's style of playing was rather simplistic and close to that of other early New Orleans cornetists, such as near-contemporaries Freddie Keppard and Buddy Petit. Much more important to Armstrong's career than musical tuition was the fact that his association with Oliver opened many doors that might otherwise have remained closed. Of special importance was the fact that through Oliver, the younger man was given the chance to take his talent out of the constrictions of one city and into the wide world beyond the bayous of Louisiana. In 1919 Oliver had been invited to take a band to Chicago (and before leaving, recommended his young protégé as his replacement with Kid Ory), and by 1922 his was the most popular ensemble in the Windy City. Back in New Orleans, Armstrong's star continued to rise even though he declined to stay with Ory when the latter was invited to take his band to Los Angeles. Armstrong, chronically shy, preferred to stay in the place that he knew; but when Oliver sent word for him to come to Chicago, he went. The reason he overcame his earlier reluctance to travel was in part his ambition and also the fact that he trusted Oliver implicitly. From the moment of Armstrong's arrival in Chicago the local musical scene was tipped onto its ear; musicians raved about the duets of the King and the young pretender and if the lay members of the audience did not know exactly what it was that they were hearing, they certainly knew that it was something special.

For two years Oliver and Armstrong made musical history and, had it not been for the piano player in the band, they might well have continued doing so for many more years. The piano player was Lillian Hardin, who took a special interest in the young cornetist and became the second major influence in his life. By 1924 Armstrong and Hardin were married and her influence had prompted him to quit Oliver's band and soon afterwards to head for New York. In New York, Armstrong joined Fletcher Henderson's orchestra, bringing to that band a quality of solo playing far exceeding anything the city had heard thus far in jazz. His musical ideas, some of which were harmonies he and Oliver had developed, were also a spur to the writing of Henderson's staff arranger, Don Redman. Armstrong stayed with Henderson for a little over a year, returning to Chicago in 1925 at his wife's behest to star as the 'World's Greatest Trumpeter' with her band. Over the next two or three years he recorded extensively, including the first of the famous Hot Five and Hot Seven sessions and as accompanist to the best of the blues singers, among them Bessie Smith, Clara Smith and Trixie Smith. He worked ceaselessly, in 1926 doubling with the orchestras of Carroll Dickerson and Erskine Tate, and becoming, briefly, a club owner with two of his closest musical companions, Earl Hines and Zutty Singleton. By the end of the decade Armstrong was in demand across the country, playing important engagements in Chicago, New York, Washington, Los Angeles (but not New Orleans, a city to which he hardly ever returned).

By the 30s, Armstrong had forsaken the cornet for the trumpet. He frequently worked with name bands yet equally often travelled alone, fronting whichever house band was available at his destination. He worked and recorded in Los Angeles with Les Hite's band (in which the drummer was Lionel Hampton), and in New York with Chick Webb. In 1932 and 1933 he made his first visits to Europe, playing to largely ecstatic audiences, although some, accustomed only to hearing him on record, found his stage mannerisms – the mugging and clowning, to say nothing of the sweating – rather difficult to accommodate. From 1935 onwards Armstrong fronted the Luis Russell orchestra, eclipsing the remarkable talents of the band's leading trumpeter, Henry 'Red' Allen. In 1938 Louis and Lillian were divorced and he married Alpha Smith. However, by 1942 he had married again, to Lucille Wilson, who survived him. In some respects, the swing era passed Louis Armstrong by, leading some observers to suggest that his career was on a downward slide from that point on. Certainly, the big band Armstrong fronted in the 30s was generally inferior to many of its competitors, but his playing was always at least as strong as that of any of the other virtuoso instrumentalist leaders of the era. His musical style, however, was a little out of step with public demand, and by the early 40s he was out of vogue. Since 1935 Armstrong's career had been in the hands of Joe Glaser, a tough-talking, hard-nosed extrovert whom people either loved or hated. Ruthless in his determination to make his clients rich and famous, Glaser promoted Armstrong intensively. When the big band showed signs of flagging, Glaser fired everyone and then hired younger, more aggressive (if not always musically appropriate) people to back his star client. When this failed to work out, Glaser took a cue from an engagement at New York's Town Hall at which Armstrong fronted a small band to great acclaim. Glaser set out to form a new band that would be made up of stars and which he planned to market under the name Louis Armstrong And His All Stars. It proved to be a perfect format for Armstrong and it remained the setting for his music for the rest of his life – even though changes in personnel gradually made a nonsense of the band's hyperbolic title.

With the All Stars, Armstrong began a relentless succession of world tours with barely a night off, occasionally playing clubs and festivals but most often filling concert halls with adoring crowds. The first All Stars included Jack Teagarden, Barney Bigard, Earl Hines and Big Sid Catlett; replacements in the early years included Trummy Young, Edmond Hall, Billy Kyle and William 'Cozy' Cole. Later substitutes, when standards slipped, included 'Big Chief' Russell Moore, Joe Darensbourg, and Barrett Deems. Regulars for many years were bassist Arvell Shaw and singer Velma Middleton. The format and content of the All Stars shows (copied to dire and detrimental effect by numerous bands in the traditional jazz boom of the 50s and 60s) were predictable, with solos being repeated night after night, often note for note. This helped to fuel the contention that Armstrong was past his best. In fact, some of the All Stars' recordings, even those made with the lesser bands, show that this was not the case. The earliest All Stars are excitingly presented on *Satchmo At Symphony Hall* and *New Orleans Nights*, while the later bands produced some classic performances on *Louis Armstrong Plays*

W.C. Handy and *Satch Plays Fats*. On all these recordings Armstrong's own playing is outstanding. However, time inevitably took its toll and eventually even Armstrong's powerful lip weakened. It was then that another facet of his great talent came into its own. Apparent to any who cared to hear it since the 20s, Armstrong was a remarkable singer.

By almost any standards but those of the jazz world, his voice was beyond redemption, but through jazz it became recognized for what it was: a perfect instrument for jazz singing. Armstrong's throaty voice, his lazy-sounding delivery, his perfect timing and effortlessly immaculate rhythmic presentation, brought to songs of all kinds a remarkable sense of rightness. Perfect examples of this form were the riotous '(I Want) A Butter And Egg Man' through such soulfully moving lyrics as '(What Did I Do To Be So) Black And Blue', 'Do You Know What It Means To Miss New Orleans', and countless superb renditions of the blues. He added comic absurdities to 'Baby, It's Cold Outside' and over-sentimentality to 'What A Wonderful World', which in 1968 gave him a UK number 1 hit. He added texture and warmth and a rare measure of understanding often far exceeding anything that had been put there by the songs' writers. Additionally, he was one of the first performers to sing scat (the improvisation of wordless vocal sounds in place of the formal lyrics), and certainly the first to do so with skill and intelligence and not through mere chance (although he always claimed that he began scatting when the sheet music for 'Heebie Jeebies' fell on the floor during a 1926 recording session and he had to improvise the words). It was in his late years, as a singer and entertainer rather than as a trumpet star, that Armstrong became a world figure, known by name, sight and sound to tens of millions of people of all nationalities and creeds, who also loved him in a way that the urchin kid from the wrong side of the tracks in turn-of-the-century New Orleans could never have imagined. Armstrong's world status caused him some problems with other black Americans, many of whom believed he should have done more for his fellow blacks. He was openly criticized for the manner in which he behaved, whether on stage or off, some accusing him of being an Uncle Tom and thus pandering to stereotypical expectations of behaviour. Certainly, he was no militant, although he did explode briefly in a fit of anger when interviewed at the time of the Civil Rights protests over events in Little Rock in 1958. What his critics overlooked was that, by the time of Little Rock, Armstrong was almost 60 years old, and when the Civil Rights movement hit its full stride he was past the age at which most of his contemporaries were slipping contentedly into retirement. To expect a man of this age to wholeheartedly embrace the Civil Rights movement, having been born and raised in conditions even fellow blacks of one or two generations later could scarcely comprehend, was simply asking too much. For almost 50 years he had been an entertainer – he would probably have preferred and used the term 'hustler' – and he was not about to change.

Louis Armstrong toured on until almost the very end, recovering from at least one heart attack (news reports tended to be very cagey about his illnesses – doubtless Joe Glaser saw to that). He died in his sleep at his New York home on 6 July 1971. With only a handful of exceptions, most trumpet players who came after Armstrong owe some debt to his pioneering stylistic developments. By the early 40s, the date chosen by many as marking the first decline in Armstrong's importance and ability, jazz style was undergoing major changes. Brought about largely by the work of Charlie Parker and his musical collaborators, chief among whom was trumpeter Dizzy Gillespie, jazz trumpet style changed and the Armstrong style no longer had immediate currency. However, his influence was only sidetracked; it never completely disappeared, and in the post-bop era the qualities of technical proficiency and dazzling technique that he brought to jazz were once again appreciated for the remarkable achievements they were. In the early 20s Louis Armstrong had become a major influence on jazz musicians and jazz music; he altered the way musicians thought about their instruments and the way that they played them. There have been many virtuoso performers in jazz since Armstrong first came onto the scene, but nobody has matched his virtuosity or displayed a comparable level of commitment to jazz, a feeling for the blues, or such simple and highly communicable *joie de vivre*. Louis Armstrong was unique. The music world is fortunate to have received his outstanding contribution.

● ALBUMS: With such a discography it is often a problem to decide if the release is a compilation or a regular album. Bearing in mind that Armstrong 'best of' albums and compilations have been appearing since the advent of the long-playing record, you will appreciate our problem.

Armstrong Classics 10-inch album (Brunswick 1950) ★★★, *New Orleans To New York* 10-inch album (Decca 1950) ★★★, *New Orleans Days* 10-inch album (Decca 1950) ★★★, *Jazz Concert* 10-inch album (Decca 1950) ★★★, *Satchmo Serenades* 10-inch album (Decca 1952) ★★★, *Town Hall Concert '48* 10-inch album (Decca 1951) ★★★, *Louis Armstrong Plays The Blues* 10-inch album (Riverside 1953) ★★★, *Louis Armstrong With King Oliver's Creole Jazz Band 1923* 10-inch album (Riverside 1953) ★★★, *Louis Armstrong And The Mills Brothers* 10-inch album (Decca 1954) ★★★★, *Louis Armstrong-Gordon Jenkins* 10-inch album (Decca 1954) ★★★, *Latter Day Louis* 10-inch album (Decca 1954) ★★★, *Satchmo At Symphony Hall* (Decca 1954) ★★★★, *Louis Armstrong Plays W.C. Handy* (Columbia 1954) ★★★★, *Louis Armstrong And His All Stars Live At The Crescendo Club, Los Angeles Volumes 1 And 2* (Decca 1955) ★★★, *Sings The Blues* (RCA Victor 1954) ★★★★, *Satch Plays Fats* (Columbia 1955) ★★★, *Louis Armstrong Plays W.C. Handy Volume 2* 10-inch album (Columbia 1955) ★★★, *Satchmo Sings* (Decca 1955) ★★★, *Ambassador Satch* (Columbia 1956) ★★★, *Satchmo The Great* film soundtrack

(Columbia 1956) ★★, *Louis Armstrong And His All Stars Live At Pasadena* ii (Decca 1956) ★★★, with Ella Fitzgerald *Ella And Louis* (Verve 1956) ★★★★★, with Fitzgerald *Porgy And Bess* (Verve 1956) ★★★★★, with Fitzgerald *Ella And Louis Again* (Verve 1956) ★★★★★, *Town Hall Concert* (RCA Victor 1957) ★★★, *Louis And The Angels* (Decca 1957) ★★★, *Satchmo On Stage* (Decca 1957) ★★, *Louis Under The Stars* (Verve 1957) ★★★, *Louis Armstrong Meets Oscar Peterson* (Verve 1957) ★★★, *Louis And The Good Book* (Decca 1958) ★★★, *Satchmo In Style* (Decca 1958) ★★★, *I've Got The World on A String* (Verve 1959) ★★★, with Bing Crosby *Bing And Satchmo* (MGM 1960) ★★★★, *A Rare Batch Of Satch* (RCA Victor 1961) ★★★, *Louis Armstrong And Duke Ellington: The Great Reunion* (Roulette 1961) ★★★, *Louis Armstrong And Duke Ellington: Together Again* (Roulette 1961) ★★★★, *I Love Jazz* (Decca 1962) ★★★, *Hello, Dolly!* (Kapp 1964) ★★★★, *What A Wonderful World* (ABC 1967) ★★★★, *Disney Songs The Satchmo Way* (Disney 1968) ★★, *Louis 'Country & Western' Armstrong* (Columbia 1970) ★, *The Great Chicago Concert 1956* (Columbia 1980) ★★★.

● COMPILATIONS: *The Louis Armstrong Story Volumes 1-4* (Columbia 1951) ★★★★★, *Louis Armstrong Plays King Oliver* (Audio Fidelity 1960) ★★★★, *Satchmo 1930-34* (Decca 1962) ★★★, *The Essential Armstrong* (Verve 1963) ★★★★, *The Best Of Louis Armstrong* (Verve 1963) ★★★★, *Louis Armstrong In The 30s And 40s* (RCA Victor 1964) ★★★★, *King Oliver's Creole Jazz Band* 1923-1924 recordings (Milestone) ★★★★, *Louis Armstrong And The Fletcher Henderson Orchestra* 1924-1926 recordings (VJM 1979) ★★★★, *Louis Armstrong & Sidney Bechet* 1924-1925 recordings (Jazz Masters 1983) ★★★★, *Louis In Los Angeles* 1930-1931 recordings (Swaggie 1983) ★★★, *Young Louis Armstrong* 1930-1933 recordings (RCA 1983) ★★★, *The Louis Armstrong Legend Volumes 1-4* 1925-1929 recordings (Retrospect 1985) ★★★★, *Louis Armstrong VSOP Volumes 1-8* 1925-1932 recordings (Columbia 1988) ★★★, *The Hot Fives And Hot Sevens Volumes 1-4* 1925-28 recordings (Columbia 1988-1990) ★★★★, *Satchmo Style* 1929-1930 recordings (DRG 1988) ★★★, *Louis Armstrong And His Orchestra* 1935-1941 recordings (Swaggie 1988) ★★★★, *The Ultimate Collection* (RCA 1994) ★★★★★, *The Essential Recordings Of Louis Armstrong: West End Blues 1926-1933* (Indigo 1995) ★★★★, *Butter And Eggman* 1929-1959 recordings (Tomato/Rhino 1995) ★★★, *American Legends Volume 5* (Laserlight 1996) ★★★, *Christmas Through The Years* (RCA Victor 1996) ★★★, *This Is Louis* (Camden 1997) ★★★, *The Complete RCA Victor Recordings* 4-CD box set (RCA Victor 1997) ★★★★★, with Ella Fitzgerald *The Complete Ella Fitzgerald & Louis Armstrong On Verve* 3-CD box set (Verve 1997) ★★★★★, with King Oliver, Bessie Smith *High Society* (Tradition/Rykodisc 1997) ★★★★, *Now You Has Jazz* (Rhino 1998) ★★★★★, *Master Of Jazz: Louis In Chicago, 1962* (Storyville 1998) ★★★, *Satchmo Sings & Satchmo Serenades* (Universal/MCA 1998) ★★★, *Louis And The Angels & Louis And The Good Book* (Universal/MCA 1998)

★★★, *Midnights At V-Disc* 40s recordings, reissue (Jazz Unlimited 1998) ★★★, *Louis Armstrong Sings* 1927-55 recordings (Columbia 1998) ★★★, *Jazz Greats* 1933-70 recordings (RCA Victor 1998) ★★, *Louis Armstrong Vol. 8* 1941-42 recordings (Ambassador 1998) ★★★, *Chronological* 1946-47 recordings (Classics 1998) ★★★, *Louis Armstrong Vol. 1 (Revised)* 1935 recordings (Ambassador 1998) ★★★, with Crosby *Fun With Bing And Louis 1949-51* (Jasmine 1998) ★★★, with Fitzgerald *Sings Gershwin's Our Love Is Here To Stay* (Verve 1998) ★★★, *An American Icon* 3-CD set, 1946-1954 recordings (Hip-O 1999) ★★★, *Hot Fives And Sevens* 4-CD box set (JSP 1999) ★★★★★, *West End Blues: The Very Best Of The Hot Fives & Hot Sevens* (MCI 2000) ★★★★, *Ken Burns Jazz: The Definitive Louis Armstrong* (Verve 2000) ★★★★, *Sugar: The Best Of The Complete RCA-Victor Recordings* (BMG 2001) ★★★★★.

● VIDEOS: *Wonderful World* (Kay Jazz 1988), *Satchmo* (CMV Enterprises 1989), *Louis Armstrong* (Stylus Video 1990), *Good Years Of Jazz Volume 1* (Storyville 1990), *Louis Armstrong On Television* (Virgin Vision 1991).

● FURTHER READING: *Satchmo: My Life In New Orleans*, Louis Armstrong. *Salute To Satchmo*, Max Jones, John Chilton and Leonard Feather. *Louis Armstrong: A Self-Portrait*, Richard Meryman. *The Louis Armstrong Story, 1900-1971*, M. Jones and J. Chilton. *Boy From New Orleans: Louis 'Satchmo' Armstrong*, Hans Westerberg. *Louis Armstrong: An American Genius*, James Lincoln Collier. *With Louis And The Duke*, B. Bigard. *Satchmo, The Genius Of Louis Armstrong*, Gary Giddins. *Louis Armstrong: An Extravagant Life*, Laurence Bergreen. *Louis Armstrong: The Definitive Biography*, Ilse Strorb. *Louis Armstrong In His Own Words: Selected Writings*, Louis Armstrong.

● FILMS: *Pennies From Heaven* (1936), *Every Day's A Holiday* (1937), *Artists And Models* (1938), *Dr Rhythm* (1938), *Going Places* (1939), *The Birth Of The Blues* (1941), *Cabin In The Sky* (1943), *Hollywood Canteen* (1944), *Atlantic City* (1944), *Jam Session* (1944), *New Orleans* (1947), *A Song Is Born* (1948), *Glory Alley* (1951), *Here Comes The Groom* (1951), *The Strip* (1951), *The Glenn Miller Story* (1954), *High Society* (1956), *Satchmo The Great* (1957), *The Five Pennies* (1959), *The Beat Generation* (1959), *Jazz On A Summer's Day* (1961), *Paris Blues* (1961), *When The Boys Meet The Girls* (1962), *A Man Called Adam* (1966), *Hello Dolly* (1969).

ARNAZ, DESI

b. Desiderio Alberto Arnez y de Acha III, 2 March 1917, Santiago, Cuba, d. 2 December 1986, Del Mar, California, USA. Arnaz came to the USA in the early 20s and began singing and playing bongo and conga drums with Xaviar Cugat and others before forming his own band. Arnaz achieved sufficient popularity to be offered musical spots in movies. While working on one of these, *Dance, Girl, Dance* (1940), he met and subsequently married Lucille Ball. In the late 40s, Ball appeared on radio in a popular series, *My Favourite Husband*, in which she co-starred with actor Richard Denning. In the early 50s, Ball decided to adapt the show for television with her real-life husband as producer, and she also decided that Arnaz should play her television husband – two decisions frowned upon by executives at CBS Records and Philip Morris (cigarette makers and potential sponsors for the show). Their reluctance stemmed from the fact that as a producer Arnaz was an unknown quantity and as an actor he was a potential liability because of his pronounced Cuban accent. In the event, Ball and Arnaz prevailed but had to make concessions. These included taking a salary reduction, though as compensation CBS made the multi-million-dollar blunder of allowing the couple to retain 100% residuals. The new show, I Love Lucy, was a runaway success and made a fortune for Desilu, the company Ball and Arnaz had formed to produce the show. I Love Lucy ran until 1959 and the following year the couple were divorced, although they continued as business partners. After I Love Lucy, Ball starred in The Lucy Show which was produced by Arnaz. In 1962, Ball bought out Arnaz's share of their company and for a while ran Desilu on her own, producing such popular television shows as Star Trek and Mission: Impossible. Arnaz made a few movie appearances in the mid-50s, including the popular The Long, Long Trailer with Ball, but then drifted into retirement. Later, he returned for occasional cameo roles, produced the NBC television series The Mothers-In-Law (1967), which starred Eve Arden and Kaye Ballard, and published his autobiography. His daughter, Lucie Arnaz, gained favourable reviews for her singing in New York clubs in the early 90s. In 1993, she, and her husband, Laurence Luckinbill, were the executive producers of Lucy And Desi: A Home Movie, 'their own version of Lucy and Desi's entwined careers', which was shown in the USA on NBC Television.

● FURTHER READING: The Book, Desi Arnaz. Desilu: The Story Of Lucille Ball And Desi Arnaz, Coyne Steven Sanders and Tom Gilbert.
● FILMS: The Long Long Trailer (1954), Forever Darling (1956), The Escape Artist (1982).

ARNOLD, BILLY BOY

b. 16 September 1935, Chicago, Illinois, USA. Arnold first played blues harmonica with Bo Diddley's group in 1950 and became a well-known figure in Chicago blues throughout the following two decades. Among those he accompanied were Johnny Shines and Otis Rush. With a serviceable singing voice and a harmonica style influenced by John Lee 'Sonny Boy' Williamson, Arnold recorded as a solo artist for local labels Cool ('Hello Stranger', 1952) and Vee Jay Records. In 1958 he led a group that included Mighty Joe Young and recorded for Mighty H. However, none of Arnold's records were as successful as the mid-50s hits of Bo Diddley such as 'Pretty Thing' and 'Hey Bo Diddley', to which he contributed the keening harp phrases. The most renowned of Arnold's own tracks is 'I Wish You Would' (Vee Jay), which was adopted by UK R&B group the Yardbirds in the 60s. During the mid-60s blues boom, he cut an album for Prestige/Bluesville,

recorded with pianist Johnny Jones (a 1963 session that remained unreleased for 17 years), and there was also a later album for Vogue. Not forgotten by European blues enthusiasts, Arnold toured there in 1975 as part of the Blues Legends package, recording albums for Peter Shertser's UK-based Red Lightnin'. He made a more prominent comeback in the early 90s, recording some excellent sides for Alligator Records.

● ALBUMS: More Blues On The South Side (Prestige/ Bluesville 1963) ★★★, Blow The Back Off It (Red Lightnin' 1975) ★★★, Sinner's Prayer (Red Lightnin' 1976) ★★★, with Johnny Jones Checkin' It Out aka Johnny Jones & Billy Boy Arnold 1963 recording (Red Lightnin'/Alligator 1979) ★★★, Ten Million Dollars (Evidence 1984) ★★★, Back Where I Belong (Alligator 1993) ★★★, Eldorado Cadillac (Alligator 1995) ★★★, Live At The Venue 1980 recording (Catfish 2000) ★★★, Boogie N' Shuffle (Stony Plain 2001) ★★★.
● COMPILATIONS: Blowin' The Blues Away (Culture Press 1998) ★★★, Catfish (Catfish 1999) ★★★.

ARNOLD, EDDY

b. Richard Edward Arnold, 15 May 1918, on a farm near Madisonville, Chester County, Tennessee, USA. Arnold's father and mother played fiddle and guitar, respectively, and he learned guitar as a child. His father died on Eddy's 11th birthday and he left school to work on the farm. By the end of the year the bank foreclosed, and the farm was sold but the family stayed as sharecroppers. Deciding that such a thing would not happen to him again he turned his thoughts to music and began playing at local dances. In 1936, working with a fiddle-playing friend, Speedy McNatt, he made his debut on local radio WTJS Jackson and during the next few years played various cities including Memphis, Louisville and St. Louis. Between 1940 and 1943 he was a member of Pee Wee King's Golden West Cowboys, appearing with them on the Grand Ole Opry and touring with the Opry's travelling Camel Caravan Show. Late in 1943, as 'The Tennessee Plowboy', he launched his solo career, playing six days a week on WSM. Signed by RCA Records he made his country chart debut in 1945 with 'Each Minute Seems A Million Years' and soon replaced Roy Acuff as country music's most popular and prolific singer. Between 1945 and 1955 he had 21 number 1 singles among his 68 US country chart hits. Sentimental ballads, incorporating the plaintive steel guitar work of Little Roy Wiggins, were the norm and many, such as the million-sellers 'I'll Hold You In My Heart (Till I Can Hold You In My Arms)', 'Anytime', 'Bouquet Of Roses' and 'Just A Little Lovin' Will Go A Long Way', also became Top 30 US pop chart hits. Perhaps his best-remembered recording from this decade is 'Cattle Call'.

During the late 40s he varied his image: although still retaining the nickname, he became a country crooner, wearing a tuxedo and bow tie. Colonel Tom Parker became his manager and was so successful with his promotion that Arnold was soon a nationally known star. Some of Parker's publicity stunts were unique for their time, such as the occasion when he travelled to a disc jockey convention in Nashville astride an elephant, bearing a cloth saying 'Never Forget Eddy Arnold'. Arnold began his solo *Grand Ole Opry* career as host of the *Ralston Purina* segment in 1946 but in 1948, due to Parker's unacceptable demands on the WSM management for shares of gate receipts, he left, being replaced on the roster by another country crooner, George Morgan. In 1948, with the exception of Jimmy Wakely's recording of 'One Has My Heart', Arnold's recordings held the number 1 position in the country charts for the whole year. Arnold eventually tired of Parker's management and apparently sacked him; he has said it was because 'I am a very conservative man', but few believed that was the sole reason.

During the 50s, he appeared on all major radio and television shows and became the first country singer to host his own network television show, *Eddy Arnold Time*. He also became one of the first country singers to play at Carnegie Hall and later appeared in concerts with major symphony orchestras. It is impossible to categorize his new style as either country or pure pop. Many of his early fans objected to it but the television and cabaret performances won him countless new fans from the wider audience and he easily maintained his popularity and chart successes. After 1954, his nickname no longer appeared on the records and he moved to MGM Records in 1972, but returned to RCA four years later. Between 1956 and 1983 he took his tally of US country chart hits to 145, and his number 1 singles to 28 (and 92 of the entries had made the Top 10!). Again, many recordings achieved crossover success, including 'Tennessee Stud', 'What's He Doing In My World' and his biggest US pop hit, 'Make The World Go Away', which reached number 6 in 1965 and the next year repeated the feat in the UK pop charts. Several of his albums also achieved Top 10 status in the US album charts. He appeared in several movies, including starring roles in *Feudin' Rhythm* and *Hoedown*, and he even received a mention in *Jailhouse Rock*. He was elected to the Country Music Hall Of Fame in 1966 and by the 80s he had semi-retired to his home near Nashville. RCA have assessed that his record sales are in excess of 85 million. It is quite astonishing that Elvis Presley *et al*. are automatically regarded as the most successful chart acts. Arnold's chart success eclipses everybody and is unlikely ever to be beaten.

● ALBUMS: *Anytime* (RCA 1952) ★★★★, *All-Time Hits From The Hills* (RCA 1952) ★★★★, *All-Time Favorites* (RCA 1953) ★★★★, *An American Institution (10th Anniversary Album)* (RCA 1954) ★★★, *Chapel On The Hill* (RCA 1954) ★★★, *Wanderin' With Eddy Arnold* (RCA 1955) ★★★, *Anytime* (RCA 1955) ★★★★, *A Dozen Hits* (RCA 1956) ★★★, *A Little On The Lonely Side* (RCA 1956) ★★★, *When They Were Young* (RCA 1957) ★★★, *My Darling, My Darling* (RCA 1957) ★★★, *Praise Him, Praise Him (Fanny Crosby Hymns)* (RCA 1958) ★★, *Have Guitar, Will Travel* reissued as *Eddy Arnold Goes Travelin'* (RCA 1959) ★★★★, *Eddy*

Arnold (RCA 1959) ★★★★, *Thereby Hangs A Tale* (RCA 1959) ★★★, *Eddy Arnold Sings Them Again* (RCA 1960) ★★★, *More Eddy Arnold* (RCA 1960) ★★★★, *You Gotta Have Love* (RCA 1960) ★★★, *Christmas With Eddy Arnold* (RCA 1961) ★★, *Let's Make Memories Tonight* (RCA 1961) ★★★, *One More Time* (RCA 1962) ★★★★, *Our Man Down South* (RCA 1963) ★★★, *Country Songs I Love To Sing* (RCA 1963) ★★★, *Faithfully Yours* (RCA 1963) ★★★, *Cattle Call* (RCA 1963) ★★★★, *Pop Hits From The Country Side* (RCA 1964) ★★★, *Eddy's Songs* (RCA 1964) ★★★, with Needmore Creek Singers *Folk Song Book* (RCA 1964) ★★★, *Sometimes I'm Happy, Sometimes I'm Blue* (RCA 1964) ★★★, *The Easy Way* (RCA 1965) ★★★, *I'm Throwing Rice (At The Girl I Love)* (RCA 1965) ★★★, *My World* (RCA 1965) ★★★, *Somebody Liked Me* (RCA 1966) ★★★, *I Want To Go With You* (RCA 1966) ★★★, *The Last Word In Lonesome* (RCA 1966) ★★★, *Lonely Again* (RCA 1967) ★★★, *Turn The World Around* (RCA 1967) ★★★, *The Everloving World Of Eddy Arnold* (RCA 1968) ★★★★, *Romantic World Of Eddy Arnold* (RCA 1968) ★★★★, *Walkin' In Love Land* (RCA 1968) ★★★, *Songs Of The Young World* (RCA 1969) ★★★, *The Warmth Of Eddy Arnold* (RCA 1969) ★★★, *The Glory Of Love* (RCA 1969) ★★★, *This Is Eddy Arnold* (RCA 1970) ★★★★, *Standing Alone* (RCA 1970) ★★★, *Love And Guitars* (RCA 1970) ★★★, *Then You Can Tell Me Goodbye* (RCA 1971) ★★★, *Welcome To My World* (RCA 1971) ★★★, *Loving Her Was Easier* (RCA 1971) ★★★, *Portrait Of My Woman* (RCA 1971) ★★★, *Chained To A Memory* (MGM 1972) ★★★, *Eddy Arnold (Sings For Housewives & Other Lovers)* (MGM 1972) ★★, *Lonely People* (MGM 1972) ★★★, *I Love How You Love Me* (MGM 1973) ★★★, *The World Of Eddy Arnold* (MGM 1973) ★★★★, *Christmas Greetings From Nashville* (MGM 1973) ★★★, *So Many Ways/If The Whole World Stopped Lovin'* (MGM 1973) ★★★, *Eddy Arnold Sings Love Songs* (MGM 1974) ★★★, *I Wish That I Had Loved You Better* (MGM 1974) ★★★, *Misty Blue* (MGM 1974) ★★★, *She's Got Everything I Need* (MGM 1974) ★★★, *The Wonderful World Of Eddy Arnold* (MGM 1975) ★★★★, *Eddy* (MGM 1976) ★★★, *Eddy Arnold's World Of Hits* (MGM 1976) ★★★★, *I Need You All The Time* (RCA 1977) ★★★, *Somebody Loves You* (RCA 1979) ★★★, *A Legend And His Lady* (RCA 1980) ★★★, *Man For All Seasons* (RCA 1981) ★★★, *Country Music – Eddy Arnold* (RCA 1981) ★★★, *Don't Give Up On Me* (RCA 1982) ★★★, *Close Enough To Love* (RCA 1983) ★★★, *Anytime* (RCA 1988) ★★★, *Christmas With Eddy Arnold* (RCA 1990) ★★, *Hand-Holdin' Songs* (RCA 1990) ★★★, *You Don't Miss A Thing* (RCA 1991) ★★★, *Last Of The Love Song Singers: Then & Now* (RCA 1993) ★★★, *Seven Decades Of Hits* (Curb 2000) ★★.

● COMPILATIONS: *The Best Of Eddy Arnold* (RCA 1967) ★★★, *Living Legend* (K-Tel 1974) ★★★★, *Country Gold* (RCA 1975) ★★★, *Pure Gold-Eddy Arnold* (RCA 1975) ★★★, *Eddy Arnold's Best* (RCA 1979) ★★★, *20 Of The Best* (RCA 1982) ★★★, *Eddy Arnold – A Legendary Performer* (RCA 1983) ★★★, *Collector's Series* (RCA 1987) ★★★, *All Time Favourites* (RCA 1987) ★★★★, *Best Of Eddy Arnold*

(Curb 1990) ★★★, *The Essential Eddy Arnold* (RCA 1996) ★★★★, *Strictly From The Hills* (Bronco Buster 1998) ★★★★, *The Tennessee Plowboy And His Guitar* 5-CD box set (Bear Family 1998) ★★★★.
● FURTHER READING: *It's A Long Way From Chester County*, Eddy Arnold.
● FILMS: *Feudin' Rhythm* (1949), *Hoedown* (1950).

ARNOLD, MALCOLM

b. 21 October 1921, Northampton, England. A composer, conductor, arranger and trumpet player, Arnold became aware of music at the age of four, and taught himself to play trumpet – his inspiration was Louis Armstrong. He began his career in 1941 as an instrumentalist with the London Philharmonic Orchestra, and returned to the orchestra in 1946 after brief service in World War II, and a spell with the BBC Symphony Orchestra. During these times he was also composing; one of his best-known pieces, 'Sea Shanties', was written in 1943. He became a full-time composer in the early 50s, and soon won much critical acclaim as 'one of the great hopes of UK music'. His work schedule was exhausting; from 1951-56 he is said to have written the music for over 70 films, as well as three operas, ballet music, concertos and other classical and light works. One of his more unusual compositions was the 'Grand Overture' for a Gerald Hoffnung concert, in which the more conventional instruments of the orchestra were augmented by three vacuum cleaners and an electric polisher. His film scores, many of which complemented classic UK productions, include *The Sound Barrier* (1952), *The Holly And The Ivy*, *The Captain's Paradise*, *Hobson's Choice*, *Prize Of Gold*, *I Am A Camera*, *Trapeze*, *Tiger In The Smoke*, *The Deep Blue Sea*, *Island In The Sun*, *The Bridge On The River Kwai* (one of the film's six Oscars went to Arnold), *Blue Murder At St. Trinians*, *The Inn Of The Sixth Happiness* (the film theme won an Ivor Novello Award in 1959), *The Key*, *The Root Of Heaven*, *Dunkirk*, *Tunes Of Glory*, *The Angry Silence*, *No Love For Johnnie*, *The Inspector*, *Whistle Down The Wind*, *The Lion*, *Nine Hours To Rama*, *The Chalk Garden*, *The Heroes Of Telemark*, *The Thin Red Line*, *Sky West And Crooked*, and *The Reckoning* (1969).
During the 60s Arnold was ignored, even reviled, by critics and sections of the concert and broadcasting establishment. He was dismissed as 'a clown', and his work was criticized as being 'out of phase' with contemporary trends in music. Arnold developed alcohol problems, suffered several nervous breakdowns, and attempted suicide more than once. He continued to write, when he was able, and was particularly interested in brass band music, but his work generally remained unappreciated. His ninth and final symphony, written in 1986, still had not received an official premiere by 1991, when low-key celebrations for his 70th birthday involved a concert at London's Queen Elizabeth Hall, which included his double violin concerto, commissioned by Yehudi Menuhin in 1962. In 1993, Malcolm Arnold received a knighthood in the Queen's New Year honours list.

● ALBUMS: *Malcolm Arnold Film Music* (Chandos 1992) ★★★★, *Arnold Overtures* (Reference Recordings 1992) ★★★★.
● FURTHER READING: *Malcolm Arnold: A Catalogue Of His Music*, A. Poulton.

AROUND THE WORLD IN 80 DAYS – VARIOUS ARTISTS

Producer Mike Todd persuaded more than 40 major stars, including Frank Sinatra, Marlene Dietrich and Ronald Colman, to contribute cameo roles to this 1957 widescreen treatment of Jules Verne's classic story in which David Niven as Phileas Fogg and his 'man', Passepartout, played by the Mexican comedian Cantiflas, circumnavigate the globe. They were accompanied by veteran composer Victor Young's breathtakingly beautiful musical themes which thrilled record-buyers to such an extent that this album stayed at number 1 in the USA for 10 weeks, although it did not reach the UK charts. The composer's Academy Award for his work was a fitting end to a distinguished career that ended a few months after the film's release.
● Tracks: *Around The World (main theme); Around The World Part II; Entrance Of The Bull March (medley); Epilogue; India Country Side; Invitation To A Bull Fight (medley); Land Ho; Pagoda Of Pillagi; Paris Arrival; Passepartout; Prairie Sail Car; Sky Symphony*.
● First released 1957
● UK peak chart position: did not chart
● USA peak chart position: 1

AT NEWPORT – DUKE ELLINGTON

This concert marked the so-called rebirth of Duke Ellington. Of course, it was the jazz audience that had lost sight of the band. However, *At Newport* saw the end of his temporary obscurity. Irritated by the place on the programme and his musicians' habitual tardiness, Ellington began the second set in a do-or-die mood. They did not die. Wonderful solos by Clark Terry, Johnny Hodges and Paul Gonsalves links the two parts of 'Diminuendo In Blue' and 'Crescendo In Blue', and makes this an evening that will live forever in the annals of jazz. Ellington had obviously intended to blow the audience away with the set. He succeeded beyond his wildest dreams.
● Tracks: *Newport Jazz Festival Suite – a) Festival Junction b) Blues To Be There c) Newport Up; Jeep's Blues; Diminuendo And Crescendo In Blue.*
● First released 1957
● UK peak chart position: did not chart
● USA peak chart position: 14

ATOMIC MR BASIE, THE – COUNT BASIE

An inspired collaboration that worked so well, it is surprising that Count Basie and Neal Hefti did not form a long-term Frank Sinatra/Nelson Riddle partnership. Hefti later found solace in writing musical opuses such as 'The Batman Theme'! Great for his bank balance, but little aid to his credibility. This, however, is a magnificent record that should always be played in its entirety. Basie rarely sounded so fresh and crisp. For a 1958 album, this is a staggering record. 'Splanky', in particular, spits out with an incredible force and their reading of 'Li'l Darlin' is definitive. The original engineer Bob Arnold deserves a special mention. The CD remastering is fabulous and comes with five bonus tracks.

● Tracks: *The Kid From Red Bank; Duet; After Supper; Flight Of The Foo Birds; Double-O; Teddy The Toad; Whirly-Bird; Midnite Blue; Splanky; Fantail; Li'l Darlin'; Silks And Satins; Sleepwalker's Serenade; Sleepwalker's Serenade (alternate take); The Late Late Show; The Late Late Show (vocal version).*
● First released 1958
● UK peak chart position: did not chart
● USA peak chart position: did not chart

ATWELL, WINIFRED

b. 1914, Tunapuna, Trinidad, d. February 1983, Sydney, Australia. Atwell began playing piano at the age of four, gave classical recitals when six and played concerts at the Services Club, Trinidad. She went to New York and studied with Alexander Borovsky before moving to London for tuition with Harold Craxton. Supplementing her income from classical music by playing boogie-woogie gained her a contract with Decca Records and throughout the 50s she had great success with a series of 'knees up' singalong medleys and 'rags', mostly on her old honky-tonk, 'other' piano. The first of these, 'Black And White Rag', was later selected as the signature tune for *Pot Black*, BBC Television's first regular snooker programme. Other 50s Top 10 hits were 'Britannia Rag', 'Coronation Rag', 'Flirtation Waltz', 'Let's Have A Party', 'Let's Have A Ding Dong', 'Make It A Party', 'Let's Have A Ball', 'Piano Party', and two chart-toppers, 'Let's Have Another Party' and 'The Poor People Of Paris'. Atwell's dubbing of John Mills' piano playing in the 1956 film *It's Great To Be Young*, included a jumping version of 'The Original Dixieland One Step'. Interrupting the pop, there was also the 'back to her roots' single, 'Rachmaninoff's 18th Variation On A Theme By Paganini', which went to number 9 in the UK chart. Thereafter, she continued to combine the two musical forms. At her peak she was a huge UK star, but in the 60s her career declined and in the 70s she went to live in Australia, where she died in 1983.

● ALBUMS: *Boogie With Winifred Atwell* (Decca 1955) ★★★★, *Around The World Of Winifred Atwell In Eighty Tunes* (Decca 1972) ★★★, *Seven Rags, Seven Boogies* (Eclipse 1975) ★★★, *It's Ragtime* (RCA 1982) ★★★, *Winifred Atwell Plays 50 All-Time Greats* (President 1983) ★★★★, *Winifred Atwell, Piano Party* (Flashback 1984) ★★★★, *Winnie's Piano Party* (President 1989) ★★★.
● COMPILATIONS: *Big Ben Boogie* (Gema 1995) ★★★★, *The Best Of Winifred Atwell* (Spectrum 2000) ★★★★.

AURIC, GEORGES

b. 15 February 1899, Lodève, Hérault, France, d. 23 July 1983, Paris, France. A composer of many classical pieces including an opera and ballet, and choral and instrumental music. From 1930 up to the early 60s, he contributed the scores to French films such as *Quand J'Ètais, A Nous La Liberté, Orphée* and *Belles De Nuit*. He also wrote the music for numerous English-speaking films, including several classic Ealing comedies. His scores included *Dead Of Night, Caesar And Cleopatra, Hue And Cry, It Always Rains On Sunday, Another Shore, Corridors Of Mirrors, Silent Dust, Passport To Pimlico, The Queen Of Spades, The Spider And The Fly, Cage Of Gold, The Galloping Major, The Lavender Hill Mob, Moulin Rouge, Roman Holiday, The Wages Of Fear, Father Brown, Rififi, The Witches Of Salem, Gervaise, The Picasso Mystery, Bonjour Tristesse, Heaven Knows Mr Allison, Heaven Fell That Night, The Innocents, The Mind Benders, Thomas The Impostor, Therese And Isabelle* and *The Christmas Tree*. The haunting theme from *Moulin Rouge* (1952), with a lyric by Bill Engvick ('Whenever we kiss, I worry and wonder/Your lips may be here, but where is your heart?'), became a hit in the USA for Percy Faith and his Orchestra, with the vocal by Felicia Sanders. A record of the title music from *Bonjour Tristesse* (1957), with words added by the film's screenwriter, Arthur Laurents, was popular for Gogi Grant. Auric published his autobiography in 1974.

AUTRY, GENE

b. Orvin Gene Autry, 29 September 1907, near Tioga, Texas, USA, d. 2 October 1998, Studio City, California, USA. The eldest of four children of Delbert Autry, a poor tenant farmer, who moved his family many times over the years, before eventually arriving at Ravia, Oklahoma. His grandfather, a Baptist minister, taught him to sing when he was a child so that he could perform in his church choir and at other local events. Autry also learned to ride at an early age and worked the fields with his father. He grew up listening to cowboy songs and received his first guitar at the age of 12 (initially he studied the saxophone but chose the guitar so that he could sing as well). He graduated from school in 1924 and found work as a telegraph operator for the Frisco Railroad in Chelsea, Oklahoma. He used to take his guitar to work and one night his singing was heard by the famous entertainer Will Rogers, who stopped to send a telegram. He suggested that Autry should look for a job in radio. After trying unsuccessfully to find work in New York, he returned to Oklahoma and began to appear on KVOO Tulsa as The Oklahoma Yodeling Cowboy. After hearing recordings of Jimmie Rodgers, he became something of a Rodgers clone as he tried to further his career. In 1929, he made his first RCA-Victor Records recordings, 'My Dreaming Of You' and 'My Alabama Home', on which he was accompanied by Jimmy Long (a fellow telegrapher) and Johnny Marvin and Frankie Marvin. Further recordings followed for ARC Records under the direction of Art Satherley, some being released on various labels for chain store sales. It was because of releases on Conqueror for Sears that Autry found himself given the opportunity to join WLS in Chicago. In

1931, he became a featured artist on the *National Barn Dance*, as well as having his own *Conqueror Record Time*. Before long, Gene Autry 'Roundup' guitars and songbooks were being sold by Sears. Interestingly, WLS portrayed him as a singing cowboy even though, at this time, few of his songs were of that genre. Between 1931 and 1934, he was a hillbilly singer, who still at times sounded like Rodgers. In fact, most experts later rated him the best of the Rodgers impersonators. He began to include his own songs and such numbers as 'The Gangster's Warning' and 'My Old Pal Of Yesterday' became very popular.

Late in 1931, he recorded 'That Silver Haired Daddy Of Mine' as a duet with Jimmy Long, with whom he had co-written the song. The song eventually became Autry's first million-selling record. By 1934, he was well known as a radio and recording personality. Having for some time been portrayed as a singing cowboy by the publicity departments of his record companies, he now took his first steps to make the publicity come true. He was given a small part in the Ken Maynard film *In Old Santa Fe*, and soon afterwards starred in a strange 12-episode western/science fiction serial called *The Phantom Empire*. In 1935, Republic Pictures signed him to a contract and *Tumbling Tumbleweeds* became his first starring western film. His previous singing cowboy image was now reality. He sang eight songs in the film including the title track, 'That Silver Haired Daddy' and 'Ridin' Down The Canyon'. Further films followed in quick succession and by 1940 Autry ranked fourth among all Hollywood money-making stars at the box office. In January 1940, Gene Autry's *Melody Ranch* radio show, sponsored by the Wrigley Gum Company, first appeared on CBS Records and soon became a national institution, running until 1956. Helped out by such artists as Pat Buttram, Johnny Bond and the Cass County Boys, Autry regularly righted wrongs, sang his hits and as a result of the programme, built himself a new home in the San Fernando Valley called Melody Ranch.

Quite apart from the radio shows and films, he toured extensively with his stage show. It featured roping, Indian dancers, comedy, music, fancy riding from Autry, and smart horse tricks by Champion. By 1941, he was respected and famous all over the USA The little town of Berwyn, Oklahoma, even changed its name to Gene Autry, Oklahoma. His songs such as 'Be Honest With Me', 'Back In The Saddle Again' (which became his signature tune), 'You're The Only Star In My Blue Heaven', 'Goodbye, Little Darlin' Goodbye' (later recorded by Johnny Cash) and many more, became tremendously popular. In 1942, his income took a severe cut when he enlisted in the Air Force, being sworn in live on a *Melody Ranch* programme. He spent some time working on recruitment but then became a pilot in Air Ferry Command and saw service in the Far East, India and North Africa. During this period, he co-wrote with Fred Rose his classic song 'At Mail Call Today'. After his release from the services, he resumed his acting and recording career. Between 1944 and

1951, he registered 25 successive Top 10 country hits, including 'Here Comes Santa Claus' (later recorded by Elvis Presley), 'Rudolph, The Red-Nosed Reindeer', 'Peter Cottontail' and 'Frosty The Snow Man', each of which sold 1 million copies. He also had six US Top 10 pop chart success in the same period. He left Republic in 1947 and formed his own Flying A Productions, which produced his later films for release by Columbia Pictures. When he made his last B-movie western, *Last Of The Pony Riders*, in 1953, he had 89 feature films to his credit. Contrary to prevailing belief, there never was a feud between Autry and his replacement at Republic, Roy Rogers – it was purely the invention of Republic's publicity department.

During the 50s, he became very successful in business and purchased many radio and television stations. Between 1950 and 1956, he produced 91 episodes of *The Gene Autry Show* for CBS-TV. His company also produced many other television series, including *The Range Rider*, *The Adventures Of Champion* and *Annie Oakley*. His business interest became even more involved during the 60s, when apart from owning various radio and television companies, he became the owner of the California Angels major league baseball team. *Melody Ranch* reappeared as a television programme in the 60s and ran for seven years on Autry's KTLA station. It was syndicated to stations across the country and although Autry did not appear as a regular, he did make guest appearances. In 1986, Nashville Network decided to screen his Republic and Columbia B-movie westerns under the title of *Melody Ranch Theatre* with Autry himself doing opening and closing announcements. During his long career, Autry had three horses to fill the role of Champion. The original died in 1947. Champion III, who appeared in the Gene Autry television series and also as the star of the *Adventures Of Champion* television series, died in 1991 at the age of 42. There was also a personal appearance Champion and a pony known as Little Champ. During his career he regularly sported a custom-made C.F. Martin guitar, with beautiful ornamental pearl inlay, together with his name. Autry was elected to the Country Music Hall Of Fame in 1969 for his songwriting abilities as well as his singing and acting. In 1980, he was inducted into the Cowboy Hall Of Fame Of Great Westerners. At the time of his induction, he was described as 'one of the most famous men, not only in America but in the world'. Autry sold the final 10 acres of his Melody Ranch film set in 1991. The ranch, in Placerita Canyon, California, which was used for the making of such classic westerns as *High Noon* and the television series *Gunsmoke*, is scheduled to become a historical feature.

● ALBUMS: *Stampede* 10-inch album (Columbia 1949) ★★★, *Western Classics* 10-inch album (Columbia 1949) ★★★, *Western Classics Volume 2* 10-inch album (Columbia 1949) ★★★, *Easter Favorites* 10-inch album reissued as *Gene Autry Sings Peter Cottontail* (Columbia 1949) ★★, *Champion* 10-inch album (Columbia 1950) ★★★, *Merry Christmas With Gene Autry* 10-inch album

(Columbia 1950) ★★, *The Story Of The Nativity* 10-inch album (Columbia 1955) ★★, *Little Johnny Pilgrim & Guffy The Goofy Gobbler* 10-inch album (Columbia 1955) ★, *Rusty The Rocking Horse & Bucky, The Bucking Bronco* 10-inch album (Columbia 1955) ★, *Gene Autry & Champion Western Adventures* (Columbia 1955) ★★, *At The Rodeo* (Columbia 1958) ★★★, *Christmas With Gene Autry* (Challenge 1958) ★★, with Art Carney, Rosemary Clooney *Christmas Favorites* (Harmony 1964) ★★★★, *Great Western Hits* (Harmony 1965) ★★★, *Melody Ranch* (Melody Ranch 1965) ★★★, with Carney, Clooney *Sings Peter Cottontail (First Easter Record For Children)* (Harmony 1965) ★, *Back In The Saddle Again* (Harmony 1966) ★★★, *Gene Autry Sings* (Harmony 1966) ★★★, *Rudolph The Red-Nosed Reindeer* (Grand Prix 1968) ★, *Live From Madison Square Garden* (Republic 1968) ★★, *Melody Ranch – A Radio Adventure* (Radiola 1975) ★★, *South Of The Border, All American Cowboy* (Republic 1976) ★★★, *Cowboy Hall Of Fame* (Republic 1976) ★★★, *50th Anniversary Album* (Republic 1978) ★★★, *Christmas Classics* (Starday 1978) ★★, *Sounds Like Jimmie Rodgers* (ACM 1985) ★★★.

● COMPILATIONS: *Gene Autry's Greatest Hits* (Columbia 1961) ★★★, *Gene Autry's Golden Hits* (RCA Victor 1962) ★★★★, *Country Music Hall Of Fame* (Columbia 1970) ★★★, *Back In The Saddle Again* (Sony 1977) ★★★, *22 All Time Favorites* (GRT 1977) ★★★, *Columbia Historic Edition* (Columbia 1982) ★★★, *Golden Hits* (Good Music 1985) ★★★, *Christmas Favorites* (Columbia 1989) ★★★, *Greatest Hits* (Sony 1992) ★★★★, *The Essential 1933-46* (Columbia/Legacy 1992) ★★★★, *South Of The Border* (Castle 1994) ★★★, *Portrait Of An Artist* (Sound Exchange 1995) ★★★★, *Blues Singer 1929-1931: Booger Rooger Saturday* (Columbia/Legacy 1996) ★★★, *Sing, Cowboy, Sing! The Gene Autry Collection* 3-CD box set (Rhino 1997) ★★★★, *The Singing Cowboy, Chapter One: Gene Autry With The Legendary Singing Groups Of The West* (Varèse Sarabande 1997) ★★★, *Private Buckaroo* (Bronco Buster 1998) ★★★, *20 Greatest Movie Hits* (Varèse Sarabande 1999) ★★★, *Love Songs* (Varèse Sarabande 1999) ★★★, *The Complete 1950s Television Recordings* (Varèse Sarabande 2000) ★★★.

● FURTHER READING: *Back In The Saddle Again*, Gene Autry with Mickey Herskowitz. *The Gene Autry Book*, David Rothel.

● FILMS: *In Old Santa Fe* (1934), *Tumbling Tumbleweeds* (1935), *Sagebrush Troubador* (1935), *Melody Trail* (1935), *The Phantom Empire* (1935), *The Singing Vangabond* (1936), *Singing Cowboy* (1936), *Ride, Ranger, Ride* (1936), *Red River Valley* (1936), *The Old Corral* (1936), *Guns And Guitars* (1936), *Comin' Round The Mountain* (1936), *The Big Show* (1936), *Yodelin' Kid From Pine Ridge* (1937), *Springtime In The Rockies* (1937), *Round-Up Time In Texas* (1937), *Rootin' Tootin' Rhythm* (1937), *Public Cowboy No. 1* (1937), *Oh Susanna* (1937), *Git Along, Little Dogies* (1937), *Boots And Saddles* (1937), *Manhattan Merry-Go-Round* (1937), *Rhythm Of The Saddle* (1938), *The Old Barn Dance* (1938), *Gold Mine In The Sky* (1938), *Man From Music Mountain* (1938), *Prairie Moon* (1938), *Western Jamboree* (1938), *South Of The Border* (1939), *Rovin' Tumbleweeds* (1939), *Mountain Rhythm* (1939), *Mexicali Rose* (1939), *In Old Monterey* (1939), *Home On The Prairie* (1939), *Colorado Sunset* (1939), *Blue Montana Skies* (1939), *Unusual Occupations* (1940), *Shooting High* (1940), *Rancho Grande* (1940), *Carolina Moon* (1940), *Men With Steel Faces* (1940), *Gaucho Serenade* (1940), *Ride, Tenderfoot, Ride* (1940), *Melody Ranch* (1940), *Under Fiesta Stars* (1941), *Sunset In Wyoming* (1941), *The Singing Hill* (1941), *Sierra Sue* (1941), *Ridin' On A Rainbow* (1941), *Down Mexico Way* (1941), *Back In The Saddle* (1941), *Stardust On The Sage* (1942), *Home In Wyomin'* (1942), *Heart Of The Rio Grande* (1942), *Cowboy Serenade* (1942), *Call Of The Canyon* (1942), *Bells Of Capistrano* (1942), *Sioux City Sue* (1946), *Twilight On The Rio Grande* (1947), *Trail To San Antone* (1947), *Saddle Pals* (1947), *Robin Hood Of Texas* (1947), *The Last Round Up* (1947), *The Strawberry Roan* (1948), *Loaded Pistols* (1948), *Sons Of New Mexico* (1949), *Rim Of The Canyon* (1949), *Riders Of The Whistling Pines* (1949), *Riders In The Sky* (1949), *The Cowboy And The Indians* (1949), *The Big Sombrero* (1949), *Mule Train* (1950), *Indian Territory* (1950), *Cow Town* (1950), *The Blazing Sun* (1950), *Beyond The Purple Hills* (1950), *Whirl Wind* (1951), *Valley Of Fire* (1951), *Texans Never Cry* (1951), *Silver Canyon* (1951), *The Hills Of Utah* (1951), *Gene Autry And The Mounties* (1951), *Wagon Team* (1952), *The Old West* (1952), *Night Stage To Galveston* (1952), *Blue Canadian Rockies* (1952), *Barbed-Wire* (1952), *Apache Country* (1952), *Winning Of The West* (1953), *Saginaw Trail* (1953), *Pack Train* (1953), *On Top Of Old Smoky* (1953), *Last Of The Pony Riders* (1953), *Goldtown Ghost Riders* (1953), *Alias Jesse James* (1959).

AVALON, FRANKIE

b. Francis Avallone, 18 September 1940, Philadelphia, Pennsylvania, USA. This photogenic 50s teen idol started as a trumpet-playing child prodigy. His first recordings in 1954 were the instrumentals 'Trumpet Sorrento' and 'Trumpet Tarantella' on X-Vik Records (an RCA Records subsidiary). In the mid-50s, he appeared on many television and radio shows including those of Paul Whiteman, Jackie Gleason and Ray Anthony. He joined Rocco And The Saints and was seen singing with them in the 1957 movie *Jamboree* (retitled *Disc Jockey Jamboree* in the UK). Avalon signed to Chancellor Records and in 1958 his third single for them, 'DeDe Dinah', reached the US Top 10. It was the first of his 25 US chart entries, many of which were written by his hard-working manager, Bob Marcucci. Despite the fact that he had a weak voice and his musical talent was often questioned, Avalon quickly became one of the top stars in the USA and managed two chart-toppers in 1959, 'Venus' and 'Why', which were his only UK Top 20 entries. Avalon had to wait until his 21st birthday in 1961 to receive the $100,000 he had earned to date, and by that time he had passed his peak as a singer and turned his attention to acting. This career move proved successful, with appearances in many movies, including a string of beach flicks alongside fellow 50s pop star Annette and a memorable appearance as Teen Angel in the highly successful 1978 movie, *Grease*.

Avalon later recorded with little success on United Artists Records, Reprise Records, Metromedia, Regalia, Delite, Amos and Bobcat. Apart from his movie and occasional television appearances, Avalon still performs on the supper-club circuit, and in 1985 toured in *The Golden Boys Of Bandstand*. He now runs the highly successful Frankie Avalon Products, selling a line of health supplement products. Alongside fellow Chancellor Records artist Fabian, he is often dismissed by rock critics, yet remains one of the American public's best-loved 50s teen-idols.

● ALBUMS: *Frankie Avalon* (Chancellor 1958) ★★, *The Young Frankie Avalon* (Chancellor 1959) ★★, *Swingin' On A Rainbow* (Chancellor 1959) ★★, *Young And In Love* (Chancellor 1960) ★★, *Summer Scene* (Chancellor 1960) ★★, *And Now About Mr. Avalon* (Chancellor 1961) ★★, *Italiano* (Chancellor 1962) ★, *You Are Mine* (Chancellor 1962) ★★, *Christmas Album* (Chancellor 1962) ★★, *Cleopatra Plus 13 Other Great Hits* (Chancellor 1963) ★★, *Songs From Muscle Beach Party* film soundtrack (United Artists 1964) ★★, *I'll Take Sweden* film soundtrack (United Artists 1965) ★★, *I Want You Near Me* (Metromedia 1970) ★, *You're My Life* (Delite 1978) ★.

● COMPILATIONS: *A Whole Lotta Frankie* (Chancellor 1961) ★★, *Frankie Avalon's 15 Greatest Hits* (United Artists 1964) ★★★, *16 Greatest Hits* (ABC 1973) ★★★, *Best Of Frankie Avalon* (Creole 1984) ★★★, *The Collection* (Castle 1990) ★★, *The Fabulous Frankie Avalon* (Ace 1991) ★★★, *The Best Of Frankie Avalon* (Varèse Sarabande 1995) ★★★, *Greatest Hits* (Curb 1995) ★★★, *The EP Collection* (See For Miles 2000) ★★★.

● FILMS: *Jamboree* aka *Disc Jockey Jamboree* (1957), *Guns Of The Timberland* (1959), *The Alamo* (1960), *Saiyu-ki* aka *The Enchanted Monkey* voice only (1960), *Voyage To The Bottom Of The Sea* (1961), *Sail A Crooked Ship* (1961), *El Valle De Las Espadas* aka *The Castilian* (1962), *Panic In Year Zero!* aka *End Of The World* (1962), *Operation Bikini* aka *The Seafighters* (1963), *Drums Of Africa* (1963), *Beach Party* (1963), *Muscle Beach Party* (1964), *Bikini Beach* (1964), *Pajama Party* aka *The Maid And The Martian* (1964), *Beach Blanket Bingo* (1965), *Ski Party* (1965), *How To Stuff A Wild Bikini* (1965), *I'll Take Sweden* (1965), *Sergeant Deadhead* (1965), *Dr. Goldfoot And The Bikini Machine* (1965), *Fireball 500* (1966), *Thunder Alley* aka *Hell Drivers* (1967), *The Million Eyes Of Sumuru* (1967), *Skidoo* (1968), *Horror House* aka *The Dark* (1969), *The Take* (1974), *Grease* (1978), *Blood Song* aka *Dream Slayer* (1982), *Back To The Beach* (1987), *Troop Beverly Hills* (1989), *The Stöned Age* aka *Tack's Chicks* (1994), *Casino* (1995).

B

BAILEY, PEARL

b. Pearl Mae Bailey, 29 March 1918, Newport News, Virginia, USA, d. 17 August 1990, Philadelphia, Pennsylvania, USA. Pearlie Mae, as she was known, was an uninhibited performer, who mumbled her way through some songs and filled others with outrageous asides and sly innuendoes. She entered the world of entertainment as a dancer but later sang in vaudeville, graduating to the New York nightclub circuit in the early 40s. After working with the Noble Sissle Orchestra, she became band-vocalist with Cootie Williams, with whom she recorded 'Tess' Torch Song', previously sung by Dinah Shore in the movie *Up In Arms*. Bailey received strong critical acclaim after substituting for Sister Rosetta Tharpe in a show, and was subsequently signed to star in the 1946 Harold Arlen/Johnny Mercer Broadway musical, *St. Louis Woman*. A year later her slurred version of 'Tired' was the highlight of the movie *Variety Girl*, and she gave several other outstanding performances in films such as *Carmen Jones* (1954), *St. Louis Blues* (1958) and *Porgy And Bess* (1959).

During her stay with Columbia Records (1945-50), Bailey recorded a series of duets with Frank Sinatra, trumpeter Oran 'Hot Lips' Page and comedienne Moms Mabley. She also recorded some solo tracks with outstanding arrangers/conductors, including Gil Evans and Tadd Dameron. Upon joining the Coral Records label in 1951, she employed Don Redman as her regular musical director, the association lasting for 10 years. In 1952, she had her biggest hit record, 'Takes Two To Tango'. In that same year she married drummer Louie Bellson and he took over from Redman as her musical director in 1961. Although few of her records sold in vast quantities, Bailey had always been a crowd-pulling live performer and, following her early stage triumph in *St. Louis Woman*, she was later cast in other shows including *The House Of Flowers*, *Bless You All*, *Arms And The Girl* and an all-black cast version of *Hello, Dolly!*. She also starred in several US television specials, playing down the *double entendre* that caused one of her albums, *Sings For Adults Only*, to be 'restricted from air-play'. In 1991 Pearl Bailey was posthumously inducted into the New York Theater Hall Of Fame.

● ALBUMS: *Pearl Bailey Entertains* 10-inch album (Columbia 1950) ★★★★, *Say Si Si* 10-inch album (Coral 1953) ★★★, *I'm With You* 10-inch album (Coral 1953) ★★★, *The One And Only Pearl Bailey* (Mercury 1956) ★★★★, *Birth Of The Blues* (Coral 1956) ★★★★, *The One And Only Pearl Bailey Sings* (Mercury 1957) ★★★, *Cultured Pearl* (Coral 1957)

★★★, *The Intoxicating Pearl Bailey* (Mercury 1957) ★★★★, *Pearl Bailey A Broad* (Roulette 1957) ★★★★, *St. Louis Blues* (Roulette 1958) ★★★★, *Gems By Pearl Bailey* (Vocalion 1958) ★★★★, *Sings For Adults Only* (Roulette 1959) ★★★★, *Sings Porgy & Bess And Other Gershwin Melodies* (Roulette 1959) ★★★★, *More Songs For Adults Only* (Roulette 1960) ★★★, *Songs Of The Bad Old Days* (Roulette 1960) ★★★, *Naughty But Nice* (Roulette 1960) ★★★, *Sings Songs Of Harold Arlen* (Roulette 1961) ★★★★, *Happy Songs* (Roulette 1962) ★★★, *Come On, Let's Play With Pearlie Mae* (Roulette 1962) ★★★, *About Good Little Girls And Bad Little Boys* (Roulette 1963) ★★★, *C'est La Vie* (Roulette 1963) ★★, *The Songs Of Academy Award Winner James Van Heusen* (Roulette 1964) ★★★★, *Les Poupees De Paris* (RCA Victor 1964) ★★★, *Searching The Gospel* (Roulette 1966) ★★★, *The Real Pearl* (Project 3 1967) ★★.
● COMPILATIONS: *The Best Of Pearl Bailey* (Roulette 1961) ★★★★, *The Best Of: The Roulette Years* (Roulette 1991) ★★★★, *16 Most Requested Songs* (Columbia 1991) ★★★★, *Ain't She Sweet! 23 Of Her Greatest Hits* (Jasmine 2000) ★★★, *Cocktail Hour* (Columbia 2001) ★★★.
● FURTHER READING: *The Raw Pearl*, Pearl Bailey. *Talking To Myself*, Pearl Bailey.
● FILMS: *Variety Girl* (1947), *Isn't It Romantic?* (1948), *Carmen Jones* (1954), *That Certain Feeling* (1956), *St. Louis Blues* (1958), *Porgy And Bess* (1959), *All The Fine Young Cannibals* (1960), *The Landlord* (1970), *Tubby The Tuba* voice only (1976), *Norman ... Is That You?* (1976), *The Fox And The Hound* voice only (1981).

BAKER, CHET

b. Chesney Henry Baker, 23 December 1929, Yale, Oklahoma, USA, d. 13 May 1988, Amsterdam, the Netherlands. One of the more lyrical of the early post-war trumpeters, Baker's fragile sound epitomized the so-called 'cool' school of west coast musicians who dominated the American jazz scene of the 50s. Baker studied music while in the army, and soon after his discharge in 1951 he was playing with Charlie Parker. He gained international prominence as a member of Gerry Mulligan's pianoless quartet, with their dynamic reading of 'My Funny Valentine' becoming a notable hit. When the quartet disbanded in 1953, Baker, after another short stint with Parker, formed his own group, which proved to be extremely popular. Baker kept this band together for the next three years, but he was not cut out for the life of a bandleader, nor was he able to withstand the pressures and temptations that fame brought him. He succumbed to drug addiction and the rest of his life was a battle against dependency. Inevitably, his music frequently fell by the wayside, as did his occasional acting career.
In the 80s, in control of his life, although not fully over his addiction, he was once again a regular visitor to international jazz venues and also made a few incursions into the pop world, guesting, for example, on Elvis Costello's 'Shipbuilding'. Probably his best work from this later period comes on a series of records he made for the Danish SteepleChase label with a trio that comprised Doug Raney and Niels-Henning Ørsted Pedersen. By this time his clean-cut boyish good looks had vanished beneath a mass of lines and wrinkles – fellow trumpeter Jack Sheldon, told by Baker that they were laugh-lines, remarked, 'Nothing's that funny!'. In his brief prime, Baker's silvery filigrees of sound, albeit severely restricted in tonal and emotional range, brought an unmistakable touch to many fine records; however, his lack of self-esteem rarely allowed him to assert himself or to break through the stylistic bounds imposed by exemplars such as Miles Davis. The 1988 movie, *Let's Get Lost*, charts the closing years of the erratic life of this largely unfulfilled musician, who died when he fell, or possibly jumped, from an Amsterdam hotel window. A commemorative plaque was erected in 1999, which would indicate an accident.
● ALBUMS: *Chet Baker Quartet* 10-inch album (Pacific Jazz 1953) ★★★, *Chet Baker Quartet Featuring Russ Freeman* 10-inch album (Pacific Jazz 1953) ★★★, *Chet Baker Ensemble* 10-inch album (Pacific Jazz 1954) ★★★★, *Chet Baker & Strings* (Columbia 1954) ★★★★, *Chet Baker Sings* 10-inch album (Pacific Jazz 1954) ★★★★, *Chet Baker Sextet* 10-inch album (Pacific Jazz 1954) ★★★, *Chet Baker Sings And Plays With Bud Shank, Russ Freeman And Strings* (Pacific Jazz 1955) ★★★★, *Jazz At Ann Arbor* (Pacific Jazz 1955) ★★★, *Chet Baker In Europe* (Pacific Jazz 1956) ★★★, *Chet Baker And Crew* (Pacific Jazz 1956) ★★★, with Art Pepper *Playboys* reissued as *Picture Of Health* (Pacific Jazz 1957) ★★★, *At The Forum Theater* (Fresh Sound 1957) ★★★, *Grey December* (Pacific Jazz 1957) ★★★, *The Route* (Pacific Jazz 1957) ★★★, *Chet Baker Cools Out* (Boblicity 1957) ★★★, *Chet Baker Big Band* (Pacific Jazz 1957) ★★★, *It Could Happen To You – Chet Baker Sings* (Riverside 1958) ★★★★, *Pretty/Groovy* (World Pacific 1958) ★★★, *Chet Baker In New York* (Riverside 1959) ★★★★, *Chet* (Riverside 1959) ★★★★, *Chet Baker Plays The Best Of Lerner And Loewe* (Riverside 1959) ★★★, *Chet Baker In Milano* (Jazzland 1959) ★★★, *Chet Baker And Orchestra* (Jazzland 1960) ★★★, *Chet Baker With Fifty Italian Strings* (Jazzland 1960) ★★★, *Chet Baker Quintette* (Crown 1962) ★★★, *Chet Is Back* aka *The Italian Sessions* (RCA 1962) ★★★, *Baby Breeze* (Limelight 1964) ★★★, *Baker's Holiday* (Limelight 1965) ★★★, *Chet Baker Sings & Plays Billie Holiday* (EmArcy 1965) ★★★, *Quietly There* (World Pacific 1966) ★★★, *Into My Life* (World Pacific 1967) ★★★, *Smokin' With The Chet Baker Quintet* 1965 recording (Prestige 1967) ★★★★, *Cool Burnin' With The Chet Baker Quintet* 1965 recording (Prestige 1967) ★★★★, *Boppin' With The Chet Baker Quintet* 1965 recording (Prestige 1967) ★★★★, *Groovin' With The Chet Baker Quintet* 1965 recording (Prestige 1967) ★★★★, *Comin' On With The Chet Baker Quintet* 1965 recording (Prestige 1967) ★★★★, *Polka Dots And Moonbeams* (Jazzland 1967) ★★★, *You Can't Go Home Again* (A&M 1972) ★★★★, *She Was Too Good To Me* (CTI 1974) ★★★, *Once Upon A Summer Time* (Artist

House 1977) ★★★, *Flic Ou Voyou* (Cobra 1977) ★★★, *The Incredible Chet Baker Plays And Sings* (Carosello 1977) ★★★, *Two A Day* (Dreyfus 1978) ★★★, *Live At Nick's* (Criss Cross 1978) ★★★, *The Touch Of Your Lips* (SteepleChase 1979) ★★★, *No Problem* (SteepleChase 1979) ★★★, *Daybreak* (SteepleChase 1979) ★★★, *This Is Always* (SteepleChase 1979) ★★★, with Wolfgang Lackerschmid *Chet Baker/Wolfgang Lackerschmid* (Inakustik 1979) ★★★, *Someday My Prince Will Come* (SteepleChase 1979) ★★★, *Chet Baker Live In Sweden* (Dragon 1983) ★★★, *The Improviser* (Cadence 1983) ★★★, *Chet At Capolinea* (Red 1983) ★★★, *Everything Happens To Me* (Timeless 1983) ★★★, *Blues For A Reason* (Criss Cross 1984) ★★★★, *Sings Again* (Timeless 1984) ★★★, *Chet's Choice* (Criss Cross 1985) ★★★, *My Foolish Heart* (IRD 1985) ★★★, *Misty* (IRD 1985) ★★★, *Time After Time* (IRD 1985) ★★★, *Live From The Moonlight* (Philology 1985) ★★★, *Diane* (SteepleChase 1985) ★★★, *Strollin'* (Enja 1985) ★★★, *Candy* (Sonet 1985) ★★★, *As Time Goes By* (Timeless 1986) ★★★, *Night Bird: Live At Ronnie Scott's* (WH 1986) ★★★, *Live At Rosenheimer* (Timeless 1988) ★★★, *When Sunny Gets Blue* (SteepleChase 1988) ★★★, *Little Girl Blue* (Philology 1988) ★★★, *Straight From The Heart* (Enja 1988) ★★★, *Let's Get Lost* film soundtrack (RCA 1989) ★★★, *Live At Fat Tuesday's* (Fresh Sound 1991) ★★★★, *Live In Buffalo* (New Note 1993) ★★★, *... In Tokyo* (Evidence 1996) ★★★, *Chet Baker In Bologna* 1985 recording (Dreyfus 1996) ★★★, *I Remember You* (Enja 1997) ★★★★, with Stan Getz *Quintessence Vol 1* 1983 recording (Concord Jazz 1999) ★★, *Autumn In New York* 1960 recording (Castle Pie 2000) ★★★, *This Time The Dream's On Me: Chet Baker Quartet Live, Volume 1* (Blue Note 2000) ★★★★, *Out Of Nowhere: Chet Baker Quartet Live, Volume 2* (Blue Note 2000) ★★★★, *My Old Flame: Chet Baker Quartet Live, Volume 3* (Blue Note 2001) ★★★★.
● COMPILATIONS: *The Complete Pacific Jazz Live Recordings Of The Chet Baker Quartet With Russ Freeman* box set (Mosaic 1986) ★★★★, *Let's Get Lost* (Pacific Jazz 1990) ★★★★, *The Pacific Years* (Pacific Jazz 1994) ★★★★, *The Legacy: Volume One* (Enja 1995) ★★★, *The Complete Pacific Jazz Recordings Of The Gerry Mulligan Quartet With Chet Baker* 4-CD box set (Pacific Jazz 1996) ★★★★, *Young Chet* (Blue Note 1996) ★★★★, *Jazz Profile* (Blue Note 1997) ★★★★, *Songs For Lovers* 1953-57 recordings (Pacific 1997) ★★★, *The Art Of The Ballad* (Prestige 1998) ★★★★, *Why Shouldn't You Cry?* (Enja 1998) ★★★, *Plays It Cool* (Metro 2000) ★★★, *1955-56 In Paris: Barclay Sessions* (Verve 2000) ★★★★.
● VIDEOS: *Live At Ronnie Scott's* (Rhino Home Video 1988).
● FURTHER READING: *As Though I Had Wings: The Lost Memoir*, Chet Baker. *Young Chet*, William Claxton (photographer). *Chet Baker: His Life And Music*, J. De Valk.
● FILMS: *Hell's Horizon* (1955), *Urlatori Alla Sbarra* aka *Howlers Of The Dock* (1959), *Stolen Hours* (1963), *Let's Get Lost* (1988).

BAKER, KENNY
b. 1 March 1921, Withernsea, Yorkshire, England, d. 7 December 1999, Chichester, West Sussex, England. After taking piano lessons at an early age Baker took up the trumpet and played in brass bands. He moved to London in the late 30s to become a professional musician and joined Sandy Powell's Concert Party. During the next few years he established himself as an outstanding technician, capable of playing in any jazz or dance band. In the early 40s, he played in the bands of Lew Stone and George Chisholm before joining Ted Heath in 1944. He remained with Heath until 1949, and was featured on many recording sessions and countless concerts. In the early 50s, he was regularly heard on BBC radio, leading his own band, the Baker's Dozen, on a weekly late-night show that lasted throughout the decade. In the 60s, he led his own groups and recorded film soundtracks, all the time building his reputation as one of the best trumpet/cornet/flügelhorn players in the world, even though he only rarely played outside the UK. At the end of the decade he was featured in Benny Goodman's UK band. Baker's career continued throughout the 70s, with appearances as co-leader of the Best of British Jazz touring package, and with Ted Heath recreations and the bands led by Don Lusher and other former colleagues. In the early 80s, Baker turned down an invitation to take over leadership of the Harry James band after the latter's death. He continued to play concerts and club dates and also featured on television, usually off-camera, playing soundtracks for Alan Plater's popular UK television series, *The Beiderbecke Affair* and *The Beiderbecke Tapes*. In 1989, he took part in a major recording undertaking that set out to recreate the classic recordings of Louis Armstrong using modern recording techniques. Baker took the Armstrong role, comfortably confounding the date on his birth certificate with his masterful playing. In 1993, he undertook a highly successful series of dates at Ronnie Scott's Birmingham club. He was playing as well as ever, and no passing of years had diminished his devastating style. Baker was a fiery soloist with a remarkable technical capacity that he never used simply for gimmick or effect. He was also one of the UK's greatest contributors to the international jazz scene.
● ALBUMS: *Kenny Baker's Half-Dozen* (Dormouse 1957) ★★★★, *Date With The Dozen* (Dormouse 1957) ★★★, *Presents The Half-Dozen* (Dormouse 1958) ★★★, *Baker Plays McHugh* (1958) ★★★, *The Phase 4 World Of Kenny Baker* (Decca 1977) ★★★, *The Boss Is Home* (Big Bear 1994) ★★★, with Warren Vaché Jnr. *Ain't Misbehavin'* (Zephyr 1998) ★★★★.
● FURTHER READING: *Kenny Baker*, Robert G. Crosby.

BAKER, LAVERN
b. Delores Williams, 11 November 1929, Chicago, Illinois, USA, d. 10 March 1997, Manhattan, New York City, New York, USA. Baker was a pioneering voice in the fusion of R&B and rock 'n' roll in the 50s. In 1947 she was discovered in a Chicago

nightclub by bandleader Fletcher Henderson. Although still in her teens, the singer won a recording contract with the influential OKeh Records, where she was nicknamed 'Little Miss Sharecropper' and 'Bea Baker'. Having toured extensively with the Todd Rhodes Orchestra, Baker secured a prestigious contract with Atlantic Records, with whom she enjoyed a fruitful relationship. 'Tweedle Dee' reached both the US R&B and pop charts in 1955, selling in excess of one million copies, and the artist was awarded a second gold disc two years later for 'Jim Dandy'. In 1959, she enjoyed a number 6 pop hit with 'I Cried A Tear' and throughout the decade Baker remained one of black music's leading performers. Although eclipsed by newer acts during the 60s, the singer enjoyed further success with 'Saved', written and produced by Leiber And Stoller, and 'See See Rider', both of which inspired subsequent versions, notably by the Band and the Animals.

Baker's final chart entry came with 'Think Twice', a 1966 duet with Jackie Wilson, as her 'classic' R&B intonation grew increasingly out of step with the prevalent soul/Motown Records boom. After leaving Atlantic, Baker is probably best known for 'One Monkey Don't Stop No Show'. In the late 60s, while entertaining US troops in Vietnam, she became ill, and went to the Philippines to recuperate. She stayed there in self-imposed exile for 22 years, reviving her career at New York's Village Gate club in 1991. During the following year she undertook a short UK tour, but audience numbers were disappointing for the only female, along with Aretha Franklin, who had, at that time, been elected to the US Rock And Roll Hall Of Fame. She replaced Ruth Brown in the Broadway musical *Black And Blue* in the early 90s, but ill health from diabetes, together with the amputation of both her legs, made her final years miserable. Baker had a stunning voice that with little effort could crack walls, and yet her ballad singing was wonderfully sensitive.

● ALBUMS: *LaVern* (Atlantic 1956) ★★★, *LaVern Baker* (Atlantic 1957) ★★★★, *Rock And Roll With LaVern* (Atlantic 1957) ★★★★, *Sings Bessie Smith* (Atlantic 1958) ★★★, *Blues Ballads* (Atlantic 1959) ★★★★, *Precious Memories* (Atlantic 1959) ★★★, *Saved* (Atlantic 1961) ★★★, *See See Rider* (Atlantic 1963) ★★★, *I'm Gonna Get You* (C5 1966) ★★, *Live In Hollywood '91* (Rhino 1991) ★★★★, *Woke Up This Mornin'* (DRG 1992) ★★★.

● COMPILATIONS: *The Best Of LaVern Baker* (Atlantic 1963) ★★★★, *Real Gone Gal* (Charly 1984) ★★★, *Soul On Fire: The Best Of LaVern Baker* (Atlantic 1993) ★★★★, *Rock & Roll* (Sequel 1997) ★★★★.

BALLARD, HANK, AND THE MIDNIGHTERS
b. Henry Ballard, 18 November 1936, Detroit, Michigan, USA. His truck-driving father died when Ballard was seven years old and he was sent to Bessemer, Alabama, to live with relations. The strict religious and gospel upbringing caused him to run away, and by the age of 15, Ballard was working on an assembly line at Ford Motors in

Detroit. His cousin, Florence Ballard, became a member of the Detroit girl group the Supremes. Hank Ballard's singing voice was heard by Sonny Woods of the Royals, who was amused by his mixture of Jimmy Rushing and Gene Autry. He was asked to replace frontman Lawson Smith during the latter's army service. The Royals, who also included Henry Booth and Charles Sutton, had been recommended to King Records by Johnny Otis and had previously recorded 'Every Beat Of My Heart', later an R&B hit for Gladys Knight And The Pips. In 1953, Ballard's first session with the Royals led to their first US R&B Top 10 entry, 'Get It', which he also wrote.

Ballard composed the newly renamed Midnighters' 1954 R&B chart-topper, 'Work With Me Annie', although its sexual innuendoes were too strong for some radio stations to broadcast. Its popularity spawned sequels ('Annie Had A Baby', 'Annie's Aunt Fannie') as well as answer records (the Platters' 'Annie Doesn't Work Here Anymore'). Etta James' 'Roll With Me, Henry' was modified by Georgia Gibbs to 'Dance With Me, Henry', while Hank himself responded with 'Henry's Got Flat Feet (Can't Dance No More)'! The group also had success with 'Sexy Ways', 'Don't Change Your Pretty Ways', 'Open Up Your Back Door' and 'Tore Up Over You'. In 1955, the Drifters had converted a gospel song into 'What'cha Gonna Do?' and, in 1957, Hank Ballard And The Midnighters (as the group was now known) used the same melody for 'Is Your Love For Real?'. They then modified the arrangement and changed the lyrics to 'The Twist'. Not realizing the song's potential, it was released as the b-side of 'Teardrops On Your Letter', a number 4 US R&B hit. Shortly afterwards, 'The Twist' was covered by Chubby Checker, who embellished Ballard's dance steps and thus created a new craze. As a result of 'The Twist', Hank Ballard And The Midnighters received exposure on pop radio stations and made the US pop charts with such dance hits as 'Finger Poppin' Time' (number 7), 'Let's Go, Let's Go, Let's Go' (number 6), 'The Hoochi Coochi Coo' (number 23), 'Let's Go Again (Where We Went Last Night)' (number 39), 'The Continental Walk' (number 33) and 'The Switch-A-Roo' (number 26). On the strength of Chubby Checker's success, their original version of 'The Twist' made number 28 on the US pop charts.

In the mid-60s Hank Ballard split with the other members, but he retained the group's title, which has enabled him to work with numerous musicians using the Midnighters name. For some years he worked with James Brown, who has paid tribute to him on record. In the late 80s, Ballard recorded a double album at the Hammersmith Palais in London. In 1990 he was inducted into the Rock And Roll Hall Of Fame. The best of his most recent recordings is 1998's *From Love To Tears*, which features the excellent 'Two Bad Boys'.

● ALBUMS: as The Midnighters *Sing Their Hits* 10-inch album (Federal 1954) ★★★, as The Midnighters *The Midnighters, Volume 2* (Federal 1955) ★★, *Singin' And Swingin'* (King 1959) ★★★, *The One And Only Hank Ballard* (King 1960) ★★★,

Mr. Rhythm And Blues (Finger Poppin' Time) (King 1960) ★★★★, *Spotlight On Hank Ballard* (King 1961) ★★★★, *Let's Go Again* (King 1961) ★★★★, *Dance Along* (King 1961) ★★★, *The Twisting Fools* (King 1962) ★★★, *Jumpin' Hank Ballard* (King 1962) ★★★, *The 1963 Sound Of Hank Ballard* (King 1963) ★★★, *A Star In Your Eyes* (King 1964) ★★, *Those Lazy, Lazy Days* (King 1964) ★★★, *Glad Songs, Sad Songs, Shout Songs* (King 1965) ★★, *Sings 24 Great Songs* (King 1966) ★★★, *You Can't Keep A Good Man Down* (King 1969) ★★, *Live At The Palais* (Charly 1987) ★★, *Naked In The Rain* (After Hours 1993) ★★, *From Love To Tears* (Pool Party 1998) ★★.
● COMPILATIONS: *Biggest Hits* (King 1963) ★★★, *24 Hit Tunes* (King 1966) ★★★, *20 Original Hits* (King 1977) ★★★, *What You Get When The Gettin' Gets Good* (Charly 1985) ★★★, *Sexy Ways: The Best Of Hank Ballard And The Midnighters* (Rhino 1993) ★★★★, *The EP Collection* (See For Miles 2000) ★★★★, *Dancin' And Twistin'* (Ace 2000) ★★★, *Let 'Em Roll* (King 2000) ★★★★.

BAND WAGON, THE

Taking the title from a highly successful 1931 Broadway revue that had a score by Arthur Schwartz and Howard Dietz, but no plot, Betty Comden and Adolph Green provided the screenplay for arguably the best and wittiest backstage film musical of them all. Released in 1953, the film's story dealt with an ageing, has-been hoofer, Tony Hunter (Fred Astaire), whose New York comeback is being masterminded and written by Lily and Lester Marton (Oscar Levant and Nanette Fabray), two characters reputedly based on Comden and Green themselves. Ballerina Gabrielle Gerard (Cyd Charisse) reluctantly agrees to become Hunter's co-star, and Jeffrey Cordova (Jack Buchanan), the reigning theatrical virtuoso and super-egotist, is called in to direct, but his extravagant efforts result in something nearer *Faust* than *Funny Face*. However, all is not lost: after the cast have revamped the show (with the help of Cordova, who turns out to be a nice, modest – even insecure – guy underneath), it promises to run for years. Schwartz and Dietz's score was full of marvellous songs, including 'A Shine On Your Shoes', 'By Myself' (Astaire), 'I Guess I'll Have To Change My Plan' (Astaire-Buchanan), the ingenious 'Triplets' (Astaire-Buchanan-Fabray), 'New Sun In The Sky' (Charisse, dubbed by India Adams), and several others involving the principals and chorus, such as 'I Love Louisa', 'Louisiana Hayride', 'You And The Night And The Music', 'Dancing In The Dark' and 'Something To Remember Me By'. The one new number was 'That's Entertainment', which, along with Irving Berlin's 'There's No Business Like Show Business', attempts to explain why, despite Noël Coward's reservations, the show must always go on. Charisse and Astaire's dancing was a dream, especially in the ethereal 'Dancing In The Dark' sequence and the 'Girl Hunt' ballet. Much of the credit for the film's outstanding success was due to director Vincente Minnelli, choreographer

Michael Kidd, and producer Arthur Freed, whose special musicals unit at MGM had created yet another winner.

BARBER, CHRIS

b. 17 April 1930, Welwyn Garden City, Hertfordshire, England. In the 40s Barber studied trombone and bass at the Guildhall School of Music, eventually choosing the former as his principal instrument (although he occasionally played bass in later years). In the late 40s he formed his first band, which, unusually, was formed as a co-operative. Also in the band were Monty Sunshine (b. 8 April 1928, London, England), Ron Bowden and Lonnie Donegan (b. Anthony Donegan, 29 April 1931, Glasgow, Scotland; banjo/vocals). By the early 50s the band had gained a considerable following but it was nevertheless decided to invite Ken Colyer (b. 18 April 1928, Great Yarmouth, Norfolk, England, d. 8 March 1988) to join. The move was musically promising but proved to be unsuccessful when the personalities involved clashed repeatedly. Eventually, Colyer left and was replaced by Pat Halcox (b. 17 March, 1930, London, England; trumpet). The vocalist Ottilie Patterson (b. Anna-Ottilie Patterson, 31 January 1932, Comber, County Down, Northern Ireland) joined in 1954 when she was Barber's girlfriend, (they married in 1959).
In the mid-50s Barber also tried his hand at skiffle and his own Chris Barber Skiffle Group featured during this time Ron Bowden (drums), Dickie Bishop (vocals), and the powerful but nasal vocalist/guitarist Johnny Duncan (b. John Franklin Duncan, 7 September 1932, Oliver Springs, near Knoxville, Tennessee, USA, d. 15 July 2000, Taree, New South Wales, Australia). Barber played upright bass during this time, an instrument on which he is equally adept. Many years later, Paul McCartney's recording of Bishop's composition 'No Other Baby' was one of the highlights of his rock 'n' roll set, *Run Devil Run*.
Aided by a remarkably consistent personnel, the Barber band was soon one of the UK's leading traditional groups and was well placed to take advantage of the surge of interest in this form of jazz in the late 50s and early 60s. Barber experienced a 'freak' hit in the pop charts in 1959 when his arrangement of Sydney Bechet's 'Petite Fleur' became a huge hit (No. 3 in the UK). The track was issued from a 1957 album to catch the boom that trad was experiencing. The clarinet solo was beautifully played by Monty Sunshine and remains a classic of the era. The decline in popularity of 'trad', which came on the heels of the beat group explosion, had a dramatic effect on many British jazz bands, but Barber's fared much better than most. This was owing in part to his astute business sense and also his keen awareness of musical trends and a willingness to accommodate other forms without compromising his high musical standards. In the 60s Barber changed the name of the band to the Chris Barber Blues and Jazz Band. Into the traditional elements of the band's book he incorporated ragtime but

also worked with such modern musicians as Joe Harriott. Among his most important activities at this time was his active promotion of R&B and the blues, which he underlined by bringing major American artists to the UK, often at his own expense. Through such philanthropy he brought to the attention of British audiences the likes of Sister Rosetta Tharpe, Brownie McGhee, Louis Jordan and Muddy Waters. Not content with performing the older blues styles, Barber also acknowledged the contemporary interest in blues evinced by rock musicians and audiences and hired such players as John Slaughter and Pete York (ex-Spencer Davis Group), who worked happily beside long-serving sidemen Halcox, Ian Wheeler, Vic Pitt and others.

In the 70s, Barber focused more on mainstream music, showing a special affinity for small Duke Ellington-styled bands, and toured with visitors such as Russell Procope, Wild Bill Davis, Trummy Young and John Lewis. He also maintained his contact with his jazz roots and, simultaneously, the contemporary blues scene by touring widely with his *Take Me Back To New Orleans* show, which featured Dr. John. As a trombone player, Barber's work is enhanced by his rich sound and flowing solo style. It is, however, as bandleader and trendspotter that he has made his greatest contribution to the jazz scene, both internationally and, especially, in the UK. He happily entered his fifth decade as a bandleader with no discernible flagging of interest, enthusiasm, skill or, indeed, of his audience. In 1991 he was awarded the OBE, the same year as *Panama!* was released, featuring the excellent trumpet playing of Wendell Brunious.

● ALBUMS: *Live In 1954-55* (London 1955) ★★★★, *Here Is Chris Barber* (Atlantic 1958) ★★★, *Ragtime* (Columbia 1960) ★★★, *Chris Barber At The London Palladium* (Columbia 1961) ★★★, *Trad Tavern* (Columbia 1962) ★★★★, *Getting Around* (Storyville 1963) ★★★, *Battersea Rain Dance* (Marmalade 1968) ★★★, *Live In East Berlin* (Black Lion 1968) ★★★, *Get Rolling!* (Polydor 1971) ★★★, *Sideways* (1974) ★★★, *Echoes Of Ellington* (Black Lion 1976) ★★★, *The Grand Reunion Concert* (Timeless 1976) ★★★, *Take Me Back To New Orleans* (Black Lion 1980) ★★★, *Creole Love Call* (Timeless 1981) ★★★, *Mardi Gras At The Marquee* (Timeless 1983) ★★★, with Kenny Ball, Acker Bilk *Ball, Barber And Bilk Live At The Royal Festival Hall* (Cambra 1984) ★★★, *Live In 85* (Timeless 1986) ★★★, *Concert For The BBC* (Timeless 1986) ★★★, *In Budapest* (Storyville 1987) ★★★★, *When Its Thursday Night In Egypt* (Sonet 1988) ★★★, *Classics Concerts In Berlin* 1959 recording (Chris Barber Collection 1988) ★★★, *Stardust* (Timeless 1988) ★★★, *Get Yourself To Jackson Square* (Sonet 1990) ★★★, *Echoes Of Ellington Volume I* (Timeless 1991) ★★★★, *Echoes Of Ellington Volume II* (Timeless 1991) ★★★★, *In Concert* (Timeless 1991) ★★★, with Wendell Brunious *Panama!* (Timeless 1991) ★★★★, *Who's Blues* (L&R 1991) ★★★, *Chris Barber And His New Orleans Friends* (Timeless 1992) ★★, *With The Zenith Hot Stompers* (Timeless 1993) ★★, *Chris Barber 40 Years Jubilee*

(Timeless 1995) ★★★★, *Elite Syncopations* 1960 recording (Lake 1994) ★★, *That's It Then* (Timeless 1997) ★★★, with Sister Rosetta Tharpe *Chris Barber's Jazz Band With Sister Rosetta Tharpe, 1957* (Lake 2000) ★★★.

● COMPILATIONS: with Kenny Ball, Acker Bilk *The Best Of Ball, Barber And Bilk* (Pye Golden Guinea 1962) ★★★★, *30 Years, Chris Barber* (Timeless 1985) ★★★★, *Can't We Get Together? (1954-84)* (Timeless 1986) ★★★★, *Best Sellers* (Storyville 1987) ★★★, *Everybody Knows* (Compact Collection 1987) ★★★, *The Best Of Chris Barber (1959-62)* (PRT 1988) ★★★★, *The Entertainer* (Polydor 1988) ★★★★, *The Ultimate* (Kaz 1989) ★★★★, *Essential Chris Barber* (Kaz 1990) ★★★★, *Petite Fleur* (Spectrum 1995) ★★★★, *The Pye Jazz Anthology: Chris Barber And His Jazz Band* (Castle 2001) ★★★★.

● VIDEOS: *Music From The Land Of Dreams Concert* (Storyville 1990), *In Concert* (Virgin Vision 1991).

BART, LIONEL

b. Lionel Begleiter, 1 August 1930, London, England, d. 3 April 1999, London, England. The comparative inactivity of Bart for many years tended to cloud the fact that he was one of the major songwriters of twentieth-century popular song. The former East-End silk-screen printer, was at the very hub of the rock 'n' roll and skiffle generation that came out of London's Soho club scene in the mid-50s. As a member of the Cavemen with Tommy Steele he later became Steele's main source of non-American song material. In addition to writing the pioneering 'Rock With The Cavemen' he composed a series of glorious singalong numbers, including 'A Handful Of Songs', 'Water Water' and the trite but delightfully innocent 'Little White Bull'. Much of Bart's work was steeped in the English music-hall tradition, diffused with a strong working-class pride, and it was no surprise that he soon graduated into writing songs for full-length stage shows. *Lock Up Your Daughters* and *Fings Ain't Wot They Used T'Be* were two of his early successes, both appearing during 1959, the same year he wrote the classic 'Living Doll' for Cliff Richard. 'Living Doll' was a fine example of simplicity and melody working together perfectly. Bart could mix seemingly incompatible words such as 'gonna lock her up in a trunk, so no big hunk can steal her away from me', and they would come out sounding as if they were meant to be together. Bart was also one of the first writers to introduce mild politics into his lyrics, beautifully transcribed with a topical yet humorously ironic innocence, for example: 'They've changed our local Palais into a bowling alley and fings ain't wot they used to be.' As the 60s dawned Bart unconsciously embarked on a decade that saw him reach dizzy heights of success and made him one of the musical personalities of the decade. During the first quarter of the year he topped the charts with 'Do You Mind' for Anthony Newley, a brilliantly simple and catchy song complete with Bart's own finger-snapped accompaniment. The best was yet to come when that year he launched *Oliver!*, a musical based on Dickens' *Oliver Twist*. This became a phenomenal triumph, and remains one of the most successful musicals of all time. Bart's knack of simple melody, combined with unforgettable lyrics, produced many classics, including the pleading 'Who Will Buy', the rousing 'Food Glorious Food' and the poignant 'As Long As He Needs Me' (also a major hit for Shirley Bassey, although she reputedly never liked the song). Bart was a pivotal figure throughout the swinging London scene of the 60s, although he maintained that the party actually started in the 50s. Bart befriended Brian Epstein, the Beatles, the Rolling Stones, became an international star following *Oliver!*'s success as a film (winning six Oscars), and, although he was homosexual, was romantically linked with Judy Garland and Alma Cogan. Following continued, although lesser, success with *Blitz!* and *Maggie May*, Bart was shaken into reality when the London critics damned his 1965 musical *Twang!!*, based upon the life of Robin Hood. Bart's philanthropic nature made him a prime target for business sharks and he lost much of his fortune as a result.

By the end of the 60s the cracks were beginning to show; his dependence on drugs and alcohol increased and he watched many of his close friends die in tragic circumstances – Cogan with cancer, Garland through drink and drugs and Epstein's supposed suicide. In 1969, *La Strada* only had a short run in New York before Bart retreated into himself, and for many years maintained a relatively low profile, watching the 70s and 80s pass almost as a blur, only making contributions to *The Londoners* and *Costa Packet*. During this time the gutter press was eager for a kiss-and-tell story but Bart remained silent, a credible action considering the sums of money he was offered. During the late 80s Bart finally beat his battle with alcohol and ended the decade a saner, wiser and healthier man. His renaissance started in 1989 when he was commissioned by a UK building society to write a television jingle. The composition became part of an award-winning advertisement, featuring a number of angelic children singing with Bart, filmed in pristine monochrome. The song 'Happy Endings' was a justifiable exhumation of a man who remained an immensely talented figure and whose work ranks with some of the greatest of the American 'musical comedy' songwriters.

In the early 90s his profile continued to be high, with revivals by the talented National Youth Theatre of *Oliver!*, *Maggie May* and *Blitz!* (the latter production commemorating the 50th anniversary of the real thing), and the inclusion of one of his early songs, 'Rock With The Caveman', in the blockbuster movie *The Flintstones*, in a version by Big Audio Dynamite. In December 1994 Lionel Bart's rehabilitation was complete when producer Cameron Mackintosh presented a major new production of *Oliver!* at the London Palladium, initially starring Jonathan Pryce. In a gesture rare in the cutthroat world of showbusiness, Mackintosh returned a portion of the show's rights to the composer (Bart had sold them during the bad old days), thereby assuring him an 'income for life'. With *Oliver!* set to make its North American debut in Toronto, Bart died in April 1999 shortly after overseeing the first major revival of *Fings Ain't Wot They Used T'Be* at the Queen's Theatre, Hornchurch, in England. He spent his last few years living alone in his apartment in Acton, West London and died after losing his battle with cancer. He had been able to experience a just and well-deserved reappraisal during his last years, with *Oliver* destined to continue in perpetuity.

● FURTHER READING: *Bart!: The Unauthorized Life & Times, Ins & Outs, Ups & Downs Of Lionel Bart*, David Roper.

BARTHOLOMEW, DAVE

b. 24 December 1920, Edgard, Louisiana, USA. Dave Bartholomew was one of the most important shapers of New Orleans R&B and rock 'n' roll during the 50s. A producer, arranger, songwriter, bandleader and artist, Bartholomew produced and co-wrote most of Fats Domino's major hits for Imperial Records. Bartholomew started playing the trumpet as a child, encouraged by his father, a dixieland jazz tuba player. He performed in marching bands throughout the 30s and then on a Mississippi riverboat band led by Fats Pichon beginning in 1939, and learned songwriting basics during a stint in the US Army. Upon his return to New Orleans in the late 40s he formed his first band, which became one of the city's most popular. He also backed Little Richard on some early recordings. Bartholomew worked for several labels, including Specialty Records, Aladdin Records and De Luxe, for whom he had a big hit in 1949 with 'Country Boy'. In the same year he started a long-term association with Imperial as a producer and arranger. The previous year Bartholomew had discovered Domino in New Orleans' Hideaway Club and he introduced him to Imperial. They collaborated on 'The Fat Man', which, in 1950, became the first of over a dozen hits co-authored by the pair and produced by Bartholomew. Others included 'Blue Monday', 'Walking To New Orleans', 'Let The Four Winds Blow', 'I'm In Love Again', 'Whole Lotta Loving', 'My Girl Josephine' and 'I'm Walkin'', the latter also becoming a hit for Ricky Nelson. Bartholomew's other credits include Smiley Lewis' 'I Hear You Knocking' (later a hit for Dave Edmunds) and 'One Night' (later a hit for Elvis Presley, with its lyrics tamed), Lloyd Price's 'Lawdy Miss Clawdy', and records for Shirley And Lee, Earl King, Roy Brown, Huey 'Piano' Smith, Bobby Mitchell, Chris Kenner, Robert Parker, Frankie Ford and Snooks Eaglin. In 1963, Imperial was sold to Liberty Records, and Bartholomew declined an invitation to move to their Hollywood base, preferring to stay in New Orleans. In 1972, Chuck Berry reworked 'My Ding-A-Ling', a song Bartholomew had penned in 1952, and achieved his only US number 1 single.

Although Bartholomew, who claims to have written over 4,000 songs, recorded under his own name, his contribution has been primarily as a backstage figure. He recorded a dixieland album in 1981 and in the 90s was still leading a big band at occasional special events such as the New Orleans Jazz & Heritage Festival. He was inducted into the Rock And Roll Hall Of Fame in 1991.

● ALBUMS: *Fats Domino Presents Dave Bartholomew* (Imperial 1961) ★★★, *New Orleans House Party* (Imperial 1963) ★★★, *Dave Bartholomew And The Maryland Jazz Band* (GHB 1995) ★★★, *New Orleans Big Beat* (Landslide 1998) ★★★.

● COMPILATIONS: *Jump Children* (Pathé Marconi 1984) ★★, *The Monkey* (Pathé Marconi 1985) ★★★, *The Best Of Dave Bartholomew: The Classic New Orleans R&B Band Sound* (Stateside 1989) ★★★★, *In The Alley* (Charly 1991) ★★★, *The Spirit Of New Orleans: The Genius Of Dave Bartholomew* (EMI 1993) ★★★★, *1947-1950* (Melodie 2001) ★★★.

BASIE, COUNT

b. William Allen Basie, 21 August 1904, Red Bank, New Jersey, USA, d. 26 April 1984, Hollywood, California, USA. Bandleader and pianist Basie grew up in Red Bank, just across the Hudson River from New York City. His mother gave him his first lessons at the piano, and he used every opportunity to hear the celebrated kings of New York keyboard – James P. Johnson, Willie 'The Lion' Smith and especially Fats Waller. Ragtime was all the rage, and these keyboard professors ransacked the European tradition to achieve ever more spectacular improvisations. The young Basie listened to Fats Waller playing the organ in Harlem's Lincoln Theater and received tuition from him. Pianists were in demand to accompany vaudeville acts, and Waller recommended Basie as his successor in the Katie Crippen And Her Kids troupe, and with them he toured black venues throughout America (often referred to as the 'chitlin' circuit'). Stranded in Kansas City after the Gonzel White tour collapsed, Basie found it 'wide-open'. Owing to the *laissez-faire* administration of Democrat leader Tom Pendergast, musicians could easily find work, and jazz blossomed alongside gambling and prostitution (many people trace the origins of modern jazz to these circumstances). Basie played accompaniment for silent movies for a while, then in 1928 joined Walter Page's Blue Devils, starting a 20-year-long association with the bassist. When the Blue Devils broke up, Basie joined Bennie Moten, then in 1935, started his own band at the Reno Club and quickly lured Moten's best musicians into its ranks. Unfettered drinking hours, regular broadcasts on local radio and Basie's feel for swing honed the band into quite simply the most classy and propulsive unit in the history of music. Duke Ellington's band may have been more ambitious, but for sheer unstoppable *swing* Basie could not be beaten. Impresario John Hammond recognized as much when he heard them on their local broadcast. In January 1937 an augmented Basie band made its recording debut for Decca Records. By this time the classic rhythm section – Freddie Green

(guitar), Walter Page (bass) and Jo Jones (drums) – had been established. The horns – which included Lester Young (tenor saxophone) and Buck Clayton (trumpet) – sounded magnificent buoyed by this team and the goadings of Basie's deceptively simple piano. Basie frequently called himself a 'non-pianist'; actually, his incisive minimalism had great power and influence – not least on Thelonious Monk, one of bebop's principal architects.

In 1938, the band recorded the classic track 'Jumpin' At The Woodside', a Basie composition featuring solos by Earle Warren (alto saxophone) and Herschel Evans (clarinet), as well as Young and Clayton. The track could be taken as a definition of swing. Basie's residency at the Famous Door club on New York's West 52nd Street from July 1938 to January 1939 was a great success, CBS broadcasting the band over its radio network (transcriptions of these broadcasts have recently been made available – although hardly hi-fi, they are fascinating documents, with Lester Young playing clarinet as well as tenor). This booking was followed by a six-month residency in Chicago. It is this kind of regular work – spontaneity balanced with regular application – that explains why the recorded sides of the period are some of the great music of the century. In 1939 Basie left Decca for Columbia Records, with whom he stayed until 1946. Throughout the 40s the Count Basie band provided dancers with conducive rhythms and jazz fans with astonishing solos: both appreciated his characteristic contrast of brass and reeds. Outstanding tenors emerged: Don Byas, Buddy Tate, Lucky Thompson, Illinois Jacquet, Paul Gonsalves, as well as trumpeters (Al Killian and Joe Newman) and trombonists (Vic Dickenson and J.J. Johnson). On vocals Basie used Jimmy Rushing for the blues material and Helen Humes for pop and novelty numbers. Economic necessity pared down the Basie band to seven members at the start of the 50s, but otherwise Basie maintained a big band right through to his death in 1984. In 1954 he made his first tour of Europe, using arrangements by Ernie Wilkins and Neal Hefti. In June 1957 Basie broke the colour bar at New York's Waldorf-Astoria Hotel; his was the first black band to play there, and they stayed for a four-month engagement. The 1957 *The Atomic Mr. Basie* set Hefti's arrangements in glorious stereo sound and was acknowledged as a classic. Even the cover made its mark: in the 70s Blondie adapted its period nuclear-chic to frame singer Deborah Harry.

In 1960, Jimmy Rushing left the band, depriving it of a popular frontman, but the European tours continued – a groundbreaking tour of Japan in 1963 was also a great success. Count Basie was embraced by the American entertainment industry and appeared in the movies *Sex And The Single Girl* and *Made In Paris*. He became a regular television guest alongside the likes of Frank Sinatra, Fred Astaire, Sammy Davis Jnr. and Tony Bennett. Arranging for Basie was a significant step in the career of Quincy Jones (later famous as Michael Jackson's producer). The onslaught of the

Beatles and rock music in the 60s was giving jazz a hard time; Basie responded by giving current pop tunes the big band treatment, and Jones arranged *Hits Of The 50s And 60s*. Its resounding commercial success led to a string of similar albums arranged by Billy Byers; the brass adopted the stridency of John Barry's James Bond scores and, unlike the work of the previous decades, these records now sound dated. In 1965, Basie signed to Sinatra's Reprise Records, and made several recordings and appearances with him.

By 1969 most of Basie's original sidemen had left the band, though Freddie Green was still with him. Eddie 'Lockjaw' Davis (tenor) was now his most distinguished soloist. The arranger Sammy Nestico provided some interesting compositions, and 1970 saw the release of *Afrique*, an intriguing and unconventional album arranged by Oliver Nelson with tunes by *avant garde* saxophonists such as Albert Ayler and Pharoah Sanders. In 1975, after recording for a slew of different labels, Basie found a home on Pablo Records (owned by Norman Granz, organizer of the Jazz At The Philharmonic showcases). This produced a late flowering as, unlike previous producers, Granz let Basie do what he does best – swing the blues – rather than collaborate with popular singers. In 1983, the death of his wife Catherine, whom he had married 40 years earlier while he was with the Bennie Moten band, struck a heavy blow and he himself died the following year.

The later compromises should not cloud Basie's achievements: during the 30s he integrated the bounce of the blues into sophisticated ensemble playing. His piano work showed that rhythm and space were more important than technical virtuosity: his composing gave many eminent soloists their finest moments. Without the Count Basie Orchestra's sublimely aerated versions of 'Cherokee' it is unlikely that Charlie Parker could ever have created 'Koko'. Modern jazz stands indubitably in Basie's debt. For newcomers to the work of Basie the *Original American Decca Recordings* is an unbeatable starting point.

● ALBUMS: *Dance Parade* 10-inch album (Columbia 1949) ★★★★, *Count Basie At The Piano* 10-inch album (Decca 1950) ★★★, with Lester Young *Lester Young Quartet And Count Basie Seven* 10-inch album (Mercury 1950) ★★★★, with Young *Count Basie And Lester Young* 10-inch album (Jazz Panorama 1951) ★★★★, *Count Basie and the Kansas City 7* (Mercury 1952) ★★★, *Count Basie And His Orchestra Collates* (Mercury 1952) ★★★, *Jazz Royalty* 10-inch album (EmArcy 1954) ★★★, *Count Basie And His Orchestra* (Decca 1954) ★★★★, *The Old Count And The New Count – Basie* 10-inch album (Epic 1954) ★★★, *Basie Jazz* (Clef 1954) ★★★★, *Rock The Blues* 10-inch album (Epic 1954) ★★★★, *Count Basie Sextet* (Clef 1954) ★★★, *Count Basie Big Band* (Clef 1954) ★★★★, *Count Basie Dance Session 1* (Clef 1954) ★★★, *Count Basie i* (RCA Victor 1955) ★★★★, *Lester Leaps In* (Epic 1955) ★★★, *Let's Go To Prez* (Epic 1955) ★★★★, *Count Basie Dance Session 2* (Clef 1955) ★★★, *Basie's Back In Town* (Epic 1955) ★★★, *Classics* (Columbia 1955) ★★★, *A Night At Count Basie's*

(Vanguard 1955) ★★★, *Count Basie Swings/Joe Williams Sings* (Clef 1955) ★★★★, *The Greatest! Count Basie Swings/Joe Williams Sings Standards* (Verve 1956) ★★★★, *Basie Bash* (Columbia 1956) ★★★★, *Basie* (Clef 1956) ★★★★, *Blues By Basie* 1939-1950 recordings (Columbia 1956) ★★★★, with Ella Fitzgerald, Williams *One O'Clock Jump* (Columbia 1956) ★★★★, *Count Basie ii* (Brunswick 1956) ★★★, *The Count* (Clef 1956) ★★★★★, *The Swinging Count* (Clef 1956) ★★★, *The Band Of Distinction* (Clef 1956) ★★★, *Basie Roars Again* (Clef 1956) ★★★★, *The King Of Swing* (Clef 1956) ★★★, *Basie Rides Again* (Clef 1956) ★★★, *Basie In Europe* (Clef 1956) ★★★, *Count Basie iii* (American Record Society 1956) ★★★, *April In Paris* (Verve 1957) ★★★★★, *Basie's Best* (American Record Society 1957) ★★★★, *Count Basie In London* (Verve 1957) ★★★★, *Count Basie At Newport* (Verve 1957) ★★★★★, *The Atomic Mr Basie* (Roulette 1957) ★★★★★, *Basie Plays Hefti* (Roulette 1958) ★★★★, *Sing Along With Basie* (Roulette 1958) ★★★, *Dizzy Gillespie And Count Basie At Newport* (Verve 1958) ★★★★, *Hall Of Fame* (Verve 1958) ★★★, with Tony Bennett *Basie Swings, Bennett Sings* (Roulette 1958) ★★★★, *One More Time* (Roulette 1959) ★★★★, *Breakfast Dance And Barbecue* (Roulette 1959) ★★★, with Billy Eckstine *Basie/Eckstine Inc.* (Roulette 1959) ★★★★, *Chairman Of The Board* (Roulette 1959) ★★★, with Williams *Memories Ad Lib* (Roulette 1959) ★★★, *Everyday I Have The Blues* (Roulette 1959) ★★★★, *Tony Bennett In Person* (Columbia 1959) ★★★, *Dance With Basie* (Roulette 1959) ★★★★, *Not Now I'll Tell You When* (Roulette 1960) ★★★, *Just The Blues* (Roulette 1960) ★★★★, *String Along With Basie* (Roulette 1960) ★★★, *Kansas City Suite: The Music Of Benny Carter* (Roulette 1960) ★★★★, *Count Basie/Sarah Vaughan* (Roulette 1960) ★★★★, *The Count Basie Story* (Roulette 1961) ★★★★, *The Essential Count Basie* (Verve 1961) ★★★★, *First Time! The Count Meets The Duke* (Columbia 1961) ★★★★, *Basie At Birdland* (Roulette 1961) ★★★★, with Bennett *Bennett And Basie Strike Up The Band* (Roulette 1962) ★★, *The Legend* (Roulette 1962) ★★★, *Count Basie And The Kansas City 7* (Impulse! 1962) ★★★, *The Best Of Basie Volume 2* (Roulette 1962) ★★★, *Count Basie Live In Sweden* (Roulette 1962) ★★★, with Fitzgerald *Ella And Basie!* (Verve 1963) ★★★★, *Easin' It* (Roulette 1963) ★★★, *This Time By Basie!* (Reprise 1963) ★★★, *On My Way And Shouting Again* (Verve 1963) ★★★★, *Li'l Ol' Groovemaker ... Basie* (Verve 1963) ★★★, *More Hits Of The 50s And 60s* reissued as *Frankly Basie: Count Basie Plays The Hits Of Frank Sinatra* (Verve 1963) ★★★, *Basie Land* (Verve 1964) ★★★, *Our Shining Hour* (Verve 1964) ★★★, *Basie Picks The Winners* (Verve 1965) ★★★, with Arthur Prysock *Prysock/Basie* (Verve 1965) ★★★, *Pop Goes The Basie* (Reprise 1965) ★★★, *Basie's Bounce* (Affinity 1965) ★★★, *Basie's Beatle Bag* (Verve 1966) ★★★, *Basie's Swingin' Voices Singin'* (ABC-Paramount 1966) ★★★, *Basie Meets Bond* (United 1966) ★★★, *Inside Outside* (Verve 1966) ★★★, *Basie's Beat* (Verve 1967) ★★★★, *Broadway ... Basie's Way* (Command 1967) ★★★, *Hollywood ... Basie's Way* (Command 1967)

★★★, *Live In Antibes 1968* (Esoldun 1968) ★★★★, *Standing Ovation* (Dot 1968) ★★★, *High Voltage* (Verve 1970) ★★★, *Afrique* (Doctor Jazz 1971) ★★★, *At The Chatterbox* 1937 recordings (Jazz Archives 1974) ★★★, *Basie Jam, Vol. 1* (Pablo 1974) ★★★, with Big Joe Turner *The Bosses* (Pablo 1974) ★★★, *For The First Time* (Pablo 1974) ★★★, with Oscar Peterson *Satch And Josh* (Pablo 1975) ★★★, with Zoot Sims *Basie And Zoot* (Pablo 1975) ★★★★, *Basie Jam At Montreux '75* (Pablo 1975) ★★★, *Fun Time: Count Basie Big Band At Montreux '75* (Pablo 1975) ★★★, *The Basie Big Band* (Pablo 1975) ★★★, *For The Second Time* (Pablo 1975) ★★★, *I Told You So* (Pablo 1976) ★★★★, *Basie Jam, Vol. 2* (Pablo 1976) ★★★, *Basie Jam, Vol. 3* (Pablo 1976) ★★★, *Prime Time* (Pablo 1977) ★★★★, *Kansas City, Vol. 5* (Pablo 1977) ★★★, with Dizzy Gillespie *The Gifted Ones* (Pablo 1977) ★★★, *Basie Jam: Montreux '77* (Pablo 1977) ★★★, *Basie Big Band: Montreux '77* (Pablo 1977) ★★★, with Peterson *Satch And Josh ... Again* (Pablo 1977) ★★★, with Peterson *Yessir, That's My Baby* (Pablo 1978) ★★★, with Peterson *Night Rider* (Pablo 1978) ★★★, with Peterson *The Timekeepers* (Pablo 1978) ★★★, *Live In Japan* (Pablo 1978) ★★★, with Fitzgerald *A Classy Pair* (Pablo 1979) ★★★, with Fitzgerald *A Perfect Match: Basie And Ella* (Pablo 1979) ★★★, with Joe Pass, Fitzgerald *Digital III At Montreux* (Pablo 1979) ★★★, *On The Road* (Pablo 1980) ★★★, *Get Together* (Pablo 1980) ★★★, *Kansas City, Vol. 7* (Pablo 1980) ★★★, *Kansas City Shout* (Pablo 1980) ★★★, *Warm Breeze* (Pablo 1981) ★★★, *Farmers Market Barbecue* (Pablo 1982) ★★★, *Me And You* (Pablo 1983) ★★★, *88 Basie Street* (Pablo 1983) ★★★, *Mostly Blues ... And Some Others* (Pablo 1983) ★★★, *Fancy Pants* (Pablo 1984) ★★★, with Roy Eldridge *Loose Walk* 1972 recording (Pablo 1992) ★★★★, *Live At The Sands* 1966 recording (Reprise 1999) ★★★★.

● COMPILATIONS: with Bennie Moten *Count Basie In Kansas City* 1929-1932 recordings (Camden 1959) ★★★★, *Basie's Basement* 1929-1932 recordings (Camden 1959) ★★★★, *Verve's Choice – The Best Of Count Basie* (Verve 1963) ★★★★, *The World Of Count Basie* 3-LP set (Roulette 1964) ★★★, *Super Chief* 1936-1942 recordings (Columbia 1972) ★★★, *Good Morning Blues* 1937-1939 recordings (MCA 1977) ★★★, *Basie And Friends* 1974-1981 recordings (Pablo 1982) ★★★★, *Birdland Era, Volumes 1 & 2* (Duke 1986) ★★★★, *The Essential Count Basie, Volume 1* 1936-1939 recordings (Columbia 1987) ★★★★, *The Essential Count Basie, Volume 2* 1939-1940 recordings (Columbia 1987) ★★★★, *The Essential Count Basie, Volume 3* 1940-1941 recordings (Columbia 1988) ★★★★, *The Swing Machine* (Giants Of Jazz 1992) ★★★, *The Best Of Count Basie* (Pablo 1992) ★★★, *The Complete American Decca Recordings (1937-1939)* 3-CD set (Decca 1992) ★★★★★, *The Best Of Count Basie* 1937-1939 recordings (Decca 1992) ★★★★, *The Best Of Count Basie: The Roulette Years* (Roulette 1992) ★★★★, *Live 1956/1957/1959/1961* recordings, 3-CD box set (Sequel 1993) ★★★★, *The Complete Atomic Basie* (Roulette 1994) ★★★★★, *Count Basie And His Great Vocalists* 1939-1945 recordings (Columbia/Legacy 1995) ★★★★, *The*

Golden Years 1972-1983 recordings, 4-CD box set (Pablo 1996) ★★★★, *One O'Clock Jump: The Very Best Of Count Basie* (Collectables 1998) ★★★, *Swingsation* (GRP 1998) ★★★, *The Complete Roulette Studio Count Basie* 10-CD box set (Mosaic) ★★★★★, *The Complete Roulette Live Recordings Of Count Basie And His Orchestra (1958-1962)* 8-CD box set (Mosaic) ★★★★, *The Last Decade* 1974/1977/1980 recordings (Artistry) ★★★, *On The Upbeat* 1937-1945 recordings (Drive Archives) ★★★, *Rock-A-Bye Basie, Vol. 2* 1938-1940 recordings (Vintage Jazz Classics) ★★★★, *The Jubilee Alternatives* 1943-1944 recordings (Hep) ★★★, *Ken Burns Jazz: The Definitive Count Basie* (Verve 2001) ★★★★, *Jump King Of Swing* (Arpeggio 2001) ★★, *Blues By Basie* (Columbia 2001) ★★★.

● VIDEOS: *Count Basie And Friends* (Verve Video 1990), *Swingin' The Blues* (Verve Video 1993), *Ralph Gleason's Jazz Casual: Count Basie* (Rhino Home Video 1999).

● FURTHER READING: *Count Basie And His Orchestra: Its Music and Its Musicians*, Raymond Horricks. *Count Basie*, Alun Morgan. *Count Basie: A Biodiscography*, Chris Sheridan. *Good Morning Blues: The Autobiography Of Count Basie*, Albert Murray.

● FILMS: *Policy Man* (1938), *Choo Choo Swing* (1942), *Reveille With Beverly* (1943), *Stage Door Canteen* (1943), *Top Man* (1943), *Ebony Parade* (1947), *Basin Street Revue* (1956), *Cinderfella* (1960), *Sex And The Single Girl* (1964), *Made In Paris* (1966), *Blazing Saddles* (1974), *The Last Of The Blue Devils* (1979).

BAXTER, LES

b. 14 March 1922, Mexia, Texas, USA, d. 15 January 1996, Palm Springs, California, USA. Baxter studied piano at the Detroit Conservatory before moving to Los Angeles for further studies at Pepperdine College. Abandoning a concert career as a pianist he turned to popular music as a singer, and at the age of 23 he joined Mel Tormé's Mel-Tones, singing on Artie Shaw records such as 'What Is This Thing Called Love'. He then turned to arranging and conducting for Capitol Records in 1950 and was responsible for the early Nat 'King' Cole hits, 'Mona Lisa' and 'Too Young'. In 1953 he scored his first movie, the sailing travelogue *Tanga Tika*. With his own orchestra he released a number of hits including 'Ruby' (1953), 'Unchained Melody' (1955) and 'The Poor People Of Paris' (1956). He also achieved success with concept albums of his own orchestral suites, *Le Sacre Du Sauvage*, *Festival Of The Gnomes*, *Ports Of Pleasure* and *Brazil Now*, the first three for Capitol and the fourth on Gene Norman's Crescendo label. Baxter had obvious skill in writing Latin music for strings, but he did not restrict his activities to recording. As he once told *Soundtrack!* magazine, 'I never turn anything down'.

In the 60s he formed the Balladeers, a besuited and conservative folk group that at one time featured a slim and youthful David Crosby. He operated in radio as musical director of *Halls Of Ivy* and the Bob Hope and Abbott & Costello shows; he also worked on movie soundtracks and later composed and conducted scores for Roger Corman's Edgar Allan Poe films and other horror stories and teenage musicals, including *Comedy Of Terrors*, *Muscle Beach Party*, *The Dunwich Horror* and *Frogs*. When soundtrack work reduced in the 80s he scored music for theme parks and seaworlds. In the 90s Baxter was widely celebrated, alongside Martin Denny (for whom he had written 'Quiet Village') and Arthur Lyman Group, as one of the progenitors of what had become known as the 'exotica' movement. In his 1996 appreciation for *Wired* magazine, writer David Toop remembered Baxter thus: 'Baxter offered package tours in sound, selling tickets to sedentary tourists who wanted to stroll around some taboo emotions before lunch, view a pagan ceremony, go wild in the sun or conjure a demon, all without leaving home hi-fi comforts in the white suburbs.'

● ALBUMS: *Le Sacre Du Sauvage* 10-inch album (Capitol 1952) ★★★, *Music Of Prince Di Candriano* (Capitol 1953) ★★★, *Festival Of the Gnomes* (Capitol 1953) ★★★, *Music Out Of The Moon* 10-inch album (Capitol 1953) ★★★, *Music For Peace Of Mind* 10-inch album (Capitol 1953) ★★★, *Le Sacre Du Savage* (Capitol 1954) ★★★, *Thinking Of You* (Capitol 1954) ★★★, *The Passions* (Capitol 1954) ★★★, *Arthur Murray Modern Waltzes* (Capitol 1955) ★★★, *Kaleidoscope* (Capitol 1955) ★★★, *Tamboo!* (Capitol 1956) ★★★, *Caribbean Moonlight* (Capitol 1956) ★★★, *Skins!* (Capitol 1957) ★★★, *Round The World* (Capitol 1957) ★★★, *Midnight On The Cliffs* (Capitol 1957) ★★★, *Ports Of Pleasure* (Capitol 1957) ★★★, *Space Escapade* (Capitol 1958) ★★★, *Selections From South Pacific* (Capitol 1958) ★★★, *Love Is A Fabulous Thing* (Capitol 1958) ★★★, *Wild Guitars* (Capitol 1959) ★★★, *African Jazz* (Capitol 1959) ★★★, *Young Pops* (Capitol 1960) ★★★, *The Sacred Idol* film soundtrack (Capitol 1960) ★★★, *Cry Of Teen Drums* (Capitol 1960) ★★★, *Barbarian* film soundtrack (American International 1960) ★★, *Broadway '61* (Capitol 1961) ★★★, *Alakazam The Great* film soundtrack (Vee Jay 1961) ★★★, *Jewels Of The Sea* (Capitol 1961) ★★★, *The Sensational! Les Baxter* (Capitol 1962) ★★★, *Academy Award Winners 1963 (And Other Outstanding Motion Picture Themes)* (Reprise 1963) ★★★, *Brazil Now!* (Reprise 1967) ★★★, *Hell's Belles* film soundtrack (Sidewalk 1969) ★★★, *The Dunwich Horror* film soundtrack (American International 1970) ★★★, *Bora Bora* film soundtrack (American International 1970) ★★, *The Banshee* (Citadel 1970) ★★★.

● COMPILATIONS: *Baxter's Best* (Capitol 1960) ★★★, *Lost Episodes* (Dionysus 1995) ★★★, *The Exotic Moods Of Les Baxter* (Capitol 1996) ★★★★.

BÉCAUD, GILBERT

b. François Silly, 24 October 1927, Toulon, France, d. 18 December 2001, Paris, France. A popular singer-songwriter in France in the 50s and 60s, rivalling other popular balladeers such as Charles Trenet and Charles Aznavour, Bécaud studied music at the Conservatoire de Nice and started writing songs in his early teens. His first collaborator was lyricist Pierre Delanoe, and one of their first successes was 'Je T'ai Dans La Peau'

for Edith Piaf in 1950. He served as an accompanist for Piaf, and other artists such as Jacques Pills. Later he sang in cabaret, and made his first stage appearance in 1952 at Versailles. Two years later a dramatic performance at the Olympia Music Hall gained him the title of 'Monsieur 100,000 Volts', and elevated him to national stardom.

In the early 50s Bécaud had hit records with 'Les Croix', 'Quand Tu Danses' and 'Mes Mains'. Subsequent successes included 'Dimanche A Orly', 'Et Maintenant', 'Le Jour Où La Pluie Viendra', 'Couventine', 'Heureuse-ment, Y'a Les Copains', 'Viens Danser', 'Quand Il Est Mort Le Poète', and 'Tu Le Regretteras'. In 1958 'The Day The Rains Came', a reworking of 'Le Jour Où La Pluie Viendra' written with Delanoe and Carl Sigman, became a UK number 1 for Jane Morgan. Four years later Morgan also recorded 'Et Maintenant' as 'What Now My Love', although it was Shirley Bassey's dramatic version that had the most chart impact. The song was revived by Sonny And Cher in 1966 and was later covered by many other artists including Frank Sinatra. In the following year, Vikki Carr's emotive rendering of 'It Must Be Him' ('Seul Sur Son Étoile'), written with veteran lyricist Mack David, made both the US and UK Top 5.

A few years earlier, Bécaud's 'Je T'Appartiens' became an international success for the Everly Brothers under the title of 'Let It Be Me' (with Delanoe and Mann Curtis). Bécaud himself had a UK hit in 1975 with 'A Little Love And Understanding', written with Marcel Stellman. He also collaborated with Neil Diamond on the hit singles 'Love On The Rocks' and 'September Morn'', and composed extensively for films. His other collaborators included Louis Amade, Maurice Vidalin and the English librettist and lyricist Julian More, with whom he worked on *Madame Roza*, the 1987 Broadway musical based on Romain Gary's novel *La Vie Devant Soi*. Georgia Brown starred as a 'crusty, retired prostitute who raises the illegitimate offsprings of hookers', but not for long – the show closed after only 12 performances.

An indefatigable live performer, Bécaud sang in six languages and sold millions of records all over the world. He was happiest on stage at the Olympia in Paris, where he topped the bill over 40 times. Bécaud died of cancer in December 2001, at home on his beloved houseboat on the river Seine in Paris.

● ALBUMS: *Et Maintenant ... Gilbert Bécaud* (EMI 1964) ★★★★, *Gilbert Bécaud* (EMI 1968) ★★★, *Bécaud Olympia '70* (EMI 1970) ★★, *A Little Love And Understanding* (Decca 1975) ★★★.

● COMPILATIONS: *Collection* (EMI Germany 1983) ★★★, *Disque D'or, Volumes 1 & 2* (EMI France 1983) ★★★★, *40 Ans De Chansons* (EMI 1999) ★★★★.

● FILMS: *Le Pays D'Où Je Viens* (1956), *Casino De Paris* (1957), *Croquemitoufle* (1959), *Les Petits Matins* (1962), *Canzoni Nel Mondo* (1963), *Monte Carlo: C'est La Rose* (1968), *Un Homme Libre* (1973), *Toute Une Vie* (1974), *Gilbert Bécaud* (1990).

BELAFONTE AT CARNEGIE HALL – HARRY BELAFONTE

Harry Belafonte was just about at the peak of his popularity when he made this double-album set in a venue that, in the 50s, was usually the home of classical performers rather than pop artists. His magnetic personality and an impressive mixture of material that ranges from international folk songs such as 'Hava Nageela', 'Sylvie', 'Day-O' and 'Jamaican Farewell', to the traditional 'Danny Boy' and even a sea shanty, 'Shenandoah', ensured a stay of 86 weeks in the US chart and a Gold Disc award. The album also won a Grammy for Best Engineering Contribution.

● Tracks: *Darlin' Cora; Sylvie; John Henry; Take My Mother Home; Jamaica/Farewell; Man Piaba, All My Trials, Man Smart; Matilda*
● First released 1959
● UK peak chart position: did not chart
● USA peak chart position: 3

BELAFONTE, HARRY

b. Harold George Belafonte Jnr., 1 March 1927, Harlem, New York City, New York, USA. In recent years, the former 'King Of Calypso' has become better known for his work with UNICEF and his enterprise with the charity organization USA For Africa. Prior to that, Belafonte had an extraordinarily varied life. His early career was spent as an actor, until he had time to demonstrate his silky smooth and gently relaxing singing voice. He appeared as Joe in Oscar Hammerstein's *Carmen Jones*; an adaptation of *Carmen* by Bizet, and in 1956 he was snapped up by RCA-Victor Records. Belafonte was then at the forefront of the calypso craze, which was a perfect vehicle for his happy-go-lucky folk songs. Early hits included 'Jamaica Farewell', 'Mary's Boy Child' and the classic transatlantic hit 'Banana Boat Song' with its unforgettable refrain: 'Day-oh, dayyy-oh, daylight come and me wanna go home'. *Calypso* became the first ever album to sell a million copies, and spent 31 weeks at the top of the US charts. Belafonte continued throughout the 50s with incredible success. He was able to cross over into many markets appealing to pop, folk and jazz fans, as well as to the ethnic population with whom he became closely associated, particularly during the civil rights movement. He appeared in many movies including *Island In The Sun*, singing the title song, and *Odds Against Tomorrow*. His success as an album artist was considerable; between 1956 and 1962 he was hardly ever absent from the album chart. *Belafonte At Carnegie Hall* spent over three years in the charts, and similar success befell *Belafonte Returns To Carnegie Hall*, featuring Miriam Makeba, the Chad Mitchell Trio and Odetta, with a memorable recording of 'There's A Hole In My Bucket'.

Throughout the 60s Belafonte was an ambassador of human rights and a most articulate speaker at rallies and on television. His appeal as a concert hall attraction was immense; no less than seven of his albums were recorded in concert. Although his appearances in the bestseller lists had stopped

by the 70s he remained an active performer and recording artist, and continued to appear on film, although in lightweight movies such as *Buck And The Preacher* and *Uptown Saturday Night*. In the mid-80s he was a leading light in the USA For Africa appeal and sang on 'We Are The World'. His sterling work continued into the 90s with UNICEF. Belafonte was one of the few black artists who broke down barriers of class and race, and should be counted alongside Dr. Martin Luther King as a major figure in achieving equal rights for blacks in America through his work in popular music. He researched and produced an impressive box set of early African recordings in 2001: *The Long Road To Freedom: An Anthology Of Black Music* proved to be another landmark in an impressive career.

● ALBUMS: *Mark Twain And Other Folk Favorites* (RCA Victor 1955) ★★★, *Belafonte* (RCA Victor 1956) ★★★★, *Calypso* (RCA Victor 1956) ★★★★, *An Evening With Belafonte* (RCA Victor 1957) ★★★★, *Belafonte Sings Of The Caribbean* (RCA Victor 1957) ★★★, *Belafonte Sings The Blues* (RCA Victor 1958) ★★★, *Love Is A Gentle Thing* (RCA Victor 1959) ★★★, with Lena Horne *Porgy And Bess* film soundtrack (RCA Victor 1959) ★★★★, *Belafonte At Carnegie Hall* (RCA Victor 1959) ★★★★, *My Lord What A Mornin'* (RCA Victor 1960) ★★★, *Belafonte Returns To Carnegie Hall* (RCA Victor 1960) ★★★, *Swing Dat Hammer* (RCA Victor 1960) ★★★, *At Home And Abroad* (RCA Victor 1961) ★★★, *Jump Up Calypso* (RCA Victor 1961) ★★★★, *The Midnight Special* (RCA Victor 1962) ★★★, *The Many Moods Of Belafonte* (RCA Victor 1962) ★★★, *To Wish You A Merry Christmas* (RCA Victor 1962) ★★★, *Streets I Have Walked* (RCA Victor 1963) ★★★, *Belafonte At The Greek Theatre* (RCA Victor 1964) ★★★, *Ballads Blues And Boasters* (RCA 1964) ★★, with Miriam Makeba *An Evening With Belafonte/Makeba* (RCA 1965) ★★★, with Nana Mouskouri *An Evening With Belafonte/Mouskouri* (RCA 1966) ★★★, *In My Quiet Room* (RCA 1966) ★★★, *Calypso In Brass* (RCA 1967) ★★, *Belafonte On Campus* (RCA 1967) ★★, *Homeward Bound* (RCA 1970) ★★, *Play Me* (RCA 1976) ★★★, *Turn The World Around* (Columbia 1977) ★★, *Loving You Is Where I Belong* (Columbia 1981) ★★, *Paradise In Gazankulu* (EMI-Manhattan 1988) ★★, *Belafonte '89* (EMI 1989) ★★.

● COMPILATIONS: *Pure Gold* (RCA 1975) ★★★★, *A Legendary Performer* (RCA 1978) ★★★, *The Very Best Of Harry Belafonte* (RCA 1982) ★★★★, *20 Golden Greats* (Deja Vu 1985) ★★★, *Collection* (Castle 1987) ★★★, *Banana Boat Song* (Entertainers 1988) ★★★, *All Time Greatest Hits, Volume 1* (RCA 1989) ★★★★, *All Time Greatest Hits, Volume 2* (RCA 1989) ★★★, *All Time Greatest Hits, Volume 3* (RCA 1989) ★★★, *Day-O And Other Hits* (RCA 1990) ★★★.

● FURTHER READING: *Belafonte*, A.J. Shaw.
● FILMS: *Bright Road* (1953), *Carmen Jones* (1954), *Island In The Sun* (1957), *The World, The Flesh And The Devil* (1959), *Odds Against Tomorrow* (1959), *The Angel Levine* (1970), *Buck And The Preacher* (1972), *Uptown Saturday Night* (1974), *Free To Be …*

You & Me (1974), *A Veces Miro Mi Vida* (1982), *Roots Of Rhythm* narrator (1984), *We Shall Overcome* narrator (1989), *The Player* (1992), *Prêt-À-Porter* aka *Ready To Wear* (1994), *White Man's Burden* (1995), *Kansas City* (1996).

BELL, FREDDIE, AND THE BELLBOYS

This early US rock 'n' roll six-piece outfit was led by singer Freddie Bell (b. 29 September 1931, South Philadelphia, Pennsylvania, USA). Their 'big band' style of rock 'n' roll included a version of Willie Mae Thornton's 'Hound Dog' for the Teen label in 1955. Elvis Presley saw them performing the song live in April 1956 and recorded his own version in July. The Bellboys achieved another landmark by appearing in the first rock 'n' roll movie – *Rock Around The Clock* – in 1956. They were also the first US rock act to tour the UK, supporting Tommy Steele in 1956. Their best-known number was also released that year, 'Giddy Up A Ding Dong', and became a number 4 hit in the UK. Other singles included 'The Hucklebuck', 'Teach You To Rock' and 'Rockin' Is My Business'. Another film appearance was in the 1964 pop exploitation movie *Get Yourself A College Girl* (*The Swinging Set* in the UK), where Roberta Linn sang with them. The Animals, the Dave Clark Five and the Standells also featured. On the strength of a few hits Bell has sustained a career for over 40 years. Now performing as the Freddie Bell Show, he has a residency in Las Vegas for most of the year and tours the world in the remaining weeks.

● ALBUMS: *Rock 'n' Roll All Flavours* (Mercury 1958) ★★★, *Bells Are Swinging* (20th Century 1964) ★★.
● COMPILATIONS: *Rockin' Is Our Business* (Bear Family 1996) ★★★.
● FILMS: *Rock Around The Clock* (1956), *Rumble On The Docks* (1956), *Get Yourself A College Girl* aka *The Swinging Set* (1964).

BELVIN, JESSE

b. 15 December 1932, San Antonio, Texas, USA, d. 6 February 1960, Fairhope, Arkansas, USA. Raised in Los Angeles, Belvin became a part of the city's flourishing R&B scene while in his teens. He was featured on 'All The Wine Is Gone', a 1950 single by Big Jay McNeely, but his career was then interrupted by a spell in the US Army. 'Earth Angel', a collaboration with two fellow conscripts, was recorded successfully by the Penguins, while Belvin enjoyed a major hit in his own right with 'Goodnight My Love', a haunting, romantic ballad adopted by disc jockey Alan Freed as the closing theme to his highly influential radio show. He also recorded with fellow songwriter Marvin Phillips as Jesse & Marvin, achieving a Top 10 R&B hit in 1953 with 'Dream Girl'. In 1958 Belvin formed part of the opportunistic vocal quintet, the Shields, who recorded the national Top 20 hit 'You Cheated' for Dot Records. That same year the singer was signed to RCA Records, who harboured plans to shape him in the mould of Nat 'King' Cole and Billy Eckstine. Further hits, including 'Funny' and 'Guess Who' – the latter of

which was written by his wife and manager Jo Ann – offered a cool, accomplished vocal style suggestive of a lengthy career, but Belvin died, along with his wife, following a car crash in February 1960.

● ALBUMS: *The Casual Jesse Belvin* (Crown 1959) ★★★★, *The Unforgettable Jesse Belvin* (Crown 1959) ★★★★, *Just Jesse Belvin* (RCA Victor 1959) ★★★, *Mr. Easy* (RCA Victor 1960) ★★★, *True To Myself* (Warners 1996) ★★★.
● COMPILATIONS: *Yesterdays* (RCA 1975) ★★★, *Memorial Album* (Ace 1984) ★★★★, *Hang Your Tears Out To Dry* (Earth Angel 1987) ★★★, *Jesse Belvin: The Blues Balladeer* (Specialty 1990) ★★★★, *Goodnight My Love* (Ace 1991) ★★★★, *Golden Classics* (Collectables 1997) ★★★.

BENEKE, TEX

b. Gordon Beneke, 12 February 1914, Fort Worth, Texas, USA, d. 31 May 2000, Costa Mesa, California, USA. Starting out on soprano saxophone, Beneke switched to tenor, working with various bands in the south-west. In 1938, he joined Glenn Miller where, in addition to featured tenor, he was also a regular vocalist. Beneke sang with engaging charm, if limited ability, on such classic hits as 'I Gotta Gal In Kalamazoo', 'Don't Sit Under The Apple Tree', and 'Chattanooga Choo Choo'. Strongly influenced by the driving, big-toned tradition of Texas tenors, Beneke's playing added a jazz flavour to many Miller dance hits, including 'In The Mood' and 'String Of Pearls', on which he duetted with fellow tenor Al Klink. At the outbreak of World War II, Beneke worked with Miller's singing group, the Modernaires, then joined the US Navy where he played in a navy band. After the war, following Miller's death, Beneke was invited by Miller's executors to direct the Miller orchestra. In 1950, he relinquished this role but continued to lead his own band which, not surprisingly, played Miller-style music and enjoyed several chart hits on the RCA-Victor Records label. He continued leading bands into the 90s, bringing unfailing good humour and enthusiasm to a somewhat overexposed corner of popular music.

● COMPILATIONS: *With No Strings* 1949-51 recordings (Hep Jazz 1981) ★★★★, *Beneke On Broadway* (Bulldog 1982) ★★★, *Shooting Star* 1948 recordings (Magic 1983) ★★★, *Memories* 1949 recordings (First Heard 1984) ★★★, *Loose Like* 1946 recordings (Hep Jazz 1988) ★★★, *Tex Beneke Salutes Glenn Miller* 40s recordings (Jazz Band 1990) ★★★★, with the Glenn Miller Orchestra *1946 Live In Hi-Fi At The Hollywood Palladium* (Jazz Hour 1997) ★★★, *The Best Of Tex Beneke* 1946-49 recordings (Collector's Choice 1998) ★★★★, *Tex Beneke-Glenn Miller Orchestra* 40s recording (Pulse 2000) ★★★, *Tex Beneke And The Glenn Miller Orchestra: But Beautiful* 1946-50 recordings (Pegasus 2000) ★★★.
● VIDEOS: *Tex Beneke And The Glenn Miller Orchestra* (Kay Jazz 1988).
● FILMS: *Sun Valley Serenade* (1941), *Orchestra Wives* (1942).

BENNY GOODMAN STORY, THE

Hollywood biopics almost always present the same paradox: if the subject is interesting enough to make a film of his/her life, why meddle with the facts? Goodman, portrayed by Steve Allen, but providing his own playing for the soundtrack, had a rags-to-riches life story that simultaneously fulfilled the American Dream and every screenwriter's wildest fantasy. Unfortunately, in real life, Goodman was a single-minded perfectionist who became a household name and a millionaire before he had reached 30. In other words, all he did was practise obsessively and perform, which did not make for good visual drama. Hence, the reality of his dedication was jettisoned in favour of a sloppy story about a home-loving boy who made good. In the course of the film, Goodman periodically whines to his Ma, 'Don't be that way'. This allows the introduction of the tune of that name as the dutiful son's grateful acknowledgement to his mother, thus overlooking the fact that Edgar Sampson wrote the song for another bandleader, Chick Webb. Goodman's not inconsiderable streak of ruthlessness was also overlooked. Nevertheless, the film has some nice musical moments from Allen/Goodman, Teddy Wilson, Lionel Hampton and Gene Krupa in the small group numbers. The specially assembled big band includes Buck Clayton, Stan Getz, Conrad Gozzo, Urbie Green, Manny Klein and Murray McEachern and plays very well, even though it does not sound much like the real Goodman band of the late 30s. Ben Pollack and Kid Ory also appear, as does Harry James (in a close-up solo feature but not in long-shot – contractual reasons were suggested, specifically, too little money). For all this 1955 film's flaws, among which is the famous 1938 Carnegie Hall concert attended by 'longhairs' – in real life the seats were packed with swing-era fans and jitterbugs – it remains one of the least embarrassing of the earlier jazz biopics.

BERRY, CHUCK

b. Charles Edward Anderson Berry, 18 October 1926, San Jose, California, USA (although Berry states that he was born in St. Louis, Missouri). A seminal figure in the evolution of rock 'n' roll, Chuck Berry's influence as songwriter and guitarist is incalculable. His cogent songs captured adolescent life, yet the artist was 30 years old when he commenced recording. Introduced to music as a child, Berry learned guitar while in his teens, but this period was blighted by a three-year spell in Algoa Reformatory following a conviction for armed robbery. On his release Berry undertook several blue-collar jobs while pursuing part-time spots in St. Louis bar bands. Inspired by Carl Hogan, guitarist in Louis Jordan's Timpani Five, and Charlie Christian, he continued to hone his craft and in 1951 purchased a tape recorder to capture ideas for compositions. The following year Berry joined Johnnie Johnson (piano) and Ebby Hardy (drums) in the house band at the Cosmopolitan Club. Over the ensuing months the trio became a popular attraction, playing a mixture of R&B, country/hillbilly songs and standards, particularly those of Nat 'King' Cole, on whom Berry modelled his cool vocal style. The guitarist also fronted his own group, the Chuck Berry Combo, at the rival Crank Club, altering his name to spare his father's embarrassment at such worldly pursuits.

In 1955, during a chance visit to Chicago, Berry met bluesman Muddy Waters, who advised the young singer to approach the Chess Records label. Berry's demo of 'Ida May', was sufficient to win a recording contract and the composition, retitled 'Maybellene', duly became his debut single. This ebullient performance was a runaway success, topping the R&B chart and reaching number 5 on the US pop listings. Its lustre was partially clouded by a conspiratorial publishing credit that required Berry to share the rights with Russ Fratto and disc jockey Alan Freed, in deference to his repeated airplay. This situation remained unresolved until 1986. Berry enjoyed further US R&B hits with 'Thirty Days' and 'No Money Down', but it was his third recording session that proved even more productive, producing a stream of classics, 'Roll Over Beethoven', 'Too Much Monkey Business' and 'Brown-Eyed Handsome Man'. The artist's subsequent releases read like a lexicon of pop history – 'School Days' (a second R&B number 1), 'Rock And Roll Music' (all 1957), 'Sweet Little Sixteen', 'Reelin' And Rockin', 'Johnny B. Goode', 'Around And Around' (all 1958), 'Little Queenie', 'Back In The USA', 'Let It Rock' (all 1959), 'Bye Bye Johnny', 'Jaguar And Thunderbird' (all 1960), 'Nadine', 'You Never Can Tell', No Particular Place To Go' and 'The Promised Land' (all 1964) are but a handful of the peerless songs written and recorded during this prolific period. In common with contemporary artists, Berry drew from both country and R&B music, but his sharp, often piquant, lyrics, clarified by the singer's clear diction, introduced a new discipline to the genre. Such incomparable performances not only defined rock 'n' roll, they provided a crucial template for successive generations.

Both the Beatles and Rolling Stones acknowledged their debt to Berry. The former recorded two of his compositions, taking one, 'Roll Over Beethoven', into the US charts, while the latter drew from his empirical catalogue on many occasions. This included 'Come On', their debut single, 'Little Queenie', 'You Can't Catch Me' and 'Around And Around', as well as non-Berry songs that nonetheless aped his approach. The Stones' readings of 'Route 66', 'Down The Road Apiece' and 'Confessin' The Blues' were indebted to their mentor's versions, while Keith Richards' rhythmic, propulsive guitar figures drew from Berry's style. Elsewhere, the Beach Boys rewrote 'Sweet Little Sixteen' as 'Surfin' USA' to attain their first million-seller, while countless other groups scrambled to record his songs, inspired by their unique combination of immediacy and longevity. Between 1955 and 1960, Berry seemed unassailable. He enjoyed a run of 17 R&B Top 20 entries, appeared in the movies Go, Johnny, Go!, Rock Rock Rock and Jazz On A Summer's Day, the last of which documented the artist's performance at the 1958 *Newport Jazz Festival*, where he demonstrated the famed 'duckwalk' to a bemused audience. However, personal impropriety undermined Berry's personal and professional life when, on 28 October 1961, he was convicted under the Mann Act of 'transporting an underage girl across state lines for immoral purposes'. Berry served 20 months in prison, emerging in October 1963 just as 'Memphis, Tennessee', recorded in 1958, was providing him with his first UK Top 10 hit. He wrote several compositions during his incarceration, including 'Nadine', 'No Particular Place To Go', 'You Never Can Tell' and 'Promised Land', each of which eventually reached the UK Top 30. Such chart success soon waned as the R&B bubble burst, and in 1966 Berry sought to regenerate his career by moving from Chess to Mercury Records. However, an ill-advised *Golden Hits* set merely featured re-recordings of old material, while attempts to secure a contemporary image on *Live At The Fillmore Auditorium* (recorded with the Steve Miller Band) and *Concerto In B. Goode* proved equally unsatisfactory.

He returned to Chess Records in 1969 and immediately re-established his craft with the powerful 'Tulane'. *Back Home* and *San Francisco Dues* were cohesive selections and in-concert appearances showed a renewed purpose. Indeed, a UK performance at the 1972 Manchester Arts Festival not only provided half of Berry's *London Sessions* album, but also his biggest-ever hit. 'My Ding-A-Ling', a mildly ribald *double entendre* first recorded by Dave Bartholomew, topped both the US and UK charts, a paradox in the light of his own far superior compositions, which achieved lesser commercial plaudits. It was his last major hit, and despite several new recordings, including *Rockit*, a much-touted release on Atco Records, Berry became increasingly confined to the revival circuit. He gained an uncomfortable reputation as a hard, shrewd businessman and disinterested performer, backed by pick-up bands with whom he refused to rehearse. Tales abound within the rock fraternity of Berry's refusal to tell the band which song he was about to launch into. Pauses and changes would come about by the musicians watching Berry closely for an often disguised signal. Berry has insisted for years upon pre-payment of his fee, usually in cash, and he will only perform an encore after a further negotiation for extra payment.

Berry's continued legal entanglements resurfaced in 1979 when he was sentenced to a third term of imprisonment following a conviction for income tax evasion. Upon release he embarked on a punishing world tour, but the subsequent decade proved largely unproductive musically and no new recordings were undertaken. In 1986, the artist celebrated his 60th birthday with gala performances in St. Louis and New York. Keith Richards appeared at the former, although relations between the two men were strained, as evinced in the resultant documentary *Hail! Hail! Rock 'N' Roll*, which provided an overview of Berry's career. Berry was inducted into the Rock

And Roll Hall Of Fame the same year. Sadly, the 90s began with further controversy and reports of indecent behaviour at the singer's Berry Park centre. Although the incident served to undermine the individual, Berry's stature as an essential figure in the evolution of popular music cannot be overestimated.

● ALBUMS: *After School Session* (Chess 1958) ★★★★ *One Dozen Berrys* (Chess 1958) ★★★★★, *Chuck Berry Is On Top* (Chess 1959) ★★★★, *Rockin' At The Hops* (Chess 1960) ★★★★, *New Juke-Box Hits* (Chess 1961) ★★★, *Chuck Berry Twist* (Chess 1962) ★★★, *More Chuck Berry* UK release (Pye 1963) ★★★, *Chuck Berry On Stage* (Chess 1963) ★★, *The Latest And The Greatest* (Chess 1964) ★★★, *You Never Can Tell* (Chess 1964) ★★★, with Bo Diddley *Two Great Guitars* (Chess 1964) ★★★, *St. Louis To Liverpool* (Chess 1964) ★★★★, *Chuck Berry In London* (Chess 1965) ★★★, *Fresh Berry's* (Chess 1965) ★★★, *Golden Hits* new recordings (Mercury 1967) ★★, *Chuck Berry In Memphis* (Mercury 1967) ★★★, *Live At The Fillmore Auditorium* (Mercury 1967) ★★, *From St. Louis To Frisco* (Mercury 1968) ★★, *Concerto In B. Goode* (Mercury 1969) ★★, *Back Home* (Chess 1970) ★★, *San Francisco Dues* (Chess 1971) ★★, *The London Chuck Berry Sessions* (Chess 1972) ★★, *Bio* (Chess 1973) ★★, *Chuck Berry* (Chess 1975) ★★, *Live In Concert* (Magnum 1978) ★★★, *Rockit* (Atco 1979) ★★★★, *Rock! Rock! Rock 'N' Roll!* (Atco 1980) ★★, *Hail! Hail! Rock 'N' Roll* film soundtrack (MCA 1987) ★★, *Live* 1982 recording (Columbia River 2000) ★★.

● COMPILATIONS: *Chuck Berry's Greatest Hits* (Chess 1964) ★★★★★, *Chuck Berry's Golden Decade* (Chess 1967) ★★★★★, *Golden Decade, Volume 2* (Chess 1973) ★★★★, *Golden Decade, Volume 3* (Chess 1974) ★★★★, *Motorvatin'* (Chess 1977) ★★★, *Spotlight On Chuck Berry* (PRT 1980) ★★★, *The Great Twenty-Eight* (Chess/MCA 1982) ★★★★★, *Chess Masters* (Chess 1983) ★★★, *Reelin' And Rockin' (Live)* (Aura 1984) ★★, *Rock 'N' Roll Rarities* (Chess/MCA 1986) ★★, *More Rock 'N' Roll Rarities* (Chess/MCA 1986) ★★★, *Chicago Golden Years* (Vogue 1988) ★★★, *Decade '55 To '65* (Platinum 1988) ★★★, *Chess Box* 3-CD box set (Chess/MCA 1989) ★★★★, *Missing Berries: Rarities, Volume 3* (Chess/MCA 1990) ★★★, *The Chess Years* 9-CD box set (Charly 1991) ★★★★★, *On The Blues Side* (Ace 1993) ★★★★, *Oh Yeah!* (Charly 1994) ★★★, *Poet Of Rock 'N' Roll* 4-CD box set (Charly 1995) ★★★★★, *His Best Volume 1* (Chess 1997) ★★★★, *The Best Of Chuck Berry: The Millennium Collection* (PolyGram 1999) ★★★★, *Chuck Berry: The Anthology* (MCA 2000) ★★★★.

● VIDEOS: *The Legendary Chuck Berry* (Channel 5 1987), *Hail Hail Rock 'N' Roll* (CIC Video 1988), *Live At The Roxy* (Old Gold 1990), *Rock 'N' Roll Music* (BMG Video 1991).

● FURTHER READING: *Chuck Berry: Rock 'N' Roll Music*, Howard A. De Witt. *Chuck Berry: Mr Rock 'N' Roll*, Krista Reese. *Chuck Berry: The Autobiography*, Chuck Berry. *Long Distance Information: Chuck Berry's Recorded Legacy*, Fred Rothwell.

● FILMS: *Rock, Rock, Rock* (1956), *Mister Rock And*

Roll (1957), *Go, Johnny, Go!* (1958), *Jazz On A Summer's Day* (1959), *Alice In Den Städten* aka *Alice In The Cities* (1974), *American Hot Wax* (1978), *Class Reunion* (1982), *Hail! Hail! Rock 'N' Roll* (1987).

BEVERLEY SISTERS

This close-harmony UK vocal group consisted of three sisters; Joy Beverley (b. 1929) and twins Teddie and Babs (b. 1932) were all born in London, England, daughters of the singing comedy duo Coram and Mills. The girls discovered they could sing harmony on school hymns, with Teddie singing the low parts, ('down in her boots', as she puts it). They started recording in the early 50s with songs such as 'Ferry Boat Inn', 'My Heart Cries For You', and 'Teasin'', and later had hits with 'I Saw Mommy Kissing Santa Claus', 'Little Drummer Boy' and 'Little Donkey'. During 1953 they performed in the USA, appeared in a record-breaking theatre season in Blackpool, played at the London Palladium with Bob Hope and presented their own television series, *Three Little Girls In View*. Their act was particularly suited to cabaret because of its risqué element ('sassy, but classy', according to Ed Sullivan). Songs such as 'We Like To Do Things Like That', 'It's Illegal, It's Immoral Or It Makes You Fat' and 'He Like It, She Like It', inevitably led to one entitled 'We Have To Be So Careful All The Time'. They wore identical outfits, on and off stage, and at one time bought the house next door to their own in order to store all their clothes. Enormously popular in the UK during the 50s, they were still a top act into the 60s, until they retired in 1967 to raise their children. Joy, who was married to ex-England football captain Billy Wright, had two daughters, Vicky and Babette, and Teddie had one girl, Sasha. In the 80s, the three young girls formed a pop group, the Little Foxes.

In 1985, while watching their daughters perform at Peter Stringfellow's Hippodrome nightspot in London, the Beverley Sisters themselves were booked to appear there on Mondays, the 'Gay Night'. They received extraordinary receptions, with the audience singing along on the old specialities such as 'Sisters' and 'Together'. Personal appearances and cabaret dates followed; a new album, *Sparkle*, was issued and some of their stage outfits were exhibited at the Victoria & Albert museum in London. The comeback endured into the 90s, with two more albums and a 30-date UK tour in 1995.

● ALBUMS: *A Date With The Bevs* (Philips 1955) ★★★, *The Enchanting Beverley Sisters* (Columbia 1960) ★★★, *Those Beverley Sisters* (Ace Of Clubs 1960) ★★★, *The World Of The Beverley Sisters* (Decca 1971) ★★★★, *Together* (MFP 1985) ★★★, *Sparkle* (K-Tel 1985) ★★★, *Sisters Sisters – An Evening With The Beverley Sisters* (Pickwick 1993) ★★★, *Bless 'Em All* (Pickwick 1995) ★★★.

BIG BOPPER

b. Jiles Perry Richardson, 24 October 1930, Sabine Pass, Texas, USA, d. 3 February 1959, USA. After working as a disc jockey in Beaumont, Richardson won a recording contract with Mercury Records, releasing two unsuccessful singles in 1957. The following year, under his radio moniker 'The Big Bopper', he recorded the ebullient 'Chantilly Lace', a rock 'n' roll classic, complete with blaring saxophone and an insistent guitar run. However, it was scheduled to be the b-side, backed with the satirical 'The Purple People Eater Meets The Witch Doctor'; the disc was a transatlantic hit. The follow-up, 'Big Bopper's Wedding', underlined the singer's love of novelty and proved popular enough to win him a place on a tour with Buddy Holly and Ritchie Valens. On 3 February 1959, a plane carrying the three stars crashed, leaving no survivors. Few of Richardson's recordings were left for posterity, though there was enough for a posthumous album, *Chantilly Lace*, which included the rocking 'White Lightning'. In 1960, Johnny Preston offered the ultimate valediction by taking the Big Bopper's composition 'Running Bear' to number 1 on both sides of the Atlantic.

● ALBUMS: *Chantilly Lace* (Mercury 1959) ★★★.
● COMPILATIONS: *Hellooo Baby! The Best Of The Big Bopper 1954-1959* (Rhino 1989) ★★★.
● FURTHER READING: *Chantilly Lace: The Life & Times Of J.P. Richardson*, Tim Knight.

BIG MAYBELLE

b. Mabel Louise Smith, 1 May 1924, Jackson, Tennessee, USA, d. 23 January 1972, Cleveland, Ohio, USA. Maybelle was discovered singing in church by Memphis bandleader Dave Clark in 1935. When Clark disbanded his orchestra to concentrate on record promotion, Smith moved to Christine Chatman's orchestra with whom she first recorded for Decca Records in 1944. Three years later, Smith made solo records for King and in 1952 she recorded as Big Maybelle when producer Fred Mendelsohn signed her to OKeh Records, a subsidiary of CBS Records. Her blues shouting style (a female counterpart to Big Joe Turner) brought an R&B hit the next year with 'Gabbin' Blues' (a cleaned-up version of the 'dirty dozens' on which she was partnered by songwriter Rose Marie McCoy). 'Way Back Home' and 'My Country Man' were also bestsellers. In 1955, she made the first recording of 'Whole Lotta Shakin' Goin' On', which later became a major hit for Jerry Lee Lewis. Big Maybelle was also a star attraction on the chitlin' circuit of black clubs, with an act that included risqué comedy as well as emotive ballads and brisk boogies. Leaving OKeh for Savoy, her 'Candy' (1956) brought more success and in 1959, she appeared in *Jazz On A Summer's Day*, the film of the Newport Jazz Festival. Despite her acknowledged influence on the soul styles of the 60s, later records for Brunswick Records, Scepter and Chess Records made little impact until she signed to the Rojac label in 1966. There she was persuaded to record some recent pop hits by the Beatles and Donovan and had some minor chart success of her own with versions of 'Don't Pass Me By' and '96 Tears'. The latter was composed by Rudy Martinez, who also recorded it with his band ? And The Mysterians. Big Maybelle's career was marred by frequent drug problems, which contributed to her early death from a diabetic coma.

● ALBUMS: *Big Maybelle Sings* (Savoy 1958) ★★★★, *Blues, Candy And Big Maybelle* (Savoy 1958) ★★★★, *What More Can A Woman Do?* (Brunswick 1962) ★★★, *The Gospel Soul Of Big Maybelle* (Brunswick 1964) ★★★★, *The Great Soul Hits Of Big Maybelle* (Brunswick 1964) ★★★★, *Gabbin' Blues* (Scepter 1965) ★★★, *Saga Of The Good Life And Hard Times* (Rojac 1966) ★★★, *Got A Brand New Bag* (Rojac 1967) ★★★, *The Last Of Big Maybelle* (Paramount 1973) ★★★.

● COMPILATIONS: *The OKeh Sessions* (Charly 1983) ★★★★, *Roots Of R&B And Early Soul* (Savoy Jazz 1985) ★★★★, *Candy* (Savoy 1995) ★★★.

BIHARI BROTHERS

The Bihari family moved in 1941 from Oklahoma to Los Angeles where eldest brother Jules went into business as a supplier and operator of juke-boxes for the black community. The next step was to ensure the supply of suitable blues and R&B recordings to feed the juke-boxes, and with Joe and Saul, he founded the Modern Music Company in 1945. As well as recording west coast artists such as Jimmy Witherspoon and Johnny Moore's Three Blazers, the brothers worked with local producers in Houston, Detroit and Memphis who supplied Modern with more rough-hewn blues material by such artists as Lightnin' Hopkins, John Lee Hooker and B.B. King. In 1951, the fourth Bihari brother, Lester, set up the Meteor label in Memphis. Meteor was responsible for some of Elmore James's earliest records as well as rockabilly by Charlie Feathers. Other Modern group labels included RPM (for which Ike Turner produced Howlin' Wolf), Blues & Rhythm and Flair.

During the early 50s, the Bihari brothers released a wide range of material, even aiming at the pop charts by covering R&B titles from other labels. Among its successes were Etta James' 'Wallflower', 'Stranded In The Jungle' by the Cadets, 'Eddie My Love' by the Teen Queens and Jessie Belvin's 'Goodnight My Love'. The arranger/producer of many Modern tracks was Maxwell Davis. However, by the late 50s, the Modern group turned its attention towards reissuing material on the Crown budget-price label, which also included a series of big-band tribute albums masterminded by Davis. When the company found itself in financial difficulties, the Biharis released recordings by Z.Z. Hill, Lowell Fulson and B.B. King on the Kent Records label, but the death of Saul Bihari in 1975 and Joe's departure from the company led to a virtual cessation of recording, and the remaining brothers concentrated on custom pressing at their vinyl record plant. In 1984, the year of Jules Bihari's death, the family sold the catalogues of Modern, Flair, Kent, Crown and RPM. Seven years later, the labels passed into the hands of a consortium of Virgin Records (USA), Ace Records (Europe) and Blues Interactions (Japan). These companies continued an extensive reissue programme that the Ace label had initiated as licensee of the Modern group in the early 80s.

BINGE, RONALD

b. 15 July 1910, Derby, England, d. 6 September 1979, Ringwood, Hampshire, England. Binge was responsible for creating in 1951 the 'cascading strings' sound that made the Mantovani Orchestra famous throughout the world. This was achieved purely by clever scoring, dividing the violins into several parts, each allotted a different melody-note in turn, which they sustain and then fade out, until called upon to move elsewhere. Binge's inspiration came from his love of church music, particularly Monteverdi. Composers of sacred music had to allow for the long reverberation inevitable in cathedrals, and this is reflected in their writing. The first big success was 'Charmaine', followed by many others that made Mantovani's albums million-sellers, especially in the USA. Binge's association with Mantovani dates from 1935 when he played in, and did all the arrangements for, Mantovani's Tipica Orchestra. During war service in the RAF he spent some time in Blackpool, teaming up with Sidney Torch and his RAF Orchestra to present concerts for recruits. In later years Binge often provided arrangements for Torch's many broadcasts. Much of Binge's post-war work involved orchestrating numerous popular songs of the day for broadcasting, as well as theatrical assignments; Binge scored Noël Coward's musical *Pacific 1860*, which opened at London's Theatre Royal Drury Lane in December 1946, with Mary Martin in the starring role. Binge gradually began to concentrate more on composing, and an early success was 'Elizabethan Serenade', first recorded by Mantovani in 1951, and later a big seller for other orchestras, notably Ron Goodwin. It won an Ivor Novello Award in 1957. In 1954 Binge adapted his 'cascade' effect with solo cornets for his 'Concert Carillon'. Like many of his contemporaries, he contributed numerous works to the London publishers' mood music libraries, which serve the special requirements of radio, television and films. Other compositions of note include 'Miss Melanie', 'Madrugado', 'The Red Sombrero', 'Faire Frou Frou', 'Caribbean Calypso', 'Dance Of The Snowflakes', 'The Fire God', 'Song Of Canterbury', 'Tales Of The Three Blind Mice', 'Thames Rhapsody', 'Trade Winds', 'Venetian Carnival', 'Man In A Hurry', 'The Watermill', 'High Stepper' and 'Sailing By', which for many years was the close-down music on BBC Radio 4. The BBC International Festival Of Light Music in 1956 commissioned Binge to compose his 'Concerto For Saxophone', which received its first performance with Michael Krein as soloist. Another major work was 'Saturday Symphony' (1966-68). Binge conducted them both in a recording by the South German Radio Orchestra. His scores for the cinema include *Desperate Moment* (1953), *Our Girl Friday* (1953), *The Runaway Bus* (1954) and *Dance Little Lady* (1954).

● ALBUMS: *Concerto For Saxophone And Orchestra/ Saturday Symphony* (Rediffusion 1971) ★★★, *British Light Music – Ronald Binge* (Marco Polo 1994) ★★★★.

BIRTH OF THE COOL – MILES DAVIS

Although this album is credited to Miles Davis, the importance of Gerry Mulligan's playing and, especially, his stellar compositions 'Jeru', 'Rocker' and the gorgeous 'Venus De Milo', make this album special. Although it is generally considered to be less accomplished than *Kind Of Blue*, this collection is, in some ways more important. It would be churlish to say this was the birth of the cool, but the songs recorded by the legendary nonet and collected together here certainly mark the birth of something significant. Hearing all the tracks on the newly available CD version makes it more complete, and therefore, more necessary than ever. It is an indispensable album, now superseded by the *Complete Birth Of The Cool*.

● Tracks: Move; Jeru; Moon Dreams; Venus De Milo; Budo; Deception; Godchild; Boplicity; Rocker; Israel; Rouge.
● First released 1954
● UK peak chart position: did not chart
● USA peak chart position: did not chart

BLACK, STANLEY

b. 14 June 1913, London, England. At the age of seven Black began learning the piano and later studied at the Mathay School of Music. His first composition, when he was aged 12, was broadcast by the BBC Symphony Orchestra. In 1929 he won an arranging contest sponsored by the then jazz weekly, *Melody Maker*, and became known as a promising jazz pianist, recording with visiting Americans Coleman Hawkins, Louis Armstrong and Benny Carter, plus the British bands of Lew Stone and Harry Roy. In 1938, he went to South America with Roy's orchestra, and became fascinated with Latin-American music, a subject on which he became an expert. He started recording for Decca Records in 1944, and in the same year became conductor of the BBC Dance Orchestra, a position that lasted until 1952. Black took part in many vintage radio shows including *Hi Gang* and *Much Binding In The Marsh*. He also composed signature tunes for several radio programmes, including the legendary *Goon Show*. He also broadcast with ensembles ranging from full symphony orchestras and the BBC Dance Orchestra to a quartet or sextet in his own programmes, such as *Black Magic* and *The Musical World Of Stanley Black*. Black has worked on over a hundred films either as score composer or musical director, and in many cases as both. His credits include *It Always Rains On Sunday* (1948), *The Long And The Short And The Tall* (1961), the Cliff Richard musicals *The Young Ones* (1961) and *Summer Holiday* (1962), and all of the late Mario Zampi's screwball comedies, such as *Laughter In Paradise* (1951), *The Naked Truth* (1957) and *Too Many Crooks* (1958). His albums have sold in huge quantities, not only in the UK, but also in the USA, New Zealand and Japan. In 1994 he joined Stéphane Grappelli in a Charity Gala Performance at the Barbican Hall in London. His many honours include an OBE and Life Fellowship of the International Institute of Arts and Letters. In 1995 he was made life president of the Celebrities

Guild of Great Britain.
● ALBUMS: *Exotic Percussion* (Phase 4 1962) ★★★, *Spain* (Phase 4 1962) ★★★, *Film Spectacular* (Phase 4 1963) ★★★★, *Film Spectacular, Volume Two* (Phase 4 1963) ★★★★, *'Bolero'/Polovtsian Dances* (Phase 4 1964) ★★, *Grand Canyon Suite* (Phase 4 1964) ★★★, *Music Of A People* (Phase 4 1965) ★★★, *Russia* (Phase 4 1966) ★★★, *Capriccio* (Phase 4 1965) ★★★, *Film Spectacular, Volume Three* (Phase 4 1966) ★★★★, *Broadway Spectacular* (Phase 4 1966) ★★★, *Gershwin Concert* (Phase 4 1966) ★★★, *Blockbusters From Broadway* (Phase 4 1967) ★★★★, *Tchaikovsky Concert* (Phase 4 1967) ★★, *Sputniks For Orchestra* (Phase 4 1967) ★★★, *Spectacular Dances For Orchestra* (Phase 4 1967) ★★★, *France* (Phase 4 1967) ★★★, *Dimensions In Sound* (Phase 4 1968) ★★★★, *Overture* (Phase 4 1968) ★★★, *Cuban Moonlight* (Eclipse 1969) ★★★, *Great Rhapsodies For Orchestra* (Phase 4 1970) ★★★, *Plays For Latin Lovers* (Eclipse 1970) ★★★, with the London Symphony Orchestra *Grieg Concert* (Phase 4 1971) ★★, *Tribute To Charlie Chaplin* (Phase 4 1972) ★★★, *Tropical Moonlight* (Eclipse 1972) ★★★, *Film Spectacular, Volume Four – The Epic* (Phase 4 1973) ★★★, *Cuban Moonlight, Volume Two* (Eclipse 1973) ★★★, with the London Festival Orchestra *Spirit Of A People* (Phase 4 1974) ★★★, *Film Spectacular, Volume Five – The Love Story* (Phase 4 1975) ★★★★, *Twelve Top Tangos* (Eclipse 1976) ★★, *Black Magic* (Phase 4 1976) ★★★, *Film Spectacular, Volume Six – Great Stories From World War II* (Phase 4 1976) ★★★, *Sounds Wide Screen* (Phase 4 1977) ★★★, *Satan Superstar* (Phase 4 1978) ★★★, *Digital Magic* (Decca 1979) ★★★, *Great Love Stories* (Decca 1988) ★★★, *ITV Themes* (Hallmark 1988) ★★★, *S'Wonderful* (President 1990) ★★★, *Nice 'N' Easy* (Decca 1992) ★★★.
● COMPILATIONS: *Film World Of Stanley Black* (Decca 1970) ★★★★, *Latin World Of Stanley Black* (Decca 1973) ★★★, *Focus On Stanley Black* (Decca 1978) ★★★★.

BLACKWELL, OTIS

b. 1931, Brooklyn, New York, USA. The author of 'Great Balls Of Fire', 'Fever' and 'All Shook Up', Blackwell was one of the greatest songwriters of the rock 'n' roll era. He learned piano as a child and grew up listening to both R&B and country music. Victory in a talent contest at Harlem's Apollo Theatre led to a recording contract with the Joe Davis label. His first release was his own composition 'Daddy Rolling Stone', which became a favourite in Jamaica where it was recorded by Derek Martin. The song later became part of the Who's 'Mod' repertoire. During the mid-50s, Blackwell also recorded in a rock 'n' roll vein for RCA Records and Groove before turning to writing songs for other artists. His first successes came in 1956 when Little Willie John's R&B hit with the sultry 'Fever' was an even bigger pop success for Peggy Lee. Subsequently, 'All Shook Up' (first recorded by David Hill on Aladdin Records) began a highly profitable association with Elvis Presley, who was credited as co-writer. The rhythmic tension of the song perfectly fitted Elvis' stage persona and it became his first UK number 1. It was followed by 'Don't Be Cruel' (1956), 'Paralysed' (1957), and the more mellow 'Return To Sender' (1962) and 'One Broken Heart For Sale'. There was a distinct similarity between Blackwell's vocal style and Presley's, which has led to speculation that Elvis adopted some of his songwriter's mannerisms.

The prolific Blackwell (who wrote hundreds of songs) also provided hits for Jerry Lee Lewis ('Breathless' and his most famous recording, 'Great Balls Of Fire', 1958), Dee Clark ('Hey Little Girl' and 'Just Keep It Up', 1959), Jimmy Jones ('Handy Man', 1960) and Cliff Richard ('Nine Times Out Of Ten', 1960). As the tide of rock 'n' roll receded, Blackwell recorded R&B material for numerous labels including Atlantic Records, MGM Records and Epic. In later years, he was in semi-retirement, making only occasional live appearances.

● ALBUMS: *Singin' The Blues* (Davis 1956) ★★, *These Are My Songs* (Inner City 1978) ★★.
● COMPILATIONS: *Otis Blackwell 1953-55* (Flyright 1994) ★★★.

BLACKWELL, ROBERT 'BUMPS'

b. Robert A. Blackwell, 23 May 1918, Seattle, Washington, USA (of mixed French, Negro and Indian descent), d. 9 March 1985, USA. An arranger and studio bandleader with Specialty Records, Blackwell had led a band in Seattle. After arriving in California in 1949, he studied classical composition at the University of California, Los Angeles, and within a few years was arranging and producing gospel and R&B singles for the likes of Lloyd Price and Guitar Slim. Previously, he had written a series of stage revues – *Blackwell Portraits* – very much in the same vein as the *Ziegfeld Follies*. His Bumps Blackwell Jnr. Orchestra featured, at various times, Ray Charles and Quincy Jones. He also worked with Lou Adler and Herb Alpert before taking over the A&R department at Specialty Records, where he first came into contact with Little Richard. His boss, Art Rupe, sent him to New Orleans in 1955 where he recorded 'Tutti Frutti' and established a new base for rock 'n' roll. Blackwell was a key producer and songwriter in the early days of rock 'n' roll, particularly with Little Richard. He was responsible for tracking down the latter and buying his recording contract from Peacock in 1955. Blackwell helped to rewrite 'Tutti Frutti' in a cleaned-up version more appropriate to white audiences, which he recorded at Richard's first Specialty session in New Orleans. As well as being involved with the writing of some of Richard's hits, he also produced some of his early work, and became his personal manager. Along with John Marascalco he wrote 'Ready Teddy', 'Rip It Up', and, with Enotris Johnson and Richard Penniman (Little Richard), 'Long Tall Sally'. He also helped to launch the secular careers of former gospel singers Sam Cooke and Wynona Carr. After leaving Specialty, he was involved in setting up Keen Records, which furthered the careers of Sam Cooke and Johnny 'Guitar' Watson, among others.

In 1981 he co-produced the title track of Bob Dylan's *Shot Of Love*, before his death from pneumonia in 1985.

BLEYER, ARCHIE

b. 12 June 1909, Corona, New York, USA, d. 20 March 1989, Sheboygan, Wisconsin, USA. A bandleader, musical arranger and founder of Cadence Records, Bleyer began playing the piano at the age of seven. He enlisted at Columbia College in 1927, intending to become an electrical engineer, but switched to music in his second year, afterwards leaving to become a musical arranger. After organizing a local band, he went to New York in the late 30s and conducted for several Broadway shows. He also composed the jazz piece 'Business In Q', which was performed by various 'hot' bands in the 30s, and he became one of the best-known writers of stock arrangements for music publishers. In the 40s Bleyer joined CBS radio as a musical conductor, and worked extensively on the *Arthur Godfrey Show*, remaining with it when it transferred to television in the 50s. He left the show in 1953, and formed Cadence Records. He had immediate success with artists such as Julius LaRosa ('Eh Cumpari'), the Chordettes ('Mr Sandman', number 1), several chart-toppers for the Everly Brothers and Andy Williams ('Canadian Sunset', 'Butterfly' and 'Are You Sincere'). He also provided the orchestral backing for several of his artists, including Janette Davis, Marion Marlowe, Alfred Drake and Arthur Godfrey, whose husky baritone can be heard on the album *Arthur Godfrey's TV Calendar Show*. Bleyer also had hits with his own orchestra during the mid-50s, including 'Hernando's Hideaway' (from *The Pajama Game*), and the Top 20 novelty number 'The Naughty Lady Of Shady Lane'. He continued to work into the early 60s, but retired from showbusiness in the late 60s, dissolving the Cadence label. He died in 1989 of Parkinson's Disease.

● ALBUMS: *Moonlight Serenade* (Cadence 1962) ★★★.
● COMPILATIONS: *Golden Classics* (Collectables 1997) ★★★.

BLUEJEAN BOP! – GENE VINCENT

In May 1956, the two and a half minutes of 'Be Bop A Lula' marked the astonishing recording debut of Gene Vincent, and the following month Vincent was back in Owen Bradley's studio in Nashville for his first album, *Bluejean Bop!*. Producer Ken Nelson flipped the echo switch to maximum and created a space-age sound for 'Who Slapped John?', in particular. Vincent's voice was softer than most rock 'n' rollers and his tender versions of 'Ain't She Sweet?' and 'Up A Lazy River' demonstrated his potential as an all-round entertainer. His country roots are covered in 'Waltz Of The Wind', but it is the extraordinary rock 'n' roll numbers such as 'Bluejean Bop' and 'Bop Street' (don't be fooled by the slow start!) that make the album so remarkable and created a guitar hero out of Cliff Gallup. Gene Vincent rocks, the Bluecaps roll, and the result is uninhibited magic.

● Tracks: *Bluejean Bop; Jezebel; Who Slapped John?; Ain't She Sweet?; I Flipped; Waltz Of The Wind; Jump Back, Honey, Jump Back; That Old Gang Of Mine; Jumps, Giggles, And Shouts; Up A Lazy River; Bop Street; Peg O' My Heart.*
● First released 1956
● UK peak chart position: did not chart
● USA peak chart position: 16

BOBBETTES

The first all-female R&B group to have a major pop hit record was not the Chantels, as is popularly believed, but the Bobbettes. Their 'Mr. Lee' beat the Chantels' 'He's Gone' to the charts by one month and outranked it in the US pop charts. The Bobbettes formed in 1955 in Harlem, New York City, USA, at PS 109, where they attended school. Consisting of Emma Pought, her sister Jannie, Laura Webb, Helen Gathers and Reather Dixon, the group was originally called the Harlem Queens. The girls were aged between 11 and 13 years old at the time of the group's formation. In 1957 they appeared on a local television programme, which led to an audition for Atlantic Records. 'Mr. Lee' was a song the girls had written in honour of their fifth-grade teacher, although the lyrics were not as kind in their original version (in fact, their second chart single was titled 'I Shot Mr. Lee'). The infectious 'Mr. Lee' was released in the summer of 1957 and ascended to number 6 in the US chart. Follow-up singles on Atlantic did not chart; the Bobbettes' subsequent singles were issued on the Triple-X, Gone, Jubilee, Diamond and RCA Records labels. Although their last chart success was in 1961, four of the original members were still performing together in the late 80s.
● COMPILATIONS: *Mr Lee & Other Big Hits* (Revival 1989) ★★★.

BOSTIC, EARL

b. Eugene Earl Bostic, 25 April 1913, Tulsa, Oklahoma, USA, d. 28 October 1965, Rochester, New York, USA. The romantic and smooth sound of Bostic's band, usually featuring the vibes of Gene Redd, piano of Fletcher Smith, bass of Margo Gibson, drums of Charles Walton, guitar of Alan Seltzer, and the marvellous alto saxophone of Bostic, was one of the great and distinctive sounds of both R&B and pop music, and his records became perennials on the juke-boxes during the 50s. Bostic was best known for his alto saxophone sound but he also played tenor saxophone, flute and clarinet on his records. Bostic was formally trained in music, having received a degree in music theory from Xavier University. He moved to New York City and formed a jazz combo in 1938. In the early 40s he was playing in the Lionel Hampton band. He left Hampton in 1945 to form a combo, recording tracks for Majestic, but did not make much of an impression until he signed with New York-based Gotham in 1948. He had immediate success with 'Temptation' (US R&B number 10). During the 50s he recorded prolifically for Cincinnati-based King Records, and had two big singles, 'Sleep' (US R&B number 6)

and 'Flamingo' (US R&B number 1), in 1951. The smooth but perky performance on the latter became his signature tune and made him something of a Beach Music artist in the Carolinas.

● ALBUMS: *The Best Of Earl Bostic* (King 1956) ★★★★, *Bostic For You* (King 1956) ★★★, *Alto-Tude* (King 1956) ★★★, *Dancetime* (King 1957) ★★★★, *Let's Dance With Earl Bostic* (King 1957) ★★★★, *Invitation To Dance* (King 1957) ★★★, *C'mon & Dance With Earl Bostic* (King 1958) ★★★★, *Bostic Rocks-Hits From The Swing Age* (King 1958) ★★★, *Bostic Showcase Of Swinging Dance Hits* (King 1958) ★★★, *Alto Magic In Hi-Fi* (King 1958) ★★, *Sweet Tunes Of The Fantastic 50's* (King 1959) ★★★, *Workshop* (King 1959) ★★★, *Sweet Tunes Of The Roaring 20's* (King 1959) ★★, *Sweet Tunes Of the Swinging 30's* (King 1959) ★★★, *Sweet Tunes Of The Sentimental 40's* (King 1959) ★★, *Musical Pearls* (King 1959) ★★★, *Hit Tunes Of The Big Broadway Shows* (King 1960) ★★, *25 Years Of Rhythm And Blues Hits* (King 1960) ★★★, *By Popular Demand* (King 1962) ★★★, *Earl Bostic Plays Bossa Nova* (King 1963) ★★, *Jazz As I Feel It* (King 1963) ★★, *The Best Of Earl Bostic* (King 1964) ★★★, *New Sound* (King 1964) ★★★, *The Great Hits Of 1964* (King 1964) ★★★, *The Song Is Not Ended* (Philips 1967) ★★★, *Harlem Nocturne* (King 1969) ★★, *Sax'O Boogie* (Oldie Blues 1984) ★★, *Blows A Fuse* (Charly 1985) ★★★, *That's Earl, Brother* (Spotlite 1985) ★★★, *Bostic Rocks* (Swingtime 1987) ★★★, *Dance Time* (Sing 1988) ★★★, *Bostic For You* (Sing 1988) ★★★, *Dance Music From The Bostic Workshop* (Charly 1988) ★★★, *Flamingo* (Charly 1995) ★★★.
● COMPILATIONS: *The EP Collection* (See For Miles 1999) ★★★, *The EP Collection, Volume 2* (See For Miles 2001) ★★★.

BOSWELL, CONNEE

b. 3 December 1907, Kansas City, Missouri, USA, d. 11 October 1976, New York City, New York, USA. An outstanding singer with enormous but often uncredited influence, Boswell claimed to have been inspired by singers as diverse as Bessie Smith and Enrico Caruso. According to outside sources, Connee and her sisters, Martha and Helvetia, were both influenced and encouraged by the New Orleans cornetist Emmett Hardy. In her work it is possible also to discern the effect of the stylistic advances being made by Ethel Waters and Louis Armstrong. Certainly, she was interested in the blues and when she made her first record as a pre-teenager she sang a blues written by Martha. The sisters formed a close-harmony singing group, the Boswell Sisters, but Connee's career extended far beyond this. Despite being in a wheelchair since contracting polio at the age of four, she grew up to be a determined, talented performer, carving a highly successful solo career after the sisters' act folded in 1935. A skilled musician, adept on saxophone, trombone, cello and piano, she worked extensively in radio, television and films. Essentially a two-beat singer, with a calculatedly casual sound, she considerably affected the manner in which later singers approached their work. Although few acknowledge their debt to Connee Boswell, the fact that one who did was Ella Fitzgerald suggests that her influence is widespread throughout popular music, even if her emulators do not always realize the original source of their inspiration. She worked steadily into the 60s, mostly on television. A rare opportunity to enjoy her work on CD came in 1998 with the reissue of her 1958 album celebrating the 50th anniversary of songwriter Irving Berlin's career.

● ALBUMS: *The Star Maker* 10-inch album (Decca 1951) ★★★, *Connee Boswell* 10-inch album (Decca 1951) ★★★, *Singing The Blues* 10-inch album (Decca 1951) ★★★, *Connee* (Decca 1956) ★★★, *Connee Boswell & The Original Memphis 5* (RCA Victor 1956) ★★★, *Connee Boswell Sings Irving Berlin* (Design 1958) ★★★★.

● COMPILATIONS: with the Boswell Sisters *Sand In My Shoes* 1935-1941 recordings (MCA) ★★★★.

BOSWELL, EVE

b. Eva Keleti, 11 May 1922, Budapest, Hungary, d. 14 August 1998, Durban, South Africa. A singer with a vivacious style, who was especially popular in the UK during the 50s, Boswell was also an accomplished pianist and ballet dancer, and spoke four languages fluently. Educated in Lausanne, Switzerland, Boswell later studied music at the Budapest Academy. She came from a vaudeville family with whom she appeared as a teenager in a music hall juggling act known as the Three Hugos. She worked in South Africa in Boswell's Circus and married Trevor McIntosh, the stepson of one of the owners, who became her manager until his death in 1970. In the 40s, as Eve Boswell, she sang with South Africa's leading dance band, led by Roy Martin. She went to the UK in 1949 and replaced Doreen Lundy as the star vocalist in Geraldo's Orchestra. After featuring on several of the orchestra's records, including 'Again', 'Best Of All' and, somewhat curiously, 'Confidentially' (the composition and theme song of comedian Reg Dixon), she left Geraldo in 1951, and toured the UK with George & Alfred Black's revue *Happy-Go-Lucky*, and was their leading lady in the musical *The Show Of Shows*, at the Opera House, Blackpool. She also toured Korea and the Far East, entertaining British Forces, appearing regularly in the UK on the radio, television and variety circuit, and at the 1953 Royal Variety Performance.

Signed to Parlophone Records in 1950, her first record, 'Bewitched', was followed by several other successful titles, including 'Beloved, Be Faithful', 'The Little Shoemaker' and 'Ready, Willing And Able'. Her biggest hits were two up-tempo South African songs, 'Sugarbush' (1952) and 'Pickin' A Chicken', which entered the UK chart in 1955, and resurfaced twice during the following year. Although well known for lively, up-tempo material, her album *Sentimental Eve* revealed that she could handle ballads equally well, with such tracks as 'I'll Buy That Dream' and 'You'll Never Know'. She remained active in the UK during the 50s and into the 60s, then faded from the scene.

She began a new career as a vocal coach, but returned to South Africa following McIntosh's death. There she married radio producer Henry Holloway and opened a singing school.

● ALBUMS: *Sugar And Spice* (Parlophone 1956) ★★★★, *Sentimental Eve* (Parlophone 1957) ★★★, *Following The Sun Around* (Parlophone 1959) ★★★, *Sugar Bush 76* (EMI 1976) ★★.

● COMPILATIONS: *Sentimental Journey* (Conifer 1988) ★★★, *The EMI Years* (EMI 1989) ★★★.

BRENNAN, ROSE

This popular Irish band singer joined Joe Loss, the leader of one of Britain's most enduring dance bands, for a trial period of two weeks, and stayed for 15 years during the 40s and 50s. One of the many who benefited from Loss's policy of generously featuring his vocalists, Brennan was voted the top girl singer in the *New Musical Express* annual poll. Her records with Loss, on several of which she was accompanied by his vocal quintet, the Loss Chords, included 'Tulips And Heather', 'Then I'll Be There', 'Somewhere Along The Way', 'The Isle Of Innisfree', 'Why Don't You Believe Me?', 'Got You On My Mind' (with the Kordites), 'Seven Lonely Days' and 'The Spinning Wheel'. Under her own name, in the 50s, she released several cover versions of hits such as Edith Piaf's 'If You Love Me – I Won't Care (Hymn A L'Amour)', 'Let Me Go, Lover' (which was successful for several artists, including Joan Weber, Dean Martin and Teresa Brewer), and Don Cherry's 'Band Of Gold'. In 1961 she had a UK Top 40 hit of her own with 'Tall Dark Stranger'.

BRENSTON, JACKIE

b. 15 August 1930, Clarksdale, Mississippi, USA, d. 15 December 1979, Memphis, Tennessee, USA. Credited with making the 'first' rock 'n' roll record, Brenston's career quickly reached a peak as a result and then entered a 25-year decline. He had returned from army service in 1947 and learned to play saxophone from local musician Jesse Flowers. Shortly afterwards, he met Ike Turner who was recruiting for his band the Kings Of Rhythm. Their local fame prompted B.B. King to recommend them to Sam Phillips in Memphis. Both Turner and Brenston made singles on 5 March 1951 and both were sold to Chess Records, but it was 'Rocket 88' that became a hit, due in part to the distorted sound of Willie Kizart's guitar. Subsequent singles, including 'My Real Gone Rocket' and 'Hi-Ho Baby', failed to reproduce that sound and after two solid years of touring behind his hit, Brenston's career began to languish. He worked in Lowell Fulson's band for a couple of years and then rejoined Turner's Kings Of Rhythm, with whom he recorded two singles for Federal and, in 1961, one for Sue Records. Brenston recorded one last single, 'Want You To Rock Me', with Earl Hooker's band. He worked for a time in the Shakers, the band of St. Louis bass player Sid Wallace, but by then alcohol had taken over his life and was a contributory factor to his fatal heart attack. In an interview, he spoke his own epitaph: 'I had a hit record and no sense.'

● COMPILATIONS: *Rocket 88* (Chess 1989) ★★★, with Ike Turner *Trailblazer* (Charly 1991) ★★★.

BRENT, TONY

b. Reginald Bretagne, 13 August 1926, Bombay, India, d. 19 June 1993, Sydney, Australia. Brent was a popular singer in the UK during the 50s, having moved there on Boxing Day 1947. Two years later he won a talent contest at the Kingston Regal Theatre singing 'Some Enchanted Evening', which led to work with Ambrose and Cyril Stapleton's BBC Showband. Contrary to disinformation spread at the time by his agent, and subsequently repeated by his record company, he had not arrived in England from the USA, nor had he sang with former Glenn Miller accompanist Tex Beneke and his band. In 1952 he made his chart debut with a cover version of one of Sammy Kaye's last hits, 'Walkin' To Missouri', and began to tour the variety circuit and appear on television. His other chart entries through until 1959 included 'Make It Soon', 'Got You On My Mind', 'Cindy, Oh Cindy', 'Dark Moon', 'The Clouds Will Soon Roll By', 'Girl Of My Dreams' and 'Why Should I Be Lonely?'. He additionally duetted with Billie Anthony on a recording of the similarly titled 'I Get So Lonely'. Brent also released two sets of standards, *Off Stage* and *Tony Takes Five*. His EPs included *Time For Tony* and *Tony Calls The Tune*. He was subsequently overwhelmed by the 60s beat group scene and retreated to the clubs. Eventually, he resumed his travels, and left the UK for Australia, where he died of a heart attack in 1993.

● ALBUMS: *Off Stage* (Columbia 1958) ★★★★, *Tony Takes Five* (Columbia 1960) ★★★.

BREWER, TERESA

b. Theresa Breuer, 7 May 1931, Toledo, Ohio, USA. A child prodigy, Brewer first appeared on radio at the age of two and sang on the *Major Bowes' Amateur Hour* between 1938 and 1943. She was a veteran radio and club performer by the time she joined London Records in 1949. The attractive and strong-voiced teenager topped the US chart in 1950 with her debut hit 'Music! Music! Music!', on which she was backed by the Dixieland All Stars. She joined Coral Records in 1952 and continued hitting the US Top 10 with records such as 'Ricochet', 'Jilted' and the number 1 'Till I Waltz Again With You'. In 1953 she made her film debut in *Those Redheads From Seattle* with Guy Mitchell. Her first transatlantic Top 10 hit was her version of 'Let Me Go Lover' in 1955, which she followed with two more in 1956, 'A Tear Fell' and 'A Sweet Old-Fashioned Girl'. As rock 'n' roll took over, Brewer's sales declined and like many other MOR pop stars of the time she reverted to covering R&B hits for the white record-buying public. In this vein she had some success with tracks including 'Pledging My Love', 'Tweedle Dee' and 'You Send Me'. Brewer had a brief flirtation with country-styled material in the early 60s and then joined the lucrative nightclub and Las Vegas circuit. She later recorded for Philips Records, Signature, Project 3, Doctor Jazz, Red Baron and Amsterdam, the latter label being owned by her producer husband Bob Thiele. In the 70s she established herself as a jazz singer, recording with Stéphane Grappelli, Count Basie and Duke Ellington among others. In all, Brewer accumulated 38 US chart hits, but by the late 50s, when rock was firmly established, there was no place in the charts for this sweet, old-fashioned girl.

● ALBUMS: *Teresa Brewer* 10-inch album (London 1951) ★★★★, *Till I Waltz Again With You* 10-inch album (Coral 1953) ★★★★, *A Bouquet Of Hits From Teresa Brewer* 10-inch album (Coral 1954) ★★★★, *Music Music Music* (Coral 1955) ★★★, *Teresa* (Coral 1956) ★★★★, *For Teenagers In Love* (Coral 1957) ★★★, *At Christmas Time* (Coral 1957) ★★★, *Miss Music* (Coral 1957) ★★★, *Time For Teresa* (Coral 1958) ★★★, *Heavenly Lover* (Coral 1959) ★★★, *When Your Lover Has Gone* (Coral 1959) ★★★, *Teresa Brewer And The Dixieland Band* (Coral 1959) ★★★, *My Golden Favorites* (Coral 1960) ★★★, *Naughty, Naughty, Naughty* (Coral 1960) ★★★, *Ridin' High* (Coral 1960) ★★★, *Aloha From Teresa* (Coral 1961) ★★★, *Songs Everybody Knows* (Coral 1961) ★★★, *Don't Mess With Tess* (Coral 1962) ★★★, *Here's Teresa Brewer* (Vocalion 1963) ★★★, *Moments To Remember* (Philips 1963) ★★★, *Teresa Brewer* (Vocalion 1963) ★★★, *Terrific Teresa Brewer!* (Wing 1963) ★★★, *Golden Hits Of 1964* (Philips 1964) ★★★, *Goldfinger, Dear Heart And Other Great Movie Songs* (Philips 1964) ★★, *Gold Country* (Philips 1965) ★★★, *Songs For Our Fighting Men* (Philips 1965) ★★, *Texas Leather And Mexican Lace* (Philips 1966) ★★★, *Singin' A Doo Dah Song* (Amsterdam 1972) ★★★, with Duke Ellington *It Don't Mean A Thing If It Ain't Got That Swing* (Flying Dutchman 1973) ★★★, *Music, Music, Music* (Amsterdam 1973) ★★★, with Count Basie *Songs Of Bessie Smith* (Flying Dutchman 1973) ★★★, *Teresa Brewer In London With Oily Rags* (Amsterdam 1973) ★★★, with Bobby Hackett *What A Wonderful World* (Flying Dutchman 1973) ★★★, *Good News* (Signature 1974) ★★★, *Unliberated Woman* (Signature 1975) ★★★, *Teresa Brewer's New Album* (Image 1977) ★★★, with Earl 'Fatha' Hines *We Love You Fats* (Doctor Jazz 1978) ★★★★, *A Sophisticated Lady* (Columbia 1981) ★★★, *Come Follow The Band* (Project 3 1982) ★★★, *I Dig Big Band Singers* (Doctor Jazz 1983) ★★★, with Stéphane Grappelli *On The Road Again* (Doctor Jazz 1983) ★★★, *Teresa Brewer In London* (Signature 1984) ★★, *Live At Carnegie Hall & Montreux, Switzerland* (Doctor Jazz 1984) ★★, *American Music Box Vol. 1: The Songs Of Irving Berlin* (Doctor Jazz 1985) ★★★★, with Mercer Ellington *The Cotton Connection* (Doctor Jazz 1985) ★★★, *Midnight Cafe* (Doctor Jazz 1986) ★★★, with Svend Asmussen *On The Good Ship Lollipop* (Doctor Jazz 1987) ★★★, *Teenage Dance Party* (Bear Family 1987) ★★★, *Memories Of Louis* (Red Baron 1991) ★★★★, *Softly I Swing* (Red Baron 1992) ★★★, *American Music Box Vol. 2: The Songs Of Harry Warren* (Red Baron 1993) ★★★,

Chicago Style (Premium 1995) ★★★.
● COMPILATIONS: *Teresa Brewer's Greatest Hits* (Philips 1962) ★★★★, *The Best Of Teresa Brewer* (Coral 1965) ★★★★, *Greatest Hits* (RCA 1975) ★★★★, *World Of Teresa Brewer* (London 1976) ★★★, *Remember Teresa Brewer* (Fontana 1977) ★★★, *Spotlight On Teresa Brewer* (Philips 1978) ★★★★, *Brewer's Best* (Philips 1981) ★★★ *Golden Greats* (MCA 1985) ★★★★, *Portrait* (RCA 1986) ★★★, *Golden Hits* (Pickwick 1988) ★★★★, *16 Most Requested Songs* (Columbia 1991) ★★★, *The Very Best Of Teresa Brewer* (Sound Waves 1993) ★★★★, *Music! Music! Music! The Best Of Teresa Brewer* (Varèse Sarabande 1995) ★★★★.
● FILMS: *Those Redheads From Seattle* (1953).

BROOKS, HADDA

b. Hadda Hopgood, 29 October 1916, Los Angeles, California, USA. Brooks began taking piano lessons as a young child of four, later studying classical music in Los Angeles and Chicago. In 1945 record executive Jules Bihari, just establishing Modern Records, heard Brooks' playing and signed her. Her first single, 'Swinging The Boogie', was issued in 1945, and Brooks was billed as 'Queen Of The Boogie' (a film of the same name was made in 1947). The follow-up, 'Rockin' The Boogie', set the style for the rest of her career, although the many boogies she recorded – often modern arrangements of classical music such as 'Humoresque' or 'Hungarian Rhapsody No. 2' – were usually backed with fine vocal blues or ballads. Although not trained in the blues, she became somewhat typecast as a boogie-woogie pianist, and counted Count Basie (who backed her on a single) and actor Humphrey Bogart (who cast her in a film) among her admirers. In 1951 she became the first black woman to host her own television show in California, as well as recording for London and OKeh Records. She toured with the Harlem Globetrotters in her spare time before moving to Australia for most of the 60s. In semi-retirement, she still retains a few select engagements each year at certain Los Angeles restaurants and hotels. In recent years she has occasionally released material on the small Rob Ray, Alwin and Kim labels, but in the 90s her recorded profile was high, with a distribution agreement through Virgin Records. In her 80th year she released a credible album, *Time Was When*.
● ALBUMS: with Pete Johnson *Boogie Battle* (Crown 1977) ★★★, *Queen Of The Boogie* (Oldie Blues 1984) ★★★, *Romance In The Dark* (Jukebox Lil 1989) ★★★, *That's My Desire* (Flair/Virgin 1994) ★★★, *Time Was When* (PointBlank 1996) ★★★.
● COMPILATIONS: *I've Got News For You* (PointBlank 1999) ★★★.

BROONZY, 'BIG' BILL

b. William Lee Conley Broonzy, 26 June 1893 (some sources give 1898), Scott, Mississippi, USA, d. 14 August 1958, Chicago, Illinois, USA. Broonzy worked as a field hand, and it was behind the mule that he first developed his unmistakable, hollering voice, with its remarkable range and flexibility. As a child he made himself a violin, and learned to play under the guidance of an uncle. For a time, he worked as a preacher, before settling finally into the secular life of the blues singer. After service in the army at the end of World War I, he moved to Chicago, where he learned to play guitar from Papa Charlie Jackson. Despite his late start as a guitarist, Broonzy quickly became proficient on the instrument, and when he first recorded in the late 20s, he was a fluent and assured accompanist in both ragtime and blues idioms. His voice retained a flavour of the countryside, in addition to his clear diction, but his playing had the up-to-date sophistication and assurance of the city dweller. The subjects of his blues, too, were those that appealed to blacks who, like him, had recently migrated to the urban north, but retained family and cultural links with the south. As such, Broonzy's music exemplifies the movement made by the blues from locally made folk music to nationally distributed, mass media entertainment. He was sometimes used as a talent scout by record companies, and was also favoured as an accompanist; up to 1942 he recorded hundreds of tracks in this capacity, as well as over 200 issued, and many unissued, titles in his own right. His own records followed trends in black tastes; by the mid-30s they were almost always in a small-group format, with piano, and often brass or woodwind and a rhythm section, but his mellow, sustained guitar tones were always well to the fore.

Despite his undoubted 'star' status – not until 1949 was it necessary to put his full name on a race record: just 'Big Bill' was enough – the questionable financial practices of the record industry meant that his income from music did not permit a full-time career as a musician until late in his life. After World War II, Broonzy had lost some of his appeal to black audiences, but by this time he had shrewdly moved his focus to the burgeoning white audience, drawn from jazz fans and the incipient folk song revival movement. He had played Carnegie Hall in 1938 (introduced as a Mississippi ploughhand!), and in 1951 was one the blues' first visitors to Europe. He recorded frequently, if from a narrowed musical base, changing his repertoire radically to emphasize well-known, older blues such as 'Trouble In Mind', blues ballads such as 'John Henry', popular songs such as 'Glory Of Love' and even protest numbers, including the witty 'When Do I Get To Be Called A Man'. He became a polished raconteur, and further developed his swinging, fluent guitar playing, although on slow numbers he sometimes became rather mannered, after the fashion of Josh White. Broonzy was greatly loved by his new audience, and revered by the younger Chicago blues singers. In 1955 he published an engaging, anecdotal autobiography, compiled by Yannick Bruynoghe from his letters. It should be noted that Broonzy had learned to write only in 1950, taught by students at Iowa State University, where he worked as a janitor. Broonzy was a proud, determined man, and a pivotal figure in blues, both when it was the music of black Americans, and as it became available to whites the world over. His reputation suffered after his death, as his later recordings were deemed as having pandered to white tastes. The importance of his earlier contribution to black music was not fully understood. Broonzy was an intelligent and versatile entertainer, and his immense talent was always at the service of his audience and their expectations.

● ALBUMS: *Treat Me Right* (Tradition 1951) ★★★, *Blues Concert* (Dial 1952) ★★, *Folk Blues* (EmArcy 1954) ★★★, *Big Bill Broonzy Sings* (Period 1956) ★★★, *Big Bill Broonzy* (Folkways 1957) ★★★★, *Country Blues* (Folkways 1957) ★★★★, *Big Bill Broonzy Sings And Josh White Comes A-Visiting* (Period 1958) ★★★, *Last Session Parts 1-3* (Verve 1959) ★★★, *Remembering Big Bill Broonzy: The Greatest Minstrel Of The Authentic Blues* (Mercury 1963) ★★★.

● COMPILATIONS: *The Big Bill Broonzy Story* 5-LP box set (Verve 1959) ★★★★, *Memorial* (Mercury 1963) ★★★★, *Remembering Big Bill Broonzy* (Mercury 1964) ★★★★, *Big Bill And Sonny Boy* (1964) ★★★★, *Trouble In Mind* (1965) ★★★, *Big Bill's Blues* (Epic 1969) ★★★★, *Feelin' Low Down* (GNP Crescendo 1973) ★★★, *Midnight Steppers* (Bluetime 1986) ★★★, *Big Bill Broonzy Volumes 1-3* (Document 1986) ★★★★, *The Young Bill Broonzy 1928-1935* (Yazoo 1988) ★★★★, *The 1955 London Sessions* (Sequel 1990) ★★★, *Remembering Big Bill Broonzy* (Beat Goes On 1990) ★★★★, *Good Time Tonight* (Columbia 1990) ★★★, *Do That Guitar Rag 1928-35* (Yazoo 1992) ★★★, *I Feel So Good* (Indigo 1994) ★★★, *Baby Please Don't Go* (Drive Archive 1995) ★★★, *Black, Brown & White* (Evidence 1995) ★★★, *Stayin' Home With The Blues* (Spectrum 1998) ★★★, *Warm, Witty & Wise* (Columbia 1998) ★★★★, *Treat Me Right* (Tradition 1998) ★★★★, *Absolutely The Best* (Fuel 2000) ★★★★, *Play Your Hand* (Arpegio 2001) ★★★.

● FURTHER READING: *Big Bill Blues: Big Bill Broonzy's Story As Told To Yannick Bruynoghe*, Yannick Bruynoghe. *Hit The Right Lick: The Recordings Of Big Bill Broonzy*, Chris Smith.

BROWN, BUSTER

b. Wayman Glasco, 15 August 1911, Cordele, Georgia, USA, d. 31 January 1976, Brooklyn, New York, USA. Brown played harmonica at local clubs and made a few recordings, including 'I'm Gonna Make You Happy' in 1943. Brown moved to New York in 1956 where he was discovered by Fire Records owner Bobby Robinson while working in a chicken and barbecue joint. In 1959, he recorded the archaic-sounding blues, 'Fannie Mae', whose tough harmonica riffs took it into the US Top 40. His similar-sounding 'Sugar Babe' (1961) was covered in the UK by Jimmy Powell. In later years he recorded for Checker and for numerous small labels including Serock, Gwenn and Astroscope.

● ALBUMS: *New King Of The Blues* (Fire 1959) ★★★, *Get Down With Buster Brown* (Fire 1962) ★★★, *Raise A Ruckus Tonite* (1976) ★★★, *Good News* (Charly 1988) ★★★.

BROWN, CHARLES

b. 13 September 1922, Texas City, Texas, USA, d. 21 January 1999, USA. Brown's mother died only six months after he was born and he was raised by his grandparents. Despite learning piano and church organ at the insistence of his grandparents while a child, Brown became a teacher of chemistry. In 1943, living in Los Angeles, he realized that he could earn more money working as a pianist-singer. He was hired to play at singer Ivie Anderson's Chicken Shack club, but with the requirement that he play 'nothing degrading like the blues'. At that time, the top small group in Los Angeles was the Nat 'King' Cole Trio, but when Cole moved on, the Three Blazers, led by Johnny Moore (guitarist brother of Oscar Moore) and whom Brown had just joined, moved into the top spot. By 1946 the band was a national favourite, with hit records including Brown's 'Driftin' Blues', and appearances at New York's Apollo Theatre. In 1948 the group broke up, although Moore continued to lead a band with the same name, but he was now on his own and virtually unknown as a solo performer. In the early 50s a string of successful records, including his own compositions 'Merry Christmas Baby', 'Black Night' and 'Seven Long Days', boosted his career. Additionally, his work was recorded by such artists as B.B. King, Ray Charles, Sam Cooke, Amos Milburn and Fats Domino, with whom Brown recorded 'I'll Always Be In Love With You' and 'Please Believe Me'.

Brown was heavily influenced by Robert Johnson, Louis Jordan, and especially by Pha Terrell, the singer with the Andy Kirk band. His singing evolved into a highly melodic ballad style that still showed signs of his blues roots. He aptly defined himself as a 'blue ballad singer', combining the velvety sound of Cole with the tough cynicism of Leroy Carr and Lonnie Johnson. One follower was Ray Charles, who, early in his career, modelled his singing on an amalgam of Brown's and Cole's styles. In contrast to Cole, Brown's star waned, despite successful records such as 'Please Come Home For Christmas', and by the end of the 60s he was working in comparative obscurity at Los Angeles nightspots. An appearance at the 1976 San Francisco Blues Festival boosted his reputation, but the pattern remained pretty much unaltered into the 80s before he rebuilt his career with a succession of albums for Bullseye Blues. Brown's lasting reputation was confirmed by the guest artists he attracted to these recordings, including Bonnie Raitt, Dr. John and John Lee Hooker, while English singer Elvis Costello wrote 'I Wonder How She Knows' for him. Brown carried on touring into the 90s, providing superb live entertainment, backed by his outstanding guitar player and musical director, Danny Caron. Ill health curtailed his appearances, but Brown received some belated reward with a lifetime achievement award from the Rhythm & Blues Foundation and a heritage fellowship from the National Endowment for the Arts. He died a few days after a major tribute concert was held in his honour and just two months before he was to have been inducted into the Rock And Roll Hall Of Fame.

● ALBUMS: *Mood Music* 10-inch album (Aladdin 1955) ★★★★, *Driftin' Blues* (Score 1958) ★★★, *More Blues With Charles Brown* (Score 1958) ★★★★, *Charles Brown Sings Million Sellers* (Imperial 1961) ★★★, *Charles Brown Sings Christmas Songs* (King 1961) ★★★★, *The Great Charles Brown* (King 1963) ★★★, *Ballads My Way* (Mainstream 1965) ★★★, *One More For The Road* (Alligator 1986) ★★★, *All My Life* (Bullseye Blues 1990) ★★★, *Someone To Love* (Bullseye Blues 1992) ★★★, *Just A Lucky So And So* (Bullseye Blues 1994) ★★★, *These Blues* (Verve 1994) ★★★, *Charles Brown's Cool Christmas Blues* (Bullseye Blues 1994) ★★★, *Blues N' Brown* 1971 recording (Jewel 1995) ★★★, *Honey Dripper* (Verve 1996) ★★★★, *So Goes Love* (Verve 1998) ★★★, *In A Grand Style* (Bullseye 1999) ★★★★, *Since I Fell For You* (Garland 2000) ★★.

● COMPILATIONS: *Legend* (Bluesway 1970) ★★★★, with Johnny Moore's Three Blazers *Sunny Road* (Route 66 1980) ★★★, with Johnny Moore's Three Blazers *Race Track Blues* (Route 66 1981) ★★★, with Johnny Moore's Three Blazers *Sail On Blues* (Jukebox Lil 1989) ★★★, *Driftin' Blues (The Best Of Charles Brown)* (Capitol 1992) ★★★, *The Complete Aladdin Recordings Of Charles Brown* (Mosaic 1994) ★★★★, with Johnny Moore's Three Blazers *Drifting And Dreaming* (Ace 1995) ★★★★.

BROWN, CLARENCE 'GATEMOUTH'

b. 18 April 1924, Vinton, Louisiana, USA (some sources give Orange, Texas, where he was raised from the age of three weeks). Brown's father was a musician who taught him to play guitar and fiddle, and during his youth he heard the music of Tampa Red, Bob Wills, Count Basie, and others. He toured the south as a drummer with a travelling show before being drafted into the army. On his discharge he worked as a musician in San Antonio, Texas, where he honed his guitar skills sufficiently to impress Don Robey, who offered him a spot at his club in Houston. It was here that Gatemouth's big break came, when he took over a show from T-Bone Walker, after Walker was taken ill. He was so well received that Robey took him to Los Angeles to record for the Aladdin label on 21 August 1947. In 1948 he set up his own Peacock label, for which Brown recorded until 1961. Many of these records are classics of Texas guitar blues, and were enormously influential. During the 60s Gatemouth broadened his stylistic base to include jazz and country, best exemplified by his 1965 Chess Records recordings made in Nashville. These were pointers to the direction in which Brown's music was later to develop. In the 70s he recorded a mixed bag of albums for the French Black And Blue label (including a Louis Jordan tribute set), a couple of Cajun/country/rock hybrids and a good blues album for Barclay Records. In the 80s, Rounder Records successfully showcased Gatemouth's versatile approach by matching him with a big, brassy band. He has also recorded for Alligator Records, Verve Records and Blue Thumb Records in recent years. Brown

sometimes showcases his fiddle-playing to the detriment of his still excellent blues guitar picking, but he remains a fine singer and an extremely talented instrumentalist, whatever genre of music he turns his attention to.

● ALBUMS: *The Blues Ain't Nothing* (Black And Blue 1971) ★★★★, *Sings Louis Jordan* (Black And Blue 1972) ★★★, *The Drifter Rides Again* (Barclay 1973) ★★★, *The Bogalusa Boogie Man* (Barclay 1974) ★★★, *San Antonio Ballbuster* (Red Lightnin' 1974) ★★★, *Cold Strange* (Black And Blue 1977) ★★★, *Blackjack* (Music Is Medicine 1977) ★★★, *Double Live At The Cowboy Bar* (Music Is Medicine 1978) ★★★, with Roy Clark *Makin' Music* (MCA 1979) ★★★, *Alright Again* (Rounder 1981) ★★★, *One More Mile* (Rounder 1983) ★★★, *Atomic Energy* (Blues Boy 1983) ★★★, *Pressure Cooker* 70s recording (Alligator 1985) ★★★, *Texas Guitarman – Duke-Peacock Story, Vol. 1* (Ace 1986) ★★★★, *Real Life* (Rounder 1987) ★★★, *Texas Swing* early 80s recording (Rounder 1987) ★★★, *The Nashville Session 1965* (Chess 1989) ★★★, *Standing My Ground* (Alligator 1989) ★★★, *No Looking Back* (Alligator 1992) ★★★, *Just Got Lucky* Black And Blue recordings (Evidence 1993) ★★★★, *The Man* (Gitanes Jazz/Verve 1994) ★★★, *Long Way Home* (Verve 1995) ★★★, *Live* 1980 recordings (Charly 1995) ★★★, *Gate Swings* (Verve 1997) ★★★★, *American Music, Texas Style* (Blue Thumb/GRP 1999) ★★★★, *Back To Bogalusa* (Blue Thumb 2001) ★★★.

● COMPILATIONS: *Original Peacock Recordings* (Rounder 1988) ★★★★, *The Best Of Clarence 'Gatemouth' Brown: A Blues Legend* (Verve 1995) ★★★★.

BROWN, LES

b. Lester Raymond Brown, 14 March 1912, Reinerton, Pennsylvania, USA, d. 4 January 2000, USA. By 1932, when he entered Duke University at Durham, North Carolina, Brown had already attended Ithaca College and the New York Military Academy and had studied harmony, arranging and composing, as well as becoming proficient on soprano saxophone, clarinet and bassoon. At Duke in 1935, he joined the university's dance band, the Duke Blue Devils, became its leader and built a substantial local reputation and recorded some sides for Decca Records. In 1937 he moved to New York where he worked as an arranger for Jimmy Dorsey and Isham Jones. In 1938 he formed his own band for an engagement at the Hotel Edison on Broadway and signed a recording contract with Bluebird Records. By 1940 the band was playing the Arcadia Ballroom and deputizing for Charlie Barnet at the Lincoln Hotel. During this spell, Brown lured Doris Day away from the Bob Crosby band to work for his.

Although the draft damaged many bands, Brown managed to find replacements and his popularity gained strength even when Day left. In 1943 he persuaded the singer to rejoin and this time they had a massive hit with 'Sentimental Journey'. The band's style remained rooted in easy swinging dance music, with deceptively simple arrangements by Frank Comstock and Skippy

Martin (whose chart for 'I've Got My Love To Keep Me Warm' was another hit). Nevertheless, at the end of 1946 Brown felt that he had not achieved the measure of success he wanted, and so folded his Band Of Renown – but he still had a contract (which he had temporarily forgotten) to play the Hollywood Palladium in March 1947. He re-formed the band and was promptly hired as resident orchestra for Bob Hope's weekly radio show. Brown remained with the show when it transferred to television, and also toured the world on the comedian's many trips to entertain US troops who were stationed overseas. A 1949 concert tour with Hope and Day broke all sales records.

During subsequent decades Les Brown and his Band Of Renown remained popular on television and in public appearances; 1987 saw a succession of concerts celebrating his 50 years as a bandleader. In 1996 he was officially named as the leader of the longest playing musical organization in the history of popular music and entered the *Guinness Book Of World Records*. He was also the first president of the Los Angeles chapter of NARAS (the National Academy of Recording Arts and Sciences), in which capacity he helped televise the Grammy Awards. Brown died of lung cancer in January 2000.

● ALBUMS: *Les Brown From The Cafe Rouge* i (Joyce 1944) ★★★, *One Night Stand With Les Brown* i (Joyce 1945) ★★★, *Les Brown From The Cafe Rouge* ii (Joyce 1945) ★★★, *One Night Stand With Les Brown* ii (Joyce 1949) ★★★, *Over The Rainbow* 10-inch album (Coral 1951) ★★★, *That Sound Of Renown* 10-inch album (Coral 1951) ★★★★, *You're My Everything* 10-inch album (Coral 1952) ★★★★, *Musical Weather Vane* 10-inch album (Coral 1952) ★★★, *Les Brown Concert At The Palladium* (Coral 1953) ★★★, *I've Got My Love To Keep Me Warm* 10-inch album (Columbia 1955) ★★★, *The Cool Classics* 10-inch album (Columbia 1955) ★★★, *College Classics* (Capitol 1955) ★★, *The Les Brown All Stars* (Capitol 1955), *Les Brown's In Town* (Capitol 1956), *Composer's Holiday* (Capitol 1957), *Dance To South Pacific* (Capitol 1958) ★★, with Vic Schoen Band *Suite For Two Bands* (Kap 1959) ★★★, *Swing Song Book* (Coral 1959) ★★★, *Jazz Song Book* (Coral 1959) ★★★, *New Horizons* (Daybreak 1972) ★★★, *Les Brown Today* (Harmonia Mundi 1974) ★★, *The Century Masters* (Century 1977) ★★★, *Les Brown At The Aurex Festival, Tokyo* (1983) ★★★, *Digital Swing* (Fantasy 1987) ★★★, *Les Brown And His Band Of Renown Live At The University Of Wisconsin, Whitewater* (Coss 2000) ★★★.

● COMPILATIONS: *The 1943 Band* (Fanfare 1979) ★★★, *Sentimental Thing* 1946-53 recordings (First Heard 1979) ★★★, *Les Brown And His Orchestra, Volumes 1, 2 & 3* 1944-49 recordings (Decca 1979) ★★★, *The Duke Blue Devils* 30s recordings (Golden Era 1982) ★★★, *The 1946 Band* (Circle 1986) ★★★, *Les Brown And His Band Of Renown, Volumes 1-4* 1944-57 recordings (Columbia 1990) ★★★★, *The Great Les Brown* (Hindsight 1994) ★★★, *Les Brown And His Great Vocalists* (Sony 1995) ★★★★, *The Complete Doris Day With Les Brown* 2-CD set (Sony Music Special Products 1997) ★★★.

BROWN, RUTH

b. 30 January 1928, Portsmouth, Virginia, USA. Brown started her musical career singing gospel at an early age in the church choir led by her father. In 1948 she was singing with a band led by her husband Jimmy in Washington, DC, when Willis Conover (from the radio show *Voice Of America*) recommended her to Ahmet Ertegun of the newly formed Atlantic Records. Ertegun signed her, despite competition from Capitol Records, but on the way up to New York for an appearance at the Apollo Theatre, she was involved in a car crash. Hospitalized for nine months, her medical bills were paid by Atlantic and she rewarded them handsomely with her first big hit, 'Teardrops From My Eyes', in 1950. More hits followed with '5-10-15 Hours' (1952) and 'Mama, He Treats Your Daughter Mean' (1953). Atlantic's first real star, Brown became a major figure in 50s R&B, forming a strong link between that music and early rock 'n' roll. Her records were characterized by her rich and expressive singing voice (not unlike that of Dinah Washington) and accompaniment by breathy saxophone solos (initially by Budd Johnson, later by Willis Jackson). Between 1949 and 1955 her songs were on the charts for 129 weeks, including five number 1s.

Brown's concentration upon R&B has not kept her from associations with the jazz world; very early in her career she sang briefly with the Lucky Millinder band, and has recorded with Jerome Richardson and the Thad Jones-Mel Lewis big band. She also brought a distinctively soulful treatment to varied material such as 'Yes Sir, That's My Baby', 'Sonny Boy', 'Black Coffee' and 'I Can Dream, Can't I?'. In 1989 she won a Tony Award for her performance in the Broadway show *Black And Blue*, and was receiving enthusiastic reviews for her nightclub act in New York, at Michael's Pub and The Blue Note, into the following decade. Brown was also to be heard broadcasting as host of National Public Radio's Harlem Hit Parade, and was inducted into the Rock And Roll Hall Of Fame in 1993. The following year she undertook a European tour, much to the delight of her small but loyal group of fans. On that tour she was recorded live at Ronnie Scott's club for an album that appeared on their own Jazzhouse label. Towards the end of the decade she recorded two excellent albums for the Bullseye Blues label.

Rightly fêted as a post-war pioneer of R&B music, Brown is also recognized as a leading advocate of performer rights. Her own struggle to recoup royalties from her Atlantic material led to the formation of the non-profit Rhythm & Blues Foundation. This organization helps other artists who find themselves in the same situation as Brown, who was forced into menial labour to earn a living after her run of hits ended at the start of the 60s.

● ALBUMS: *Ruth Brown Sings Favorites* 10-inch album (Atlantic 1952) ★★★, *Ruth Brown* (Atlantic 1957) ★★★★, *Late Date With Ruth Brown* (Atlantic 1959) ★★★★, *Miss Rhythm* (Atlantic 1959)

★★★★, *Along Comes Ruth* (Philips 1962) ★★★★, *Gospel Time* (Philips 1962) ★★★, *Ruth Brown '65* (Mainstream 1965) ★★★, *Black Is Brown And Brown Is Beautiful* (Rhapsody 1969) ★★★, *Thad Jones & Mel Lewis Featuring Miss Ruth Brown* (Solid State 1969) ★★★★, *Sugar Babe* (President 1977) ★★★, *Takin' Care Of Business* (Stockholm 1980) ★★★, *The Soul Survives* (Flair 1982) ★★, *Brown Sugar* (Topline 1986) ★★★, *Sweet Baby Of Mine* (Route 66 1987) ★★, *I'll Wait For You* (Official 1988) ★★, *Blues On Broadway* (Fantasy 1989) ★★★, *Fine And Mellow* (Fantasy 1992) ★★★, *The Songs Of My Life* (Fantasy 1993) ★★★, *Live In London* (Jazzhouse 1995) ★★, *R + B = Ruth Brown* (Bullseye Blues 1997) ★★★★, *A Good Day For The Blues* (Bullseye Blues 1999) ★★★, *Here's That Rainy Day* (Garland 1999) ★★.
● COMPILATIONS: *The Best Of Ruth Brown* (Atlantic 1963) ★★★★, *Rockin' With Ruth* 1950-1960 recordings (Charly 1984) ★★★★, *Brown Black And Beautiful* (SDEG 1990) ★★★, *Miss Rhythm: Greatest Hits And More* (Atlantic 1993) ★★★★, *You Don't Know Me* (Indigo 1997) ★★★★.
● FURTHER READING: *Miss Rhythm, The Autobio-graphy Of Ruth Brown*, Ruth Brown with Andrew Yule.
● FILMS: *Under The Rainbow* (1981), *Hairspray* (1988), *True Identity* (1991).

BROWN, SANDY

b. Alexander Brown, 25 February 1929, Izatnagar, Bareilly, India, d. 15 March 1975, London, England. Raised in Edinburgh from the age of six, Brown began playing clarinet with Al Fairweather and Stan Greig, fellow-students at the Royal High School. He made his first important impression on the UK jazz scene in the mid-50s, when the Fairweather-Brown All Stars were formed. This was the period of the trad jazz boom, and Brown's skilful yet impassioned clarinet playing was one of that era's highlights. Unlike many of his fellow trad bandleaders, Brown's interests were ever-expanding, and any bands under his leadership were home to adventurous musical souls, such as Brian Lemon and Tony Coe. Through the 50s and 60s Brown pursued musical excellence, making a string of classic albums, including *McJazz* and *The Incredible McJazz*, and working with such diverse jazz personalities as George Chisholm and Kenny Wheeler. In addition to his playing activity, he was a perceptive and witty writer (*The McJazz Manuscripts*), and was heavily involved in running an architectural practice that specialized in building acoustic recording studios. His health began to fail in the 70s, although he was able to visit the USA where he recorded with Earle Warren. His death came when he still had much to offer the jazz world.
● ALBUMS: *Fifty-Fifty Blues* (1956) ★★★, *Sandy's Sidemen* (1956) ★★★, *McJazz* (1957) ★★★, *Doctor McJazz* (1960) ★★★★, *The Incredible McJazz* (1962) ★★★★, *Hair At Its Hairiest* (1968) ★★★, *Barrelhouse And Blues* (1969) ★★★, with the Brian Lemon Trio *In The Evening* (Hep Jazz 1971) ★★★, with Earle Warren *Everybody Loves Saturday Night* (1974) ★★★, *Splanky* (Spotlite 1983) ★★★★, *Clarinet Opening* (CSA 1988) ★★★.
● COMPILATIONS: *Sandy's Sidemen* 1955-56 recordings (Lake 2000) ★★★.
● FURTHER READING: *The McJazz Manuscripts*, Sandy Brown.

BRYANT, BOUDLEAUX

b. Diadorius Boudleaux Bryant, 13 February 1920, Shellman, Georgia, USA, d. 30 June 1987, USA. With his wife Felice Bryant, he formed one of the greatest songwriting teams in country music and pop history. From a musical family, Boudleaux learned classical violin and piano from the age of five. During the early 30s his father organized a family band with Boudleaux and his four sisters and brothers, playing at county fairs in the Midwest. In 1937 Boudleaux moved to Atlanta, playing with the Atlanta Symphony Orchestra as well as jazz and country music groups. For several years he went on the road, playing in radio station bands in Detroit and Memphis before joining Hank Penny's Radio Cowboys, who performed over the airwaves of WSB Atlanta. In 1945 he met and married Felice Scaduto and the pair began composing together. The earliest recordings of Bryant songs included the Three Sons with 'Give Me Some Sugar, Sugar Baby, And I'll Be Your Sweetie Pie', but the first break came when they sent 'Country Boy' to Nashville publisher Fred Rose of Acuff-Rose. When this became a hit for Jimmy Dickens, the duo moved to Nashville as staff writers for Acuff-Rose. Among their numerous successes in the 50s were 'Have A Good Time' (a pop success for Tony Bennett in 1952), 'Hey Joe' (recorded by Carl Smith and Frankie Laine in 1953) and the Eddy Arnold hits 'I've Been Thinking' and 'The Richest Man' (1955). In 1957, Rose's son Wesley Rose commissioned the Bryants to switch to teenage material for the Everly Brothers.
Beginning with 'Bye Bye Love', they supplied a stream of songs that were melodramatic vignettes of teen life. Several of them were composed by Boudleaux alone. These included the wistful 'All I Have To Do Is Dream', the tough and vengeful 'Bird Dog', 'Devoted To You' and 'Like Strangers'. At this time he wrote what has become his most recorded song, 'Love Hurts'. This sorrowful, almost self-pitying ballad has been a favourite with the country rock fraternity, through notable versions by Roy Orbison and Gram Parsons. There have also been less orthodox rock treatments by Jim Capaldi and Nazareth. From the early 60s, the Bryants returned to the country sphere, composing the country standard 'Rocky Top' as well as providing occasional hits for artists such as Sonny James ('Baltimore') and Roy Clark ('Come Live With Me'). Shortly before Boudleaux's death in June 1987, the Bryants were inducted into the Songwriters' Hall Of Fame.
● ALBUMS: *Boudleaux Bryant's Best Sellers* (Monument 1963) ★★★, with Felice Bryant *All I Have To Do Is Dream* aka *A Touch Of Bryant* (CMH 1979) ★★.

BRYANT, FELICE

b. Felice Scaduto, 7 August 1925, Milwaukee, Wisconsin, USA. The lyricist of some of the Everly Brothers' biggest hits, Felice Bryant was a member of one of the most famous husband-and-wife songwriting teams in pop and country music. Recordings of their 750 published songs have sold over 300 million copies in versions by over 400 artists as diverse as Bob Dylan and Lawrence Welk. Of Italian extraction, Felice was already writing lyrics when she met Boudleaux Bryant while working as an elevator attendant in a Milwaukee hotel. A violinist with Hank Penny's band, Boudleaux had composed instrumental pieces and after their marriage in 1945 the duo began to write together. The success of 'Country Boy' for Jimmy Dickens led them to Nashville where they were the first full-time songwriters and pluggers. During the 50s, the Bryants' country hits were often covered by pop artists such as Al Martino, Frankie Laine and Tony Bennett. Then, in 1957, they switched to composing teenage pop material for the Everly Brothers. Felice and Boudleaux proved to have a sharp eye for the details of teen life and among the hits they supplied to the close-harmony duo were 'Bye Bye Love', 'Wake Up Little Susie', 'Problems', 'Poor Jenny' and 'Take A Message To Mary'. They also composed 'Raining In My Heart' (for Buddy Holly) and the witty 'Let's Think About Living' (Bob Luman). After the rock 'n' roll era had subsided, the Bryants returned to the country scene, composing prolifically throughout the 60s and 70s in bluegrass and American Indian folk material. Their most enduring song from this period has been 'Rocky Top', a hymn of praise to the state of Tennessee. First recorded by the Osborne Brothers in 1969, it was adopted as a theme song by the University of Tennessee. In the late 70s, Felice and Boudleaux recorded their own compositions for the first time.

● ALBUMS: with Boudleaux Bryant *All I Have To Do Is Dream* aka *A Touch Of Bryant* (CMH 1979) ★★.

BRYANT, JIMMY

b. 2 June 1929, Tarrant, Birmingham, Alabama, USA. Bryant began singing at the age of five and six years later was touring Florida with the Dixie Boys Choir. He was educated at Birmingham-Southern College and the Birmingham Conservatory of Music before receiving a scholarship in composition at the New England Conservatory of Music. In 1953 he began working in New York City as an arranger, orchestrator, singer and after three years moved to California where he worked as a string bass player in various hotels and clubs, including Puccini's, which was then owned by Frank Sinatra. During this period, he also worked as a group singer, making records, movies, and appearing on television. In this capacity he performed with many leading entertainers of the period, including Sinatra, Nat 'King' Cole, Dean Martin, Fred Astaire, Bing Crosby, Dinah Shore, Doris Day and Rosemary Clooney. In 1959 he ghosted the singing voice of actor Richard Beymer, who played the role of Tony in the film version of *West Side Story*, famously singing 'Maria'. Another 'unknown' credit, also heard by millions, is Bryant's singing in the group that performed the theme for the 60s television series *Batman* – 'that's actually me singing the G above high C at the end!'

During the following decades Bryant worked as an orchestrator, arranger, composer, most notably for John Williams and James Horner, and orchestrated hundreds of television shows and television movies, and in 1990 won an EMMY Achievement Award for orchestrating *Stephen King's 'It'*. He composed and orchestrated many projects for various Disney theme parks and also orchestrated and arranged for numerous production shows in Las Vegas, as well as the Lido de Paris, in Paris. For several years he had a company, Jimmy Bryant Creative Music Service, and composed music for radio and television commercials; he wrote jingles for clients including motor companies, wine and beer makers. The most prominent of these was the theme for a Toyota advertisement written in 1973. Entitled 'Come Run With Me', it was developed into a full song and recorded by Al Martino and the Brady Bunch, among others. In the late 90s, when many of his age might have decided to drift into leisurely retirement, Bryant was hard at work on a new major project, this time for Tokyo Disneyland.

BRYDEN, BERYL

b. 11 May 1920, Norwich, Norfolk, England, d. 14 July 1998, London, England. In the mid-40s Bryden was active in local jazz circles, organizing concerts and club dates and singing with various bands. In London in the late 40s she sang and played washboard with many of the important bands of the British trad-jazz explosion, including those of George Webb, Freddy Randall, Alex Welsh, Humphrey Lyttelton and Chris Barber. She made her recording debut in 1948 on Randall's 'Hurry Me Down', and formed her own Beryl's Backroom Boys to reproduce the music of the pre-bop era. Despite all this activity and a growing following, singing was only a part-time occupation for her, and it was not until the early 50s that she became a full-time performer. In the 50s and 60s her career was perhaps stronger in mainland Europe than the UK, and she played with visiting Americans including Sidney Bechet and Mary Lou Williams. In 1954 she played washboard on a cover version of Lead Belly's 'Rock Island Line' from Barber's *New Orleans Joy* album. Featuring skiffle singer Lonnie Donegan on vocals, the single went on to sell two million copies and reached the US Top 10. Bryden achieved her biggest hit, 'Gimme A Pigfoot And A Bottle Of Beer', in 1961 during the short-lived 'trad' boom. She waited until the early 70s before visiting the USA.

In the 70s she toured extensively, sometimes as a solo artist or with her Jazzaholics Anonymous group, other times in the company of jazz musicians such as Pete Allen and Monty Sunshine. A robust performer of songs from the classic period of the blues and vaudeville, Bryden's popularity with audiences was matched by the

fellow-feeling she induced in her musical companions (a quality singers often lack). Apart from performing, Bryden also developed a second-string career as a good jazz photographer. Her retirement in the 80s was not taken too seriously, either by her fellow artists or by Bryden herself. In the early 90s she was still on the road and delighting her many fans and friends, before her death from cancer in 1998.
● ALBUMS: *Way Down Yonder In New Orleans* (1975) ★★★, *Basin Street Blues* (Columbia 1991) ★★★, *Big Daddy* (Columbia 1991) ★★★★, *Two Moods Of Beryl Bryden* (Audiophile 1994) ★★★★.

BUCKLEY, LORD

b. Richard Myrle Buckley, 5 April 1906, Stockton, California, USA, d. 12 November 1960, New York, USA. A celebrated humorist and raconteur, Lord Buckley began his career in Chicago's speakeasies where, it is said, he enjoyed the patronage of mobster Al Capone. He assimilated the patois of Black America, infusing his monologues with a bewildering succession of images and phrases that owed their inspiration to jazz or bop prose. The artist sustained comprehension by adapting well-known subject matter – Mark Anthony's eulogy in Shakespeare's *Julius Caesar* began 'Hipsters, Flipsters and Finger-Poppin' Daddies', while in another sketch Jesus Christ was referred to as 'The Naz'. Buckley was a true eccentric. Resplendent with his waxed moustache and sporting a pith helmet, the comedian challenged contemporary convention and even founded his own religion, the Church Of The Living Swing. For a time his career was overseen by later Byrds manager Jim Dickson. The enterprise substituted belly dancers for altar boys and was raided by the Chicago vice squad. A voracious appetite for artificial stimulants eventually took its toll, and despite rumours that the cause of his death was a beating by Black Muslims, Lord Buckley's death in 1960 is recorded as the result of prolonged drug and alcohol abuse. In the early 80s, Chris 'C.P.' Lee, the leading member of UK comic rock group Alberto Y Lost Trios Paranioas, staged a one-man show in tribute to Buckley's legacy.
● ALBUMS: *Hipsters, Flipsters And Finger-Poppin' Daddies, Knock Me Your Lobes* 10-inch album (RCA Victor 1955) ★★★★, *Euphoria* 10-inch album (Vaya 1955) ★★★, *Euphoria, Volumes 1 & 2* (Vaya 1957) ★★★, *The Way Out Humour Of Lord Buckley* reissued as *Lord Buckley In Concert* (World Pacific 1959) ★★★.
● COMPILATIONS: *The Best Of Lord Buckley* (Crestview 1963) ★★★★, *Blowing His Mind (And Yours, Too)* (World Pacific 1966) ★★★, *Buckley's Best* (World Pacific 1968) ★★★, *Bad Rapping Of The Marquis De Sade* (World Pacific 1969) ★★★, *A Most Immaculately Hip Aristocrat* (Straight 1970) ★★★.
● FURTHER READING: *The Hiparama Of The Classics*, Lord Buckley.

BUDDY HOLLY STORY, THE – BUDDY HOLLY

Few artists had exercised such a profound influence in such a short space of time. Buddy Holly's untimely death robbed pop of a performer adept as a solo act and as leader of his group, the Crickets. He wrote, or co-wrote, most of his own material at a time when many singers relied on outside material, and his sparse, but effective, guitar style proved highly influential, particularly on British beat groups. *The Buddy Holly Story* abounds with songs now indisputably pop classics and confirms Holly's status as a major figure. The Beatles, Tex-Mex music and the singer-songwriter genre each owe Holly a debt, which is itself a lasting tribute to the quality of his work.
● Tracks: *Raining In My Heart; Early In The Morning; Peggy Sue; Maybe Baby; Everyday; Rave On; That'll Be The Day; Heartbeat; Think It Over; Oh Boy; It's So Easy; It Doesn't Matter Any More.*
● First released 1959
● UK peak chart position: 2
● USA peak chart position: 11

BURGESS, SONNY

b. Albert Burgess, 28 May 1931, Newport, Arkansas, USA. As a child Burgess earned the name 'Sonny' as a result of his father also being called Albert. Inspired by the *Grand Ole Opry* show transmitted over WSM's airwaves, he set about learning to play a catalogue-purchased guitar. He joined his first country band while at high school, eventually moving from the role of supporting guitarist to lead the band. After graduation, Burgess joined the backing band of local singer Fred Waner (later a successful solo singer as Freddie Hart), along with Johnny Ray Hubbard (bass) and Gerald Jackson (drums) who had been with his high school group. Military service in Germany then intervened, but Burgess still found an opportunity to perform, eventually forming a band that successfully auditioned for the overseas forces' version of the *Grand Ole Opry*. Returning to Arkansas after his discharge in 1953, he found work at a box factory but also formed a new group, the Moonlighters, with Hubbard, Kern Kennedy and Russ Smith. After their first handful of performances at local venues the young mandolin player Joe Lewis also joined. Although their original sound was up-tempo country, the rise of Elvis Presley in the mid-50s soon led them to incorporate many of his best-known songs into their set. In 1955 the Moonlighters supported Presley at Newport's Silver Moon club. Jack Nance then joined the group in time for its name change to the Pacers.

Finally, in May 1956, Burgess decided it was time to record the band, journeying to Sun Records Studios in Memphis to audition for Sam Phillips. 'Red Headed Woman'/'We Wanna Boogie' duly became their first single release for Sun, selling a respectable 90,000 copies, its popularity spreading outside of the local community. Their first major tour of the Midwest followed, before the Pacers took an engagement as Roy Orbison's backing band. Their second single, 'Restless'/'Ain't Got A Thing', followed in January 1957. Shortly afterwards, they slimmed to a trio when Lewis left to join Conway Twitty and Smith departed for Jerry Lee Lewis' band. Further singles, including

'One Broken Heart' and 'Ain't Gonna Do It', followed, as did touring engagements with Orbison. The Pacers continued to release singles, including 'My Bucket's Got A Hole In It', but were unable to secure that elusive hit. The line-up also shifted again. The 1958 model of the band saw Burgess supported by J.C. Caughron (guitar), Bobby Crafford (drums) and Kern Kennedy on piano. Further recording sessions took place, resulting in the release of several singles including 'Oh Mama!', 'What'cha Gonna Do' and 'One Night'. Burgess later cited the recording of the latter song as the main inspiration behind Presley's version – certainly the similarities between their respective interpretations are remarkable. However, by the end of 1957 the Pacers were out of contract with Sun, and the group had to content itself with touring commitments. A final single, 'Sadie's Back In Town', was released on Sam Phillips' Phillips International, after which the Pacers broke up.

Burgess remained in the music business with a new, but largely unrecorded group, Kings IV, until 1970, at which time he returned home to Newport. Between 1974 and 1986 he stayed away from the music business, preferring to work as a travelling salesman. Renewed interest in the 90s led to Rounder Records signing him and in 1996 a remarkably fresh-sounding Burgess was heard on *Sonny Burgess* (subtitled *has still got it*). An excellent choice of tracks included 'Bigger Than Elvis' and Bruce Springsteen's 'Tiger Rose'. His vital contributions to both the development of rockabilly and the Sun Records' story offers a testimony to his status denied him in simple chart placings. It would appear that recognition has come 40 years too late.

● ALBUMS: *We Wanna Boogie* (Rounder 1990) ★★★, with Dave Alvin *Tennessee Border* (Hightone 1992) ★★★, *Sonny Burgess (has still got it)* (Rounder 1996) ★★★.
● COMPILATIONS: *The Classic Recordings 1956-1959* (Bear Family 1991) ★★★, *The Arkansas Wild Man* 1956-60 recordings (Charly 1995) ★★★★, *Arkansas Rock 'n' Roll* (Stomper Time 2000) ★★★.

BURNETTE, DORSEY

b. 28 December 1932, Memphis, Tennessee, USA, d. 19 August 1979, Canoga Park, California, USA. Living a full life, Burnette was a member of a classic 50s rock 'n' roll act, had his own hit soloist act in the 60s and became a country singer in the 70s. He helped to form the highly respected Johnny Burnette Trio with younger brother Johnny in 1953, but after appearing in the movie *Rock Rock Rock* in 1956, Dorsey left the trio. He recorded with Johnny as The Texans (on Infinity and Jox) and wrote major hits for Ricky Nelson, including 'It's Late' and 'Waitin' In School'. As a soloist, he recorded for Abbott, Cee-Jam, and then Era, where he had his two biggest solo hits, 'Tall Oak Tree' and 'Hey Little One', in 1960, both classics of their kind and both showcasing his deep, rich, country-style voice. He then recorded without luck on Lama, Dot Records, Imperial Records, Reprise Records, Mel-O-Day, Condor,

Liberty Records, Merri, Happy Tiger, Music Factory, Smash (where he re-recorded 'Tall Oak Tree'), Mercury Records and Hickory. In the 70s he had 15 Top 100 country hits (none making the Top 20) on Capitol Records, Melodyland, Calliope and Elektra Records, with whom he had only recently signed when he died of a heart attack in August 1979. His son Billy Burnette is also a recording artist.
● ALBUMS: *Tall Oak Tree* (Era 1960) ★★, *Dorsey Burnette Sings* (Dot 1963) ★★, *Dorsey Burnette's Greatest Hits* (Era 1969) ★★★, *Here & Now* (Capitol 1972) ★★★, *Dorsey Burnette* (Capitol 1973) ★★★, *Things I Treasure* (Calliope 1977) ★★.
● COMPILATIONS: *Great Shakin' Fever* (Bear Family 1992) ★★★.
● FILMS: *Rock Rock Rock* (1956).

BURNETTE, JOHNNY

b. 28 March 1934, Memphis, Tennessee, USA, d. 1 August 1964, Clear Lake, California, USA. Having attended the same high school as Elvis Presley, Johnny moved into the rockabilly genre by forming a trio with his brother Dorsey Burnette on string bass and schoolfriend Paul Burlison on guitar. Allegedly rejected by Sun Records owner Sam Phillips, the group recorded 'Go Mule Go' for Von Records in New York and were subsequently signed to Coral Records, where they enjoyed a minor hit with 'Tear It Up'. After touring with Carl Perkins and Gene Vincent, the trio underwent a change of personnel in November 1956 with the recruitment of drummer Tony Austin. That same month, the trio featured in Alan Freed's movie *Rock Rock Rock*. During this period, they issued a number of singles, including 'Honey Hush', 'The Train Kept A-Rollin'', 'Lonesome Train', 'Eager Beaver Baby', 'Drinking Wine, Spo-Dee-O-Dee' and 'If You Want It Enough', but despite the quality of the songs their work was unheralded. By the autumn of 1957, the trio broke up and the Burnette brothers moved on to enjoy considerable success as songwriters. Writing as a team, they provided Ricky Nelson with the hits 'It's Late', 'Believe What You Say' and 'Just A Little Too Much'. After briefly working as a duo, the brothers parted for solo careers. Johnny proved an adept interpreter of teen ballads, whose lyrics conjured up innocent dreams of wish fulfilment. Both 'Dreamin'' and 'You're Sixteen' were transatlantic Top 10 hits, perfectly suited to Burnette's light but expressive vocal. A series of lesser successes followed with 'Little Boy Sad', 'Big Big World', 'Girls' and 'God, Country And My Baby'. With his recording career in decline, Burnette formed his own label Magic Lamp in 1964. In August that year, he accidentally fell from his boat during a fishing trip in Clear Lake, California and drowned. Among the family he left behind was his son Rocky Burnette, who subsequently achieved recording success in the 70s.
● ALBUMS: as the Johnny Burnette Trio *Johnny Burnette And The Rock 'N' Roll Trio* 10-inch album (Coral 1956) ★★★★, *Dreamin'* (Liberty 1961) ★★★, *You're Sixteen* (Liberty 1961) ★★★, *Johnny*

Burnette (Liberty 1961) ★★★, *Johnny Burnette Sings* (Liberty 1961) ★★★, *Burnette's Hits And Other Favourites* (Liberty 1962) ★★★, *Roses Are Red* (Liberty 1962) ★★★.
● COMPILATIONS: *The Johnny Burnette Story* (Liberty 1964) ★★★★, with the Rock 'n' Roll Trio *Tear It Up* (Solid Smoke/Coral 1968) ★★★, *Tenth Anniversary Album* (United Artists 1974) ★★★, *We're Having A Party* (Rockstar 1988) ★★★, *Rock 'N' Roll Masters: The Best Of Johnny Burnette* (Liberty 1989) ★★★★, *You're Sixteen: The Best Of Johnny Burnette* (Capitol 1992) ★★★★, *25 Greatest Hits* (MFP 1998) ★★★, *Dreamin': The Very Best Of Johnny Burnette* (Collectables 1999) ★★★.
● FILMS: *Rock Rock Rock* (1956).

BURNS, RALPH

b. 29 June 1922, Newton, Massachusetts, USA, d. 21 November 2001, USA. After studying music at the New England Conservatory in Boston, Burns worked with several late swing-era bands, including Charlie Barnet's, as both pianist and arranger. His best-known period was as a member of Woody Herman's First Herd, during which time he was not only one quarter of a superb rhythm section (the others being Billy Bauer, Chubby Jackson and Dave Tough), but also arranged some of the band's most successful numbers (in some cases formalizing classic head arrangements, like that of 'Apple Honey'). In 1945 Burns decided to concentrate on writing and arranging, and contributed some exciting charts for Herman's Four Brothers band. He also composed some longer works, among which are 'Lady McGowan's Dream' and 'Summer Sequence', both recorded by Herman. When the record company decided to reissue 'Summer Sequence', they requested that a further section be added to the original three-part suite to fill the fourth side of a pair of 78 rpm releases. Burns obliged, and although some years had elapsed since the recording of the first three parts and the Herman band's personnel and style had substantially altered, he was able to recapture the mood successfully. The new piece, entitled 'Early Autumn', became a favourite of many jazz players, including Stan Getz.
Freelancing in the 50s and 60s, Burns gradually moved away from jazz and into the film studios, although even here, as in *New York, New York* (1977), he was sometimes able to make use of his extensive knowledge of the jazz world. He won Academy Awards for his work on *Cabaret* (1972) and *All That Jazz* (1979), and continued to score for a mixture of feature and television movies such as *Lenny, Piaf, Lucky Lady, Movie Movie, Make Me An Offer, Urban Cowboy, Golden Gate, Pennies From Heaven*, (with Marvin Hamlisch), *Annie, Kiss Me Goodbye, My Favourite Year, Star 80, Ernie Kovacs-Between The Laughter, A Chorus Line; Moving Violations, The Christmas Star, In The Mood, Bert Rigby, You're A Fool, Sweet Bird Of Youth, All Dogs Go To Heaven*, and *The Josephine Baker Story*.
● ALBUMS: *Free Forms* 10-inch album (Mercury 1952) ★★★★, *Ralph Burns Among The JATP's* (Norgran 1955) ★★★, *Spring Sequence* 10-inch

album (Period 1955) ★★★, *Bijou* 10-inch album (Period 1955) ★★, *Jazz Studio 5* (Decca 1956) ★★★★, with Mary Lou Williams *Composers – Pianists* (Jazztone 1956) ★★★, with Beverly Kenney *Come Swing With Me* (Roost 1956) ★★★, *The Masters Revisited* (Decca 1957) ★★★, *The Swinging Seasons* (MGM 1958) ★★★★, *New York's A Song* (Decca 1959) ★★★, *Very Warm For Jazz* (Decca 1959) ★★★, *Porgy And Bess* (Decca 1959) ★★★, *Where There's Burns There's Fire* (Warwick 1961) ★★, *Ralph Burns Conducts* 1951-1954 recordings (Raretone 1988) ★★★, *Bijou* 1955 recordings (Fresh Sounds 1988) ★★★.

BURNS, RAY

b. 1923, England, d. 2001. A popular singer in the UK in the 50s, Burns entered showbusiness straight after demobilization from the RAF in 1945. In the early days he was encouraged by Issy Bonn, and was spotted by Ambrose at the Blue Lagoon Club, and recorded with his Orchestra in 1949. After singing with Jack Nathan's band at the Coconut Grove and other nightspots such as Selby's and the Stork Club, he spent some time with Dave Shand's Orchestra, before signing for Columbia Records in 1953. His early sides included 'Mother Nature And Father Time' and 'Lonely Nightingale'. He had two chart entries in 1955, 'Mobile' (written by US songwriters Bob Wells and David Holt) and 'That's How A Love Song Was Born' (composed by the British team of record producer Norman Newell and Philip Green). His other releases during the 50s included 'Begorrah', 'Rags To Riches', 'I Can't Tell A Waltz From A Tango', 'Why?', 'A Smile Is Worth A Million Tears', 'Blue Star', 'Wonderful! Wonderful!', 'Meanwhile, Back In My Arms' and 'Condemned For Life (With A Rock And Roll Wife)'.

BURTON, JAMES

b. 21 August 1939, Shreveport, Louisiana, USA. One of the most distinguished of rock and country rock guitar players, Burton toured and recorded with Ricky Nelson, Elvis Presley and numerous other artists. His first recording was the highly influential 'Suzie-Q', sung by Dale Hawkins in 1957. Burton also performed with country singer Bob Luman before moving to Los Angeles where he was hired to work with Nelson, then the latest teen sensation. For six years he toured and recorded with Nelson, perfecting a guitar sound known as 'chicken pickin'. This was achieved by damping the strings for staccato-sounding single-string riffs and solos. Among the best examples of this style are 'Hello Mary Lou', 'Never Be Anyone Else But You' and the more frantic, rockabilly-flavoured 'Believe What You Say'.
During the late 60s and early 70s, Burton was much in demand as a session guitarist, working with Dale Hawkins on a comeback album as well as various artists including Buffalo Springfield, Judy Collins, John Phillips, Joni Mitchell, Michael Nesmith and Longbranch Pennywhistle, an outfit featuring future Eagles member Glenn

Frey. Burton also played dobro on albums by P.F. Sloan and John Stewart. In addition, Burton's powerful, rockabilly-influenced guitarwork made a major contribution to the harsher country sound developed at this time by Merle Haggard. Burton made two albums of his own during these years, one in collaboration with steel guitarist Ralph Mooney. During the 70s, Burton's work took him in contrasting directions. With pianist Glen D. Hardin (a former Crickets member), he was a mainstay of Elvis Presley's touring and recording band from 1969-77, but he also played a leading role in the growing trend towards country/rock fusion. Burton's most significant performances in this respect came on the albums of Gram Parsons. After Parsons' death, Burton and Hardin toured with Emmylou Harris and backed her on several solo albums. As a session guitarist, Burton played on albums by Jesse Winchester, Ronnie Hawkins, John Denver, Elvis Costello, Rodney Crowell, Phil Everly, J.J. Cale and Nicolette Larson, and toured with Jerry Lee Lewis. As a result of an accident in 1995, Burton lost the use of his hands and had to receive treatment to enable him to play the guitar again. He returned to work remarkably quickly, playing with Lewis and the Elvis Tribute Band and appearing on albums by Travis Tritt and the Tractors. He was inducted into the Rock And Roll Hall Of Fame in 2001.

● ALBUMS: with Ralph Mooney *Corn Pickin' And Slick Slidin'* (Capitol 1966) ★★★, *The Guitar Sound Of James Burton* (A&M 1971) ★★★.

BYGRAVES, MAX

b. Walter Bygraves, 16 October 1922, London, England. Performing as a soloist in his school choir and employing Max Miller impressions in the RAF, with music hall dates in the late 40s, led Bygraves quickly to his recording debut and first Royal Command Performance in 1950. His debut record, with the Carrol Gibbons Band, contained impressions of Al Jolson, and was followed by a string of novelty hits through the 50s such as 'Cowpuncher's Cantata', 'Heart Of My Heart', 'Gilly Gilly Ossenfeffer Katzenellen Bogen By The Sea', 'Meet Me On The Corner', 'You Need Hands'/'Tulips From Amsterdam', 'Jingle Bell Rock' and 'Fings Ain't Wot They Used To Be'. On the popular BBC radio show *Educating Archie*, scripted by comedian Eric Sykes, he gave a receptive nation catchphrases such as 'a good idea son!' and 'bighead!'. Bygraves became enormously popular on stage and television with his clever mix of song and patter, defying the dramatic changes in music and entertainment taking place in the 60s. In the early 70s with Pye Records musical director Cyril Stapleton and the Tony Mansell Singers, Bygraves recorded an album of standard songs in medley form, called *Sing Along With Max*. It was the first of an amazingly successful series for which he has now earned over 30 Gold Discs. Surprisingly, he has never successfully adapted his 'song and dance' image to films, although he has played several, mainly dramatic, roles to substantial critical acclaim, including *A Cry From The Streets* and *Spare The*

Rod. As early as the late 50s he formed his own music publishing company, Lakeview Music. It was intended to publish his own songs, including 'You Need Hands'. However, he bought the publishing rights to a 16-song show score for £350 because he liked one of the numbers. The show was Lionel Bart's *Oliver!*, and in the 80s Bygraves is said to have sold the rights to Essex Music for a quarter of a million pounds.

In 1982 he received the OBE, and 10 years later, celebrated his 70th birthday by attending a lunch given in his honour by the Variety Club, and including in his theatre act a cheeky topical parody of the old number 'They're Changing Guard At Buckingham Palace', entitled 'They're Changing *Wives* At Buckingham Palace'. In 1994 Max Bygraves released 'The Bells Of Arnhem', a powerful and emotional 50th anniversary commemoration of the men in Britain's World War II Airborne Forces who were defeated in the nine-day massacre that came to be known as 'A Bridge Too Far'. The song was written by Les Reed and Geoff Stephens, and all proceeds from the recording went to Airborne Forces charities.

● ALBUMS: *Songs For Young In Heart* (Decca 1959) ★★★, *Max Bygraves* (Hallmark 1971) ★★★, *Max* (Hallmark 1972) ★★★, *Sing Along With Max* (Pye 1972) ★★★★, *Sing Along With Max, Volume 2* (Pye 1972) ★★★★, *Singalongamax, Volume 3* (Pye 1973) ★★★★, *Singalongamax, Volume 4* (Pye 1973) ★★★★, *Singalongapartysong* (Pye 1973) ★★★, *You Make Me Feel Like Singing A Song* (Pye 1974) ★★★, *Singalongaxmas* (Pye 1974) ★★, *I Wanna Sing You A Story* (Pye 1975) ★★★, *Viva Congalongamax* (Pye 1975) ★★, *Singalongamovies* (Pye 1975) ★★, *Smile* (Pye 1976) ★★★, *Golden Greats Of The 20s* (Pye 1977) ★★★, *Golden Greats Of The 30s* (Pye 1977) ★★, *Golden Greats Of The 40s* (Pye 1977) ★★★, *Golden Greats Of The 50s* (Pye 1977) ★★★, *Lingalongamax* (Ronco 1978) ★★, with Victor Silvester *Song And Dance Men* (Pye 1978) ★★★, *Golden Greats Of The 60s* (Pye 1979) ★★, *Discolongamax* (Pye 1979) ★★, *Lingalongamax, Volume 2* (Pye 1980) ★★, with Acker Bilk *Twogether* (Piccadilly 1980) ★★, *Maximemories* (Celebrity 1981) ★★★, *You're My Everything* (Monarch 1982) ★★, *Max Sings While Ted Swings* (President 1983) ★★★★, with Silvester *Together: Max Bygraves And Victor Silvester* (PRT 1985) ★★★, *Singalong A Christmas* (Hallmark 1988) ★★, *Singalongawaryears* (Parkfield 1989) ★★★, *Singalongawaryears, Volume 2* (Parkfield 1989) ★★★.

● COMPILATIONS: *World Of Max Bygraves* (Decca 1969) ★★★, *World Of Max Bygraves, Volume 2* (Decca 1969) ★★★, *Unbeatable Bygraves* (Decca 1974) ★★★, *100 Golden Greats* (Ronco 1976) ★★★★, *Focus On Max Bygraves* (Decca 1978) ★★★, *Max Bygraves At His Very Best* (Golden Hour 1979) ★★★, *Spotlight On Max Bygraves, Volume 1* (PRT 1981) ★★★, *Spotlight On Max Bygraves, Volume 2* (PRT 1982) ★★★, *100 Minutes Of Max Bygraves* (PRT 1982) ★★★, *Happy Hits* (Spot 1983) ★★★, *Best Of Max* (Spot 1984) ★★★, *Classics* (MFP 1984) ★★★, *Collection* (PRT 1986) ★★★, *The Singalong Collection* (PRT 1987) ★★★, *An*

Hour Of Max Bygraves (Hour Of Pleasure 1988) ★★★★, *Singalong Years* (Ariola 1990) ★★★, *Tulips From Amsterdam* (Deram 1990) ★★★★, *The EMI Years* (EMI 1991) ★★★.
● VIDEOS: *Singalongawaryears* (Parkfield Publishing 1989).
● FURTHER READING: *I Wanna Tell You A Story*. Max Bygraves, *I Wanna Tell You A Funny Story*, Max Bygraves. *After Thoughts*, Max Bygraves. *Max Bygraves: In His Own Words*, Max Bygraves.

CADETS/JACKS

This Los Angeles, California, USA-based vocal unit, who recorded for Modern Records as the Cadets and for RPM as the Jacks, is an example of a house group, used by a record company to record cover hits or songs in styles of other groups. As the Cadets, the group had a hit with the novelty jump 'Stranded In The Jungle' (number 4 R&B, number 15 pop), in 1956, and as the Jacks with the ballad 'Why Don't You Write Me' (number 4 R&B, number 82 pop) in 1955. 'Stranded' was a cover of a record by the original Jayhawks and 'Why Don't You Write Me' was a cover of a record by the Feathers. The unit came together as the gospel group Santa Monica Soul Seekers, with the members including Ted Taylor (first tenor), Lloyd McCraw (baritone), and Will 'Dub' Jones (b. Will J. Jones, 14 May 1928, Shreveport, Louisiana, USA, d. 16 January 2000, Long Beach, California, USA; bass). Willie Davis (first tenor) and Aaron Collins (second tenor) replaced Taylor, who established a successful solo career as a hard soul singer during the 60s, when the group was signed to Modern Records in 1955. After leaving the label two years later, Davis and Collins kept the group together under the name Cadets, recording several singles for minor labels without success. In 1961 Collins and Davis, with several new members, recorded as the Flares and had a hit with 'Foot Stompin''.
● ALBUMS: as the Jacks *Jumpin' With The Jacks* (RPM 1956) ★★★, as the Cadets *Rockin' N' Reelin With The Cadets* (Crown 1957) ★★★, as the Jacks *Jumpin' With The Jacks* (Crown 1960) ★★★, as the Jacks *The Jacks* (Crown 1963) ★★★, as the Cadets *The Cadets* (Crown 1963) ★★★.
● COMPILATIONS: *The Best Of The Jacks* (Relic 1975) ★★★, *The Best Of The Cadets* (Relic 1975) ★★★, *The Cadets Meet The Jacks* (Ace 1987) ★★★.

CAHN, SAMMY

b. Samuel Cohen, 18 June 1913, New York City, New York, USA, d. 15 January 1993, Los Angeles, California, USA. The son of Jewish immigrant parents from Galicia, Poland, Cahn grew up on Manhattan's Lower East Side. Encouraged by his mother, he learned to play the violin, joined a small orchestra that played at bar mitzvahs and other functions, and later worked as a violinist in Bowery burlesque houses. At the age of 16 he wrote his first lyric, 'Like Niagara Falls, I'm Falling For You', and persuaded a fellow member of the orchestra, Saul Chaplin, to join him in a songwriting partnership. Their first published effort was 'Shake Your Head From Side To Side', and in the early 30s they wrote special material for vaudeville acts and bands. In 1935 the duo had their first big hit when the Jimmy Lunceford orchestra recorded their 'Rhythm Is Our Business'. The following year Andy Kirk topped the US Hit Parade with the duo's 'Until The Real Thing Comes Along', and Louis Armstrong featured their 'Shoe Shine Boy' in the revue *Connie's Hot Chocolates Of 1936*. In the following year Cahn and Chaplin had their biggest success to date when they adapted the Yiddish folk song 'Beir Mir Bist Du Schöen'. It became the top novelty song of the year and gave the Andrews Sisters their first million-seller. The team followed this with 'Please Be Kind', a major seller for Bob Crosby, Red Norvo and Benny Goodman. During this time Cahn and Chaplin were also under contract to Warner Brothers Records, and soon after that commitment ended they decided to part company.

In 1942, Cahn began a very productive partnership with Jule Styne, with their first chart success, 'I've Heard That Song Before'. Just as significant was Cahn's renewed association with Frank Sinatra, whom he had known when the singer was with Tommy Dorsey. Cahn and Styne wrote the score for the Sinatra movies *Step Lively* (1944), ('Come Out, Wherever You Are' and 'As Long As There's Music'), *Anchors Aweigh* (1945) ('I Fall In Love Too Easily', 'The Charm Of You' and 'What Makes The Sunset?') and *It Happened In Brooklyn* (1947) ('Time After Time', 'It's The Same Old Dream' and 'It's Gotta Come From The Heart'). Sinatra also popularized several other 40s Cahn/Styne songs, including 'I'll Walk Alone', 'Saturday Night Is The Loneliest Night In The Week', 'The Things We Did Last Summer', 'Five Minutes More', and the bleak 'Guess I'll Hang My Tears Out To Dry', which appeared on his 1958 album, *Only The Lonely*. Other hits included 'It's Been A Long, Long Time', associated with Harry James and his vocalist Kitty Kallen, 'Let It Snow! Let It Snow! Let It Snow!' (Vaughn Monroe) and 'There Goes That Song Again' (Kay Kyser and Russ Morgan). Cahn and Styne wrote the scores for several other movies, including *Tonight And Every Night* (1945), two Danny Kaye vehicles, *Wonder Man* (1945) and *The Kid From Brooklyn* (1946), and *West Point Story* (1950). They also provided the songs for *Romance On The High Seas* (1948), the movie in which Doris Day shot to international stardom, singing 'It's Magic' and 'Put 'Em In A Box, Tie It With A Ribbon'. The two songwriters also wrote the Broadway show *High Button Shoes* (1947), starring Phil Silvers (later Sgt. Bilko) and Nanette Fabray, which ran for 727 performances and introduced songs such as 'I Still Get Jealous', 'You're My Girl' and 'Papa, Won't You Dance With Me'.

After *High Button Shoes* Cahn went to California, while Styne stayed in New York. Cahn collaborated with Nicholas Brodszky for a time in the early 50s, writing movie songs for Mario Lanza including 'Be My Love', 'Wonder Why', 'Because You're Mine', 'Serenade' and 'My Destiny'. The collaboration also composed 'I'll Never Stop Loving You' for the Doris Day movie *Love Me Or Leave Me* (1955). Cahn and Styne reunited briefly

in 1954, ostensibly to write the score for the movie *Pink Tights*, to star Sinatra and Marilyn Monroe, but the project was shelved. Soon afterwards, Cahn and Styne were asked to write the title song for *Three Coins In The Fountain*. The result, a big hit for Sinatra and for the Four Aces, gained Cahn his first Academy Award. Cahn and Styne eventually worked with Monroe when they wrote the score for the comedy *The Seven Year Itch* (1955).

In the same year Cahn started his last major collaboration – with Jimmy Van Heusen and, some would say, with Frank Sinatra as well. They had immediate success with the title song of the Sinatra movie *The Tender Trap* (1955), and won Academy Awards for songs in two of his movies, 'All The Way', from *The Joker Is Wild* (1957) and 'High Hopes', from *A Hole In The Head* (1959). A parody of 'High Hopes' was used as John F. Kennedy's presidential campaign song in 1960. Among the many other numbers written especially for Sinatra were 'My Kind Of Town' (from *Robin And The Seven Hoods*, 1964) and the title songs for his bestselling albums *Come Fly With Me*, *Only The Lonely*, *Come Dance With Me!*, *No One Cares*, *Ring-A-Ding-Ding!* and *September Of My Years*. Cahn and Van Heusen also produced his successful Timex television series during 1959-60. They won another Oscar for 'Call Me Irresponsible' (from *Papa's Delicate Condition*, 1963), Cahn's fourth Academy Award from over 30 nominations, and contributed to many other movies including 'The Second Time Around' (from *High Time*) and the title songs from *A Pocketful Of Miracles*, *Where Love Has Gone*, *Thoroughly Modern Millie* and *Star*. The songwriters also supplied the score for a television musical version of Thorton Wilder's play *Our Town*, which introduced 'Love And Marriage' and 'The Impatient Years'. In the mid-60s they wrote the scores for two Broadway musicals, *Skyscraper* ('Everybody Has The Right To Be Wrong' and 'I'll Only Miss Her When I Think Of Her') and *Walking Happy*, while in 1969 Cahn worked with Styne again on another musical, *Look To The Lilies* ('I, Yes, Me! That's Who!').

Cahn's other collaborators included Axel Stordahl and Paul Weston ('Day By Day' and 'I Should Care'), Gene De Paul ('Teach Me Tonight'), Arthur Schwartz ('Relax-Ay-Voo'), George Barrie ('All That Love To Waste') and Vernon Duke ('That's What Makes Paris Paree', and 'I'm Gonna Ring The Bell Tonight'). In 1972 Cahn was inducted into the Songwriters Hall of Fame after claiming throughout his lifetime that he only wrote songs so that he could demonstrate them. Two years later he mounted his 'one man show', *Words And Music*, on Broadway, and despite his voice being described by a New York critic as that of 'a vain duck with a hangover', the nostalgic mixture of his songs, sprinkled with amusing memories of the way they were created, won the Outer Circle Critics Award for the best new talent on Broadway. Later in 1974, he repeated his triumph in England, and then re-staged the whole show all over again in 1987. After over six decades of 'putting *that* word to *that* note', as he termed it, Sammy Cahn died of congestive heart failure in January 1993.

● ALBUMS: *An Evening With Sammy Cahn* (EMI 1972) ★★★.

● FURTHER READING: *I Should Care: The Sammy Cahn Story*, Sammy Cahn. *Sammy Cahn's Rhyming Dictionary*, Sammy Cahn.

● FILMS: *Boardwalk* (1979).

CAIOLA, AL

b. Alexander Emil Caiola, 7 September 1920, Jersey City, New Jersey, USA. A highly respected studio guitarist, Caiola has played with many renowned musical directors such as Percy Faith, Hugo Winterhalter and Andre Kostelanetz. After serving as musical arranger and conductor for United Artists Records, Caiola released several singles on RCA during the 50s, including 'Delicado', a Brazilian song written by Walter Azevedo, which became a hit for Percy Faith, Stan Kenton, Ralph Flanagan and Dinah Shore. Caiola also released *Serenade In Blue* and *Deep In A Dream*, recorded by his Quintet. In 1961 he entered the US Top 40 charts with the movie theme *The Magnificent Seven* and *Bonanza*, the title music from the popular western television series; he had his own television show for a short time in the USA. Still active, Caiola has recorded over 75 albums.

● ALBUMS: include *Deep In A Dream* (Savoy/London 1955) ★★, *Serenade In Blue* (Savoy/London 1956) ★★★, *High Strung* (RCA Victor 1959) ★★★, *Music For Space Squirrels* (Atco 1960) ★★, with Don Arnone *Great Pickin'* (Chancellor 1960) ★★★, *Salute Italia* (Roulette 1960) ★★, *Percussion Espanol* (Time 1960) ★★★, *Spanish Guitars* (Time 1960) ★★★, *Gershwin And Guitars* (Time 1961) ★★★, *Soft Guitars* (Time 1962) ★★★, *Cleopatra And All That Jazz* (United Artists 1963) ★★★, *Tuff Guitar* (United Artists 1964) ★★, *Music To Read James Bond By* (United Artists 1965) ★★★, *Sounds For Spies And Private Eyes* (United Artists 1965) ★★★.

CALL ME MADAM

Ethel Merman enjoyed her greatest film triumph when she recreated her original role in this 1953 adaptation of Irving Berlin's hit Broadway show. Although she was never considered to be as effective on the screen as she was on stage, the part of the extrovert oil-heiress Sally Adams, the brand new Ambassador to the mythical Duchy of Lichtenburg, suited her down to the ground. In Arthur Sheekman's screenplay, which was faithfully based on Howard Lindsay and Russell Crouse's witty and sometimes satirical libretto, Merman flirted with one of the tiny principality's highest officials, Cosmo Constantine (George Sanders), while enquiring 'Can You Use Any Money Today?'. This was only one of the charming and amusing numbers in a Berlin score that arrived in Hollywood from New York almost intact, although inevitably the reference to 'panties' in Merman's *tour de force*, 'The Hostess

With The Mostes' On The Ball', which had presumably been acceptable to Broadway theatregoers, was removed for worldwide consumption. Merman was also firing on all cylinders with 'That International Rag', 'You're Just In Love' (with Donald O'Connor, who played her press attaché Ken Gibson) and 'The Best Thing For You' (with Sanders). The latter artist was more than adequate on the gentle 'Marrying For Love', and O'Connor had his moments on 'What Chance Have I With Love?', 'Something To Dance About' and the lively 'It's A Lovely Day Today', the last two with Vera-Ellen, whose singing was dubbed by Carole Richards. O'Connor and Vera-Ellen made a charming couple, and their dances together, which were choreographed by Robert Alton, were sublime. The rest of the cast included the always watchable duo, Walter Slezak and Billy De Wolfe. Musical Director Alfred Newman won an Oscar for his 'scoring of a musical picture' which was directed by Walter Lang and released by 20th Century-Fox.

CALLOWAY, CAB

b. Cabell Calloway, 25 December 1907, Rochester, New York, USA, d. 18 November 1994, Cokesbury Village, Hockessin, Delaware, USA. Involved in showbusiness from an early age, vocalist Calloway was an occasional drummer and MC, working mostly in Baltimore, where he was raised, and Chicago, where he relocated in the late 20s. He worked with his sister Blanche, and then, in 1929, he became frontman for the Alabamians. Engagements with this band took him to New York; in the same year he fronted the Missourians, a band for which he had briefly worked a year earlier. The Missourians were hired for New York's Savoy Ballroom; although the band consisted of proficient musicians, there is no doubt that it was Calloway's flamboyant leadership that attracted most attention. Dressing outlandishly in an eye-catching 'Zoot Suit' – knee-length drape jacket, voluminous trousers, huge wide-brimmed hat and a floor-trailing watch chain – he was the centre of attraction. His speech was peppered with hip phraseology and his catch phrase, 'Hi-De-Hi', echoed by the fans, became a permanent part of the language.

The popularity of the band and of its leader led to changes. Renamed as Cab Calloway And His Orchestra, the band moved into the Cotton Club in 1931 as replacement for Duke Ellington, allegedly at the insistence of the club's Mafia-connected owners. The radio exposure this brought helped to establish Calloway as a national figure. As a singer Calloway proved difficult for jazz fans to swallow. His eccentricities of dress extended into his vocal style, which carried echoes of the blues, crass sentimentality and cantorial religiosity. At his best, however, as on 'Geechy Joe' and 'Sunday In Savannah', which he sang in the 1943 movie *Stormy Weather*, he could be highly effective. His greatest popular hits were a succession of songs, the lyrics of which were replete with veiled references to drugs that, presumably, the record company executives failed to recognize. 'Minnie The Moocher' was the first of these, recorded in March 1931 with 'Kickin' The Gong Around', an expression that means smoking opium, released in October the same year. Other hits, about sexual prowess, were Fats Waller's 'Six Or Seven Times' and the Harold Arlen-Ted Koehler song 'Triggeration'.

For the more perceptive jazz fans who were patient enough to sit through the razzmatazz, and what one of his sidemen referred to as 'all that hooping and hollering', Calloway's chief contribution to the music came through the extraordinary calibre of the musicians he hired. In the earlier band he had the remarkable cornetist Reuben Reeves, trombonist Ed Swayzee, Doc Cheatham and Bennie Payne. As his popularity increased, Calloway began hiring the best men he could find, paying excellent salaries and allowing plenty of solo space, even though the records were usually heavily orientated towards his singing. By the early 40s the band included outstanding players such as Chu Berry, featured on 'Ghost Of A Chance' and 'Tappin' Off', Hilton Jefferson ('Willow Weep For Me'), Milt Hinton ('Pluckin' The Bass'), Cozy Cole ('Ratamacue' and 'Crescendo In Drums') and Jonah Jones ('Jonah Joins The Cab'). Further musicians included Ben Webster, Shad Collins, Garvin Bushell, Mario Bauza, Walter 'Foots' Thomas, Tyree Glenn, J.C. Heard and Dizzy Gillespie, making the Calloway band a force with which to be reckoned and one of the outstanding big bands of the swing era.

In later years Calloway worked on the stage in *Porgy And Bess* and *Hello, Dolly!*, and took acting roles in movies such as *The Blues Brothers* (1980). His other film appearances over the years included *The Big Broadcast* (1932), *International House* (1933), *The Singing Kid* (1937), *Manhattan Merry-Go-Round* (1937), *Sensations Of 1945* (1944), *St. Louis Blues* (1958), and *The Cincinnati Kid* (1965). Calloway enjoyed a considerable resurgence of popularity in the 70s with a Broadway appearance in *Bubbling Brown Sugar*. In the 80s he was seen and heard on stages and television screens in the USA and UK, sometimes as star, sometimes as support but always as the centre of attention. In 1993 he appeared at London's Barbican Centre, and in the same year celebrated his honorary doctorate in fine arts at the University of Rochester in New York State by leading the 9,000 graduates and guests in a singalong to 'Minnie The Moocher'. Calloway died the following year.

● ALBUMS: *Cab Calloway* 10-inch album (Brunswick 1954) ★★★★, *Cab Calloway* ii (Epic 1956) ★★★, *Hi De Hi, Hi De Ho* (RCA Victor 1958) ★★★★, *The Cotton Club Revue Of 1958* (Gone 1959) ★★★, *Blues Make Me Happy* (Coral 1962) ★★★.
● COMPILATIONS: *Club Zanzibar Broadcasts* (Unique Jazz 1981) ★★★, *Kickin' The Gong Around* (Living Era 1982) ★★★, *The Hi-De-Ho Man* (RCA 1983) ★★★★, *Cab & Co.* (RCA 1985) ★★★, *Cab Calloway Collection: 20 Greatest Hits* (Déjà Vu 1986) ★★★★, *The Cab Calloway Story*

(Déjà Vu 1989) ★★★★, *Best Of The Big Bands* (Columbia 1991) ★★★, *1941-42* (Classics 1993) ★★★★, *Jumpin' Jive* (Camden 1998) ★★★.
● FURTHER READING: *Of Minnie The Moocher And Me*, Cab Calloway. *The New Cab Calloway's Hepster's Dictionary*, Cab Calloway.
● FILMS: *Minnie The Moocher* (1932), *The Big Broadcast* (1932), *Snow-White* voice only (1933), *International House* (1933), *The Old Man Of The Mountain* (1933), *Cab Calloway's Hi-De-Ho* (1934), *Cab Calloway's Jitterbug Party* (1935), *The Singing Kid* (1937), *Manhattan Merry-Go-Round* (1937), *Meet The Maestros* (1938), *Stormy Weather* (1943), *Sensations Of 1945* (1944), *Caledonia* (1945), *Hi-De-Ho* (1947), *Ebony Parade* (1947), *Rhythm And Blues Revue* (1955), *Basin Street Revue* (1956), *St. Louis Blues* (1958), *The Cincinnati Kid* (1965), *The Blues Brothers* (1980).

CALVERT, EDDIE

b. 15 March 1922, Preston, Lancashire, England, d. 7 August 1978, Johannesburg, South Africa. Calvert's father taught him to play the trumpet, and at the age of 11, he joined the Preston Town Silver Band. In the 40s he played with Billy Ternent and Geraldo before forming his own group for nightclub engagements. By the early 50s he was touring the British variety circuit, and became known as 'The Man With The Golden Trumpet'. In 1953 he recorded a Swiss tune 'O Mein Papa' which went to number 1 in the UK and made the Top 10 in the USA. Two years later he topped the UK charts again with a cover version of the Perez Prado hit 'Cherry Pink And Apple Blossom White', and in the late 50s had more success with 'Zambesi', 'Mandy' and the theme from the Peter Sellers film *John And Julie*. Calvert had enormous success in theatres and clubs in the UK, including the London Palladium and major regional venues, until he moved to South Africa in 1968, where he was appointed liaison officer between the government and the Bantu tribe. He died there from a heart attack in 1978.
● ALBUMS: *Latin Carnival* (Columbia 1960) ★★★, *All In The Summer Evening (And Other Songs Of Faith)* (1965) ★★★, *Eddie Calvert Salutes The Trumpet Greats* (1967) ★★★.
● COMPILATIONS: *The Man With The Golden Trumpet* (One-Up 1978) ★★★, *20 Golden Trumpet Greats* (Note 1979) ★★★, *The EMI Years* (EMI 1992) ★★★★.

CAPRIS

This R&B vocal group from Philadelphia, Pennsylvania, USA, comprised Rena Hinton, Bobby Smart, Eddie Warner, Harrison Scott, and Reuben White. Their one claim to fame was 'God Only Knows' (not the Beach Boys' hit) in 1954, which featured the quivering and fetching lead of Hinton. His vocals typified the delicate high-pitched lead work of Philadelphia doo-wop groups. The Capris originally formed in the early 50s in west Philadelphia, and in 1953 established their recording configuration when original member Charlie Stroud left the group to be

replaced by Hinton. The Capris signed with Gotham in June 1954. 'God Only Knows' attracted considerable east coast play and they made radio and television appearances. The follow-ups, 'It's A Miracle' and 'It Was Moonglow', both ballads featuring the same vocal approach, were fine examples of the Philadelphia sound, but they did not sustain the group's commercial success. When some of the members entered the Air Force in early 1955, the Capris were forced to disband. The group re-formed in 1958, with Fred Hale replacing Harrison Scott. They recorded 'My Weakness', but its lack of success served to break up the group for good. Some members of the Capris later formed the Moniques.
● COMPILATIONS: *Gotham Recording Stars: The Capris* (Collectables 1990) ★★★.

CARMEN JONES

This was at least the fifth manifestation of a story that started out as a novel by Frenchman Prosper Mérimeé, then became a grand opera by Bizet, Meilhac and Halévy, a 1943 Broadway musical, a 1948 film *The Loves Of Carmen* starring Rita Hayworth and Glenn Ford, and eventually this, a full-blown film musical that was produced and directed by Otto Preminger for 20th Century-Fox in 1954. Harry Kleiner's screenplay, which was based on Oscar Hammerstein II's libretto for that 1943 musical, follows the dramatic action of its operatic source, but changes the setting of the cigarette factory in Seville to a parachute factory in Chicago, and updates the story to World War II. Don José becomes Joe (Harry Belafonte), a young soldier destined for flying school before being ruined by Carmen (Dorothy Dandridge); Escamillo, the toreador, is now Husky Miller (Joe Adams), a champion heavyweight prizefighter; Micaëla, the village maid, is transformed into Cindy Lou (Olga James), a small-town maiden who always remains faithful to her Joe; and Frasquita and the smuggler friends of Carmen are now Frankie (Pearl Bailey), Myrt (Diahann Carroll), Dink (Nick Stewart) and Rum (Roy Glenn). The singing voices of Carmen, Joe, Husky, Myrt, Rum and Dink are dubbed by Marilyn Horne, La Vern Hutcherson, Marvin Hayes, Bernice Peterson, Brock Peters and Joe Crawford, respectively. The highly emotional score, with music by Georges Bizet and lyrics by Oscar Hammerstein, was comprised of 'Dat's Love', 'You Talk Jus' Like My Maw', 'Dere's A Cafe On De Corner', 'Dis Flower', 'Beat Out Dat Rhythm On A Drum', 'Stan' Up And Fight', 'Whizzin' Away Along De Track', 'Card Song' and 'My Joe'. Herbert Ross was the choreographer and *Carmen Jones* was photographed by Sam Leavitt in Delux Color and CinemaScope.

CAROUSEL

It took more than 10 years for Richard Rodgers and Oscar Hammerstein II's second musical to transfer from Broadway to Hollywood in 1956, but the wait was more than worthwhile. The story, with its inherent dark undertones, was always going to be difficult to film, but Henry Ephron and his wife Phoebe wrote a fine screenplay. It was based on the original stage libretto, which itself had been adapted from Ferenc Molnar's play *Liliom*. It was set in Maine, New England, in 1873, and told of the tragic love affair between carousel barker Billy Bigelow (Gordon MacRae) and mill worker Julie Jordan (Shirley Jones). Out of work, and desperate to earn enough money to support his pregnant wife, Billy is persuaded by sly Jigger Craigin (Cameron Mitchell) to take part in a robbery that goes awry. He is killed in the ensuing scuffle when he falls on his own knife. Fifteen years later he is allowed to return to earth for just one day so that he can make his peace with his lovely teenage daughter. An admirable supporting cast included Barbara Ruick and Robert Rounseville as the delightful Carrie Pipperidge and Enoch Snow, Claramae Turner, Susan Luckey, Audrey Christie, Gene Lockhart and Jacques d'Amboise. The classic score remained more or less intact, from the majestic 'Carousel Waltz' through to the inspirational 'You'll Never Walk Alone'. Along the way there are other memorable numbers such as 'You're A Queer One, Julie Jordan', 'If I Loved You', 'Mr. Snow', 'June Is Bustin' Out All Over', 'When The Children Are Asleep', 'Soliloquy', 'Stonecutters Cut It On Stone', 'What's The Use Of Wond'rin'?' and 'A Real Nice Clambake'. Roger Alexander and the legendary Agnes de Mille staged the dances, and the film, which was produced by Henry Ephron for 20th Century-Fox, was photographed by Charles Clarke in DeLuxe Color and CinemaScope. The director was Henry King. Frank Sinatra was the original choice to play Billy Bigelow but he withdrew soon after filming began. However, he did record an impressive version of 'Soliloquy' which stretched to both sides of a 12-inch 78 rpm record.

CARR, PEARL, AND TEDDY JOHNSON

Both were popular solo vocalists prior to their marriage in 1955. Carr (b. Pearl Lavina Carr, 2 November 1923, Exmouth, Devon, England) worked with several popular bands and was lead singer with the Keynotes, the resident vocal group on BBC Radio's *Take It From Here*. She also appeared on radio as a comedienne and singer on *Breakfast* (and *Bedtime*) *With Braden*, and had her own series, *In The Blue Of The Evening*. Johnson (b. Edward Victor Johnson, 4 September 1920, Surbiton, Surrey, England) led his own five-piece amateur band at the age of 14 and sang and played drums professionally at the age of 17. He recorded extensively for Columbia Records in the early 50s, worked as a disc jockey for Radio Luxembourg, and regularly appeared on television on programmes such as *Crackerjack* and *Music Shop*. The couple's professional liaison proved to be extremely successful, especially during the late 50s when they became known as Britain's Mr and Mrs Music. They toured the UK variety circuit, and in 1959 made the UK Top 20 chart with the catchy 'Sing Little Birdie', a song that they had taken to second place in the Eurovision Song Contest. They had another hit in

1961 with the Italian 'Aneme E Core (How Wonderful To Know)'. More recently they have been involved in biographical stage presentations such as *The Bing Crosby Story* and *London To Hollywood Songbook*, which they devised and appeared in. In 1987 they were contemplating retirement when they accepted an offer to appear as two ageing vaudeville stars in Stephen Sondheim's *Follies*, their first West End musical. In the late 80s and early 90s Johnson continued to write and present programmes for the BBC World Service and Radio 2.

CARROLL, RONNIE

b. Ronald Cleghorn, 18 August 1934, Belfast, Northern Ireland. A singer with an extremely high baritone voice, who became known as 'The Minstrel'. Carroll has been a baker, plumber, greengrocer, milkman, car mechanic and auctioneer's assistant. He began his career in shows promoted by Ruby Murray's father, then joined Eddie Lee's *Hollywood Doubles Show*, blacking up to provide Nat 'King' Cole impressions. Cole attended his performance in Liverpool and asked, 'What are you trying to do, cripple me?'. Carroll toured the UK Variety circuit with the show, adding Billy Eckstine material to his repertoire. After BBC producer Albert Stevenson gave him his television debut, he met singer and actress Millicent Martin on a show and they were married in 1959. Carroll was signed to Philips by A&R manager Johnny Franz who had seen him at the London Metropolitan, Edgware Road. In the late 50s he had UK hits with 'Walk Hand In Hand' (1956) and 'Wisdom Of A Fool' (1957), and in the early 60s with 'Footsteps' (1960), 'Roses Are Red (My Love)' (1962 – a number 3 hit), 'If Only Tomorrow' (1962) and two songs with which he won the British heats of the Eurovision Song Contest, 'Ring-A-Ding Girl' (1962) and 'Say Wonderful Things' (1963 – Top 10). After separating from Millicent Martin in 1965, Carroll married the Olympic Sprinter June Paul. In 1972 they emigrated with their children to Grenada and opened a nightclub, but a political revolution ruined their plans, and Carroll returned to Britain in deep financial trouble. Although continuing to perform occasionally at holiday camps and Far East locations, he eventually abandoned singing for a more profitable hot sausage stall at London's Camden Market. This he later combined with helping to run the Everyman Cinema and Jazz Club in Hampstead. Having lived in that area of London for many years, in 1997 Carroll stood for Parliament on a 'Home Rule for Hampstead' ticket at the General Election. In the event, he posed little threat to the sitting member, another former refugee from showbusiness, ex-film star Glenda Jackson.
● ALBUMS: with Bill McGuffie *From Ten Till One* (Philips 1956) ★★★, *Lucky Thirteen* (Philips 1959) ★★★, *Sometimes I'm Happy, Sometimes I'm Blue* (Philips 1963) ★★★, with Millicent Martin *Mr & Mrs Is The Name* (Philips 1964) ★★, *Carroll Calling* (1965) ★★★, *Wonderful Things And Other*

Favourites (Wing 1967) ★★★, with Anna Pollack *Phil The Fluter* (Fontana 1969) ★★, with Aimi McDonald *Promises Promises* (Fontana 1970) ★★.
● COMPILATIONS: *Roses Are Red: The Ronnie Carroll Story* (Diamond 1996) ★★★★.

CARTER, BETTY

b. Lillie Mae Jones, 16 May 1930, Flint, Michigan, USA, d. 26 September 1998, New York City, New York, USA. Some historians also state her date of birth is 1929. Growing up in Detroit, Carter sang with touring jazzmen, including Charlie Parker and Dizzy Gillespie. In her late teens, she joined Lionel Hampton, using the stage name Lorene Carter. With Hampton she enjoyed a love-hate relationship; he would regularly fire her only to have his wife and business manager, Gladys Hampton, re-hire her immediately. Carter's predilection for bop earned from Hampton the mildly disparaging nickname of 'Bebop Betty', by which name she became known thereafter. In the early 50s she worked on the edge of the R&B scene, sharing stages with blues artists of the calibre of Muddy Waters. Throughout the remainder of the 50s and into the 60s she worked mostly in and around New York City, establishing a reputation as a fiercely independent and dedicated jazz singer. She took time out for tours with packages headlined by Ray Charles (with whom she recorded a highly regarded album of duets), but preferred to concentrate on her own shows and club performances. She also found time for marriage and a family. Her insistence upon certain standards in her recording sessions eventually led to the formation of her own record company, Bet-Car. During the 80s, Carter continued to perform in clubs in New York and London, occasionally working with large orchestras but customarily with a regular trio of piano, bass and drums, the ideal setting for her spectacular improvisations.
Taking her inspiration from instrumentalists such as Parker and Sonny Rollins rather than from other singers, Carter's technique drew little from the vocal tradition in jazz. Her kinship with the blues was never far from the surface, however complex and contemporary that surface might be. In performance, Carter mainly employed the lower register of her wide range. Always aurally witty Carter frequently displayed scant regard for the lyrics of the songs she sang, her inventiveness was ably displayed on performances such as 'Sounds', a vocalese excursion which, in one recorded form, lasts for more than 25 minutes. Despite such extraordinary performances and the breakneck tempos she employed on 'The Trolley Song' and 'My Favourite Things', she could sing ballads with uncloying tenderness. In concert, Carter dominated the stage, paced like a tigress from side to side and delivered her material with devastating attack. The authority with which she stamped her performances, especially in vocalese and the boppish side of her repertoire, helped to make unchallenged her position as the major jazz singer of the 80s and 90s.
● ALBUMS: *Meet Betty Carter And Ray Bryant*

(Epic 1955) ★★★★, *Social Call* (Sony 1956) ★★★, *Out There With Betty Carter – Progressive Jazz* (Peacock 1958) ★★★, *The Modern Sound Of Betty Carter* (ABC-Paramount 1960) ★★★, *I Can't Help It* (Impulse! 1961) ★★★, *Ray Charles And Betty Carter* (ABC 1961) ★★★★, *'Round Midnight* (Atco 1963) ★★★, *Inside Betty Carter* (United Artists 1963) ★★★, *Finally* (Roulette 1969) ★★★, *Live At The Village Vanguard* (Verve 1970) ★★★★, *The Betty Carter Album* (Verve 1972) ★★★, *Now It's My Turn* (Roulette 1976) ★★★, *What A Little Moonlight Can Do* (Impulse! 1977) ★★★★, *I Didn't Know What Time It Was* (Verve 1979) ★★★, *The Audience With Betty Carter* (Verve 1979) ★★★★, *Whatever Happened To Love?* (Verve 1982) ★★★★, *Look What I Got* (Verve 1988) ★★★★, *Droppin' Things* (Verve 1990) ★★★, *It's Not About The Melody* (Verve 1992) ★★★★, *Feed The Fire* (Verve 1993) ★★★, *I'm Yours, You're Mine* (Verve 1996) ★★★★.
● COMPILATIONS: *Compact Jazz* (Philips 1990) ★★★, *Priceless Jazz* (Verve 1999) ★★★.

CASSIDY, JACK

b. John Cassidy, 5 March 1927, Richmond Hill, New York, USA, d. 12 March 1976, Los Angeles, California, USA. A versatile actor and singer who, even in his later years, seemed to retain his youthful appearance, Cassidy made his Broadway debut at the age of 17 in the chorus of the 1943 Cole Porter-Ethel Merman hit musical *Something For The Boys*. More chorus work followed in *Sadie Thompson*, *The Firebrand Of Florence*, *Around The World*, *Music In My Heart*, and *Inside USA*, before Cassidy played a more prominent role, along with others on the brink of success such as Tom Ewell and Alice Pearce, in the stylish revue *Small Wonder* (1948). He was in the short-lived *Alive And Kicking* in 1950, and two years later took over the part of Seabee Richard West in *South Pacific*. Also in 1952, Cassidy had his first leading role as the suave Chick Miller in *Wish You Were Here*, a show that attracted a great deal of publicity owing to the fact that it had a swimming-pool built into the stage. Cassidy introduced the appealing title song, and also sang the underrated 'Where Did The Night Go?'. He subsequently played opposite Betty Oakes in the offbeat *Sandhog* (1954), co-starred with Carol Lawrence in a musical adaptation of James Hilton's novel *Lost Horizon* called *Shangri-La*, and appeared in various musical productions in the US regions and Europe, before returning to Broadway in 1963 with the charming *She Loves Me*. While Barbara Cook and Daniel Massey resolved their complicated relationship, Cassidy, playing the unctuous 'resident ladies man' Steven Kodaly, pursued Barbara Baxley with 'Ilona' and 'Grand Knowing You'. His performance was rewarded with the 1964 Tony Award for Supporting/ Featured Actor in a musical.

During the remainder of the 60s, Cassidy had another ultra-smooth role as Hollywood leading man Byron Prong in *Fade Out-Fade In* (1964), was egotistical columnist Max Mencken in the comic strip spoof *It's A Bird, It's A Plane, It's Superman* (1966), and played Irishman Phineas Flynn in the

Civil War musical *Maggie Flynn* (1968). In the title role of the latter show was Shirley Jones, the former star of films such as *Oklahoma!*, *Carousel* and *The Music Man*, who was Cassidy's second wife. Cassidy himself also appeared in a number of films, notably as John Barrymore in *W.C. Fields And Me* and as Damon Runyon in *The Private Files Of J. Edgar Hoover*. After his Broadway career declined, he worked in regional theatre, both straight and musical, and appeared on television and in nightclubs. He died at the age of 49 in a fire at his Los Angeles apartment. Three of his sons, Patrick Cassidy and Shaun Cassidy (from his marriage to Shirley Jones), along with David Cassidy (from his earlier marriage to Evelyn Ward), are also in showbusiness.
● FILMS: *Look In Any Window* (1961), *The Chapman Report* (1962), *FBI Code 98* (1964), *Guide For The Married Man* (1967), *The Cockeyed Cowboys Of Calico County* (1970), *Bunny O'Hare* (1971), *The Eiger Sanction* (1975), *W.C. Fields And Me* (1976), *The Private Files Of J. Edgar Hoover* (1978).

CHACKSFIELD, FRANK

b. 9 May 1914, Battle, Sussex, England, d. 9 June 1995. After early training on the piano and organ, Chacksfield led small groups in the late 30s before becoming arranger for the *Stars In Battledress* entertainment unit in World War II. His first radio broadcast was *Original Songs At The Piano* from Glasgow, and during the late 40s he worked with comedian Charlie Chester's *Stand Easy*, making his recording debut accompanying Chester's resident singer, Frederick Ferrari. He also conducted for the Henry Hall and Geraldo orchestras, and later formed his own band, the Tunesmiths. In 1953, he had a hit with the novelty 'Little Red Monkey', with composer Jack Jordan on the clavioline. Later that year, with a 40-piece orchestra featuring a large string section, Chacksfield made the Top 10 in the UK and US charts with Charles Chaplin's 'Terry's Theme From *Limelight*', repeating the process in 1954 with his version of 'Ebb Tide'. Both records, with their richly scored arrangements, became million-sellers. He had further success in the 50s with 'In Old Lisbon', 'Donkey Cart', 'Flirtation Waltz', 'Memories Of You', and another Chaplin theme, 'Smile'. He had his own weekly radio programme for a time, and in later years continued to broadcast regularly in programmes such as *Friday Night Is Music Night*. His many albums reflected music from all over the world, as well as featuring the work of various popular composers.
● ALBUMS: *The Ebb Tide* (Decca 1960) ★★★, *The New Ebb Tide* (Decca 1964) ★★★, *New Limelight* (Phase 4 1965) ★★★, *All Time Top TV Themes* (Phase 4 1965) ★★★, *Beyond The Sea* (Phase 4 1965) ★★★★, *Great Country And Western Hits* (Phase 4 1966) ★★, *Film Festival* (Phase 4 1968) ★★★, *South Sea Island Magic* (Eclipse 1969) ★★, *Tango* (Eclipse 1970) ★★, *New York* (Phase 4 1970) ★★★★, *Plays The Beatles Songbook* (Phase 4 1970) ★★★, *Plays Simon And Garfunkel/Jim Webb* (Phase 4 1971) ★★, *Mediterranean Moonlight* (Eclipse

1971) ★★★★, *Plays Bacharach* (Phase 4 1972) ★★★, *The World Of Immortal Classics* (Decca 1972) ★★★, *Music Of Cole Porter* (Phase 4 1972) ★★★, *Opera's Golden Moments* (Phase 4 1973) ★★, *Music For Christmas* (Decca 1973) ★★★, *The World Of Immortal Serenades* (Decca 1973) ★★★, *Music Of Noël Coward* (Eclipse 1974) ★★★, *Romantic Europe* (Eclipse 1974) ★★★, *The Glory That Was Gershwin* (Phase 4 1974) ★★★★, *The Incomparable Jerome Kern* (Phase 4 1975) ★★★★, *Plays Rodgers And Hart* (Phase 4 1975) ★★★★, *The World Of Immortal Strauss Waltzes* (Decca 1975) ★★★, *The World Of Operatic Melodies* (Decca 1976) ★★★, *Plays Lerner And Loewe* (Phase 4 1976) ★★★, *Plays Irving Berlin* (Phase 4 1976) ★★★, *Vintage '52* (Phase 4 1977) ★★★, *Plays Hoagy Carmichael* (Phase 4 1977) ★★★, *Hawaii* (Goldcrown 1978) ★★★, *The Unmistakable Frank Chacksfield* (Rim 1979) ★★★, *Could I Have This Dance?* (Dansan 1981) ★★★, *Chariots Of Fire* (Premier 1984) ★★★, *Love Is In The Air* (Premier 1984) ★★★, *Nice 'N' Easy* (Premier 1984) ★★★, *A Little More Love* (Premier 1987) ★★★, *Thanks For The Memories (Academy Award Winners 1934-55)* (Eclipse 1991) ★★★.
● COMPILATIONS: *The World Of Frank Chacksfield* (Decca 1969) ★★★★, *The World Of Frank Chacksfield, Volume Two* (Decca 1971) ★★★★, *Focus On Frank Chacksfield* (Decca 1977) ★★★, *Stardust* (Contour 1981) ★★★, *Limelight And Other Favourites* (President 1985) ★★★.

CHAKACHAS

This Belgian septet were led by Gaston Boogaerts (bass guitar) with a flux of personnel usually including a female singer, horns and Latin percussion. Launched by a European smash with 'Eso Es El Amor' in 1958, a consequent crowded booking schedule guaranteed a steady growth of popularity throughout the continent – even in the UK where their opportunist 'Twist Twist' sneaked into the Top 50 in 1962. Five years later, constant touring took its toll, causing Boogaerts to resume his former occupation as a painter. Nevertheless, he continued to supervise the group's record dates. During 1970 sessions for an album, he earmarked 'Jungle Fever' (composed by William Albimoor) as a potential hit single. This judgement proved correct when, featuring vocalist Kary and saxophonist Victor Ingeveld, it took most European markets by storm and even reached number 8 in the USA. The true benefit of this episode, however, was the broadening of the outfit's work spectrum, especially into the lucrative US supper clubs, and they received invitations to perform on television for the first time in years.

CHAMPS

Best known for the classic 1958 rock 'n' roll near-instrumental 'Tequila', a US number 1 song, the Champs were formed in Los Angeles, California, USA, in December 1957. The five musicians initially comprising the group were Dave Burgess (rhythm guitar), Danny Flores (saxophone, piano), Cliff Hills (bass), Buddy Bruce (lead

guitar) and Gene Alden (drums). The musicians were united by Joe Johnson, co-owner of Challenge Records, for the purpose of providing backing for the Kuf-Linx vocal group. With time left after that session, the musicians recorded three instrumentals written by Burgess. Flores, who also went under the name Chuck Rio, as he was already contracted to the RPM label, taught the others 'Tequila' from a riff on which he had worked for performance at club dates in Los Angeles. The recording was considered a 'throwaway' by the musicians, who did not even stay to hear the final playback. Issued in January 1958 under the name Champs (in honour of Champion, a horse owned by Challenge founder Gene Autry), 'Tequila' was planned as the b-side to 'Train To Nowhere'. Radio stations preferred 'Tequila' and the Champs' version battled for chart positions with a cover version of the song by Eddie Platt; the latter's version reached number 20 in the US charts while the Champs' made number 1. With the song a success, there was a need for them to tour, so a new line-up was formed including Flores, Burgess, Alden and new members Dale Norris (guitar) and Joe Burnas (bass). Flores and Alden left in late 1958 and were replaced by Jim Seals (saxophone), Dash Crofts (drums) and Dean Beard (piano). Seals And Crofts remained with the group until its termination, before forming the Dawnbreakers and then re-emerging in the late 60s as a popular acoustic music duo. The Champs placed a further seven singles in the charts through 1962, none of which came close to matching the debut's success. Further personnel changes occurred throughout their history, most notably the replacement of Burgess by young guitarist Glen Campbell in 1960. The Champs disbanded in 1964.
● ALBUMS: *Go Champs Go* (Challenge 1958) ★★★, *Everybody's Rockin' With The Champs* (Challenge 1959) ★★★, *Great Dance Hits Of Today* (Challenge 1962) ★★★, *All American Music With The Champs* (Challenge 1962) ★★★.
● COMPILATIONS: *Wing Ding!* (Ace 1994) ★★★, *The Early Singles* (Ace 1996) ★★★, *The Champs: The EP Collection . . . Plus* (See For Miles 2001) ★★★.

CHANNING, CAROL

b. 31 January 1921, Seattle, Washington, USA. An actress and singer with a style and appearance that are difficult to define, she has been described as 'a blonde, wide-eyed, long-legged, husky voiced, scatty personality' – among other things. The daughter of a Christian Science teacher, Channing moved with her family to San Francisco at an early age, and later attended Bennington College in Vermont, where she majored in drama and dance. In 1941 she appeared in Marc Blitzstein's labour opera *No For An Answer*, but only for three Sunday nights. In the same year she served as an understudy in *Let's Face It!* on Broadway, and had a small part in *Proof Through The Night* (1942). After playing nightclubs around New York, she returned to San

Francisco in 1946 and won a part in the Hollywood revue *Lend An Ear*. Her performance in the Broadway version of the show led to her triumph as Lorelei Lee in *Gentlemen Prefer Blondes*, in which she introduced several memorable numbers including 'A Little Girl From Little Rock' and 'Diamonds Are A Girl's Best Friend'. In 1954, she replaced Rosalind Russell in *Wonderful Town*, and in the next year, had her first big flop with *The Vamp*. In the late 50s her nightclub act was so successful that it was turned into a one-woman revue entitled *Show Girl*, which played on Broadway in 1961. Three years later, she had her biggest success in *Hello, Dolly!*, as the matchmaker Dolly Levi, with a Jerry Herman score that included 'So Long, Dearie', 'Before The Parade Passes By', and the insinuating title song. She won a Tony Award for outstanding performance, but Barbra Streisand was preferred for the movie version. Channing's larger-than-life personality is perhaps more suited to the stage than film, although she was hilarious in *Thoroughly Modern Millie* (1967). Other film credits include *Paid In Full*, *The First Travelling Saleslady*, *Skidoo* and *Shinbone Alley* (voice only). In 1974 she was back on Broadway in *Lorelei*, which, as the title suggests, was a compilation of the best scenes from *Gentlemen Prefer Blondes*. It lasted for 320 performances and had a reasonable life on the road. At that stage of her career, with suitable musical comedy roles hard to come by, Channing continued to work mostly on US television and in nightclubs, but in 1987 she co-starred with Mary Martin in James Kirkwood's aptly named show *Legends!*. A year later she embarked on a concert tour of locations such as Kansas City and San Diego, accompanied at each stop by the local symphony orchestra. In 1990 she appeared at the Desert Inn, Las Vegas, and two years later toured with Rita Moreno in *Two Ladies Of Broadway*. In 1995, Carol Channing received a special Lifetime Achievement Tony Award, and was back where she belongs, on Broadway starring in a major revival of her greatest success, *Hello, Dolly!*
● ALBUMS: *Carol Channing* (Vanguard 1959) ★★★, *Previous Hits* (Vanguard 1959) ★★★, *Carol Channing Entertains* (Command 1965) ★★★★, *Jazz Baby* (DRG 1994) ★★★, and Original Cast and soundtrack recordings.
● FILMS: *Paid In Full* (1950), *The First Travelling Saleslady* (1956), *Thoroughly Modern Millie* (1967).

CHANTELS

Regarded as the first true 'girl group', this New York vocal quintet – Arlene Smith (b. 5 October 1941, New York, USA), Sonia Goring, Rene Minus, Lois Harris and Jackie Landry – were all members of a high-school choir when they auditioned for producer Richard Barrett in 1957. The group made its recording debut for End Records with 'He's Gone' following two months of rehearsal, and this plaintive offering set the tone for the Chantels' subsequent work. Their impassioned style culminated with 'Maybe', wherein Smith's heart-wrenching plea carried an inordinate passion.

Barely 16 years old on its release, the singer's emotional delivery belied her youth. The single reputedly sold in excess of one million copies and reached R&B number 2 and the pop Top 20, but pirated pressings were prevalent in many American states, undermining the group's potential. Subsequent releases failed to match its quality and the Chantels grew disenchanted with their management and label. Harris had already dropped out of the line-up and Smith embarked on a solo career under the tutelage of Phil Spector, while Barrett continued to produce the remaining trio with different singers in place of the former vocalist. The Chantels enjoyed two further US Top 30 pop hits with 'Look In My Eyes' and 'Well I Told You', but they lacked the distinctiveness of the earlier releases.
● ALBUMS: *The Chantels* aka *We Are The Chantels* (End 1958) ★★★, *The Chantels On Tour* (Carlton 1961) ★★, *There's Our Song Again* (End 1962) ★★★, *The Chantels Sing Their Favorites* (Forum 1964) ★★★.
● COMPILATIONS: *The Best Of The Chantels* (Rhino 1990) ★★★.

CHARISSE, CYD

b. Tulla Ellice Finklea, 8 March 1923, Amarillo, Texas, USA. An elegant, long-legged dancer who appeared in several outstanding film musicals of the 40s and 50s, Finklea took ballet classes from an early age, and was enrolled in the renowned Fanchon and Marco Dance Studio in Hollywood at the age of 12. One of the teachers there was Frenchman Nico Charisse, and four years later, during which time she performed at intervals with the famed Ballet Russes, they were married. Her connections with the Ballet Russes gained Charisse a part in the Columbia film *Something To Shout About* (1943), which led to a contract with MGM. One of the studio's top producers, Arthur Freed, is said to have been responsible for changing her name to Cyd (she had been known as Sid by her friends since childhood). During the late 40s and early 50s she made effective contributions to several straight films, and a number of musicals, which included *Ziegfeld Follies*, *The Harvey Girls*, *Till The Clouds Roll By*, *Fiesta* (in which Ricardo Montalban made his debut), *The Unfinished Dance*, *On An Island With You*, *Words And Music*, *The Kissing Bandit*, *Singin' In The Rain* (with Gene Kelly) and *Easy To Love* (1953). Also in 1953 she had what was arguably her best role in *The Band Wagon* with Fred Astaire and Jack Buchanan.
By this time she was at her peak both as an actress and a dancer (although her singing was invariably dubbed in films), and her excellent work during the remaining years of the 50s included *Brigadoon*, *It's Always Fair Weather* and *Invitation To The Dance* (all with Kelly), *Meet Me In Las Vegas* (with Dan Dailey), and *Silk Stockings* (with Astaire). The latter was her last musical, although she did appear in the occasional dance sequence in films such as *Black Tights* (1960) and *The Silencers* (1966). Her subsequent screen work has been confined to guest appearances and television

features. After the break-up of her first marriage in the early 40s, she married the popular singer Tony Martin in 1948, and he travelled with her to London in 1986 when she played the role of Lady Hadwell in a new production of David Heneker's musical *Charlie Girl*. Even then, when she was in her 60s, those famous legs were still the main subject of discussion. Impresario Harold Fielding said: 'They are her trademark, so we're going to insure them for a million, maybe two.' A substantial sum of money must also have changed hands in 1988 when Cyd Charisse agreed to appear in a video to promote a pop single by the two-man group the Blue Mercedes. Their record of 'I Want To Be Your Property' reached the top of the US dance charts. In a rather different vein, four years later Miss Charisse made her Broadway debut when she took over the role of fading ballerina Grushinskaya in the hit musical *Grand Hotel*. Asked about her age, which has always been a subject of some dispute (born 1921 or 1923), she would only say: 'Oh, I feel young!'

● FURTHER READING: *The Two Of Us*, Tony Martin and Cyd Charisse.

● FILMS: *Something To Shout About* (1943), *Mission To Moscow* (1943), *Till The Clouds Roll By* (1946), *Three Wise Fools* (1946), *The Harvey Girls* (1946), *Ziegfeld Follies* (1946), *The Unfinished Dance* (1947), *Fiesta* (1947), *Words And Music* (1948), *On An Island With You* (1948), *The Kissing Bandit* (1948), *Tension* (1949), *East Side West Side* (1949), *Mark Of The Renegade* (1951), *Singin' In The Rain* (1952), *The Wild North* (1952), *The Band Wagon* (1953), *Easy To Love* (1953), *Sombrero* (1953), *Deep In My Heart* (1954), *Brigadoon* (1954), *It's Always Fair Weather* (1955), *Meet Me In Las Vegas* (1956), *Silk Stockings* (1957), *Invitation To The Dance* (1957), *Party Girl* (1958), *Twilight For The Gods* (1958), *Black Tights* (1960), *Five Golden Hours* (1961), *Call Her Mom* (1962), *Two Weeks In Another Town* (1962), *Assassination In Rome* (1963), *The Silencers* (1966), *Maroc 7* (1967), *Warlords Of Atlantis* (1978), *Portrait Of An Escort* (1980), *Swimsuit* (1989), *Visioni Private* aka *Private Screening* (1989).

CHARLES, RAY

b. Ray Charles Robinson, 23 September 1930, Albany, Georgia, USA. Few epithets sit less comfortably than that of genius; Ray Charles has borne this title for over 30 years. As a singer, composer, arranger and pianist, his prolific work deserves no other praise. Born in extreme poverty, Charles was slowly blinded by glaucoma until, by the age of seven, he had lost his sight completely. Earlier, he had been forced to cope with the tragic death of his brother, whom he had seen drown in a water tub. He learned to read and write music in braille and was proficient on several instruments by the time he left school. His mother Aretha died when Charles was 15, and he continued to have a shared upbringing with Mary Jane (the first wife of Charles's absent father). Charles drifted around the Florida circuit, picking up work where he could, before moving across the country to Seattle. Here he continued

his itinerant career, playing piano at several nightclubs in a style reminiscent of Nat 'King' Cole and a vocal similar to Charles Brown.

Charles began recording in 1949 and this early, imitative approach was captured on several sessions. Three years later, Atlantic Records acquired his contract, but initially the singer continued his 'cool' direction, revealing only an occasional hint of the passions later unleashed. 'It Should've Been Me', 'Mess Around' and 'Losing Hand' best represent this early R&B era, but Charles's individual style emerged as a result of his work with Guitar Slim. This impassioned, almost crude blues performer sang with a gospel-based fervour that greatly influenced Charles's thinking. He arranged Slim's million-selling single, 'Things That I Used To Do', on which the riffing horns and unrestrained voice set the tone for Charles's own subsequent direction. This effect was fully realized in 'I Got A Woman' (1954), a song soaked in the fervour of the Baptist Church, but rendered salacious by the singer's abandoned, unrefined delivery. Its extraordinary success, commercially and artistically, inspired similarly compulsive recordings, including 'This Little Girl Of Mine' (1955), 'Talkin' 'Bout You' (1957) and the lush and evocative 'Don't Let The Sun Catch You Crying' (1959), a style culminating in the thrilling call and response of 'What'd I Say' (1959). This acknowledged classic is one of the all-time great encore numbers performed by countless singers and bands in stadiums, clubs and bars all over the world. However, Charles was equally adept at slow ballads, as his heartbreaking interpretations of 'Drown In My Own Tears' and 'I Believe To My Soul' (both 1959) clearly show. Proficient in numerous styles, Charles's recordings embraced blues, jazz, standards and even country, as his muscular reading of 'I'm Movin' On' attested.

In November 1959 Charles left the Atlantic label for ABC Records, where he secured both musical and financial freedom. Commentators often cite this as the point at which the singer lost his fire, but early releases for this new outlet simply continued his groundbreaking style. 'Georgia On My Mind' (1960) and 'Hit The Road Jack' (1961) were, respectively, poignant and ebullient, and established the artist as an international name. This stature was enhanced further in 1962 with the release of the massive-selling album *Modern Sounds In Country And Western Music*, a landmark collection that produced the million-selling single 'I Can't Stop Loving You'. Its success defined the pattern for Charles's later career; the edges were blunted, the vibrancy was stilled as Charles's repertoire grew increasingly inoffensive. There were still moments of inspiration: 'Let's Go Get Stoned' and 'I Don't Need No Doctor' brought glimpses of a passion now too often muted, while *Crying Time*, Charles's first album since kicking his heroin habit, compared favourably with any Atlantic release. This respite was, however, temporary and as the 60s progressed so the singer's work became less compulsive and increasingly MOR. Like most artists, he attempted cover versions of Beatles songs and had substantial hits with versions of 'Yesterday' and 'Eleanor Rigby'. Two 70s releases, *A Message From The People* and *Renaissance*, did include contemporary material in Stevie Wonder's 'Living In The City' and Randy Newman's 'Sail Away', but subsequent releases reneged on this promise.

Charles' 80s work included more country-flavoured collections and a cameo appearance in the movie *The Blues Brothers*, but the period is better marked by the singer's powerful appearance on the USA For Africa release, 'We Are The World' (1985). It brought to mind a talent too often dormant, a performer whose marriage of gospel and R&B laid the foundations for soul music. His influence is inestimable, and his talent widely acknowledged and imitated by formidable white artists such as Steve Winwood, Joe Cocker, Van Morrison and Eric Burdon. Charles has been honoured with countless awards during his career including induction into the Rock And Roll Hall Of Fame in 1986, and receiving the Grammy Lifetime Achievement Award in 1987. It was fitting that, in 1992, an acclaimed documentary, *Ray Charles: The Genius Of Soul*, was broadcast by PBS television. *My World* was a return to form, and was particularly noteworthy for his cover versions of Paul Simon's 'Still Crazy After All These Years' and Leon Russell's 'A Song For You', which Charles made his own through the power of his outstanding voice. *Strong Love Affair* continued in the same vein with a balance of ballads matching the up-tempo tracks; however, it was clear that low-register, slow songs such as 'Say No More', 'Angelina' and 'Out Of My Life' should be the focus of Charles' concentration. In 2000 Charles returned to jazz with an excellent contribution to Steve Turre's *In The Spur Of The Moment*.

No record collection should be without at least one recording by this 'musical genius'. His ability to cross over into other musical territories is enviable. He has performed rock, jazz, blues and country with spectacular ease, but it is 'father of soul music' that remains his greatest title.

● ALBUMS: *Hallelujah, I Love Her So* aka *Ray Charles* (Atlantic 1957) ★★★, *The Great Ray Charles* (Atlantic 1957) ★★★★, with Milt Jackson *Soul Brothers* (Atlantic 1958) ★★★★, *Ray Charles At Newport* (Atlantic 1958) ★★★★, *Yes Indeed* (Atlantic 1959) ★★★, *Ray Charles* (Hollywood 1959) ★★★★, *The Fabulous Ray Charles* (Hollywood 1959) ★★★, *What'd I Say* (Atlantic 1959) ★★★, *The Genius Of Ray Charles* (Atlantic 1959) ★★★★★, *Ray Charles In Person* (Atlantic 1960) ★★★★, *The Genius Hits The Road* (ABC 1960) ★★★★, *Dedicated To You* (ABC 1961) ★★★, *Genius + Soul = Jazz* (Impulse! 1961) ★★★★★, *The Genius After Hours* (Atlantic 1961) ★★★★, with Betty Carter *Ray Charles And Betty Carter* (ABC 1961) ★★★★, *The Genius Sings The Blues* (Atlantic 1961) ★★★★, with Jackson *Soul Meeting* (Atlantic 1961) ★★★★, *Do The Twist With Ray Charles* (Atlantic 1961) ★★★, *Modern Sounds In Country And Western Music* (ABC 1962) ★★★★★, *Modern Sounds In Country And Western Volume 2* (ABC 1962) ★★★★, *Ingredients In A Recipe For Soul*

(ABC 1963) ★★★★, *Sweet And Sour Tears* (ABC 1964) ★★★, *Have A Smile With Me* (ABC 1964) ★★★, *Ray Charles Live In Concert* (ABC 1965) ★★★, *Country And Western Meets Rhythm And Blues* aka *Together Again* (ABC 1965) ★★★, *Crying Time* (ABC 1966) ★★★, *Ray's Moods* (ABC 1966) ★★★, *Ray Charles Invites You To Listen* (ABC 1967) ★★★, *A Portrait Of Ray* (ABC 1968) ★★★, *I'm All Yours, Baby!* (ABC 1969) ★★, *Doing His Thing* (ABC 1969) ★★★, *My Kind Of Jazz* (Tangerine 1970) ★★★, *Love Country Style* (ABC 1970) ★★, *Volcanic Action Of My Soul* (ABC 1971) ★★★, *A Message From The People* (ABC 1972) ★★★★, *Through The Eyes Of Love* (ABC 1972) ★★★, *Jazz Number II* (Tangerine 1972) ★★★, *Ray Charles Live* (Atlantic 1973) ★★★, *Come Live With Me* (Crossover 1974) ★★, *Renaissance* (Crossover 1975) ★★, *My Kind Of Jazz III* (Crossover 1975) ★★, *Live In Japan* (Atlantic 1975) ★★★, with Cleo Laine *Porgy And Bess* (RCA 1976) ★★★, *True To Life* (Atlantic 1977) ★★, *Love And Peace* (Atlantic 1978) ★, *Ain't It So* (Atlantic 1979) ★★, *Brother Ray Is At It Again* (Atlantic 1980) ★★, *Wish You Were Here Tonight* (Columbia 1983) ★★, *Do I Ever Cross Your Mind* (Columbia 1984) ★★, *Friendship* (Columbia 1985) ★★★★, *The Spirit Of Christmas* (Columbia 1985) ★★, *From The Pages Of My Mind* (Columbia 1986) ★★, *Just Between Us* (Columbia 1988) ★★, *Seven Spanish Angels And Other Hits* (Columbia 1989) ★★, *Would You Believe* (Warners 1990) ★★, *My World* (Warners 1993) ★★★, *Strong Love Affair* (Qwest/Warners 1996) ★★, *Berlin, 1962* (Pablo 1996) ★★★★.

● COMPILATIONS: *The Ray Charles Story* (Atlantic 1962) ★★★, *Ray Charles' Greatest Hits* (ABC 1962) ★★★★, *A Man And His Soul* (ABC 1967) ★★★, *The Best Of Ray Charles 1956-58* (Atlantic 1970) ★★★★, *A 25th Anniversary In Show Business Salute To Ray Charles* (ABC 1971) ★★★★, *The Right Time* (Atlantic 1987) ★★★, *A Life In Music 1956-59* (Atlantic 1982) ★★★★, *Greatest Hits Volume 1 1960-67* (Rhino 1988) ★★★★, *Greatest Hits Volume 2 1960-72* (Rhino 1988) ★★★★, *Anthology* (Rhino 1989) ★★★★, *The Collection* ABC recordings (Castle 1990) ★★★, *Blues Is My Middle Name* 1949-52 recordings (Double Play 1991) ★★★, *The Birth Of Soul: The Complete Atlantic R&B '52-'59* (Rhino/Atlantic 1991) ★★★★★, *The Living Legend* (Atlantic 1993) ★★★, *The Best Of The Atlantic Years* (Rhino/Atlantic 1994) ★★★, *Classics* (Rhino 1995) ★★★, *Genius & Soul* 5-CD box set (Rhino 1997) ★★★★★, *Standards* (Rhino 1998) ★★★★, *The Complete Country & Western Recordings, 1959-1986* 4-CD box set (Rhino 1998) ★★★★★, *The Definitive Ray Charles* (WSM 2001) ★★★★.

● FURTHER READING: *Ray Charles*, Sharon Bell Mathis. *Brother Ray, Ray Charles' Own Story*, Ray Charles and David Ritz. *Ray Charles: Man And Music*, Michael Lydon.

● FILMS: *Blues For Lovers* aka *Ballad In Blue* (1964), *The Blues Brothers* (1980).

CHARMS

This popular R&B act of the mid-50s was formed in Cincinnati, USA, by Otis Williams (lead), Richard Parker (bass), Joseph Penn (baritone),

Donald Peak (tenor) and Rolland Bradley (tenor). 'Heaven Only Knows' was released by Deluxe Records, followed by 'Happy Are We', 'Bye-Bye Baby', 'Quiet Please' and 'My Baby Dearest Darling', all of which failed to secure significant success. However, their September 1954 cover version of the Jewels' 'Hearts Of Stone' took them into the US charts and by January of the following year the song had peaked at number 15 (number 1 in the R&B charts), despite competing versions by both the Jewels and the Fontane Sisters. December 1954 produced two follow-ups: 'Mambo Sha-Mambo' and another cover version, this time the Five Keys' 'Ling, Ting, Tong', were released concurrently, the latter keeping stride with the Five Keys' original version and reaching number 26 on the *Billboard* charts. The policy of outgunning the opposition over 'hot new songs' soon became a Charms trait, but it was not always so successful. An attempt to hijack Gene And Eunice's 'Ko Ko Mo (I Love You So)' in February 1955 failed, and saw the group return to writing originals. 'Two Hearts' was written by Otis Williams and King Records' A&R head Henry Glover, but was in turn covered within a week by Pat Boone, who took it to US number 16.

The Charms then toured as part of the Top Ten R&B Show package with the Moonglows, Clovers and others. After asking for a pay rise from Deluxe the entire group, with the exception of Otis Williams, was sacked. Williams was joined by Rollie Willis, Chuck Barksdale (b. 11 January 1935, Chicago, Illinois, USA; ex-Dells) and Larry Graves. This version of the Charms was imaginatively renamed 'Otis Williams And His New Group'. Some things, though, did not change. The success of 'Gum Drop' was usurped by a *Billboard* Top 10 version by the Crew-Cuts. Meanwhile, the remaining four-fifths of the original Charms had left for Miami, where they filed suit against Deluxe over their continued use of the brand name. Deluxe countered by issuing two singles under the name Otis Williams And His Charms, while Parker, Penn, Peak and Bradley released 'Love's Our Inspiration' for their new label, Chart Records. Without Otis Williams there was little residual interest, especially as Williams' incarnation of the Charms went on to score two significant hits in 'That's Your Mistake' and 'Ivory Tower'. However, both Barksdale (back to the Dells) and Graves quit, with Winfred Gerald, Matt Williams (no relation) and Lonnie Carter taking their places. A poor chart run was then ended with the release of another cover version, this time of the Lovenotes' 'United', in June 1957. It was their last significant success, despite a continuing and prolific relationship with Deluxe, and then King Records, until 1963. Only 'Little Turtle Dove' and 'Panic', both from 1961, scraped the lower reaches of the charts. Ironically, by this time Lonnie Carter had joined the original Charms, who had now become the Escos. Williams then transferred to OKeh Records but without success, before signing to Stop Records as a solo country artist. The Charms' complicated but fascinating history ended with the move.

CHERRY, DON

b. 11 January 1924, Wichita, Texas, USA. Cherry sang briefly with the post-war orchestras of Jan Garber, Victor Young and Tommy Dorsey. His first solo hits for Decca Records in 1950/51 were 'Thinking Of You' from the Fred Astaire/Vera-Ellen movie *Three Little Words*, 'Vanity' and 'Belle, Belle, My Liberty Belle', the latter beaten to the upper reaches of the US chart by Guy Mitchell's version. Switching to Columbia Records, Cherry had a massive seller in 1955 with the Bob Musel and Jack Taylor ballad, 'Band Of Gold' (not to be confused with another song with the same title which was a hit in 1970 for Freda Payne). The unusual choral backing on the Cherry record signified trombonist/ arranger Ray Conniff's first arrangement for Columbia. After further US success in 1956 with 'Wild Cherry', 'Ghost Town' and 'Namely You', Cherry, always a keen amateur golfer, launched an assault on the US professional circuit, but was still recording occasionally on the Monument label well into the 60s. In the mid-80s, he was still telling golf stories in-between songs such as 'The Wind Beneath My Wings' and 'Band Of Gold', in his Las Vegas nightclub act.
● ALBUMS: with Ray Conniff And His Orchestra *Swingin' For Two* (Columbia 1956) ★★★, *Don Cherry* (Monument 1967) ★★.

CHEVALIER, MAURICE

b. Maurice Auguste Chevalier, 12 September 1888, Menilmontant, nr. Paris, France, d. 1 January 1972, Paris, France. The ninth of 10 children eventually reduced by death to three males, Chevalier's early ambitions to become an acrobat were thwarted by injury. He toured local cafes and music halls as a singer and broad comedian, and later performed at the Eldorado in Paris. His big break came when he signed a three-year contract with the *Folies Bergère*, and worked with his idol, Mistinguett. In 1913 he was drafted into the French Army, was captured, and then sent to Alten Grabow prisoner-of-war camp where he learnt to speak English. After the war he developed a more sophisticated act, wearing a tuxedo for his solo spot, and the straw boater that soon became his trademark. In-between the triumphs at the Folies Bergère, Casino de Paris and the Empire in Paris, Chevalier suffered a serious mental breakdown. When he recovered he went to England in 1927 and appeared in the revue *White Birds*. Two years later he made his first Hollywood movie, *Innocents Of Paris*, in which he introduced 'Louise', a song forever associated with him ('every little breeze seems to whisper Louise'). He also sang his famous French version of 'Yes, We Have No Bananas'.
Chevalier then starred in several movies, directed by Ernst Lubitsch including Lubitsch's first talkie, *The Love Parade* (1929). It was also the first of four movies that Chevalier made with Jeanette MacDonald. Following *The Smiling Lieutenant* (1931) with Claudette Colbert, and *One Hour With You* (1932), Chevalier made what has been described as 'one of the great films of the decade'. *Love Me Tonight*, directed by Rouben Mamoulian

and co-starring MacDonald, was innovative in several ways, especially in its integration of plot and music. It also contained 'Mimi', another speciality Chevalier song. He then appeared in *The Merry Widow* (1934, MGM) and *Folies Bergère* (1935, United Artists) in 1935 before returning to France, as one of the world's leading entertainers. During World War II Chevalier lived mostly in seclusion, emerging twice to perform in response to German demands, once in exchange for the release of 10 French prisoners. Rumours and accusations of collaboration with the enemy were emphatically disproved. After the war he projected a more mature image in the movie *Le Silence Est D'or* (1947) directed by René Clair, which won the Grand Prize at the Brussels Film Festival. During the same period, Chevalier toured Europe and the USA with his 'one man show'. Semi-retired during the early 50s, he returned to Hollywood to play a series of character roles in movies such as *Love In The Afternoon* (1957), *Gigi* (1958), *Can-Can* (1959), *Fanny* (1961), *In Search Of The Castaways* (1962) and *I'd Rather Be Rich* (1964). *Gigi* was one of the highlights of Chevalier's career. His idiosyncratic versions of 'Thank Heaven For Little Girls', 'I'm Glad I'm Not Young Anymore', and a duet with Hermione Gingold, 'I Remember It Well', charmed the Academy of MPAS into awarding *Gigi* nine Oscars, including Best Picture. At the age of 70, Chevalier received a special Academy Award for his contribution to the world of entertainment for over half a century. During the 60s he appeared frequently on US television with his own 'specials' such as *The World Of Maurice Chevalier*, and travelled widely with his 'one man show' until 1968, when, from the stage of the Theatre des Champs Elysees in Paris, he announced his retirement. His honours included the Croix de Guerre (1917), the Belgian Order of Leopold (1943), the Légion d'Honneur (1938) and the Order Mérite National (1964).

● ALBUMS: *Maurice Chevalier Sings Broadway* (MGM 1959) ★★★★, *A Tribute To Al Jolson* (MGM 1959) ★★★, *Life Is Just A Bowl Of Cherries* (MGM 1960) ★★★★, *Thank Heaven For Little Girls* (MGM 1960) ★★★★, *Thank Heaven For Maurice Chevalier* (RCA Victor 1960) ★★★, *Maurice Chevalier Sings Lerner, Loewe And Chevalier* (MGM 1962) ★★★, *Paris To Broadway* (MGM 1963) ★★★★, *Maurice Chevalier* (Time 1963) ★★★.

● COMPILATIONS: *Sings* (Retrospect 1969) ★★★★, *The World Of Maurice Chevalier* (Decca 1971) ★★★★, *You Brought A New Kind Of Love To Me* (Monmouth Evergreen 1979) ★★★, *Encore Maurice* (Living Era 1982) ★★★, *Bonjour D'Amour* (Karussell 1982) ★★★, *Ma Pomme* (EMI France 1983) ★★★, *The Golden Age Of Maurice Chevalier* (Golden Age 1984) ★★★★, *Bravo Maurice* (Living Era 1986) ★★★, *The Maurice Chevalier Collection* (Deja Vu 1987) ★★★★, *Maurice Chevalier's Paris* (Compact Selection 1988) ★★★, *On Top Of The World* (Flapper 1990) ★★★, *Maurice Chevalier* (ASV 1997) ★★★.

● FURTHER READING: *The Man In The Straw Hat*, Maurice Chevalier. *With Love*, Maurice Chevalier. *I Remember It Well*, Maurice Chevalier. *Maurice Chevalier: His Life 1888-1972*, James Harding. *Thank Heaven For Little Girls: The True Story Of Maurice Chevalier's Life*, Edward Behr.

● FILMS: *Trop Crédule* (1908), *Par Habitude* (1911), *Un Mariée Récalcitrante* (1911), *Une Mariée Qui Se Fait Attendre* (1911), *La Valse Renversante* (1914), *Une Soirée Mondaine* (1917), *Le Mauvais Garçon* (1921), *Le Match Criqui-Ledoux* (1922), *L'Affaire De La Rue Lourcine* (1923), *Gonzague* (1923), *Jim Bougne Boxeur* (1924), *Par Habitude* remake (1924), *Bonjour New York!* (1928), *Innocents Of Paris* (1929), *The Love Parade* (1929), *Playboy Of Paris* (1930), *The Big Pond* (1930), *Paramount On Parade* (1930), *The Smiling Lieutenant* (1931), *The Stolen Jools (The Slippery Pearls)* (1931), *El Cliente Seductor* (1931), *Love Me Tonight* (1932), *Make Me A Star* (1932), *One Hour With You* (1932), *Toboggan (Battling Georges)* (1932), *The Way To Love* (1933), *Bedtime Story* (1933), *The Merry Widow* (1934), *Folies Bergère* (1935), *The Beloved Vagabond* (1936), *Avec Le Sourire* (1936), *L'Homme Du Jour* (1936), *Break The News* (1938), *Pièges* (1939), *Le Silence Est D'Or* (1945), *Le Roi* (1946), *Paris 1900* (1950), *Ma Pomme* (1950), *Schlager-Parade* (1953), *J'Avais Sept Filles* (1954), *Cento Anni D'Amore* (1954), *Love In The Afternoon* (1957), *Rendezvous With Maurice Chevalier* series of six (1957), *Gigi* (1958), *Count Your Blessings* (1959), *Can-Can* (1959), *Pepe* (1960), *A Breath Of Scandal* (1960), *Un, Deux, Trois, Quatre!* (1960), *Fanny* (1961), *In Search Of The Castaways* (1962), *Jessica* (1962), *A New Kind Of Love* (1963), *I'd Rather Be Rich* (1964), *Panic Button* (1964), *Monkeys Go Home!* (1966).

CHORDETTES

Formed in 1946 in Sheboygan, Wisconsin, USA, the Chordettes were a female singing group whose career extended into the rock era. Initially envisioning themselves as a female barbershop quartet the members were Dorothy Schwartz (lead), Janet Ertel (d. 4 November 1988, Black River, Wisconsin, USA; bass), Carol Buschman (baritone) and Jinny Lockard (tenor). In 1949 the group came to the attention of Arthur Godfrey, whose national *Talent Scouts* radio programme was a popular means for acts to break through to a wider audience. Godfrey offered the Chordettes a permanent spot on the show and they were signed to Columbia Records, for whom they recorded a series of 10-inch EPs. In 1953 the group left Godfrey and signed to Cadence Records, operated by Godfrey's musical director, Archie Bleyer (Ertel married Bleyer in 1954). Their first recording for Cadence, 'Mr. Sandman', in 1954, became a million-seller, logging seven weeks at number 1 in the US charts. It featured Lynn Evans, who had replaced Schwartz, as lead singer, and Margie Needham, who had replaced Lockard. The Chordettes remained with Cadence until the early 60s, gaining three other Top 10 hits: 'Born To Be With You' (1956), 'Just Between You And Me' (1957) and 'Lollipop' (1958). The group disbanded in the mid-60s. Janet Bleyer died at the age of 75 in 1988.

● ALBUMS: *Harmony Time* 10-inch album (Columbia 1950) ★★★★, *Harmony Time, Volume 2* 10-inch album (Columbia 1951) ★★, *Harmony Encores* 10-inch album (Columbia 1952) ★★★, *Your Requests* 10-inch album (Columbia 1953) ★★★, *Listen* (Columbia 1956) ★★, *The Chordettes* (Cadence 1957) ★★★, *Close Harmony* (Cadence 1957) ★★★★, *Never On Sunday* (Cadence 1962) ★★.

● COMPILATIONS: *The Chordettes* (Ace 1983) ★★★, *The Best Of The Chordettes* (Ace 1985) ★★★, *Mainly Rock 'N' Roll* (Ace 1990) ★★★★, *The Fabulous Chordettes* (Ace 1991) ★★★.

CHORDS

The original members were brothers Carl (d. 23 January 1981; lead tenor) and Claude Feaster (baritone), Jimmy Keyes (d. 22 July 1995; tenor), Floyd McRae (tenor), William Edwards (bass) and pianist Rupert Branker, all schoolfriends from the Bronx, New York, USA. The Chords, who evolved out of three other groups, the Tunetoppers, the Keynotes and the Four Notes, were one of the first acts signed to the Atlantic Records subsidiary label Cat. Their debut disc was a doo-wop version of the then current Patti Page hit 'Cross Over The Bridge'. On the b-side of this 1954 release, Cat grudgingly issued one of the group's own songs, 'Sh-Boom', which became a milestone in rock 'n' roll music. This fun piece of nonsense took the USA by storm and featured the joyous but contentious lyric, 'Ah, life could be a dream, sh-boom, sh-boom!'. Some claim that this was rock 'n' roll's first 'drug song'! It shot into the US Top 10, a unique occurrence in those days for an R&B record, while a watered-down cover version by Canada's Crew-Cuts had the honour of being America's first number 1 rock 'n' roll hit.

The song created such a furore that even ace satirist Stan Freberg's cruel take-off of the Chords' record also made the Top 20. Since a group on Gem Records was already using the same name, the group quickly became the Chordcats. They tried to follow the monster novelty hit with other similar tracks, such as the follow-up 'Zippety-Zum', but with no success. Some personnel changes and another new name, the inevitable Sh-Booms, also failed to return them to the charts. The Chords, who were probably the first R&B group to appear on USA television nationwide, also recorded on Vik, Roulette (under the name Lionel Thorpe), Atlantic and Baron, among others. They occasionally reunited to play 'oldies' shows until lead singer Carl died in 1981.

CHRISTY, JUNE

b. Shirley Luster, 20 November 1925, Springfield, Illinois, USA, d. 21 June 1990, Sherman Oaks, California, USA. Christy first came to prominence with the bands of Boyd Raeburn and Stan Kenton, although her chirpy singing style sometimes sat oddly with the earnestly progressive experiments of her employers. Her bright, bubbling personality glowed through her performances and she was especially effective on up-tempo swingers. However, she was also adept on reflective ballads and was never afraid to have fun with a song. With Kenton she had successes in all of these areas. One of her first recordings with the band was 'Tampico', which became a million-seller; another was 'How High The Moon'. During the late 40s she was one of the band's main attractions. Kenton and his chief arranger, Pete Rugolo, responded by providing effective settings for her voice which, while of limited range, was engaging and her performances were always highly professional. In January 1947 she married Kenton's tenor saxophonist Bob Cooper, with whom she made some fine recordings backed by his small group. After leaving Kenton in 1948 Christy worked as a solo artist, making many successful recordings for Capitol Records, including three US Top 20 albums, *Something Cool* (imaginatively arranged for her by Rugolo), *The Misty Miss Christy* and *June – Fair And Warmer!*. After many years in retirement, she died in June 1990 of kidney failure.

● ALBUMS: *Something Cool* 10-inch album (Capitol 1954) ★★★★, with Stan Kenton *Duets* (Capitol 1955) ★★★★, *The Misty Miss Christy* (Capitol 1956) ★★★★, *June – Fair And Warmer!* (Capitol 1957) ★★★, *Gone For The Day* (Capitol 1957) ★★★, *June's Got Rhythm* (Capitol 1958) ★★★★, *The Song Is June!* (Capitol 1959) ★★★★, *June Christy Recalls Those Kenton Days* (Capitol 1959) ★★★, *Ballads For Night People* (Capitol 1959) ★★★, with Kenton *The Road Show, Volumes 1 & 2* (Capitol 1960) ★★★, with Kenton *Together Again* (Capitol 1960) ★★★, *The Cool School* (Capitol 1960) ★★★, *Off Beat* (Capitol 1961) ★★★, *Do-Re-Mi* film soundtrack (Capitol 1961) ★★, *That Time Of Year* (Capitol 1961) ★★★, *Big Band Specials* (Capitol 1962) ★★, *The Intimate June Christy* (Capitol 1962) ★★★★, *Something Broadway, Something Latin* (Capitol 1965) ★★, *Impromptu* (Interplay 1977) ★★★, *Willow Weep For Me* (Interplay 1979) ★★★, *Interlude* (Discovery 1985) ★★★, *The Uncollected June Christy 1944* recordings (Hindsight 1986) ★★, *The Uncollected June Christy Vol II 1956* recordings (Hindsight 1987) ★★, with Johnny Guarnieri *A Friendly Session Vol 1 1949* transcription (Jasmine 1998) ★★★.

● COMPILATIONS: *This Is June Christy!* (Capitol 1958) ★★★★, *The Best Of June Christy* (Capitol 1962) ★★★★, *The Capitol Years* (Capitol 1989) ★★★★, *A Lovely Way To Spend An Evening* (Jasmine 1989) ★★★, *The Best Of June Christy: The Jazz Sessions 1949-1962* recordings (Capitol 1996) ★★★★, with Peggy Lee *The Complete Peggy Lee And June Christy Capitol Transcription Sessions* 5-CD box set (Mosaic 1999) ★★★★.

CLANTON, JIMMY

b. 2 September 1940, Baton Rouge, Louisiana, USA. Pop vocalist Clanton celebrated his 18th birthday with his co-written debut hit, the R&B ballad 'Just A Dream', at number 4 in the US Hot 100. His smooth singing style appealed to the teen market and his subsequent releases were aimed in that direction. These included 'My Own True Love', which used the melody of 'Tara's Theme' from *Gone With The Wind*. The title track of the movie *Go, Johnny, Go!*, in which he starred, gave him another US Top 5 smash and the ballad 'Another Sleepless Night' reached the UK Top 50 in July 1960. His most famous record, 'Venus In Blue Jeans', co-written by Neil Sedaka, gave him his last US Top 10 hit, in late 1962. The song became a bigger hit in the UK, when Mark Wynter took his version into the Top 5. Clanton went on to become a DJ in Pennsylvania.

● ALBUMS: *Just A Dream* (Ace 1959) ★★★, *Jimmy's Happy* (Ace 1960) ★★★, *Jimmy's Blue* (Ace 1960) ★★★, *My Best To You* (Ace 1961) ★★★, *Teenage Millionaire* (Ace 1961) ★★★, *Venus In Bluejeans* (Ace 1962) ★★★.

● COMPILATIONS: *The Best Of Jimmy Clanton* (Philips 1964) ★★★.

● FILMS: *Go, Johnny, Go!* (1958).

CLARK, DICK

b. Richard Wagstaff Clark, 30 November 1929, Mount Vernon, New York, USA. Clark became a showbusiness giant via the US television dance programme *American Bandstand*, the longest-running variety show in television history. As its host for over 30 years, Clark brought rock 'n' roll music and dancing into millions of American homes. He has been nicknamed 'America's Oldest Living Teenager'. Clark's career began in 1947, upon his graduation from high school. After working at minor jobs at his uncle's radio station, WRUN (Utica, New York), Clark debuted on the air at WAER, the radio station at Syracuse University, which he attended. Further radio jobs followed, until Clark took his first television job, as a newscaster, in 1951. He returned to radio upon moving to Philadelphia's WFIL, but by 1956 WFIL's television outlet needed a replacement host for its *Bandstand* show. Clark was offered the position and started his new job on 9 July 1956. *Bandstand*'s format was simple: play current hit records and invite local teenagers to come in and dance to them. The programme was a surprise success and a year later the ABC network decided to broadcast it nationally, changing the name to *American Bandstand* on 5 August 1957.

Clark continued to host, bringing in guest artists – particularly top rock 'n' roll performers of the day – and the programme became a national phenomenon. Record promoters coveted airplay on *Bandstand*, as its power to 'break' records was unparalleled, and managers clamoured to land their artists on the programme to 'lip-sync' their latest hits. Many artists, particularly such Philadelphia-based singers as Fabian, Bobby Rydell, Chubby Checker and Frankie Avalon, largely owed their success to *Bandstand* exposure. Bobby Darin, Paul Anka and Connie Francis were also regulars. By this time Clark's own power within the music industry had grown, and when in 1959-60 the US government cracked down on so-called 'payola', the practice of disc jockeys accepting money or gifts in exchange for airplay, Clark was called to Washington to testify. He claimed innocence and was cleared with his reputation intact, although he divested himself of

some $8 million in music business-related investments.

Clark had formed a production company early in his career, and in the mid-60s began producing other music television programmes, such as *Where The Action Is* and *Happening*. He also produced television game shows and films (including *Psych-Out* and *Because They're Young*). Clark's later creations include the *American Music Awards*, the *Country Music Awards* and television films about the Beatles and Elvis Presley – ironically, the only two major pop artists never to appear on *American Bandstand*. He also arranged tours called the Caravan of Stars, which took top musical stars on one-night-stand concerts throughout the USA in the early 60s. In 1964 *Bandstand* moved to Los Angeles from Philadelphia, and eventually it was scaled down from a daily to a weekly show. It continued until the late 80s, featuring contemporary artists such as Madonna, Prince and Cyndi Lauper. Clark remained an enormously powerful and influential figure in the entertainment industry into the 90s.

● FURTHER READING: *Rock, Roll & Remember*, Dick Clark and Richard Robinson.

● FILMS: *Because They're Young* (1960).

CLARK, SANFORD

b. 24 October 1935, Tulsa, Oklahoma, USA. Clark is best recalled for his 1956 Top 10 single and only chart success, 'The Fool'. He moved to Phoenix, Arizona, during his teens and there was heard by guitarist Al Casey, who introduced the young singer to local disc jockey and producer Lee Hazlewood. They recorded Hazlewood's song 'The Fool' (which was credited to the producer's wife Naomi Shackleford under the pseudonym Naomi Ford) and it was released first on the small MCI label, created specifically for this record's release. After it received local attention, the national Dot Records picked up distribution and the song shot to number 7 in the USA; it also reached the country and R&B charts. Clark had one further chart single with the follow-up, 'The Cheat'. In 1960, he joined the US Air Force and although he released numerous further singles on Dot and other labels into the mid-60s, none were hits. He recorded more tracks with Hazlewood in 1968 and 1982, although neither liaison was successful.

● ALBUMS: *Return Of The Fool* (LHI 1969) ★★★.

● COMPILATIONS: *The Fool* (Ace 1983) ★★★★, *Rockin' Rollin', Volumes 1 & 2* (Bear Family 1986) ★★★★, *Shades* 1982 recordings (Bear Family 1993) ★★★★.

CLEFS

Formed at high school in Arlington, Virginia, USA, in 1951 by Scotty Mansfield (lead), Fred Council (baritone), Gerald Bullock (bass), Pavel Bess (tenor) and Frank Newman (second tenor), this R&B vocal group's early performances were limited to fraternity parties and school hops. For the recording of their first demo a year later, Leroy Flack (brother of Roberta Flack) had replaced Bullock on bass, with James Sheppard adding further tenor support. Through manager Lillian Claiborne they were brought to the attention of Chess Records, who subsequently released their cover version of the Ink Spots' 'We Three'. Afterwards they returned to the local club circuit, losing one member (Flack) in 1955, at which time Bess took over bass duties. One further single emerged before they were offered a contract with Peacock Records in Houston, Texas. However, the Clefs declined, opting to pursue their fortunes with the more musically sympathetic Vee Jay Records. However, 1955's 'I'll Be Waiting' failed to provide any degree of success. Their name was then changed to Scotty Mann And The Masters, but 'Just A Little Bit Of Loving' also failed to work the miracle for them, in light of which they returned solely to live performances and, finally, more secure day jobs. This turn of events had become inevitable when Vee Jay failed to release them from contract, despite not wishing to release any new material by the band in either incarnation.

CLINE, PATSY

b. Virginia Patterson Hensley, 8 September 1932, Gore, near Winchester, Virginia, USA, d. 5 March 1963, Camden, Tennessee, USA. Her father, Sam Hensley, already had two children from a previous marriage when he married Hilda, Patsy's mother – a woman many years his junior. Hilda was only 16 when Patsy was born and they grew up like sisters. At the age of four, Patsy was influenced by a film of Shirley Temple and, without tuition, learned tap-dancing and showed an interest in music that was encouraged by the piano-playing of her step-sister. In spite of financial hardships, her parents gave her a piano for her seventh birthday, which she soon learned to play by ear. Hilda could never understand her daughter's affinity with country music, since neither she nor Sam was interested in the genre. At the age of 10, Patsy was eagerly listening to broadcasts from the *Grand Ole Opry* and informing everyone that one day she too would be an *Opry* star. In the early 40s, the Hensleys relocated to Winchester, where Patsy became interested in the country show on WINC presented by Joltin' Jim McCoy. Apart from playing records, he also fronted his own band in live spots on the show.

At the age of 14, Patsy contacted McCoy and told him she wanted to sing on his show. He was impressed by her voice and Virginia Hensley quickly became a regular singer with his Melody Playboys. She also became associated with pianist William 'Jumbo' Rinker with whom she sang at local venues, and she left school to work in Gaunt's Drug Store to help the family finances. In 1948, Wally Fowler, a noted *Grand Ole Opry* artist whose gospel show was broadcast live on WSM, appeared at the Palace Theatre in Winchester. Cline brazenly manoeuvred herself backstage on the night and confronted Fowler. Taken aback by her approach, he sarcastically suggested that perhaps she was 'Winchester's answer to Kitty

Wells', but nevertheless let her sing for him. She sang unaccompanied and impressed Fowler so much that he included her in that night's show. Having sought Hilda's permission for her to audition for WSM in Nashville, a few weeks later, Patsy went to see Jim Denny, the manager of the *Grand Ole Opry*. Accompanied by the legendary pianist Moon Mullican, she impressed Denny who asked her to remain in Nashville so that he could arrange an *Opry* appearance. However, without money, although too embarrassed to admit it, and accompanied by the two younger children, Hilda pleaded that they must return to Winchester that day. Before they left, Roy Acuff, who had heard her singing from an adjoining studio, asked her to sing on his *Noon Time Neighbours* broadcast that day. Her hopes that she would hear from Denny, however, were not realized and Patsy returned to the drug store and singing locally.

In 1952, she met Bill Peer, a disc jockey and musician, who had run bands for some years, and who was at the time touring the Tri-State Moose Lodge circuit with his band, the Melody Boys And Girls. He hired Patsy as lead vocalist and on 27 September 1952, she made her first appearance with him at the Brunswick Moose Club in Maryland. Peer did not think the name Virginia was suitable and, wrongly assuming that her second name was Patricia, he billed her as Patsy Hensley. On 27 February 1953, Patsy married Gerald Cline, whom she had met at a show only a few weeks earlier. On the night of her marriage, Patsy appeared on stage for the first time as Patsy Cline. Although Cline's name was known over a considerable area, Peer was aware that she needed national exposure, and concentrated his efforts on seeking a recording contract for her. A demo tape attracted attention and on 30 September 1954, she signed a two-year contract with Four-Star, a Pasadena-based independent company, once owned by Gene Autry, whose president was now William A. McCall, a man not highly regarded by many in the music business. The contract stated that all Patsy Cline's recordings would remain Four-Star property – in effect, she could only record songs that McCall published and, being a non-writer herself, she was obliged to record any material she chose.

Cline made her first four recordings on 1 June 1955 under the production of pianist, guitarist and arranger Owen Bradley, in his 'Quonset' hut studios in Nashville. 'A Church, A Courtroom And Then Goodbye', penned by Eddie Miller and W.S. Stevenson, was the chosen song, but it failed to reach the country charts (W.S. Stevenson was a pseudonym used by McCall, seemingly for his own songs, but it is known that, on occasions, he applied the name to songs that were written by other writers, such as Donn Hecht, who were under contract to his label). Cline made further recordings on 5 January and 22 April 1956, including the toe-tapping 'I Love You Honey' and the rockabilly 'Stop, Look And Listen'. The anticipated country chart entries did not occur and she became despondent. Her private life took a new turn in April 1956, when she met Charlie Dick, who became her second husband when her marriage to Gerald Cline ended in 1957. In an effort to secure a country hit, McCall commissioned songwriter Hecht, who suggested 'Walkin' After Midnight', a blues-styled number that he had initially written for Kay Starr, who had turned it down. Cline did not like the song either, claiming it was 'nothing but a little old pop song'. Under pressure from Decca (who leased her records from Four-Star), she recorded it, on 8 November 1956, in a session that also included 'A Poor Man's Roses (Or A Rich Man's Gold)' and 'The Heart You Break May Be Your Own'. On 28 January 1957, although preferring 'A Poor Man's Roses', she sang 'Walkin' After Midnight' on the Arthur Godfrey *Talent Scouts* show. On 11 February, Decca released the two songs in a picture sleeve on 78 rpm and it immediately entered both country and pop charts. Cline first sang 'Walkin' After Midnight' on the *Opry* on 16 February. The song finally peaked as a number 2 country and number 12 pop hit, while 'A Poor Man's Roses' also reached number 14 on the country chart. It was later estimated that the record sold around three-quarters of a million copies.

In July 1959, she recorded two fine gospel numbers, 'Life's Railroad To Heaven' and 'Just A Closer Walk With Thee', but although Decca released various records the follow-up chart hit did not materialize. In truth, Decca had only 11 songs, recorded between February 1958 and November 1960, from which to choose. It was possible Cline chose to record the minimum number necessary under the terms of her Four-Star contract in the hope McCall would drop her, thus enabling her to pick up a promised Decca contract. The first song she recorded under her new association with Decca, on 16 November 1960, was 'I Fall To Pieces' by Hank Cochran and Harlan Howard. It quickly became a country number 1 and also peaked at number 12 on the pop charts. In August 1961 she completed a four-day recording session that included 'True Love', 'The Wayward Wind', 'San Antonio Rose' and her now legendary version of 'Crazy'. Willie Nelson, who had written the song, had demoed it almost as a narration. With Owen Bradley's persuasion, she produced her own stunning interpretation in one take. The recording was a number 2 country and a number 9 pop hit. In 1962, 'She's Got You' was an even bigger country hit, spending five weeks at number 1, while peaking at number 14 in the pop charts. It also became her first entry in the Top 50 UK pop charts.

Meanwhile, her marriage to Charlie Dick was becoming more stormy. She had long ago discarded her cowgirl outfits for more conventional dress and she seemed indifferent to her weight problem. Her wild and promiscuous lifestyle included an enduring affair with Faron Young. Her last recording session took place on 7 February 1963, when she recorded 'He Called Me Baby', 'You Took Him Off My Hands' and 'I'll Sail My Ship Alone'. The latter, ironically, was a song written by Moon Mullican, the pianist who had played for her *Opry* audition in 1948. Cline appeared in Birmingham, Alabama, with Tex Ritter and Jerry Lee Lewis on 2 March 1963, following which she agreed with other artists to appear in a charity show in Kansas City the next day, a show staged for the widow of Jack Call, a noted disc jockey on KCMK, known as Cactus Jack, who had died in a car crash. The weather was bad on 4 March but early on the afternoon of 5 March, in spite of further adverse weather forecasts, Cline, together with country singers Cowboy Copas and Hawkshaw Hawkins, set off on the five-hundred-mile flight to Nashville in a small aircraft piloted by Randy Hughes, the son-in-law of Copas and Cline's lover and manager. Hughes first landed at Little Rock to avoid rain and sleet and then at Dyersburg to refuel, where he was warned of bad weather in the area. They encountered further bad weather and, although the exact reason for the crash is unknown, the life of Patsy Cline came to an end some 50 minutes later, when the aircraft came down in woodland about a mile off Highway 70, near Camden, Tennessee.

At the time of her death, Cline's recording of 'Leaving On Your Mind' was in both country and pop charts and before the year was over, both 'Sweet Dreams' and 'Faded Love' became Top 10 country and minor pop hits. It has been suggested that Patsy Cline was not an outstanding performer of up-tempo material, but it is an undisputed fact that she could extract every possible piece of emotion from a country weepie. Her versions of 'Walkin' After Midnight', 'I Fall To Pieces', 'Crazy', 'She's Got You' and 'Sweet Dreams' represent five of the greatest recordings ever made in country music. Those in any doubt of Patsy Cline's standing should consult the *Billboard* back-catalogue country chart – at one point her *Greatest Hits* album stood at number 1 for over four years, in addition to over 10 million sales and 13 years actually on the chart!

● ALBUMS: *Patsy Cline* (Decca 1957) ★★★★, *Patsy Cline Showcase* (Decca 1961) ★★★★, *Sentimentally Yours* (Decca 1962) ★★★★, *In Memoriam* (Everest 1963) ★★★★, *Encores* (Everest 1963) ★★★, *A Legend* (Everest 1963) ★★★, *Reflections* (Everest 1964) ★★★, *A Portrait Of Patsy Cline* (Decca 1964) ★★★★, *That's How A Heartache Begins* (Decca 1964) ★★★, *Today, Tomorrow, Forever* (Hilltop 1964) ★★★, *Gotta Lot Of Rhythm In My Soul* (Metro 1965) ★★★, *Stop The World And Let Me Off* (Hilltop 1966) ★★★, *The Last Sessions* (MCA 1980) ★★★★, *Try Again* (Quicksilver 1982) ★★★, *Sweet Dreams* film soundtrack (1985) ★★★, *Live At The Opry* (MCA 1988) ★★★, *Live – Volume Two* (MCA 1989) ★★★, *The Birth Of A Star* (Razor & Tie 1996) ★★★, *Live At The Cimarron Ballroom* 1961 recording (MCA 1997) ★★★★.

● COMPILATIONS: *Patsy Cline's Golden Hits* (Everest 1962) ★★★, *The Patsy Cline Story* (Decca 1963) ★★★★, *Patsy Cline's Greatest Hits* (Decca 1967) ★★★★, *Country Great* (Vocalion 1969) ★★★, *Greatest Hits* (MCA 1973) ★★★★, *Golden Greats* (MCA 1979) ★★★★, *20 Golden Greats* (Astan 1984) ★★★, *20 Classic Tracks* (Starburst 1987) ★★★, *12*

Greatest Hits (MCA 1988) ★★★★, *Dreaming* (Platinum Music 1988) ★★★, *20 Golden Hits* (Deluxe 1989) ★★★, *Walkin' Dreams: Her First Recordings, Volume One* (Rhino 1989) ★★★★, *Hungry For Love: Her First Recordings, Volume Two* (Rhino 1989) ★★★★, *Rockin' Side: Her First Recordings, Volume Three* (Rhino 1989) ★★★★, *The Patsy Cline Collection* 4-CD box set (MCA 1991) ★★★★★, *The Definitive* (MCA 1992) ★★★, *Discovery* (Prism Leisure 1994) ★★★, *Premier Collection* (Pickwick 1994) ★★★, *The Patsy Cline Story* (MCA 1994) ★★★★, *Thinking Of You* (Summit 1995) ★★★, *Today, Tomorrow And Forever* 2-CD set (Parade 1995) ★★★, *Through The Eyes Of ... An Anthology* (Snapper 1998) ★★★★, *The Ultimate Collection* (UTV 2000) ★★★★, *A Star Is Born* (Yeaah! 2001) ★★★, *The Essential Collection* (Universal 2001) ★★★★.
● VIDEOS: *The Real Patsy Cline* (Platinum Music 1989), *Remembering Patsy* (1993).
● FURTHER READING: *Patsy Cline: Sweet Dreams*, Ellis Nassour. *Honky Tonk Angel: The Intimate Story Of Patsy Cline*, Ellis Nassour. *Patsy: The Life And Times Of Patsy Cline*, Margaret Jones. *I Fall To Pieces: The Music And The Life Of Patsy Cline*, Mark Bego. *Singing Girl From Shenandoah Valley*, Stuart E. Brown. *Love Always, Patsy: Patsy Cline's Letters To A Friend*, Cindy Hazen and Mike Freeman.

CLOONEY, ROSEMARY

b. 23 May 1928, Maysville, Kentucky, USA. Although her heyday was back in the 50s, this popular singer and actress remained close to the peak of her powers into the 1990s. Rosemary and her sister Betty sang at political rallies in support of their paternal grandfather. When Rosemary was 13 the Clooney children moved to Cincinnati, Ohio, and appeared on radio station WLW. In 1945 they auditioned successfully for tenor saxophonist Tony Pastor and joined his band as featured vocalists, travelling the country doing mainly one-night shows. Rosemary made her first solo record in 1946 with 'I'm Sorry I Didn't Say I'm Sorry When I Made You Cry Last Night'. After around three years of touring, Betty quit, and Rosemary stayed on as a soloist with the band. She signed for Columbia Records in 1950 and had some success with children's songs such as 'Me And My Teddy Bear' and 'Little Johnny Chickadee', before coming under the influence of A&R manager Mitch Miller, who had a penchant for folksy, novelty dialect songs.

In 1951 Clooney's warm, husky melodious voice registered well on minor hits, 'You're Just In Love', a duet with Guy Mitchell, and 'Beautiful Brown Eyes'. Later that year she topped the US chart with 'Come On-A My House' from the off-Broadway musical *The Son*, with a catchy harpsichord accompaniment by Stan Freeman. During the next four years Clooney had a string of US hits including 'Tenderly', which became her theme tune, 'Half As Much' (number 1), 'Botcha-Me', 'Too Old To Cut The Mustard' (a duet with Marlene Dietrich), 'The Night Before Christmas Song' (with Gene Autry), 'Hey There' and 'This Ole House' (both number 1 hits), and 'Mambo

Italiano'. UK hits included 'Man', with the b-side, 'Woman', sung by her then husband, actor/producer/director José Ferrer, and the novelty, 'Where Will The Dimple Be'. Her last singles hit was 'Mangos', in 1957. Her own US television series regularly featured close harmony vocal group the the Hi-Lo's, leading to their communal album *Ring Around Rosie*. Clooney's film career started in 1953 with *The Stars Are Singing* and was followed by three films the next year, *Here Come The Girls* with Bob Hope, *Red Garters* (1954) with Guy Mitchell and the Sigmund Romberg biopic, *Deep In My Heart*, in which she sang 'Mr And Mrs' with Ferrer. In the same year she teamed with Bing Crosby in *White Christmas*. Highly compatible, with friendly, easy-going styles, their professional association was to last until Crosby died, and included, in 1958, the highly regarded album *Fancy Meeting You Here*, a musical travelogue with special material by Sammy Cahn and James Van Heusen, arranged and conducted by Billy May.

Semi-retired in the 60s, Clooney's psychiatric problems were chronicled in her autobiography, *This For Remembrance*, later dramatized for television as *Escape From Madness*. Her more recent work has been jazz-based, and included a series of tributes to the 'great' songwriters such as Harold Arlen, Cole Porter and Duke Ellington, released on the Concord Jazz label. In 1991, Clooney gave an 'assured performance' in concert at Carnegie Hall, and duetted with her special guest artist, Linda Ronstadt. Her 1998 album, *A Seventieth Birthday Celebration*, with guest stars k.d. lang and Ronstadt, contains some of the best from the Concord Jazz years. It opens and closes with two new selections – 'Secret Of Life' and 'Love Is Here To Stay'. Late in 1999, Clooney published the second volume of her memoirs, and received excellent reviews when she became the first star to appear at Michael Feinstein's new supper club at New York's Regency Hotel. Clooney has continued to play US clubs, including her much appreciated annual stint at the Rainbow & Stars in New York. She has also made occasional appearances in the popular US medical drama *ER*. In January 2002 she underwent surgery for lung cancer.

● ALBUMS: *Hollywood's Best* (Columbia 1952/55) ★★★, *Deep In My Heart* film soundtrack (MGM 1954) ★★★, *Rosemary Clooney* 10-inch album (Columbia 1954) ★★★, *White Christmas* 10-inch album (Columbia 1954) ★★★★, *Red Garters* film soundtrack (Columbia 1954) ★★★, *Tenderly* 10-inch album (Columbia 1955) ★★★★, *Children's Favorites* 10-inch album (Columbia 1956) ★★, *Blue Rose* (Columbia 1956) ★★★, *A Date With The King* 10-inch album (Columbia 1956) ★★★, *On Stage* 10-inch album (Columbia 1956) ★★, *My Fair Lady* 10-inch album (Columbia 1956) ★★, *Clooney Tunes* (Columbia 1957) ★★★, with the Hi-Lo's *Ring A Round Rosie* (Columbia 1957) ★★★★, *Swing Around Rosie* (Coral 1958) ★★★★, with Bing Crosby *Fancy Meeting You Here* (RCA Victor 1958) ★★★★, *Rosemary Clooney In Hi-Fidelity* (Harmony 1958) ★★★, *The Ferrers At Home* (1958) ★★★,

Hymns From The Heart (MGM 1959) ★★, *Oh Captain!* (MGM 1959) ★★, *Rosemary Clooney Swings Softly* (MGM 1960) ★★★★, *A Touch Of Tabasco* (RCA Victor 1960) ★★★, *Clap Hands, Here Comes Rosie* (RCA Victor 1960) ★★★, *Rosie Solves The Swingin' Riddle* (RCA Victor 1961) ★★★★, *Country Hits From The Heart* (RCA Victor 1963) ★★, *Love* (Reprise 1963) ★★★, *Thanks For Nothing* (Reprise 1964) ★★★, with Crosby *That Travelin' Two Beat* (Capitol 1965) ★★★, *Look My Way* (United Artists 1976) ★★★, *Nice To Be Around* (United Artists 1977) ★★★, *Here's To My Lady* (Concord Jazz 1979) ★★★, *With Love* (Concord Jazz 1981) ★★★, *Sings The Music Of Cole Porter* (Concord Jazz 1982) ★★★★, *Sings Harold Arlen* (Concord Jazz 1983) ★★★★, *My Buddy* (Concord Jazz 1983) ★★★, *Sings The Music Of Irving Berlin* (Concord Jazz 1984) ★★★★, *Rosemary Clooney Sings Ballads* (Concord Jazz 1985) ★★★★, *Our Favourite Things* (Dance Band Days 1986) ★★★, *Mixed Emotions* (Columbia 1986) ★★★, *Sings The Lyrics Of Johnny Mercer* (Concord Jazz 1987) ★★★★, *Sings The Music Of Jimmy Van Heusen* (Concord Jazz 1987) ★★★★, *Show Tunes* (Concord Jazz 1989) ★★★, *Everything's Coming Up Rosie* (Concord Jazz 1989) ★★★, *Sings Rodgers, Hart And Hammerstein* (Concord Jazz 1990) ★★★, *Rosemary Clooney Sings The Lyrics Of Ira Gershwin* (Concord Jazz 1990) ★★★★, *For The Duration* (Concord Jazz 1991) ★★★, *Girl Singer* (Concord Jazz 1992) ★★★, *Do You Miss New York?* (Concord Jazz 1993) ★★★, *Still On The Road* (Concord Jazz 1994) ★★★★, *Demi-Centennial* (Concord Jazz 1995) ★★★, *Dedicated To Nelson* (Concord Jazz 1995) ★★★★, *Mothers & Daughters* (Concord Jazz 1997) ★★★, *White Christmas* (Concord Jazz 1997) ★★, with the Count Basie Orchestra *At Long Last* (Concord Jazz 1998) ★★★, *Rosemary Clooney 70: A Seventieth Birthday Celebration* (Concord Jazz 1998) ★★★, with John Pizzarelli *Brazil* (Concord Jazz 2000) ★★★, with Big Kahuna And The Copa Cat Pack *Sentimental Journey: The Girl Singer And Her New Big Band* (Concord Jazz 2001) ★★★.
● COMPILATIONS: *Rosie's Greatest Hits* (Columbia 1957) ★★★★, *Rosemary Clooney Showcase Of Hits* (Columbia 1959) ★★★★, *Greatest Hits* (Columbia 1983) ★★★★, *The Best Of Rosemary Clooney* (Creole 1984) ★★★★, *The Rosemary Clooney Songbook* (Columbia 1984) ★★★★, *Come On-A My House* 7-CD box set (Bear Family 1997) ★★★★, *Songs From The Girl Singer: A Musical Autobiography* (Concord Jazz 1999) ★★★★, *The Songbook Collection* 6-CD set (Concord Jazz 2000) ★★★★.
● FURTHER READING: *This For Remembrance*, Rosemary Clooney. *Girl Singer*, Rosemary Clooney with Joan Barthel.
● FILMS: *The Stars Are Singing* (1953), *Here Come The Girls* (1953), *Red Garters* (1954), *White Christmas* (1954), *Deep In My Heart* (1954).

CLOVERS

This US R&B vocal ensemble formed in Washington, DC, in 1946, and built a career recording smooth ballads and bluesy jumps for New York independent Atlantic Records, in the process becoming one of the most popular vocal groups of the 50s. By the time the group first recorded for Rainbow Records in early 1950, the Clovers consisted of John 'Buddy' Bailey (b. 1930, Washington, DC, USA; lead), Matthew McQuater (tenor), Harold Lucas (baritone) and Harold Winley (bass), with instrumental accompaniment from Bill Harris (b. 14 April 1925, Nashville, North Carolina, USA, d. 5 December 1988; guitar). Later in the year the Clovers joined the fledgling Atlantic label. In 1952 Charles White (b. 1930, Washington, DC, USA), who had earlier experience in the Dominoes and the Checkers, became the Clovers' new lead, replacing Buddy Bailey who was drafted into the US Army. In late 1953 Billy Mitchell took over from White. Bailey rejoined the group in 1954 but Mitchell remained and the two alternated the leads. Whoever was the lead, from 1951-56 the Clovers achieved a consistent sound and remarkably consistent success. They had three US number 1 R&B hits with 'Don't You Know I Love You', 'Fool, Fool, Fool' (both 1951) and 'Ting-A-Ling' (1952), plus four number 2 R&B hits with 'One Mint Julep', 'Hey, Miss Fannie' (both 1952), 'Good Lovin'' (1953) and 'Lovey Dovey' (1954). The best-known of the remaining 11 other Top 10 hits for Atlantic was 'Devil Or Angel', a song frequently covered, most notably by Bobby Vee. The Clovers only made the US pop charts with 'Love, Love, Love' (number 30, 1956) and 'Love Potion No. 9' (number 23, 1959). The latter, one of Leiber And Stoller's best songs, was recorded for United Artists Records, the only label other than Atlantic that saw the Clovers reach the charts. In 1961 the Clovers split into rival groups led, respectively, by Buddy Bailey and Harold Lucas, and the hits dried up. Various permutations of the Clovers continued to record and perform for years afterwards, particularly in the Carolinas where their brand of music was popular as 'beach music'.
● ALBUMS: *The Clovers* (Atlantic 1956) ★★★★, *Dance Party* (Atlantic 1959) ★★★★, *In Clover* (Poplar 1959) ★★, *Love Potion Number Nine* (United Artists 1959) ★★★, *Clovers Live At CT's* (1989) ★★.
● COMPILATIONS: *The Original Love Potion Number Nine* (Grand Prix 1964) ★★★★, *Their Greatest Recordings - The Early Years* (Atco 1975) ★★★★, *The Best Of The Clovers: Love Potion Number Nine* (EMI 1991) ★★★★, *Down In The Alley* (Atlantic 1991) ★★★, *Dance Party* (Sequel 1997) ★★★★, *The Very Best Of The Clovers* (Atlantic 1998) ★★★★.

COASTERS

The illustrious career of the Coasters, the pre-eminent vocal group of the early rock 'n' roll era, was built on a remarkable body of cleverly comic R&B songs for Atco Records fashioned by their producers, Leiber And Stoller. Under their direction, the Coasters exchanged the crooning of ballads favoured by most groups of the era for robust and full-throated R&B shouting. The group came together in Los Angeles, California, USA in October 1955 from remnants of the Robins, who had a dispute with their producers/songwriters, Jerry Leiber and Mike Stoller. The original Coasters comprised two ex-Robins, Carl Gardner (b. Carl Edward Gardner, 29 April 1928, Tyler, Texas, USA; lead) and Bobby Nunn (b. Ulysses B. Nunn, 20 September 1925, Birmingham, Alabama, USA, d. 5 November 1986, Los Angeles, California, USA; bass), plus Leon Hughes (b. Thomas Leon Hughes, 26 August 1932, Los Angeles County, California, USA; tenor), and Billy Guy (b. 20 June 1936, Itasca, Texas, USA; lead and baritone). Hughes was replaced briefly in 1957 by Young Jessie (b. Obie Donmell Jessie, 28 December 1936, Dallas, Texas, USA), who in turn was replaced by ex-Flairs Cornell Gunter (b. 14 November 1938, Los Angeles, California, USA, d. 26 February 1990, Las Vegas, Nevada, USA). In January 1958, Nunn was replaced by ex-Cadets Will 'Dub' Jones (b. Will J. Jones, 14 May 1928, Shreveport, Louisiana, USA, d. 16 January 2000, Long Beach, California, USA). At the start of the following year original guitar player Adolph Jacobs (b. Herman Adolph Jacobsen, 27 April 1931, Oakland, California, USA) was replaced by Albert 'Sonny' Forriest (b. Elbert McKinley Forriest, 21 May 1934, Pendleton, North Carolina, USA, d. 10 January 1999, Capital Heights, Maryland, USA), who became a contracted member of the line-up. Ex-Cadillacs Earl 'Speedo' Carroll (b. Gregory Carroll, 2 November 1937, New York City, New York, USA) replaced Gunter in mid-1961.

The Coasters first charted with 'Down In Mexico' (US R&B Top 10) in 1956, but the superb double-sided hit from 1957, 'Searchin'' (US R&B number 1 and pop number 3) and 'Young Blood' (US R&B number 2 and pop Top 10) established the group as major rock 'n' roll stars (in the UK, 'Searchin'' reached number 30). The classic line-up of Gardner, Guy, Gunter and Jones enjoyed three more giant hits, namely 'Yakety Yak' (US R&B and pop number 1 in 1958), 'Charlie Brown' (US R&B and pop number 2 in 1959), and 'Poison Ivy' (US R&B number 1 and pop Top 10 in 1959). In the UK, 'Yakety Yak' went to number 12, 'Charlie Brown' to number 6, and 'Poison Ivy' to number 15, the group's last chart record in the UK. By this time, they were generally regarded as one of the wittiest exponents of teenage growing problems to emerge from the rock 'n' roll era. By the mid-60s, however, the lustre had worn off, as the hits increasingly emphasized the comic lyrics to the detriment of the music. The Coasters parted company with Atco in 1966, and renewed their partnership with Leiber And Stoller (who had left the label in 1963) with several sides for the CBS Records subsidiary, Date Records. After a one-off single for Turntable (1969's 'Act Right'), the long-serving Gardner and Guy enjoyed a brief comeback in late 1971, when a reworking of 'Love Potion Number Nine' for the King label broke into the *Billboard* Hot 100.

The Coasters have continued in the subsequent decades as an oldies act, fracturing into several different groups playing the nostalgia circuit although most authorities accept the Carl Gardner led Coasters as the genuine article. Personnel in the durable Gardner's line-up has included Vernon Harrell (baritone), Ronnie Bright (b. 18 October 1938, New York, USA; bass, ex-Valentines), Jimmy Norman (b. 12 August 1937, Nashville, Tennessee, USA; baritone), Thomas 'Curley' Palmer (b. 1927, Dallas, Texas, USA; guitar), Alvin Morse (tenor), and his son Carl 'Mickey' Gardner Jnr. (baritone). Sadly, all of the original members, except Jacobs, have at various times attempted to cash in on the Coasters name. Bobby Nunn launched the Coasters, Mark II, and when he died from congestive heart failure in 1986 his group carried on under the leadership of Billy Richards Jnr. Leon Hughes formed his own tribute group, the Original Coasters. Billy Guy, who worked with the Gardner led Coasters up until 1973, has been involved with the World Famous Coasters and Billy Guy's Coasters. Cornell Gunter (who changed the spelling of his surname to Gunther in later years) was shot dead on 26 February 1990. He had also formed his own version of the Coasters, known as the Fabulous Coasters, after leaving the group in June 1961. Gardner, Guy, Jones and Gunter's induction into the Rock And Roll Hall Of Fame in January 1987 went some of the way towards restoring the group's tarnished image.

● ALBUMS: *The Coasters* (Atco 1957) ★★★★, *The Coasters' Greatest Hits* (Atco/London 1959) ★★★★★, *One By One* (Atco 1960) ★★★★, *Coast Along With The Coasters* (Atco/London 1962) ★★★, *On Broadway* (King/London 1973) ★★★.
● COMPILATIONS: *That Is Rock & Roll* (Clarion 1965) ★★, *Their Greatest Recordings: The Early Years* (Atco/Atlantic 1971) ★★★★, *16 Greatest Hits* (Trip 1975) ★★★, *20 Great Originals* (Atlantic 1978) ★★★, *What Is The Secret Of Your Success?* (Mr. R&B 1980) ★★★, *The Coasters* (Warners/Pioneer 1980) ★★★★, *Wake Me, Shake Me* (Warners/Pioneer 1981) ★★★★, *All About The Coasters* (Warners/Pioneer 1982) ★★★, *Young Blood* aka *The Ultimate Coasters* (Atlantic 1982) ★★★★, *Thumbin' A Ride* (Edsel 1984) ★★★, *20 Greatest Hits* (Highland-DeLuxe 1987) ★★★★, *Poison Ivy: The Best Of The Coasters* (Atco 1991) ★★★★, *50 Coastin' Classics* (Rhino/Atlantic 1992) ★★★★★, *Yakety Yak* (Rhino 1993) ★★★, *The Very Best Of The Coasters* (Rhino 1994) ★★★★★, *Spotlight: The Coasters & More – 20 All Time Greats* (Javelin 1996) ★★★, *Yakety Yak: 17 Classic Tracks* (MasterTone 1997) ★★★, *The Coasters* (Time-Life 1999) ★★★, *Charlie Brown* aka *The Clown Princes Of Rock N Roll* (Mr. R&B/Millennium 2000) ★★★★.
● FURTHER READING: *The Coasters*, Bill Millar.

COCHRAN, EDDIE

b. Edward Raymond Cochrane, 3 October 1938, Albert Lea, Minnesota, USA, d. 17 April 1960, Chippenham, Wiltshire, England. Recent information states he was raised in Minnisota, but without sight of the birth certificate, it is still possible he was born in Oklahoma City. Although Cochran's career was brief, during which time he had only had one major hit in the USA and topped the UK charts only once, he is now regarded as one of the finest ever rock 'n' roll artists and an outstanding rhythm guitarist.

Cochran formed his first proper group when he was 15, and known as the melody boys he started a musical partnership with his school friend Connie 'Guybo' Smith (b. 1939, Los Angeles, California, USA; bass) that would last throughout his short life. By now the young Cochran had already become a formidable player, using a chunky electric picking style similar to Chet Atkins. He formed a duo with non-relative Hank Cochran (b. Garland Petty Cochran, 2 August 1935, Greenville, Mississippi, USA; guitar/vocals), and they went out as the Cochran Brothers. He soon became an outstanding rockabilly guitarist with his now trademark Gretsch 6120 guitar, and he was soon finding plenty of work as a session player. Artists like Cochran and his friend Glen Glenn, were in transition during the mid-50s, moving out of country inspired rockabilly, into a harder rock 'n' roll sound.

Cochran's early recordings on the Ekko label sank without a trace, but in 1956 his cameo performance of 'Twenty Flight Rock' in the movie *The Girl Can't Help It* gave this handsome James Dean lookalike the career boost he needed, and he was signed by Liberty Records. Strangely, his new record company decided to release a ballad, 'Sittin' In The Balcony', which became a US Top 20 hit. The following year after a couple of minor hits ('Drive In Show' and 'Jeannie Jeannie Jeannie') the first of his classic anthems was released. The song 'Summertime Blues' (USA number 8, UK number 18), has now been recorded and performed by dozens of artists, and is now one of the most famous rock songs of all time. This lyric of teenage angst is timeless and features many perceptive observations of frustration, for example: 'Well my ma and papa told me son, you gotta make some money, if you wanna use the car to go a-riding next Sunday'. The repeated chorus 'Sometimes I wonder what I'm a gonna do, but there ain't no cure for the Summertime Blues' perfectly encapsulated American teenage feelings. Additionally, the infectious riff has been copied down the ages, as the simple chord progression E,A,B,E sounds *great* to every guitar novice. The Who's lengthy and gutsy version on *Live At Leeds* is probably the most famous other than Cochran's. The following year, another timeless classic appeared, originally titled 'Let's Get Together', 'C'mon Everybody', had a similarly infectious riff; this time Cochran brilliantly conveyed the relief of finishing a hard day's work and preparing for a night out: 'Well c'mon everybody and let's get together tonight, I've got some money in my jeans and I'm really gonna spend it right', followed by the repeated and long-anticipated chorus, 'Whooah c'mon everybody'. This gem of a record ably showed how 50s rock 'n' roll could be uplifting, musically brilliant and yet contain simple, honest and enduring lyrics.

Cochran toured the UK in 1960 and became an immediate favourite, on radio, television, due to the lengthy Larry Parnes package tour all over Britain. He was due to return to his home in California for a brief recording session, and come back to the UK for a tour extension. He travelled by taxi after a gig at Bristol, intending to fly home in a day or two. He was tragically killed in Chippenham, Wiltshire, when his taxi went out of control and crashed after veering off the road. Although he was sitting in the back seat, Cochran's body was thrown clear and he died a few hours later in hospital. The driver was subsequently prosecuted with a fine, a driving ban and a token prison sentence. His close friend and co-star Gene Vincent broke a collar bone in the accident. His girlfriend, songwriter Sharon Sheeley, was badly injured. She was co-writer of his posthumous hit 'Something Else', which became a major hit for the Sex Pistols in 1979. His biggest record was the inappropriately titled 'Three Steps To Heaven', which topped the UK chart shortly after his untimely death. Surprisingly it failed to dent the chart in the USA. 'Weekend' was another posthumous hit, and the last of his classics, another tale of simple youthful enthusiasm for life, and the anticipated wild weekend: 'Friday night and everything's right for the weekend, boy its great for staying out late at the weekend'.

In 1963 ex-Tornados bassist Heinz launched his solo career with the Joe Meek-produced tribute 'Just Like Eddie'. Heinz was only one of the many artists who have been influenced by Cochran. His reputation continues to grow as his slim catalogue of recordings is constantly repackaged to a perennial audience. In recent years Tony Barrett of Rockstar Records in the UK, has uncovered many tapes of early Cochran demos, outtakes and unreleased gems. The whole catalogue has been released on this enterprising label, dedicated to keeping Cochran's name alive. It is remarkable that in a chart career of little over two years, Cochran made such a big impression, and like Buddy Holly he continues to be cited as a major influence. The recent excellent biography *Don't Forget Me*, which uses some of Rob Finnis' thorough research, has also invited a reappraisal of his career. He was a dedicated musician and one of the greatest exponents of 'progressive' rock 'n' roll.

● ALBUMS: *Singing To My Baby* (Liberty 1957) ★★★, *The Eddie Cochran Memorial Album* (Liberty 1960) ★★★, *Never To Be Forgotten* (Liberty 1962) ★★★, *Cherished Memories* (Liberty 1962) ★★★★, *My Way* (Liberty 1964) ★★★, *On The Air* (United Artists 1972) ★★★, *The Many Sides Of Eddie Cochran* (Rockstar 1975) ★★★, *The Young Eddie Cochran* (Rockstar 1982) ★★★, *Words And Music* (Rockstar 1985) ★★★, *Portrait Of A Legend* (Rockstar 1985) ★★★, *The Many Styles Of Eddie Cochran* (Conifer 1985) ★★★, *The Hollywood Sessions* (Rockstar 1986) ★★★, *Thinkin' About You* (Rockstar 1989) ★★★, with Hank Cochran *Eddie And Hank: The Cochran Brothers* (Rockstar 1991) ★★★, *L.A. Sessions* (Rockstar 1992) ★★★, *Mighty Mean* (Rockstar 1995) ★★★★, *Cruisin' The Drive In* (Rockstar 1996) ★★★, *One Minute To One* (Rockstar 1996) ★★★, *Rockin' It Country Style* (Rockstar 1997) ★★, *Rock & Roll TV Show* (Carlton 1997) ★★★, *Don't Forget Me* (Rockstar 1998) ★★★★, with Gene Vincent *The Town Hall Party*

TV Shows (Rockstar 1999) ★★.
● COMPILATIONS: *Summertime Blues* (Sunset 1966) ★★★★, *The Very Best Of Eddie Cochran* (Liberty 1970) ★★★★, *Legendary Masters* (United Artists 1971) ★★★★, *The Very Best Of Eddie Cochran: 15th Anniversary Album* (United Artists 1975) ★★★, *The Singles Album* (United Artists 1979) ★★★★, *20th Anniversary Album* 4-LP box set (United Artists 1980) ★★★★, *The 25th Anniversary Album* (Liberty 1985) ★★★★, *Rock 'N' Roll Legend* (Rockstar 1987) ★★★, *The Early Years* (Ace 1988) ★★★★, *C'mon Everybody* (Liberty 1988) ★★★★, *The Eddie Cochran Box Set* 4-CD box set (Liberty 1988) ★★★★, *The EP Collection* (See For Miles 1989) ★★★★, *Greatest Hits* (Curb 1990) ★★★★, *Rare 'N' Rockin'* (Music Club 1997) ★★★, *Legends Of The 20th Century* (EMI 1999) ★★★.
● VIDEOS: *The Town Hall Party TV Shows 1959* (Rockstar 2001).
● FURTHER READING: *The Eddie Cochran Nostalgia Book*, Alan Clark. *Eddie Cochran: Never To Be Forgotten*, Alan Clark. *The Legend Continues*, Alan Clark. *Don't Forget Me: The Eddie Cochran Story*, Julie Mundy and Darrel Higham.
● FILMS: *The Girl Can't Help It* (1956), *Go, Johnny, Go!* (1958).

COGAN, ALMA

b. 19 May 1932, London, England, d. 26 October 1966, London, England. After appearing in the stage shows *Sauce Tartare* and *High Button Shoes*, Cogan was spotted by A&R representative Wally Ridley and signed to HMV Records. Although she began her career as a balladeer, her breakthrough came with the novelty hit 'Bell Bottom Blues', which reached the Top 5 in the UK in 1954. A cover version of Kitty Kallen's 'Little Things Mean A Lot' followed quickly and during that same year Cogan appeared with Frankie Vaughan on a couple of unsuccessful singles. Her lone UK number 1 occurred in the spring of 1955 with 'Dreamboat' and the following Christmas she was back with the novelty 'Never Do A Tango With An Eskimo'. A duet with Ronnie Hilton appeared on the b-side of his chart-topper 'No Other Love', and throughout this period Cogan earnestly covered a string of US hits including Jewel Akens' 'The Birds And The Bees' and Frankie Lymon And The Teenagers' 'Why Do Fools Fall In Love?'.

By the end of the 50s, she had notched up 18 UK chart entries, more than any female singer of her era. The press were fascinated by her amazing collection of dresses; at one time it was rumoured that she never wore any dress more than once, and her home in Essex was reputedly full of hundreds of voluminous frocks. Meanwhile, she was succeeding as a top variety star and enjoyed the luxury of her own television programme. Another duet, this time with Ocher Nebbish, appeared on one of her b-sides. Nebbish was, in fact, famed composer Lionel Bart, who not only cast Alma in *Oliver!*, but planned to marry her, much to the astonishment of the showbiz community. The unlikely nuptials never occurred, and by the 60s, Cogan was no longer a chart regular. Always a candidate for the cover version game, she recorded

the bouncy 'Tell Him' but lost out to Billie Davis. Paul McCartney made a surprise appearance playing tambourine on the b-side of one of her singles and she repaid the compliment by cutting 'Eight Days A Week', a belated shot at chart fame that narrowly missed. In March 1966, doctors discovered that the singer had cancer. During a period of convalescence she wrote a number of songs under the pseudonym Al Western, including Ronnie Carroll's 'Wait For Me' and Joe Dolan's 'I Only Dream Of You'. At the peak of the popularity of the *Man From UNCLE* television series, she recorded a tribute disc to its star, David McCallum, 'Love Ya Illya', by the pseudonymous Angela And The Fans, received extensive airplay and only narrowly missed the charts in 1966. That autumn, while working in Sweden, Cogan collapsed and was sent home. On 26 October 1966, she lost her fight against cancer and died at London's Middlesex Hospital. In 1992, she was the subject of a 30-minute documentary as part of BBC Television's *The Lime Grove Story* and again in 2001 with *Juke Box Heroes* confirming her continuing importance of a past era of pop
● ALBUMS: *I Love To Sing* (HMV 1958) ★★★, *With You In Mind* (Columbia 1961) ★★★, *How About Love* (Columbia 1962) ★★★.
● COMPILATIONS: *The Alma Cogan Collection* (One-Up 1977) ★★★, *The Second Collection* (One-Up 1978) ★★★, *The Very Best Of Alma Cogan* (MFP 1984) ★★★, *With Love In Mind* (MFP 1986) ★★★, *A Celebration* (Capitol 1987) ★★★, *The Almanac* (MFP 1990) ★★★, *The EMI Years* (EMI 1991) ★★★★, *The A-Z Of Alma* 3-CD box set (EMI 1994) ★★★★, *The Girl With The Laugh In Her Voice* 4-CD box set (EMI 2001) ★★★.
● FURTHER READING: *Alma Cogan*, Sandra Caron. *Alma Cogan*, Gordon Burn.

COLE, NAT 'KING'

b. Nathaniel Adams Coles, 17 March 1916, Montgomery, Alabama, USA, d. 15 February 1965, Santa Monica, California, USA. Cole was born into a family that held a key position in the black community; his father was pastor of the First Baptist Church. In 1921 the family migrated to Chicago, part of the mass exodus of blacks seeking a better life in the booming industrial towns of the north. He learned piano by ear from his mother, who was choir director in the church, from the age of four. When he was 12 years old he took lessons in classical piano, 'everything from Bach to Rachmaninoff'. Jazz was all-pervasive in Chicago, and Cole's school was a musical hotbed, producing musicians of the stature of Ray Nance, Eddie South and Milt Hinton. Cole's first professional break came touring with the show *Shuffle Along*, a revival of the first all-black show to make it to Broadway, which he joined with his bass-playing brother, Eddie. Stranded in Los Angeles when the show folded, Cole looked for club work and found it at the Century Club on Santa Monica Boulevard. It was a hangout for musicians and the young pianist made a splash: 'All the musicians dug him,' said Robert 'Bumps' Blackwell, 'that cat could play! He was unique.'

In 1939 Cole formed an innovative trio with Oscar Moore on guitar and Wesley Prince on bass, eschewing the noise of drums. Like Fats Waller in the previous generation, Cole managed to combine pleasing and humorous ditties with piano stylings that were state-of-the-art. Times had moved on, and Cole had a suave sophistication that expressed the new aspirations of the black community. In 1943 he recorded his 'Straighten Up And Fly Right' for Capitol Records – it was an instant hit and Cole's future as a pop success was assured. In 1946 'The Christmas Song' added strings, starting a process that would lead to Cole emerging as a middle-of-the-road singer, accompanied by leading arrangers and conductors including Nelson Riddle, Gordon Jenkins, Ralph Carmichael, Pete Rugolo and Billy May. In the 40s Cole made several memorable sides with the Trio, including 'Sweet Lorraine', 'It's Only A Paper Moon', '(Get Your Kicks) On Route 66' and '(I Love You) For Sentimental Reasons'. By 1948, and 'Nature Boy' (a US number 1), on which Cole was accompanied by Frank DeVol's Orchestra, the move away from small-group jazz, towards his eventual position as one of the most popular vocalists of the day, was well underway.

Absolute confirmation came in 1950, when Cole, with Les Baxter conducting Nelson Riddle's lush arrangement of 'Mona Lisa', spent eight weeks at the top of the US chart with what was to become one of his most celebrated recordings. Throughout the 50s the singles hits continued to flow, mostly with ballads such as 'Too Young', 'Faith Can Move Mountains', 'Because You're Mine', 'Unforgettable', 'Somewhere Along The Way', 'Funny (Not Much)', 'Pretend', 'Can't I?', 'Answer Me, My Love', 'Smile', 'Darling, Je Vous Aime Beaucoup', 'The Sand And The Sea', 'A Blossom Fell', 'When I Fall In Love' and 'Star Dust' (said to be composer Hoagy Carmichael's favourite version of his song). No doubt because of his jazz grounding, Cole was equally at home with the more up-tempo 'Orange Coloured Sky', backed by Stan Kenton And His Orchestra, 'Walkin' My Baby Back Home', 'Night Lights' and 'Ballerina'. In the same period, his bestselling albums included *After Midnight* (with the Trio), *Love Is The Thing*, which was at the top of the US chart for eight weeks, *Just One Of Those Things*, *Cole Espanol* and *The Very Thought Of You*.

During the 50s he was urged to make films, but his appearances were few and far between, including character parts in *Blue Gardenia*, *China Gate* and *Night Of The Quarter Moon*. Cole's most effective film role came in 1958 when he played W.C. Handy in *St. Louis Blues*. He also appeared on screen with Stubby Kaye, singing the linking ballads in the spoof western *Cat Ballou* (1965), but it was clear that his enormous appeal lay in concerts and records. One of his lesser-known albums, *Welcome To The Club*, featured the [Count] Basie Orchestra, without the Count himself (for contractual reasons), and included Cole's superior readings of 'She's Funny That Way', 'Avalon' and 'Look Out For Love'. The title track was composed by Noel Sherman, who, with his brother Joe, wrote

'Mr Cole Won't Rock And Roll', an amusing piece performed by the singer in his concert show, 'Sights And Sounds', which played over 100 cities in the early 60s. It was not so much rock 'n' roll that concerned Cole's purist fans around that time: they had acute reservations about another of the Sherman Brothers' numbers, 'Ramblin' Rose' (1962), the singer's first big hit in four years, which came complete with a 'twangy C&W feeling'. They also objected to 'Those Lazy-Hazy-Crazy Days Of Summer' ('unabashed corn'), which also made the Top 10 in the following year. Cole himself felt that he was 'just adjusting to the market: as soon as you start to make money in the popular field, they scream about how good you were in the old days, and what a bum you are now'.

Performing as part of his most agreeable musical association during the early 60s, *Nat King Cole Sings/George Shearing Plays*, Cole went back to 1940 for Ian Grant and Lionel Rand's 'Let There Be Love'. His version became a hit single in many parts of the world, and remains a particularly fondly remembered 'classic' performance. In a way, he was back to where he had started at the time the song was written: singing with a small jazz group – albeit this time with George Shearing's polite piano and the inevitable 'String Choir'. During the years of Cole's enormous popularity in the 'easy listening' field, jazz fans had to turn out to see him in the clubs to hear his glorious piano – an extension of the Earl Hines style that had many features of the new, hip sounds of bebop. If Cole had not had such an effective singing voice he might well have been one of bebop's leaders. Bebop was an expression of black pride, but so was Cole's career, creating opportunities for all kinds of 'sepia Sinatras' (Charles Brown, Sammy Davis Jnr., etc.) who proved that whites had no monopoly on sophistication. Cole bore the brunt of racism, meeting objections when he bought a house in fashionable Beverly Hills, and becoming the first black television presenter (he abandoned the role in 1957, protesting that the agencies would not find him a national sponsor). Though his position entailed compromises that gained him the hostility of civil rights activists in the early 60s, he was a brave and decent figure in a period when racial prejudice was at its most demeaning.

Before his death from lung cancer in 1965, Cole was planning a production of James Baldwin's play *Amen Corner*, showing an interest in radical black literature at odds with his image as a sentimental crooner. Nat Cole's voice, which floats butter-won't-melt vowel sounds in an easy, dark drawl, is one of the great moments of black music, and no matter how sugary the arrangements he always managed to sing as if it mattered. In 1991 his daughter Natalie Cole revived his 'Unforgettable', singing a duet with his recorded vocal. Despite the questionable taste of beyond-the-grave duets, Cole's piano intro was a startling reminder of the extraordinary harmonic creativity he brought to the pop music of his time. Perhaps, like Louis Armstrong, the most moving aspect of his legacy is the way his music cuts across the usual boundaries – chart-watchers and jazzheads, rock 'n' rollers and MOR fans can all have a good time with his music.

● ALBUMS: *The King Cole Trio* 10-inch album (Capitol 1950) ★★★, *The King Cole Trio Volume 2* 10-inch album (Capitol 1950) ★★★, *The King Cole Trio Volume 3* 10-inch album (Capitol 1950) ★★★, *At The Piano* 10-inch album (Capitol 1950) ★★★, *The King Cole Trio Volume 4* 10-inch album (Capitol 1950) ★★★, *Harvest Of Hits* 10-inch album (Capitol 1950) ★★★, with Buddy Rich, Lester Young *The Lester Young Trio* 10-inch album (Mercury 1951) ★★★★, *Penthouse Serenade* 10-inch album (Capitol 1952) ★★★★, *Unforgettable* (Capitol 1952) ★★★★, with Red Callender, Young *King Cole-Lester Young-Red Callender Trio* reissued as *Lester Young-Nat King Cole Trio* (Aladdin/Score 1953) ★★★★, *Nat 'King' Cole Sings For Two In Love* 10-inch album (Capitol 1953) ★★★, *8 Top Pops* (Capitol 1954) ★★★, *Tenth Anniversary Album* (Capitol 1955) ★★★, *Vocal Classics* (Capitol 1955) ★★★, *Instrumental Classics* (Capitol 1955) ★★★, *The Piano Style of Nat King Cole* (Capitol 1956) ★★★, *In The Beginning* (Decca 1956) ★★, *Ballads Of The Day* (Capitol 1956) ★★★, *After Midnight* (Capitol 1957) ★★★★, *Love Is The Thing* (Capitol 1957) ★★★★, *This Is Nat 'King' Cole* (Capitol 1957) ★★★★, *Just One Of Those Things* (Capitol 1957) ★★★, *St. Louis Blues* film soundtrack (Capitol 1958) ★★, *Cole Espanol* (Columbia 1958) ★★, *The Very Thought Of You* (Capitol 1958) ★★★★, *Welcome To The Club* (Capitol 1959) ★★★, *To Whom It May Concern* (Capitol 1959) ★★★, *A Mis Amigos* (Capitol 1959) ★★, *Tell Me All About Yourself* (Capitol 1960) ★★★, *Every Time I Feel The Spirit* (Capitol 1960) ★★★, *Wild Is Love* (Capitol 1960) ★★★, *The Magic Of Christmas* (Capitol 1960) ★★, *The Touch Of Your Lips* (Capitol 1961) ★★★★, *String Along With Nat 'King' Cole* (Capitol 1961) ★★★★, *Nat 'King' Cole Sings/George Shearing Plays* (Capitol 1962) ★★★★, *Ramblin' Rose* (Capitol 1962) ★★★, *Sings The Blues* (Capitol 1962) ★★★, *Dear Lonely Hearts* (Capitol 1962) ★★★, *Where Did Everyone Go?* (Capitol 1963) ★★★, *Those Lazy-Hazy-Crazy Days Of Summer* (Capitol 1963) ★★★, *Sings The Blues Volume 2* (Capitol 1963) ★★★, *The Christmas Song* (Capitol 1963) ★★★, *I Don't Want To Be Hurt Anymore* (Capitol 1964) ★★★, *My Fair Lady* (Capitol 1964) ★★★, *L-O-V-E* (Capitol 1965) ★★★, *Songs From 'Cat Ballou' And Other Motion Pictures* (Capitol 1965) ★★★, *Looking Back* (Capitol 1965) ★★★, *Nat 'King' Cole At The Sands* (Capitol 1966) ★★★, *At JATP* (Verve 1966) ★★★, *At JATP 2* (Verve 1966) ★★★, *The Great Songs!* 1957 recording (Capitol 1966) ★★★★, with Dean Martin *White Christmas* (Capitol 1971) ★★★, *Christmas With Nat 'King' Cole* (Stylus 1988) ★★★.

● COMPILATIONS: *The Nat King Cole Story* 3-LP box set (Capitol 1961) ★★★★, *The Best Of Nat King Cole* (Capitol 1968) ★★★★, *20 Golden Greats* (Capitol 1978) ★★★★, *Greatest Love Songs* (Capitol 1982) ★★★★, *Trio Days* (Affinity 1984) ★★★, *The Complete Capitol Recordings Of The Nat King Cole Trio* 18-CD box set (Mosiac 1990) ★★★★★, *The Unforgettable Nat 'King' Cole* (EMI 1991) ★★★★, *The Nat King Cole Gold Collection* (1993) ★★★★, *World War II Transcriptions* (1994) ★★★, *The Best*

Of The Nat 'King' Cole Trio 3-CD set (Capitol Jazz 1998) ★★★★, *The Ultimate Collection* (EMI 1999) ★★★★.

● VIDEOS: *Nat King Cole* (Missing In Action 1988), *Unforgettable* (PMI 1988), *Nat King Cole Collection* (Castle Music Pictures 1990), *Nat King Cole 1942-1949* (Verve Video 1990), *Nat King Cole* (Virgin Vision 1992).

● FURTHER READING: *Nat King Cole: The Man And His Music*, Jim Haskins & Kathleen Benson. *Unforgettable: The Life And Mystique Of Nat King Cole*, Leslie Gourse. *Nat King Cole*, Daniel Mark Epstein.

COLEMAN, CY

b. Seymour Kaufman, 14 June 1929, New York, USA. A pianist, singer, producer and composer of popular songs and scores for films and the Broadway stage. The youngest of the five sons of emigrants from Russia, Coleman was born and brought up in the Bronx, where his mother owned two tenement buildings. He began to pick out tunes on the piano when he was four years old, irritating his father, a carpenter, to such an extent that he nailed down the lid of the instrument. However, a local teacher was so impressed by Coleman's piano playing that she provided free lessons in classical music. Between the ages of six and nine, Coleman performed in New York at the Town Hall, Steinway Hall and Carnegie Hall. While continuing his classical studies at the High School of Music and Art and the New York College of Music, from which he graduated in 1948, Coleman decided to change course and pursue a career in popular music. After a stint at Billy Reed's Little Club, he spent two years as a cocktail-lounge pianist at the exclusive Sherry Netherland Hotel in Manhattan, and played piano for several television programmes, including *The Kate Smith Show* and *A Date In Manhattan*.

In 1950 he appeared with his trio, and singer Margaret Phelan, in the RKO short *Package Of Rhythm*. During the early 50s Coleman began to play in jazz clubs in New York and elsewhere, developing what he called a 'kind of bepoppy style'. By then he had been composing songs for several years. One of his earliest collaborators was Joseph Allen McCarthy, whose father, also named Joseph, wrote the lyrics for shows such as *Irene*, *Kid Boots* and *Rio Rita*. One of their first efforts, 'The Riviera', was included several years later on Johnny Mathis' *Live It Up*, while 'I'm Gonna Laugh You Right Out Of My Life' was recorded by singer-pianist Buddy Greco. Another, 'Why Try To Change Me Now?', received a memorable reading from Frank Sinatra in 1952. In the following year Coleman contributed 'Tin Pan Alley' to the Broadway show *John Murray Anderson's Almanac*, and around the same time, he wrote several songs for a Tallulah Bankhead vehicle, *Ziegfeld Follies*, which never made it to Broadway. From the late 50s until 1962, Coleman had a 'stormy' working relationship with lyricist Carolyn Leigh. Together they wrote several popular numbers such as 'Witchcraft' (Frank Sinatra), 'The Best Is Yet To Come' (Mabel Mercer), 'A Moment Of Madness'

(Sammy Davis Jnr.), 'When In Rome' (Vikki Carr/Barbra Streisand), 'You Fascinate Me So' (Mark Murphy), 'Playboy's Theme', 'The Rules Of The Road', 'It Amazes Me', 'I Walk A Little Faster' and 'Firefly'. The latter was written in 1958 for Coleman and Leigh's musical based on the memoirs of stripper Gypsy Rose Lee. The project was later abandoned, but the song became a hit for Tony Bennett, who was instrumental in bringing their work before the public, and included two of their songs in his famous Carnegie Hall concert in 1962. Two years before that, the team wrote the music and lyrics for the Broadway musical *Wildcat*. The score included the show-stopper 'What Takes My Fancy', plus 'That's What I Want For Janie', 'Give A Little Whistle', 'You've Come Home', 'El Sombrero', and the march 'Hey, Look Me Over'. The latter became a hit for Peggy Lee. Coleman and Lee collaborated to write 'Then Is Then And Now Is Now'.

In 1962, Coleman and Leigh were back on Broadway with *Little Me*. The libretto, by Neil Simon, was based on a successful novel by Patrick Dennis, and traced the life of Belle Poitrine. Sid Caesar played all seven of her lovers, from the 16-year-old Noble Eggleston to the geriatric skinflint Mr. Pinchley. The score included 'Love You', 'Deep Down Inside', 'The Other Side Of The Tracks', 'Real Live Girl' and the show-stopper 'I've Got Your Number'. Despite a favourable reception from the critics, *Little Me* did not fulfil its potential, and folded after only 257 performances. In 1964, it was acclaimed in London, where comedian and song and dance man Bruce Forsyth played the lead, and a revised version was presented in the West End in 1984, starring the UK television comic Russ Abbott. After *Little Me*, Coleman and Leigh went their separate ways, collaborating briefly again in 1964 for 'Pass Me By', which was sung by the British writer-performer Digby Wolfe, over the opening titles of the Cary Grant movie *Father Goose*. In the same year, Coleman wrote the catchy 'Take a Little Walk' with Buddy Greco, before teaming with the lyricist and librettist Dorothy Fields.

Fields was 25 years older than Coleman, with an impressive track record of standard songs for films and shows, written with composers such as Jimmy McHugh, Jerome Kern and Arthur Schwartz, plus the book for Irving Berlin's smash hit musical *Annie Get Your Gun*. In 1966 the new combination had their own Broadway hit with the score for *Sweet Charity*, a musical version of Federico Fellini's film *Nights Of Cabiria*. The accent was very much on dancing in this 'sentimental story of a New York dancehall hostess, and her desperate search for love'. The Coleman-Fields score included 'Baby, Dream Your Dream', 'Big Spender', 'If My Friends Could See Me Now', 'There's Gotta Be Something Better Than This', 'Where Am I Going?' and 'I'm A Brass Band'. The show ran for 608 performances on Broadway, and for 14 months in London, where it starred Juliet Prowse. The lead in the 1969 movie version was taken by Shirley Maclaine, and it also featured Sammy Davis Jnr. as a hippie evangelist

singing 'The Rhythm Of Life', and Stubby Kaye leading the ensemble in 'I Love To Cry At Weddings'. Coleman was nominated for an Academy Award for his musical score. After failing to have several other projects mounted, such as a biography of Eleanor Roosevelt and a stage adaptation of the 1939 James Stewart movie *Mr. Smith Goes To Washington*, Coleman and Fields were back on Broadway in 1973 with *Seesaw*, based on William Gibson's 50s comedy *Two For The Seesaw*. The score included 'Welcome To Holiday Inn', 'Poor Everybody Else' and the blockbusters 'It's Not Where You Start (It's Where You Finish)' and 'Nobody Does It Like Me'. The latter became successful outside the show as a cabaret number for artists such as Shirley Bassey and comedienne Marti Caine.

After Dorothy Fields' death in 1974, it was another three years before Coleman returned to Broadway with *I Love My Wife*, with book and lyrics by Michael Stewart. Adapted from Luis Rego's farce 'about two suburban couples and their bumbling attempt to engage in wife swapping', the production ran for 857 performances. It featured a small onstage orchestra whose members sang, dressed in fancy clothes, and commented on the show's action. Coleman won the Drama Desk Award for a score which included 'Hey There, Good Times', 'Something Wonderful I've Missed', 'Sexually Free', 'Lovers On A Christmas Eve', 'Everybody Today Is Turning On' and the title song. Less than a year after the opening of *I Love My Wife*, Coleman contributed to *On The Twentieth Century*, which was based on a 30s play by Ben Hecht and Charles MacArthur, with lyrics and libretto by Betty Comden and Adolph Green. The production included the songs 'I Rise Again', 'Together', 'Never', 'She's A Nut' and 'Our Private World'. The show ran for over a year, and earned six Tony Awards, including best score of a musical. Coleman's next project, with lyricist Barbara Fried, was *Home Again*, which 'followed an Illinois family from the Depression to the Watergate scandal'. It closed in Toronto during April 1979, two weeks before it was set to open on Broadway. In complete contrast, *Barnum* (1980), a musical treatment of the life of showman P.T. Barnum, was a smash hit. Coleman's music and Michael Stewart's lyrics were 'catchy and clever, and occasionally very beautiful'. British actor Jim Dale received rave notices for his endearing performance in the title role, which called for him to sing and be a clown, ride a unicycle and walk a tightrope. The part of his wife was played by Glenn Close, on the brink of her 80s movie stardom. The score included 'There's A Sucker Born Ev'ry Minute', 'One Brick At A Time', 'The Colours Of My Life' and 'Come Follow The Band'. *Barnum* ran for 854 performances and captured three Tonys and two Grammies for the Broadway Cast album. Its subsequent run of almost two years at the London Palladium was a triumph for Michael Crawford. During the early 80s Coleman mounted Broadway revivals of *Little Me* and *Sweet Charity* which won four Tonys, including best revival of a play or musical. In 1988 Coleman wrote the music and lyrics, in collaboration with A.E. Hotchner, for *Let 'Em Rot*. It failed to reach New York, and when Coleman did return to Broadway in April 1989 with *Welcome To The Club*, that show was censured by the critics, and only ran for a few performances.

It proved to be a temporary setback, for in December of that year, Coleman had one of the biggest hits of his career with *City Of Angels*, utilizing David Zippel's lyrics, and a book by Larry Gelbart that 'both satirized and celebrated the film *noire* genre and the hard boiled detective fiction of the 1940s'. The show garnered six Tonys, three Outer Critics Circle Awards and eight Drama Desk Awards, among them those for best musical, best music and lyrics. The production included the songs 'With Every Breath I Take', 'The Tennis Song', 'What You Don't Know About Women', 'You're Nothing Without Me' and 'Double Talk'. *City Of Angels* ran at the Virginia Theatre in New York for 878 performances. Meanwhile, Coleman had turned his attention to *The Will Rogers Follies*, which related 'the life story of America's favourite humorist in the style of a *Ziegfeld Follies*' (1991). With Keith Carradine in the title role, Peter Stone's book called for 'a mutt act, a world champion roper, four kids, 12 sisters, a ranchful of cowboys, Gregory Peck (his voice only), and girls wearing spangles, and, of course, girls wearing not much of anything at all', which was put together by director-choreographer Tommy Tune. For the lyrics to his pastiche melodies, Coleman turned again to Comden and Green for 'Never Met A Man I Didn't Like', 'Let's Go Flying', 'Willamania', 'It's A Boy!', 'The Powder Puff Ballet', 'Give A Man Enough Rope' and 'Marry Me Now/I Got You'. Despite initial notices citing 'lapses of taste' and 'a paltry case for a cultural icon', the show ran for 1,420 performances, and gained Tony Awards for best musical and original score.

Taste could well have been an issue once more with Coleman's 1997 Broadway project, *The Life*. Based around New York's 42nd Street, habitat of hookers and their pimps, the show had lyrics by Ira Gasman, who collaborated with Coleman and David Newman on the book. Among the best numbers in Coleman's 'most driving big-beat score since *Sweet Charity*', were 'Check It Out!', 'The Oldest Profession', 'My Body', 'Use What You Got', 'Mr. Greed', 'People Magazine', and 'Why Don't They Leave Us Alone'. *The Life* won two Tony Awards, as well as Drama Desk, Outer Critics Circle and Drama League honours. In 1998, *Exactly Like You*, 'a courtroom drama' on which Coleman collaborated with co-lyricist and librettist A.E. Hotchner, had its world premiere at Goodspeed-at-Chester, Connecticut.

In parallel with his Broadway career, Coleman has written several film scores, although they have generally failed to match the critical acclaim of his stage work. His music for *Family Business* was termed by one critic as 'one of the most appalling music scores in recent memory'. Coleman's other film work has included *Father Goose* (1964), *The Troublemaker* (1964), *The Art Of Love* (1965), *The Heartbreak Kid* (1972), *Blame It On Rio* (1984),

Garbo Talks (1984) and *Power* (1986). He has also worked in television, where he conceived and co-produced Shirley Maclaine's special *If They Could See Me Now* (1974), and produced her *Gypsy In My Soul* (1976), both Emmy-winning presentations. Coleman has also performed with many symphony orchestras, including those of Milwaukee, Detroit, San Antonio, Indianapolis and Fort Worth, and has been a director of ASCAP, and a governor of the Academy of Television Arts And Sciences and the Dramatists Guild. He was inducted into the Songwriters' Hall of Fame, and has served as a member of the Academy of Motion Picture Arts and Sciences and the New York State Advisory Committee on Music. His honours include the La Guardia Award for Outstanding Achievement in Music and the Irvin Feld Humanitarian award from the National Conference of Christians and Jews.

● ALBUMS: as a pianist and vocalist *Cy Coleman* 10-inch album (Benida 1955) ★★★, *Jamaica*, *Playboy's Penthouse*, *Piano Artistry* (all 50s), *Cool Coleman* (Westminster 1958) ★★★★, *Flower Drum Song* (1959) ★★★, *Why Try To Change Me* (1959) ★★★, *If My Friends Could See Me Now* (1966) ★★★, *Barnum* (Rhapsody 1981) ★★★, *Coming Home* (DRG 1988) ★★★.

COLTRANE, JOHN

b. John William Coltrane, 23 September 1926, Hamlet, North Carolina, USA, d. 17 July 1967, New York, USA. Coltrane grew up in the house of his maternal grandfather, Rev. William Blair (who gave him his middle name), a preacher and community spokesman. While he was taking clarinet lessons at school, his school band leader suggested his mother buy him an alto saxophone. In 1939 his grandfather and then his father died, and after finishing high school he joined his mother in Philadelphia. He spent a short period at the Ornstein School of Music and the Granoff Studios, where he won scholarships for both performance and composition, but his real education began when he started gigging. Two years' military service was spent in a navy band (1945-46), after which he toured in the King Kolax and Eddie 'Cleanhead' Vinson bands, playing goodtime, rhythmic big-band music. It was while playing in the Dizzy Gillespie Big Band (1949-51) that he switched to tenor saxophone. Coltrane's musical roots were in acoustic black music that combined swing and instrumental prowess in solos, the forerunner of R&B. He toured with Earl Bostic (1952), Johnny Hodges (1953-54) and Jimmy Smith (1955). However, it was his induction into the Miles Davis band of 1955 – rightly termed the Classic Quintet – that brought him to notice. Next to Davis' filigree sensitivity, Coltrane sounds awkward and crude, and Davis received criticism for his choice of saxophonist. The only precedent for such modernist interrogation of tenor harmony was John Gilmore's playing with Sun Ra.

Critics found Coltrane's tone raw and shocking after years in which the cool school of Lester Young and Stan Getz had held sway. It was generally acknowledged, however, that his ideas were first rate. Along with Sonny Rollins, he became New York's most in-demand hard bop tenor player: 1957 saw him appearing on 21 important recordings, and enjoying a brief but fruitful association with Thelonious Monk. That same year he returned to Philadelphia, kicking his long-time heroin habit, and started to develop his own music (Coltrane's notes to the later *A Love Supreme* refer to a 'spiritual awakening'). He also found half of his 'classic' quartet: at the Red Rooster (a nightclub that he visited with trumpeter Calvin Massey, an old friend from the 40s), he discovered pianist McCoy Tyner and bassist Jimmy Garrison.

After recording numerous albums for the Prestige label, Coltrane signed to Atlantic Records and, on 15 August 1959, he recorded *Giant Steps*. Although it did not use the talents of his new friends from Philadelphia, it featured a dizzying torrent of tenor solos that harked back to the pressure-cooker creativity of bebop, while incorporating the muscular gospel attack of hard bop. Pianist Tommy Flanagan (later celebrated for his sensitive backings for singers such as Ella Fitzgerald and Tony Bennett) and drummer Art Taylor provided the best performances of their lives. Although this record is rightly hailed as a masterpiece, it encapsulated a problem: where could hard bop go from here? Coltrane knew the answer; after a second spell with Davis (1958-60), he formed his best-known quartet with Tyner, Garrison and the amazing polyrhythmic drummer Elvin Jones. Jazz has been recovering ever since.

The social situation of the 60s meant that Coltrane's innovations were simultaneously applauded as *avant garde* statements of black revolution and efficiently recorded and marketed. The Impulse! label, to which he switched from Atlantic in 1961, has a staggering catalogue that includes most of Coltrane's landmark records, plus several experimental sessions from the mid-60s that still remain unreleased (although they missed *My Favorite Things*, recorded in 1960 for Atlantic, in which Coltrane helped re-establish the soprano saxophone as an important instrument). Between 1961 and his death in 1967, Coltrane made music that has become the foundation of modern jazz. For commercial reasons, Impulse! Records had a habit of delaying the release of his music; fans emerged from the live performances in shock at the pace of his evolution. A record of *Ballads* and an encounter with Duke Ellington in 1962 seemed designed to deflect criticisms of coarseness, although Coltrane later attributed their relatively temperate ambience to persistent problems with his mouthpiece. *A Love Supreme* was more hypnotic and lulling on record than in live performance, but nevertheless a classic.

After that, the records became wilder and wilder. The unstinting commitment to new horizons led to ruptures within the group. Elvin Jones left after Coltrane incorporated a second drummer (Rashied Ali). McCoy Tyner was replaced by Alice McLeod (who married Coltrane in 1966). Coltrane was especially interested in new saxophone players and *Ascension* (1965) made space for Archie Shepp, Pharoah Sanders, Marion Brown and John Tchicai. Eric Dolphy, although he represented a different tradition of playing from Coltrane (a modernist projection of Charlie Parker), had also been a frequent guest player with the quartet in the early 60s, touring Europe with them in 1961. *Interstellar Space* (1967), a duet record, pitched Coltrane's tenor against Ali's drums, and provides a fascinating hint of new directions.

Coltrane's death in 1967 robbed *avant garde* jazz of its father figure. The commercial ubiquity of fusion in the 70s obscured his music and the 80s jazz revival concentrated on his hard bop period. Only Reggie Workman's Ensemble and Ali's Phalanx carried the huge ambition of Coltrane's later music into the 90s. As soloists, however, few tenor players have remained untouched by his example. It is interesting that the saxophonists Coltrane encouraged did not sound like him; since his death, his 'sound' has become a mainstream commodity, from the Berklee College Of Music style of Michael Brecker to the 'European' variant of Jan Garbarek. New stars such as Andy Sheppard have established new audiences for jazz without finding new ways of playing. Coltrane's music – like that of Jimi Hendrix – ran parallel with a tide of mass political action and consciousness. Perhaps those conditions are required for the creation of such innovative and intense music. Nevertheless, Coltrane's music reached a wide audience, and was particularly popular with the younger generation of listeners who were also big fans of rock music. *A Love Supreme* sold sufficient copies to win a gold disc, while the Byrds used the theme of Coltrane's tune 'India' as the basis of their hit single 'Eight Miles High'. Perhaps by alerting the rock audience to the presence of jazz, Coltrane can be said to have – inadvertently – prepared the way for fusion. Coltrane's work has some challenging moments and if you are not in the right mood, he can sound irritating. What is established without doubt is his importance as a true messenger of music. His jazz came from somewhere inside his body. Few jazz musicians have reached this nirvana, and still have absolute control over their instrument.

● ALBUMS: with Paul Chambers *High Step* 1955-1956 recordings (Blue Note 1956) ★★★, with Elmo Hope *Informal Jazz* reissued as *Two Tenors* (Prestige 1956) ★★★, with various artists *Tenor Conclave* (Prestige 1957) ★★★, *Dakar* (Prestige 1957) ★★★, *Coltrane* reissued as *The First Trane* (Prestige 1957) ★★★, *John Coltrane With The Red Garland Trio* reissued as *Traneing In* (Prestige 1957) ★★★, with various artists *Wheelin' And Dealing* (Prestige 1957) ★★★, *Blue Train* (Blue Note 1957) ★★★★★, with Thelonious Monk *Thelonious Monk With John Coltrane* (Jazzland 1957) ★★★★, with Miles Davis *Miles And Coltrane* (Columbia 1958) ★★★★, *Lush Life* (Prestige 1958) ★★★, *Soultrane* (Blue Note 1958) ★★★★, *John Coltrane* (Prestige 1958) ★★★★, *Settin' The Pace* (Prestige 1958) ★★★, with Paul Quinichette *Cattin' With Coltrane And Quinichette* (Prestige

1959) ★★★, *Coltrane Plays For Lovers* (Prestige 1959) ★★★, *The Believer* (Prestige 1959) ★★★, *Black Pearls* (Prestige 1959) ★★, *The Stardust Session* (Prestige 1959) ★★★, *Standard Coltrane* (Prestige 1959) ★★★, *Bahia* (Prestige 1959) ★★★, *Giant Steps* (Atlantic 1959) ★★★★★, *Coltrane Jazz* (Atlantic 1960) ★★★★, with Don Cherry *The Avant-Garde* (Atlantic 1960) ★★★, with Milt Jackson *Bags And Trane* (Atlantic 1961) ★★★★, *My Favorite Things* (Atlantic 1961) ★★★★, *Olé Coltrane* (Atlantic 1961) ★★★, *Africa/Brass: Volumes 1 & 2* (Impulse! 1961) ★★★★, with Kenny Burrell *Kenny Burrell With John Coltrane* (New Jazz 1962) ★★★★, *Live At The Village Vanguard* (Impulse! 1962) ★★★, *Coltrane Plays The Blues* (Atlantic 1962) ★★★★, *Coltrane Time* originally released as Cecil Taylor's *Hard Driving Jazz* (United Artists 1962) ★★★, *Coltrane* (Impulse! 1962) ★★★★, with Duke Ellington *Duke Ellington And John Coltrane* (MCA/Impulse! 1962) ★★★★, *Ballads* (Impulse! 1962) ★★★★, with Johnny Hartman *John Coltrane And Johnny Hartman* (Impulse! 1963) ★★★★, *Coltrane Live At Birdland* (Impulse! 1963) ★★★, *Impressions* (Impulse! 1963) ★★★★, *Coltrane's Sound* 1960 recording (Atlantic 1964) ★★★★, *Crescent* (Impulse! 1964) ★★★, with Cannonball Adderley *Cannonball And Coltrane* (Limelight 1964) ★★★, *The Last Trane* (Prestige 1965) ★★★, *A Love Supreme* (Impulse! 1965) ★★★★★, *The John Coltrane Quartet Plays* (Impulse! 1965) ★★★, with Archie Shepp *New Thing At Newport* (Impulse! 1965) ★★★, *Ascension – Edition 1* (Impulse! 1965) ★★★★, *Transition* (Impulse! 1965) ★★★★, *Ascension – Edition 2* (Impulse! 1966) ★★★★, *Kulu Se Mama* (Impulse! 1966) ★★★, *Meditations* (Impulse! 1966) ★★★★, *Expression* (Impulse! 1967) ★★★, *Live At The Village Vanguard Again!* (Impulse! 1967) ★★★, *Om* (Impulse! 1967) ★★, *Selflessness* 1963, 1965 recordings (Impulse! 1969) ★★★, *Sun Ship* 1965 recording (1971) ★★★, *Dear Old Stockholm* (Impulse! 1965) ★★★, *Live In Seattle* 1965 recording (Impulse! 1971) ★★★, *Africa Brass, Volume Two* 1961 recording (1974) ★★★★, *Interstellar Space* 1967 recording (Impulse! 1974) ★★★, *First Meditations – For Quartet* 1965 recording (Impulse! 1977) ★★★, *The Other Village Vanguard Tapes* 1961 recording (1977) ★★★, *Afro-Blue Impressions* 1962 recording (Pablo 1977) ★★★, *The Paris Concert* 1962 recording (Pablo 1979) ★★★, *The European Tour* 1962 recording (Pablo 1980) ★★★, *Bye Bye Blackbird* 1962 recording (1981) ★★★, *Live At Birdland – Featuring Eric Dolphy* 1962 recording (Impulse! 1982) ★★★, *Stellar Regions* 1967 recording (Impulse! 1995) ★★★, *The Olatunji Concert: The Last Live Recording* (Impulse! 2001) ★★★.

● COMPILATIONS: *The Best Of John Coltrane* (Atlantic 1969) ★★★★, *The Best Of John Coltrane – His Greatest Years (1961-1966)* (MCA/Impulse! 1972) ★★★★, *The Best Of John Coltrane – His Greatest Years, Volume 2 (1961-1967)* (MCA/Impulse! 1972) ★★★★, *The Mastery Of John Coltrane, Volumes 1-4* (1978) ★★★★, *The Art Of John Coltrane (The Atlantic Years)* (Pablo 1983) ★★★★, *The Gentle Side Of John Coltrane* (Impulse!

1992) ★★★★, *The Major Works Of John Coltrane* (Impulse! 1992) ★★★★, *The Impulse! Years* (Impulse! 1993) ★★★★, *The Heavyweight Champion: The Complete Atlantic Recordings* 7-CD box set (Rhino/Atlantic 1995) ★★★★★, *The Complete 1961 Village Vanguard Recordings* 4-CD box set (Impulse! 1997) ★★★★, *The Classic Quartet – Complete Impulse! Studio Recordings* 8-CD box set (Impulse! 1998) ★★★★★, *The Bethlehem Years* (Charly 1998) ★★★, *The Very Best Of John Coltrane* (Rhino 2000) ★★★★, with Miles Davis *The Complete Columbia Recordings 1955-1961* (Columbia/Legacy 2000) ★★★★, *Ken Burns Jazz: The Definitive John Coltrane* (Verve 2000) ★★★, *Coltrane For Lovers* (Impulse 2001) ★★★.

● CD ROM: *John Coltrane – The Ultimate Blue Train* (Blue Note 1997).

● VIDEOS: *The World According To John Coltrane* (1993), *Ralph Gleason's Jazz Casual: John Coltrane* (Rhino Home Video 1999).

● FURTHER READING: *The Style Of John Coltrane*, William Shadrack Cole. *Trane 'N' Me*, Andrew Nathaniel White. *About John Coltrane*, Tim Gelatt (ed.). *John Coltrane, Discography*, Brian Davis. *The Artistry Of John Coltrane*, John Coltrane. *Chasin' The Trane*, J.C. Thomas. *Coltrane*, Cuthbert Ormond Simpkins. *As Serious As Your Life: John Coltrane And Beyond*, Valerie Wilmer. *John Coltrane*, Brian Priestley. *John Coltrane*, Bill Cole. *Ascension: John Coltrane And His Quest*, Eric Nisenson. *John Coltrane: A Sound Supreme*, John Selfridge.

COLYER, KEN

b. 18 April 1928, Great Yarmouth, Norfolk, England, d. 8 March 1988, France. Of all the musicians involved in the British Revivalist movement of the late 40s and early 50s, trumpeter Colyer was the only one to achieve the status of a jazz legend. He achieved this through a gritty determination to adhere to what he believed to be the true spirit of jazz. Colyer first demonstrated his obsession with the great traditions of New Orleans jazz in the early 50s. He joined the Merchant Navy in order to visit the USA, where he promptly jumped ship and headed for the Crescent City. In New Orleans he sat in with local grandmasters, including George Lewis and Emile Barnes, before the authorities caught up with him and he was deported. Before his visit to the USA, Colyer had already worked with the Crane River Jazz Band and the Christie Brothers Stompers, but his American exploits had made him a big name in the UK and he was invited to front the co-operative band formed a little earlier by Chris Barber and Monty Sunshine. Although this unit was working regularly and building a reputation, Barber and Sunshine felt that Colyer's fame would be an asset. For a while this assumption proved correct, but personality clashes developed, particularly when Colyer appeared to lose sight of the fact that the band he was leading was not his own but was a collective venture. In 1954 Barber took over the reins and Colyer formed his own band, which, with various personnel changes, he continued to lead for the next 30 years. Among the many musicians who worked under Colyer's leadership were Acker Bilk, Diz Disley, Ian Wheeler and Sammy Rimington. Conceding that his technique was limited, Colyer overcame any deficiencies in style through an unflinching determination not to be swayed by changing public tastes or commercial considerations, although he did play guitar and sing in a skiffle group in the mid-50s. In 1957 he returned to the USA and joined the George Lewis band, arranging their trips to Europe. His last significant work was as part of the touring jazz show *New Orleans Mardi Gras*. Colyer defeated cancer, and the temporary retirement this necessitated, playing on into the 80s. A year after he died, a commemorative blue plaque was placed on the wall of the 100 Club in London, and many of his former colleagues took part in a concert organized by the Ken Colyer Trust. A hugely important figure in British jazz.

● ALBUMS: *Ken Colyer In New Orleans* (Vogue 1954) ★★★★, *New Orleans To London* (Decca 1954) ★★★★, *In The Beginning ...* (1954) ★★★★, *Back To The Delta* (Decca 1954) ★★★★, *Ken Colyer's Jazzmen* (Tempo 1956) ★★★, *Club Session With Colyer* (Decca 1957) ★★★, *A Very Good Year* (1957) ★★★, *In Gloryland* (Decca 1958) ★★★, *In Hamburg* (Decca 1959) ★★★, *Plays Standards* (Decca 1959) ★★★, *Sensation* (Lake 1960) ★★★, *This Is Jazz* (Columbia 1960) ★★★, *This Is Jazz Volume 2* (Columbia 1961) ★★★, *When I Leave The World Behind* (Lake 1963) ★★★, *Out Of Nowhere* (1965) ★★★, *Wandering* (KC 1965) ★★★, *Live At The Dancing Slipper* (1969) ★★★, *Ken Colyer And His Handpicked Jazzmen* (1972) ★★★, *Watch That Dirty Tone Of Yours* (Joy 1974) ★★★, *Spirituals, Volumes 1 & 2* (Joy 1974) ★★★, *Swinging And Singing* (1975) ★★★, *Painting The Clouds With Sunshine* (Black Lion 1979) ★★★, *Darkness On The Delta* (Black Lion 1979) ★★★, *Ken Colyer With John Petters' New Orleans Allstars* (1985) ★★★, with Max Collie, Cy Laurie *New Orleans Mardi Gras* (1985) ★★★, *Too Busy* (CMJ 1985) ★★★, with Acker Bilk *It Looks Like A Big Time Tonight* (Stomp 1988) ★★★.

● COMPILATIONS: *The Decca Years, Volume 1 (1955-59)* (Lake 1985) ★★★★, *The Decca Years, Volume 2 (1955-59)* (Lake 1986) ★★★★, *The Decca Years, Volume 3 (1955-59)* (Lake 1987) ★★★★, *The Decca Years, Volume 4 (Skiffle Sessions 1954-57)* (Lake 1987) ★★★★, *The Decca Years, Volume 5 (Lonesome Road)* (Lake 1988) ★★★★, *The Decca Years, Volume 6 (In The Beginning)* (Lake 1988) ★★★★, *The Guv'nor (1959-61)* (Polydor 1989) ★★★★.

● FURTHER READING: *When Dreams Are In The Dust (The Path Of A Jazzman)*, Ken Colyer.

COMDEN, BETTY

b. 3 May 1915, New York City, New York, USA. After graduating with a degree in science, Betty Comden strove to find work as an actress. During this period, the late 30s, she met Adolph Green (b. 2 December 1915, New York, USA), who was also seeking work in the theatre. Unsuccessful in their attempts to find acting jobs, Comden and Green formed their own troupe, together with another struggling actress, Judy Holliday. In the absence of suitable material, Comden and Green began creating their own and discovered an ability to write librettos and lyrics. At first their success was only limited, but in the early 40s they were invited by a mutual friend, Leonard Bernstein, to work on the book and lyrics of a musical he planned to adapt from his ballet score *Fancy Free*. The show, in which Comden and Green also appeared, was retitled *On The Town* (1944), and became a huge success; Comden and Green never looked back. *On The Town* was followed by *Billion Dollar Baby* (1945, music by Morton Gould) and an assignment in Hollywood for the musical films *Good News* (1947), *The Barkleys Of Broadway* (1949), *On The Town* and *Take Me Out To The Ball Game* (both 1949). In the 50s and 60s Comden and Green were back on Broadway, collaborating with Bernstein again on *Wonderful Town* (1953), and with Jule Styne on *Two On The Aisle*, *Peter Pan*, *Say, Darling*, *Do Re Mi*, *Subways Are For Sleeping*, *Fade Out-Fade In*, *Halleluja, Baby!*, and most notably, *Bells Are Ringing* (1956), in which the leading role was played by their former associate Judy Holliday.

Among their films were *Singin' In The Rain* (1952), for which they wrote the screenplay, incorporating the songs of Nacio Herb Brown, and *The Band Wagon* (1953), again contributing the screenplay which was peppered with the songs of Arthur Schwartz and Howard Dietz. For *It's Always Fair Weather* (1955) they wrote the screenplay and lyrics (music by André Previn) and later in the 50s and into the 60s wrote screenplays for *Auntie Mame* (1958) and *Bells Are Ringing* (1960), among others. From the late 50s they also performed their own accomplished two-person stage show. After writing the libretto for *Applause* (1970) they continued to make sporadic returns to the musical stage with *Lorelei* (1974), *On The Twentieth Century* (1978), *A Doll's Life* (1982) and *The Will Rogers Follies* (1991).

Among their best-known songs are 'Just In Time', 'Make Someone Happy', 'Lonely Town', 'Some Other Time', 'Never Never Land', 'It's Love', 'Long Before I Knew You', 'Lucky To Be Me', 'New York, New York', 'The Party's Over' and 'The Right Girl For Me'. Regarded as the longest-running creative partnership in theatre history, Comden and Green have gained several Tony Awards, a Grammy and Kennedy Center Awards. They have also been elected to the Songwriters' Hall Of Fame and the Theatre Hall Of Fame. Albums celebrating their work have been released by Sally Mayes and Blossom Dearie, among others. In 1993, 40 years after they wrote one of their most famous numbers, 'Ohio', for *On The Town*, the Governor of that US State threw an opulent anniversary party, *The Show Must Go On: Fifty Years Of Comden And Green*, in their honour. As well as seeing their musical *On The Town* return to Broadway, they continued to receive tributes and awards throughout the 90s, including the ASCAP Richard Rodgers Lifetime Achievement Award and the Stage Directors And Choreographers President's Award for Outstanding Contribution To The

Theatre. A revue of their songs, *Make Someone Happy*, opened the Bay City season in 1997, and a year later they wrote a new book and English dialogue for the Metropolitan Opera's revival of Johann Strauss' *Die Fledermaus*. In 1999, a two-night Carnegie Hall tribute to Comden and Green featured an all-star line-up which included Faith Prince, Lilias White, Elaine Stritch, and Brian Stokes Mitchell (*Ragtime*).
● ALBUMS: *A Party With Betty Comden And Adolph Green* (Broadway Angel 1993) ★★★★, *Comden And Green Perform Their Own Songs* 1955 recordings (DRG 1998) ★★★★.
● FURTHER READING: *Betty Comden And Adolph Green: A Bio-Bibliography*, Alice M. Robinson. *Off Stage*, Betty Comden. *The New York Musicals Of Comden & Green*, Mike Nichols and Aldolph Green.

COME DANCE WITH ME – FRANK SINATRA
On Frank Sinatra's great records of the 50s and early 60s equal billing must be given to the conductors/arrangers. Sinatra was able to let loose and blossom with the confidence that the great songs he had chosen, together with his voice, would be enhanced by the orchestration. This album is another in a series of quite brilliant arrangements, this time by Billy May, giving new life to Johnny Mercer's 'Something's Gotta Give', Irving Berlin's 'Cheek To Cheek' and George Weiss's 'Too Close For Comfort'. In keeping with other Sinatra reissues the CD has four bonus tracks including two duets with Keely Smith.
● Tracks: Come Dance With Me; Something's Gotta Give; Just In Time; Dancing In The Dark; Too Close For Comfort; I Could Have Danced All Night; Saturday Night (Is The Loneliest Night Of The Week); Day In, Day Out; Cheek To Cheek; Baubles, Bangles And Beads; Song Is You; Last Dance; It All Depends On You; Nothing In Common; Same Old Song And Dance; How Are Ya' Fixed For Love.
● First released 1959
● UK peak chart position: 2
● USA peak chart position: 2

COME FLY WITH ME – FRANK SINATRA
A mildly conceptual album that has lasted, with a choice of songs that takes the listener around the world in 45 minutes. Some of Frank Sinatra's finest moments are on this album, notably with Sammy Cahn and Jimmy Van Heusen's uplifting 'Come Fly With Me' and 'It's Nice To Go Trav'ling'. This was Sinatra's first album arranged and conducted by Billy May, a relationship that produced further classic orchestrations. Once again the CD purchaser will greatly benefit from three bonus tracks with Nelson Riddle in charge; 'Chicago', 'South Of The Border' and 'I Love Paris'. Happy-go-lucky fare that we all need an infusion of from time to time.
● Tracks: Come Fly With Me; Around The World; Isle Of Capri; Moonlight In Vermont; Autumn In New York; On The Road To Mandalay; Let's Get Away From It All; April In Paris; London By Night; Brazil; Blue Hawaii; It's Nice To Go Trav'ling.
● First released 1958
● UK peak chart position: 2
● USA peak chart position: 1

COMO, PERRY
b. Pierino Como, 18 May 1912, Canonsburg, Pennsylvania, USA, d. 12 May 2001, Jupiter Inlet Beach Colony, Florida, USA. Como was an accomplished popular singer with a warm baritone voice, whose repertoire included ballads, novelty numbers and singalongs. Born into a large Italian-American family in Canonsburg, he left his home-town barber shop in 1933 and toured with the local band of Freddie Carlone. His big break came in 1936 when he joined trombonist Ted Weems' band and featured on their *Beat The Band* radio show. He left the band when it broke up in 1942, and the following year signed for RCA Records. After minor hits with 'Long Ago And Far Away', 'I'm Gonna Love That Gal' and 'If I Loved You', he topped the US charts in 1945 with "Till The End Of Time', based on Chopin's 'Polonaise In A-Flat Major'.
A comparatively late starter in hit parade terms, he made up for lost time in the late 40s with a string of US hits including 'Did You Ever Get That Feeling In The Moonlight?', '(A Hubba-Hubba-Hubba) Dig You Later', 'I'm Always Chasing Rainbows' (adapted from another Chopin theme), 'You Won't Be Satisfied (Until You Break My Heart)', 'Prisoner Of Love' (number 1), 'All Through The Day', 'They Say It's Wonderful', 'Surrender' (number 1), 'Chi-Baba, Chi-Baba, (My Baby Go To Sleep)' (number 1), 'When You Were Sweet Sixteen', 'I Wonder Who's Kissing Her Now' (a 1939 recording when Como was with Ted Weems), 'Because' (a 1902 song, originally sung by Enrico Caruso), 'Far Away Places', 'Forever And Ever', 'A-You're Adorable' (a number 1, with the Fontane Sisters), 'Some Enchanted Evening' (number 1) and 'A Dreamer's Holiday'. He also featured regularly on radio programmes, such as his own *Supper Club* series, and made four films, *Something for The Boys* (1944), loosely based on the Cole Porter Broadway show, *Doll Face* (1945), *If I'm Lucky* (1946), and the star-studded Richard Rodgers/Lorenz Hart biopic, *Words And Music* (1948).
The 50s were even more fruitful years for Como, mainly because of the apparent ease with which he adapted to television. His easy, relaxed singing style coupled with an engaging sense of humour proved ideal for the relatively new medium. He had made his television debut in 1948 on NBC's *The Chesterfield Supper Club*, and two years later began his own show with CBS, *The Perry Como Show*. Later retitled *Perry Como's Kraft Music Hall*, his new weekly show ran on NBC from 1955-63 and is still regarded as the best television show of its kind, and featured his theme song 'Sing Along With Me'. It also inspired the albums *We Get Letters* and *Saturday Night With Mr. C*. Andy Williams' successful television show owed much to the Como style. In the early 50s, despite the onset of rock 'n' roll, the hits continued with 'Hoop-Dee-Doo' (number 1) and 'You're Just In Love' (both with the Fontane Sisters), 'Patricia', 'A Bushel And

A Peck', 'If', 'Maybe' (with Eddie Fisher), 'Don't Let The Stars Get In Your Eyes' (number 1 in the USA and UK), 'Wild Horses' (adapted From Robert Schumann's 'Wild Horseman'), 'Say You're Mine Again', 'No Other Love' (based on the theme from the 1954 documentary *Victory At Sea*), 'You Alone', 'Wanted' (number 1) and 'Papa Loves Mambo'. During the latter half of the 50s, with the advantage of the television showcase, he still registered strongly in the USA with 'Ko Ko Mo (I Love You So)', 'Tina Marie', 'Hot Diggity (Dog Ziggity Boom)' (number 1), 'Juke Box Baby', 'More', 'Glendora', 'Round And Round' (number 1), 'Catch A Falling Star' (number 1), 'Magic Moments' (an early Burt Bacharach and Hal David song), and 'Kewpie Doll'. He also made the UK Top 10 several times, with 'Magic Moments' topping the charts in 1958.

Semi-retired during the 60s, he emerged in 1970 to play 'live' for the first time for over 20 years, an event celebrated by the album *In Person At The International Hotel Las Vegas*. He then, somewhat surprisingly, embarked on a series of world tours, and had his first hit singles for over a decade with the Mexican ballad 'It's Impossible', composed by Armando Manzanero, with a new lyric by Sid Wayne, 'And I Love You So' and 'For The Good Times'. At this time Como's record sales were estimated at over 60 million, including 20 gold discs. To many, Como's laid-back approach and many popular television specials, particularly at Christmas, bordered on parody. In the late 80s he performed occasionally in Las Vegas, and received generous media tributes in 1992 on the occasion of his 80th birthday.

After a spell of ill health Como died in May 2001 having suffered from Alzheimer's disease. His immense commercial success was undeniable, and is perhaps one of the reasons when male song stylists are discussed, that he is too often underrated. It is hoped that he will be remembered in the history of popular music, not only for his warming voice but for his incredibly relaxed aura, both in front of the television camera and in the company of a live audience. It is unlikely that the great Perry Como ever broke into a sweat.

● ALBUMS: *Perry Como Sings Merry Christmas Music* 10-inch album (RCA Victor 1951) ★★★, *TV Favorites* 10-inch album (RCA Victor 1952) ★★★, *A Sentimental Date With Perry Como* 10-inch album (RCA Victor 1952) ★★★, *Supper Club Favorites* 10-inch album (RCA Victor 1952) ★★★, *Hits From Broadway Shows* 10-inch album (RCA Victor 1953) ★★★, *Around The Christmas Tree* 10-inch album (RCA Victor 1953) ★★★, *I Believe* 10-inch album (RCA Victor 1953) ★★★, *So Smooth* (RCA Victor 1955) ★★★, *We Get Letters* (RCA Victor 1957) ★★★, *Dream Along With Me* (RCA Camden 1957) ★★★, *Saturday Night With Mr. C.* (US) *Dear Perry* (UK) (RCA Victor 1958) ★★★, *When You Come To The End Of The Day* (RCA Victor 1958) ★★★, *Como Swings* (RCA Victor 1959) ★★★, *Season's Greetings From Perry Como* (RCA Victor 1959) ★★★, *For The Young At Heart* (RCA Victor 1961) ★★★, *Sing To Me Mr. C.* (RCA Victor 1961) ★★★,

By Request (RCA Victor 1962) ★★★, *The Best Of Irving Berlin's Songs From Mr. President* (RCA Victor 1962) ★★★, *The Songs I Love* (RCA Victor 1963) ★★★, *The Scene Changes* (RCA Victor 1965) ★★, *Lightly Latin* (RCA Victor 1966) ★★, *In Italy* (RCA Victor 1966) ★★★, *The Perry Como Christmas Album* (RCA Victor 1968) ★★★, *Look To Your Heart* (RCA Victor 1968) ★★★, *Seattle* (RCA Victor 1969) ★★★, *In Person At The International Hotel Las Vegas* (RCA Victor 1970) ★★★, *It's Impossible* (RCA Victor 1970) ★★★, *I Think Of You* (RCA Victor 1971) ★★★, *And I Love You So* (RCA Victor 1973) ★★★, *Perry* (RCA Victor 1974) ★★★, *Just Out Of Reach* (RCA Victor 1975) ★★, *The Best Of British* (RCA 1977) ★★★, *Where You're Concerned* (RCA Victor 1978) ★★★, *Perry Como* (RCA Victor 1980) ★★★, *Live On Tour* (RCA Victor 1981) ★★, *So It Goes* (RCA Victor 1983) ★★, *Today* (RCA Victor 1987) ★★★, *Take It Easy* (RCA Victor 1990) ★★★, *The Perry Como Shows 1943: Volume 1* (Intermusic 1995) ★★★, *The Perry Como Shows 1943: Volume 2* (Intermusic 1995) ★★★, *The Perry Como Shows 1943: Volume 3* (Intermusic 1995) ★★★.

● COMPILATIONS: *Evergreens By Perry Como* 10-inch album (HMV 1952) ★★★, *Como's Golden Records* 10-inch album (RCA Victor 1955) ★★★★, *I Believe* (RCA Victor 1956) ★★★, *Relaxing With Perry Como* (RCA Victor 1956) ★★★, *A Sentimental Date With Perry Como* (RCA Victor 1956) ★★★, *Sings Hits From Broadway Shows* (RCA Victor 1956) ★★★, *Sings Merry Christmas Music* (RCA Victor 1956) ★★★, *Dream Along With Me* (RCA Camden 1957) ★★★, *Sings Just For You* (RCA Camden 1958) ★★★, *Wednesday Night Music Hall* (RCA Camden 1959) ★★★, *Dreamer's Holiday* (RCA Camden 1960) ★★★, *Make Someone Happy* (RCA Camden 1962) ★★★, *An Evening With Perry Como* (RCA Camden 1963) ★★★, *Perry At His Best* (RCA Victor 1963) ★★★★, *Love Makes The World Go 'Round* (RCA Camden 1964) ★★★, *Somebody Loves Me* (RCA Camden 1965) ★★★, *No Other Love* (RCA Camden 1966) ★★★, *Hello Young Lovers* (RCA Camden 1967) ★★★, *You Are Never Far Away* (RCA Camden 1968) ★★★, *Home For The Holidays* (RCA 1968) ★★★★, *The Lord's Prayer* (RCA Camden 1969) ★★★, *Easy Listening* (RCA Camden 1970) ★★★, *This Is Perry Como* (RCA Victor 1970) ★★★★, *Door Of Dreams* (RCA Camden 1971) ★★★, *Here Is Perry Como* (RCA 1971) ★★★, *The Shadow Of Your Smile* (RCA Camden 1972) ★★★, *This Is Perry Como, Volume 2* (RCA Victor 1972) ★★★, *Dream On Little Dreamer* (RCA Camden 1973) ★★★, *The Sweetest Sounds* (RCA Camden 1974) ★★★, *Pure Gold* (RCA Victor 1975) ★★★, *Perry Como: 40 Greatest* (K-Tel 1975) ★★★★, *Memories Are Made Of Hits* (RCA 1975) ★★★★, *The First Thirty Years* 4-LP box set (RCA 1975) ★★★, *The Best Of Perry Como* 7-LP set (Reader's Digest 1975) ★★★, *A Legendary Performer* (RCA 1976) ★★★★, *By Special Request* (Sylvania/BMG 1976) ★★★, *Season's Greetings* (RCA Victor 1976) ★★★, *Especially For You* (RCA Victor 1977) ★★★, *Perry Como* (K-Tel 1977) ★★★, *The Perry Como Christmas Collection* (Pickwick 1979) ★★★, *I Wish It Could Be Christmas Forever*

(RCA Victor 1982) ★★★, *40 Golden Years* limited edition (RCA Victor 1983) ★★★★, *Love Moods* (Pair 1983) ★★★, *16 Million Hits* (RCA Germany 1983) ★★★★, *For The Good Times: 20 Greatest Love Songs* (Telstar 1984) ★★★, with the Ted Weems Orchestra *The Young Perry Como (1936-41)* (MCA 1984) ★★, *Perry Como* (Time-Life 1985) ★★★, *The Best Of Times* (RCA 1986) ★★★, *Jukebox Baby* (Bear Family 1988) ★★★, *Collection* (Castle 1988) ★★★★, *The Living Legend* (RCA 1992) ★★★, *Yesterday & Today: A Celebration In Song* 3-CD set (RCA 1993) ★★★★, *A Portrait Of Perry Como* (MCI 1999) ★★★.
● VIDEOS: *The Best Of Perry Como* (Warner Music Video 1991), *The Best Of Perry Como Volume 2* (Warner Music Video 1992), *Perry Como's Christmas Concert* (Teal 1994), *Perry Como's Christmas Classics* (Haber Video 1996).
● FILMS: *Something For The Boys* (1944), *Doll Face* aka *Come Back To Me* (1945), *If I'm Lucky* (1946), *Words And Music* (1948).

COMPAGNONS DE LA CHANSON

This French male vocal group were Edith Piaf's original accompanists, and featured on one of her best-known numbers, 'Les Trois Cloches', composed by Jean Villard in 1945. Later, they recorded it under their own name, and when an English lyric by Bert Reisfeld was added in 1948, the song was retitled 'The Three Bells' ('The Jimmy Brown Song)'. Their re-recorded Anglicized version reached the UK chart in 1959. Apparently, it was their version, sung on the *Ed Sullivan Show* in 1951, that inspired US group the Browns to record it, thereby giving themselves a number 1 hit. Composer Jean Villard used the same melody in 1945 for 'While The Angelus Was Ringing', which had a lyric by the American songwriter Dick Manning.

CONWAY, RUSS

b. Trevor Herbert Stanford, 2 September 1925, Bristol, Avon, England, d. 15 November 2000, Eastbourne, East Sussex, England. Conway not only played the piano as a young boy, but won a scholarship to join the choir at the Bristol Cathedral School. He was conscripted into the Royal Navy in 1942 and, during a varied career, was awarded the DSM (Distinguished Service Medal) for service during campaigns in the Mediterranean and Aegean sea and lost part of a finger while using a bread slicer. A spell in the post-war Merchant Navy was finally ended by a recurrent stomach ulcer, after which Conway began playing piano in nightclubs. His big break came when he started working as rehearsal pianist for choreographer Irving Davies and audition pianist for Columbia Records (UK) record producer Norman Newell. He later served as accompanist for star singers such as Dennis Lotis, Gracie Fields and Joan Regan. Signed to Columbia, his first hit, 'Party Pops', in 1957, was an instrumental medley of standard songs.
It was the first of 20 UK chart entries featuring his catchy piano-playing through to 1963, including two number 1 singles, 'Side Saddle' and 'Roulette',

and Top 10 entries 'China Tea', 'Snowcoach', 'More And More Party Pops', and 'Toy Balloons' all of which were his own compositions. He headlined several times at the London Palladium, had his own television show (*Russ Conway And A Few Friends*) and regularly guested on others, including the Billy Cotton Band Show on BBC television where his cross-talk and vocal duets with the host revealed a genuine flair for comedy and an acceptable light baritone voice.
During the 60s his career was marred by ill health, a nervous breakdown while on stage and a mild stroke which prevented him from working during 1968-1971. In subsequent decades, still an anachronism, his combination of lively tunes, light classical themes and shy smile consistently proved a big draw abroad and in the UK, where he promoted his own nostalgia package shows and charity concerts. After fighting stomach cancer for five years, in June 1994 Conway was told by doctors that he was in good health. Two years earlier he had been awarded the Lord Mayor of Bristol's Medal for his contributions to popular music and the cancer fund he set up after learning that he had the disease. Despite trapping his thumb in the door of his Rolls Royce car in 1995, Conway remained active until finally succumbing to cancer in November 2000.
● ALBUMS: *Pack Up Your Troubles* (Columbia 1958) ★★★, *Songs To Sing In Your Bath* (Columbia 1958) ★★★, *Family Favourites* (Columbia 1959) ★★★, *Time To Celebrate* (Columbia 1959) ★★★, *My Concerto For You* (Columbia 1960) ★★★, *Party Time* (Columbia 1960) ★★★, *At The Theatre* (Columbia 1961) ★★★, *At The Cinema* (Columbia 1961) ★★★, *Happy Days* (Columbia 1961) ★★★, *Concerto For Dreamers* (Columbia 1962) ★★★, *Russ Conway's Trad Party* (Columbia 1962) ★★★, *Something For Mum* (Columbia 1963) ★★★, *Enjoy Yourself* (Columbia 1964) ★★★, *Concerto For Lovers* (Columbia 1964) ★★★, *Once More It's Party Time* (Columbia 1965) ★★★, *Pop-A-Conway* (Columbia 1966) ★★★, *Concerto For Memories* (Columbia 1966) ★★★, *Russ Hour* (Columbia 1966) ★★★, *New Side Of Russ Conway* (Chapter 1 1971) ★★★, *The One And Only* (MFP 1979) ★★★, *Always You And Me* (MFP 1981) ★★★, *A Long Time Ago* (Churchill 1986) ★★★.
● COMPILATIONS: *Songs From Stage And Screen* (Golden Hour 1974) ★★★, *The Very Best Of Russ Conway* (EMI 1976) ★★★★, *24 Piano Greats* (Ronco 1977) ★★★, *The Two Sides Of Russ Conway* (Platinum 1986) ★★★, *Greatest Hits* (Hour Of Pleasure 1986) ★★★★, *The Magic Piano Of Russ Conway* (Ditto 1988) ★★★, *The EMI Years: The Best Of Russ Conway* (EMI 1989) ★★★★, *The EP Collection* (See For Miles 1991) ★★★, *A Walk In The Black Forest: The Best Of Russ Conway* (Castle Pulse 1999) ★★★.
● FILMS: *It's All Happening* (1963).

CORNELL, DON

b. 1924, New York City, New York, USA. During the late 30s Cornell sang and played guitar with several bands, including Lennie Hayton, Red Nichols and Mickey Alpert, before joining Sammy

Kaye, mainly as a guitar player, in 1942. He stayed with Kaye until 1950, with a break for military service, and sang on several of the band's hits, including 'I Left My Heart At The Stage Door Canteen', 'Tell Me A Story' and 'It Isn't Fair' (a million-seller), all for RCA-Victor Records. His first solo success, 'I Need You So', was also on that label, but his move to Coral Records in 1951 produced several winners including 'I'll Walk Alone', 'I', (the shortest song title ever charted), 'Heart Of My Heart', accompanied by Alan Dale and ex-Glenn Miller vocalist Johnny Desmond, and two more gold discs with 'I'm Yours' and 'Hold My Hand'. The latter song was featured in the 1954 movie *Susan Slept Here*, starring Dick Powell and Debbie Reynolds, and was nominated for an Academy Award, only to be beaten by 'Three Coins In The Fountain'. Later in the 50s Cornell had several US Top 30 entries including 'Stranger In Paradise', 'Most Of All', 'The Bible Tells Me So', 'Love Is A Many-Splendored Thing' and 'Young Abe Lincoln'. After that the hits dried up, but Cornell's seemingly effortless high baritone voice remained in demand for club and theatre work.

● ALBUMS: *Don Cornell For You* (Vogue Coral 1954) ★★★, *Let's Get Lost* (Coral 1956) ★★★, *For Teenagers Only!* (Coral 1957) ★★★, *Don Cornell* (1959) ★★, *Don Cornell Sings Love Songs* (Signature 1962) ★★, *I Wish You Love* (1966) ★★★.

● COMPILATIONS: *Don Cornell's Great Hits* (Dot 1959) ★★★.

COSTA, DON

b. 10 June 1925, Boston, Massachusetts, USA, d. 19 January 1983, New York, USA. The youngest of five children, Costa taught himself to play the guitar by the age of eight, and at 15 was a member of the CBS radio orchestra in Boston. In his spare time he loved to dance the jitterbug. After starting as a musical arranger in radio in the 40s, Costa moved into the recording business as an A&R executive, working with new and established artists, and choosing their material. In 1957, while at ABC-Paramount, he launched Paul Anka's career, and later worked with a variety of artists including Little Anthony, Dean Martin, Frankie Avalon, Barbra Streisand, Steve Lawrence and the Osmonds. In the 60s he formed DCP (Don Costa Productions) and collaborated with Frank Sinatra as producer, arranger and conductor on several albums including *Sinatra & Strings*, *My Way* and *Cycles*. In 1973, with Gordon Jenkins, Costa conducted Sinatra's television special *Ol' Blue Eyes Is Back*. He is reputed to have conducted and arranged over 200 hit records in his career, working with many kinds of music including C&W, jazz, rock, disco and film music. In 1960 he entered the US Top 30 singles chart with 'Theme From *The Unforgiven* (The Need For Love)' and the Academy Award-winning song 'Never On Sunday'. His own film scores include *Rough Night In Jericho* (1967), *Madigan* (1968) and *The Impossible Years* (1968). Among his many successful albums were *101 Strings Play Million Seller Hits*, *Theme From The Misfits*, *I'll Walk The Line* and *Never On Sunday*. One of his last albums,

Out Here On My Own, was recorded with his daughter Nikka, and they were also working on another at the time of his death.

● ALBUMS: *Don Costa Conducts His 15 Hits* (ABC-Paramount 1961) ★★★.

CRAYTON, PEE WEE

b. Connie Curtis Crayton, 18 December 1914, Liberty Hill, Texas, USA, d. 25 June 1985, Los Angeles, California, USA. After learning to play ukulele and banjo as a child, Crayton took up the guitar in his mid-twenties. He was inspired by Charlie Christian and T-Bone Walker, the latter of whom taught Crayton the basics of electric guitar playing. His tutelage was completed at the side of another legendary guitarist, John Collins, and he began playing with local bands before graduating to Ivory Joe Hunter's bay area band in 1946. After making his recording debut with Hunter for Pacific Records, he recorded his first efforts under his own name and these were later issued on 4 Star Records after his success with Modern Records. In 1947 Crayton formed a trio, and after an obscure release on the tiny Gru-V-Tone label, began recording for Modern between 1948 and 1951, finding success with 'Blues After Hours', 'Texas Hop', and, his biggest hit 'I Love You So'. Soon after he switched to Aladdin and Recorded In Hollywood for one-off sessions. Imperial Records took Crayton to New Orleans in 1954-55 to record with Dave Bartholomew's band, and the following year he moved to Detroit to record for Fox and Vee Jay Records in nearby Chicago. During this period he was admired by and became the inspiration for young local guitarist Kenny Burrell. Moving back to Los Angeles in 1960, he recorded an unissued session for Kent Records (Modern) and subsequently recorded single sessions for the Jamie/Guyden, Smash and Edco labels, before leaving the music business in 1964 for five years, after recording the obscure *Sunset Blues Band* for Liberty's Sunset subsidiary. Rediscovered in the blues boom of the late 60s, he recommenced his recording career with an unissued session for Blue Horizon Records, a well-received album for Vanguard entitled *Things I Used To Do*, and an explosive appearance with Johnny Otis' band at the 1970 *Monterey Festival*. The five years or so before his death coincided with another resurgence of interest in blues and R&B, and this saw Crayton reaching an even wider audience with albums recorded for his friend Otis, solo albums, and albums with Big Joe Turner on Pablo, new blues projects for the Murray Brothers, through Ace Records initiating a large-scale reissue programme of his Modern Records classics from the late 40s/early 50s.

● ALBUMS: *Pee Wee Crayton* (Crown 1959) ★★★★, *After Hours* (1960) ★★★, *Sunset Blues Band* (Sunset 1965) ★★★, *Things I Used To Do* (Vanguard 1970) ★★★, *Monterey Festival* (1970) ★★★★, *Great Rhythm & Blues* (Blues Spectrum 1973) ★★★, *Blues Guitar Genius* (1980) ★★★, *Great R&B Oldies* (1982) ★★★, with Big Joe Turner *Every Day I Have The Blues* (1982) ★★★★, *Peace Of Mind* (1982) ★★★, *Rocking Down Central*

Avenue (1982) ★★★, *Make Room For Pee Wee* (Murray Brothers 1983) ★★, *Early Hours* (Murray Brothers 1987) ★★, *Blues Before Dawn* (1986) ★★★, *Memorial Album* (1986) ★★★, *After Hours Boogie* (1988) ★★★, *Blues After Dark* (1988) ★★★★, *Blues After Hours* (1988) ★★★.
● COMPILATIONS: *The Modern Legacy Volume 1* (Ace 1996) ★★★★, *The Complete Aladdin And Imperial Recordings* (Capitol 1996) ★★★★, *Early Hour Blues* (Blind Pig 1999) ★★★★.

CRESTS

Formed in New York City, USA, in 1956, the Crests soon became one of the most successful of the 'integrated' doo-wop groups of the period, after being discovered by Al Browne. Headed by the lead tenor of Johnny Mastro (b. Johnny Mastrangelo, 7 May 1930, USA), the rest of the band comprised Harold Torres, Talmadge Gough, J.T. Carter and Patricia Van Dross. By 1957 they were recording for Joyce Records and achieved their first minor pop hit with 'Sweetest One'. Moving to the new Coed label, the Crests (without Van Dross) recorded their signature tune and one of doo-wop's enduring classics, '16 Candles', a heartfelt and beautifully orchestrated ballad. It became a national pop hit at number 2 in the *Billboard* charts, paving the way for further R&B and pop successes such as 'Six Nights A Week', 'The Angels Listened In' and 'Step By Step'. At this time the band were almost permanently on the road. Following 'Trouble In Paradise' in 1960, the band's final two chart singles would be credited to The Crests featuring Johnny Mastro. However, this was evidently not enough to satisfy their label, Coed, whose priority now was to launch the singer as a solo artist. Mastro's decision to go solo in 1960 (subsequently calling himself Johnny Maestro) weakened the band, although they did continue with James Ancrum in his stead. Their former vocalist made the charts with 'Model Girl', still for Coed, in the following year, before re-emerging as leader of Brooklyn Bridge, an 11-piece doo-wop group who are best remembered for their 1968 single 'The Worst That Could Happen'. After 'Little Miracles' failed to break the *Billboard* Top 100 (the first such failure for the Crests in 10 singles), Gough moved to Detroit and a job with General Motors. He was replaced by Gary Lewis. However, the Crests were now entangled in legal disputes with Coed over the ownership of their name. They eventually moved to Selma, although the songs made available to the group were now of significantly inferior quality, including 'You Blew Out The Candles', a blatant attempt to revisit the success of '16 Candles'. The band continued to tour throughout the 60s, though Torres had left to become a jeweller, leaving a core of Carter, Lewis and Ancrum. Later line-ups were organized by Carter for lounge sessions (although there are no recordings from this period), and in June 1987 the original line-up (minus Van Dross) was re-formed for a show in Peepskill, New York.
● COMPILATIONS: *The Best Of The Crests* (Coed 1960) ★★★★, *Crests Sing All Biggies* (Coed 1985) ★★★, *16 Fabulous Hits* (Coed 1988) ★★★, *Best Of The Crests* (Rhino 1990) ★★★★, *Best Of The Rest* (Coed 1991) ★★★.

CREW-CUTS

Formed in Toronto, Ontario, Canada, in 1952, the Crew-Cuts were a white vocal quartet that had success in the early 50s by covering black R&B songs. Their version of 'Sh-Boom', originally a number 2 R&B hit for the Chords in 1954, became a number 1 pop hit for the Crew-Cuts, staying in that position for nine weeks and helping to usher in the rock 'n' roll era. The group was comprised of Rudi Maugeri (b. 27 January 1931; baritone), Pat Barrett (b. 15 September 1931; tenor), John Perkins (b. 28 August 1931; lead) and his brother Ray Perkins (b. 28 November 1932; bass), all born in Toronto. The group met at Toronto's Cathedral School, where they all sang in the choir, and decided to form a barber shop-style group. Initially called the Canadaires, the group received its first break in Cleveland, Ohio, USA, where they appeared on Gene Carroll's television programme. After that show they were introduced to the influential local disc jockey Bill Randle, who suggested the name change (after a popular short-cropped hairstyle). Randle introduced the group to Mercury Records, who signed them. Their first recording, an original composition called 'Crazy 'Bout Ya Baby', made the Top 10 in the US charts. Mercury suggested covering 'Sh-Boom' and its massive success led to further cover versions of R&B records by the group, including the Penguins' 'Earth Angel', Nappy Brown's 'Don't Be Angry' and the Nutmegs' 'Story Untold'. The success of the Crew-Cuts and other white cover artists helped pave the way for recognition and acceptance of the black originators. In addition to 'Sh-Boom', other Top 10 placings were 'Earth Angel' (1955), 'Ko Ko Mo (I Love You So)' (1955) and 'Gum Drop' (1955). The Crew-Cuts placed 14 singles in the charts throughout 1957, moving to RCA Records in 1958; they disbanded in 1963.
● ALBUMS: *The Crew-Cuts On The Campus* (Mercury 1954) ★★★, *The Crew-Cuts Go Longhair* (Mercury 1956) ★★★, *Crew-Cut Capers* (Mercury 1957) ★★★, *Music Ala Carte* (Mercury 1957) ★★★, *Rock And Roll Bash* (Mercury 1957) ★★★, *Surprise Package* (RCA Victor 1958) ★★★, *The Crew-Cuts Sing!* (RCA Victor 1959) ★★★, *You Must Have Been A Beautiful Baby* (RCA Victor 1960) ★★★, *The Crew Cuts Sing Out!* (RCA Victor 1960) ★★★, *The Crew Cuts Have A Ball And Bowling Tips* (RCA Victor 1960) ★★★, *The Crew Cuts* (RCA Victor 1962) ★★★, *High School Favorites* (RCA Victor 1962) ★★★, *Sing The Masters* (RCA Victor 1962) ★★★, *The Crew-Cuts Sing Folk* (RCA Victor 1963) ★★.

CRICKETS

An R&B vocal group from the Bronx section of New York City, New York, USA, the members were Grover 'Dean' Barlow (lead), Harold Johnson (tenor, guitar), Eugene Stapleton (tenor), Leon Carter (baritone) and Rodney Jackson (bass). The Crickets' only hit was with 'You're Mine' (number

10 R&B) on the MGM Records label in 1953. Their lack of success probably stemmed from their pop sound, a sound that was typical for black groups during the 40s when the Ink Spots, Deep River Boys, and Charioteers held sway. However, during 1953-55, when the Crickets were recording, the more bluesy Clovers, Dominoes, and Five Royales were storming up the charts, so to both listeners and radio programmers the Crickets, with their pretty singing and tasteful but thin arrangements, may have sounded dated. Veteran record man Joe Davis produced their sessions both for the MGM label and for his own Davis label. It is fortunate for posterity that Davis was there, because what may not have been commercial in 1953 sounded fabulous decades later to record collectors, making Crickets records prized collector items. The ballads, such as 'Be Faithful', 'You're Mine' and the jump 'My Little Baby's Shoes', were the most desired and the most rewarding.
● COMPILATIONS: *Dreams & Wishes* (Relic 1992) ★★★.

CROSBY, BING
b. Harry Lillis Crosby, 3 May 1903, Tacoma, Washington, USA, d. 14 October 1977, La Moraleja, Madrid, Spain. One of the most popular vocalists of all time, Crosby picked up his nickname through a childhood love of a strip-cartoon character in a local newspaper. After first singing with a jazz band at high school, he sang at university with a friend, Al Rinker. The duo decided to take a chance on showbusiness success, quit school and called on Rinker's sister, Mildred Bailey, in the hope that she could help them find work. Their hopes were fulfilled and they were soon hired by Paul Whiteman. With the addition of Harry Barris they formed the singing trio the Rhythm Boys, and quickly became one of the major attractions of the Whiteman entertainment package. The popularity of the trio on such recordings as 'Mississippi Mud' and 'I'm Coming Virginia', and an appearance in the film *The King Of Jazz* (1930), gave Crosby an edge when he chose to begin a solo career.
The late 20s saw a great increase in the use of microphones in public auditoriums and the widespread use of more sophisticated microphones in recording studios. This allowed singers to adopt a more confidential singing style, which became known as 'crooning'. Of the new breed of crooners, Crosby was by far the most popular and successful. Although never a jazz singer, Crosby worked with many jazzmen, especially during his stint with Whiteman, when his accompanists included Jimmy and Tommy Dorsey, Joe Venuti and Bix Beiderbecke. This early experience, and a sharp awareness of the rhythmic advances of Louis Armstrong, brought Crosby to the forefront of popular American singers in an era when jazz styles were beginning to reshape popular music. Another contributory factor to his rise was the fact that the new singing style was very well suited to radio, which at the time dominated the entertainment industry. He made numerous film appearances and many

hundreds of records, several of them massive hits. Indeed, sales of his records eclipsed those of any earlier recording artist and by the 40s, these had helped to establish Crosby as the world's biggest singing star. In contrast, his films were usually frothy affairs and he displayed only limited acting ability. However, in the early 40s his film career took an upswing with a series of comedies in which he co-starred with Bob Hope and Dorothy Lamour, while some good light dramatic roles advanced his career still further.
Throughout the 50s Crosby continued to work in radio and television, and made regular concert appearances and still more records. During his radio and television career Crosby often worked with other leading entertainers, among them Al Jolson, Connee Boswell, Dinah Shore, Judy Garland, Armstrong, Hope and his brother, Bob Crosby. By the mid-60s he was content to take things a little easier, although he still made records and personal appearances. Despite his carefree public persona, Crosby was a complex man, difficult to know and understand. As a singer, his seemingly lazy intonation often gave the impression that anyone could sing the way he did, itself a possible factor in his popularity. Nevertheless, his distinctive phrasing was achieved by a good ear, selective taste in building his repertoire, and an acute awareness of what the public wanted. Although his countless fans may well regard it as heresy, Crosby's way with a song was not always what songwriters might have wanted. Indeed, some of Crosby's recordings indicate scant regard for the meanings of lyrics and, unlike Frank Sinatra, for instance, he was never a major interpreter of songs. Despite this casual disregard for the niceties of music and lyrics, many of Crosby's best-known recordings remain definitive by virtue of the highly personal stylistic stamp he placed upon them. Songs such as 'Pennies From Heaven', 'Blue Skies', 'White Christmas', 'The Bells Of St Mary's', 'Moonlight Becomes You', 'Love In Bloom', 'How Deep Is The Ocean', 'The Blue Of The Night' and 'Temptation' became his own. Although Sinatra is the major male song-stylist of American popular music, and also the one who most influenced other singers, every vocalist who followed Crosby owes him a debt for the manner in which his casual, relaxed approach completely altered audience perceptions of how a singer should behave. Towards the end of his life, Crosby's star had waned but he was still capable of attracting sell-out crowds for his occasional public appearances, even though he preferred to spend as much time as he could on the golf course. It was while playing golf in Spain that he collapsed and died.
● ALBUMS: *Merry Christmas* (Decca 1945) ★★★, *Going My Way* film soundtrack (Decca 1945) ★★★, *The Bells Of St. Mary's* film soundtrack (Decca 1946) ★★★, *Don't Fence Me In* (Decca 1946) ★★★, *The Happy Prince* (Decca 1946) ★★★, *Road To Utopia* (Decca 1946) ★★★, *Stephen Foster Songs* (Decca 1946) ★★★, *What So Proudly We Hail* (Decca 1946) ★★★, *Favorite Hawaiian Songs Volumes 1 & 2* (Decca 1946) ★★★, *Blue Skies*

(Decca 1946) ★★★, *St. Patrick's Day* (Decca 1947) ★★★, *Merry Christmas* (Decca 1948) ★★★, *Emperor Waltz* (Decca 1948) ★★★, *St. Valentine's Day* (Decca 1948) ★★★, *Stardust* (Decca 1948) ★★★, *A Connecticut Yankee* (Decca 1949) ★★★, *South Pacific* (Decca 1949) ★★★, *Christmas Greetings* (Decca 1949) ★★★, *Hits From Musical Comedies* (Decca 1949) ★★★, *Jerome Kern Songs* (Decca 1949) ★★★, with Andrews Sisters *Merry Christmas* (Decca 1949) ★★★, *El Bingo* (Decca 1950) ★★★, *Drifting And Dreaming* (Decca 1950) ★★★, *Auld Lang Syne* (Decca 1950) ★★★, *Showboat Selections* (Decca 1950) ★★★, *Cole Porter Songs* (Decca 1950) ★★★, *Songs By Gershwin* (Decca 1950) ★★★, *Holiday Inn* film soundtrack (Decca 1950) ★★★, *Blue Of The Night* (Decca 1950) ★★★, *Cowboy Songs* (Decca 1950) ★★★, *Cowboy Songs, Volume 2* (Decca 1950) ★★★, *Bing Sings Hits* (Decca 1950) ★★★, *Top O' The Morning* (Decca 1950) ★★★★, *Mr. Music* (Decca 1950) ★★★, *The Small One/The Happy Prince* film soundtrack (Decca 1950) ★★★, with Connee Boswell *Bing And Connee* (Decca 1951) ★★★, *Hits From Broadway Shows* (Decca 1951) ★★★, *Go West, Young Man* (Decca 1951) ★★★, *Way Back Home* (Decca 1951) ★★★, *Bing Crosby* (Decca 1951) ★★★, *Bing And The Dixieland Bands* (Decca 1951) ★★★, *Yours Is My Heart Alone* (Decca 1951) ★★★, *Country Style* (Decca 1951) ★★★, *Down Memory Lane* (Decca 1951) ★★★, *Down Memory Lane, Volume 2* (Decca 1951) ★★★, *Beloved Hymns* (Decca 1951) ★★★, *Bing Sings Victor Herbert* (Decca 1951) ★★★, *Ichabod Crane* (Decca 1951) ★★★, *Collector's Classics* (Decca 1951) ★★★, *Two For Tonight* (Decca 1951) ★★★, *Rhythm Of The Range* film soundtrack (Decca 1951) ★★★, *Waikiki Wedding* film soundtrack (Decca 1951) ★★★, *The Star Maker* film soundtrack (Decca 1951) ★★★, *The Road To Singapore* film soundtrack (Decca 1951) ★★★, *When Irish Eyes Are Smiling* (Decca 1952) ★★★, *Just For You* (Decca 1952) ★★★, *The Road To Bali* film soundtrack (Decca 1952) ★★, *Song Hits Of Paris/Le Bing* (Decca 1953) ★★★, *Country Girl* (Decca 1953) ★★★, *Some Fine Old Chestnuts* (Decca 1954) ★★★, *A Man Without A Country* (Decca 1954) ★★★★, *White Christmas* film soundtrack (Decca 1954) ★★★★, *Lullabye Time* (Decca 1955) ★★★, *Shillelaghs And Shamrocks* (Decca 1956) ★★★, *Home On The Range* (Decca 1956) ★★★, *Blue Hawaii* (Decca 1956) ★★★, *High Tor* film soundtrack (Decca 1956) ★★★, *Anything Goes* film soundtrack (Decca 1956) ★★★, *Songs I Wish I Had Sung The First Time Around* (Decca 1956) ★★★, *Twilight On The Trail* (Decca 1956) ★★★, *A Christmas Sing With Bing Around The World* (Decca 1956) ★★★, *High Society* film soundtrack (Capitol 1956) ★★★★, *Bing Crosby Sings While Bergman Swings* (Verve 1956) ★★★, *New Tricks* (Decca 1957) ★★, *Ali Baba And The Forty Thieves* (Grand Award 1957) ★★★, *Christmas Story* (Grand Award 1957) ★★★, *Bing With A Beat* (RCA Victor 1957) ★★★, *Around The World* (Decca 1958) ★★★, *Bing In Paris* (Decca 1958) ★★★, *That Christmas Feeling* (Decca 1958) ★★★, with Rosemary Clooney *Fancy Meeting You Here* (RCA Victor 1958) ★★★★, *Paris Holiday* film soundtrack (United Artists 1958) ★★★, *In A Little Spanish Town* (Decca 1959) ★★★, *Ichabod* (Decca 1959) ★★★, *Young Bing Crosby* (RCA Victor 1959) ★★★, with Louis Armstrong *Bing And Satchmo* (MGM 1960) ★★★, *High Time* film soundtrack (RCA Victor 1960) ★★★, *Join Bing And Sing Along: 33 Great Songs* (Warners 1960) ★★★, *Join Bing And Sing Along: 101 Gang Songs* (Warners 1960) ★★★★, *Join Bing In A Gang Sing Along* (Warners 1961) ★★★, *My Golden Favorites* (Decca 1961) ★★★, *Easy To Remember* (Decca 1962) ★★★, *Pennies From Heaven* (Decca 1962) ★★★, *Pocket Full Of Dreams* (Decca 1962) ★★★, *East Side Of Heaven* (Decca 1962) ★★★, *The Road Begins* (Decca 1962) ★★★, *Only Forever* (Decca 1962) ★★★, *Swinging On A Star* (Decca 1962) ★★★, *Accentuate The Positive* (Decca 1962) ★★★, *But Beautiful* (Decca 1962) ★★★, *Sunshine Cake* (Decca 1962) ★★★, *Cool Of The Evening* (Decca 1962) ★★★, *Zing A Little Zong* (Decca 1962) ★★★, *Anything Goes* (Decca 1962) ★★★, *Holiday In Europe* (Decca 1962) ★★★, *The Small One* (Decca 1962) ★★★, *The Road To Hong Kong* film soundtrack (Liberty 1962) ★★★, *A Southern Memoir* (London 1962) ★★★★, *Join Bing And Sing Along: 51 Good Time Songs* (Warners 1962) ★★★, *On The Happy Side* (Warners 1962) ★★★, *I Wish You A Merry Christmas* (Warners 1962) ★★★, *Bing Sings The Great Standards* (MGM 1963) ★★★, *Songs Everybody Knows* (Decca 1964) ★★★, *Return To Paradise Islands* (Reprise 1964) ★★★, with Frank Sinatra, Fred Waring *America, I Hear You Singing* (Reprise 1964) ★★, *Robin And The Seven Hoods* film soundtrack (Reprise 1964) ★★★, with Clooney *That Travellin' Two-Beat* (Capitol 1965) ★★★, *Bing Crosby* (MGM 1965) ★★★, *Great Country Hits* (Capitol 1965) ★★★, *Thoroughly Modern Bing* (Stateside 1968) ★★★, *Hey Jude/Hey Bing!!* (Amos 1969) ★★★, *Wrap Your Troubles In Dreams* (RCA 1972) ★★★, *Bingo Viejo* (London 1975) ★★★, *The Dinah Shore-Bing Crosby Shows* (Sunbeam 1975) ★★★, *That's What Life Is All About* (United Artists 1975) ★★★, with Fred Astaire *A Couple Of Song And Dance Men* (United Artists 1975) ★★★, *Feels Good, Feels Right* (Decca 1976) ★★★, *Live At The London Palladium* (K-Tel 1976) ★★★, *"On The Air"* (Spokane 1976) ★★★★, *At My Time Of Life* (United Artists 1976) ★★★★, *Beautiful Memories* (United Artists 1976) ★★★★, *Kraft Music Hall December 24, 1942* (Spokane 1978) ★★★.

● COMPILATIONS: *Crosby Classics, Volume 1* (Columbia 1949) ★★★, *Crosby Classics, Volume 2* (Columbia 1950) ★★★, *Bing Crosby Volumes 1 & 2* (Brunswick 1950) ★★★, *Bing – A Musical Autobiography* 5-LP box set (Decca 1954) ★★★, *Old Masters* 3-LP set (Decca 1954) ★★★, *Der Bingle* (Columbia 1955) ★★★, *Crosby Classics* (Columbia 1955) ★★★, *The Voice Of Bing In The 30s* (Brunswick 1955) ★★★, *A Musical Autobiography Of Bing Crosby 1927-34* (Decca 1958) ★★★, *A Musical Autobiography Of Bing Crosby 1934-41* (Decca 1958) ★★★, *A Musical Autobiography Of Bing Crosby 1941-44* (Decca 1958) ★★★, *A Musical Autobiography Of Bing Crosby 1944-47* (Decca 1958) ★★★, *A Musical Autobiography Of Bing Crosby,*

1947-53 (Decca 1958) ★★★, *The Very Best Of* (MGM 1964) ★★★, *The Best Of Bing Crosby* (Decca 1965) ★★★, *The Bing Crosby Story – Volume 1: Early Jazz Years 1928-32* (Columbia 1968) ★★★, *Bing Crosby Remembered: A CSP Treasury* (Fairway 1977) ★★★, *Bing Crosby's Greatest Hits* (MCA 1977) ★★★★, *Seasons* (Polydor 1977) ★★★, *A Legendary Performer* (RCA 1977) ★★★★, *Crosby Classics Volume 3* (Capitol 1977) ★★★★, *A Bing Crosby Collection Volumes 1 & 2* (Columbia 1978) ★★★★, *Christmas With Bing* (Reader's Digest 1980) ★★★, *Bing In The Hall* (Spokane 1980) ★★★, *Music Hall Highlights* (Spokane 1981) ★★★, *Rare 1930-31 Brunswick Recordings* (MCA 1982) ★★★, *Bing In The Thirties Volumes 1-8* (Spokane 1984-88) ★★★★, *The Radio Years Volumes 1-4* (GNP Crescendo 1985-87) ★★★★, *Bing Crosby Sings Again* (MCA 1986) ★★★, *10th Anniversary Album* (Warwick 1987) ★★★★, *Bing Crosby 1929-34, Classic Years Volume 1* (BBC 1987) ★★★★, *Chronological Bing Crosby Volumes 1-10* (Jonzo 1985-88) ★★★★, *The Crooner: The Columbia Years 1928-34* (Columbia 1988) ★★★★, *The Victor Masters Featuring Bing Crosby (Paul Whiteman And His Orchestra)* (RCA 1989) ★★★★, *The All Time Best Of* (Curb 1990) ★★★, *Bing Crosby And Some Jazz Friends* (MCA/GRP 1991) ★★★★, *The Jazzin' Bing Crosby* (Charly 1992) ★★★★, *16 Most Requested Songs Legacy* (Columbia 1992) ★★★★, *The Quintessential Bing Crosby* (1993) ★★★★, *The EP Collection* (1993) ★★★★, *Bing Crosby And Friends* (1993) ★★★, *His Legendary Years* 4-CD box set (MCA 1993) ★★★★, *Only Forever* (Empress 1994) ★★★, *The Complete United Artists Sessions – Special Collectors Edition* 3-CD set (EMI 1997) ★★★, with the Andrews Sisters *The Essential Collection* (Half Moon 1998) ★★★, *Christmas Is A Comin'* (MCA 1998) ★★★.

● VIDEOS: *A Bing Crosby Christmas* (VCI 1997).

● FURTHER READING: *Bing: The Authorized Biography*, Charles Thompson. *The One & Only Bing*, Bob Thomas. *The Complete Crosby*, Charles Thompson. *Bing Crosby: The Hollow Man*, Donald Shepherd. *Bing Crosby: A Discography, Radio Programme List & Filmography*, Timothy A. Morgereth. *A Pocketful Of Dreams: The Early Years 1903-1940*, Gary Giddins.

● FILMS: *King Of Jazz* (1930), *Reaching For The Moon* (1930), *Confessions Of A Co-Ed* (1931), *The Bif Broadcast* (1932), *College Humor* (1933), *Too Much Harmony* (1933), *Going Hollywood* (1933), *Here Is My Heart* (1934), *She Loves Me Not* (1934), *We're Not Dressing* (1934), *The Big Broadcast Of 1936* (1935), *Two For Tonight* (1935), *Mississippi* (1935), *Pennies From Heaven* (1936), *Rhythm On The Range* (1936), *Anything Goes* (1936), *Double Or Nothing* (1937), *Waikiki Wedding* (1937), *Sing You Sinners* (1938), *Doctor Rhythm* (1938), *The Star Maker* (1939), *East Side Of Heaven* (1939), *Paris Honeymoon* (1939), *Rhythm On The River* (1940), *If I Had My Way* (1940), *Road To Singapore* (1940), *Birth Of The Blues* (1941), *Road To Zanzibar* (1941), *My Favorite Blonde* cameo (1942), *Star-Spangled Rhythm* (1942), *Road To Morocco* (1942), *Holiday Inn* (1942), *Dixie* (1943), *The Princess And The Pirate* (1944), *Here Comes The Waves* (1944), *Going*

My Way (1944), *The Bells Of St. Mary's* (1945), *Duffy's Tavern* (1945), *Blue Skies* (1946), *Road To Utopia* (1946), *My Favorite Brunette* cameo (1947), *Variety Girl* (1947), *Road To Rio* (1947), *Welcome Stranger* (1947), *The Emperor Waltz* (1948), *Top O' The Morning* (1949), *A Connecticut Yankee In King Arthur's Court* (1949), *Mr. Music* (1950), *Riding High* (1950), *Here Comes The Groom* (1951), *Son Of Paleface* cameo (1952), *The Greatest Show On Earth* cameo (1952), *Road To Bali* (1952), *Just For You* (1952), *Scared Stiff* cameo (1953), *Little Boy Lost* (1953), *The Country Girl* (1954), *White Christmas* (1954), *High Society* (1956), *Anything Goes* remake (1956), *Man On Fire* (1957), *Alias Jesse James* cameo (1959), *Say One For Me* (1959), *Pepe* cameo (1960), *Let's Make Love* cameo (1960), *High Time* (1960), *The Road To Hong Kong* (1962), *Robin And The Seven Hoods* (1964), *Cinerama's Russian Adventure* narration (1966), *Stagecoach* (1966), *That's Entertainment!* on-screen narration (1974).

CRUDUP, ARTHUR 'BIG BOY'

b. 24 August 1905, Forest, Mississippi, USA, d. 28 March 1974, Nassawadox, Virginia, USA. During the 40s and early 50s Arthur Crudup was an important name in the blues field, his records selling particularly well in the south. For much of his early life Crudup worked in various rural occupations, not learning to play the guitar until he was 32. His teacher was one 'Papa Harvey', a local bluesman, and although Crudup's guitar style never became adventurous, it formed an effective backdrop for his high, expressive voice. Allegedly, Crudup was playing on the sidewalk in Chicago when he was spotted by the music publisher and general 'Mr Fixit' for the blues in the Windy City, Lester Melrose. Like many others with his background, Big Boy's first recordings were his most countrified; 'If I Get Lucky' and 'Black Pony Blues' were recorded in September 1941 and probably sold largely to the same group of resident and ex-patriot southerners who were buying records by Tommy McClennan and Sleepy John Estes.

During the next 12 years he recorded approximately 80 tracks for Victor, including songs that became blues standards. 'Mean Old Frisco' was later picked up by artists as diverse as Brownie McGhee (1946) and B.B. King (1959), and was one of the first blues recordings to feature an electric guitar. He recorded 'Dust My Broom' in 1949 and the following year moonlighted for the Trumpet label in Jackson, Mississippi, under the name 'Elmer James'. Despite attempts to update his sound by the introduction of piano, harmonicas and saxophones, by 1954 Big Boy's heyday was over. When he was contracted to record an album of his hits for Fire in 1962, the project had to be delayed until the picking season was over, Crudup having given up music and gone back to working on the land. Two of Crudup's compositions, 'That's All Right' and 'My Baby Left Me' were recorded by Elvis Presley, who also sang his 'I'm So Glad You're Mine', but it is not likely that Crudup benefited much from this. A second career bloomed for Big Boy with the interest in blues among the white audience in the mid-60s, beginning with an album for Bob Koester's Delmark label. This prompted appearances at campuses and clubs in the USA and Crudup even journeyed to Europe – always encouraged to perform in a country style. It appears likely that, with his superior lyrics and wide cross-racial popularity, Big Boy Crudup gave more to the blues than he ever received in return. His three sons George, James and Jonas recorded as the Malibus and more recently as the Crudup Brothers.

● ALBUMS: *Mean Ol' Frisco* (Fire 1957) ★★★★, *Look On Yonders Wall* (Delmark 1968) ★★★, *Crudup's Mood* (Delmark 1970) ★★★, *Meets The Master Blues Bassists* (Delmark 1994) ★★★.

● COMPILATIONS: *The Father Of Rock And Roll* (RCA Victor 1971) ★★★, *After Hours* (Camden 1997) ★★★.

DALE, ALAN

b. Aldo Sigismondi, 9 July 1926, Brooklyn, New York, USA. Formerly with Carmen Cavallaro, Alan Dale first graced the US charts when his rich baritone vocal style provided Ray Bloch And His Orchestra with the 'swing' hit 'Kate (Have I Come Too Early Too Late)' in 1947. In the following year he duetted with Connie Haines on 'At The Darktown Strutters' Ball'. In 1951 he hosted his own US television series, which led to more success, most notably with 'Heart Of My Heart' (with Johnny Desmond and Don Cornell) and 'East Side, West Side' (with Desmond and Buddy Greco). In 1955 he again made the US Top 20 with 'Cherry Pink And Apple Blossom White' and an adaptation of a Cuban mambo-cha-cha 'Me Lo Dijo Adela', entitled 'Sweet And Gentle'.

● FILMS: *Don't Knock The Rock* (1956).

DAMONE, VIC

b. Vito Farinola, 12 June 1928, Brooklyn, New York, USA. A romantic balladeer with a strong, smooth baritone voice, Damone took singing lessons while working as an usher and elevator operator at New York's Paramount Theater. After appearing with *Arthur Godfrey's Talent Scouts*, he sang at La Martinique Club, a venue known as a nursery for young vocalists. When he started recording for Mercury Records in 1947, his first chart successes included 'I Have But One Heart', 'You Do' and 'Say Something Sweet To Your Sweetheart' (with Patti Page). In 1949 he had two million-sellers: 'Again', from the Ida Lupino movie *Roadhouse*; and 'You're Breaking My Heart'. In the late 40s Damone also had his own CBS radio show, *Saturday Night Serenade*. His movie career started in 1951 when he featured in *Rich, Young And Pretty*, the first in a series of musicals with soprano Jane Powell. These included *Athena* (1953), the Sigmund Romberg biopic *Deep In My Heart* (1954) and *Hit The Deck* (1955). Damone also appeared in *The Strip* (1951), a musical mystery melodrama, which featured Mickey Rooney, and jazz stars Jack Teagarden, Louis Armstrong, Earl 'Fatha' Hines and Barney Bigard; and a screen adaptation of the stage musical *Kismet* (1955), co-starring with Howard Keel, Anne Blythe and Dolores Gray.

His many record hits during the 50s included 'Tzena, Tzena, Tzena' (adapted from an Israeli song), 'Cincinnati Dancing Pig', 'My Heart Cries for You', 'My Truly, Truly Fair', 'Here In My Heart' (a UK number 1 for Al Martino), 'April In Portugal', 'Eternally' (the theme from Charlie Chaplin's movie *Limelight*), 'Ebb Tide', 'On The Street Where You Live' (Damone's third million-seller) and 'An Affair To Remember' (one of

prolific film composer Harry Warren's last songs). He was also in the album charts with *That Towering Feeling!*, and had his own television series in 1956-57. Like many other singers of his kind, Damone suffered from the changing musical climate of the 60s and 70s, although he did make some well-regarded albums such as *Linger Awhile With Vic Damone* and *On the Swingin' Side*, and had a US Top 30 single in 1965 with 'You Were Only Fooling (While I Was Falling In Love)'. He made a remarkable comeback in the UK in the early 80s, chiefly because his back-catalogue was plugged incessantly by BBC Radio 2 presenter David Jacobs. Suddenly, he was in fashion again. Most of his old albums were reissued, and many of his hit singles, and others, were repackaged on *Vic Damone Sings The Great Songs*. Throughout the 80s he recorded several new albums, promoting them in the UK via regular concert tours. In 1987 he was married, for the third time, to actress Diahann Carroll. In 1991 Damone played Michael's Pub in New York, his first club appearance in the city for more than 10 years.
● ALBUMS: *Vic Damone* 10-inch album (Mercury 1950) ★★★, *Song Hits* 10-inch album (Mercury 1950) ★★★, *Christmas Favorites* 10-inch album (Mercury 1951) ★★★, *Rich, Young And Pretty* film soundtrack (MGM 1951) ★★★, *Vic Damone And Others* 10-inch album (Mercury 1952) ★★★, *The Night Has A Thousand Eyes* 10-inch album (Mercury 1952) ★★★★, *Vocals By Vic* 10-inch album (Mercury 1952) ★★★, *April In Paris* 10-inch album (Mercury 1952) ★★★, *Athena* film soundtrack (Mercury 1954) ★★★, *Deep In My Heart* film soundtrack (MGM 1954) ★★★, *That Towering Feeling!* (Columbia 1956) ★★★, *The Stingiest Man In Town* film soundtrack (Columbia 1956) ★★★, *Yours For A Song* (Mercury 1957) ★★★, *All Time Song Hits* (Mercury 1957) ★★★, *My Favorites* (Mercury 1957) ★★★, *The Gift Of Love* film soundtrack (Columbia 1958) ★★★★, *Closer Than A Kiss* (Philips 1958) ★★★, *Angela Mia* (Columbia 1959) ★★★, *This Game Of Love* (Philips 1959) ★★★, *On The Swingin' Side* (Columbia 1961) ★★★★, *Linger Awhile With Vic Damone* (Capitol 1962) ★★★, *Strange Enchantment* (Capitol 1962) ★★★, *The Lively Ones* (Capitol 1962) ★★★, *My Baby Loves To Swing* (Capitol 1963) ★★★★, *The Liveliest* (Capitol 1963) ★★★, *On The Street Where You Live* (Capitol 1964) ★★★, *You Were Only Fooling* (Warners 1965) ★★★, *Arrivederci Baby* film soundtrack (RCA Victor 1966) ★★★, *Stay With Me* (RCA 1976) ★★★, *Damone's Feeling 1978* (Rebecca 1979) ★★★, *Now* (RCA 1981) ★★★, *Make Someone Happy* (RCA 1981) ★★★, *Now And Forever* (RCA 1982) ★★★, *Vic Damone Sings The Great Songs* (Columbia 1983) ★★★, *The Damone Type Of Thing* (RCA 1984) ★★★, *Christmas With Vic Damone* (Audio Fidelity 1984) ★★★, *The Best Of Vic Damone, Live* (Ranwood 1989) ★★★.
● COMPILATIONS: *Vic Damone's Best* (RCA 1980) ★★★★, *20 Golden Pieces* (Bulldog 1982) ★★★★, *Magic Moments With Vic Damone* (RCA 1985) ★★★★, *Didn't We?* (Castle 1986) ★★★, *The Capitol*

Years (Capitol 1989) ★★★, *16 Most Requested Songs* (Columbia 1992) ★★★★, *The Best Of Vic Damone: The Mercury Years* (Mercury 1996) ★★★★.
● FILMS: *The Strip* (1951), *Rich, Young And Pretty* (1951), *Athena* (1954), *Deep In My Heart* (1954), *Hit The Deck* (1955), *Kismet* (1955), *The Gift Of Love* voice (1958), *Hell To Eternity* (1960), *Spree* (1967).

DANIELS, BILLY

b. 12 September 1915, Jacksonville, Florida, USA, d. 7 October 1988. Daniels began his career as a singing waiter before working with dance bands and in vaudeville. In the late 30s he became popular in clubs and on radio. In 1943, during a club appearance, he performed 'That Old Black Magic', giving the song a highly dramatic, visually exciting treatment it had never before received, and from that time onwards, the singer and the song were inseparable. At his best in a cabaret setting, Daniels was a natural for television and from 1950, in partnership with pianist Bennie Payne, appeared regularly in the USA and UK. He made a few film appearances and was also in the television production of *Night Of The Quarter Moon*. P.J. Proby used much of Daniels' vocal technique with his epic ballads during the 60s. In 1975 he worked with Pearl Bailey in Hello, Dolly! and two years later starred in London in the UK version of *Bubbling Brown Sugar*. He also appeared with Sammy Davis Jnr. in the revival of Golden Boy. Offstage, Daniels frequently associated with underworld characters. He was stabbed in one incident and was once charged with a shooting. Late in his life he suffered ill health and twice underwent heart bypass surgery before his death in 1988.
● ALBUMS: *Around That Time* (50s) ★★★, *At The Stardust Las Vegas* (50s) ★★, *Love Songs For A Fool* (50s) ★★★, *You Go to My Head* (1957) ★★★★, *The Masculine Touch* (1958) ★★★, *At the Crescendo* (1959) ★★★, *Dance To The Magic* (1959) ★★★, *Bubbling Black Magic* (Polydor 1978) ★★★.
● COMPILATIONS: *The Magic Of Billy Daniels* (MFP 1976) ★★★.

DANKWORTH, JOHN

b. John Philip William Dankworth, 20 September 1927, London, England. Dankworth started playing clarinet as a child and in the early 40s was a member of a traditional jazz band. In the mid-40s he studied at the Royal Academy of Music and extended his knowledge of jazz by taking work on transatlantic liners, so that he could hear leading jazzmen in New York. Among his influences at this time was Charlie Parker, and Dankworth began to concentrate on alto saxophone. He was an active participant in the London bebop scene of the late 40s and early 50s, often playing at the Club 11. In 1950 he formed his own band, the Johnny Dankworth Seven, which included Jimmy Deuchar and Don Rendell. Three years later he formed a big band, playing his own, sometimes innovative, arrangements. The band's singer was Cleo Laine whom Dankworth married in 1958. For his big band Dankworth drew upon the best available modern jazzmen; at one time or another, artists such as Rendell, Dick Hawdon, Kenny Wheeler, Danny Moss, Peter King, Dudley Moore and Kenny Clare were in its ranks. Dankworth's writing, especially for the big band, demonstrated his considerable arranging skills, although for many fans it is the performances by the Seven that linger longest in fond memory. In the 60s Dankworth was in demand for film work, which, together with the growing popularity of Laine, led to a shift in policy. In the early 70s Dankworth became Laine's musical director, touring extensively with her and making many records. Dankworth's musical interests extend beyond jazz and he has composed in the classical form, including a nine-movement work, 'Fair Oak Fusions', written for cellist Julian Lloyd Webber. He has also experimented with third-stream music. His deep interest in music education led in 1969 to the founding of the Wavendon Allmusic Plan, which has continued to attract performers, students and audiences from around the world to concerts, classes, courses and lectures. Although a reliable performer on alto, it is as an arranger and tireless promoter of music that Dankworth has made his greatest contributions to the international jazz scene. In 1974, in recognition of his work, he became a Companion of the British Empire.

● ALBUMS: *Five Steps To Dankworth* (Parlophone 1957) ★★★★, *London To Newport* (Top Rank 1960) ★★★, *Jazz Routes* (Columbia 1961) ★★★, *Curtain Up* (Columbia 1963) ★★★, *What The Dickens!* (Fontana 1963) ★★, *Zodiac Variations* (Fontana 1965) ★★★, *Modesty Blaise* (Fontana 1966) ★★★, *Fathom* film soundtrack (Stateside 1967) ★★, *The $1,000,000 Collection* (Fontana 1968) ★★★, *Full Circle* (1972) ★★★, *Lifeline* (1973) ★★★, *Movies 'N' Me* (1974) ★★, *And The Philharmonic* (Boulevard 1974) ★★, with Cleo Laine *A Lover And His Lass* (Esquire 1976) ★★★★, *Sepia* (1979) ★★★, *Fair Oak Fusions* (1982) ★★★, *Metro* (Repertoire 1983) ★★★, *Gone Hitchin'* (Sepia 1983) ★★★, *Octavius* (Sepia 1983) ★★★, *Symphonic Fusions* (Pickwick 1985) ★★★, *Innovations* (Pickwick 1987) ★★★, *Live At Ronnie Scott's* (Total 1992) ★★★, with Alec Dankworth *Generation Big Band* (Jazz House 1994) ★★★★, *Moon Valley* (ABCD 1998) ★★★.

● COMPILATIONS: *Johnny Dankworth Seven And Orchestra* 1953-57 recordings (Retrospect 1983) ★★★★, *Featuring Cleo Laine* 1953-1958 recordings (Retrospect 1984) ★★★, with others *Bop At Club 11* 1949 recordings (Esquire 1986) ★★, *The John Dankworth Big Band, Vintage Years 1953-1959* (Sepia 1990) ★★★★, with Humphrey Lyttelton *All That Jazz* (MFP 1990) ★★★★, *The Roulette Years* (Roulette 1991) ★★★★.

● FURTHER READING: *Jazz In Revolution*, John Dankworth.

DANNY AND THE JUNIORS

This Philadelphia-based, Italian-American vocal quartet comprised lead vocalist Danny Rapp (b. 10 May 1941, d. 4 April 1983), first tenor Dave White, second tenor Frank Mattei and baritone Joe Terranova. Formed in 1955 as the Juvenairs, their song 'Do The Bop' came to the attention of Dick Clark, who suggested the title change 'At The Hop'. They took his advice and released the song in 1957, initially with few sales. However, after they sang it on Clark's television show *Bandstand*, it was picked up by ABC-Paramount and shot to the top of the US chart for five weeks. Despite comments from the British music press that the group was amateur and imitative, it made the UK Top 3 and sold over two million copies worldwide. They followed it with their only other US Top 20 hit, the similar-sounding and prophetically titled 'Rock 'n' Roll Is Here To Stay'. In 1960 they signed to Dick Clark's Swan Records where they gained their fourth and last US Top 40 hit, 'Twistin' U.S.A.' (they re-recorded it unsuccessfully for the UK as 'Twistin England'). They recorded songs about such dance crazes as the Mashed Potato, Pony, Cha Cha, Fish, Continental Walk and Limbo, but could not repeat their earlier success, even when they released 'Back To The Hop' in 1961. Later in the 60s they also appeared on Guyden, Mercury Records and Capitol Records, where they re-recorded 'Rock 'n' Roll Is Here To Stay' in 1968. Dave White left the group in the early 60s to concentrate on writing and production and composed a number of hits, including 'You Don't Own Me' for Lesley Gore and '1-2-3' and 'Like A Baby' for Len Barry, before recording a solo album on Bell in 1971. In the 70s they played the 'oldies' circuit with a line-up that included Fabian's ex-backing singer Jimmy Testa. In 1976 a reissue of their classic 'At The Hop' returned them to the UK Top 40. After a few quiet years, leader Rapp was found dead in Arizona in 1983, having apparently committed suicide.

● COMPILATIONS: *Rockin' With Danny And The Juniors* (MCA 1983) ★★, *Back To Hop* (Roller Coaster 1992) ★★.

DAVIS, MILES

b. Miles Dewy Davis, 25 May 1926, Alton, Illinois, USA, d. 28 September 1991, Santa Monica, California, USA. Davis was born into a comparatively wealthy middle-class family and both his mother and sister were capable musicians. He was given a trumpet for his thirteenth birthday by his dentist father, who could not have conceived that his gift would set his son on the road to becoming a giant figure in the development of jazz. Notwithstanding his outstanding talent as master of the trumpet, Davis' versatility encompassed flügelhorn and keyboards together with a considerable gift as a composer. This extraordinary list of talents earned Davis an unassailable reputation as the greatest leader/catalyst in the history of jazz. Such accolades were not used lightly, and he can justifiably be termed a 'musical genius'. Davis quickly progressed from his high school band into Eddie Randall's band in 1941, after his family had moved to St. Louis. He studied at the Juilliard School of Music in New York in 1945 before joining Charlie 'Bird' Parker, with whom he had previously played in the Billy Eckstine band. In 1947 Davis had topped a *Down Beat* poll and by

1948 he had already played or recorded with many jazz giants, most notably Coleman Hawkins, Dizzy Gillespie, Benny Carter, Max Roach, George Russell, John Lewis, Illinois Jacquet and Gerry Mulligan. The following year was to be a landmark for jazz; Davis, in collaboration with arranger Gil Evans, whose basement apartment Davis rehearsed in, made a series of 78s for Capitol Records that were eventually released as one long-player in 1954, the highly influential *Birth Of The Cool*. Davis had now refined his innovative style of playing, which was based upon understatement rather than the hurried action of the great bebop players. Sparse and simple, instead of frantic and complicated, it was becoming 'cool'. The *Birth Of The Cool* sessions between January 1949 and March 1950 featured a stellar cast, mostly playing and recording as a nonet, including Lee Konitz (saxophone), Kenny Clarke (drums), Mulligan (baritone saxophone), Kai Winding (trombone), Roach (drums). Davis was on such a creative roll that he could even pass by an invitation to join Duke Ellington!

During the early 50s Davis became dependent on heroin and his career was effectively put on hold for a lengthy period. This spell of drug dependency lasted until as late as 1954, although he did record a few sessions for Prestige during this time. The following year his seminal quintet/sextets included, variously, Red Garland, John Coltrane, Percy Heath, Thelonious Monk, Milt Jackson, Paul Chambers, Philly Joe Jones, Horace Silver, J.J. Johnson, Lucky Thompson, Cannonball Adderley, Bill Evans and Sonny Rollins. Among their output was the acclaimed series of collections released on the Prestige label, *Walkin'*, *Cookin'*, *Relaxin'*, *Workin'* and *Steamin'*. During this time Davis was consistently voted the number 1 artist in all the major jazz polls. No longer totally dependent on drugs by this time, he set about collaborating with Gil Evans once again, now that he had signed with the prestigious Columbia Records. The orchestral albums made with Evans between 1957 and 1960 have all become classics: *Miles Ahead*, (featuring pianist Wynton Kelly and drummer Art Taylor), *Porgy And Bess* and the sparsely beautiful *Sketches Of Spain* (influenced by composer Joaquin Rodrigo). Evans was able to blend lush and full orchestration with Davis' trumpet, allowing it the space and clarity it richly deserved. Davis went on further.

By 1957 he had assembled a seminal sextet featuring a spectacular line-up, including Coltrane, Chambers, Bill Evans, Jimmy Cobb and Cannonball Adderley. Two further landmark albums during this fertile period (1957-1959), were the aptly titled *Milestones*, followed in 1959 by the utterly fabulous *Kind Of Blue*. The latter album is cited by most critics as the finest in jazz history. More than 40 years later all his albums are still available, and form an essential part of any jazz record collection, but *Kind Of Blue* is at the top of the list. 'So What', the opening track, has been covered by dozens of artists, with recent offerings from guitarist Ronny Jordan, Larry Carlton, saxophonist Candy Dulfer and reggae star

Smiley Culture, who added his own lyrics and performed it in the movie *Absolute Beginners*. Ian Carr, Davis' leading biographer, perceptively stated of *Kind Of Blue* in 1982: 'The more it is listened to, the more it reveals new delights and fresh depths'. Davis was finding that as Coltrane grew as a musician their egos would clash. Davis would always play simple and sparingly, Coltrane began to play faster and more complicated pieces that soloed for far too long. Shortly before their inevitable final split, an incident occurred which has been passed down and repeated by musicians and biographers. Davis, who had a dry sense of humour and did not tolerate fools, had chastised Coltrane for playing too long a solo. Coltrane replied apologetically that; 'Sorry Miles, I just get carried away, I get these ideas in my head which just keep coming and coming and sometimes I just can't stop'. Davis laconically replied; 'Try taking the motherfucker out of yo' mouth'. Another repeated anecdote (this time from Adderley); Miles; 'Why did you play so long, man?', Coltrane; 'It took that long to get it all in'.

In 1959, following an incident outside a New York club during which Davis was provoked and arrested for loitering, he was taken to the police headquarters and arrived covered in blood from a large cut in his head. Davis took out a lawsuit against the New York Police, which he subsequently and wisely dropped after they had accepted he was wrongfully arrested. This incident deeply upset Davis. However, he entered the 60s comfortably as the leading innovator in jazz, and shrugged off attempts from John Coltrane to dethrone him in the jazz polls. Davis chose to keep to his sparse style, allowing his musicians air and range. In 1964, while the world experienced Beatlemania, Davis created another musical landmark when he assembled a line-up to match the classic sextet. The combination of Herbie Hancock, Wayne Shorter, Ron Carter and Tony Williams delivered the monumental *E.S.P.* in 1965. He continued with this acoustic line-up through another three recordings, including *Miles Smiles* and ending with *Nefertiti*. By the time of *Filles De Kilimanjaro*, Davis had gradually electrified his various groups and taken bold steps towards rock music, integrating multiple electric keyboards and utilizing a wah-wah pedal connected to his electrified trumpet. Additionally, his own fascination with the possibilities of electric guitar, as demonstrated by Jimi Hendrix, assumed an increasing prominence in his music. Young US west coast rock musicians had begun to produce a form of music based upon improvisation (mostly through the use of hallucinogenics). This clearly interested Davis, who recognized the potential of blending traditional rock rhythms with jazz, although he was often contemptuous of some white rock musicians at this time. The decade closed with his band being accepted by rock fans. Davis appeared at major festivals with deliriously stoned audiences appreciating his line-up, which now featured the brilliant electric guitarist John McLaughlin, of whom Davis stated in deference to black musicians: 'Show me a black who can play like him, and I'd have him instead'.

Other outstanding musicians Davis employed included Keith Jarrett, Airto Moreira, Chick Corea, Dave Holland, Joe Zawinul, Billy Cobham and Jack DeJohnette. Two major albums from this period were *In A Silent Way* and *Bitches Brew*, which unconsciously invented jazz rock and what was later to be called fusion. These records were marketed as rock albums, and consequently appeared in the regular charts.

By the early 70s Davis had alienated himself from the mainstream jazz purists by continuing to flirt with rock music. In 1975, after a succession of personal upheavals including a car crash, further drug problems, a shooting incident, more police harassment and eventual arrest, Davis, not surprisingly, retired. During this time he became seriously ill, and it was generally felt that he would never play again, but, unpredictable as ever, Davis returned healthy and fit six years later with the comeback album, *The Man With The Horn*. He assembled a new band and received favourable reviews for live performances. Among the personnel were guitarist John Scofield and the young saxophonist Bill Evans. On the predominantly funk-based *You're Under Arrest*, he tackled pure pop songs, and although unambitious by jazz standards, tracks such as Cyndi Lauper's 'Time After Time' and Michael Jackson's 'Human Nature' were given Davis' brilliant master touch. The aggressive disco album *Tutu* followed, featuring his trumpet played through a synthesizer. A soundtrack recording for the Dennis Hopper movie *The Hot Spot* found Davis playing the blues alongside Taj Mahal, John Lee Hooker, Tim Drummond and slide guitarist Roy Rogers.

During his final years Davis settled into a comfortable pattern of touring the world and recording, able to dictate the pace of his life with the knowledge that ecstatic audiences were waiting for him everywhere. Following further bouts of ill health, during which times he took to painting, Davis was admitted to hospital in California and died in September 1991. The worldwide obituaries were neither sycophantic nor morose; great things had already been said about Davis for many years. Django Bates stated that his own favourite Davis recordings were those between 1926 and mid-1991. Ian Carr added, in his impressive obituary, with regard to Davis' music: 'unflagging intelligence, great courage, integrity, honesty and a sustained spirit of enquiry always in the pursuit of art – never mere experimentation for its own sake'. Miles Davis' influence on rock music is considerable; his continuing influence on jazz is inestimable.

● ALBUMS: *Bopping The Blues* 1946 recording (Black Lion) ★★, *Cool Boppin'* 1948-1949 recordings (Fresh Sounds) ★★★, *Young Man With A Horn* 10-inch album (Blue Note 1952) ★★★, *The New Sounds Of Miles Davis* 10-inch album (Prestige 1952) ★★★★, *Blue Period* 10-inch album (Prestige 1953) ★★★, *Miles Davis Plays Al Cohn Compositions* 10-inch album (Prestige 1953) ★★★, *Miles Davis Quintet* 10-inch album (Prestige 1953) ★★★★, *Miles Davis Quintet Featuring Sonny Rollins* 10-inch album (Prestige 1953) ★★★, *Miles Davis Volume 3* 10-inch album (Blue Note 1954) ★★★, *Miles Davis Sextet* 10-inch album (reissued as *Walkin'*) (Prestige 1954) ★★★★, *Jeru* 10-inch album (Capitol 1954) ★★★★★, *Birth Of The Cool* 1949-50 recordings (Capitol 1954) ★★★★★, *Miles Davis All Stars Volume 1* 10-inch album (Prestige 1955) ★★★★, *Miles Davis All Stars Volume 2* 10-inch album (Prestige 1955) ★★★★, *Miles Davis Volume 1* (Blue Note 1955) ★★★, *Miles Davis Volume 2* (Blue Note 1955) ★★★★, *Hi-Hat All Stars* 1955 recording (Fresh Sound) ★, *Blue Moods* (Debut 1955) ★★★, *Musings Of Miles* reissued as *The Beginning* (Prestige 1955) ★★★, with Sonny Rollins *Dig Miles Davis/Sonny Rollins* reissued as *Diggin'* (Prestige 1956) ★★★★, *Collectors Item* (Prestige 1956) ★★★, *Miles – The New Miles Davis Quintet* reissued as *The Original Quintet* (Prestige 1956) ★★★, *Blue Haze* 1953-54 recordings (Prestige 1956) ★★★, *Miles Davis And Horns* reissued as *Early Miles* (Prestige 1956) ★★★, *Miles Davis And Milt Jackson Quintet/Sextet* reissued as *Odyssey* (Prestige 1956) ★★★, *Cookin' With The Miles Davis Quintet* (Prestige 1957) ★★★★, *Relaxin' With The Miles Davis Quintet* (Prestige 1957) ★★★★, *Bags Groove* 1954 recording (Prestige 1957) ★★★★, *Round About Midnight* 1955-56 recordings (Columbia 1957) ★★★★, *Miles Ahead* (Columbia 1957) ★★★★★, *Miles Davis And The Modern Jazz Giants* 1954-56 recordings (Prestige 1958) ★★★, with John Coltrane *Miles And Coltrane* 1955-58 recordings (Columbia 1958) ★★★, *Milestones* (Columbia 1958) ★★★★, *Porgy And Bess* (Columbia 1958) ★★★★★, *'58 Miles* (Columbia 1958) ★★★★, *Jazz Track (Ascenseur Pour L'Échafaud)* soundtrack (Fontana 1958) ★★★, *Mostly Miles* 1958 recording (Phontastic) ★★, *Workin' With The Miles Davis Quintet* (Prestige 1959) ★★★★, *Kind Of Blue* (Columbia 1959) ★★★★★, *Sketches Of Spain* (Columbia 1960) ★★★★, *On Green Dolphin Street* 1960 recording (Jazz Door 1960) ★★★, *Jazz At The Plaza* (Columbia 1960) ★★, *Live In Zurich* (Jazz Unlimited 1960) ★★★, *Live In Stockholm 1960* reissued as *Miles Davis In Stockholm Complete* (Royal Jazz 1960) ★★★, *Steamin' With The Miles Davis Quintet* (Prestige 1961) ★★★★, *Friday Night At The Blackhawk Vol 1* (Columbia 1961) ★★★★, *Saturday Night At The Blackhawk Volume 2* (Columbia 1961) ★★★★, *Someday My Prince Will Come* (Columbia 1961) ★★★★, with Teddy Charles, Lee Konitz *Ezz-Thetic* (New Jazz 1962) ★★★, with Dizzy Gillespie, Fats Navarro *Trumpet Giants* (New Jazz 1962) ★★★★, *Miles Davis At Carnegie Hall* (Columbia 1962) ★★★★, *Seven Steps To Heaven* (Columbia 1963) ★★★, *Quiet Nights* (Columbia 1963) ★★★, with Thelonious Monk *Miles And Monk At Newport* 1958 and 1963 (Columbia 1964) ★★★, *Miles Davis In Europe* (Columbia 1964) ★★★, *My Funny Valentine: Miles Davis In Concert* (Columbia 1965) ★★★★, *E.S.P.* (Columbia 1965) ★★★★, *Miles Davis Plays For Lovers* (Prestige 1965) ★★★, *Jazz Classics* (Prestige 1965) ★★★, *'Four' And More – Recorded Live In Concert*

(Columbia 1966) ★★★, *Miles In Antibes* (Columbia 1966) ★★★, *Miles Smiles* (Columbia 1966) ★★★, *Sorcerer* (Columbia 1967) ★★★, *Nefertiti* (Columbia 1968) ★★★, *Miles In The Sky* (Columbia 1968) ★★★, *Miles Orbits* (Columbia Record Club 1968) ★★★, *In A Silent Way* (Columbia 1969) ★★★★★, *Double Image* (Moon 1969) ★★★, *Filles De Kilimanjaro* (Columbia 1969) ★★★★, *Paraphernalia* (JMY 1969) ★★★, *Bitches Brew* (Columbia 1970) ★★★★★, *Miles Davis At The Fillmore* (Columbia 1970) ★★★★, *A Tribute To Jack Johnson* (Columbia 1971) ★★★★, *What I Say? Volumes 1 & 2* (JMY 1971) ★★★, *Live-Evil* (Columbia 1971) ★★★, *On The Corner* (Columbia 1972) ★★★, *In Concert* (Columbia 1972) ★★★, *Tallest Trees* (Prestige 1973) ★★★, *Black Beauty* 1970 recording (Columbia 1974) ★★★★, *Big Fun* 1969-70-72 recordings (Columbia 1974) ★★★, *Get Up With It* 1970-74 recordings (Columbia 1974) ★★★, *Jazz At The Plaza Volume 1* (1974) ★★★, *Agharta* (Columbia 1976) ★★★★, *Pangaea* (Columbia 1976) ★★★, *Live At The Plugged Nickel* 1965 recording (Columbia 1976) ★★★★, *Water Babies* (Columbia 1977) ★★★, *The Man With The Horn* (Columbia 1981) ★★★, *A Night In Tunisia* (Star Jazz 1981) ★★★, *We Want Miles* (Columbia 1982) ★★★, *Star People* (Columbia 1983) ★★★, *Blue Christmas* (Columbia 1983) ★★★, *Heard 'Round the World* 1964 concert recordings (Columbia 1983) ★★★, *At Last! Miles Davis And The Lighthouse All Stars* 1953 recording (Boplicity 1985) ★★★, *Decoy* (Columbia 1984) ★★★, *You're Under Arrest* (Columbia 1985) ★★★★, *Tutu* (Warners 1986) ★★★★, *Music From Siesta '88* (Warners 1988) ★★★★, *Amandla* (Warners 1989) ★★★, *Aura* 1985 recording (Columbia 1989) ★★★★, *The Hot Spot* (Antilles 1990) ★★★, with Michel Legrand *Dingo* (Warners 1991) ★★★, *Doo-Bop* (Warners 1992) ★★★, *The Complete Concert 1964: My Funny Valentine And 'Four' And More* (Columbia 1992) ★★★★, with Quincy Jones *Miles And Quincy Jones Live At Montreux* 1991 recording (Reprise 1993) ★★★★, *Live Around The World* (Warners 1996) ★★★, *Miles Davis Live And Electric: Live Evil* (Columbia/Legacy 1997) ★★★★, *Miles Davis Live And Electric: Miles Davis At The Fillmore East* (Columbia/Legacy 1997) ★★★★, *Miles Davis Live And Electric: Black Beauty, Miles Davis Live At The Fillmore West* (Columbia/Legacy 1997) ★★★★, *Miles Davis Live And Electric: Dark Magus, Live At Carnegie Hall* 1974 recording (Columbia/Legacy 1997) ★★★★, *Miles Davis Live And Electric: Miles Davis In Concert, Live At The Philharmonic Hall* (Columbia/ Legacy 1997) ★★★★, *The Complete Birth Of The Cool* (Capitol 1998) ★★★★★, *The Complete Bitches Brew Sessions* 4-CD box set (Columbia/Legacy 1998) ★★★★★, *Miles Davis At Carnegie Hall: The Complete Concert* 1961 recording (Columbia/Legacy 1998) ★★★★, *At Fillmore East (March 7 1970): It's About That Time* (Columbia/Legacy 2000) ★★★, *Jazz At The Plaza* 1958 recording (Columbia 2001) ★★.
● COMPILATIONS: *Miles Davis' Greatest Hits* (Prestige 1957) ★★★★, *Greatest Hits* (Columbia 1969) ★★★★, *Basic Miles – The Classic Performances Of Miles Davis* 1955-1958 recordings

(Columbia 1973) ★★★★, *Circle In The Round* 1955-1970 recordings (Columbia 1979) ★★★, *Directions* unreleased recordings 1960-1970 (Columbia 1981) ★★★, *Chronicle: The Complete Prestige Recordings* (Prestige 1987) ★★★★, *The Columbia Years 1955-1985* (Columbia 1988) ★★★★, *Ballads* 1961-1963 recordings (Columbia 1988) ★★★★, *Mellow Miles* 1961-1963 recordings (Columbia 1989) ★★★, *First Miles* (Savoy 1989) ★★★, *The Essence Of Miles Davis* (Columbia 1991) ★★★★, *Collection* (Castle 1992) ★★★★, *The Complete Live At The Plugged Nickel 1965* 8-CD box set (Columbia 1995) ★★★★★, *Highlights From The Plugged Nickel 1965* (Columbia 1995) ★★★★, *Ballads And Blues* (Blue Note 1996) ★★★★, *Miles Davis Acoustic: This Is Jazz No. 8* (Legacy 1996) ★★★, with Gil Evans *Miles Davis/Gil Evans: The Complete Columbia Studio Recordings* 6-CD/11-LP box set (Columbia/Mosaic 1996) ★★★★★, *Miles Davis Plays Ballads; This Is Jazz No. 22* (Legacy 1997) ★★★★, *The Complete Studio Recordings Of The Miles Davis Quintet 1965-June 1968* 7-CD/10-LP box set (Columbia/Mosaic 1998) ★★★★, *Love Songs* (Columbia 1999) ★★★, with John Coltrane *The Complete Columbia Recordings 1955-1961* (Columbia/Legacy 2000) ★★★★, *Blue Miles* (Columbia 2000) ★★★★, *Young Miles* 4-CD box set (Proper 2001) ★★★★, *The Essential Miles Davis* (Columbia 2001) ★★★★★, *Complete In A Silent Way Sessions* 3-CD box set (Columbia 2001) ★★★★.
● VIDEOS: *Miles Davis And Jazz Hoofer* (Kay Jazz 1988), *Miles In Paris* (Warner Music Video 1990), *Miles Davis And Quincy Jones: Live At Montreux* (Warner Music Video 1993).
● FURTHER READING: *Milestones: 1. Miles Davis, 1945-60*, Jack Chambers. *Milestones: 2. Miles Davis Since 1960*, Jack Chambers. *Miles: The Autobiography*, Miles Davis with Quincy Troupe. *Miles Davis*, Barry McRae. *Miles Davis: A Critical Biography*, Ian Carr. *Miles Davis For Beginners*, Daryl Long. *The Man In The Green Shirt: Miles Davis*, Richard Williams. *Miles Davis: The Early Years*, Bill Cole. *'Round About Midnight: A Portrait Of Miles Davis*, Eric Nisenson. *The Miles Davis Companion*, Gary Carner (ed.). *Milestones: The Music And Times Of Miles Davis*, Jack Chambers. *A Miles Davis Reader*, Bill Kirchner (ed.). *Kind Of Blue: The Making Of The Miles Davis Masterpiece*, Ashley Kahn. *The Making Of Kind Of Blue: Miles Davis And His Masterpiece*, Eric Nisenson. *Miles And Me*, Quincey Troupe. *Miles Davis: Complete Discography*, Nasuki Nakayama. *Miles Beyond: The Electric Explorations Of Miles Davis 1967-1999*, Paul Tingen. *Miles Davis And American Culture*, Gerald Early (ed.).
● FILMS: *Dingo* (1991).

DAVIS, SAMMY, JNR.

b. 8 December 1925, Harlem, New York, USA, d. 16 May 1990, Los Angeles, California, USA. A dynamic and versatile all-round entertainer, Davis was a trouper in the old-fashioned tradition. The only son of two dancers in a black vaudeville troupe, called Will Mastin's Holiday In Dixieland, Davis made his professional debut with the group at the age of three, as 'Silent Sam, The Dancing Midget'. While still young he was coached by the legendary tap-dancer Bill 'Bojangles' Robinson. Davis left the group in 1943 to serve in the US Army, where he encountered severe racial prejudice for the first, but not the last, time. After the war he rejoined his father and adopted uncle in the Will Mastin Trio. By 1950 the Trio were headlining at venues such as the Capitol in New York and Ciro's in Hollywood with stars including Jack Benny and Bob Hope, but it was Davis who was receiving the standing ovations for his singing, dancing, drumming, comedy and apparently inexhaustible energy.

In 1954 he signed for Decca Records, and released two albums, *Starring Sammy Davis Jr.* (number 1 in the US chart), featuring his impressions of stars such as Dean Martin, Jerry Lewis, Johnnie Ray and Jimmy Durante, and *Just For Lovers*. He also made the US singles chart with 'Hey There' from *The Pajama Game*, and in the same year he lost his left eye in a road accident. When he returned to performing in January 1955 wearing an eye patch, he was greeted even more enthusiastically than before. During that year he reached the US Top 20 with 'Something's Gotta Give', 'Love Me Or Leave Me' and 'That Old Black Magic'. In 1956 he made his Broadway debut in the musical *Mr Wonderful*, with music and lyrics by Jerry Bock, Larry Holofcener and George Weiss. Also in the show were the rest of the Will Mastin Trio, Sammy's uncle and Davis Snr. The show ran for nearly 400 performances, and produced two hits, 'Too Close For Comfort', and the title song, which was very successful for Peggy Lee. Although generally regarded as the first popular American black performer to become acceptable to both black and white audiences, Davis attracted heavy criticism in 1956 over his conversion to Judaism, and later for his marriage to Swedish actress Mai Britt. He described himself as a 'one-eyed Jewish nigger'.

Apart from a few brief appearances when he was very young, Davis started his film career in 1958 with *Anna Lucasta*, and was critically acclaimed the following year for his performance as Sporting Life in *Porgy And Bess*. By this time Davis was a leading member of Frank Sinatra's 'inner circle', called, variously, the 'Clan' or the 'Rat Pack'. He appeared with Sinatra in three movies, *Ocean's Eleven* (1960), *Sergeants 3* (1962), and *Robin And The 7 Hoods* (1964), but made, perhaps, a greater impact when he co-starred with another member of the 'Clan', Shirley MacLaine, in the Cy Coleman and Dorothy Fields film musical *Sweet Charity*. The 60s were good times for Davis, who was enormously popular on records and television, but especially 'live', at Las Vegas and in concert. In 1962 he made the US chart with the Anthony Newley/Leslie Bricusse number 'What Kind Of Fool Am I?', and thereafter featured several of their songs in his act. He sang Bricusse's nominated song, 'Talk To The Animals', at the 1967 Academy Awards ceremony, and collected the Oscar on behalf of the songwriter when it won. In 1972, he had a million-selling hit record with another Newley/Bricusse song, 'The Candy

Man', from the film *Willy Wonka And The Chocolate Factory*.

He appeared again on Broadway in 1964 in *Golden Boy*, Charles Strouse and Lee Adams' musical adaptation of Clifford Odet's 1937 drama of a young man torn between the boxing ring and his violin. Also in the cast was Billy Daniels. The show ran for 569 performances in New York, and went to London in 1968. During the 70s Davis worked less, suffering, allegedly, as a result of previous alcohol and drug abuse. He entertained US troops in the Lebanon in 1983, and five years later undertook an arduous comeback tour of the USA and Canada with Sinatra and Dean Martin. In 1989 he travelled further, touring Europe with the show *The Ultimate Event*, along with Liza Minnelli and Sinatra. While he was giving everything to career favourites such as 'Birth Of The Blues', 'Mr Bojangles' and 'That Old Black Magic', he was already ill, although it was not apparent to audiences. After his death in 1990 it was revealed that his estate was almost worthless. In 1992, an all-star tribute, led by Liza Minnelli, was mounted at the Royal Albert Hall in London, the city that had always welcomed him. Proceeds from the concert went to the Royal Marsden Cancer Appeal. Few all-round entertainers in the history of popular song and showbusiness have retained such a long-standing appeal.

● ALBUMS: *Starring Sammy Davis Jr.* (Decca 1955) ★★★, *Just For Lovers* (Decca 1955) ★★★, *Mr. Wonderful* film soundtrack (Decca 1956) ★★, *Here's Looking At You* (Decca 1956) ★★★, with Carmen McRae *Boy Meets Girl* (Epic 1957) ★★★, *Sammy Swings* (Decca 1957) ★★★★, *It's All Over But The Swingin'* (Decca 1957) ★★★★, *Mood To Be Wooed* (Decca 1958) ★★★, *All The Way And Then Some* (Decca 1958) ★★★★, *Sammy Davis Jr. At Town Hall* (Decca 1959) ★★★★, *Porgy And Bess* (Decca 1959) ★★★, *I Got A Right To Swing* (Decca 1960) ★★★★, *Sammy Awards* (Decca 1960) ★★★, *What Kind Of Fool Am I And Other Show-Stoppers* (Reprise 1962) ★★★★, *Sammy Davis Jr. At The Cocoanut Grove* (Reprise 1963) ★★★★, *Johnny Cool* film soundtrack (United Artists 1963) ★★★, *As Long As She Needs Me* (Reprise 1963) ★★★, *Sammy Davis Jr. Salutes The Stars Of The London Palladium* (Reprise 1964) ★★★, *The Shelter Of Your Arms* (Reprise 1964) ★★★, *Golden Boy* film soundtrack (Capitol 1964) ★★, with Count Basie *Our Shining Hour* (Verve 1965) ★★★, *That's All!* (Reprise 1965) ★★★, *A Man Called Adam* film soundtrack (Reprise 1966) ★★, *I've Gotta Be Me* (Reprise 1969) ★★★, *Sammy Davis Jr. Now* (MGM 1972) ★★★, *Portrait Of Sammy Davis Jr.* (MGM 1972) ★★★, *It's A Musical World* (MGM 1976) ★★★, *The Song And Dance Man* (20th Century 1977) ★★★★, *Sammy Davis Jr. In Person 1977* (RCA 1983) ★★★, *Closest Of Friends* (Vogue 1984) ★★★.

● COMPILATIONS: *The Best Of Sammy Davis Jr.* (MCA 1982) ★★★, *Collection* (Castle 1989) ★★★, *The Great Sammy Davis Jr.* (MFP 1989) ★★★, *Capitol Collectors Series* (Capitol 1990) ★★★, *The Decca Years* (MCA 1990) ★★★★, *The Wham Of Sam* (Warners 1995) ★★★, *That Old Black Magic*

(MCA 1995) ★★★, *I've Gotta Be Me: The Best Of Sammy Davis Jr. On Reprise* (Reprise 1996) ★★★★, *Yes I Can!* 4-CD box set (Reprise/Rhino 2000) ★★★.

● VIDEOS: with Liza Minnelli, Frank Sinatra *The Ultimate Event!* (Video Collection 1989), *Mr Bojangles* (Decca/PolyGram Music Video 1991).

● FURTHER READING: *Yes I Can: The Story Of Sammy Davis Jr.*, Sammy Davis Jnr. *Hollywood In A Suitcase*, Sammy Davis Jnr. *Why Me: The Autobiography Of Sammy Davis Jr.*, Sammy Davis Jnr. with Burt Boyar.

● FILMS: *The Benny Goodman Story* (1956), *Anna Lucasta* (1958), *Porgy And Bess* (1959), *Pepe* (1960), *Ocean's Eleven* (1960), *The Threepenny Opera* (1962), *Convicts Four* (1962), *Sergeants 3* (1962), *Johnny Cool* (1963), *Robin And The 7 Hoods* (1964), *A Man Called Adam* (1966), *Movin' With Nancy* (1968), *Salt And Pepper* (1968), *Sweet Charity* (1969), *One More Time* (1970), *Save The Children* concert film (1973), *James Dean, The First American Teenager* (1975), *Gone With The West* (1975), *Sammy Stops The World* (1978), *The Cannonball Run* (1981), *Heidi's Song* (1982), *Cracking Up* (1983), *Cannonball Run II* (1984), *That's Dancing!* (1985), *Moon Over Parador* (1988), *Tap* (1989).

DAY, BOBBY

b. Robert Byrd, 1 July 1932, Fort Worth, Texas, USA, d. 27 July 1990, USA. Day moved to Los Angeles in 1947 and shortly afterwards formed the Flames, who recorded under a variety of names on numerous labels throughout the 50s. Oddly, it took until 1957 before they achieved their first and biggest hit as the Hollywood Flames with Day's song 'Buzz, Buzz, Buzz'. Simultaneously, the group were climbing the US charts as Bobby Day And The Satellites with another of his songs, 'Little Bitty Pretty One' on Class Records, although a cover version by Thurston Harris became a bigger hit. Day, who first recorded solo in 1955, took lone billing again in 1958 for the double-sided US number 2 hit 'Rockin' Robin' and 'Over And Over'. Despite releasing a string of further outstanding R&B/rock singles in the 50s, this distinctive singer-songwriter never returned to the Top 40. In the early 60s he formed Bob And Earl with ex-Hollywood Flame Earl Nelson, although he was replaced before the duo's hit 'Harlem Shuffle'. He later recorded without success under various names on Rendezvous, RCA Records and Sureshot and his own Bird Land label. He temporarily relocated to Australia before settling in Florida. Although his records were no longer selling, his songs were often revived, with Dave Clark taking 'Over And Over' to the top in 1965, Michael Jackson taking 'Rockin' Robin' to number 2 in 1972 and the Jackson Five reaching the Top 20 with the catchy 'Little Bitty Pretty One' in 1972. Day's long-awaited UK debut in 1989 was warmly received, although sadly he died of cancer in July 1990.

● ALBUMS: *Rockin' With Robin* (Class 1958) ★★★.

● COMPILATIONS: *The Original Rockin' Robin* (Ace 1991) ★★★, *The Best Of Bobby Day* (Varèse Sarabande 2001) ★★★.

DAY, DENNIS

b. Eugene McNulty, 21 May 1917, New York City, New York, USA, d. 22 June 1988, Brentwood, California, USA. Day was a popular singer, from the late 30s to the 60s, whose distinctive Irish tenor voice and flair for comedy gained him a prestigious spot on the top rated Jack Benny radio show. Day graduated from St. Patrick's Cathedral High School, and attended Manhattan College, planning to study law. He first appeared on Benny's show in 1939, replacing another tenor, Kenny Baker. After military service during World War II, Lewis became the comedian's regular foil, and moved with him to television in the 50s, and until the show ended in the mid-60s. He would continually frustrate Benny with his clowning, and favourite line: 'Oh, Mr. Benny'; to which the comedian would invariably reply: 'Oh, for heaven's sake. Sing Dennis!'. He also had his own show for a while on NBC, and appeared frequently on other programmes such as *Max Leiberman Presents*, *Hour Glass*, *All Star Review* and Milton Berle's *Texaco Star Theatre*. In the late 40s and early 50s Day had hits with 'Mamselle', 'Clancy Lowered The Boom', 'Dear Hearts And Gentle People', 'Goodnight, Irene', 'Mona Lisa', 'All My Love' and 'Mister And Mississippi'. He was also well known for his renditions of Irish favourites such as 'Peg O' My Heart', 'Too-Ra-Loo-Ra-Loo-Ral', 'McNamara's Band' and 'Danny Boy'. Day's film appearances included *Buck Benny Rides Again* (1940, with Jack Benny), *The Powers Girl* (1942), *I'll Get By* (1950), *Golden Girl* (1951) and *The Girl Next Door* (1953). He also provided the voice of 'Johnny Appleseed' for the cartoon *Melody Time*, along with Frances Langford, Ethel Smith and the Andrews Sisters. By the late 60s he had more or less retired from showbusiness, but continued to perform occasionally at conventions and fairs. He was a zealous supporter, and vice president of the Muscular Dystrophy Association. He died shortly after being critically injured in a fall at his home in March 1988.

● ALBUMS: *Here's Dennis Day!* (50s) ★★★, *Shillelaghs* (60s) ★★★, *Sings Songs From My Wild Irish Rose* (1967) ★★★, *At Hollywood's Moulin Rouge* (60s) ★★★.

● COMPILATIONS: *America's Favorite Irish Tenor* (Starline 1989) ★★★.

DAY, DORIS

b. Doris Von Kappelhoff, 3 April 1922, Cincinnati, Ohio, USA. One of popular music's premier post-war vocalists and biggest names, Kappelhoff originally trained as a dancer, before turning to singing at the age of 16. After changing her surname to Day, she became the featured singer with the Bob Crosby Band. A similarly successful period with the Les Brown Band saw her record a single for Columbia Records, 'Sentimental Journey', which sold in excess of a million copies. Already an accomplished businesswoman, it was rumoured that she held a substantial shareholding in her record company. After securing the female lead in the 1948 film *Romance On The High Seas*, in which she introduced Sammy Cahn and Jule

Styne's 'It's Magic', she enjoyed a stupendous movie career. Her striking looks, crystal-clear singing voice and willingness to play tomboy heroines, as well as romantic figures, brought her a huge following. In common with other female singers of the period, she was occasionally teamed with the stars of the day and enjoyed collaborative hits with Frankie Laine ('Sugarbush') and Johnnie Ray ('Let's Walk That A-Way').

She appeared in nearly 40 movies over two decades, including It's A Great Feeling (1949), Young Man With A Horn (1950), Tea For Two (1950), West Point Story (1950), Lullaby Of Broadway (1951), On Moonlight Bay (1951), Starlift (1951), I'll See You In My Dreams (1951), April In Paris (1952), By The Light Of The Silvery Moon (1953), Calamity Jane (1953), Young At Heart (1954), Love Me Or Leave Me (1955), The Man Who Knew Too Much (1956), The Pajama Game (1957), Pillow Talk (1959) and Jumbo (1962). These films featured some of her best-known hits. One of her finest performances was in the uproarious romantic western Calamity Jane, which featured her enduringly vivacious versions of 'The Deadwood Stage' and 'Black Hills Of Dakota'. The movie also gave her a US/UK number 1 single with the yearningly sensual 'Secret Love' (later a lesser hit for Kathy Kirby). Day enjoyed a further UK chart topper with the romantically uplifting 'Whatever Will Be, Will Be (Que Sera, Sera)'. After a gap of nearly six years, she returned to the charts with the sexually inviting movie theme 'Move Over Darling', co-written by her producer son Terry Melcher. Her Hollywood career ended in the late 60s and thereafter she was known for her reclusiveness. After more than 20 years away from the public's gaze, she emerged into the limelight in 1993 for a charity screening of Calamity Jane in her home-town of Carmel, California.

Two years later she made further appearances to promote The Love Album, which was recorded in 1967 but had been 'lost' since that time and never released. An earlier effort to remind her fans of the good old days came in the early 90s, when Leo P. Carusone and Patsy Carver's songbook revue Definitely Doris began its life as a cabaret at New York's Duplex. The show subsequently had its 'world premiere' at the King's Head Theatre, Islington, north London, before returning to the USA and entertaining audiences at Boston's 57 Theatre with a host of memorable numbers such as 'Ten Cents A Dance', 'Secret Love', 'When I Fall In Love', 'It's Magic', and the rest. In 1998, a British-born celebration of Doris Day and her work starred popular singer Rosemary Squires, who created the project with Helen Ash, wife of musician Vic Ash. History has made her an icon; her fresh-faced looks, sensual innocence and strikingly pure vocal style effectively summed up a glamorous era of American music.

● ALBUMS: You're My Thrill (Columbia 1949) ★★, Young Man With A Horn film soundtrack (Columbia 1950/54) ★★, Tea For Two film soundtrack (Columbia 1950) ★★, Lullaby Of Broadway film soundtrack (Columbia 1951) ★★, On Moonlight Bay film soundtrack (Columbia 1951)

★★★, I'll See You In My Dreams film soundtrack (Columbia 1951) ★★★, By The Light Of The Silvery Moon film soundtrack (Columbia 1953) ★★★, Calamity Jane film soundtrack (Columbia 1953) ★★★★, Young At Heart (Columbia 1954) ★★★★, Lights Camera Action (Columbia 1955) ★★★, Boys And Girls Together (Columbia 1955) ★★★, with Peggy Lee Hot Canaries (Columbia 1955) ★★★, Lullaby Of Broadway (Columbia 1955) ★★★★, Day Dreams (Columbia 1955) ★★★, Day In Hollywood (Columbia 1955) ★★★, Love Me Or Leave Me film soundtrack (Columbia 1955) ★★★★, Day By Day (Columbia 1957) ★★★★, Day By Night (Columbia 1957) ★★★, The Pajama Game film soundtrack (Columbia 1957) ★★★★, Hooray For Hollywood (Columbia 1958) ★★★, Cuttin' Capers (Columbia 1959) ★★★, Show Time (Columbia 1960) ★★★, What Every Girl Should Know (Columbia 1960) ★★★, Listen To Day (Columbia 1960) ★★★, Bright & Shiny (Columbia 1961) ★★★, I Have Dreamed (Columbia 1961) ★★★, Love Him! (Columbia 1964) ★★★, Sentimental Journey (Columbia 1965) ★★★, Latin For Lovers (Columbia 1965) ★★, The Love Album 1967 recordings (Columbia 1994) ★★★★.
● COMPILATIONS: Doris Day's Greatest Hits (Columbia 1958) ★★★★, Golden Greats (Warwick 1978) ★★★, The Best Of Doris Day (Columbia 1980) ★★★★, It's Magic 6-CD box set (Bear Family 1993) ★★★★, Hit Singles Collection (Telstar 1994) ★★★★, Personal Christmas Collection (1994) ★★★, The Magic Of Doris Day (Sony 1994) ★★★★, Move Over Darling 8-CD set (Bear Family 1997) ★★★, The Complete Doris Day With Les Brown 2-CD set (Sony Music Special Products 1997) ★★★, The Magic Of The Movies (Columbia 1999) ★★★.
● VIDEOS: Magic Of Doris Day (Warner Home Video 1989).
● FURTHER READING: Doris Day: Her Own Story, Doris Day and A.E. Hotcher. Doris Day, Eric Braun.
● FILMS: Romance On The High Seas (1948), It's A Great Feeling (1949), My Dream Is Yours (1949), West Point Story (1950), Tea For Two (1950), Young Man With A Horn (1950), Starlift cameo (1951), I'll See You In My Dreams (1951), On Moonlight Bay (1951), Lullaby Of Broadway (1951), Storm Warning (1951), April In Paris (1952), The Winning Team (1952), Calamity Jane (1953), By The Light Of The Silvery Moon (1953), Lucky Me (1954), Young At Heart (1954), Love Me Or Leave Me (1955), Julie (1956), The Man Who Knew Too Much (1956), The Pajama Game (1957), Teacher's Pet (1958), Tunnel Of Love (1958), Pillow Talk (1959), It Happened To Jane (1959), Midnight Lace (1960), Please Don't Eat The Daisies (1960), That Touch Of Mink (1962), Jumbo (1962), Lover Come Back (1962), Move Over Darling (1963), The Thrill Of It All (1963), Send Me No Flowers (1964), Do Not Disturb (1965), The Glass Bottom Boat (1966), Caprice (1967), With Six You Get Eggroll (1968), Where Were You When The Lights Went Out? (1968), The Ballad Of Josie (1968).

DAY, JILL
b. Yvonne Page, 5 December 1930, Brighton, Sussex, England, d. 16 November 1990, Kingston, Surrey, England. Originally a band singer, Day

graduated to become the main vocalist in the Geraldo orchestra. By 1954 she had topped the bill at the London Palladium and co-starred in the West End production of *The Talk Of The Town*. Screen appearances followed in *Always The Bride* and *All For Mary*. Although she registered no chart hits, her name became synonymous with a number of ballads including 'I'm Old Fashioned', 'Mangoes', 'A Holiday Affair' and 'I've Got My Love To Keep Me Warm'. Diminutive but tough, she was known for her fierce temper, made worse by her inexorable slide into alcoholism. Although various comebacks were mooted, including a prestigious part in the musical *Follies*, her singing career declined during the 60s. In 1963 she made the headlines when she emptied a tureen of peas over a waiter at the Pigalle theatre-restaurant, complaining that he clattered plates and cutlery during her act. Later she owned racehorses, and her business ventures included a theatrical agency and a baby-clothes company. She died of cancer in 1990.

DE CASTRO SISTERS

Peggy De Castro (b. Dominican Republic), Babette De Castro (b. Havana, Cuba) and Cherie De Castro (b. New York, USA) formed this close-harmony vocal trio who were extremely popular on record in the USA during the 50s, with a mixture of ballads and novelty numbers, and also in nightclubs, with a slick and flamboyant (some say flashy) act. They were raised in Cuba, on their father's sugar plantation, and began singing as a group when they moved to New York. Signed to the small Abbott label, they had a smash hit in 1954 with 'Teach Me Tonight', written by Sammy Cahn and Gene De Paul, which sold over five million copies. In 1955 they made the US charts again, with 'Boom Boom Boomerang'. Other important 50s titles included 'Too Late Now', 'Snowbound For Christmas', 'It's Yours', 'Who Are They To Say', 'Cuckoo In The Clock', 'Give Me Time' and 'Cowboys Don't Cry'. In 1959, they re-recorded their original hit as 'Teach Me Tonight Cha Cha', perhaps a sign that their appeal, at least on record, was fading. Despite the rapidly changing musical climate, they released *Sing* and *Rockin' Beat* in the early 60s. More than 25 years later, in 1988, the De Castro Sisters hit the comeback trail at Vegas World, Las Vegas. Reliving 50s joys while also strutting to later anthems such as 'New York, New York', they made up for tired vocal cords with an abundance of showbiz flair.
● ALBUMS: *The De Castros Sing* (Capitol 1960) ★★★, *The De Castro Sisters* (Abbott 1960) ★★, *The Rockin' Beat* (Capitol 1961) ★★★, *At The Stardust* (1965) ★★.

DEEP RIVER BOYS

A leading black vocal quartet of the 40s and 50s who, like their counterparts, the Charioteers, the Golden Gate Quartet, and the Delta Rhythm Boys, represented the jubilee and smooth ballad styles of the period. The Deep River Boys were formed by students at Hampton Institute in 1936 and consisted of lead Harry Douglass (b. 6 May 1916,

Bridgeville, Delaware, USA, d. 5 June 1999, New York, USA), bass Edward Ware, second tenor George Lawson and first tenor Vernon Gardner. Pianist Charlie Ford joined the group in 1937 and with his coaching and arrangements, the Deep River Boys proved a sensation, becoming regulars on network radio for the next few years. Ford was replaced in 1940 by Ray Duran (b. Horacio Duran, 1910, d. 1980), who in turn was replaced by Cameron Williams in 1943. The Deep River Boys began recording in 1940, and continued regularly for the next 15 years to record alternately for Victor and for Joe Davis' Beacon and Jay Dee labels. Appearances in 'soundies' (the 40s version of videos) further spread their name to the public. Although hit records proved elusive, songs associated with the group included 'That Chick's Too Young To Fry' (1946), 'Recess In Heaven' and 'Truthfully' (1952). The Deep River Boys' first visit to the UK was in 1949, launching their popularity in Europe, which in the 50s superseded their success in the USA, where the rise of R&B made their music seem dated. In the UK they achieved a chart record in 1956 with 'That's Right', which went to number 29 for one week. In 1950 Lawson left the group, and in 1955 Duran came back to replace Williams as pianist. Following the departure in 1956 of originals Ware and Gardner, Harry Douglass kept the group going through a bewildering number of personnel changes, but following the death of Duran in 1980, he retired.
● ALBUMS: *The Deep River Boys Sing Songs Of Jubilee* 10-inch album (Waldorf Music Hall 1955) ★★★★, *The Deep River Boys Sing Spirituals* 10-inch album (Waldorf Music Hall 1955) ★★★, *Presenting The Deep River Boys* (X 1956) ★★★★, *Midnight Magic* (Que 1957) ★★★, and *The Amazing The Deep River Boys, The Sensational Voices Of The Deep River Boys, Presenting Harry Douglass & The Deep River Boys, The International Inn Presents...*, *Old And New Songs, Golden Negro Spirituals*.
● COMPILATIONS: *Rock A Beatin' Boogie* (See For Miles 1985) ★★★★.

DEL-VIKINGS

Formed by members of the US Air Force in 1955 at their social club in Pittsburg, Ohio, the Del-Vikings' place in history is primarily secured by their status as the first successful multiracial rock 'n' roll band, but their recorded legacy also stands the test of time. Another fact overlooked by many archivists is that they were in fact, at inception, an all-black troupe. They were formed at Pittsburgh airport in 1956 by Clarence Quick (bass), Corinthian 'Kripp' Johnson (b. 1933, USA, d. 22 June 1990; lead and tenor), Samuel Patterson (lead and tenor), Don Jackson (baritone) and Bernard Robertson (second tenor). They were invited to record by producer Joe Averback, but Air Force assignments in Germany dragged away both Patterson and Robertson, who were replaced by Norman Wright and Dave Lerchey, the latter the band's first white member. 'Come Go With Me' became the lead-off track on their debut single for Averback's Fee Bee Records, but was then nationally licensed to Dot Records. It reached number 4 in the *Billboard* charts in February 1957, the highest position thus far achieved by a mixed-race group. That mix was further refined when Jackson became the third member to be transferred to Air Force duties in Germany, at which time he was replaced by a second white member, Donald 'Gus' Backus.

The group's second record, 'Down In Bermuda', was ignored, but 'Whispering Bells' was afforded a better reception, reaching number 9 in the US charts. Strange circumstances surrounded the subsequent disappearance of Johnson from the group; when their manager Al Berman took the Del-Vikings to Mercury Records, he was able to break their contract with Fee Bee because the musicians were under-age when they signed, apart from Johnson, who was legally bound being 21 years of age. William Blakely replaced him in the new line-up, which debuted with 'Cool Shake' in May 1957 (this entered the charts at about the same time as 'Whispering Bells', causing considerable confusion). Kripp Johnson retaliated by forming his own Del-Vikings with Arthur Budd, Eddie Everette, Chuck Jackson and original member Don Jackson, who had returned from his service endeavours in Germany. They released two singles, 'Willette' and 'I Want To Marry You', to little commercial recognition. Luniverse Records also muddied the picture by releasing an album of eight Del-Vikings songs that the group had originally placed with them in 1956 before Averback had signed them to Fee Bee. In order to clarify the situation, the next release on Dot Records was credited to the Dell-Vikings And Kripp Johnson, but this did not prevent Mercury Records suing to ensure that any use of the Del-Vikings name, whatever its spelling, belonged to it. Some of the confusion was abated when Kripp Johnson was able to rejoin the Del-Vikings when his contract with Fee Bee ran out in 1958 (by which time Donald Backus had become the fourth member of the group to lose his place due to an Air Force posting to Germany). Kripp sang lead on the group's last two Mercury singles, 'You Cheated' and 'How Could You'. Although recordings by the 'original Del-Vikings' were less forthcoming from this point, the group, now all discharged from the Air Force, toured widely throughout the 60s. They signed to a new label, ABC-Paramount Records, in 1961, and began in promising style with 'Bring Back Your Heart'. Several excellent releases followed, but none revisited the chart action of old. The 70s saw them record a handful of one-off singles as they toured widely, including stints in Europe and the Far East.

● ALBUMS: *Come Go With The Del Vikings* (Luniverse 1957) ★★★, *They Sing – They Swing* (Mercury 1957) ★★★, *A Swinging, Singing Record Session* (Mercury 1958) ★★, *Newies And Oldies* (1959) ★★★, *The Del Vikings And The Sonnets* (Crown 1963) ★★★, *Come Go With Me* (Dot 1966) ★★★.

● COMPILATIONS: *Del Vikings* (Buffalo Bop 1988) ★★★, *Cool Shake* (Buffalo Bop 1988) ★★★, *Collectables* (Mercury 1988) ★★★, *In Harmony* (Fireball 1998) ★★★.

DELANEY, ERIC

b. 22 May 1924, London, England. Delaney came from a musical family and learnt to play the piano while still at school. He switched to the drums at the age of 10, and studied tympani at the Guildhall School of Music in London during 1946-47. After playing in other bands, including the one led by Geraldo, Delaney formed his own unit in 1954, which was built around his 'Siamese twin drum kit', revolving stage, and a distinctive percussion sound. The record catalogues of the day listed him as a 'swing drummer'. His novel recording of 'Oranges And Lemons' gave the band its first boost, and it toured the UK Variety circuit in 1955, and in the following year played in the Royal Command Performance at the London Palladium, besides visiting the USA. Typical of the band's repertoire were 'Roamin' In The Gloamin'', 'Hornpipe Boogie', 'Cockles And Muscles', 'Say Si Si', 'Fanfare Jump' and the album *Cha-Cha-Cha Delaney*, all of which appeared on the UK Pye label. In 1960, Delaney switched to Parlophone Records and made an album *Swingin' Thro' The Shows*, produced by George Martin. In the 80s he was still touring with a small group, predominantly in the north of England. In 1991, sporting a 'Yul Brynner' haircut, Delaney announced his return to work following a three-month hiatus prompted by a condition he described as 'Lumbar Sacral Spondylosis'.

● ALBUMS: *Cha-Cha-Cha Delaney* (Pye 1959) ★★★, *Swingin' Thro' The Shows* (Parlophone 1960) ★★★.

DENE, TERRY

b. Terence Williams, 20 December 1938, London, England. Dene was discovered singing in the famous Soho coffee bar the 2 I's. His big break came when he appeared on the BBC Television show *6.5 Special* in April 1957. After being rejected by EMI Records, he was signed by Decca Records' A&R man Dick Rowe and his version of Marty Robbins' 'A White Sports Coat (And A Pink Carnation)' became the first of his three UK Top 20 hits between 1957 and 1958. His other big hits were 'Start Movin'', a cover version of the Sal Mineo original, and another Marty Robbins song, 'The Stairway Of Love'. Fame brought him many problems and in 1958 he was fined for both drunkenness and vandalism. A one-time screen extra, he also starred in the unsuccessful 1958 British pop film *The Golden Disc*. Often referred to as 'Britain's Elvis', this singer – with an admitted history of mental disturbance – was inducted into the army with the full press treatment in 1959. A large battalion of media representatives was also present when he was released as 'medically unfit' just two months later. The end of his short marriage to singer Edna Savage continued to give him the kind of publicity that destroyed what was left of his career. He next joined Larry Parnes' stable of stars, but the legendary impresario could not salvage Dene's career. After abandoning pop music, he became a street-singing evangelist, recording three gospel albums. He spent five years living in Sweden and in 1974 a book and album, both called *I Thought Terry Dene Was Dead*, were issued. In the 80s he returned to singing and rock 'n' roll with members of his original group, the Dene-Aces, which included Brian Gregg, writer of the classic 'Shakin' All Over'. Despite the fact that Dene was not a great rock 'n' roll original, he was welcomed back like a true legend by many UK fans.

● ALBUMS: *I Thought Terry Dene Was Dead* (Decca 1974) ★★★.
● COMPILATIONS: *The Real Terry Dene* (Rollercoaster 1998) ★★★.
● FURTHER READING: *I Thought Terry Dene Was Dead*, Dan Wooding.
● FILMS: *The Golden Disc* (1958).

DENNIS, JACKIE

b. 1942, Edinburgh, Scotland. Dennis was discovered by UK comedians Mike and Bernie Winters, when he was performing at an American Air Force base in Prestwick. They brought him to the attention of top agent Eve Taylor and she instantly booked him on the *6.5 Special* television show. Dennis's impact was immediate and he was quickly added to the cast of the *6.5 Special* film; it was even announced that he was to start filming *The Jackie Dennis Story*. The future looked very bright indeed in 1958 for the lively, kilt-wearing, 15-year-old pop singer, whose first record 'La Dee Dah', a cover version of Billy And Lillie's US hit, had leapt into the UK Top 20 just two weeks after its release. Television and live bookings flooded in and he was even invited to the USA to appear in Perry Como's top-rated television show, where he was introduced as 'Britain's Ricky Nelson'. Despite all this, record buyers did not purchase his subsequent releases in any quantity and he faded from the public eye just as quickly as he had arrived.

DIAMONDS

The members of this vocal group from New York, New York, USA were lead Harold Wright (d. April 1996), first tenor Myles Hardy, and bass Daniel Stevens. The Diamonds had moderate success in the early 50s specializing in deep-sounding ballads. The group was formed in 1948 as a trio – Wright, Hardy, and Stevens – but in 1950 they added a guitarist, Ernest Ward, who also sang tenor. The group was discovered by Bobby Schiffman of the Apollo Theatre and he gave them their start by having them play the amateur shows at his theatre. As their manager he helped them sign with Atlantic Records, which was enjoying great success with the Clovers at the time. The company released three singles by the group, the best remembered being 'A Beggar For Your Kisses'. The unit broke up by 1954, and Wright joined the Regals, who recorded four tracks for Aladdin. When the other Regals became Sonny Till's new Orioles group, Wright formed the Metronones, which recorded four tracks for Cadence.

DICKENSON, VIC

b. 6 August 1906, Xenia, Ohio, USA, d. 16 November 1984, New York City, New York, USA.

A self-taught musician, Dickenson's early experience came playing trombone in the territory bands of Speed Webb and Zack Whyte. By the 30s he was ready for the big time and worked with bands led by Luis Russell, Claude Hopkins, Benny Carter and Count Basie. Throughout the 40s he was active mostly with small groups, including those of Sidney Bechet, Frankie Newton, Eddie Heywood (for a long spell), and as leader of his own groups. This pattern continued into the 50s and 60s when he worked with Bobby Hackett, Red Allen and others. Although rooted in the more traditional jazz style, Dickenson's big band experience, allied to his instinctive melodic grace, made him an ideal musician to enter the mainstream. Indeed, his record albums of the early and mid-50s, especially dates with Ruby Braff, were important milestones in the emergence of this strand of jazz. In addition to his mastery of his instrument, Dickenson brought a refreshing sense of humour to his playing, inserting little musical asides that help to make his work readily identifiable.

● ALBUMS: *The Vic Dickenson Septet, Volume 1* 10-inch album (Vanguard 1953) ★★★★, *The Vic Dickenson Septet, Volume 2* 10-inch album (Vanguard 1953) ★★★★, *Vic Dickenson Septet, Volume 3* 10-inch album (Vanguard 1953) ★★★★, *The Vic Dickenson Septet, Volume 4* 10-inch album (Vanguard 1954) ★★★★, *Vic's Boston Story* (Storyville 1957) ★★★, with Joe Thomas *Mainstream* (Atlantic 1958) ★★★, *Yacht Club Swing* (1964) ★★★, with Bobby Hackett *This Is My Bag* (1968) ★★★, *Bobby Hackett, Vic Dickenson, Maxine Sullivan At The Fourth Manassas Jazz Festival* (Jazzology 1969) ★★★, with Bobby Hackett *Bobby Hackett-Vic Dickenson Septet* (1973) ★★★, *Jive At Five* (1975) ★★★, *Gentleman Of The Trombone* (1975) ★★★, *Vic Dickenson In Holland* (1975) ★★★, *Plays Bessie Smith – Trombone Cholly* (1976) ★★★, *The Vic Dickenson Quintet* (1976) ★★★, *Vic Dickenson In Sessions* (1978) ★★★, with Joe Thomas *Mainstream* (Koch 1999) ★★.
● COMPILATIONS: *The Essential Vic Dickenson* (Vanguard 1998) ★★★★.
● FURTHER READING: *Ding! Ding! A Bio-Discographical Scrapbook On Vic Dickenson*, Manfred Selchow.

DIXIE HUMMINGBIRDS

This gospel group, originally fronted by baritone James Davis, were formed in 1928 in Greenville, South Carolina, USA. In the 30s and 40s they sang hymns, spirituals and jubilees with little accompaniment except for their precise and warm harmonies. Baritone Ira Tucker (b. 17 May 1925, Spartanburg, North Carolina, USA) joined the line-up in 1938, and was later established as the flamboyant showman of the group, introducing a dramatic live act that had a lasting influence on many soul singers. Their 1939-49 recordings for labels including Apollo and Gotham are best heard on the *In The Storm Too Long* compilation, which captures the intricate vocal interplay of Tucker and Paul Owens. From

1952 onwards, the group recorded a series of compelling albums for Don Robey's Peacock Records, the compassion and emotive timbre of which matched the power of Mahalia Jackson and Rev. James Cleveland, with outstanding teamwork rather than individual flair their greatest asset. The line-up on such classics as 'Wading Through Blood And Water', 'Let's Go Out To The Program', 'Christian Testimonial', 'Nobody Knows The Trouble I See', and 'Our Prayer For Peace' comprised Tucker, Davis, Beachey Thompson (b. 1915, d. 1994), William Bobo (d. 1976), and Owens' replacement, the honey-throated James Walker (b. 1926, d. 1992).

With the advent of the 60s they began to embrace secular music, fusing their traditional gospel with jazz, blues and even rock, and appearing at the 1966 Newport Folk Festival. Their most famous appearance outside of the church circuit came in 1973 when they backed Paul Simon at the Muscle Shoals Studio on his recording of 'Loves Me Like A Rock'. The death of bass vocalist Bobo in 1976 brought an end to the classic line-up. Two years later the group was inducted into the Philadelphia Hall Of Fame. Founder member James Davis retired in 1984, while Walker and Thompson died in 1992 and 1994 respectively. In the late 90s, Tucker was still performing with a line-up comprising Paul Owens, Howard Carroll, and Carl Davis, and celebrated the group's 70th anniversary with the *Music In The Air* album. The Dixie Hummingbirds' natural market was always within the gospel community, where recordings such as 'Somebody Is Lying', 'You Don't Have Nothing If You Don't Have Jesus' and 'The Devil Can't Harm A Praying Man' are still venerated.

● ALBUMS: *A Christian Testimonial* (Peacock 1959) ★★★★, *In The Morning* (Peacock 1962) ★★★, *Prayer For Peace* (Peacock 1964) ★★★, *Every Day And Every Hour* (Peacock 1966) ★★★, *Live* (Mobile Fidelity 1976) ★★, *Dixie Hummingbirds* (Gospel Heritage 1988) ★★★, *Music In The Air: The 70th Anniversary All-Star Tribute* (House Of Blues 1999) ★★★.

● COMPILATIONS: *In The Storm Too Long* 1939-1949 recordings (Golden Jubilee 1985) ★★★, *The Best Of The Dixie Hummingbirds* (MCA 1988) ★★★★, *Dixie Hummingbirds 1939-47* (Document 1996) ★★★, *Thank You For One More Day: The 70th Anniversary Of The Dixie Hummingbirds* (MCA 1998) ★★★★, *Looking Back: A Retrospective* (Platinum 1998) ★★★, *Up In Heaven: The Very Best Of The Dixie Hummingbirds & The Angelics* (Collectables 1998) ★★★.

DIXON, FLOYD

b. 8 February 1929, Marshall, Texas, USA. Dixon, aka J. Riggins Jnr., began playing piano and singing as a child, absorbing every influence from gospel and blues to jazz, and even hillbilly. In 1942 his family moved to Los Angeles and he came into contact with fellow ex-Texan Charles Brown who, sensing Dixon's potential, introduced him to his brand of cool, jazzy night club blues as singer and pianist with Johnny Moore's Three Blazers. When the Blazers split up, Dixon was the natural choice for a substitute Charles Brown, and he made early recordings in the Brown style with both Eddie Williams (the Blazers' bass player) for Supreme and with Johnny Moore's new Blazers for Aladdin and Combo. His own trio recorded extensively for Modern, Peacock and Aladdin labels between 1947 and 1952; later, they played in a harder R&B style for Specialty Records, Cat and Checker Records, and in the late 50s and 60s for a host of tiny west coast and Texas independent labels. In 1975 Dixon made a comeback, beginning with a tour of Sweden, and became the first artist to be featured on Jonas Bernholm's celebrated Route 66 reissue label. Dixon was commissioned to write 'Olympic Blues' for the 1984 Los Angeles games. In the 90s he surfaced on the Alligator Records label.

● ALBUMS: *Opportunity Blues* (Route 66 1980) ★★★, *Houston Jump* (Route 66 1980) ★★★, *Empty Stocking Blues* (Route 66 1985) ★★★★, *Hitsville Look Out, Here's Mr. Magnificent* (1986) ★★★, *Wake Up And Live* (Alligator 1996) ★★★.

● COMPILATIONS: *Marshall Texas Is My Home* (Ace 1991) ★★★, *Cowtown Blues* (Ace 2000) ★★★.

DIXON, REGINALD

b. 1905, Sheffield, England, d. 9 May 1985, Blackpool, Lancashire, England. The son of a craftsman in the local Sheffield steel industry, as a teenager Dixon played the organ in a Methodist church and provided the accompaniment for silent films. In 1930 he accepted the position of organist at the Tower Ballroom in Blackpool, and stayed there – except for a spell in the RAF during World War II – for 40 years, until his retirement. Heralded by his much-loved signature tune 'Oh, I Do Like To Be Beside The Seaside', he came to be known as 'Mr. Blackpool', and was almost as famous as the Tower itself. However, his reputation also reached other areas of the UK through his frequent broadcasts and recordings of medleys of familiar popular tunes and light classical pieces.

● ALBUMS: *Presenting Reginald Dixon* (Columbia 1963) ★★★★, *Happy Memories Of Blackpool* (Encore 1964) ★★★, *Mr. Blackpool* (Columbia 1964) ★★★★, *Sing Along At The Tower* (Columbia 1966) ★★★, *Gala Night At The Tower* (Encore 1966) ★★★, *Great Organ Favourites* (Columbia 1967) ★★★, *At Your Request* (Columbia 1967) ★★★, *Meet Mr. Blackpool* (Columbia 1968) ★★★, *Beside The Seaside* (Columbia 1969) ★★★★, *Farewell Mr. Blackpool* (Columbia 1970) ★★★, *At The Movies* (One-Up 1976) ★★★, *Isn't This A Lovely Day* (EMI 1980) ★★★, *At The Wurlitzer Organ* (Ideal 1981) ★★★★, *Over The Waves* (EMI 1981) ★★★, *Blackpool Nights* (EMI 1985) ★★★★, *Fascinating Rhythm* (Burlington Records 1988) ★★★, *At The Organ Of The Tower Ballroom, Blackpool* (Ideal 1991) ★★★.

● COMPILATIONS: *World Of Reginald Dixon* (Decca 1969) ★★★★, *Magic Of Reginald Dixon* (MFP 1987) ★★★.

DIXON, WILLIE

b. 1 July 1915, Vicksburg, Mississippi, USA, d. 29 January 1992, Burbank, California, USA. At an early age Dixon was interested in both words and music, writing lyrics and admiring the playing of Little Brother Montgomery. As an adolescent, Dixon sang bass with local gospel groups, had some confrontation with the law, and hoboed his way to Chicago, where he became a boxer. He entered music professionally after meeting Baby Doo Caston, and together they formed the Five Breezes, whose 1940 recordings blend blues, jazz, pop and the vocal group harmonies of the Inkspots and the Mills Brothers. During World War II, Dixon resisted the draft, and was imprisoned for 10 months. After the war, he formed the Four Jumps Of Jive before reuniting with Caston in the Big Three Trio, who toured the Midwest and recorded for Columbia Records. The trio featured vocal harmonies and the jazz-influenced guitarwork of Ollie Crawford. Dixon's performing activities lessened as his involvement with Chess Records increased. By 1951 he was a full-time employee, as producer, A&R representative, session musician, talent scout, songwriter, and occasionally, name artist.

Apart from an interlude when he worked for Cobra in a similar capacity, Dixon remained with Chess until 1971. The relationship, however, was ultimately complex; he was forced to regain control of his copyrights by legal action. Meanwhile, Dixon was largely responsible for the sound of Chicago blues on Chess and Cobra, and of the black rock 'n' roll of Chuck Berry and Bo Diddley. He was also used on gospel sessions by Duke/Peacock, and his bass playing was excellent behind Rev. Robert Ballinger. Dixon's productions of his own songs included Muddy Waters' 'Hoochie Coochie Man', Howlin' Wolf's 'Spoonful', Diddley's 'You Can't Judge A Book By The Cover', Otis Rush's 'I Can't Quit You Baby' (a triumph for Dixon's and Rush's taste for minor chords), and Koko Taylor's 'Wang Dang Doodle', among many others. In the early 60s, Dixon teamed up with Memphis Slim to play the folk revival's notion of blues, and operated as a booking agent and manager, in which role he was crucial to the American Folk Blues Festival Tours of Europe. Many British R&B bands recorded his songs, including the Rolling Stones and Led Zeppelin, who adapted 'You Need Love'. After leaving Chess, Dixon went into independent production with his own labels, Yambo and Spoonful, and resumed a recording and performing career. He also administered the Blues Heaven Foundation, a charity that aimed to promote awareness of the blues, and to rectify the financial injustices of the past. Willie Dixon claimed, 'I am the blues'; and he was, certainly, hugely important in its history, not only as a great songwriter, but also as a producer, performer and mediator between artists and record companies.

● ALBUMS: *Willie's Blues* (Bluesville 1959) ★★★, *Memphis Slim & Willie Dixon At The Village Gate* (1960) ★★★★, *I Am The Blues* (Columbia 1970) ★★★, *Peace* (Yambo 1971) ★★★, *Catalyst* (Ovation 1973) ★★★, *Mighty Earthquake And Hurricane* (Chase 1983) ★★★, *I Feel Like Steppin' Out* (1986) ★★★, *Hidden Charms* (Bug 1988) ★★★, *Blues Dixonary* (1993) ★★★, *Across The Borderline* (1993) ★★★.

● COMPILATIONS: *Collection* (Deja Vu 1987) ★★★, *The Chess Box* box set (Chess 1988) ★★★★, *The Original Wang Dang Doodle – The Chess Recordings & More* (MCA/ Chess 1995) ★★★★, *Poet Of The Blues* (Columbia/ Legacy 1998) ★★★★, *The Songs Of Willie Dixon* tribute album (Telarc 1999) ★★.

● FURTHER READING: *I Am The Blues*, Willie Dixon.

DJANGO REINHARDT

This movie was a good examination of the work of the first European to achieve international status in jazz. Directed by Paul Paviot, this 1958 film features several musicians associated with Reinhardt, including his brother, Joseph, and Stéphane Grappelli.

DOGGETT, BILL

b. 16 February 1916, Philadelphia, Pennsylvania, USA, d. 13 November 1996, New York City, New York, USA. In 1938 pianist Doggett formed his first band, partly drawing his sidemen from the band of Jimmy Goreham, with whom he had played for the past few years. Later that year he worked with Lucky Millinder, with whom he also played in the early 40s – Millinder having taken over leadership of Doggett's band. During this period Doggett wrote many arrangements for various bands, including Lionel Hampton and Count Basie, and also worked as staff arranger and accompanist with the popular vocal group the Ink Spots. He made a number of recordings with Buddy Tate and Illinois Jacquet, then worked with Willie Bryant, Johnny Otis and Louis Jordan. In the mid-40s he began playing organ, and when he formed his own R&B band in 1951, concentrated on this instrument. He had big hits with 'Honky Tonk', which reached number 1 in the R&B charts and number 2 in the US charts in 1956, and was in the Top 10 for 14 weeks with 'Slow Walk'. He showed his versatility by arranging and conducting Ella Fitzgerald's 1963 album *Rhythm Is Our Business*. Doggett continued leading a swinging R&B-orientated band into the 80s.

● ALBUMS: *Bill Doggett – His Organ And Combo* 10-inch album (King 1955) ★★★, *Bill Doggett – His Organ And Combo Volume 2* 10-inch album (King 1955) ★★★, *All-Time Christmas Favorites* 10-inch album (King 1955) ★, *Sentimentally Yours* 10-inch album (King 1956) ★★★, *Moondust* (King 1957) ★★, *Hot Doggett* (King 1957) ★★, with Earl Bostic *C'mon And Dance With Earl Bostic* (King 1958) ★★★★, *As You Desire* (King 1958) ★★★, *A Salute To Ellington* (King 1958) ★★★, *Goin' Doggett* (King 1958) ★★★, *The Doggett Beat For Dancing Feet* (King 1958) ★★★, *Candle Glow* (King 1958) ★★★, *Dame Dreaming* (King 1958) ★★★, *Everybody Dance To The Honky Tonk* (King 1958) ★★★, *Man With A Beat* (King 1958) ★★★, *Swingin' Easy* (King 1959) ★★★, *Dance Awhile With Doggett* (King

1959) ★★, *Hold It* (King 1959) ★★★, *High And Wide* (King 1959) ★★★, *Big City Dance Party* (King 1959) ★★★, *Bill Doggett On Tour* (King 1959) ★★★, *Bill Doggett Christmas* (King 1959) ★★, *For Reminiscent Lovers, Romantic Songs* (King 1960) ★★★, *Back Again With More Bill Doggett* (King 1960) ★★★, *Focus On Bill Doggett* (King 1960) ★★, *Bonanza Of 24 Songs* (King 1960) ★★★, *The Many Moods Of Bill Doggett* (King 1963) ★★, *American Songs In The Bossa Nova Style* (King 1963) ★★, *Impressions* (King 1964) ★★★, *Honky Tonk Popcorn* (King 1969) ★★★, *Midnight Slows Volume 9* (Black And Blue 1978) ★★★.
● COMPILATIONS: *The Best Of Bill Doggett* (King 1964) ★★★, *Bonanza Of 24 Hit Songs* (King 1966) ★★★, *14 Original Greatest Hits* (King 1988) ★★★.

DOMINO, FATS

b. Antoine Domino, 26 February 1928, New Orleans, Louisiana, USA. From a large family, Domino learned piano from local musician Harrison Verrett who was also his brother-in-law. A factory worker after leaving school, Domino played in local clubs such as the Hideaway. It was there in 1949 that bandleader Dave Bartholomew and Lew Chudd of Imperial Records heard him. His first recording, 'The Fat Man', became a Top 10 R&B hit the next year and launched his unique partnership with Bartholomew who co-wrote and arranged dozens of Domino tracks over the next two decades.
Like that of Professor Longhair, Domino's playing was derived from the rich mixture of musical styles to be found in New Orleans. These included traditional jazz, Latin rhythms, boogie-woogie, Cajun and blues. Domino's personal synthesis of these influences involved lazy, rich vocals supported by rolling piano rhythms. On occasion his relaxed approach was at odds with the urgency of other R&B and rock artists and the Imperial engineers would frequently speed up the tapes before Domino's singles were released. During the early 50s, Domino gradually became one of the most successful R&B artists in America. Songs such as 'Goin' Home' and 'Going To The River', 'Please Don't Leave Me' and 'Don't You Know' were bestsellers and he also toured throughout the country. The touring group included the nucleus of the band assembled by Dave Bartholomew for recordings at Cosimo Matassa's studio. Among the musicians were Lee Allen (saxophone), Frank Field (bass) and Walter 'Papoose' Nelson (guitar). By 1955, rock 'n' roll had arrived and young white audiences were ready for Domino's music. His first pop success came with 'Ain't That A Shame' in 1955, although Pat Boone's cover version sold more copies. 'Bo Weevil' was also covered, by Teresa Brewer, but the catchy 'I'm In Love Again', with its incisive saxophone phrases from Allen, took Domino into the pop Top 10. The b-side was an up-tempo treatment of the 20s standard, 'My Blue Heaven', which Verrett had sung with Papa Celestin's New Orleans jazz band. Domino's next big success also came with a pre-rock 'n' roll song, 'Blueberry Hill'. Inspired by Louis Armstrong's 1949 version, Domino used his Creole drawl to

perfection. Altogether, Fats Domino had nearly 20 US Top 20 singles between 1955 and 1960. Among the last of them was the majestic 'Walking To New Orleans', a Bobby Charles composition that became a string-laden tribute to the sources of his musical inspiration. His track record in the Billboard R&B lists, however, is impressive, with 63 records reaching the charts. He continued to record prolifically for Imperial until 1963, maintaining a consistently high level of performance.
There were original compositions such as the jumping 'My Girl Josephine' and 'Let the Four Winds Blow' and cover versions of country songs (Hank Williams' 'Jambalaya (On The Bayou)') as well as standard ballads such as 'Red Sails In The Sunset', his final hit single in 1963. The complex off-beat of 'Be My Guest' was a clear precursor of the ska rhythms of Jamaica, where Domino was popular and toured in 1961. The only unimpressive moments came when he was persuaded to jump on the twist bandwagon, recording a banal number titled 'Dance With Mr Domino'. By now, Lew Chudd had sold the Imperial company and Domino switched labels to ABC Paramount. There he recorded several albums with producers Felton Jarvis and Bill Justis, but his continuing importance lay in his tours of North America and Europe, which recreated the sound of the 50s for new generations of listeners. The quality of Domino's touring band was well captured in a 1965 live album for Mercury from Las Vegas with Roy Montrell (guitar), Cornelius Coleman (drums) and the saxophones of Herb Hardesty and Lee Allen. Domino continued this pattern of work into the 70s, breaking it slightly when he gave the Beatles' 'Lady Madonna' a New Orleans treatment. He made further albums for Reprise (1968) and Sonet (1979), the Reprise sides being the results of a reunion session with Dave Bartholomew.
Official recognition of Domino's contribution to popular music came in the late 80s. In 1986 he was inducted into the Rock And Roll Hall Of Fame, and won Hall Of Fame and Lifetime Achievement awards at the 1987 Grammy's. In 1991 EMI, which now owns the Imperial catalogue, released a scholarly box set of Domino's remarkable recordings. Two years later, Domino was back in the studio recording his first sessions proper for 25 years, resulting in his *Christmas Is A Special Day* set. 'People don't know what they've done for me', he reflected. 'They always tell me, "Oh Fats, thanks for so many years of good music". And I'll be thankin' them before they're finished thankin' me!' He remains a giant figure of R&B and rock 'n' roll, both musically and physically.
● ALBUMS: *Carry On Rockin'* (Imperial 1955) ★★★★, *Rock And Rollin' With Fats* (Imperial 1956) ★★★★, *Rock And Rollin'* (Imperial 1956) ★★★★, *This Is Fats Domino!* (Imperial 1957) ★★★★, *Here Stands Fats Domino* (Imperial 1958) ★★★★, *Fabulous Mr D* (Imperial 1958) ★★★★, *Let's Play Fats Domino* (Imperial 1959) ★★★★, *Fats Domino Swings* (Imperial 1959) ★★★★★, *Million Record Hits* (Imperial 1960) ★★★★, *A Lot Of Dominos*

(Imperial 1960) ★★★★, *I Miss You So* (Imperial 1961) ★★★, *Let The Four Winds Blow* (Imperial 1961) ★★★★, *What A Party* (Imperial 1962) ★★★, *Twistin' The Stomp* (Imperial 1962) ★★★, *Just Domino* (Imperial 1962) ★★★, *Here Comes Fats Domino* (ABC-Paramount 1963) ★★★, *Walkin' To New Orleans* (Imperial 1963) ★★★★, *Let's Dance With Domino* (Imperial 1963) ★★★, *Here He Comes Again* (Imperial 1963) ★★★, *Fats On Fire* (ABC 1964) ★★★, *Fats Domino '65* (Mercury 1965) ★★★, *Getaway With Fats Domino* (ABC 1965) ★★★, *Fats Is Back* (Reprise 1968) ★★★, *Cookin' With Fats* (United Artists 1974) ★★★, *Sleeping On The Job* (Sonet 1979) ★★, *Live At Montreux* (Atlantic 1987) ★★★, *The Domino Effect* (Charly 1989) ★★★, *Christmas Is A Special Day* (Right Stuff/EMI 1994) ★★.

● COMPILATIONS: *The Very Best Of Fats Domino* (Liberty 1970) ★★★★, *Rare Domino's* (Liberty 1970) ★★★, *Rare Domino's Volume 2* (Liberty 1971) ★★★, *Fats Domino – His Greatest Hits* (MCA 1986) ★★★, *My Blue Heaven – The Best Of Fats Domino* (EMI 1990) ★★★★, *They Call Me The Fat Man: The Legendary Imperial Recordings* 4-CD box set (EMI/Imperial 1991) ★★★★★, *Out Of Orleans* 8-CD box set (Bear Family 1993) ★★★★★, *The EP Collection Volume 1* (See For Miles 1995) ★★★★, *The Early Imperial Singles 1950-52* (Ace 1996) ★★★★, *The EP Collection Volume 2* (See For Miles 1997) ★★★★, *The Imperial Singles Volume 3* (Ace 1999) ★★★★, *Legends Of The 20th Century* (EMI 1999) ★★★.

● FILMS: *The Girl Can't Help It* (1956), *Jamboree* aka *Disc Jockey Jamboree* (1957), *The Big Beat* (1957).

DOMINOES
(see Ward, Billy, And The Dominoes)

DONEGAN, LONNIE
b. Anthony Donegan, 29 April 1931, Glasgow, Scotland. Donegan, as 'The King Of Skiffle', became a more homogeneous UK equivalent to Elvis Presley than Tommy Steele. Steeped in traditional jazz and its by-products, he was a guitarist in a skiffle band before a spell in the army found him drumming in the Wolverines Jazz Band. After his discharge, he played banjo with Ken Colyer and then Chris Barber. With his very stage forename a tribute to a black bluesman, both units allowed him to sing a couple of blues-tinged American folk tunes as a 'skiffle' break. His version of Lead Belly's 'Rock Island Line', issued from Barber's *New Orleans Joys* in 1954 as a single after months in the domestic hit parade, was also a US hit. Donegan's music inspired thousands of teenagers to form amateur skiffle combos, with friends playing broomstick tea-chest bass, washboards and other instruments fashioned from household implements. The Beatles, playing initially as the Quarry Men, were the foremost example of an act traceable to such roots.

Playing with his own group, Donegan was a prominent figure in skiffle throughout its 1957 prime; he possessed an energetic whine far removed from the gentle plumminess of other native pop vocalists. Donegan could dazzle with his virtuosity on 12-string acoustic guitar and his string of familiar songs has rarely been surpassed: 'Don't You Rock Me Daddy-O', 'Putting On The Style' ('putting on the agony, putting on the style'), 'Bring A Little Water Sylvie', 'Grand Coulee Dam', 'Does Your Chewing Gum Lose Its Flavour On The Bedpost Over Night' and 'Jimmy Brown The Newsboy', were only a few of Donegan's gems. He arguably made the traditional song 'Cumberland Gap' his own (his first UK number 1), and 1959's 'Battle Of New Orleans' was the finest ever reading. He delved more deeply into Americana to embrace bluegrass, spirituals, Cajun and even Appalachian music, the formal opposite of jazz. However, when the skiffle boom diminished, he broadened his appeal – to much purist criticism – with old-time music hall/pub singalong favourites, and a more pronounced comedy element. His final chart-topper was with the uproarious 'My Old Man's A Dustman', which sensationally entered the UK charts at number 1 in 1960. The hit was an adaptation of the ribald Liverpool folk ditty 'My Old Man's A Fireman On The Elder-Dempster Line'. He followed it with further comedy numbers including 'Lively' in 1960. Two years later, Donegan's Top 20 run ended as it had started, with a Lead Belly number ('Pick A Bale Of Cotton'). However, between 1956 and 1962 he had numbered 34 hits. He finished the 60s with huge sales of two mid-price *Golden Age Of Donegan* volumes, supplementing his earnings in cabaret and occasional spots on BBC Television's *The Good Old Days*.

The most interesting diversion of the next decade was Adam Faith's production of *Putting On The Style*. Here, at Paul McCartney's suggestion, Donegan remade old smashes backed by an extraordinary glut of artists who were lifelong fans, including Rory Gallagher, Ringo Starr, Leo Sayer, Zoot Money, Albert Lee, Gary Brooker, Brian May, Nicky Hopkins, Elton John and Ron Wood. While this album brushed 1978's UK album list, a 1982 single, 'Spread A Little Happiness', was also a minor success – and, as exemplified by the Traveling Wilburys' 'skiffle for the 90s', the impact of Donegan's earliest chart entries continues to exert an influence on pop music. Although no longer enjoying the best of health, Donegan continues to entertain. He has long been an influential legend and the man who personifies British skiffle music. In the early 90s he was touring occasionally with his old boss, Chris Barber, and in 1995 he was presented with an Ivor Novello Award for Outstanding Contribution To British Music. In 1998, Donegan recorded his first new album in 20 years. Among the highlights on *Muleskinner Blues* was a duet with Van Morrison and revitalized versions of several Donegan staples such as 'Rock Island Line' and 'Alabamy Bound'. In the late 90s his playing is as sharp as ever but what is of greater note is his voice. Not only has he maintained the power of his high treble, but he now has a baritone range that can shake the floor. Donegan is a remarkable survivor; without doubt he is the king of British skiffle but also a hugely influential figure in the development of popular music in the UK.

● ALBUMS: *Showcase* (Pye Nixa 1956) ★★★, *Lonnie* (Pye Nixa 1957) ★★★, *Tops With Lonnie* (Pye 1958) ★★★★, *Lonnie Rides Again* (Pye 1959) ★★★, *More Tops With Lonnie* (Pye 1961) ★★★★, *Sings Hallelujah* (Pye 1962) ★★★, *The Lonnie Donegan Folk Album* (Pye 1965) ★★★★, *Lonniepops-Lonnie Donegan Today* (Decca 1970) ★★★, *Lonnie Donegan Meets Leineman* (1974) ★★, *Lonnie Donegan* (1975) ★★, *Lonnie Donegan Meets Leineman-Country Roads* (1976) ★★, *Putting On The Style* (Chrysalis 1978) ★★★, *Sundown* (Chrysalis 1979) ★★★, *Jubilee Concert* (Cube 1981) ★★, *Muleskinner Blues* (BMG 1998) ★★★★.

● COMPILATIONS: *Golden Age Of Donegan* (Golden Guinea 1962) ★★★★, *Golden Age Of Donegan Volume 2* (Golden Guinea 1963) ★★★★, *Golden Hour Of Golden Hits* (Golden Hour 1973) ★★★, *Golden Hour Of Golden Hits, Volume 2* (Golden Hour 1974) ★★★, *The Lonnie Donegan File* (Pye 1977) ★★★★, *The Hits Of Lonnie Donegan* (MFP 1978) ★★★, *Greatest Hits: Lonnie Donegan* (Ditto 1983) ★★★★, *Rare And Unissued Gems* (Bear Family 1985) ★★★, *Rock Island Line* (Flashback 1985) ★★★★, *The Hit Singles Collection* (PRT 1987) ★★★★, *The Best Of Lonnie Donegan* (Pickwick 1989) ★★★★, *The Collection: Lonnie Donegan* (Castle 1989) ★★★★, *The EP Collection* (See For Miles 1992) ★★★, *Putting On The Styles* 3-CD box set (1992) ★★★★, *More Than 'Pye In The Sky'* 8-CD box set (Bear Family 1994) ★★★★, *Talking Guitar Blues: The Very Best Of Lonnie Donegan* (Sequel 1999) ★★★★.

● FURTHER READING: *Skiffle: The Inside Story*, Chas McDevitt. *The Skiffle Craze*, Mike Dewe.

DONEN, STANLEY

b. 13 April 1924, Columbia, South Carolina, USA. The director and choreographer for a string of classic MGM musicals of the 50s, Donen was fascinated by film and theatre from an early age. After graduating from high school he worked on Broadway in the chorus of the Richard Rodgers and Lorenz Hart musical Pal Joey (1940), which starred Gene Kelly, and he assisted Kelly on the choreography for Best Foot Forward (1941) and also appeared in the chorus. Signed to MGM, during the 40s he worked as choreographer, co-choreographer and/or co-director of occasional sequences (often uncredited) on musicals such as Cover Girl, *Hey Rookie*, *Jam Session*, *Kansas City Kitty*, Anchors Aweigh, *Holiday In Mexico*, No Leave, No Love, Living In A Big Way, This Time For Keeps, A Date With Judy, The Kissing Bandit and Take Me Out To The Ball Game. In 1949 Donen made his official directorial debut as Gene Kelly's co-director on the acclaimed, ground-breaking musical On The Town, and they worked together on several more memorable films, including Singin' In The Rain, It's Always Fair Weather and The Pajama Game. Donen also brought his skill as a director of breathtakingly fresh and exuberant sequences to pictures such as Wedding Bells, *Give A Girl A Break* (also choreographed with Gower Champion), Deep In My Heart, Seven Brides For

Seven Brothers, Funny Face and Damn Yankees (1958). By that time the golden age of movie musicals was over, and, with the exception of *The Little Prince* (1974), Donen concentrated on directing (and producing) dramatic and light-comedy films such as Indiscreet, *The Grass Is Greener*, Arabesque, *Two For The Road*, Bedazzled, Staircase, *Lucky Lady*, Movie, Movie, Saturn 3, and Blame It On Rio (1984). Since then, Donen has been rumoured to be trying to bring biographies of Judy Garland and Marlene Dietrich to the screen, but to date nothing has materialized. In 1988 he produced the Academy Awards show, and five years later made his directorial debut on Broadway in the Jule Styne musical The Red Shoes. After the original director, Susan Schulman, bowed out in the early stages of production, Donen took over. Unfortunately, unlike those earlier MGM musicals, there was no happy ending and the show closed after three days. However, in 1998 Donen received an Honorary Academy Award 'in appreciation of a body of work marked by grace, elegance, wit and visual innovation'.

DON'T KNOCK THE ROCK

The same production team responsible for *Rock Around The Clock* made this 1956 film. Alan Dale played the part of rock 'n' roll singer Arnie Haynes, accused by parents of corrupting impressionable minds when he returns to his home-town. Disc jockey Alan Freed enjoyed a prominent role as Haynes' agent. When a riot breaks out at a concert headlined by Bill Haley And His Comets, the pair stage another show to convince the adults the music is no more controversial than previous fashions. The Treniers and Dave Appell And His Applejacks make appearances, but the film's highlight comes courtesy of Little Richard who contributes explosive versions of 'Long Tall Sally', 'Tutti Frutti' and 'Rip It Up'. His performances saved this hurriedly produced film from oblivion.

DOOTONES

The origins of vocal group the Dootones can be traced to Fremont High School in Los Angeles, California, USA, where singer and multi-instrumentalist H.B. Barnum played in a jazz band with his drumming friend Ronald Barrett. The Dootones were subsequently formed in 1954 when the duo added Charles Gardner and Marvin Wilkins. Their initial employment was as backing singers/musicians to the Meadowlarks and Penguins. They were titled the Dootones in 1955 by their manager, Dootsie Williams, and made their debut with 'Teller Of Fortune' in April. A pop-orientated take on R&B, it attracted local airplay, while further exposure came with Californian tours with Etta James and Jackie Wilson. Afterwards, Williams put the quartet together with Vernon Green, formerly of the Medallions, for a Canadian tour, and made his intentions to remodel the band as the new Medallions clear. The existing Dootones were evidently unhappy with this turn of events, and disbanded without issuing any further recordings. Barrett teamed up with the

Meadowlarks, Gardner persevered with Green as yet another version of the Medallions, while Barnum joined the Robins, later working as an arranger with artists including Ray Charles and Lou Rawls. Charles Gardner became a minister in Pasadena. The Dootones recorded 'Down The Road' in 1962. Originally recorded in 1955, it backed a track entitled 'Sailor Boy' by a second, entirely different version of the Dootones assembled by Dootsie Williams. That formation had earlier released a single entitled 'Strange Love Affair'.

DORSEY, JIMMY

b. 29 February 1904, Shenandoah, Pennsylvania, USA, d. 12 June 1957, New York City, New York, USA. Musically active as a small child under the tutelage of his father, who was a coal miner turned music teacher, Dorsey switched from brass to reed instruments while still in his early teens. Concentrating on clarinet and alto saxophone, he played in various bands, mostly with his brother, Tommy Dorsey. Their co-led group, Dorsey's Novelty Six, later renamed Dorsey's Wild Canaries, was one of the first jazz bands to broadcast on the radio. Dorsey later joined the California Ramblers. Sometimes with his brother, sometimes alone, Dorsey played in a number of leading bands, including those led by Jean Goldkette, Paul Whiteman, Red Nichols and Ted Lewis. He also recorded frequently, often in company with Nichols and his Goldkette/ Whiteman colleague, Bix Beiderbecke. He continued to associate with his brother, and in 1934 they formed the Dorsey Brothers Orchestra, which became extremely popular. Unfortunately for the band, the brothers frequently disagreed, sometimes violently, and after one such argument, on the stand at the Glen Island Casino in May 1935, Tommy walked out leaving Jimmy to run the band on his own.

One of the most accomplished of the white bands of the swing era, Jimmy Dorsey's band retained a strong jazz element but also catered to popular demands. Particularly successful in this respect was a series of hit records devised by arranger Tutti Camarata. In an attempt to present all aspects of the band's work in one three-minute radio spot, Camarata made an arrangement of a song which featured first the band's male singer, Bob Eberly, in ballad mood, then the leader with an up-tempo jazz solo on alto, and finally, a wailing sensual vocal chorus by the band's other singer, Helen O'Connell (b. 23 May 1920, Lima, Ohio, USA, d. 9 September 1993, San Diego, California, USA). The first song treated in this manner was 'Amapola', followed by 'Yours' and then 'Green Eyes', which was a runaway hit, as was the later 'Tangerine'. Records like these ensured Dorsey's success and, by the mid-40s, his was one of the most popular of the big bands. This ensured Dorsey's survival over the hard winter of 1946/7, a time which saw many big bands fold, but the 50s proved difficult too, and in 1953 he was reunited with his brother who promptly renamed his own still-successful band as the Dorsey

Brothers Orchestra. Jimmy remained with the band until Tommy's death, by which time he too was terminally ill, dying only a few months after his brother. An outstanding technician, Jimmy Dorsey was one of the finest jazz saxophonists of his era and a major influence on many of his contemporaries and successors.

● ALBUMS: *Latin American Favorites* 10-inch album (Decca 1950) ★★, *Contrasting Music, Volume 1* 10-inch album (Coral 1950) ★★★★, *Contrasting Music, Volume 2* 10-inch album (Coral 1950) ★★★, *Gershwin Music* 10-inch album (Coral 1950) ★★★, *Dixie By Dorsey* 10-inch album (Columbia 1950) ★★★, *Dorseyland Band* 10-inch album (Columbia 1950) ★★★, as the Dorsey Brothers *Dixieland Jazz* 10-inch album (Decca 1951) ★★★, as the Dorsey Brothers *Jazz Of The Roaring Twenties* 10-inch album (Riverside 1953) ★★★★, as the Dorsey Brothers *The Dorsey Brothers With The California Ramblers* 10-inch album (Riverside 1955) ★★★, as the Dorsey Brothers *A Backward Glance* (Riverside 1956) ★★★, as the Dorsey Brothers *The Fabulous Dorseys In Hi-Fi Volumes 1 & 2* (Columbia 1958) ★★★★.

● COMPILATIONS: *Mostly 1940* 1939-40 recordings (Circle 1984) ★★★, as the Dorsey Brothers *Spotlighting The Fabulous Dorseys* 1942-45 recordings (Giants Of Jazz 1984) ★★★★, *Contrasts* recorded 1945 (Decca 1987) ★★★★, *The Early Years* 1936-41 recordings (Bandstand 1988) ★★★, *Don't Be That Way* 1935-40 recordings (Bandstand 1988) ★★★, *The Uncollected Jimmy Dorsey Volumes 1-5* 1939-50 recordings (Hindsight 1989) ★★★, *The Essential V-Discs* 1943-45 (Sandy Hook) ★★★★.

● FURTHER READING: *Tommy And Jimmy: The Dorsey Years*, Herb Sanford.

● FILMS: *The Fabulous Dorseys* (1947).

DORSEY, TOMMY

b. 19 November 1905, Shenandoah, Pennsylvania, USA, d. 26 November 1956, Greenwich, Connecticut, USA. Like his older brother, Jimmy Dorsey, Tommy was taught as a small child by his father, a music teacher. He first learned to play trumpet, but switched to trombone while still very young. He played in various bands, often with his brother, their co-led group known first as Dorsey's Novelty Six, later renamed Dorsey's Wild Canaries. With his brother, Dorsey later played in a number of leading bands, including those led by Jean Goldkette and Paul Whiteman. He also recorded frequently, often in the company of leading jazzmen of the day. In 1934 he and Jimmy formed the Dorsey Brothers Orchestra, which became extremely popular. Despite, or perhaps because of, their close relationship, the brothers frequently argued, sometimes violently, and after one such disagreement, in May 1935, Tommy walked out leaving Jimmy to take over leadership of the orchestra. Tommy then took over the excellent danceband led by Joe Haymes.

Highly ambitious, Dorsey set about turning the band, which was already a sound and well-disciplined unit, into the finest dance orchestra of the era. Over the years he employed first rate arrangers, including Axel Stordahl, Carmen Mastren, Paul Weston and, most influential of all in ensuring the band's success and musical stature, Sy Oliver. Dorsey also engaged the services of several strong jazz players, including Bunny Berigan, Buddy Rich, Johnny Mince, Yank Lawson, Pee Wee Erwin, Buddy De Franco, Gene Krupa, Charlie Shavers and Bud Freeman. Alert to the demands of audiences, Dorsey also employed some of the finest singers ever to work with the big bands. An early find was Jack Leonard, who sang on one of the band's big hits, 'Marie', and others included Edythe Wright, Jo Stafford, Connie Haines and Dick Haymes. The latter was the able replacement for the best singer Dorsey hired, Frank Sinatra. Although Sinatra had already begun to establish a reputation with Harry James, it was his stint with Dorsey that made him into an international singing star and helped to make the Dorsey band one of the most popular of the swing era – in many ways the band and musical sound which most aptly epitomizes this period in American popular music.

Dorsey's popularity was enough to ensure his band's survival after the great days of the 40s were over, and he was one of the few to move into television. Nevertheless, the 50s were difficult times and in 1953, he was happy to be reunited with his brother, whose own outfit had folded. Tommy Dorsey gave Jimmy a featured spot and renamed his band as the Dorsey Brothers Orchestra. Despite his popularity, to say nothing of his determination to succeed and his sometimes arrogant self-confidence, Dorsey was always reticent about his ability as a jazz player, although some of his early recordings display a gifted musician with a strong sense of style. Like his brother, Tommy Dorsey was an outstanding technician and brought trombone playing to new heights of perfection. His smooth playing was ideally suited to ballads and his solos on countless records were often exemplary. Even with the advent of later generations of outstanding trombone technicians, few have matched his skill and none have surpassed him in his own particular area of expertise. A noted heavy eater, Tommy Dorsey choked to death in his sleep.

● ALBUMS: *Tommy Dorsey Plays Howard Dietz* 10-inch album (Decca 1951) ★★★, *In A Sentimental Mood* 10-inch album (Decca 1951) ★★★★, as the Dorsey Brothers *Dixieland Jazz* 10-inch album (Decca 1951) ★★★, *Tenderley* 10-inch album (Decca 1952) ★★★★, *Your Invitation To Dance* 10-inch album (Decca 1952) ★★★, as the Dorsey Brothers *Jazz Of The Roaring Twenties* 10-inch album (Riverside 1953) ★★★★, *Tommy Dorsey Broadcasts For The American National Guard* (1953) ★★★, as the Dorsey Brothers *The Dorsey Brothers With The California Ramblers* 10-inch album (Riverside 1955) ★★★, *Tommy Dorsey Plays Cole Porter And Jerome Kern* (RCA Victor 1956) ★★★★, as the Dorsey Brothers *A Backward Glance* (Riverside 1956) ★★★, *Tommy Dorsey At The Statler Hotel* (1956) ★★★, as the Dorsey Brothers *The Fabulous Dorseys In Hi-Fi Volumes 1 & 2* (Columbia 1958) ★★★★.

● COMPILATIONS: with Frank Sinatra *The Dorsey/ Sinatra Sessions* 1940-42 recordings (RCA 1972) ★★★★, *One Night Stand With Tommy Dorsey* recorded 1940 (Sandy Hook 1979) ★★★, *The Sentimental Gentleman* 1941-42 recordings (RCA 1980) ★★★★, *At The Fat Man's* 1946-48 recordings (Hep Jazz 1981) ★★★, *Solid Swing* 1949-50 recordings (First Heard 1984) ★★★, as the Dorsey Brothers *Spotlighting The Fabulous Dorseys* 1942-45 recordings (Giants Of Jazz 1984) ★★★★, *The Indispensable Tommy Dorsey Volumes 1/2* 1935-36 recordings (RCA 1987) ★★★★, *The Indispensable Tommy Dorsey Volumes 3/4* 1936-37 recordings (RCA 1987) ★★★★, *The Indispensable Tommy Dorsey Volumes 5/6* 1937-38 recordings (RCA 1987) ★★★★, *The Indispensable Tommy Dorsey Volumes 7/8* 1938-39 recordings (RCA 1987) ★★★★, *The Legend, Volumes 1-3* (RCA 1987) ★★★★, *Carnegie Hall V-Disc Session, April 1944* (Hep Jazz 1990) ★★★, *The Clambake Seven: The Music Goes Round And Round* 1935-47 recordings (Bluebird 1991) ★★★★, with Sinatra *The Song Is You* 5-CD box set (Columbia 1994) ★★★★, *Dance With Dorsey* (Parade 1995) ★★★, *The Sky Fell Down* 1940s recordings (Traditional Line 2000) ★★★.

● FURTHER READING: *Tommy And Jimmy: The Dorsey Years*, Herb Sanford.

● FILMS: *The Fabulous Dorseys* (1947).

DOUGLAS, SHIRLEY
(see McDevitt, Chas)

DREAM WEAVERS

A vocal group consisting of three college students, based in Miami, Florida, USA. The Dream Weavers were born out of necessity when Wade Buff and Eugene Atkinson were unable to find an artist to record their composition 'It's Almost Tomorrow'. After exposure on the college radio station, their own self-financed recording was picked up by Decca Records and entered the US Top 10 in 1955. It did even better in the UK, climbing to the top of the charts in the following year. Subsequently, the Dream Weavers had a minor hit with Sammy Fain and Paul Francis Webster's 'A Little Love Can Go A Long, Long Way', from the film *Ain't Misbehavin'*, but then disappeared without a trace. 'It's Almost Tomorrow' also charted in the USA for Jo Stafford, Snooky Lanson and David Carroll in the 50s, and was a UK hit for Mark Wynter in 1963.

DRIFTING COWBOYS

Country star Hank Williams had been using the name the Drifting Cowboys since the late 30s, and he employed an existing group, the Alabama Rhythm Boys, as the Drifting Cowboys in 1943. The line-up only became consistent after Hank Williams appeared at the *Grand Ole Opry* in 1949 and realized the need for a permanent band. He employed Jerry Rivers (b. 25 August 1928, Miami, Florida, USA, d. 4 October 1996, Hermitage, Tennessee, USA; fiddle), Bob McNett (b. 16 October 1925, Roaring Branch, Pennsylvania, USA; guitar), Hillous Butrum (b. 21 April 1928, Lafayette, Tennessee, USA; bass) and Don Helms (b. 28 February 1927, New Brockton, Alabama,

USA; steel guitar). There were no drums as the instrument was not favoured in country circles. In 1951, McNett and Butrum were replaced, respectively, by Sammy Pruett, who had been in the Alabama Rhythm Boys with Helms, and Howard Watts. Williams used the Drifting Cowboys on his sessions, sometimes augmenting the musicians with Chet Atkins. His simply chorded songs did not need elaborate embellishment, and the Drifting Cowboys' backings perfectly complemented the material. The group disbanded after Williams' death. Helms worked with the Wilburn Brothers and formed the powerful Wil-Helm Agency. Helms and Rivers also worked in Hank Williams Jnr.'s band, the Cheatin' Hearts. Rivers wrote a biography *Hank Williams – From Life To Legend* (Denver, 1967/ updated in 1980). In 1976 the original line-up re-formed for radio shows with compere Grant Turner and comedian the Duke of Paducah. They had a minor success with 'Rag Mop' and recorded a tribute to Hank Williams, 'If The Good Lord's Willing'. Hank Williams Jnr. and Don Helms recorded a duet, 'The Ballad Of Hank Williams', which was based on 'The Battle Of New Orleans' and indicated how volatile Williams was. The Drifting Cowboys first appeared in the UK in 1979, and in 1991 appeared at Wembley's country music festival with Williams' illegitimate daughter, Jett Williams.

● ALBUMS: *We Remember Hank Williams* (1969) ★★★★, with Jim Owen *A Song For Us All – A Salute To Hank Williams* (Epic 1977) ★★★, *The Drifting Cowboys' Tribute To Hank Williams* (Epic 1979) ★★★, *Best Of Hank Williams' Original Drifting Cowboys* (Epic 1979) ★★★★, *Classic Instrumentals* (1981) ★★, *One More Time Around* (1982) ★★★.

DUKE WORE JEANS, THE

Taking its cue from the plot of *The Prince And The Pauper*, this 1958 film starred Tommy Steele as the son of a Cockney pearly king who trades lifestyles with his double, the Hon. Tony Whitecliffe. Inevitably, the former falls in love with an aristocrat. *The Duke Wore Jeans* has little to commend it other than being a vehicle for Steele's chirpy personality. He contributed eight songs to the soundtrack, including 'Happy Guitar', which reached number 20 in the UK charts when issued as a single. If Steele was ever a bona fide rock 'n' roll singer, this film marked his transformation into an all-round entertainer. *The Duke Wore Jeans* was retitled *It's All Happening* for the US market. The same title was used for a British 1963 feature film starring Steele, which was known as *The Dream Maker* in America.

DUNCAN, JOHNNY, AND THE BLUE GRASS BOYS

b. John Franklin Duncan, 7 September 1932, Oliver Springs, near Knoxville, Tennessee, USA, d. 15 July 2000, Taree, New South Wales, Australia. Duncan sang from an early age in a church choir and then, when aged 13, he joined a gospel quartet. At 16, he left Tennessee for Texas and

while there, he formed a country group. Duncan was drafted into the US army in 1952 and posted in England. He married an English woman, Betty, in 1953. After his demobilization, they went to the USA. Betty returned home for Christmas 1955 and, as she fell ill and needed an operation, Duncan worked in the UK for his father-in-law. He met jazz bandleader Chris Barber, who was looking to replace Lonnie Donegan. Donegan had formed his own skiffle group, a fashion he had started with Barber's band. Barber was impressed by Duncan's nasal vocal delivery and physical resemblance to Donegan and immediately recruited him, and he joined them the following night at London's Royal Festival Hall. In 1957 Duncan left the band and called his own group the Blue Grass Boys in homage to Bill Monroe, but they were all British – Denny Wright (guitar), Jack Fallon (bass), Danny Levan (violin) and Lennie Hastings (drums). Although promoted as a skiffle artist, Duncan was a straight country performer, both in terms of arrangements and repertoire. 'Last Train To San Fernando', a Trinidad calypso he re-arranged, steamed up the UK charts, but the communication cord was pulled just before it reached the top. The b-side, 'Rock-A-Billy Baby', was equally strong. Duncan was featured on BBC Television's *6.5 Special* and hosted radio programmes for the BBC and Radio Luxembourg, but he only had two more Top 30 entries, 'Blue Blue Heartache' and 'Footprints In The Snow', which both reached number 27. Duncan subsequently worked as a country singer in UK clubs and encouraged local talent. In 1974 he emigrated to Melbourne, Australia, and continued to work there until his death from cancer in 2000.

● ALBUMS: *Johnny Duncan's Tennessee Songbag* (Columbia 1957) ★★★, *Johnny Duncan Salutes Hank Williams* (Columbia 1958) ★★★, *Beyond The Sunset* (1961) ★★★, *Back In Town* (1970) ★★, *The World Of Country Music* (Decca 1973) ★★★.

● COMPILATIONS: *Last Train To San Fernando* 4-CD box set (Bear Family 1997) ★★★★.

DUNING, GEORGE

b. 25 February 1908, Richmond, Indiana, USA, d. 27 February 2000, San Diego, California, USA. A composer and conductor for films, from the 40s through to the 80s. Duning studied at the University of Cincinnati, and the Cincinnati Conservatory Of Music, becoming a jazz and symphonic trumpet player. He was a sideman and chief arranger for the Kay Kyser Band in the early 40s when Kyser was one of the biggest attractions in the business. Around the same time, he began to arrange and orchestrate music for films, and in 1946 he collaborated with Irving Gertz to write the score for *The Devil's Mask*. Between then and 1950, he scored some 21 features for Columbia, a mixture of thrillers, melodramas, westerns and comedies. These included *Mysterious Intruder*; *Johnny O'Clock* and *To The Ends Of Earth*, starring Dick Powell, *The Guilt Of Janet James*; *I Love Trouble*; *The Man From Colorado*; *Shockproof*; *The Dark Past*; *The Undercover Man* and *And Baby Makes Three*. Duning also scored *Down To Earth* and *The Gallant Blade*, both starring Larry Parks, and Parks appeared once more in *Jolson Sings Again*, for which Duning gained the first of five Oscar nominations. Three of the others were awarded to Duning in the 50s for his work on *From Here To Eternity*, *The Eddie Duchin Story* and *Picnic* (1955). The latter's theme music, used extremely effectively on the soundtrack in conjunction with the 1934 melody 'Moonglow', became a US number 1 for Morris Stolloff and his orchestra, and a substantial hit for pianist George Cates. A lyric was added by Steve Allen. Duning's other scores during the 50s and 60s included *Lorna Doone*, *Man In The Saddle*, *Scandal Sheet*; *Last Of The Commanches*, *Salome*, *Houseboat*; *Bell, Book And Candle*, *Cowboy*, *The World Of Suzie Wong*, *The Devil At 4 O'Clock*, *Toys In The Attic*, *My Blood Runs Cold* and *Any Wednesday*. In the 60s and 70s, apart from the occasional feature such as *Arnold* (1973), *Terror In The Wax Museum* (1976) and *The Man With Bogart's Face* (1980), which was George Raft's last film, Duning concentrated on writing for television. He scored several films such as *Then Came Bronson*, *Quarantined*, *But I Don't Want To Get Married!*, *Yuma*, *Black Noon*, *Climb An Angry Mountain*, *The Woman Hunter*, *Honour Thy Father*, *The Abduction Of Saint Anne*, *The Top Of The Hill*, *The Dream Merchants* and *Goliath Waits* (1981); he also contributed music to numerous television series, including *Star Trek*, *The Partridge Family* and *Houseboat*.

DUPREE, CHAMPION JACK

b. William Thomas Dupree, 4 July 1910, New Orleans, Louisiana, USA, d. 21 January 1992, Hanover, Germany. Orphaned in infancy, Dupree was raised in the Colored Waifs Home for Boys until the age of 14. After leaving, he led a marginal existence, singing for tips, and learning piano from musicians such as Willie 'Drive-'em-down' Hall. Dupree also became a professional boxer, and blended fighting with hoboing throughout the 30s, before retiring from the ring in 1940, and heading for New York. Initially, he travelled only as far as Indianapolis, where he joined with musicians who had been associates of Leroy Carr. Dupree rapidly became a star of the local black entertainment scene, as a comedian and dancer as well as a musician. He acquired a residency at the local Cotton Club, and partnered comedienne Ophelia Hoy. In 1940, Dupree made his recording debut, with music that blended the forceful, barrelhouse playing and rich, Creole-accented singing of New Orleans with the more suave style of Leroy Carr. Not surprisingly, a number of titles were piano/guitar duets, although on some, Jesse Ellery's use of amplification pointed the way forward. A few songs covered unusual topics, such as the distribution of grapefruit juice by relief agencies, or the effects of drugs.

Dupree's musical career was interrupted when he was drafted into the US Navy as a cook; even so he managed to become one of the first blues singers to record for the folk revival market while on leave in New York in 1943. Dupree's first wife died while he was in the navy, and he took his

discharge in New York, where he worked as a club pianist, and formed a close musical association with Sonny Terry and Brownie McGhee. His own post-war recording career commenced with a splendid series of solo recordings for Joe Davis, on some of which the influence of Peetie Wheatstraw is very evident. More typical were the many tracks with small groups recorded thereafter for a number of labels from 1946-53, and for King between April 1953 and late 1955. As ever, these recordings blend the serious with the comic, the latter somewhat tastelessly on songs such as 'Tongue Tied Blues' and 'Harelip Blues'. 'Walking The Blues', a comic dialogue with Teddy 'Mr Bear' McRae, was a hit on King, and the format was repeated on a number of titles recorded for RCA's Vik and Groove. In 1958, Dupree made his last American recordings until 1990; 'Blues From The Gutter' appears to have been aimed at white audiences, as was Dupree's career thereafter. In 1959, he moved to Europe, and lived in Switzerland, England, Sweden and Germany, touring extensively and recording prolifically, with results that varied from the excellent to the mediocre. This served both as a stamp of authenticity and as a licensed jester to the European blues scene. The tracks on *One Last Time* are drawn from his final recording session before his death in 1992.

● ALBUMS: *Blues From The Gutter* (Atlantic 1959) ★★★★, *Natural And Soulful Blues* (Atlantic 1960) ★★★, *Champion Of The Blues* (Atlantic 1961) ★★★, *Sings The Blues* (King 1961) ★★★, *Women Blues Of Champion Jack Dupree* (Folkways 1961) ★★★, *Cabbage Greens* (OKeh 1963) ★★★, *The Blues Of Champion Jack Dupree* (1963) ★★★, with Jimmy Rushing *Two Shades Of Blue* (Ember 1964) ★★, *Trouble Trouble* (Storyville 1965) ★★★, *Portraits In Blues* (Storyville 1965) ★★★, *From New Orleans To Chicago* (Decca 1966) ★★★, featuring Mickey Baker *Champion Jack Dupree And His Blues Band* (Decca 1967) ★★★, *Champion Jack Dupree* (Storyville 1967) ★★, *Scoobydoobydoo* (Blue Horizon 1969) ★★★, *When You Feel The Feeling* (Blue Horizon 1969) ★★★, *The Incredible Champion Jack Dupree* (Sonet 1970) ★★, *Legacy Of The Blues* (Sonet 1972) ★★, *Blues From Montreux* (Atlantic 1972) ★★★, *Rub A Little Boogie* (Krazy Kat 1982) ★★, *Junker Blues* (Travelin' Man 1985) ★★★, *Shake Baby Shake* (Detour 1987) ★★★, *Legacy Of The Blues Volume 3* (Sonet 1987) ★★★★, *Live At Burnley* (JSP 1989) ★★★, *Blues For Everybody* (Charly 1990) ★★★, *1945-1946 (The Joe Davis Sessions)* (Flyright 1990) ★★★, *Back Home In New Orleans* (Bullseye Blues 1990) ★★★, *Forever And Ever* (Bullseye Blues 1991) ★★★, *Home* (1993) ★★★, *One Last Time* (1993) ★★★, *Won't Be A Fool No More ... Plus* (See For Miles 1994) ★★★, *The Blues Of Champion Jack Dupree Volume 2* (Storyville 1996) ★★★★, *Get Back Jack, Do It Again* (Catfish 1998) ★★★★.

DURHAM, EDDIE

b. 19 August 1906, San Marcos, Texas, USA, d. 6 March 1987, New York City, New York, USA. As a child Durham worked in travelling shows with other musical members of his large family. In the mid-20s he worked in a number of southwest territory bands including Walter Page's Blue Devils from where he, and several others, moved to the Bennie Moten band. Up to this point Durham had been playing both guitar and trombone and now added arranging to his arsenal of skills. During the 30s he played in, and arranged for, the bands of Willie Bryant, Jimmie Lunceford and Count Basie. In the following decade he arranged for several noted swing bands including Artie Shaw's, and also worked closely with the one of the outstanding but neglected bands of the late 40s, the International Sweethearts Of Rhythm. Later in his career Durham arranged more and played less, but did return to the stage in the 70s and 80s with Eddie Barefield, Buddy Tate and other comrades from his Basie days. Durham's contributions to jazz are extensive and include helping develop and refine the electrically amplified guitar. More important still were his loosely swinging arrangements exemplified by such Basie classics as 'Moten Swing' and the popular 'In The Mood' for Glenn Miller. He was also co-composer of 'Topsy' which became an unexpected hit for Cozy Cole in 1958.

● ALBUMS: *Eddie Durham* (RCA 1973) ★★★, *Blue Bone* (JSP 1981) ★★★.

DUTCH SWING COLLEGE BAND

This outfit's polished, cleverly arranged repertoire was still heard in concert more than half a century after its formation by Peter Schilperoort (clarinet, saxophones) in 1945. Among musicians that have passed through its ranks are Wout Steenhuis (guitar), Jan Morks (clarinet), Kees Van Dorser (trumpet), Oscar Klein (trumpet), and Rod Mason (cornet). Famous US musicians visiting Europe proudly 'sat in' with the band. Schilperoort became established as the Netherlands' foremost ambassador of trad jazz, following the foundation of his long-standing partnership with Arie Ligthart (banjo/ guitar) in 1952. Yet, after embracing saxophonists and even amplification, the combo were to deviate further from the prescribed New Orleans precedent via adaptations of rock 'n' roll, country, and military marches, to achieve acceptance in the generalized pop field. By the 70s, Schilperoort started his own DSC Productions record company, and was knighted by Queen Juliana of the Netherlands.

● ALBUMS: *Dixieland Goes Dutch* (Epic 1955) ★★★★, *Dixie Gone Dutch* (Philips 1962) ★★★★, *On Tour* (Philips 1981) ★★, *Digital Dixie* (Philips 1982) ★★★, *Music For The Millions* (Philips 1983) ★★★, *The Bands Best* (Verve 1984) ★★★, *Swing Studio Sessions* (Philips 1985) ★★★, *When The Swing Comes Marching In* (Philips 1985) ★★★, *40 Years 1945-1985, At Its Best* (Timeless 1986) ★★★★, *Digital Anniversary* (Philips 1986) ★★★, *With Guests Volume 1* (Polydor 1987) ★★, *Digital Date* (Philips 1988) ★★★, *Dutch Samba* (Timeless 1989) ★★, *1960* (Philips 1990) ★★★, *Jubilee Concert* (Philips 1991) ★★★, *The Old Fashioned Way* (Jazz Hour 1993) ★★★.

EAGER, VINCE

One of the many UK rock/pop artists of the late 50s Eager was one of the more promising singers in the Larry Parnes stable of stars. Launched in the spring of 1958 and christened Eager because of his enthusiastic personality, the vocalist was featured on several prestigious television shows, most notably Jack Good's pioneering *Oh Boy*. He seemed a strong bet to follow Parnes' other acts, Tommy Steele and Marty Wilde, into the UK charts but, despite a series of singles written by such name writers as Floyd Robinson, Marty Robbins, Conway Twitty and Gene Pitney, chart success proved·elusive. Eager also received regular star billing on the BBC Television series *Drumbeat*, but his career prospects receded when he split with Parnes. In later years, he featured in the stage production of the musical *Elvis*.

● ALBUMS: *Vince Eager Plays Tribute To Elvis Presley* (Avenue 1972) ★.

ECKSTINE, BILLY

b. William Clarence Eckstein, 8 July 1914, Pittsburgh, Pennsylvania, USA, d. 8 March 1993, Pittsburgh, Pennsylvania, USA. Eckstine possessed one of the most distinctive voices in popular music, a deep tone with a highly personal vibrato. He began singing at the age of 11 but until his late teens was undecided between a career as a singer or football player. He won a sporting scholarship but soon afterwards broke his collar bone and decided that singing was less dangerous. He worked mostly in the north-eastern states in the early 30s and towards the end of the decade joined the Earl 'Fatha' Hines band in Chicago. Although far from being a jazz singer, opting instead for a highly sophisticated form of balladry, Eckstine clearly loved working with jazz musicians and in particular the young experimenters who drifted into the Hines band in the early 40s, among them Wardell Gray, Dizzy Gillespie and Charlie Parker. While with Hines he developed into a competent trumpeter and, later, valve trombonist, having first mimed as a trumpet player in order to circumvent union rules.

In 1943, acting on the advice and encouragement of Budd Johnson, Eckstine formed his own band. Although his original intention was to have a band merely to back his vocals, Eckstine gathered together an exciting group of young bebop musicians and thus found himself leader of what constituted the first true bebop big band. During the band's four-year existence its ranks were graced by Gray, Parker, Gillespie, Gene Ammons, Dexter Gordon, Miles Davis, Kenny Dorham, Fats Navarro and Art Blakey, playing arrangements by

Gillespie, Johnson, Tadd Dameron, Gil Fuller and Jerry Valentine. Eckstine also hired the Hines band's other singer, Sarah Vaughan. In 1947 the band folded but had already served as an inspiration to Gillespie, who formed his own bebop big band that year. Eckstine's commercial recordings during the life of the big band were mostly ballads which he wrapped in his deep, liquid baritone voice, and with his bandleading days behind him he continued his career as a successful solo singer. He gained a huge international reputation as a stylish balladeer. During his long career Eckstine had many hit records, including 'Jelly, Jelly', recorded in 1940 with Hines, 'Skylark', 'Everything I Have Is Yours', 'I Apologize' (stylistically covered by P.J. Proby to great success), 'Prisoner Of Love', 'A Cottage For Sale', 'No One But You' (number three in the UK charts in 1954), 'Gigi' (number eight in 1959), and several duets with Vaughan, the best-known being 'Passing Strangers', which, although recorded a dozen years earlier, reached number 17 in the 1969 charts. He went on to record for Motown, Stax and A&M. In later years Eckstine recorded a new single with Ian Levine as part of his Motown revival project on the Motor City label.

● ALBUMS: Live At Club Plantation, Los Angeles (1945) ★★★, Billy Eckstine Sings (National 1949) ★★★, Songs By Billy Eckstine (MGM 1951) ★★★, Favorites (MGM 1951) ★★★, Billy Eckstine Sings Rodgers And Hammerstein (MGM 1952) ★★★★, The Great Mr B (King 1953) ★★★, Tenderly (MGM 1953) ★★★★, Earl Hines With Billy Eckstine 10-inch album (RCA Victor 1953) ★★★, I Let A Song Go Out Of My Heart (MGM 1954) ★★★, Blues For Sale (EmArcy 1954/55) ★★★★, The Love Songs Of Mr B (EmArcy 1954/55) ★★★, Mr B With A Beat (MGM 1955) ★★★, Rendezvous (MGM 1955) ★★★, I Surrender Dear (EmArcy 1955) ★★★★, That Old Feeling (MGM 1955) ★★★★, Prisoner Of Love (Regent 1957) ★★★, The Duke The Blues And Me (Regent 1957) ★★★, My Deep Blue Dream (Regent 1957) ★★★★, You Call It Madness (Regent 1957) ★★★, Billy Eckstine's Imagination (EmArcy 1958) ★★★★, Billy's Best (Mercury 1958) ★★★, Sarah Vaughan And Billy Eckstine Sing The Best Of Irving Berlin (Mercury 1958) ★★★★, with Sarah Vaughan Billy And Sarah (Lion 1959) ★★★★, with Count Basie Basie/Eckstine Inc. (Roulette 1959) ★★★★, Golden Saxophones (London 1960) ★★★, I Apologize (1960) ★★★★, Mr B (Audio Lab 1960) ★★★, Broadway Bongos And Mr B (Mercury 1961) ★★★, No Cover No Minimum (Mercury 1961) ★★★, Billy Eckstine & Quincy Jones At Basin St. East (Mercury 1962) ★★★, Don't Worry 'Bout Me (Mercury 1962) ★★★, Once More With Feeling (Mercury 1962) ★★★, Everything I Have Is Yours (Metro 1965) ★★★, Prime Of My Life (Motown 1965) ★★, My Way (Motown 1966) ★★, For Love Of Ivy (Motown 1969) ★★★, Gentle On My Mind (Motown 1969) ★★, Feel The Warm (Enterprise 1971) ★★, Stormy (Stax 1971) ★★, If She Walked Into My Life (Stax 1974) ★★, Something More (Stax 1981) ★★, Billy Eckstine Sings With Benny Carter (1986) ★★★, I'm A Singer (Kim 1987) ★★.

● COMPILATIONS: The Best Of Billy Eckstine (Lion 1958) ★★★, The Golden Hits Of Billy Eckstine (Mercury 1963) ★★★★, Golden Hour: Billy Eckstine (Golden Hour 1975) ★★★★, with Sarah Vaughan (coupled with a Dinah Washington and Brook Benton collection) Passing Strangers (Mercury 1978) ★★★, Greatest Hits (Polydor 1984) ★★★★, Billy Eckstine Orchestra 1945 (Alamac 1985) ★★★, Mr B And The Band – Savoy Sessions (Savoy 1986) ★★★.

EDISON, HARRY 'SWEETS'

b. 10 October 1915, Columbus, Ohio, USA, d. 27 July 1999, Columbus, Ohio, USA. A trumpeter who was inspired by Louis Armstrong, Edison gained valuable early experience with a number of territory bands, including the excellent Jeter-Pillars Orchestra. After a short spell with Lucky Millinder, Edison joined the Count Basie band in 1938, where he remained until Basie folded his big band in 1950. Edison then began a long career as leader of small groups, a solo artist, and studio musician; he also worked occasionally with bandleaders such as Buddy Rich. He toured with Jazz At The Philharmonic and in the 50s his work came to the attention of millions who never knew his name when he performed exquisite trumpet obligati with the Nelson Riddle orchestra behind the vocals of Frank Sinatra. In the 60s he worked occasionally with Basie again but was mostly heard as a soloist, touring extensively on the international club and festival circuit. He also recorded with the saxophonists Jimmy Forrest and Eddie 'Lockjaw' Davis. In performance Edison often favoured playing with a Harmon mute and, while he had many imitators, few matched his laconic wit and inventiveness. Indeed, his trademark of repeated single notes is something no other trumpeter has been able to use to such good effect. On his numerous recording dates he was teamed with most of the big names in jazz and continually defied his advancing years. In November 1989 he appeared as featured soloist with the Frank Wess-Harry Edison Orchestra at the Fujitsu-Concord Jazz Festival in Japan.

● ALBUMS: Harry Edison Quartet reissued as The Inventive Harry Edison (Pacific Jazz 1953) ★★★, with Buddy Rich Buddy And Sweets (Norgran 1955) ★★★, with Lester Young Pres And Sweets (Norgran 1955) ★★★★, Sweets (Clef 1956) ★★★★, Blues For Basie (Verve 1957) ★★★★, Gee Baby, Ain't I Good To You? (Verve 1958) ★★★, with Buck Clayton Harry Edison Swings Buck Clayton And Vice-Versa (Verve 1958) ★★★, The Swinger (Verve 1958) ★★★, with Roy Eldridge, Dizzy Gillespie Tour De Force (Verve 1958) ★★★, Mr. Swing (Verve 1959) ★★★, Sweetenings (Roulette 1959) ★★★, with Eldridge, Young Going For Myself (Verve 1959) ★★★★, with Eldridge, Young Laughin' To Keep From Cryin' (Verve 1959) ★★★★, Patented By Edison (Roulette 1960) ★★★, with Ben Webster Ben Webster-Sweets Edison (Columbia 1962) ★★★★, with Eddie 'Lockjaw' Davis Jawbreakers (Riverside 1962) ★★★★, Sweets For The Taste Of Love (Vee Jay 1964) ★★★, Sweets For

The Sweet (Sue 1965) ★★★, *When Lights Are Low* (Liberty 1966) ★★★, with Davis *Sweet And Lovely* (Black & Blue 1975) ★★★, with Davis *Edison's Lights* (Pablo 1976) ★★★, with Davis *Harry 'Sweets' Edison And Eddie 'Lockjaw' Davis, Vol. 1* (Storyville 1976) ★★★, with Davis *Harry 'Sweets' Edison And Eddie 'Lockjaw' Davis, Vol. 2* (Storyville 1976) ★★★, with Davis *Simply Sweets* (Pablo 1978) ★★★, with Zoot Sims *Just Friends* (Pablo 1979) ★★★, *'S Wonderful* (Pablo 1983) ★★★, *For My Pals* (Pablo 1988) ★★★, with Spike Robinson *"Jusa Bit 'O' Blues" Volume 1* (Capri 1988) ★★★, with Robinson *"Jusa Bit 'O' Blues" Volume 2* (Capri 1988) ★★★, *Can't Get Out Of This Mood* (Orange Blue 1989) ★★★, *Swing Summit* (Candid 1990) ★★★, *Live At The Iridium* (Telarc 1998) ★★★.
● COMPILATIONS: *Best Of Harry Edison* (Pablo 1982) ★★★★.
● FILMS: *Jammin' The Blues* (1944).

EDWARDS, TOMMY
b. 17 February 1922, Richmond, Virginia, USA, d. 22 October 1969, Virginia, USA. This jazz/pop/R&B singer-songwriter began his professional career in 1931. He wrote the hit 'That Chick's Too Young To Fry' for Louis Jordan in 1946. A demo recording of his own 'All Over Again' later won Edwards an MGM Records contract. Early releases included 'It's All In The Game' (US number 18 in 1951), a tune based on a 1912 melody by future US Vice-President Charles Gates Dawes. Edwards re-recorded the song in 1958 in a 'beat-ballad' arrangement, hitting number 1 on both sides of the Atlantic and eventually selling 3.5 million. The song was an indisputable classic of its era, highlighted by Edwards' strong, masterful vocal. The song was covered many times and provided hits for Cliff Richard (1963-64) and the Four Tops (1970) and was a notable album track by Van Morrison (1979). Edwards himself enjoyed five more hits during the next two years, including 'Love Is All We Need' and remakes of earlier successes 'Please Mr. Sun' and 'Morning Side Of The Mountain'.
● ALBUMS: *For Young Lovers* (MGM 1958) ★★★, *Tommy Edwards Sings* (Regent 1959) ★★, *It's All In The Game* (MGM 1959) ★★★★, *Step Out Singing* (MGM 1960) ★★★★, *You Started Me Dreaming* (MGM 1960) ★★★, *Tommy Edwards In Hawaii* (MGM 1960) ★, *Golden Country Hits* (MGM 1961) ★, *Stardust* (MGM 1962) ★★★, *Soft Strings And Two Guitars* (MGM 1962) ★★★, *Tommy Edwards* (1965) ★★.
● COMPILATIONS: *Tommy Edwards' Greatest Hits* (MGM 1961) ★★★, *The Very Best Of Tommy Edwards* (MGM 1963) ★★★, *It's All In The Game: The Complete Hits* (Epic 1995) ★★★★.

ELLA AND LOUIS – ELLA FITZGERALD AND LOUIS ARMSTRONG
An inspired collaboration, masterminded by producer Norman Granz. Both artists were riding high at this stage in their careers. Granz assembled a stellar quartet of Oscar Peterson (piano), Buddy Rich (drums), Herb Ellis (guitar) and Ray Brown (bass). Equally inspired was the choice of material, with the gruffness of Armstrong's voice blending like magic with Fitzgerald's stunningly silky delivery. Outstanding are Irving Berlin's 'Cheek To Cheek' and 'Isn't This A Lovely Day', and everything else works like a dream, with the gold star going to Ira and George Gershwin's 'They Can't Take That Away From Me'. Gentle and sincere, this is deserving of a place in every home.
● Tracks: *Can't We Be Friends; Isn't This A Lovely Day; Moonlight In Vermont; They Can't Take That Away From Me; Under A Blanket Of Blue; Tenderly; A Foggy Day; Stars Fell On Alabama; Cheek To Cheek; The Nearness Of You; April In Paris*.
● First released 1957
● UK peak chart position: did not chart
● USA peak chart position: 12

ELLA FITZGERALD SINGS THE COLE PORTER SONGBOOK – ELLA FITZGERALD
One of Ella Fitzgerald's great assets was also, paradoxically, one of her failings as a jazz singer. Throughout her long career her voice was that of an innocent girl. This immaturity of sound, allied as it was to consummate musical mastery, weakened her jazz performances, especially in the blues where emotional intensity is of paramount importance. As if sensing this, Norman Granz heard in Fitzgerald's voice the ideal vehicle for a selection of readings from the Great American Songbook. Her coolly detached approach to lyrics is nowhere better displayed than on this album of songs by one of the most sophisticated American songwriters.
● Tracks: *All Through The Night; Anything Goes; Miss Otis Regrets; Too Darn Hot; In The Still Of The Night; I Get A Kick Out Of You; Do I Love You?; Always True To You In My Fashion; Let's Do It; Just One Of Those Things; Ev'ry Time We Say Goodbye; All Of You; Begin The Beguine; Get Out Of Town; I Am In Love; From This Moment On; I Love Paris; You Do Something To Me; Riding High; Easy To Love; It's All Right With Me; Why Can't You Behave; What Is This Thing Called Love; You're The Top; Love For Sale; It's D'Lovely; Night And Day; Ace In The Hole; So In Love; I've Got You Under My Skin; I Concentrate On You; Don't Fence Me In*.
● First released 1956
● UK peak chart position: did not chart
● USA peak chart position: 15

ELLA FITZGERALD SINGS THE GEORGE AND IRA GERSHWIN SONGBOOK – ELLA FITZGERALD
The paradox of Ella Fitzgerald's prominence in the history of jazz singing and her lack of emotional intensity is much less apparent on this album. George Gershwin's affinity with jazz, and the corresponding delight jazz musicians take in performing his material, allow the singer to fly with the music. As for brother Ira's lyrics, they receive their due as cheerful, tender and always delightful examples of the lyricist's art. The Songbook series remains one of Ella Fitzgerald's major contributions – among many – to American popular music and this in particular is one of the

best of the sizeable bunch.

● Tracks: *Including – Sam And Delilah; But Not For Me; My One And Only; Let's Call The Whole Thing Off; I've Got Beginners Luck; Oh, Lady Be Good; Nice Work If You Can Get It; Things Are Looking Up; Just Another Rhumba; How Long Has This Been Going On; S'wonderful; The Man I Love; That Certain Feeling; By Strauss; Who Cares; Someone To Watch Over Me; Real American Folk Song; They All Laughed; Looking For A Boy; My Cousin From Milwaukee; Somebody From Somewhere; A Foggy Day; Clap Yo' Hands; For You, For Me, Forever More; Stiff Upper Lip; Strike Up The Band; Soon; I've Got A Crush On You; Bidin' My Time; Aren't You Kind Of Glad We Did?; Of Thee I Sing; Half It, Dearie' Blues; I Was Doing All Right; He Loves And She Loves; Love Is Sweeping The Country; Treat Me Rough; Love Is Here To Stay; Slap That Bass; Isn't It A Pity; Shall We Dance.*

● First released 1959
● UK peak chart position: did not chart
● USA peak chart position: 111

ELLA FITZGERALD SINGS THE RODGERS AND HART SONGBOOK – ELLA FITZGERALD

Richard Rodgers' tuneful music and Lorenz Hart's wittily amusing lyrics form a very special part of American popular music. So too does Ella Fitzgerald, and their meeting – under the benign influence of Norman Granz – is a high-water mark in the story of popular singing. The singer's unworldly and ingenuous charm suits the material and transports the listener to times without care; until, that is, the occasional tartness of a Hart lyric reminds us that life is not always a song. Along with the rest of the Songbook series, this is popular vocal music at its best and sets standards never previously attained.

● Tracks: *Have You Met Miss Jones?; You Took Advantage Of Me; Ship Without A Sail; To Keep My Love Alive; Dancing On The Ceiling; The Lady Is A Tramp; With A Song In My Heart; Manhattan; Johnny One Note; I Wish I Were In Love Again; Spring Is Here; It Never Entered My Mind; This Can't Be Love; Thou Swell; My Romance; Where Or When; Little Girl Blue; Give It Back To The Indians; Ten Cents A Dance; There's A Small Hotel; I Didn't Know What Time It Was; Everything I've Got; I Could Write A Book; Blue Room; My Funny Valentine; Bewitched; Mountain Greenery; Wait Till You See Her; Lover; Isn't It Romantic?; Here In My Arms; Blue Moon; My Heart Stood Still; I've Got Five Dollars.*

● First released 1957
● UK peak chart position: did not chart
● USA peak chart position: 11

ELLINGTON, DUKE

b. Edward Kennedy Ellington, 29 April 1899, Washington, DC, USA, d. 24 May 1974, New York City, New York, USA. Ellington began playing piano as a child but, despite some local success, took up a career as a signpainter. In his teens he continued to play piano, studied harmony, composed his first tunes and was generally active in music in Washington. Among his childhood friends were Sonny Greer, Artie Whetsol and Otto Hardwicke; from 1919 he played with them in various bands, sometimes working outside the city. In 1923 he ventured to New York to work with Elmer Snowden, and the following year formed his own band, the Washingtonians. Also in 1924, in collaboration with lyricist Joe Trent, he composed the *Chocolate Kiddies* revue. By 1927, Ellington's band had become established in east coast states and at several New York nightclubs. At the end of the year he successfully auditioned for a residency at Harlem's Cotton Club. The benefits arising from this engagement were immeasurable: regular radio broadcasts from the club ensured a widespread audience and Ellington's tours and recording sessions during the period of the residency, which ended early in 1931, built upon the band's popularity.

In the early 30s the band consolidated its reputation with extended tours of the USA, appearances in films and visits to Europe, which included performances in London in 1933. Towards the end of the decade the band returned for further seasons at the Cotton Club. Throughout the 30s and early 40s the band recorded extensively and to great acclaim; they continued to tour and record with little interruption during the rest of the 40s and into the early 50s but, although the quality of the music remained high, the band became significantly less popular than had once been the case. An appearance at the 1956 Newport Jazz Festival revived their popularity, and during the rest of the 50s and the following decade Ellington toured ceaselessly, playing concerts around the world. Ellington had always been a prolific writer, composing thousands of tunes including 'It Don't Mean A Thing (If It Ain't Got That Swing)', 'Sophisticated Lady', 'In A Sentimental Mood', 'Prelude To A Kiss', 'Concerto For Cootie (Do Nothin' Till You Hear From Me)', 'Cotton Tail', 'In A Mellotone', 'I Got It Bad And That Ain't Good', 'Don't Get Around Much Anymore', 'I'm Beginning To See The Light' and 'Satin Doll'. In later years he also composed film scores, among them *The Asphalt Jungle* (1950), *Anatomy Of A Murder* (1959), *Paris Blues* (1960) and *Assault On A Queen* (1966).

More importantly, he began to concentrate upon extended works, composing several suites and a series of sacred music concerts, the latter mostly performed in churches and cathedrals. Over the years the personnel of Ellington's orchestra proved remarkably stable, several of his sidemen remaining with him for decades. The ceaseless touring continued into the early 70s, with Ellington making few concessions to the advancing years. After his death in 1974 the orchestra continued for a time under the direction of his son, Mercer Ellington, but despite the continuing presence of a handful of survivors, such as Harry Carney, who had been in the band virtually without a break for 47 years, the spirit and guiding light was gone. From this moment, Ellington lived on through an immense recorded legacy and in the memories of musicians and an army of fans.

Ellington was born into relatively comfortable circumstances. His father had been a butler, even working for some time at the White House. The family was deeply religious and musical, and Ellington himself was very close to his parents. He reported that he was 'pampered and spoiled rotten', and of his parents he wrote: 'My mother was beautiful but my father was only handsome.' His mother was a piano player; under her influence, Ellington had music lessons from a teacher called Mrs. Clinkscales. In later life, he whimsically commented that one of the first things she taught him was never to share the stage with Oscar Peterson. Perhaps more influential than Mrs. Clinkscales were the piano players he heard in the pool-rooms, where, like any self-respecting, under-age, sharp-suited adolescent-about-town, he found his supplementary education among a diversity of gamblers, lawyers, pickpockets, doctors and hustlers. 'At heart,' he said, 'they were all great artists.' He paid special tribute to Oliver 'Doc' Perry, a pianist who gave him lessons of a less formal but more practical nature than those of Mrs. Clinkscales – 'reading the leads and recognizing the chords'. Ellington became a professional musician in his teens. One of his first engagements was playing 'mood' music for a travelling magician and fortune teller, improvising to suit the moment, whether serious or mystical. In 1914 he wrote his first compositions: 'Soda Fountain Rag' and 'What You Gonna Do When The Bed Breaks Down?'. By the age of 18 he was leading bands in the Washington area, having learned that the bandleader, as 'Mr. Fixit', generally earned more money than the other members of the band. Thus, by the age of 20, he was pianist, composer and bandleader: the essential Duke Ellington was formed, and would later blossom into one of the most influential musicians in jazz, although with characteristic perversity, he insisted that he wrote folk music, not jazz.

By the time of the band's debut at the Cotton Club, in addition to Greer and Hardwicke, Ellington had recruited key players such as Bubber Miley, his first great 'growling' trumpet player; the trombonist Joe 'Tricky Sam' Nanton; the bassist Wellman Braud and Carney, whose baritone saxophone formed the rich and sturdy foundation of the band's reed section for its entire history. Perhaps just as crucial was Ellington's meeting with Irving Mills, who became his manager. For a black musician to survive, let alone prosper, in the America of the 20s and 30s, a tough white manager was an essential safeguard. In 1927 came the first classic recordings of 'Black And Tan Fantasy' and 'Creole Love Call', the latter with the legendary vocal line by Adelaide Hall. In these, and in up-tempo numbers such as 'Hot And Bothered', the Ellington method was fully formed. The conventional way to praise a big band was to say that they played like one man. The quality of the Ellington bands was that they always played like a bunch of highly talented and wildly disparate individuals, recalling the 'great artists' of the pool-room.

The Cotton Club provided an ideal workshop and laboratory for Ellington. Situated in Harlem, its performers were exclusively black, its clientele exclusively white and in pursuit of dusky exotic pleasures. Ellington, who enjoyed being a showman, gave the audience what it wanted: music for showgirls and boys to dance to, in every tempo from the slow and sultry to the hot and hectic, coloured with so-called 'jungle sounds'. Although this was a racial slur, Ellington had the skill and wit to transcend it, creating music that met the specification but disarmingly turned it inside-out. The music winked at the audience. Moving into the 30s, the band's repertoire was enriched by pieces such as 'Rockin' In Rhythm', 'Old Man Blues', 'The Mooche' and, of course, 'Mood Indigo'. Its personnel now included Juan Tizol on trombone, Cootie Williams, de facto successor to Miley on trumpet, and the sublime Johnny Hodges on alto saxophone, whose lyricism, tempered with melancholy, became a crucial element in the Ellington palette. Hodges became the most striking example of the truism 'once an Ellingtonian, always an Ellingtonian'. Like Williams and Tizol, he would leave the band to become a leader in his own right or briefly a sideman in another band, only to return.

The 30s saw the first attempts at compositions longer than the conventional three minutes (the length of a gramophone record), starting with 'Creole Rhapsody' in 1931. The period also saw, to oversimplify the situation, a move into respectability. Critics and musicians from the serious side of the tracks had begun to take notice. People as diverse as Constant Lambert, Percy Grainger, Leopold Stokowski and Igor Stravinsky recognized the extraordinary and unique gifts of Ellington. Phrases such as 'America's greatest living composer' crept into print. Ellington continued to refer to himself, gracefully and demurely, as 'our piano player'. To be sure, his composing methods, from all accounts, were radically different from those of other title contenders. He would scribble a few notes on the back of an envelope, or memorize them, and develop the piece in rehearsal. The initial themes were often created by musicians in the band – hence the frequent shared composer credits: 'The Blues I Love To Sing' with Miley, 'Caravan' with Tizol, and 'Jeep's Blues' with Hodges. 'Bluebird Of Delhi', from the 1966 'The Far East Suite', was based on a phrase sung by a bird outside Billy Strayhorn's room. Strayhorn joined the band in 1939, as arranger, composer, occasional piano player, friend and musical alter ego. A small, quiet and gentle man, he became a vital element in the Ellington success story. His arrival coincided with that of the tenor saxophone player Ben Webster, and the brilliant young bass player Jimmy Blanton, who died in 1943, aged 23. By common consent, the Webster/Blanton band produced some of the finest music in the Ellington canon, exemplified by 'Jack The Bear', with Blanton's innovative bass solo, and 'Just A-Settin' And A-Rockin', where Webster demonstrates that the quality of jazz playing lies in discretion and timing rather than vast numbers of notes to the square inch.

Duke Ellington was elegantly dismissive of analysis; too much talk, he said, stinks up the place. However, he was more than capable of sensitive examination of his own music. Of the haunting and plaintive 'Mood Indigo', he said: 'Just a story about a little girl and a little boy. They are about eight and the girl loves the boy. They never speak of it, of course, but she just likes the way he wears his hat. Every day he comes to her house at a certain time and she sits in her window and waits. Then one day he doesn't come. 'Mood Indigo' just tells how she feels.' The story, and the tune it describes, are characteristically Ellingtonian: they bear the hallmark of true sophistication, which is audacious simplicity. His music is never cluttered, and travels lightly and politely.

Ellington's output as a composer was immense. The late Derek Jewell, in his indispensable biography of the man, estimated that he wrote at least 2,000 pieces, but, because of his cavalier way with pieces of paper, it may have been as many as 5,000. Among them were many tunes that have become popular standards – 'Sophisticated Lady', 'In A Sentimental Mood', 'Don't Get Around Much Anymore' and 'I'm Beginning To See The Light' are just a selected handful. Their significance, aside from the musical, was that their royalty income effectively subsidized the band, particularly during the post-war period when the big bands virtually disappeared under successive onslaughts from inflation, the growth of television, the decline of the dancehalls and, most significantly, the arrival of rock 'n' roll. Even Ellington was not immune to these pressures and in the early 50s, looking handsome suddenly became hard work.

The turning-point came at the Newport Jazz Festival on 7 July 1956, when morale was low. The previous year had seen embarrassing attempts at cashing in on commercial trends with recordings of 'Twelfth Street Rag Mambo' and 'Bunny Hop Mambo', plus a summer season at an aquashow, with a string section and two harpists. The first set at Newport was equally embarrassing. Ellington arrived onstage to find four of his musicians missing. The band played a few numbers, then departed. They returned around midnight, at full strength, to play the 'Newport Jazz Festival Suite', composed with Strayhorn for the occasion. Then Ellington, possibly still rankled by the earlier behaviour of the band, called 'Diminuendo And Crescendo In Blue', a piece written almost 20 years earlier and by no means a regular item on their usual concert programme. In two sections, and linked by a bridge passage from, on this occasion, the tenor saxophone player Paul Gonsalves, the piece was a revelation. Gonsalves blew 27 choruses, the crowd went wild, the band played four encores, and the news travelled around the world on the jazz grapevine; it was also reported in detail in *Time* magazine, with a picture of the piano player on the cover. After Newport and until his death, Ellington's life and career became a triumphal and global procession, garlanded with awards, honorary degrees, close encounters with world leaders and, more importantly, further major compositions. 'Such Sweet Thunder', his Shakespearean suite written with Strayhorn, contains gems such as 'Lady Mac' – 'Though she was a lady of noble birth, we suspect there was a little ragtime in her soul' – and 'Madness In Great Ones', dedicated to Hamlet with the laconic remark 'in those days crazy didn't mean the same thing it means now'.

Further collaborations with Strayhorn included an enchanting reworking of Tchaikovsky's 'The Nutcracker Suite' and 'The Far East Suite' – still adorned with dazzling contributions from various of the now-elder statesmen in the band: Hodges, Gonsalves and Carney in the reeds, Lawrence Brown, Britt Woodman and Tizol among the trombones, and Ray Nance and Cat Anderson in the trumpet section. Astonishingly, the band that recorded the *70th Birthday Concert* in England in 1969 included Carney, Hodges and Williams 40 years after they first joined Ellington, and on the record they still sounded like a group of kids having a good night on the town. The freshness and energy of the band as it tackled material played hundreds of times before, was extraordinary.

There was another side to the story. Ellington had always been a religious man, and in his later years he turned increasingly to the writing and performance of sacred music. The origins of this can be traced back to 'Come Sunday', from the 1945 suite 'Black, Brown And Beige', and beyond that to 'Reminiscing In Tempo', written 10 years earlier, following the death of his mother, of which he said: 'My mother's death was the greatest shock. I didn't do anything but brood. The music is representative of all that. It begins with pleasant thoughts. Then something awful gets you down. Then you snap out of it and it ends affirmatively.' From a man who was dismissive of analysis, this represented a very shrewd assessment not only of the piece in question, but of his entire output. Working within the framework of the conventional big band line-up – five reeds, four trumpets, three trombones, bass, drums and a remarkable piano player – he produced music of extraordinary diversity. His themes were startling in their simplicity, as if he had picked them off trees, and in a way, he did. The tonal qualities of the band – the unique Ellington sound – were based on a celebration of its individuals. The music might be lyrical or triumphant, elegiac or celebratory and the blues were never far away, yet it always ended affirmatively. To borrow a phrase from Philip Larkin, writing about Sidney Bechet, Duke Ellington's life and music added up to A Resounding Yes. In 1999, Ellington was awarded a Special Citation Pulitzer Prize commemorating the centenary of his birth and recognizing his 'musical genius' in the medium of jazz.

● ALBUMS: *Carnegie Hall Concert* (1943) ★★★★, *The Hollywood Bowl Concert Volumes 1 & 2* (1947) ★★★★, *Mood Ellington* 10-inch album (Columbia 1949) ★★★★, *Liberian Suite* 10-inch album

(Columbia 1949) ★★★★, *Ellingtonia, Volume 1* 10-inch album (Brunswick 1950) ★★★★, *Ellingtonia, Volume 2* 10-inch album (Brunswick 1950) ★★★★, *Masterpieces By Ellington* (Columbia 1951) ★★★, *Ellington Uptown* (Columbia 1951) ★★★, *Duke Ellington Volumes 1-3* 10-inch albums (Jazz Panorama 1951) ★★★★, *Duke Ellington* (RCA-Victor 1951) ★★★★, *The Duke Is On The Air – From The Blue Note* (1952) ★★★★, *This Is Duke Ellington And His Orchestra* (RCA-Victor 1952) ★★★★, *Duke Ellington Plays the Blues* (RCA-Victor 1953) ★★★★, *Premiered By Ellington* 10-inch album (Capitol 1953) ★★★, *Ellington Plays Ellington* 10-inch album (Capitol 1953) ★★★★, *Early Ellington* (Brunswick 1954) ★★★, *The Music Of Duke Ellington* (Columbia 1954) ★★★★, *Duke Ellington Plays* 10-inch album (Allegro 1954) ★★★, *Ellington '55* (Capitol 1954) ★★★, *The Duke Plays Ellington* (Capitol 1954) ★★★★, *Seattle Concert* (RCA-Victor 1954) ★★★, *Duke's Mixture* 10-inch album (Columbia 1955) ★★★, *Dance To The Duke* (Capitol 1955) ★★★, *Duke And His Men* (RCA-Victor 1955) ★★★, *Blue Light* (Columbia 1955) ★★★★, *Here's The Duke* 10-inch album (Columbia 1956) ★★★★, *Historically Speaking, The Duke* (Bethlehem 1956) ★★★, *Duke Ellington Presents* (Bethlehem 1956) ★★★, *Birth Of Big Band Jazz* (Riverside 1956) ★★★★, *Al Hibbler With the Duke* 10-inch album (Columbia 1956) ★★★, with Johnny Hodges *Ellington At Newport '56* (Columbia 1956) ★★★★★, *Ellington Showcase* (Capitol 1956) ★★★, *A Drum Is A Woman* (Columbia 1957) ★★★, *Such Sweet Thunder* (Columbia 1957) ★★★, *In A Mellotone* (RCA-Victor 1957) ★★★★, *Ellington Indigos* (Columbia 1958) ★★★★★, *Duke Ellington At His Very Best* (RCA-Victor 1958) ★★★★, *Newport 1958* (Columbia 1958) ★★★★★, *Black, Brown And Beige* (Columbia 1958) ★★★★, *The Cosmic Scene* (Columbia 1958) ★★★, *Duke Ellington At The Bal Masque* (Columbia 1959) ★★★, *Duke Ellington Jazz Party* (Columbia 1959) ★★★, with Hodges *Back To Back: Duke Ellington And Johnny Hodges Play The Blues* (Verve 1959) ★★★★, with Hodges *Side By Side* (Verve 1959) ★★★★, *Festival Session* (Columbia 1959) ★★★, *Ellington Moods* (SeSac 1959) ★★★, *Anatomy Of A Murder* soundtrack (Columbia 1959) ★★★★, *The Ellington Suites: The Queen's Suite* (1959) ★★★, *Swinging Suites By Edward E. And Edward G. (Suite Thursday/Peer Gynt)* (Columbia 1960) ★★★, with Hodges *The Nutcracker Suite* (Columbia 1960) ★★★, *Piano In The Background* (Columbia 1960) ★★★, *Blues In Orbit* (Columbia 1960) ★★★★, *Paris Blues* (1961) ★★★, *The Indispensable Duke Ellington* (RCA-Victor 1961) ★★★, with Count Basie *Ellington/Basie – First Time! The Count Meets The Duke* (Columbia 1962) ★★★, with Charles Mingus, Max Roach *Money Jungle* (United Artists 1962) ★★★★, *All American* (Columbia 1962) ★★★, *Midnight In Paris* (Columbia 1962) ★★★, with John Coltrane *Duke Ellington And John Coltrane* (MCA/Impulse! 1962) ★★★★, *Afro-Bossa* (Reprise 1963) ★★★★, with Coleman Hawkins *Duke Ellington Meets Coleman Hawkins* (MCA/Impulse! 1963) ★★★★★, *The Symphonic Ellington* (Reprise 1963) ★★★, *Piano In The Foreground* (Columbia 1963) ★★★, with Svend Asmussen *Jazz Violin Session* (Reprise 1963) ★★★★, with Billy Strayhorn *Piano Duets: Great Times!* (Riverside 1963) ★★★, *Duke Ellington's Concert Of Sacred Music* (RCA-Victor 1964) ★★★, *Hit's Of The 60s* (Reprise 1964) ★★, *Daybreak Express* (RCA-Victor 1964) ★★★, *Jumpin' Pumpkins* (RCA-Victor 1965) ★★, *Johnny Come Lately* (RCA-Victor 1965) ★★, *Mary Poppins* (Reprise 1965) ★, *Pretty Woman* (RCA-Victor 1965) ★★, *Flaming Youth* (RCA-Victor 1965) ★★, *Ellington '66* (Reprise 1965) ★★★, *Will Big Bands Ever Come Back?* (Reprise 1965) ★★★, *Concert In The Virgin Islands* (Reprise 1965) ★★★, with Boston Pops Orchestra *The Duke At Tanglewood* (RCA-Victor 1966) ★★★, with Ella Fitzgerald *Ella At Duke's Place* (Verve 1966) ★★★★★, with Fitzgerald *The Stockholm Concert* (1966) ★★★, with Fitzgerald *Ella And Duke At The Côte D'Azure* (Verve 1966) ★★★, *The Popular Duke Ellington* (RCA-Victor 1966) ★★★, *Concert Of Sacred Music* (RCA-Victor 1966) ★★★, with Hodges *The Far East Suite* (RCA-Victor 1967) ★★★★, *Soul Call* (Verve 1967) ★★★, *And His Mother Called Him Bill* (RCA-Victor 1968) ★★★★★, with Frank Sinatra *Francis A. And Edward K.* (Reprise 1968) ★★★, *Second Sacred Concert* (Prestige 1968) ★★★, *70th Birthday Concert* (1969) ★★★, *The Latin American Suite* (Fantasy 1969) ★★★, *The New Orleans Suite* (Atlantic 1970) ★★★★, *Afro-Eurasian Eclipse* (Fantasy 1971) ★★★, with Ray Brown *This One's For Blanton* (Pablo 1972) ★★★, *Third Sacred Concert* (Prestige 1973) ★★★, *Eastbourne Performance* (RCA 1973) ★★, *Yale Concert* (Fantasy 1973) ★★★, with Teresa Brewer *It Don't Mean A Thing . . .* (Columbia 1973) ★★★★, *The Duke's Big 4* (Pablo 1974) ★★★★, *The Duke Ellington Carnegie Hall Concerts-January, 1943* (Prestige 1977) ★★★★, *The Duke Ellington Carnegie Hall Concerts-December, 1944* (Prestige 1977) ★★★★, *The Duke Ellington Carnegie Hall Concerts-January, 1946* (Prestige 1977) ★★★★, *The Duke Ellington Carnegie Hall Concerts-December, 1947* (Prestige 1977) ★★★★, *The Unknown Session* 1960 recording (Columbia 1979) ★★★, *In Concert At The Pleyel Paris* 1958 recording (Magic 1990) ★★★, *The Far East Suite: Special Mix* (Bluebird 1995) ★★★★, *Berlin '65/Paris '67* (Pablo 1998) ★★★, *Duke's Joint* 1945 live performances (RCA/Buddah 1999) ★★, *Ellington At Newport: The Complete Concert* (Columbia Legacy 1999) ★★★★★.

● COMPILATIONS: *Ellington's Greatest* (RCA-Victor 1954) ★★★★, *Duke Ellington Volume 1 – In The Beginning* (Decca 1958) ★★★★, *Duke Ellington Volume 2 – Hot In Harlem* (Decca 1959) ★★★★, *Duke Ellington Volume 3 – Rockin' In Rhythm* (Decca 1959) ★★★★, *The Best Of Duke Ellington* (Capitol 1961) ★★★★, *The Ellington Era Volume 1* 3-LP box set (Columbia 1963) ★★★★, *The Ellington Era Volume 2* 3-LP box set (Columbia 1964) ★★★★, *Duke Ellington's Greatest Hits* (Reprise 1966) ★★★★, *Duke Ellington – The Pianist* 1966-74 recordings (Fantasy 1974) ★★★★, *The Ellington Suites* (Pablo 1976) ★★★★, *The Intimate Ellington* (Pablo 1977) ★★★, *The All-Star Road Band, Volume 1* (Columbia 1983) ★★★★, *The All-Star Road Band, Volume 2* (Columbia 1983) ★★★★, *The*

Indispensable Duke Ellington Volumes 1-12 (RCA 1983-87) ★★★, *The Intimacy Of The Blues* 1970 recordings (Fantasy 1986) ★★★★, *The Blanton-Webster Band* 1940-42 recordings (RCA Bluebird 1987) ★★★★★, *Black, Brown And Beige* (RCA Bluebird 1988) ★★★★, *Four Symphonic Works* (Music Master 1989) ★★★★, *The Best Of Duke Ellington* (Columbia 1989) ★★★, *Braggin' In Brass – The Immortal 1938 Year* (Portrait 1989) ★★★★, *The Brunswick Era, Volume 1* (MCA 1990) ★★★★, with Blanton and others *Solos, Duets And Trios* 1932-67 recordings (RCA Bluebird 1990) ★★★★, *The OKeh Ellington* (Columbia 1991) ★★★★, *Small Groups, Volume 1* (Columbia/Legacy 1991) ★★★★, *The Essence Of Duke Ellington* (Columbia/Legacy 1991) ★★★★★, *The Complete Capitol Recordings Of Duke Ellington* 5-CD box set (Mosaic 1996) ★★★★★, *Jazz Profile* (Blue Note 1997) ★★★★, *1945, Vol. 2* (Classics 1998) ★★★, *The Centennial Edition: The Complete RCA Victor Recordings* 24-CD box set (RCA Victor 1999) ★★★★★, *The Essential Collection 1927-1962* (Columbia 2000) ★★★★, *Complete Columbia & RCA Studio Sessions With Ben Webster Featuring Jimmy Blanton* 40s recordings (Definitive 2000) ★★★★★, *Ken Burns Jazz: The Definitive Duke Ellington* (Columbia/Legacy 2000) ★★★★, *The Reprise Studio Recordings* 5-CD box set (Mosaic 2000) ★★★.

● VIDEOS: *Duke Ellington* (Virgin Vision 1992), *On The Road With Duke Ellington* (Direct Cinema 1995).

● FURTHER READING: *Duke Ellington: Young Music Master*, Martha E. Schaaf. *Sweet Man, The Real Duke Ellington*, Don R. George. *Duke Ellington*, Ron Franki. *Duke Ellington*, Barry Ulanov. *The World Of Duke Ellington*, Stanley Dance. *Music Is My Mistress*, Duke Ellington. *Celebrating The Duke*, Ralph J. Gleason. *Duke: A Portrait Of Duke Ellington*, Derek Jewell. *Duke Ellington In Person*, Mercer Ellington. *Duke Ellington: His Life And Music*, Peter Gammond. *Duke Ellington: Life And Times Of A Restless Genius Of Jazz*, James Lincoln Collier. *Duke Ellington: The Early Years*, Michael Tucker. *Duke Ellington: Jazz Composer*, Ken Rattenbury. *The Duke Ellington Reader*, Mark Tucker. *Beyond Category: The Life And Genius Of Duke Ellington*, John Edward Hasse. *The Duke Ellington Primer*, Dempsey J. Travis. *Reminiscing In Tempo: A Portrait Of Duke Ellington*, Stuart Nicholson. *Jump For Joy: Jazz At Lincoln Center Celebrates The Ellington Centennial*, Veronica Byrd, James Ty Cumbie, Tiffany A. Ellis and Rob Gibson (ed.). *The King Of All, Sir Duke*, Peter Lavezzoli.

ELLINGTON, RAY

b. Harry Brown, 1915, London, England, d. 28 February 1985. Ellington began playing drums as a teenager and by 1937 was proficient enough to replace Joe Daniels in Harry Roy's popular band. He remained with Roy for almost five years, although his personal musical taste tended more towards the new jazz styles, and soon after the end of World War II he was playing bop in London clubs. He led his own quartet at this time and made a number of records, and sometimes accompanied visiting American jazzmen. His quartet in the late 40s comprised Dick Katz (piano), Coleridge Goode (bass) and Lauderic Caton guitar who was replaced by Laurie Deniz, and they were able to play swing, jumping R&B and popular jazz. In the early 50 Ellington began to incorporate comedy and novelty material into his repertoire but the group's musical base was always strongly bop-influenced. Throughout the 50s the quartet was regularly featured on *The Goon Show* on BBC Radio, usually with Ellington singing, and he also took small acting roles in the programme. By the 60s and with the passing of *The Goon Show*, Ellington was much less in demand, but he continued playing until shortly before his death in February 1985. His son, Lance Ellington, played trombone with the National Youth Jazz Orchestra and also sang as a member of the pop duo Coffee And Cream.

● ALBUMS: *Goon Show Hits* (BBC 1958) ★★★★, *You're The Talk Of The Town* (Gold Star 1975) ★★.
● COMPILATIONS: *The Three Bears* 1948-49 recordings (Avid 2001) ★★★★.

ELVIS - ELVIS PRESLEY

While Private Elvis Presley was gaining his stripes in Germany, RCA was desperate for new material. They kept the pot boiling by taking his first UK album, *Rock 'n' Roll No.1*, substituting three tracks and adding two more. Although critics sometimes regard his Sun tracks in a different light to his RCA ones, they sit well together. 'I Was The One', the b-side of 'Heartbreak Hotel' and one of Elvis's favourite songs, could easily have been recorded at Sun. 'Lawdy, Miss Clawdy', written and originally recorded by Lloyd Price, remains one of Presley's best-ever performances: the lyrics do not mean much but there is tremendous commitment from Elvis. Lloyd Price's original version had Fats Domino on piano: this one had Elvis himself. Elvis always enjoyed his recording sessions and you can sense this on the good-natured 'Money Honey'.

● Tracks: *That's All Right; Lawdy, Miss Clawdy; Mystery Train; Playing For Keeps; Poor Boy; Money Honey; I'm Counting On You; My Baby Left Me; I Was The One; Shake, Rattle And Roll; I'm Left, You're Right, She's Gone; You're A Heartbreaker; Trying To Get You; Blue Suede Shoes.*
● First released 1959
● UK peak chart position: did not chart
● USA peak chart position: 1

ELVIS PRESLEY - ELVIS PRESLEY

Although five tracks remained from the Sun cellar this is usually known as Elvis Presley's first RCA album, and what a lucky company they were, probably unaware that they had signed the greatest ever donor to their company pension scheme. No rock aficionado should be unaware of the tracks, although the album has long been replaced with compilations. It still is nominated by the majority of the cognoscenti who are old enough to remember this album plopping down on their Dansettes. It was a vitally important album although now doomed by the age of CD, as there are much better compilations with many more tracks.

● Tracks: *Blue Suede Shoes; I Love You Because; Tutti Frutti; I'll Never Let You Go; Money Honey; I'm Counting On You; I Got A Woman; One-Sided Love Affair; Just Because; Tryin' To Get To You; I'm Gonna Sit Right Down And Cry Over You; Blue Moon.*
● First released 1956
● UK peak chart position: did not chart
● USA peak chart position: 1

ERTEGUN, AHMET

b. 1923, Istanbul, Turkey. The son of the Turkish ambassador to Washington, USA, Ahmet Ertegun moved to New York upon his father's death in 1944. Although a philosophy graduate, he was drawn towards a musical career via his passion for jazz and blues, of which he was an inveterate collector. With friend and partner Herb Abramson, he founded two unsuccessful labels, Quality and Jubilee, before inaugurating Atlantic Records in 1947. Early releases featured recordings by jazz artists Errol Garner and Tiny Grimes, but Ertegun decided to pursue an R&B-styled policy and the label enjoyed its first notable hit with Granville 'Stick' McGhee's 'Drinking Wine, Spo-Dee-O-Dee', which Ertegun produced. He continued to fulfil that role when Jerry Wexler arrived at Atlantic. The pair were responsible for producing early seminal releases for Clyde McPhatter and the Drifters, including 'Money Honey' and 'Such A Night'. Ahmet also proved himself a skilled composer, co-penning 'Chains Of Love' and 'Sweet Sixteen', the first two hits for 1949 signing Big Joe Turner. Many of his subsequent compositions were credited to the anagrammatical pseudonym, 'Nutgere'.

During the 50s Atlantic established itself as a leading independent through the signings of Ray Charles and Bobby Darin. Ertegun and Wexler produced Ray Charles together, while Ahmet took sole charge for Darin, notably on his first hit, 'Splish Splash'. The label was quick to capitalize on the long-player format and Ertegun passed responsibility for transferring 78s to the new medium to his older brother, Nesuhi. The Coasters and a revitalized Drifters ensured Atlantic's success rate was maintained and with many contemporaries now experiencing financial difficulties, Ertegun entered the 60s as a music industry survivor. Indeed, in 1965 he assisted producer/songwriter Bert Berns in establishing the Bang Records label. Although Jerry Wexler is credited with shaping Atlantic's mid-60s policies, in particular his arrangements with Stax Records and Fame, Ertegun signed white 'southern-styled' acts Dr. John, Delaney And Bonnie and Jessie Davis to the label. However, his greatest achievement was a deliberate decision to broaden Atlantic's R&B image with pop and rock signings. Ertegun brought Sonny And Cher to the company, a faith repaid immediately when 'I Got You Babe' became one of the bestselling singles of 1965. That same year he launched the (Young) Rascals, who gained 17 US Top 20 hits until leaving for Columbia Records in 1969.

Meanwhile, another Ertegun acquisition, Vanilla Fudge, found success with their dramatic rearrangements of popular songs, notably 'You Keep Me Hangin' On'. He introduced Neil Young and Stephen Stills to the public via Buffalo Springfield, who struck gold with 'For What It's Worth' and won critical acclaim for three excellent albums. Ertegun kept faith with Stills upon the quintet's disintegration, trading band member Richie Furay for David Crosby and securing a release for the Hollies' Graham Nash. The resultant 'supergroup', Crosby, Stills And Nash, became one of the era's leading attractions. However, Iron Butterfly did not receive the same critical approbation, although *In-A-Gadda-Da-Vida* was, for a spell, the biggest-selling album in history. Ertegun's vision proved equally astute with respect to UK acts. A licensing agreement with Polydor Records ensured Atlantic had first option on its British roster. He took up the Bee Gees and Cream, as well as the solo careers of the latter's ex-members following their split. Eric Clapton proved an important coup. Ertegun signed Led Zeppelin directly to US Atlantic; his faith was rewarded when the quartet became one of rock's most successful bands. Ahmet also took up the rights to the soundtrack of the Woodstock Festival, and in 1970, he persuaded the Rolling Stones that Atlantic was the natural home for their own record label. By this point, however, his company's autonomy had been affected.

In 1967 Ertegun and Wexler allowed Warner Brothers Records to purchase Atlantic stock in return for an executive position in a conglomerate known as WEA Records with the acquisition of Elektra Records. Although Ertegun has remained at his label's helm, it has since lost its distinctive qualities. He has concurrently pursued other interests and a passion for soccer led to his becoming a director of the New York Cosmos, to which he attracted such luminaries as Pele and Franz Bekenbauer. Even if his profile is less apparent than in previous years, Ahmet Ertegun has left an indelible mark on the development of popular music through his entrepreneurial and musical gifts. He was inducted into the Rock And Roll Hall Of Fame in 1987.

EVANS, GIL

b. Ian Ernest Gilmore Green, 13 May 1912, Toronto, Canada, d. 20 March 1988, Cuernavaca, Mexico. Although self-taught, Evans became extraordinarily proficient as a pianist and composer, though his greatest talent lay in his abilities as an arranger. He formed his first band in 1933 in California, where he was raised. He wrote most of the arrangements, a duty he retained when the band was later fronted by popular singer Skinnay Ennis. Up to this point Evans' work had followed the orthodox line demanded of commercial dancebands, but his musical ambitions lay in other areas. A long stint as chief arranger for Claude Thornhill during the 40s gave him the opportunity he needed to explore different sounds and unusual textures. Thornhill's predilection for soft and slowly shifting pastel patterns as a background for his delicate piano proved to be an interesting workshop for Evans, who would always remark on this experience as being influential upon his later work. Towards the end of his stay with Thornhill, Evans was writing for very large ensembles, creating intense moody music.

However, by this time, he was eager to try something new, feeling that the music he was required to write for the band was becoming too static and sombre. During this same period, Gerry Mulligan was a member of the Thornhill band and was also writing arrangements. Both he and Evans had become fascinated by the developments of the radical new beboppers such as Charlie Parker and Miles Davis, and in 1948 the two men embarked upon a series of arrangements for Davis' nine-piece band. These records, subsequently released under the generic title *Birth Of The Cool*, proved very influential in the 50s. Despite the quality of the material Evans was creating at this point in his career, he did not meet with much commercial or critical success. Towards the end of the 50s Evans again worked with Davis, helping to create landmark albums such as *Miles Ahead* and *Sketches Of Spain*. His writing for Davis was a highly effective amalgam of the concepts developed during his Thornhill period and the needs of the increasingly restrained trumpet style Davis was adopting. Evans' use in these and later arrangements for his own band of such instruments as tubas and bass trombones broadened the range of orchestral colours at his disposal and helped him to create a highly distinctive sound and style. As with many other gifted arrangers and composers, Evans' real need was for a permanent band for the expression of his ideas, but this proved difficult to achieve. Such groups as he did form were in existence for only short periods, although some, fortunately, made records of his seminal works. He continued to write, composing many extended works, often uncertain if they would ever be performed. However, in the early 70s he was able to form a band which played regularly and the music showed his ready absorption of ideas and devices from the current pop music scene.

After a number of international tours during the 70s, his work became more widely known and his stature rose accordingly. So too did his popularity when it became apparent to audiences that his was not esoteric music but was readily accessible and showed a marked respect for the great traditions of earlier jazz. By the late 70s, the music Evans was writing had developed a harder edge than hitherto; he was making extensive use of electronics and once again was happily absorbing aspects of pop. In particular, he arranged and recorded several Jimi Hendrix compositions. His creativity showed no signs of diminishing as the 80s dawned and he continued a punishing round of concert tours, record dates, radio and television appearances, all the while writing more new material for his band. One of his final commissions was with Sting, arranging a fine version of Hendrix's 'Little Wing'. One of the outstanding arrangers and composers in jazz, Evans was particularly adept at creating complex scores which held at their core a simple and readily understandable concept. Throughout his career, his writing showed his profound respect for the needs of jazz musicians to make their own musical statements within an otherwise formally conceived and structured work. Perhaps this is why so many notable musicians – including Steve Lacy, Elvin Jones, Lew Soloff, George Adams, Ron Carter and David Sanborn – were happy to play in his bands over the years. As a result Evans' work, even at its most sophisticated, maintained an enviable feeling of freedom and spontaneity that few other arrangers of his calibre were able to achieve.

● ALBUMS: *There Comes A Time* (RCA Victor 1955) ★★★★, *Gil Evans Plus 10* reissued as *Big Stuff* (Prestige 1957) ★★★★, *New Bottles Old Wine* (Pacific Jazz 1958) ★★★★, *Great Jazz Standards* (World Pacific 1959) ★★★, with Johnny Coles *Out Of The Cool* (Impulse! 1960) ★★★★★, *Into The Hot* (Impulse! 1961) ★★★, *America's Number 1 Arranger* (Pacific Jazz 1961) ★★★, *The Individualism Of Gil Evans* (Verve 1964) ★★★★, with Kenny Burrell *Guitar Forms* (Verve 1965) ★★★★, *Blues In Orbit* (Enja 1971) ★★★, *Svengali* (Atlantic 1973) ★★★, *The Gil Evans Orchestra Featuring Kenny Burrell And Phil Woods* 1963 recording (Verve 1973) ★★★, *The Gil Evans Orchestra Plays The Music Of Jimi Hendrix* (Bluebird 1974) ★★★★, *Synthetic Evans* (Zeta 1976) ★★★, *Live '76* (Zeta 1976) ★★★, *Priestess* (Antilles 1977) ★★★, *Tokyo Concert* (Westwind 1977) ★★★, *Gil Evans At The Royal Festival Hall* (Westwind 1978) ★★★, *The Rest Of Gil Evans At The Royal Festival Hall* (Westwind 1978) ★★★, *Little Wing* (DIW 1978) ★★★, *Parabola* (Horo 1979) ★★★, *Live At New York Public Theatre Volumes 1 and 2* (Blackhawk 1980) ★★★, *The British Orchestra* (Mole 1983) ★★★, *Live At Sweet Basil Volumes 1 & 2* (Electric Bird 1984) ★★★, *Farewell* (Electric Bird 1987) ★★★, with Helen Merrill *Helen Merrill/Gil Evans* (EmArcy 1988) ★★★, with Steve Lacy *Paris Blues* (Owl 1988) ★★★, *Sting And Bill Evans/Last Session* (Jazz Door 1988) ★★★, *Lunar Eclypse* 1981 recordings (New Tone 1993) ★★★.

● COMPILATIONS: with Tadd Dameron *The Arrangers Touch* 1953/1956/1957 recordings (Prestige 1975) ★★★★, *Jazz Masters* 1964/1965 recordings (Verve 1994) ★★★★, *Giants Of Jazz: The Gil Evans Orchestra 1957-1959 recordings* (Sarabandas 1994) ★★★★, with Miles Davis *Miles Davis/Gil Evans: The Complete Columbia Studio Recordings* 6-CD/11-LP box set (Columbia/Mosaic 1996) ★★★★★, *Gil Evans* (GRP 1998) ★★★.

● FURTHER READING: *Svengali, Or The Orchestra Called Gil Evans*, Raymond Horricks. *Gil Evans: Out Of The Cool*, Stephanie Stein Crease.

EVERLY BROTHERS

Don (b. Isaac Donald Everly, 1 February 1937, Brownie, Kentucky, USA) and Phil (b. Phillip Everly, 19 January 1939, Chicago, Illinois, USA), the world's most famous rock 'n' roll duo, had already experienced a full career before their first record, 'Bye Bye Love', was released. As sons of popular country artists Ike and Margaret, they were pushed into the limelight from an early age.

They regularly appeared on their parents' radio shows throughout the 40s and accompanied them on many tours. In the mid-50s, as rockabilly was evolving into rock 'n' roll, the boys moved to Nashville, the Mecca for such music. Don had a minor hit when Kitty Wells recorded his composition 'Thou Shalt Not Steal' in 1954. In 1957 they were given a Felice and Boudleaux Bryant song that was finding difficulty being placed. They took 'Bye Bye Love' and made it their own; it narrowly missed the US number 1 position and reached number 6 in the UK. The brothers then embarked on a career that made them second only to Elvis Presley in the rock 'n' roll popularity stakes. Their blend of country and folk did much to sanitize and make respectable a phenomenon towards which many parents still showed hostility. America, then a racially segregated country, was not ready for its white teenagers to listen to black-based rock music. The brothers' clean looks and even cleaner harmonies did much to change people's attitudes.

They quickly followed this initial success with more irresistible Bryant songs, 'Wake Up Little Susie', 'All I Have To Do Is Dream', 'Bird Dog', 'Problems', 'So Sad' and the beautiful 'Devoted To You'. The brothers were supremely confident live performers, both with their trademark Gibson Dove and later, black J50 guitars. By the end of the 50s they were the world's number 1 vocal group. Amazingly, their career gained further momentum when, after signing with the newly formed Warner Brothers Records for $1 million, they delivered a song that was catalogued WB1. This historical debut was the superlative 'Cathy's Clown', written by Don. No Everly record had sounded like this before; the echo-laden production and the treble-loaded harmonies ensured that it stayed at number 1 in the USA for five weeks. In the UK it stayed on top for over two months, selling several million and making it one of the most successful records of all time. The brothers continued to release immaculate records; many of them reached the US Top 10, although in England their success was even greater, with two further number 1 hits during 1961. Again the echo and treble dominated in two more classics, 'Walk Right Back' and a fast-paced reworking of the former Bing Crosby hit 'Temptation'. At the end of 1961 they were drafted into the US Marines, albeit for only six months, and resumed by embarking on a European tour. Don became dependent on drugs, and the pressures from constant touring and recording began to show; during one historic night at London's East Ham Granada, England, a nervous Phil performed solo. The standard 'food poisoning/exhaustion' excuse was used. What was not known by the doting fans was that Don had attempted a suicidal drug overdose twice in 48 hours. Phil completed the tour solo. Don's addiction continued for another three years, although they were able to work during part of this time.

The advent of the beat boom pushed the brothers out of the spotlight and while they continued to make hit records, none approached their previous achievements. The decline was briefly halted in 1965 with two excellent major UK hits, 'The Price Of Love' and 'Love Is Strange'. The former, a striking chart-topper, recalled their early Warner sound, while the latter harked back even earlier, with a naïve but infectious call-and-answer spoken segment. In 1966 they released *Two Yanks In England*, a strong album that contained eight songs by Nash/Clarke/Hicks of the Hollies; surprisingly, the album failed to chart. The duo were recognized only for their superb singles, and many of their albums were less well-received. *Stories We Could Tell*, recorded with an array of guest players, threatened to extend their market into the rock mainstream, but it was not to be. After a few years of declining fortunes and arrival at the supper-club circuit, the brothers parted acrimoniously. Following a show at Knotts Berry Farm, California, in 1973, during which a drunken Don insulted Phil, the latter walked off, smashed one of his beloved Gibsons and vowed, 'I will never get on a stage with that man again'. The only time they met over the next 10 years was at their father's funeral. Both embarked on solo careers with varying degrees of accomplishment. Their country-flavoured albums found more favour with the Nashville audience of their roots. Don and his band, the Dead Cowboys, regularly played in Nashville, while Phil released the critically acclaimed *Star Spangled Springer*. Inexplicably, the album was a relatively poor seller, as were several follow-ups. Phil made a cameo appearance in the movie *Every Which Way But Loose*, performing with actress Sondra Locke. While Don maintained a steady career, playing with ex-Heads, Hands And Feet maestro Albert Lee, Phil concentrated on writing songs. 'She Means Nothing To Me' was a striking duet with Cliff Richard which put the Everly name back in the UK Top 10. Rumours began to circulate of a reunion, which was further fuelled by an UK television advertisement for an Everly Brothers compilation. In June 1983 they hugged and made up and their emotional reconciliation was made before an ecstatic, wet-eyed audience at London's Royal Albert Hall. The following year *EB84* was released and gave them another major hit with Paul McCartney's 'Wings Of A Nightingale'. In 1986 they were inducted into the Rock And Roll Hall Of Fame and the following year Phil gave Don a pound of gold and a handmade guitar for his 50th birthday. They now perform regularly together, with no pressure from record companies. Don lives quietly in Nashville and tours with his brother for a few months every year. A major reissue programme, with alternative takes was undertaken by Warners in 2001. The Everly Brothers' influence on a generation of pop and rock artists is inestimable; they set a standard for close harmony singing that has rarely been bettered and is still used as a blueprint for many of today's harmony vocalists.

● ALBUMS: *The Everly Brothers* (Cadence 1958) ★★★★, *Songs Our Daddy Taught Us* (Cadence 1959) ★★★★, *The Everly Brothers' Best* (Cadence 1959) ★★★, *It's Everly Time* (Warners 1960) ★★★, *The Fabulous Style Of The Everly Brothers* (Cadence

1960) ★★★★, *A Date With The Everly Brothers* (Warners 1960) ★★★★, *Both Sides Of An Evening* (Warners 1961) ★★★, *Folk Songs Of the Everly Brothers* (Cadence 1962) ★★★, *Instant Party* (Warners 1962) ★★★, *Christmas With The Everly Brothers And The Boys Town Choir* (Warners 1962) ★★, *The Everly Brothers Sing Great Country Hits* (Warners 1963) ★★★, *Gone Gone Gone* (Warners 1965) ★★★★, *Rock 'N' Soul* (Warners 1965) ★★★, *Beat 'N' Soul* (Warners 1965) ★★★, *In Our Image* (Warners 1966) ★★★, *Two Yanks In England* (Warners 1966) ★★★, *The Hit Sound Of The Everly Brothers* (Warners 1967) ★★★, *The Everly Brothers Sing* (Warners 1967) ★★★, *Roots* (Warners 1968) ★★★★, *The Everly Brothers Show* (Warners 1970) ★★★, *End Of An Era* (Barnaby/Columbia 1971) ★★★, *Stories We Could Tell* (RCA-Victor 1972) ★★★, *Pass The Chicken And Listen* (RCA-Victor 1973) ★★, *The Exciting Everly Brothers* (RCA 1975) ★★★, *Living Legends* (Warwick 1977) ★★★, *The New Album* previously unissued Warners material (Warners 1977) ★★★, *The Everly Brothers Reunion Concert* (Impression 1983) ★★★★, *Nice Guys* previously unissued Warners material (Magnum Force 1984) ★★, *EB84* (Mercury 1984) ★★★, *In The Studio* previously unissued Cadence material (Ace 1985) ★★★, *Born Yesterday* (Mercury 1985) ★★★, *Some Hearts* (Mercury 1988) ★★★, *Live In Paris* 1963 recording (Big Beat 1997) ★★★, *Live At The Olympia* 10-inch album (Big Beat 1997) ★★★. Solo: Don Everly *Don Everly* (A&M 1971) ★★, *Sunset Towers* (Ode 1974) ★★, *Brother Juke Box* (Hickory 1976) ★★★. Phil Everly *Star Spangled Springer* (RCA 1973) ★★★, *Phil's Diner (There's Nothing Too Good For My Baby)* (Pye 1974) ★★, *Mystic Line* (Pye 1975) ★★, *Living Alone* (Elektra 1979) ★★, *Phil Everly* (Capitol 1983) ★★.
● COMPILATIONS: *The Golden Hits Of The Everly Brothers* (Warners 1962) ★★★★, *15 Everly Hits* (Cadence 1963) ★★★, *The Very Best Of The Everly Brothers* (Warners 1964) ★★★★, *The Everly Brothers' Original Greatest Hits* (Columbia 1970) ★★★★★, *The Most Beautiful Songs Of The Everly Brothers* (Warners 1973) ★★★, *Don's And Phil's Fabulous Fifties Treasury* (Janus 1974) ★★★, *Walk Right Back With The Everlys* (Warners 1975) ★★★★, *The Everly Brothers Greatest Hits Collection* (Pickwick 1979) ★★★, *The Sensational Everly Brothers* (Reader Digest 1979) ★★, *Cathy's Clown* (Pickwick 1980) ★★★, *The Very Best Of The Everly Brothers* (Marks & Spencer 1980) ★★, *The Everly Brothers* (Warners 1981) ★★★, *Rock 'N' Roll Forever* (Warners 1981) ★★★, *Love Hurts* (K-Tel 1982) ★★, *Rip It Up* (Ace 1983) ★★★, *Cadence Classics (Their 20 Greatest Hits)* (Rhino 1985) ★★★★, *The Best Of The Everly Brothers* (Rhino 1985) ★★★, *All They Had To Do Is Dream* US only (Rhino 1985) ★★★, *Great Recordings* (Ace 1986) ★★★, *The Everly Brothers Collection* (Castle 1988) ★★★, *The Very Best Of The Everly Brothers* (Pickwick 1988) ★★★, *Hidden Gems* Warners material (Ace 1989) ★★★, *The Very Best Of The Everly Brothers Volume 2* (Pickwick 1990) ★★, *Perfect Harmony* box set (Knight 1990) ★★★, *Classic Everly Brothers* 3-CD box set (Bear Family 1992) ★★★★, *The Golden Years Of The Everly Brothers* (Warners 1993)

★★★★, *Heartaches And Harmonies* 4-CD box set (Rhino 1995) ★★★★★, *Walk Right Back: On Warner Bros. 1960 To 1969* 2-CD set (Warners 1996) ★★★★, *All I Have To Do Is Dream* (Carlton 1997) ★★★, *The EP Collection* (See For Miles 1998) ★★★, *The Masters* (Eagle 1998) ★★★, *The Very Best Of The Cadence Era* (Repertoire 1999) ★★★, *Devoted To You: Love Songs* (Varèse Sarabande 2000) ★★★★, *The Complete Cadence Recordings: 1957-1960* (Varèse Sarabande 2001) ★★★★.
● VIDEOS: *Rock 'N' Roll Odyssey* (MGM 1984).
● FURTHER READING: *Everly Brothers: An Illustrated Discography*, John Hosum. *The Everly Brothers: Walk Right Back*, Roger White. *Ike's Boys*, Phyllis Karpp. *The Everly Brothers: Ladies Love Outlaws*, Consuelo Dodge. *For-Everly Yours*, Peter Aarts and Martin Alberts.

EXCELLO RECORDS

The Excello Records label was launched in August 1952 as a subsidiary of the Nashboro Record Distributing Co., that had been set up a year earlier to tap into the insatiable demand for black southern gospel music. The founder was Ernie Young (b. Ernest L. Young, 2 December 1892, Giles County, Tennessee, USA), a jukebox operator and electronics/record retailer. He started the business from 177 Third Avenue North, Nashville, Tennessee – the home of The Record Mart (later renamed Ernie's Record Mart), a store that was to play a vital role in the Excello story.
The early Excello releases covered blues, R&B, gospel, hillbilly, even pop music. The first hits were all in the southern markets: 'Banana Split' (Kid King's Combo), 'Bus Station Blues' (Louis Brooks And His Pinetoppers), and 'Baby Let's Play House' (Arthur Gunter), subsequently covered by a young Elvis Presley as his fourth single for Sun Records. The flow of royalties from Presley's recording to the publishing arm Excellorec Music helped to underpin Young's business operations. In 1955 and 1956 there were further R&B chart hits: 'Rollin' Stone' (the Marigolds, led by Johnny Bragg), 'It's Love Baby (24 Hours A Day)' (Louis Brooks And His Hi-Toppers, featuring young vocalist Earl Gaines), and 'Pleadin' For Love' (Larry Birdsong, a protégé of local producer Ted Jarrett). Until then, most of the Excello releases had been recorded in Young's small, makeshift studio in the Ernie's Record Mart building.
Young had the foresight to sponsor nightly shows over Nashville's powerful 50,000-watt Radio WLAC, hosted by John Richbourg (John R). Record orders started flooding into Ernie's Record Mart. Young hit upon the great idea of making up five-pack specials of 45s at a discount price (at one time $2.98). These packs contained not only the latest R&B hits, but also at least one Excello record with every order. Young applied the same principle to his gospel 'specials' by including Nashboro 45s in every pack. With good profit margins on the record packs, Young needed the assurance of regular Excello product. In 1955, he began releasing swamp blues recordings by an ambitious Crowley, Louisiana producer, Jay Miller, who had already written the big country hit 'It Wasn't God Who

Made Honky Tonk Angels' for Kitty Wells. The first Miller artist signed to Excello was Lightnin' Slim. By 1957, there was a string of high quality Miller swamp blues recordings from Lightnin' Slim, Lonesome Sundown, Lazy Lester and Guitar Gable. Miller was renowned for giving his artists colourful pseudonyms. The swamp bluesman who epitomized the laid-back Excello blues sound of mellow harmonicas and moody bass rhythms was about to make his debut record, James Moore aka Slim Harpo. Curiously, 'I'm A King Bee', despite its subsequent impact, never made the R&B charts of the day. With white teenagers listening to R&B records in ever increasing numbers, the cross-over from R&B to rock 'n' roll was now an established trend. Excello broke into the Top 100 charts for the first time in spring 1957 with 'Little Darlin'' by the Gladiolas (led by Maurice Williams). However, the age of white cover versions was not over and Canadian group the Diamonds, proceeded to spend a full half-year on the charts. Later, in 1960, with his new group, Maurice Williams And The Zodiacs were to make a startling comeback with 'Stay', a number 1 national hit for Herald.

In May 1957, Young had launched another subsidiary label, Nasco Records, which quickly became the pop arm of the Nashboro group. In 1958, local teen vocal group the Crescendos scored a big national hit with 'Oh Julie' at number 5 during an 18-week stay. The group could not find a follow-up record and became quintessential one-hit-wonders. The only other Nasco record to chart during a three-year lifespan was 'Prisoner's Song' by Jay Miller session drummer Warren Storm, with a Louisiana swamp pop sound. By the early 60s both Excello and Nashboro were releasing more than 20 singles per year, and were starting to issue long-playing albums by Lightnin' Slim, Slim Harpo and Nashville R&B artist Roscoe Shelton. Hit singles, though, were still all important. Producer Jay Miller obliged with 'Rainin' In My Heart' by Slim Harpo that peaked at number 34 on the *Billboard* Hot 100 chart in May 1961, and even higher at number 24 on the *Cash Box* chart. The gloss of the 'Rainin' In My Heart' hit quickly dissipated when Miller was unable to coax Slim Harpo to record a follow-up owing to a royalty dispute. Even so, Miller was able to step up his blues output for Excello from Lightnin' Slim, Lonesome Sundown and Lazy Lester and introduced new blues artists from the Baton Rouge area such as Silas Hogan, Jimmy Anderson and Moses 'Whispering' Smith.

In 1963, EMI Records of London licensed an album of mostly then-recent Excello singles entitled *Authentic R&B* on the Stateside label, compiled by Guy Stevens. The effect of this album on the British Beat era bands and fans was considerable. Miller healed the rift with Slim Harpo and in 1966 Harpo hit the charts again with the charismatic dance record 'Baby Scratch My Back,' which made number 1 R&B and touched number 16 on the Hot 100 charts. 'Baby Scratch My Back' subsequently was voted number 3 R&B record of 1966, this in an era when Motown Records dominated the airwaves.

'Baby Scratch My Back' was the last hit enjoyed by Ernie Young. In summer 1966 he retired at the age of 73. He sold the Nashboro Record Company to the Crescent Company conglomerate, which installed Shannon Williams as vice-president in charge of the Nashboro Group. The new owners disposed of the Ernie's Record Mart building and developed the Woodland Sound Studios complex, in the old Woodland Theatre Building. Jack Funk and Bud Howell were also involved in the management of the new music division. Jay Miller was to sever his relationship forever when the Crescent team signed Slim Harpo direct to Excello, upon the expiration of Miller's personal contract with Harpo.

With southern soul music at its Otis Redding-inspired peak, Excello contracted an impressive roster of soul artists, including Freddie North (their promo man), Z.Z. Hill, Bobby Powell, Kip Anderson, and Maceo And The King's Men. The Nashville arranger and producer Bob Holmes was brought in to oversee acts such as Slim Harpo and the Kelly Brothers. The soul releases were being allocated between Excello, A-Bet and a new affiliate, Mankind. Excello managed two minor soul hits with Jerry Washington from South Carolina, but the only soul hit of significance for the Nashboro Group was 'She's All I Got' by Freddie North (produced by Jerry Williams, aka Swamp Dogg) on Mankind in 1971. The Nashboro operation was hit badly by the change in format in WLAC Radio from R&B to Top 40 that saw the departure of old-style disc jockeys John R. and Hoss Allen (temporarily in his case). The final Excello release was in 1975. A-Bet continued until 1977 and even had modest hits by Oliver Sain and Skip Mahoney And The Casuals. Shannon Williams continued releasing gospel singles and albums on the Nashboro, Kenwood, Crescent and Creed labels until 1980. Meanwhile, in 1978, the Crescent Company had sold the Nashboro music complex to AVI, headed by record man Ray Harris and Ed Cobb (of the Four Preps).

To the world at large Excello and Nashboro were dormant throughout the 80s. The catalogues were revived in the early 90s when AVI granted licenses to Ace Records in England and P-Vine in Japan. The AVI stock was acquired in 1993 by former Motown executive Harry Anger, who embarked on an extensive CD reissue campaign. Then in 1997 the Excello and Nashboro masters were purchased by the Universal Music Group, and the Excellorec publishing catalogue was sold to Music Sales.

Excello Records will always be remembered as Ernie Young's brainchild. He was a smart businessman who had the vision to exploit the developing R&B and gospel record markets of the 50s and the 60s. In so doing, he has bequeathed a wealth of southern music on record. It is a tribute to him as founder, to Jay Miller as the main producer, and to the artists and their music that the Excello Records story lives on.

● COMPILATIONS: *The Excello Story Volumes 1-4* (Hip-O 1999) ★★★★.

● FURTHER READING: *South To Louisiana: The Music Of The Cajun Bayous*, John Broven.

EXPRESSO BONGO

This 1959 comedy feature began life as a stage play loosely based on the rise of British rock 'n' roll star Tommy Steele. Written by Wolf Mankowitz and directed by Val Guest, *Expresso Bongo* starred Laurence Harvey as an unscrupulous Soho agent, determined to make his protégé, ably played by Cliff Richard, into an international success. The film manages to convey some of the exploitative nature of early pop and the nascent teenage subculture spearheaded by the legendary 2I's coffee bar. However, the cynicism of Mankowitz meant the funny moments lacked warmth and the film now merely offers period charm. Although mild-mannered by the standards of today, *Expresso Bongo* was given an X-certificate, confirming the moody, threat-to-society image Richard initially bore. It did nothing to hinder his popularity, however, and in 1960 a soundtrack EP reached the number 14 position in the UK singles chart while the film's finest song, 'A Voice In The Wilderness', peaked at number 2.

FABIAN

b. Fabiano Forte Bonaparte, 6 February 1943, Philadelphia, Pennsylvania, USA. Fabian, almost despite himself, was among the more endurable products of the late 50s when the North American charts were infested with a turnover of vapid boys-next-door – all hair cream, doe eyes and coy half-smiles – groomed for fleeting stardom. Fabian was 'discovered' by two local talent scouts, Peter De Angelis and Bob Marucci, in Frankie Avalon's Teen And Twenty youth club in 1957. Enthralled by the youth's good looks, the pair shortened his name and contracted him to their own label Chancellor Records where a huge budget was allocated to project him as a tamed Elvis Presley. Accompanied by the Four Dates, Fabian's first two singles – 'I'm In Love' and 'Lilly Lou' – were only regional hits, but a string of television performances on Dick Clark's nationally-broadcast *American Bandstand* plus a coast-to-coast tour had the desired effect on female teenagers, and Fabian found himself suddenly in *Billboard*'s Top 40 with 'I'm A Man,' composed by the top New York songwriting team Doc Pomus/Mort Shuman, who also delivered more lucrative hits in 'Turn Me Loose' and 'Hound Dog Man', the main theme from Fabian's silver screen debut of the same name. More substantial movie roles came Fabian's way after his recording career peaked with 1959's million-selling 'Tiger' and *Hold That Tiger*. As well as the predictable teen-pics with their vacuous storylines and mimed musical sequences, he coped surprisingly well as John Wayne's sidekick in 1960's *North To Alaska* and with Bing Crosby and Tuesday Weld in *High Time*. Fabian's decline was as rapid as his launch after Congress pinpointed him as an instance of one of the exploited puppets in the payola scandal. Questioned at the time, Fabian made matters worse by honestly outlining the considerable electronic doctoring necessary to improve his voice on record. Reverb was required to cover his limited vocal range. His first serious miss came in 1960 with 'About This Thing Called Love' and an irredeemable downward spiral mitigated by 1962's 'Kissin' And Twistin'' and other small hits. Nevertheless, he could be seen in films such as the 1962 war epic *The Longest Day*, but more commensurate with his talent were productions such as and 1964's *Ride The Wild Surf* and *Fireball 500* (a 1966 hot-rod epic with his old friend Frankie Avalon). Fabian's limited vocal range should not be held against him: he became a puppet and he danced; out of it he traded a doomed musical career for a credible movie career.

● ALBUMS: *Hold That Tiger* (Chancellor 1959)

★★, *The Fabulous Fabian* (Chancellor 1959) ★★, *The Good Old Summertime* (Chancellor 1960) ★★, *Fabian Facade* (Chancellor 1961) ★★, *Rockin' Hot* (Chancellor 1961) ★★, *Fabian's 16 Fabulous Hits* (Chancellor 1962) ★★.
● COMPILATIONS: *The Best Of Fabian* (Varèse Sarabande 1996) ★★★, *Turn Me Loose: Very Best Of Fabian* (Collectables 1999) ★★★.
● FILMS: *Hound-Dog Man* (1959), *North To Alaska* aka *Go North* (1960), *High Time* (1960), *Love In A Goldfish Bowl* (1961), *Mr. Hobbs Takes A Vacation* (1962), *Five Weeks In A Balloon* (1962), *The Longest Day* (1962), *Ride The Wild Surf* (1964), *Dear Brigitte* (1965), *Ten Little Indians* (1966), *Spie Vengono Dal Semifreddo* aka *Dr. Goldfoot And The Girl Bombs* (1966), *Fireball 500* (1966), *Thunder Alley* aka *Hell Drivers* (1967), *The Wild Racers* (1968), *Maryjane* (1968), *The Devil's 8* (1969), *A Bullet For Pretty Boy* (1970), *Little Laura And Big John* (1973), *The Day The Lord Got Busted* aka *Soul Hustler* (1976), *Disco Fever* (1978), *Kiss Daddy Goodbye* aka *Caution, Children At Play* (1981), *Get Crazy* aka *Flip Out* (1983), *Up Close & Personal* (1996).

FACENDA, TOMMY
b. 10 November 1939, Norfolk, Virginia, USA. Facenda became known for one single he recorded in 1959 for Atlantic Records, 'High School USA' Facenda, nicknamed 'Bubba', first gained a foothold in the music business in 1957 as a back-up singer for Gene Vincent. He was performing at a club in 1958 when discovered by Frank Guida (who later discovered and managed Gary 'U.S.' Bonds). Facenda first recorded a single, 'Little Baby', for Nasco Records in 1958, but it did not reach the charts. Guida then wrote 'High School USA', which included the names of several schools in the section of Virginia in which Facenda worked. It was released on Legrand Records and when Guida noticed that local high school students were buying the record to hear the name of their school, he had Facenda re-record the vocals 28 times (some accounts put the number at 46), each version mentioning the names of schools in a different region of the USA. It was released on Atlantic and reached number 28 but Facenda was unable to come up with another hit. Two volumes of the album *High School USA* were issued during the 80s on the revived Legrand, each including 14 versions of the title track. He later retired from the music business and became a firefighter.
● ALBUMS: *High School USA, Volume 1* (Legrand 1984) ★★★, *High School USA, Volume 2* (Legrand 1984) ★★.

FAIN, SAMMY
b. Samuel Feinberg, 17 June 1902, New York, USA, d. 6 December 1989, Los Angeles, California, USA. A prolific composer of Broadway shows and films for over 40 years, early in his career he worked for music publisher Jack Mills, and as a singer/pianist in vaudeville and radio. His first published song, with a lyric by Irving Mills and Al Dubin in 1925, was 'Nobody Knows What A Red Haired Mama Can Do', and was recorded, appropriately, by Sophie Tucker. In 1926 he met Irving Kahal (b. 5 March 1903, Houtzdale, Pennsylvania, USA), who was to be his main collaborator until Kahal's death in 1942. Almost immediately they had hits with 'Let A Smile Be Your Umbrella' and 'I Left My Sugar Standing In The Rain'. In 1929 their song, 'Wedding Bells Are Breaking Up That Old Gang Of Mine' was a hit for another singer/pianist, Gene Austin, and surfaced again 25 years later, sung by the Four Aces.
Fain contributed songs to several early musical films including *The Big Pond* (1930) in which Maurice Chevalier introduced 'You Brought A New Kind Of Love To Me', the Marx Brothers' comedy, *Monkey Business* (1931) 'When I Take My Sugar To Tea', *Footlight Parade* (1933) 'By A Waterfall', *Goin' To Town* (1935) in which Mae West sang 'Now I'm A Lady' and 'He's A Bad, Bad Man But He's Good Enough For Me' and *Dames* (1934) which featured the song 'When You Were A Smile On Your Mother's Lips And A Twinkle In Your Daddy's Eye' – and in which Fain actually appeared as a songwriter. Fain's 30s Broadway credits included *Everybody's Welcome*, *Right This Way* (featuring 'I'll Be Seeing You' and 'I Can Dream, Can't I?'), *Hellzapoppin'* (reputedly the most popular musical of the 30s) and *George White's Scandals Of 1939* ('Are You Havin' Any Fun?' and 'Something I Dreamed Last Night'). During the 40s and 50s Fain collaborated with several lyricists including Lew Brown, Jack Yellen, Mitchell Parish, Harold Adamson, E.Y. 'Yip' Harburg, Bob Hilliard and Paul Francis Webster. In 1945 he worked with Ralph Freed, brother of the more famous lyricist and movie producer, Arthur Freed. Fain and Freed's 'The Worry Song' was interpolated into the Sammy Cahn/Jule Styne score for the Frank Sinatra/Gene Kelly movie *Anchors Aweigh* (1945), to accompany Kelly's famous dance sequence with the animated Jerry the mouse.
Fain's greatest Hollywood success was in the 50s. He wrote the scores for two Walt Disney classics: *Alice In Wonderland* (1951), 'I'm Late' with Bob Hilliard; and *Peter Pan* (1953), 'Your Mother And Mine' and 'Second Star To The Right' with Sammy Cahn. Also with Cahn, Fain wrote some songs for the *Three Sailors And a Girl* (1953) movie ('The Lately Song' and 'Show Me A Happy Woman And I'll Show You A Miserable Man'). In 1953 Fain, in collaboration with Paul Francis Webster, won his first Academy Award for 'Secret Love', from their score for the Doris Day/Howard Keel movie, *Calamity Jane*. His second Oscar, the title song for the film *Love Is A Many Splendored Thing* (1955), was also written in partnership with Webster, as were several other film title songs including 'A Certain Smile', 'April Love', and 'Tender Is The Night', which were all nominated for Academy Awards. Other Fain/Webster movie songs included 'There's A Rising Moon (For Every Falling Star)' from *Young At Heart* (1954) and 'A Very Precious Love' from *Marjorie Morningstar* (1958), both sung by Doris Day. Fain's last four Broadway musicals were *Flahooley* (1951) written with Harburg ('Here's To Your Illusions' and 'He's Only Wonderful'), *Ankles Aweigh* (1955) with Dan

Shapiro, *Christine* (1960), with Webster, and *Something More* (1964) with Alan And Marilyn Bergman. Fain continued to write films songs through to the 70s. He also made some vocal records, and had a US chart entry as early as 1926 with Al Dubin and Joe Burke's, 'Painting The Clouds With Sunshine'. He was inducted into the Songwriters Hall Of Fame in 1971, and served on the board of directors of ASCAP from 1979 until his death from a heart attack in December 1989.

FAITH, PERCY

b. 7 April 1908, Toronto, Ontario, Canada, d. 9 February 1976, Ericino, California, USA. During the 30s Faith worked extensively on radio in Canada, and moved to the USA in 1940 to take up a post with NBC. During the 50s he was musical director for Columbia Records, for whom he made a number of popular albums, mostly of mood music. He worked with Tony Bennett, with whom he had three million-selling singles, and, from 1950, also had several hits in his own right, including 'Cross My Fingers', 'All My Love', 'On Top Of Old Smoky' (vocal by Burl Ives), 'Delicado', 'Song From The Moulin Rouge (Where Is Your Heart)' (US number 1 in 1953), 'Return To Paradise' (1953), and 'Theme From A Summer Place', which reached number 1 in the US and number 2 in the UK charts in 1960. In Hollywood in the 50s Faith had composed several background film scores, including *Love Me Or Leave Me* (1955), the highly acclaimed biopic of singer Ruth Etting, which starred Doris Day. His film credits in the 60s included *Tammy Tell Me True* (1961), *I'd Rather Be Rich* (1964), *The Third Day* (1965) and *The Oscar* (1966). For *The Love Goddesses*, Faith wrote the title song with Mack David. His other compositions included 'My Heart Cries For You' (with his main collaborator Carl Sigman), which was a big hit for Guy Mitchell, Dinah Shore, Vic Damone and others in 1951. Faith died of cancer in February 1976. In the mid-90s there was renewed interest in his work, particularly in Japan, where many of his albums were reissued. New performances of his arrangements have been conducted by Nick Perito for a series of CDs.

● ALBUMS: *Continental Music* (Columbia 1956) ★★★, *Passport To Romance* (Columbia 1956) ★★★, *Music From My Fair Lady* (Columbia 1957) ★★★★, *Touchdown!* (Columbia 1958) ★★★, *North & South Of The Border* (Columbia 1958) ★★★, *Music Of Victor Herbert* (Columbia 1958) ★★★, *Viva!* (Columbia 1959) ★★★, *Hallelujah* (Columbia 1959) ★★★, *Porgy And Bess* (Columbia 1959) ★★★, *Music Of George Gershwin* (Columbia 1959) ★★★★, *A Night With Sigmund Romberg* (Columbia 1959) ★★★, *Malaguena* (Columbia 1959) ★★★, *Bouquet* (Columbia 1959) ★★★★, *Music From South Pacific* (Columbia 1960) ★★, *Bon Voyage!* (Columbia 1960) ★★★, *Continental Souvenirs* (Columbia 1960) ★★★, *Jealousy* (Columbia 1960) ★★★★, *A Night With Jerome Kern* (Columbia 1960) ★★★, *Camelot* (Columbia 1961) ★★★★, *Carefree* (Columbia 1961) ★★★, *Mucho Gusto! More Music Of Mexico* (Columbia 1961) ★★, *Tara's Theme* (Columbia 1961) ★★★, *Bouquet Of Love* (Columbia

1962) ★★★★, *Subways Are For Sleeping* (Columbia 1962) ★★★, *The Music Of Brazil!* (Columbia 1962) ★★★, *Hollywood's Themes* (Columbia 1963) ★★★★, *American Serenade* (Columbia 1963) ★★★, *Exotic Strings* (Columbia 1963) ★★★, *Shangri-La!* (Columbia 1963) ★★★, *Great Folk Themes* (Columbia 1964) ★★★, *More Themes For Young Lovers* (Columbia 1964) ★★★, *Latin Themes* (Columbia 1965) ★★★, *Broadway Bouquet* (Columbia 1965) ★★★, *Themes For The 'In' Crowd* (Columbia 1966) ★★★, *The Academy Award Winner And Other Great Movie Themes* (Columbia 1967) ★★★★, *Today's Themes For Young Lovers* (Columbia 1967) ★★★, *For Those In Love* (Columbia 1968) ★★★, *Angel Of The Morning (Hit Themes For Young Lovers)* (Columbia 1968) ★★, *Those Were The Days* (Columbia 1969) ★★, *Windmills Of Your Mind* (Columbia 1969) ★★, *Love Theme From 'Romeo And Juliet'* (Columbia 1969) ★★★, *Forever Young* (Columbia 1970) ★★, *Leaving On A Jet Plane* (Columbia 1970) ★★, *Held Over! Today's Great Movie Themes* (Columbia 1970) ★★★, *The Beatles Album* (Columbia 1970) ★★, *A Time For Love* (Columbia 1971) ★★★, *I Think I Love You* (Columbia 1971) ★★, *Black Magic Woman* (Columbia 1971) ★★, *Jesus Christ, Superstar* (Columbia 1971) ★★, *Joy* (Columbia 1972) ★★★, *Day By Day* (Columbia 1972) ★★★.

● COMPILATIONS: *Moods* (Ditto 1983) ★★★, *Images* (Knight 1990) ★★★, *Music From the Movies* (Sony 1994) ★★★.

FEATHER, LEONARD

b. 13 September 1914, London, England, d. 22 September 1994, Los Angeles, California, USA. After studying piano, Feather advanced his musical interests by teaching himself arranging and in the early 30s produced a number of record sessions, contributing charts and scores. Among the musicians for whom he worked in such capacities was Benny Carter and he was instrumental in persuading Henry Hall to hire Carter for the BBC Dance Orchestra. In the mid-30s Feather went to the USA and during the next decade he continued to work in record production, sometimes supplying original material for artists such as Louis Armstrong, Lionel Hampton ('Blowtop Blues') and Dinah Washington ('Evil Gal Blues'). Feather also branched into concert promotion and produced numerous recording sessions. Additionally, he continued to compose songs for artists such as Sarah Vaughan, Ella Fitzgerald, Cannonball Adderley and Sonny Stitt. Despite all these endeavours, most of his considerable efforts in the cause of jazz were gradually concentrated into writing on the subject for several magazines, including *Esquire* and *Down Beat*, and he also wrote a jazz column for the *Los Angeles Times*. He was the author of several jazz books, notably *Encyclopedia Of Jazz* and his autobiography, *The Jazz Years: Ear Witness To An Era*. He was also a frequent broadcaster on jazz on radio and television. His daughter Lorraine is an accomplished singer.

● ALBUMS: all as producer *Leonard Feather's*

Swinging Swedes (1951-54) ★★★, Winter Sequence 10-inch album (MGM 1954) ★★★, Swingin' On The Vibories (ABC-Paramount 1956) ★★, Leonard Feather Presents Bop reissued as Leonard Feather Presents 52nd Street (Mode 1957) ★★★, Hi-Fi Suite (MGM 1957) ★★★, Oh, Captain! (MGM 1958) ★★★, Seven Ages Of Jazz (1958) ★★★, Swedish Punch (1959) ★★★, Leonard Feather's Encyclopedia Of Jazz All Stars (1967) ★★★★, Leonard Feather Presents (VSOP 1988) ★★★, Night Blooming (Mainstream 1991) ★★★.

● FURTHER READING: The Jazz Years: Ear Witness To An Era, Leonard Feather. The Encyclopedia Of Jazz various editions, Leonard Feather.

FEATHERS, CHARLIE

b. Charles Arthur Feathers, 12 June 1932, Holly Springs, Mississippi, USA, d. 29 August 1998, Memphis, Tennessee, USA. The work of rockabilly legend Feathers became more elevated during each revival of interest in the genre. Feathers was an enigmatic superstar, although in reality his influence totally overshadowed his commercial success. His upbringing on a farm, being taught guitar by a cotton-picking black bluesman and leaving home to work on an oilfield, gave Feathers a wealth of material for his compositions. In the early 50s, together with Jody Chastain (b. 1933, USA, d. 28 July 1999), and Jerry Huffman, he performed as the Musical Warriors. He was an early signing to Sam Phillips' Sun Records. He recorded his first song, 'Defrost Your Heart', in 1955, and claimed to have co-written Elvis Presley's debut, 'Blue Moon Of Kentucky'. He did, however, co-write Presley's first hit, 'I Forgot To Remember To Forget'. Over the years he continued to record for a number of labels, still unable to break through the barrier between 'cult' and 'star'. Among his early rockabilly sides was 'One Hand Loose' on King, regarded by many collectors as one of the finest examples of its kind.

His highly applauded performance at London's famous Rainbow theatre in 1977 gave his career a significant boost in Europe and brought him a new audience, notably the fans who were following Dave Edmunds and his crusade for 'rockabilly'. Feathers' later recordings suffered from the problem of being aided by younger musicians who were merely in awe of his work, and his best material was from the 50s. Influential but spartan, full of whoops and growls, but ultimately, irresistible country rock, Feather's 'light comedy' style was an 'invisible influence' over many decades, from Big Bopper in the 50s to Hank Wangford in the 80s. His 1991 release contained a reworked version of his classic 'I Forgot To Remember To Forget'. He performed with his son and daughter on guitar and vocals, respectively. A remarkable crop of unissued demos appeared in 1995 as Tip Top Daddy and further highlighted the originality of the man who defined country rockabilly long before Garth Brooks was born, and yet never received widespread recognition for his contribution.

● ALBUMS: Live In Memphis (Barrelhouse 1979)

★★★, Charlie Feathers (Elektra 1991) ★★★.
● COMPILATIONS: Rockabilly Mainman (Charly 1978) ★★★, The Legendary 1956 Demo Session (Zu Zazz 1986) ★★, Jungle Fever (Kay 1987) ★★★, Wild Wild Party (Rockstar 1987) ★★★, The Living Legend (Redita 1988) ★★★, Rock-A-Billy (Zu Zazz 1991) ★★★, Tip Top Daddy (Norton 1995) ★★★, Rock-A-Billy (Bear Family 1999) ★★★★.

FENDER, LEO

Along with Les Paul and Adolph Rickenbacker, Leo Fender (b. 10 August 1909, Anaheim, California, USA, d. 21 March 1991, USA) was one of the key names in the development of the electric guitar in the middle of the twentieth century. He first came to the attention of the musical instrument manufacturing industry when he was working with 'Doc' Kauffman producing guitar amplifiers in the mid-40s. He had developed a new smaller pick-up and designed a solid body guitar based on the Hawaiian steel, with which to demonstrate it. Although the pick-up itself was quite revolutionary, local musicians were more intrigued with the guitar, and so Fender decided to concentrate his efforts in that direction. In 1946 he left Kauffman and formed the Fender Electrical Instrument Company. The idea of a solid body guitar had been in the forefront of manufacturer's minds since the advent of electrical amplification which meant that hollow sound boxes were no longer essential. It was Fender, along with Californian neighbours Les Paul and Paul Bigsby, who spearheaded the forthcoming wave of electric guitars.

In 1948 Fender launched the Broadcaster (later called the Telecaster) which remained virtually unchanged for the next 30 or so years; there were a few variations such as the Esquire (1954), the Thinkline (1969), the Deluxe (1972) and the Custom (1972). Famous rock 'n' roll guitarist James Burton favours a Telecaster, as does Bruce Welch of the Shadows, Steve Cropper, Roy Buchanan and Bruce Springsteen. Fender's next major instrument was the Stratocaster, developed in 1953 with his chief engineer Leo Tavares, and put into production the following year. Like the Telecaster, the Stratocaster was virtually untouched in design over the next few decades and became a favourite of Buddy Holly, Hank B. Marvin, Eric Clapton, Rory Gallagher, Mark Knopfler and the master – Jimi Hendrix, to name just a few of thousands. In 1990 a Stratocaster once owned by Hendrix was sold at auction for almost £200,000. The design, shape, feel and colour of the Stratocaster became an art form, and arguably, the accepted icon for the electric guitar. In 1955 Fender contracted a virus that would dog him for the next decade.

In the mid-60s, convinced that he had little time to live, Leo decided to order his affairs. The Fender Electrical Instrument Company was sold to CBS in January 1965 for $13 million, shortly after which Fender made a complete recovery. CBS employed him as a consultant and he continued to help to design and develop new guitars. Later he formed the CLF Research Company before returning to consultancy work for Music Man guitars, started by former Fender employees Thomas Walker and Forrest White. In the 80s he formed G&L (George and Leo) Guitars with long time associate George Fullerton. They continued to make popular instruments, although names like the F100-1 series were less appealing than their forebears. Leo Fender died in the spring of 1991 aged 82. As well as the guitars mentioned, the Fender name is also attached to the Musicmaster (1956), the Jazzmaster (1958), the Jaguar (1961), and the Starcaster (1975). He also moved into electric basses in 1951 with the Precision and then the Jazz Bass (1960), Bass VI (1962) and the Telecaster Bass (1968).

● FURTHER READING: *The Fender Book: A Complete History Of Fender Electric Guitars*, Tony Bacon and Paul Day. *Fender Custom Shop Guitar Gallery*, Richard Smith. *50 Years Of Fender*, Tony Bacon.

FERRARI, FREDERICK

b. 20 July 1912, Manchester, Lancashire, England, d. 19 April 1994, London, England. Usually known simply as 'the voice' because of his superb tenor, Ferrari was among the most popular of the post-war variety club and radio acts. He took his name – and his love for singing – from his Italian father. After appearing in small concert parties around the Manchester area, his career began in earnest when he joined the army in 1941. Although ultimately the army life helped to advance his singing ambitions (via the khaki entertainment troupe *Stars In Battledress*), his call-up actually scotched an engagement with the Carl Rosa Opera Company. Together with top comedian Charlie Chester, Ferrari went on to appear in over 2,000 service shows both at home and overseas, performances often highlighted by the rendering of his signature tune, 'Love Descended Like An Angel', written for him by Chester. After the war, Ferrari joined Chester in his popular radio show *Stand Easy*, before returning to variety (still as a huge star) in the early 50s. In addition to seaside residencies, he regularly performed at the London Palladium and made an appearance in front of the Queen. Alongside charity work he continued to be a popular attraction at functions and shows long after the variety halls closed.

FIELDING, HAROLD

b. 4 December 1916, Woking, Surrey, England. A leading producer of stage musicals from the 50s through to the 80s, Fielding has presented, or co-presented, some of the West End's favourite shows. When he was 10 years old he resisted parental pressure to play the piano, and instead took up the violin, studying in Paris with virtuoso Szigeti. By the time he was 12, Fielding was himself a concert performer, touring as a supporting artist to the diva Tetrazzini. When he was in his early 20s, the impresario who was presenting him died, and Fielding took over the tour management. In a short space of time, he was presenting hundreds of concerts throughout the UK, including his Sunday Concert Series at

Blackpool Opera House, which endured for many years. He also mounted a series called *Music For Millions* in collaboration with his wife, Maisie. Among the artists appearing in his productions were Richard Tauber, Grace Moore, Benjamino Gigli, Rawicz and Landauer, Jeanette MacDonald, Paul Robeson, Gracie Fields, and the London Philharmonic Orchestra.

Subsequent promotions in the popular music field would include Johnnie Ray, Danny Kaye, Nat 'King' Cole, and Frank Sinatra. In January 1949, while returning from the USA after negotiating a contract for the Philadelphia Symphony Orchestra to visit England, Fielding was involved in the famous pick-a-back air crash. A light aircraft collided with the roof of his Constellation airliner, and the dead pilot fell into Fielding's lap. The Constellation made a perfect landing, and, having survived that kind of crash, from then on Fielding believed that flying was the safest form of travel. By the late 50s, with government-sponsored concerts affecting his business, Fielding turned to the legitimate theatre. He had already collaborated with Charles B. Cochran and Jack Hylton, one of his associations with Hylton resulting in the first ever arena concert festival at Harringay, London. They also promoted a classical ballet season. Just prior to Christmas 1958, Fielding launched himself as a solo producer with a spectacular presentation of Richard Rodgers and Oscar Hammerstein II's *Cinderella* at the London Coliseum. Originally conceived for US television, Fielding blended pantomime material with the musical comedy aspect of the piece, and cast rock 'n' roll star Tommy Steele as Buttons. *Cinderella* was followed by another Coliseum extravaganza, *Aladdin*, and from then on Fielding lived a rollercoaster existence – producing or co-producing many of the West End's biggest hits, and some of its biggest disasters.

The Music Man, starring Van Johnson, and Noël Coward's *Sail Away*, led in 1963 to one of Fielding's most fondly remembered shows, *Half A Sixpence*, a musicalization of H.G. Wells' novel, *Kipps*, starring Tommy Steele. However, the success of *Half A Sixpence* in London and New York paled in comparison with *Charlie Girl* (1965, 2,202 performances), which was followed by several more profitable productions in the shape of *Sweet Charity*, *Mame*, *The Great Waltz*, *Show Boat*, *I Love My Wife*, *Irene*, stage versions of the popular movies *Hans Andersen* and *Singin' In The Rain* (both with Tommy Steele), as well as *Barnum* (Michael Crawford). At the time, Fielding's 1971 *Show Boat* was the longest-running to date with 910 performances (Hal Prince's 1994 production clocked up 951). Like all the great showmen since Florenz Ziegfeld, Fielding was fond of making extravagant gestures. When Ginger Rogers arrived in the UK to appear in *Mame* (1969), he ensured that the event made the front pages by transporting her from Southampton to London in a special train filled with pressmen, and an orchestra playing tunes from the show. There was also a portable movie theatre showing her old films. The Ziegfeld reference would probably send a shiver up the now-venerable producer's spine, because *Ziegfeld* (1988), with a book by Ned Sherrin, was one of his shows, along with *Man Of Magic*, *You're A Good Man, Charlie Brown*, *Phil The Fluter*, *Gone With The Wind*, *Beyond The Rainbow*, *On The Twentieth Century*, *The Biograph Girl*, and the 1986 revival of *Charlie Girl* with Cyd Charisse, which failed to set the London theatrical scene alight. He was reported to have lost £1.3 million on *Ziegfeld*, and that sum rose to £1.7 million four years later when Petula Clark's American Civil War musical, *Someone Like You*, folded after only a month, ensuring that Harold Fielding Limited went into voluntary liquidation.

Since then, understandably, Fielding has not been a major force, partly due to ill health, although he was associated with the West End transfer of *Mack And Mabel* from the Leicester Haymarket Theatre in 1995, which resulted in the show's long-awaited London premiere. Over the years, he has presented a whole range of entertainment, including revues, plays, and variety shows featuring outstanding performers such as The Two Ronnies (Corbett and Barker), Petula Clark, Julie Andrews, Peter Sellers, Benny Hill, Marlene Dietrich, Eartha Kitt, and Shirley Bassey, but it is for his often lavish and immensely likeable musicals that he will be remembered. In 1986 he 'passed' on the opportunity to present the UK version of *La Cage Aux Folles* because 'it wasn't a family show', yet more than 10 years previously he had been associated with the notorious 'sexual musical', *Let My People Come*. A much-loved personality, he belongs to the tradition of great British showman such as Hylton, Bernard Delfont, and Lew Grade. He risked his own money rather than that of theatrical 'angels', and in 1996 received a Gold Badge from BASCA (British Academy of Songwriters. Composers and Authors) in recognition of his special contribution to Britain's entertainment industry.

FIELDS, ERNIE

b. 26 August 1905, Nacogdoches, Texas, USA. This trombonist, arranger and bandleader fronted his own outfit in the Tulsa, Oklahoma area from the 30s, and recorded for various labels, including Vocalian, Frisco, Bullet and Gotham. During the 50s he became an arranger for pop and rock sessions, and ran his own R&B band. In 1958 he became co-founder of the Rendezvous label, and had a million-seller with his swinging revival of the 1939 Glenn Miller favourite, 'In The Mood'. He followed that with his own individual interpretations of other standards, such as 'Chattanooga Choo Choo' and 'The Charleston', but without the same success. He was also involved with the Rendezvous act, B. Bumble And The Stingers, who had hits with 'Bumble Boogie' and 'Nut Rocker', before Rendezvous folded in the early 60s.

FIESTAS

Formed in Newark, New Jersey, USA, *c*.1958, the Fiestas were known for their R&B hit 'So Fine', released on Old Town Records the following year.

The group consisted of Tommy Bullock (lead vocals), Eddie Morris (tenor), Sam Ingalls (baritone) and Preston Lane (bass). Two conflicting stories about the group's signing to Old Town have circulated throughout the years. One has the Fiestas recording a demo tape in Newark, which studio owner Jim Gribble brought to the attention of Old Town's Hy Weiss. The other simply has Weiss overhearing the group singing and liking them enough to take them on. The result was the group's only hit, a soulful dance number which reached number 11 in the US charts. Only one other single made the charts, but the Fiestas stayed with Old Town until 1965. Tommy Bullock formed a duo with Cleveland Horne, Tommy and Cleve, and they had a hit in 1966 with 'Boogaloo Baby' (Checker). Numerous personnel changes kept the Fiestas working into the 70s.

● COMPILATIONS: *The Oh So Fine Fiestas* (Ace 1993) ★★★★.

FINEGAN, BILL

b. 3 April 1917, Newark, New Jersey, USA. Pianist Finegan's first successes were the arrangements he wrote for the Tommy Dorsey band, but his real breakthrough came in 1938 when he became a staff arranger for Glenn Miller. Throughout the late 30s and early 40s, Finegan wrote extensively for films, but continued to provide charts for Miller, Dorsey, Horace Heidt and others. At the start of the 50s Finegan was studying at the Paris Conservatoire and began corresponding with fellow-arranger Eddie Sauter, who was then hospitalized with tuberculosis. Out of this correspondence emerged a decision to form an orchestra of their own that would play music other leaders might well regard as uncommercial. In 1952 the 21-piece Sauter-Finegan Orchestra made its appearance. With so many musicians, several of whom doubled and even trebled on other instruments, the tonal palette was huge and the two arrangers took full advantage of this. The band was hugely successful with memorable records such as 'The Doodletown Fifers' and 'Sleigh Ride' (based upon music by Prokofiev). On this latter title the sound effect of horses' hooves on hard-packed snow was created by Finegan beating his chest. Later, he wryly remarked, 'this is probably my finest effort on wax – or snow'. In the late 50s Finegan worked mostly in radio and television, but in the 70s returned to big band arranging with charts for the Glenn Miller reunion orchestra and for Mel Lewis, who continued to use his work into the 80s.

● ALBUMS: all by Sauter-Finegan Orchestra *New Directions In Music* 10-inch album (RCA-Victor 1953) ★★★★, *Inside Sauter-Finegan* (RCA-Victor 1954) ★★★, *The Sound Of Sauter-Finegen* (RCA-Victor 1954) ★★★, *Sons Of Sauter-Finegan* (RCA-Victor 1955) ★★★, *Concert Jazz* (RCA-Victor 1955) ★★★, *New Directions In Music* (RCA 1956) ★★★, *Adventure In Time* (RCA-Victor 1956) ★★★, *Under Analysis* (RCA-Victor 1957) ★★★★, *One Night Stand With The Sauter-Finegan Orchestra* (RCA-Victor 1957) ★★★, *Straight Down The Middle* (RCA-

Victor 1957) ★★★, *Inside Sauter-Finegan Revisited* (RCA-Victor 1961) ★★★, *Sleigh Ride* (RCA-Victor 1961) ★★★★, *The Return Of The Doodletown Fifers* (Capitol 1985) ★★★.

FINGS AIN'T WOT THEY USED T'BE

This show originally opened on 17 February 1959 at the Theatre Royal, Stratford East, London, home of the *avant garde* director Joan Littlewood and her 'repertory company'. During two separate runs there it was completely revised and remodelled, and transferred to the Garrick Theatre in the West End on 11 February 1960. Set in the drab and dreary world of London's Soho district, with its prostitutes, pimps and small-time criminals, Frank Norman's book (Norman was an ex-convict) told of Fred Cochran (Glynn Edwards), one of life's losers, who runs a sleazy gambling club – a haven for the local low-life. He can only dream of owning a big-time venue, but a large win on the horses means that he can at least have his place decorated by the camp decorator Horace Seaton (Wallas Eaton). Unfortunately, the reopening night party is ruined when Fred is beaten up for not providing the police with their usual slice of payola. There is a good deal more trouble and strife before Fred ends up with a knees-up *al fresco* wedding to his girlfriend Lily Smith (Miriam Karlin). The local milieu is populated by a variety of characters such as the crooked copper Sergeant Collins (Tom Chatto), plus two more members of the constabulary, played by Yootha Joyce and George Sewell, a civilian crook, Redhot (Edward Carrick), Tosher (James Booth), the area's premier ponce, and several 'ladies of the night', including Rosie (Barbara Windsor) and Betty (Toni Palmer). Lionel Bart, who had provided just the lyrics for *Lock Up Your Daughters* at the Mermaid Theatre in 1959, wrote both words and music for this exhilarating piece. His songs, which so accurately captured the show's spirit and atmosphere, included 'G'Night Dearie', 'Layin' Abaht', 'Where It's Hot', 'Contempery', 'Meatface', 'The Ceilin's Comin' Dahn', 'Where Do Little Birds Go?', 'The Student Ponce', 'Big Time', 'Polka Dots', 'Cop A Bit Of Pride' and 'Cochran Will Return'. The popular comedian-singer Max Bygraves took a cleaned-up version of the title song into the UK Top 5, and the personality pianist Russ Conway also had a minor hit with the tune. The critics were not enthusiastic about the show, but audiences loved it, and *Fings Ain't Wot They Used T'Be* enjoyed a two-year run of 897 performances. This established Lionel Bart as a real force in the London musical theatre, and won the *Evening Standard Award* for best musical. Early in 1999, Bart was involved with the first major revival of 'Fings' at the Queen's Theatre, Hornchurch, in England. Bob Carlton (*Return To The Forbidden Planet*) directed a cast which included Steve Edwin (Cochran), Anthony Psaila (Seaton), Diana Croft (Lily), Tony Hunt (Collins), Phil Hearne (Redhot), Richard Brightiff (Tosher), Nina Lucking (Rosie), and Liz Marsh (Betty).

FISHER, EDDIE

b. Edwin Jack Fisher, 10 August 1928, Philadelphia, Pennsylvania, USA. Fisher was a 'bobby sox idol', one of the most popular US singers of the 50s, with a strong, melodic voice. He sang with the bands of Buddy Morrow and Charlie Ventura at the age of 18, and his nickname was 'Sonny Boy' because of his affection for Al Jolson songs. In 1949 he gained nationwide exposure on Eddie Cantor's radio show. Signed to RCA-Victor Records, and accompanied by Hugo Winterhalter, Fisher had a string of US Top 10 hits through to 1956, including 'Thinking Of You', 'A Man Chases A Girl (Until She Catches Him)', 'Turn Back The Hands Of Time', 'Tell Me Why', 'I'm Yours', 'Maybe'/'Watermelon Weather' (duets with Perry Como), 'Wish You Were Here' (number 1), 'Lady Of Spain', 'I'm Walking Behind You' (number 1), 'Oh My Pa-Pa' (number 1), 'I Need You Now' (number 1), 'Count Your Blessings', 'Heart', 'Dungaree Doll' and 'Cindy, Oh Cindy'. Five of those won gold discs. He also made the US Top 40 album charts in 1955 with *I Love You*. His career was interrupted from 1952-53 when he served in the US Armed Forces Special Services, and spent some time in Korea. After his discharge he became immensely popular singing in top nightclubs, and on his own television series, *Coke Time* and *The Chesterfield Supper Club*, with George Gobel. In 1956 he co-starred with his first wife, Debbie Reynolds, in the film musical *Bundle Of Joy*; and had a straight role in *Butterfield 8* (1960), in which his second wife, Elizabeth Taylor, won an Academy Award for Best Actress. During the 60s, beset by drug and financial problems, he switched record labels and recorded *Eddie Fisher At The Winter Garden* for his own Ramrod Records, and *Eddie Fisher Today!* for Dot Records. He returned to RCA and had a minor singles hit in 1966 with 'Games That Lovers Play', which became the title of a bestselling album. His last album for RCA was a Jolson tribute, *You Ain't Heard Nothing Yet*. During the late 60s he married and divorced actress Connie Stevens, and in the 70s attempted several unsuccessful comebacks. In 1990, following extended periods of treatment at the Betty Ford Centre, Fisher announced that he was finally cured of his drug problems and intended to resume work. His daughter by Debbie Reynolds, actress Carrie Fisher, appeared in the hit movies *Star Wars*, *The Empire Strikes Back*, *Return Of The Jedi*, and *When Harry Met Sally*.

● ALBUMS: *Fisher Sings* 10-inch album (RCA-Victor 1952) ★★★, *I'm In The Mood For Love* (RCA-Victor 1952/55) ★★★, *Christmas With Fisher* 10-inch album (RCA-Victor 1952) ★★, *Irving Berlin Favorites* 10-inch album (RCA-Victor 1954) ★★★, *May I Sing To You?* (RCA-Victor 1954/55) ★★★, *I Love You* (RCA-Victor 1955) ★★★, *Academy Award Winners* (RCA-Victor 1955) ★★★★, *Bundle Of Joy* film soundtrack (RCA-Victor 1956) ★★, *Thinking Of You* (RCA-Victor 1957) ★★★, *As Long As There's Music* (RCA-Victor 1958) ★★★, *Scent Of Mystery* film soundtrack (Ramrod 1960) ★★, *Eddie Fisher At The Winter Garden* (Ramrod 1963) ★★, *Eddie Fisher Today!* (Dot 1965) ★★, *When I Was Young*

(RCA 1965) ★★, *Games That Lovers Play* (RCA 1966) ★★, *People Like You* (RCA 1967) ★★, *You Ain't Heard Nothing Yet* (RCA 1968) ★★.
● COMPILATIONS: *The Best Of Eddie Fisher* 10-inch album (RCA-Victor 1954) ★★★, *Eddie Fisher's Greatest Hits* (RCA-Victor 1962) ★★★, *His Greatest Hits* (RCA 1965) ★★★, *The Very Best Of Eddie Fisher* (MCA 1988) ★★★.
● VIDEOS: *A Singing Legend* (1994).
● FURTHER READING: *The Eddie Fisher Story*, Myrna Greene. *My Life, My Loves*, Eddie Fisher. *Been There, Done That*, Eddie Fisher with David Fisher.
● FILMS: *All About Eve* (1950), *Bundle Of Joy* (1956), *Butterfield 8* (1960).

FITZGERALD, ELLA

b. Ella Jane Fitzgerald, 25 April 1917, Newport News, Virginia, USA, d. 15 June 1996, Beverly Hills, California, USA. Following the death of her father, Fitzgerald was taken to New York City by her mother. At school she sang with a glee club and showed early promise, but preferred dancing to singing. Even so, chronic shyness militated against her chances of succeeding as an entertainer. Nevertheless, she entered a talent contest as a dancer, but owing to last-minute nerves, she was unable to dance and was therefore forced to sing. Her unexpected success prompted her to enter other talent contests, and she began to win frequently enough to persevere with her singing. Eventually, she reached the top end of the talent show circuit, singing at the Harlem Opera House where she was heard by several influential people. In later years many claimed to have 'discovered' her, but among those most likely to have been involved in trying to establish her as a professional singer with the Fletcher Henderson band were Benny Carter and Charles Linton. These early efforts were unsuccessful, however, and she continued her round of the talent shows.

An appearance at Harlem's Apollo Theatre, where she won, was the most important stepping-stone in her career. She was heard by Linton, who sang with the Chick Webb band at the Savoy Ballroom. Webb took her on, at first paying her out of his own pocket, and for the fringe audience she quickly became the band's main attraction. She recorded extensively with Webb, with a small group led by Teddy Wilson, with the Ink Spots and others, and even recorded with Benny Goodman. Her hits with Webb included 'Sing Me A Swing Song', 'Oh, Yes, Take Another Guess', 'The Dipsy Doodle', 'If Dreams Come True', 'A-Tisket, A-Tasket' (a song on which she collaborated on the lyric), 'F.D.R. Jones' and 'Undecided'. After Webb's death in 1939 she became the nominal leader of the band, a position she retained until 1942. Fitzgerald then began her solo career, recording numerous popular songs, sometimes teaming up with other artists, and in the late 40s signing with Norman Granz. It was Granz's masterly and astute control of her career that helped to establish her as one of America's leading jazz singers. She was certainly the most popular jazz singer with non-

jazz audiences, and through judicious choice of repertoire, became the foremost female interpreter of the Great American Popular Song Book. With Granz she worked on the 'songbook' series, placing on record definitive performances of the work of America's leading songwriters, and she also toured extensively as part of his Jazz At The Philharmonic package.

Fitzgerald had a wide vocal range, but her voice retained a youthful, light vibrancy throughout the greater part of her career, bringing a fresh and appealing quality to most of her material, especially 'scat' singing. However, it proved less suited to the blues, a genre that, for the most part, she wisely avoided. Indeed, in her early work the most apparent musical influence was Connee Boswell. As a jazz singer, Fitzgerald performed with elegantly swinging virtuosity and her work with accompanists such as Ray Brown, to whom she was married for a time (they had an adopted son, Ray Brown Jnr, a drummer), Joe Pass and Tommy Flanagan was always immaculately conceived. However, her recordings with Louis Armstrong reveal the marked difference between Fitzgerald's approach and that of a singer for whom the material is secondary to his or her own improvisational skills. For all the enviably high quality of her jazz work, it is as a singer of superior popular songs that Fitzgerald remains most important and influential. Her respect for her material, beautifully displayed in the 'songbook' series, helped her to establish and retain her place as the finest vocalist in her chosen area of music. Due largely to deteriorating health, by the mid-80s Fitzgerald's career was at a virtual standstill, although a 1990 appearance in the UK was well received by an ecstatic audience. In April 1994 it was reported that both her legs had been amputated because of complications caused by diabetes. She lived a reclusive existence at her Beverly Hills home until her death in 1996. Fitzgerald's most obvious counterpart among male singers was Frank Sinatra and, with both singers now dead, questions inevitably arise about the fate of the great popular songs of the 30s and 40s. While there are still numerous excellent interpreters in the 90s, and many whose work has been strongly influenced by Fitzgerald, the social and artistic conditions that helped to create America's First Lady of Song no longer exist, and it seems highly unlikely, therefore, that we shall ever see or hear her like again.

● ALBUMS: *Souvenir Album* 10-inch album (Decca 1950) ★★★, *Ella Fitzgerald Sings Gershwin Songs* 10-inch album (Decca 1950) ★★★★, *Songs In A Mellow Mood* (Decca 1954) ★★★★, *Lullabies Of Birdland* (Decca 1955) ★★★, *Sweet And Hot* (Decca 1955) ★★★, *Ella Fitzgerald Sings The Cole Porter Songbook* (Verve 1956) ★★★★★, *Ella Fitzgerald Sings The Rodgers And Hart Songbook* (Verve 1956) ★★★★★, with Count Basie, Joe Williams *One O' Clock Jump* (Columbia 1956) ★★★★, with Louis Armstrong *Ella And Louis* (Verve 1956) ★★★★★, with Armstrong *Porgy And Bess* (Verve 1956) ★★★★★, with Armstrong *Ella And Louis Again* (Verve 1956) ★★★★★, *Like*

Someone In Love (Verve 1957) ★★★★★, Ella Fitzgerald Sings The Duke Ellington Songbook 4-LP box set (Verve 1957) ★★★★★, Ella Fitzgerald Sings The Gershwin Songbook (Verve 1957) ★★★★, Ella Sings Gershwin (Decca 1957) ★★★★, Ella And Her Fellas (Decca 1957) ★★★, Ella Fitzgerald At The Opera House (Verve 1958) ★★★★, Ella Fitzgerald Sings The Irving Berlin Songbook (Verve 1958) ★★★★★, First Lady Of Song (Decca 1958) ★★, Miss Ella Fitzgerald And Mr Nelson Riddle Invite You To Listen And Relax (Decca 1958) ★★★, Ella Fitzgerald And Billie Holiday At Newport (Verve 1958) ★★★, For Sentimental Reasons (Decca 1958) ★★★, Ella Fitzgerald Sings The George And Ira Gershwin Songbook 5-LP box set (Verve 1959) ★★★★★, Ella Swings Lightly (Verve 1959) ★★★★★, Ella Sings Sweet Songs For Swingers (Verve 1959) ★★★, Hello Love (Verve 1959) ★★★, Get Happy! (Verve 1959) ★★★★, Mack The Knife – Ella In Berlin (Verve 1960) ★★★★, Ella Wishes You A Swinging Christmas (Verve 1960) ★★★★, The Intimate Ella (Decca 1960) ★★★★, Golden Favorites (Decca 1961) ★★★, Ella Returns To Berlin (Verve 1961) ★★★, Ella Fitzgerald Sings The Harold Arlen Songbook (Verve 1961) ★★★★★, Clap Hands, Here Comes Charlie! (Verve 1962) ★★★★, Ella Swings Brightly With Nelson (Verve 1962) ★★★★★, Ella Swings Gently With Nelson (Verve 1962) ★★★★★, Rhythm Is My Business (Verve 1962) ★★★, Ella Fitzgerald Sings The Jerome Kern Songbook (Verve 1963) ★★★★★, These Are The Blues (Verve 1963) ★★★★, Ella Sings Broadway (Verve 1963) ★★★, with Basie Ella And Basie! (Verve 1963) ★★★★, Ella At Juan-Les-Pins (Verve 1964) ★★★, Hello, Dolly! (Verve 1964) ★★★, Stairway To The Stars (Decca 1964) ★★★, Early Ella (Decca 1964) ★★★, A Tribute To Cole Porter (Verve 1964) ★★★, Ella Fitzgerald Sings The Johnny Mercer Songbook (Verve 1965) ★★★★★, with Duke Ellington Ella At Duke's Place (Verve 1966) ★★★★, with Ellington The Stockholm Concert (1966) ★★★, with Ellington Ella And Duke At The Côte D'Azure (Verve 1966) ★★★, Ella In Hamburg (Verve 1966) ★★★, The World Of Ella Fitzgerald (Metro 1966) ★★★, Whisper Not (Verve 1966) ★★★, Brighten The Corner (Capitol 1967) ★★★, Misty Blue (Columbia 1968) ★★★, Ella 'Live' (Verve 1968) ★★★, 30 By Ella (Columbia 1968) ★★★, Sunshine Of Your Love/Watch What Happens (Prestige 1969) ★★★, Ella (Reprise 1969) ★★★, Things Ain't What They Used To Be (Reprise 1970) ★★★, Ella Fitzgerald At Carnegie Hall (Columbia 1973) ★★★, with Joe Pass Take Love Easy (Pablo 1973) ★★★, Ella In London (Pablo 1974) ★★★, Fine And Mellow (Pablo 1974) ★★★, Ella – At The Montreux Jazz Festival 1975 (Pablo 1975) ★★★, with Oscar Peterson Ella And Oscar (Pablo 1975) ★★★, with Pass Fitzgerald And Pass ... Again (Pablo 1976) ★★★, Ella Fitzgerald With The Tommy Flanagan Trio (Pablo 1977) ★★★, Lady Time (Pablo 1978) ★★★, Dream Dancing (Pablo 1978) ★★★, with Basie A Classy Pair (Pablo 1979) ★★★, with Basie A Perfect Match: Basie And Ella (Pablo 1979) ★★★, with Pass, Basie Digital III At Montreux (Pablo 1979) ★★★, Ella Fitzgerald Sings The Antonio Carlos Jobim Songbook (Pablo 1981)

★★★, The Best Is Yet To Come (Pablo 1982) ★★★, with Pass Speak Love (Pablo 1982) ★★, Nice Work If You Can Get It (Pablo 1983) ★★★, Easy Living (Pablo 1986) ★★★, All That Jazz (Pablo 1990) ★★★, A 75th Birthday Tribute (Pablo 1993) ★★★.
● COMPILATIONS: The Best Of Ella (Decca 1958) ★★★, The Best Of Ella Fitzgerald (Verve 1964) ★★★★, The Best Of Ella Fitzgerald Volume 2 (Verve 1969) ★★★, shared with Billie Holiday, Lena Horne, Sarah Vaughan Billie, Ella, Lena, Sarah! (Columbia 1980) ★★★★★, The Best Of Ella Fitzgerald (Pablo 1988) ★★★★, The Pablo Years (Pablo 1993) ★★★★, Oh Lady Be Good! Best Of The Gershwin Songbook (Verve 1995) ★★★★, Ella: The Legendary Decca Recordings 4-CD box set (Decca 1995) ★★★, Ella Fitzgerald: Priceless Jazz (GRP 1997) ★★★, The Complete Ella Fitzgerald & Louis Armstrong On Verve 3-CD box set (Verve 1997) ★★★★★, Unforgettable Ella (Carlton 1998) ★★★, Ultimate Ella Fitzgerald (Verve 1998) ★★★★★, Something To Live For (Verve 1999) ★★★★, The Last Decca Years: 1949-1954 (GRP 1999) ★★★, with Joe Pass Sophisticated Lady (Pablo 2001) ★★★.
● VIDEOS: Something To Live For (Winstar 1999).
● FURTHER READING: Ella: The Life And Times Of Ella Fitzgerald, Sid Colin. Ella Fitzgerald: A Life Through Jazz, Jim Haskins. Ella Fitzgerald, Stuart Nicholson. First Lady Of Song, Mark Fidelman.
● FILMS: Pete Kelly's Blues (1955), St. Louis Blues (1958).

FIVE KEYS

This US R&B vocal group helped shape the rhythm and blues revolution of the early 50s. The ensemble was formed as the Sentimental Four in Newport News, Virginia, USA, in the late 40s, and originally consisted of two sets of brothers – Rudy West (b. 25 July 1932, Newport News, Virginia, USA) and Bernie West (b. 4 February 1930, Newport News, Virginia, USA), and Ripley Ingram (b. 1930, d. 23 March 1995, Newport News, Virginia, USA) and Raphael Ingram. After Raphael Ingram left and Maryland Pierce and Dickie Smith became members in 1949, the name of the group was changed to Five Keys. With Pierce doing the lead work, the Five Keys joined Los Angeles-based Aladdin Records in 1951, and the same year had a hit with a remake of the old standard 'Glory Of Love', which became a US R&B number 1. Despite recording an appealing combination of old standards and R&B originals, further chart success on Aladdin eluded the Five Keys. In 1952 Rudy West went into the army, and was replaced by Ulysses K. Hicks, and in 1954 Dickie Smith left and was replaced with Ramon Loper. This new line-up of Five Keys was signed to Capitol Records, which brought the group to stardom, albeit with some modification in their style from a deep rhythm and blues sound to a more pop vein with greater instrumentation in support. The group's first hit for Capitol was the novelty pop jump 'Ling, Ting, Tong' (US R&B number 5 and pop Top 30 in 1955). Following the first Capitol recording session, Rudy West rejoined the Five Keys in October 1954, replacing the ailing Hicks, who died a few months later. Further hits on Capitol included some spectacular R&B ballads: the Chuck Willis-composed 'Close Your Eyes' (R&B number 5, 1955), 'The Verdict' (R&B number 13, 1955) and 'Out Of Sight, Out Of Mind' (R&B number 12 and pop Top 30 in 1956). The Capitol material also featured old standards, such as a marvellous remake of the Ink Spots' 'The Gypsy' (1957). Rudy West retired in 1958. An unsuccessful period at King Records from 1958-61 produced more personnel changes and no hits, and few songs that could compete with the new rock 'n' roll sounds. Periodic sessions were recorded by various reunion groups in subsequent years, but the basic legacy of the Five Keys rests in their Aladdin, Capitol Records and King Records sessions.

● ALBUMS: *The Best Of The Five Keys* (Aladdin 1956) ★★★, *The Five Keys On The Town* (Score 1957) ★★, *The Five Keys On Stage* (Capitol 1957) ★, *The Five Keys* (King 1960) ★★★, *Rhythm And Blues Hits Past And Present* (King 1960) ★★★, *The Fantastic Five Keys* (Capitol 1962) ★★★.

● COMPILATIONS: *The Five Keys* (King 1978) ★★, *The Five Keys And The Nitecaps* (Detour 1988) ★★★, *The Five Keys: Capitol Collector's Series* (Capitol 1989) ★★★, *Dream On* (Charly 1991) ★★★, *The Five Keys: The Aladdin Years* (EMI 1991) ★★★.

FIVE PENNIES, THE

This schmaltzy biopic of 20s cornet player Red Nichols was released by Paramount in 1959. Danny Kaye plays Nichols, and Barbara Bel Geddes is the wife who, following his early success, stays with him through the emotional traumas of their daughter's illness, until he re-emerges from depression and returns to his beloved world of jazz. On-screen musicians include Shelly Manne (in the role of Dave Tough, the second time in the same year he played the part of the drummer), Bobby Troup, Ray Anthony (in the role of Jimmy Dorsey, despite his being a trumpet player), and Louis Armstrong and his All Stars, who at that time included Peanuts Hucko, Billy Kyle and Trummy Young. Kaye and Armstrong mug their way through a vocal and trumpet duet of 'When the Saints Go Marching In', with Nichols himself dubbing for Kaye. Period songs such as 'Runnin' Wild' (Joe Grey-Leo Wood-A. Harrington Gibbs), 'Out Of Nowhere' (Edward Heyman-Johnny Green), 'After You've Gone' (Henry Creamer-Turner Layton), and 'Indiana' (Ballard MacDonald-James F. Hanley), are supplemented by three new ones written by Kaye's wife, Sylvia Fine – 'The Five Pennies', 'Lullaby In Ragtime' and 'Goodnight Sleep Tight', the last two of which are presented in a charming contrapuntal setting. Leith Stevens won an Oscar nomination for his 'scoring for a musical film', and there were other nominations for Daniel L. Fapp's impressive Vistavision and Technicolor cinematography, and Fine's title song. Melville Shavelson directed the picture, and he and Jack Rose wrote the script.

5 ROYALES

The 5 Royales were hugely successful exponents of southern vocal R&B throughout the 50s, although they started their career in a different style as the Royal Sons Gospel Group of Winston-Salem, North Carolina, USA. This quintet variously featured Clarence (b. 19 March 1928, Winston-Salem, North Carolina, USA, d. 6 May 1995, Los Angeles, California, USA), Curtis and Lowman Pauling (d. 26 December 1973, Brooklyn, New York, USA), Otto Jeffries, Johnny Tanner, Obediah Carter (d. July 1994, Winston-Salem, North Carolina, USA), Johnny Moore and William Samuels.

The Paulings had started out supporting Lowman Pauling Snr., on local North Carolina stages, while his namesake son reputedly built his first guitar out of cigar-boxes. Lowman Pauling Jnr. was the group's musical arranger and springboard, while Tanner usually handled lead vocals. At the suggestion of local radio producer Robert Woodward, the group contacted New York label Apollo Records, headed by Bess Berman and Carl Le Bowe. There the group sang spirituals as the Royal Sons Quintet, until Le Bowe re-christened them 5 Royales for the purposes of recording R&B music. Having elected to pursue the latter style, Johnny Holmes, the final member of the Royal Sons who graced their 'Bedside Of A Neighbor' debut, departed. This left a core 5 Royales line-up of Lowman Pauling (guitar), Johnny Tanner (lead), Johnny Moore (tenor), Obediah Carter (tenor) and Otto Jeffries (baritone). Typical of their background, their first single, 'Give Me One More Chance' (coupled with 'Too Much Of A Little Bit'), was a spiritual standard energized into a raunchy R&B number. By 1953 Eugene Tanner (b. 1936, d. 29 December 1994, Winston-Salem, North Carolina, USA; baritone/bass) had replaced Jeffries, the oldest member of the group by over 10 years, who was no longer capable of performing their energetic stage routines, instead becoming manager. Together they achieved their first major success with 'Baby Don't Do It', which made number 1 in the US R&B charts in January 1953. The follow-up single, 'Help Me Somebody', stayed at number 1 on the same chart for five weeks, while the group's powerful and frequent live performances, now completely divorced from their gospel background, built them a formidable reputation. Their new found fame also resulted in a lawsuit when they discovered that the Royals of Detroit were the first of several groups to impersonate them.

The 5 Royales made their first appearance at the Apollo in January 1953, performing for a week alongside Willy Mabon and Gene Ammons. 'Crazy, Crazy, Crazy' and 'Too Much Lovin'' were also sizeable R&B hits, although it was the latter's b-side, 'Laundromat Blues', with its sexually suggestive lyric, that provoked most attention. By 1954 the group had signed to King Records, following Le Bowe's defection to that label. However, the 5 Royales were never as successful again. Though over 40 singles were issued under their name up to 1965, usually of good quality, they seldom reached the charts. 'Tears Of Joy' and 'Think', both from 1957, were two notable exceptions. 'Think' was their first national US pop chart success, at number 66, although 'Dedicated To The One I Love', later covered by the Shirelles and Mamas And The Papas, also reached number 81 on the same chart in 1961. This was a revised version of a Chester Mayfield composition, 'I Don't Want You To Go', which Mayfield had written while a member of fellow North Carolina R&B group the Casanovas, also signed to Apollo. Their membership included William Samuels, Lowman Pauling's brother-in-law and formerly of the Royal Sons himself. However, after leaving King Records in 1960 the group failed to reach the charts again, despite recording for several labels with variable line-ups. Lowman Pauling left the group between stints at Home Of The Blues Records and Todd Records, replaced by Robert 'Pee Wee' Burris on guitar. Tanner also departed in December 1963, and was replaced by Eudell Graham. Graham, who became the focus of the touring 5 Royales, was later jailed for armed robbery.

The 5 Royales' influence on R&B proved fundamental to the music of James Brown, with whom the group had frequently worked in their heyday. Lowman Pauling, whose uninhibited guitar style was also a major influence on the style of Eric Clapton, died in 1973 while working as a custodian at a Brooklyn synagogue. Clarence Pauling, who left the Royal Sons before they became the 5 Royales, re-christened himself Clarence Paul and later became the A&R director at Motown Records where he helped shape the careers of Stevie Wonder and Marvin Gaye.

● ALBUMS: *The Rockin' 5 Royales* (Apollo 1956) ★★★, *Dedicated To You* (King 1957) ★★★, *The 5 Royales Sing For You* (King 1959) ★★★, *The Five Royales* (King 1960) ★★.

● COMPILATIONS: *24 All Time Hits* (King 1966) ★★★, *Sing Baby Don't Do It* (Relic 1987) ★★★, *Sing Laundromat Blues* (Relic 1987) ★★★, *Monkey, Hips And Rice: The 5 Royales Anthology* (Rhino 1997) ★★★★, *All Righty! The Apollo Recordings 1951-1955* (Westside 1999) ★★★★.

FIVE SATINS

This R&B vocal group was formed in New Haven, Connecticut, USA, in 1955. The Five Satins' first hit, 'In The Still Of The Nite' (US R&B number 3 and pop Top 30 in 1956), was one of the definitive songs of the early rock 'n' roll era, with its strong chanting of doo-wop riffs in the background and impassioned lead work. The group on this record consisted of lead Fred Parris, Al Denby, Ed Martin, bass Jim Freeman and pianist Jessie Murphy. Parris, who wrote the song, brought valuable experience to the Five Satins, having formed the Scarlets (Parris, Denby, Bill Powers, Sylvester Hopkins and Nate Mosely) in 1953, a group that hit regionally with 'Dear One' in 1954. The long-cherished national success for Parris was initially denied him, as he was in the army stationed in Japan when 'In The Still Of The Nite' became a hit, and the wonderful follow-up, 'To The Aisle'

(US R&B number 5 and pop Top 30 in 1957), featured a reorganized group with Bill Baker (b. Auburn, Alabama, USA, d. 10 August 1994, New Haven, Connecticut, USA) as lead. Parris returned from Japan in 1958 and again reorganized the Five Satins, recruiting tenor Richie Freeman (b. December 1940), second tenor West Forbes (b. 1937), Sylvester Hopkins and Lou Peeples. This group was not able to secure another big hit, although 'Shadows' (US R&B number 27, 1959) kept their name visible. Their profile was significantly enhanced with the release of Art Laboe's first *Oldies But Goodies*, which included 'In The Still Of The Nite'. As a result, the song helped to create the doo-wop revival in the early 60s and re-entered the national pop chart in 1961. The Five Satins broke up in the early 60s, but re-formed and became a perennial on the live circuit in the 70s. The new group consisted of Parris, Richie Freeman, Jimmy Curtis and Nate Marshall. Under the name Black Satin, they had a number 49 R&B hit in 1975 with 'Everybody Stand And Clap Your Hands (For The Entertainer)'. Another hit followed in 1982 with the medley 'Memories Of Days Gone By', before Parris and his various personnel returned to the oldies circuit.

● ALBUMS: *The 5 Satins Sing* (Ember 1957) ★★★, *Encore, Volume 2* (Ember 1960) ★★★.

● COMPILATIONS: *The Best Of The 5 Satins* (Celebrity Show 1971) ★★★.

FLAMINGOS

This R&B vocal group, formed in Chicago, Illinois, USA, in 1951, was renowned for producing the tightest and most gorgeous harmonies of the rock 'n' roll era. For much of their history they consisted of Zeke Carey (b. 24 January 1933, Bluefield, Virginia, USA), Jake Carey (b. 9 September 1926, Pulaski, Virginia, USA), Paul Wilson (b. 6 January 1935, Chicago, Illinois, USA, d. May 1988) and Johnny Carter (b. 2 June 1934, Chicago, Illinois, USA). The group's first lead was Sollie McElroy (b. 16 July 1933, Gulfport, Mississippi, USA, d. 15 January 1995), who brought the group regional fame on 'Golden Teardrops' for the Chance label in 1954. He was replaced by Nate Nelson (b. 10 April 1932, Chicago, Illinois, USA, d. 10 April 1984) who brought the group into the rock 'n' roll era with the magnificent ballad 'I'll Be Home', a number 5 R&B hit in 1956 on Chess Records. There then followed a period of disarray, in which Carter and Zeke Carey were lost to the draft. The Flamingos brought into the group Tommy Hunt (b. 18 June 1933, Pittsburgh, Pennsylvania, USA) and Terry Johnson (b. 12 November 1935, Baltimore, Maryland, USA) and moved to New York where they signed with End Records in 1958.

At this stage of their career the Flamingos had their biggest US hits, 'Lovers Never Say Goodbye' (R&B number 25 in 1958), 'I Only Have Eyes For You' (R&B number 3 and pop number 11 in 1959), 'Nobody Loves Me Like You' (R&B number 23 and pop Top 30 in 1960), the latter song written by Sam Cooke. One of the group's last outstanding records was 'I Know Better' (1962), a Drifters' sound-alike that captured top spots in many markets. During the early 60s the Flamingos lost the rest of their original members, except for Jake and Zeke Carey. The cousins managed to achieve some minor hits during the soul era, notably 'Boogaloo Party', which was the group's only UK chart hit when it reached number 26 in 1969 (three years earlier it was a US R&B number 22 hit). The Flamingos' last US chart record was 'Buffalo Soldier' 1970 (R&B Top 30). Nate Nelson died in 1984 and Paul Wilson in 1988. Sollie McElroy, after leaving the Flamingos in 1955, joined the Moroccos, with whom he recorded for three years, and Johnny Carter joined the Dells in 1960.

● ALBUMS: *The Flamingos* (Checker 1959) ★★★, *Flamingo Serenade* (End 1959) ★★★, *Flamingo Favorites* (End 1960) ★★★, *Requestfully Yours* (End 1960) ★★★, *The Sound Of The Flamingos* (End 1962) ★★★, *The Spiritual And Folk Moods Of The Flamingos* (End 1963) ★★, *Their Hits – Then And Now* (Philips 1966) ★★, *Flamingos Today* (Ronze 1971) ★★★.

● COMPILATIONS: *Collectors Showcase: The Flamingos* (Constellation 1964) ★★★, *Flamingos* (Chess 1984) ★★★★, *The Chess Sessions* (Chess 1987) ★★★, *The Doo Bop She Bop: The Best Of The Flamingos* (Rhino 1990) ★★★★, *The Flamingos: I Only Have Eyes For You* (Sequel 1991) ★★★, *The Flamingos Meet The Moonglows: 'On The Dusty Road Of Hits': The Complete 25 Chance Sides* (Vee Jay 1993) ★★★.

● FILMS: *Go Johnny Go* (1958).

FLANAGAN AND ALLEN

Bud Flanagan (b. Reuben Weintrop [Robert Winthrop], 14 October 1896, Whitechapel, London, England, d. 20 October 1968, Kingston, Surrey, England) and Chesney Allen (b. William Ernest Allen, 5 April 1896, London, England, d. 13 November 1982, Midhurst, Sussex, England). One of Britain's best-loved comedy-singing duos during their heyday in the 30s and 40s. Allen was the straight man, with a neat, well tailored image complete with trilby, while comedian Flanagan wore a voluminous mangy fur coat and a battered straw hat. The son of Jewish refugees from Poland, Flanagan took a job as a call boy at the Cambridge Music Hall when he was 10, and made his first stage appearance at the London Music Hall – as conjuror Fargo, the Boy Wizard – in 1908. After winning singing competitions sponsored by the popular musical hall artist Dora Lyric, Flanagan made up his young mind to run away to America, and, at the age of 14, found himself washing dishes in the galley of the S.S. *Majestic* bound for New York. Once there, he worked as a Western Union messenger, newspaper vendor, and prizefighter (billed as 'Luke McGlook from England'), before forming a vaudeville double act with Dale Burgess. They toured the US, and appeared in Australia, New Zealand, and South Africa, before Flanagan returned to England just after the outbreak of World War I, and enlisted in the Royal Artillery. Posted to Northern France, where he first met Chesney Allen briefly, he took his future stage name from a particularly obnoxious, anti-Semitic

Sergeant-Major Flanagan. After his release in 1919, he worked with various stage partners and was a taxi driver for a spell in the early 20s, before taking over from Stan Stanford as Chesney Allen's partner in Florrie Forde's revue and pantomime company in 1924. Allen, whose father was a master builder, had been articled to a solicitor before opting for a stage career. As well as performing in Forde's shows, he was also her manager. When Forde decided to retire, Flanagan and Allen's first inclination was to follow their main interest and start up as bookmakers, but they accepted D.J. Clarke's offer of a week in variety at the Argyle Theatre, Birkenhead, in January 1931. Their performances were so well received, especially their rendering of Flanagan's composition, 'Underneath The Arches', that they were swiftly booked for the Holborn Empire and the London Palladium. Flanagan and Allen also appeared at the Palladium in their first Royal Variety Performance in 1932. Flanagan's impulsive appeal for 'three cheers' for their majesties King George V and Queen Mary at the end of the show, marked the beginning of his long reign as an affectionately regarded 'court jester'. Also on the bill that year were the comic duo, Nervo And Knox, and that pair's subsequent appearances with Flanagan And Allen, Eddie Gray, Caryll And Mundy, and Naughton And Gold in the Palladium's *Crazy Month* revues, saw the birth of the legendary Crazy Gang. The team was reduced to seven after Billy Caryll lost a leg and died. In the 30s, as well as touring in variety and appearing together in their own shows such as *Give Me A Ring*, *Happy Returns*, *Life Begins At Oxford Circus*, and *Swing Is In The Air*, Flanagan And Allen were part of the Crazy Gang (although in most cases the artists were each billed separately) in popular revues such as *Round About Regent Street*, *O-Kay For Sound*, *London Rhapsody*, *These Foolish Things*, and *The Little Dog Laughed* (1939). During World War II Flanagan And Allen entertained the troops with ENSA, and were seen in the revues *Top Of The World*, *Black Vanities* and *Hi-Di-Hi*. They also starred in a series of comedy films – sprinkled occasionally with songs – which had begun in the 30s with *A Fire Has Been Arranged*, *Underneath The Arches*, *Okay For Sound*, *Alf's Button Afloat*, and *The Frozen Limit*, and continued in the early 40s with *Gasbags*, *We'll Smile Again*, *Theatre Royal*, *Here Comes The Sun*, and *Dreaming* (1944).

Chesney Allen's ill health brought the illustrious partnership to an end in 1946, and in the same year Flanagan appeared in Robert Nesbitt's revue, *The Night And The Laughter*, before rejoining the re-formed Crazy Gang in 1947 for *Together Again* at the Victoria Palace. It ran for more than two years, and similar productions such as *Knights Of Madness*, *Ring Out The Bells*, *Jokers Wild*, *These Foolish Kings*, and *Clown Jewels* (1959), also enjoyed extended stays, keeping the same theatre fully occupied during the 50s. In the latter show, Flanagan introduced Ralph Reader's 'Strollin'', a perfect addition to the catalogue of songs indelibly identified with Flanagan And Allen, which included 'The Umbrella Man', 'Run, Rabbit, Run',

'Home Town', 'Hey, Neighbour', 'We're Gonna Hang Out The Washing On The Siegfried Line', 'Dreaming', 'Forget-Me-Not Lane', 'Music, Maestro, Please', 'Franklin D. Roosevelt Jones' 'On The Outside Looking In', 'The Oi Song', and, of course, 'Underneath The Arches'. Flanagan received the OBE in 1959, and after the Crazy Gang's farewell show, *Young In Heart*, closed in 1962, he concentrated mainly on his bookmaking and other business interests. However, in 1968 he was persuaded to sing Jimmy Perry and Derek Taverner's 'Who Do You Think You Are Kidding Mr. Hitler' to be used over the opening titles of the brand new television comedy series, *Dad's Army*. Although he died just a few weeks after the first show was transmitted, his voice is still heard in 90s re-runs. Following his early retirement from the stage, Chesney Allen became the managing director of a theatrical and variety agency, and was the Crazy Gang's manager for a time. He joined Flanagan for two more films, *Life Is A Circus* and *Dunkirk*, in 1958, and made a nostalgic appearance at the 1980 Royal Variety Performance. He also took part in the cast recording of *Underneath The Arches*, a celebration of Flanagan And Allen, starring Roy Hudd (as Flanagan) and Christopher Timothy (as Allen), which played at London's Prince of Wales Theatre in 1982.

● COMPILATIONS: *Favourites* (Decca 1953) ★★★★, *Successes* (Columbia 1953) ★★★★, *Down Forget-Me-Not Lane* (Decca 1962) ★★★★, *The Flanagan And Allen Story* (Encore 1963) ★★★★, *We'll Smile Again* (Ace Of Clubs 1965) ★★★★, *Best Of* (Encore 1978) ★★★★, *Yesterday's Dreams* (Decca 1981) ★★★★, *Arches and Umbrellas* (Flapper 1990) ★★★★, *Underneath The Arches* (MFP 1991) ★★★★.

● FURTHER READING: *My Crazy Life* Bud Flanagan.

FLANAGAN, RALPH

b. 7 April 1919, Loranie, Ohio, USA. Flanagan played piano with several local bands during his teen years, eventually becoming pianist-arranger with Sammy Kaye in 1940. He was a member of the Merchant Marines during World War II and later provided arrangements for Charlie Barnet, Sammy Kaye, Gene Krupa, Blue Barron, Alvino Rey, Tony Pastor and many other bands. He also worked with a number of singers including Mindy Carson and Perry Como. He struck lucky when Herb Hendler, who worked for a minor record label, commissioned him to provide an album devoted to cover versions of Glenn Miller favourites. The resulting record sold so well that when Hendler moved to a job at RCA-Victor, he persuaded that company (which owned all the original Miller masters) to release further tracks by Flanagan. This time, he grafted Miller-style arrangements onto material not formerly associated with the Miller band. The ploy paid off and the records sold prolifically, encouraging Flanagan to form a full-time orchestra in early 1950 and to take it out on the road. The band was heavily influenced by Miller, and their vocal group, the Singing Winds, emulated the sounds of the

Pied Pipers. Flanagan's band also boasted a good male vocalist named Harry Prime, filling the Ray Eberle role. As a result, the band quickly became one of the biggest crowd-pullers on the big-band circuit, hit records coming with 'Rag Mop', 'Nevertheless' and 'Harbour Lights' in 1950, followed by 'Slow Poke', and his own composition 'Hot Toddy'. The success of the Flanagan band sparked off a whole Miller revival, with such former Miller-men as Ray Anthony and Jerry Gray, plus many others who had never even met Miller, organizing bands that echoed the Miller sound. Most of these imitators gradually faded, although Flanagan was still an active leader/arranger in the early 60s.

● COMPILATIONS: *Hot Toddy* (1988) ★★★, *On The Beat* (Golden Era 1989) ★★★.

FLANDERS AND SWANN

The son of an actor father, and a mother who had been a concert-violinist before she married, Michael Flanders (b. 1 March 1922, London, England, d. 14 April 1975), was brought up in a musical household. He learned to play the clarinet and made his stage debut at the age of seven in a singing contest with *Uncle Mac's Minstrel Show*. At Westminster School in London, where Peter Ustinov was one of his classmates, he started to write and stage revues. His search for a pianist led him to Donald Swann (b. Donald Ibrahim Swann, 30 September 1923, Llanelli, Wales, d. 23 March 1994, London, England), and their first revue together was *Go To It*. At Oxford University in 1940 Flanders played in and directed several productions for the Dramatic Society and made his professional debut as Valentine in Shaw's *You Never Can Tell*, at the Oxford Playhouse. In 1943, while serving in the Royal Navy Volunteer Reserve, having survived the infamous convoys to Russia, he was struck down by poliomyelitis. Three years later he was discharged from hospital, in a wheelchair, and with a full beard which he retained for the rest of his life.

Unable to resume a normal acting career, Flanders turned to writing and broadcasting. He contributed lyrics to several West End revues, in collaboration with Swann, including *Penny Plain* (1951), *Airs On A Shoestring* (1953) and *Fresh Airs* (1956). Flanders also appeared extensively on radio, and later, television, in programmes ranging from sports commentary to poetry readings, and including a spell of two years as chairman of *The Brains Trust*. His translation of Stravinsky's *Soldier's Tale* (with Kitty Black) became the standard English version, and his concert performance of it with Peter Ustinov and Sir Ralph Richardson was a surprise sell-out at the Royal Festival Hall in 1956. After successfully entertaining their friends at parties with their own songs, Flanders and Swann decided to perform professionally, so on New Year's Eve 1956, they opened their own two-man show, *At The Drop Of A Hat*, at the intimate New Lindsey Theatre, Notting Hill, west London, moving three weeks later into the West End's Fortune Theatre. The show was a smash hit and ran for over two years. It was reported that Princess Margaret attended a performance, and returned the following week with the Queen and the Duke of Edinburgh. With Flanders' urbane image contrasting with Swann's almost schoolboy enthusiasm, they introduced songs such as 'The Hippopotamus ('Mud, Mud, Glorious Mud')', 'Misalliance', 'A Gnu', and 'Madeira M'Dear?'. Two albums from the show were released, the earlier mono recording being preferable to the later stereo issue from the last night of the London run. In 1959 the show opened on Broadway, billed as 'An After-Dinner Farrago', and later toured the USA, Canada and the UK. In 1963 at the Haymarket Theatre, London, they presented a fully revised version entitled *At The Drop Of Another Hat*, which included songs such as 'The Gas-Man Cometh', 'First And Second Law' and 'Bedstead Men'. During 1964/5 they toured Australia, New Zealand and Hong Kong, before returning to the West End in 1965, and yet again, to New York in the following year.

Meanwhile, Flanders was still continuing with his other work, writing, broadcasting and performing theatrical speech recitals. He published *Creatures Great And Small*, a children's book of verses about animals and, together with Swann, released an album of animal songs entitled *The Bestiary Of Flanders And Swann*. Flanders was awarded the OBE in 1964. After the partnership broke up in 1967, Swann, who was born of Russian parents, continued to compose. In the 50s he had written the music for revues such as *Pay The Piper* and *Wild Thyme*, but in later years his music reflected his religious beliefs (he was a Quaker) and his love of Greece, and many other interests. He was still working right up to the time he died from cancer in 1994. In that same year, a musical celebration of the works of Michael Flanders and Donald Swann, entitled *Under Their Hats*, was presented at the King's Head Theatre in London.

● ALBUMS: *At The Drop Of A Hat* (Parlophone 1957) ★★★★, *The Bestiary Of Flanders And Swann* (Parlophone 1961) ★★★, *At The Drop Of Another Hat* (Parlophone 1964) ★★★.
● COMPILATIONS: *A Review Of Revues* (EMI 1975) ★★★, *Tried By Centre Court* (Note 1977) ★★★, *The Complete Flanders & Swann* 3-CD set (EMI 1991) ★★★★.
● VIDEOS: *The Only Flanders And Swann Video* (PMI 1992).
● FURTHER READING: all by Donald Swann *The Space Behind The Bars. Swann's Way Out. Swann's Way-A-Life In Song* (autobiography).

FLATT AND SCRUGGS

Lester Flatt (b. 28 June 1914, Overton County, Tennessee, USA, d. 11 May 1979, Nashville, Tennessee, USA; guitar) and Earl Scruggs (b. 6 January 1924, Cleveland County, North Carolina, USA; banjo). These influential musicians began working together in December 1945 as members of Bill Monroe's Bluegrass Boys. In February 1948 they left to form the Foggy Mountain Boys with Jim Shumate (fiddle), Howard Watts aka Cedric Rainwater (bass fiddle) – both ex-Bill Monroe – and, latterly, Mac Wiseman (tenor vocals, guitar).

They became an established feature of Virginia's WCYB radio station and undertook recording sessions for the Mercury Records label before embarking on a prolonged tour of the south. Here they forged a more powerful, ebullient sound than was associated with their chosen genre and in November 1950 Flatt and Scruggs joined Columbia/CBS Records, with whom they remained throughout their career together. Three years later they signed a sponsorship agreement with Martha White Mills which engendered a regular show on Nashville's WSM and favoured slots on their patron's television shows. Josh Graves (dobro) was then added to the line-up which in turn evolved a less frenetic sound and reduced the emphasis on Scruggs' banjo playing. Appearances on the nationally syndicated *Folk Sound USA* brought the group's modern bluegrass sound to a much wider audience, while their stature was further enhanced by an appearance at the 1960 Newport Folk Festival. Flatt and Scruggs were then adopted by the college circuit where they were seen as antecedents to a new generation of acts, including the Kentucky Colonels, the Hillmen and the Dillards. The Foggy Mountain Boys performed the theme song, 'The Ballad Of Jed Clampett', to the popular *Beverly Hillbillies* television show in the early 60s while their enduring instrumental, 'Foggy Mountain Breakdown', was heavily featured in the movie *Bonnie And Clyde*. Bluegrass students suggested that this version lacked the sparkle of earlier arrangements and declared that the group lacked its erstwhile vitality. By 1968 Earl Scruggs' sons, Randy and Gary, had been brought into the line-up, but the banjoist nonetheless grew dissatisfied with the constraints of a purely bluegrass setting. The partnership was dissolved the following year. While Flatt formed a new act, the Nashville Grass, his former partner added further members of his family to found the Earl Scruggs Revue. Plans for a reunion album were thwarted by Flatt's death in May 1979. They were inducted into the Country Music Hall Of Fame in 1985.

● ALBUMS: *Foggy Mountain Jamboree* (Columbia 1957) ★★★★, *Country Music* (Mercury 1958) ★★★, *Lester Flatt And Earl Scruggs* (Mercury 1959) ★★★★, *Songs Of Glory* (Columbia 1960) ★★★, *Flatt And Scruggs And The Foggy Mountain Boys* (Harmony 1960) ★★★, *Foggy Mountain Banjo* (Columbia 1961) ★★★★, *Songs Of The Famous Carter Family* (Columbia 1961) ★★★, *Folk Songs Of Our Land* (Columbia 1962) ★★★★, *Flatt And Scruggs At Carnegie Hall* (Columbia 1962) ★★★, *The Original Sound Of Flatt And Scruggs* (Mercury 1963) ★★★, *Hard Travelin'/The Ballad Of Jed Clampett* (Columbia 1963) ★★★★, *Recorded Live At Vanderbilt University* (Columbia 1964) ★★★, *The Fabulous Sound Of Flatt And Scruggs* (Columbia 1964) ★★★, *The Versatile Flatt And Scruggs* (Columbia 1965) ★★★, *Pickin' Strummin' And Singin'* (Columbia 1965) ★★★, one side is Jim And Jesse *Stars Of The Grand Ol' Opry* (Starday 1966) ★★, *Town & Country* (Columbia 1966) ★★★, *When The Saints Go Marching In*

(Columbia 1966) ★★★, with Doc Watson *Strictly Instrumental* (Columbia 1967) ★★, *Hear The Whistle Blow* (Columbia 1967) ★★, *The Original Theme From Bonnie & Clyde* (Mercury 1968) ★★, *Bill Monroe With Lester Flatt & Earl Scruggs: The Original Bluegrass Band* (Decca 1978) ★★★.
● COMPILATIONS: *Flatt And Scruggs Greatest Hits* (Columbia 1966) ★★★, *The Original Foggy Mountain Breakdown* (Mercury 1968) ★★★★, *World Of Flatt And Scruggs* (Columbia 1973) ★★★, *The Golden Era 1950-1955* (Rounder 1977) ★★★★, *Blue Ridge Cabin Home* (Rebel 1979) ★★★★, *Columbia Historic Edition* (Columbia 1982) ★★★, *20 All Time Great Recordings* (Columbia 1983) ★★★, *Country And Western Classics* 3-LP box set (Time-Life 1982) ★★★, *Mercury Sessions, Volume 1* (Mercury 1987) ★★★★, *Mercury Sessions, Volume 2* (Mercury 1987) ★★★, *You Can Feel It In Your Soul* (County 1988) ★★★, *Don't Get Above Your Raisin'* (Rounder 1992) ★★★, *The Complete Mercury Sessions* (Mercury 1992) ★★★★, *1949 - 1959* 4-CD box set (Bear Family 1992) ★★★★, *1959 - 1963* 5-CD box set (Bear Family 1992) ★★★★, *1964 – 69, Plus* 6-CD box set (Bear Family 1996) ★★★★, *Tis Sweet To Be Remembered: The Essential Flatt & Scruggs* (Legacy/Columbia 1997) ★★★★.

FLEETWOODS

One of America's most popular doo-wop groups in the late 50s comprised Gary Troxell (b. 28 November 1939, Centralia, Washington, DC, USA), Gretchen Christopher (b. 29 February 1940, Olympia, Washington, DC, USA) and Barbara Ellis (b. 20 February 1940, Olympia, Washington, USA). They met while seniors at high school in the girls' home town. Originally a female duo, they recruited Troxell initially to play trumpet. The girls had composed a song, while independently, Troxell had written a hook that went something like: 'Mmm Dooby Doo, Dum Dim Dum Doo Dum'; they put them together and 'Come Softly To Me' was born. Their first moniker, Two Girls And A Guy, was changed by a Seattle record distributor Bob Reisdorff, who became their manager and founded Dolphin Records (later called Dolton) which released the single. Chart fame was instant for the distinctive trio and the haunting and catchy song (on which the vocal was recorded *a cappella*) shot to the top of the US charts and made the UK Top 10 despite a hit cover version by Frankie Vaughan and the Kaye Sisters. Their third release, 'Mr. Blue', a Dwayne Blackwell song originally written for the Platters, was also a US number 1 (in the UK two cover versions took the honours) and made Troxell one of the leaders in the teen-idol stakes. In the midst of their success he was drafted into the navy, his place being taken when necessary by subsequent solo star Vic Dana. Despite Troxell's absence, the US hits continued and they totalled nine Top 40 hits between 1959 and 1963, including the number 10 hit 'Tragedy', a revival of the Thomas Wayne song. The unmistakable close-harmony trio surfaced again in 1973 when they signed with the noted producer Jerry Dennon, but no hits

resulted from this brief collaboration.
● ALBUMS: *Mr. Blue* (Dolton 1959) ★★★★, *The Fleetwoods* (Dolton 1960) ★★★★, *Softly* (Dolton 1961) ★★★★, *Deep In A Dream* (Dolton 1961) ★★★, *The Best Of The Oldies* (Dolton 1962) ★★★★, *Goodnight My Love* (Dalton 1963) ★★★, *The Fleetwoods Sing For Lovers By Night* (Dolton 1963) ★★★, *Before And After* (Dolton 1965) ★★, *Folk Rock* (Dolton 1966) ★★.
● COMPILATIONS: *The Fleetwoods' Greatest Hits* (Dolton 1962) ★★★★, *In A Mellow Mood* (Sunset 1966) ★★★, *The Best Of The Fleetwoods* (Rhino 1990) ★★★★, *Come Softly To Me: The Best Of The Fleetwoods* (EMI 1993) ★★★★.

FONTANA, D.J.

b. Dominic James Fontana, 1934, USA. Fontana says that his cousin's drums were the only instruments to hand when he was young so he played them. He started in cocktail lounges and became the drummer for the country music radio show, *The Louisiana Hayride*. He was placed behind a curtain as many country fans (and musicians!) were suspicious of the instrument. Fontana impressed Elvis Presley who appeared on the show with Scotty Moore (guitar) and Bill Black (double bass) on 16 October 1954, and he became a part of Presley's touring band on a regular basis the following year. The drummer on Presley's Sun Records recordings was Johnny Bernero, but, starting with 'Heartbreak Hotel', Fontana recorded with Presley when he moved to RCA Records in 1956. He played on 'Hound Dog', 'Don't Be Cruel', 'Jailhouse Rock' and the majority of his early hits. On December 1968's *Elvis TV Special*, Fontana played a guitar case as there was no rooms for drums on the stage: 'Who cares?' he said, 'I'd done it before. That sound on 'All Shook Up' is the back of a guitar case, not a drum.' He played drums on Ringo Starr's Nashville album, *Beaucoups Of Blues* and also played for a stripper in the Robert Altman movie, *Nashville*. He has written his memoirs, *D.J. Fontana Remembers Elvis*, and in recent years, he has made several appearances including UK tours with Scotty Moore and Charlie Gracie. In 1997, Fontana linked up with Moore and guest artists including the Band, Steve Earle, Jeff Beck and Keith Richards to record *All The King's Men*.
● ALBUMS: with Scotty Moore *All The King's Men* (Sweetfish/Polydor 1997) ★★★.
● VIDEOS: *Scotty Moore & D.J. Fontana Live In Concert* (1993).

FONTANE SISTERS

The line-up of this close-harmony 50s US vocal group, whose initial success was achieved by making cover versions of black R&B records, comprised Marge Rosse (b. New Milford, New Jersey, USA; lead), Bea Rosse (b. New Milford, New Jersey, USA; low harmony) and Geri Rosse (b. New Milford, New Jersey, USA; harmony). Their mother was a choral director and organist. After leaving high school they joined an all-girl troupe and went on an eight-month tour. Later, they were joined by their brother Frank on guitar, and appeared on radio and in theatres and clubs. After Frank was killed in World War II, the girls re-formed in 1944 as a trio and worked for several years on Perry Como's radio and television shows; they also backed him on several records, including the US number 1 hits 'You're Adorable' and 'Hoop-Dee-Doo'. Signed to RCA-Victor Records in 1949, they had several minor hits in the early 50s, including 'Tennessee Waltz', 'Let Me In' (with Texas Jim Robertson) and 'Cold, Cold Heart'. In 1954 they switched to Dot Records, a label that specialized in making cover versions of established hits, and came under the influence of Dot's musical director, Billy Vaughn, who, with his orchestra, provided the backing for most of their successful records. Early that year, they made the US charts with 'Happy Days And Lonely Nights', a 1929 song by Fred Fisher and Billy Rose, and in December 1954 they went to number 1 with 'Hearts Of Stone'. The original version was the debut disc of the R&B Cincinnati group Otis Williams And The Charms. Other successful cover versions of black artists' records included 'Rock Love', 'Rollin' Stone' (original by the Marigolds) and 'Eddie My Love' (originally by the Teen Queens). Other 'white' cover versions included Boyd Bennett And His Rockets' 'Seventeen', which the Fontanes took to number 3 in the US chart, and 'Daddy-O', a song said to have been inspired by a character in the 1955 movie *Blackboard Jungle*, and which was originally a US Top 20 hit for Bonnie Lou. The Fontanes' 1957 version of 'Banana Boat Song' also made the Top 20, but was prevented from rising higher by a version by the Tarriers; another version, by Steve Lawrence, was his first chart entry. By the late 50s, with more and more black artists reaching the charts themselves, the Fontanes faded from their position as one of the top girl groups of the 50s. Their last two hits, 'Chanson D'Amour' and 'Jealous Heart', came in 1958.

● ALBUMS: *The Fontanes Sing* (Dot 1956) ★★★, *A Visit With The Fontane Sisters* (Dot 1957) ★★★, *Tips Of My Fingers* (1963) ★★.

● COMPILATIONS: *Rock Love* (Charly 1984) ★★★, *Rock Again Love* (Charly 1986) ★★★, *Hearts Of Stone* (Varèse Sarabande 1994) ★★★★.

FORD, FRANKIE

b. Francis Guzzo, 4 August 1939, Gretna, Louisiana, USA. A rocker from a suburb of New Orleans, Frankie Ford is second cousin to that other New Orleans legend Dr. John. His first major appearance was on *Ted Mack's Amateur Hour Talent Show*, where he sang with Carmen Miranda and Sophie Tucker. After winning a scholarship to South Eastern College, Hammond, he started his first band with schoolfriends. By 1958 he was singing with the Syncopators, when he was asked to audition for Ace Records. Subsequently, he released his first single, 'Cheatin' Woman', as Frankie Ford. Fellow musician Huey 'Piano' Smith (b. 26 January 1934, New Orleans, Louisiana, USA) had previously recorded with his group the Clowns a self-penned

song called 'Sea Cruise', but Ace persuaded him to let Ford record a new vocal over Bobby Marcham's original. They also added a few extra effects such as paddle-steamer whistle blows, which altered the song enough for Ford to claim a co-writing credit. Released under the title Frankie Ford with Huey 'Piano' Smith and his Clowns, it sold over a million copies and docked in the national Top 20.

It was perceived in retrospect as a rock 'n' roll classic, and was revived by Jerry Lee Lewis, Herman's Hermits, Sha Na Na, John Fogerty and Shakin' Stevens. Both 'Sea Cruise' and its follow-up, 'Alimony', were taken from original tapes recorded by composer Huey Smith with the Clowns; the lead vocals were then erased and Ford's singing superimposed. As Morgus And The Ghouls, Ford and the Clowns also recorded 'Morgus The Magnificent', a novelty tribute to a local television personality. There was also an unissued homage to Fats Domino, written and recorded by Ford and Dave Bartholomew. Ford left Ace in 1960 to form his own Spinet Records and signed to Liberty Records in 1960, but never repeated the success of 'Sea Cruise'. He also formed a 'supergroup' with Huey Smith, Robert Parker (hitmaker of 'Barefootin'') and Dr. John (under various pseudonyms due to contractual problems), and they recorded various New Orleans favourites. He continued to record for obscure labels throughout the 70s. In 1971, he opened a club in New Orleans' French Quarter where he became a cabaret fixture and tourist attraction. Moreover, he still looked youthful enough to play his younger self in the 1977 movie *American Hot Wax*, set in the late 50s. As part of a package, he toured the UK in 1985 along with Rick Nelson, Bobby Vee and Bo Diddley. Ford resents the term one-hit-wonder, and rightly pointed out that his four recordings of 'Sea Cruise' have now sold over 30 million copies worldwide.

● ALBUMS: *Let's Take A Sea Cruise With Frankie Ford* (Ace 1959) ★★★, *Frankie Ford* (Briarmeade 1976) ★★, *Hot & Lonely* (Ace 1995) ★★, *Christmas* (Avanti 1999) ★★.

● COMPILATIONS: *New Orleans Dynamo* (Ace 1984) ★★★, *Ooh-Wee Baby! The Very Best Of Frankie Ford* (Westside 1997) ★★★, *Sea Cruise: The Very Best Of Frankie Ford* (Music Club 1998) ★★★, *Cruisin' With Frankie Ford: The Imperial Sides And London Sessions* (Ace 1998) ★★★.

● FILMS: *American Hot Wax* (1977).

FORD, MARY

(see Paul, Les)

FORD, TENNESSEE ERNIE

b. Ernest Jennings Ford, 13 February 1919, Bristol, Tennessee, USA, d. 17 October 1991, Reston, Virginia, USA. It is difficult to categorize a performer with so many varied achievements, but Ford can be summarized as a master interpreter of melodic songs and hymns. The fact that he was able to combine singing with his strong faith gave America's best-loved gospel singer great satisfaction. When only four years old, he was singing 'The Old Rugged Cross' at family gatherings, and from an early age, he wanted to be an entertainer. He pestered the local radio station until they made him a staff announcer in 1937 and he also took singing lessons. He subsequently worked for radio stations WATL in Atlanta and WROL in Knoxville, where he announced the attack on Pearl Harbor. He joined the US Army Air Corps in 1942 and married a secretary, Betty Heminger, whom he met at the bombardier's school. After the war, they moved to California and he worked as an announcer and a disc jockey of hillbilly music for KXFM in San Bernardino. He rang cowbells and added bass harmonies to the records he was playing and so developed a country yokel character, Tennessee Ernie. He continued with this on KXLA Pasadena and he became a regular on their *Hometown Jamboree*, which was hosted by bandleader Cliffie Stone. He was also known as the Tennessee Pea-Picker, using the catchphrase 'Bless your pea-pickin' hearts' and appearing on stage in bib overalls and with a blacked-out tooth. Lee Gillette, an A&R man for Capitol Records, heard Ford singing along with a record on air and asked Stone about him. His first record, in 1949, was 'Milk 'Em In The Morning Blues'. Ford began his chart success with 'Tennessee Border', 'Country Junction' and 'Smokey Mountain Boogie', a song he wrote with Stone. 'Mule Train', despite opposition from Frankie Laine, Gene Autry and Vaughn Monroe, was a national hit and a US country number 1. An attempt to write with Hank Williams did not lead to any completed songs, but Ford wrote 'Anticipation Blues' about his wife's pregnancy and it reached the US charts in 1949. Capitol teamed him with many of their female artists including Ella Mae Morse, Molly Bee and the Dinning Sisters, and his most successful duets were 'Ain't Nobody's Business But My Own' and 'I'll Never Be Free', a double-sided single with Kay Starr. The duet just missed gold record status, but he secured one, also in 1950, with his own song, 'Shotgun Boogie', which capitalized on the boogie craze and can be taken as a forerunner of rock 'n' roll. Its UK popularity enabled him to top a variety bill at the London Palladium in 1953. Ford recalls, 'When somebody told me that 'Give Me Your Word' was number 1 in your charts, I said, "When did I record that?" because it wasn't big in America and I had forgotten about it!' Ford also had success with 'The Cry Of The Wild Goose' and the theme for the Marilyn Monroe movie *The River Of No Return*, while the superb musicians on his records included Joe 'Fingers' Carr, who was given equal billing on 'Tailor Made Woman' in 1951, Speedy West and Jimmy Bryant.

Ford hosted a US daytime television show for five days a week and, in 1955, Capitol informed him that he would be in breach of contract if he did not record again soon. He chose a song he had been performing on the show, Merle Travis' 'Sixteen Tons'. Ford says, 'The producer, Lee Gillette, asked me what tempo I would like it in. I snapped my fingers and he said, "Leave that in." That snapping on the record is me.' 'Sixteen Tons' topped both the US and the UK charts, and Ford was also one of many who recorded 'The Ballad Of Davy Crockett', the theme of a Walt Disney western starring Fess Parker, which made number 3 in the UK. His half-hour US television show, *The Ford Show* (guess the sponsor), ran from 1956-61. He closed every television show with a hymn, which led to him recording over 400 gospel songs. One album, *Hymns*, made number 2 in the US album charts and was listed for over five years. He has shared his billing with the Jordanaires on several albums including *Great Gospel Songs*, which won a Grammy in 1964. Ford says, 'Long before I turned pro, it was a part of my life. There are many different types of gospel music, ranging from black music to the plain old Protestant hymns. I've shown that you don't have to sing them with a black robe on.' Ford had further US hits with 'That's All', 'In The Middle Of An Island' and 'Hicktown' but, for many years, he concentrated on gospel. In 1961 he decided to spend more time with his family and moved to a ranch in the hills of San Francisco. He recorded albums of well-known songs, both pop and country; he rated *Country Hits – Feelin' Blue* and *Ernie Sings And Glen Picks*, an album that showcased his deep, mellow voice alongside Glen Campbell's guitar, among his best work. Many collectors seek original copies of his earlier albums of Civil War songs. Ford, who was elected to the Country Music Hall of Fame in 1990, remarked, 'People say to me, "Why don't you record another 'Sixteen Tons'?" And I say, "There is no other 'Sixteen Tons'"'

● ALBUMS: *This Lusty Land* (Capitol 1956) ★★★, *Hymns* (Capitol 1956) ★★★, *Spirituals* (Capitol 1957) ★★★, *C-H-R-I-S-T-M-A-S* (Capitol 1957) ★★, *Tennessee Ernie Ford Favourites* (Capitol 1957) ★★★, *Ol' Rockin' 'Ern* (Capitol 1957) ★★★, *The Folk Album* (Capitol 1958) ★★★, *Nearer The Cross* (Capitol 1958) ★★★, *The Star Carol* (Capitol 1958) ★★★, with the Jordanaires *Gather 'Round* (Capitol 1959) ★★★★, with the Jordanaires *A Friend We Have In Jesus* (Capitol 1960) ★★★, *Sing A Hymn With Me* (Capitol 1960) ★★★, *Sixteen Tons* (Capitol 1960) ★★★★, *Sing A Spiritual With Me* (Capitol 1960) ★★, *Come To The Fair* (Capitol 1960) ★★★, *Sings Civil War Songs Of The North* (Capitol 1961) ★★★★, *Sings Civil War Songs Of The South* (Capitol 1961) ★★★★, *Ernie Ford Looks At Love* (Capitol 1961) ★★, *Hymns At Home* (Capitol 1961) ★★★, *Here Comes The Tennessee Ernie Ford Mississippi Showboat* (Capitol 1962) ★★, *I Love To Tell The Story* (Capitol 1962) ★★★, *Book Of Favourite Hymns* (Capitol 1962) ★★, *Long, Long Ago* (Capitol 1963) ★★★, with the San Quentin Prison Choir *We Gather Together* (Capitol 1963) ★★★, with the Roger Wagnor Chorale *The Story Of Christmas* (Capitol 1963) ★★, with the Jordanaires *Great Gospel Songs* (Capitol 1964) ★★★★, *Country Hits – Feeling Blue* (Capitol 1964) ★★★★, *Let Me Walk With Thee* (Capitol 1965) ★★, *Sing We Now Of Christmas* (Capitol 1965) ★★★, *My Favourite Things* (Capitol 1966) ★★★,

Wonderful Peace (Capitol 1966) ★★, *God Lives* (Capitol 1966) ★★, *Aloha From Tennessee Ernie Ford* (Capitol 1967) ★★★, *Faith Of Our Fathers* (Capitol 1967) ★★, with Marilyn Horne *Our Garden Of Hymns* (Capitol 1967) ★★, with Brenda Lee *The Show For Christmas Seals* (Decca 1968) ★★★, *The World Of Pop And Country Hits* (Capitol 1968) ★★★★, *O Come All Ye Faithful* (Capitol 1968) ★★★, *Songs I Like To Sing* (Capitol 1969) ★★★, *New Wave* (Capitol 1969) ★★★, *Holy Holy Holy* (Capitol 1969) ★★★, *America The Beautiful* (Capitol 1970) ★★★, *Sweet Hour Of Prayer* (Capitol 1970) ★★★, *Tennessee Ernie Ford Christmas Special* (Capitol 1970) ★★★, *Everything Is Beautiful* (Capitol 1970) ★★★, *Abide With Me* (Capitol 1971) ★★★, *Mr. Words And Music* (Capitol 1972) ★★★, *It's Tennessee Ernie Ford* (Capitol 1972) ★★★, *Country Morning* (Capitol 1973) ★★★, *Ernie Ford Sings About Jesus* (Capitol 1973) ★★, *Precious Memories* (Capitol 1975) ★★★, with Glen Campbell *Ernie Sings And Glen Picks* (Capitol 1975) ★★★, *Tennessee Ernie Ford Sings His Great Love* (Capitol 1976) ★★★, *For The 83rd Time* (Capitol 1976) ★★★, *He Touched Me* (Capitol 1977) ★★, with the Jordanaires *Swing Wide Your Golden Gate* (Capitol 1978) ★★★★, *Tell The Old, Old Story* (Capitol 1981) ★★★, *There's A Song In My Heart* (Word 1982) ★★★, *Sunday's Still A Special Day* (Capitol 1984) ★★★, *Keep Looking Up* (Word 1985) ★★★.

● COMPILATIONS: *Tennessee Ernie Ford Deluxe Set* (Capitol 1968) ★★★, *The Very Best Of Tennessee Ernie Ford* (MFP 1983) ★★★, *16 Tons Of Boogie/The Best Of Tennessee Ernie Ford* (Rhino 1989) ★★★★, *All Time Greatest Hymns* (Curb 1990) ★★★★, *Capitol Collectors Series* (Capitol 1991) ★★★, *Country Gospel Classics, Volumes 1 & 2* (Capitol 1991) ★★★, *Sings Songs Of The Civil War* (Capitol 1991) ★★★, *Red, White & Blue* (Capitol 1991) ★★★, *Sixteen Tons* (Capitol 1995) ★★★★, *The Tennessee Ernie Ford Collection (1949-1965)* (Razor & Tie 1997) ★★★★, *The EP Collection* (See For Miles 2001) ★★★★.

FORTUNE, LANCE

b. Chris Morris, 1940, Birkenhead, Cheshire, England. Until he received a guitar at Christmas 1956, this grammar school student had studied classical piano. Morris sacrificed a scholarship at a Welsh university to work as an odd-job man at the famous London coffee bar, the 2I's, and it was there that he was heard singing by top manager and impresario Larry Parnes in 1959. Although he did not manage him, Parnes rechristened him Lance Fortune (a name he had previously given to Clive Powell, a singer and pianist, whom he later renamed Georgie Fame). Fortune recorded his first single 'Be Mine', an Adam Faith-styled pop song, backed by John Barry's musicians, which was released by Pye and eventually climbed to number 4 in the UK. During the time it took to reach the charts in Britain, Fortune toured with his idol, Gene Vincent. He also managed to put the follow-up 'This Love I Have For You' into the Top 30 but it was his last taste of success – long-term fame was not on the cards for Mr. Fortune.

FOSSE, BOB

b. Robert Louis Fosse, 23 June 1927, Chicago, Illinois, USA, d. 23 September 1987, Washington, DC, USA. A director, choreographer, dancer and actor for films and stage, Fosse was renowned particularly for his innovative and spectacular staging, with the emphasis very firmly on the exhilarating dance sequences. He studied ballet, tap and acrobatic dance from an early age, and, while still a youngster, performed with a partner as the Riff Brothers in vaudeville and burlesque houses. After graduating from high school in 1945, he spent two years in the US Navy before moving to New York and studying acting at the American Theatre Wing. He then toured in the chorus of various productions before making his Broadway debut as a dancer in the revue *Dance Me A Song* (1950). He worked on television and in theatres and clubs for a time until Hollywood beckoned, and he moved to the west coast to appear in three films, *Give A Girl A Break*, *The Affairs Of Dobie Gillis* and *Kiss Me, Kate* (1953). On his return to New York, he gained his big break when author and director George Abbott hired him as a choreographer for *The Pajama Game* (1954). The show was a massive hit, and Fosse was much in demand – for a time at least. He met Gwen Verdon while working on *Damn Yankees* in 1955, and they were married in 1960.

He choreographed *Bells Are Ringing* in 1956, and worked with Verdon again on *New Girl In Town* a year later. From then on, with the exception of *How To Succeed In Business Without Really Trying* (1961), he directed his shows as well as staging the dancing. Fosse's dual role is considered by critics to be a major factor in the success of highly popular productions such as *Redhead* (1959), *Little Me* (1962), *Sweet Charity* (1966), *Pippin* (1972), *Chicago* (1975) and *Dancin'* (1978). Throughout all this time he moved back and forwards between New York and Hollywood, working on films such as *My Sister Eileen* (1955), *The Pajama Game* (1957) and *Damn Yankees* (1958), all three of which were well received. However, *Sweet Charity* (1968), which Fosse controlled completely in his role as director and choreographer, was hammered by many critics for Shirley MacLaine's over-the-top performance, and particularly for the director's self-indulgent cinematography, with its looming close-ups, zooms and blurred focus effects. Fosse was in the wilderness for some time, but all was forgiven four years later when *Cabaret*, starring Liza Minnelli and Joel Grey, won eight Academy Awards, one of which went to Fosse. It was a box-office smash, and Fosse also satisfied most of the purists by confining the dance sequences to appropriate locations such as a beer garden and nightclub, rather than flooding the streets of Berlin with terpsichorean tourists.

In the early 70s Fosse was applauded for his direction of *Lenny*, a film biography of the comedian Lennie Bruce, which starred Dustin Hoffman. In the light of Fosse's recent heart problems, his record as a workaholic, and his lifelong obsession with perfection, many observers thought that *All That Jazz* (1979) was intended to be Fosse's own film autobiography, with its ghoulish, self-indulgent examination of life and death. However, no one denied the brilliance of the dance routines or the outstanding performance of Roy Scheider in the leading role. In 1983 Fosse wrote and directed his last film, *Star 80*, which also had a lurid, tragic theme. Three years later, he wrote, staged and choreographed his final Broadway musical, *Big Deal* – which was, in fact, far less than its title suggested. It represented an inappropriate end to a brilliant career, in which Fosse had created some of the most imaginative and thrilling dance routines ever seen on Broadway or in Hollywood, winning eight Tony Awards in the process. In 1987 he revived one of his most successful shows, *Sweet Charity*, and died shortly before the curtain went up on the night of 23 September. A fascinating documentary entitled *Bob Fosse – Steam Heat*, was made by the US company WNET/Thirteen in 1990. The source of one of his greatest triumphs, *Chicago*, was revived to great acclaim on Broadway and in the West End in 1996/7. Anne Reinking's choreography was created, with great respect and affection, 'in the style of Bob Fosse'. His incredibly wit and vitality were remembered again early in 1999, when a retrospective of his dance numbers entitled *Fosse* opened on Broadway. The show was directed by Richard Maltby Jnr. and Ann Reinking, and choreographed by Reinking and Chet Walker.

● FURTHER READING: *Razzle Dazzle: The Life And Works Of Bob Fosse*, Kevin Boyd Grubb. *Bob Fosse's Broadway*, Margery Beddow.

FOSTER, FRANK

b. 23 September 1928, Cincinnati, Ohio, USA. Although he began his musical career playing alto saxophone, Foster showed commendable foresight in deciding to change to tenor saxophone and flute, declaring his intention of following his own path and not the one sign-posted by Charlie Parker. In the late 40s he played with several like-minded spirits in the Detroit area, among them Wardell Gray and Snooky Young, before serving in the armed forces. In 1953 he joined Count Basie and became a significant member of the band as soloist, arranger and composer ('Shiny Stockings'). After 11 years with Basie he joined Elvin Jones, another of the musicians with whom he had played in Detroit early in his career. In the mid-60s he formed a big band which continued to play intermittently over the next decade. He also played with the Thad Jones-Mel Lewis Jazz Orchestra and co-led a small group with former Basie section-mate Frank Wess. In the mid-80s Foster began a long stint as frontman for the reactivated Basie band, with which he toured the USA and Europe. Foster's arrangements have always shown his affinity with post-war big-band writing and his work for Basie was an important factor in the success of that particular edition of the band. As a soloist, Foster's early decision to go his own way paid dividends as he developed a distinctively acerbic tone which, while reflecting an awareness of his contemporaries, was very

much his own.

● ALBUMS: *Frank Foster Quintet* 10-inch album (Blue Note 1954) ★★★, with Paul Quinichette *Jazz Studio 1* (Decca 1954) ★★★, with Elmo Hope *Hope Meets Foster* reissued as *Wail Frank Wail* (Prestige 1956) ★★★★, *Basie Is Our Boss* (Argo 1963) ★★★★, *Fearless Frank Foster* (Prestige 1967) ★★★, *Soul Outing!* (Prestige 1967) ★★★, *Manhattan Fever* (Blue Note 1968) ★★★, *The Loud Minority* (Mainstream 1974) ★★★, *Giants Steps* (1975) ★★★★, *Here And Now* (Catalyst 1976) ★★★, *12 Shades Of Black* (Leo 1978) ★★★, *Shiny Stockings* (Denon 1978) ★★★★, *Roots, Branches And Dances* (1978) ★★★★, *Ciquito Loco: Live At The HNITA Jazz Club* (1979) ★★★, *A Blues Ain't Nothing But A Trip* (1979) ★★★, *The House That Love Built* (Steeple Chase 1982) ★★, *Two For The Blues* (Pablo 1983) ★★★, *Frankly Speaking* (Concord Jazz 1984) ★★, with James Moody *Sax Talk* (1993) ★★★, *Leo Rising* (Arabesque 1997) ★★★★.

FOUR ACES

A close-harmony vocal group of the pre-rock 'n' roll era, the quartet was founded in Pennsylvania, USA, in 1949 by baritone lead singer Al Alberts (b. Chester, Pennsylvania, USA). With Dave Mahoney, Lou Silvestri and Sol Vocare, he recorded a single on the local Victoria label in 1951. 'Sin (Not A Sin)' sold a million copies and the Four Aces were signed to Decca Records. Alberts and Martin Gold co-wrote 'Tell Me Why', which began a string of hit singles during the mid-50s. Among them were the 1952 revival of Hoagy Carmichael and Frank Loesser's 1938 song 'Heart And Soul', 'Stranger In Paradise' (from the stage musical *Kismet*), 'Mister Sandman' (1954), 'Heart' and 'Melody Of Love' (1955). The group's only number 1 record was the Oscar-winning 'Love Is A Many-Splendored Thing', the title song from the 1955 movie starring Jennifer Jones and William Holden. The Four Aces also recorded versions of the theme from *Three Coins In The Fountain* and 'The World Outside' from the movie *Suicide Squadron*. In 1956, the group suffered a double blow as Alberts left to follow a solo career and rock 'n' roll arrived. The Four Aces tried various strategies to survive, including covering a Pat Boone song 'Friendly Persuasion (Thee I Love)' and jumping on the calypso and rock bandwagons with 'Bahama Mama' and 'Rock And Roll Rhapsody'. However, few of these records were even minor hits and by the end of the 50s the Four Aces had disappeared from view. Alberts did little better, although 'Willingly' (1958) was only a minor success.

● ALBUMS: *The Four Aces* 10-inch album (Decca 1952) ★★★★, *The Mood For Love* (Decca 1955) ★★★, *Merry Christmas* (Decca 1956) ★★★, *Sentimental Souvenirs* (Decca 1956) ★★★, *Heart And Soul* (Decca 1957) ★★★, *She Sees All The Hollywood Hits* (Decca 1957) ★★★, *Written On The Wind* film soundtrack (Decca 1957) ★★, *Shuffling Along* (Decca 1957) ★★, *Hits From Hollywood* (Decca 1958) ★★★, *The Swingin' Aces* (Decca 1959) ★★, *Hits From Broadway* (Decca 1959) ★★, *Beyond The Blue Horizon* (Decca 1959) ★★.

● COMPILATIONS: *The Golden Hits Of The Four Aces* (Decca 1960) ★★★★, *Record Oldies* (United Artists 1963) ★★★★, *The Best Of The Four Aces* (Spectrum 2001) ★★★.
● FILMS: *The Big Beat* (1957).

FOUR ESQUIRES

Bill Courtney (lead singer) and backing vocalists Walter Gold, Robert Golden and Frank Mahoney were students at the University of Boston, Massachusetts, USA, in the early 50s who harmonized for their own amusement to whatever instrumental accompaniment they could muster. Though popular locally, they waited until they were sufficiently schooled before becoming professional entertainers. After London Records signed them in March 1956, 'Look Homeward Angel' was a turntable hit, but it was eclipsed by Johnnie Ray's version. Their workmanlike 'Love Me Forever' (augmented with a female session vocalist's obligato), was overshadowed by a US cover version by Eydie Gorme and one in Britain by Marion Ryan. Nevertheless, it clawed into each country's Top 30 and, unhindered by competition, so did 1958's 'Hideaway' in the USA. While able to fill moderate-sized auditoriums and becoming a reliable support act in bigger venues, the Esquires clocked up no further chart entries and had disbanded by the early 60s.

FOUR FRESHMEN

Formed at Arthur Jordan Conservatory of Music in Indianapolis, Indiana, USA, in 1948, the Four Freshmen were a ground-breaking vocal group who influenced the Hi-Lo's, the Beach Boys, Manhattan Transfer and countless other close-harmony outfits. The group originally consisted of lead vocalist Bob Flanigan (b. 22 August 1926, Greencastle, Indiana, USA), his cousins Ross Barbour (b. 31 December 1928, Columbus, Indiana, USA) and Don Barbour (b. 19 April 1929, Columbus, Indiana, USA, d. 5 October 1961), and Hal Kratzsch (b. Warsaw, Indiana, USA, d. 18 November 1970). Prior to the formation of the Four Freshmen, the Barbour brothers and Kratzsch, along with lead singer Marvin Pruitt, had been in a barbershop quartet called Hal's Harmonizers, each member playing an instrument. The same line-up formed a more jazz-oriented second group, called the Toppers, in 1948. Pruitt left that same year, at which point Flanigan returned from Florida, where he had spent the summer. Inspired by Mel Tormé's Mel-Tones, the new group, renamed the Four Freshmen, was discovered in September 1949 by Woody Herman.
In 1950 Stan Kenton saw the quartet in concert in Dayton, Ohio, and arranged for them to audition for Capitol Records, who signed them. Their first hit single came in 1952, 'It's A Blue World', which reached number 30 in the USA. Spring 1953 saw a personnel change when Kratzsch left, replaced by Ken Errair (b. 23 January 1930, d. 14 June 1968). Errair also departed in 1955, replaced by Ken Albers. By that time the group had logged two more Top 40 hits, 'It Happened Once Before' and 'Mood Indigo'. Three final chart singles were

issued in 1955-56, including the number 17 'Graduation Day', later covered by the Beach Boys. The group had seven album hits, including the Top 10 *Four Freshmen And 5 Trombones* in 1956 and *4 Freshmen And 5 Trumpets* the following year. Further personnel changes marked the group's career. Don Barbour left in 1960, replaced by Bill Comstock (who left in 1972). Ross Barbour stayed on until 1977 and Ken Albers in 1982. Flanigan remained with the group into the early 90s. Don Barbour was killed in a car crash in 1961, Kratzsch died of cancer in 1970 and Errair died in a plane crash in 1968. Flanigan continues to act as manager and agent for the present day line-up, who are able to reproduce the original sound almost note perfect. They won the *Down Beat* readers poll in 2000 for best vocal group, over 50 years since they were formed.
● ALBUMS: *Voices In Modern* (Capitol 1955) ★★★★, *Four Freshmen And 5 Trombones* (Capitol 1956) ★★★★, *Freshmen Favorites* (Capitol 1956) ★★★, *4 Freshmen And 5 Trumpets* (Capitol 1957) ★★★, *Four Freshmen And Five Saxes* (Capitol 1957) ★★★, *Voices In Latin* (Capitol 1958) ★★, *The Four Freshmen In Person* (Capitol 1958) ★★★, *Voices In Love* (Capitol 1958) ★★★, *Freshmen Favorites Volume 2* (Capitol 1959) ★★★, *Love Lost* (Capitol 1959) ★★, *The Four Freshmen And Five Guitars* (Capitol 1960) ★★, *Voices And Brass* (Capitol 1960) ★★, *Road Show* (Capitol 1960) ★★★, *First Affair* (Capitol 1960) ★★★, *Freshmen Year* (Capitol 1961) ★★, *Voices In Fun* (Capitol 1961) ★★, *Stars In Our Eyes* (Capitol 1962) ★★, *Got That Feelin'* (Capitol 1963) ★★, *More With 5 Trombones* (Capitol 1964) ★★★, *Time Slips Away* (Capitol 1964) ★★★, *Still Fresh* (Gold 1999) ★★★.
● COMPILATIONS: *The Best Of The Four Freshmen* (Capitol 1962) ★★★★, *The EP Collection* (See For Miles 2000) ★★★★.

FOUR KNIGHTS

The singing of Gene Alford was framed by the backing harmonies of Oscar Broadway, Clarence Dixon and John Wallace (who also strummed guitar). From regular performances in the late 40s on radio stations local to their native Charlotte, North Carolina, USA, the Knights graduated to television, providing musical interludes on nationally broadcast situation comedies starring Arthur Godfrey and Red Skelton. This exposure aided the combo's procurement of a Capitol contract and much airplay for their debut single, 1951's 'It's No Sin', on which Broadway's bass grumblings were conspicuous. In 1953, they reached the national hit parade with 'Oh Happy Day' – lush with orchestral accompaniment – and the following year, came up with the million-selling 'I Get So Lonely', a clever up-tempo reworking of a hillbilly ballad. After 'O Falling Star' slipped from the charts, the quartet teamed up with Nat 'King' Cole for a 1956 smash with 'That's All There Is To That' – and so it was for the Four Knights, who never had another hit.
● ALBUMS: *Spotlight Songs* (Capitol 1953/56) ★★★, *The Four Knights* (Coral 1959) ★★★, *Million $ Baby* (Coral 1960) ★★★.

FOUR LADS

The line-up comprised Frank Busseri (b. Toronto, Canada; baritone), Bernard Toorish (b. Toronto, Canada; second tenor), James Arnold (b. Toronto, Canada; first tenor) and Connie Codarini (b. Toronto, Canada; bass). A versatile vocal quartet, popular in US clubs and theatres, and on television and records, especially during the 50s. The Lads formed their group while attending St. Michael's Choir School in Toronto. Aided by 'Dad' Wilson, a member of the Golden Gate Quartet, the Lads played a try-out engagement at Le Ruban Bleu in New York, stayed for some 30 weeks, and then toured extensively. They were signed by Columbia Records as a background group, and in 1951 accompanied Johnnie Ray on his first big hit, 'Cry', which sold over two million copies. Their first solo success was in 1952 with 'Mocking Bird', followed by 'He Who Has Love', 'Down By The Riverside', 'Istanbul (Not Constantinople)', 'Gilly Gilly Ossenfeffer Katzenellen Bogen By The Sea' and 'Skokiaan', a South African song. In 1955 they had one of their biggest hits with 'Moments To Remember', written by Robert Allen and Al Stillman.

The songwriters also provided the Lads with several other successful singles such as 'No, Not Much', 'Who Needs You', 'Enchanted Island' and 'There's Only One Of You'. Allen and Stillman also contributed to Johnny Mathis' early success with numbers such as 'Chances Are' and 'It's Not For Me To Say'. Other Four Lads' US Top 20 entries, through until 1958, included 'The Bus Stop Song (A Paper Of Pins)', 'A House With Love In It', 'Put A Light In The Window' and 'Standing On The Corner', from Frank Loesser's Broadway show *The Most Happy Fella*. In 1957, the group recorded the album *The Four Lads Sing Frank Loesser*, which featured medleys from three of his successful scores: *Where's Charley?*, *Hans Christian Andersen* and *Guys And Dolls*. Other successful albums were their US Top 20 entry, *On The Sunny Side*, with the Claude Thornhill Orchestra, *Breezin' Along*, conducted by Ray Ellis and *Four On The Aisle*, a collection of extended medleys from the musical shows *Annie Get Your Gun*, *Babes In Arms* and *Kiss Me, Kate*. A modified version of the group continued to work in the following decades, with Arnold and Busseri performing with two new members. Toorish was to be found singing with the Vince Mastro Quartet, and later became an insurance underwriter. He reactivated the Four Lads following their induction into the Juno Awards Hall Of Fame in 1984, and continues to lead the group (of which he is the only remaining original member) on the oldies circuit.
● ALBUMS: *Stage Show* 10-inch album (Columbia 1954) ★★★, *On The Sunny Side* (Columbia 1956) ★★★★, *The Stingiest Man In Town* film soundtrack (Columbia 1956) ★★, *The Four Lads With Frankie Laine* (Columbia 1956) ★★★, *The Four Lads Sing Frank Loesser* (Columbia 1957) ★★★, *Breezin' Along* (Columbia 1959) ★★★★, *Four On The Aisle* (Columbia 1959) ★★★, *The Four Lads Swing Along* (Columbia 1959) ★★★, *High Spirits!* (Columbia 1959) ★★, *Love Affair* (Columbia 1960) ★★★, *Everything Goes* (Columbia 1960) ★★★, *Dixieland Doin's* (Columbia 1961) ★★★★, *Hits Of The 60's* (Columbia 1962) ★★★, *Oh, Happy Day* (Columbia 1963) ★★★, *This Year's Top Movie Hits* (Columbia 1964) ★★★, *Songs Of World War I* (Columbia 1964) ★★.
● COMPILATIONS: *The Four Lads' Greatest Hits* (Columbia 1958) ★★★★, *Twelve Hits* (Columbia 1961) ★★★★.

FOUR PREPS

Formed in the early 50s in Hollywood, California, USA, the Four Preps were a vocal group consisting of Bruce Belland, Glen Larson, Marvin Inabnett and Ed Cobb (d. 1999, Honolulu, Hawaii, USA). Recording for Capitol Records, they placed 13 singles in the US charts between 1956 and 1964, two of which made the Top 5 in 1958. The quartet began singing together during their high-school years, influenced by the Mills Brothers, Four Aces, and Four Freshmen acts. Impressed by a demo tape the group recorded Mel Shauer, manager of Les Paul And Mary Ford, took the group under his wing and arranged a recording contract with Capitol. Their first session, in late 1956, yielded 'Dreamy Eyes', which was a minor hit, but the follow-up, '26 Miles (Santa Catalina)', written by Belland and Larson years earlier, reached number 2, and their next single, 'Big Man', made number 3.

Subsequent singles failed to reach the US Top 10 although the group did achieve a Top 10 album, *Four Preps On Campus*, in 1961 during the height of the folk music revival in the USA. The group's final charting single, 1964's 'A Letter To The Beatles', parodied Beatlemania but was allegedly withdrawn from distribution by Capitol upon the request of the Beatles' management. The group continued until 1967. Cobb went on to join the group Piltdown Men, and later to produce such records as the Standells' 'Dirty Water'; he also wrote 'Tainted Love', a hit for Soft Cell in 1982. In 1988, the Four Preps were back on the road, with two of the original members, Belland and Cobb, being joined by David Somerville, former lead singer of the Diamonds and Jim Pike, founder of the Lettermen.
● ALBUMS: *The Four Preps* (Capitol 1958) ★★★★, *The Things We Did Last Summer* (Capitol 1958) ★★★★, *Dancing And Dreaming* (Capitol 1959) ★★★, *Early In The Morning* (Capitol 1960) ★★, *Those Good Old Memories* (Capitol 1960) ★★★, *Four Preps On Campus* (Capitol 1961) ★★★, *Campus Encore* (Capitol 1962) ★★★, *Campus Confidential* (Capitol 1963) ★★, *Songs For A Campus Party* (Capitol 1963) ★★, *How To Succeed In Love!* (Capitol 1964) ★★.
● COMPILATIONS: *Best Of The Four Preps* (Capitol 1967) ★★★★, *Capitol Collectors Series* (Capitol 1989) ★★★★.

FOUR TUNES

The Four Tunes, like many African-American groups of the 40s and early 50s, were a pop rather than a R&B ensemble. The group had its origin in the Brown Dots, and were formed by Ivory 'Deek'

Watson after he left the Ink Spots in 1945. The remainder of the group was Pat Best, Jimmy Gordon and Jimmy Nabbie. While still with the Brown Dots, Best, Gordon and Nabbie joined with Danny Owens in 1946 to record on the Manor label as the Sentimentalists, changing their name shortly afterwards to the Four Tunes. They backed Savannah Churchill on her 1947 hit 'I Want To Be Loved (But Only By You)', but did not attain any national hits of their own while with Manor. In 1948 they finally left the Brown Dots and a year later signed with RCA Records. Their two big chart hits came after they signed with Jubilee in 1953 with 'Marie' (number 2 R&B, number 13 pop) from 1953, and 'I Understand (Just How You Feel)' (number 7 R&B, number 6 pop) from 1954. The Four Tunes made their last recordings in 1956 and finally broke up in 1963. Their musical legacy was remembered in 1961 when the G-Clefs had a big hit with 'I Understand (Just How You Feel)' and in 1965 when the Bachelors had success with 'Marie'.
● ALBUMS: *The Four Tunes: 12 X 4* (Jubilee 1957) ★★★.
● COMPILATIONS: *The Complete Jubilee Sessions* (Sequel 1992) ★★★.

FRANCIS, CONNIE

b. Concetta Rosa Maria Franconero, 12 December 1938, Newark, New Jersey, USA. A popular singer of tearful ballads and jaunty up-tempo numbers, Francis was one of the most successful female artists of the 50s and 60s. She began playing the accordion at the age of four, and was singing and playing professionally when she was 11. After winning an *Arthur Godfrey Talent Show*, she changed her name, at Godfrey's suggestion. Signed for MGM Records in 1955, her first record was a German import, 'Freddy', which was also recorded by Eartha Kitt and Stan Kenton. 'Majesty Of Love', her 10th release, a duet with Marvin Rainwater, was her first US chart entry. In 1957 she was persuaded by her father, against her will, to record one of his favourites, the 1923 song 'Who's Sorry Now', by Harry Ruby, Bert Kalmar and Ted Snyder. It went to number 4 in the US charts and number 1 in the UK, and was the first of a string of hits through to 1962. These included reworkings of more oldies, such as 'My Happiness', 'Among My Souvenirs' and 'Together'. Among her more jaunty, upbeat songs were 'Stupid Cupid' (another UK number 1 coupled with 'Carolina Moon') and 'Where The Boys Are' by the new songwriting team of Neil Sedaka and Howard Greenfield. Her other US Top 10 entries included 'Lipstick On Your Collar', 'Frankie', 'Mama', 'Everybody's Somebody's Fool' (her first US number 1), 'My Mind Has A Heart Of Its Own' (another US number 1), 'Many Tears Ago', 'Breakin' In A Brand New Broken Heart', 'When The Boy In Your Arms (Is The Boy In Your Heart)', 'Don't Break The Heart That Loves You' (US number 1), 'Second Hand Love' and 'Vacation'. Francis made her film debut in 1960 with *Where The Boys Are*, and followed it with similar 'frothy' comedy musicals such as *Follow*

The Boys (1963), *Looking For Love* (1964) and *When The Boys Meet The Girls* (1965). Outdated by the 60s beat boom, she worked in nightclubs in the late 60s, and did much charity work for UNICEF and similar organizations, besides entertaining US troops in Vietnam. She also extended her repertoire, and kept her options open by recording albums in several languages, including French, Spanish and Japanese, and one entitled, *Connie Francis Sings Great Jewish Favorites*. Late 70s issues included more country music selections.

In 1974 she was the victim of a rape in her motel room after performing at the Westbury Theatre, outside New York. She later sued the motel for negligence, and was reputedly awarded damages of over three million dollars. For several years afterwards she did not perform in public, and underwent psychiatric treatment for long periods. She returned to the Westbury in 1981, to an enthusiastic reception, and resumed performing in the USA and abroad, including appearances at the London Palladium in 1989, and in Las Vegas in the same year, where she received a standing ovation after a mature performance ranging from her opening number, 'Let Me Try Again', to the climactic, 'If I Never Sing Another Song'. While at the Palladium, her speech became slurred and she was suspected of being drunk. In 1991 she had trouble speaking on a US television show, and, a year later, collapsed at a show in New Jersey. She was diagnosed as suffering from 'a complex illness', and of 'having been toxic for 18 years'. After drastically reducing her daily lithium intake, in 1993 she signed a new recording contract with Sony, buoyed up by the fact that her 1959 hit, 'Lipstick On Your Collar', was climbing high in the UK charts, triggered by its use as the title track of playwright Dennis Potter's television drama.

● ALBUMS: *Who's Sorry Now?* (MGM 1958) ★★★★, *The Exciting Connie Francis* (MGM 1959) ★★★★, *My Thanks To You* (MGM 1959) ★★★★, *Christmas In My Heart* (MGM 1959) ★★★, *Italian Favorites* (MGM 1960) ★★★, *More Italian Favorites* (MGM 1960) ★★★, *Rock 'N' Roll Million Sellers* (MGM 1960) ★★★, *Country And Western Golden Hits* (MGM 1960) ★★, *Spanish And Latin American Favorites* (MGM 1960) ★★★, *Connie Francis At The Copa* (MGM 1961) ★★, *Connie Francis Sings Great Jewish Favorites* (MGM 1961) ★★, *Songs To A Swingin' Band* (MGM 1961) ★★, *Never On Sunday And Other Title Songs From Motion Pictures* (MGM 1961) ★★★, *Folk Song Favorites* (MGM 1961) ★★★, *Do The Twist* (MGM 1962) ★★★, *Second Hand Love And Other Hits* (MGM 1962) ★★★, *Country Music Connie Style* (MGM 1962) ★★★, *Modern Italian Hits* (MGM 1963) ★★★, *Follow The Boys* film soundtrack (MGM 1963) ★★★, *German Favorites* (MGM 1963) ★★, *Award Winning Motion Picture Hits* (MGM 1963) ★★, *Great American Waltzes* (MGM 1963) ★★★, *In The Summer Of His Years* (MGM 1964) ★★★, *Looking For Love* film soundtrack (MGM 1964) ★★, with Hank Williams Jnr. *Great Country Favorites* (MGM 1964) ★★, *A New Kind Of Connie*

(MGM 1964) ★★★, *Connie Francis Sings For Mama* (MGM 1965) ★★★, *When The Boys Meet The Girls* film soundtrack (MGM 1965) ★★★, *Movie Greats Of The Sixties* (MGM 1966) ★★★, *Live At The Sahara In Las Vegas* (MGM 1966) ★★, *Love Italian Style* (MGM 1967) ★★★, *Happiness* (MGM 1967) ★★, *My Heart Cries For You* (MGM 1967) ★★★, *Hawaii Connie* (MGM 1968) ★★, *Connie And Clyde* (MGM 1968) ★★, *Connie Sings Bacharach And David* (MGM 1968) ★★★, *The Wedding Cake* (MGM 1969) ★★★, *Connie Francis Sings Great Country Hits, Volume Two* (MGM 1973) ★★, *Sings The Big Band Hits* (MGM 1977) ★★, *I'm Me Again – Silver Anniversary Album* (MGM 1981) ★★★, *Connie Francis And Peter Kraus, Volumes 1 & 2* (MGM 1984) ★★★, *Country Store* (MGM 1988) ★★, *Live At Trump's Castle* (Click 1996) ★★★.
● COMPILATIONS: *Connie's Greatest Hits* (MGM 1960) ★★★★, *More Greatest Hits* (MGM 1961) ★★★★, *Mala Femmena And Connie's Big Hits From Italy* (MGM 1963) ★★★, *The Very Best Of Connie Francis* (MGM 1963) ★★★★, *The All Time International Hits* (MGM 1965) ★★★★, *20 All Time Greats* (Polydor 1977) ★★★★, *Connie Francis In Deutschland* 8-LP box set (Bear Family 1988) ★★★★, *The Very Best Of Connie Francis* (Polydor 1988) ★★★, *The Singles Collection* (PolyGram 1993) ★★★, *White Sox, Pink Lipstick ... And Stupid Cupid* 5-CD box set (Bear Family 1993) ★★★★, *Souvenirs* 4-CD box set (Polydor/ Chronicles 1996) ★★★★, *On Guard With Connie Francis* (Jazz Band 1996) ★★★, *Where The Boys Are: Connie Francis In Hollywood* (Rhino/Turner 1997) ★★★, *Kissin' And Twistin': Going Where The Boys Are* 5-CD box set (Bear Family 1997) ★★★, *The Best Of Connie Francis: The Millennium Collection* (Polydor 1999) ★★★★.
● VIDEOS: *The Legend Live* (Prism Video 1990).
● FURTHER READING: *Who's Sorry Now?*, Connie Francis.
● FILMS: *Jamboree* aka *Disc Jockey Jamboree* (1957), *Where The Boys Are* (1960), *Follow The Boys* (1963), *Looking For Love* (1964), *When The Boys Meet The Girls* (1965).

FRANK SINATRA SINGS FOR ONLY THE LONELY – FRANK SINATRA
Asked to reveal the mood of this album prior to its release, Frank Sinatra (tongue-in-cheek) said: 'Put it this way – we discarded 'Gloomy Sunday' (the 'suicide' song) because it was too swingin'!' Bleak, it certainly is, but with the singer at the height of his powers singing a classy set of saloon songs, superbly arranged and conducted by Nelson Riddle, this is still the number 1 album of all time for many a Sinatra aficionado. Even in the 90s he was compelled to include one of the tracks, 'One For My Baby', complete with the distinctive piano introduction, in every concert performance. Even the album's cover, with its sad clown-face picture, won a Grammy Award.
● Tracks: *Only The Lonely; Angel Eyes; What's New?; It's A Lonesome Old Town; Willow Weep For Me; Good-bye; Blues In The Night; Guess I'll Hang My Tears Out To Dry; Ebb Tide; Spring Is Here; Gone With The Wind; One For My Baby.*

● First released 1958
● UK peak chart position: 5
● USA peak chart position: 1

FRANKLIN, C.L., REV.
b. Clarence LaVaughn Franklin, 22 January 1915, Sunflower County, Mississippi, USA, d. 24 July 1984. Although his own career was eclipsed by that of his daughter, Aretha Franklin, the Rev. C.L. Franklin was a popular religious recording artist in his own right. Franklin began singing in church at the age of 12 and began preaching two years later. He attended college and gained a ministerial degree, preaching in Mississippi, New York and Tennessee before being named pastor of the New Bethel Baptist Church in Detroit, Michigan, USA, in 1946. He began recording 78s featuring his sermons, for the J-V-B label in 1953, some of which were leased to Chess Records for more widespread distribution. He recorded over a dozen singles for the label. Each summer, daughter Aretha would accompany her father on the road, where he participated in gospel revues; much of her exposure to the gospel singing style came during those tours. In the 60s the Rev. Franklin became active in the civil rights movement and helped organize the 1963 March on Washington, at which Dr. Martin Luther King delivered his famous 'I have a dream' speech. Also the father of Erma Franklin and Carolyn Franklin, the Rev. Franklin was shot by burglars entering his home in 1979. He lapsed into a coma from which he never recovered.

FRANZ, JOHNNY
b. John Charles Franz, 23 February 1922, London, England, d. 29 January 1977, London, England. An extremely successful and highly regarded pianist, and A&R producer for Philips Records in the UK. Franz began to study the piano when he was 13, and two years later, he joined the music publishers Francis, Day and Hunter. In parallel with his day job, Franz worked in the evenings with artists such as Jack Jackson, George Elrick and Nat Allen. He also served as accompanist to harmonica soloist Ronald Chesney, on the latter's radio series. In 1940 Franz played the piano for the band singer Bernard Hunter's first stage appearance, at Collins Music Hall, and, by the late 40s, had established a reputation as one of the leading accompanists in Britain, working with Adelaide Hall, Benny Lee and visiting American star Vivian Blaine. One of his most enduring associations was with Anne Shelton, and they were part of an entertainment 'package' that was flown on a round trip of 1,500 miles to play three dates in the American zone of Nurembourg, West Germany, in 1950. Ironically, not long afterwards, Franz was a passenger in a Rapide small aircraft that up-ended on a runway in Jersey, and he was reluctant ever to fly again. In 1954, after spending 17 years with Francis, Day and Hunter, while also discovering and coaching new talent, Franz was appointed the A&R Manager of Philips Records in 1954. His previous background meant that he was ideally suited to the job. He was able to select

the right kind of material for his roster of artists, routine them, and explain to the musical arrangers precisely the sound that he wanted to hear on the finished records. Blessed with perfect pitch, he could also spot a clinker in the string section from the other side of the control room. In the late 50s Franz was responsible for the output of some of the most successful artists in the UK, such as Frankie Vaughan, Shirley Bassey, Harry Secombe, the Beverley Sisters, the Kaye Sisters, Robert Earl, Ronnie Carroll, Susan Maughan, Julie Rogers and, of course, Anne Shelton. It was his idea, when recording Shelton's 1956 chart-topper 'Lay Down Your Arms', to add the sound of martial marching feet by having one of the studio staff shuffle about in a sand tray. In complete contrast, he worked with the risqué American cabaret star Ruth Wallis, and also produced the sophisticated *Mel Tormé Meets The British*, which was arranged by Wally Stott, one of Franz's key conductor-arrangers along with Ivor Raymonde and Peter Knight. In the late 50s, Marty Wilde was at the forefront of Philips's assault on the charts, as Franz adapted to the radical musical changes that were happening all around him. Early in the 60s he nurtured the vocal instrumental group the Springfields, from which emerged one of the decade's superstars, Dusty Springfield, with a string of hits that included the million-sellers 'I Only Want To Be With You' (written by her musical director, Ivor Raymonde, with Mike Hawker) and 'You Don't Have To Say You Love Me'. The Four Pennies were another successful Franz act around that time, with their UK number 1 'Juliet'; so too were the Walker Brothers, who introduced the pop world to another 60s icon, Scott Walker. The sound that Franz created for Walker Brothers hits such as 'Make It Easy On Yourself', 'My Ship Is Coming In' and 'The Sun Ain't Gonna Shine Any More', is sometimes called 'Phil Spectorish'. This had shades of truth, although the two producers were very different in appearance and style: Franz could easily have been mistaken for a bank manager – albeit one who chain-smoked and devoured copious amounts of tea. As well as producing Scott Walker's chart hits 'Jackie', 'Joanna' and 'Lights Of Cincinnati', Franz's influence was also apparent on *Sings Songs From His T.V. Series*, which, with show numbers such as 'I Have Dreamed', 'The Song Is You' and 'If She Walked Into My Life', showed Walker to be a romantic balladeer of the old school. In a way, it was the 'old pals' act' that brought much of the best commercial material Franz's way. His contacts in the music publishing business, such as Cyril Shane, ensured that Philips were offered many potential hit songs, some of them from abroad. Dusty Springfield's 'I Only Want To Be With You' came to London from the 1965 San Remo Song Festival, and in 1973, Franz placed 'Welcome Home' ('Vivre'), a French number with an English lyric by Bryan Blackburn, with *Opportunity Knocks* winners Peters And Lee. It gave them a UK number 1, and they hit the top spot again in the same year with *We Can Make It*, the first of their four Top 10 albums in the 70s.

Among the most fondly remembered television and recording performers of the decade, the duo were a part of the final flourish in the life of a man who has been called 'the last of the great pro's'. Johnny Franz died in 1977 at the age of 55, in a Chelsea hospital.

FREBERG, STAN

b. Stanley Victor Freberg, 7 August 1926, Los Angeles, California, USA. Stan Freberg was a satirist who experienced great popularity during the early 50s in the USA. Freberg pioneered the style of satire and parody later used on such television programmes as *Saturday Night Live*. He performed on radio and television acted, wrote books as well as his own comedy material, worked in advertising and was even an accomplished puppeteer. Freberg grew up the son of a Baptist minister in Pasadena, California. His first showbusiness experience was at the age of 11 as an assistant to his uncle, a magician. Freberg became enthralled with the radio during his youth. As well as performing, he wrote and produced student shows and became his high school's speech champion, going on to win a statewide competition. He was awarded a drama scholarship but turned it down to work with Mel Blanc, who provided the voices of Warner Brothers cartoon characters such as Bugs Bunny and Porky Pig. Freberg provided voice-overs for other characters.

In the mid-40s he appeared on radio for the first time and soon became a regular on such programmes as the *Jack Benny Show* and on the Armed Forces Radio Network. He spent two years in the army and then joined a small orchestra, Red Fox And His Musical Hounds, as comedian, guitarist. He and actor Daws Butler (later the voice of Yogi Bear and Huckleberry Hound) then wrote and performed for the cartoon show *Time For Beany*, an Emmy-winning programme which served as inspiration to *Muppets* creator Jim Henson. In 1951 Freberg signed to Capitol Records and recorded 'John And Marsha', a spoof of soap operas in which the only lyrics were the two names of the title, repeated dramatically throughout the record. The record became a US hit, and was followed by parodies of Cole Porter's 'I've Got You Under My Skin', Johnnie Ray's 'Cry' and others. In 1953 Freberg scored a number 1 record with 'St. George And The Dragonet', a parody of the *Dragnet* television series.

As the rock 'n' roll era began in 1954 Freberg lampooned such hits as 'Sh-Boom' and 'The Great Pretender', with orchestration by Billy May, who remains Freberg's arranger, conductor in the 90s. In 1956 Freberg took on Elvis Presley's 'Heartbreak Hotel' and British skiffle artist Lonnie Donegan's 'Rock Island Line', while the following year found him satirizing Harry Belafonte's 'Banana Boat Day-O'. Other Freberg targets were Lawrence Welk, Mitch Miller and the television medium itself. In 1957 Freberg was given his own 17-week radio programme, some of which was collected on the Grammy-winning album *The Best Of The Stan Freberg Shows*. Freberg's 1958 single

'Green Chri\$tma\$' brilliantly attacked the commercialization of Christmas and was subsequently banned by many radio stations. His final chart hit, 1960's 'The Old Payola Roll Blues (Side 1)' was another controversial release. Freberg continued to release albums throughout the 60s, his most successful being 1961's *Stan Freberg Presents The United States Of America*. He remained active as an advertising writer in the 90s and still lends his voice to advertisement and voice-overs, and the occasional cartoon, such as the CBS television animation anthology *Toon Night* (1991).

● ALBUMS: *Comedy Caravan* (1956) ★★★★, *A Child's Garden Of Freberg* (Capitol 1957) ★★★★, *The Best Of The Stan Freberg Show* (Capitol 1958) ★★★★, *Stan Freberg With The Original Cast* (Capitol 1959) ★★★, *Presents The United States Of America* (Capitol 1961) ★★★★, *Face The Funnies* (Capitol 1962) ★★★, *Madison Avenue Werewolf* (Capitol 1962) ★★★★, *Mickey Mouse's Birthday Party* (Capitol 1963) ★★★, *Underground Show #1* (Capitol 1966) ★★★.

● COMPILATIONS: *The Best Of Stan Freberg* (Capitol 1964) ★★★★, *The Capitol Years* (Capitol 1989) ★★★★, *Capitol Collectors Series* (Capitol 1990) ★★★★, *The Tip Of The Freberg: The Stan Freberg Collection 1951-1998* 4-CD box set (Rhino 1999) ★★★.

● FURTHER READING: *It Only Hurts When I Laugh*, Stan Freberg.

FREED, ALAN

b. 15 December 1922, Johnstown, Pennsylvania, USA, d. 20 January 1965, Palm Springs, California, USA. Freed was one of several key individuals who helped to create the audience for rock 'n' roll. As an influential disc jockey, he made enemies among the music business establishment by championing the cause of black artists but his career ended tragically when he was found to be guilty of payola in 1962. The son of European immigrants, he played trombone in a high school band named the Sultans Of Swing. After US Army service, he secured his first radio job in 1946, playing classical records. He moved on to Akron, Ohio, to play contemporary pop material and in 1951 joined WJW Cleveland. There Freed hosted a show sponsored by local record store owner Leo Mintz, consisting of R&B originals rather than white pop cover versions. Entitled *Moondog's Rock 'N' Roll Party*, the show attracted large audiences of white teenagers who swamped a 1952 concert by the Moonglows, a group Freed had discovered and signed to his own short-lived Champagne label. A near riot at the Moondog Coronation Ball the same year resulted in pressure from the local authorities, and Freed moved to New York and WINS in 1953. He was stopped from using the Moondog title after litigation with the blind Manhattan street musician Moondog (Louis Hardin). Still a champion of black artists such as Chuck Berry and Fats Domino, Freed hosted major live shows at the Paramount Theatre and in 1956-58 appeared in the movies *Rock Around The Clock*, *Rock Rock Rock*, *Don't Knock The Rock* and *Go*

Johnny Go. However, with the rise of Bill Haley, Elvis Presley and Pat Boone (whose cover versions he frequently ignored), Freed's power as a disc jockey was weakened. In particular, he became a target of opponents of rock 'n' roll such as Columbia Records' A&R chief Mitch Miller, and when Freed refused to play Columbia releases he was fired by WINS. He then joined WABC and hosted a televised *Dance Party* show on WNEW-TV based on Dick Clark's *American Bandstand*. Freed's arrest on a charge of inciting a riot at a Boston concert left him ill prepared to deal with the accusations of payola levelled by a Congressional investigation in 1959. It emerged that independent labels had offered cash or publishing rights to Freed in return for the airplay they were denied by the prejudices of other radio stations. In 1962 Freed was found guilty of bribery and this was followed by charges of tax evasion. He died of uremic poisoning in January 1965.

● ALBUMS: *The Big Beat* 10-inch album (MGM 1956) ★★★, *Alan Freed's Rock 'N Roll Dance Party, Volume 1* (Coral 1956) ★★★, *Alan Freed's Rock 'N Roll Dance Party, Volume 2* (Coral 1956) ★★★, *Go Go Go – Alan Freed's TV Record Hop* (Coral 1957) ★★★, *Rock Around The Block* (Coral 1958) ★★★, *Alan Freed Presents The King's Henchmen* (Coral 1958) ★★★, *The Alan Freed Rock & Roll Show* (Brunswick 1959) ★★★, *Alan Freed's Memory Lane* (End 1962) ★★.

● FURTHER READING: *Big Beat Heat: Alan Freed And The Early Years Of Rock 'n' Roll*, John A. Jackson.

● FILMS: *Rock Around The Clock* (1956), *Don't Knock The Rock* (1956), *Rock Rock Rock* (1956), *Mister Rock And Roll* (1957), *Go Johnny Go* (1958).

FREEMAN, BOBBY

b. 13 June 1940, San Francisco, California, USA. Freeman is generally recognized as his home city's first rock 'n' roll star by virtue of 'Do You Want To Dance'. This 1958 smash hit was later immortalized by the Beach Boys and Cliff Richard. The singer enjoyed further success in 1964 with 'C'mon And Swim', a dance-craze novelty song produced, and co-written, by Sly Stone. Freeman later elected to pursue his singing career at a local topless club, but later appearances at the annual San Francisco Bay Area Music ('Bammy') awards showed him an able performer.

● ALBUMS: *Do You Wanna Dance?* (Jubilee 1958) ★★, *Twist With Bobby Freeman* (Jubilee 1962) ★★, *C'mon And S-W-I-M* (Autumn 1964) ★★, *The Lovable Style Of Bobby Freeman* (King 1965) ★★, *Get In The Swim With Bobby Freeman* (Josie 1965) ★★.

● COMPILATIONS: *The Best Of Bobby Freeman* (Sequel 1992) ★★★.

FREEMAN, ERNIE

b. 16 August 1922, Cleveland, Ohio, USA, d. 16 May 1981. A noted pianist, arranger and producer, Freeman enjoyed a series of minor hits during the late 50s and early 60s. His chart entries included 'Dumplins' (1957) and 'Indian Love Call' (1959), but his biggest success came with a cover version of Bill Justis' smash 'Raunchy'. Although the original reached the US Top 3, Freeman's interpretation peaked at number 12. He recorded as B. Bumble And The Stingers on all of this act's releases, bar 'Nut Rocker', before embarking on a successful session career. Freeman appeared on material by Frank Sinatra, Dean Martin and Connie Francis, and later became musical director with the Reprise Records label, a post he held for 10 years. Freeman retired during the 70s and died as the result of a heart attack.

● ALBUMS: *Ernie Freeman Plays Irving Berlin* (Imperial 1957) ★★, *Jivin' Around* (Imperial 1957) ★★★, *Ernie Freeman Plays: Dreaming With Freeman* (Imperial 1958) ★★★, *Dark At The Top Of The Stairs* (Imperial 1959) ★★★, *Twistin' Time* (Imperial 1960) ★★★, *The Stripper* (Imperial 1962) ★★, *Limbo Dance Party* (Liberty 1963) ★★, *Comin' Home, Baby* (Liberty 1963) ★★★, *Ernie Freeman Hit Maker* (Dunhill 1968) ★★.

● COMPILATIONS: *Raunchy: Ernie Freeman And His Combo* (Ace 1997) ★★★★.

FRIZZELL, LEFTY

b. William Orville Frizzell, 31 March 1928, Corsicana, Navarro County, Texas, USA, d. 19 July 1975, Nashville, Tennessee, USA. The eldest of eight children of an itinerant oilfield worker, Frizzell was raised mainly in El Dorado, Arkansas, but also lived in sundry places in Texas and Oklahoma. Greatly influenced by his parents' old 78s of Jimmie Rodgers, he sang as a young boy and when aged 12, he had a regular spot on KELD El Dorado. Two years later he was performing at local dances at Greenville and further exposure on other radio stations followed as the family moved around. At the age of 16, he was playing the honky tonks and clubs in places such as Waco and Dallas and grew into a tough character himself, performing the music of Jimmie Rodgers, plus some of his own songs. Some accounts suggest that it was at this time that he became known as Lefty after fighting in a Golden Gloves boxing match, but this appears to have been later publicity hype by Columbia Records. Both his father and his wife steadfastly denied the story, maintaining that Lefty actually gained the nickname when he beat the school bully during his schooldays. It is further claimed that it was a schoolfriend and guitarist called Gene Whitworth who first called him Lefty (he was actually always known as Sonny to his family).

In 1945, he was married, and his wife Alice became the inspiration for several of his songs over the 30 years the marriage lasted. More and more frequently, his drinking landed him in trouble with the authorities, and he was inspired to write his famous song, 'I Love You A Thousand Ways', while spending a night in a Texas country jail. He made his first recordings for Columbia in 1950, and had immediate success when 'If You've Got The Money, I've Got The Time' and 'I Love You A Thousand Ways' both became US country number 1 hits. He became close friends with Hank Williams, who suggested Frizzell should join the *Grand Ole Opry*. Frizzell replied, 'Look, I

got the number-one song, the number-two song, the number-seven song, the number-eight song on the charts and you tell me I need to join the *Opry*'; Williams thought for a while, and commented, 'Darned if you ain't got a hell of an argument'. The following year he had seven Top 10 entries, which included three more number 1 hits, 'I Want To Be With You Always' (which also gained Top 30 status in the US pop charts), 'Always Late (With Your Kisses)' and 'Give Me More More More (Of Your Kisses)'. Further Top 10s followed and as Merle Haggard later sang in his song 'The Way It Was in '51', 'Hank and Lefty crowded every jukebox'. In 1952, Frizzell did join the *Grand Ole Opry* but left after a few months, stating that he did not like it.

In 1953, Frizzell moved from Beaumont, Texas, to Los Angeles, where he became a regular on *Town Hall Party*. He had by now become accepted as a national entertainer and he recorded regularly, although the hits became less frequent. His hard-drinking lifestyle was partly to blame, and certainly he and Williams suffered similar troubles. Charles Wolfe quotes Frizzell as once saying: 'All Hank thought about was writing. He did record a number he wrote because I was having trouble with my better half, called 'I'm Sorry for You, My Friend'.' Some time later, the friendship between the two men was damaged when Frizzell refused to allow Williams to record 'What Am I Gonna Do With All This Love I Have For You', Frizzell intending to record it himself, although, for some reason, he never did so.

Lefty Frizzell became upset about material not being released by Columbia and in 1954, he broke up his band and stopped writing songs; tired of the way he had been exploited, his behaviour became more unpredictable. He was joined in California by his brother David Frizzell, and for a time they toured together. Eventually he charted again with his version of Marty Robbins' 'Cigarettes And Coffee Blues' and in 1959, he enjoyed a number 6 US country hit with 'The Long Black Veil'. The *Town Hall Party* had closed in 1960 and late in 1961, Frizzell decided to move to Nashville. He played bookings wherever he could and made further recordings, achieving minor hits that included 'Don't Let Her See Me Cry'. His career received a welcome boost in 1964 when 'Saginaw, Michigan' became a country number 1 and also entered the US pop charts. This song must rate as one of country music's finest ballads and Frizzell's version has rightly become a standard and worthy of a place in any collection. Twelve more chart entries followed between 1964 and 1972, but only 'She's Gone Gone Gone' reached the Top 20. In the late 60s, he became despondent that Columbia was not releasing his material; the label issued some albums but released few singles that were potential chart hits.

In 1968, he even recorded with June Stearns as Agnes And Orville but, concerned at the lack of promotion of his own material, his drinking worsened. In 1972, after 22 years with the label, he left Columbia and joined ABC Records. The change seemed to work wonders – he set about recording material for albums, resumed playing concerts all over the USA and appeared on network television. He charted with such songs as 'I Can't Get Over You To Change My Life', 'I Never Go Around Mirrors' and 'Railroad Lady', and his album releases proved very popular. His superb song 'That's The Way Love Goes' (his own recording was only issued as a b-side) became a US country number 1 for Johnny Rodriguez in 1974 and Merle Haggard in 1984. Frizzell developed high blood pressure, but refused to take medication to treat the condition since he thought the medicine would interfere with his alcohol consumption. Even in the depths of his drinking, he remained humorous, which led writer Bob Oermann to describe him as 'a loveable, punch-drunk, boozy, puddin'-headed, bear-like kind of a guy who never really got along with Nashville or the *Opry*'. He spent much time between concerts fishing at his home just outside Nashville. He was 47 (although he looked older), and aside from the blood pressure, seemed to be in reasonable health. It therefore came as a surprise to most when, on the morning of 19 July 1975, he suffered a massive stroke and died later that evening of the resulting haemorrhage.

Lefty Frizzell was a great songwriter and one of the best stylists that the world of country music has ever seen. His singing was distinctive, with a unique style of pronunciation and a laid-back delivery and gentle vibrato that may have appeared lazy, but was in fact part of a carefully designed pattern that he alone mastered. The bending of words as emphasized in 'Alway-yayys Lay-yate' (Always Late) and similar songs led to him being described as a genius for phrasing. John Pugh once described his singing as 'a compelling, ethereal, transcendent vocal quality that has produced some of the most hauntingly beautiful sounds ever to emanate from a pair of human vocal chords'. His influence is evident on later performers such as Merle Haggard, John Anderson, Stoney Edwards, Randy Travis and George Strait, who, although not perhaps intentionally trying to imitate their mentor, are readily identifiable as students of Frizzell. Since his death many artists have recorded tribute songs, while some have even recorded complete albums, including Willie Nelson (*To Lefty From Willie*) and brother David Frizzell (*David Sings Lefty*). Lefty Frizzell was elected to the Nashville Songwriters' Association International Hall Of Fame in 1972 and inducted into the Country Music Hall Of Fame in 1982.

● ALBUMS: *The Songs Of Jimmie Rodgers* 10-inch album (Columbia 1951) ★★★★, *Listen To Lefty* 10-inch album (Columbia 1952) ★★★★, shared with Carl Smith and Marty Robbins *Carl, Lefty & Marty* (Columbia 1956) ★★★★, *The One And Only Lefty Frizzell* (Columbia 1959) ★★★★, *Lefty Frizzell Sings The Songs Of Jimmie Rodgers* (Harmony 1960) ★★★★, *Saginaw, Michigan* (Columbia 1964) ★★★, *The Sad Side Of Love* (Columbia 1965) ★★★, *Lefty Frizzell's Country Favorites* (Harmony 1966) ★★★, *Lefty Frizzell Puttin' On* (Columbia 1967) ★★★, *Mom And Dad's Waltz (& Other Great Country Hits)*

(Harmony 1967) ★★★, *Signed Sealed And Delivered* (Columbia 1968) ★★★, *The Legendary Lefty Frizzell* aka *Lefty* (ABC 1973) ★★★, *The Legend Lives On* (Columbia 1983) ★★★, *The Legendary Last Sessions* (MCA 1986) ★★★ *Lefty Goes To Nashville* (Rounder 1988) ★★★.

● COMPILATIONS: *Lefty Frizzell's Greatest Hits* (Columbia 1966) ★★★★, *Remembering ... The Greatest Hits Of Lefty Frizzell* (Columbia 1975) ★★★, *The ABC Collection* (ABC 1977) ★★★★, *Treasures Untold: The Early Recordings Of Lefty* (Rounder 1980) ★★★, *Lefty Frizzell* (Columbia Historic Edition 1982) ★★★, *American Originals* (Columbia 1990) ★★★, *The Best Of Lefty Frizzell* (Rhino 1991) ★★★★, *His Life – His Music* 14-LP box set (Bear Family 1984) ★★★★ reissued as *Life's Like Poetry* 12-CD box set (Bear Family 1992) ★★★★, *That's The Way Love Goes: The Final Recordings Of Lefty Frizzell* (Varèse Sarabande 1997) ★★★, *Look What Thoughts Will Do: The Essential, 1950-1963* (Columbia 1997) ★★★★.

● FURTHER READING: *Lefty Frizzell His Life – His Music*, Charles Wolfe. *The Honky Tonk Life Of Country Music's Greatest Singer*, Daniel Cooper.

FULLER, JESSE 'LONE CAT'

b. 12 March 1896, Jonesboro, Georgia, USA, d. 29 January 1976, Oakland, California, USA. A veteran of tent shows, Fuller fashioned himself a unique one-man band of six-string bass (played with his right foot), a combination of kazoo, harmonica and microphone fixed to a harness around his neck, a hi-hat cymbal (played with the left foot) and a 12-string guitar. Fuller was also known for preceding many of his songs with a spoken intro. He came to fame in the late 50s as a result of appearances on US television, where he followed Ramblin' Jack Elliot's lionization via his recording of 'San Francisco Bay Blues'. In the 50s he made three albums of original and traditional material and by the mid-60s became a darling of the 'coffee-house circuit' after Bob Dylan cited him as one of his influences. Similar success followed in the UK resulting from Donovan's performance of 'San Francisco Bay Blues' on UK Independent Television's *Ready, Steady, Go!* music show in 1965. Although Fuller's output was meagre, his influence has been considerable. Eric Clapton provoked renewed interest with an excellent version of 'San Francisco Bay Blues' on his *MTV Unplugged* album in 1992. Original Blues Classics have reissued his albums on CD with the original covers. Although often repetitive his originality is irresistible.

● ALBUMS: *Workin' On The Railroad* 10-inch album (World Songs 1954) ★★★, *Frisco Bound* (Cavalier 1955/58) ★★★★, *Jazz, Folk Songs, Spirituals & Blues* (Good Time Jazz 1958) ★★★★, *The Lone Cat* (Good Time Jazz 1961) ★★★★, *San Francisco Bay Blues* (Folklore 1964) ★★★★, *Favorites* (Stateside 1965) ★★★★, *Move On Down The Line* (Topic 1965) ★★★.

FULSON, LOWELL

b. 31 March 1921, Tulsa, Oklahoma, USA, d. 6 March 1999, Los Angeles, California, USA. Blues guitarist Lowell Fulson (whose surname was often mistakenly misspelled Fulsom) recorded steadily from 1946 onwards, and performed regularly on the US and European club circuits into the 90s. One of the founding fathers of West Coast blues, Fulson blended the rural blues of his home state with the modern sounds of urban California. Fulson was raised in Atoka, close to the Texas border, and began his career performing with string bands and backing country blues vocalist Alger 'Texas' Alexander in the late 30s. During World War II he was stationed in Oakland, California, where he met record producer Bob Geddins. Following his discharge from the US Navy, Fulson recorded for several labels under the direction of Geddins, including Big Town, Down Town, Gilt Edge and Trilon. His first hit came in 1950 on the Swing Time label when he reworked Memphis Slim's 'Nobody Loves Me' into 'Every Day I Have The Blues'. At that time his 12-piece orchestra included a young Ray Charles on piano and tenor saxophonist Stanley Turrentine.

Fulson recorded for Aladdin Records in 1953 and then switched to Checker Records, a subsidiary of Chess Records, the following year. His first side for that company, 'Reconsider Baby', was later covered by Elvis Presley and became a blues standard. Fulson stayed with Checker Records into the early 60s and then moved to Kent Records, who changed the spelling of his name. Now recording in a more contemporary and commercial soul-blues vein, Fulson's biggest hits for Kent were 'Black Nights' in 1965 and 'Tramp' a year later. The latter song, co-written with Jimmy McCracklin, was later a duet hit for Otis Redding and Carla Thomas. In 1968 Fulson signed with Jewel Records and then recorded for a succession of small labels including Crazy Cajun and Granite. He reappeared on the international circuit in the mid-80s, his sound and voice seemingly undiminished by the passing years. By the early 90s his early work often appeared on reissues, while much of his new material was only released on minor labels, such as France's Blue Phoenix Records. However, in 1993 the artist received five W.C. Handy Awards, and was inducted into the Blues Hall Of Fame, both for himself and his song, 'Reconsider Baby'. He continued working up until 1997. An excellent remastered and expanded version of *I've Got The Blues* was released in 2001.

● ALBUMS: *In A Heavy Bag* (Jewel 1965) ★★★★, *I've Got The Blues* (Jewel 1965) ★★★★, *Lowell Fulson* (Kent 1965) ★★★★, *Soul* (Kent 1966) ★★★★, *Tramp* (Kent 1967) ★★★, *Lowell Fulson Now!* (Kent 1969) ★★★, *Let's Go Get Stoned* (United Artists 1971) ★★★, *The Ol' Blues Singer* (Jet 1976) ★★★, *Lovemaker* (Big Town 1978) ★★★, *Think Twice Before You Speak* (JSP 1984) ★★★, *Blue Days, Black Nights* (Ace 1986) ★★★, *I Don't Know My Mind* (Bear Family 1987) ★★★, *Baby Won't You Jump With Me* (Crown Prince 1988) ★★★, *Hold On* (Bullseye 1993) ★★★, *Them Update Blues* (Bullseye 1995) ★★★, *Blue Shadows* 1981 recording (Stony Plain 1998) ★★★.

● COMPILATIONS: *Man Of Motion* (Charly 1981) ★★★, *Everyday I Have The Blues* (Night Train 1984) ★★★★, *Lowell Fulson 1946-57* (Blues Boy 1987) ★★★, *San Francisco Blues* (Black Lion 1993) ★★★, *Reconsider Baby* (Charly 1993) ★★★, *Sinner's Prayer* (Night Train 1996) ★★★★, *The Complete Chess Masters* (MCA/Chess 1998) ★★★★, *The Crazy Cajun Recordings* (Crazy Cajun 1998) ★★★, *I've Got The Blues (... And Then Some!): The Jewel Recordings 1969-71* (Westside 2001) ★★★.

G-CLEFS

This US doo-wop-styled vocal group consisted of brothers Teddy, Chris, Timmy and Arnold Scott and friend Ray Gibson, all from Roxbury, Massachusetts, USA. The quintet, who began singing gospel, were spotted by Pilgrim Records' Jack Gould and in 1956 their first release, 'Ka-Ding-Dong' (on which Freddy Cannon is reputed to have played guitar), reached the R&B Juke Box Top 10 and the US Top 40 pop chart. It probably would have been a bigger hit but for cover versions by two name acts, the Diamonds and Hilltoppers. Following another release on Pilgrim and two on Paris they decided to put their singing careers on ice and finish their schooling. After the youngest member Arnold left school in 1960 they re-formed and, with help from Gould, joined Terrace Records. Their first release, a version of the Four Tunes' song 'I Understand' cleverly combined with the chorus of 'Auld Lang Syne', gave them their only US Top 10 entry and five months later (around New Year) their sole UK Top 20 hit. The follow-up 'A Girl Has To Know' charted, but later releases including ones on Loma, Regina and Veep brought them no further success. Freddie And The Dreamers had a UK Top 5 hit with a version of their arrangement of 'I Understand' in 1964.

GARLAND, JUDY

b. Frances Ethel Gumm, 10 June 1922, Grand Rapids, Minnesota, USA, d. 22 June 1969, Chelsea, London, England. The Gumms were a theatrical family. Parents Frank and Ethel had appeared in vaudeville as Jack and Virginia Lee, and later, with the addition of their first two daughters, Mary Jane and Virginia, they appeared locally as 'The Four Gumms'. 'Baby Frances' joined the troupe when she was just over two years of age, and it was quickly apparent that with her arrival, even at that early age, the Gumm family had outgrown their locale. The family moved to Los Angeles, where all three girls were enrolled in a dance school. When Frank Gumm bought a run-down theatre in Lancaster, a desert town north of Los Angeles, the family moved again. Domestic problems beset the Gumm family throughout this period and Frances' life was further disrupted by Ethel Gumm's determined belief in her youngest daughter's showbusiness potential. The act had become the Gumm Sisters, although Baby Frances was clearly the one audiences wanted to see and hear. In 1933 Ethel Gumm returned to Los Angeles, taking the girls with her. Frances was again enrolled in a theatrical school.

A visit to Chicago was an important step for the girls, with the youngest once more attracting the most attention; here too, at the urging of comedian George Jessell, they changed their name to the Garland Sisters. On their return to Los Angeles in 1934 the sisters played a successful engagement at Grauman's Chinese Theater in Hollywood. Soon afterwards, Frances was personally auditioned by Louis B. Mayer, head of MGM. Deeply impressed by what he saw and heard, Mayer signed the girl before she had even taken a screen test. With another adjustment to her name, Frances became Judy Garland. She made her first notable film appearance in *Every Sunday* (1936), a short musical film that also featured Deanna Durbin. Her first major impact on audiences came with her third film, *Broadway Melody Of 1938*, in which she sang 'Dear Mr Gable' (to a photograph of Clark Gable), segueing into 'You Made Me Love You'. She was then teamed with MGM's established child star Mickey Rooney, a partnership that brought a succession of popular films in the 'Andy Hardy' series. By now, everyone at MGM knew that they had a star on their hands. This fact was triumphantly confirmed with her appearance in *The Wizard Of Oz* (1939), in which she sang 'Over The Rainbow', the song with which she would subsequently always be associated. Unfortunately, this period of frenzied activity came at a time when she was still developing physically.

Like many young teenagers, she tended to put on weight, which was something film-makers could not tolerate. Undoubtedly, they did not want a podgy celebrity, and continuity considerations could not allow their star to change appearance during the course of the film. Regardless of the reason, she was prescribed some drugs for weight control, others to ensure she was bright and perky for the long hours of shooting, and still more to bring her down at the end of the day so that she could sleep. This was long before the side effects of amphetamines (which she took to suppress her appetite) were understood, and no one at the time was aware that the pills she was consuming in such huge quantities were highly addictive. Added to the growing girl's problems were emotional difficulties that had begun during her parents' stormy relationship and were exacerbated by the pressures of her new life. In 1941, against the wishes and advice of her mother and the studio, she married David Rose and soon afterwards became pregnant, but was persuaded by her mother and Mayer to have an abortion. With her personal life already on a downward spiral, Garland's successful film career conversely took a further upswing. In 1942 she appeared in *For Me And My Gal*, then made *Presenting Lily Mars*, *Thousands Cheer*, *Girl Crazy* (all 1943), *Meet Me In St. Louis* (1944), *The Harvey Girls*, *Ziegfeld Follies* and *Till The Clouds Roll By* (all 1946). Garland's popularity extended beyond films into radio and records, but her private life was still in disarray.

In 1945 she divorced Rose and married Vincente Minnelli, who had directed her in *Meet Me In St Louis*. In 1946 her daughter, Liza Minnelli, was born. The late 40s brought more film successes with *The Pirate*, *Easter Parade*, *Words And Music* (all 1948) and *In The Good Old Summertime* (1949). Although Garland's career appeared to be in splendid shape, in 1950 her private life was fast deteriorating. Pills, alcohol and severe emotional disturbances led to her failing to appear before the cameras on several occasions and resulted in the ending of her contract with MGM. In 1951 her marriage to Minnelli also dissolved and she attempted suicide. Her subsequent marriage to Sid Luft and his handling of her career brought an upturn both emotionally and professionally. She made a trip to Europe, appearing at the London Palladium to great acclaim. On her return to the USA she played the Palace Theater in New York for a hugely successful 19-week run. Her film career resumed with a dramatic/singing role in *A Star Is Born* (1954), for which she was nominated for an Oscar. By the late 50s, her problems had returned, and in some cases, had worsened. She suffered nervous and emotional breakdowns, and made further suicide attempts. A straight dramatic role in *Judgement At Nuremberg* (1961), for which she was again nominated for an Oscar, enhanced her reputation. However, her marriage was in trouble, although she and Luft made repeated attempts to hold it together (they had two children, Lorna and Joey).

Despite the personal traumas and the professional ups and downs, Garland achieved another huge success with a personal appearance at New York's Carnegie Hall on 23 April 1961, the subsequent album of the concert winning five Grammy Awards. A 1963 television series was disappointing and, despite another good film performance in a dramatic role in *A Child Is Waiting*, and a fair dramatic/singing appearance in *I Could Go On Singing* (both 1963), her career remained plagued with inconsistencies. The marriage with Luft ended in divorce, as did a subsequent marriage. Remarried again in 1969, Garland attempted a comeback in a season at London's Talk Of The Town nightclub, but suffered the indignity of having bread sticks and other objects thrown at her when she turned up late for some performances. On 22 June 1969 she was found dead, apparently from an accidental overdose of sleeping pills. She was at her best in such films as *Meet Me In St. Louis* and *The Wizard Of Oz* and on stage for the superb Carnegie Hall concert, and had she done nothing else, she would have earned a substantial reputation as a major singing star. To her powerful singing voice she added great emotional depths, which came not only through artifice but from the often cruel reality of her life. When the catalogue of personal tragedies was added to Garland's performing talent she became something else, a cult figure, and a showbusiness legend. She was a figure that only Hollywood could have created and yet, had she been a character in a melodrama, no one would have believed such a life was possible.

● ALBUMS: *Till The Clouds Roll By* film soundtrack (MGM 1950/55) ★★★, *Easter Parade* film soundtrack (MGM 1950/55) ★★★, *Words And Music* film soundtrack (MGM 1950/55) ★★★, *Summer Stock/The Pirate* film soundtracks (MGM 1950/55) ★★★, *Judy Garland Sings* (MGM 1951) ★★★, *Judy At The Palace* (Decca 1951) ★★★, *The Wizard Of Oz* (Decca 1951) ★★★★★, *Girl Crazy* film soundtrack (Decca 1953) ★★★, *If You Feel Like Singing Sing* (MGM 1955) ★★★, *Judy Garland's Greatest Performances* (Decca 1955) ★★★, *Miss Show Business* (Capitol 1955) ★★★, *Judy Garland With The MGM Orchestra* (MGM 1956) ★★★, *The Wizard Of Oz* (MGM 1956) ★★★★, *Judy* (Capitol 1956) ★★★, *Meet Me In St Louis/The Harvey Girls* film soundtracks (Decca 1957) ★★★, *Alone* (Capitol 1957) ★★★, *A Star Is Born* (Columbia 1958) ★★★★, *Judy In Love* (Capitol 1958) ★★★, *In Love* (Capitol 1958) ★★★, *Garland At The Grove* (Capitol 1959) ★★★, with John Ireland *The Letter* (Capitol 1959) ★★★, *Judy! That's Entertainment* (Capitol 1960) ★★★, *Judy At Carnegie Hall* (Capitol 1961) ★★★★★, *Pepe* film soundtrack (Colpix 1961) ★★, *The Star Years* (MGM 1961) ★★★, *The Magic Of Judy Garland* (Decca 1961) ★★★, *The Hollywood Years* (MGM 1962) ★★★, *Gay Purr-ee* film soundtrack (Warners 1962) ★★, *The Garland Touch* (Capitol 1962) ★★★, *I Could Go On Singing* film soundtrack (Capitol 1963) ★★★★, *Our Love Letter* (Capitol 1963) ★★★, *Just For Openers* (Capitol 1964) ★★★, with Liza Minnelli *'Live' At The London Palladium* (Capitol 1965) ★★★★, *Judy Garland* (1965) ★★★, *Judy Garland At Home At The Palace* (ABC 1967) ★★★, *The Last Concert 20-7-68* (Paragon 1984) ★★★, *Judy Garland Live!* recorded 1962 (Capitol 1989) ★★★, *Judy Garland On Radio: 1936-44, Volume One* (Vintage Jazz Classics 1993) ★★★.

● COMPILATIONS: *The Very Best Of Judy Garland* (MGM 1962) ★★★, *The Hits Of Judy Garland* (Capitol 1963) ★★★★, *The Best Of Judy Garland* (Decca 1964) ★★★, *The Judy Garland DeLuxe Set* 3-LP box set (Capitol 1957) ★★★★, *The ABC Years* (ABC 1976) ★★★, *The Young Judy Garland 1938-42* (MCA 1983) ★★★, *Golden Greats* (MCA 1985) ★★★, *Collection* (Castle 1986) ★★★, *The Capitol Years* (Capitol 1989) ★★★★, *Great MGM Stars* (MGM 1991) ★★★, *The One And Only* 3-CD box set (Capitol 1991) ★★★, *The Complete Decca Masters (Plus)* 4-CD box set (MCA 1994) ★★★★, *Child Of Hollywood* (CDS 1994) ★★★, *Collectors' Gems From The M-G-M Films* (R2 1997) ★★★, *The Best Of Judy Garland* (Half Moon 1998) ★★★, *Over The Rainbow: The Very Best Of Judy Garland* (MCA 2001) ★★★★.

● VIDEOS: *Best Of Judy Garland* (World Of Video 1988), *Judy Garland In Concert* (RCA/Columbia 1988).

● FURTHER READING: *Judy: The Films And Career Of Judy Garland*, Joe Morella and Edward Epstein. *The Other Side Of The Rainbow: With Judy Garland On The Dawn Patrol*, Mel Tormé. *Weep No More, My Lady: An Intimate Biography Of Judy Garland*, Mickey Deans. *Judy With Love*, Lorna Smith. *Judy*, Gerold Frank. *Rainbow: The Stormy Life Of Judy Garland*, Christopher Finch. *Judy Garland: A Mortgaged Life*, Anne Edwards. *Little Girl Lost: The Life And Hard Times Of Judy Garland*, Al DiOrio. *The Young Judy*, David Dahl and Barry Kehoe. *Judy & Liza*, James Spada and Karen Swenson. *Judy: Portrait Of An American Legend*,

Thomas J. Watson and Bill Chapman. *The Complete Judy Garland*, Emily R. Coleman. *Rainbow's End: The Judy Garland Show*, Coyne Stephen Sanders. *Judy Garland*, David Shipman. *Me And My Shadows: Living With The Legacy Of Judy Garland*, Lorna Luft.
● FILMS: *The Big Revue* aka *Starlet Revue* (1929), *Pigskin Parade* aka *Harmony Parade* (1936), *Every Sunday* (1936), *Broadway Melody Of 1938* (1937), *Thoroughbreds Don't Cry* (1937), *Love Finds Andy Hardy* (1938), *Everybody Sing* (1938), *Listen, Darling* (1938), *The Wizard Of Oz* (1939), *Babes In Arms* (1939), *Andy Hardy Meets Debutante* (1940), *Strike Up The Band* (1940), *Little Nellie Kelly* (1940), *If I Forgot About You* (1940), *Life Begins For Andy Hardy* (1941), *Ziegfeld Girl* (1941), *Babes On Broadway* (1941), *For Me And My Gal* (1942), *We Must Have Music* (1942), *Thousands Cheer* (1943), *Presenting Lily Mars* (1943), *Girl Crazy* aka *When The Girls Meet The Boys* (1943), *Meet Me In St. Louis* (1944), *The Clock* aka *Under The Clock* (1945), *Ziegfeld Follies* (1946), *The Harvey Girls* (1946), *Till The Clouds Roll By* (1947), *Easter Parade* (1948), *Words And Music* (1948), *The Pirate* (1948), *In The Good Old Summertime* (1949), *Moments In Music* (1950), *Summer Stock* (1950), *A Star Is Born* (1954), *Pepe* (1960), *Judgement At Nuremberg* (1961), *Gay Purr-ee* voice only (1962), *A Child Is Waiting* (1963), *I Could Go On Singing* (1963).

GARNER, ERROLL

b. Erroll Louis Garner, 15 June 1921, Pittsburgh, Pennsylvania, USA, d. 2 January 1977, Los Angeles, California, USA. A self-taught pianist, Garner played on the radio at the age of 10 and within a few more years was playing professionally in his home-town. Among the bands with which he played during this period were those led by Leroy Brown and, reputedly, Fate Marable. In 1944 Garner moved to New York and began working in nightclubs, including the Rendezvous and the Melody Bar. He became a popular and successful performer in these establishments, but also enjoyed playing at the more jazz-orientated venues along 52nd Street, such as Tondelayo's and the Three Deuces. For a short time, he worked in a trio led by Slam Stewart, but soon formed his own trio.
For the rest of his life, with only occasional exceptions, Garner worked as leader of a trio or as a soloist. Throughout the 50s, 60s and early 70s, he toured the USA, playing prestigious club and hotel engagements, appearing at festivals and on radio and television. He also visited Europe and the UK, where he appeared on television, and in 1962 he had an album in the UK charts. During these years, Garner recorded numerous albums, some of them, such as the classic *Concert By The Sea*, becoming virtual fixtures in the catalogue. Although Garner taught himself to play, he never learnt to read music, yet he contrived to create several jazz tunes, including one, 'Misty', that became a standard when Johnny Burke added a lyric. Slight echoes of the full sound of Earl 'Fatha' Hines occasionally appear in Garner's playing, as do touches that suggest he had absorbed the work

of the stride piano players, yet throughout the bulk of his vast output, Garner remains unique. Playing consistently to a very high standard, he developed certain characteristics that bear few resemblances to other pianists. Notably, these include a plangent left-hand, block-chorded pulse, a dancing pattern of seemingly random ideas played with the right hand in chords or single notes, and playful introductions, which appear as independent miniature compositions, only to sweep suddenly, with apparent spontaneity and complete logic, into an entirely different song. Sumptuously romantic on ballads, and fleet and daring on up-tempo swingers, Garner's range was wide. Nicknamed 'The Elf', more, perhaps, for his diminutive stature than for the impish good humour of those introductions, Garner was the first jazz pianist since Fats Waller to appeal to the non-jazz audience, and the first jazzman ever to achieve popular acclaim from this audience without recourse to singing or clowning. Dudley Moore acknowledges much of his style to Garner, and 'swinging 60s piano jazz' owes a massive debt to him. Stylistically, Garner is in a category of which he is, so far, the only true member. Since his death in January 1977, there has been no sign that any other pianist other than Keith Jarrett is following his independent path in jazz.
● ALBUMS: *Free Piano Improvisations Recorded By Baron Timme Rosenkrantz At One Of His Famous Gaslight Jazz Sessions* reissued as *Early Erroll* (Dial 1949), ★★★ *Piano Moods* (Columbia 1950) ★★, *Rhapsody* (Atlantic 1950) ★★, *Erroll Garner Volume 1* (Dial 1950) ★★★, *Erroll Garner Playing Piano Solos, Volume 1* (Savoy 1950) ★★★, *Erroll Garner Playing Piano Solos, Volume 2* (Savoy 1950) ★★★, *Erroll Garner Playing Piano Solos, Volume 3* (Savoy 1950) ★★★, *Erroll Garner Playing Piano Solos, Volume 4* (Savoy 1951) ★★★, *Gone With Garner* (Mercury 1951) ★★★, *Gems* (Columbia 1951) ★★, *Erroll Garner At The Piano* (Mercury 1951) ★★★, *Erroll Garner At The Piano* (Atlantic 1951) ★★★, *Passport To Fame* (Atlantic 1952) ★★★, *Solo Flight* (Columbia 1952) ★★★, *Piano Solos Volume 2* (Atlantic 1952) ★★★, *Overture To Dawn Volume 1* (Blue Note 1952) ★★★★, *Overture To Dawn Volume 2* (Blue Note 1952) ★★★★, *Piano Stylist* reissued as *Piano Variations* (King 1952) ★★★, *Separate Keyboards* (Savoy 50s) ★★, *Long Ago And Far Away* (Columbia 50s) ★★★, *Erroll Garner At The Piano* (Savoy 1953) ★★★, *Erroll Garner At The Piano* (Columbia 1953) ★★★, *Overture To Dawn Volume 3* (Blue Note 1953) ★★★, *Overture To Dawn Volume 4* (Blue Note 1953) ★★★, *Overture To Dawn Volume 5* (Blue Note 1953) ★★★, *Erroll Garner Plays For Dancing* (Columbia 1953) ★★★, *Body And Soul* (Columbia 1953) ★★★★, *Mambo Moves Garner* (Mercury 1954) ★★, *Solitaire* (Mercury 1954) ★★★, *Garnering* (EmArcy 1954) ★★★★, *Contrasts* (EmArcy 1954) ★★★, *Afternoon Of An Elf* (Mercury 1955) ★★, *Garnerland* (Columbia 1955) ★★★, *Penthouse Serenade* (Savoy 1955) ★★★, *Serenade To Laura* (Savoy 1955) ★★★, *Gone Garner Gonest* (Columbia 1955) ★★★, *Erroll!* (EmArcy 1956) ★★★★, *The Greatest Garner* (Atlantic 1956) ★★★★, *He's Here! He's Gone! He's*

Garner (Columbia 1956) ★★★, Concert By The Sea (Columbia 1956) ★★★★★, with Art Tatum Giants Of The Piano (Roost 1956) ★★★, Most Happy Piano (Columbia 1957) ★★★, Other Voices (Columbia 1957) ★★, Soliloquy (Columbia 1957) ★★★, Erroll Garner (Ron-lette 1958) ★★★, Encores In Hi-Fi (Columbia 1958) ★★★, Paris Impressions (Columbia 1958) ★★★★, Paris Impressions Volume 2 (Columbia 1958) ★★★★, Perpetual Motion (Atlantic 1959) ★★★, The One And Only Erroll Garner (Columbia 1960) ★★★, Swinging Solos (Columbia 1960) ★★★, Dreamstreet (ABC-Paramount 1961) ★★★, The Provocative Erroll Garner (Columbia 1961) ★★★★, Closeup In Swing (ABC-Paramount 1961) ★★★, Informal Piano Improvisations (Baronet 1962) ★★★, Misty (Mercury 1962) ★★★★, The Concert Garner In England (1963) ★★★★, One World Concert (Reprise 1963) ★★★, Seeing Is Believing (Mercury 1964) ★★★, A Night At The Movies (1965) ★★★, Now Playing (MGM 1966) ★★★, Campus Concert (MGM 1966) ★★★, That's My Kick (MGM 1967) ★★★, Up In Erroll's Room (MGM 1967) ★★★, Feeling Is Believing (Mercury 1969) ★★★.
● COMPILATIONS: Historical First Recordings (1944) ★★★★, Overture To Dawn (1944) ★★★, Passport To Fame (1944) ★★★, Early Erroll: 1945 Stride Volumes 1 & 2 (1945) ★★★★, Gemini (Decca 1978) ★★★, The Great Garner (Atlantic 1979) ★★★, Complete Savoy Sessions Volume 1 1945-49 recordings (RCA 1986) ★★★, Yesterdays (1945-49) ★★★, The Elf (1945-49) ★★★, Cocktail Time (1947) ★★★, Body & Soul (1951-52) ★★★★, Erroll Garner Plays Gershwin And Kern (1958-65) ★★★, Complete Savoy Sessions Volume 2 1949 recordings (RCA 1986) ★★★, Jazz Portraits (Jazz Portraits 1993) ★★★, Dreamstreet/One World Concert (Telarc 1996) ★★★★, Gershwin & Kern/Magician (Telarc 1996) ★★★, That's My Kick/Gemini (Telarc 1996) ★★★, A Night At The Movies/Up In Erroll's Room (Telarc 1996) ★★★, Erroll Garner 6-CD box set (Telarc 1999) ★★★★, The Complete Savoy Master Takes (Savoy 1999) ★★★, Erroll Garner On Dial: The Complete Sessions 1946-48 recordings (Spotlite 1999) ★★★, Memories Of You 1945-47 recordings (Memoir 1999) ★★★★.
● FURTHER READING: Erroll Garner: The Most Happy Piano, James M. Doran.

GAYNOR, MITZI

b. Francesca Mitzi Gerber, 4 September 1930, Chicago, Illinois. USA. This vivacious and extremely talented actress, singer and dancer, reputedly of Hungarian descent, graced several good movie musicals in the 50s, and is probably best remembered as the girl who tried to 'wash that man (Rossano Brazzi) right out of her hair' in South Pacific (1958). After taking ballet lessons from an early age, Gaynor danced with the Los Angeles Civic Light Opera while in her early teens, and made a strong impression with Betty Grable and Dan Dailey in her first movie, My Blue Heaven (1950). This was followed by one or two straight parts, and a few musicals such as Golden Girl, Bloodhounds Of Broadway, Down Among The Sheltering Palms and The 'I Don't Care' Girl (1953),

which were not as satisfying. The situation improved as the 50s progressed and she had excellent roles in There's No Business Like Show Business, Anything Goes, The Birds And The Bees, The Joker Is Wild and Les Girls (1957). She was good, too, in South Pacific, but although it remains, to date, the fourth highest-grossing screen musical of the period in the USA, she was reportedly personally disaffected with the experience. Her particular genre of film musicals was becoming extinct, and, like so many others, she worked more often in television and had her own top-rated specials during the 60s. She also toured in stage musical revivals, and, as an accomplished actress, continued to play the occasional comic or dramatic movie role. Gaynor also built up a polished and highly regarded concert and cabaret act. As recently as 1987 she was acclaimed for her nightclub performances, which included a section devoted to Irving Berlin and Fred Astaire, a satirical version of Harry Von Tilzer and Arthur Lamb's nineteenth century song 'A Bird In A Gilded Cage', and a rousing singalong 'God Bless America' finale. Two years later she embarked on an 11-month, 36-city tour of the USA in a revival of Cole Porter's 1934 show Anything Goes, the first time in her long career that she had been on the road in a book musical. The Daily News, commenting on a New York performance of hers in the late 90s, wrote: 'She is what showbusiness is all about.'
● ALBUMS: Mitzi (Verve 1959) ★★★, Mitzi Gaynor Sings The Lyrics Of Ira Gershwin (Verve 1959) ★★★, and soundtrack recordings.
● FILMS: My Blue Heaven (1950), Take Care Of My Little Girl (1951), Golden Girl (1951), Bloodhounds Of Broadway (1952), We're Not Married! (1952), The I Don't Care Girl (1953), Down Among The Sheltering Palms (1953), Three Young Texans (1954), There's No Business Like Show Business (1954), Birds And The Bees (1956), Anything Goes (1956), The Joker Is Wild (1957), Les Girls (1957), South Pacific (1958), Happy Anniversary (1959), Surprise Package (1960), For Love Or Money (1963).

GELDRAY, MAX

b. Max van Gelder, 1916, Amsterdam, Netherlands. Geldray was born into a musical family and reputed to be one of the first harmonica players in Europe. His mother was a classically trained pianist, and the young Geldray inherited his father's ability to play an instrument by ear. He bought his first harmonica when he was aged 16, and taught himself to play it. Influenced by hearing jazz greats such as Louis Armstrong on the radio, Geldray formed his own eight-piece group, which soon evolved into a quartet, the Hollander Boys. They were spotted by the English comedian and impresario Tom Moss, and travelled to the UK where they toured the variety theatres. On his return to Holland Geldray went solo, and played at the Boeuf sur la Toit Club in Brussels, and with the Johnny Fresco Band in Ostend. It was there that he met the French bandleader Ray Ventura, who took him to Paris in the late 30s. Geldray was billed as the

'special attraction' with Ventura's orchestra, which was considered to be one of the top bands in Europe, and he became something of a celebrity, often jamming with the legendary jazz guitarist Django Reinhardt. Just after the outbreak of World War II, Geldray fled to Britain and joined the Princess Irene Brigade. He also did numerous broadcasts for the BBC, and appeared in a special Royal Command Performance at Windsor Castle to celebrate Princess Elizabeth's 16th birthday. In 1945 he rejoined Ray Ventura in Paris for a time, and then returned to Britain and subsequently provided the musical interludes (and, as 'the world's worst actor', spoke a few lines) in the radio series that started out as *Crazy People*, but was soon retitled *The Goon Show*, starring Spike Milligan, Harry Secombe, Peter Sellers and (initially) Michael Bentine. Geldray and his harmonica were ever-present in more than 200 episodes from 1951 until the series ended in 1960. In the early 60s, after working in Australia and on cruise ships, Geldray moved to the USA, but was reunited with his former colleagues in *The Last Goon Show Of All* in 1972. On returning to America, he took work outside the music business before eventually retiring to Palm Springs, California, emerging only to play the occasional gig. In more recent years Geldray has done extensive voluntary work for the local Stroke Centre and the Betty Ford Centre for drugs and alcohol rehabilitation.
● ALBUMS: *Goon With The Wind* (Parlophone 60s) ★★★.
● FURTHER READING: *Goon With The Wind*, Max Geldray with John R. Vance.

GENE KRUPA STORY, THE

This film, made in 1959, is another jazz biopic that misses its target by a mile. Sal Mineo portrays Gene Krupa as a sulky rebel, quite unlike the real-life drummer. Despite other shortcomings, Mineo convincingly played on-screen drums to Krupa's ghosted backing, and, to his credit, the actor later acknowledged the film's mediocrity. On the strength of this telling of Krupa's tale, no one could have imagined that he was a heart-throb idol of millions and one of the greatest showbiz attractions of his era; but then, any film on Krupa that manages to omit Benny Goodman is more than a little short on veracity. Shot in black and white, the film's director was Don Weis. Musically, there are low and high points. Among the former is a scrappy jam session with Red Nichols; the best of the latter is a wonderful version of 'Memories Of You' sung by Anita O'Day. Shelly Manne appears as Dave Tough (he also played the late drummer in *The Five Pennies*). Krupa's return to the stage after a drugs bust that put him in jail and cost him his highly popular band is quite well represented, with Tommy Pederson playing the role of Tommy Dorsey who hired Krupa in 1944. In 1989 a projected remake was abandoned when a leading Hollywood star, interested in the role of Krupa, had to bow out to meet other obligations. (Alternative title: *Drum Crazy*).

GENTLE, JOHNNY

b. John Askew, 1941, Liverpool, England. Askew was a merchant seaman who sang as a semi-professional before he was spotted and rechristened by the celebrated 50s svengali, Larry Parnes. Beginning with 1959's 'Boys And Girls Were Meant For Each Other' on Philips Records, this square-jawed hunk's singles all missed the UK chart but he was often seen on British television pop series such as *Oh Boy* and *Drumbeat* and was, therefore, guaranteed a period of well-paid one-nighters. His backing groups for these included fellow Merseysiders the Beatles and Cass And The Cassanovas with entertainments that embraced mutually familiar rock 'n' roll standards and the simpler sides of Gentle's singles, such as the self-penned 'Wendy'. Without a recording contract in 1963, Gentle replaced Gordon Mills in the Viscounts before retiring from showbusiness by the mid-60s.

GERALDO

b. Gerald Walcan Bright, 10 August 1904, London, England. d. 4 May 1974, Vevey, Switzerland. A child prodigy, Geraldo played piano and organ, and studied at the Royal Academy of Music in London. After leading several small groups he formed his own Light Orchestra under the name of Gerald Bright and played a five-year residency at the Hotel Majestic, St Anne's-on-Sea making his first broadcast from there. He disbanded the orchestra at the peak of its success, and toured South America to study authentic Latin-American rhythms. On his return to London in 1930 he changed his name to Geraldo, took his flamboyantly garbed Gaucho Tango Orchestra into the Savoy Hotel and stayed there for 10 years, reputedly making over 2,000 broadcasts. Throughout his career he was extremely popular on BBC radio. His theme song, 'Hello, Again', heralded such shows as *Geraldo's Guest House, Romance In Rhythm, Milestones Of Melody, Dancing Through The Music Shop, Band Box*, and many more. He also recorded prolifically, at first for Decca Records, and then for an assortment of labels including Parlophone Records.
Soon after the orchestra's appearance in the Royal Command Performance of 1933, Geraldo changed his image and formed a conventional dance orchestra, Geraldo and His Sweet Music. At the outbreak of World War II he was appointed Supervisor of Bands for ENSA, and toured Europe, the Middle East and North Africa with his own orchestra. The 40s are generally considered to be the period in which he led his best orchestras, and are remembered on *50 Hits Of The Naughty 40s*, a double album released on Pickwick Records in the UK. All the selections are claimed to be private recordings made for Geraldo, and owned by his widow, Manja. During most of the 40s and the early 50s Geraldo's Orchestra was the most prominent in the UK. The music also became somewhat jazzier, due perhaps to the inclusion in the orchestra of musicians such as Harry Hayes, George Evans, and Leslie 'Jiver' Hutchinson.
In the late 30s Geraldo launched his *Sunday Night*

Swing Club sessions at London's St Martin's Theatre, and in the early 40s played a 'swing' concert at London's Stoll Theatre to an enthusiastic audience of some 3,000. He made several records in the style of USA big bands of the era. After the war Geraldo, besides leading his own orchestra, became engaged in band management, particularly in supplying ensembles to perform on the big Cunard ocean liners. These groups were nicknamed 'Geraldo's Navy', and included many young UK jazz musicians, eager to get to the USA and taste the exciting sounds emanating from the clubs on New York's 52nd Street. Geraldo's was the first band to play on UK's infant television service after the war, and later, after he had retired from bandleading in the mid-50s, he became musical director for Scottish Television.

He kept his name in the public eye by occasionally assembling a group of musicians and playing concerts in a nostalgic style, which was attracting audiences as late as 1970 at London's Royal Festival Hall. Over the years, most of the UK's top musicians played with Geraldo's orchestra, including Andy McDevitt, Ivor Mairants, Nat Temple, George Evans, Harry Roche, Ted Heath, Max Goldberg, Alfie Noakes, Freddie Clayton, Joe Ferrie, Dougie Robinson and many others. His popular vocalists included Dorothy Carless, Johnny Green, Doreen Villiers, Carol Carr, Jill Day, Rosemary Squires, Dick James, Denny Vaughan, Bob Dale, and even, for a brief while in the early days, Al Bowlly. Geraldo died from a heart attack while on holiday in Switzerland. In 1993 a new Geraldo Orchestra, directed by trombonist Chris Dean, toured the UK provinces. One of the stars of the original band, drummer Eric Delaney, was featured prominently, along with vocalist Eleanor Keenan and Russell Stone.

● COMPILATIONS: *Geraldo And His Orchestra* (1974) ★★★, *Hello Again...Again* (1976) ★★★, *50 Hits Of The Naughty 40s* (1977) ★★★, *Gerry's Music Shop* (1980) ★★★, *Featuring Al Bowlly '1939 Recordings'* (1980) ★★★, *Heart And Soul* (1983) ★★★, with the Gaucho Tango Orchestra *Jealousy* (1983) ★★★, *Serenade In The Night* (1984) ★★★, *Geraldo: The Man And His Music* (1984) ★★★, *The Golden Age Of Geraldo* (1986) ★★★★, *Tip Top Tunes* (1986) ★★★, *Take The A Train* (1988) ★★★, *Geraldo And His Music With Cyril Grantham* (1988) ★★★, *The Man And His Music* (1992) ★★★, *The Dance Band Years* (Pulse 1997) ★★★.

GIBSON, DON

b. 3 April 1928, Shelby, North Carolina, USA. If loneliness meant world acclaim, then Gibson, with his catalogue of songs about despair and heartbreak, would be a superstar. Gibson learnt the guitar from an early age and started performing while still at school. He worked some years around the clubs in Knoxville and he built up a reputation via local radio. His first records were made as part of the Sons Of The Soil for Mercury Records in 1949. His first recorded composition was 'Why Am I So Lonely?'. Gibson

recorded for RCA Records, Columbia Records and MGM Records (where he recorded the rockabilly 'I Ain't A-Studyin' You, Baby' in 1957), but with little chart success. However, Faron Young took his forlorn ballad 'Sweet Dreams' to number 2 in the US country charts in 1956. It has since been associated with Patsy Cline and also recorded by Emmylou Harris, Don Everly, Roy Buchanan, Reba McIntyre and Elvis Costello. 'I Can't Stop Loving You' was a US country hit for Kitty Wells and then, in 1962, a transatlantic number 1 for Ray Charles. In 1991, the song was revived by Van Morrison with the Chieftains. 'I Can't Stop Loving You' was also one side of the hit single (US number 7 pop, number 1 country) that marked his return to RCA in 1958. The other side, 'Oh Lonesome Me', which Gibson had originally intended for George Jones, is also a much-recorded country classic. Gibson actually sings 'Ole lonesome me' but a clerk misheard his vocal. Chet Atkins' skilful productions appealed to both pop and country fans and this single was followed by 'Blue Blue Day' (number 20 pop/number 1 country), 'Give Myself A Party', 'Don't Tell Me Your Troubles', 'Just One Time' and his own version of 'Sweet Dreams'. In 1961 Gibson made his UK chart debut with 'Sea Of Heartbreak', which was followed by the similar-sounding 'Lonesome Number One'. The sadness of his songs matched Roy Orbison's, who recorded an album *Roy Orbison Sings Don Gibson* in 1967 and had a hit single with 'Too Soon To Know'. His own bleak *King Of Country Soul*, which includes some country standards, is highly regarded. Gibson lost his impetus through his alcohol and drug dependency, but he recorded successful duets with both Dottie West and Sue Thompson. He had a US country number 1 with 'Woman (Sensuous Woman)' in 1972. Further hits with 'One Day At A Time' and 'Bring Back Your Love To Me' marked the end of Gibson's chart success, but he has continued performing throughout the subsequent decades.

● ALBUMS: *Oh Lonesome Me* (RCA Victor 1958) ★★★★, *Songs By Don Gibson* (Lion 1958) ★★, *No One Stands Alone* (RCA Victor 1959) ★★★, *That Gibson Boy* (RCA Victor 1959) ★★★, *Look Who's Blue i* (RCA Victor 1960) ★★★, *Sweet Dreams* (RCA Victor 1960) ★★★★, *Girls, Guitars And Gibson* (RCA Victor 1961) ★★★★, *Some Favourites Of Mine* (RCA Victor 1962) ★★★, *I Wrote A Song* (RCA Victor 1963) ★★★, *God Walks These Hills* (RCA Victor 1964) ★★, *Too Much Hurt* (RCA Victor 1965) ★★★, *Don Gibson* (RCA Victor 1965) ★★★, *The Fabulous Don Gibson* (RCA Victor 1965) ★★★, *A Million Blue Tears* (RCA Victor 1965) ★★★, *Hurtin' Inside* (RCA Victor 1966) ★★★, *Don Gibson With Spanish Guitars* (RCA Victor 1966) ★★, *Great Country Songs* (RCA Victor 1966) ★★★★, *All My Love* (RCA Victor 1967) ★★★, *The King Of Country Soul* (RCA Victor 1968) ★★★, *More Country Soul* (RCA Victor 1968) ★★★, *I Love You So Much It Hurts* (RCA Victor 1968) ★★★, *My God Is Real* (RCA Victor 1969) ★★, with Dottie West *Dottie And Don* (RCA Victor 1969) ★★★, *Don Gibson Sings All-Time Country Gold* (RCA Victor 1969) ★★★, *Hits –*

The Don Gibson Way (RCA Victor 1970) ★★★, *A Perfect Mountain* (Hickory 1970) ★★★, *Hank Williams As Sung By Don Gibson* (Hickory 1971) ★★★, *Country Green* (Hickory 1972) ★★★, *Woman (Sensuous Woman)* (Hickory 1972) ★★★, *Sample Kisses* (Hickory 1972) ★★★, *Am I That Easy To Forget?* (Hickory 1973) ★★★, with Sue Thompson *The Two Of Us Together* (Hickory 1973) ★★★, *Touch The Morning/That's What I'll Do* (Hickory 1973) ★★★, with Sue Thompson *Warm Love* (Hickory 1973) ★★★, *Just Call Me Lonesome* (Hickory 1973) ★★★, *Snap Your Fingers* (Hickory 1974) ★★★, *Bring Back Your Love To Me* (Hickory 1974) ★★★, *Just One Time* (Hickory 1974) ★★★, *I'm The Loneliest Man/There She Goes I Wish Her Well* (Hickory 1975) ★★★, with Sue Thompson *Oh How Love Changes* (Hickory 1975) ★★★, *Don't Stop Loving Me* (Hickory 1975) ★★★, *I'm All Wrapped Up In You* (Hickory 1976) ★★★, *If You Ever Get To Houston (Look Me Down)* (Hickory 1977) ★★★, *Starting All Over Again* (Hickory 1978) ★★★, *Look Who's Blue* ii (Hickory 1978) ★★★.

● COMPILATIONS: *20 Of The Best* (RCA 1982) ★★★, *Rockin' Rollin' Gibson, Volume l* (Bear Family 1984) ★★★★, *Rockin' Rollin' Gibson, Volume 2* (Bear Family 1984) ★★★★, *Collector's Series* (RCA 1985) ★★, *Don Gibson And Los Indios Tabajaras* (Bear Family 1986) ★★, *Don Gibson – The Early Days* (Bear Family 1986) ★★, *Collection: Don Gibson* (Castle 1987) ★★★, *A Legend In His Time* (Bear Family 1988) ★★★, *All Time Greatest Hits* (RCA 1990) ★★★★, *The Singer: The Songwriter, 1949-60* (Bear Family 1991) ★★★, *The Singer: The Songwriter 1961-66* 4-CD box set (Bear Family 1993) ★★★★.

● FURTHER READING: *Don Gibson – A Legend In His Own Time*, Richard Weize and Charles Wolfe.

GIGI

The golden era of MGM film musicals was drawing to a close when this most delightful of films was released in 1958. The original story, by the French novelist Colette, had previously been adapted into a non-musical film in 1948 starring Daniele Delormé and Gaby Morlay, and a play that was subsequently performed in New York and London. Alan Jay Lerner's screenplay for this musical treatment was set in Paris at the turn of the century and tells of the young, strong-willed Gigi (Leslie Caron), who is being brought up by her grandmother, Mamita (Hermione Gingold), and her great-aunt Alicia (Isabel Jeans) to be a courtesan, but breaks with that family tradition – and actually marries her suitor, Gaston Lachailles (Louis Jourdan). Watching over this somewhat shocking situation is Honoré Lachailles (Maurice Chevalier), Gaston's grandfather and a good friend of Mamita. He is also a gentleman with much experience in the delights of romance, and, therefore, is appalled when Gaston, his well-heeled grandson, who, permanently surrounded by lovely ladies and all the other good things in life, suddenly declares that 'It's A Bore'. This was just one of Alan Jay Lerner and Frederick Loewe's memorable songs that were so skilfully integrated into the charming story. Other highlights included

Chevalier's 'Thank Heaven For Little Girls' ('Those little eyes so helpless and appealing/One day will flash, and send you crashing through the ceiling'), 'The Parisians' (Caron), 'Waltz At Maxim's' (Jourdan), 'The Night They Invented Champagne' (Caron-Jourdan-Mamita), 'Say A Prayer For Me Tonight' (Caron), 'I'm Glad I'm Not Young Anymore' (Chevalier) and 'Gigi (Gaston's Soliloquy)' (Jourdan). For many, the most endearing moment came when Honoré and Mamita reminisced about old times with 'I Remember It Well' (He: 'You wore a gown of gold.' She: 'I was all in blue.' He: 'Am I getting old?' She: 'Oh, no – not you.'). Vincente Minnelli directed the film which was mostly shot on location in Paris, and the producer was Arthur Freed. It was magnificently photographed in Metrocolor and CinemaScope by Joseph Ruttenberg, and he won one of the picture's Academy Awards, along with those for Cecil Beaton's sumptuous costumes and best picture, director, writer (Lerner), art direction-set direction (William A. Horning and Preston Ames; Henry Grace and Keogh Gleason), film editing (Adrienne Fazan), best song ('Gigi'), and scoring of a musical picture (André Previn). At the same awards ceremony Maurice Chevalier received a special Oscar 'for his contributions to the world of entertainment for more than half a century'. *Gigi* was one of the Top 10 highest-grossing films of the 50s in the USA, but subsequent stage productions did not appeal. The 1973 Broadway production starring Alfred Drake, Agnes Moorhead, Maria Karnilova and Daniel Massey only ran for three months, and West End audiences saw *Gigi* for seven months in 1985-86.

GILLESPIE, DIZZY

b. John Birks Gillespie, 21 October 1917, Cheraw, South Carolina, USA, d. 6 January 1993, Englewood, New Jersey, USA. Born into a large family, Gillespie began playing trombone at the age of 12 and a year or so later took up the trumpet. Largely self-taught, he won a musical scholarship but preferred playing music to formal study. In 1935 he quit university and went to live in Philadelphia, where he began playing in local bands. It was during this period that he acquired the nickname by which he was to become universally known. The name Dizzy resulted from his zestful behaviour and was actually bestowed by a fellow trumpeter, Fats Palmer, whose life Gillespie saved when Palmer was overcome by fumes in a gas-filled room during a tour with the Frankie Fairfax band. Gillespie's startling technical facility attracted a great deal of attention and in 1937 he went to New York to try out for the Lucky Millinder band. He did not get the job but stayed in town and soon afterwards was hired for a European tour by Teddy Hill, in whose band he succeeded his idol, Roy Eldridge. Back in the USA in 1939, Gillespie played in various New York bands before returning to Hill, where he was joined by drummer Kenny Clarke, in whom he found a kindred spirit, who was similarly tired of big band conventions.

When Hill folded his band to become booking

manager for Minton's Playhouse in New York, he gave free rein to young musicians eager to experiment and among the regulars were Clarke, Thelonious Monk, Joe Guy and, a little later, Gillespie. In the meantime, Gillespie had joined the Cab Calloway Band, which was then riding high in popular esteem. While with Calloway, Gillespie began to experiment with phrasing that was out of character with what was until this time accepted jazz trumpet parlance. He also appeared on a Lionel Hampton record date, playing a solo on a tune entitled 'Hot Mallets' which many observers believe to be the first recorded example of what would later be called bebop. The following year, 1940, Gillespie met Charlie Parker in Kansas City, during a tour with the Calloway band, and established musical rapport with the man with whom he was to change the face and sound of jazz. In 1941 Gillespie was fired by Calloway following some on-stage high jinks which ended with Gillespie and his boss embroiled in a minor fracas. Gillespie returned to New York where he worked with numerous musicians, including Benny Carter, Millinder, Charlie Barnet and Earl Hines, in whose band he again met Parker and also singer Billy Eckstine.

Gillespie had begun to hang out, after hours, at Minton's and also at Clark Monroe's Uptown House. He led his own small band for club and record dates, both appealing to a small, specialized, but growing, audience. Amongst his influential recordings of the period were 'Salt Peanuts' and 'Hot House'. In 1944 Gillespie joined the big band Eckstine had just formed: originally intended as a backing group for Eckstine's new career as a solo singer, the outfit quickly became a forcing house for big band bebop. Apart from Gillespie, the sidemen Eckstine hired at various times included Gene Ammons, Sonny Stitt, Wardell Gray, Dexter Gordon, Fats Navarro, Howard McGhee and Miles Davis. Subsequently, Gillespie formed his own big band, which enjoyed only limited commercial success but which was, musically, an early peaking of the concept of big band bebop. He also began playing and recording regularly with Parker in a quintet that the two men co-led. During this period Gillespie was constantly in excellent musical company, playing with most of the major voices in bop and many of those swing era veterans who tried, with varying levels of success, to adapt to the new music. In the big band, Gillespie had employed at one time or another during its two separate periods of existence James Moody, Cecil Payne, Benny Bailey, Al McKibbon, Willie Cook, Big Nick Nicholas, John Lewis, Milt Jackson, Ray Brown and Clarke. In his small groups he recorded with Don Byas, Al Haig and others, but it was in the band he co-led with Parker that Gillespie did his most influential work. The other members of the quintet varied, but initially included Haig, Curley Russell and 'Big' Sid Catlett and, later, Haig, Jackson, Brown and Stan Levey. These small bands brought Gillespie to the fascinated attention of countless musicians; from their performances evolved the establishment of bop as a valid form of

jazz, with its necessary renewal of a music which had begun to fall prey to the inroads of blandness, sanitization and formulaic repetitiveness that accompanied the commercial successes of the swing era.

Gillespie was feverishly active as a composer too. And, despite his youth he was fast becoming an *eminence grise* to beboppers. Aided by his stable private life and a disdain for the addictive stimulants increasingly favoured by a small but well-publicized coterie of bebop musicians, he was the epitome of the successful businessman. That he combined such qualities with those of musical explorer and adventurer made him one of the more dominant figures in jazz. Moreover, in his work with Chano Pozo (who joined Gillespie's orchestra in 1947) and later Machito he was one of the pioneers of US-based Latin jazz. Most important of all, his personal demeanour helped bop rise above the prevailing tide of contemptuous ignorance which, in those days, often passed for critical comment.

Gillespie's busy career continued into the 50s; he recorded with J.J. Johnson, John Coltrane, Jackson, Art Blakey, Wynton Kelly and others. Many of his record dates of this period were on his own label, Dee Gee Records. With his big band folded, Gillespie toured Europe, returning to New York in 1952 to find that his record company was on the skids. He was already undergoing some difficulties as he adjusted his playing style to accommodate new ideas and the shift from large to small band. In 1953, during a party for his wife, the members of a two-man knockabout act fell on his trumpet. The instrument was badly bent but when Gillespie tried to play it he found that, miraculously, he preferred it that way. The upward 45-degree angle of the bell allowed him to hear the notes he was playing sooner than before. In addition he found that when he was playing from a chart, and therefore was looking down, the horn was pointing outwards towards microphone or audience. He liked all these unexpected benefits and within a few weeks had arranged to have a trumpet especially constructed to incorporate them. By the end of 1953 the temporary hiatus in Gillespie's career was over. A concert in Toronto in this year featured Gillespie and Parker with Bud Powell, Charles Mingus and Max Roach in a group which was billed, and in some quarters received, as The Quintet Of The Year. Although all five musicians did better things at other times, collectively it was an exciting and frequently excellent session. Significantly, it was an occasion which displayed the virility of bop at a time when, elsewhere, its fire was being gently doused into something more palatable for the masses.

Gillespie then began working with Norman Granz's Jazz At The Philharmonic and he also began a long series of recording dates for Granz, in which he was teamed with a rich and frequently rewarding mixture of musicians. In 1956 Gillespie's standing in jazz circles was such that Adam Clayton Powell Jnr. recommended him to President Dwight D. Eisenhower as the ideal man to lead an orchestra on a State Department-sponsored goodwill tour of Africa, the Middle East and Asia. The tour was a great success, even if Gillespie proved unwilling to play up its propagandist element, and soon after his return to the USA he was invited to make another tour, this time to South America. The all-star band assembled for these tours was maintained for a while and was also recorded by Granz. By the end of the 50s Gillespie was again leading a small group and had embarked upon a ceaseless round of club, concert, festival and recording dates that continued for the next three decades. He continued to work on prestigious projects, which included, in the early 70s, a tour with an all-star group featuring Blakey, Monk, Stitt, McKibbon and Kai Winding. Throughout the 70s and during the 80s he was the recipient of many awards, and his earlier status as an absurdly young *eminence grise* was succeeded by his later role as an elder statesman of jazz even though when the 70s began, he was still only in his early 50s.

By the middle of the 70s Gillespie was once again at a point in his career where a downturn seemed rather more likely than a further climb. In the event, it was another trumpet player who gave him the nudge he needed. Jon Faddis had come into Gillespie's life as an eager fan, but in 1977 was teamed with his idol on a record date at the Montreux festival where their planned performance was abruptly altered when the scheduled rhythm section ended up in the wrong country. Hastily assembling a substitute team of Milt Jackson, Ray Brown, Monty Alexander and drummer Jimmie Smith, the two trumpeters played a highly successful set which was recorded by Norman Granz. Subsequently, Gillespie and Faddis often played together, making a great deal of memorable music, with the veteran seemingly sparked into new life. In the early 80s Gillespie recorded for television in the USA as part of the *Jazz America* project, appeared in London with a new quintet featuring Paquito D'Rivera, and played at the Nice, Knebworth and Kool festivals in duets with, respectively, such varied artists as Art Farmer, Chico Freeman and Art Blakey.

He showed himself eager to experiment although sometimes, as with his less-than-wonderful teaming with Stevie Wonder, his judgement was somewhat awry. In 1987 he celebrated his 70th birthday and found himself again leading a big band, which had no shortage of engagements and some excellent players, including Faddis and Sam Rivers. He was also fêted during the JVC Festival at the Saratoga Springs Performing Arts Center, where he brilliantly matched horns with Faddis and new pretender, Wynton Marsalis. He was not always in the spotlight, however. One night in Los Angeles he went into a club where Bill Berry's LA Big Band was working and sat in, happily playing fourth trumpet. As the 90s began Gillespie was still performing, usually occupying centre stage, but also happy to sit and reminisce with old friends and new, to sit in with other musicians, and to live life pretty much the way he had done for more than half a century. It was a shock to the music world on 6 January 1993 when it was announced that Dizzy was no longer with us, perhaps we had selfishly thought that he was immortal.

In the history of the development of jazz trumpet, Gillespie's place ranked second only to that of Louis Armstrong. In the history of jazz as a whole he was firmly in the small group of major innovators who reshaped the music in a manner so profound that everything that follows has to be measured by reference, conscious or not, to their achievements. Just as Armstrong had created a new trumpet style which affected players of all instruments in the two decades following his emergence in Chicago in 1922, so did Gillespie, in 1940, redirect trumpet players and all other jazz musicians along new and undefined paths. He also reaffirmed the trumpet's vital role in jazz after a decade (the 30s) in which the saxophone had begun its inexorable rise to prominence as the instrument for change. In a wider context Gillespie's steadying hand did much to ensure that bop would survive beyond the impractical, errant genius of Parker. In much of Gillespie's earlier playing the dazzling speed of his execution frequently gave an impression of a purely technical bravura, but as time passed it became clear that there was no lack of ideas or real emotion in his playing. Throughout his career, Gillespie rarely failed to find fresh thoughts; and, beneath the spectacular high note flourishes, the raw excitement and the exuberant vitality, there was a depth of feeling akin to that of the most romantic balladeers. He earned and will forever retain his place as one of the true giants of jazz. Without his presence, the music would have been not only different but much less than it had become.

● ALBUMS: *Modern Trumpets* (Dial 1950) ★★★★, *Dizzy Gillespie Plays/Johnny Richards Conducts* 10-inch album (Discovery 1950) ★★★, *Dizzy Gillespie* reissued as *School Days* (Dee Gee 1952) ★★★, *Dizzy Gillespie Volume 1* 10-inch album (Atlantic 1952) ★★★★, *Dizzy Gillespie Volume 2* 10-inch album (Atlantic 1952) ★★★★, *Pleyel Concert 1953* (Vogue 1953) ★★★, *Horn Of Plenty* 10-inch album (Blue Note 1953) ★★★★, *Dizzy Gillespie With Charlie Christian* 10-inch album (Esoteric 1953) ★★★★★, *Dizzie Gillespie With Strings* (Clef 1953) ★★★, *Dizzy In Paris* 10-inch album (Contemporary 1953) ★★★★, *Dizzy Over Paris* reissued as *Concert In Paris* (Roost 1953) ★★★★, *Dizzy Gillespie Orchestra* 10-inch album (Allegro 1954) ★★★, *Dizzie Gillespie And His Original Big Band* 10-inch album (Gene Norman 1954) ★★★, *Dizzier And Dizzier* (RCA Victor 1954) ★★★, *The Dizzy Gillespie-Stan Getz Sextet #1* 10-inch album (Norgran 1954) ★★★★, *The Dizzy Gillespie-Stan Getz Sextet #2* 10-inch album (Norgran 1954) ★★★★, *Afro* (Norgran 1954) ★★★, *Dizzy Gillespie Plays* 10-inch album (Allegro 1954) ★★★, *Dizzy And Strings* reissued as *Diz Big Band* (Norgran 1955) ★★★, with Stan Getz *Diz And Getz* (Verve 1955) ★★★★, with Roy Eldridge *Roy And Diz* (Clef 1955) ★★★★, with Eldridge *Roy And Diz, Volume 2* (Clef 1955) ★★★★, *Dizzy Gillespie* (Allegro 1955)

★★★, *Groovin' High* (Savoy 1955) ★★★, with Jimmy McPartland *Hot Vs. Cool* (MGM 1955) ★★★★, *Dizzy Gillespie And His Orchestra* reissued as *Jazz Recital* (Norgran 1956) ★★★, *Dizzy Gillespie* (American Recording Society 1956) ★★★, *Big Band Jazz* (American Recording Society 1956) ★★★, with Eldridge *Trumpet Battle* (Clef 1956) ★★★, with Eldridge *The Trumpet Kings* (Clef 1956) ★★★, *The Champ* (Savoy 1956) ★★★, *The New Continent* (Limelight 1956) ★★★, *For Musicians Only* (Verve 1956) ★★★, *World Statesman* (Norgran 1956) ★★★, *Dizzy At Home And Abroad* (Atlantic 1957) ★★★★, *The Dizzy Gillespie Story* (Savoy 1957) ★★★, *Dizzy In Greece* (Verve 1957) ★★★, *Manteca* (Verve 1958) ★★★, *Dizzy Gillespie And Stuff Smith* (Verve 1958) ★★★★, with Slim Gaillard *Gaillard And Gillespie* (Ultraphonic 1958) ★★★, with Harry 'Sweets' Edison, Eldridge *Tour De Force* (Verve 1958) ★★★, *Birk's Works* (Verve 1958) ★★★★, *Dizzy Gillespie At Newport* (Verve 1958) ★★★★, *Dizzy Gillespie And Count Basie At Newport* (Verve 1958) ★★★★, with Sonny Rollins, Sonny Stitt *Duets* reissued as *Dizzy, Rollins & Stitt* (Verve 1958) ★★★★, with Charlie Parker *Diz 'N' Bird In Concert* (Roost 1959) ★★★★, *The Ebullient Mr. Gillespie* (Verve 1959) ★★★, *Have Trumpet, Will Excite!* (Verve 1959) ★★★★, *The Greatest Trumpet Of Them All* (Verve 1959) ★★★, *A Portrait Of Duke Ellington* (Verve 1960) ★★★★, *Gillespiana: The Carnegie Hall Concert* (Verve 1960) ★★★★, with Count Basie *First Time! The Count Meets The Duke* (Columbia 1961) ★★★★, *An Electrifying Evening With The Dizzy Gillespie Quintet* (Verve 1961) ★★★★, *Perceptions* (Verve 1961) ★★★, *Jazz Recital* (Verve 1961) ★★★, with Miles Davis, Fats Navarro *Trumpet Giants* (New Jazz 1962) ★★★★, *Jazz On The French Riviera* (Philips 1962) ★★★, *Dateline Europe* (Reprise 1963) ★★★, *New Wave!* (Philips 1963) ★★★, *Something Old, Something New* (Philips 1963) ★★★, *Dizzy Goes Hollywood* (Philips 1964) ★★★, *Dizzy Gillespie And The Double Six Of Paris* (Philips 1964) ★★★★, *The Cool World* film soundtrack (Philips 1964) ★★★, *Jambo Caribe* (Limelight 1964) ★★★, *The New Continent* (Limelight 1965) ★★★, *The Essential Dizzy Gillespie* (Verve 1964) ★★★, *Angel City* (Moon 1965) ★★★, *Gil Fuller And The Monterey Jazz Festival Orchestra With Dizzy Gillespie* (Pacific Jazz 1965) ★★★, with Eldridge *Soul Mates* (Verve 1966) ★★★★, *A Night In Tunisia* (Verve 1966) ★★★★, *Swing Low, Sweet Cadillac* (Impulse! 1967) ★★★, *Reunion Big Band* (MPS 1968) ★★★★, *Live At The Village Vanguard* (Solid State 1969) ★★★★, *My Way* (Solid State 1969) ★★, *Cornacopia* (Solid State 1969) ★★★, *The Real Thing* (Perception 1970) ★★★, *Giants* (Perception 1970) ★★★, *Portrait Of Jenny* (Perception 1970) ★★★, *Dizzy Gillespie And The Dwike Mitchell-Willie Ruff Duo* (Mainstream 1971) ★★★, *Giants Of Jazz* (Atlantic 1973) ★★★★, *The Giant* (Accord 1973) ★★★, *Dizzy Gillespie's Big Four* (Pablo 1974) ★★★★, with Machito *Afro-Cuban Jazz Moods* (Pablo 1975) ★★★★, with Eldridge *Jazz Maturity ... Where It's Coming From* (Pablo 1975) ★★★, with Eldridge *The Trumpet Kings At Montreux '75* (Pablo 1975) ★★★★, *Dizzy's Party* (Pablo 1976) ★★★, *Free Ride* (Pablo 1977)

★★★, with Count Basie *The Gifted Ones* (Pablo 1977) ★★★, *Montreux '77* (Pablo 1977) ★★★, *Trumpet Summit Meets Oscar Peterson Big Four* (Pablo 1980) ★★★, *Digital At Montreux, 1980* (Pablo 1980) ★★★, *Musician-Composer-Raconteur* (Pablo 1981) ★★, with Arturo Sandoval *To A Finland Station* (Pablo 1982) ★★★, *New Faces* (GRP 1984) ★★★, *Arturo Sandoval And His Group With Dizzy Gillespie* (Egrem 1985) ★★★, *Closer To The Source* (Atlantic 1985) ★★, *Dizzy Gillespie Meets Phil Woods Quintet* (Timeless 1987) ★★★, *Live At The Royal Festival Hall* (Enja 1990) ★★★, *Symphony Sessions* (Pro Arte 1990) ★★, with Max Roach *Max & Dizzy – Paris 1989* (A&M 1990) ★★★, *The Winter In Lisbon* film soundtrack (Milan 1990) ★★★, *To Diz With Love: Diamond Jubilee Recordings* (Telarc 1992) ★★★, *To Bird With Love: Live At The Blue Note* (Telarc 1992) ★★★, *Bird Songs: The Final Recordings* 1991 recording (Telarc 1997) ★★★, the Dizzy Gillespie Alumni All-Stars *Dizzy's 80th Birthday Party!* (Shanachie 1998) ★★★, *On The Sunny Side Of The Street* 1953 recording (Moon 1998) ★★★, *Angel City* 1965 recording (Moon 1998) ★★, *Tour De Force* 1969 recording (Moon 1998) ★★, with Sonny Stitt *Diz Meets Stitt* 1974 recording (Moon 1998) ★★★, *Dizzy In South America Vol 1* 1956 recordings (Red Anchor 1998) ★★★★, *Dizzy In South America Vol 2* 1956 recordings (Consolidated Artists 2000) ★★★.

● COMPILATIONS: *Shaw Nuff* 1945-46 recordings (Musicraft) ★★★★, *One Bass Hit* 1946 recordings (Musicraft) ★★★★★, with Dwike Mitchell, Willie Ruff *Enduring Magic* 1970-85 recordings (Black Hawk) ★★★★, *Dizzy Gillespie 1946-1949* (RCA 1983) ★★★★, *Dee Gee Days* 1951-52 recordings (Savoy 1985) ★★★, *Dizzy's Diamonds: The Best Of The Verve Years* 1950-64 recordings (Verve 1993) ★★★★, *Birk's Works: Verve Big Band Sessions* 1956-57 recordings (Verve 1993) ★★★★, *Dizzy Songs* (Vogue 1993) ★★★★, *The Complete RCA Victor Recordings* 1937-49 recordings (RCA 1996) ★★★★★, *Dizzier And Dizzier* 1946-49 recordings (RCA 1997) ★★★, *Talkin' Verve* (Verve 1997) ★★★, *Jivin' In Be Bop* 1947 recordings (Moon 1998) ★★★, *Good Bait* 40s recordings (Moon 1998) ★★★, *Dizzy Gillespie 1945-6* (Classics 1998) ★★★, *Dizzy Gillespie 1947-1949* (Classics 2000) ★★★★, *Ken Burns Jazz: The Definitive Dizzy Gillespie* (Verve 2001) ★★★★, *Matrix: The Perception Sessions* (Castle 2001) ★★★★, *The Dizzy Gillespie Story 1939-1950* 4-CD box set (Proper 2001) ★★★★.

● VIDEOS: *A Night In Chicago* (View Video 1995), *Ralph J. Gleason's Jazz Casual: Dizzy Gillespie* (Rhino 2000).

● FURTHER READING: *Dizzy: To Be Or Not To Bop*, Dizzy Gillespie and Al Fraser. *Dizzy Gillespie: His Life And Times*, Barry McRae. *Dizzy Gillespie*, M James. *The Trumpets Of Dizzy Gillespie, 1937-1943*, Jan Evensmo. *Dizzy Gillespie And The Be-Bop Revolution*, Raymond Horricks. *Waiting for Dizzy*, Gene Lees. *Dizzy: John Birks Gillespie In His 75th Year*, Lee Tanner (ed.). *Groovin' High: The Life Of Dizzy Gillespie*, Alyn Shipton. *Dizzy Gillespie: The Bebop Years 1937-1952*, Ken Vail.

GIRL CAN'T HELP IT, THE

Perhaps the finest film of the rock 'n' roll era, this 1956 outing has much to recommend it. In a plot liberally borrowed from Judy Holliday's *Born Yesterday*, struggling agent Tom Ewell is charged by mobster Edmund O'Brien to further the career of his girlfriend (Jayne Mansfield). Risqué (for 1956) references to the latter's physical attributes aside – a running gag throughout – the film is fired by comedy veteran Frank Tashlin's script and direction which, for once, matches the pace and rhythm of the musical interludes. Gene Vincent contributes a memorable 'The Girl Can't Help It', the fledgling talent of Eddie Cochran is heard on 'Twenty Flight Rock' and Fats Domino adds a superb 'Blue Monday'. However, the star is undoubtedly Little Richard, who tears through the title song, 'She's Got It' and 'Ready Teddy'. *The Girl Can't Help It* not only showcased such acts without condescension, it was the first rock 'n' roll film shot in colour. However, the film's strength does not solely rest on these pivotal figures. Tom Ewell is superb as the long-suffering agent, and his hallucinations about a former client immortalized Julie London's 'Cry Me A River'. Edmund O'Brien relished his rare excursion into comedy and the gangster-inspired composition he sang, 'Rock Around The Rock Pile', acted as a thinly veiled sideswipe at exploitative releases made to cash in on fads. Few films embraced rock 'n' roll with similar understanding and respect.

GLEASON, JACKIE

b. Herbert John Gleason, 26 February 1916, Brooklyn, New York, USA, d. 24 June 1987. Gleason was primarily a comedian, starring on stage, screen and television, but he also recorded a number of albums in the 50s and 60s. He established his persona with early films such as *Orchestra Wives* (1942) and several appearances on Broadway (*Artists And Models*, *Follow The Girls* and *Along Fifth Avenue*). However, stardom came with the dawn of the 50s. The formative television series *The Life Of Riley* led to *Cavalcade Of Stars* in 1949, from which Gleason, alongside Art Carney, launched a series of sketches and basic comedy routines. He then fronted a variety/new talent CBS programme *Stageshow* before Tommy and Jimmy Dorsey took over. The programme was notable for introducing Elvis Presley to a television audience. The enormously popular television show *The Honeymooners* followed in 1955, before a series of films leading into the 60s. Notable among these were *The Hustler* (1961), alongside Paul Newman, for which Gleason was nominated for an Oscar as Best Supporting Actor, and *Requiem For A Heavyweight*, the first major play by *The Twilight Zone*'s creator Rod Serling. Gleason also appeared as Buford T. Justice, a law officer prone to mishap in the Burt Reynolds vehicle *Smokey And The Bandit* in 1977. By this time his recording career had largely ended. He had previously written the score for *Gigot* (1962), and his own television theme, 'Melancholy Serenade'. In addition there were several 'mood music' albums on Capitol, which represented his most successful material, and a projected ballet. A string of Top 10 US albums between 1956 and 1957 featured Bobby Hackett and Pee Wee Erwin in his studio orchestras.

● ALBUMS: *Music For Lovers Only* (Capitol 1952/53) ★★★, *Lover's Rhapsody* 10-inch album (Capitol 1953) ★★★, *Music To Make You Misty* (Capitol 1954) ★★★★, *Tawny* (Capitol 1954) ★★, *And 'Awaaay We Go!* TV soundtrack (Capitol 1954/55) ★★, *Music Martinis And Memories* (Capitol 1954) ★★★, *Music To Remember Her* (Capitol 1955) ★★, *Lonesome Echo* (Capitol 1955) ★★★★, *Romantic Jazz* (Capitol 1955) ★★★, *Music To Change Her Mind* (Capitol 1956) ★★★, *Night Winds* (Capitol 1956) ★★★★, *Merry Christmas* (Capitol 1956) ★★, *Music For The Love Hours* (Capitol 1957) ★★★★, *Velvet Brass* (Capitol 1957) ★★★★, *Jackie Gleason Presents 'Oooo!'* (Capitol 1957) ★★★, *The Torch With The Blue Flame* (Capitol 1958) ★★★, *Riff Jazz* (Capitol 1958) ★★★, *Take Me Along* film soundtrack (RCA Victor 1959) ★★★, *Aphrodisia* (Capitol 1960) ★★★, *The Gentle Touch* (Capitol 1961) ★★★, *Gigot* film soundtrack (Capitol 1962) ★★★, *Movie Themes – For Lovers Only* (Capitol 1963) ★★, *Today's Romantic Hits: For Lovers Only* (Capitol 1963) ★★, *Today's Romantic Hits: For Lovers Only, Volume 2* (Capitol 1964) ★★, *Silk 'N' Brass* (Capitol 1966) ★★★, *How Sweet It Is For Lovers* (Capitol 1966) ★★★, *A Taste Of Brass For Lovers Only* (Capitol 1967) ★★.

● COMPILATIONS: *Close-Up* (Capitol 1969) ★★★, *The Romantic Moods Of ...* (Capitol 1997) ★★★.

● FURTHER READING: *The Great One: The Life And Legend Of Jackie Gleason*, William A. Henry III. *Jackie Gleason: An Intimate Portrait Of The Great One*, W.J. Weatherby.

● FILMS: *The Hustler* (1961), *Blood Money* (1962), *Gigot* (1962), *Requiem For A Heavyweight* (1963), *Soldier In The Rain* (1964), *Skidoo* (1968), *How To Commit Marriage* (1969), *Don't Drink The Water* (1969), *Smokey And The Bandit* (1977).

GLENN MILLER STORY, THE

Competently directed by Anthony Mann, and featuring a fine James Stewart performance as Miller (portrayed as much more warm-hearted than the real man), this 1953 biopic does not pass up any opportunity for a cliché. Miller's search for a 'new sound' is hounded to death (scratch any ex-sideman of Miller and one would hear a different version of how he achieved it), but the storyline omits the obvious, if dull, solution that it was all a matter of a workmanlike arranger sticking to his trade. The cross-country slogs on a tour of one-night shows are well presented and the studio-assembled band accurately recreates Miller's music. Stewart copes well with his on-screen trombone miming, and off-screen, Joe Yukl (and possibly Murray McEachern) provides the sound. Miller's disappearance, just before Christmas 1944, is tied into a mythical 'gift' to his wife of an arrangement of her favourite tune, 'Little Brown Jug'. In fact, Miller's hit recording of this tune came some years before his death, but in this way, the film can end without a dry eye in the house. In a jazz club sequence, the 1953 edition of the Louis Armstrong All Stars, including Barney Bigard, William 'Cozy' Cole and Trummy Young, teams up with a handful of 30s swing stars, including Gene Krupa and Babe Russin, to knock spots off 'Basin Street Blues'.

GO, JOHNNY, GO!
Disc jockey Alan Freed, who reputedly coined the phrase 'rock 'n' roll', took part in several 50s genre films, including *Rock Around The Clock* and *Rock Rock Rock*. He assumed the lead role in this 1958 feature, playing to type as a DJ searching for singer Johnny Melody, whose demo recordings proved highly popular with Freed's audience. Chuck Berry also enjoys a (brief) acting part, but is clearly more comfortable performing the title song, plus 'Little Queenie' and 'Memphis, Tennessee', the last of which became a UK Top 10 entry five years later. Rising star Richie Valens contributes 'Ooh My Head' in what would be his only film appearance, while other notable cameos include the Flamingos' 'Jump Children', Eddie Cochran's 'Teenage Heaven', Jackie Wilson's 'You'd Better Know It' and Harvey Fuqua's 'Don't Be Afraid To Love Me'. New Orleans-based singer Jimmy Clanton, who played Melody, provides four songs for the soundtrack, including 'My Own True Love', a US Top 40 entry in 1959. The film did not propel Clanton to stardom, although the singer did enjoy several subsequent hit singles, including 'Go Jimmy Go' (clearly based on his starring feature) and 'Venus In Blue Jeans'.

GOLDNER, GEORGE
b. 1919, near Turtle Bay, Manhattan, USA, d. 15 April 1970. Goldner's long association with New York music circles began in the early 50s. Although initially employed at Tico, a label specializing in Latin music, he switched to R&B in 1953 with the formation of Rama. Its roster included vocal groups the Crows and Harptones, establishing a pattern for Goldner's subsequent outlets, Gee, Gone/End and Roulette. Drawing on New York's profligate street-corner harmony acts, the entrepreneur launched the careers of Frankie Lymon And The Teenagers, Little Anthony And The Imperials and the Chantels, but subsequently sold his interests in each of the companies. Goldner re-emerged in 1964, partnering songwriters/producers Jerry Leiber and Mike Stoller in Red Bird Records. The label enjoyed a highly successful initial period with hits by the Dixie Cups, Jelly Beans and Shangri-Las, and Goldner later bought out his partners when they tired of administrative roles. Despite a promotional acumen, he was unable to maintain the outlet's position and it folded in 1966. In keeping with many contemporaries faced with a new generation of self-sufficient acts, Goldner was unable to exert the same influence in pop's post-Beatles history and later dropped out of music altogether.

GOODMAN, BENNY
b. 30 May 1909, Chicago, Illinois, USA, d. 20 June 1986, New York City, New York, USA. Born into a large, impoverished family of immigrants, Goodman experienced hard times while growing up. Encouraged by his father to learn a musical instrument, Goodman and two of his brothers took lessons; as the youngest and smallest he learned to play the clarinet. These early studies took place at the Kehelah Jacob Synagogue and later at Hull House, a settlement house founded by reformer Jane Addams. From the start, Goodman displayed an exceptional talent and he received personal tuition from James Sylvester and then the renowned classicist Franz Schoepp (who also taught Buster Bailey around the same time). Before he was in his teens, Goodman had begun performing in public and was soon playing in bands with such emerging jazz artists as Jimmy McPartland, Frank Teschemacher and Dave Tough. Goodman's precocious talent allowed him to become a member of the American Federation of Musicians at the age of 14 and that same year he played with Bix Beiderbecke. By his mid-teens Goodman was already established as a leading musician, working on numerous engagements with many bands to the detriment of his formal education. In 1925 he was heard by Gil Rodin, who was then with the popular band led by Ben Pollack. Goodman was hired by Pollack, then working in California, and the following year made a triumphal return to Chicago as featured soloist with the band. Goodman remained with Pollack until 1929, when he became a much in-demand session musician in New York, making many hundreds of record and radio dates. Keenly ambitious and already a determined perfectionist, Goodman continued to develop his craft until he was perhaps the most skilled clarinet player in the country, even if he was virtually unknown to the general public.

During the late 20s and early 30s Goodman played in bands led by Red Nichols, Ben Selvin, Ted Lewis, Sam Lanin and others, sometimes for club, dance hall and theatre engagements and often on record sessions. In 1934 his ambitions led him to form a large dance band, which was successful in being hired for a residency at Billy Rose's Music Hall. After a few months, this date collapsed when Rose was replaced by someone who did not like the band but Goodman persisted and late that same year was successful in gaining one of three places for dance bands on a regular radio show broadcast by NBC. The show, entitled *Let's Dance*, ran for about six months. By this time Goodman was using arrangements by leading writers of the day such as Fletcher Henderson and Spud Murphy, and including in his band musicians such as Bunny Berigan, trombonists Red Ballard and Jack Lacey, saxophonists Toots Mondello and Hymie Schertzer, and in the rhythm section George Van Eps and Frank Froeba, who were quickly replaced by Allan Reuss and Jess Stacy. Goodman's brother, Harry, was on bass, and the drummer was Stan King, who was soon replaced by the more urgent and exciting Gene Krupa. The band's singer was Helen Ward, one of the most popular band singers of the day. When the *Let's Dance* show ended, Goodman took the band on a nation-wide tour.

Prompted in part by producer John Hammond Jnr. and also by his desire for the band to develop, Goodman made many changes to the personnel, something he would continue to do throughout his career as a big band leader, and by the time the tour reached Los Angeles, in August 1935, the band was in extremely good form. Despite the success of the radio show and the band's records, the tour had met with mixed fortunes and some outright failures. However, business picked up on the west coast and on 21 August 1935 the band played a dance at the Palomar Ballroom in Los Angeles. They created a sensation and the massive success that night at the Palomar is generally credited as the time and place where the showbusiness phenomenon which became known as the 'swing era' was born.

After an extended engagement at the Palomar the band headed back east, stopping over in Chicago for another extended run, this time at the Joseph Urban Room at the Congress Hotel. Earlier, Goodman had made some trio recordings using Krupa and pianist Teddy Wilson. The records sold well and he was encouraged by Helen Oakley, later Helen Oakley Dance, to feature Wilson in the trio at the hotel. Goodman eventually was persuaded that featuring a racially mixed group in this manner was not a recipe for disaster and when the occasion passed unremarked, except for musical plaudits, he soon afterwards employed Wilson as a regular member of the featured trio. In 1936 he added Lionel Hampton to form the Benny Goodman Quartet and while this was not the first integrated group in jazz it was by far the one with the highest profile. Goodman's big band continued to attract huge and enthusiastic audiences. In the band now were leading swing era players such as Harry James, Ziggy Elman, Chris Griffin, Vernon Brown, Babe Russin and Arthur Rollini.

Goodman had an especially successful date at the Paramount Theatre in New York, beginning on 3 March 1937, and his records continued to sell very well. On 16 January 1938 the band played a concert at Carnegie Hall, sealing its success and Goodman's reputation as the 'King of Swing.' Soon after the Carnegie Hall date the band's personnel underwent significant changes. Krupa left to form his own band, soon followed by Wilson and James. Goodman found replacements and carried on as before although, inevitably, the band sounded different. In the early 40s he had a particularly interesting personnel, which included Cootie Williams, 'Big' Sid Catlett, Georgie Auld and, in the small group (which was now a septet although labelled as the Benny Goodman Sextet), Charlie Christian. Other Goodman musicians of this period included Jimmy Maxwell and Mel Powell, while his singer, who had followed Ward, Martha Tilton and Helen Forrest, was Peggy Lee. With occasional fallow periods, which usually coincided with the persistent back trouble with which he

was plagued, Goodman continued to the end of the 40s, dabbling with bop by way of a small group which featured musicians such as Doug Mettome, Åke 'Stan' Hasselgård, Wardell Gray and, fleetingly, Fats Navarro and with big bands which included Mettome, Gray, Stan Getz, Don Lamond and Jimmy Rowles.

Goodman soon ended his flirtation with bop, but the release, in 1953, of a long-playing album made from acetates cut during the 1938 Carnegie Hall concert and forgotten during the intervening years revitalized interest in him and his career. He reformed a band for a concert tour which brought together many of the old gang; but a decision to enhance the tour's chances of success by also featuring Louis Armstrong and his All Stars was an error. The two stars clashed at rehearsals and during the out-of-town warm up concert. By the time the package was ready for its opening at Carnegie Hall, Goodman was in hospital, whether for a genuine illness, or because of a sudden attack of diplomacy, no one is quite sure. In 1955 he recorded the soundtrack for a feature film, *The Benny Goodman Story*, and a soundtrack album was also released which featured Wilson, Hampton, Krupa, James, Getz and other former sidemen. During the rest of the 50s and in succeeding decades, Goodman made many appearances with small groups and with occasional big bands, but his days as a leader of a regular big band were over. Even as a small group leader, his bands tended to be one-off only affairs, although he did regularly associate with musicians for whom he had high regard, among them Ruby Braff and Urbie Green.

In Europe he led a big band for an appearance at the 1958 World's Fair in Brussels and in 1962 took a band to the USSR for a visit sponsored by the US State Department. Later, he fronted other big bands, including two formed from British musicians for concert tours in 1969 and again in 1970. From the late 60s he began appearing at regular reunions of the quartet with Wilson, Hampton and Krupa. These reunions, along with club and television dates, occasional tours to Europe and the Far East, occupied the 70s. This decade also saw, on 16 January 1978, a Carnegie Hall date which attempted to recreate the magic of his first appearance there, 30 years before. Goodman continued to record and play concert and other dates into the early 80s. In the last few years of his life and ensconced in his apartment on west 44th, Manhattan he lived quietly and is well-remembered with great affection by the local community.

From the earliest days of his career Goodman was marked out as a hot clarinettist. Although he had an early regard for Ted Lewis, it was the playing of such musicians as Teschemacher and Jimmy Noone that most influenced him. By the start of the 30s, however, Goodman was very much his own man, playing in a highly distinctive style and beginning to influence other clarinettists. His dazzling technique, allied to his delight in playing hot jazz, made him one of the most exciting players of his day. Without question, he was the most technically proficient of all musicians regularly playing jazz clarinet. On the many records he made during this period Goodman almost always soloed, yet he rarely made an error, even on unused takes. During the swing era, despite the rising popularity of Artie Shaw and a handful of others, Goodman retained his popularity, even though his jazz style became noticeably less hot as the decade progressed. His dabblings with bop were never fully convincing, although in his playing of the 40s and later there are signs that he was aware of the changes being wrought in jazz. There are also fleeting stylistic nods towards Lester Young, whose playing he clearly admired.

From the late 30s Goodman had become steadily more interested in classical music and periodically appeared and recorded in this context, often performing pieces which he had specially commissioned. The classical pursuits led him to adopt a different embouchure thus altering the sound of all his playing, and further attenuating the gap some felt had arisen between the current Goodman style and the hot jazz playing of his youth. As a musician Goodman was a perfectionist, practising every day until the end of his life (in his biography of Goodman, James Lincoln Collier reports that, at the time of his death, the clarinettist, alone at home, appeared to have been playing a Brahms Sonata). As with so many perfectionists, Goodman expected his employees to adhere to his own high standards. Many were similarly dedicated musicians, but they were also individualistic, and in some cases had egos which matched his own. Inevitably, there were many clashes; over the years a succession of Goodman stories have emerged which suggest that he was a man who was totally preoccupied with his music to the exclusion of almost everything else including social niceties.

Goodman's achievements in this particular field of American popular music are virtually matchless. He rose from poverty to become a millionaire before he was 30 years old, a real rags to riches story. He was, for a while, the best-known and most popular musician in the USA. And if the title King of Swing rankled with many musicians and was clearly inappropriate when his work is compared with that of such peers as Armstrong and Duke Ellington, Goodman's band of the late 30s was a hard-driving outfit which contrasted sharply with many other white bands of the period and at its best was usually their superior. The trio and quartet brought to small group jazz a sophistication rarely heard before, and seldom matched since; but which nevertheless included much hot music, especially from the leader. It was, perhaps, in the sextet, with Christian, Williams, Auld and others that Goodman made his greatest contribution to jazz. All the tracks recorded by this group before Christian's untimely death are classics of the form. His encouragement of musicians like Christian, Wilson and Hampton not only helped Goodman to promote important careers in jazz but also did much to break down racial taboos in showbusiness and American

society. The fact that he was never an innovator means Goodman was not a great jazzman in the sense that Armstrong, Ellington, Charlie Parker and others were. Nevertheless, he was a major figure in jazz and played an important role in the history of twentieth century popular music.

● ALBUMS: *Benny Goodman On The Air* (Sunbeam 1935) ★★★★, *Benny Goodman And Peggy Lee* (Columbia 1949) ★★★, *Dance Parade* (Columbia 1949) ★★★, *Goodman Sextet Session* (Columbia 1949) ★★★★, *Let's Hear The Melody* (Columbia 1950) ★★★, *Chicago Jazz Classics* (Brunswick 1950) ★★★, *Session For Six* (Capitol 1950) ★★★, *Dance Parade Vol 2* (Columbia 1950) ★★★★, *Carnegie Hall Jazz Concert* (Columbia 1950) ★★★★, *King Of Swing* 6-LP box set (Columbia 1950) ★★★★, with Jack Teagarden *Goodman & Teagarden* 10-inch album (Jazz Panorama 1951) ★★★★, *Benny Goodman* (RCA Victor 1951) ★★★, *Benny Goodman Plays For The Fletcher Henderson Fund* (Tax 1951) ★★★, *1937-38 Jazz Concert No 2* (Columbia 1952) ★★★, *Easy Does It* (Capitol 1952) ★★★, *Immortal Performances* (RCA Victor 1952) ★★★★, *The Benny Goodman Trio* (Capitol 1952) ★★★★, *The Benny Goodman Band* (Capitol 1953) ★★★, *The Golden Era: Combos* (Columbia 1953) ★★★★, *The Goodman Touch* (Capitol 1953) ★★★★, *The Golden Era: Bands* (Columbia 1953) ★★★★, *Presents Eddie Sauter Arrangements* (Columbia 1954) ★★★★, *Benny Goodman 1937-1939* (RCA Victor 1954) ★★★★★, *Small Combo 1947* (Capitol 1954) ★★★★, *Benny Goodman 1927-1934* (Brunswick 1954) ★★★★, *Benny Goodman Featuring Jack Teagarden* 10-inch album (Jolly Rogers 1954) ★★★★, *The Golden Age Of Benny Goodman* (RCA Victor 1955) ★★★★, *The Benny Goodman Story* (Coral 1955) ★★★★, *The Great Benny Goodman* (Columbia 1956) ★★★, *Trio, Quartet, Quintet* (RCA Victor 1956) ★★★★, *The Vintage Benny Goodman* (Columbia 1956) ★★★★, *This Is Benny Goodman* (RCA Victor 1956) ★★★★, *Benny Goodman In Brussels Vol 1* (Columbia 1958) ★★★★, *Mostly Sextets* (Capitol 1958) ★★★, *Benny Goodman In Brussels Vol 2* (Columbia 1958) ★★★★, *The Superlative Goodman* (Verve 1958) ★★★, *Happy Session* (Columbia 1959) ★★★, *The Benny Goodman Tentet And Sextet* (1959) ★★★, *Benny Goodman Swings Again* (Columbia 1960) ★★★, *The Kingdom Of Swing* (RCA Victor 1960) ★★★, *Swing Swing Swing* (RCA Camden 1960) ★★★, *Benny Goodman In Moscow* (RCA Victor 1962) ★★★, *Hello Benny* (Capitol 1964) ★★★, with Lionel Hampton, Gene Krupa, Teddy Wilson *Together Again!* (RCA Victor 1964) ★★★, *The Essential Benny Goodman* (Verve 1964) ★★★, *Made In Japan* (Capitol 1964) ★★★★, *B.G. The Small Groups* (RCA Victor 1965) ★★★, *Live In Las Vegas* (1967) ★★★, *London Date* (Philips 1969) ★★★★, *Benny Goodman Today* (Decca 1970) ★★★, *Live In Stockholm* (Decca 1970) ★★★, *On Stage With Benny Goodman And His Sextet* (Decca 1972) ★★★★, *Seven Come Eleven* (CBS 1975) ★★★, *The King* (Century 1978) ★★★, *Carnegie Hall Reunion Concert* (Decca 1978) ★★★★, *King Of Swing* (East World 1980) ★★★★, *In Stockholm 1959* (Phontastic 1988) ★★★, *Breakfast Ball* 1934 recording (Decca

1988) ★★★, *The Famous 1938 Carnegie Hall Jazz Concert* (Columbia/Legacy 1998) ★★★★.
● COMPILATIONS: *The Hits Of Benny Goodman* (Capitol 1961) ★★★, *Benny Goodman's Greatest Hits* (Columbia 1966) ★★★, *BG With Ben Pollack 1926-31* recordings (Sunbeam 1980) ★★★, *The Rare BG* (1927-29) ★★★, *The Formative Years* (1927-34) ★★★★, *Benny Goodman's Boys 1928-29* recordings (Sunbeam 1980) ★★★, *The Hotsy Totsy Gang With Benny Goodman* (1928-30) ★★★, *Benny Goodman On The Side* (1929-31) ★★★, *Red Nichols Featuring Benny Goodman* (1929-31) ★★★, *Ben Selvin And His Orchestra Featuring Benny Goodman Vols 1, 2, 3* (1929-33) ★★★, *Benny Goodman In A Melotone Manner* (1930-31) ★★★, *Ted Lewis And His Band Featuring Benny Goodman* (1931-32) ★★★, *Benny Goodman Accompanies The Girls* (1931-33) ★★★, *Benny Goodman: The Early Years* (1931-35) ★★★★, *BG With Chick Bullock And Steve Washington* (1933) ★★★, *BG With Adrian Rollini And His Orchestra* (1933-34) ★★★, *The 'Let's Dance' Broadcasts Vols 1-3* 1934-35 recordings (Sunbeam 1982) ★★★★, *The Alternate Goodman Vols 1-9* (Nostalgia 1982) ★★★★, *The Rhythm Makers Vols 1, 2, 3* 1935 recordings (Sunbeam 1982) ★★★★, *The Indispensable Benny Goodman Vols 1/2* 1935-36 recordings (RCA Victor 1984) ★★★★, *The Complete Small Combinations Vols 1/2* 1935-37 recordings (RCA Victor 1984) ★★★★, *This Is Benny Goodman* (1935-39) ★★★★, *Benny Goodman From The Congress Hotel Vols 1-4* (1936) ★★★, *The Indispensable Benny Goodman Vols 3/4* 1936-37 recordings (RCA Victor 1984) ★★★★, *BG – The Camel Caravan Vols 1 & 2* 1937 recordings (Sunbeam 1984) ★★★, *Benny Goodman At The Manhattan Room Vols 1-11* 1937 recordings (Sunbeam 1985) ★★★, *Benny Goodman Trio And Quartet Live* (1937-38) ★★★★, *The Complete Small Combinations Vols 3/4* 1937-39 recordings (RCA Victor 1985) ★★★★, *Swingtime* (1938) ★★★, *Solo Flight: Charlie Christian With The Benny Goodman Sextet And Orchestra* (1939-41) ★★★★, *Charlie Christian With The Benny Goodman Sextet And Orchestra* (1939-41) ★★★, *Benny And Big Sid 'Roll 'Em'* (Honeysuckle Rose 1941) ★★★, *Benny Goodman On V-Disc* (1941-46) ★★★★, *The Forgotten Year* 1943 transcriptions (Swing Treasury 1980) ★★★, *Permanent Goodman Vols. 1 & 2 20s* recordings (Phontastic 80s) ★★★, *Camel Caravan Broadcasts Vols 1-3* 1939 recordings (Phontastic 80s) ★★★, *Alternate Takes Vols 1-12* 1939-40 recordings (Phontastic 80s) ★★★, *Different Version Vols. 1-5* 1940-45 recordings (Phontastic 80s) ★★★, *Dance & Swing* 1945-46 recordings (Phontastic 80s) ★★★, *Benny Goodman On The Fitch Bandwagon* (1944-45) ★★★, *Benny Goodman Featuring Jess Stacy* (1944-47) ★★★, *Live 1945 Broadcasts* (1945) ★★★, *Benny Goodman In Sweden* (1950) ★★★, *The Benny Goodman Yale Archives Vols-1-3* (1955-86) ★★★★, *Benny Goodman* (Flapper 1991) ★★★, *The Birth Of Swing 1935-36* (Bluebird 1992) ★★★★, *King Of Swing (1935-5)* (Giants Of Jazz 1992) ★★★★, *Air Checks 1937-1938* (Sony 1993) ★★★, *Swing Sessions* 1946 recording (Hindsight 1996) ★★★★, *The Complete RCA Victor Small Group Recordings* 3-CD box set (BMG/RCA Victor 1997)

★★★, *Live 1938 At The Carnegie Hall, Complete* (Legacy 1999) ★★★★, *Benny Rides Again 1940-47* recordings (Vocalion 1999) ★★★, *Benny Goodman 1939* (Classics 1999) ★★★, *The Breakdown Sessions Vol 1* 1944 recordings (Slipped Disc 1999) ★★★, *The Radio Years 1940-41, Vol 1* (Jazz Unlimited 1999) ★★★, *The Complete Capitol Trios 1947-54* recordings (Capitol 2000) ★★★, *Complete RCA Victor Small Group Master Takes* 1935-39 recordings (Definitive Records 2000) ★★★★, with Helen Forrest *The Original Recordings Of The 40s* (Columbia 2001) ★★★★.
● FURTHER READING: *The Kingdom Of Swing*, Benny Goodman and Irving Kolodin. *Benny Goodman: Listen To His Legacy*, D. Russell Connor. *Benny Goodman And The Swing Era*, James Lincoln Collier. *Swing, Swing, Swing: The Life And Times Of Benny Goodman*, Ross Firestone. *BG On The Record: A Bio-Discography Of Benny Goodman*, D. Russell Connor and W. Hicks Warren. *Benny, King Of Swing*, Benny Goodman. *Benny Goodman*, Bruce Crowther.

GOODWIN, RON

b. Ronald Alfred Goodwin, 17 February 1925, Plymouth, Devon, England. An important composer, conductor and arranger, from an early age Goodwin was deeply interested in all things musical, but began his working life outside the business. Eventually, he took a job as a music copier with a firm of music publishers. He also studied trumpet and arranging at the Guildhall School of Music in London, and played trumpet professionally with Harry Gold and wrote arrangements for the bands of Ted Heath and Geraldo. Goodwin made several records, arranging and conducting the backing music for singers, including Petula Clark, and also worked in radio. He has composed music in the classical form, including his 'Drake 400 Concert Suite' and 'New Zealand Suite', but it is as a writer for films that he made his greatest impact.
After first writing for documentaries, from the 60s through to the 80s he composed the scores – and generally served as the musical director – for numerous feature films, including *Whirlpool*, *The Witness*, *I'm All Right Jack*, *In The Nick*, *Village Of The Damned*, *The Trials Of Oscar Wilde*, *The Man With The Green Carnation*, *The Man At The Carleton Tower*, *The Clue Of The New Pin*, *Partners In Crime*, *Invasion Quartet*, a series of 'Miss Marple' films starring Margaret Rutherford (*Murder, She Said*, *Murder At The Gallop*, *Murder Most Foul* and *Murder Ahoy*), *The Day Of The Triffids*, *Follow The Boys*, *Of Human Bondage*, *Children Of The Damned*, *633 Squadron*, *A Home Of Your Own*, *Those Magnificent Men In Their Flying Machines*, *Operation Crossbow*, *The Alphabet Murders*, *That Riviera Touch*, *The Trap* (used as the theme for the London Marathon), *Mrs. Brown*, *You've Got A Lovely Daughter*, *Where Eagles Dare*, *Battle Of Britain*, *The Executioner*, *Frenzy*, *One Of Our Dinosaurs Is Missing*, *Escape From The Dark*, *Ride A Wild Pony*, *Candleshoe*, *Force 10 From Navarone*, *The Spaceman And King Arthur*, *Clash Of Loyalties* and *Valhalla*. He has won several Ivor

Novello Awards, including the Entertainment Music Award in 1972, and a Life Achievement Award in 1993. In the 70s Goodwin made concert tours of the UK with an orchestra performing his own film scores. He has continued to broadcast on radio, and has worked extensively in Canada.
● ALBUMS: *Film Favourites* (Parlophone 1954) ★★★★, *Music To Set You Dreaming* (Parlophone 1956) ★★★, *Out Of This World* (Parlophone 1958) ★★★★, *Adventure And Excitement/Music For An Arabian Night* (Parlophone 1958) ★★★, *Decline And Fall ... Of A Birdwatcher* film soundtrack (Stateside 1968) ★★, *Monte Carlo Or Bust* film soundtrack (Paramount 1969) ★★★, *Legend Of The Glass Mountain* (Studio 2 1970) ★★★, *Spellbound* (Studio 2 1973) ★★★, *Elizabethan Serenade* (MFP 1975) ★★★, *I'll See You In My Dreams* (Studio 2 1976) ★★★, *Escape From The Dark* film soundtrack (EMI 1976) ★★, *Rhythm And Romance* (Studio 2 1977) ★★★, with the New Zealand Symphony Orchestra *Going Places* (Studio 2 1978) ★★★, *Christmas Wonderland* (One-Up 1978) ★★★, with the Bournemouth Symphony Orchestra *Ron Goodwin And The Bournemouth Symphony Orchestra* (Chandos 1980) ★★★, *Drake 400 Concert Suite* (Chandos 1980) ★★★, *Sounds Superb* (MFP 1981) ★★★, with the Royal Philharmonic Orchestra *Projections* (EMI 1983) ★★★, *Fire And Romance* (EMI 1984) ★★★, with the New Zealand Symphony Orchestra *New Zealand Suite* (Columbia 1984) ★★★, *Ron Goodwin Plays Bacharach And David* (Ideal 1984) ★★★, *The Love Album* (MFP 1985) ★★★, with the Bournemouth Symphony Orchestra *My Kind Of Music* (Chandos 1989) ★★★.
● COMPILATIONS: *This Is Ron Goodwin* (EMI 1973) ★★★, *Very Best Of Ron Goodwin* (Studio 2 1977) ★★★, *First 25 Years* (Studio 2 1978) ★★★★.

GOONS

Mutating from Britain's radio show *Crazy People* in 1951, the high summer of the BBC Home Service's *Goon Show* was reflected in UK hit parade entries in 1956 for its spin-off double a-sides, 'I'm Walking Backwards For Christmas'/'Bluebottle Blues' and 'Bloodnok's Rock 'N' Roll'/'Ying Tong Song' – which encapsulated the offbeat humour, topical parodies and musical interludes (under the baton of bandleader Ray Ellington) of the radio series starring Spike Milligan, Peter Sellers, Harry Secombe and, briefly, Michael Bentine. As well as ushering in the strata of English comedy that culminated in the late 60s with *Monty Python's Flying Circus*, aspects of the Goons became apparent in the stylistic determination of the Scaffold, the Bonzo Dog Doo-Dah Band and, less directly, the Beatles – particularly in their first two films and in John Lennon's literary output. In reciprocation, a cod-Shakespearian recitation of 'A Hard Day's Night' was among Sellers' solo successes. However, Secombe – whose chart career began before that of the Goons – enjoyed greater success with sonorous ballads, almost topping the British list in 1967 with 'This Is My Song'. Nevertheless, Secombe's next – and last – Top 10 entry came six years later with a reissue of the Goons' 'Ying Tong Song', shortly after the

troupe's one-off radio and television reunion recorded during the BBC's 50th anniversary celebrations.
● ALBUMS: *The Best Of The Goon Shows* (Parlophone 1959) ★★★★, *The Best Of The Goon Shows Volume 2* (Parlophone 1960) ★★★★, *The Last Goon Show Of All* (BBC 1972) ★★★, there are also many BBC spoken word cassettes of *The Goon Show*.

GORDON, BARRY

b. 21 December 1948, Brookline, Massachusetts, USA, A precocious Barry Gordon found himself at the number 6 position in the US charts at the age of seven with a novelty song, 'Nuttin' For Christmas'. His first television appearance came at the age of three, followed by numerous other guest slots on programmes hosted by stars such as Jackie Gleason. MGM Records signed Gordon to sing the 'Christmas Song', written by Sid Tepper and Roy Bennett, which quickly reached the Top 10. Within weeks cover versions were released by such artists as Stan Freberg, Homer And Jethro, Fontane Sisters and Joe Ward, who reached number 20 with his version. Gordon placed only one other single in the charts, another novelty tune called 'Rock Around Mother Goose', in 1956. He went on to act on television and the stage and was still active in those areas in the mid-80s.

GORDON, DEXTER

b. 27 February 1923, Los Angeles, California, USA, d. 25 April 1990, Philadelphia, Pennsylvania, USA. Gordon began his musical career studying clarinet; by his mid-teens he had switched to tenor saxophone, on which instrument he played with Lionel Hampton in 1940. He stayed with Hampton for a little over two years, recording with the band and gaining in stature so that no less an artist than Coleman Hawkins could nominate him, in 1941, as one of his favourite tenor players. Gordon then worked with Lee Young, his own small group, Fletcher Henderson, Louis Armstrong and Billy Eckstine. By late 1944 Gordon had absorbed many of the new developments in jazz and his exposure to numerous eager beboppers in the Eckstine band soon won him over completely. In the next few years he played frequently on both the east and west coasts, comfortably ignoring the artificial but effective dividing line in the bop of the early 50s. Amongst his playing partners of this period was Wardell Gray, with whom he made several important and much-imitated records. During the rest of the 50s Gordon's career was disrupted by his addiction to narcotics, but by the 60s he was off drugs and playing better than ever. Throughout the 60s and into the 70s he toured extensively, becoming especially popular in Europe where he mostly resided. He returned to the USA in 1976 and continued to record, attracting considerable attention with his mature yet evolving style. His personal life was then in some disarray due to a second broken marriage and a drink problem. He reached a turning point in 1986 when he secured an acting role in a feature film. He had previously dabbled with acting in the early 60s, but the leading role in a major film was a very different matter. He rose to the challenge and the film, 'Round Midnight, was widely considered an artistic and commercial success with Gordon being nominated for an Academy Award for his portrayal of an alcoholic saxophonist.

One of the outstanding tenor saxophonists in jazz, Gordon's early influences gave him a deeply felt appreciation of swing. Although he was rightly regarded as a major figure in bop, his playing always displayed his awareness of the swing era cadences. In his up tempo performances, especially in his duets and duels with Gray, there is a thrusting aggression to his playing. On ballads he could be tough or tender, able to enhance any tune through his unique combination of experience and inspiration. His recordings stand as eloquent testimony to a man who influenced many musicians. Perhaps because he was not at his best in his later years (one drummer who worked with him then described the experience as 'a crash course in playing slow'), Gordon was largely ignored by record companies during the 80s, recording only the soundtrack album for 'Round Midnight between 1982 and his death in 1990. However, in 1985 Blue Note Records, for whom he had made many of his finest records in the 60s, did release the double Nights At The Keystone, comprising live recordings from 1978-79, and later added more material from the same sessions to make up a three-volume CD set with the same title, which was reissued in 1990.

● ALBUMS: Dexter Gordon Quintet (Dial 1950) ★★★★, All Star Series – Dexter Gordon (Savoy 1951) ★★★★, New Trends In Modern Jazz Vol. 3 (Savoy 1952) ★★★★, Daddy Plays The Horn (Bethlehem 1955) ★★★, Dexter Blows Hot And Cool (Dootone 1956) ★★★, with Howard McGhee The Chase (Jazztone 1956) ★★★, The Resurgence Of Dexter Gordon (Jazzland 1960) ★★★, Doin' Alright (Blue Note 1961) ★★★★, Dexter Calling (Blue Note 1961) ★★★★, Go (Blue Note 1962) ★★★★, A Swingin' Affair (Blue Note 1962) ★★★★, Cry Me A River (SteepleChase 1962) ★★, Our Man In Paris (Blue Note 1963) ★★★★, One Flight Up (Blue Note 1964) ★★★★, Cheese Cake (SteepleChase 1964) ★★, King Neptune (SteepleChase 1964) ★★★, I Want More (SteepleChase 1964) ★★★, It's You Or No One (SteepleChase 1964) ★★, Billie's Bounce (SteepleChase 1964) ★★, Love For Sale (SteepleChase 1964) ★★, Clubhouse (Blue Note 1965) ★★★, Gettin' Around (Blue Note 1965) ★★★★, with Booker Ervin Settin' The Pace (Prestige 1967) ★★★★, The Montmartre Collection (1967) ★★★, Take The 'A' Train (Black Lion 1967) ★★, Both Sides Of Midnight (Black Lion 1967) ★★★, Body And Soul (Black Lion 1967) ★★, Live At The Amsterdam Paradiso (1969) ★★★, with Slide Hampton A Day In Copenhagen (MPS 1969) ★★★, The Tower Of Power/More Power (Prestige 1969) ★★★, with Karin Krog Some Other Spring (1970) ★★★, with Gene Ammons The Chase! (Prestige 1970) ★★★, At Montreux (Prestige 1970) ★★★, The Panther (1970) ★★, with Jackie McLean The Meeting (SteepleChase 1973) ★★★, Blues A La Suisse (Prestige 1973) ★★★, with McLean The

Source (SteepleChase 1974) ★★★, The Apartment (SteepleChase 1974) ★★, Bouncin' With Dex (SteepleChase 1975) ★★★, Stable Mable (Steeple-Chase 1975) ★★★, Homecoming (Columbia 1976) ★★, Lullaby For A Monster (SteepleChase 1977) ★★, Biting The Apple (SteepleChase 1977) ★★★, Sophisticated Giant (1977) ★★★, More Than You Know (SteepleChase 1977) ★★, Something Different (SteepleChase 1977) ★★★, Midnight Dream (West Wind 1977) ★★★, Nights At The Keystone Vol 1-3 (Blue Note 1979) ★★★, Gotham City (1981) ★★★, American Classic (1982) ★★★, 'Round Midnight: Soundtrack (1986) ★★★, A Gordon Cantata recorded 1978 (West Wind 1993) ★★★, Live At Carnegie Hall: Complete (Columbia/Legacy 1998) ★★★★, The Squirrel 1967 live recording (Blue Note 1998) ★★★, In A Soulful Mood 1955, 1962-69 recordings (Music Club 1999) ★★★, The Jumpin' Blues (Prestige 1970) ★★, Those Were The Days 1971 recording (Moon 1999) ★★, with Ben Webster Baden 1972 (TCB 1999) ★★★.

● COMPILATIONS: Dexter Rides Again 1945-47 recordings (Savoy 1958) ★★★, Best Of Dexter Gordon: The Blue Note Years (Blue Note 1988) ★★★★, Ballads (Blue Note 1992) ★★★★, The Complete Blue Note Sixties Sessions 6-CD box set (Blue Note 1996) ★★★★, The Art Of The Ballad 1969-73 recordings (Prestige 1998) ★★★★, with Wardell Gray Citizens Bop 40s recordings (Black Lion 1998), In A Soulful Mood (Music Club 1999) ★★★, Settin' The Pace 1945-47 recordings (Savoy 1999) ★★★★.

● VIDEOS: The Dexter Gordon Quartet (Rhapsody 1995), More Than You Know (Academy Video 1998).

● FURTHER READING: Long Tall Dexter, Stan Britt.

GORDON, ROSCO

b. 23 December 1933, Memphis, Tennessee, USA. A self-taught boogie-woogie styled pianist with no acknowledged influences other than a presumed awareness of the work of Amos Milburn and Little Willie Littlefield. Gordon was part of the Beale Streeters group in the late 40s, alongside Johnny Ace, B.B. King and later, Bobby Bland. Ike Turner, then a freelance producer and talent scout, recognized the potential of Gordon's powerful singing and recorded him for Modern. He was still a teenager when he first recorded at Sam Phillips' Memphis Recording Service in January 1951. Phillips sold masters to both Chess Records in Chicago and RPM in Los Angeles, and thus, Gordon's 'Booted' appeared on both labels, a possible factor in its becoming the number 1 R&B hit in the spring of 1952. The follow-up, 'No More Doggin'', was another Top 10 R&B hit and typified what became known as 'Rosco's Rhythm', a loping boogie shuffle rhythm that predated and perhaps influenced Jamaican ska and blue-heat music. Gordon signed to Phillips' own Sun Records label in 1955, recording a regional hit, 'The Chicken', which led to his appearance in the film Rock Baby, Rock It two years later. Moving to New York, he formed the duo Rosco and Barbara, making singles for Old Town. Many tracks recorded during this time remained unissued until the 70s and 80s. His most well-known song reached number 2 in the R&B charts and was recorded in 1960 for the Chicago-based label Vee Jay Records. With its catchy sax-driven riff, 'Just A Little Bit' captured the imaginations of British R&B groups as well as black record buyers. A version by Merseybeat band the Undertakers was a minor hit in 1964. Further records for ABC, Old Town, Jomada, Rae-Cox and Calla made little impression and in 1970, Gordon created his own label, Bab-Roc, issuing records by himself and his wife Barbara. An album of new compositions plus remakes of his hits was recorded for Organic Productions in 1971 but never released. A brief visit to England in 1982 brought an onstage reunion with B.B. King at London's 100 Club. At that time he was financing recordings from his own cleaning business. *Memphis Tennessee*, a newly recorded batch of songs appeared in 2001, with musical support from Duke Robillard. It is a great pity that Gordon left it so long to deliver a new album of such quality.

● ALBUMS: *Memphis Tennessee* (Stony Plain 2001) ★★★★.

● COMPILATIONS: *The Legendary Sun Performers: Rosco Gordon* (Charly 1977) ★★★, *Best Of Rosco Gordon Volume 1* (Ace 1980) ★★★★, *Rosco Gordon Volume 2* (Ace 1982) ★★★★, *Keep On Diggin'* (Mr R&B 1981) ★★★, *The Memphis Masters* (Ace 1982) ★★★, *Rosco Rocks Again* (JSP 1983) ★★★, *Bootin' Boogie* (1990) ★★★, *Lets Get High* (Charly 1990) ★★★, *Bootin': The Best Of The RPM Years* (Ace 1998) ★★★★,

● FILMS: *Rock Baby, Rock It* (1957).

GORME, EYDIE

b. Edith Gorme, 16 August 1931, New York City, New York, USA. The youngest of three children, Gorme's parents were of Turkish and Spanish origin, and since Spanish was the family language, she grew up speaking it fluently. At the age of three she made her radio debut, singing in a children's programme from a department store. While at the William Howard Taft High School in the Bronx, Gorme was voted 'the prettiest, peppiest cheerleader', starred in the school musicals, and sang with her friend Ken Greengrass' band at the weekends. On leaving school, she worked as a Spanish interpreter with the Theatrical Supply Export Company, before deciding to concentrate on a singing career, with Greengrass as her manager. Her first break came in 1950 when she successfully auditioned for bandleader Tommy Tucker, and toured with him for two months. When that tour ended she spent a year with Tex Beneke before going out on her own, appearing in nightclubs, and on radio and television. After being turned down several times by Arthur Godfrey's talent scouts ('the fourth time I tried, they locked the office door when they saw me coming up the stairs'), Gorme signed for Coral Records in 1952. Her singles included 'Frenesi', 'I've Gotta Crow', 'Tea For Two' and 'Fini', which entered the US Top 20. She also hosted her own radio show, *Cita Con Eydie* (*A Date With Eydie*), which was transmitted to Spanish-speaking countries via the *Voice Of America*. In September 1953, she became a permanent member of Steve Allen's top-rated *Tonight* show, on which she sang, and wrote and performed sketches with another regular, Steve Lawrence. They also introduced Allen's composition 'This Could Be The Start Of Something (Big)', which became associated with them as their singing partnership blossomed into romance. Lawrence was the son of Eastern European parents and had sung in the choir at his cantor father's synagogue. Lawrence *did* make it onto the *Arthur Godfrey Talent Show*, in 1952, and had made an impression with his version of Tony Martin's hit 'Domino'.

An important and influential figure in both Gorme and Lawrence's recording careers was conductor, arranger and producer Don Costa. In February 1956, Gorme deputized at short notice for Billy Daniels at New York's Copacabana nightclub, and was so well received that she returned in July to headline with her own show. In January 1957, she made her Broadway debut in the *Jerry Lewis Stage Show* at the Palace Theatre, and in December, Gorme and Lawrence were married in Las Vegas. Gorme's success in the US singles chart up to this period had included 'Too Close For Comfort', 'Mama, Teach Me To Dance' (both 1956), 'Love Me Forever' (1957) and the number 11 hit 'You Need Hands' (1958).

During the summer of 1958 the couple starred in their own weekly one-hour musical variety television show, as a replacement for Steve Allen. Shortly afterwards, Lawrence was inducted into the US Army for two years. Gorme embarked on a country-wide nightclub tour until 1960 when she was reunited with Lawrence at the Copacabana and the Coconut Grove, Los Angeles, and the Sands and Sahara Hotels in Las Vegas. In 1960 they won a Grammy Award for *We Got Us*, their first complete duet album, which was followed by several others, including *Two On The Aisle*, a set of Broadway show numbers and *At The Movies*. In the singles chart, the couple's most successful joint efforts included 'I Want To Stay Here' (1963) and 'I Can't Stop Talking About You' (1964). Eydie received a Grammy Award for Best Popular Female Vocalist for her version of 'If He Walked Into My Life', from Jerry Herman's musical *Mame*. In 1968, the couple appeared on Broadway in *Golden Rainbow*, a musical adaptation of Arnold Schulman's play *A Hole In the Head*, with words and music by Walter Marks. One of the songs, 'I've Gotta Be Me', became the title of a Lawrence album, and also became a regular part of Sammy Davis Jnr.'s repertoire. In 1969, Gorme and Lawrence recorded their first musical, *What It Was, Was Love*, written for them by Gordon Jenkins.

During the 70s and 80s, the couple continued to record and appear regularly on television. Several of their 'specials', commemorating the music of composers such as Cole Porter and George and Ira Gershwin, won awards; *Steve And Eydie Celebrate Irving Berlin* gained a record-breaking seven Emmys. In 1987, they were in a television production of *Alice In Wonderland*, written by Steve Allen, playing the parts of Tweedledum and

Tweedledee. In 1989, they released *Alone Together*, on their own GL label. It was for their live performances, however, that they received the most applause. During the 80s, they appeared at venues such as Carnegie Hall in 1981 and 1983, the Universal Amphitheatre, in Los Angeles, Harrah's, Tahoe, and the 1,400-seater Bally's at Las Vegas. Their skilful blend of classy songs (or, as they put it, 'no punk, no funk, no rock, no schlock'), coupled with a brand of humour that has been honed for over 30 years, make them one of the few consistently successful acts of their kind in the world. In 1991, they saw quite a lot of that world, when they joined Frank Sinatra on his year long *Diamond Jubilee Tour*, to commemorate his 75th birthday.

● ALBUMS: *Delight* (Coral 1957) ★★, *Eydie Gorme* (ABC-Paramount 1957) ★★★, *Eydie Swings The Blues* (ABC-Paramount 1957) ★★★★, *Eydie Gorme Vamps The Roaring '20s* (ABC-Paramount 1958) ★★★★, *Eydie In Love ...* (ABC-Paramount 1958) ★★★★, *Love Is A Season* (ABC-Paramount 1958) ★★★, *Eydie Sings Showstoppers* (ABC-Paramount 1959) ★★★★, *Eydie Gorme On Stage* (ABC-Paramount 1959) ★★★★, *Eydie Gorme In Dixieland* (ABC-Paramount 1960) ★★, *Come Sing With Me* (United Artists 1961) ★★★, *I Feel So Spanish* (United Artists 1962) ★★★, *Blame It On The Bossa Nova* (Columbia 1963) ★★★★, *Let The Good Times Roll* (Columbia 1963) ★★★, *Gorme Country Style* (Columbia 1964) ★, *Amor* (Columbia 1964) ★★★, *More Amor* (Columbia 1965) ★★, *Don't Go To Strangers* (Columbia 1966) ★★★, with the Trio Los Panchos *Navidad Means Christmas* (Columbia 1966) ★★, *Softly, As I Love You* (Columbia 1967) ★★★, *Tonight I'll Say A Prayer* (RCA 1970) ★★★, *Tomame O Dejame* (President 1985) ★★★, *Come In From The Rain* (President 1985) ★★★, *Sings/Canta* (Sound 1987) ★★★.
With Steve Lawrence *We Got Us* (ABC-Paramount 1960) ★★★★, *Steve And Eydie Sing The Golden Hits* (ABC-Paramount 1960) ★★★, *Cozy* (United Artists 1961) ★★★, *Two On The Aisle* (United Artists 1963) ★★★, *Our Best To You* (ABC-Paramount 1964) ★★★, *Together On Broadway* (Columbia 1967) ★★★, *What It Was, Was Love* (RCA 1969) ★★★, *Real True Lovin'* (RCA 1969) ★★★, *Tonight I'll Say A Prayer* (RCA 1970) ★★★, *We Can Make It Together* (Ember 1975) ★★★, *Our Love Is Here To Stay* (United Artists 1977) ★★★, *I Still Believe In Love* (President 1985) ★★★, *Alone Together* (GL 1989) ★★★, *Since I Fell For You* (GL 1993) ★★★.
● COMPILATIONS: *The Very Best Of Eydie Gorme* (ABC-Paramount 1961) ★★★, *Eydie Gorme's Greatest Hits* (Columbia 1967) ★★★.
With Steve Lawrence *The Very Best Of Eydie And Steve* (United Artists 1962) ★★★, *The Golden Hits Of Eydie And Steve* (United Artists 1962) ★★★, *The Best Of Steve And Eydie* (Columbia 1977) ★★★, *20 Golden Performances* (Columbia 1977) ★★★.

GOULD, MORTON
b. 10 December 1913, Richmond Hill, New York, USA, d. 21 February 1996, Orlando, Florida, USA.

Gould was one of the most important figures in American music of the twentieth century. His composition 'Pavane' (from his 'American Symphonette No. 2') has become a light-music standard. By the age of 21 he was conducting and arranging a weekly series of orchestral radio shows, which allowed him to introduce many of his lighter works to a wider public. Equally at home in the popular and classical fields, his compositions included 'American Salute', 'Latin-American Symphonette', 'Spirituals For Orchestra', 'Interplay For Piano And Orchestra', 'Tap Dance Concerto', 'Dance Variations For Two Pianos And Orchestra', 'Jekyll And Hyde Variations', plus five symphonies and numerous works for symphonic band. Among many special commissions were 'Fall River Legend', 'Inventions For Four Pianos And Wind Orchestra', 'Declaration', 'St Lawrence Suite', 'Festive Music', 'Venice', 'Columbia', 'Soundings', 'Cheers' (commissioned by the Boston Symphony for Arthur Fiedler's 50th anniversary), 'Burchfield Gallery', 'Celebration '81', 'Housewarming', 'Cello Suite', 'Concerto Concertante', 'Centennial Symphony For Band' and 'Troubador Music For Four Guitars'. Gould's musical scores for Broadway included *Billion Dollar Baby* (1945) and *Arms And The Girl* (1950). For the cinema he scored *Delightfully Dangerous*, *Cinerama Holiday* and *Windjammer*. Ballets included Jerome Robbins' *Interplay*, Agnes De Mille's *Fall River Legend*, George Balanchine's *Clarinade* and Eliot Field's *Santa Fe Saga* and *Halftime*.
His television work included a *CBS World War 1* documentary series, *F. Scott Fitzgerald In Hollywood* for ABC, the four-part mini-series *Holocaust* (1978) and a role as musical host for the National Educational Network series *The World Of Music With Morton Gould*. His list of recordings is extensive and he received many Grammy nominations. In 1966 his RCA Red Seal recording of Charles Ives with the Chicago Symphony won the NARAS Grammy Award as the best classical recording of the year. In lighter vein, Gould's mood albums by his own orchestra from the 40s and 50s are collector's items. He also recorded with the London Symphony, London Philharmonic, the American Symphony Orchestra and the Louisville Orchestra. Gould travelled widely in the USA and throughout the world as a guest conductor, and was the recipient of numerous awards from fellow musicians. In March 1986 he became President of the American Society of Composers, Authors and Publishers (ASCAP), holding the post until 1994. Much of his music featured a strong patriotic American flavour, partly explaining why his own compositions were not better known outside the USA. In 1995, at the age of 81, Morton Gould won his first Pulitzer Prize in music for his work 'Stringmusic'. He died suddenly at a hotel in Orlando, Florida, while attending the Disney Institute as artist-in-residence.
● ALBUMS: *After Dark* (Columbia 1949) ★★★, *South Of The Border* (Columbia) ★★★, *Rhapsodies For Piano And Orchestra* (Columbia) ★★★, *Soft*

Lights And Sweet Music (Columbia) ★★★, *Strike Up The Band* (Columbia) ★★★, *Christmas Music For Orchestra* (Columbia) ★★★, *Interplay For Piano And Orchestra – Music Of Morton Gould* (Columbia) ★★★, *Family Album/Tap Dance Concerts* (Columbia) ★★★, *Manhattan Moods* (Columbia) ★★★, *Victor Herbert Serenades* (Columbia) ★★★, *Symphonic Serenade* (Columbia) ★★★, *Starlight Serenade* (Columbia) ★★★, *Music At Midnight* (Columbia) ★★★, *Morton Gould Showcase* (Columbia) ★★★, *Music Of Morton Gould* (Columbia) ★★★, *Curtain Time* (Columbia 1951) ★★★, *Morton Gould Programme* (Columbia 1951) ★★★, *The Months (Tchaikovsky)* (Columbia) ★★★, *Movie Time* (Columbia) ★★★, *Memories* (Columbia) ★★★, *Wagon Wheels* (Columbia) ★★★, *Famous Operettas* (Columbia) ★★★, *Oklahoma! And Carousel Suites* (RCA 1955) ★★★, *An American In Paris/Porgy And Bess Suite* (RCA 1956) ★★★, *Music For Summertime* (RCA 1956) ★★★, *Where's The Melody* (RCA 1958) ★★★, *Moon, Wind And Stars* (RCA 1958) ★★★, *World's Best Loved Waltzes* (RCA) ★★★, *Pendagrass* (Columbia) ★★★, *High-Fi Band Concert* (Columbia) ★★★, *Brass And Percussion* (RCA) ★★★, *Blues In The Night* (RCA 1957) ★★★, *Temptation* (RCA 1957) ★★★, *Batons And Bows* (RCA 1958) ★★★, *Coffee Time* (RCA 1958) ★★★, *Jungle Drums* (RCA 1960) ★★★, *Doubling In Brass* (RCA 1961) ★★★, *Beyond The Blue Horizon* (RCA 1961) ★★★, *Kern And Porter Favorites* (RCA 1961) ★★★, *Sousa Forever!* (RCA 1961) ★★★, *Love Walked In* (RCA 1961) ★★★, *Moonlight Sonata* (RCA 1961) ★★★, *Goodnight Sweetheart* (RCA 1962) ★★★, *Finlandia* (RCA 1963) ★★★, *More Jungle Drums* (RCA 1964) ★★★, *Spirituals For Strings* (RCA 1965) ★★★, *World War I* (RCA 1965) ★★★, *Spirituals For Orchestra* (RCA 1965) ★★★, *Latin Lush And Lovely* (RCA 1966) ★★★, *Two Worlds Of Kurt Weill* (RCA 1966) ★★★, *Charles Ives Orchestra Set No. 2* (RCA 1967) ★★★, *Morton Gould Makes The Scene* (RCA 1967) ★★★, with Larry Adler *Discovery* (RCA 1969) ★★★★, *Musical Christmas Tree* (RCA 1969) ★★★, *Holocaust* (RCA 1978) ★★★, *Gould Conducts Gould* (RCA 1978) ★★★, *The Louisville Orchestra First Edition Series: Morton Gould* (Albany 1988) ★★★.

GRACIE, CHARLIE

b. Charles Anthony Graci, 14 May 1936, Philadelphia, Pennsylvania, USA. When guitarist and songwriter Charlie Gracie recorded the original version of the rock 'n' roll song 'Butterfly' in 1957, he faced stiff competition from Andy Williams' cover version. Gracie's Elvis Presley-like vocal took the song to number 5 in the US charts and Top 20 in the UK, but Williams' charted higher, number 1 in the UK and USA. They both sold over a million copies. He started out appearing as a teenager on Paul Whiteman's top-rated American television show. Gracie's subsequent singles were styled to suit his voice, including the ballads 'Fabulous' and 'Wanderin' Eyes', both Top 10 smashes in the UK in the same year. For many years he has been a legend rather than a performing artist. Often controversial, he has changed record labels countless times and still regularly performs in the USA and Europe. In the UK he has a fiercely loyal following, probably owing to the fact that he was the first ever rock 'n' roller to tour the UK in the 50s.

● ALBUMS: *The Cameo Parkway Sessions* (London 1978) ★★★, *Charlie Gracie's Early Recordings* (Revival 1979) ★★★, *Rockin' Philadelphia* (Magnum Force 1982) ★★★, *Amazing Gracie* (Charly 1982) ★★★, *Live At The Stockton Globe 1957* (Rollercoaster 1983) ★★, *Boogie Boogie Blues And Other Rarities* (Revival 1990) ★★.

● COMPILATIONS: *Best Of Charlie Gracie* (Revival 1988) ★★★, *It's Fabulous* (Stomper Time 1995) ★★★, *It's Fabulous It's Charlie Gracie* (Cotton Town Jubilee 1995) ★★★.

● FILMS: *Jamboree* aka *Disc Jockey Jamboree* (1957).

GRANAHAN, GERRY

b. 17 June 1939, Pittston, Pennsylvania, USA. Granahan was associated with the 50s groups Dicky Doo And The Don'ts and the Fireflies and also recorded under his own name. Granahan started out as a disc jockey in his home-town before switching to a music career. At the age of 17 he began recording demos for Elvis Presley at the latter's Gladys Music firm. He recorded an unreleased single under the name Jerry Grant in 1957. The following year he co-wrote a song called 'No Chemise, Please' and recorded it under his name for Sunbeam Records; it reached number 23 in the summer of 1958. That same year Granahan also reached the US charts as a member of the Fireflies, who just missed the Top 20 with the ballad 'You Were Mine', on Ribbon Records, and led Dicky Doo And The Don'ts, a quintet that charted five times on Swan Records, first and most notably with 'Click Clack', a novelty rock 'n' roll song Granahan co-wrote with Dave Alldred, ex-drummer of Jimmy Bowen and the Rhythm Orchids. In later years Granahan became a producer for such artists as Shirley Ellis, Linda Scott, the Dave Clark Five, Jay And The Americans, Patty Duke and Farrante And Teicher, and ran his own Caprice label, whose roster at one time included Linda Scott, the Angels, James Ray and Santo And Johnny (the latter actually signed to the related Canadian-American label). In the early 90s he was running his own GPG Studios based in Warwick, Rhode Island.

● ALBUMS: *Gerry Granahan's King-Sized Hits Volumes 1 and 2.* (Caprice) ★★★.

GRANT, GOGI

b. Myrtle Audrey Arinsberg, 20 September 1924, Philadelphia, Pennsylvania, USA. Pop vocalist Grant was apparently named after a New York restaurant called Gogi's La Rue, which was frequented by Dave Kapp, head of A&R at RCA Records. She had previously recorded, without success, as Audrey Brown and Audrey Grant, but as Gogi Grant she hit the US Top 10 in 1955 with the ballad 'Suddenly There's A Valley'. Her biggest hit came a year later with a sad ballad about lost love, 'The Wayward Wind', which shot to number

1 in the USA and reached the Top 10 in the UK. After signing to RCA Victor she was heavily marketed as an easy-listening singer. She provided all the vocals for actress Ann Blyth's portrayal of 1920s torch singer Helen Morgan in the 1957 biopic *The Helen Morgan Story*.

● ALBUMS: *Suddenly There's Gogi Grant* (Era 1956) ★★★, *The Helen Morgan Story* film soundtrack (RCA Victor 1957) ★★★, *Welcome To My Heart* (RCA Victor 1958) ★★★, *Torch Time* (RCA Victor 1959) ★★, *Kiss Me Kate* (RCA Victor 1959) ★★, *Granted . . . It's Gogi* (RCA Victor 1960) ★★, *If You Want To Get To Heaven, Shout* (Liberty 1960) ★★, *The Wayward Wind* (Era 1960) ★★★.

● FILMS: *The Big Beat* (1957).

GRANZ, NORMAN

b. 6 August 1918, Los Angeles, California, USA, d. 22 November 2001, Geneva, Switzerland. A lifelong love of jazz led to Granz's early involvement in music as both film-maker and concert promoter. Together with photographer Gjon Mili, he made *Jammin' The Blues* (1944), still regarded as one of the best jazz short films ever made. Granz also promoted jazz sessions at Los Angeles clubs, insisting upon desegregated audiences. In 1944 he staged a jazz concert at the Philharmonic Auditorium in Los Angeles, an event whose title was shortened to fit the available advertising space. The abbreviated version, Jazz At The Philharmonic, or JATP, became synonymous with concert-hall jam sessions featuring the very best jazz talent. A few of the saxophonists who played at JATP in its formative years were Lester Young, Coleman Hawkins, Charlie Parker, Benny Carter, Charlie Ventura, Illinois Jacquet, Willie Smith and Joe 'Flip' Phillips. Granz insisted on desegregated audiences and first-class travel and hotel accommodation – things of which jazz musicians, especially those who were black, had previously only dreamed. From the start, Granz recorded his concerts and eventually began releasing them, often on labels he owned or controlled, among them Clef, Norgran, Verve Records and Pablo. On recording sessions, Granz arranged for the return to the studios of several musicians who had been neglected by the major record companies. Among those whose careers were resuscitated was Art Tatum, whom Granz recorded with a wide range of musical partners and also in an extensive series of solo albums. Granz became personal manager for some of the artists he promoted, notably Ella Fitzgerald, with whom he recorded the remarkable 'Song Book' sequence of albums, and Oscar Peterson. Granz was also responsible for recording much of Billie Holiday's later work. He received the *Down Beat* lifetime achievement award in 1989.

In appraising Granz's remarkable career it is astonishing to wade through the cavalcade of names he not only knew well but with whom he formed productive working partnerships. The back catalogue of Verve Records alone is a testament to his greatness and undiminished enthusiasm for popular music.

GRAY, DOLORES

b. 7 June 1924, Chicago, Illinois, USA. A dynamic, full-bloodied singer, early in her career Gray sang on radio with Milton Berle and Rudy Vallee. Making her Broadway debut in Cole Porter's *Seven Lively Arts* (1944), she went on to appear in *Are You With It* and *Sweet Bye And Bye* in 1946, and was then chosen by Richard Rodgers and Oscar Hammerstein II for the lead in their London production of *Annie Get Your Gun*. That historic opening night in 1947, on her 23rd birthday, she took London by storm with a performance that almost matched Ethel Merman's triumph in the role on Broadway. She was back there herself in 1951 with *Two On The Aisle*, and followed this two years later with *Carnival In Flanders*, for which she won a Tony Award as the outstanding actress in a musical. MGM signed her for *It's Always Fair Weather* (1955) in which she shared the spotlight with Gene Kelly, Dan Dailey Michael Kidd, and Cyd Charisse, and excelled with her vibrant versions of 'Music Is Better Than Words' and 'Thanks A Lot But No Thanks'. She was rewarded with a starring role in *Kismet*, followed by *The Opposite Sex* in 1956, but because film musicals were on the wane, MGM had only the comedy *Designing Woman* to offer, and she returned to Broadway in *Destry Rides Again*. Gray worked steadily in television and clubs and made singles for Capitol showing that she was no mere stage belter but a sensitive interpreter of standards. Apart from the splendid *Warm Brandy*, so far she has been heard only on soundtrack and Original Cast albums. After taking over from Angela Lansbury in the 1973 London production of *Gypsy*, in 1987 she returned to the West End in the role of Carlotta Campion, singing that memorable anthem, 'I'm Still Here', in Stephen Sondheim's *Follies*.

● ALBUMS: *Warm Brandy*. (Capitol 1957) ★★★★.

GREAT CARUSO, THE

This lavishly produced biopic of the celebrated Italian opera singer was released by MGM in 1951. Mario Lanza, making his third screen appearance, was the perfect choice to play the lead in a screenplay by Sonia Levian and William Ludwig that, in certain areas of Caruso's life, was somewhat economical with the truth. For instance, the existence of one of his wives was totally ignored in the haste to condense drastically his rise to fame, and to feature as much music on the screen as possible. It was all rather false, and even the hit song that emerged from the film, 'The Loveliest Night Of The Year', was not actually associated with Caruso, being a Mexican instrumental piece, 'Over The Waves' (Juventino Rosas), adapted by Irving Aaronson and lyricist Paul Francis Webster. As for the remainder of the musical fare, it was a collection of songs and operatic excerpts that included 'Last Rose Of Summer' (Thomas Moore-Richard Alfred Milliken), 'Sextet' (Donizetti), 'La Donna E Mobile' (Verdi), 'Celeste Aida' (Verdi), 'Ave Maria' (Bach-Charles Gounod), 'Sweethearts' (Victor Herbert-Robert B. Smith), 'Vesti La Guibba' (Leoncavallo) and 'M'Appari' (Flotow). Anne Blyth played Dorothy Benjamin, Caruso's wife, and among the rest of the cast were Dorothy Kirsten, Jarmila Novotna, Richard Hageman, Eduard Franz, Carl Benton, Ludwig Donath, Ian Wolfe and Mae Clarke.

Joseph Ruttenbergs' Technicolor photography enhanced the whole spectacular affair, which was produced by Joe Pasternak and directed by Richard Thorpe. Musical directors Johnny Green and Peter Herman Adler were nominated for Oscars, and Douglas Shearer won one for sound recording. *The Great Caruso* grossed over $4.5 million in North America (a great deal of money in those days), and proved to be the most popular of Mario Lanza's brief film career (he made only seven films).

GRECO, BUDDY

b. Armando Greco, 14 August 1926, Philadelphia, Pennsylvania, USA. A singer and pianist known for his swinging, ultra-hip interpretations of classy songs. The son of a music critic who had his own radio show on station WPEN, Buddy himself appeared on WPEN at the age of five, initially making his mark as a singer and actor. Later on, like his two brothers, he studied to become a pianist, practising and playing at the Philadelphia Settlement House, a 10-block complex of recreational and hobby facilities, where so many of the city's youthful musicians congregated. Greco led his own trio during 1944-49, and recorded a major hit version of Carmen Lombardo's 'Ooh! Look-A-There, Ain't She Pretty?', though the singer received only $32 for recording the single. Heard by Benny Goodman while playing at Philadelphia's Club 13, he was offered a job by the bandleader and subsequently became pianist-vocalist-arranger with the Goodman orchestra, appearing with Goodman's sextet at the London Palladium in 1949, embarking on several tours with the band and his vocals gracing such Goodman sides as 'It Isn't Fair', 'Don't Worry 'Bout Me', 'The Land of Oo-Bla-Dee' and 'Brother Bill'.

By 1951 Greco had become a solo act once more, gaining a regular spot on the *Broadway Open House* television show and providing Coral Records with a hit single in 'I Ran All The Way Home'. He also won many lucrative nightclub engagements, one of which provided the bestselling album *Buddy Greco At Mister Kelly's*, a superb document of his appearances at the Chicago club in 1955. Greco's biggest hit was still to come, a non-stop, grab-at-the-lyrics version of Richard Rodgers and Lorenz Hart's 'The Lady Is A Tramp', cut for Epic Records in 1960. This track sold over a million copies worldwide and gave Buddy his first UK chart entry. During the late 60s and 70s Greco became increasingly associated with the British showbusiness scene, playing dates at London's Talk Of The Town, appearing on the Royal Command Performance and recording an instrumental album with the London Symphony Orchestra. This well-travelled and appreciated performer claims to have played every major club in the world on at least two occasions, and was still

touring round some of them again in the late 80s. In the early 90s he re-established himself in Britain with some well-received cabaret appearances at London's Café Royal.

● ALBUMS: *Buddy Greco At Mr. Kelly's* (Coral 1956) ★★★, *Broadway Melodies* (Kapp 1956) ★★★, *My Buddy* (Epic 1959) ★★★, *Songs For Swinging Losers* (Columbia 1960) ★★★, *Buddy's Back In Town* (Columbia 1961) ★★★, *I Like It Swinging* (Columbia 1961) ★★★, *Let's Love* (Columbia 1962) ★★★, *Buddy And Soul* (Columbia 1963) ★★★, *Buddy's Back In Town* (Columbia 1963) ★★★, *Sings For Intimate Moments* (Columbia 1963) ★★★, *Soft And Gentle* (Columbia 1963) ★★★, *One More Time* (Columbia 1964) ★★★, *On Stage* (Columbia 1964) ★★★, *Modern Sounds Of Hank Williams* (Columbia 1965) ★★, *I Love A Piano* (Columbia 1966) ★★★, *Let The Sunshine In* (Wand 1970) ★★, *Live At Pullen's Talk Of North, April 1974* (Pye 1974) ★★★, *For Once In My Life* (Bulldog 1982) ★★★, *Moving On (It's Magic)* (Prestige 1990) ★★★, *Route 66* (Capitol 1994) ★★★, *MacArthur Park* (Candid 1996) ★★, *Live Buddy Greco* (Dolphin 1998) ★★, *Jazz Grooves* (Candid 1999) ★★★.

● COMPILATIONS: *Golden Hour Presents Buddy Greco* (Golden Hour 1978) ★★★, *Greatest Hits* (Columbia 1984) ★★★, *Talkin' Verve* (Verve 2001) ★★★.

GRÉCO, JULIETTE

b. 1927, Montpelier, France. An actress and inimitable singer of the *chanson*, Gréco was born the daughter of a police chief and a mother who became a Resistance worker in 1939. After spending some time in prison during the Occupation when she was 15, Gréco took acting lessons, and began to dress in men's black clothing – heavy overcoats and trousers, with polo neck sweaters – and cut her hair in a fringe. In the mid-40s she became a leading member of the philosopher Jean-Paul Sartre's intellectual Existentialist movement, which flourished in cafés such as Le Boeuf sur le Toit and Café Flore on Paris's Left Bank. Sartre encouraged her to sing, and with her slightly raw-edged voice, attractive appearance and impressive stage presence, she soon became immensely popular in the world of cabaret. Among her most memorable – and usually sad – songs are Hubert Giraud and Jean Drejec's 'Sous Le Ciel De Paris' ('Under Paris Skies'), Jacques Brel's 'J'arrive' and 'Je Suis Bien', along with several written by Joseph Kosma and Jacques Prevert, including 'Les Feuilles Mortes', which, with an English lyric by Johnny Mercer, became the wistful 'Autumn Leaves'. After appearing in a few French films from 1949 onwards, in the late 50s she embarked on a brief Hollywood career sponsored by Darryl F. Zanuck, starring in *The Sun Also Rises*, *Roots Of Heaven*, *Crack In The Mirror* and *The Big Gamble*. Afterwards, she returned to her *chansons*, and has continued to sing ever since. Her popularity in Britain has waned since the 50s, but she did perform in London in 1989 for the first time in 10 years. In the previous year, she married her musical director and accompanist Gérard Jouannest. Her previous husbands, Philippe

Lemaire and Michel Piccoli, were both actors.
● ALBUMS: *Juliette Greco* (Philips 1954) ★★★, *Gréco* (Philips 1957) ★★, *Les Grandes Chansons* (Philips 1961) ★★★★, *Juliette Gréco Showcase* (Philips 1962) ★★★, *La Femme* (Philips 1968) ★★, *Juliette Gréco* (French Decca 1972) ★★★, *Je Vous Attends* (French Decca 1974) ★★, *Le Disque D'Or* (Phonogram 1974) ★★, *Un Jour D'ete Et Quelques Nuits* (1999) ★★★.
● COMPILATIONS: *Greatest Hits* (Impact 1977) ★★★.
● FILMS: including *Au Royaume Des Cieux* (1949), *Orpheus* (1950), *The Green Glove* (1952), *Quand Tu Liras Cette Lettre* (1953), *Paris Does Strange Things* (1956), *The Sun Also Rises* (1957), *Bonjour Tristesse* (1958), *Naked Earth* (1958), *Roots Of Heaven* (1959), *Whirlpool* (1959), *Crack In The Mirror* (1960), *The Big Gamble* (1961), *Where The Truth Lies* (1962), *Uncle Tom's Cabin* (1965), *The Night Of The Generals* (1967).

GRENFELL, JOYCE

b. Joyce Irene Phipps, 10 February 1910, London, England, d. 30 November 1979, London, England. An actress, singer and author, and a brilliant exponent of the monologue and witty song. The daughter of American parents – her mother's sister was Nancy Astor – Joyce Phipps used to describe herself as 'three fourths American'. She became interested in the theatre at an early age, and spent a term at RADA before marrying Reginald Grenfell in 1929. Subsequently, she worked for a time in commercial art, contributed to *Punch* and *Country Life*, and spent over three years as radio critic for the *Observer*. After impressing the humorist Steven Potter with her own charming recollection of a lecture that she had recently attended at a Women's Institute, she was engaged by the theatrical producer Herbert Farjeon for *The Little Revue* (1939). In the early 40s she appeared in other Farjeon revues, *Diversion, Diversion No. 2* and *Light And Shade*, and then, in 1944, toured extensively with ENSA, in the Near and Far East, and in India, entertaining the troops in British forces' hospitals, with comic monologues and songs. Two years later she was awarded the OBE. In *Sigh No More* (1945), at London's Piccadilly Theatre, Grenfell dressed as a schoolgirl for Noël Coward's witty 'That Is The End Of The News', and, in the same show, introduced 'Du Maurier', a song she had written with composer Richard Addinsell. They collaborated again on material for the revues, *Tuppence Coloured* (1947) and *Penny Plain* (1951), in which Grenfell also appeared. It was the beginning of a significant and enduring professional relationship. By the late 40s and early 50s, Grenfell was working more and more in radio – as a panellist on *We Beg To Differ*, and as the British host of *Transatlantic Quiz*. She made a couple of propaganda films during the war, but her movie career proper began in 1943 with a comedy, *The Demi-Paradise*, which starred Laurence Olivier and Margaret Rutherford. Grenfell appeared with Rutherford again, in *The Happiest Days Of Your Life* (1949), which also starred the lugubrious Alastair Sim. He and Grenfell managed to emerge

unscathed from the *St. Trinians* film series. during the late 50s. Grenfell's other film roles, some of them highly telling cameos, included appearances in *Here Comes The Bride, The Galloping Major, Pickwick Papers, The Million Pound Note* and *The Americanization Of Emily*. It was on stage, however, that she really came into her own. In 1954 she wrote the book and lyrics, with Addinsell's music, for *Joyce Grenfell Requests The Pleasure*, which ran for nearly a year in London before transferring to Broadway in the following year. In America, Grenfell developed her one-woman show, toured US cities, and appeared on the *Ed Sullivan Show* several times in the late 50s. One Sullivan date saw her on the same bill with Elvis Presley ('a pasty-faced plump boy', as she recalled). She presented her solo effort in London for the first time in 1957, at the Lyric theatre, under the title of *Joyce Grenfell – A Miscellany*, and later took the show to Australia where it was called *Meet Joyce Grenfell*. Throughout the 60s she continued to tour extensively at home and abroad, and went back to Australia three times. In the early 70s she lost the sight in one eye and retired from the stage. During the next six years she published two volumes of autobiography, *Joyce Grenfell Requests The Pleasure* and *In Pleasant Places*, before cancer affected her other eye, and she died in 1979. Always an effective broadcaster, from 1966 she was an essential panel-member on television's *Face The Music*, a general knowledge quiz about music, and had her own television series on UK's BBC2 for a time. As a performer she was unique, and impossible to pigeonhole. Despite her 'terribly English' image, she was incredibly popular around the world, particularly in America. With the gentle 'I'm Going To See You Today', which became her theme, the pomp of 'Stately As A Galleon', and many other favourites such as 'Maude', 'Nursery School', 'A Terrible Worrier', 'Time', 'Three Brothers', 'It's Almost Tomorrow', and two recorded duets with Norman Wisdom, 'Narcissus' and 'I Don't 'Arf Love You', she presented a refined, humorous, perceptive, yet never unkind, view of society. One of her best-remembered pieces is 'I Like Life', which accords with her own philosophy: 'I am not interested in the pursuit of happiness, but only in the discovery of joy'. Her companion on that journey, Reginald Grenfell, who edited some of her books, died in 1993. In 1988, the revue *Re: Joyce!*, 'a diverting and engaging mixture of anecdotal biography and quintessential sketch material', starring Maureen Lipman with Denis King, opened in London and continued to be presented at intervals into the 90s.
● ALBUMS: *Requests The Pleasure* (1955) ★★★★, *At Home* (1957) ★★★★,
● COMPILATIONS: *The Collection* (One-Up 1976) ★★★★, *George Don't Do That* (Starline 1977) ★★★★, *The New Collection* (EMI 1978) ★★★, *The Second Collection* (Encore 1979) ★★★★, *Joyce Grenfell Talking* (Cube 1981) ★★★★, *Keepsake* (Retrospect 1986) ★★★, *Re: Joyce* (EMI 1988) ★★★, *Maureen Lipman and Denis King Re: Joyce!* stage cast (EMI 1989) ★★, *Songs And Monologues Of Joyce Grenfell* (EMI 1991) ★★★★, *Joyful Joyce* (1991) ★★★★, *Requests The Pleasure* 3-CD set

(BBC 1992) ★★★★, *More Joyful Joyce* (1994) ★★★.
● FURTHER READING: *George – Don't Do That...* (sketches and songs). *Stately As A Galleon* (sketches and songs). *Time Of My Life – Entertaining The Troops: Her Wartime Journals*, Joyce Grenfell. *Joyce Grenfell Requests The Pleasure*, Joyce Grenfell. *In Pleasant Places*, Joyce Grenfell. *Darling Ma: Letters To Her Mother, 1932-1944*, edited by James Roose-Evans. *Joyce: By Herself And Her Friends*, edited by Reggie Grenfell and Richard Garnett. *Joyce And Ginnie: The Letters Of Joyce Grenfell And Virginia Graham*, edited by Janie Hampton.

GRIFFITH, ANDY

b. Andrew Samuel Griffith, 1 June 1926, Mount Airy, North Carolina, USA. Andy Griffith was an actor best known for the 60s comedy show which was named after him. He attended the University of North Carolina where he studied to be a preacher, but switched his interests to pursue drama and music. With his southern drawl, Griffith easily landed roles requiring a southerner, and he starred in the 1955 Broadway production of *No Time For Sergeants*. His most acclaimed film role was the 1957 *A Face In The Crowd*. He made his move to television in 1960 with *The Andy Griffith Show*, which also starred Don Knotts and child actor Ron Howard, who would go on to fame as a director as an adult. The show ran until 1968 and spun off a sequel titled *Mayberry R.F.D.* In the late 80s Griffith starred in a successful programme titled *Matlock*, in which he played a lawyer. Griffith's recording career was not nearly as celebrated as his acting, yet he did record a number of albums and singles (in addition to comedy records and soundtracks from his television shows). He had one charting single in 1955, 'Make Yourself Comfortable', on Capitol Records, which reached number 26 in the USA.
● ALBUMS: *Andy Griffith Shouts The Blues And Old Timey Songs* (1959) ★★★, *The World's Favorite Hymns* (1973) ★★★★.

GUYS AND DOLLS

Producer Sam Goldwyn pulled off quite a coup when he cast Frank Sinatra and Marlon Brando in this 1955 screen version of the smash-hit Broadway show. In Joseph L. Mankiewicz's screenplay, which was based on Abe Burrows' libretto and Damon Runyan's short story *The Idyll Of Miss Sarah Brown*, Sinatra plays Nathan Detroit, the operator of the oldest established permanent floating crap game in New York. Constantly harassed by Inspector Brannigan (Robert Keith), and his fiancé of 14 years, Miss Adelaide (Vivian Blaine), Nathan bets 'the highest roller in town', Sky Masterson (Brando), that he cannot transport Salvation Army stalwart Sarah Brown (Jean Simmons), from the Save Our Souls Mission in New York, to Havana. Against all the odds, Sky and Sarah make the trip, but Nathan subsequently loses nothing – except his precious freedom – when he and Adelaide, along with Sky and Sarah, make it a double wedding in Times Square. There was a rumour that Sinatra wanted to play the Brando role because, in the original, Nathan does

not have a solo number. In the event, composer Frank Loesser gave him a new song, 'Adelaide', and he also wrote another new one for Brando, 'A Woman In Love', because the actor reportedly could not handle the tender 'I've Never Been In Love Before'. In fact, both he and Jean Simmons were surprisingly good on 'I'll Know' and 'If I Were A Bell'. The rest of the magnificent score – arguably Loesser's masterpiece – included 'Fugue For Tinhorns' (Sinatra-Silver-Danny Dayton), 'The Oldest Established' (Sinatra-Silver-Kaye-ensemble), 'Pet Me Poppa' (which replaced 'A Bushel And A Peck') (Blaine and chorus), 'Adelaide's Lament' (Blaine), 'Guys And Dolls' (Sinatra-Silver-Kaye), 'Take Back Your Mink' (Blaine and chorus), 'Luck Be A Lady' (Brando), 'Sue Me' (Sinatra-Blaine) and 'Sit Down, You're Rockin' The Boat'. The latter number was performed by the irrepressible Stubby Kaye, recreating his Broadway role of Nicely-Nicely Johnson. Other veterans of the stage show, playing two of the loveable Runyanesque rogues, were Johnny Silver (Benny Southstreet) and B.S. Pully (Big Jule), along with the marvellous Vivian Blaine and choreographer Michael Kidd. Also in the cast were Sheldon Leonard, George E. Stone, Regis Toomey, Kathryn Givney, Veda Ann Borg and Alan Hokanson. Directed by Mankiewicz, and photographed in Eastman Color and CinemaScope for MGM, *Guys And Dolls* was derided by the critics, but welcomed by the cinema-going public who made it one of the top box-office successes of the 50s.

GYPSY

Based on stripper Gypsy Rose Lee's autobiography, this legendary show opened at the Broadway Theatre in New York on 21 May 1959. Arthur Laurents' book follows Rose (Ethel Merman), the ruthless and ambitious show-biz mother, who is determined that her Baby June (Jacqueline Mayro) will be a star no matter what. Unfortunately for Rose, when she grows older, June (Lane Bradbury) evades her mother's clutches and defects to get married. Unfazed, Rose disregards the advice of manager and long-time fiancé Herbie (Jack Klugman), switches her fanatical attention to June's sister, Louise (Sandra Church), and eventually transforms her from a shy young girl into the classy stripper Gypsy Rose Lee. Laurents suggested that Stephen Sondheim, fresh from his lyrical success with *West Side Story*, should provide the score but Merman turned him down, preferring to rely on the experience of composer Jule Styne. Laurents eventually persuaded Sondheim to write lyrics only, and the overall result was a triumph. The score is among the most highly regarded in Broadway musical history, and includes 'Let Me Entertain You', 'Together Wherever We Go', 'Small World', 'If Mama Was Married', 'All I Need Is The Girl', 'You Gotta Have A Gimmick', 'Mr. Goldstone', and Merman's blockbusters, 'Everything's Coming Up Roses' and 'Rose's Turn'. Also cast were Maria Karnilova (Tessie Tura), Paul Wallace (Tulsa), Mort Marshall (Uncle Jocko), Lane Bradbury (June), Joe Silver (Weber), Peg Murray (Miss Cratchitt), and Michael

Parks (LA). The David Merrick production, which gave Merman one of her most satisfying roles, both in vocal and acting terms, was directed and choreographed by Jerome Robbins, and ran for 702 performances. The 1973 London version, with Angela Lansbury as Rose, Barrie Ingham (Herbie), and Zan Charisse (Louise) was directed by Arthur Laurents, and lasted for 300 performances. This production transferred to Broadway in the following year (120 performances) with Rex Robbins taking over as Herbie. In 1989 *Gypsy* returned to Broadway once again (476 performances), with television star Tyne Daly in the leading role, along with Jonathan Hadary (Herbie) and Crista Moore (Louise). Daly won a Tony Award for best actress, and there was another for best musical revival. A unique opportunity to view this wonderful musical at leisure came in 1993, when *Gypsy*, starring Bette Midler (Rose), Peter Riegert (Herbie), and Cynthia Gibb (Louise), was shown on US television and later released on video. It purported to be the first film of a complete stage musical to retain the original text, with no material added or altered. The 1998 Paper Mill Playhouse, New Jersey, production had Betty Buckley as Rose, Deborah Gibson (Louise), and Lenny Wolpe (Herbie). The 1962 film version starred Rosalind Russell (Rose), Natalie Wood (Louise), and Karl Malden (Herbie).

HALEY, BILL, AND HIS COMETS

b. William John Clifton Haley, 6 July 1925, Highland Park, Michigan, USA, d. 9 February 1981, Harlingen, Texas, USA. Haley was one of the great pioneers of rock 'n' roll and was the first artist to take the new musical form to the world stage. His roots were in country music and he began his career as a yodelling cowboy. After playing in such country groups as the Downhomers and the Range Drifters, he formed the Four Aces Of Western Swing in 1948. At that point, his repertoire included compositions by both Red Foley and Hank Williams. His next group was the Saddlemen, who played a stirring mixture of western swing, mixed with polka. In 1951, he recorded the R&B hit 'Rocket 88', which indicated how far he had already travelled in assimilating the styles of rock 'n' roll. Haley's fusion of country, R&B and a steady beat was to provide the backbone of the musical genre that he immortalized. The jive talk used on the following year's 'Rock The Joint', coupled with the distinctive slap bass playing on the record, continued the experiment.

In 1953, Haley abandoned the cowboy image and formed a new group, Bill Haley And His Comets. The line-up of the group would change frequently over the years, but Haley himself was a constant. Their first single, the exuberant 'Crazy Man Crazy', crossed over into the national charts and was the first rock 'n' roll Top 20 US hit. After signing to Decca Records in May 1954, Haley recorded a series of songs with Danny Cedrone (d. 1954; lead guitar), Joey D'Ambrosia (saxophone), Billy Williamson (steel guitar), Johnny Grande (piano), Marshall Lytle (bass) and Dick Richards (drums) that were historically crucial in bringing rock 'n' roll to the world. 'Rock Around The Clock' was a staggering achievement, a single whose timing, vocal, spine-tingling guitar breaks and inspired drumming were quite unlike any other commercial recordings up until that time. Amazingly, it was initially issued as a b-side and, even when the sides were flipped, it initially became only a minor hit. Haley returned to the studio to record a follow-up: 'Shake Rattle And Roll'. This was another seminal work, whose jive-style lyrics and brilliant employment of saxophone and upright bass brought a new sound into the US Top 20. Haley enjoyed further, though less important hits, during the next year with 'Dim, Dim The Lights' and 'Mambo Rock'. Then, in the spring of 1955, his career took a dramatic upswing when the previously issued 'Rock Around The Clock' was included in the controversial film *The Blackboard Jungle*. Suddenly, the world woke up to the importance of 'Rock Around The Clock' and it became a veritable rock 'n' roll anthem and rallying cry. It soared to the top of the US charts for a lengthy spell and achieved the same feat in the UK. When *The Blackboard Jungle* was shown in Britain, enthusiastic youths jived in the aisles and ripped up their seats in excitement.

Haley was crowned the king of rock 'n' roll and dominated the US/UK chart listings throughout 1955/6 with such songs as 'Rock-A-Beatin' Boogie', 'See You Later Alligator', 'The Saints Rock 'N' Roll', 'Razzle Dazzle', 'Burn That Candle', 'Rip It Up' and 'Rudy's Rock'. The latter was an instrumental that focused attention on Haley's saxophone player, the excellent Rudy Pompilli (d. 5 February 1976), who often played onstage lying on his back. His brother, Al Pompilli, was another important component in the group, renowned for his acrobatic displays on the stand-up bass. Haley's exciting stage act provoked hysteria among the youth population, which soon became pandemic. In February 1957, he travelled to England, the first rock 'n' roll star to tour abroad. He was mobbed when his train arrived in London and there were rabid scenes of fan mania when he performed at the Dominion Theatre, London. Inevitably, the moral pundits criticized such performances but Haley proved himself an adept apologist and emphasized the point by recording the protest 'Don't Knock The Rock', the title theme of an Alan Freed film.

Haley's star burned brightly for a couple of years, but his weakness was his age and image. At the age of 32, he was a little too old to be seen as the voice of teendom and his personality was more avuncular than erotic. Once Elvis Presley exploded onto the scene, Haley seemed a less authentic rock 'n' roll rebel and swiftly lost his standing among his young audience. He was still respected as a kind of elder statesman of rock – the man who first brought the music to the masses. Not surprisingly, he maintained his popularity by constantly touring, and his recordings veered from Latin dance excursions to novelty and straight country. He was always called upon to carry the rock 'n' roll mantle whenever there was a nostalgic outbreak of 50s revivalism. It is a testament to the power of Haley's influence that 'Rock Around The Clock' returned to the UK Top 20 on two separate occasions: in 1968 and 1974. His music effectively transcended the generation gap by reaching new listeners over three decades. By the late 70s, Haley was reportedly ill and drinking heavily. He returned to England in November 1979 for a memorable performance at the *Royal Variety Show*. The following year reports filtered through that he was suffering from a brain tumour. On 9 February 1981, he died of a heart attack in Harlingen, Texas, USA. His inestimable influence on rock 'n' roll still continues, and he was posthumously inducted into the Rock And Roll Hall Of Fame in 1987.

● ALBUMS: *Rock With Bill Haley And The Comets* (Essex 1955) ★★, *Shake, Rattle And Roll* 10-inch album (Decca 1955) ★★★, *Rock Around The Clock* (Decca 1956) ★★★★, with various artists *Music*

For The Boyfriend (Decca 1956) ★★, *Rock 'N Roll Stage Show* (Decca 1956) ★★★★, *Rocking The Oldies* (Decca 1957) ★★, *Rockin' Around The World* (Decca 1958) ★★★, *Rocking The Joint* (Decca 1958) ★★★, *Bill Haley's Chicks* (Decca 1959) ★★★★, *Strictly Instrumental* (Decca 1960) ★★, *Bill Haley And His Comets* (Warners 1960) ★★★, *Bill Haley's Jukebox* (Warners 1960) ★★★, *Twistin' Knights At The Round Table* (Roulette 1962) ★★★, *Bill Haley And The Comets* (Vocalion 1963) ★★, *Rip It Up* (MCA 1968) ★★★, *Scrapbook/Live At The Bitter End* (Kama Sutra 1970) ★, *Travelin' Band* (Janus 1970) ★★★, *Golden King Of Rock* (Hallmark 1972) ★★★, *Just Rock And Roll Music* (Sonet 1973) ★★★, *Live In London '74* (Atlantic 1974) ★★, *Rock Around The Country* (Hallmark 1974) ★★.

● COMPILATIONS: *Bill Haley's Greatest Hits* (Decca 1967) ★★★, *King Of Rock* (Ember 1968) ★★★, *Mister Rock 'n' Roll* (Ember 1969) ★★★, *The Bill Haley Collection* (Pickwick 1976) ★★★, *R-O-C-K* (Sonet 1976) ★★★, *Armchair Rock 'N' Roll* (MCA 1978) ★★★, *Everyone Can Rock 'N' Roll* (Sonet 1980) ★★★, *A Tribute To Bill Haley* (MCA 1981) ★★★, *The Essential Bill Haley* (Charly 1984) ★★★, *Hillbilly Haley* (Rollercoaster 1984) ★★★, *Boogie With Bill Haley* (Topline 1985) ★★★, *Greatest Hits* (MCA 1985) ★★★, *Golden Greats* (MCA 1985) ★★★, *From The Original Master Tapes* (MCA 1985) ★★★, *The Original Hits '54-'57* (Hallmark 1987) ★★★, *Greatest Hits* (Connoisseur 1988) ★★★, *Rip It Up Rock 'N' Roll* (Connoisseur 1988) ★★★, *Golden CD Collection* (Bulldog 1989) ★★★, *Bill Haley's Rock 'N' Roll Scrapbook* (Sequel 1990) ★★★, *The Decca Years And More* 5-CD box set (Bear Family 1991) ★★★.

● FURTHER READING: *Sound & Glory*, John Von Hoelle and John Haley.

● FILMS: *Don't Knock The Rock* (1956).

HALL, ROBIN, AND JIMMIE MACGREGOR

This folk duo from Scotland featured Robin Hall (b. 27 June 1937, Edinburgh, Scotland, d. 18 November 1998, Glasgow, Scotland; vocals, bodhrán) and Jimmie MacGregor (b. 10 March 1930, Springburn, Glasgow, Scotland; vocals, guitar). Hall had studied at the Royal Scottish Academy Of Music And Dramatic Art from 1955-58. There followed a brief spell as an actor in repertory theatre, plus some solo gigs and radio work. He met and teamed up with MacGregor at the 1959 World Youth Festival in Vienna. In contrast, MacGregor came from a working-class family, and was involved in the folk revival of the 50s. He learned a great number of songs at the famous house parties that took place at the time, with everyone singing and harmonizing. MacGregor's first influences were not Scottish at all, and were, in fact, Burl Ives and black American blues man Josh White. MacGregor built up a repertoire of Ives songs with the first guitar he bought. His next big influence was Ewan MacColl and 'Ballads And Blues'. MacGregor graduated after four years at art school, and worked as a studio potter and teacher. He often hitchhiked to London to visit what few folk clubs there were at the time.

Eventually, he settled in London, joining Chas McDevitt's skiffle group, but he left a few weeks before they had the hit record 'Freight Train'. There followed a series of solo performances and membership of various groups, including the Steve Benbow Folk Four. After meeting Hall in Vienna, the two were given much encouragement by Paul Robeson who was playing at the same concert. Hall's solo album of child ballads from the Gavin Greig collection, *Last Leaves Of Traditional Ballads*, is now a collector's item. The duo were popular on television, making their first appearance on BBC Television's *Tonight*, and appeared five nights weekly for 14 years. In 1960, Decca Records released the single 'Football Crazy', which received a great deal of airplay and attendant publicity. Hall and MacGregor also appeared regularly on radio, and are remembered for the series *Hullabaloo*, which started on 28 September 1963, on ABC television. They went on to tour the world, and record more than 20 albums, appearing on countless radio and television programmes. One series for which they became known was *The White Heather Club*, which they hosted for five years. They also recorded with Shirley Bland and Leon Rosselson as the Galliards. After 21 years together, it was Hall who called a halt to the duo's career. He had always been nervous and had never really liked performing. There were several reunion concerts, the last in 1994.

After the split, Hall went into broadcasting for the BBC World Service, as well as writing, arranging and producing records. In addition to script writing, he also took up journalism as a music and drama critic. In 1977, he won two national radio awards, best presenter and best documentary, for a documentary on Radio Clyde, *The Sing Song Streets*, a programme about Glasgow told through songs, stories and children's games. The programme was written, produced and presented by Hall. MacGregor wrote three folk songbooks, did some solo work, and wrote a book on the West Highland Way, which became the basis of a successful television series. Subsequently, he has made six outdoor television series, and written five accompanying books. His own radio show for BBC Scotland, *MacGregor's Gathering*, has been running now for many years. In 1993 MacGregor was awarded the OBE.

● ALBUMS: with the Galliards *Scottish Choice* (1961) ★★★★, with the Galliards *A Rovin'* (1961) ★★★, *Scotch And Irish* (Eclipse 1962) ★★★★, *Tonight And Every Night* (1962) ★★★★, *Two Heids Are Better Than Yin* (Eclipse 1963) ★★★, *The Next Tonight Will Be-Robin Hall And Jimmie MacGregor* (1964) ★★★★, *By Public Demand* (1964) ★★★ *The Red Yo-Yo* (1966) ★★★, *Songs Of Grief And Glory* (1967) ★★★, *One Over Eight* (1969) ★★, *We Belong To Glasgow* (1970) ★★, *Scottish Choice* (Eclipse 1971) ★★★, *Kids Stuff* (Eclipse 1974) ★★★, *Scotland's Best* (Decca 1975) ★★★, *Songs For Scotland* (Beltona 1977) ★★★.
Solo: Robin Hall *Last Leaves Of Traditional Ballads* (Collector 1959) ★★★.

HAMILTON, ROY

b. 16 April 1929, Leesburg, Georgia, USA, d. 20 July 1969, New Rochelle, New York, USA. Hamilton's booming baritone voice made him a 50s hitmaker singing gospel-flavoured pop songs. In the late 40s Hamilton honed his singing skills in a church choir and as a member of its offshoot quartet, the Searchlight Singers. He won a talent contest at the Apollo Theatre in 1947, but it was not until 1953 that he was discovered singing in a New Jersey club by Bill Cook, an influential local disc jockey who became the singer's manager. Hamilton's very first record for Columbia Records' subsidiary Epic, 'You'll Never Walk Alone', became an R&B number 1 and national US Top 30 hit in 1954, and it shot Hamilton to fame (the song would also later become a UK hit for Gerry And The Pacemakers in 1963). There followed for Hamilton a long string of singles that reached both R&B and pop audiences, notably 'If I Loved You', 'Ebb Tide' and 'Hurt' (all three 1954), and 'Unchained Melody' (an R&B number 1, 1955). Hamilton's songbook was built from the most popular entertainments of the day; 'You'll Never Walk Alone' and 'If I Loved You' were two Rodgers And Hammerstein songs taken from their musical *Carousel*, and 'Unchained Melody' came from a Warner Brothers film, *Unchained*. Hamilton retired during 1956-58 owing to exhaustion, but when he came back he had adopted the harder gospel sound of his youth to compete with rock 'n' roll and the emerging soul sound. Best reflecting the change in style were the singles 'Don't Let Go' (1958) and his last hit record, 'You Can Have Her' (1961), plus the album *Mr. Rock And Soul* in 1962. The Epic label treated Hamilton as a major pop star and issued 16 albums by the artist. During the mid-60s, his career sank while recording with MGM Records and then RCA Records, and he died not long after suffering a stroke in 1969.
● ALBUMS: *Roy Hamilton* (Epic 1956) ★★★, *You'll Never Walk Alone* (Epic 1956) ★★★, *The Golden Boy* (Epic 1957) ★★★, *With All My Love* (Epic 1958) ★★★, *Why Fight The Feeling?* (Epic 1959) ★★, *Come Out Swingin'* (Epic 1959) ★★★, *Have Blues, Must Travel* (Epic 1959) ★★, *Roy Hamilton Sings Spirituals* (Epic 1960) ★★★★, *Soft 'N' Warm* (Epic 1960) ★★★, *You Can Have Her* (Epic 1961) ★★★, *Only You* (Epic 1961) ★★★, *Mr. Rock And Soul* (Epic 1962) ★★★, *The Great Golden Grooves* (MGM 1963) ★★, *Warm Soul* (MGM 1963) ★★★, *Sentimental, Lonely And Blue* (MGM 1964) ★★, *The Impossible Dream* (RCA 1966) ★★★.
● COMPILATIONS: *Roy Hamilton At His Best* (Epic 1960) ★★★, *Roy Hamilton's Greatest Hits* (Epic 1962) ★★★, *Unchained* (Charly 1988) ★★★, *Golden Classics* (Collectables 1991) ★★★.

HAMILTON, RUSS

b. Ronald Hulme, 1933, Liverpool, England. This singer-songwriter was the first Liverpool artist to make the US Top 10 in the 50s. In 1956, this Korean War veteran (he was in the Royal Air Force) entertained children as a Redcoat at Butlins Holiday Camps in Blackpool and Brighton, and when at the latter, he formed a skiffle group and recorded his first single for Oriole. The a-side, 'We Will Make Love', written after splitting up with girlfriend Pat Hichin, made number 2 in the UK, staying in the Top 10 for 15 weeks. The b-side, 'Rainbow', which he says took only a couple of minutes to write, made him a US one-hit-wonder and shot to number 7, becoming the biggest hit to date there by a UK male artist. In the summer of 1957 he was a transatlantic star, commuting between the USA and Clacton, Essex, where he was entertaining Butlins holidaymakers at one of their camps. His follow-up, 'Wedding Ring', again written about Miss Hitchin, gave him his last UK chart entry. He joined MGM Records in 1960, but even recording in Nashville did not help him return to the charts. Despite having such a spectacular start to his career, it seemed that either Hamilton's face, distinctive lisp, or seemingly unfashionable ballad singing style, no longer fitted.

● ALBUMS: *Rainbow* (Kapp 1957) ★★, *We Will Make Love* (Oriole 1959) ★★.

HAMMERSTEIN, OSCAR, II

b. Oscar Greeley Clendenning Hammerstein, 12 July 1895, New York City, New York, USA, d. 23 August 1960, Doylestown, Pennsylvania, USA. Hammerstein was born into a family with long-standing theatrical associations. His father, William Hammerstein, was manager of New York's Victoria theatre, and an uncle, Arthur Hammerstein, was a Broadway producer. Most famous of all his ancestors was his grandfather, Oscar Hammerstein I, who had made a fortune in industry before becoming one of New York's leading theatrical impresarios and founder of the Manhattan Opera. Although he studied law, the young Oscar's background inevitably affected him and, while still at school, he wrote for shows. He was doubtless also influenced by some of his fellow students, who included future songwriters Lorenz Hart and Howard Dietz. Oscar's showbusiness career began when he was employed by his uncle as assistant stage manager. Soon afterwards, he collaborated with Otto Harbach, Frank Mandel, and composer Herbert Stothart on *Tickle Me* (1920). Subsequently, he and Harbach teamed up again to write the book and lyrics to the season's biggest hit, *Wildflower* (1923), which had music by Stothart and Vincent Youmans. Hammerstein, Harbach and Stothart then had further success, working with Rudolph Friml on *Rose-Marie* (1924), which proved to be a classic of American operetta. Two of the show's most memorable songs were 'Rose-Marie' and 'Indian Love Call'. Hammerstein and Harbach's next composing partner was Jerome Kern, and their liaison resulted in *Sunny* (1925), which had the appealing 'Sunny' and 'Who' in its score.

In the following year, Hammerstein worked with George Gershwin on *Song Of The Flame*, and the year after that with Harbach and Sigmund Romberg on *The Desert Song*, which produced lasting successes such as 'The Desert Song' and 'One Alone'. Hammerstein teamed up again with Kern in 1927 for *Show Boat*, writing lyrics for such immortal numbers as 'Why Do I Love You?', 'Can't Help Lovin' Dat Man', 'Only Make Believe' and 'Ol' Man River'. In 1928 he rejoined Harbach and Friml to gain further acclaim with *The New Moon*, which featured 'Lover, Come Back To Me' and 'Softly As In A Morning Sunrise'. He continued to work with Kern, and during the next few years their shows were full of songs that became standards, among them 'The Song Is You', 'I've Told Ev'ry Little Star' and 'All The Things You Are'.

In the early 30s Hammerstein was lured to Hollywood, where he met with only limited success. Although some of the films on which he worked were box-office failures, he nevertheless co-authored several timeless songs, including, 'When I Grow Too Old To Dream' (with Romberg) and 'I Won't Dance' (with Harbach and Kern), the latter for the 1935 Fred Astaire-Ginger Rogers film *Roberta*. Other songs written with Kern for films were 'Can I Forget You', 'The Folks Who Live On The Hill', 'I'll Take Romance' and 'The Last Time I Saw Paris', which won an Oscar in 1941. In the early 40s Hammerstein's career took a new direction, and the ups and downs of the past were forgotten with the first of a series of smash-hit Broadway shows written with a new partner. He had worked briefly with Richard Rodgers in 1928 and again in 1935, but now, with Rodgers' regular collaborator Lorenz Hart a victim of alcoholism and depression, a new partnership was formed. Rodgers and Hammerstein's first score was for *Oklahoma!* (1943), which was followed by *Carousel* (1945), *Allegro* (1947), *South Pacific* (1949), *The King And I* (1951), *Me And Juliet* (1953), *Pipe Dream* (1955), *Flower Drum Song* (1958) and *The Sound Of Music* (1959). Collectively, these shows were among the most successful in the history of the American musical theatre, with *Oklahoma!* running for 2,212 performances and winning a Pulitzer Prize – as did *South Pacific*, which ran for 1,925 performances.

In addition to their stage successes, Rodgers and Hammerstein wrote the score for the film *State Fair* (1945), which included the Oscar-winning song 'It Might As Well Be Spring', and the television show *Cinderella* (1957). A brief list of songs from their stage musicals includes such well-loved hits as 'Oh, What A Beautiful Mornin'', 'People Will Say We're In Love', 'The Surrey With The Fringe On Top', 'If I Loved You', 'You'll Never Walk Alone', 'Some Enchanted Evening', 'Younger Than Springtime', 'Bali Ha'i', 'Hello, Young Lovers', 'Shall We Dance?', 'No Other Love' and 'Climb Ev'ry Mountain'. Between *Oklahoma!* and *Carousel*, Hammerstein wrote a new book and lyrics for Georges Bizet's opera *Carmen*. The new show, *Carmen Jones*, opened on Broadway in 1943 and was a great success. It was transferred to the screen in 1954 and, most recently, was revived in London's West End in 1991. One of Broadway's most successful lyricists, Hammerstein wrote with engaging simplicity, a trait that set him well apart from his predecessor Hart. His remarkable contribution to America's theatrical tradition was

profound, and his irreproachable standards represented the culmination of the traditional, operetta-based style of musical comedy. In 1993, the 50th anniversary of Rodgers and Hammerstein's first collaboration on 'America's most loved musical' was celebrated by the publication of *OK! The Story Of Oklahoma!* and *The Rodgers And Hammerstein Birthday Book*. In addition, the revue *A Grand Night For Singing*, which was packed with their songs, played for a brief spell in New York.
● FURTHER READING: *Some Enchanted Evening: The Story Of Rodgers and Hammerstein*, J.D. Taylor. *The Rodgers And Hammerstein Story*, Stanley Green. *The Sound Of Their Music: The Story Of Rodgers And Hammerstein*, Frederick Nolan. *OK! The Story Of Oklahoma!*, Max Wilk. *Rodgers And Hammerstein Birthday Book*, compiled by Bert Fink. *The Wordsmiths: Oscar Hammerstein & Alan Jay Lerner*, Stephen Citron.

HAMMOND, JOHN, JNR.

b. John Henry Hammond II, 15 December 1910, New York City, USA, d. July 1987. Hammond became a jazz fan as a child and in the early 30s was a record reviewer for *Melody Maker*. He used his inherited wealth to finance recordings at a time when economic depression had made record companies unwilling to invest in jazz, and produced Billie Holiday's first session as well as tracks by Teddy Wilson, Bessie Smith, Mildred Bailey and Artie Shaw. In 1936 a chance hearing of a broadcast by Count Basie from Kansas City (Hammond was listening on his car radio outside a Chicago hotel where Benny Goodman was appearing) led him actively to promote Basie's career. In 1938/9, Hammond devised and organized the *Spirituals To Swing* concerts at New York's Carnegie Hall. These were designed to show the full breadth of black American music and featured gospel (Sister Rosetta Tharpe), blues (Big Bill Broonzy), New Orleans jazz (Sidney Bechet) and contemporary dance music (Benny Goodman, who married Hammond's sister, Alice). In the early 40s, he worked for Columbia Records and after army service moved to Keynote, Mercury Records and Vanguard Records as a staff producer. Hammond returned to Columbia in 1958 and was chiefly responsible for signing such folk revival artists as Pete Seeger and Bob Dylan, who was known at the company as 'Hammond's folly' in the early years of his contract. Hammond was the producer of Dylan's first two albums. While chiefly involved with jazz and blues – he supervised reissues of Bessie Smith and Robert Johnson, and was a founder of the Newport Jazz Festival – Hammond continued to bring new artists to Columbia during the 60s and 70s, most notably Leonard Cohen, George Benson and Bruce Springsteen. His son, John Hammond III (often confusingly titled John Hammond Jnr. himself, which leads to his father being mistakenly identified as Hammond Snr.), is a noted white blues singer whose recording career began in the mid-60s.

HANK WILLIAMS SINGS – HANK WILLIAMS

Like one Hank Williams album and you will like the lot, and this 10-inch album was the first. All Williams' trademarks are in these eight songs: devotion to your mother, loveless marriages (his own is reflected in 'A House Without Love'), the deep religious convictions of the southern states and the problems of living up to those beliefs. Numerous interpretations have turned 'I Saw The Light' into a standard and far too many musicians have followed Hank down that 'Lost Highway'.
A House Without Love; Wedding Bells; The Mansion On The Hill; Wealth Won't Save Your Soul; I Saw The Light; Six More Miles To The Graveyard; Lost Highway; I've Just Told Mama Goodbye.
● First released 1952
● UK peak chart position: did not chart
● USA peak chart position: did not chart

HANS CHRISTIAN ANDERSEN

This extremely popular, but critically slated, musical biopic of the legendary Danish storyteller was produced by Samuel Goldwyn in 1952. Estimates vary as to how many prospective screenplays were rejected by the producer (and the Danish authorities) before Moss Hart came up with the final draft. Eschewing all pretensions of biographical accuracy, this 'fairy tale about a great spinner of fairy tales' set in 1830, told of a simple cobbler (Danny Kaye) who falls in love with a beautiful ballerina (Jeanmaire) after he has made some shoes for her. When his love is rejected, he returns to his home-town and eventually makes a fortune from writing children's stories. Kaye, whose renowned zany style has made him a controversial choice for the leading role, toned down the histrionics and gave a brilliant performance. He was assisted in no small part by a marvellous Frank Loesser score, much of which was inspired by Andersen's original tales. It included several endearing numbers, such as 'Thumbelina', 'No Two People', 'I'm Hans Christian Andersen', 'The King's New Clothes', 'Wonderful Copenhagen', 'Anywhere I Wander', 'The Ugly Duckling' and 'The Inchworm'. The delightful ballet sequences were choreographed by Roland Petit, who made an appearance in one of them. Also in the cast were Farley Granger, Joey Walsh, John Brown, Philip Tonge, Erik Bruhn and John Qualen. The director was Charles Vidor, and the film was beautifully photographed in Technicolor by Harry Stradling. It grossed $6 million in the USA, and went on to become one of the most celebrated film musicals of the decade. A successful stage production, entitled *Hans Andersen*, with a new book by Beverley Cross and some additional songs from Marvin Laird, was presented at the London Palladium in 1974 and 1977. It starred Tommy Steele on both occasions, and in the later production his leading lady was Sally Ann Howes. Around 20 years later, two entirely different musicals with the same theme, *Hans Christian Andersen* (music: Sebastian, book: Flemming Enevold) and *H.C. Andersen* (Tove Lind and Tommy Jervidal) premiered in Denmark.

HANSON, JOHN

b. John Stanley Watts, 31 August 1922, Oshawa, Ontario, Canada, d. 4 December 1998, Shepperton, Surrey, England. A singer, actor and producer, Watts moved to the UK with his parents in 1925 and was brought up in Dumfries, Scotland. He sang as a boy soprano in his local choir and made several broadcasts in the early 30s. When he left school he became a production engineer before making his professional debut in 1946 in *Night Of A Thousand Stars* in Birmingham. Taking his mother's maiden name of Hanson, he made his name initially on radio programmes such as *Songs From The Shows*, and appeared with the orchestras of Geraldo and Mantovani, and Troise And His Mandoliers. Hanson later became a regular on *Friday Night Is Music Night*, *Fred Hartleys' Hour* and *Ray's A Laugh*. It was Mantovani who gave Hanson his first opportunity on television and he eventually had his own series, *John Hanson Sings*, which was introduced by 'A Song Of Romance', one of his own compositions.

In 1957 he began to organize and appear in touring revivals of romantic musicals from the past. He played the Red Shadow in *The Desert Song*, and the role became indelibly associated with him. It was followed by *The Student Prince*, *The Vagabond King*, *Lilac Time*, *Rose Marie*, and *The Maid Of The Mountains*. In Britain the beat boom was well under way, but Hanson – who by then was being termed 'the last of the matinee idols' – continued to bring a glorious taste of nostalgia to eager and appreciative audiences throughout the UK. In 1965 he took the leading role in *The World Of Ivor Novello* and a year later appeared in *When You're Young* (originally known as *Smilin' Through*), for which he wrote the book, music, and lyrics. In 1967 he made his West End debut in *The Desert Song* which was succeeded by *The Student Prince*. Both London productions transferred to Blackpool for summer seasons in 1969/70. In 1972 at the Prince of Wales Theatre he played John Carteret in his own *Smilin' Through*. Over the next few years he continued to tour in nostalgic productions such as *Lilac Time*, *Rose Marie*, *The Dancing Years*, and *Glamorous Night*. After producing and directing a farewell tour of *The Desert Song* in 1976/7, he devoted most of his time to concerts and summer seasons, and was still active until the mid-80s when he was forced to retire through ill health.

● ALBUMS: *The Student Prince-Vagabond King* (1961) ★★★★, *Lilac Time-Maid Of the Mountains* (1964) ★★★, *In Musical Comedy* (1964) ★★★, *The Music Of Ivor Novello* (1965) ★★★★, *Songs Of Romance* (1965) ★★★, with Vanessa Lee *This Is London* (1966) ★★★, *Encores* (1966) ★★★, *When You're Young* (1966) ★★★, *The Desert Song-New Moon* (1967) ★★, *Rodgers And Hammerstein Favourites* (1968) ★★★, *My Songs Of Love For You* (1969) ★★★, *Desert Song-Student Prince* (1970) ★★★, *Great Songs From Great Films* (1970) ★★★, *Smilin' Through* (1972) ★★★, *Lilac Time-Maid Of The Mountain* (1973) ★★★, *Sings Friml Favourites* (1973) ★★★, *I'll Sing You A Thousand Love Songs* (1973) ★★★, *The Dancing Years-White Horse Inn* (Philips 1975) ★★, *Sings 20 Showtime Greats* (K-Tel 1977) ★★★.

● COMPILATIONS: *Showcase* (1968) ★★★, *Favourites* (Philips 1974) ★★★, *Sings Songs From His Hit Shows* (Philips 1976) ★★★, *Spotlight On John Hanson* (Philips 1977) ★★★.

● FURTHER READING: *Me And My Red Shadow: The Autobiography Of John Hanson*, John Hanson.

HARPTONES

An R&B vocal group formed in 1953 in Harlem, New York City, New York, USA. The members were lead Willie Winfield, first tenor Nick Clark, second tenor William Dempsey, baritone Bill 'Dicey' Galloway, bass Billy Brown and pianist/arranger Raoul J. Cita. The Harptones were one of the smoothest and most polished R&B vocal groups to emerge during the early rock 'n' roll era. Although considered a part of the doo-wop phenomenon, they rarely employed nonsense syllables. Instead, the chorus would answer in words employing a special 'opened mouth harmony' devised by Cita. The Harptones were giants on the east coast but virtually unknown elsewhere in the country. Among their best numbers (all ballads) are 'A Sunday Kind Of Love' (1954), 'My Memories Of You' (1954) and 'Life Is But A Dream'' (1955); none of their jump songs were particularly convincing. By 1956, with the death of Brown, the group was beginning to break up, and during this time Jimmy Beckum appeared on many of the tracks recorded for George Goldner's Rama/Gee complex. Top notch songs during this period included 'On Sunday Afternoon' and 'Shrine Of St. Cecilia'. Their final recordings were released in 1957. During the 70s and 80s Winfield and Cita made up various permutations of a Harptones group to play the east coast oldies circuit.

● COMPILATIONS: *The Paragons Meet The Harptones* (Musicnote 1963) ★★★, *The Harptones Featuring Willie Winfield* (Relic 1971) ★★★, *Echoes Of A Rock Era* 12 tracks by the Harptones, 12 by the Crows (Roulette 1972) ★★★, *The Harptones Featuring Willie Winfield Volume 2* (Relic 1973) ★★★, *Golden Classics: The Goldner Recordings, 1956-57* (Collectables 1991) ★★★★, *A Sunday Kind Of Love* (Relic 1992) ★★★.

HARRIS, MAX

b. 15 September 1918, Bournemouth, Dorset, England. A pianist, composer and prolific conductor-arranger for radio and television programmes. As a boy, he had private tuition on the piano up to the Royal Academy Of Music Advanced Grade, and gave piano lessons himself, while still a teenager. He served as pianist-arranger with the Jack Parnell orchestra, played gigs with top sidemen such as Tommy Whittle and George Chisholm, and made his first broadcast in 1950 on the BBC's *Jazz Club*. During the 50s he arranged for BBC Radio's *Show Band Show*, conducted by Cyril Stapleton, which featured top US artists such as Frank Sinatra. He has also worked on many of Britain's top-rated radio and television comedy shows and was involved in a special radio tribute to the Queen Mother on her 80th birthday. His compositions have included the title themes and/or incidental music for radio and television programmes such as *Round The Horne*, *Young At Heart*, *Father Charlie*, *Mickey Dunne*, *Doomwatch*, *Poldark*, *Horseman Riding By*, *The Spies*, *Open All Hours*, *Mind Your Language*, *Porridge*, *Sherlock Holmes*, *On The Buses* and *Doctor's Daughters*. His 'Gurney Slade Theme', from ATV's quirky *The Strange World Of Gurney Slade* (1960-61), starring Anthony Newley, made the UK Top 20, and won an Ivor Novello Award. Harris gained another 'Ivor' in 1964, when his 'Bombay Duck', from the *Kipling* television series, was adjudged 'The Year's Outstanding Orchestral/Instrumental Composition'. He also won the Designer and Graphics Association Award in 1980 for his work on *The Pink Medicine Show*. Besides his own recordings, he has served as arranger and musical director for many top artists, such as Ted Heath, Ella Fitzgerald, Dick Haymes, Owen Brannigan, and a series of four albums which brought legendary musicians Yehudi Menuhin and Stéphane Grappelli together on record for the first time.

HARRIS, WEE WILLIE

'Discovered' in London's famous coffee bar club the 2I's – shrine of early UK pop – he was promoted by his manager as the kingdom's very own Jerry Lee Lewis – though he was less a teen-idol than a television gimmick in loud attire and hair dyed a funny colour – usually shocking pink, green or orange – for regular appearances on the television pop show *6.5 Special*. Nor was he above banal publicity stunts, including a 'feud' with blue-rinsed Larry Page, another 50s hopeful. Though Harris composed 'Rockin' At The 2 I's' as a debut single, he relied mostly on US cover versions – albeit delivered with more enthusiasm than many other native contemporaries. Nevertheless, home consumers preferred the original versions of 'Riot In Cell Block No. 9' (the Robins) and 'Wild One' (Bobby Rydell), though they were unlikely to have heard Timmie Rogers' 'Back To School Again' or Gerry Granahan's 'No Chemise, Please' before Harris rehashed them. Although a less enduring clown than Screaming Lord Sutch, he resurfaced as a nostalgia act in the late 70s after Ian Dury mentioned his name in the lyrics of 1979's 'Reasons To Be Cheerful (Part Three)'.
● COMPILATIONS: *Goes Ape* (Ace 1986) ★★.

HARRISON, WILBERT

b. 5 January 1929, Charlotte, North Carolina, USA, d. 26 October 1994, Spencer, North Carolina, USA. Although Harrison first recorded as early as 1953, it was not until the end of the decade that the singer established his reputation with a superb jump blues-styled adaptation of the perennial 'Kansas City'. This memorable single eventually rose to number 1 in the US pop and R&B charts, despite the attention of several competing versions. The singer then unleashed a series of similarly excellent releases including the compulsive 'Let's Stick Together', which was revived many years later by Bryan Ferry. Harrison continued to record, rather unsuccessfully, throughout the 60s, until 'Let's Work Together', a regenerated reading of that former release, returned him to the public eye. Harrison subsequently appeared in London with Creedence Clearwater Revival, but the song ultimately became better known with Canned Heat's hit version, a number 2 in the UK and a number 17 in the USA. Its originator, meanwhile, made several excellent albums in the wake of his new-found popularity, but was unable to gain any consistent commercial appeal.
● ALBUMS: *Kansas City* (Sphere Sound 1965) ★★★, *Let's Work Together* (Sue 1970) ★★★, *Shoot You Full Of Love* (Juggernaut 1971) ★★, *Anything You Want* (Wet Soul 1971) ★★, *Wilbert Harrison* (Buddah 1971) ★★, *Soul Food Man* (Chelsea 1976) ★★, *Lovin' Operator* (Charly 1985) ★★, *Small Labels* (Krazy Kat 1986) ★★, *Listen To My Song* (Savoy Jazz 1987) ★★.
● COMPILATIONS: *Kansas City* (Relic 1990) ★★★★.

HART, MOSS

b. 24 October 1904, New York, USA, d. 20 December 1961, Palm Springs, California, USA. A distinguished librettist, director, and playwright who was particularly renowned for his work with George S. Kaufman. Hart is reported to have written the book for the short-lived *Jonica* in 1930, but his first real Broadway musical credit came three years later when he contributed the sketches to the Irving Berlin revue *As Thousands Cheer*. Subsequent revues for which he co-wrote sketches included *The Show Is On*, *Seven Lively Arts* and *Inside USA*. During the remainder of the 30s Hart wrote the librettos for *The Great Waltz* (adapted from the operetta *Waltzes Of Vienna*), *Jubilee*, *I'd Rather Be Right* (with Kaufman) and *Sing Out The News* (which he also co-produced with Kaufman and Max Gordon). In 1941 he wrote one of his wittiest and most inventive books for *Lady In Dark*, which starred Gertrude Lawrence, and gave Danny Kaye his first chance on Broadway. Thereafter, as far as the musical theatre was concerned, apart from the occasional revue, Hart concentrated mostly on directing, and sometimes producing, shows such as Irving Berlin's *Miss Liberty*, and Alan Jay Lerner and Frederick Loewe's smash hits *My Fair Lady* and *Camelot*. He won a Tony Award for his work on *My Fair Lady*. His considerable output for the straight theatre included *Light Up The Sky*, *The Climate Of Eden*, *Winged Victory*, and (with Kaufman) *Once In A Lifetime*, *You Can't Take It With You* (for which they both won the Pulitzer Prize) and *The Man Who Came To Dinner*. Hart also wrote the screenplays for two film musicals, *Hans Christian Andersen* (1952) and the 1954 remake of *A Star Is Born*, starring Judy Garland. His absorbing autobiography, *Act One*, was filmed in 1963 with George Hamilton as Hart and Jason Robards as Kaufman.
● FURTHER READING: *Act One*, Moss Hart.

HARTMAN, JOHNNY

b. John Maurice Hartman, 13 July 1923, Chicago, Illinois, USA, d. 15 September 1983, New York City, New York, USA. Having started to sing while still at school, Hartman went on to study at musical college. He became a professional following the end of the World War II and first attracted widespread attention singing with Earl Hines in 1947 and two years later with Erroll Garner. His rich, deep baritone lent itself to a range of material and he comfortably accommodated country music alongside popular songs of the day (which meant he was able to make the breakthrough into television), although his first and lasting preference was for jazz. Within a jazz context he inclined towards modernism, performing and recording with Dizzy Gillespie, John Coltrane, and Sir Roland Hanna. He was nominated for a Grammy in 1981 for his album *Once In Every Life*. Hartman veered from jazz to smooth easy listening and pop in his later years.

● ALBUMS: *Songs From The Heart* (Bethlehem 1956) ★★★★, *Just You Just Me* (Regent 1956) ★★★, *All Of Me* (Bethlehem 1956) ★★★, *The Debonair Mr Harman* (Bethlehem 1956) ★★★★, with John Coltrane *John Coltrane And Johnny Hartman* (Impulse! 1963) ★★★★, *I Just Dropped By To Say Hello* (Impulse! 1963) ★★★, *The Voice That Is!* (Impulse! 1964) ★★★, *The Unforgettable Johnny Hartman* (ABC 1966) ★★, *Today* (Perception 1973) ★★★, *I've Been There* (Perception 1975) ★★, *Live At Sometime* (Trio 1977) ★★, *Once In Every Life* (Bee Hive 1980) ★★★, *This One's For Tedi* (Bee Hive 1980) ★★★, *And I Thought About You* 1959 recording (Roost 1997) ★★★, *Thank You For Everything* 1978 recording (Audiophile 1998) ★★★.

● COMPILATIONS: *Collection 1947-1972* (Hip-O 1998) ★★★★.

HAWKINS, COLEMAN

b. Coleman Randolph Hawkins, 21 November 1904, St. Joseph, Missouri, USA, d. 19 May 1969, New York City, New York, USA. Coleman Hawkins (aka 'Bean' and 'Hawk') is a colossus of the tenor saxophone, and hence of jazz. He was the first to use the instrument as a serious means of expression and continued to be open to new developments for 40 years. Starting piano lessons at the age of five, he later learned cello and took up tenor saxophone when he was nine years old. Within a few years he was playing dances and appearing in Kansas and Chicago. He attended Washburn College in Topeka and toured as a member of Mamie Smith's Jazz Hounds in 1921. He joined Fletcher Henderson's Orchestra in 1924, a sophisticated New York dance band then coming to terms with the new jazz music – hot and improvised – that Louis Armstrong, who had also joined Henderson in 1924, had brought from New Orleans by way of Chicago. Released in 1926, 'The Stampede' featured Hawkins' first notable solo.

In his 10 years with the band he transformed the tenor saxophone – previously a novelty instrument for blues and hokum records – from rather quaint imitations of Armstrong's staccato style into a vehicle for the powerful and suave solos that were the essence of swing. 'St Louis Shuffle' (1927), 'Sugar Foot Stomp' (1931) and 'Hocus Pocus' (1934) are three brilliant sides that trace this evolution. By 1934 jazz had become a global music. Coleman Hawkins left Fletcher Henderson and travelled to Europe, where he was welcomed by the local players. He recorded with Jack Hylton in England. Excluded from a Hylton tour of Germany in 1935 by the Nazis' new racial laws, he joined Theo Masman's Ramblers Dance Orchestra and recorded with them for Decca Records. In 1937 he met up with Django Reinhardt and recorded some memorable music (Stéphane Grappelli was relegated to piano), and he also played with fellow exile Benny Carter. When war broke out in 1939 Hawkins returned to the USA. There his supremacy on tenor saxophone had been challenged by the languid yet harmonically sophisticated playing of Lester Young, but his recording of the Johnny Green, Edward Heyman, Robert Sour, Frank Eyton collaboration 'Body & Soul' (on 11 October 1939) was a massive hit and established him as a national figure, his confessional, tender-but-tough tenor the epitome of jazz. In 1940 he toured with his own 16-piece, appearing at premier New York jazz spots the Arcadia and the Savoy Ballroom, but the days of the big band were numbered.

In December 1943 his small combo recordings – 'How Deep Is The Ocean', 'Stumpy' and an irresistible swinger called 'Voodte' – represented the apex of swing, though the sense of headlong abandon was akin to the new music of bebop. Bebop was black America's first *avant garde* art form, featuring innovations many established musicians felt moved to denounce, but Hawkins loved it. He led an early bebop recording session in February 1944 – featuring Don Byas, Dizzy Gillespie and Max Roach. In 1943 he had formed a sextet with Thelonious Monk, Don Byas and trumpeter Benny Harris and a year later gave Monk his recording debut. Most of 1944 and 1945 were spent on the west coast with a band that included Sir Charles Thompson and Howard McGhee. As featured soloist on Norman Granz's *Jazz At The Philharmonic* tours, trips to Europe followed in 1950 and 1954.

The popularity of Stan Getz's interpretation of Lester Young made Hawkins and his ripe sound unfashionable in the 50s, but his strength as a player – and his openness of mind – never left him. In 1957 Thelonious Monk repaid the compliment by inviting him to join his septet, and the application of Hawkins' big, swinging tenor to Monk's paradoxical compositions yielded wonderful results on tunes such as 'Off Minor'. Playing next to young turks such as John Coltrane, Hawkins showed that he still had something to contribute. The classic *The Hawk Flies High* (1957) showed what Hawkins could accomplish in a mainstream setting, while a reunion with his ex-Henderson colleague Henry 'Red' Allen in the same year showed he could also shine in a more traditional context. In the 60s Hawkins kept playing, recording with new tenor star Sonny Rollins. The list of his engagements in that decade is testament to the catholic taste that an established elder statesman can afford: Pee Wee Russell, Duke Ellington, Bud Powell, Tommy Flanagan, Eric Dolphy, even an appearance on Max Roach's inflammatory *We Insist! Freedom Now* suite and at a 1966 'Tenors Titan' concert that also featured Rollins, Coltrane, Zoot Sims and Yusef Lateef. He played on the last JATP tour (1967) and toured with Oscar Peterson in 1968, though by that point he was increasingly prone to bouts of depression and drinking, exacerbated by a refusal to eat. His death from pneumonia in 1969 marked the end of an era; he was a jazz master whose life work stretched across five decades of the music's history.

● ALBUMS: *Originals With Hawkins* 10-inch album (Stinson 1950) ★★★★, *Coleman Hawkins All Stars* 10-inch album (Apollo 1951) ★★★, *Coleman Hawkins Favorites* 10-inch album (Advance 1951) ★★★★, *King Of The Tenor Sax* reissued as *Meditations* (Commodore 1952) ★★★★, *Classics In Jazz* 10-inch album (Capitol 1952) ★★★★, *Tenor Sax* 10-inch album (Brunswick 1953) ★★★★, *The Bean* 10-inch album (EmArcy 1954) ★★★, *The Hawk Talks* 10-inch album (Savoy 1954) ★★★★, *Improvisations Unlimited* (Concert Hall 1955) ★★★, *Accent On The Tenor Sax* (Urania 1955) ★★★, *Hawk in Flight* (RCA Victor 1955) ★★★★, *The Hawk Returns* (Savoy 1955) ★★★, *Coleman Hawkins And His Orchestra* (American Record Society 1956) ★★★, *Coleman Hawkins: A Documentary* (Riverside 1956) ★★★, *Hawk In Hi-Fi* (RCA Victor 1956) ★★★, *The Hawk In Paris* (Vik 1957) ★★★, *Gilded Hawk* (Capitol 1957) ★★★, *The Hawk Flies High* (Riverside 1957) ★★★, with Roy Eldridge *At The Opera House* (Verve 1957) ★★★★, *The High And Mighty Hawk* (Felsted 1958) ★★★, *Coleman Hawkins With The Basie Sax Section* (World Wide 1958) ★★★, *Soul* (Prestige 1959) ★★★, *Hawk Eyes* (Prestige 1959) ★★★, *Coleman Hawkins Encounters Ben Webster/Blue Saxophones* (Verve 1959) ★★★★, *Coleman Hawkins And His Confreres With The Oscar Peterson Trio* (Verve 1959) ★★★★, *Coleman Hawkins Plus The Red Garland Trio* (Swingville 1960) ★★★, *At Ease With Coleman Hawkins* (Moodsville 1960) ★★★, *The Coleman Hawkins All Stars* (Swingville 1960) ★★★, *Night Hawk* (Prestige 1961) ★★★, *The Hawk Swings* (Crown 1961) ★★★★, *Things Ain't What They Used To Be* (Swingville 1961) ★★★, *The Hawk Blows At Midnight* (Decca 1961) ★★★, *Years Ago* (Swingville 1961) ★★★, *The Hawk Relaxes* (Moodsville 1961) ★★★, with Pee Wee Russell *Jazz Reunion* (Candid 1961) ★★★, *Good Old Broadway* (Moodsville 1962) ★★★, *The Jazz Version Of No Strings* (Moodsville 1962) ★★★, *On The Bean* (Continental 1962) ★★★, *In A Mellow Tone* (Original Jazz Classics 1962) ★★★, *Jazz At The Metropole* (Philips 1962) ★★★, with Howard McGhee, Lester Young *A Date With Greatness* (Imperial 1962) ★★★★, *Duke Ellington Meets Coleman Hawkins* (MCA/Impulse! 1963) ★★★★, *Desafinado: Bossa Nova & Jazz Samba* (Impulse! 1963) ★★★, *Today And Now* (Impulse! 1963)

★★★, *Make Someone Happy* (Moodsville 1963) ★★★, *Hawkins! Alive! At The Village Gate* (Verve 1963) ★★★, with Clark Terry *Eddie Costa Memorial Concert* (Colpix 1963) ★★★, with Earl Hines *Grand Reunion* (Limelight 1965) ★★★★, *Wrapped Tight* (Impulse! 1965) ★★★, with Frank Hunter *The Hawk And The Hunter* (Mira 1965) ★★★, *Supreme* 1966 concert recording (Enja 1995) ★★★, *The Gentle Hawk* 60s recordings (BMG 1998) ★★★, with Sonny Rollins *Sonny Meets Hawk!* 1963 recording (RCA Victor 1998) ★★★★, with Benny Carter *Jammin' The Blues* 1965-66 recordings (Moon 1998) ★★★, *Jamestown NY 1958* (Uptown 1999) ★★, with Milt Jackson *Beanbags* 1959 recording (Koch 1999) ★★★, *Lausanne 1949: Swiss Radio Days Jazz Series: Vol 13* (TCB 2001) ★★.

● COMPILATIONS: *The Genius Of Coleman Hawkins* (Verve 1958) ★★★★, *The Essential Coleman Hawkins* (Verve 1964) ★★★★, *Body And Soul* (Bluebird 1988) ★★★★, *The Complete Recordings 1929-31* (RCA 1992) ★★★★, *April In Paris* 1939-56 recordings (Bluebird 1992) ★★★★, *The Indispensable Body And Soul* 1961 recordings (RCA 1993) ★★★★, *The Complete Recordings 1929-1940* (Charly 1993) ★★★, *A Retrospective 1929-1963* (Bluebird 1995) ★★★★, *In The Groove* (Indigo 1996) ★★★, *The Tenor For All Seasons* (Jazz Classics 1997) ★★★★, *His Best Recordings, 1923-1945* (Best Of Jazz 1998) ★★★, *Ultimate* (Verve 1998) ★★★★, *The Bebop Years* 40s recordings, 4-CD box set (Properbox 2000) ★★★.

● FURTHER READING: *Coleman Hawkins Volume 1 1922-44, Volume 2 1945-57*, Jean François Villetard. *The Song Of The Hawk*, John Chilton. *Coleman Hawkins*, Burnett James.

HAWKINS, DALE

b. Delmar Allen Hawkins, 22 August 1936, Goldmine, Louisiana, USA. Born into a musical family where his father Delmar, and later, his younger brother Jerry were both musicians. The latter recorded three unsuccessful singles. Dale Hawkins was one of the earliest exponents of rockabilly, and this underrated singer-guitarist was discovered in 1955 by Shreveport record distributor Stan Lewis and signed by the Chicago-based Chess Records label. Among his earliest singles was the Bobby Charles composition 'See You Soon Baboon', an answer record to Bill Haley's 'See You Later Alligator' (which was also written by Charles), but Hawkins' biggest hit was the excellent Howlin' Wolf-influenced 'Suzie-Q', with Roy Buchanan on lead guitar. It reached the US Top 30 in 1957 and was later covered by numerous artists, including the Everly Brothers, the Rolling Stones and Creedence Clearwater Revival, for whom the song was a Top 20 hit in 1968. Hawkins and his Hawks recorded further hard-rocking tracks such as 'La-Do-Dada' and 'Class Cutter' over the next few years, featuring guitarists Scotty Moore and James Burton. Hawkins left Chess in 1961 and made occasional records for a number of other labels, including ABC Records, Roulette Records, Atlantic Records, Bell Records and Paula but during the 60s he concentrated on production, creating Top 10 hits for Bruce Channel ('Hey Baby', 1962 and 'Keep On' in 1968) and the Five Americans ('Western Union', 1967). Hawkins returned to recording with a pleasant country-rock album for Bell in 1969 which contained versions of Leiber And Stoller's 'Hound Dog' and Jimmy Reed's 'Baby What You Want Me To Do'. Among the artists Hawkins produced in the 70s was Texas rock band Rio Grande.

● ALBUMS: *Suzie-Q* (Chess 1958) ★★★, *Let's Twist At The Miami Beach Peppermint Lounge* (Roulette 1962) ★★, *L.A., Memphis & Tyler, Texas* (Bell 1969) ★★, *Oh! Suzie-Q* (Checker 1973) ★★★, *Daredevil* (Norton 1997) ★★★, *Wildcat Tamer* (Mystic 1999) ★★.

● COMPILATIONS: *Oh! Suzie-Q, The Best Of Dale Hawkins* (MCA 1995) ★★★★, *Rock 'N' Roll Tornado* (Ace 1998) ★★★★.

HAWKINS, 'SCREAMIN' JAY'

b. Jalacy Hawkins, 18 July 1929, Cleveland, Ohio, USA, d. 12 February 2000, Neuilly-sur-Seine, France. Reportedly raised in Cleveland by a tribe of Blackfoot Indians, young Jalacy became interested in music at an early age, teaching himself piano at the age of six and, having mastered the keyboard, he then learned to play saxophone in his early teens. Hawkins was also an adept young boxer, winning an amateur *Golden Gloves* contest and becoming Middleweight Champion of Alaska in 1949. He judged music to be the easier option, and became a professional musician, playing piano with artists such as Gene Ammons, Arnett Cobb, Illinois Jacquet, James Moody, Lynn Hope, and on one occasion, Count Basie. In 1950, Hawkins began developing an act based more on his almost operatic bass-baritone voice, and the following year he joined Tiny Grimes' Rocking Highlanders as pianist and occasional vocalist, making his recording debut with the band for Gotham Records in 1952 (the record was withdrawn after three weeks) and for Atlantic Records in 1953 (the results remain unissued). Leaving Grimes, Hawkins was befriended by blues shouter Wynonie Harris, who brought the young musician to New York City as his protégé.

At this point, Hawkins' fortunes began to take an upswing, first with his debut records under his own name for the Timely label, followed by superior efforts for Mercury/Wing and Grand Records. In 1956, Screamin' Jay (as he was now known) signed with Columbia Records' reactivated OKeh Records subsidiary and enjoyed enormous success with his manic – and apparently drunken – rendition of his own 'I Put A Spell On You', which he had recorded earlier as a ballad for Grand Records. Released in October 1956, the original version was quickly withdrawn as a result of the public outrage caused by the 'suggestive and cannibalistic' sound effects provided by Hawkins. A suitably truncated substitution was soon made. Despite these efforts, an air-play ban remained in force, but the record sold over a million copies regardless, becoming a classic of rock music and invoking hundreds of cover versions from Nina Simone to the Alan Price Set and Creedence Clearwater Revival. Remaining with OKeh until 1958, Hawkins ran the gamut of his weird-but-wonderful repertoire with recordings of straight R&B songs such as 'Little Demon' and 'Person To Person', tongue-in-cheek, semi-operatic standards such as 'I Love Paris' and 'Temptation', and the unclassifiable and uniquely bizarre 'Hong Kong', 'Alligator Wine' and 'There's Something Wrong With You'.

To enhance this ghoulish strangeness, on his tours with rock 'n' roll package shows, Hawkins was encouraged by Alan Freed to use macabre props such as skulls, snakes and shrunken heads and to begin his act from the inside of a coffin. Again, uproar followed, resulting in a largely unrepresentative album release and, worse still, Hawkins' only 50s movie appearance in *Mister Rock And Roll* being cut out in case parents boycotted the release. Shunned by the mass media, Hawkins spent most of the 60s playing one-nighters and tired rock 'n' roll revival gigs, making the occasional one-off recording agreement with tiny independent labels. *The Night And Day Of Screaming Jay Hawkins*, recorded in London for producer Shel Talmy's Planet label, was more conservative in tone. A brace of late 60s albums extended his idiosyncratic reputation and it was during these sessions that Hawkins recorded the original 'Constipation Blues', a lavatorial performance destined to become an intrinsic part of his stage act.

He enjoyed a cameo role in 1978's much-praised *American Hot Wax*, and later won a starring role as the laconic hotel desk clerk in Jim Jarmusch's *Mystery Train*. Hawkins later collaborated with modern garage band the Fleshtones. A 1991 release, *Black Music For White People*, which included readings of two Tom Waits compositions, 'Ice Cream Man' and 'Heart Attack And Vine', as well as a rap interpretation of 'I Put A Spell On You', revealed a largely undiminished power. His influence on other performers, notably Screaming Lord Sutch, Arthur Brown and Alice Cooper, should not be underestimated. Touring and recording steadily through the 80s and 90s, Hawkins formed a new band, the Fuzztones, and made successful tours of Europe and the USA. His 1998 album, *At Last*, was a notable return to form. Hawkins died in February 2000 from an aneurysm following intestine surgery.

● ALBUMS: *At Home With Screamin' Jay Hawkins* (Epic 1958) ★★★, *I Put A Spell On You* (Epic 1959) ★★★★, *The Night & Day Of Screamin' Jay Hawkins* (Planet 1965) ★★★, *What That Is* (Philips 1969) ★★, *Screamin' Jay Hawkins* (Philips 1970) ★★★, *A Portrait Of A Man & His Woman* (Hot Line 1972) ★★★, *Frenzy* (Edsel 1982) ★★, *Real Life* (Charly 1983) ★★, *Live And Crazy* (Midnight Music 1986) ★★★, *Feast Of The Mau Mau* (Edsel 1988) ★★, *Real Life* (Charly 1989) ★★★, *Black Music For White People* (Demon 1991) ★★★, *Stone Crazy* (Demon 1993) ★★★, *Somethin' Funny Goin' On* (Demon 1994) ★★★, *At Last* (Last Call 1998) ★★★★, *Live Olympia, Paris 1998* (Last Call 1999) ★★★.

● COMPILATIONS: *I Put A Spell On You* (Direction 1969) ★★★, *Screamin' The Blues* (Red Lightnin' 1982) ★★★★, *Frenzy* (Edsel 1986) ★★★, *I Put A Spell On You* (Charly 1989) ★★★, *Spellbound! 1955-1974* (Bear Family 1990) ★★★★, *Voodoo Jive: The Best Of Screamin' Jay Hawkins* (Rhino 1990) ★★★, *Cow Fingers & Mosquito Pie* (Epic 1991) ★★★★, *1952-1955* (Magpie 1991) ★★★, *From Gotham And Grand* (SJH 1992) ★★★, *Portrait Of A Man: A History Of Screamin' Jay Hawkins* (Edsel 1995) ★★★, *Alligator Wine* (Music Club 1997) ★★★, *Best Of The Bizarre Sessions: 1990-1994* (Manifesto 2000) ★★★.

● FILMS: *Mister Rock And Roll* (1957), *American Hot Wax* (1978), *Joey* (1985), *Two Moon Junction* (1988), *Mystery Train* (1989), *A Rage In Harlem* (1991), *Perdita Durango* aka *Dance With The Devil* (1997), *Peut-être* aka *Maybe* (1999).

HEATH, TED

b. 30 March 1900, Wandsworth, London, England, d. 18 November 1969, Virginia Water, Surrey, England. After playing tenor horn at the age of six, Heath later switched to trombone and throughout the 20s and 30s played with top orchestras such as Jack Hylton, Al Sarita, Sydney Lipton, and in the early 40s with Geraldo. On 7 May 1945 (VJ Day), he formed his own band, some of the early finance being provided by royalties from the songs 'That Lovely Weekend' and 'I'm Gonna Love That Guy', written by Heath and his wife Moira. Kenny Baker, Jack Parnell, Ronnie Chamberlain and Don Lusher were just some of the top musicians who played for him, plus vocalists Paul Carpenter and Beryl Davis. In 1946 the band provided the musical background for the first major UK movie musical, *London Town*. Taking a big chance, Heath hired the London Palladium for a *Sunday Night Swing Session*, which proved to be so successful, that it ran for several years. The addition of singers Lita Roza, Dennis Lotis and Dickie Valentine in the early 50s gave the band more teenage appeal, and they appeared in three more films, *Dance Hall* (1950), *It's A Wonderful World* (1956) and *Jazz Boat* (1960). Their theme, 'Listen To My Music', introduced many specialities including 'Opus One', 'The Champ', 'Dragnet', 'Skin Deep', 'Hot Toddy' and 'Swingin' Shepherd Blues'. The Heath band was the first unit to go to the USA when Musicians' Union restrictions were relaxed and Anglo-American exchanges began in 1955, and subsequently toured there many times.

Heath died in 1969. Many of the original personnel continued to play together usually under the direction of Jack Parnell or Don Lusher and made a 'farewell' concert tour in autumn 2000. An important series of biographical programmes was broadcast on BBC Radio 2 in 1993. The band compared favourably with even America's top units, and it is generally accepted as being the best swing band that Britain ever produced.

● ALBUMS: *Ted Heath And His Orchestra* 10-inch album (London) ★★★, featuring Winifred Atwell *Black And White Magic* 10-inch album (London) ★★★★, *Tempo For Dancers* (Decca 1951) ★★★, *Listen To My Music* (Decca 1952) ★★★, *Selection* (Decca 1952) ★★★, *At The London Palladium* (Decca 1953) ★★★★, *Strike Up The Band* (Decca 1953) ★★★★, *Ted Heath's Fats Waller Album* (Decca 1954) ★★★, *100th London Palladium Concert* (Decca 1954) ★★★★, *Gershwin For Moderns* (Decca 1954) ★★★, *Kern For Moderns* (Decca 1956) ★★★, *At The London Palladium Volume 4* (Decca 1956) ★★★, *Rodgers For Moderns* (Decca 1956) ★★★, *A Yank In Europe* (London 1956) ★★★, *Spotlight On Sidemen* (London 1957) ★★★, *Showcase* (London 1957) ★★★, *Tribute To The Fabulous Dorseys* (London 1957) ★★★, featuring Atwell *Rhapsody In Blue* (London 1957) ★★★, *At Carnegie Hall* (Decca 1957) ★★★★, *First American Tour* (Decca 1957) ★★★, *Hits I Missed* (Decca 1958) ★★★, *Olde Englyshe* (Decca 1958) ★★, *The Instruments Of The Orchestra* (Decca 1958) ★★★, *Swings In Hi-Fi Stereo* (Decca 1958) ★★★★, *Things To Come* (London 1958) ★★★, *Our Kind Of Jazz* (1958) ★★★, *Shall We Dance* (London 1959) ★★★, *Pop Hits From The Classics* (London 1959) ★★★, *Focus On Ted Heath* (1959) ★★★, *Big Band Blues* (London 1959) ★★★, *Swing Session* (Decca 1959) ★★★★, *Plays The Great Film Hits* (Decca 1959) ★★★, *My Very Good Friends The Band Leaders* (Decca 1960) ★★★, *The Big Band Dixie Sound* (London 1960) ★★★, *The Hits Of The Twenties* (London 1960) ★★★, *Ted Heath In Concert* (London 1960) ★★★, *Songs For The Young At Heart* (London 1960) ★★★, *The Hits Of The 30s* (London 1960) ★★★, *Latin Swingers* (London 1961) ★★, *Big Band Beat* (Richmond 60s) ★★★, featuring Atwell *Ted Heath Plays Gershwin* (Richmond 60s) ★★★, *Ted Heath Plays The Music Of Fats Waller* (Richmond 60s) ★★★★, *Big Band Gershwin* (Richmond 60s) ★★★, *Big Band Kern* (Richmond 60s) ★★★, *Big Band Rodgers* (Richmond 60s) ★★★, *Big Band Percussion* (Phase 4 1962) ★★★, *Big Band Bash* (Phase 4 1963) ★★★, *Satin Saxes And Bouncing Brass* (Phase 4 1963) ★★★, *Big Band Spirituals* (Phase 4 1964) ★★★, *Coast To Coast* (Phase 4 1964) ★★★, *Palladium Revisited* (Phase 4 1964) ★★★, with Edmundo Ros *Heath Versus Ros* (Phase 4 1964) ★★★, *The Sound Of Music* (Phase 4 1965) ★★, with Ros *Heath Versus Ros, Round Two* (Phase 1967) ★★, *Ted Heath Recalls The Fabulous Dorseys* (Eclipse 1969) ★★★★, *Fever* (Phase 4 1966) ★★★, *Beatles, Bach And Bacharach* (Phase 4 1971) ★★, *Salute To Glenn Miller* (Phase 4 1973) ★★★★, *Big Band Themes Remembered, Volume One* (Phase 4 1974) ★★★★, *Big Band Themes Remembered, Volume Two* (Phase 4 1974) ★★★, *Salutes The Duke* (Phase 4 1975) ★★★★, *Ted Heath At The London Palladium 1953* (Eclipse 1976) ★★★★, *Salutes Benny Goodman* (Decca 1976) ★★★★, *Smooth 'N' Swinging* 1959-62 recordings (Decca 1981) ★★★, *Get With the Swing* (President 1999) ★★★.

● COMPILATIONS: *Big Band World Of Ted Heath* (Decca 1970) ★★★★, *The World Of Big Band Blues* (Decca 1972) ★★★, *Swing Meets Latin* (Decca 1974) ★★★, with Dennis Lotis, Lita Roza *The Ted Heath Years* (Decca 1977) ★★★★, *Focus On Ted Heath* (Phase 4 1978) ★★★★, *All Time Top Twelve* (Decca 1979) ★★★, *Ted Heath At The BBC* (BBC 1983) ★★★★, *Big Band Favourites* (Decca 1984)

★★★★, *Big Band Bash, Volumes 1-4* (Echo Jazz 1988) ★★★★, *The Golden Age Of Ted Heath Volumes 1-3* (Horatio Nelson 1990) ★★★★, *The Very Best Of Ted Heath Volume 1* (Horatio Nelson 1995) ★★★★, *Euphoria* 1944-49 recordings (Jasmine 1999) ★★★, *Listen To My Music Vols 1-3* 1944-48 recordings (Hep 1997-99) ★★★.

HEFTI, NEAL

b. 29 October 1922, Hastings, Nebraska, USA. One of the most influential big band arrangers of the 40s and 50s, Hefti's early charts were played by the Nat Towles band in the late 30s. His material was also used by Earl Hines; however, his first real taste of the big time came when he joined Charlie Barnet in 1942 and then moved into the Woody Herman band in 1944. Both engagements were as a member of the trumpet section, but his writing became steadily more important than his playing. For Herman he arranged many of the band's most popular recordings, including 'The Good Earth' and 'Wild Root', and was co-arranger with Ralph Burns of 'Caldonia'. In 1946 Hefti's charts were among those used by the ill-fated Billy Butterfield big band and by Charlie Ventura's equally short-lived band. In the late 40s he wrote for what was one of the best of Harry James' bands; in the mid-50s, along with Ernie Wilkins and Nat Pierce, he helped to give the Count Basie band the new distinctive, tighter style that led to a wholesale re-evaluation of big band music, especially in the UK. *Atomic Basie* was composed by Hefti and it features among others the classic 'Li'l Darlin'' and 'Splanky'. The album remains one of Basie's finest works and Hefti's peak. Throughout the 50s and 60s Hefti was heavily involved in composing for films and television (including the theme for the US *Batman* television series), and while much of his work in these quarters was geared to the demands of the medium, there were many moments when he was able to infuse his work with echoes of his jazz heritage. Throughout those years and into the 70s Hefti periodically formed big bands either for club, concert or record dates. The tradition of precise, disciplined arranging, of which Hefti was one of the more important exponents, continues to make itself heard in the work of Sam Nestico, which has proved immensely popular with college and university bands on both sides of the Atlantic.

● ALBUMS: *Swingin' On A Coral Reef* 10-inch album (Coral 1953) ★★★, *Music Of Rudolph Friml* 10-inch album (X 1954) ★★★, *Pardon My Doo-wah* (Epic 1954) ★★, *Hot 'N' Hearty* (1955) ★★★, *Singing Instrumentals* (Epic 1956) ★★★, *Light And Right!!* (Columbia 1960) ★★, *Themes From TV's Top 12* (Reprise 1962) ★★, *Boeing Boeing* film soundtrack (RCA Victor 1966) ★★, *Batman Theme* (RCA Victor 1966) ★★, *Hefti In Gotham City* (RCA Victor 1966) ★★, *Duel At Diablo* film soundtrack (United Artists 1966) ★★★, *Barefoot In The Park* film soundtrack (London 1967) ★★★, *The Odd Couple* film soundtrack (Dot 1968) ★★★, *Batman Theme And 19 Hefti Bat Songs* (Razor & Tie 1998) ★★★.

HENDERSON, JOE 'MR PIANO'

b. 2 May 1920, Glasgow, Scotland, d. 4 May 1980, London, England. A pianist and composer, Henderson formed his own band to play at school dances before turning professional at the age of 13. In the early 50s he served as accompanist for former child actress and singer Petula Clark, who featured frequently in the UK charts, and subsequently recorded several of her ex-pianist's compositions. Henderson himself became extremely popular on the UK variety circuit, alongside other solo piano acts, such as Winifred Atwell, Russ Conway and – much later – Bobby Crush. He survived the radical changes in popular music that began to take place in the 50s, and still retained an audience. He also featured in *Bumper Bundle* on Radio Luxembourg, and had his own television series *Sing Along With Joe* and *Mr. Piano Plays*. Henderson's first hits came in 1955 with 'Sing It With Joe' and 'Sing It Again With Joe'. These consisted of short piano medleys of jolly standards, such as 'Margie' and 'Somebody Stole My Gal'. In 1958 he had another UK Top 20 hit with 'Trudie', accompanied by the Beryl Stott Chorus. It was the best-known of his mostly bright, catchy compositions, and won an Ivor Novello Award for 'The Year's Best Selling And Most Performed Item'. He earned another 'Ivor' the following year for the movie title song 'Jazzboat', 'The Year's Most Outstanding Composition In The "Jazz" Or "Beat" Idiom'. *Jazzboat* was one of three films that Henderson scored that starred Anthony Newley. The others were *Idle On Parade*, the film that launched Newley's singing career (he co-wrote some of the songs) and *Let's Get Married*. Henderson's other compositions, published by his own company, included 'Why Don't They Understand?' (a US and UK chart hit for country singer George Hamilton IV), 'Chick', 'Treble Chance' (his last Top 30 entry, in 1959), 'Dear Daddy' (with lyrics by Jack Fishman, featured on *Ruby Murray Successes*), 'Matchbox Samba', 'Coffee Bar Jive', 'What A Day We'll Have', 'I'd Have A Long Way To Go', 'When You're Away', 'Dream Of Paradise', 'First Theme', 'I Need You', 'Somebody' and 'Crinoline Waltz'. His other recordings included Charles Chaplin's 'Smile', Leroy Anderson's 'Forgotten Dreams', 'The Theme From The Threepenny Opera (Moritat)' and a lively version of the novelty 'Don't Ring-A Da Bell'. On the latter he played harpsichord, while the vocal was by the British actress Shani Wallis, who went on to play Nancy in the movie of Lionel Bart's *Oliver!* A very likeable and genial personality, Henderson continued to entertain for many years after the hits dried up, particularly in the seaside summer season, at top venues such as Blackpool and Bournemouth.

● ALBUMS: *Joe 'Mr. Piano' Henderson* (1961) ★★★★, *Dancing Cheek To Cheek* (60s) ★★★, *Bumper Bundle* (60s) ★★★★, *The Hits Of 1968* (1968) ★★, *Secret Love Hits Of The 50s* (Columbia 1972) ★★★, *Sing-A-Long With Joe* (Spark 1973) ★★, *Swing-A-Long With Joe 'Mr. Piano' Henderson* (Spark 1974) ★★★, *40 All Time Singalong Party Hits* (Warwick 1975) ★★★, *Joe Henderson Recalls The Unforgettable 50s* (One-Up 1975) ★★★★.

HENDERSON, LYLE 'SKITCH'

b. Lyle Russell Cedric Henderson, 27 January 1918, Halstad, Minnesota, USA. After studying at the Juilliard School of Music in New York, Henderson undertook further studies with Arnold Schoenberg. Despite his classical training, Henderson began playing piano in dance bands, some of which he also led. In the early 40s he accompanied leading artists such as Judy Garland and Bing Crosby, for whom he acted as musical director on radio. Crosby was also responsible for Henderson's unusual nickname, derived from Sketch Kid (because he made piano sketches for orchestras). After serving in the Army Air Corps during the war Henderson set up his own big band, but by the early 50s had become Frank Sinatra's MD. Later, he went into the studios of NBC. From 1954 to 1957 he was musical director for the Steve Allen television show and, from 1962 to 1966, for Johnny Carson's *Tonight* show. His sidemen in the bands he led on these shows included leading session musicians, among them Doc Severinsen, Snooky Young and Clark Terry, and he used arrangements by distinguished writers such as Neal Hefti and Ernie Wilkins. In 1971 Henderson returned to his musical roots, becoming conductor of the Tulsa Symphony Orchestra; he was later musical director for the New York production of Kurt Weill's *Street Scene*.
● ALBUMS: *Skitch ... Tonight!* (Columbia 1965) ★★★.

HERE'S LITTLE RICHARD – LITTLE RICHARD

The enigmatic Little Richard turned rock 'n' roll inside-out with a succession of highly expressive recordings during the mid-50s. Fuelled by an unfettered New Orleans backbeat, he combined gospel fervour and orgasmic delight in equal doses, singing without recourse to convention, hammering the piano keys with barely checked passion. *Here's Little Richard* abounds with essential performances that define an era and few collections offer such unremitting excitement. The pace barely relents, while almost every track has become an integral part of pop history, either in their own right, or through the countless cover versions they have inspired. It is an exceptional album from an exceptional legend.
● Tracks: *Tutti Frutti; True, Fine Mama; Ready Teddy; Baby; Slippin' And Slidin'; Long Tall Sally; Miss Ann; Oh Why?; Rip It Up; Jenny Jenny; She's Got It; Can't Believe You Wanna Leave.*
● First released 1957
● UK peak chart position: did not chart
● USA peak chart position: 13

HERRMANN, BERNARD

b. 29 June 1911, New York, USA, d. 24 December 1975, Los Angeles, USA. One of the most highly regarded composers and arrangers of background music for films, from the early 40s through to the 70s. Herrmann studied at New York University and the Juilliard School of Music, before joining CBS broadcasting in 1933. While serving as a composer conductor for radio documentaries and

dramas he became associated with Orson Welles, and began his film career by scoring Welles' legendary *Citizen Kane*, for which he was nominated for an Academy Award in 1941. He did win the Oscar that year, not for *Citizen Kane*, but for his music to *All That Money Can Buy* (also known as *The Devil And Danny Webster* amongst other titles), generally thought of as among his best work. His other early scores included another Welles classic, *The Magnificent Ambersons, Jane Eyre, Hangover Square, Anna And The King Of Siam, The Ghost And Mrs Muir, The Day The Earth Stood Still, Five Fingers, Beneath The 12 Mile Reef, King Of The Khyber Rifles, Garden Of Evil, The Egyptian* (with Alfred Newman), *The Man In The Grey Flannel Suit, Prince Of Players* and *The Kentuckian* (1955). Herrmann then proceeded to make several films with Alfred Hitchcock – he became known as the director's favourite movie composer. They included thrillers such as *The Man Who Knew Too Much, The Wrong Man, Vertigo, North By Northwest, Psycho* and *Marnie*. He was also a consultant on Hitchcock's sinister *The Birds*. Herrmann was 'gravely wounded' when Hitchcock rejected his score for *Torn Curtain* in favour of one by John Addison; this decision terminated their relationship.

His other dramatic scores included *A Hatful Of Rain, The Naked And The Dead, Journey To The Centre Of The Earth, The Three Worlds Of Gulliver, Mysterious Island, Cape Fear, Tender Is The Night, Joy In The Morning, Sisters, It's Alive.* Between 1965 and 1975, Herrmann spent much of his time based in Britain, and composed the background music for a good many European productions, such as *Jason And The Argonauts, Fahrenheit 451, The Bride Wore Black, Twisted Nerve, The Battle Of Nereveta, The Night Digger* and *Endless Night.* At the end of his career, as at the beginning, Herrmann was nominated for an Academy Award twice in the same year. This time, however, neither *Taxi Driver* nor *Obsession* won the Oscar for Original Score, and Herrmann died, the day after he completed recording the music for Martin Scorsese's *Taxi Driver* in 1975. The many recordings of his vast output include *Classic Fantasy Film Scores* conducted by Herrmann, *Citizen Kane – Classic Film Scores Of Bernard Herrmann* with the National Philharmonic Orchestra, and *From Citizen Kane To Taxi Driver* (1993) on which Elmer Bernstein conducts the Royal Philharmonic Orchestra. In 1992, an hour-long, analytical documentary, *Music For The Movies: Bernard Herrmann*, which included home movies, interviews, and a scene from Hitchcock's *Torn Curtain* accompanied by Herrmann's original, rejected music, was shown on US television.
● COMPILATIONS: *Citizen Kane: The Essential Bernard Herrmann Film Music Collection* (Silva Screen 1999) ★★★★.
● FURTHER READING: *Bernard Herrmann*, E. Johnson. *A Heart At Fire's Center: The Life And Music Of Bernard Herrmann*, Steven C. Smith.

HI-LO'S

The name of this outstanding North American vocal unit derived from the contrast in height between its tallest members – leader/arranger Eugene Thomas Puerling (b. 31 March 1929, Milwaukee, Wisconsin) and Robert Morse (b. 27 July 1927, Pasadena, Texas) – and diminutive Clark Burroughs (b. 3 March 1930, Los Angeles, California) and Robert Strasen (b. 1 April 1928, Strasbourg, France). While developing their sophisticated close-harmony style, they lived in the same Chicago house, making ends meet with menial jobs and engagements at weekends and evenings. Through the offices of bandleader Jerry Fielding, they recorded for several labels while building a reputation as a versatile, technically accomplished act via a Las Vegas hotel season, a tour supporting Judy Garland and replacing the Four Esquires as resident musical turn on comedian Red Skelton's networked television series. Before Strasen was replaced by Dan Shelton in 1958, the four teamed up on disc with the Marty Paich Dek-tette – and Rosemary Clooney with 1957's 'Ring Around Rosie' (with Morse's counter-tenor prominent). This breakthrough assisted the passage of *Now Hear This* into the album Top 20. Further collections – some devoted to specific stylistic genres – sold steadily if less remarkably.

After the Hi-Lo's disbanded in 1964, Puerling and Shelton found employment producing advertising jingles with vocalists Len Dresslar and Bonnie Herman with whom they formed Singers Unlimited in 1966. An impressed Oscar Peterson recommended them to Germany's BASF/MPS company, which released several Singers albums including *Sentimental Journey* and, accompanied by Robert Farnon's orchestra, 1978's *Eventide*. That same year, the Shelton line-up of the Hi-Lo's reformed as a recording entity and were affectionately welcomed at performances in nostalgia revues. The Hi-Lo's had a profound influence on the harmony sound of the Four Freshmen and the Beach Boys.

● ALBUMS: *Listen!* (Starlite 1955/56) ★★★, *The Hi-Lo's, I Presume* (Starlite 1955/56) ★★★, *The Hi-Lo's Under Glass* (Starlite 1956) ★★★, *The Hi-Lo's On Hand* (Starlite 1956) ★★★, *The Hi-Lo's And The Jerry Fielding Band* (Kapp 1956) ★★★, *The Hi-Lo's In Stereo* (Omega 50s) ★★★★, *Suddenly It's The Hi-Lo's* (Columbia 1957) ★★★, *Now Hear This* (Columbia 1957) ★★★, with Rosemary Clooney *Ring A Round Rosie* (Columbia 1957) ★★★★, *The Hi-Lo's ... And All That Jazz* (Philips 1959) ★★★, *Broadway Playbill* (Columbia 1959) ★★, *All Over The Place* (Columbia 1960) ★★★, *The Hi-Lo's Happen To Folk* (Columbia 1962) ★★★, *This Time It's Love* (Columbia 1962) ★★★, *The Hi-Lo's Happen To Bossa Nova* (Reprise 1963) ★★, *Back Again* (1978) ★★.

HIGGINS, CHUCK

b. Charles Williams Higgins, 17 April 1924, Gary, Indiana, USA. Higgins was an R&B singer best known for his recording 'Pachuko Hop' in 1952. The son of a preacher who also played trombone,

Higgins learned to play the trumpet at the age of 10. In 1940 he moved to Los Angeles, where he played the trumpet in his high-school band. While attending the Los Angeles Music Conservatory, Higgins formed a band with pianist Frank Dunn, saxophonist Johnny Parker and others on bass and drums. After a series of personnel changes, Higgins took over the saxophone position and wrote 'Pachuko Hop', featuring a squealing solo on that instrument. It became a highlight of his stage show and was heard by Vernon 'Jake' Porter, owner of Combo Records. Porter released the single ('pachuko' was a slang word denoting a Mexican-American dressed fashionably in baggy pants, with a long key chain), with the b-side 'Motorhead Baby', another raw R&B rocker (and later the inspiration for the nickname of Frank Zappa sideman James 'Motorhead' Sherwood, and subsequently, the heavy metal band Motorhead). Although the record was not a big seller outside the Los Angeles area, it made Higgins a local favourite and he secured concert bookings with Charlie Parker, Nat 'King' Cole, Johnny Ace, Little Richard and the Orioles. Among Higgins' band members at the time were Jimmy Nolen and Johnny 'Guitar' Watson, who then left for a successful blues solo career. Higgins enlisted Daddy Cleanhead to take most of the lead vocals on recordings and as Higgins never signed an exclusive recording contract, his records were released on numerous labels, including Aladdin Records, Caddy, Lucky, Recorded in Hollywood, Specialty Records and Dootone. Primarily an instrumentalist, Higgins also recorded some music featuring singers. He retired from performing in the early 60s and went on to teach music at Los Angeles high schools and colleges. He attempted a comeback briefly in the mid-70s, performing in a disco style, but achieved no success. Two albums recorded in the late 70s returned him to his earlier style and attracted a small European following. In 1983 he toured the UK and later returned to performing in his original style at Los Angeles nightclubs during the 80s. A collection of his early rare singles, *Yak A Dak*, was released on the Swedish Saxophonograph label in 1990.

● ALBUMS: *Pachuko Hop* (Combo 1956) ★★★, *Rock 'N' Roll Versus Rhythm And Blues* (Dootone 1959) ★★★, *Motor Head Chuck* (1977) ★★★, *Chuck Higgins Is A Ph.D.* (1979) ★★.

● COMPILATIONS: *Yak A Dak* (Saxophonograph 1990) ★★★, *Pachuko Hop* (Ace/Specialty 1992) ★★★★.

HIGH SOCIETY

This enjoyable musical adaptation of Philip Barry's stylish play, *The Philadephia Story*, which was filmed (without songs) in 1940 with Katharine Hepburn, Cary Grant and James Stewart, was released by MGM in 1956. Apart from some changes in characterization and locales, John Patrick's screenplay, which was set in swanky Newport, Rhode Island, stayed fairly close to the original and concerns Tracey Lord (Grace Kelly), who is set to marry an insufferable snob, George

Ketteridge (John Lund), when her former husband, C.K. Dexter Haven (Bing Crosby), returns to his house next door, ostensibly to organize a jazz festival. This situation is further complicated by the arrival of Mike Connor (Frank Sinatra) and Liz Imbrie (Celeste Holm), two reporters from *Spy* magazine, which has been allowed access to the wedding because it is in possession of certain information regarding the (alleged) philandering of Tracey's father, Seth Lord (Sidney Blackmer). Louis Calhern is especially amusing as Tracey's uncle, and also in the cast were Lydia Reed, Margalo Gillmore, Richard Keene, Hugh Boswell, and jazz giant Louis Armstrong who played – who else but himself? By the end of the film Tracey comes to her senses, sends George off in a huff, and remarries Dexter. It is obvious that Mike and Liz will be making their own arrangements soon. Cole Porter's score contained several pleasing numbers such as 'High Society Calypso' (Armstrong), 'Now You Has Jazz' (Crosby-Armstrong), 'Little One' (Crosby), 'Who Wants to Be A Millionaire?' (Sinatra-Holm), 'You're Sensational' (Sinatra), 'I Love You, Samantha' (Crosby) and 'Well, Did You Evah?' (Crosby-Sinatra). Bing Crosby and Grace Kelly's record of 'True Love' made the Top 5 in both the UK and US charts, and Sinatra's version of 'Mind If I Make Love To You?' remains one of his most endearing recorded performances. The director-choreographer was Charles Walters, and, in a decade that produced a feast of film musicals, *High Society* grossed nearly six million dollars.

A 1987 UK stage adaptation of the movie, starring Trevor Eve (Dexter), Stephen Rea (Mike), Natasha Richardson (Tracey), Angela Richards (Liz), Ronald Fraser (Uncle Willie) and Robert Swales (George), had a revised book by Richard Eyre, and interpolated into the score some of Porter's other numbers, including 'Give Him The Oo-La-La', 'Hey, Good Lookin'', 'Most Gentlemen Don't Like Love' and 'In The Still Of The Night'. Another version, adapted by Carolyn Burns, dipped further into the Porter song catalogue, and toured the English provinces in 1996. A year later, an American *High Society* started out in San Francisco on its journey to Broadway, where it opened in April 1998. This staging, with Melissa Errico (Tracey), Daniel McDonald (Dexter), Stephen Bogardus (Mike), Randy Graff (Liz), Marc Kudisch (George) and John McMartin (Uncle Willie), supplemented the original film score with Porter numbers such as 'I Love Paris', 'Just One Of Those Things', 'It's All Right With Me' and 'Let's Misbehave'. Additional lyrics were credited to Susan Birkenhead, and Arthur Kopit (*Phantom*) provided the book.

HILLIARD, BOB

b. 21 January 1918, New York, USA, d. 1 February 1971, Hollywood, California, USA. A prolific lyricist from the mid-40s into the 60s, the first of many Hilliard hit songs came in 1946 when he collaborated with Dick Miles on 'The Coffee Song'. It became successful for Frank Sinatra, who remembered it again many years later, and

included it on *Ring-A-Ding-Ding*, the first album for his own Reprise label. In 1947, Hilliard and Carl Sigman contributed 'The Big Brass Band From Brazil' and 'Civilization' to the Broadway musical *Angel With Wings*. 'Civilization' was sung by Elaine Stritch in the show, and became a massive hit for Danny Kaye and the Andrews Sisters, Ray McKinley and Louis Prima. Hilliard's other 40s successes included 'A Strawberry Moon', 'Careless Hands' (with Sigman – revived by Des O'Connor in 1967) and 'Dear Hearts And Gentle People' (with Sammy Fain), which was a hit for Bing Crosby, Dennis Day, Gordon MacRae and others. In the 50s Hilliard collaborated with Jule Styne on the scores for two Broadway musicals, *Michael Todd's Peep Show* ('Stay With The Happy People') and *Hazel Flagg* ('Ev'ry Street's A Boulevard (In Old New York)' and 'How Do You Speak To An Angel?'). His film work around this time included several songs, with Sammy Fain, for Walt Disney's *Alice In Wonderland* (1952, 'It's Late', 'Very Good Advice'). Among Hilliard's other 50s songs were 'Dearie' (with Dave Mann), 'Be My Life's Companion', 'Jealous Eyes', 'Bouquet Of Roses', 'Downhearted' (a hit for Eddie Fisher), 'Sweet Forgiveness', 'Somebody Bad Stole De Wedding Bells' (with Mann) and 'Moonlight Gambler' (with Phil Springer). In 1959 Hilliard had a hit with another novelty song, 'Seven Little Girls Sitting In The Back Seat' (with Lee Pockriss), recorded by Paul Evans in the US, and the Avons in the UK. In the early 60s, with the advent of the beat boom, his output declined, although he had some success with 'Tower Of Strength' (with Burt Bacharach), 'You're Following Me', 'My Summer Love', 'My Little Corner Of The World' (with Pockriss) and 'Our Day Will Come' (with Mort Garson), which was a US number 1 for Ruby And The Romantics. Hilliard's other songs included 'Don't You Believe It', 'Any Day Now', 'Red Silk Stockings And Green Perfume', 'The Thousand Islands Song', 'Chocolate Whiskey And Vanilla Gin', 'Castanets And Lace', and 'Baby Come Home'. Among his many collaborators were Dick Sanford and Sammy Mysels.

HILLTOPPERS

This vocal quartet formed at the Western Kentucky College in Bowling Green, Kentucky, USA, comprised lead Jimmy Sacca (b. Hazard, Kentucky, USA), baritone Billy Vaughn (b. 12 April 1931, Glasgow, Kentucky, USA), tenor Seymour Speigelman and bass Don McGuire. Sacca and Vaughn formed the group to record 'Trying' in 1952 and named it after their college nickname. Dot Records signed the band, re-recorded 'Trying' in the college auditorium, and it reached the US Top 10 (making the UK charts in 1956). Over the next five years the group, who wore college sweaters and beanies on stage, scored a further nine US Top 20 singles, the biggest being 'P.S. I Love You' in 1953, 'Only You' in 1955 and 'Marianne' in 1957. Vaughn left in 1955 and had a very successful career as musical director for Dot and as an orchestra leader. In the UK, where the Platters' original version of 'Only You' was not released until 1956, they reached number 3 with their recording and were in the Top 20 for six months. They were one of the most successful early 50s vocal groups, but like many other acts they could not survive in a rock 'n' roll world and disbanded in 1963. Since then Sacca has occasionally played dates with new sets of Hilltoppers.

● ALBUMS: *Tops In Pops* (London 1957) ★★★, *The Towering Hilltoppers* (London 1957) ★★★, *Love In Bloom* (Dot 1958) ★★.

● COMPILATIONS: *P.S. I Love You – The Best Of* (Varèse Vintage 1994) ★★★.

HILTON, RONNIE

b. Adrian Hill, 26 January 1926, Hull, England, d. 21 February 2001, Hailsham, East Sussex, England. Hilton left school at the age of 14 and worked in an aircraft factory during the war before joining the Highland Light Infantry. He was demobilized in 1947 and returned to factory work as a fitter in Leeds. He sang with the Johnny Addlestone band at the Starlight Roof in Leeds from 1950 and was heard by A&R manager Wally Ridley and signed to HMV Records. At this point he underwent surgery for a hair lip, changed his name, and in July 1954 made his debut as Ronnie Hilton. His first appearance on stage was at the Dudley Hippodrome, and soon afterwards he got his own radio series. For the next 10 years he was one of the most popular vocalists in the UK and specialized in romantic ballads. His hits included 'I Still Believe', 'Veni Vidi Vici', 'A Blossom Fell', 'Stars Shine In Your Eyes', 'The Yellow Rose Of Texas', 'Young And Foolish', 'No Other Love' (a UK number 1 in 1956), 'Who Are We', 'A Woman In Love', 'Two Different Worlds', 'Around The World', 'Wonderful, Wonderful', 'Magic Moments', 'I May Never Pass This Way Again', 'The World Outside', 'The Wonder Of You', 'Don't Let The Rain Come Down (Crooked Little Man)', and the novelty, 'A Windmill In Old Amsterdam'. Since his last hit in 1965 he remained in demand, especially in the north of England, performing summer seasons and tours with nostalgia packages that include contemporaries such as Russ Conway, Dennis Lotis and Rosemary Squires. Financial problems and a stroke in 1976 hindered his activities, but Hilton bounced back as the presenter of *Sounds Of The Fifties* for BBC Radio 2. In 1989, he was awarded a gold medal for services to popular music by the British Academy of Song Composers.

● ALBUMS: *I'm Beginning To See The Light* (EMI 1959) ★★★.

● COMPILATIONS: *The Very Best Of Ronnie Hilton: 16 Favourites Of The 50s* (MFP 1984) ★★★, *The EMI Years: The Best Of Ronnie Hilton* (EMI 1989) ★★★★, *Ronnie Hilton* (Hour Of Pleasure 1990) ★★★.

HODGES, EDDIE

b. 5 March 1947, Hattiesburg, Mississippi, USA. In the mid-50s child star Hodges appeared in television programmes *The Jackie Gleason Show* and *Name That Tune* and was seen on Broadway 405 times in the hit musical *The Music Man*. In 1959 he starred alongside Frank Sinatra and Edward G. Robinson in the film *A Hole In The Head* and can be heard on Sinatra's hit from the film, 'High Hopes'. He also had a major role in the film of *Huckleberry Finn*, starred with Hayley Mills in *Summer Magic* and even had his own television show, *The Secret World Of Eddie Hodges*. His youthful revival of the Isley Brothers' 'I'm Gonna Knock On Your Door' on Cadence, not only took him into the US Top 20 in 1961 but also gave the 14-year-old an Australian and Canadian chart-topper and a small UK hit. He returned to the US Top 20 with an endearing song written by Phil Everly, '(Girls, Girls, Girls) Made To Love' in 1962. He had releases on Columbia in 1963 and MGM in 1964 before 'New Orleans' on Aurora in 1965 gave him his last US chart entry. It seems that, for Hodges, maturity brought a halt to his recording career.

HOGG, SMOKEY

b. Andrew Hogg, 27 January 1914, Westconnie, Texas, USA, d. 1 May 1960, McKinney, Texas. USA. Born in north-east Texas, Smokey came from a clan that included blues singers Lightnin' Hopkins and John Hogg. He learned to play the guitar and piano early in life under the instruction of his father, Frank. One of seven children, he looked upon music as a means of escape from labour in the fields. He sang around Dallas and Greenville and was popular enough to be known as Little Peetie Wheatstraw after his idol. He played in clubs with men such as B.K. Turner (Black Aces) and D.C. Bender. In 1937 he recorded two tracks for Decca Records, which, although much valued by collectors, made no impression on the blues-buying public of the time. During World War II he was drafted and served in the US Army, but by 1947 he was in Los Angeles, where he recorded for the Exclusive label, again without much success. His breakthrough came after he had moved back to Texas where he recorded 'Too Many Drivers', released under the Modern label in 1947. Back in Los Angeles, but still for Modern, he recorded his biggest hit, 'Little School Girl'. Now established, he began, like many of his contemporaries, to hop from label to label, recording for Specialty, Imperial, SIW, Mercury and many smaller concerns. He enjoyed a good deal of popularity, especially with older fans, and this allowed him to survive the initial impact of rock 'n' roll. Hogg's work seems to be something of an acquired taste and collectors are divided quite violently when judging its worth. He had no such problems with his black audience when his rural blues were sung to a small (often saxophone-led) band accompaniment and were appearing on labels from Texas to the coast.

● ALBUMS: including *Smokey Hogg* (1962) ★★★, *I'm So Lonely* (1964) ★★★, *Original Folk Blues* (1967) ★★★, *Sings The Blues* (1971) ★★★, with Earl Hooker, Lightnin' Hopkins *Hooker, Hopkins And Hogg* (Specialty 1973) ★★★, *U Better Watch That Jive* (1974) ★★, *Going Back Home* (Krazy Kat 1984) ★★, *Everybody Needs Help* (1986) ★★.

● COMPILATIONS: *Angels In Harlem* 1949-58 recordings (Ace 1992) ★★★, *Deep Ellum Rambler* (Ace 2001) ★★★★.

HOLIDAY, BILLIE

b. Eleanora Harris (aka Fagan), 7 April 1915, Philadelphia, Pennsylvania, USA, d. 17 July 1959, New York City, New York, USA. 'Lady Day' taught herself to sing during her early teens in Baltimore, Maryland, where she was brought up until moving to New York in 1929. Factual inaccuracies and elements of myth and exaggeration have clouded the picture of her formative years despite the best efforts of researchers to present her career story in a properly ordered manner. Not until Stuart Nicholson's immaculately researched book appeared in 1995 was a detailed and reliable account of these years made available. Nicholson's research revealed that some of the statements made by the singer in her 1956 autobiography, *Lady Sings The Blues*, were true, despite having been dismissed as exaggeration by other writers. Holidays' teenage parents, Sadie Harris (aka Fagan) and probable father, Clarence Holiday, probably never married, and it seems unlikely that they lived together for any length of time. Holiday, a banjo and guitar player is remembered principally for his work with Fletcher Henderson's band in the early 30s. He remains a somewhat shadowy figure who left his daughter in the care of Fagan or other relatives. As a musician with touring bands in the later 20s Holiday would often be away from home, and during the stay with Henderson, which lasted until 1932, the guitarist severed connections with the Fagans. However Billie proved hard to shake off after joining her mother in New York's Harlem district, and when rent on their apartment was overdue, she confronted Clarence at the Roseland Ballroom – where Henderson's orchestra enjoyed a lengthy 'residency' – and extorted money by threatening to show him up publicly.

Fragments of information about Holiday's deprived, cruelly exploited and extravagantly ill-fated early history prove she had learned how to survive extreme poverty, race prejudice and the injustice of black ghetto life by the time she was 15 or 16. Also, they hint at a more influential relationship between father and daughter (no matter how tenuous it might have been) than Holiday revealed in print. Clarence, a more than competent guitarist with a reputation for 'good time' in a rhythm section, seemed surrounded by paradox. Through the 30s, even after his barely noted death early in 1937, compilers of books which included record reviews and personnel listings employed the spellings Haliday or Halliday, and there is evidence that Billie used that name occasionally until persuaded to sing professionally as Billie Holiday. For jazz historians the interest lies in tracking down a link between her father's fine, relaxed sense of rhythm and her own astonishing command of time and swing: *laid-back* swing of a type not previously heard on records by singers. Since Holiday had very little schooling and no formal musical training, her extraordinary creative gifts were intuitive in the first place. She developed her singing in obscure New York speakeasies and Harlem nightclubs such as Pods' and Jerry's Log Cabin, the Yeah

Man, Monette Moore's Supper Club, the Hot-Cha, Alabama Grill and Dickie Wells' place. She even sang at the local Elks club in order to pick up a few dollars in tips. Poverty was the spur, the initial incentive, but the dedication she then displayed to the mastering of jazz-craft is not easy to explain. No amount of theorizing will help to a real understanding of her seemingly instinctive gift for music-making. She was a perfectionist in her fashion, depending upon her excellent ear, innate taste and honesty of purpose to make up artistically for her small voice and range. This integrity, so far as vocal sound and style went, is the more baffling because of the insecurity and brutal ugliness of her early life. She had already survived rape at age 11 and a period in care which followed this attack. In New York she endured a brief stint as a prostitute for which she and her mother were arrested in 1929. For this she served 100 days at the workhouse on Blackwell's Island on the East River (later known as Welfare Island). It has frequently been stated that fame and success depend largely on an artist or performer being in the right place at the right time. In Holiday's case, the lucky break came when she found herself by sheer chance singing in front of the well-connected record producer and talent spotter John Hammond Jnr. Hammond had stopped off at the 133rd Street club with the intention of listening to singer Monette Moore. Instead of the blues singer, a performer who had been recording since 1923, he heard the unknown girl deputizing for Monette (absent, playing in a Broadway show) and was immediately impressed. 'She sang popular songs in a manner that made them completely her own', Hammond wrote later in his autobiography, praising her excellent memory for lyrics and sense of phrasing. He also gave Holiday the first press notice of her career. In April 1933 it appeared in the *Melody Maker*, and Hammond wrote: 'This month there has been a real find in the person of a singer called Billie Halliday' (she had by now adopted the first name of film actress Billie Dove, a childhood favourite whom she regarded as the epitome of glamour). Hammond represented a real break in Holiday's long run of bad luck because he had the power and willingness to forward the careers of those he thought worthy of special aid. The enthusiasm of his initial reaction to the promising youngster was shown in his description, 'She is incredibly beautiful and sings as well as anybody I ever heard', printed in the 1933 *Melody Maker*. Living up to his reputation, Hammond 'got into the habit of bringing people uptown to hear Billie'. Benny Goodman shared his opinion of Holiday and agreed to record with her. In the course of three sessions during November and December 1933, two songs were recorded with Goodman in charge of a nine-man studio group most of whom were strangers to the already nervous Holiday. 'Your Mother's Son-in-Law' was the first record she ever made; 'Riffin' The Scotch', a lightweight novelty concoction, was the second. Neither was successful as a showcase for her – nor, in truth, designed to be – because her role in the proceedings presented Holiday as band vocalist in a setting which stressed the instrumental prowess of Goodman, trombonist Jack Teagarden and other soloists. However, the singer managed to stamp her imprint on the vocal refrains and, for a young black performer with no experience of recording and, in her words, 'afraid to sing in the mike', came across as reasonably confident. For the Lady (she had earned that nickname on the Harlem club circuit for her regal sense of dignity, and it was amended by Lester Young who added a typically personal touch, calling her Lady Day), expecting little she was not disappointed. Royalties were not routinely paid to recording artists in those days, and Holiday remembered receiving a flat fee of about 35 dollars for her work. Having a record on the market was no great deal; she placed little value on either song, not bothering to include them in her club or stage programmes or future recording repertoire.

Holiday continued her round of club dates, as well as being heard in the film *Symphony In Black*, made with Duke Ellington and released in 1935. Her career was given a boost when she won a week's engagement at the Apollo Theatre, Harlem's most famous and, for up-and-coming artists, formidable entertainment centre. Holiday, then just 20 years old, appeared with pianist Bobbie Henderson and her notices were, at best, mildly critical. Clearly, her relaxed, seemingly lazy, behind-the-beat style did not appeal to the Apollo's often vociferous patrons. Nevertheless, when the entire show was held over for a second week, at which time she appeared with Ralph Cooper's orchestra, her notices improved thanks to her capacity to adapt. By this time, Holiday had settled on the spelling of her name (earlier, her given name, Eleanora, was also subject to variation).

By mid-July the singer had returned to the recording studio for a session organized by Hammond and directed by Teddy Wilson. In Wilson, an accomplished musician and sensitive pianist, Holiday had found the sympathetic partner she needed to reveal the full range of her talents. The four songs picked for this groundbreaking record date were above average – 'I Wished On The Moon' and 'Miss Brown To You' were film numbers – and the easygoing jam-session atmosphere suited Holiday admirably. She responded to Wilson's masterly accompaniments and solo playing, and to the brilliance of Goodman, Roy Eldridge and Ben Webster, and similar jazz aces on subsequent recordings. They in turn seemed to be spurred by the rhythmic thrust and innovative magic of her singing. Here was a rising star (since 10 July 1936 she had achieved own-name status on the Vocalion Records label) who could invest ordinary popular songs with the emotional kick of a first-rate blues or ballad composition. The records also paid off sufficiently well to satisfy the marketing men.

Following appearances at a few slightly more prestigious venues than hitherto, Holiday sang with the bands of Count Basie (1937-38) and Artie Shaw (1938). She enjoyed the company of the bandsmen, and had an affair with Basie's guitarist Freddie Green. In spite of this rapport, the period with Basie was not a consistently happy one for Holiday, who encountered setbacks on the road and rejection by management people who disliked her 'way-out' style, or criticism from friends advising her to tailor her singing to the perceived requirements of the orchestra. As usual, Lady Day refused to compromise. She quit the Basie band, or was fired, in February of 1938 and, reservations about the touring life notwithstanding, joined Shaw almost at once and was on the road again, this time with a white band. She ran into trouble with racists, especially in the 'Jim Crow' Southern states, and before the end of the year had left Shaw. It was to be her final appearance as a band member: from now on she would be presented as a solo artist.

She continued making records and it seems likely that those closest to her heart were those recorded in association with Wilson, her beloved Lester Young and trumpeter Buck Clayton. And there is an emerging consensus that the inspirational partnership of Holiday and Young – musical and emotional – led to a batch of the finest vocal interpretations of her life. Undeniably, these discs and others made between 1935 and 1942 are among the finest in jazz. Early in 1939, Holiday's career took a giant step upwards. Again Hammond proffered a helping hand, as did Barney Josephson who dreamed of running a racially integrated nightclub in New York's Greenwich Village. Hammond was the one who invested in the project and, asked to advise on appropriate attractions for liberal patrons, recommended Holiday. She opened at Café Society with Frankie Newton's band that January and had her first taste of stardom at the Café whose slogan read 'The wrong place for the right people'. Holiday stayed there for nearly nine months, during which time she was given a song-poem, 'Strange Fruit', an anti-lynching protest written by Abel Merropol, a white Jewish schoolteacher who used the pseudonym Lewis Allan. The song gave Holiday a real hit record and new and international fame as a purveyor of socially significant ballads. The track continued to be identified with Holiday who, on 20 April 1939, made a record of this controversial title for the Commodore label, her own having refused to record it. Opinion divided sharply on the merits of 'Strange Fruit' as a jazz vehicle, and the effect it had upon her instinctive taste and artistry. Critics feared it could lead to a self-consciousness which would destroy the strangely innocent qualities of earlier days.

Unfortunately as the sound of jazz progressed into the 40s and 50s Holiday responded positively, if unwisely, to some changes in the musical and social climate. Already an eager drinker, smoker of tobacco and marijuana, eater, dresser and shopper with a sexual appetite described as 'healthy-plus', she embraced the hard-drug culture of the 40s as to the manner born. She was having troublesome love affairs, nothing new to her, but on 25 August 1941 married Jimmy Monroe. It was a union that did nothing to ease her situation, being an on-off affair which lasted until their divorce in 1957. Nobody now can say when exactly, and by whom, but Holiday was turned on to opium and then heroin. The details are unimportant; the addiction hardly affected her singing at first, although her behaviour grew increasingly unpredictable, and she gained a reputation for unreliability. At last she was earning real money, as much as $1,000 weekly, it was reported, and about half that sum was going to pay for her 'habit'. Nevertheless, she now had the public recognition she craved. In the first *Esquire* magazine poll (1943) the critics voted her best vocalist, topping Mildred Bailey and Ella Fitzgerald in second and third places respectively. Holiday was a stellar act, in spite of drug problems, and one accompanist spoke years later of her 'phenomenal musicianship.' The series of 78s – 36 titles made for Decca Records with a wide variety of more commercially acceptable accompaniments, including strings on a dozen or so sides and a vocal group on two – rank with the mature Holiday's most accomplished performances, technically speaking, although the revolutionary approach had become more calculating and mannered. To compensate, she turned up the emotional heat, depending on her imagination to deliver the right touch. Among these 78s, recorded between October 1944 and March 1950, are a number of gems of jazz singing – among them 'Lover Man', 'Porgy', 'Good Morning Heartache', 'You Better Go Now' and, as a welcome example of Lady Day back to top form as a commanding, exuberant, mistress of swing phrasing, the mid-tempo blues-drenched 'Now Or Never'. To round off this set, assembled on three *The Lady Sings* albums, she exhibits another facet of her craft by duetting comfortably with Armstrong on 'My Sweet Hunk O' Trash' and sharing space on a second Armstrong track.

At this stage of her life Holiday experienced regular bouts of depression, pain and ill health. In 1947 she was sentenced to a long term in the Federal Reformatory, West Virginia, her arraignment coming, surprisingly, at the behest of her manager, Joe Glaser. The attendant publicity disastrously affected her confidence while drugs slowly weakened her physique. Running her own big band with husband Joe Guy in 1945 had cost Holiday a sum reckoned to be $35,000, and that blow was followed by the death of her mother. Another disappointment to Holiday's professional aspirations was her failure to secure a film break, after pinning her hopes on the part she was offered in the jazz film, *New Orleans* (1946). Both Holiday and her idol, Armstrong, had roles involving a great deal of music-making – much of it left in the cutting room – but the purported jazz story turned out to be a nonsensical fantasy; and worse, Holiday and Armstrong were cast as servants. She was quoted later as saying: 'I fought my whole life to keep from being somebody's damn maid. It was a real drag . . . to end up as a make-believe maid'. The picture failed but gave her valuable international exposure, and jazz fanciers were pleased to see and hear sequences featuring Holiday Armstrong, Kid Ory, Woody

Herman and other musicians. For Holiday it was goodbye to the movies.

From the 50s on, Holiday and trouble seemed often to be inseparable, and as a consequence of her criminal record on drugs, Holiday's cabaret card was withdrawn by the New York Police Department. This prevented her appearance at any venue where liquor was on sale, and effectively ruled out New York nightclubs. In her eyes it amounted to an absolute injustice and one that diminished her out-of-town earning capacity. She appeared in England during 1954 to great acclaim, and in 1956, her outspoken autobiography (written with William Dufty) brought increased fame, or notoriety. In 1957, Holiday was still making good money but by the following year the drink and drugs crucially influenced her vocal control, and the 'hoarsely eloquent voice' had increased in hoarseness at the expense of the eloquence. However, one further segment of the Holiday discography deserves attention: the body of work on the Clef-Verve label (produced or master-minded by Norman Granz) which placed her in a jazz setting and encouraged her to shine when she and the small-group accompaniment felt right. These recordings (1952-57) include a number of satisfying performances, and several worthy of high praise. As for the final albums with the Ray Ellis Orchestra, they are, for the majority of jazz fanciers, a painfully acquired taste, although certain tracks, most notably 'You've Changed' on *Lady In Satin* are immensely moving on their own terms. It was clear that her voice was shot, yet the treble-laden croak she often lapses into is still somehow a brilliant and moving record.

Billie Holiday paid a second and last visit to Europe late in 1958, and came to London to make a television appearance on Granada's *Chelsea At Nine* show in February 1959. Back in America, however, her condition worsened and at the end of May she was taken to hospital suffering from heart and liver disease. Harried still by the police (she had been arrested twice already for possession, in 1949 and 1956), and placed under arrest in her private room, she was charged with 'possession' and put under police guard – the final cruelty the system could inflict upon her. Thus the greatest of jazz singers died in humiliating circumstances at 3.10 am on 17 July 1959 with $750 in notes taped to one leg – an advance on a series of promised articles. Even at the end squabbles had begun between a lawyer, virtually self-appointed, and her second husband, Louis McKay, whom she had married on 28 March 1957. She did not live to rejoice in the flood of books, biographical features, critical studies, magazine essays, album booklets, discographies, reference-book entries, chapters in innumerable jazz volumes, films and television documentaries which far exceed any form of recognition she experienced in her lifetime.

In defiance of her limited vocal range, Billie Holiday's use of tonal variation and vibrato, her skill at jazz phrasing, and her unique approach to the lyrics of popular songs, were but some of the elements in the work of a truly original artist. Her clear diction, methods of manipulating pitch, improvising on a theme, the variety of emotional moods ranging from the joyously optimistic, flirtatious even, to the tough, defiant, proud, disillusioned and buoyantly barrelhouse, were not plucked out of the air, acquired without practice. Holiday paid her dues in a demanding milieu. That she survived at all is incredible; that she should become the greatest jazz singer there has ever been – virtually without predecessor or successor – borders on the miraculous. Today she is revered beyond her wildest imaginings in places which, in her lifetime, greeted her with painfully closed doors. Sadly, she would not have been surprised. As she wrote in her autobiography: 'There's no damn business like showbusiness. You had to smile to keep from throwing up'. Any new student coming to popular music or Jazz will at some point be directed to the work of Holiday. Unquestionably they will be moved and probably they will be amazed.

● ALBUMS: *Billie Holiday, Volume 1* 10-inch album (Commodore 1950) ★★★, *Billie Holiday, Volume 2* 10-inch album (Commodore 1950) ★★★, *Billie Holiday Sings* 10-inch album (Columbia 1950) ★★★, *Favorites* 10-inch album (Columbia 1951) ★★★, *Lover Man* 10-inch album (Decca 1951) ★★★, *Billie Holiday Sings* 10-inch album (Mercury 1952) ★★★, *Billie Holiday Sings* reissued as *Solitude – Songs By Billie Holiday* (Clef 1953) ★★★, *An Evening With Billie Holiday* 10-inch album (Clef 1953) ★★★, *Billie Holiday* 10-inch album (Clef 1954) ★★★, *Billie Holiday At Jazz At The Philharmonic* 10-inch album (Clef 1954) ★★★, *Music For Torching* (Clef 1955) ★★★, with Teddy Wilson *Lady Day* (Columbia 1955) ★★★★, *A Recital By Billie Holiday* reissue of *An Evening With Billie Holiday* and *Billie Holiday* (Clef 1956) ★★★, *The Lady Sings* (Decca 1956) ★★★★, *Velvet Mood* (Clef 1956) ★★★, *Lady Sings The Blues* (Clef 1956) ★★★★, *Body And Soul* (Verve 1957) ★★★, *Songs For Distingué Lovers* (Verve 1958) ★★★★, *Stay With Me* (Verve 1958) ★★★, *The Blues Are Brewin'* (Decca 1958) ★★★★, *Lady In Satin* (Columbia 1958) ★★★★, *All Or Nothing At All* (Verve 1959) ★★★★, *In Europe 1954* (Kangourou Swing 2000) ★★★, *In Europe 1958* (Kangourou Swing 2000) ★★★.

● COMPILATIONS: *The Unforgettable Lady Day* (Verve 1959) ★★★★, *The Essential Billie Holiday* (Verve 1961) ★★★★, *The Golden Years* 3-LP box set (Columbia 1962) ★★★★, *Billie's Blues* (United Artists 1962) ★★★★, *Rare Live Recordings* (Ric 1964) ★★★, *The Commodore Recordings* (Mainstream 1965) ★★★, with Teddy Wilson *Once Upon A Time* (Mainstream 1965) ★★★, *Lady* (Verve 1966) ★★★, *The Golden Years, Volume 2* (Columbia 1966) ★★★★, *Billie Holiday's Greatest Hits* Columbia material (Columbia 1967) ★★★★, *Billie Holiday's Greatest Hits* Decca material (Decca 1968) ★★★, *The Billie Holiday Story* Decca material (Decca 1972) ★★★★, *Strange Fruit* (Atlantic 1973) ★★★, *Lady In Autumn: The Best Of The Verve Years* (Verve 1973/91) ★★★★★, *The Original Recordings* (Columbia 1973) ★★★★,

shared with Ella Fitzgerald, Lena Horne, Sarah Vaughan *Billie, Ella, Lena, Sarah!* (Columbia 1980) ★★★★, *The Silver Collection* (Verve 1984) ★★★★, *Billie Holiday At Monterey 1958* (1986) ★★★, *The Billie Holiday Collection* (Déjà Vu 1988) ★★★, *Billie's Blues 1942, 1951, 1954* recordings (Blue Note 1988) ★★★★, *The Quintessential Billie Holiday Volume 1* 1933-1935 recordings (Columbia 1991) ★★★★, *The Quintessential Billie Holiday Volume 2* 1936 recordings (Columbia 1991) ★★★★, *The Quintessential Billie Holiday Volume 3* 1936-1937 recordings (Columbia 1991) ★★★★, *The Quintessential Billie Holiday Volume 4* 1937 recordings (Columbia 1991) ★★★★, *The Quintessential Billie Holiday Volume 5* 1937-1938 recordings (Columbia 1991) ★★★★, *The Quintessential Billie Holiday Volume 6* 1938 recordings (Columbia 1991) ★★★★, *The Quintessential Billie Holiday Volume 7* 1938-1939 recordings (Columbia 1991) ★★★★, *The Quintessential Billie Holiday Volume 8* 1939-1940 recordings (Columbia 1991) ★★★★, *The Quintessential Billie Holiday Volume 9* 1940-1942 recordings (Columbia 1991) ★★★★, *Billie Holiday: The Legacy Box 1933-1958* Columbia material (Columbia 1991) ★★★, *The Complete Decca Recordings* 1944-1950 recordings (Decca 1991) ★★★★, *1933-1937* (Classics 1991) ★★★, *1937-1939* (Classics 1991) ★★★, *1939-1940* (Classics 1991) ★★★, *1940-1942* (Classics 1991) ★★★, *1944* (Classics 1995) ★★★, *The Essential Billie Holiday: Songs Of Lost Love* 50s material (Verve 1992) ★★★★, *Billie's Best* Verve material (Verve 1992) ★★★★, *The Early Classics* (Pearl Flapper 1992) ★★★, *The Complete Billie Holiday On Verve 1945-1959* 10-CD box set (Verve 1993) ★★★★, *16 Most Requested Songs* Columbia material (Columbia 1993) ★★★★, *Collection* (Castle 1993) ★★★, *Verve Jazz Masters 12: Billie Holiday* (Verve 1994) ★★★★, *Great American Songbook* (PolyGram 1994) ★★★, *Masters Of Jazz, Volume 3* 1944-49 recordings (Storyville) ★★★★, *Greatest Hits* (MCA 1995) ★★★★, *Fine And Mellow (1935-1941)* (Indigo 1995) ★★★, *Lady Sings The Blues: Original Sessions 1937-1947* (Accord 1995) ★★★, *Verve Jazz Masters 47: Billie Holiday Sings Standards* 1945-59 recordings (Verve/PolyGram 1995) ★★★, *All Or Nothing At All* comprises *Distingué Lovers, Body And Soul, All Or Nothing At All* albums (Verve 1996) ★★★★, *Love Songs* Columbia material (Sony 1996) ★★★★, *American Legends: Billie Holiday* Columbia/ Decca material (Laserlight 1996) ★★★, *This Is Jazz No. 15: Billie Holiday* Columbia material (Sony 1996) ★★★★, *Billie Holiday 1935-1938* (Fat Boy 1996) ★★★, *Golden Hits* (Intercontinental 1996) ★★★, *Lady Day's 25 Greatest 1933-1944* (ASV/Living Era 1996) ★★★, *The Complete Commodore Recordings* 1939, 1944 recordings (GRP 1997) ★★★★, *Priceless Jazz Collection* Decca material (GRP 1997) ★★★, *Ultimate Billie Holiday* (Verve 1997) ★★★★, *Gold Collection* (Fine Tune 1998) ★★, *The Incomparable Billie Holiday Vols 1-5* 1930s recordings (ABM 1999) ★★, *Complete Edition Vol. 15* 1945-46 recordings (Media 7 1999) ★★★, *The Very Best Of Billie Holiday* 1936-59 recordings (Verve 1999) ★★★, *Radio And TV Broadcasts* 1949-52 transcriptions

(ESP 1999) ★★★, *Radio And TV Broadcasts* 1953-56 transcriptions (ESP 1999) ★★★, *Ken Burns Jazz: The Definitive Billie Holiday* (Verve 2000) ★★★★, *Lady Sings The Blues* 1954, 57 recordings (The Entertainers 2000) ★★★, *Lady Day – The Best Of Billie Holiday* (Sony 2001) ★★★★, *Lady Day: The Complete Billie Holiday On Columbia (1933-1944)* 10-CD box set (Columbia/Legacy 2001) ★★★★.

● VIDEOS: *Lady Day: The Many Faces Of Billie Holiday* (1991).

● FURTHER READING: *Billie's Blues,* John Chilton. *Lady Sings The Blues,* Billie Holiday with William Duffy, *Billie Holiday,* Stuart Nicholson. *Wishing On The Moon: The Life & Times Of Billie Holiday,* Donald Clarke. *Divas: Billie Holiday,* Chris Ingham. *Lady Day: The Many Faces Of Billie Holiday,* Robert O'Meally, *Strange Fruit: Billie Holiday, Cafe Society, And An Early Cry For Civil Rights.* David Margolick.

HOLLIDAY, JUDY

b. Judith Tuvim, 21 June 1922, New York, USA, d. 7 June 1965, New York, USA. An actress and singer with an endearing quality and a warm, unique comic style, Holliday's first attempt to break into showbusiness was with Orson Welles and John Houseman at the Mercury Theatre, but she only succeeded in getting a job there as a telephone operator – ironic considering her later memorable role in the musical theatre. Holliday joined some more young hopefuls, Betty Comden, Adolph Green, John Frank and Alvin Hammer, in a nightclub act called the Revuers, who attracted a good deal of attention. In 1945 she made her Broadway debut in the play *Kiss Them For Me,* and a year later was acclaimed for her performance in the Garson Kanin comedy *Born Yesterday.* She had taken over the dizzy blonde role after the producers' original choice, Jean Arthur, withdrew during the Philadelphia try-out. In 1950 Holliday won an Academy Award when she recreated her part for the Columbia film version. In the previous year she had almost stolen the glory from stars Katharine Hepburn and Spencer Tracey in *Adam's Rib,* which also had a screenplay by Kanin and his wife Ruth Gordon. In 1956 Holliday returned to Broadway in the musical *Bells Are Ringing.* The book and lyrics were by her old friends, Comden and Green (music by Jule Styne), and Holliday played Ella Peterson, a telephone operator who cannot help becoming emotionally involved with the clients who subscribe to Susanswerphone, the answering service where she works. *Bells Are Ringing* was a smash hit, and Holliday introduced several of its delightful songs, including 'The Party's Over', 'Drop That Name', 'Just In Time' and 'Long Before I Knew You' (both with Sydney Chaplin), and the immortal 'I'm Goin' Back (To The Bonjour Tristesse Brassiere Company)'. Her unforgettable performance won her Tony and New York Drama Critics awards.

In 1948 she had married musician David Oppenheim, who became head of the classical division of Columbia Records, but they divorced in 1957. Holliday's subsequent partner was another musician, a giant of the jazz world, Gerry Mulligan. He played one of her boyfriends in the 1960 screen adaptation of *Bells Are Ringing,* in which she co-starred with Dean Martin, and they also wrote songs together. Four of the best of these, 'What's The Rush?', 'Loving You', 'It Must Be Christmas' and 'Summer's Over', were included among the standards on an album they recorded in 1961. In spite of its tender and poignant quality, and the presence of accompanying luminaries such as Bob Brookmeyer, Mel Lewis and Al Klink, Holliday was reported to be unhappy with the result, and the album was not released until 1980. In 1960 she was out of town with the play *Laurette,* based on the life of the former Broadway star Laurette Taylor, when she found that she was unable to project her voice properly. It was the first sign that she had cancer. After surgery, she returned to New York in 1963 with the musical *Hot Spot,* but it folded after only 43 performances. She died just two weeks before her forty-third birthday.

● ALBUMS: with Gerry Mulligan *Holliday With Mulligan* 1961 recording (DRG 1980) ★★★★, and Original Cast and soundtrack recordings.

● FURTHER READING: *Judy Holliday,* W. Holtzman. *Judy Holliday,* G. Carey.

● FILMS: *Greenwich Village* (1944), *Something For The Boys* (1944), *Winged Victory* (1944), *Adam's Rib* (1949), *Born Yesterday* (1950), *The Marrying Kind* (1952), *It Should Happen To You* (1954), *Phffft* (1954), *The Solid Gold Cadillac* (1956), *Full Of Life* (1956), *Bells Are Ringing* (1960).

HOLLIDAY, MICHAEL

b. Michael Milne, 26 November 1928, Liverpool, England, d. 29 October 1963, Croydon, Surrey, England. A popular singer in the UK during the 50s, influenced by, and very similar in style and tone to Bing Crosby. After entertaining his shipmates in the Merchant Navy, Holliday made his first public appearance as a singer when his ship docked in New York. He won a talent contest on the stage of Radio City Music Hall, one of the world's largest theatres. In the absence of offers to star in a big Broadway musical, he returned to the UK, was released from the navy, and obtained work as a singer-guitarist with the Eric Winstone Band, touring UK holiday camps. He was signed to Columbia Records by Norrie Paramor in 1955, and during the next couple of years, covered several US artists' hits such as 'The Yellow Rose Of Texas' (Mitch Miller), 'Sixteen Tons' (Tennessee Ernie Ford) and 'Hot Diggity (Dog Ziggity Boom)' (Perry Como), while also reaching the UK Top 30 with 'Nothin' To Do', 'Ten Thousand Miles' and 'The Gal With The Yaller Shoes', from the 1956 movie *Meet Me In Las Vegas.* In 1958 he had some success with 'In Love', 'Stairway Of Love' and the 1929 number 'I'll Always Be In Love With You', and topped the UK chart with 'The Story Of My Life', an early composition by Burt Bacharach and Hal David. On the b-side of that record was one of Holliday's own compositions, 'Keep Your Heart'. Early in 1960 he had another number 1 with 'Starry Eyed', but after 'Skylark' and 'Little Boy Lost' later in the year, the singles hits dried up. On his albums such as *Mike* and *Holliday Mixture*, he ignored the contemporary music scene, and sang old standards – as he did on television. With his casual, easy-going style, he was a natural for the small screen, and had his own *Relax With Mike* series, on which he duetted with himself on a tape recorder, in the days when those machines were a domestic novelty in the UK. His only appearance on the larger screen was in the movie *Life Is A Circus* (1962), with one of Britain's best-loved comedy teams, the Crazy Gang. Unfortunately, his relaxed image seems to have been a façade, concealing professional and personal problems. When Holliday died in a Croydon hospital the cause of death was reported to have been an overdose of drugs.

● ALBUMS: *Hi!* (Columbia 1958) ★★★, *Mike* (Columbia 1959) ★★★, *Holliday Mixture* (Columbia 1960) ★★★, *Happy Holiday* (Columbia 1961) ★★, *To Bing From Mike* (Columbia 1962) ★★★.

● COMPILATIONS: *The Best Of Michael Holliday* (Columbia 1964) ★★★, *Story Of My Life* (One-Up 1973) ★★★, *The Very Best Of Michael Holliday* (MFP 1984) ★★★, with Edna Savage *A Sentimental Journey* (See For Miles 1988) ★★★, *The EMI Years: The Best Of Michael Holliday* (EMI 1989) ★★★★, *30th Anniversary Collection* (EMI 1994) ★★★★.

HOLLY, BUDDY

b. Charles Hardin Holley, 7 September 1936, Lubbock, Texas, USA, d. 3 February 1959. Holly was one of the first major rock 'n' roll groundbreakers, and one of its most influential artists. He wrote his own songs, recorded with a self-contained guitar-bass-drums combo, experimented in the studio and even changed the image of what a rock singer could look like: until he came along, the idea of a bespectacled rock idol was unthinkable. Holly's hiccuping vocal style and mature, melodic compositions inspired many of the rockers who would emerge in the 60s and 70s, from the Beatles and Bob Dylan to the Hollies. Later, British singer-songwriter Elvis Costello would emerge with an unabashed Holly-inspired physical appearance. Like many other early rock 'n' rollers, Holly's musical influences included both C&W music and 'race' music, or R&B. He made his first stage appearance at the age of five, joining with his brothers Larry and Travis in a talent contest; he won $5. During his childhood, Holly learned to play guitar, violin and piano, taking formal lessons but teaching himself boogie-woogie rhythms on the piano. At 12 years old he was entertaining friends with Hank Williams songs and in 1949 formed a bluegrass duo, Buddy And Bob, with friend Bob Montgomery. He learned to play banjo and mandolin during this period. Holly made his first recording on a home tape recorder in 1949, a song called 'My Two Timin' Woman'.

By 1952 Buddy And Bob had become popular around Lubbock; recording two songs together at Holly's home that year and another in 1953. In September of that year Buddy And Bob appeared on KDAV radio, performing two numbers. Adding

Larry Welborn on bass, they were given their own programme, *The Buddy And Bob Show*. They performed country material primarily, but occasionally included an R&B song by artists such as Hank Ballard. KDAV disc jockey Hipockets Duncan became the trio's manager and secured work for them in the West Texas area. Further recording took place at KDAV but none of it was released. In 1954 the trio added fiddler Sonny Curtis and steel guitarist Don Guess to the group, and together made more recordings in Lubbock and at Nesman Recording Studio in Wichita Falls, Texas. That year the group, now including drummer Jerry Allison, opened concerts for Bill Haley And His Comets and Elvis Presley in Texas. Holly was impressed by Presley and began thinking about performing in the new rock 'n' roll style. However, in the meantime he continued to play country.

In December 1955 Nashville agent Eddie Crandall requested of KDAV disc jockey Dave Stone that Holly and his group record four demo songs, believing he could secure them a contract with Decca Records. The group, now minus Montgomery, sent five songs, and Decca brought them to Nashville where they recorded four songs produced by Owen Bradley at Bradley's Barn Studio on 26 January 1956. Decca issued 'Blue Days, Black Nights', backed with 'Love Me', under the name Buddy Holly And The Three Tunes (the Crickets were not contracted to Decca at this time), in April. Several other records were recorded in two sessions for Decca during the autumn of 1956, but Holly, dissatisfied with Decca's insistence that he continue to play country music, together with the loss of his group to insensitive sessionmen, left the label in September. Later that year, Holly, Allison and Welborn went to Clovis, New Mexico, where they recorded two songs with Norman Petty at his NorVaJak studio. Upon returning to Lubbock, Holly formed the Crickets with Allison and Niki Sullivan on rhythm guitar. On 25 February 1957 they went back to Clovis and recorded a rock 'n' roll version of Holly's 'That'll Be The Day', a song from their period in Nashville.

The song was a revelation and contained one of the most gripping vocals and distinctive galloping riffs of any record released during the 50s. Joe B. Mauldin joined as the Crickets' bass player following those sessions. A number of record companies turned down the song until it was issued by Brunswick Records in May, ironically a division of Decca, of which Coral Records was another subsidiary, although artistically independent. With Petty as manager, the single underwent heavy promotion until it reached number 1 in September 1957. It also reached number 1 in the UK. Just as the record was being released, the Crickets performed at such venues as the Apollo Theatre in New York and the Howard Theater in Washington, DC, winning over predominantly black audiences and helping to further break down racial barriers in rock. They spent the next three months touring the USA.

The group recorded prolifically in 1957, including

such indisputable classics as 'Words Of Love', 'Maybe Baby', 'Not Fade Away', 'Everyday', 'Peggy Sue' (named after Allison's girlfriend) and 'Oh Boy'. Holly was innovative in the studio, making much use of newly available production techniques, such as overdubbing vocals and double-tracking guitar parts. The vocals on 'Peggy Sue' were a typical example of Holly's technique. Although simple in structure and execution, Holly somehow managed to recite the words 'Peggy Sue' differently in every line, as if fascinated by the very syllables of her name. A seemingly straightforward song like 'Everyday' is similarly transformed by the ingenious use of a celeste (played by Petty's wife, Vi) and the decision to include Jerry Allison slapping his knee, in place of drums. Brunswick continued to issue recordings under the Crickets name while Holly signed on as a solo artist to Coral Records. Despite this, most releases featured the entire group, often with other musicians (Vi Petty on piano) and a vocal group (the Picks). Of these releases, 'Peggy Sue' reached number 3 in the USA and 'Oh Boy' number 10 during 1957. Contrary to the legend, Holly and the Crickets only charted 11 times in the USA during their brief career.

No albums charted during Holly's lifetime. The Crickets closed 1957 with an appearance on the influential *Ed Sullivan Show* and again in January 1958, by which time Holly had left the group. In late January the Crickets recorded 'Rave On' in New York and then toured Australia for six days. Further Clovis recording sessions, including 'Well All Right' occupied February. This was followed by a UK tour beginning on 2 March at the Trocadero in London, which also included appearances on the UK television programmes *Sunday Night At The London Palladium* and *Off The Record*. The UK tour finished on 25 March at the Hammersmith Gaumont. Holly and the group enjoyed immense popularity in Britain, with nine top 10 singles. 'Maybe Baby' became the fourth Holly/Crickets single to chart in the USA in March, eventually peaking at number 17 (and number 4 in the UK). The group returned to the USA in late March and immediately embarked on a US tour instigated by disc jockey Alan Freed, also featuring such popular artists as Jerry Lee Lewis and Chuck Berry. Coral released the frantic 'Rave On' in May and although it reached only number 37 in the USA, it made number 5 in the UK. Following the tour, on 19 June, Holly recorded two songs written by Bobby Darin in New York without the Crickets; they remained unreleased but signalled an impending rift between Holly and the group. While in New York Holly met Maria Elena Santiago, whom he married two months later. During that summer Holly returned to Petty's studio in Clovis and recorded 'Heartbeat', 'Love's Made A Fool Of You' and 'Wishing'. Guitarist Tommy Allsup played on the latter two and was subsequently asked to join the Crickets. During September sessions in Clovis, extra musicians including saxophonist King Curtis and guitarist Phil Everly joined Holly. Waylon Jennings, then unknown, provided backing vocals on one track;

during the same period, Holly produced Jennings' debut single. By September three more Holly/Crickets singles had charted in the USA, but none fared very well.

Holly and the Crickets toured the north-east and Canada during October, by which time there was apparently friction between the Hollys and the Pettys. Buddy and Maria Holly travelled separately from the group between dates. During the trip, Holly decided to try recording with strings, but prior to returning to New York for that session in October 1958, he announced to manager/producer Petty that he was leaving him. To Holly's surprise the other Crickets chose to leave Holly and remain with Petty; Holly allowed them use of the group's name and they continued to record without him (Sonny Curtis joined the group after Holly's death). Meanwhile, on 21 October, Holly, producer Dick Jacobs and studio musicians (including a string section) recorded 'True Love Ways', 'It Doesn't Matter Anymore' (written by Paul Anka), 'Raining In My Heart' and 'Moondreams'. They were held for later release while 'It's So Easy' was released; it failed to chart in the USA. 'Heartbeat' was issued in December and became the last Holly single to chart in the USA during his lifetime. The superb 'It Doesn't Matter Anymore' was released posthumously and its lyrics betrayed an unintended elegiac mood in light of the singer's fate. The song provided Holly with his only UK number 1 hit and served as a perfect memorial. The flip-side, 'Raining In My Heart', was equally inventive, with a touching melody reinforced by the orchestral arrangement in which strings were used to startling effect to suggest tearful raindrops.

In December 1958 Holly, now living in New York with his wife, recorded six songs at home on his tape recorder, presumably to be re-recorded in the studio at a later date. During Christmas Holly returned to Lubbock and appeared on radio station KLLL with Jennings. Back in New York during January 1959 he made other demos at home by himself. That month he began assembling a band to take on the 'Winter Dance Party' tour of the US Midwest. Allsup was hired on guitar, Jennings on bass and Carl Bunch on drums. They were billed as the Crickets despite the agreement to give Holly's former bandmates that name. Also starring Ritchie Valens, the Big Bopper, Dion And The Belmonts and the unknown Frankie Sardo, the tour began on 23 January 1959 in Milwaukee, Wisconsin. On the afternoon of 1 February the tour played in Green Bay, Wisconsin, but an evening show was cancelled owing to bad weather. The 2 February date at the Surf Ballroom in Clear Lake, Iowa, went ahead. It was following this show that Holly, Valens and the Big Bopper chartered a small plane to take them to the next date in Moorhead, Minnesota, rather than travel on the tour bus, which had a defective heater and had previously broken down several times. In the dark early hours of a freezing cold morning and as a result of the snowy weather, the plane crashed minutes after take-off, killing all three stars and the pilot. (The tour actually continued after their deaths, with Bobby Vee, Jimmy Clanton and Frankie Avalon filling in.)

Holly's popularity increased after his death, and his influence continues to this day. Even as late as the 80s unreleased material was still being released. Several of the posthumous releases fared particularly well in the UK. In 1962 Norman Petty took the demos Holly had recorded at home in 1958 and had the instrumental group the Fireballs play along to them, creating new Buddy Holly records from the unfinished tapes. In 1965, *Holly In The Hills*, comprised of the early Buddy and Bob radio station recordings, was released and charted in the UK. Compilation albums also charted in both the USA and the UK, as late as the 70s. During the 70s the publishing rights to Holly's song catalogue were purchased by Paul McCartney, who began sponsoring annual Buddy Holly Week celebrations. A Buddy Holly Memorial Society was also formed in the USA to commemorate the singer. In 1978, a film called *The Buddy Holly Story*, starring actor Gary Busey as Holly, premiered; members of the Crickets, in particular, denounced it as containing many inaccurate scenes. The following year, a six-record boxed set called *The Complete Buddy Holly* was released in the UK (it was issued in the USA two years later).

A 1983 release, *For The First Time Anywhere*, contained original Holly recordings prior to overdubbing. As of the early 90s a group called the Crickets, which included at least one original member (and usually more), was still touring. In 1990, *Buddy*, a musical play that had previously been staged in London, opened on Broadway in New York. Buddy Holly's legacy lives on, not only with tributes such as these, but in the dozens of cover versions of his songs that have been recorded over the years. Holly was an initial inductee into the Rock And Roll Hall Of Fame in 1986. To have a catalogue of songs of this calibre behind him at the age of 22 was remarkable. How would he have approached the 60s and subsequent decades? Such was the quality of his work that few could doubt that he would have lasted the course.

● ALBUMS: *The 'Chirping' Crickets* (Brunswick 1957) ★★★★, *Buddy Holly* (Coral 1958) ★★★★, *That'll Be The Day* (Decca 1958) ★★★★, *The Buddy Holly Story* (Coral 1959) ★★★★, *The Buddy Holly Story, Volume 2* (Coral 1960) ★★★★, *Buddy Holly And The Crickets* (Coral 1963) ★★★★, *Reminiscing* (Coral 1963) ★★★★, *Showcase* (Coral 1964) ★★★★, *Holly In The Hills* (Coral 1965) ★★★★, *The Great Buddy Holly* (Vocalion 1967) ★★★★, *Giant* (Coral 1969) ★★★★, *Remember* (Coral 1971) ★★★, *Good Rockin'* (Vocalion 1971) ★★★, *A Rock And Roll Collection* (Decca 1972) ★★★, *The Nashville Sessions* (MCA 1975) ★★★★, *Western And Bop* (Coral 1977) ★★★, *For The First Time Anywhere* (MCA 1983) ★★★, *From The Original Master Tapes* (MCA 1985) ★★★★, *Something Special From Buddy Holly* (Rollercoaster 1986) ★★★, *Buddy Holly And The Picks Original Voices Of The Crickets* (Ace 1993) ★★.

● COMPILATIONS: *The Best Of Buddy Holly* (Coral 1966) ★★★★, *Buddy Holly's Greatest Hits* (Coral 1967) ★★★, *Rave On* (MFP 1975) ★★★, *20 Golden Greats* (MCA 1978) ★★★★★, *The Complete Buddy Holly* 6-LP box set (Coral 1979) ★★★★, *Love Songs* (MCA 1981) ★★★, *Legend* (MCA 1985) ★★★★, *Buddy Holly Rocks* (Charly 1985) ★★★, *Buddy Holly* (Castle 1986) ★★★, *True Love Ways* (Telstar 1989) ★★★★, *Words Of Love* (PolyGram 1993) ★★★★, *The Singles Collection 1957-1960* (Pickwick 1994) ★★★, *The Very Best Of Buddy Holly* (Dino 1996) ★★★★, *The Ultimate EP Collection* (See For Miles 2001) ★★★★.

● FURTHER READING: *Buddy Holly*, Dave Laing. *Buddy Holly: A Biography In Words Photographs And Music*, Elizabeth Peer and Ralph Peer. *Buddy Holly: His Life And Music*, John Goldrosen. *The Buddy I Knew*, Larry Holley. *The Buddy Holly Story*, John Goldrosen. *Buddy Holly And The Crickets*, Alan Clark. *Buddy Holly: 30th Anniversary Memorial Series No 1*, Alan Clark. *The Legend That Is Buddy Holly*, Richard Peters. *Buddy Holly, Alan Mann's A-Z*, Alan Mann. *Buddy Holly: A Biography*, Ellis Amburn. *Remembering Buddy*, John Goldrosen and John Beecher. *Buddy The Biography* (UK) *Rave On* (USA), Phillip Norman. *Memories Of Buddy Holly*, Jim Dawson and Spencer Leigh.

HOLLYWOOD FLAMES

Formed as the Flames in 1949, this R&B group went through a variety of name changes – Four Flames, Hollywood Four Flames, Jets, Ebbtides and Satellites – during its career. However, it was as the Hollywood Flames that they had their biggest success, the 1957 hit 'Buzz Buzz Buzz'. The song was written by founding member Bobby Byrd, who also had a solo career as Bobby Day. The vocal on the song was not by Day, however, but by group member Earl Nelson, who also recorded as Jackie Lee and as half of Bob And Earl. The other members of the group at the time of the hit, which reached number 11 in the US pop charts and number 5 in the R&B charts, were founding member David Ford and baritone Curtis Williams, co-writer of the hit 'Earth Angel' and a former member of the group that recorded it, the Penguins. 'Buzz Buzz Buzz' was released on Ebb Records, run by Lee Rupe, wife of Specialty Records owner Art Rupe. Released in November 1957, the single spent 17 weeks in the charts. Follow-up singles were issued under Day's name, but by 1959 Ebb had folded. The group continued to record with various personnel for several years.

● COMPILATIONS: *The Hollywood Flames* (Specialty 1992) ★★★.

HOMER AND JETHRO

Homer (b. Henry D. Haynes, 27 July 1920, d. 7 August 1971, Chicago, Illinois, USA) and Jethro (b. Kenneth C. Burns, 10 March 1920, d. 4 February 1989, Evanston, Illinois, USA) were both from Knoxville, Tennessee, USA. They went to the same school and learned to play stringed instruments as young children. In 1932, they began to work together as musicians on WNOX Knoxville, where they performed in a quartet known as the String Dusters. With Homer on guitar and Jethro on mandolin, they mainly played instrumental pop music and any vocals were usually performed as a trio. Somewhat bored with the regular format, they developed a comedy act that they used backstage. They began to present comedy versions of popular songs by maintaining the melody but changing the lyrics, and before long, they were encouraged to perform them live on the radio. They were given the names of Homer and Jethro by the programme director, Lowell Blanchard. The act quickly proved a popular part of the String Dusters' routine. In 1936, they left the group to work solely as Homer and Jethro but stayed at WNOX until 1939. They then became regulars on the *Renfro Valley Barn Dance* in Kentucky, but in 1941, they were both called up for military service. In 1945, they were back together as regulars on the *Midwestern Hayride* on WLW Cincinnati, and between 1946 and 1948, they recorded their humorous songs for the local King label.

In 1949, after a move to RCA Records, they had Top 10 US country chart success with a recording with June Carter of 'Baby It's Cold Outside'. In the late 1940s, they toured with their own tent show but eventually joined Red Foley on KWTO Springfield. In 1949, they toured the USA as part of orchestra leader Spike Jones' show and in 1951, while in Chicago with Jones, they were invited to become regulars on the *National Barn Dance* on WLS, where they remained until 1958. During the 50s and 60s, they toured extensively, their humour proving very popular in many varied venues, including Las Vegas. Their biggest country chart hit came in 1953, when 'How Much Is That Hound Dog In The Window' reached number 2. In 1959, they had a US pop Top 20 hit with 'The Battle Of Kookamonga', their parody of Johnny Horton's hit 'Battle Of New Orleans'. Proving that no song was safe from the couple's attentions in 1964, they had their last chart entry with their version of the Beatles' 'I Want To Hold Your Hand'. They also made commercials for Kellogg's Cornflakes during the 60s, which made them household names in the USA, but might have prompted a drop in sales had they been shown in Britain. The zany comedy tended to overshadow the fact that the duo were fine musicians. They made instrumental albums and in 1970, they recorded with Chet Atkins (Jethro's brother-in-law) as the Nashville String Band (it was not until the album had reached the charts that RCA revealed the identities of the musicians). Atkins rated Homer as one of the best rhythm guitarists he ever knew. He was also a good enough vocalist to have pursued a singing career but had no interest in doing so.

Jethro was also noted as an excellent mandolin player and one who, even in his early days, did much to make the instrument acceptable in jazz music. The partnership came to an end after 39 years on 7 August 1971, when Homer suffered a heart attack and died. Jethro was deeply affected by Homer's death but eventually returned to work as a musician. In the late 70s, he toured and recorded with Steve Goodman. Jethro died of cancer at his home in February 1989. Homer and Jethro's parodies included such titles as 'The Ballad Of Davy Crew-Cut' and 'Hart Brake Motel', and few could match album titles such as *Songs My Mother Never Sang, Ooh! That's Corny* (named after their catchphrase) or, bearing in mind they had been steadily turning out albums for 16 years, to suddenly decide to call one simply *Homer & Jethro's Next Album*. They never enjoyed success in the UK but were an institution in the USA.

● ALBUMS: Homer & Jethro *Fracture Frank Loesser* 10-inch album (RCA Victor 1953) ★★★, *The Worst Of Homer & Jethro* (RCA Victor 1957) ★★★★, *Barefoot Ballads* (RCA Victor 1957) ★★★, *Life Can Be Miserable* (RCA Victor 1958) ★★★★, *Musical Madness* (Audio Lab 1958) ★★★, *They Sure Are Corny* (King 1959) ★★★★, *At The Country Club* (RCA Victor 1960) ★★★, *Songs My Mother Never Sang* (RCA Victor 1961) ★★★, *Homer & Jethro At The Convention* (RCA Victor 1962) ★★★, *Homer & Jethro Strike Back* (Camden 1962) ★★★, *Playing It Straight* (RCA Victor 1962) ★★★, *Cornier Than Corn* (King 1963) ★★★★, *Zany Songs Of The 30s* (RCA Victor 1963) ★★★, *Homer & Jethro Go West* (RCA Victor 1963) ★★★, *Ooh, That's Corny!* (RCA Victor 1963) ★★★, *The Humorous Side Of Country Music* (Camden 1963) ★★★, *Cornfucius Say* (RCA Victor 1964) ★★★, *Fractured Folk Songs* (RCA Victor 1964) ★★★, *Homer & Jethro Sing Tenderly And Other Love Ballads* (RCA Victor 1965) ★★★, *The Old Crusty Minstrels* (RCA Victor 1965) ★★★, *Songs To Tickle Your Funny Bone* (Camden 1966) ★★★, *Wanted For Murder* (RCA Victor 1966) ★★★, *Any News From Nashville* (RCA Victor 1966) ★★★, *It Ain't Necessarily Square* (RCA Victor 1967) ★★★, *Nashville Cats* (RCA Victor 1967) ★★★, *24 Great Songs In The Homer & Jethro Style* (King 1967) ★★★★, *Something Stupid* (RCA Victor 1967) ★★★, *Songs For The 'Out' Crowd* (RCA Victor 1967) ★★★, *The Playboy Song* (Camden 1968) ★★★, *There's Nothing Like An Old Hippie* (RCA Victor 1968) ★★, *Homer & Jethro Live At Vanderbilt University* (RCA Victor 1968) ★★★, *Cool Crazy Christmas* (RCA Victor 1968) ★★, *Homer & Jethro's Next Album* (RCA Victor 1969) ★★★, *The Far Out World Of Homer & Jethro* (RCA Victor 1972) ★★★. With The Nashville String Band *Down Home* (RCA Victor 1970) ★★★, *Identified* (RCA Victor 1970) ★★★, *Strung Up* (RCA Victor 1971) ★★★.

By Jethro Burns: with Curly Chalker, Eldon Shamblin, Joe Venuti *S'Wonderful (4 Giants Of Swing)* (Flying Fish 1977) ★★★, *Jethro Burns* (Flying Fish 1977) ★★★, *Jethro Burns Live* (Flying Fish 1978) ★★★, with Tiny Moore *Back To Back* (Flying Fish 1980) ★★★, *Tea For One* (Flying Fish 1982) ★★★, with Red Rector *Old Friends* (Flying Fish 1983) ★★★.

● COMPILATIONS: *The Best Of Homer & Jethro* (RCA Victor 1966) ★★★, *Country Comedy* (Camden 1971) ★★★, *Assault On The Rock 'N' Roll Era* (Bear Family 1989) ★★★, *The Best Of* (RCA 1992) ★★★, *America's Favorite Song Butchers: The Weird World Of Homer & Jethro* (Razor & Tie 1997) ★★★★.

HORNE, LENA

b. 30 June 1917, Brooklyn, New York, USA. Horne is a dynamic performer, of striking appearance and elegant style. The daughter of an actress and a hotel operator, she was brought up mainly by her paternal grandmother, Cora Calhoun Horne. She made her professional debut at the age of 16 as a singer in the chorus at Harlem's Cotton Club, learning from Duke Ellington, Cab Calloway, and Harold Arlen, the composer of a future big hit, 'Stormy Weather'. From 1935-36 she was featured vocalist with the all-black Noble Sissle's Society Orchestra (the same Noble Sissle who, with Eubie Blake, wrote several hit songs including 'Shuffle Along' and 'I'm Just Wild About Harry') and later toured with the top swing band of Charlie Barnet, singing numbers such as 'Good For Nothin' Joe' and 'You're My Thrill'. Sometimes, when Barnet's Band played the southern towns, Horne had to stay in the band bus. She made her Broadway debut in 1934 as 'A Quadroon Girl' in *Dance With Your Gods*, and also appeared in Lew Leslie's *Blackbirds Of 1939*, in which she sang Mitchell Parish and Sammy Fain's 'You're So Indifferent' – but only for the show's run of nine performances. After a spell at the Café Society Downtown in New York, she moved to Hollywood's Little Troc Club and was spotted by Roger Edens, musical supervisor for MGM Pictures, and former accompanist for Ethel Merman, who introduced her to producer Arthur Freed. In her first film for MGM, *Panama Hattie* (1942), which starred Merman, Horne sang Cole Porter's 'Just One Of Those Things', and a rhumba number called 'The Sping'. To make her skin appear lighter on film, the studio used a special make-up called 'Light Egyptian'. Horne referred to herself as 'a sepia Hedy Lamarr'. Her next two films, *Cabin In The Sky* and *Stormy Weather*, both made in 1943, are generally regarded as her best. In the remainder of her 40s and 50s movie musicals (which included *Thousands Cheer*, *Swing Fever*, *Broadway Rhythm*, *Two Girls And A Sailor*, *Ziegfeld Follies*, *Till The Clouds Roll By*, *Words And Music*, *Duchess Of Idaho* and *Meet Me In Las Vegas*), she merely performed guest shots that were easily removable, without spoiling the plot, for the benefit of southern-state distributors.

Her 40s record hits included her theme song, 'Stormy Weather', and two other Arlen songs, "Deed I Do' and 'As Long As I Live'. She also recorded with several big swing era names such as Artie Shaw, Calloway and Teddy Wilson. During World War II, she became the pin-up girl for many thousands of black GIs and refused to appear on US tours unless black soldiers were admitted to the audience. In 1947 she married pianist, arranger and conductor Lennie Hayton, who also became her manager and mentor until his death in 1971. For a time during the 50s Lena Horne was blacklisted, probably for her constant involvement with the Civil Rights movement, but particularly for her friendship with alleged Communist sympathizer Paul Robeson. Ironically, she was at the peak of her powers at that time, and although she was unable to appear much on television and in films, she continued to make records and appear in nightclubs, which were regarded as her special forte. Evidence of that was displayed on *Lena Horne At The Waldorf Astoria*. The material on this classic album ranged from the sultry 'Mood Indigo', right through to the novelty 'New Fangled Tango'. *Lena At The Sands* featured a medley of songs by Richard Rodgers/Oscar Hammerstein II, Jule Styne and E.Y. 'Yip' Harburg. Other US Top 30 chart albums included *Give The Lady What She Wants* and *Porgy And Bess*, with Harry Belafonte. Horne also made the US Top 20 singles charts in 1955 with 'Love Me Or Leave Me', written by Gus Kahn and Walter Donaldson for Ruth Etting to sing in the 1928 Broadway show *Whoopee*.

In 1957 Horne had her first starring role on Broadway when she played Savannah, opposite Ricardo Montalban, in the Arlen/Harburg musical *Jamaica*. In the 60s, besides the usual round of television shows and records, she appeared in a dramatic role, with Richard Widmark, in *Death Of A Gunfighter* (1969). After Hayton's death in 1971 she worked less, but did feature in *The Wiz*, an all-black film version of *The Wizard Of Oz*, starring Diana Ross and Michael Jackson, and in 1979 she received an honorary doctorate degree from Harvard University. In May 1981, she opened on Broadway in her own autobiographical show, *Lena Horne: The Lady And Her Music*. It ran at the Nederland Theatre to full houses for 14 months, a Broadway record for a one-woman show. Horne received several awards including a special Tony Award for 'Distinguished Achievement In The Theatre', a Drama Desk Award, New York Drama Critics' Special Award, New York City's Handel Medallion, Dance Theatre of Harlem's Emergence Award, two Grammy Awards and the NAACP Springarn Award. She took the show to London in 1984, where it was also acclaimed. In 1993, after not having sung in public for several years, Lena Horne agreed to perform the songs of Billy Strayhorn at the US JVC Jazz Festival. She included several of the same composer's songs on her 1994 album *We'll Be Together Again*, and, in the same year, surprised and delighted her fans by appearing in concert at Carnegie Hall. In 1996 she won a Grammy for the best vocal jazz performance on her album *An Evening With Lena Horne*. In 1998, she sang a superb version of 'Stormy Weather' on US television's top-rated *Rosie O'Donnell Show*, and introduced what is said to be her fortieth album, *Being Myself*.

● ALBUMS: *Lena Horne Sings* 10-inch album (MGM 1952) ★★★, *This Is Lena Horne* 10-inch album 10-inch album (RCA Victor 1952) ★★★★, *Moanin' Low* 10-inch album (Tops 1954) ★★, *It's Love* (RCA Victor 1955) ★★★, *Stormy Weather* (RCA Victor 1956) ★★★★, *Lena And Ivie* (Jazztone 1956) ★★★, *Lena Horne At The Waldorf Astoria* (RCA Victor 1957) ★★★★, *Jamaica* film soundtrack (RCA Victor 1957) ★★, *Give The Lady What She Wants* (RCA Victor 1958) ★★★, with Harry Belafonte *Porgy And Bess* film soundtrack (RCA Victor 1959) ★★★★, *Songs Of Burke And Van Heusen* (RCA Victor 1959) ★★★, *Lena Horne At The Sands* (RCA Victor 1961) ★★★★, *Lena On The*

Blue Side (RCA Victor 1962) ★★★, *Lena ... Lovely And Alive* (RCA Victor 1963) ★★★, *Lena Goes Latin* (RCA Victor 1963) ★★★, with Gabor Szabo *Lena And Gabor* (Gryphon 1970) ★★★, *Lena* (RCA 1974) ★★★, *Lena, A New Album* (RCA 1976) ★★★, *Lena Horne: The Lady And Her Music* stage cast (Qwest 1981) ★★★, *We'll Be Together Again* (Blue Note 1994) ★★★, *An Evening With Lena Horne: Live At The Supper Club* (Blue Note 1995) ★★★★, *Being Myself* (Blue Note 1998) ★★★★.
● COMPILATIONS: *Twenty Golden Pieces Of Lena Horne* (Bulldog 1979) ★★★, *Lena Horne* (Jazz Greats 1979) ★★★, *Lena Horne And Pearl Bailey* (Jazz Greats 1979) ★★★, shared with Ella Fitzgerald, Billie Holiday, Sarah Vaughan *Billie, Ella, Lena, Sarah!* (Columbia 1980) ★★★★, *Lena Horne And Frank Sinatra* (Astan 1984) ★★★, *The Fabulous Lena Horne* (Cambra 1985) ★★★, *The Fabulous Lena Horne 1936-46* recordings (ASV 1997) ★★★, *Being Myself* (Blue Note 1998) ★★★★, *The Irrepressible Lena Horne* (ABM 1999) ★★.
● FURTHER READING: *In Person*, Lena Horne. *Lena*, Lena Horne with Richard Schikel. *Lena: A Personal And Professional Biography*, J. Haskins and K. Benson.
● FILMS: *The Duke Is Tops* (1938), *Panama Hattie* (1942), *I Dood It* (1943), *Swing Fever* (1943), *Stormy Weather* (1943), *Thousands Cheer* (1943), *Cabin In The Sky* (1943), *Two Girls And A Sailor* (1944), *Broadway Rhythm* (1944), *Till The Clouds Roll By* (1946), *Ziegfeld Follies* (1946), *Words And Music* (1948), *Duchess Of Idaho* (1950), *Meet Me In Las Vegas* (1956), *Death Of A Gunfighter* (1969), *The Wiz* (1978).

HORTON, JOHNNY

b. 3 April 1925, Los Angeles, California, USA, d. 5 November 1960, Texas, USA. Horton was raised in Tyler, Texas, where his sharecropping family settled in search of work. He learned the guitar from his mother and, due to his athletic prowess, won scholarships at Baylor University and later the University of Seattle. For a time he worked in the fishing industry but began his singing career on KXLA Pasadena in 1950, quickly acquiring the nickname of 'The Singing Fisherman'. He recorded for Cormac in 1951 and then became the first artist on Fabor Robinson's Abbott label. In 1952 he moved to Mercury Records but was soon in conflict with the company about the choice of songs. He married Hank Williams' widow, Billie Jean, in September 1953, who encouraged him to better himself. With Tillman Franks as his manager, Horton moved to Columbia Records, and their co-written 'Honky Tonk Man' marked his debut in the US country charts. Horton recorded 'Honky Tonk Man' the day after Elvis Presley recorded 'Heartbreak Hotel' and Presley's bass player, Bill Black, was on the session. The song was successfully revived by Dwight Yoakam in 1986, while George Jones revived another song recorded that day, 'I'm A One Woman Man', in 1989. Other fine examples of Horton's rockabilly talents are 'All Grown Up' and the hard-hitting 'Honky Tonk Hardwood Floor'.

In 1959, Horton switched direction and concentrated on story songs, often with an historical basis, and had his first US country number 1 with a Tillman Franks song, 'When It's Springtime In Alaska'. This was followed by his version of Jimmie Driftwood's 'The Battle Of New Orleans', which became a number 1 pop and country hit in the USA. Lonnie Donegan's 'Battle Of New Orleans' made number 2 in the UK, but Horton's number 16 was respectable, especially in view of the fact that his version was banned by the BBC for referring to 'the bloody British'. Horton's next record was another historical song, 'Johnny Reb', backed with the up-tempo novelty, 'Sal's Got A Sugar Lip'. Told simply to cover Horton's latest record, Donegan mistakenly covered 'Sal's Got A Sugar Lip' – and still managed to have a hit! Horton's 'Sink The Bismarck', inspired by the film, made number 3 in the US charts, while he sang the title song of the John Wayne film *North To Alaska* and took it to number 4 in the USA and number 23 in the UK. It also topped the US country charts for five weeks.

On 5 November 1960, Horton died on the way to hospital after a head-on collision with a pick-up truck near Milano, Texas. Tillman Franks received head and chest injuries that required hospital treatment and guitarist Tommy Tomlinson suffered a very serious leg injury which, because of his diabetes, failed to heal and a few months later the leg was amputated. He later played guitar for a time with Claude King but never really recovered from the crash (the driver of the other vehicle, James Davis, aged 19, also died). Billie Jean (who later stated that before he left for the last time, Horton kissed her on exactly the same place on the same cheek that Hank Williams had kissed her when he set off for his final trip) became a country star's widow for the second time in 10 years. Horton, who has been described as the last major star of the *Louisiana Hayride*, is buried in Hillcrest Cemetery, Bossier City, Louisiana. Much of his up-tempo material did not appeal to the traditionalists but somebody once wrote that 'he was ten years older than most of the rockabillies but with his cowboy hat hiding a receding hairline, he more or less looked the part'. However, his 'saga' songs have certainly guaranteed that he is not forgotten.
● ALBUMS: *Honky Tonk Man* (Columbia 1957) ★★★, *Done Rovin'* (Briar International 1958) ★★, *Free And Easy Songs* (Sesac 1959) ★★, *The Fantastic Johnny Horton* (Mercury 1959) ★★★, *The Spectacular Johnny Horton* (Columbia 1960) ★★★, *Johnny Horton Makes History* (Columbia 1960) ★★★, *Honky Tonk Man* (Columbia 1962) ★★★, *Johnny Horton* (Dot 1962) ★★★, *I Can't Forget You* (Columbia 1965) ★★★, *The Voice Of Johnny Horton* (Hilltop 1965) ★★★, *Johnny Horton On The Louisiana Hayride* (Columbia 1966) ★★★, *All For The Love Of A Girl* (Hilltop 1968) ★★, *The Unforgettable Johnny Horton* (Harmony 1968) ★★★, *Johnny Horton On The Road* (Columbia 1969) ★★, *The Battle Of New Orleans* (Harmony 1971) ★★★.
● COMPILATIONS: *Johnny Horton's Greatest Hits*

(Columbia 1961) ★★★, *America Remembers Johnny Horton* (Columbia Special Products 1980) ★★★, *Rockin' Rollin' Johnny Horton* (Bear Family 1981) ★★★★, *American Originals* (Columbia 1989) ★★★★, *The Early Years* 7-LP box set (Bear Family 1991) ★★★, *Johnny Horton 1956-1960* 4-CD box set (Bear Family 1991) ★★★★, *Honky Tonk Man: The Essential Johnny Horton 1956-1960* (Columbia/Legacy 1996) ★★★★, *Somebody's Rockin'* (Bear Family 1996) ★★★, *Johnny Horton: The Collection* (Connoisseur 2001) ★★★.
● FURTHER READING: *Johnny Horton: Your Singing Fisherman*, Michael LeVine.

HOUSTON, CISCO

b. Gilbert Vandine Houston, 18 August 1918, Wilmington, Delaware, USA, d. 25 April 1961, San Bernadino, California, USA. This folk singer is best remembered for his work as a travelling companion for Woody Guthrie, although his own recordings form a vital part of the folk revival of the 50s. Houston's family moved to California in 1919, where he showed an early interest in the theatre. Having spent his early years in a variety of simple jobs, he found himself, like many others in the 30s, unemployed. He left home with his brother to travel across America in pursuit of work, renaming himself Cisco after a small town near Sacramento. Houston wanted to become a comedian, but obtained only secondary roles in a few Hollywood movies. He subsequently became involved in theatre work and a number of folk festivals, as well as union meetings and political gatherings, and travelled with Woody Guthrie and actor Will Geer. In 1940 Houston joined the US merchant marines with Guthrie and performed for the benefit of fellow seamen. It was after the war that the two returned to New York and Houston began touring, performing at concerts and recording for the Folkways label.
In 1948, he appeared in the Broadway musical *The Cradle Will Rock*. During the 50s, he recorded for Decca Records and hosted his own nationally broadcast show, although this was later cancelled when the network grew wary of Houston's left-wing views. In 1959, the US State Department sent Houston, together with Marilyn Childs, Sonny Terry and Brownie McGhee, to India on a cultural exchange. By this time Houston knew that cancer of the stomach was threatening his life. Despite this fact, he appeared on television on the CBS show *Folk Sound, USA*, and performed at the 1960 Newport Folk Festival. He also made several recordings for the Vanguard Records label. Houston made his last appearance in Pasadena at a folk concert, in spite of his painful illness, and died in April 1961. His passing was widely commemorated in song, most memorably by Tom Paxton ('Fare Thee Well Cisco').
● ALBUMS: *900 Miles And Other Railroad Ballads* (Folkways 1952) ★★★, *Sings Cowboy Ballads* (Folkways 1952) ★★★, *Hard Travelin'* (Folkways 1954) ★★★, *Sings Folk Songs* (Folkways 1955) ★★★, *The Cisco Special* (Vanguard 1960) ★★★, *Sings The Songs Of Woody Guthrie* (Vanguard 1961) ★★★★, *I Ain't Got No Home* (Vanguard 1962)

★★★, *Songs Of The Open Road* (Folkways 1964) ★★★★, *Passing Through* (Verve/ Folkways 1965) ★★★.
● COMPILATIONS: *The Folkways Years 1944-1961* (Smithsonian/Folkways 1994) ★★★★, *Best Of The Vanguard Years* (Vanguard/Ace 2000) ★★★★.
● FURTHER READING: *900 Miles: The Ballads, Blues And Folksongs Of Cisco Houston*, Moses Asch and Irwin Silber (eds.).

HOWLIN' WOLF

b. Chester Arthur Burnett, 10 June 1910, West Point, Mississippi, USA, d. 10 January 1976, Hines, Illinois, USA. Howlin' Wolf was one of the most important of the southern expatriates who created the post-war blues out of their rural past and moulded it into the tough 'Chicago sound' of the 50s. He was one of six children born to farmer Dock Burnett and his wife Gertrude, and spent his earliest years around Aberdeen, Mississippi, where he sang in the local Baptist church. In 1923 he relocated to Ruleville, Mississippi, and 10 years later moved again to work on Nat Phillips' plantation at Twist, Arkansas. By this time he was working in music, appearing at local parties and juke-joints. He had been inspired by performers such as Charley Patton and Tommy Johnson, both of whom he had met, and he took much of the showmanship of his act from them, although his hoarse, powerful voice and eerie 'howling' were peculiarly his own. Other seminal Mississippi figures, Robert Johnson and Son House, also proved influential. During this period he enjoyed many nicknames such as 'Big Foot' and 'Bull Cow' but it was as Howlin' Wolf that his fame grew. He was a huge man with a commanding presence and threatening aspect, whom contemporary Johnny Shines once likened to a wild animal, saying that he (Shines) was scared to lay his hand on him.
Throughout the 30s Wolf combined farming with working in music, sometimes travelling in the company of people such as Shines, Robert Johnson, and Sonny Boy 'Rice Miller' Williamson. Williamson, who courted and married Wolf's half-sister Mary, taught his new brother-in-law to play some harmonica and Wolf also experimented with the guitar. Wolf's first marriage had been to a sister of singer Willie Brown and it was during this time that he married his second wife, Lillie Handley. It was a union that lasted until his death. During 1941-44 Wolf was drafted into the army but once he had left, he formed his own group and gained sufficient fame to be approached by KWEM, a west Memphis radio station that was competing for local black listeners and recognized Wolf's potential. For KWEM, Wolf worked as a disc jockey as well as performing himself, and this brought him to the attention of Sam Phillips, who was recording material in Memphis and leasing it to others for sale in the black communities of the northern and western areas of the USA. Phillips, who considered Wolf to be one of the greatest talents he knew, originally made separate agreements with the Bihari Brothers in California and Chess

Records of Chicago to issue Wolf's recordings. The success of the early recordings led to something of a war between these two camps, with each trying to attract him under their own aegis. On the evidence of some of the songs that he recorded at the time, it seems that Wolf was tempted to take a 'stroll out west', but in the event he went to Chicago, 'the onliest one who drove out of the south like a gentleman'.

In Memphis, Wolf, whose recording sessions were often under the direction of Ike Turner, had been lucky to employ the talents of guitarist Willie Johnson, who refused to move north, and in Chicago that good fortune continued as he worked first with Jody Williams and then the unique Hubert Sumlin. The raw delta sound of Wolf's earlier records assured him of a ready-made audience once he reached Chicago, and he quickly built a powerful reputation on the club circuit, extending it with such classic records as 'Smokestack Lightning' and 'Killing Floor'. Like his great rival Muddy Waters, he maintained his audience, and a Chess recording contract, through the lean times of rock 'n' roll and into the blues boom of the 60s. He came to Europe with the AFBF in 1964 and continued to return over the next 10 years. The Rolling Stones and the Yardbirds did much to publicize Wolf's (and Waters') music, both in Europe and white America, and as the 60s progressed, the newer artists at Chess saw their target audience as the emerging white 'love and peace' culture and tried to influence their material to suit it. Wolf's music was a significant influence on rock and many of his best-known songs – 'Sitting On Top Of The World', 'I Ain't Superstitious', 'Killing Floor', 'Back Door Man' and 'Little Red Rooster' – were recorded by acts as diverse as the Doors, Cream, the Rolling Stones, the Yardbirds and Manfred Mann. Few, however, rivalled the power or sexual bravura displayed on the originals and only Don Van Vliet (Captain Beefheart) came close to recapturing his aggressive, raucous voice.

A compelling appearance on the teen-orientated *Shindig* television show (at the behest of the Rolling Stones) was a rare concession to commerciality. His label's desire for success, akin to the white acts he influenced, resulted in the lamentable *The Howlin' Wolf Album*, which the artist described as 'dog shit'. This ill-conceived attempt to update earlier songs was outshone by *The London Howlin' Wolf Sessions*, on which Wolf and long-serving guitarist Hubert Sumlin were joined by an array of guests, including Eric Clapton, Steve Winwood, and Rolling Stones members Bill Wyman and Charlie Watts. Wolf, along with others like Muddy Waters, resisted this move but were powerless to control it. They were, of course, men in their 50s, set in their ways but needing to maintain an audience outside the dwindling Chicago clubs. Fortunately, Wolf outlived this trend, along with that for piling well-known artists together into 'super bands'. Wolf continued to tour but his health was declining. After a protracted period of illness Howlin' Wolf died of cancer in the Veterans Administration

Hospital in 1976. His influence has survived the excesses of the 'swinging 60s' and is to be seen today in the work of many of the emerging black bluesmen such as Roosevelt 'Booba' Barnes.

● ALBUMS: *Moaning In The Moonlight* (Chess 1959) ★★★★, *Howlin' Wolf* aka *The Rocking Chair Album* (Chess 1962) ★★★★, *Howlin' Wolf Sings The Blues* (Crown 1962) ★★★, *The Real Folk Blues* (Chess 1966) ★★★★, *Big City Blues* (Custom 1966) ★★★, *Original Folk Blues* (Kent 1967) ★★★, *More Real Folk Blues* (Chess 1967) ★★★★, *This Is Howlin' Wolf's New Album* aka *The Dog Shit Album* (Cadet 1969) ★★, *Evil* (Chess 1969) ★★★, *Message To The Young* (Chess 1971) ★★, *The London Sessions* (Chess 1971) ★★★, *Live And Cookin' At Alice's Revisited* (Chess 1972) ★★, *Howlin' Wolf AKA Chester Burnett* (Chess 1972) ★★★, *The Back Door Wolf* (Chess 1973) ★★★★, *Change My Way* (Chess 1975) ★★★, *Ridin' In The Moonlight* (Ace 1982) ★★★, *Live In Europe 1964* (Sundown 1988) ★★★, *Memphis Days Volume 1* (Bear Family 1989) ★★★, *Memphis Days Volume 2* (Bear Family 1990) ★★★, *Howlin' Wolf Rides Again* (Ace 1991) ★★★.

● COMPILATIONS: *Going Back Home* (Chess 1970) ★★★, *Chess Blues Masters* (Chess 1976) ★★★★★, *The Legendary Sun Performers* (Charly 1977) ★★★, *Chess Masters* (Chess 1981) ★★★★, *Chess Masters 2* (Chess 1982) ★★★★, *Chess Masters 3* (Chess 1983) ★★★, *The Wolf* (Blue Moon 1984) ★★★, *Golden Classics* (Astan 1984) ★★★, *The Howlin' Wolf Collection* (Deja Vu 1985) ★★★★, *His Greatest Hits* (Chess 1986) ★★★, *Cadillac Daddy: Memphis Recordings, 1952* (Rounder 1987) ★★★, *Howlin' For My Baby* (Sun 1987) ★★★, *Shake For Me – The Red Rooster* (Vogue 1988) ★★★, *Smokestack Lightnin'* (Vogue 1988) ★★★, *Red Rooster* (Joker 1988) ★★★, *Moanin' And Howlin'* (Charly 1988) ★★★, *Howlin' Wolf* 5-LP box set (Chess 1991) ★★★★, *Going Down Slow* 5-CD box set (Roots 1992) ★★★★, *Gold Collection* (1993) ★★★, *The Wolf Is At Your Door* (Fan 1994) ★★★, *The Complete Recordings 1951-1969* 7-CD box set (Charly 1994) ★★★★, *The Genuine Article – The Best Of* (MCA 1994) ★★★★, *The Very Best Of Howlin' Wolf* 3-CD set (Charly 1995) ★★★★, *His Best* (Chess 1997) ★★★★, various artists *A Tribute To Howlin' Wolf* (Telarc 1998) ★★★.

HUGHES, DAVID
b. 11 October 1929, Birmingham, England, d. 19 October 1972. A ballad singer with a fine tenor voice, who had success in the popular field in the UK during the 50s and early 60s, before he went on to become a star in opera. After studying at the Royal Academy, Hughes made his West End debut in the romantic musical *Belinda Fair* (1949). During the 50s, he was a regular on radio and television in programmes such as *The Passing Show*, *Come To Charlie*, *Henry Hall's Guest Night*, *Presenting David Hughes*, *TV Starlight*, *Sunday Night At The London Palladium*, *Spring Song*, *Boy Meets Girls* (from Paris), and his own series, *Make Mine Music*. He also appeared with Ginger Rogers, Lizbeth Webb and Brian Reece in a television

version of the 1948 West End musical *Carissima*, and was back on the London stage himself in 1956 in *Summer Song*. Hughes was also popular on the UK variety circuit, and had several successful records, including 'By The Fountains Of Rome', which won an Ivor Novello Award as The Most Outstanding Song Of The Year in 1956, for its writers Matyas Seiber and Norman Newell. Around this time, with his good looks and romantic delivery, he was dubbed 'Mr. Hearthrob'. In 1962, he appeared in *Scapa*, a musical version of the 1950 hit comedy *Seagulls Over Sorrento*, and shortly afterwards decided to forsake the world of pop, for light music and opera. In 1964, he made an album of sixteenth-century songs, which led to appearances at Glyndebourne the following year, and eventually with the Sadler's Wells Company. From then on, encouraged by the legendary Sir John Barbarolli, he sang many leading roles in opera, including Lieutenant Pinkerton in *Madame Butterfly*, in the UK and abroad.

● ALBUMS: *Songs You Love* (1968) ★★★, *Favourite Opera And Operetta Arias* (1970) ★★★, *World Of Great Classic Love Songs* (1973) ★★★.

HUNTER, IVORY JOE

b. 10 October 1911, Kirbyville, Texas, USA, d. 8 November 1974. Although Hunter was a well-known figure in Texas through his radio shows, it was not until the 40s, when he moved to the west coast, that his career flourished. He established his own record companies, Ivory and Pacific, the latter of which provided the outlet for Hunter's first R&B chart-topper, 'Pretty Mama Blues'. Hunter continued his success with several singles recorded with sidemen from the Duke Ellington Orchestra before one of his most enduring compositions, 'I Almost Lost My Mind', became a second R&B number 1 in 1950. A re-recorded version also proved popular when the singer moved to the Atlantic label later in the decade, but Pat Boone's opportunistic cover version was a greater commercial success. However, a further fine Hunter original, 'Since I Met You Baby', then swept to the top of the R&B chart in 1956 and to number 12 in the national pop chart. Unhappy at being labelled an R&B act, this talented and prolific artist was equally adept with pop, ballad and spiritual styles and in later years became a popular C&W attraction, so much so that a benefit concert was held for him at Nashville's *Grand Ole Opry* shortly before his death in 1974, as a result of lung cancer.

● ALBUMS: *I Get That Lonesome Feeling* (1957) ★★★, *Ivory Joe Hunter* (Sound 1957) ★★★, *Ivory Joe Hunter* (Atlantic 1958) ★★★, *Ivory Joe Hunter Sings The Old And The New* (Atlantic 1958) ★★★, *Ivory Jo Hunter* (Sage 1959) ★★★, *The Fabulous Ivory Joe Hunter* (1961) ★★★, *This Is Ivory Joe Hunter* (1964) ★★★, *The Return Of Ivory Joe Hunter* (Epic 1971) ★★★, *I've Always Been Country* (1974) ★★★.

● COMPILATIONS: *Sixteen Of His Greatest Hits* (1958) ★★★★, *Ivory Joe Hunter's Greatest Hits* (1963) ★★★, *7th Street Boogie* (Route 66 1980) ★★★, *The Artistry Of Ivory Joe Hunter* (Bulldog

1982) ★★★, *This Is Ivory Joe* (Ace 1984) ★★★★, *I Had A Girl* (Route 66 1987) ★★★, *Jumping At The Dewdrop* (Route 66 1987) ★★★, *Since I Met You Baby* (Mercury 1988) ★★★, *I'm Coming Down With The Blues* (Home Cooking 1989) ★★★, *Sings 16 Greatest Hits* (1992) ★★★★.

HUNTER, TAB

b. Arthur Gelien, 11 July 1931, New York City, New York, USA. This blond-haired, blue-eyed pop vocalist/actor used his mother's maiden name, Gelien, until he was spotted in 1948, working at a stable, by talent scout Dick Clayton. He introduced him to Rock Hudson's Hollywood agent Harry Wilson, who said 'We've got to tab you something', then named him Tab Hunter. He made his screen debut in the 1950 film *The Lawless* and two years later co-starred with Linda Darnell in the British film *Saturday Island* (US title: *Island Of Desire*). In late 1956 he received a phone call from Randy Wood, president of Dot Records, asking him to record a song recently cut by US country star Sonny James, the lilting ballad 'Young Love'. Both versions made the US charts, Hunter reaching number 1 and James peaking at number 2. Hunter also topped the UK chart, but James lagged behind at number 11. He continued recording for Dot and hit with the slightly up-tempo '99 Ways', which narrowly missed the US Top 10 but made the UK Top 5 (1957). In the following year he appeared in the film version of the Broadway show *Damn Yankees*, with Gwen Verdon and Ray Walston. As Warner Brothers had him under contract to make films, they resented him recording for Dot and established their own record label in 1958. He signed, with moderate success, and in 1960 starred in his own NBC US television series. He continued his acting and appeared opposite Fabian in the 1964 'beach party' film *Ride The Wild Surf*. He was still acting in the 80s, notably with the late Divine in *Polyester* and *Lust In The Dust*, and also in the *Grease* sequel, *Grease 2*. In the late 80s Hunter moved to Mexico to write, and set up a film production company, one of the fruits of which was the 'family' picture *Dark Horse* (1992).

● ALBUMS: *Tab Hunter* (Warners 1958) ★★, *When I Fall In Love* (Warners 1959) ★★, *R.F.D. Tab Hunter* (Warners 1960) ★★, *Young Love* (Dot 1961) ★★.

● FILMS: *The Lawless* (1950), *Saturday Island* (1952), *Island Of Desire* (1952), *The Steel Lady* (1953), *Gun Belt* (1953), *Return To Treasure Island* (1953), *Track Of The Cat* (1954), *Battle Cry* (1955), *The Sea Chase* (1955), *The Girl He Left Behind* (1956), *The Burning Hills* (1956), *Gunman's Walk* (1958), *Damn Yankees* (1958), *Hell Bent For Glory* (1958), *That Kind Of Woman* (1959), *They Came To Cordura* (1959), *The Pleasure Of His Company* (1961), *Operation Bikini* (1963), *Ride The Wild Surf* (1964), *The Golden Arrow* (1964), *War Gods Of The Deep* (1965), *The Loved One* (1965), *Birds Do It* (1966), *Hostile Guns* (1967), *The Fickle Finger Of Fate* (1967), *Shotgun* (1968), *The Last Chance* (1968), *Legion Of No Return* (1969), *Sweet Kill* (1970), *The Life And Times Of Judge Roy Bean*

(1972), *Timber Tramps* (1973), *Won Ton Ton, The Dog Who Saved Hollywood* (1976), *Polyester* (1981), *Pandemonium* (1982), *Grease 2* (1982), *Lust In The Dust* (1985), *Out Of The Dark* (1988), *Cameron's Closet* (1989), *Dark Horse* (1992), *Wild Bill: Hollywood Maverick* (1996).

HUSKY, FERLIN

b. 3 December 1925, on a farm near Flat River, Missouri, USA. Husky learned to play guitar as a child and during World War II served in the US Merchant Navy. His mother wanted him to be a preacher and his father a farmer, but after discharge, he found radio work as an announcer and disc jockey but gradually turned to performing while at KXLW St. Louis. In the late 40s he moved to California, where he appeared on the Los Angeles *Hometown Jamboree* and played clubs in the Bakersfield area. Believing that Ferlin Husky, his real name, was unsuitable, he first called himself Tex Preston, then changed again to Terry Preston. He also developed an alter ego country philosopher character, Simon Crum, whom he introduced into his act. (A few years later, Sheb Wooley also adopted a similar practice with his character Ben Colder, who sought to entertain with his supposed humorous parodies on popular and country songs.) In the early 50s, he recorded for Capitol and worked with Tennessee Ernie Ford. In 1953, as Ferlin Huskey, he recorded 'A Dear John Letter' with Jean Shepard, which became a smash US country number 1, as well as reaching number 4 on the US pop charts. An answer version called 'Forgive Me John', also had success in both charts. Following success with his self-penned 'Hank's Song' (a tribute to Hank Williams), Huskey finally dropped the name of Terry Preston. In 1957, now minus the 'e' again, Husky joined the *Grand Ole Opry* and achieved another smash hit number 1 with his million-selling recording of 'Gone', which, ironically, he had first recorded unsuccessfully as Preston five years earlier. In 1960, he charted a further country number 1 with the gospel/country 'Wings Of A Dove', which also became a Top 20 pop hit. He recorded 'The Drunken Driver', a tear-jerking narrative about a father who runs over his son, which has been rated a classic by some and one of the worst recordings ever made by others. He became a popular entertainer on many network television shows, including hosting the *Arthur Godfrey Show* and appearing as a dramatic actor on *Kraft TV Theatre*. While not always singing traditional country material, he maintained his country popularity through the character of Simon Crum. In this guise, he demonstrated a great talent for impersonating other country stars, presenting rustic comedy, and even managed a number 2 country hit with 'Country Music's Here To Stay'. He recorded an album of pop songs called *Boulevard Of Broken Dreams* in 1957 and also recorded several rock 'n' roll singles such as 'Wang Dang Do'. Husky has appeared in several films including *Mr. Rock & Roll* and *Country Music Holiday*. From the 60s to the mid-70s, he toured extensively with his band, the Hush Puppies, and had regular country chart entries including 'Once', 'Just For You', 'True True Lovin'' and 'Freckles And Polliwog Days'. He moved to ABC Records in 1973 and achieved a country chart entry, 'An Old Memory Got In My Eye', in 1975. Husky has been married six times and has nine children, one of whom is called Terry Preston. In 1977 he had a heart operation but he recovered and continued to perform, and later recorded once more.

● ALBUMS: with Jean Shepard *Ferlin Husky And Jean Shepard* (Capitol 1955) ★★★, *Ferlin Husky's Songs Of The Home And Heart* (Capitol 1956) ★★★, *Boulevard Of Broken Dreams* (Capitol 1957) ★★, *Born To Lose* (Capitol 1959) ★★★, *Ferlin Husky – Country Tunes From The Heart* (King 1959) ★★★, *Sittin' On A Rainbow* (Capitol 1959) ★★★, *Gone* (Capitol 1960) ★★★, *Easy Livin'* (King 1960) ★★★, *Ferlin's Favorites* (Capitol 1960) ★★★, *Some Of My Favorites* (Capitol 1960) ★★★, *Walkin' & Hummin'* (Capitol 1961) ★★★, *Memories Of Home* (Capitol 1963) ★★★, *The Heart & Soul Of Ferlin Husky* (Capitol 1963) ★★★, *The Unpredictable Simon Crum* (Capitol 1963) ★★, *By Request* (Capitol 1964) ★★★, *True True Lovin'* (Capitol 1965) ★★★, *I Could Sing All Night* (Capitol 1966) ★★★, *Songs Of Music City, USA* (Capitol 1966) ★★★, *Christmas All Year Long* (Capitol 1967) ★★, *What Am I Gonna Do Now* (Capitol 1967) ★★★, *Where No One Stands Alone* (Capitol 1968) ★★★, *Just For You* (Capitol 1968) ★★★, *White Fences And Evergreen Trees* (Capitol 1969) ★★★, *That's Why I Love You So Much* (Capitol 1969) ★★★, *Your Love Is Heavenly Sunshine* (Capitol 1970) ★★★, *Your Sweet Love Lifted Me* (Capitol 1970) ★★★, *One More Time* (Capitol 1971) ★★★, *Just Plain Lonely* (Capitol 1972) ★★★, *Sweet Honky Tonk* (1973) ★★★, *True True Lovin'* (1973) ★★★, *Champagne Ladies & Blue Ribbon Babies* (ABC 1974) ★★★, *Freckles & Polliwog Days* (ABC 1974) ★★★, *Mountain Of Everlasting Love* (ABC 1974) ★★, *The Foster & Rice Songbook* (ABC 1975) ★★, *Ferlin Husky* (1982) ★★★, *Live* (1983) ★★.

● COMPILATIONS: *Hits Of Ferlin Husky* (Capitol 1963) ★★★★, *The Best Of Ferlin Husky* (Capitol 1969) ★★★, *Collector's Series* (Capitol 1989) ★★★★, *Greatest Hits* (Curb 1990) ★★★★, *Vintage* (Capitol 1996) ★★★★.

HUTTON, BETTY

b. 26 February 1921, Battle Creek, Michigan, USA. A dynamic and vivacious singer and actress, while still a small child Hutton began singing in the streets to help support her impoverished family. By her early teens she was already beginning to make a name for herself when she was hired by Vincent Lopez, then leader of a popular radio band. In 1940, by then known as 'The Blonde Bombshell' in recognition of her fizzing vitality, Hutton appeared on Broadway in *Panama Hattie*, and the following year was snapped up by Hollywood. During the 40s she appeared in a string of popular musicals including *Star Spangled Rhythm, Happy Go Lucky, Let's Face It, And The Angels Sing, Here Comes The Waves, Incendiary*

Blonde, Duffy's Tavern, The Stork Club, Cross My Heart, The Perils Of Pauline, Dream Girl and *Red Hot And Blue*. However, it was her sensational performance in the title role of *Annie Get Your Gun* in 1950 that established her as a major star. It gained her an international reputation, which she enhanced with roles in *Let's Dance* (1950), *The Greatest Show On Earth* and *Somebody Loves Me* (both 1952). Subsequent contractual difficulties with the studio resulted in her career coming to an abrupt halt, and although she made a brief appearance in the 1957 film *Spring Reunion*, she was declared bankrupt in 1967. In 1971, the last of her four marriages, to trumpeter Pete Candoli, ended in divorce, and after suffering a nervous breakdown and problems with drugs and alcohol, she worked for several years as a cook and housekeeper in a rectory in Portsmouth, Long Island. She made a triumphant comeback in 1980 when she took over the role of Miss Hannigan in the hit Broadway musical *Annie*. Later, she enrolled as a student at a New England college, before settling in Los Angeles. Her sister, Marion, two years her senior, was also a singer who worked with Glenn Miller's civilian band. In 1994 Capitol issued a collection of some of her most entertaining tracks, and a year later ex-Sugarcubes lead singer Björk included one of Hutton's specialities, 'It's Oh So Quiet', on her *Post* album.

● ALBUMS: *Square In The Social Circle* 10-inch album (Capitol 1950) ★★★, *Annie Get Your Gun* film soundtrack (MGM 1950/55) ★★★, *Somebody Loves Me* film soundtrack (RCA 1952) ★★★, *Satins And Spurs* TV soundtrack (Capitol 1954) ★★, *At The Saints And Sinners Ball* (Warners 1959) ★★★.
● COMPILATIONS: *Great Ladies Of Song: Spotlight On Betty Hutton* (Capitol 1994) ★★★.
● FILMS: *The Fleet's In* (1942), *Star Spangled Rhythm* (1942), *The Miracle Of Morgan's Creek* (1943), *Let's Face It* (1943), *Here Comes The Waves* (1944), *And The Angels Sing* (1944), *Incendiary Blonde* (1945), *The Stork Club* (1946), *Cross My Heart* (1946), *The Perils Of Pauline* (1947), *Dream Girl* (1948) *Annie Get Your Gun* (1950), *Let's Dance* (1951), *Somebody Loves Me* (1952), *The Greatest Show On Earth* (1952), *Spring Reunion* (1957).

HYMAN, DICK

b. 8 March 1927, New York City, New York, USA. After studying classical music, Hyman broadened his interests to encompass jazz and many other areas of music. In the late 40s he played piano in and around his home-town, working with Red Norvo and Benny Goodman and leading bop musicians, including founding fathers Charlie Parker and Dizzy Gillespie. Early in the 50s he began a long career as a studio musician, playing piano, arranging, composing and leading orchestras. He was staff pianist at WMCA and WNBC-New York from 1951-57, and music director of *Arthur Godfrey And His Friends* from 1958-62. His work in the studios did not keep him from actively participating in jazz dates, many of which he himself organized. He enjoyed a US Top 10 hit single in 1956 with 'Moritat (A Theme From "The Three Penny Opera")', credited to The

'Unforgettable' Sound Of The Dick Hyman Trio. Hyman also became deeply interested in the history of jazz and especially the development of jazz piano. He demonstrated his interest in radio broadcasts and concert performances, with his enormously eclectic taste allowing him to range from ragtime to freeform with complete confidence. Through performances and recordings with the New York Jazz Repertory Company, he encouraged interest in the music of Jelly Roll Morton, Fats Waller, James P. Johnson and Louis Armstrong. He also formed a small group, the Perfect Jazz Repertory Quintet.

During his freeform period he played electric piano and later added the organ and synthesiser to the instruments at his command. From the late 50s through to the early 70s Hyman worked as a musician, arranger and composer for Enoch Light's Grand Award, Command Records and Project 3 labels, though as he was still contracted to other labels during this period many of his recordings were released under a pseudonymous title. The surprise 1969 US Top 40 hit 'The Minotaur', credited to Dick Hyman And His Electric Eclectics, was the first single ever to be entirely performed on a synthesiser.

From the mid-70s onwards, Hyman returned to a more traditional style on solo dates and duo albums with Ruby Braff such as *Cincinnati Fats* and *Manhattan Jazz*. Hyman also recorded with Braff using, however improbably in a jazz context, a Wurlitzer organ. Unusual though it might have been, *A Pipe Organ Recital Plus One* was a critical and popular success. As a composer, Hyman has written for large and small ensembles and composed several movie scores, including *Scott Joplin* (1977), *Stardust Memories* (1980), *Zelig* (1983), *Broadway Danny Rose* (1984), *Purple Rose Of Cairo* (1985), *Moonstruck* (1987), *Mighty Aphrodite* (1995), *Everyone Says I Love You* (1996), and *Sweet And Lowdown* (1999). He has also worked as artistic director of the Jazz In July concerts in New York. A master of jazz piano, his performances not only display his extraordinary virtuoso technique but also demonstrate his deep understanding and abiding love for the great traditions of the music.

● ALBUMS: *60 Great All Time Songs, Volume 3* (MGM 1957) ★★★, *Provocative Piano* (Command 1960) ★★★, *Provocative Piano, Vol. 2* (Command 1961) ★★★, *The Dick Hyman Trio* (Command 1961) ★★★, *Electrodynamics* (Command 1963) ★★★, *Fabulous* (Command 1963) ★★★, *Keyboard Kaleidoscope* (Command 1964) ★★★, *The Man From O.R.G.A.N.* (Command 1965) ★★, *Happening!* (Command 1966) ★★★, *Brasilian Impressions* (Command 1966) ★★★, *Mirrors – Reflections Of Today ...* (Command 1967) ★★★, *Moog – The Electric Eclectics Of Dick Hyman* (Command 1968) ★★★★, *The Age Of Electronicus* (Command 1969) ★★★, *Concerto Electro* (Command 1970) ★★★, *The Sensuous Piano Of 'D'* (Project 3 1970) ★★★, *Fantomfingers* (Project 3 1970) ★★★, *Piano Solos* (Project 3 1972) ★★★, *Genius At Play* (Monmouth Evergreen 1973) ★★★, *Traditional Jazz Piano* (Project 3 1973) ★★★, *Some*

Rags, Some Stomps And A Little Blues (Columbia 1974) ★★★★, *Satchmo Remembered* (Atlantic 1974) ★★★, *Scott Joplin: The Complete Works For Piano* (RCA 1975) ★★★★, *A Waltz Dressed In Blue* (RCA 1977) ★★★, *Charleston* (Columbia 1977) ★★, *Come And Trip It* (New World 1978) ★★★, *Themes And Variations On 'A Child Is Born'* (Chiaroscuro 1978) ★★★, *The Music Of Jelly Roll Morton* (Smithsonian 1978) ★★★, *Dick Hyman And The Perfect Jazz Repertory Quintet Plays Irving Berlin* (World Jazz 1979) ★★★, *Dick Hyman Piano Solos* (Monmouth 1979) ★★★, with Ruby Braff *Cincinnati Fats* (Concord Jazz 1981) ★★★★, with Braff *A Pipe Organ Recital Plus One* (Concord Jazz 1982) ★★★, with Braff *Fireworks* (Inner City 1983) ★★★, *Kitten On The Keys: The Music Of Zez Confrey* (RCA 1983) ★★, with Dick Wellstood *I Wish I Were Twins* (Swingtime 1983) ★★★, *Eubie!* (Seven Star 1984) ★★★, with Braff *America The Beautiful* (George Wein Collection 1984) ★★★, with Braff *Manhattan Jazz* (Music Masters 1985) ★★★, *Gulf Coast Blues* (Omega 1986) ★★, with Wellstood *Stridemonster!* (Unisson 1986) ★★★★, *The Kingdom Of Swing & The Republic Of Oop Bop Sh'Bam* (Music Masters 1987) ★★, *Face The Music: A Century Of Irving Berlin* (Music Masters 1988) ★★★, *Live From Toronto's Cafe Des Copains* (Music & Arts 1988) ★★★, *Plays Fats Waller* (Reference 1989) ★★★, *Music Of 1937* (Concord Jazz 1989) ★★★★, *Plays Harold Arlen* (Reference 1989) ★★★, *Blues In The Night* (Music Masters 1990) ★★★, with Braff *Music From My Fair Lady* (Concord Jazz 1990) ★★, *16 Classic Rags* (RCA 1991) ★★★, with Braff *Younger Than Swingtime: Music From South Pacific* (Concord Jazz 1991) ★★★, *All Through The Night* (Music Masters 1991) ★★★, *Plays Duke Ellington* (Reference 1992) ★★★, *The Gershwin Songbook: Jazz Variations* (Music Masters 1992) ★★★, *Dick Hyman/Ralph Sutton* (Concord Jazz 1993) ★★★, *From The Age Of Swing* (Reference 1994) ★★★, *Swing Is Here* (Reference 1996) ★★★, *Ruby Braff & Dick Hyman Play Nice Tunes* (Arbors 1996) ★★★, *Cheek To Cheek* (Arbors 1997) ★★★, with Bob Wilber *A Perfect Match* (Arbors 1998) ★★★, *In Recital* (Reference 1998) ★★★★, with Derek Smith *Dick And Derek At The Movies* (Arbors 1998) ★★★, *Dick Hyman's Century Of Jazz Piano* (Orchard 2000) ★★★★.

IDLE ON PARADE

Taking inspiration from Elvis Presley's induction into the US Army, Anthony Newley starred as the drafted pop star Jeep Jones in this 1959 British feature. Comedy stalwarts Sid James and Lionel Jeffries were also cast, but this jaundiced film owed more to television's *The Army Game* than rock 'n' roll. The soundtrack material, including 'Idle Rock-A-Boogie' and 'Saturday Night Rock-A-Boogie', consisted of little more than poorly formed pastiches, lacking neither the charm of Newley's Goons-inspired hits, 'Strawberry Fair' and 'That Noise', nor the wistfulness of his two UK chart-toppers, 'Why' and 'Do You Mind'. The four-track *Idle On Parade* EP nonetheless reached number 13 in the UK singles chart, reflecting the singer's popularity rather than the success of the film itself. Newley later became a celebrated songwriter for West End and Broadway productions, having bade farewell to his pop-styled inclinations.

IMPALAS

With sweet-voiced lead singer Joe 'Speedo' Frazier (b. 5 September 1943, New York City, New York, USA), this New York doo-wop group had an overnight success with their first record, '(Sorry) I Ran All The Way Home'. From the Carnesie section of Brooklyn, the rest of the Impalas were Richard Wagner, Lenny Renda and Tony Calouchi. They were discovered by disc jockey Alan Freed and Artie Zwirn, who co-wrote the bright, brash novelty tune with Gino Giosasi (of the Gino and Gina vocal duo). With an arrangement by Ray Ellis, '(Sorry) I Ran All The Way Home' was released in 1959 on the MGM Records subsidiary label Cub, reaching number 2 in America and entering the UK Top 30. The follow-up, 'Oh What A Fool' was a smaller hit. The Impalas made later records for Hamilton and 20th Century Fox before splitting up. Frazier went on to sing with Love's Own in 1973.
● ALBUMS: *Sorry I Ran All The Way Home* (Cub 1959) ★★★.

IMPERIAL RECORDS

Formed in Los Angeles, California, USA, by Lew Chudd in 1947, Imperial emerged as one of the most influential independent R&B labels of the 50s. Despite the company's devotion to the R&B market, for many years their only major hit was by the C&W artist Slim Whitman, with 'Indian Love Call' in 1952. Having secured the New Orleans R&B bandleader Dave Bartholomew as house producer, a former Bartholomew band member, Fats Domino, was signed to record for the label, and his first release, 'The Fat Man' became a US R&B chart hit. The subsequent and consistent success of Domino's career in the national US chart between 1955 and 1962 was, for some time, crucial to Imperial's ability to promote other R&B artists, such as Roy Brown ('Let The Four Winds Blow'), Smiley Lewis ('I Hear You Knocking'), Chris Kenner ('Sick And Tired') and Ernie Freeman ('Raunchy'). In 1957 Chudd found his new pop star in Rick Nelson, who provided the label with a string of 16 hits up until 1962. An effort to cash in on Phil Spector's Teddy Bears success with 'To Know Him Is To Love Him' (having been recorded on the Dore label) came to nought, except that the group did release their only (and very rare) album on the Imperial label. Other US hits during this period were supplied by Garry Mills (a 1960 Top 30 hit with 'Look For A Star – Part 1') and the rock 'n' roll drummer Sandy Nelson, with his instrumental hits 'Let There Be Drums' (1961) and 'Drums Are My Beat' (1962). Throughout this time the label was well served by the steady success of Slim Whitman, particularly in the UK, where the Imperial label was licensed to London Records.

In the early 60s Chudd acquired the New Orleans label Minit Records. He sold the company to Liberty Records in 1963, after which Imperial concentrated more on the mainstream pop market, releasing many British acts in the USA, including Billy J. Kramer (a Top 10 hit with 'Little Children'/'Bad To Me' in 1964), Georgie Fame (a Top 30 hit in 1965 with 'Yeh Yeh') and the Hollies (notably, two Top 10 hits in 1966 with 'Bus Stop' and 'Stop Stop Stop'). Cher had begun her solo career with Imperial, achieving five US Top 40 hits between 1965 and 1967, including 'Bang Bang (My Baby Shot Me Down)' (number 2) and 'You Better Sit Down Kids' (number 9), and former rock 'n' roll singer-turned-MOR act Johnny Rivers had an impressive string of 13 hit singles from 1964-67, including the number 1 'Poor Side Of Town' in 1966. A link with the R&B past was maintained with Irma Thomas's Top 20 hit 'Wish Someone Would Care' (1964) and with Mel Carter's three Top 40 hits during 1965-66, which included the Top 10 'Hold Me, Thrill Me, Kiss Me' (1965). Songwriter Jackie DeShannon's occasional excursion into the recording studio rewarded Imperial with two Top 10 hits with the classic Burt Bacharach song 'What The World Needs Now Is Love' (1965) and 'Put A Little Love In Your Heart' (1969). Classics IV rounded off the label's list of Top 10 hits during 1968-69 with 'Spooky' (number 3), 'Stormy' (number 5) and 'Traces' (number 2). By the end of the 60s, the machinations of the corporate music industry had forced Liberty and Imperial to merge with the United Artists Records label who, in turn, were swallowed up by the giant EMI Records conglomerate in 1979. Chudd died on 15 June 1998.

● COMPILATIONS: *Imperial Rockabillies* (1977) ★★★★, *Imperial Rockabillies Volume 2* (1979) ★★★, *Imperial Rockabillies Volume 3* (1980) ★★★, *Imperial Musicians 1951-1962: The Rhythm In Rhythm & Blues* (1987) ★★★★.

IN THE WEE SMALL HOURS - FRANK SINATRA

As ever, Frank Sinatra's collaboration with his best arranger, Nelson Riddle is wholly successful, this time a magnificent statement in understated orchestration. Emotional and romantic Sinatra gently eases himself through another 16 classics of great American popular song. Although he fails to swing he never ceases to move the listener, and images of comfy sofas, scotch on the rocks and hi-fi radiograms spring to mind as the listener wallows in songs by Duke Ellington, Richard Rodgers and Lorenz Hart, Jimmy Van Heusen, Harold Arlen and E.Y. 'Yip' Harburg, and Cole Porter. Mellow, rich and pure, and now universally acclaimed as one of the best albums Sinatra ever recorded. Top the glass up before your tears melt the ice.

● Tracks: *In the Wee Small Hours Of The Morning; Mood Indigo; Glad To Be Unhappy; I Get Along Without You Very Well; Deep In A Dream; I See Your Face Before Me; Can't We Be Friends?; When Your Lover Has Gone; What Is This Thing Called Love; Last Night When We Were Young; I'll Be Around; Ill Wind; It Never Entered My Mind; Dancing On The Ceiling; I'll Never Be The Same; This Love Of Mine.*
● First released 1955
● UK peak chart position: did not chart
● USA peak chart position: 2

INK SPOTS

The original line-up consisted of Jerry Franklin Daniels (b. 1916, d. 7 November 1995, Indianapolis, Indiana, USA; lead tenor, guitar), Orville 'Hoppy' Jones (b. 17 February 1905, Chicago, Illinois, USA, d. 18 October 1944; bass), Charlie Fuqua (d. 1979; baritone, guitar) and Ivory 'Deek' Watson (d. 1967; second tenor). Most sources state that this enormously popular black vocal quartet was formed in the early 30s when they were working as porters at the Paramount Theatre in New York. Early in their career the Ink Spots played 'hot' numbers, and travelled to England in the mid-30s where they performed with the Jack Hylton Band. When they returned to the USA, Daniels became ill and was replaced by Bill Kenny (b. 1915, d. 23 March 1978). The new combination changed their style, slowed down the tempos, and had a big hit in 1939 with 'If I Didn't Care', which featured Kenny's impressive falsetto and a deep-voiced spoken chorus by bass singer Jones. This record set the pattern for their future success, mixed with only a few slightly more up-tempo items, such as 'Java Jive', 'Your Feet's Too Big', and two of several collaborations with Ella Fitzgerald, 'Cow-Cow Boogie' and 'Into Each Life Some Rain Must Fall'. The latter sold more than a million copies.

Throughout the 40s their US hits included 'Address Unknown' (number 1), 'My Prayer', 'Bless You', 'When The Swallows Come Back To Capistrano', 'Whispering Grass', 'We Three' (number 1), 'Do I Worry?', 'I Don't Want To Set The World On Fire', 'Don't Get Around Much Any More', 'I'll Get By', 'Someday I'll Meet You Again', 'I'm Making Believe' (number 1) and 'I'm Beginning To See

The Light' (both with Ella Fitzgerald), 'The Gypsy' (number 1 and a million-seller), 'Prisoner Of Love', 'To Each His Own' (number 1 and another million-seller), 'It's A Sin To Tell A Lie', 'You Were Only Fooling (While I Was Falling In Love)' and 'You're Breaking My Heart' (1949). The group were also popular on radio, in theatres, and made guest appearances in movies such as *The Great American Broadcast* and *Pardon My Sarong*. Orville Jones died in 1944 and was replaced by Bill Kenny's twin brother Herb (b. Herbert Cornelius Kenny, 1915, d. 11 July 1992, Columbia, Maryland, USA). A year later, founder member Watson recruited Jimmie Nabbie (b. 1920, Tampa, Florida, USA, d. 15 September 1992, Atlanta, Georgia, USA) as lead tenor, and then Watson himself was replaced by Billy Bowen. Subsequent personnel changes were many and varied. There was some confusion in 1952 when two different groups began using the Ink Spots' name, Charlie Fuqua and Bill Kenny each owning 50 per cent of the title. Fuqua's Ink Spots consisted of himself, Watson, Harold Jackson, and high tenor Jimmy Holmes. Other members included Isaac Royal, Leon Antoine and Joseph Boatner (d. 8 May 1989, Laconia, New Hampshire, USA). In the early 50s the Ink Spots had further chart success with 'Echoes', 'Sometime' and 'If', and Bill Kenny also had US hits in his own name, including 'It Is No Secret' (with the Song Spinners) and '(That's Just My Way Of) Forgetting You'.

It is said that, over the years, many other groups worked under the famous name, including one led by Al Rivers (d. 17 February 1993, aged 65) who sang with the Ink Spots in the late 40s and 50s, and another fronted by Stanley Morgan (d. 21 November 1989, aged 67), an occasional guitar player with the quartet in the 30s. In 1988 the original group's first hit, 'If I Didn't Care', was awarded a Grammy, and a year later the Ink Spots were inducted into the Rock And Roll Hall Of Fame. Jimmie Nabbie's Ink Spots appeared extensively worldwide for many years through to the early 90s, until Nabbie's death in 1992 following double bypass heart surgery. Gregory Lee took over as frontman when the group co-starred with Eartha Kitt in the UK tour of *A Night At The Cotton Club*, during which, according to one critic, 'they reproduced the sedate four-part harmonies with skill and just enough spontaneity to satisfy their long-term fans'. In 1995, when the Ink Spots were in cabaret at London's Café Royal, the line-up was Grant Kitchings (lead tenor), Sonny Hatchett (second lead tenor), Ellis Smith (baritone and guitar) and Harold Winley (bass). The latter is said to have worked with the group for more than 40 years.

● ALBUMS: *America's Favorite Music* 10-inch album (Waldorf Music 1950) ★★★, *The Ink Spots Volume 1* 10-inch album (Decca 1950) ★★★★, *The Ink Spots Volume 2* 10-inch album (Decca 1950) ★★★★, *Precious Memories* 10-inch album (Decca 1951) ★★★, *Street Of Dreams* 10-inch album (Decca 1954) ★★★★, *The Ink Spots* (Decca 1955) ★★★, *Time Out For Tears* (Decca 1956) ★★★, *Torch Time* (Decca 1958) ★★★, *Something Old,*

Something New (King 1958) ★★★, *Sincerely Yours* (King 1958) ★★★, *Songs That Will Live Forever* (King 1959) ★★★, *The Ink Spots Favorites* (Verve 1960) ★★★, *Lost In A Dream* (Verve 1965) ★★★, *Stanley Morgan's Ink Spots In London* (1977) ★★★, *Just Like Old Times* (Open Sky 1982) ★★★.

● COMPILATIONS: *Golden Favourites* (Decca 1962) ★★★★, *The Best Of The Ink Spots* (Decca 1965) ★★★★, *The Ink Spots Greatest, Volumes. 1 & 2* (Grand Award 1956) ★★, *The Best Of The Ink Spots* (MCA 1980) ★★★★, *Golden Greats: Ink Spots* (MCA 1986) ★★★, *Swing High! Swing Low!* (Happy Days 1989) ★★★. In addition, there are a great many compilations available under the title of *Greatest Hits* or *Best Of*.

IVES, BURL

b. Burl Icle Ivanhoe Ives, 14 June 1909, Hunt Township, Jasper County, Illinois, USA, d. 14 April 1995, Anacortes, Washington, USA. One of the world's most celebrated singers of folk ballads, with a gentle, intimate style, Ives was also an actor on the stage and screen, and an anthologist and editor of folk music. The son of tenant farmers in the 'Bible Belt' of Illinois, he was singing in public for money with his brothers and sisters when he was four years old. Many of the songs they sang originated in the British Isles, and were taught to them by their tobacco-chewing grandmother. After graduating from high school in 1927 Ives went to college with the aim of becoming a professional football coach. Instead, he left college early, in 1930, and hitch-hiked throughout the USA, Canada and Mexico, supporting himself by doing odd jobs and singing to his own banjo accompaniment, picking up songs everywhere he went. After staying for a time in Terre Haute, Indiana, attending the State Teachers College, he moved to New York and studied with vocal coach Ekka Toedt, before enrolling for formal music training at New York University.

Despite this classical education, he was determined to devote himself to folk songs. In 1938 he played character roles in several plays, and had a non-singing role on Broadway in the Richard Rodgers and Lorenz Hart musical *The Boys From Syracuse*, followed by a four-month singing engagement at New York's Village Vanguard nightclub. He then toured with another Rodgers and Hart show, *I Married An Angel*. In 1940 Ives performed on radio, singing his folk ballads to his own guitar accompaniment on programmes such as *Back Where I Come From*, and was soon given his own series entitled *Wayfaring Stranger*. The introductory 'Poor Wayfaring Stranger', one of America's favourite folk songs, and by then already over 100 years old, became his long-time theme. Drafted into the US Army in 1942, Ives sang in Irving Berlin's military musical revue *This Is The Army*, both on Broadway and on tour. In 1944, after medical discharge from the forces, Ives played a long stint at New York's Cafe Society Uptown nightclub, and also appeared on Broadway with Alfred Drake in *Sing Out Sweet Land*, a 'Salute To American Folk And Popular Music'. For his performance, Ives received the

Donaldson Award as Best Supporting Actor. During the following year, he made a concert appearance at New York's Town Hall, and played a return engagement in 1946. Also in that year he made his first movie, *Smoky*, with Fred MacMurray and Anne Baxter, and appeared with Josh White in a full-length feature about folk music. Ives' other movies, in which he played characters ranging from villainous to warmly sympathetic, included *So Dear To My Heart* (1948), *East Of Eden* (1955) and *Cat On A Hot Tin Roof* (1958), in which he played Big Daddy, recreating his highly acclaimed Broadway performance in the Tennessee Williams play; he also appeared in *Wind Across The Everglades* (1958), *Desire Under The Elms* (1958) and *The Big Country* (1958), for which he received an Oscar as the Best Supporting Actor; and *Our Man In Havana* (1960). In 1954 Ives appeared as Cap'n Andy Hawkes in a revival of Jerome Kern and Oscar Hammerstein II's *Show Boat* at the New York City Center. In the 60s and 70s he appeared regularly on US television, sometimes in his dramatic series, such as *OK Crackerby* and *The Bold Ones*, and several musical specials. In the 80s, he continued to contribute character roles to feature films and television, and performed in concerts around the world.

Back in 1948, his first chart record, 'Blue Tail Fly', teamed him with the Andrews Sisters. The song, written by Dan Emmett in 1846, had been in the Ives repertoire for some years. Other US Top 30 hits through to the early 60s included 'Lavender Blue (Dilly Dilly)', 'Riders In The Sky (Cowboy Legend)', 'On Top Of Old Smoky', 'The Wild Side Of Life', 'True Love Goes On And On', 'A Little Bitty Tear', 'Funny Way Of Laughin'' and 'Call Me Mr. In-Between'. Many other songs became associated with him, such as 'Foggy Foggy Dew', 'Woolie Boogie Bee', 'Turtle Dove', 'Ten Thousand Miles', 'Big Rock Candy Mountain', 'I Know An Old Lady (Who Swallowed A Fly)', 'Aunt Rhody' and 'Ballad Of Davy Crockett'. Ives published several collections of folk ballads and tales, including *America's Musical Heritage – Song Of America*, *Burl Ives Song Book*, *Tales Of America*, *Burl Ives Book Of Irish Songs*, and for children, *Sailing On A Very Fine Day*. In 1993, in the distinguished company of Tom Paxton, Pete Seeger, Theodore Bikel, the Chad Mitchell Trio, Oscar Brand and Paul Robeson Jnr., Burl Ives performed in an emotional and nostalgic concert at the 92nd Street 'Y' Theatre in New York. Ives died in April 1995.

● ALBUMS: *The Wayfaring Stranger* 10-inch album (Stinson 1949) ★★★★, *Ballads And Folk Songs Volume 1* 10-inch album (Decca 1949) ★★★★, *Ballads And Folk Songs Volume 2* 10-inch album (Decca 1949) ★★★★, *The Return Of The Wayfaring Stranger* 10-inch album (Columbia 1949) ★★★★, *Ballads, Folk And Country Songs* 10-inch album (Decca 1949) ★★★★, *More Folksongs* 10-inch album (Columbia 1950) ★★★, *Christmas Day In The Morning* 10-inch album (Decca 1952) ★★★, *Folk Songs Dramatic And Dangerous* 10-inch album (Decca 1953) ★★★★, *Women: Folk Songs About The Fair* 10-inch album (Decca 1954) ★★★, *Children's Favorites* 10-inch album (Columbia 1954) ★★★, *Coronation Concert* (Decca 1956) ★★★, *The Wild Side Of Life* (Decca 1956) ★★★★, *Men* (Decca 1956) ★★★, *Down To The Sea In Ships* (Decca 1956) ★★★★, *Women* (Decca 1956) ★★, *In The Quiet Of Night* (Decca 1956) ★★★, *Burl Ives Sings For Fun* (Decca 1956) ★★, *Burl Ives Sings Songs For All Ages* (Columbia 1957) ★★, *Christmas Eve With Ives* (Decca 1957) ★★, *Songs Of Ireland* (Decca 1958) ★★★, *Old Time Varieties* (Decca 1958) ★★★, *Captain Burl Ives' Ark* (Decca 1958) ★★★, *Australian Folk Songs* (Decca 1958) ★★★, *Cheers* (Decca 1959) ★★★, *Little White Duck* (Fontana 1960) ★★, *Burl Ives Sings Irving Berlin* (1961) ★★, *The Versatile Burl Ives!* (Decca 1962) ★★, *It's Just My Funny Way Of Laughin'* (Decca 1962) ★★★, *Songs Of The West* (Brunswick 1962) ★★★, *Sunshine In My Soul* (Brunswick 1963) ★★★, *Singin' Easy* (Brunswick 1963) ★★★, *Walt Disney Presents Burl Ives – Animal Folk* (1964) ★★, *Pearly Shells* (Decca 1964) ★★★, *Rudolph The Red Nosed Reindeer* (Decca 1966) ★, *Something Special* (Brunswick 1966) ★★★, *Times They Are A-Changin'* (Columbia 1968) ★★, *Animal Folk* (Castle Music 1974) ★★, *Chim Chim Cheree* (Castle Music 1974) ★, with the Korean Children Choir *Faith And Joy* (Sacred/Word 1974) ★, *How Great Thou Art* (Word 1974) ★★, *Songs I Sang In Sunday School* (Sacred/Word 1974) ★★, *I Do Believe* (Word 1974) ★★★, *Shall We Gather At The River* (Sacred/Word 1978) ★★★, *Talented Man* (Bulldog 1978) ★★★, *Live In Europe* (Polydor 1979) ★★★, *Bright And Beautiful* (Word 1979) ★★, *Christmas At The White House* (Caedmon 1979) ★★, *Stepping In The Light* (Word 1984) ★★★, *Love And Joy* (Word 1984) ★★★, and the 50s film and audio series *Historical America In Song* for *Encyclopedia Britannica*.

● COMPILATIONS: *The Best Of Burl Ives* (MCA 1965) ★★★, *Junior Choice* (MFP 1979) ★★, *The Best Of Burl's For Boys And Girls* (MCA 1980) ★★, *A Little Bitty Tear: The Nashville Years 1961-65* (Bear Family 1993) ★★★, *The Best Of Burl Ives: The Millennium Collection* (Chronicles 2001) ★★★.

● FURTHER READING: *Wayfaring Stranger*, Burl Ives.

● FILMS: *Smoky* (1946), *So Dear To My Heart* (1948), *East Of Eden* (1955), *Cat On A Hot Tin Roof* (1958), *Wind Across The Everglades* (1958), *Desire Under The Elms* (1958), *The Big Country* (1958), *Our Man In Havana* (1960), *The Brass Bottle* (1964), *Rocket To The Moon* (1967).

JACKSON, MAHALIA

b. 16 October 1911, New Orleans, Louisiana, USA,
d. 27 January 1972, Evergreen Park, Illinois, USA.
For many commentators, Mahalia Jackson
remains the definitive exponent of gospel music.
At the age of four she sang at the Plymouth Rock
Baptist Church and later joined the Mount Moriah
Baptist Church junior choir. She mixed the singing
styles of the Baptists with the Sanctified Church,
which produced a powerful rhythm and beat, and
fell under the influence of gospel artists Roberta
Martin and Willie Mae Ford Smith. Coupled with
the expressions of Bessie Smith and Ma Rainey,
which in her teens Jackson had begun to observe,
she developed the beginnings of a deep soulful
blues style. In 1927, Mahalia moved from New
Orleans to Chicago; after her first Sunday church
service, where she had given a impromptu
performance of her favourite song, 'Hand Me
Down My Favourite Trumpet, Gabriel', she was
invited to join the Greater Salem Baptist Church
Choir and began touring the city's churches and
surrounding areas with the Johnson Singers.
After several years with the Johnsons, Mahalia
began to forge a solo career. During this time, as
well as singing in church, she sang at political
rallies and in 1937 became a song demonstrator of
the talents of gospel songwriter Thomas A.
Dorsey. That same year she recorded four tracks
for Decca Records, to little commercial success,
and was dropped soon afterwards. Jackson then
toured extensively – in the intervening time she
qualified as a beautician to safeguard her future –
and recorded again, this time for the Apollo label
in 1946, which included the first use in gospel
music of the Hammond organ rather than the
usual lone piano. These recordings, most of which
feature a simple backdrop, show a singer of
peerless quality, whose prudent use of slow
hymns allowed space for her voice to develop its
seemingly effortless inflections. Pianist Mildred
Falls, who remained with Jackson throughout her
career, added a measured, complimentary
background. The success of the Apollo pressings,
in particular 'Move On Up A Little Higher',
culminated in 1954 with Jackson hosting and
starring in her own Sunday night radio show for
CBS, bringing black gospel music to a mass white
audience. That same year she began recording for
CBS which resulted in a number of tight
productions and a departure from the almost
improvisational feel of previous sessions.
Although these releases lacked the simplicity of
earlier work, they became a huge success; in 1956
she brought the studio audience at the *Ed Sullivan
Show* to its feet. She later triumphed at the rain-
soaked Newport Jazz Festival in 1958. Jackson

became an ambassador for gospel music, and
embarked on several successful European tours.
Despite endless entreaties, she resisted crossing
over into jazz or blues and pop for many years,
although she did perform with Duke Ellington in
his 'Black, Brown And Beige' suite. She sang at
one of the inaugural balls for President John F.
Kennedy in 1960, and often performed at Dr.
Martin Luther King's rallies. In 1968 she sang at
King's funeral, where she gave an emotional
rendition of Dorsey's 'Precious Lord, Take My
Hand'. Towards the end of her career Jackson did
bow to pressure to record more secular songs and
included, among others, 'What The World Needs
Now Is Love' and Dion's classic anthem,
'Abraham, Martin And John'. Mahalia gave her last
public performance in Germany in October 1971,
and died of heart failure in 1972.

● ALBUMS: *Mahalia Jackson* (Vogue 1952) ★★★,
Newport 1958 (Columbia 1958) ★★★★, *Great
Gettin' Up Morning* (Columbia 1959) ★★★, *Just As
I Am* (Kenwood 1960) ★★★★, *The Power And The
Glory* (Columbia 1960) ★★, *Come On Children Let's
Sing* (Columbia 1960) ★★★, *I Believe* (Columbia
1961) ★★★, *Sweet Little Jesus Boy* (Columbia 1961)
★★★, *Every Time I Feel The Spirit* (Columbia 1961)
★★★, *Great Songs Of Love And Faith* (Columbia
1962) ★★★, *Silent Night – Songs For Christmas*
(Columbia 1962) ★★, *Make A Joyful Noise Unto
The Lord* (Columbia 1962) ★★★, *Bless This House*
(Columbia 1963) ★★★, *Let's Pray Together*
(Columbia 1964) ★★★, *In The Upper Room*
(Kenwood 1965) ★★★, *Mahalia* (Kenwood 1965)
★★★★, *No Matter How You Pray* (Kenwood 1965)
★★★, *Mahalia Sings* (Kenwood 1966) ★★★★, *The
Old Rugged Cross* (Kenwood 1966) ★★★, *My Faith*
(Columbia 1967) ★★★★, *In Concert* (Columbia
1968) ★★★, *A Mighty Fortress* (Columbia 1968)
★★★, *Sings The Best-Loved Hymns Of Dr. Martin
Luther King, Jr.* (Columbia 1968) ★★★, *You'll Never
Walk Alone* (1968) ★★★, *Christmas With Mahalia*
(Columbia 1968) ★★, *Sings America's Favorite
Hymns* (Columbia 1971) ★★★, *Right Out Of The
Church* (Columbia 1976) ★★★.

● COMPILATIONS: *Best Of Mahalia Jackson*
(Kenwood) ★★★★, *1911 – 1972* (Kenwood)
★★★★, *Mahalia Jackson's Greatest Hits* (Columbia
1963) ★★★, *The Great Mahalia Jackson* (Columbia
1972) ★★, *The World's Greatest Gospel Singer*
(Columbia 1975) ★★★, *How I Got Over* (Columbia
1976) ★★★★, *Gospel* (Vogue 1977) ★★★, *The
Warm And Tender Soul Of Mahalia Jackson* (Joker
1981) ★★★, *20 Greatest Hits* (Astan 1984) ★★★,
The Mahalia Jackson Collection (Deja Vu 1985)
★★★, *When The Saint's Go Marching In* (Columbia
1987) ★★★★, *The Mahalia Jackson Story* (Deja Vu
1989) ★★★, *Gospels, Spirituals & Hymns*
(Columbia/Legacy 1991) ★★★, *Gospels, Spirituals
& Hymns Vol. 2* (Columbia/Legacy 1992) ★★★,
How I Got Over: The Apollo Sessions, 1946-1954 3-
CD set (Westside 1998) ★★★★.

● VIDEOS: *Mahalia* (Hendring Music Video
1990).

● FURTHER READING: *Just Mahalia, Baby*,
Laurraine Goreau. *Got To Tell It: Mahalia Jackson
Queen Of Gospel*, Jules Schwerin.

JACKSON, MILT 'BAGS'

b. 1 January 1923, Detroit, Michigan, USA, d. 9 October 1999, New York City, New York, USA. Jackson's first professional engagement, at the age of 16, was in his hometown, playing the vibraphone alongside tenor saxophonist Lucky Thompson (one year his junior). Jackson benefited from the 40s loose attitude towards band personnel, spending six years accompanying visiting musicians, as well as studying at Michigan State University. In 1945, Dizzy Gillespie heard him and invited him to join his band for a west coast tour. Later moving to New York, the brilliant young vibes player found himself much in demand, playing and recording with Howard McGhee and Thelonious Monk (including Monk's classic 1951 session for Blue Note Records). A spell with Woody Herman (1949-50) and more work with Gillespie established him as the pre-eminent player on his instrument. Jackson's recording debut as a leader was for Gillespie's Dee Gee label in 1951. He also had the depth of experience to play with both Ben Webster and Charlie Parker. In 1954, the Milt Jackson Quartet transformed itself into the Modern Jazz Quartet, with pianist John Lewis becoming musical director. For the next 20 years, Milt Jackson led a Dr Jeckyll and Mr Hyde existence, playing the consummately sophisticated music of the MJQ, all dressed in their famous tuxedoes, and leading his own dates in the swinging company of Coleman Hawkins, Lucky Thompson or Horace Silver. In 1961, Jackson accompanied Ray Charles on *Soul Meeting*, on which the soul singer restricted himself to electric piano and alto saxophone. Sleevenote writers loved to debate how happy Jackson could be with the MJQ's starchy charts. Certainly when he broke up the group in 1974, it was due to what he considered its financial exploitation rather than musical antagonism. Often the vibes were an instrument associated with the hot, swinging proto-R&B of big band leaders Lionel Hampton and Johnny Otis. By slowing the vibrato and giving the right-hand mallet sweeping lines like a saxophone, Jackson gave the instrument sensuality and soul. Not until the appearance of Bobby Hutcherson in the mid-60s did anyone come up with an alternative modern approach to playing it. Jackson's harmonic sense was unerringly inventive and he also kept his ears open for new talent. He championed guitarist Wes Montgomery and recorded with him for Riverside Records (*Bags Meets Wes*). Jackson was a strong force in the reintegration of bebop with swing values and musicians, the very definition of what came to be known as 'mainstream' jazz. His own quintets included players such as Cedar Walton, Jimmy Heath and James Moody. The 70s were a hard period for jazz players, but even in the dated arrangements of Bob James on a record like *Olinga* (recorded in 1974 for CTI) his caressing, ebullient vibes playing shone through. The 80s jazz revival was reflected by the MJQ re-forming and appearing at countless jazz festivals. In 1985, Jackson toured Europe under his own name. The Pablo record label continued to document his music into the 90s. He died of liver cancer in October 1999.

● ALBUMS: *In The Beginning* 1948 recordings (Original Jazz Classics) ★★★, *Milt Jackson* 10-inch album (Dee Gee 1952) ★★★, *Wizard Of The Vibes* reissued as *Milt Jackson* (Blue Note 1952) ★★★★, *Milt Jackson* reissued as *Meet Milt Jackson* (Savoy 1954) ★★★★, *Milt Jackson Quintet* 10-inch album (Prestige 1954) ★★★★, *Milt Jackson* reissued as *Soul Pioneers* (Prestige 1955) ★★★★, *Opus De Jazz* (Savoy 1955) ★★★, *Roll Em Bags* (Savoy 1955) ★★★, *The Jazz Skyline* (Savoy 1956) ★★★, *Jackson's-ville* (Savoy 1956) ★★★, *Ballads & Blues* (Atlantic 1956) ★★★★, *Plenty, Plenty Soul* (Atlantic 1957) ★★★★, *Bags & Flutes* (Atlantic 1958) ★★★, with Ray Charles *Soul Brothers* (Atlantic 1958) ★★★★, with Coleman Hawkins *Bean Bags* (Atlantic 1959) ★★★★, *Bags' Opus* (United Artists 1959) ★★★★, *Ballad Artistry* (Atlantic 1960) ★★★, with John Coltrane *Bags And Trane* (Atlantic 1961) ★★★★, with Charles *Soul Meeting* (Atlantic 1961) ★★★★, with Wes Montgomery *Bags Meets Wes* (Riverside 1962) ★★★★, *Statements* (Impulse! 1962) ★★★, *Big Bags* (Riverside 1962) ★★★★, *Invitation* (Riverside 1963) ★★★★, *Jazz n' Samba* (Impulse! 1964) ★★★, *In A New Setting* (Limelight 1964) ★★★, with Ray Brown *Much In Common* (Verve 1964) ★★★★, *Ray Brown-Milt Jackson* (Verve 1965) ★★★★, *At The Museum Of Modern Art* (Limelight 1965) ★★★★, *Born Free* (Limelight 1966) ★★★, *For Someone I Love* (Riverside 1966) ★★★, *'Live' At The Village Gate* (Riverside 1967) ★★★, *Memphis Jackson* (Impulse! 1967) ★★★, *Bags And Brass* (Riverside 1968) ★★★, *Milt Jackson And The Hip String Quartet* (Verve 1969) ★★★, *Sunflower* (CTI 1973) ★★★, *Goodbye* (CTI 1973) ★★★, *Olinga* (CTI 1974) ★★, *Montreux '75* (Pablo 1975) ★★★, *The Big 3* (Pablo 1975) ★★★, *Feelings* (Pablo 1976) ★★★, with Joe Pass, Ray Brown , Mickey Roker *Quadrant* (Pablo 1977) ★★★, *Soul Fusion* (Pablo 1977) ★★★★, *Montreux '77* (Pablo 1977) ★★★, with Brow *Live-Montreux '77* (Pablo 1978) ★★★, *Milt Jackson + Count Basie + The Big Band, Vols 1 And 2* (Pablo 1978) ★★★, *Soul Believer* (Pablo 1978) ★★, *All Too Soon: The Duke Ellington Album* (Pablo 1980) ★★★, *Night Mist* (Pablo 1980) ★★★, *Big Mouth* (Pablo 1981) ★★★, *Ain't But A Few Of Us Left* (Pablo 1982) ★★★, *Jackson, Johnson, Brown & Company* (Pablo 1983) ★★★, *Soul Route* (Pablo 1984) ★★, *It Don't Mean A Thing If You Can't Tap Your Foot To It* (Pablo 1985) ★★★, *Brother Jim* (Pablo 1986) ★★, *A London Bridge* 1982 recording (Pablo 1986) ★★★, *Bebop* (East West 1988) ★★★, *Milt Jackson Meets The Clayton-Hamilton Jazz Orchestra: Explosive!* (Qwest 1990) ★★★★, *Mostly Duke* 1982 recording (Pablo 1991) ★★★, *Memories Of Thelonious Sphere Monk* 1982 recording (Pablo 1991) ★★★, *The Harem* (Music Masters 1991) ★★★, *Reverence And Compassion* (Qwest 1993) ★★★, *The Prophet Speaks* (Qwest 1994) ★★★, *Burnin' In The Woodhouse* (Qwest 1995) ★★★, *Sa Va Bella (For Lady Legends)* (Qwest 1997) ★★, with Oscar Peterson, Brown *The Very Tall Band Live At The Blue Note* (Telarc 1999) ★★★.

● COMPILATIONS: *The Complete Milt Jackson* (Prestige 1969) ★★★★, *The Best Of Milt Jackson* (Pablo 1982) ★★★★.

JACOBS, DICK

b. 29 March 1918, New York, USA, d. 1988. A graduate from the city university, Jacobs was to be one of the few producers for a major US record company in the 50s who catered for rock 'n' roll consumers without finding the form personally objectionable. With his orchestra, he had a US Top 30 entry with Elmer Bernstein's jazzy main theme to 1956's *The Man With The Golden Arm* (starring Frank Sinatra) but after serving as musical director for the nationally televised Hit Parade, he became recording manager for Coral Records, a Decca Records subsidiary. Among his clients were Jackie Wilson, Bobby Darin and Buddy Holly, for whom Jacobs cut corners by duplicating the Darin arrangement of 'Early In The Morning'. By contrast, 'the most unplanned thing I have ever written' was the pizzicato string section that embroidered Holly's posthumous smash, 'It Doesn't Matter Anymore', taped in the New York's Pythian Temple studio. During the 60s, Jacobs functioned in a more administrative capacity in the music industry, working for New York's Springboard Records prior to his retirement in the late 70s.

JAFFA, MAX

b. 28 December 1911, London, England, d. 30 July 1991, London, England. A classically trained violinist, inspired and influenced by Jascha Heifetz and Fritz Kreisler, who had a long and successful career in British popular music. Born into a non-musical family, Jaffa's father presented him with a violin on his sixth birthday. At the age of nine he made his first concert appearance at the Palace Pier Theatre, Brighton, and later studied at the Guildhall School Of Music. To supplement his income, he formed a trio to play for silent movies. When he was 17 years old, he worked at the Piccadilly Hotel in London and, during a five-year stay, formed his Salon Orchestra, which made its first broadcast from the hotel in August 1929. Later that year he was released for a season to become the youngest ever leader of the Scottish Symphony Orchestra, and went on a concert tour of Scotland with Joseph Hislop.
During World War II, Jaffa flew with the Royal Air Force, and afterwards found that he was physically unable to play the violin. After reverting to the basics of the instrument, assisted by one of his original tutors, he joined the Mantovani Orchestra, eventually becoming its leader, and played on the original version of the 1951 multi-million-selling record of 'Charmaine'. Around this time, Jaffa's meeting with cellist Reginald Kilbey and pianist Jack Byfield led to the formation of the renowned Max Jaffa Trio. It was a professional association lasting over 30 years. For 27 years, from 1959-86, Max Jaffa served as musical director at Scarborough in Yorkshire, conducting the Spa Orchestra in two concerts a day, during the 17-week summer season. His wife, contralto Jean Grayston, was a regular guest artist. A prolific broadcaster, his radio and television programmes included *Music At Ten, Music For Your Pleasure,* *Melody On Strings, Max Jaffa Trio,* and the long-running, affectionately remembered *Grand Hotel,* in which he presided over the Palm Court Orchestra. A film he made in 1959, entitled *Music With Max Jaffa,* was billed intriguingly as: 'Musical: Violin, Songs and *Sword Dance*'. His honours included the Gold Medal and Principal's Prize from the Guildhall School of Music, the Freedom of Scarborough, and the OBE, which he received in 1982 for services to music. After a career lasting 70 years, he announced his retirement in 1990. A humorous and enlightened attitude to life and music was reflected in his autobiography, which was published in 1991.

● ALBUMS: *Palm Court Concert* (Columbia 1958) ★★★, *Reflections In Gold* (Valentine 1980) ★★★, *Prelude To Romance* (Valentine 1983) ★★★, *Music For A Grand Hotel* (Valentine 1986) ★★★, *Relax With The Music Of Max Jaffa* (MFP 1987) ★★★, *The Way You Look Tonight* (Warwick 1987) ★★★, *Favourite Violin Melodies* (Pickwick 1992) ★★★.
● FURTHER READING: *A Life On The Fiddle,* Max Jaffa.
● FILMS: *Music With Max Jaffa* (1959).

JAILHOUSE ROCK

Although hamstrung by mediocre films throughout much of his Hollywood career, Elvis Presley did complete some outstanding early features. In *Jailhouse Rock* he was aided by a superior plot in which the singer is taught to play guitar while serving in prison for manslaughter. Fame and egotism follow suit until his former cell-mate returns to haunt him and, eventually, prick his conscience. The film also provides an insight into record company practices during the 50s and has a visual impact many other contemporary works lacked. The highly choreographed scene that the title track accompanies has passed into pop cinema history. The Leiber And Stoller songwriting team, famed for their work with the Coasters, provided all of the soundtrack material, which ranges from the electric 'Baby I Don't Care' to the ballad-styled 'Young And Beautiful'. Taken together, the album and film represent a high-water mark in Presley's output.

JAMAL, AHMAD

b. Fritz Jones, 2 July 1930, Pittsburgh, Pennsylvania, USA. A professional pianist from before his teenage years, Jamal (who changed his name in the early 50s) managed to break through to a wider audience than most jazz artists. His trio work produced many excellent recordings and his accompanists included Israel Crosby. The most influential of his advocates was Miles Davis, who recognized Jamal's interesting rhythmic concepts as being something which he could incorporate into his own work. *Ahmad Jamal At The Pershing* during his time became one of the biggest selling jazz albums and stayed on the album charts for nearly two years. Jamal worked extensively in the USA throughout the 60s, 70s and 80s, usually in trio format but occasionally with larger backing for record dates, and also appeared with Gary Burton. Jamal is an important figure among mainstream pianists and their post-bop successors, mainly as a result of the indirect influence he has had through Davis. A lyrical, gently swinging musician, Jamal's playing is a constant delight.

● ALBUMS: *Chamber Music Of The New Jazz* (Creative/Argo 1956) ★★★, *The Ahmad Jamal Trio i* (Epic 1956) ★★★, *Count 'Em 88* (Argo 1956) ★★★, *But Not For Me/Ahmad Jamal At The Pershing* (Argo 1958) ★★★★, *Ahmad's Blues* (Impulse! 1958) ★★★★, *Ahmad Jamal, Volume IV* (Argo 1958) ★★★, *The Ahmad Jamal Trio ii* (Epic 1959) ★★★, *Jamal At The Penthouse* (Argo 1959) ★★★, *Happy Mood* (Argo 1960) ★★★, *Ahmad Jamal At The Pershing, Volume 2* (Argo 1961) ★★★, *Listen To Ahmad Jamal* (Argo 1960) ★★★, *Ahmad Jamal's Alhambra* (Argo 1961) ★★★, *Ahmad Jamal At The Blackhawk* (Argo 1961) ★★★★, *Macanudo* (Argo 1962) ★★★, *Poin'ci-an'a* (Argo 1963) ★★★, *Naked City Theme* (Argo 1964) ★★★, *The Roar Of The Greasepaint, The Smell Of The Crowd* (Argo 1965) ★★★★, *Extensions* (Argo 1965) ★★★, *Ahmad Jamal With String* (1965) ★★★, *Rhapsody* (Cadet 1966) ★★★, *Heat Wave* (Cadet 1966) ★★★, *Standard Eyes* (Cadet 1967) ★★★, *Cry Young* (Cadet 1967) ★★★, *The Bright, The Blue And The Beautiful* (Cadet 1968) ★★★, *Tranquillity* (ABC 1968) ★★, *Jamal At The Top/Poinciana Revisited* (Impulse! 1969) ★★★, *The Awakening* (MCA 1970) ★★, *Free Flight Vol. 1* (1971) ★★★, *Outertimeinnerspace* (Impulse! 1972) ★★★, *Jamal Plays Jamal* (1974) ★★★ *Live At Oil Can Harry's* (1976) ★★, *Prelude To A Kiss* (1976-78) ★★★, *Steppin' Out With A Dream* (c.1977) ★★★, *Intervals* (c.1979) ★★★, *Ahmad Jamal Live At Bubba's* (Kingdom Jazz 1980) ★★★, *Night Song* (Motown 1980) ★★★, *Ahmad Jamal In Concert* (1981) ★★, *American Classical Music* (1982) ★★★, *Digital Works* (Atlantic 1985) ★★★★, *Rossiter Road* (Atlantic 1985) ★★★, *Live At The Montreux Jazz Festival* (Atlantic 1986) ★★★★, *Goodbye Mr Evans* (Black Lion 1988) ★★★, *Crystal* (WEA 1993) ★★★, *Chicago Revisited* (Telarc 1993) ★★★, *Live In Paris 92* (Birdology 1993) ★★★, *I Remember Duke, Hoagy & Strayhorn* (Telarc 1995) ★★★, *The Essence Part 1* (Verve 1996) ★★★, *Big Byrd: The Essence Part 2* (Verve 1997) ★★★, *Ahmad Jamal With The Assai Quartet* (Roesch 1997) ★★★, *Nature: The Essence Part 3* (Atlantic 1998) ★★★, *Cross Country Tour 1958-1961* (GRP 1998) ★★★★, *Olympia 2000* (Dreyfus 2001) ★★★.

● COMPILATIONS: *Genetic Walk* (20th Century 1980) ★★★, *Ahmad Jamal 1956-66 recordings* (GRP 1998) ★★★.

JAMES, ELMORE

b. 27 January 1918, Richland, Mississippi, USA, d. 23 May 1963, Chicago, Illinois, USA. Although his recording career spanned 10 years, Elmore James is chiefly recalled for his debut release, 'Dust My Broom'. This impassioned, exciting performance, based on a virulent composition by country blues singer Robert Johnson, was marked by the artist's unfettered vocals and his searing electric slide guitar. James' formative years were spent in Mississippi juke joints where he befriended Rice

Miller (Sonny Boy Williamson), a regular performer on the US radio station KFFA's *King Biscuit Time* show. Elmore accompanied Miller for several years, and through his influence secured his initial recording contract in 1951. James then moved to Chicago where he formed the first of several groups bearing the name 'the Broomdusters'. Subsequent recordings included different variations on that initial success – 'I Believe', 'Dust My Blues' – as well as a series of compositions that proved equally influential. 'Bleeding Heart' and 'Shake Your Moneymaker' were later adopted, respectively, by Jimi Hendrix and Fleetwood Mac, while the guitarist's distinctive 'bottleneck' style resurfaced in countless British blues bands. James' style was accurately copied by Jeremy Spencer of Fleetwood Mac – the band often had 'Elmore James' segments in their act during the late 60s. Another James devotee was Brian Jones of the Rolling Stones, whose early stage name of Elmo Lewis, and bottleneck guitar work paid tribute to James. John Mayall's 'Mr. James' was a thoughtful tribute to this significant performer who sadly did not live to enjoy such acclaim. In May 1963, James suffered a fatal heart attack at the home of his cousin, Homesick James, who, along with J.B. Hutto, then assumed the late musician's mantle.

● COMPILATIONS: *Blues After Hours* (Crown 1961) ★★★★, *Original Folk Blues* (Kent 1964) ★★★★, *The Sky Is Crying* (Sphere Sound 1965) ★★★, *The Best Of Elmore James* (Sue 1965) ★★★★, *I Need You* (Sphere Sound 1966) ★★★, *The Elmore James Memorial Album* (Sue 1966) ★★★★, *Something Inside Of Me* (Bell 1968) ★★★, *The Late Fantastically Great Elmore James* (Ember 1968) ★★★, *To Know A Man* (Blue Horizon 1969) ★★★, *Whose Muddy Shoes* (Chess 1969) ★★★, *Elmore James* (Bell 1969) ★★★, *Blues In My Heart, Rhythm In My Soul* (1969) ★★★, *The Legend Of Elmore James* (United Artists 1970) ★★★, *Tough* (Blue Horizon 1970) ★★★, *Cotton Patch Hotfoots* (Polydor 1974) ★★★, *All Them Blues* (DJM 1976) ★★★, with Robert Nighthawk *Blues In D'Natural* (1979) ★★★★, *The Best Of Elmore James* (Ace 1981) ★★★, *Got To Move* (Charly 1981) ★★★, *King Of The Slide Guitar* (Ace 1983) ★★★★, *Red Hot Blues* (Blue Moon 1983) ★★★, *The Original Meteor And Flair Sides* (Ace 1984) ★★★★, *Come Go With Me* (Charly 1984) ★★★, *One Way Out* (Charly 1985) ★★★, *The Elmore James Collection* (Déjà Vu 1985) ★★★★, *Let's Cut It* (Ace 1986) ★★★, *King Of The Bottleneck Blues* (Crown 1986) ★★★★, *Shake Your Moneymaker* (Charly 1986) ★★★★, *Pickin' The Blues* (Castle 1986) ★★★, *Greatest Hits* (Blue City 1988) ★★★, *Chicago Golden Years* (Vogue 1988) ★★★, *Dust My Broom* (Instant 1990) ★★★★, *Rollin' And Tumblin' – The Best Of* (Relic 1992) ★★★★, *Elmore James Box Set* (Charly 1992) ★★★★, *The Classic Early Recordings 1951-56* 3-CD box set (Flair/Ace 1993) ★★★★, *The Best Of Elmore James: The Early Years* (Ace 1995) ★★★★, *Rollin' And Tumblin'* (Recall 1999) ★★★★, *Shake Your Moneymaker: The Best Of The Fire Sessions* (Buddha 2001) ★★★.

JENKINS, GORDON

b. 12 May 1910, Webster Groves, Missouri, USA, d. 24 April 1984, Malibu, California, USA. A distinguished songwriter, arranger and conductor, as a child Jenkins occasionally played organ at the Chicago movie theatre where his father was the regular organist. During Prohibition he played piano in a St. Louis speakeasy and was later employed by a radio station in the same city. In 1936 he became chief staff arranger for Isham Jones, producing skilful charts for this superior dance orchestra, and later composed and arranged for Woody Herman, Lennie Hayton, Vincent Lopez, Benny Goodman and André Kostalanetz. He composed Herman's theme, 'Blue Prelude' (with Joe Bishop), and 'Goodbye', which Goodman used as the closing music to hundreds of radio shows. In 1936 he conducted the orchestra for *The Show Is On* on Broadway, and in the following year settled on the west coast, working for Paramount. In 1939 he began a five-year tenure as musical director for NBC in Hollywood. In the mid-40s he worked on the Dick Haymes show and in 1945 became staff conductor for Decca Records. In the same year Jenkins wrote and recorded a long work, in effect a personal love song to New York City, entitled 'Manhattan Tower'. This piece for orchestra and singers has been performed by the Atlanta Symphony Orchestra, in revues and on television.

In 1949 Jenkins was back in New York, working on the score for the Broadway show *Along Fifth Avenue*, and at the Capitol and Paramount theatres. Among his song credits, several of which have attracted the attention of jazz musicians, are 'Homesick – That's All', 'Blue Evening', 'Married I Can Always Get', 'New York's My Home', and 'You Have Taken My Heart', 'P.S. I Love You' and 'When A Woman Loves A Man' (the last three with Johnny Mercer). In 1952 Jenkins wrote the score for *Bwana Devil*, the first 3-D feature film, and, through the years, accompanied many top artists on record, such as Martha Tilton, Louis Armstrong and Peggy Lee. His work with Frank Sinatra received much critical acclaim, notably the albums *Where Are You?* (1957) and *No One Cares* (1959), and his scores for Nat 'King' Cole included the definitive vocal arrangement of 'Star Dust' for *Love Is The Thing* (1957). Gordon Jenkins and his Orchestra had their own series of hits from 1942-53, often with various vocalists, which included 'I Don't See Me In Your Eyes Anymore', 'Again', 'Don't Cry, Joe', 'My Foolish Heart', 'Bewitched', two with the Weavers, 'Tzena, Tzena, Tzena' and 'Goodnight, Irene' (US number 1 in 1950), 'I'm Forever Blowing Bubbles', and 'So Long (It's Been Good To Know Ya)'. He won a Grammy Award in 1965 for his arrangement of Frank Sinatra's 'It Was A Very Good Year', and served as arranger and conductor on the singer's 1973 television comeback.

● ALBUMS: with Louis Armstrong *Louis Armstrong-Gordon Jenkins* 10-inch album (Decca 1954) ★★★, *The Complete Manhattan Tower* (Capitol 1956) ★★★, *Dreamer's Holiday* (Capitol 1958) ★★★, *Hawaiian Wedding* (Capitol 1962) ★★, *I Live Alone* (Capitol 1965) ★★★, *Soft Soul* (Capitol 1966) ★★★, *My Heart Sings* (Capitol 1966) ★★★, *Blue Prelude* (Capitol 1967) ★★.

JIMÉNEZ, JOSÉ ALFREDO

b. 19 January 1926, Dolores, Hidalgo, Guanajuato, Mexico, d. 23 November 1973, Mexico. The greatest ranchera composer of all time, Jiménez began singing with the trio Los Rebeldes at the same Mexico City restaurant where he worked as a waiter. His first hit as a singer-songwriter came in 1950 with 'Ella', which was included in the motion picture *Arrabalera*. From then on, Jiménez penned hit after hit, often performing them himself, but also offering them to singers as illustrious as Jorge Negrete, Pedro Infante, Lola Beltrán, Amalia Mendoza and his favourite performer, Miguel Aceves Mejía. Jiménez recorded more than 30 albums and wrote about 400 songs, dozens of which are a required part of any self-respecting mariachi repertoire. Aside from his obvious melodic genius, Jiménez became an idol in his country because he was able to distil Mexico's character and idiosyncrasies like no other songwriter. Married three times, he concentrated on lyrics where love is seen as a powerful force that sooner or later brings pain and destruction. However, in typical life-affirming fashion, this songwriter laughs in the face of adversity, and ultimately accepts life for the tragicomedy that it is. Though Jiménez died from cirrhosis of the liver in 1973, he is still regarded as a national hero. There is hardly a Mexican singer who has not, at one point or another, paid tribute to the master of the ranchera. To quote his most popular tune, Jiménez 'sigue siendo El Rey', he is still the King.

● COMPILATIONS: *Coleccion* (BMG 1998) ★★★★, *Lo Mejor De Lo Mejor* (BMG 1999) ★★★★.

● FILMS: *Ahí Viene Martín Cornona* (1952), *El Enamorado* aka *Vuelve Martín Cornona* (1952), *El Charro Inmortal* (1955), *Pura Vida* (1956), *Mis Padres Se Divorcian* (1958), *Ferias De Mexico* (1958), *Cada Quién Su Música* (1958), *El Hombre De Alazán* (1959), *Juana Gallo* aka *The Guns Of Juana Gallo* (1961), *Escuela Para Solteras* aka *Águila Con Las Hermanas* (1964), *Arrullo De Dios* (1966), *La Loco De Los Milagros* (1973).

JOHN, LITTLE WILLIE

b. William Edgar John, 15 November 1937, Cullendale, Arkansas, USA, d. 26 May 1968, Walla Walla, Washington, USA. The brother of singer Mable John, Willie was one of the most popular 50s R&B performers. His first hit, 'All Around The World', also known as 'Grits Ain't Groceries', was followed by a spectacular double-sided smash, 'Need Your Love So Bad'/'Home At Last' in 1956. The a-side of this successful coupling was later recorded by Fleetwood Mac and Gary Moore. It was followed by 'Fever'/'Letter From My Darling', both sides of which also reached the US R&B Top 10. 'Fever', written by Otis Blackwell (as 'Davenport') and Eddie Cooley, was a million-selling single in its own right, topping that particular chart in May 1956. However, the song is more closely associated with Peggy Lee, who took the song into the US and UK charts in 1958. 'Talk To Me, Talk To Me' gave Little Willie John another gold disc that year, while in 1959 he enjoyed further success with 'Leave My Kitten Alone', a favoured song of British beat groups. The singer's professional career faltered during the 60s while his private life ended in tragedy. Convicted of manslaughter in 1966, John died of a heart attack in Washington State Prison in 1968. He was posthumously inducted into the Rock And Roll Hall Of Fame in 1996.

● ALBUMS: *Fever* (King 1956) ★★★★, *Talk To Me* (King 1958) ★★★★, *Mister Little Willie John* (King 1958) ★★★★, *Action* (King 1960) ★★★★, *Sure Things* (King 1961) ★★★★, *The Sweet, The Hot, The Teen Age Beat* (King 1961) ★★★, *Come On And Join* (Ling 1962) ★★★, *These Are My Favourite Songs* (King 1964) ★★, *Little Willie John Sings All Originals* (King 1966) ★★.

● COMPILATIONS: *Free At Last* (King 1970) ★★★★, *Grits And Soul* (Charly 1985) ★★★★, *Fever* (Charly 1990) ★★★★, *Sure Things* (King 1990) ★★★, *Fever: The Best Of Little Willie John* (Rhino 1993) ★★★★.

JOHNSON, JOHNNIE

b. 8 July 1924, Fairmont, West Virginia, USA. Johnson's name may not be well known but his sound has been heard by millions: he was the piano player on most of Chuck Berry's classic Chess Records tracks. Johnson began learning to play piano at the age of seven without the benefit of lessons, influenced by jazz and boogie-woogie musicians such as Earl Hines, Meade 'Lux' Lewis and Clarence 'Pinetop' Smith. After a spell in the US Army Johnson began performing professionally in 1946, and in 1952, leading the Sir John Trio, he hired the young Berry as his guitarist. Berry soon began writing the group's songs and became its leader. Chess artist Muddy Waters suggested the group audition for that label and Berry was signed in 1955. Johnson can be heard on Berry hits such as 'Maybellene', 'Roll Over Beethoven' and 'Johnny B. Goode', which Berry has stated was written for Johnson. Johnson also played in Berry's road band but in the 60s left, working with blues guitarist Albert King, among others. Johnson led his own band in the 70s but still worked with Berry on occasion. He was featured in the 1986 Berry concert movie *Hail! Hail! Rock And Roll* and later appeared as a guest on Keith Richards' debut solo album, *Talk Is Cheap*. Johnson has recorded sparingly under his own name, releasing his first solo album in 1987.

● ALBUMS: *Blue Hand Johnnie* (Evidence 1987) ★★★, *Rockin' Eighty-Eights* (Modern Blues 1990) ★★★, *Johnnie B. Bad* (Elektra 1992) ★★★, with the Kentucky Headhunters *That'll Work* (Elektra 1993) ★★★, *Johnnie Be Back* (Music Masters 1995) ★★★.

● COMPILATIONS: *Complete Recorded Works Volumes 1-3* (Document 1995) ★★★.

● FURTHER READING: *Father Of Rock & Roll: The Story Of Johnnie "B Goode" Johnson*, Travis Fitzpatrick.

JOHNSON, SYL

b. Sylvester Thompson, 1 July 1936, Holly Springs, Mississippi, USA. Johnson was the youngest of three children and his family moved to Chicago during the late 40s. An elder brother, Mac Thompson, played bass with the Magic Sam Blues Band. Having learned guitar and harmonica, Johnson began frequenting the city's southside blues clubs, playing alongside Howlin' Wolf, Muddy Waters and Junior Wells. His first recordings were made in 1956 accompanying Billy Boy Arnold, after which Johnson appeared on sessions for Shakey Jake, Junior Wells and Jimmy Reed. In 1959 Federal released Johnson's first solo single, 'Teardrops', and he recorded unsuccessfully for several independents until signing with Twilight (later changed to Twinight) in 1967. His debut there, 'Come On Sock It To Me', reached number 12 in the R&B chart. Johnson's musical activities, however, were not solely confined to performing. He also produced several local acts including Tyrone Davis and Otis Clay, while the Deacons, his backing group, featuring brother Jimmy Johnson on guitar, enjoyed a minor hit on the singer's Shama label. Johnson was then spotted by Willie Mitchell and 'Dresses Too Short' (1968) was recorded with the Mitchell's Hi Records house band. The remaining Twinight sessions were divided between Memphis and Chicago. Johnson remained with the label until 1971, recording two albums in the process. Free to sign with Hi, he began a series of releases that matched for excellence those of labelmate Al Green. Brash, up-tempo topsides, including 'Back For A Taste Of Your Love' and 'We Did It', contrasted with the often-reflective couplings, of which 'Anyway The Wind Blows' and 'I Hear The Love Chimes' were particularly emotive. The third of his exemplary albums for Hi, *Total Explosion*, produced Johnson's only substantial R&B hit when his version of 'Take Me To The River' (1975) reached number 7. However, his final years at Hi were dogged by internal problems and towards the end of the decade he reactivated his Shama label. A contemporary blues/soul collection, *Ms Fine Brown Frame*, was licensed to Boardwalk, while a French album, *Suicide Blues*, followed in 1984. By the mid-80s, he had semi-retired from the music business and opened a string of fast-food fish restaurants. He returned to performing in 1992 and in 1994 with an excellent album *Back In The Game*. Jonny Lang appeared on his 1998 album *Bridge To A Legacy*.

● ALBUMS: *Dresses Too Short* (Twinight 1968) ★★★, *Is It Because I'm Black* i (Twinight 1970) ★★★, *Back For A Taste Of Your Love* (Hi 1973) ★★★★, *Diamond In The Rough* (Hi 1974) ★★★, *Total Explosion* (Hi 1976) ★★★★, *Uptown Shakedown* (Shama 1979) ★★★, *Brings Out The Blues In Me* (Shama 1980) ★★★, *Ms Fine Brown Frame* (Boardwalk 1983) ★★★, *Suicide Blues* (1984) ★★★, *Foxy Brown* (Shama 1988) ★★★, *Back In The Game* (Delmark 1994) ★★★★, *Bridge To A Legacy* (Antone's 1998) ★★, *Talkin' Bout Chicago* (Delmark 2000) ★★★.

● COMPILATIONS: *Brings Out The Blues In Me*

(Flyright 1986) ★★★, *Is It Because I'm Black* ii (Charly 1986) ★★★★, *The Love Chimes* (Hi 1986) ★★★, *Stuck In Chicago* (Hi 1989) ★★★, *Back For A Taste - The Syl Johnson Story (1971-78)* (Hi 1998) ★★★.

JONES, PHILLY JOE

b. Joseph Rudolph Jones, 15 July 1923, Philadelphia, Pennsylvania, USA, d. 30 August 1985, Philadelphia, Pennsylvania, USA. Jones began his drumming career in his home town, later moving to New York where he worked with many leading bebop musicians. Despite this early exposure to Charlie Parker, Dizzy Gillespie and other innovators, Jones was able to adapt to the stylistic needs of any group in which he played. Although proficient in bands led by mainstreamers such as Ben Webster and Lionel Hampton he was happiest in his many fruitful associations with modernists, among whom were Tadd Dameron, John Coltrane and Miles Davis. His tenure with Davis occupied a substantial slice of the 50s; in the following decade he played and recorded with Gil Evans, Bill Evans and led his own groups. In the late 60s he lived briefly in the UK, playing with musicians such as Kenny Wheeler and Pete King and also teaching. In the early 80s Jones formed the band Dameronia, with which to play the music of his former associate. Whether subtly encouraging or with sustained power, often working with a minimal, scaled-down drum kit, Jones was able to adjust his playing style to accommodate any group or individual.
● ALBUMS: *Blues For Dracula* (Riverside 1958) ★★★, *Drums Around The World* (Riverside 1959) ★★★, *Showcase* (Riverside 1959) ★★★, *Philly Joe's Beat* (Atlantic 1960) ★★★, *Trailways Express* (Black Lion 1968) ★★, *'Round Midnight* (1969) ★★★, *Mo' Jo* (Black Lion 1969) ★★★, *Mean What You Say* (Sonet 1977) ★★, *Philly Mignon* (Galaxy 1977) ★★★, *Drum Song* (Galaxy 1978) ★★, *Advance!* (1978) ★★, *To Tadd With Love* (Uptown 1982) ★★★, *Dameronia* (Uptown 1983) ★★★, *Look, Stop And Listen* (Uptown 1983) ★★★, *Filet De Sole* (Marge 1992) ★★★.

JONES, SHIRLEY

b. 31 March 1934, Smithton, Pennsylvania, USA. An actress and singer whose film portrayals of sweet and wholesome ingénues in the 50s contrasted sharply with her Academy Award-winning performance as Burt Lancaster's prostitute girlfriend in *Elmer Gantry* (1960). After taking singing lessons from an early age, Jones performed in stage productions before making her film debut opposite Gordon MacRae in the excellent film version of Richard Rodgers and Oscar Hammerstein II's *Oklahoma!* (1955). So successful was the collaboration that the two stars came together again a year later for another Rodgers and Hammerstein project, *Carousel*. After appearing with Pat Boone in *April Love* (1957), Jones turned in an impressive acting performance alongside James Cagney in the musical comedy-drama *Never Steal Anything Small*, joined a host of other stars in *Pepe*, and made one or two lacklustre features before partnering Robert Preston in another fine screen adaptation of a Broadway show, *The Music Man* (1962). From then on, Shirley Jones eschewed musical films for dramatic roles in big-screen features and on television. She was married for a time to the actor and singer Jack Cassidy, and she co-starred with her step-son, David Cassidy, in the top-rated television series *The Partridge Family* in the early 70s. Later in the decade she had her own show entitled *Shirley*. She continued to sing in nightclubs and concerts, and in the late 80s undertook a 14-week tour of the USA in *The King And I* with David Carradine. In the summer of 1994 she appeared with Marty Ingels in a provincial production of A.R. Gurney's two-hander *Love Letters*, and also starred in a Detroit revival of *The King And I*.

JORDANAIRES

This renowned harmony-vocal quartet is famed for their lengthy working relationship with Elvis Presley. They were founded in 1948 in Springfield, Missouri, by Bill Matthews (b. 19 September 1923, USA; first tenor), Bob Hubbard (b. 3 July 1928, USA; second tenor), Monty Matthews (b. 25 August 1927, USA; baritone), and Culley Holt (b. 2 July 1925, USA, d. 28 June 1980, USA; bass), with Bob Money (b. 4 May 1929, USA) providing piano accompaniment. They relocated to Nashville the following year and had soon secured a slot on the *Grand Ole Opry*. By the end of 1954, the line-up had undergone a series of changes and now comprised Gordon Stoker (b. 3 August 1924, USA; first tenor, but formerly the piano player who had replaced Money in 1950), Neal Matthews (b. 26 October 1929, Nashville, Tennessee, USA, d. 21 April 2000, Nashville, Tennessee, USA; second tenor), Hoyt Hawkins (b. 31 March 1927, USA, d. 23 October 1982, USA; baritone) and Hugh Jarrett (b. 11 October 1929, USA; bass). The quartet first accompanied the youthful Presley in 1956 during a performance on the pivotal *The Louisiana Hayride*. Lead vocalist Gordon Stoker was subsequently featured on Presley's first recordings for RCA-Victor Records, notably 'Heartbreak Hotel', while the remaining trio joined him on the session that produced 'Hound Dog' and 'Don't Be Cruel'. The Jordanaires also supported Presley on the *Steve Allen* and *Milton Berle* television shows, where their clean-cut, conservative appearance contrasted with the impact of the singer's explosive persona.
The quartet, featuring new bass singer Ray Walker (b. 16 March 1934, USA) since 1958, continued to accompany Presley throughout the 50s and 60s, although they were noticeably absent from December 1968's 'comeback' NBC-TV spectacular where their role was taken by girl-group the Blossoms. The Jordanaires did not feature on Presley's fruitful sessions spawning 'Suspicious Minds' and 'In The Ghetto', nor the subsequent live appearances, but returned to the fold for recordings undertaken in Nashville during June and September 1970. These marked the end of the

Jordanaires' relationship with Presley, but the quartet remained an integral part of the city's music industry. They had already contributed to *The Guitar That Changed The World!*, the solo debut by long-time Presley guitarist Scotty Moore, and were heavily featured on sessions with Johnny Cash, Kris Kristofferson, Don McLean, Tracy Nelson and Billy Swan.

The Jordanaires have released several albums in their own right, most of which feature their favoured gospel material, but their career remains inextricably linked to that of Elvis Presley. Hawkins died in 1982 and was replaced by Duane West (b. 28 April 1941, USA), who had already filled in for the ailing baritone during the previous decade. In 1996, the quartet added harmonies to alternative US rock band Ween's album *12 Golden Country Greats*. Louis Nunley (b. 15 October 1931, USA), who had stood in for Walker on several occasions in the past four decades, replaced West as baritone in 1999, and Curtis Young (b. 9 January 1943, USA) was brought into the line-up the following April when Matthews passed away. The Jordanaires continue to tour the world knowing that the audience wants to hear that remarkable smooth harmonic sound, one that has barely changed over seven decades.

● ALBUMS: *Beautiful City* 10-inch album (RCA Victor 1953) ★★★, *Peace In The Valley* aka *Church In The Wildwood* (Decca/Vocalion 1957) ★★★★, *Heavenly Spirit!* (Capitol 1958) ★★★, *Gloryland* (Capitol 1959) ★★★★, *Of Rivers And Plains* (Sesac 1959) ★★★, with Tennessee Ernie Ford *A Friend We Have In Jesus* (Capitol 1960) ★★★, *Land Of Jordan* (Capitol 1960) ★★★★, *To God Be The Glory* (Capitol 1961) ★★★, *Spotlight On The Jordanaires* (Capitol 1962) ★★★, with Tennessee Ernie Ford *Great Gospel Songs* (Capitol 1964) ★★★★, *This Land* (Columbia 1964) ★★★, *The Big Country Hits* (Columbia 1965) ★★★, *Beyond This Day* (Worldwide 1966) ★★★, *Monster Makers* (Stop 1969) ★★★, *We'd Like To Teach The World To Sing* (Ember 1972) ★★★, with Tennessee Ernie Ford *Swing Wide Your Golden Gate* (Word 1978) ★★★★, *The Jordanaires Sing Elvis' Gospel Favourites* (Magnum Force 1986) ★★★, *The Jordanaires Sing Elvis' Favourite Spirituals* (Rockhouse 1990) ★★★, *40th Anniversary* (Worldwide 1990) ★★★, *With Friends, Denmark* (Worldwide 1991) ★★★.

● COMPILATIONS: *Will The Circle Be Unbroken* (CEMA 1985) ★★★, *Golden Gospel Greats* (Time/Life 1993) ★★★★.

● FILMS: *Jailhouse Rock* (1957), *G.I. Blues* (1960), *Blue Hawaii* (1961), *Girls Girls Girls* (1962), *Fun In Acapulco* (1963), *Elvis – The Movie* (1979).

JUSTIS, BILL

b. 14 October 1927, Birmingham, Alabama, USA, d. 15 July 1982, Nashville, Tennessee, USA. Justis was a saxophonist, arranger and producer who created 'Raunchy', one of the classic rock 'n' roll instrumentals (and, coincidentally, the first song that George Harrison learned to play). He grew up in Memphis playing jazz and dance band music before joining Sam Phillips' Sun Records in 1957 as musical director. Phillips liked a tune called

'Backwoods', composed by Justis and guitarist Sid Manker, but renamed it 'Raunchy'. It was issued as a single and Justis' own honking saxophone solo made it a million-seller. Cover versions by Billy Vaughn and Ernie Freeman also sold well, while there were later recordings by the Shadows and Duane Eddy. Later singles such as 'College Man' and 'Flea Circus' (written by Steve Cropper) were unsuccessful and Justis concentrated on his arrangements for Sun artists. His most important A&R work was with Charlie Rich, whom he discovered singing ballads. Urging him to listen to Jerry Lee Lewis, Justis produced Rich's biggest rock era hit, 'Lonely Weekends', in 1960 and also co-wrote the answer record 'After The Hop' for Bill Pinky And The Turks. Leaving Sun, Justis recorded rockabilly artist Ray Smith for Sam's brother Judd Phillips and briefly ran his own label (Play Me) before working again with Rich at RCA Records. By 1963 he was with Monument Records, another significant southern label, where he produced hits by vocal group the Dixiebelles. Kenny Rogers was among those for whom he later wrote arrangements. Justis occasionally made his own instrumental albums. He died in July 1982.

● ALBUMS: *Cloud Nine* (Philips 1959) ★★★, *Bill Justis Plays 12 Big Instrumental Hits (Alley Cat/Green Onions)* (Smash 1962) ★★★, *Bill Justis Plays 12 More Big Instrumental Hits (Telstar/The Lonely Bull)* (Smash 1962) ★★★, *Twelve Top Tunes* (Smash 1963) ★★★, *Twelve Other Instrumental Hits* (Smash 1964) ★★★, *Dixieland Folk Style* (Smash 1964) ★★★, *More Instrumental Hits* (Smash 1965) ★★★, *Raunchy* (Smash 1970) ★★★, *Enchanted Sea* (Harmony 1972) ★★.

KALIN TWINS

A classic example of the one-hit-wonder syndrome, the Kalin Twins have a more interesting history than many who fall into that bracket. Herbie and Harold 'Hal' Kalin, who are twins, were born on 16 February 1934 in Port Jervis, New York State, USA (many references give their birth date as 1939 but this was a Decca Records diversion, in an attempt to make them appear younger than they were). Their first public performances came at just five years of age at a local Christmas party, and the bug stayed with them. They graduated from Port Jervis High School in June 1952, but plans to break into the music industry were delayed when Hal was drafted into the Air Force as a radio operator. They kept in touch during this period, recording and writing songs on a tape recorder and sending them back and forth. After Hal's discharge in 1956 they set about resurrecting their double act. During these early struggles a demo single was pressed, combining the compositions 'Beggar Of Love' and 'The Spider And The Fly'. The result was an audition for Decca, and their first single proper, 'Jumpin' Jack'/'Walkin' To School'. While searching through piles of writers' demo tapes to find a suitable follow-up the twins discovered a song entitled 'When', written by Paul Evans and Jack Reardon. It became their second single. However, the record company chose to plug its flip side, 'Three O'Clock Thrill', instead. It was not until disc jockeys belatedly began to play 'When' that the single took off. It reached number 5 in the *Billboard* charts but topped the UK charts for no less than five weeks (selling over two million copies worldwide). Coast to coast touring of the USA ensued before a two week engagement at the Prince Of Wales Theatre in England (later dates introduced Cliff Richard as support artist on his first national tour). The subsequent 'Forget Me Not' and 'Oh My Goodness!' both made reasonable showings in the *Billboard* charts, but neither entered the UK equivalent. Two more minor US hits followed, 'Cool' and 'Sweet Sugarlips', but their remaining Decca sides failed to sell. With the arrival of the Beatles there seemed little place in the market for the Kalin Twins' innocent harmonies, although a further single, 'Sometimes It Comes, Sometimes It Goes' for Amy Records, did appear in 1966. Disillusioned with their diminishing rewards, the brothers mutually agreed to return to their day jobs, with each pursuing college degrees. They did not perform again until 1977 when a friend booked them to appear weekly at his new night spot, the River Boat Club. This led to further one-off engagements, in which they were sometimes joined by younger sibling Jack to appear as the Kalin Brothers. A brace of singles appeared for small labels: 'Silver Seagull' and 'American Eagle' both used the same backing track. A 16-track compilation was released by Bear Family Records in 1983. They disappeared again until old support hand Cliff Richard invited them to play at his 30th Anniversary shows in 1989.

● ALBUMS: *The Kalin Twins* (Decca 1958) ★★★, *When* (Vocalion 1966) ★★★.
● COMPILATIONS: *When* (Bear Family 1983) ★★★.

KARAS, ANTON

b. 1 July 1906, Vienna, Austria, d. 9 January 1985, Vienna, Austria. The man who arguably did more to popularize the zither than anyone before or after him, is best remembered as the sound behind the famous 'The Third Man Theme' (Harry Lime). Carol Reed's classic 1949 movie, *The Third Man*, utilized Karas' music throughout, and it was no surprise that film-goers made the song and its accompanying album a number 1 hit in 1951. Although Karas was a virtuoso, he remains one of the more famous one-hit-wonders of our time.

● ALBUMS: *Anton Karas* (Decca 1951) ★★★.
● COMPILATIONS: *World Of Anton Karas* (Decca 1971) ★★★, *Folk Songs Of Austria* (Decca 1974) ★★★.
● FILMS: *Come Dance With Me* (1950), *Die Sennerin Von St. Kathrein* aka *The Cowgirl Of Saint Catherine* (1955).

KAY, CONNIE

b. Conrad Henry Kirnon, 27 April 1927, Tuckahoe, New York, USA, d. 30 November 1994, New York City, New York, USA. A self-taught drummer, in his late teens Kay played with leading bop musicians, including Miles Davis. He gained big band experience with Cat Anderson in the late 40s. In the early 50s, he was playing R&B in studio backing bands – but was mostly playing in small modern jazz groups with Lester Young, Stan Getz, Davis, Charlie Parker and others. In 1955, he took over from Kenny Clarke in the Modern Jazz Quartet, remaining with the group for the next 20 years. During these years he also performed with other artists on record dates, among them Chet Baker, Paul Desmond, Cannonball Adderley and fellow MJQ member John Lewis. He played on rock singer Van Morrison's 1968 masterpiece *Astral Weeks*. After the MJQ disbanded in 1974 Kay worked with Lewis and other jazzmen, including Benny Goodman in whose band he played at the Carnegie Hall 40th Anniversary Concert. In the late 70s he was mostly working in New York playing jazz-club dates which included several years in the house band at Eddie Condon's. In 1981, he was again a member of the MJQ when the group re-formed. Despite his wide experience in several areas of jazz, Kay was understandably best known for his highly sophisticated work with the MJQ in which context he played with great subtlety and deftly understated swing.

● COMPILATIONS: *MJQ 40* 4-CD box set (Atlantic 1992) ★★★★.

KAYE, CAB

b. Augustus Kwamlah Nii-lante Quaye, 3 September 1921, London, England, d. 13 March 2000, Amsterdam, Netherlands. The son of an English music hall artist and Ga (Ghanaian) pianist Caleb Jonas Kwamlah Quaye (who, as 'Mope Desmond', played with Sidney Bechet in London in 1921), Kaye began his singing career with Billy Cotton. As 'Young Cab', he sang and played percussion with drummer Ivor Kirchin, then in 1940 joined Ken 'Snakehips' Johnson, with whom he broadcast on several occasions until the outbreak of World War II. Injuries sustained while serving in the Merchant Navy led to hospitalization in New York, where he later toured clubs in Harlem and Greenwich Village and sat in with Roy Eldridge and Sandy Williams. Returning to England, Kaye joined clarinettist Harry Parry and accordionist Tito Burns, subsequently appearing with the big bands of Vic Lewis and Ted Heath. In the early 50s, Kaye organized a band to play dances for newly-arrived Caribbean settlers, and with it made two extended trips to Europe. In Holland, he met Charlie Parker and renewed his acquaintance with Eldridge. Kaye was a popular figure on the burgeoning London bebop scene, where he worked with Dennis Rose, the music's local *éminence gris*. Kaye found his natural audiences in the 'afterhours' milieu epitomised by the Ringside Club, Paris, where he sang with Americans such as James Moody. In 1960, he worked with Humphrey Lyttelton, then appeared at Ronnie Scott's Club before moving to West Africa. In 1961, he occupied an entertainments post in Ghana during the Nkrumah regime, then lived briefly in Nigeria before returning to England in 1973. Settling finally in Amsterdam, he opened Cab's Piano Bar. He recorded with clarinettist Keith Bird (1949), arranger Ken Moule (1954), Lyttelton (1960), and several times under his own name (1951, 1952, 1984). Kaye, by his first marriage to singer Theresa Austin, was the father of singer/conga drummer Terri Naa-Koshie Quaye and guitarist Caleb Quaye (ex-Bluesology, Hookfoot and Elton John). He was also the father of singer Finlay Quaye.

● ALBUMS: *Cab Meets Humph* (1960) ★★★, *Solo Piano* (1984) ★★★.

KAYE, DANNY

b. David Daniel Kaminski, 18 January 1913, Brooklyn, New York City, New York, USA, d. 3 March 1987, Los Angeles, California, USA. Kaye was an extraordinary entertainer and an apparently inexhaustible comedian, mimic and dancer who seemed to be able to twist his face and body into any shape he wanted. As a singer, he specialized in very fast double talk and tongue twisters, but could present a gentle ballad equally well. He was also an indefatigable ambassador for numerous charities, especially the United Nations International Children's Emergency Fund (now UNICEF), for which he travelled and worked for many years. A son of Jewish immigrant parents from Russia, Kominsky originally wanted to join the medical profession, but dropped out of high school when he was 14 years old, and hitch-hiked to Florida with his friend, Louis Eilson, where they sang for money. On their return to New York, they formed an act called Red And Blackie, and performed at private functions. During the day, Kominski worked as a soda jerk, and then as an automobile appraiser with an insurance company. The latter job was terminated after he made a mistake which is said to have cost the company some $40,000. Kominski and Eilson then obtained summer work as 'toomlers', creators of tumult or all-round entertainers, in the Borscht Circuit summer hotels and camps in the Catskill Mountains. After five years, Kominski was earning $1,000 per season.

In 1933, he joined David Harvey and Kathleen Young on the vaudeville circuit in their dancing act, the Three Terpsichoreans, and was billed for the first time as Danny Kaye. An early onstage accident in which he split his trousers, elicited much laughter from the audience and was incorporated into the act. Signed by producer A.B. Marcus, the group toured the USA for five months in the revue *La Vie Paree*, before sailing for the Orient in February 1934. It is often said that this period of playing to non-English speaking audiences in Japan, China and Malaya, was when Kaye first developed his face-making and pantomiming techniques, and his 'gibberish' singing with the occasional recognized word. Back in the USA in 1936, Kaye worked with comedian Nick Long Jnr. and toured with Abe Lyman's Band, before being booked by impresario Henry Sherek, to appear in cabaret at London's Dorchester Hotel. The engagement, in 1938, was not a success. Kaye commented: 'I was too loud for the joint'. (Ten years later in London, it would be an entirely different story.) While appearing in Max Liebman's *Sunday Night Varieties* in New York, Kaye met pianist-songwriter Sylvia Fine (b. 29 August 1913, New York, USA, d. 28 October 1991, New York, USA), who had been raised in the same Brooklyn neighbourhood, and majored in music at Brooklyn College. She became a powerful influence throughout his career, as his director, coach and critic.

Working with Liebman's Saturday night revues at Camp Taimiment in the Pennsylvania Hills, during the summer of 1939, they started their collaboration, with Fine accompanying Kaye on the piano, and writing special material that included three of his most famous numbers, 'Stanislavsky', 'Pavlova' and the story of the unstable chapeau designer, 'Anatole Of Paris'. The best of the material was assembled in *The Straw Hat Revue* in which Kaye appeared with Imogene Coca, and which opened on Broadway in September 1939. The show also featured a young dancer named Jerome Robbins. After Fine and Kaye were married in January 1940, Kaye appeared in a smash hit engagement at La Martinique nightclub in New York, which led to a part in *Lady In The Dark*, starring Gertrude Lawrence. On the first night, Kaye stopped the show with the Kurt Weill and Ira Gershwin tongue-twister 'Tchaikovsky', in which he reeled off the names of 50 real, or imagined, Russian composers in 38 seconds. After playing a return engagement at La Martinique, and a five-week stint at the Paramount Theatre, Kaye appeared again on Broadway, starring in the Cole Porter musical *Let's Face It!*, which opened in October 1941. Porter allowed Sylvia Fine and Max Liebman to interpolate some special material for Kaye, which included a 'jabberwocky of song, dance, illustration and double-talk' called 'Melody In 4-F'. Kaye had to leave the show early in 1942, suffering from nervous exhaustion, but having recovered, he toured on behalf of the war effort and is said to have sold a million dollars' worth of government bonds in six months. Rejected by the US Army because of a back ailment, he entertained troops with his two-hour shows in many theatres of operations including the South Pacific.

In 1944, Kaye made his feature film debut in *Up In Arms*, the first in a series of five pictures for Sam Goldwyn at RKO. His performance as a hypochondriac elevator boy, involving yet another memorable Fine-Liebman piece, 'Manic Depressive Pictures Presents: Lobby Number', moved one critic to hail his introduction as 'the most exciting since Garbo's'. Goldwyn was criticized, however for having Kaye's red hair dyed blonde. His remaining films for the studio included *Wonder Man*, in which he gave his impression of a sneezing Russian baritone with 'Orchi Tchornya'. This was the first of several films in which he played more than one character; *The Kid From Brooklyn* (1946), which featured 'Pavlova', *The Secret Life Of Walter Mitty* (1947), one of his best-remembered roles (six of them), and *A Song Is Born* (1948), one of his least remembered. In 1945, Kaye appeared for a year on his own CBS radio show with Harry James and Eve Arden, and during the following year the Kayes' daughter, Dena, was born. When Kaye recorded the old standard 'Dinah', he changed some of the 'i' sounds to 'e', so that the song ran: 'Denah, is there anyone fener? In the State of Carolena . . .', etc. His other hit songs included 'Tubby The Tuba', 'Minnie The Moocher', 'Ballin' The Jack', 'Bloop Bleep', 'Civilization' and 'The Woody Woodpecker Song', both with the Andrews Sisters; 'C'est Si Bon'; and 'Blackstrap Molasses', recorded with Jimmy Durante, Jane Wyman and Groucho Marx. In 1948, Kaye returned to England to appear at the London Palladium.

His enormously successful record-breaking performances began an affectionate and enduring relationship with the British public. He is said to have received over 100,000 letters in a week. His shows were attended by the Royal Family; he met both Winston Churchill and George Bernard Shaw, and was cast in wax for London's Madame Tussaud's Museum. He returned in 1949 for the first of several Royal Command Performances, and also toured provincial music-halls throughout 1952. He endeared himself to the British by singing some of their parochial songs such as the novelty 'I've Got A Lovely Bunch Of Coconuts' and 'Maybe It's Because I'm A Londoner'. During one performance at the Palladium, when a member of the audience enquired after the state of Kaye's ribs following a car accident, he ordered the lights to be lowered while he displayed the actual X-ray plates! Kaye went to Canada in 1950 and became the first solo performer to star at the Canadian National Exhibition, where he sold out the 24,000-seater stadium for each of his 14 performances.

He returned to his multiple roles in films such as *The Inspector General* (1949) and *On The Riviera* (1951), before embarking on the somewhat controversial *Hans Christian Andersen* (1952). After 16 different screenplays over a period of 15 years, and protests in the Danish press about the choice of Kaye to play their national hero, the film, with a final screenplay by Moss Hart, became a huge money-spinner. Frank Loesser's score produced several appealing songs, including 'No Two People', 'Anywhere I Wander', 'Inchworm', 'Thumbelina', 'The Ugly Duckling' and 'Wonderful Copenhagen', the latter reaching the UK Top 5. Kaye's other films during the 50s and early 60s included *Knock On Wood* (1954), said to be his favourite, in which he sang two more Fine numbers, the title song, and 'All About Me', *White Christmas* (1954), co-starring with Bing Crosby, Rosemary Clooney and Vera-Ellen, *The Court Jester* (1956), *Me And The Colonel* (1958), *Merry Andrew* (1958), *The Five Pennies* (1959), a biopic of 20s cornet player Red Nichols (including a rousing version of 'When The Saints Go Marching In' with Louis Armstrong), *On The Double* (1961) and *The Man From The Diners' Club* (1963). After a break, he came back for *The Madwoman Of Challiot* (1969), and the following year, returned to Broadway in the role of Noah, in the Richard Rodgers and Martin Charnin musical *Two By Two*. Shortly after the show opened, Kaye tore a ligament in his leg during a performance, and subsequently appeared on crutches or in a wheelchair, in which he tried to run down the other actors, adapting the show to his injury, much to the distaste of producer and composer Richard Rodgers.

During the 70s and 80s, Kaye conducted classical orchestras and appeared on several television shows including *Peter Pan*, *Pinocchio* and *Danny Kaye's Look At The Metropolitan Opera*. He also played dramatic roles on television in *Skokie* and *The Twilight Zone*, but concentrated mainly on his charity work. He had started his association with UNICEF in the early 50s, and in 1955 made a 20-minute documentary, *Assignment Children*. He eventually became the organization's ambassador-at-large for 34 years, travelling worldwide on their behalf, and entering the *Guinness Book Of Records* by visiting 65 US and Canadian cities in five days, piloting himself in his own jet plane. During his career he received many awards including the French Légion d'Honneur, the Jean Hersholt Humanitarian Award, and the Knight's Cross of the First Class of the Order of Danneborg, given by the Danish Government. Other awards included a special Academy Award in 1954, along with Tonys for his stage performances, plus Emmys for his successful 60s television series. He died in 1987, following a heart attack.

● ALBUMS: *Danny Kaye* (Columbia 1949) ★★, *Danny Kaye Entertains* (Columbia 1949) ★★★, *Gilbert And Sullivan And Danny Kaye* (Decca 1949) ★★, *Danny At The Palace* (Decca 1953) ★★★, *Mommy, Gimme A Drink Of Water* (Capitol 1958) ★★★, *The Court Jester* (Decca 1959) ★★★, *For Children* (Decca 1959) ★★, and film soundtracks.
● COMPILATIONS: *The Best Of Danny Kaye* (Decca 1962) ★★★, *The Very Best Of Danny Kaye – 20 Golden Greats* (MCA 1987) ★★★.
● FURTHER READING: *The Danny Kaye Saga*, Kurt Singer. *Nobody's Fool – The Secret Lives Of Danny Kaye*, Martin Gottfried. *The Life Story Of Danny Kaye*, D. Richards. *Fine And Danny*, Sylvia Fine.
● FILMS: *Up In Arms* (1944), *Wonder Man* (1945), *The Kid From Brooklyn* (1946), *The Secret Life Of Walter Mitty* (1947), *A Song Is Born* (1948), *The Inspector General* (1949), *On The Riviera* (1951), *Hans Christian Anderson* (1952), *Knock On Wood* (1953), *White Christmas* (1954), *Assignment Children* (1954), *The Court Jester* (1956), *Me And The Colonel* (1957), *Merry Andrew* (1958), *The Five Pennies* (1959), *On The Double* (1962), *The Man From The Diner's Club* (1963), *The Madwoman Of Challiot* (1969).

KAYE, SAMMY

b. 13 March 1910, Lakewood, Ohio, USA. Kaye began playing in bands while still at college. In the early 30s he led a band at the Statler Hotel in Cleveland and also worked in Pittsburgh. In the later years of the decade he was hired by several top New York hotels, including the Astor and the New Yorker. An adept clarinettist, Kaye also made a name for himself as a bandleader without any help from the critics who unanimously derided his corny arrangements. 'Swing and Sway with Sammy Kaye' ran the billing, but swinging was something beyond the band. Instead, they offered hotel patrons and their later radio audience simple dance music, and becoming enormously successful. The band featured numerous singers, none of them especially memorable, although the musicians Kaye hired were always competent (George T. Simon referred to them as 'magnificently trained and exceedingly unoriginal'). Pianist Ralph Flanagan was a member of the band for a while. Kaye survived the collapse of many better dancebands and his career benefited from several popular sponsored radio shows. Replete with gimmicks, including the 'So You Want To Lead A Band' spot, the show transferred to television in the early 50s, in which members of the public were invited to conduct the band. In the late 50s and early 60s Kaye made a number of well-received if uncharacteristic records, including one of dixieland music. He composed a number of popular songs, including 'Hawaiian Sunset' and 'Until Tomorrow'. In 1986, the Sammy Kaye Orchestra, complete with its current vocalist Bob Casper, was reconstituted with a new leader, Roger Thorpe, although Kaye continued as a supervisor of the band's musical activities.
● ALBUMS: *One Night Stand At The Hollywood Palladium* (1946) ★★★.
● COMPILATIONS: *One Night Stand With Sammy Kaye* (1984) ★★★, *Sammy Kaye And His Orchestra Play 22 Original Big Band Recordings* (1984) ★★★, *Sammy Kaye And His Orchestra, Volume 2 (1944-46)* (1988) ★★★, *Sammy Kaye And His Orchestra, Volume 3 (1944-48)* (1988) ★★★, *Sammy Kaye* (1993) ★★★.

KAYE SISTERS

This UK pop trio comprised Sheila Jones (b. 21 October 1936, Lewisham, London, England), Shirley 'Shan' Palmer (b. 15 August 1938, Hull, England) and Carole Young (b. 12 April 1930, Oldham, Lancashire, England). Formed in 1954 by Carmen Kaye and originally known as the Three Kayes, their big break came when they appeared on television's *In Town Tonight* in 1956. They followed this with two weeks at the London Palladium and then their debut single, a cover version of the Charms' 'Ivory Tower' on HMV, made the UK Top 20. They joined the Philips label in 1957 and their first two Top 10 hits, which came in the company of Frankie Vaughan, were cover versions of Bob Jaxon's 'Gotta Have Something In The Bank Frank' (their royalties going to the Boys Clubs, an organization with which Vaughan has been involved for many years) and the Fleetwoods' 'Come Softly To Me'. Of the many singles they released, their only solo Top 10 hit was their version of Anita Bryant's US hit 'Paper Roses' in 1960. Jones retired in the late 60s and was replaced by Gilly. They continued to work, often supporting Max Bygraves. Young left in the late 70s to pursue an acting career, and appeared in the ITV series *Albion Market* and top soap opera *Coronation Street*. 'Shan and Gilly Kaye' appeared at the 1978 Royal Command Performance, and sang together in theatres and cabaret during the 80s. The original three members were reunited in 1992 and 1993, singing numbers made famous by the Andrews Sisters in UK tours of *In The Mood*, a tribute to Glenn Miller.
● ALBUMS: *Shan, Gill And Carole* (1973) ★★.

KAYE, STUBBY

b. 11 November 1918, New York City, New York, USA, d. 14 December 1997. An actor and singer who carved himself an instant slice of musical history by stopping the show as Nicely-Nicely Johnson in the original Broadway production of *Guys And Dolls* – and then doing it all over again three years later in London. Kaye had his first break when he came first on the Major Bowes Amateur Hour on US radio in 1939. During the late 30s and early 40s he toured as a comedian in vaudeville, and made his London debut in USO shows during World War II. His role in *Guys And Dolls* (1950) was not a leading one, but he was outstanding in numbers such as 'Fugue For Tinhorns', 'The Oldest Established', 'Guys And Dolls', and the rousing 'Sit Down You're Rockin' The Boat'. He had one more big success on Broadway in 1956 as Marryin' Sam in *Li'l Abner*, and subsequently toured in revivals, played nightclubs as a comedian, and appeared on the

television series *Love And Marriage* and *My Sister Eileen*. Unlike many stage performers he moved easily into films, and appeared in a variety features including *Guys And Dolls*, *Li'l Abner*, *40 Pounds Of Trouble*, *Cat Ballou* (with Nat 'King' Cole), *Sweet Charity*, *The Cockeyed Cowboys Of Calico County*, *The Dirtiest Girl I Ever Met*, *Six Pack Annie* and *Who Framed Roger Rabbit?*. The ample figure and sunny disposition he displayed as Nicely-Nicely in 1953 endeared him to London audiences and he made frequent appearances in the UK, including one in the musical *Man Of Magic* in 1956. Eventually he settled in Britain and married Angela Bracewell, who came to fame in the 50s in her role as the hostess of the audience participation game 'Beat The Clock' in the top-rated television variety show *Sunday Night At The London Palladium*. After appearing in the West End in 1983 in the short-lived musical *Dear Anyone*, Kaye returned to Broadway two years later and won the only good notices in the musical *Grind*, a complete disaster that was described by one critic as 'art slaughter'. He continued to work in the UK and in 1986 starred as Ring Lardner in the radio play *Some Like Them Cold*. His voice also featured in 1988's partly-animated *Who Framed Roger Rabbit?* Kaye died in December 1997.
● ALBUMS: *Music For Chubby Lovers* (1962) ★★★, and Original Cast and film soundtrack recordings.

KEEL, HOWARD
b. Harry Clifford Leek, 13 April 1917, Gillespie, Illinois, USA. A popular singer in films and on the musical stage, with a rich, powerful baritone voice and commanding presence. After starting his career as a singing waiter in Los Angeles, Keel became an 'in-house entertainer' for the huge Douglas aircraft manufacturing company. In 1945, he appeared in *Carousel* on the west coast and then travelled to the UK to appear in the London production of *Oklahoma!*. At this time he was known as Harold Keel, having reversed the spelling of his last name. He subsequently changed his first name and after making a non-singing appearance in the film *The Small Voice* (1948), he returned to the USA where he landed the role of Frank Butler in the film *Annie Get Your Gun* (1950). He continued to make films, mostly musicals, including *Show Boat* (1951), *Kiss Me Kate* and *Calamity Jane* (both 1953), *Rose Marie* and *Seven Brides For Seven Brothers* (both 1954) and *Kismet* (1955). By the 60s he was touring the USA in revivals of popular shows, and appearing in non-musical low-budget western movies. In 1981 his acting career received a boost when he started to appear in the long-running television soap opera *Dallas*. This revived interest in his singing, particularly in the UK, and in 1984 he recorded his first solo album. In 1993, with tongue firmly in his cheek, he announced his farewell tour of the UK, but subsequently returned 'by public demand' for encores.
● ALBUMS: *And I Love You So* (Warwick 1984) ★★★★, *Reminiscing* (Telstar 1985) ★★★, *Live In Concert* (BBC 1989) ★★★, *The Collection* (Castle 1989) ★★★, *The Great MGM Stars* (MGM 1991)

★★★, *An Enchanted Evening With Howard Keel* (Music Club 1991) ★★★, *Close To My Heart* (Premier 1991) ★★★, and the soundtrack albums from the above musicals.
● VIDEOS: *Close To My Heart* (PMI 1991).
● FURTHER READING: *A Bio-Bibliography*, Bruce R. Leiby.
● FILMS: *The Small Voice* (1948), *Pagan Love Song* (1950), *Annie Get Your Gun* (1950), *Texas Carnival* (1951), *Three Guys Named Mike* (1951), *Show Boat* (1951), *Lovely To Look At* (1952), *Desperate Search* (1952), *Callaway Went Thataway* (1952), *Calamity Jane* (1953), *Fast Company* (1953), *I Love Melvin* (1953), *Kiss Me Kate* (1953), *Ride Vaquero!* (1953), *Deep In My Heart* (1954), *Seven Brides For Seven Brothers* (1954), *Rose Marie* (1954), *Jupiter's Darling* (1955), *Kismet* (1955), *Floods Of Fear* (1958), *The Big Fisherman* (1959), *Armoured Command* (1961), *Day Of The Triffids* (1963), *The Man From Button Willow* voice only (1965), *Waco* (1966), *Red Tomahawk* (1967), *The War Wagon* (1967), *Arizona Bushwackers* (1968).

KELLER, JERRY
b. 20 June 1938, Fort Smith, Arkansas, USA. After moving to Tulsa in 1944 Keller formed the Lads Of Note Quartet in the 50s before joining the Tulsa Boy Singers. He won a talent contest organized by bandleader Horace Heidt which earned him the vocalist job with Jack Dalton's Orchestra. He then spent nine months as a disc jockey in Tulsa before moving to New York in 1956. He recorded a series of demos for record companies before fellow performer Pat Boone introduced him to Marty Mills who became his manager. Keller recorded the self-penned 'Here Comes Summer' for the Kapp record label, and it became a US summer hit in 1959. Ironically it only entered the UK charts in late August as the warmer months lapsed into autumn, but it still went to number 1. Follow-ups such as 'If I Had A Girl', and 'Now Now Now' failed to repeat the success. In 1960, he toured the UK replacing Eddie Cochran in a package tour engagement after Cochran had died in a car crash. Despite the lack of subsequent hits as a singer, his songs charted handsomely for artists such as Andy Williams and the Cyrkle. In 1977, he appeared in the film *You Light Up My Life* and the following year in *If I Ever See You Again*.
● ALBUMS: *Here Comes Jerry Keller* (Kapp 1960) ★★.

KELLY, GENE
b. Eugene Curran Kelly, 23 August 1912, Pittsburgh, Pennsylvania, USA, d. 2 February 1996, Los Angeles, California, USA. An actor, dancer, singer, choreographer, director, producer, and one of the most innovative and respected figures in the history of the screen musical. Kelly took dance lessons at the age of eight – albeit against his will – and excelled at sports while he was at high school. During the Depression he had a variety of jobs, including gymnastics instructor, and, with his brother Fred (b. 2 June 1916, d. 15 March 2000), performed a song-and-dance act at local nightclubs. In the early 30s, he spent a few

months at law school before opening the Gene Kelly Studios of the Dance, and discovering that he had a real aptitude for teaching, which would manifest itself throughout his career in some of the most creative choreography ever seen on the big screen. In 1937, Kelly moved to New York, and gained a small part as a dancer in the musical comedy *Leave It To Me!*, in which Mary Martin also made her Broadway debut. A larger role followed in the revue *One For The Money*, and he also played Harry, the 'good natured hoofer', in the Pulitzer prize-winning comedy, *The Time Of Your Life*.

In 1940, after working in summer stock, and serving as a dance director at Billy Rose's Diamond Horseshoe club, Kelly won the title role in the new Richard Rodgers and Lorenz Hart musical, *Pal Joey*. His portrayal of the devious, unscrupulous nightclub entertainer made him a star overnight in New York, but, after choreographing another Broadway hit show, *Best Foot Forward*, he moved to Hollywood in 1942, and made his screen debut with Judy Garland in *For Me And My Gal*. He appeared in two more musicals for MGM, *Du Barry Was A Lady* and *Thousands Cheer*, before the company loaned him to Columbia for *Cover Girl* (1944). Co-starring with Rita Hayworth and Phil Silvers, the film was a major landmark in Kelly's career, and an indication of the heights he would achieve during the next 10 years. It was memorable in many respects, particularly for Kelly's sensitive rendering of Jerome Kern and Ira Gershwin's 'Long Ago And Far Away', and the 'Alter Ego' dance, during which Kelly danced with his own reflection in a shop window. Back at MGM, he was called upon to play several dramatic roles as well as appearing in *Anchors Aweigh* (1945), for which he received an Oscar nomination for best actor. In the film, as a couple of sailors on leave, Kelly and Frank Sinatra were accompanied by Kathryn Grayson, a Sammy Cahn and Jule Styne score – and Jerry – an animated mouse, who joined Kelly in a live-action/cartoon sequence that is still regarded as a classic of its kind.

After spending two years in the real US Navy during World War II, supervising training films, Kelly resumed at MGM with *Ziegfeld Follies* (1946), in which he sang and danced with Fred Astaire for the first time on screen, in 'The Babbitt And The Bromide'. Two years later he was reunited with Judy Garland for *The Pirate*, a somewhat underrated film, with a score by Cole Porter that included 'Be A Clown'. He then choreographed the 'Slaughter On Tenth Avenue' sequence in the Rodgers and Hart biopic *Words And Music*, in which he danced with Vera-Ellen, before joining Sinatra and Jules Munshin, first for the lively *Take Me Out To The Ball Game* (1949), and again for *On The Town*, 'the most inventive and effervescent movie musical Hollywood had thus far produced'. Although criticized for its truncation of the original Broadway score, *On The Town*, with its integrated music and plot, and the athletic dance sequences on the streets of New York, was acclaimed from all sides. After his triumph in *On*

The Town, Kelly went on to *Summer Stock*, with Judy Garland again, before turning to what many consider to be the jewel in MGM's musical crown – *An American In Paris* (1951). Directed by Vincente Minnelli, and set in an idealized version of Paris, Kelly and his partner, Leslie Caron, danced exquisitely to a Gershwin brothers score that included 'I Got Rhythm', 'Our Love Is Here To Stay', ''S Wonderful' and 'I'll Build A Stairway To Paradise'. The film ended with a 17-minute ballet sequence, a 'summation of Gene Kelly's work as a film dancer and choreographer, allowing him his full range of style – classical ballet, modern ballet, Cohanesque hoofing, tapping, jitterbugging, and sheer athletic expressionism'. It won eight Academy Awards, including one for best picture. Kelly received a special Oscar 'in appreciation of his versatility as an actor, singer, director, and dancer, and specifically for his brilliant achievements in the art of choreography on film'. If *An American In Paris* was MGM's jewel, then *Singin' In The Rain* (1952), was probably its financial plum – arguably the most popular Hollywood musical of them all. Produced by Arthur Freed, who also wrote the songs with Nacio Herb Brown, the film's witty screenplay, by Betty Comden and Adolph Green, dealt with the Hollywood silent movie industry trying to come to terms with talking pictures. Debbie Reynolds and Donald O'Connor joined Kelly in the joyous spoof, and sang and danced to a score that included 'You Were Meant For Me', 'Make 'Em Laugh', 'Good Mornin'' and 'Moses Supposes'. The scene in which Kelly sings the title song, while getting completely drenched, is probably the most requested film clip in the history of the musical cinema.

For *Deep In My Heart* (1955), the Sigmund Romberg biopic, Kelly went back to his roots and danced with his younger brother, Fred, in one of the film's high spots, 'I Love To Go Swimmin' With Wimmen'. Kelly's final major musical projects for MGM were *Brigadoon* (1954) and *It's Always Fair Weather* (1955). In the former, 'the magical story of a Scottish village long lost to history and coming to life once every hundred years for a single day', Kelly co-starred with Cyd Charisse and Van Johnson in a production that was criticized for being shot in Cinemascope, and in the studio, rather than on location. For the latter film in 1955, Kelly co-starred with Dan Dailey and Michael Kidd for what was essentially a satirical swipe at the cynical commercialism of the US television industry – with music.

His next project, *Invitation To The Dance* (1956), with script, choreography, and direction by Kelly, consisted of three unrelated episodes, all entirely danced, with Kelly accompanied by a classically trained troupe. A commercial failure in the USA, it was acclaimed in some parts of Europe, and awarded the grand prize at the West Berlin film festival in 1958. Following its success there, Kelly choreographed a new ballet for the Paris Opera's resident company, and was made a Chevalier of the Legion of Honor by the French government. *Les Girls* (1957) was Kelly's final MGM musical, and Cole Porter's last Hollywood score – the golden era of screen musicals was over. Subsequently, Kelly played several straight roles in films such as *Marjorie Morningstar* and *Inherit The Wind*, but spent much of his time as a director on projects such as Richard Rodgers and Oscar Hammerstein's Broadway musical *Flower Drum Song*, and 20th Century Fox's $24,000,000 extravaganza, *Hello, Dolly!* (1969), which starred Barbra Streisand, Walter Matthau and a young Michael Crawford. In 1974, he was back on the screen in *That's Entertainment!*, 'a nostalgia bash, featuring scenes from nearly 100 MGM musicals'. It became a surprise hit, and two years later, Kelly and Fred Astaire hosted the inevitable sequel, *That's Entertainment, Part 2*.

After viewing all that vintage footage, it would be interesting to have known Kelly's real opinions on a more modern musical film, such as *Xanadu* (1980), in which he appeared with Olivia Newton-John. By then, together with director Stanley Donen, the complete Arthur Freed Unit, and the rest of the talented personnel who produced most of his musicals at MGM, Kelly, with his athletic performance, choreography and direction, had completed a body of work that was only equalled by the other master of dance on film, Fred Astaire – but in a very different style. Whereas Astaire purveyed the image of a smooth man about town, with top hat, white tie and tails, Kelly preferred to appear casual in sports shirt, slacks and white socks. As he said himself: 'Astaire represents the aristocracy when he dances – I represent the proletariat!'.

● COMPILATIONS: *Nursery Songs* 10-inch album (Columbia 1949) ★★★, *Song And Dance Man* (Columbia 1954) ★★★★, *Singin' In The Rain Again* (Decca 1978) ★★, *Best Of Gene Kelly: From MGM Films* (MCA 1988) ★★★, *Great MGM Stars* (MGM 1991) ★★★, *Gotta Dance! The Best Of Gene Kelly* (Sony 1993) ★★★★, and film soundtracks.
● FURTHER READING: *Gene Kelly: A Biography*, Clive Hirschhorn. *The Films Of Gene Kelly*, Tony Thomas. *Gene Kelly*, J. Basinger. *Gene Kelly: A Celebration*, Sheridan Morley and Ruth Leon.
● FILMS: *For Me And My Gal* (1942), *Pilot No. 5* (1943), *Du Barry Was A Lady* (1943), *Thousands Cheer* (1943), *The Cross Of Lorraine* (1943), *Cover Girl* (1944), *Christmas Holiday* (1944), *Anchors Aweigh* (1945), *Ziegfeld Follies* (1946), *Living In A Big Way* (1947), *The Pirate* (1948), *The Three Musketeers* (1948), *Words And Music* (1948), *Take Me Out To The Ball Game* (1949), *On The Town* (1949), *The Black Hand* (1950), *Summer Stock* (1950), *An American In Paris* (1951), *It's A Big Country* (1952), *Singin' In The Rain* (1952), *The Devil Makes Three* (1952), *Brigadoon* (1954), *Crest Of The Wave* (1954), *Deep In My Heart* (1955), *It's Always Fair Weather* (1955), *Invitation To The Dance* (1956), *The Happy Road* (1957), *Les Girls* (1957), *Marjorie Morningstar* (1958), *The Tunnel Of Love* as director (1958), *Inherit The Wind* (1960), *Gigot* as director (1962), *Let's Make Love* (1960), *What A Way To Go* (1964), *The Young Girls Of Rochefort* (1968) *A Guide For The Married Man* as director (1967), *Hello, Dolly!* as director (1969), *The Cheyenne Social Club* as director and producer (1970), *40 Carats* (1973), *That's Entertainment!* as narrator (1974), *That's Entertainment, Part 2* as narrator (1976), *Viva Knievel!* (1977), *Xanadu* (1980), *Reporters* (1981), *That's Dancing!* (1985).

KENNEDY, JIMMY

b. 20 July 1902, Omagh, Co. Tyrone, Northern Ireland, d. 6 April 1984, Cheltenham, England. One of Britain's leading songwriters from the mid-30s through to the 50s, Kennedy's collaboration with Michael Carr, in particular, produced some of the most popular songs of the day. After graduating from Trinity College, Dublin, Kennedy spent brief periods as a teacher and a civil servant before deciding to concentrate on songwriting. His first big break came when he signed a contract with music publisher Bert Feldman, which led to him writing lyrics for songs such as 'Oh, Donna Clara' (music by J. Petersburski, 1930), 'The Teddy Bear's Picnic' (a new lyric to John W. Bratton's 1907 melody), 'My Song Goes Round The World' (Hans May, Ernst Neubach), 'Beside My Caravan' (Karel Vacek), 'Café In Vienna' (Vacek), 'Little Valley In The Mountains' (J. Dvoracek, K. Zeleny), 'Play To Me, Gypsy' (Vacek) and 'Isle Of Capri' (Will Grosz). The latter number has proved to be an enduring all-time standard: Gracie Fields' version, in particular, is fondly remembered. In 1934 Kennedy began his five-year association with Michael Carr, which resulted in several mostly memorable compositions, including 'Ole Faithful', 'Misty Islands Of The Highlands', 'The General's Fast Asleep', 'Did Your Mother Come From Ireland?', 'The Sunset Trail', 'Why Did She Fall For The Leader Of The Band?', 'Waltz Of The Gypsies', 'Cinderella, Stay In My Arms', 'A Handsome Territorial', 'Two Bouquets', and probably their best-known song, 'South Of The Border'. Kennedy and Carr also contributed to films, and London Palladium shows such as *O-Kay For Sound* ('There's A New World'), *The Little Dog Laughed* ('There's Danger In The Waltz'), and the Flanagan And Allen revue *London Rhapsody* ('Home Town' and 'Sing A Song Of London'). Towards the end of their partnership, they wrote one of the biggest morale-boosting hits of World War II, 'We're Gonna Hang Out The Washing On The Siegfried Line'. During this comparatively brief but highly productive period, Kennedy continued to collaborate with other composers on songs such as 'Red Sails In The Sunset' (Hugh Williams, 1935), 'At The Café Continental', 'Bird On The Wing' and 'Ten Pretty Girls' (all three: Will Grosz), 'Serenade In The Night' (C.A. Bixio, B. Cherubini), 'Harbour Lights' (Hugh Williams), 'The Chestnut Tree' (Tommie Connor, Hamilton Kennedy), 'My Prayer' (Georges Boulanger) and 'Oh Nicholas, Don't Be So Ridiculous' (Harry Castling, 1939). He also wrote both words and music for 'Roll Along Covered Wagon' (1935), 'The Coronation Waltz', 'There's A Boy Coming Home On Leave', 'Saint Mary's In The Twilight', 'All Our Tomorrows', and 'An Hour Never Passes' (1944), among many others, and his lyrical addition to a traditional tune resulted in 'The Cokey Cokey' (often called

'The Hokey Cokey') becoming one of the most popular party dances of all time. After serving in the army during the war, in the late 40s and early 50s Kennedy's prolific and varied output continued with songs such as 'An Apple Blossom Wedding' (Nat Simon), 'Down The Old Spanish Trail' (Kenneth Leslie Smith), 'And Mimi' (Simon), 'Pigalle' (George Ulmer, George Koger), 'French Can-Can Polka' (Jacques Offenbach), 'Down The Trail Of Aching Hearts' (Simon), 'April In Portugal (Coimbra)' (Raul Ferrao, Jose Galhardo) and 'Istanbul (Not Constantinople)' (Simon, 1953). Later, although he was still able to come up with occasional hits such as 'Love Is Like A Violin (Mon Coeur Est Un Violin)' (Miarka Laparcerie) and 'Romeo' (Robert Stolz) for Ken Dodd and Petula Clark, respectively, like so many others, Kennedy's style of songs were swamped by the rock 'n' roll revolution. In the early 60s he retreated to Switzerland, but eventually moved back home to Ireland where he devoted much of his time to writing music for dramatic plays. During his long and distinguished career, his honours included two ASCAP Awards, and Ivor Novello Awards – for Outstanding Services To British Music (1971) and Life Achievement (1980). He was also awarded an honorary doctorate by the University of Ulster (1978), and an OBE (1983). In 1984, the year of his death, the British Academy of Songwriters, Composers and Authors (BASCA) inaugurated a special annual Jimmy Kennedy Award. Further recognition came in 1997, when Kennedy was inducted into the American Songwriters' Hall Of Fame.

Like his sometime partner, Michael Carr (b. 1904, Leeds, England, d. 16 September 1968) was one of Tin Pan Alley's great characters. He spent much of his early life in Dublin before moving to America where he worked at a variety of jobs. Soon after he returned to the UK he was introduced to Jimmy Kennedy and their historic partnership began. Over the years, Carr also collaborated with others on songs such as 'Fonso My Hot Spanish (K)Night' (Leo Tower, Will Haines, 1930), 'Getting Around And About' and 'Old Timer' (both Lewis Ilda), 'The Girl With The Dreamy Eyes' (Eddie Pola), 'The Wheel Of The Wagon Is Broken' (Elton Box, Desmond Cox), 'The Little Boy That Santa Claus Forgot' (Tommie Connor, Jimmy Leach), 'Merrily We Roll Along' (Raymond Wallace), 'A Pair Of Silver Wings' (Eric Maschwitz), 'The First Lullaby' (Jack Popplewell), 'I Love To Sing' (Tommie Connor, Paul Misraki) and 'Lonely Ballerina' (Paul Lambrecht). Early in his career, he wrote, unaided, 'Dinner For One Please, James', 'Cowboy' and 'On The Outside Looking In', and in the early 60s provided the Shadows with the highly successful 'Man Of Mystery' and 'Kon-Tiki'. Just before he died in 1968, Carr wrote Des O'Connor's Top 5 hit '1-2-3 O'Leary' with Barry Mason, and Jackie Lee's first chart entry, 'White Horses', with Ben Nisbet.

KENTON, STAN

b. Stanley Newcombe Kenton, 15 December 1911, Wichita, Kansas, USA, d. 25 August 1979, Los Angeles, California, USA. After playing piano in various dance bands, including those of Everett Hoagland and Vido Musso, mostly on the west coast, Kenton decided to form his own band in 1941. Although geared partially to the commercial needs of the dancehall circuit of the time, Kenton's band, which he termed the 'Artistry In Rhythm' orchestra, also featured powerful brass section work and imaginative saxophone voicings, unlike those of his more orthodox competitors. The band developed a substantial following among the younger elements of the audience who liked their music brash and loud. During the remainder of the 40s Kenton's popularity increased dramatically, seemingly immune to the declining fortunes that affected other bands. A succession of exciting young jazz musicians came into the band, among them Buddy Childers, Art Pepper, Kai Winding, Shelly Manne, Bob Cooper and Laurindo Almeida, playing arrangements by Kenton, Gene Roland and Pete Rugolo. His singers included Anita O'Day, June Christy and Chris Connor. In the 50s, his enthusiasm undimmed, Kenton introduced a 43-piece band, his 'Innovations In Modern Music' orchestra, again featuring Pepper and Manne as well as newcomers such as Maynard Ferguson and Bud Shank. Complex, quasi-classical arrangements by Bob Graettinger and others proved less appealing, but a 1953 tour of Europe ensured Kenton's international reputation.

Reduced to a more manageable 19-piece, his New Concepts In Artistry In Rhythm band continued playing concerts and recording, using arrangements by Roland, Gerry Mulligan and Johnny Richards. Always eager to try new ideas, and to clearly label them, in the 60s Kenton introduced his 'New Era In Modern Music' orchestra, a 23-piece band using mellophoniums, and the 'Neophonic' orchestra, five pieces larger and tempting fate with neo-classical music. In the 70s he embraced rock rhythms and looked as if he might go on forever. By 1977, however, his health had begun to deteriorate and although he returned from hospitalization to lead his band until August 1978, his bandleading days were almost over. He died in August 1979.

More than most bandleaders, Kenton polarized jazz fans, inspiring either love or hatred and only rarely meeting with indifference. Almost half a century after the event it is hard to understand what all the fuss was about. Certainly the band did not swing with the grace of, for example, the Jimmie Lunceford band, but it was equally wrong to declare, as many critics did, that Kenton never swung at all. Although some of the arrangements were too monolithic for effective jazz performances, the abilities of his key soloists were seldom buried for long. Kenton's band was important in bringing together many excellent musicians and for allowing arrangers free rein to experiment in big band concepts, a practice that few other leaders of the period would tolerate.

● ALBUMS: *Stan Kenton And His Orchestra With June Christy* (1949) ★★★★, *Encores* 10-inch album (Capitol 1950) ★★★, *Innovations In Modern Music*

10-inch album (Capitol 1950) ★★★★, *Milestones* 10-inch album (Capitol 1950) ★★★, *Artistry In Rhythm* 10-inch album (Capitol 1950) ★★★★, *A Presentation Of Progressive Jazz* 10-inch album (Capitol 1950) ★★★, *One Night Stand With Stan Kenton* i (Capitol 1950) ★★★, *Stan Kenton Presents* 10-inch album (Capitol 1950) ★★★★, *Nineteen Fifty-One* (Capitol 1951) ★★★, *One Night Stand With Stan Kenton* ii (Capitol 1951) ★★★, *Carnegie Hall – October 1951* (Capitol 1951) ★★★★, *Artistry In Tango* (Capitol 1952) ★★★, *Concert In Miniature* (Capitol 1952) ★★★, *Classics* 10-inch album (Capitol 1952) ★★★, *City Of Glass* 10-inch album (Capitol 1952) ★★★★, *Concert In Miniature No 9 And 10* (Capitol 1952) ★★★, *Concert In Miniature No 11 And 12* (Capitol 1952) ★★★, *Concert In Miniature No 13 And 14* (Capitol 1952) ★★★, *New Concepts Of Artistry In Rhythm* (Capitol 1953) ★★★★, *Concert Encores* (Capitol 1953) ★★★, *Prologue This Is An Orchestra* 10-inch album (Capitol 1953) ★★★, *Popular Favorites* 10-inch album (Capitol 1953) ★★★, *Sketches On Standards* 10-inch album (Capitol 1953) ★★★, *This Modern World* 10-inch album (Capitol 1953) ★★★, *Stan Kenton Radio Transcriptions* 10-inch album (MacGregor 1953) ★★★, *Portraits Of Standards* 10-inch album (Capitol 1953) ★★★, *Artistry In Kenton* (Capitol 1954) ★★★, *Kenton Showcase – The Music Of Bill Russo* 10-inch album (Capitol 1954) ★★★, *Kenton Showcase – The Music Of Bill Holman* 10-inch album (Capitol 1954) ★★★, *Stan Kenton Festival* (Capitol 1954) ★★★, with June Christy *Duet* (Capitol 1955) ★★★★, *Contemporary Concepts* (Capitol 1955) ★★★, *Stan Kenton In Hi-Fi* (Capitol 1956) ★★★★, *Kenton In Concert* (Capitol 1956) ★★★, *Kenton In Stereo* (Capitol 1956) ★★★, *Cuban Fire!* (Capitol 1956) ★★★★, *Kenton '56* (Capitol 1956) ★★★, *Rendezvous With Kenton/At The Rendezvous Volume 1* (Capitol 1957) ★★★, *Kenton With Voices* (Capitol 1957) ★★★, *Back To Balboa* (Capitol 1958) ★★★, *Lush Interlude* (Capitol 1958) ★★★, *The Stage Door Swings* (Capitol 1958) ★★★, *On The Road* (Capitol 1958) ★★★, *The Kenton Touch* (Capitol 1958) ★★★, *The Ballad Style Of Stan Kenton* (Capitol 1958) ★★★★, *Stan Kenton At The Tropicana* (Capitol 1959) ★★★, *In New Jersey* (Capitol 1959) ★★★, *At Ukiah* (Capitol 1959) ★★★, *Viva Kenton* (Capitol 1959) ★★★, with June Christy *The Road Show, Volumes 1 & 2* (Capitol 1960) ★★★, with Ann Richards *Two Much* (Capitol 1960) ★★★, with June Christy *Together Again* (Capitol 1960) ★★★, *Standards In Silhouette* (Capitol 1960) ★★★, *Stan Kenton's Christmas* (Capitol 1961) ★★, *The Romantic Approach* (Capitol 1961) ★★★★, *Stan Kenton's West Side Story* (Capitol 1961) ★★★★, *Mellophonium Magic* (Capitol 1961) ★★★, *Sophisticated Approach* (Capitol 1961) ★★★, *Adventures In Standards* (Capitol 1961) ★★★, *Adventures In Blues* (Capitol 1961) ★★★, *Adventures In Jazz* (Capitol 1961) ★★★, *Adventures In Time* (Capitol 1962) ★★★, *Stan Kenton's Mellophonium Band* (Capitol 1962) ★★★, *Artistry In Bossa Nova* (Capitol 1963) ★★★, *Artistry In Voices And Brass* (Capitol 1963) ★★★, *Wagner* (Capitol 1964) ★★★, *Stan Kenton Conducts The Los Angeles Neophonic Orchestra* (Capitol 1965)

★★★, *Stan Kenton Conducts The Jazz Compositions Of Dee Barton* (Capitol 1968) ★★★, *Live At Redlands University* (Creative World 1970) ★★, *Live At Brigham Young University* (Creative World 1971) ★★, *Live At Butler University* (Creative World 1972) ★★, *National Anthems Of The World* (Creative World 1972) ★★, *Stan Kenton Today* (London Philharmonic 1972) ★★★, *Birthday In Britain* (Creative World 1973) ★★, *7.5 On The Richter Scale* (Creative World 1973) ★★, *Solo: Stan Kenton Without His Orchestra* (Creative World 1973) ★★, *Stan Kenton Plays Chicago* (Creative World 1974) ★★, *Fire, Fury And Fun* (Creative World 1974) ★★, *One Night Stand With Stan Kenton At The Hollywood Palladium* 1945 recordings (Joyce *c.*1975) ★★★, *One Night Stand With Nat 'King' Cole And Stan Kenton* 1947 recording (Joyce *c.*1975) ★★★, *One Night Stand At The Commodore* 1947 recording (Joyce *c.*1975) ★★★, *Kenton 1976* (Creative World 1976) ★★, *Journey Into Capricorn* (Creative World 1976) ★★, *Live At Sunset Ridge Country Club Chicago* (Magic 1977) ★★, *Live In Cologne 1976 Vols. 1 &2* (Magic 1977) ★★, *Street Of Dreams* (Creative World 1977) ★★, *Tunes And Topics* 1970 live recording (Tantara 1998) ★★★, *Intermission Riff* 1955-56 recording (Giants Of Jazz 1999) ★★★, *Live From Las Vegas Tropicana 60s* recordings (Capitol 1999) ★★★.

● COMPILATIONS: *Progressive Jazz* (1946) ★★★, *The Kenton Era (1940-53)* (Capitol 1955) ★★★★, *Stan Kenton's Greatest Hits* (Capitol 1965) ★★★★, *Stan Kenton's Greatest Hits (1943-51)* (Capitol 1983) ★★★★, *The Christy Years (1945-47)* (Creative World 1985) ★★★★, *The Fabulous Alumni Of Stan Kenton (1945-56)* (Creative World 1985) ★★★★, *Collection: 20 Golden Greats* (Deja Vu 1986) ★★★★, *Retrospective 1943-1968* 4-CD box set (Capitol 1992) ★★★★, *Best Of* (Capitol 1995) ★★★★, *The Complete Capitol Studio Recordings Of Stan Kenton 1943-47* 7-CD/10-LP box set (Mosaic 1996) ★★★★, *Broadcast Transcriptions (1941-1945)* (Music And Arts 1996) ★★★, *Live At Newport 1959-1971* (Jasmine 1999) ★★★, *The 1950s Birdland Broadcasts* (Jazz Band 1999) ★★★, *1947* (Classics 1999) ★★★, *Revelations* 4-CD box set (Tantara 2000) ★★★, *Transcription Performances Volume 2* 1945-48 recordings (Hep Jazz 2000) ★★★, *The Stan Kenton Story* 1936-47 recordings, 4-CD box set (Properbox 2000) ★★★.

● VIDEOS: *Stan Kenton And Frank Rosolino* (Kay Jazz 1988), *Stan Kenton And His Orchestra* (Kay Jazz 1988).

● FURTHER READING: *Straight Ahead: The Story Of Stan Kenton*, Carol Easton. *Stan Kenton: Artistry In Rhythm*, William F. Lee. *Stan Kenton: The Man And His Music*, Lillian Arganian.

KING AND I, THE

Yul Brynner became a legend in the 1951 Broadway show, and no other actor could even have been considered for the leading role in this 1956 screen version. Brynner's stage partner, Gertrude Lawrence, died during the Broadway run, and his co-star for this film, the British actress Deborah Kerr, proved to be an ideal replacement. She plays Anna, the widowed English governess, who is engaged by King Mongkut of Siam (Brynner) to educate his many children. In spite of their fundamental differences and principles, they fall in love, but are parted by the King's death. The film's other love story is that between one of the King's daughter's, Tuptim (Rita Moreno) and Lun Tha (Carlos Rivas), but that romance, too, is destined to end unhappily. Other parts were taken by Martin Balsam, Rex Thompson, Terry Saunders, Alan Mowbray, Patrick Adiarte, Yuriko, Michiko, Geoffrey Toone, and Charles Irwin. The highly emotional story was complemented by Richard Rodgers and Oscar Hammerstein II's magnificent score, which included 'I Whistle A Happy Tune' (Kerr), 'March Of The Siamese Children' (instrumental), 'Hello, Young Lovers' (Kerr), 'A Puzzlement' (Brynner), 'Getting To Know You' (Kerr with the children), 'We Kiss In A Shadow' (Moreno-Rivas), 'Something Wonderful' (Saunders), 'The Small House Of Uncle Thomas' (ballet) and 'Song Of The King' (Brynner). Perhaps the film's most memorable moment comes when Anna tries to teach the King how to dance, and they – awkwardly at first – and then exuberantly, whirl around the floor to the sublime 'Shall We Dance?'. Deborah Kerr's singing voice was dubbed by Marni Nixon. Ernest Lehman's screenplay was based on Hammerstein's original libretto and Margaret Landon's novel *Anna And The King Of Siam*. Jerome Robbins was the choreographer and the film, which was directed by Walter Lang, was superbly photographed by Leon Shamroy in DeLuxe Color and CinemaScope. It won Oscars for best actor (Brynner), its sumptuous costumes (Irene Shariff), sound recording, art-set decoration and scoring of a musical picture (Alfred Newman and Ken Darby), and went on to gross well over $8 million in the USA, ranking high in the Top 10 musical films of the 50s. In 1999 an animated movie version of *The King And I* was released. Voicing the characters were Christiane Noll/Miranda Richardson (Anna), Martin Vidnovic (the King), Ian Richardson (the Kralahome), Darrell Hammond (Master Little), Allen D. Hong/David Burnham (Prince Chululongkorn), Armi Arabe/Tracy Venner Warren (Tuptim), Adam Wylie (Louis Leonowens), and Sean Smith (Sir Edward Ramsay). This is the first animated original Broadway musical ever.

KING BROTHERS

Brothers Michael (b. 25 April 1935, Barking, Essex, England; guitar), Tony (b. 31 January 1937, Barking, Essex, England; bass and bass guitar) and Denis King (b. 25 July 1939, Hornchurch, Essex, England; piano, guitar) were one of Britain's top groups in the 50s. The trio, fronted by Denis, made their television debut in 1953 on *Shop Window* and were often seen on mid-50s children's programmes. In 1954, they appeared at London's famous Astor and Embassy clubs, played a season at the Windmill Theatre and performed at the Palladium in 1955. After recording unsuccessfully for World Record Club and Conquest, the old-styled young trio, who were mistakenly tagged

'Britain's Rock 'n' Roll Kids', joined Parlophone Records. In 1957, they charted with cover versions of 'A White Sports Coat (And A Pink Carnation)', 'In The Middle Of An Island' and even the Everly Brothers' 'Wake Up Little Susie' and were voted Britain's Top Vocal Group by *New Musical Express* readers. They had four more Top 40 hits in 1960-61, again with Norman Newell-produced cover versions of songs popular in the USA. The biggest of these was 'Standing On The Corner', from the musical *The Most Happy Fella*, which reached number 4 in 1960. Their final chart hit came a year later with 'Seventy-Six Trombones'. In those days, when UK vocal groups were rare, these successes helped them to regain the *NME* Vocal Group award in 1960 and collect *Melody Maker*'s similar award a year later. When they decided to record their own compositions, the hits stopped for the trio, who disliked being associated with rock 'n' roll. They were the last of the old-school vocal groups to be successful in the UK, and were perhaps fortunate to be on the scene when Britain badly needed a vocal group to call its own. They recorded for Pye in 1963, Oriole in 1964 and CBS and Page One in 1966. Denis King has since become one of the best-known television music writers in the UK, composing the themes for such successful television series as *Bouquet Of Barbed Wire*, *The Fenn St. Gang*, *Within These Walls* and *Black Beauty*, among many others.

● ALBUMS: with Geoff Love *Three Kings And An Ace* (Decca 1959) ★★★, *Kings Of Song* (1962) ★★★.

KING CREOLE

This 1958 film is, for many, the best of Elvis Presley's Hollywood career. Based on the Harold Robbins novel *A Stone For Danny Fisher*, it afforded him a first-rate plot – that of a singer performing in a New Orleans club owned by mobsters – providing Presley with a dramatic role equal to the memorable soundtrack. 'Trouble', 'Crawfish' and the title track itself rank among the finest tracks he recorded and the content ranged from compulsive rock 'n' roll numbers to melodic ballads. Presley's singing is self-assured yet unmannered and only his induction into the US Army thwarted the direction both his acting and music were taking.

KING, DAVE

b. Twickenham, Middlesex, England. A very popular comedian and singer in the UK during the 50s and 60s, at the age of 15 King was a stooge and washboard player in the bill-topping variety act, Morton Fraser's Harmonica Gang. He joined the Royal Air Force in 1950 and returned to the Gang afterwards. His big solo break came with appearances on UK television's *Showcase* and *Television Music Hall*. These resulted in West End appearances and his own television variety series. King first recorded in 1955 with producer George Martin for Parlophone and his debut hit came in 1956, with a cover of 'Memories Are Made Of This' on Decca, which gave the Dean Martin original strong competition in the UK charts. He also enjoyed success with 'You Can't Be True To Two' in 1956 and 'The Story Of My Life', which was one of three versions of the Burt Bacharach song to make the UK Top 20 in 1958. King was one of the rare UK comedians to make any impact in the USA having his own summer television series there in the late 50s. He joined Pye in 1959 but no more hits came the way of this easy-going, relaxed ballad singer whose television appearances also eventually dried up. In later years King became a respected character actor in UK films and television.

● ALBUMS: *Memories Are Made Of This* (Ace Of Hearts 1962) ★★★.

KING, SID

b. Sidney Erwin, 1936, Denton, Texas, USA. King was one of the foremost rockabilly singers of the 50s. As a teenager he formed the Western Melodymakers, which became Sid King And The Five Strings when he signed to Starday in 1954. Among the group's earliest recordings was 'Who Put The Turtle In Myrtle's Girdle', but after joining Columbia, King concentrated on more hard-rocking material. Recording in Dallas, he released a version of Roy Orbison's 'Ooby Dooby' in 1955 but though King's record was issued first, Orbison himself had the hit. He also recorded 'Sag, Drag And Fall' as well as versions of R&B hits including 'Drinking Wine, Spo-Dee-O-Dee'.

● COMPILATIONS: *Gonna Shake This Shack Tonight* (Bear Family 1984) ★★★, *Rockin' On The Radio* (Rollercoaster 1984) ★★, *Let's Get Loose* (Rockhouse 1987) ★★★.

KINGSTON TRIO

An influential part of America's folk revival, the Kingston Trio was formed in San Francisco in 1957 and was popular in the late 50s. The group consisted of Bob Shane (b. 1 February 1934, Hilo, Hawaii), Nick Reynolds (b. 27 July 1933, Coronado, California, USA) and Dave Guard (b. 19 October 1934, San Francisco, California, USA, d. 22 March 1991). The Kingston Trio had limited singles successes and are most often remembered for 'Tom Dooley' which reached number 5 in the UK charts, and number 1 in the US chart in 1958. The song, written by Guard, was based on an old folk tune from the 1800s called 'Tom Dula'. *The Kingston Trio*, from which 'Tom Dooley' came, also reached number 1 in the USA. The group had a run of successful albums in 1959, with *From The Hungry i*, a live recording, reaching number 2, and *The Kingston Trio At Large* and *Here We Go Again* both achieving top placings. Further chart-toppers followed with *Sold Out* and *String Along*. Their fresh harmonies and boyish enthusiasm endeared the trio to an America suspicious of the genre's New Left sympathies, but in the process paved the way for a generation of more committed performers. Guard was replaced by John Stewart (b. 5 September 1939, San Diego, California, USA) in May 1961, having left to pursue a solo career and form the Whiskeyhill Singers.

Close-Up was the first release featuring Stewart, who had previously been with the Cumberland

Three, and it reached number 3 in the US charts. 'San Miguel', the follow-up to 'Tom Dooley', only just managed to reach the Top 30 in the UK the following year. 'Reverend Mr. Black' achieved a Top 10 placing in the US chart in 1963. The line-up with Stewart continued until 1967 (he went on to achieve a cult following as a soloist). Shane later re-formed the group, as the New Kingston Trio, with Roger Gambill and George Grove. The group continued to enjoy widespread popularity and their output, if stylistically moribund, was certainly prolific. However, the success of more exciting folk and folk-rock acts rendered them increasingly old-fashioned, and the group was disbanded in 1968. A 1981 television reunion brought all six members together for the first time. Shane continues to lead various Kingston Trio line-ups on the oldies circuit.

● ALBUMS: *The Kingston Trio* (Capitol 1958) ★★★, *From The Hungry i* (Capitol 1959) ★★★, *The Kingston Trio At Large* (Capitol 1959) ★★★★, *Here We Go Again!* (Capitol 1959) ★★★★, *Sold Out* (Capitol 1960) ★★★, *String Along* (Capitol 1960) ★★★, *Stereo Concert* (Capitol 1960) ★★★, *The Last Month Of The Year* (Capitol 1960) ★★★, *Make Way!* (Capitol 1961) ★★★, *Goin' Places* (Capitol 1961) ★★★, *Close-Up* (Capitol 1961) ★★★, *College Concert: The Kingston Trio Recorded In Live Performance* (Capitol 1962) ★★★, *Something Special* (Capitol 1962) ★★★, *New Frontier* (Capitol 1962) ★★★, *#16* (Capitol 1963) ★★, *Sunny Side!* (Capitol 1963) ★★, *Sing A Song With The Kingston Trio* (Capitol 1963) ★★, *Time To Think* (Capitol 1963) ★★★, *Back In Town* (Capitol 1964) ★★★, *Nick Bob John* (Decca 1964) ★★, *Stay Awhile* (Decca 1965) ★★, *Somethin' Else* (Decca 1965) ★★, *Children Of The Morning* (Decca 1966) ★★, *Once Upon A Time* 1966 live recording (Tetragammatron 1969) ★★★, *American Gold* (Longines 1973) ★★★★, *Best Of The Best* (Proarté 1986) ★★.

● COMPILATIONS: *Encores* (Capitol 1961) ★★★★, *The Best Of The Kingston Trio* (Capitol 1962) ★★★★, *The Folk Era* 3-LP box set (Capitol 1964) ★★★, *The Best Of The Kingston Trio Volume 2* (Capitol 1965) ★★★★, *The Best Of The Kingston Trio Volume 3* (Capitol 1966) ★★★, *The Historic Recordings Of The Kingston Trio* (Capitol 1975) ★★★★, *Rediscover The Kingston Trio* (1985) ★★★, *The Very Best Of The Kingston Trio* (Capitol 1987) ★★★★, *Capitol Collectors Series* (Capitol 1991) ★★★, *Greatest Hits* (Curb 1991) ★★★, *The EP Collection* (See For Miles 1997) ★★★★, *The Guard Years* 10-CD box set (Bear Family 1998) ★★★, *The Stewart Years* 10-CD box set (Bear Family 2000) ★★★.

● FURTHER READING: *The Kingston Trio On Record*, Kingston Korner.

KISMET

This opulent but rather unsatisfying adaptation of the hit Broadway musical reached the screen in 1955, courtesy of Arthur Freed's renowned MGM production unit. Although the show's librettists, Charles Lederer and Luther Davis, were entrusted with the screenplay, much of the magic in this

Arabian Nights saga was somehow lost in the transfer. For some strange reason, Alfred Drake, who had enjoyed such a triumph in the stage production, was replaced by Howard Keel. He plays the public poet-turned-beggar Hajj, who lives on the streets of old Baghdad, and embarks on a hectic day-long adventure during which his daughter (Ann Blyth) is married to the young Caliph (Vic Damone), while he elopes with the lovely Lalume (Dolores Gray) after getting rid of her husband, the evil Wazir (Sebastian Cabot). Robert Wright and George Forrest's majestic score was based on themes by Alexander Borodin, and there were several memorable songs in the score, including 'Baubles, Bangles, And Beads', 'The Olive Tree', 'Stranger In Paradise', 'And This Is My Beloved', 'Not Since Ninevah', 'Fate', 'Bored', 'Sands Of Time', 'Night Of My Nights', 'Rhymes Have I' and 'Gesticulate'. While perhaps regretting the absence of Drake (he only ever made one film), there is no doubt that Keel was in fine voice and he made an adequate substitute. Also taking part were Jay C. Flippen, Monty Woolley, Jack Elam, Ted De Corsia and Aaron Spelling. Jack Cole was the choreographer, and the film was directed by Vincente Minnelli. Whatever its faults, the film did at least look beautiful, owing in no small part to the Eastman Color and Cinemascope photography of Joseph Ruttenberg. The source of *Kismet* – the 1911 play by Edward Knoblock – has also been adapted into three other, non-musical films, in 1920, 1930 and 1944.

KISS ME KATE

This film had most of the elements of a great screen musical – an outstanding score, a witty screenplay, and a fine cast. The original Broadway show from which it was adapted is generally considered to be Cole Porter's masterpiece, and this 1953 version only served to emphasize and reaffirm that view. The story of thespians Fred Graham (Howard Keel) and his ex-wife, Lilli Vanessi (Kathryn Grayson), who allow their onstage conflict in an out-of-town production of *The Taming Of The Shrew* to spill over into their own tempestuous private lives, was both hilarious and musically thrilling. The dance sequences, which were choreographed by Hermes Pan and his assistant Bob Fosse, were stunning, involving high-class hoofers such as Ann Miller, Bobby Van, Tommy Rall and Carol Haney. Most observers cite Miller's scintillating 'Too Darn Hot' as the film's high spot, but all the songs were performed memorably, including 'I Hate Men' (Grayson), 'So In Love', 'Wunderbar' and 'Kiss Me Kate' (Grayson-Keel), 'I've Come To Wive It Wealthily In Padua', 'Were Thine That Special Face' and 'Where Is The Life That Late I Led?' (Keel), 'Always True To You In My Fashion' and 'Why Can't You Behave? (Miller-Rall), 'We Open In Venice' (Keel-Grayson-Miller-Rall), 'From This Moment On' (Miller-Rall-Haney-Van-Fosse-Jeannie Coyne). One other item, which would have stopped the show every night if it had been performed in a similar fashion on stage, was 'Brush Up Your Shakespeare', in which James

Whitmore and Keenan Wynn, as a couple of affable debt-collecting gangsters, mangle the Bard, courtesy of Porter, in lines such as 'If your blonde won't respond when you flatter 'er/Tell her what Tony told Cleopaterer'. George Sidney directed, and the film was photographed in Ansco Color. Dorothy Kingsley's screenplay was based on Bella And Sam Spewack's original libretto. Some sequences appear slightly puzzling and unnerving – even unnatural – until one realizes that certain effects, such as characters throwing items towards the camera, were inserted to take advantage of the 3-D process in which the film was originally shot.

KITT, EARTHA

b. 17 January 1927, Columbia, South Carolina, USA. The daughter of a white dirt farmer and a black Cherokee mother, Kitt was born in the cotton fields of South Carolina. After being given away by her mother she was raised in Harlem, where after a period of struggle she ended up attending the High School for Performing Arts. She later joined Katherine Dunham's famed dancing troupe. At the end of a European tour Kitt decided to stay behind, taking up residence in Paris. Having added singing to her repertoire, she was a success and on her return to New York appeared at several leading nightclubs. She appeared on Broadway in *New Faces Of 1952* introducing 'Monotonous', and was later seen more widely in the film version of the show. Her other Broadway shows around this time included *Mrs. Patterson* (1954) and *Shinbone Alley* (1957). She continued to work in cabaret, theatre and television, singing in her uniquely accented manner and slinkily draping herself across any available object, animate or otherwise. She made a few more films over the years, playing a leading role in *St. Louis Blues* (1958), with Nat 'King' Cole, and in an all-black version of *Anna Lucasta* (1958), opposite Sammy Davis Jnr.

Although her highly mannered presentation of songs is best seen rather than merely heard, Kitt has made some songs virtually her own property, among them 'I Want To Be Evil', 'An Englishman Needs Time', 'Santa Baby' and 'I'm Just An Old-Fashioned Girl', a claim which is patently untrue. Her other record successes over the years have included 'Uska Dara – A Turkish Tale', 'C'est Si Bon', 'Somebody Bad Stole De Wedding Bell', 'Lovin' Spree', 'Under The Bridges Of Paris', 'Where Is My Man', 'I Love Men' and 'This Is My Life'. In 1978 Kitt appeared on Broadway with Gilbert Wright and Melba Moore in an all-black version of *Kismet* entitled *Timbuktu*. Her career continued along similar lines on both sides of the Atlantic throughout the 80s and into the 90s, although she was courted by a much younger audience (witness her collaboration on 'Cha Cha Heels' with Bronski Beat in 1989) who were suitably impressed by her irreverent coolness. In 1988 Kitt played the role of Carlotta Campion in the London production of *Follies* and sang Stephen Sondheim's legendary anthem to survival, 'I'm Still Here', which, appropriately, became the title of one of her volumes of autobiography. In the early 90s she performed her one-woman show in London and New York and appeared as a witch in the comedy/horror movie *Ernest Scared Stupid*. She also toured Britain with the Ink Spots in the revue *A Night At The Cotton Club*. In 1993 Kitt appeared in cabaret at several international venues, including London's Café Royal, and in the following year she played the role of Molly Bloom, the heroine of James Joyce's novel *Ulysses*, in 'an erotic monologue punctuated with songs by the French crooner, Charles Aznavour', which proved to be a cult hit at the Edinburgh Festival. The indefatigable Kitt remains in-demand in Hollywood, and in 2000 provided the voice for Yzma in *The Emperor's New Groove*.

● ALBUMS: *New Faces Of 1952* original cast (RCA Victor 1952) ★★★, *Songs* 10-inch album (RCA Victor 1953) ★★★, *That Bad Eartha* 10-inch album (RCA Victor 1953) ★★★★, *Down To Eartha* (RCA Victor 1955) ★★★, *Thursday's Child* (RCA Victor 1956) ★★★, *St. Louis Blues* (RCA Victor 1958) ★★★, *The Fabulous Eartha Kitt* (Kapp 1959) ★★★, *Eartha Kitt Revisited* (Kapp 1960) ★★★, *Bad But Beautiful* (MGM 1962) ★★★, *Eartha Kitt Sings In Spanish* (Decca 1965) ★★★, *C'est Si Bon* (IMS 1983) ★★★, *I Love Men* (Record Shack 1984) ★★★, *Love For Sale* (Capitol 1984) ★★, *The Romantic Eartha Kitt* (Pathe Marconi 1984) ★★, *St. Louis Blues* (RCA Germany 1985) ★★★, *That Bad Eartha* (RCA Germany 1985) ★★★, *Eartha Kitt In Person At The Plaza* (GNP 1988) ★★★★, *I'm A Funny Dame* (Official 1988) ★★★, *My Way* (Caravan 1988) ★★★, *I'm Still Here* (Arista 1989) ★★★, *Live In London* (Arista 1990) ★★★★, *Thinking Jazz* (ITM 1992) ★★★, *Back In Business* (ITM 1994) ★★★.

● COMPILATIONS: *At Her Very Best* (RCA 1982) ★★★, *Songs* (RCA 1983) ★★★, *Diamond Series: Eartha Kitt* (Diamond 1988) ★★★, *Best Of Eartha Kitt* (MCA 1990) ★★★, *The Best Of Eartha Kitt: Where Is My Man* (Hot 1995) ★★★, *Purr-Fect: Greatest Hits* (Buddah 1999) ★★★★.

● FURTHER READING: *Thursday's Child*, Eartha Kitt. *Alone With Me: A New Biography*, Eartha Kitt. *I'm Still Here*, Eartha Kitt.

● FILMS: *Casbah* (1948), *New Faces* (1954), *The Mark Of The Hawk* aka *Accused* (1957), *St. Louis Blues* (1958), *Anna Lucasta* (1958), *Saint Of Devil's Island* aka *Seventy Times Seven* (1961), *Synanon* aka *Get Off My Back* (1965), *Onkel Toms Hütte* aka *Uncle Tom's Cabin* (1969), *Up The Chastity Belt* aka *Naughty Knights* (1971), *Friday Foster* (1975), *All By Myself* (1982), *The Serpent Warriors* (1985), *The Pink Chiquitas* (1987), *Erik The Viking* (1989), *Master Of Dragonard Hill* (1989), *Living Doll* (1990), *Ernest Scared Stupid* (1991), *Boomerang* (1992), *Fatal Instinct* (1993), *Unzipped* (1995), *Harriet The Spy* (1996), *Ill Gotten Gains* voice only (1997), *I Woke Up Early The Day I Died* (1998), *The Emperor's New Groove* voice only (2000).

KNIGHT, SONNY

b. Joseph C. Smith, 1934, Maywood, Illinois, USA. Sonny Knight succeeded with one beautiful R&B ballad, 'Confidential', in the *Billboard* charts in 1956 before fading from the scene. Smith's family moved to Los Angeles in the early 50s, where he not only sang but wrote a novel. Encouraged to seek a recording contract by a girlfriend, Smith looked in the telephone book and called the first label listed, Aladdin Records. He changed his professional name to Sonny Knight and recorded unsuccessfully for Aladdin, then switching to Specialty Records. Specialty producer Robert 'Bumps' Blackwell partnered him with songwriter Dorina Morgan (wife of producer Hite Morgan), who penned 'Confidential' for Knight. The single reached number 17 in the USA, but Knight was unable to follow it up. He had two less successful singles in the mid-60s before retiring from singing.

● ALBUMS: *If You Want This Love* (1964) ★★★.
● COMPILATIONS: *Confidential* (1985) ★★★.
● FURTHER READING: *The Day The Music Died*, Sonny Knight.

KNOX, BUDDY

b. Buddy Wayne Knox, 14 April 1933 (others state 20 July), Happy, Texas, USA, d. 14 February 1999, Port Orchard, Washington, USA. Knox was one of the first 'pop-abilly' hit-makers in the 50s. In 1955, while at West Texas State University, he formed the Serenaders with bass player Jimmy Bowen and Don Lanier (guitar), later adding Don Mills (drums) and changing their name to the Rhythm Orchids. The following year Knox sang lead vocals on 'Party Doll', recorded at Norman Petty's Clovis, New Mexico studio, with Dave 'Dicky Do' Alldred on drums. First issued locally on the Blue Moon and Triple-D labels, it later became the first release on Roulette Records, formed by New York nightclub owner Maurice Levy. 'Party Doll' went to number 1 in the USA in February 1957. At the same session Bowen recorded the song's original b-side, 'I'm Stickin' With You', which Roulette issued separately under the recording credit Jimmy Bowen And The Rhythm Orchids. With his light voice skimming over the insistent rhythms, Knox was the first in a line of Texan rockers that included Buddy Holly and Roy Orbison. Both 'Rock Your Little Baby To Sleep' and the gimmicky 'Hula Love' were Top 20 hits later in 1957, when he also appeared in the film *Disc Jockey Jamboree*. Although he toured frequently with Alan Freed's package shows, 'Somebody Touched Me' (August 1958) was his only other Top 20 hit.

In 1960, Knox and Bowen moved to Los Angeles. There, recording as a solo artist, Knox turned to 'teenbeat' material such as 'Lovey Dovey', 'Ling, Ting, Tong' and 'She's Gone' (a minor UK hit in 1962) with producer Snuff Garrett. During the mid-60s he returned to country music, recording in Nashville for Reprise Records and had a hit with 'Gypsy Man', composed by ex-Crickets' Sonny Curtis. This led to film appearances in *Travellin' Light* (with Waylon Jennings) and *Sweet Country Music* (with Boots Randolph and Johnny Paycheck). Now based in Canada, Knox set up his own Sunnyhill label. He also proved popular in Europe, playing rockabilly revival shows during the 70s and early 80s to a loyal fanbase. He died in February 1999. Following an operation on his hip after a fall, it was discovered that he was suffering from cancer.

● ALBUMS: *Buddy Knox* (Roulette 1958) ★★★, *Buddy Knox And Jimmy Bowen* (Roulette 1959) ★★★, *Buddy Knox In Nashville* (United Artists 1967) ★★★, *Gypsy Man* (United Artists 1969) ★★★, *Sweet Country Music* (Rockstar 1981) ★★, *Texas Rockabilly Man* (Rockstar 1987) ★★, *Travellin' Light* (Rundell 1988) ★★.

● COMPILATIONS: *Buddy Knox's Golden Hits* (Liberty 1962) ★★★, *Rock Reflections* (Sunset 1971) ★★★, *Party Doll* (Pye 1978) ★★★, *Greatest Hits* (Rockhouse 1985) ★★★, *Liberty Takes* (Charly 1986) ★★★, *Party Doll And Other Hits* (Capitol 1988) ★★★, *The Best Of Buddy Knox* (Rhino 1990) ★★★★, with Jimmy Bowen *The Complete Roulette Recordings* (Sequel 1996) ★★★★.

● FILMS: *Jamboree* aka *Disc Jockey Jamboree* (1957).

LAINE, FRANKIE

b. Frank Paul LoVecchio, 30 March 1913, Chicago, Illinois, USA. Laine had been a chorister at the Immaculate Conception Church in his city's Sicilian quarter before entering showbusiness proper on leaving school. For nearly a decade he travelled as a singing waiter, dancing instructor (with a victory in a 1932 dance marathon as his principal qualification) and other lowly jobs, but it was as a member of a New Jersey nightclub quartet that he was given his first big break – replacing Perry Como in Freddie Carlone's touring band in 1937. This was a springboard to a post as house vocalist with a New York radio station until migration to Los Angeles, where he was 'discovered' entertaining in a Hollywood spa by Hoagy Carmichael. The songwriter persuaded him to adopt an Anglicized *nom de theatre*, and funded the 1947 session that resulted in 'That's My Desire', Laine's first smash. This was followed by 'Shine' (written in 1924) and a revival again in Louis Armstrong's 'When You're Smiling'. This was the title song to a 1950 movie starring Laine, the Mills Brothers, Kay Starr and other contributors of musical interludes to its 'backstage' plot. His later career on celluloid focused largely on his disembodied voice carrying main themes of cowboy movies such as *Man With A Star*, the celebrated *High Noon*, *Gunfight At The OK Corral* and the *Rawhide* television series. Each enhanced the dramatic, heavily masculine style favoured by Laine's producer, Mitch Miller, who also spiced the artist's output with generous pinches of country and western. This was best exemplified in the extraordinary 1949 hit 'Mule Train', one of the most dramatic and impassioned recordings of its era. Other early successes included 'Jezebel', 'Jalousie' and 'Rose, Rose, I Love You', an adaptation by Wilfred Thomas of Hue Lin's Chinese melody 'Mei Kuei'.

Laine proved a formidable international star, particularly in the UK, where his long chart run began in 1952 with 'High Noon'. The following year he made chart history when his version of 'I Believe' topped the charts for a staggering 18 weeks, a record that has never been eclipsed since, despite a valiant run of 16 weeks by Bryan Adams 28 years later. Laine enjoyed two further UK chart-toppers in 1953 with 'Hey Joe' and 'Answer Me'. Incredibly, he was number 1 for 27 weeks that year, another feat of chart domination that it is difficult to envisage ever being equalled. No less than 22 UK Top 20 hits during the 50s emphasized Laine's popularity, including such memorable songs as 'Blowing Wild', 'Granada', 'The Kid's Last Fight', 'My Friend', 'Rain Rain Rain', 'Cool Water', 'Hawkeye', 'Sixteen Tons', 'A

Woman In Love' and 'Rawhide'. Laine was also a consummate duettist and enjoyed additional hits with Johnnie Ray, Doris Day and Jimmy Boyd. After his hit-parade farewell with 1961's 'Gunslinger', he pursued a full-time career commuting around the world as a highly paid cabaret performer, with a repertoire built around selections from hit compilations, one of which (*The Very Best Of Frankie Laine*) climbed into international charts as late as 1977. New material tended to be of a sacred nature – though in the more familiar 'clippetty-clop' character was 'Blazing Saddles', featured in Mel Brooks' (the lyricist) 1974 spoof-western of the same name. By the mid-80s, he was in virtual semi-retirement in an opulent ocean-front dwelling in San Diego, California, with his wife, former actress Nanette Gray. With sales in excess of 100 million copies, Laine was a giant of his time and one of the most important solo singers of the immediate pre-rock 'n' roll period.

● ALBUMS: *Favorites* (Mercury 1949) ★★★, *Songs From The Heart* (Mercury 1949) ★★, *Frankie Laine* (Mercury 1950) ★★★, *Mr Rhythm Sings* (Mercury 1951) ★★★, *Christmas Favorites* (Mercury 1951) ★★, *Listen To Laine* (Mercury 1952) ★★★, *One For My Baby* (Columbia 1952) ★★★★, with Jo Stafford *Musical Portrait Of New Orleans* (Columbia 1954) ★★, *Mr Rhythm* (Columbia 1954) ★★★, *Songs By Frankie Laine* (Mercury 1955) ★★★★, *That's My Desire* (Mercury 1955) ★★★★, *Lovers Laine* (Columbia 1955) ★★★, *Frankie Laine Sings For Us* (Mercury 1955) ★★★, *Concert Date* (Mercury 1955) ★★★, *With All My Heart* (Mercury 1955) ★★★, *Command Performance* (Columbia 1956) ★★★, *Jazz Spectacular* (Columbia 1956) ★★, *Rockin'* (Columbia 1957) ★★, *Foreign Affair* (Columbia 1958) ★★★, *Torchin'* (Columbia 1960) ★★★, *Reunion In Rhythm* (Columbia 1961) ★★★, *You Are My Love* (Columbia 1961) ★★★, *Frankie Laine, Balladeer* (Columbia 1961) ★★★, *Hell Bent For Leather!* (Columbia 1961) ★★★, *Deuces Wild* (Columbia 1962) ★★★, *Call Of The Wild* (1962) ★★★, *Wanderlust* (1963) ★★, *I'll Take Care Of Your Cares* (ABC 1967) ★★★, *I Wanted Someone To Love* (ABC 1967) ★★★, *To Each His Own* (ABC 1968) ★★, *You Gave Me A Mountain* (ABC 1969) ★★★, with Erich Kunzel And The Cincinnati Pops Orchestra *Round Up* (1987) ★★★.

● COMPILATIONS: *Greatest Hits* (Columbia 1959) ★★★★, *Golden Hits* (Mercury 1960) ★★★★, *Golden Memories* (Polydor 1974) ★★★, *The Very Best Of Frankie Laine* (Warwick 1977) ★★★★, *American Legend* (Columbia 1978) ★★★, *Songbook* (World Records 1981) ★★★★, *All Of Me* (Bulldog 1982) ★★★, *Golden Greats* (Polydor 1983) ★★★, *The Golden Years* (Phillips 1984) ★★★, *His Greatest Hits* (Warwick 1986) ★★★, *The Uncollected* (Hindsight 1986) ★★★, *Rawhide* (Castle 1986) ★★★, *20 Of His Best* (The Collection 1987) ★★★, *Sixteen Evergreens* (Joker 1988) ★★★, *Country Store: Frankie Laine* (Country Store 1988) ★★★, *Portrait Of A Song Stylist* (Masterpiece 1989) ★★★, *21 Greatest Hits* (Westmoor 1989) ★★★★, *Memories In Gold* (Prestige 1990) ★★★, *All Time Hits* (MFP 1991) ★★★, with Jo Stafford *Goin' Like Wildfire* (Bear Family 1992) ★★★.

● FURTHER READING: *That Lucky Old Son*, Frankie Laine and Joseph F. Laredo.

LAMBERT, HENDRICKS AND ROSS

In the late 50s a group of singers began informal 'vocalese' jam sessions at the New York apartment of Dave Lambert (b. 19 June 1917, Boston, Massachusetts, USA, d. 3 October 1966, Westport, Connecticut, USA). At these sessions singers would improvise vocal lines in much the same manner as jazz instrumentalists. Ten years previously, Lambert had worked as arranger and singer in Gene Krupa's band, recording 'What's This?', an early example of a bop vocal. In 1955, Lambert teamed up with Jon Hendricks (b. 16 September 1921, Newark, Ohio, USA) to record a vocalized version of 'Four Brothers'. In 1958, Lambert and Hendricks added to their duo the highly distinctive singer Annie Ross (b. Annabelle Short Lynch, 25 July 1930, Mitcham, Surrey, England) to record the album *Sing A Song Of Basie*. The concept of the Lambert, Hendricks And Ross recordings was simple, although highly complex in execution. The singers performed wordless vocal lines, matching the brass and reed section parts of the Count Basie band's popular recordings. With this formula they enjoyed great success in the late 50s and early 60s. In 1962, Ross left the trio and was replaced by Yolanda Bavan (b. 1 June 1940, Colombo, Ceylon). Two years later Lambert also left and soon thereafter the trio concept was abandoned. Subsequently, Lambert worked briefly as a studio arranger before his tragic death in 1966, when he was hit by a passing truck. Nobody has ever matched this incredible style of vocalese. They had grace and style and made complicated singing sound effortless and natural.

● ALBUMS: *Sing A Song Of Basie* (ABC-Paramount 1958) ★★★★, *Sing Along With Basie* (Roulette 1958) ★★★★, with Zoot Sims *The Swingers!* (Affinity 1959) ★★★, *The Hottest New Group In Jazz* (Columbia 1959) ★★★★★, *Lambert, Hendricks & Ross Sing Ellington* (Columbia 1960) ★★★★, *High Flying* (Columbia 1961) ★★★★. As Lambert, Hendricks And Bavan: *Live At Basin Street East* (RCA Victor 1963) ★★★, *Lambert, Hendricks & Bavan At Newport* (RCA Victor 1963) ★★★, *Lambert, Hendricks & Bavan At The Village Gate* (RCA 1964) ★★★.

● COMPILATIONS: *Twisted: The Best Of Lambert, Hendricks And Ross* (Rhino 1992) ★★★★.

LAMPLIGHTERS

This vocal R&B outfit was formed in 1952 at Jordan High School in Los Angeles, California, USA, but was always too erratic and plagued with personal problems to be destined for success in the long haul. Leon Hughes, Matthew Nelson and Willie Ray Rockwell comprised the initial trio, who entered a talent show at Johnny Otis' Barrell House but came second to singer Thurston Harris (b. 11 July 1931, Indianapolis, Indiana, USA, d. 1990, California, USA). They set about convincing him to join forces with them, and he eventually agreed. Al Frazier, formerly vocalist with the Mellomoods, helped to choreograph their rough stage act. Their performances soon evolved into some of the most exciting and wild events on the west coast R&B circuit, with acrobatics and audience participation that predated the rock 'n' roll boom. Frazier, too, was persuaded to join the group. After losing Leon Hughes, the unit secured a contract at Federal Records, having been once more reduced to a quartet. Their debut single, a powerful ballad titled 'Part Of Me', failed to garner its just reward, though it did introduce them as the Lamplighters (Federal boss Ralph Bass had chosen the name in the absence of any band decision). A second single emerged, 'Bee Bop Wino', but its title ironically mirrored the slide of several members of the band into alcoholism. Indeed, Rockwell later died after drunkenly crashing his car into a telephone pole. In 1954, following the release of 'Sad Life', 'Smootchie', 'I Used To Cry Mercy, Mercy' and 'Salty Dog', the group embarked on a major tour, with Eddie Jones and Harold Lewis deputizing for Rockwell and Nelson. Harris quit halfway through the tour because of a disagreement over money, and that appeared to be the end of the story. However, back in Los Angeles, Frazier put together a new version of the band with Sonny Harris, Carl White and a returning Matthew Nelson. The new formation christened itself the Tenderfoots. Four singles, beginning with 'Kissing Bug' in March 1955, failed to bring any success, and they returned to the Lamplighters name after renewing their friendship with Thurston Harris. Three final singles emerged on Federal between 1955 and 1956. However, Thurston Harris's old behaviour problems resurfaced and he was soon replaced by Turner Wilson III. After this, the group changed names again to become the Sharps, while Thurston Harris enjoyed one major solo single, 'Little Bitty Pretty One' (which ironically featured the Sharps as uncredited backing band).

LANG, DON

b. Gordon Langhorn, 19 January 1925, Halifax, Yorkshire, England, d. 3 August 1992, London, England. Lang started as a dance band trombonist working with the bands of Peter Rose, Teddy Foster and Vic Lewis. It was with Lewis that he made his first recordings. He began singing with Ken Mackintosh's Band and is credited under his real name on some of their records and also one recording with the Cyril Stapleton Orchestra. Lang went solo in the mid-50s and after a couple of singles on Decca he made the UK Top 20 with a 'vocalese' (scat jazz) version of 'Cloudburst' in 1956/56 on HMV Records. Together with his Frantic Five (which included the late saxophonist Red Price) he was one of the first UK acts to get involved with rock 'n' roll and skiffle, although his jazz roots were always audible. The group appeared regularly on UK television's seminal 6.5 Special and sang the theme song over the credits. After many unsuccessful singles he charted with a cover of Chuck Berry's 'School Day' and reached the Top 10 with a version of David Seville's 'Witch

Doctor' (with the curious lyric, 'ooh ee ooh aha bing bang walla walla bing bang'). When the hits dried up for this elder statesman of UK pop, he formed a new band and played the dancehall and club circuit for many years. At times he sang alongside such notable acts as the Mike Sammes and Cliff Adams Singers and played on records like the Beatles' 'white album' (*The Beatles*). Alongside 50s acts like Wee Willie Harris and Tommy Bruce, he could still be seen on the UK rock 'n' roll circuit. For a time he returned to his first love – jazz, but for the last few years of his life he was in virtual retirement, emerging for the occasional rock 'n' roll revival show or recording session. He died of cancer in the Royal Marsden Hospital in August 1992. His son Brad has played bass for ABC and Toyah.

● ALBUMS: *Skiffle Special* (HMV 1957) ★★★, *Introducing The Hand Jive* (HMV 1958) ★★★, *Twenty Top 20 Twists* (HMV 1962) ★★.

● COMPILATIONS: *Rock Rock Rock* (1983) ★★★, with the Twisters *20 Rock 'n' Roll Twists* (1988) ★★★.

LANZA, MARIO

b. Alfredo Arnold Cocozza, 31 January 1921, Philadelphia, Pennsylvania, USA, d. 7 October 1959, Rome, Italy. An enormously popular star in film musicals and on records during the 50s, with a magnificent operatic tenor voice. The son of Italian immigrants, he took his stage name from the masculine version of his mother's maiden name, Maria Lanza. From the age of 15, Lanza studied singing with several teachers, and was introduced into society circles with the object of gaining a patron. He was signed to Columbia Artistes Management as a concert singer, but their plans to send him on an introductory tour were quashed when Lanza was drafted into the US Army in 1943. He appeared in shows, billed as 'the Service Caruso', and sang in the chorus of the celebratory Forces show *Winged Victory*. After release, he lived in New York, gave concerts and worked on radio shows. One of the audition recordings that he made for RCA Records found its way to the MGM Film Studios, and when he deputized for another tenor at the Hollywood Bowl, MGM chief Louis B. Mayer was in the audience.

Soon afterwards Lanza was signed to a seven-year MGM contract by Hungarian producer Joe Pasternak, who was quoted as saying: 'It was the most beautiful voice I had ever heard – but his bushy hair made him look like a caveman!' Lanza's contract allowed him to continue with his concert career, and in April 1948 he made his first, and last, appearance on the professional operatic stage, in two performances of *Madame Butterfly*, with the New Orleans Opera. In Lanza's first film in 1949 for MGM, *That Midnight Kiss*, he co-starred with Kathryn Grayson and pianist Jose Iturbi; the musical contained a mixture of popular standards as diverse as 'They Didn't Believe Me' and 'Down Among The Sheltering Palms', and classical pieces, including 'Celeste Aida' (from Verdi's *Aida*), which gave Lanza one of his first record hits. The film was a big box-office success, and was followed by *The Toast Of New Orleans*, also with Grayson, which, along with the operatic excerpts, contained some songs by Sammy Cahn and Nicholas Brodszky, including one of Lanza's all-time smash hits, the million-seller, 'Be My Love'. Lanza starred in the biopic *The Great Caruso* (1951), performing several arias associated with his idol. He also introduced 'The Loveliest Night Of The Year', a song adapted by Irving Aaronson from 'Over the Waves', by Juventino Rosas, with a new lyric by Paul Francis Webster; it gave Lanza his second million-selling record.

By this point, he was one of Hollywood's hottest properties, and as his career blossomed, so did his waistline. There were rumours of breakfasts consisting of four steaks and six eggs, washed down with a gallon of milk, which caused his weight to soar to 20 stone. He claimed that 'nervousness' made him eat. In 1951, Lanza embarked on a country wide tour of 22 cities, and also appeared on his own CBS radio series. Back in Hollywood, he initially rejected MGM's next project, *Because You're Mine*, because of its 'singer-becomes-a-GI' storyline. After some difficulties, the film was eventually completed, and was chosen for the 1952 Royal Film Premiere in the UK. The title song, by Cahn and Brodszky, was nominated for an Academy Award in 1952, and became Lanza's third, and last, million-selling single. He had already recorded the songs for his next MGM project, *The Student Prince*, when he walked out on the studio following a disagreement with the director. He avoided damaging breach of contract lawsuits by allowing MGM to retain the rights to his recordings for the film. British actor Edmund Purdom took his place, miming to Lanza's singing voice.

Ironically, Lanza's vocal performances for the film were considered to be among his best, and *Songs From The Student Prince And Other Great Musical Comedies* (containing 'The Drinking Song'), was number 1 in the USA for several weeks. Beset by problems with alcohol, food, tranquillizers and the US tax authorities, Lanza became a virtual recluse, not performing for over a year, before appearing on CBS Television with Betty Grable and Harry James. He was criticized in the press for miming to his old recordings on the show, but proved the voice was still intact by resuming his recording career soon afterwards. In 1956, Lanza returned to filming, this time for Warner Brothers. *Serenade*, adapted from the novel by James M. Cain, in which Lanza co-starred with Joan Fontaine, was considered by the critics to be one of his best movies. Once again, the operatic excerpts were interspersed with some romantic songs by Cahn and Brodszky, including 'Serenade' and 'My Destiny'. In 1957, tired of all the crash diets, and disillusioned by life in the USA, Lanza moved to Italy, and settled in Rome. He made one film there, *The Seven Hills Of Rome* (1958). Apart from the sight of Lanza playing an American entertainer doing impersonations of Dean Martin, Frankie Laine and Louis Armstrong, the film is probably best remembered for the inclusion of the

1955 hit song 'Arrivederci, Roma', written by Renato Rascel (Ranucci) and Carl Sigman, impressively sung in the film by Lanza, and which has become the accompaniment to many a backward glance by tourists ever since.

In 1958, Lanza visited the UK, making his first stage appearances for six years, in concert at London's Royal Albert Hall and on the Royal Variety Show. From there, he embarked on a European tour. While on the Continent, he made *For The First Time* (1959), which was the last time he was seen on film. He appeared relatively slim, and was still in excellent voice. In the autumn of 1959 he went into a Rome clinic; a week later, he died of a heart attack. Much later it was alleged that he was murdered by the Mafia because he refused to appear at a concert organized by mobster Lucky Luciano. The city of Philadelphia officially proclaimed 7 October as 'Mario Lanza Day', and subsequently established a museum that still preserves his memory in the 90s. Opinions of his voice, and its potential, vary. José Carreras is quoted as saying that he was 'turned on' to opera at the age of 16 by seeing Lanza in *The Great Caruso*, and he emphasized the singer's influence by presenting his *Homage To Mario Lanza* concert at London's Royal Albert Hall in March 1994. Arturo Toscanini allegedly described it as the greatest voice of the twentieth century. On the other hand, one critic, perhaps representing the majority, said: 'He just concentrated on the big "lollipops" of the opera repertoire, he had a poor musical memory, and would never have been an opera star.' Ironically, it was one of the world's leading contemporary opera singers, Placido Domingo, who narrated the 1981 television biography *Mario Lanza-The American Caruso*.

● ALBUMS: *The Great Caruso* (HMV 1953) ★★★★, *Operatic Arias* (HMV 1954) ★★★, *Songs Of Romance* (HMV 1955) ★★★, *Serenade* (HMV 1956) ★★★★, *Songs From The Student Prince* film soundtrack (RCA 1956) ★★★★, *Lanza On Broadway* (HMV 1957) ★★★★, *The Touch Of Your Hand* (HMV 1957) ★★★, *In A Cavalcade Of Show Tunes* (RCA 1957) ★★★, *Seven Hills Of Rome* film soundtrack (RCA 1958) ★★★, *Songs From The Student Prince/The Great Caruso* (RCA 1958) ★★★★, *Sings A Kiss And Other Love Songs* (RCA 1959) ★★★, *For The First Time* film soundtrack (RCA 1959) ★★★, *Lanza Sings Christmas Carols* (RCA 1959) ★★★, *Mario Lanza Sings Caruso Favourites/The Great Caruso* (RCA 1960) ★★★★, *You Do Something To Me* (RCA 1969) ★★★.

● COMPILATIONS: *His Greatest Hits, Volume 1* (RCA 1971) ★★★★, *Art And Voice Of Mario Lanza* (RCA 1973) ★★★, *Pure Gold* (RCA 1980) ★★★, *His Greatest Hits From Operettas And Musicals, Volumes One, Two & Three* (RCA Classics 1981) ★★★★, *The Legendary Mario Lanza* (K-Tel 1981) ★★★★, *Collection* (RCA Red Seal 1982) ★★★, *20 Golden Favourites* (RCA 1984) ★★★★, *Magic Moments With Mario Lanza* (RCA 1985) ★★★, *Forever* (RCA 1986) ★★★, *A Portrait Of Mario Lanza* (Stylus 1987) ★★★★, *Diamond Series: Mario Lanza* (Diamond Series 1988) ★★★★, *Be My Love* (RCA

1991) ★★★, *The Ultimate Collection* (RCA 1994) ★★★★, *With A Song In My Heart: The Love Collection* (Camden 1997) ★★★★.
● FURTHER READING: *Mario Lanza*, Matt Bernard. *Mario Lanza*, Michael Burrows. *Lanza – His Tragic Life*, R. Strait and T. Robinson. *Mario Lanza*, Derek Mannering.

LAURENTS, ARTHUR

b. 14 July 1918, New York, USA. A distinguished stage director, author and screenwriter, Laurents has enjoyed equal success in both the musical and legitimate theatre. His parents did not approve of his early ambitions to be a playwright, and young Laurents went alone to New York theatres in the Depression-hit early 30s. He made his name as the author of plays such as *Home Of The Brave* (1945) and *The Time Of The Cuckoo* (1952), before writing the libretto for the landmark musical *West Side Story* (1957). The 50s were troubled times for Laurents: blacklisted during the McCarthy witch hunts, he was nearly bankrupted by the lawyers fees incurred in securing the return of his passport. He and composer Leonard Bernstein auditioned Stephen Sondheim as lyricist for *West Side Story*, enabling him to make his Broadway debut. Laurents and Sondheim collaborated again in 1959 on *Gypsy* (music: Jule Styne), *Anyone Can Whistle* (1964, Laurents also directed) and *Do I Hear A Waltz?* (1965). Laurents made his debut as the director of a musical in 1962 with *I Can Get It For You Wholesale*, in which Barbra Streisand made an enormous impact, stopping the show every night with the comic 'Miss Marmelstein'. Since then, Laurents has experienced mixed fortunes. *Hallelujah, Baby!* (1967), with his libretto and a score by Jule Styne, Betty Comden and Adolph Green, was considered a failure in New York, but the first West End production of *Gypsy* in 1973, starring Angela Lansbury, which Laurents directed, was acclaimed, and subsequently transferred to Broadway. Laurents also directed another New York revival of his favourite musical in 1989, with Tyne Daly. In 1979, *The Madwoman Of Central Park West*, a one-woman entertainment that Laurents wrote with and for Phyllis Newman, played off-Broadway at the 22 Steps Theatre. After being nominated for a Tony Award for his direction of the original *Gypsy*, Laurents' staging of *La Cage Aux Folles* finally won him an Award in 1983. However, there were no Tonys awarded to *Nick And Nora* (1991); Laurents was associated with this colossal flop as author and director, but ironically, for him personally, some good came from it. Disillusioned with musical productions, he immediately launched into the creation of a series of plays, their content spanning four decades: *Jolson Sings Again*, a piece about politics and principles set in Hollywood during the McCarthy era, a comedy of manners entitled *The Radical Mystique*, *My Good Name*, and *Two Lives*. He also settled on two venues sympathetic to his work, Seattle Rep and the Manhattan Theatre Club. Laurents' other notable contributions to the straight theatre over the years have included *Invitation To A March* (1960), which had incidental music by Sondheim, *The Way We Were*, *Scream*, *A Clearing In The Woods*, and the homosexual-themed *The Enclave* (1973). One of his earliest efforts, *The Time Of The Cuckoo*, had already provided the basis for the musical *Do I Hear A Waltz?*, before it was filmed in 1955 as *Summertime*, starring Katharine Hepburn, while *The Way We Were* came to the big screen in 1973, with Barbra Streisand and Robert Redford in the leading roles. Laurents wrote the screenplay for the latter, and he also scripted *The Snake Pit* (1948), *Rope* (1948), *Caught* (1948), *Anna Lucasta* (1949, with Philip Yordan), *Anastasia* (1956), *Bonjour Tristesse* (1958) and *The Turning Point* (1977). In 1995, the York Theatre Company presented Laurents with its sixth annual Oscar Hammerstein II Award, and his many other honours have included Golden Globe, Drama Desk, National Board of Review, Writers Guild of America, National Institute of Arts and Letters, Screen Writers Guild, Sydney Drama Critics awards. He has been inducted into the Theatre Hall of Fame.

LAWRENCE, LEE

b. Leon Siroto, *c.*1921, Salford, Lancashire, England, d. February 1961, USA. A popular ballad singer in Britain during the 50s, with a fine tenor voice, rivalling that of David Whitfield. Both his parents were with the Carl Rosa Opera Company, and when he was 16, young Lawrence went to Italy to study opera for three years. He returned to England at the outbreak of World War II, and enlisted in the Royal Tank Regiment. After the war, he continued singing with ENSA before being noticed by BBC producer Roy Spear. He made his radio debut in Spear's *Beginners Please*, and continued to broadcast with the bands of Stanley Black and Sydney Lipton, among many others. He was also resident singer for a time with Cyril Stapleton's BBC Show Band, and had his own Radio Luxembourg series in 1955, on which the orchestra was conducted by Harry Gold. His first recording was 'How Can You Buy Killarney?'/'Helene', and he subsequently made the UK Top 20 with 'Crying In The Chapel' and 'Suddenly There's A Valley'. His orchestral backings were provided by top musical directors such as Stanley Black, Ray Martin, Geoff Love, Roland Shaw, and Tony Osborne. Like many other balladeers of the day, he was always in demand on the UK Variety circuit, singing numbers such as 'With These Hands', 'Blue Tango', 'A Beggar In Love', 'Tell Me Tonight', 'The Story Of Tina', 'Falling In Love With Love', 'Lonely Ballerina', and his theme 'The World Is Mine Tonight'. With rock 'n' roll taking a firm hold in Britain, Lawrence moved with his family to the USA in the late 50s, and played in cabaret and on television, and worked the renowned Borscht circuit in the Catskills until his death at the age of 40. Among his last UK releases was a fascinating single containing completely untypical material. On one side was Annisteen Allen's 'Don't Nobody Move', and on the other, 1956's opportunist 'Rock 'N' Roll Opera', a spoof that mentioned Elvis Presley,

Gene Vincent, and Tommy Steele, along with other newcomers who were preventing Lawrence ever returning to the charts.
● ALBUMS: *Presenting Lee Lawrence* (Decca 1953) ★★★, *Fascination* (President 1985) ★★★.

LAWRENCE, STEVE

b. Stephen Leibowitz, 8 July 1935, Brooklyn, New York City, New York, USA. The son of a cantor in a Brooklyn synagogue, Lawrence was in the Glee club at Thomas Jefferson High School, where he began studying piano, saxophone, composition and arranging. He made his recording debut for King Records at the age of 16. The record, 'Mine And Mine Alone', based on 'Softly Awakes My Heart' from *Samson & Delilah*, revealed an remarkably mature voice and style. Influenced by Frank Sinatra, but merely a copyist, Lawrence's great range and warmth earned him a break on Steve Allen's *Tonight* television show, where he met, sang with and later married Eydie Gorme. He recorded for Coral Records and had his first hit in 1957 with 'The Banana Boat Song'. It was the infectious 'Party Doll' which gave him a Top 5 hit in 1957 and he followed that same year with four further, although lesser successes, namely 'Pum-Pa-Lum', 'Can't Wait For Summer', 'Fabulous' and 'Fraulein'. During his US Army service (1958-60) he sang with military bands on recruiting drives and bond rallies.
Back home he and Eydie embarked on a double act, their most memorable hit being 'I Want To Stay Here' in 1963. As Steve And Eydie they made albums for CBS Records, ABC Records and United Artists Records, including *Steve And Eydie At The Movies*, *Together On Broadway*, *We Got Us*, *Steve And Eydie Sing The Golden Hits* and *Our Love Is Here To Stay*, the latter a double album of great George Gershwin songs, which was the soundtrack of a well-received television special. Lawrence, on his own, continued to have regular hits with 'Portrait Of My Love' and 'Go Away Little Girl' in 1961/2, and enjoyed critical success with albums such as *Academy Award Losers* and *Portrait Of My Love*. As an actor he starred on Broadway in *What Makes Sammy Run?*, took the lead in *Pal Joey* in summer stock, and has acted in a crime series on US television. During the 70s and 80s he continued to record and make television appearances with Gorme, with the couple gaining a record-breaking seven Emmys for their *Steve And Eydie Celebrate Irving Berlin* special. The couple also joined Frank Sinatra on his *Diamond Jubilee Tour* in 1991.
● ALBUMS: *About That Girl* (Coral 1956) ★★★, *Songs By Steve Lawrence* (Coral 1957) ★★★, *Here's Steve Lawrence* (Coral 1958) ★★★, *All About Love* (Coral 1959) ★★★, *Steve Lawrence* (King 1959) ★★★, *Swing Softly With Me* (ABC-Paramount 1960) ★★★★, *The Steve Lawrence Sound* (United Artists 1960) ★★★★, *Steve Lawrence Goes Latin* (United Artists 1960) ★★, *Portrait Of My Love* (United Artists 1961) ★★★★, *Winners!* (Columbia 1963) ★★★★, *Come Waltz With Me* (Columbia 1963) ★★★, *People Will Say We're In Love* (United Artists 1963) ★★★, *Steve Lawrence Conquers*

Broadway (United Artists 1963) ★★★, *Songs Everybody Knows* (Coral 1963) ★★★, *Academy Award Losers* (Columbia 1964) ★★★★, *What Makes Sammy Run* film soundtrack (Columbia 1964) ★★, *The Steve Lawrence Show* (Columbia 1965) ★★★, *We're All Alone* (President 1985) ★★★.
With Eydie Gorme *We Got Us* (ABC-Paramount 1960) ★★★★, *Steve And Eydie Sing The Golden Hits* (ABC-Paramount 1960) ★★★, *Cozy* (United Artists 1961) ★★★, *Two On The Aisle* (United Artists 1963) ★★★, *Our Best To You* (ABC-Paramount 1964) ★★★, *Together On Broadway* (Columbia 1967) ★★★, *What It Was, Was Love* (RCA 1969) ★★★, *Real True Lovin'* (RCA 1969) ★★★★, *Tonight I'll Say A Prayer* (RCA 1970) ★★★, *We Can Make It Together* (Ember 1975) ★★★, *Our Love Is Here To Stay* (United Artists 1977) ★★★, *I Still Believe In Love* (President 1985) ★★★, *Alone Together* (GL 1989) ★★★, *Since I Fell For You* (1993) ★★★.
● COMPILATIONS: *The Best Of Steve Lawrence* (ABC-Paramount 1960) ★★★, *The Very Best Of Steve Lawrence* (United Artists 1962) ★★★, *The Best Of Steve Lawrence* (Taragon 1995) ★★★.
With Eydie Gorme *The Very Best Of Eydie And Steve* (United Artists 1962) ★★★, *The Golden Hits Of Eydie And Steve* (United Artists 1962) ★★★, *The Best Of Steve And Eydie* (Columbia 1977) ★★★, *20 Golden Performances* (1977) ★★★.

LAZY LESTER

b. Leslie Johnson, 20 June 1933 (or 1923), Torras, Louisiana, USA. Blues harmonica player and vocalist Lazy Lester recorded numerous singles for Excello Records in the late 50s and early 60s. Forming his first band in 1952, the musician's first significant job was as a sideman for bluesman Lightnin' Slim. Owing to his slow-moving, laid-back approach, Johnson received his performing name during this period from record producer Jay Miller, who was known for his 'swamp pop' sound. Miller recorded Lester and placed him with the Nashville-based Excello in 1958. Lester's first solo single was 'Go Ahead' (1956), and his first local hit was 'Sugar Coated Love'/'I'm A Lover Not A Fighter'. The latter was covered in the UK by the Kinks. Lester continued to record as a leader until 1965. He also played harmonica for such artists as the blues-rock guitarist Johnny Winter (an early recording in 1961) and Lonesome Sundown. At the end of the 60s, Lester moved around the country and did not record again until 1987, for the UK Blues 'N' Trouble label. The following year he recorded *Harp & Soul* for Alligator Records, and was back touring the USA in the late 80s and 90s, enjoying new found acclaim.
● ALBUMS: *True Blues* (Excello 1966) ★★★★, *Lazy Lester Rides Again* (Blue Horizon 1987) ★★★, *Harp & Soul* (Alligator 1988) ★★★, *I'm A Lover Not A Fighter* (Ace 1994) ★★★, *All Over You* (Antones 1998) ★★★★, with Carey Bell, Raful Neal, Snooky Pryor *Superharps II* (Telarc 2001) ★★★★, *Blues Stop Knockin'* (Antone's 2001) ★★★.
● COMPILATIONS: *They Call Me Lazy* (Flyright 1977) ★★★★, *Poor Boy Blues – Jay Miller Sessions* (Flyright 1987) ★★★★.

LEE, PEGGY

b. Norma Deloris Egstrom, 26 May 1920, Jamestown, North Dakota, USA, d. 21 January 2002, California, USA. Lee was of Scandinavian descent, her grandparents being Swedish and Norwegian immigrants. She endured a difficult childhood and her mother died when she was four; when her father remarried she experienced a decidedly unpleasant relationship with her stepmother. Her father took to drink, and at the age of 14 she found herself carrying out his duties at the local railroad depot. Despite these and other hardships, she sang frequently and appeared on a local radio station. She took a job as a waitress in Fargo, where the manager of the radio station changed her name to Peggy Lee. In 1937, she took a trip to California to try her luck there but soon returned to Fargo. Another California visit was equally unsuccessful and she then tried Chicago where, in 1941, as a member of a vocal group, The Four Of Us, she was hired to sing at the Ambassador West Hotel.

During this engagement she was heard by Mel Powell, who invited Benny Goodman to hear her. Goodman's regular singer, Helen Forrest, was about to leave and Lee was hired as her replacement. She joined the band for an engagement at the College Inn and within a few days sang on a record date. A song from this period, 'Elmer's Tune', was a huge success. Among other popular recordings she made with Goodman were 'How Deep Is The Ocean?', 'How Long Has This Been Going On?', 'My Old Flame' and 'Why Don't You Do Right?'. Later, Lee married Goodman's guitarist, Dave Barbour. After she left Goodman's band in 1943, she had more successful records, including 'That Old Feeling' and three songs of which she was co-composer with Barbour, 'It's A Good Day', 'Don't Know Enough About You' and 'Mañana'. She also performed on radio with Bing Crosby. In the 50s she made several popular recordings for Decca and Capitol Records, the orchestral backings for many of which were arranged and conducted by Barbour, with whom she maintained a good relationship despite their divorce in 1952. Her 1958 hit single 'Fever' was also a collaboration with Barbour. Her *Black Coffee* album of 1953 was particularly successful, as was *Beauty And The Beat* a few years later. On these and other albums of the period, Lee was often accompanied by jazz musicians, including Jimmy Rowles, Marty Paich and George Shearing.

During the 50s Lee was also active in films, performing the title song of *Johnny Guitar* (1954), and writing songs for others including *Tom Thumb* (1958). She also made a number of on-screen appearances in acting roles, including *The Jazz Singer* (1952), and for one, *Pete Kelly's Blues* (1955), she was nominated for an Academy Award as Best Supporting Actress. However, her most lasting fame in films lies in her off-screen work on Walt Disney's *Lady And The Tramp* (1955), for which Lee wrote the song 'He's A Tramp' and provided the voice for the characters of 'Peg', the Siamese cats, and one other screen feline. Her recording successes continued throughout this period even

if, on some occasions, she had to fight to persuade Capitol to record them. One such argument surrounded 'Lover', which executives felt would compete directly with the label's then popular version by Les Paul. Lee won out and her performance of her own arrangement, played by a studio orchestra under the direction of Gordon Jenkins, was a sensation. Towards the end of the 50s, the intense level of work began to take its toll and she suffered a period of illness.

Throughout the 60s and succeeding decades Lee performed extensively, singing at concerts and on television and, of course, making records, despite being frequently plagued with poor health. Her voice, light with a delicate huskiness, offered intriguing contrasts with the large orchestral accompaniment that was usually a part of a Lee performance. Over the years her repeated use of previously successful settings for songs has tended to make her shows predictable but she remained a dedicated perfectionist in everything that she did. In the early 80s she attempted a stage show, *Peg*, but it proved unpopular and closed quickly. In the late 80s she again suffered ill health and on some of her live performances her voice was starting to betray the ravages of time. For her many fans, it did not seem to matter: to paraphrase the title of one of her songs, they just loved being there with Peg. In 1992, wheelchair-bound for the previous two years, Lee was persisting in a lawsuit, begun in 1987, against the Walt Disney Corporation for her share of the video profits from *Lady And The Tramp*. A year later, dissatisfied with the 'paltry' $2 million settlement for her six songs (written with Sonny Burke) and character voices, she was preparing to write a book about the whole affair. Meanwhile, she continued to make occasional cabaret appearances at New York venues such as Club 53. In 1993 she recorded a duet with Gilbert O'Sullivan for his album *Sounds Of The Loop*. Six years later Lee once again started litigation for unpaid royalties, this time against her former record company Decca. By 2000, Lee's career appeared to have been ended through illness with reports that she had lost the power of speech. By this point her performing career had finally been ended through a stroke suffered on 27 October 1998, and she remained in poor health until passing away at her Bel Air home in January 2002.

● ALBUMS: *Benny Goodman And Peggy Lee* (Columbia 1949) ★★★, *Rendezvous* (Capitol 1952) ★★★, *My Best To You* (Capitol 1952) ★★★, *Song In Intimate Style* (Decca 1953) ★★★, *Black Coffee* (Decca 1953) ★★★★, *Lady And The Tramp* film soundtrack (Decca 1955) ★★★★, with Ella Fitzgerald *Songs From Pete Kelly's Blues* film soundtrack (Decca 1955) ★★★, *Dream Street* (Decca 1956) ★★★, *The Man I Love* (Capitol 1957) ★★★★, *Jump For Joy* (Capitol 1958) ★★★, *Sea Shells* (Decca 1958) ★★★, *Things Are Swingin'* (Capitol 1958) ★★★★, with George Shearing *Beauty And The Beat* (Capitol 1959) ★★★★, *I Like Men!* (Capitol 1959) ★★★, *Miss Wonderful* (Capitol 1959) ★★★, *Pretty Eyes* (Capitol 1960) ★★★, *Alright, Okay, You Win* (Capitol 1960) ★★★, *Latin A La Lee!* (Capitol 1960) ★★★, *All Aglow Again*

(Capitol 1960) ★★★, *Olé A La Lee* (Capitol 1960) ★★★, *Christmas Carousel* (Capitol 1960) ★★, *At Basin Street East* (Capitol 1960) ★★★, *Blues Across Country* (Capitol 1961) ★★★, *If You Go* (Capitol 1961) ★★★, *Sugar 'N' Spice* (Capitol 1962) ★★★, *I'm A Woman* (Capitol 1963) ★★★, *Mink Jazz* (Capitol 1963) ★★★, *In Love Again* (Capitol 1963) ★★★, *Lover* (Decca 1964) ★★★, *In The Name Of Love* (Capitol 1964) ★★★, *Pass Me By* (Capitol 1965) ★★★, *That Was Then, This Is Now* (Capitol 1965) ★★★, *Big Spender* (Capitol 1966) ★★★, *Extra Special* (Capitol 1967) ★★★, *Guitars A La Lee* (Capitol 1967) ★★★, *Is That All There Is?* (Capitol 1969) ★★★, *Bridge Over Troubled Water* (Capitol 1970) ★★★, *Make It With You* (Capitol 1970) ★★★, *Let's Love* (Atlantic 1974) ★★★, *Mirrors* (A&M 1976) ★★★, *Close Enough For Love* (DRG 1979) ★★★, *Miss Peggy Lee Sings The Blues* (Music Masters 1988) ★★★, *The Peggy Lee Songbook: There'll Be Another Spring* (Music Masters 1990) ★★★, with Quincy Jones *P'S & Q'S* (Capitol 1992) ★★★, *Moments Like This* (Chesky 1992) ★★★.
● COMPILATIONS: *Bewitching-Lee!* (Capitol 1962) ★★★★, *The Best Of Peggy Lee* (MCA 1980) ★★★★, *Peggy Lee Sings With Benny Goodman (1941-43)* (Columbia 1984) ★★★★, *The Peggy Lee Collection – 20 Golden Greats* (MCA 1985) ★★★★, *Unforgettable: Peggy Lee* (Unforgettable/Castle 1987) ★★★, *The Capitol Years* (Capitol 1988) ★★★★, *Capitol Collectors Series: The Early Years* (Capitol 1990) ★★★, *All-Time Greatest Hits* (Curb 1990) ★★★, *Peggy Lee – Fever* (CEMA 1992) ★★★★, *The Best Of Peggy Lee, 1952-1956* (Music Club 1994) ★★★★, *EMI Presents The Magic Of Peggy Lee* (EMI 1997) ★★★★, *Black Coffee: The Best Of The Decca Years* (Half Moon 1998) ★★★★, *Miss Peggy Lee* 4-CD box set (Capitol 1998) ★★★★, *The Complete Peggy Lee And June Christy Capitol Transcription Sessions* 5-CD box set (Mosaic 1999) ★★★★.
● VIDEOS: *Quintessential* (Hendring Music Video 1989).
● FURTHER READING: *Miss Peggy Lee*, Peggy Lee.

LEHRER, TOM

b. Thomas Andrew Lehrer, 9 April 1928, New York City, New York, USA. Lehrer was a song satirist who also recorded a number of albums during the 50s and 60s. Having graduated from Harvard University, Lehrer then taught mathematics there. Having trained on piano, he began to perform song satires of his own for colleagues at the college. They enjoyed his songs, so Lehrer recorded a dozen of them in 1953 and had 400 copies pressed on a 10-inch album, on his own Lehrer label. An instant success on campus, Lehrer was forced to press more copies to meet the demand. He then began entertaining in clubs and writing songs for television programmes. Before the end of the 50s he had recorded three more albums on his own label and had begun to tour extensively, even gaining a following in Europe. His sense of black humour is encapsulated in the titles 'Poisoning Pigeons In The Park', 'The Old Dope Peddler' and 'The Masochism Tango' – which could be described as falling somewhere between

Mad magazine and Lenny Bruce. He stopped making live appearances in 1960 but continued to record, signing with Reprise Records in 1965. He also wrote for the US editions of the television programme *That Was The Week That Was* in 1964-65, lampooning current news events. His album *That Was The Year That Was* collected songs that had featured on the programme. He largely stopped writing in the late 60s and returned to teaching, but contributed songs to the television show *The Electric Company* in 1972. In 1980, Robin Ray and Cameron Mackintosh adapted some of his songs for the revue, *Tomfoolery*, which was still visiting the London Fringe in the early 90s. In 1998, BBC Radio 2 celebrated his 70th birthday with a special programme entitled *An Evening Wasted With Tom Lehrer*. In recent times, Lehrer continues teaching maths and has not performed for many years. Why should he, as he stated in *Billboard*; 'I'm not a performer, I just sit at the piano'. His recorded legacy continues to stay in print, and is destined to survive to a continuing refreshed audience who will want to seek out one of the finest satirists ever, and certainly an artist who had the 50s and 60s very well observed.
● ALBUMS: *Songs By Tom Lehrer* 10-inch album (Lehrer 1953) ★★★★, *More Of Tom Lehrer* (Lehrer 1959) ★★★★, *An Evening Wasted With Tom Lehrer* (Lehrer 1959) ★★★★, *Tom Lehrer Revisited* (Lehrer 1960) ★★, *That Was The Year That Was* (Reprise 1965) ★★★, *Songs By Tom Lehrer* re-recorded versions of first album's songs (Reprise 1966) ★★.
● COMPILATIONS: *Too Many Songs By Tom Lehrer* (1981) ★★★★, *Songs & More Songs By Tom Lehrer* (Rhino 1997) ★★★, *The Remains Of Tom Lehrer* 3-CD box set (Rhino 2000) ★★★★.

LEIBER AND STOLLER

Jerry Leiber (b. 25 April 1933, Baltimore, Maryland, USA) and Mike Stoller (b. 13 March 1933, New York City, New York, USA) began their extraordinary songwriting and production partnership at the age of 17. Leiber was a blues enthusiast and record store assistant, while Stoller played jazz piano. Based in Los Angeles, they provided numerous songs for the city's R&B artists during the early 50s. 'Hard Times' by Charles Brown was the first Leiber and Stoller hit, but their biggest songs of the era were 'Hound Dog' and 'K.C. Lovin'' (later renamed 'Kansas City'). Originally recorded by Big Mama Thornton, 'Hound Dog' was one of the songs that came to define rock 'n' roll after Elvis Presley performed it. 'Kansas City' had its greatest success in a version by Wilbert Harrison, and went on to become part of every UK beat group's repertoire.
In 1954, the duo set up their own Spark Records label to release material by the Robins, a vocal group they had discovered. Renamed the Coasters a year later, when Leiber and Stoller moved to New York, the group was given some of the songwriters' most clever and witty compositions. Songs such as 'Smokey Joe's Cafe', 'Searchin'', 'Yakety Yak' and 'Charlie Brown' bridged the gap between R&B and rock 'n' roll, selling millions in the mid to late 50s, while Leiber And Stoller's

innovative production techniques widened the scope of the R&B record, prompting hosts of imitators. In New York, Leiber and Stoller had a production contract with Atlantic Records, where they created hits for numerous artists. They wrote 'Lucky Lips' for Ruth Brown and 'Saved' for LaVern Baker, but their most notable productions were for the Drifters and the group's lead singer Ben E. King. Among these were 'On Broadway', 'Spanish Harlem', 'There Goes My Baby', 'I (Who Have Nothing)' and 'Stand By Me', which was an international hit when reissued in 1986. Away from Atlantic, Leiber and Stoller supplied Elvis Presley with songs including 'Jailhouse Rock', 'Baby I Don't Care', 'Loving You', 'Treat Me Nice' and 'His Latest Flame'. They also wrote hits for Perry Como, Peggy Lee ('I'm A Woman') and Dion. In 1964, the duo set up the Red Bird and Blue Cat record labels with George Goldner. Despite the quality of many of the releases (Alvin Robinson's 'Down Home Girl' was later covered by the Rolling Stones), the only big hits came from the Shangri-Las, who were produced by Shadow Morton rather than Leiber and Stoller.

Subsequently, the duo took several years away from production, purchasing the King Records group and creating the *Cabaret*-like songs for Peggy Lee's album *Mirrors* (1976). They returned to the pop world briefly in 1972, producing albums for UK acts including Stealer's Wheel and Elkie Brooks, for whom they part-wrote 'Pearl's A Singer'. During the 70s, they were in semi-retirement, developing *Only In America*, a stage show involving 30 of their compositions. Another musical based on their work – *Yakety Yak* – was presented in London with oldies band Darts. During the 80s Leiber and Stoller's songs were featured in the cartoon film *Hound Dog* and they were reported to be working on a musical. However, their public appearances seemed to be confined to awards ceremonies where they were made members of several Halls of Fame, including that of the Rock And Roll Hall Of Fame in 1987. In 1979, US critic Robert Palmer wrote a highly praised biography of the duo. The stage musical *Smokey Joe's Cafe: The Songs Of Leiber And Stoller*, which opened to rave reviews in March 1995 at New York's Virginia Theatre, featured nearly 40 songs by the duo.

● COMPILATIONS: *Leiber & Stoller Present The Spark Records Story* (Ace 2001) ★★★.
● FURTHER READING: *Baby, That Was Rock & Roll: The Legendary Leiber And Stoller*, Robert Palmer.

LERNER, ALAN JAY

b. 31 August 1918, New York, USA, d. June 1986. A lyricist and librettist, and one of the most eminent and literate personalities in the history of the Broadway musical theatre, Lerner played the piano as a child, and studied at the Juilliard School of Music, the Bedales public school in England, and Harvard University, where he took a Bachelor of Science degree in the late 30s. After working as a journalist and radio scriptwriter, he met composer Frederick Loewe at the Lamb's Club in

1942. Also a pianist, Loewe had moved to the USA in 1924, and had previously been involved in some unsuccessful musical shows. The new team's first efforts, *What's Up?* and *The Day Before Spring* (1945; 'A Jug Of Wine', 'I Love You This Morning'), did not exactly set Broadway alight, but two years later, they had their first hit with *Brigadoon*. Lerner's whimsical fantasy about a Scottish village that only comes to life every 100 years, contained 'Waitin' For My Dearie', 'I'll Go Home With Bonnie Jean', 'The Heather On The Hill', 'Come To Me, Bend To Me', 'From This Day On', and the future standard, 'Almost Like Being In Love'. A film version was made in 1954, starring Gene Kelly, Cyd Charisse and Van Johnson.

After *Brigadoon*, Lerner collaborated with Kurt Weill on the vaudeville-style *Love Life* (1948), and then spent some time in Hollywood writing the songs, with Burton Lane, for *Royal Wedding* (1951). Among them was one of the longest-ever titles, 'How Could You Believe Me When I Said I Loved You (When You Know I've Been A Liar All My Life?)', expertly manipulated by Fred Astaire and Jane Powell. Another of the numbers, 'Too Late Now', sung by Powell, was nominated for an Academy Award. In the same year, Lerner picked up an Oscar for his story and screenplay for George and Ira Gershwin's musical film *An American In Paris* (1951). Also in 1951, Lerner reunited with Loewe for the 'Gold Rush' Musical, *Paint Your Wagon*. The colourful score included 'They Call The Wind Maria', 'I Talk To The Trees', 'I Still See Elisa', 'I'm On My Way' and 'Wand'rin' Star', which, in the 1969 movie, received a lugubrious reading from Lee Marvin. Precisely the opposite sentiments prevailed in *My Fair Lady* (1956), Lerner's adaptation of *Pygmalion* by George Bernard Shaw, which starred Rex Harrison as the irascible Higgins, and Julie Andrews as Eliza ('I'm a good girl, I am'). Sometimes called 'the most perfect musical', Lerner and Loewe's memorable score included 'Why Can't The English?', 'Wouldn't It Be Lovely?', 'The Rain In Spain', 'I Could Have Danced All Night', 'On The Street Where You Live', 'Show Me', 'Get Me To The Church On Time', 'A Hymn To Him', 'Without You' and 'I've Grown Accustomed To Her Face'. 'Come To The Ball', originally written for the show, but discarded before the opening, was, subsequently, often performed, particularly by Lerner himself. After a run of 2,717 performances on Broadway, and 2,281 in London, the show was filmed in 1964, when Andrews was replaced by Audrey Hepburn (dubbed by Marni Nixon). The Broadway Cast album went to number 1 in the US charts, sold over five million copies, and stayed in the Top 40 for 311 weeks.

In 1958 Lerner was back in Hollywood, with a somewhat reluctant Loewe, for one of the last original screen musicals, the charming *Gigi*. Lerner's stylish treatment of Colette's turn-of-the-century novella, directed by Vincente Minnelli, starred Maurice Chevalier, Leslie Caron, Louis Jourdan and Hermione Gingold, and boasted a delightful score that included 'The Night They Invented Champagne', 'Say A Prayer For Me

Tonight', 'I'm Glad I'm Not Young Anymore', 'Thank Heaven For Little Girls', 'Waltz At Maxim's', 'She Is Not Thinking Of Me' and the touching 'I Remember It Well', memorably performed by Chevalier and Gingold. Lerner won one of the film's nine Oscars for his screenplay, and another, with Loewe, for the title song.

Two years later, Lerner and Loewe returned to Broadway with *Camelot*, a musical version of the Arthurian legend, based on T.H. White's *The Once And Future King*. With Julie Andrews, Richard Burton and Robert Goulet, plus a fine score that included 'C'Est Moi', 'The Lusty Month Of May', 'If Ever I Would Leave You', 'Follow Me', 'How To Handle A Woman' and the title song, the show ran on Broadway for two years. During that time it became indelibly connected with the Kennedy presidency: 'for one brief shining moment, that was known as Camelot'. The 1967 movie version was poorly received. In the early 60s, partly because of the composer's ill health, Lerner and Loewe ended their partnership, coming together again briefly in 1973 to write some new songs for a stage presentation of *Gigi*, and, a year later, for the score to the film *The Little Prince*. Lerner's subsequent collaborators included Burton Lane for *On A Clear Day You Can See Forever* (1965) ('Come Back To Me', 'On The S.S. Bernard Cohn', and others). Lerner won a Grammy Award for the title song, and maintained that it was his most frequently recorded number. He wrote with Lane again in 1979 for *Carmelina*. In the interim he collaborated with André Previn for *Coco* (1969), which had a respectable run of 332 performances, mainly due to its star, Katherine Hepburn, and with Leonard Bernstein for *1600 Pennsylvania Avenue* (1976).

Lerner's last musical, *Dance A Little Closer* (1983), which starred his eighth wife, English actress Liz Robertson, closed after one performance. They had met in 1979 when he directed her, as Eliza, in a major London revival of *My Fair Lady*. Shortly before he died of lung cancer in June 1986, he was still working on various projects, including a musical treatment of the 30s film comedy *My Man Godfrey*, in collaboration with pianist-singer Gerard Kenny, and *Yerma*, based on the play by Federico Garcia Lorca. Frederick Loewe, who shared in Lerner's triumphs, and had been semi-retired since the 60s, died in February 1988. In 1993, New Yorkers celebrated the 75th anniversary of Lerner's birth, and his remarkable and fruitful partnership with Loewe, with *The Night They Invented Champagne: The Lerner And Loewe Revue*, which played for a season at the Rainbow and Stars. Six years later the team's contribution to the recording industry was recognized by the NARAS (National Academy of Recording Arts and Science), and their Trustees' Non-Performer Grammy Awards.

● ALBUMS: *An Evening With Alan Jay Lerner* (Laureate 1977) ★★★.

● FURTHER READING: *The Musical Theatre: A Celebration*, Alan Jay Lerner. *The Street Where I Live: The Story Of My Fair Lady, Gigi And Camelot*, Alan Jay Lerner. *A Hymn To Him: The Lyrics Of Alan Jay Lerner*, Benny Green (ed.). *The Wordsmiths: Oscar Hammerstein II & Alan Jay Lerner*, Stephen Citron.

LEROLE, ELIAS, AND HIS ZIG ZAG JIVE FLUTES

This studio band was one of the most popular penny-whistle jive outfits in South Africa in the mid-50s, and released the first version of the evergreen and hypnotic 'Tom Hark' in 1956. Although a massive international hit for the group – spawning countless cover versions from Ted Heath in the 50s through to the present day – the members of the Zig Zag Jive Flutes are reputed to have received only $10 each for their efforts, while composer Aaron Lerole, Elias' brother, received the princely sum of $15 and the added accolade of having his song credited to producer Ernest Bopape. However, that was showbusiness, 50s-style, in South Africa.

LET THE GOOD TIMES ROLL

Perhaps one of the finest paeans to classic rock 'n' roll, *Let The Good Times Roll* is a sumptuous amalgamation of documentary footage and memorable concert performances. At its core was a 1972 marathon, hosted at Madison Square Gardens by New York impresario Richard Nader. Directors Sid Levin and Robert Abel blended footage from that event with television appearances, newsreels, interviews and demonstration films. Scenes from 50s genre movies *The Wild One* and *I Was A Teenage Werewolf* help to place the music in a broader cultural context, while intelligent use of split-screen techniques facilitated then-and-now scenarios. One particular clip of Little Richard, in monochrome from the 50s and in colour from the 70s, is particularly memorable. 'Good Golly Miss Molly', 'Rip It Up' and 'Lucille' are among the songs he performs as part of a cast that also includes Fats Domino, Chuck Berry, the Coasters, Danny And The Juniors, the Five Satins, Shirley And Lee, Bo Diddley, the Shirelles, Chubby Checker and Bill Haley And His Comets. 'Blueberry Hill', 'Reelin' And Rockin'', 'At The Hop', 'Poison Ivy', 'I'm A Man' and, of course, 'Rock Around The Clock', are among the songs featured in this endearing tribute to rock's first golden era.

LEVENE, SAM

b. 28 August 1905, Russia, d. 28 December 1980, New York, USA. Some sources suggest that this popular stage and screen character actor was born in New York. However, it seems more likely that he was taken to the USA in 1907, and became a naturalized citizen some 30 years later. After graduating from high school, Levene attended the American Academy of Dramatic Art in New York from 1925-27, and made his Broadway debut almost immediately in *Wall Street* (1927). The Depression made work scarce, but Levene persevered, and after making an impression in *Dinner At Eight* (1932), he established himself as a fine actor with *Three Men On A Horse* (1935). His hustling, fast-talking, streetwise style meant he was a natural choice for the role of Nathan Detroit, the operator of 'the oldest established permanent floating crap game in New York', in *Guys And Dolls* (1950). Levene reprised his role for London audiences in 1953, but was overlooked by producers of the film version, who preferred Frank Sinatra in the part. Although the remainder of his career was mostly spent in Hollywood film studios and the straight theatre, where he is particularly remembered for his performances in *The Devil's Advocate* (1961, Tony Awards nomination) and Neil Simon's 1972 hit, *The Sunshine Boys*, Levene did star in two more Broadway musicals, *Let It Ride* (1961, as Patsy) and *Café Crown* (1964, as Hymie). He continued to sigh and shrug in projects of variable quality on stage and screen until shortly before his death.

● FILMS: *Three Men On A Horse* (1936), *After The Thin Man* (1936), *Yellow Jack* (1938), *The Mad Miss Manton* (1938), *The Shopworn Angel* (1938), *Golden Boy* (1939), *Married Bachelor* (1941), *Shadow Of The Thin Man* (1941), *Grand Central Murder* (1942), *Sunday Punch* (1942), *Sing Your Worries Away* (1942), *The Big Street* (1942), *I Dood It* (1943), *Action In the North Atlantic* (1943), *Whistling In Brooklyn* (1943), *Gung Ho!* (1943), *The Purple Heart* (1944), *The Killers* (1946), *Brute Force* (1947), *Boomerang!* (1947), *Killer McCoy* (1947), *The Babe Ruth Story* (1948), *Leather Gloves* (1948), *Dial 1119* (1950), *Guilty Bystander* (1950), *Three Sailors And A Girl* (1953), *The Opposite Sex* (1956), *Sweet Smell Of Success* (1957), *A Farewell To Arms* (1957), *Designing Woman* (1957), *Slaughter On Tenth Avenue* (1957), *Kathy O* (1958), *Act One* (1963), *A Dream Of Kings* (1969), *Such Good Friends* (1971), *The Money* (1976), *God Told Me So* (1976), *Demon* (1977), *Last Embrace* (1979), *And Justice For All* (1979).

LEWIS, JERRY LEE

b. 29 September 1935, Ferriday, Louisiana, USA. The 'Killer' is the personification of 50s rock 'n' roll at its best. He is rowdy, raw, rebellious and uncompromising. The outrageous piano-pounder has a voice that exudes excitement and an aura of arrogance that becomes understandable after witnessing the seething hysteria and mass excitement at his concerts. As a southern boy, Lewis was brought up listening to many musical styles in a home where religion was as important as breathing. In 1950, he attended a fundamentalist bible school in Waxahachie, Texas, but was expelled. The clash between the secular and the religious would govern Lewis' life and art for the remainder of his career. He first recorded on *The Louisiana Hayride* in 1954 and decided that Elvis Presley's label, Sun Records, was where he wanted to be. His distinctive version of country star Ray Price's 'Crazy Arms' was his Sun debut, but it was his second single, a revival of Roy Hall's 'Whole Lotta Shakin' Goin' On' in 1957 that propelled him to international fame. The record, which was initially banned as obscene, narrowly missed the top of the US chart, went on to hit number 1 on the R&B and country charts and

introduced the fair-haired, one-man piano wrecker to a world ready for a good shaking up. He stole the show from many other stars in the film *Jamboree* in which he sang the classic 'Great Balls Of Fire', which became his biggest hit and topped the UK chart and made number 2 in the USA. He kept up the barrage of rowdy and unadulterated rock with the US/UK Top 10 single 'Breathless', which, like its predecessor, had been written by Otis Blackwell.

Problems started for the flamboyant 'god of the glissando' when he arrived in Britain for a tour in 1958, accompanied by his third wife, Myra, who was also his 13-year-old second cousin. The UK media stirred up a hornet's nest and the tour had to be cancelled after only three concerts, even though the majority of the audience loved him. The furore followed Lewis home and support for him in his homeland also waned; he never returned to the Top 20 pop chart in the USA. His last big hit of the 50s was the title song from his film *High School Confidential*, which made the UK Top 20 in 1959 and number 21 in the USA. Despite a continued high standard of output, his records either only made the lower chart rungs or missed altogether. When his version of Ray Charles' 'What'd I Say' hit the UK Top 10 in 1960 (US number 30) it looked like a record revival was on the way, but it was not to be. The fickle general public may have disowned the hard-living, hellraiser, but his hardcore fans remained loyal and his tours were sell-outs during the 60s. He joined Smash Records in 1963 and although the material he recorded with the company was generally unimaginative, there were some excellent live recordings, most notably *The Greatest Live Show On Earth* (1964).

In 1966, Lewis made an unexpected entry into rock music theatre when he was signed to play Iago in Jack Good's *Catch My Soul*, inspired by *Othello*. After a decade playing rock 'n' roll, Lewis decided to concentrate on country material in 1968. He had often featured country songs in his repertoire, so his new policy did not represent an about-face. This changeover was an instant success – country fans welcomed back their prodigal son with open arms. Over the next 13 years Lewis was one of country's top-selling artists and was a main attraction wherever he put on his 'Greatest Show On Earth'. He first appeared at the *Grand Ole Opry* in 1973, playing an unprecedented 50-minute set. He topped the country chart with records such as 'There Must Be More To Love Than This' in 1970, 'Would You Take Another Chance On Me?' in 1971 and a revival of 'Chantilly Lace' a year later. The latter also returned him briefly to the transatlantic Top 40. However, he also kept the rock 'n' roll flag flying by playing revival shows around the world and by always including his old 50s hits in his stage shows. In fact, long-time fans have always been well catered for – numerous compilations of top-class out-takes and never previously issued tracks from the 50s have regularly been released over the last 20 years. On the personal front, his life has never been short of tragedies, often compounded by his alcohol and drug problems. His family has been equally prone to tragedy.

In November 1973, his 19-year-old son, Jerry Lee Jnr., was killed in a road accident following a period of drug abuse and treatment for mental illness. Lewis' own behaviour during the mid-70s was increasingly erratic. He accidentally shot his bass player in the chest – the musician survived and sued him. Late in 1976, Lewis was arrested for waving a gun outside Elvis Presley's Gracelands home. Two years later, Lewis signed to Elektra Records for the appropriately titled *Rockin' My Life Away*. Unfortunately, his association with the company ended with much-publicized lawsuits. In 1981, Lewis was hospitalized and allegedly close to death from a haemorrhaged ulcer. He survived that ordeal and was soon back on the road. In 1982, his fourth wife drowned in a swimming pool. The following year, his fifth wife was found dead at his home following a methadone overdose. The deaths brought fresh scandal to Lewis' troubled life. Meanwhile, the IRS were challenging his earnings from the late 70s in another elongated dispute. A sixth marriage followed, along with more bleeding ulcers and a period in the Betty Ford Clinic for treatment for his pain-killer addiction.

Remarkably, Lewis' body and spirit have remained intact, despite these harrowing experiences. During his career he has released dozens of albums, the most successful being *The Session* in 1973, his sole US Top 40 album, on which many pop names of the period backed him, including Peter Frampton and Rory Gallagher. Lewis was one of the first people inducted into the Rock And Roll Hall Of Fame in 1986. In 1989, a biopic of his early career, *Great Balls Of Fire*, starring Dennis Quaid, brought him briefly back into the public eye. In 1990, a much-awaited UK tour had to be cancelled when Lewis and his sixth wife (who was not even born at the time of his fateful first tour) failed to appear. He moved to Dublin, Eire, to avoid the US tax man, but eventually returned to Memphis. In 1995, he jammed with Bruce Springsteen at the opening of the Rock And Roll Hall Of Fame building in Cleveland.

His cousin Mickey Gilley is an accomplished country artist, while another cousin, Jimmy Lee Swaggart, has emerged as one of America's premier television evangelists. Any understanding of the career of Jerry Lee Lewis is inextricably linked with the parallel rise and fall of Swaggart. They were both excellent piano players, but whereas Lewis devoted his energies to the 'devil's music', Swaggart damned rock 'n' roll from the pulpit and played gospel music. Lewis has often described his career as a flight from God, with Swaggart cast in the role of his conscience and indefatigable redeemer. The relationship, however, was more complex than that, and the spirits of these two American institutions were latterly revealed as more complementary than antithetical. When Swaggart was discovered with a prostitute in a motel, the evangelist created a scandal that surpassed even his cousin's series of dramas. Tragedy, scandal and, above all, rock 'n' roll have seldom played such an intrinsic role in one musician's life.

● ALBUMS: *Jerry Lee Lewis* (Sun 1957) ★★★★, *Jerry Lee Lewis And His Pumping Piano* (London 1958) ★★★, *Jerry Lee's Greatest* (Sun 1961) ★★★★, *Rockin' With Jerry Lee Lewis* (Design 1963) ★★★, *The Greatest Live Show On Earth* (Smash 1964) ★★★, with the Nashville Teens *Live At The Star Club, Hamburg* (Philips 1965) ★★, *The Return Of Rock* (Smash 1965) ★★★, *Country Songs For City Folks* (Smash 1965) ★★★, *Whole Lotta Shakin' Goin' On* (London 1965) ★★★★, *Memphis Beat* (Smash 1966) ★★★, *By Request – More Greatest Live Show On Earth* (Smash 1966) ★★★, *Breathless* (London 1967) ★★★, *Soul My Way* (Smash 1967) ★★★, *Got You On My Mind* (Fontana 1968) ★★★, *Another Time, Another Place* (Mercury 1969) ★★★, *She Still Comes Around* (Mercury 1969) ★★★, *I'm On Fire* (Mercury 1969) ★★★, *Jerry Lee Lewis' Rockin' Rhythm And Blues* (Sun 1969) ★★★, with Linda Gail Lewis *Together* (Mercury 1970) ★★★, *She Even Woke Me Up To Say Goodbye* (Mercury 1970) ★★★, *A Taste Of Country* (Sun 1970) ★★★, *There Must Be More To Love Than This* (Mercury 1970) ★★★, *Johnny Cash And Jerry Lee Lewis Sing Hank Williams* (Sun 1971) ★★★, *Touching Home* (Mercury 1971) ★★★, *In Loving Memories* (Mercury 1971) ★★★, *Would You Take Another Chance On Me* (Mercury 1972) ★★★, *The Killer Rocks On* (Mercury 1972) ★★★, *Old Tyme Country Music* (Sun 1972) ★★★, with Johnny Cash *Sunday Down South* (Sun 1972) ★★, *The Session* (Mercury 1973) ★★★, *Live At The International, Las Vegas* (Mercury 1973) ★★★, *Great Balls of Fire* (Hallmark 1973) ★★★, *Southern Roots* (Mercury 1974) ★★★, *Rockin' Up A Storm* (Sun 1974) ★★★, *Rockin' And Free* (Sun 1974) ★★★, *I'm A Rocker* (Mercury 1975) ★★★, *Odd Man In* (Mercury 1975) ★★★, *Jerry Lee Lewis* (Elektra 1979) ★★★, *Killer Country* (Elektra 1980) ★★★, *When Two Worlds Collide* (Elektra 1980) ★★★, with Johnny Cash, Carl Perkins *The Survivors* (Columbia 1982) ★★★, *My Fingers Do The Talking* (MCA 1983) ★★★, *I Am What I Am* (MCA 1984) ★★★, with Webb Pierce, Mel Tillis, Faron Young *Four Legends* (1985) ★★★, with Johnny Cash, Carl Perkins, Roy Orbison *Class Of '55* (America 1986) ★★★, *Interviews From The Class Of '55 Recording Sessions* (America 1986) ★★, *Keep Your Hands Off It* (Zu Zazz 1987) ★★★, *Don't Drop It* (Zu Zazz 1988) ★★★, *Live In Italy* (Magnum Force 1989) ★★, *Great Balls Of Fire!* film soundtrack (Polydor 1989) ★★★, with Carl Perkins, Elvis Presley *The Million Dollar Quartet* (RCA 1990) ★★★, *Rocket* (Instant 1990) ★★★, *Live At The Vapors Club* (Ace 1991) ★★★, *Young Blood* (Sire/Elektra 1995) ★★★, *Jerry Lee Lewis At Hank Cochran's 1987 recording* (Tomato 1996) ★★★, *Live At Gilley's* (Connoisseur Collection 2000) ★★.

● COMPILATIONS: *Golden Hits* (Smash 1964) ★★★★, *Country Music Hall Of Fame Hits Volume 1* (Smash 1969) ★★★★, *Country Music Hall Of Fame Hits Volume 2* (Smash 1969) ★★★★, *Original Golden Hits Volume 1* (Sun 1969) ★★★★, *Original Golden Hits Volume 2* (Sun 1969) ★★★, *The Best Of Jerry Lee Lewis* (Smash 1970) ★★★★, *Original Golden Hits Volume 3* (Sun 1971) ★★★, *Monsters* (Sun 1971) ★★★, *Rockin' With Jerry Lee Lewis* (Mercury 1972) ★★★★, *Fan Club Choice* (Mercury

1974) ★★★, *Whole Lotta Shakin' Goin' On* (Hallmark 1974) ★★★★, *Good Rockin' Tonight* (Hallmark 1975) ★★★, *Jerry Lee Lewis And His Pumping Piano* (Charly 1975) ★★★, *Rare Jerry Lee Lewis Volume 1* (Charly 1975) ★★★, *Rare Jerry Lee Lewis Volume 2* (Charly 1975) ★★★, *The Jerry Lee Lewis Collection* (Hallmark 1976) ★★★★, *Golden Hits* (Mercury 1976) ★★★, *The Original Jerry Lee Lewis* (Charly 1976) ★★★★, *Nuggets* (Charly 1977) ★★★★, *Nuggets Volume 2* (Charly 1977) ★★★, *The Essential Jerry Lee Lewis* (Charly 1978) ★★★★, *Shakin' Jerry Lee* (Arcade 1978) ★★★, *Back To Back* (Mercury 1978) ★★★, *Duets* (Sun 1979) ★★★, *Jerry Lee Lewis* (Hammer 1979) ★★★, *Good Golly Miss Molly* (Bravo 1980) ★★★, *Trio Plus* (Sun 1980) ★★★, *Jerry Lee's Greatest* (Charly 1981) ★★★★, *Killer Country* i (Elektra 1981) ★★★★, *Jerry Lee Lewis* (Mercury 1981) ★★★, *The Sun Years* 12-LP box set (Sun 1984) ★★★★, *18 Original Sun Greatest Hits* (Rhino 1984) ★★★★, *Milestones* (Rhino 1985) ★★★★, *The Collection* (Deja Vu 1986) ★★★★, *The Pumpin' Piano Cat* (Sun 1986) ★★★, *Great Balls Of Fire* (Sun 1986) ★★★★, *The Wild One* (Sun 1986) ★★★, *At The Country Store* (Starblend 1987) ★★★, *The Very Best Of Jerry Lee Lewis* (Philips 1987) ★★★★, *The Country Sound Of Jerry Lee Lewis* (Pickwick 1988) ★★, *The Classic Jerry Lee Lewis* 8-CD box set (Bear Family 1989) ★★★★, *The Classic Jerry Lee Lewis* (Ocean 1989) ★★★, *Killer's Birthday Cake* (Sun 1989) ★★★, *Killer's Rhythm And Blues* (Sun 1989) ★★★★, *Killer: The Mercury Years, Volume One, 1963-1968* (Mercury 1989) ★★★, *Killer: The Mercury Years, Volume Two, 1969-1972* (Mercury 1989) ★★★, *Killer: The Mercury Years, Volume Three, 1973-1977* (Mercury 1989) ★★★★, *Great Balls Of Fire* (Pickwick 1989) ★★, *The EP Collection* (See For Miles 1990) ★★★★, *The Jerry Lee Lewis Collection* (Castle 1990) ★★★, *The Best Of Jerry Lee Lewis* (Curb 1991) ★★★, *Rockin' My Life Away* (Warners 1991) ★★★★, *Pretty Much Country* (Ace 1992) ★★★, *All Killer, No Filler: The Anthology* (Rhino 1993) ★★★★, *The Complete Palomino Club Recordings* (1993) ★★★, *The EP Collection Volume 2 ... Plus* (See For Miles 1994) ★★★★, *The Locust Years . . . And The Return To The Promised Land* 8-CD box set (Bear Family 1995) ★★★★, *Sun Classics* (Charly 1995) ★★★★, *Killer Country* ii (Mercury 1995) ★★★, *The Country Collection* (Eagle 1997) ★★★, *Sings The Rock 'N' Roll Classics* (Eagle 1997) ★★★, *The Killer Collection* (Spectrum 1998) ★★★, *Mercury Smashes ... And Rockin' Sessions* 10-CD box set (Bear Family 2001) ★★★★.

● VIDEOS: *Carl Perkins & Jerry Lee Lewis Live* (BBC Video 1987), *Jerry Lee Lewis* (Fox Video 1989), *I Am What I Am* (Charly Video 1990), *The Killer* (Telstar Video 1991), *Killer Performance* (Virgin Vision 1991), *The Jerry Lee Lewis Show* (MMG Video 1991).

● FURTHER READING: *Jerry Lee Lewis: The Ball Of Fire*, Allan Clark. *Jerry Lee Lewis*, Robert Palmer. *Whole Lotta Shakin' Goin' On: Jerry Lee Lewis*, Robert Cain. *Hellfire: The Jerry Lee Lewis Story*, Nick Tosches. *Great Balls Of Fire: The True Story Of Jerry Lee Lewis*, Myra Lewis. *Rockin' My Life Away: Listening To Jerry Lee Lewis*, Jimmy Guteman.

Killer!, Jerry Lee Lewis And Charles White. *The Devil, Me, And Jerry Lee*, Linda Gail Lewis with Les Pendleton.

● FILMS: *Jamboree* aka *Disc Jockey Jamboree* (1957), *Beach Ball* (1964), *Be My Guest* (1965), *American Hot Wax* (1976).

LEWIS, MONICA

b. 5 May 1922, Chicago, Illinois, USA. Lewis was born into a musical family, a career in showbusiness was virtually inevitable. Her father, Leon Lewis, was a symphonic composer and pianist, her mother, Jessica, sang with the Chicago Opera Company and became one of the country's leading vocal coaches. Her sister, Barbara Lewis Golub, became an accomplished concert pianist; while her brother, Marlo Lewis, was the producer of the original Ed Sullivan television show, *The Toast Of The Town*. Lewis first studied voice with her mother and left college at 17 to begin a career as a vocalist on radio. While still in her teens, she had her own programme, *Monica Makes Music*, on WMCA in New York. This early radio success led to a prestigious engagement at the Stork Club, and appearances with Benny Goodman's orchestra. After appearing on radio with Frank Sinatra, Dick Powell, and Morton Gould, Lewis had recording dates with Signature Records and Decca Records. She had a number of successes, including 'A Tree In A Meadow' and 'Autumn Leaves'.

Alongside her appearances on radio and records, for more than a decade, Lewis provided the voice for the 'Chiquita Banana' character in cartoons and commercials. She had appeared on the first of Sullivan's television shows, in 1948, and then came to the attention of Hollywood. She was signed by MGM where she was groomed as a dramatic actress and the studio's answer to popular star Lana Turner. Among the movies Lewis made was *The Strip* (1951), which starred Mickey Rooney as a jazz drummer with the featured band of Louis Armstrong. She continued to play roles in films, and also provided an on and off screen singing voice, including *Everything I Have Is Yours* (1952), in which she sang the title song and danced with star Gower Champion. She also appeared frequently on television, working with Bob Hope, Milton Berle, and Dean Martin and Jerry Lewis, sharing top-billing with the latter pair for a New York club engagement. She also toured with USO shows, appearing in Korea with Danny Kaye.

Although at the height of her popularity, and headlining at leading hotels and clubs in Las Vegas, New York, San Francisco and elsewhere, Lewis, now married to movie executive Jennings Lang, retired. However, the call was too strong for a permanent absence and in the 60s, 70s and 80s she appeared in numerous television shows, including *Wagon Train*, *Peter Gunn*, *Ironside*, *Quincy*, *Falcon Crest* and *Remington Steele*. She also made occasional movie appearances, including *Charley Varrick* (1973), *Airport '77* (1977) and *The Sting II* (1983). In the mid- and late 80s, Lewis returned to the recording studio, releasing the highly praised *Never Let Me Go*. The success of this album resulted in the re-release of her 50s recordings.

A fluent interpreter of standards and the great show tunes, Lewis' singing voice is clear and true. Her warm sound, allied as it is to a subtle vibrato and underlying power, allows her to bring a distinctive touch to a wide range of material. Her son Mike Lang is a noted studio musician and composer who has played piano with several leading jazz artists. He accompanied Lewis on some of her later recordings, which he also produced.

● ALBUMS: *Sing It To The Marines* (Verve 1948) ★★★, *Never Let Me Go* (Equinox 1988) ★★★ *Monica Lewis Sings Songbook Collection 1945-1949* (Fresh Sound 1992) ★★★, *Why Did I Choose You?* (Equinox 1997) ★★★.

● COMPILATIONS: *From The Vaults Of MGM* 50s recordings (Verve 1988) ★★★, *But Beautiful* 50s recordings (Fresh Sound/Jubilee 1989) ★★★.

● FILMS: *The Strip* (1951), *Inside Straight* (1951), *Excuse My Dust* (1951), *Everything I Have Is Yours* (1952), *Affair With A Stranger* (1953), *The D.I.* aka *The Drill Instructor* (1957), *Charley Varrick* aka *Kill Charley Varrick* (1973), *Earthquake* (1974), *Airport '77* (1977), *Rollercoaster* (1977), *Nunzio* (1978), *Zero To Sixty* (1978), *The Concorde: Airport '79* (1979), *Boxoffice* (1982), *The Sting II* (1983), *Stick* (1985), *Dead Heat* (1988).

LEWIS, SMILEY

b. Overton Amos Lemons, 5 July 1913, DeQuincy, Louisiana, USA, d. 7 October 1966. While failing to gain the commercial plaudits his work deserved, this New Orleans-based artist was responsible for some of that city's finest music. He made his recording debut, as Smiling Lewis, in 1947, but his strongest work appeared during the 50s. 'The Bells Are Ringing' (1952) took him into the US R&B chart, and his biggest hit came three years later with 'I Hear You Knocking'. This seminal slice of Crescent City blues featured pianist Huey 'Piano' Smith and bandleader Dave Bartholomew, and was revived successfully in 1970 by Dave Edmunds. Smiley's career was dogged by ill luck. His original version of 'Blue Monday' was a hit in the hands of Fats Domino, while Elvis Presley took another song, 'One Night', and by altering its risqué lyric, secured a massive pop hit in the process. A further powerful Lewis performance, 'Shame, Shame, Shame', has subsequently become an R&B standard and it was even covered by the Merseybeats on their EP *On Stage* in 1964. This underrated artist continued recording into the 60s, but died of cancer in 1966.

● ALBUMS: *I Hear You Knocking* (Imperial 1961) ★★★.

● COMPILATIONS: *Caledonia's Party* (KC 1986) ★★★, *New Orleans Bounce – 30 Of His Best* (Sequel 1991) ★★★.

LEWIS, VIC

b. 29 July 1919, London, England. Lewis began playing a four-string banjo while still a child, later switching to guitar. In his teens he formed his own quartet, having developed an interest in jazz through listening to records. His quartet appeared on a talent show and soon obtained radio work on the BBC and Radio Luxembourg and also in London theatres. In the London jazz clubs Lewis met and played with artists such as Django Reinhardt, Stéphane Grappelli, George Shearing and George Chisholm. In 1938, he visited New York where he played with Joe Marsala, Marty Marsala, Joe Bushkin, Buddy Rich, Pee Wee Russell, Bobby Hackett and other noted jazzmen, even sitting in with Tommy Dorsey, Jack Teagarden and Louis Armstrong. He also made a handful of records during this trip with Hackett, Eddie Condon and Zutty Singleton in the band. He returned to England and with the outbreak of war served in the RAF where he played in a band whenever the opportunity presented itself. After the war, Lewis formed a new unit, teaming up with Jack Parnell to co-lead a small group. When Parnell moved on, Lewis continued to lead the band, which proved very popular and broadcast frequently on the BBC. In the late 40s Lewis formed a big band, employing musicians such as Ronnie Chamberlain, Bob Efford and Gordon Langhorn, that emulated the music of Stan Kenton. He also formed an orchestra that backed visiting American artists including Armstrong and Johnny Ray. On occasion, Lewis sat in with Armstrong and Kenton, playing trombone. In the 60s, Lewis switched tracks, becoming a manager and agent, handling tours by Count Basie, whom he had met in New York in 1938, Dudley Moore (his first client), Judy Garland, Carmen McRae, Johnny Mathis, Andy Williams and Nina Simone. Lewis was also deeply involved with NEMS Enterprises, working with Brian Epstein, the Beatles and Cilla Black. Lewis' activities in these areas continued through the 70s when he organized tours for Shirley Bassey and Elton John. He retained his jazz links, however, recording a bossa nova album in 1963, half in the USA with several Kenton alumni and half in London with a band featuring Tubby Hayes and Ronnie Scott. In the early 80s he began to form occasional big bands for jazz dates. He recruited visiting American stars such as Shorty Rogers and Bud Shank to perform on a series of records. As a bandleader and promoter, Lewis has been active for many decades and has brought to the UK jazz scene a great deal of enthusiasm; his activities on the pop scene were also of much value. For all that, as his autobiography hints, he would probably have given away his entire musical career for a chance to play cricket for England.

● ALBUMS: *Mulligan's Music And At The Royal Festival Hall* (1955) ★★★★, *Vic Lewis And His Bossa Nova All Stars* (1963) ★★★★, *Vic Lewis At The Beaulieu Jazz Festival* (1965) ★★★, *Vic Lewis Plays The Music Of Donovan Leith* (1968) ★★, *Vic Lewis With Maynard Ferguson* (1969) ★★★, *Don't Cry For Me Argentina* (1974) ★★, *Vic Lewis And R.P.O.* (RCA 1977) ★★★, *Back Again* (1984) ★★★, *Vic Lewis Big Bands* (1985) ★★★, *Tea Break* (1985) ★★★, *Vic Lewis And The West Coast All Stars* (1989) ★★★★, *Know It Today, Know It Tomorrow* (1993) ★★★, *Shake Down The Stars* (Candid 1993) ★★★, *Play Bill Holman* (Candid 1994) ★★★, *A Celebration Of West Coast Jazz* (Candid 1996) ★★★★.

● COMPILATIONS: *My Life, My Way* 4-LP box set (1975) ★★★, *New York, 1938* (Esquire 1986) ★★★, *Vic Lewis Jam Sessions, Volumes 1-6 (1938-49)* (Harlequin 1986) ★★★, *Vic Lewis Plays Stan Kenton (1948-54)* (Harlequin 1987) ★★★★, *The EMI Years* (EMI 1991) ★★★★, *The Golden Years 1938-46* recordings (Candid 1999) ★★★.
● FURTHER READING: *Music And Maiden Overs: My Show Business Life*, Vic Lewis with Tony Barrow.

LIBERACE

b. Wladziu Valentino Liberace, 16 May 1919, West Allis, Wisconsin, USA, d. 4 February 1987, Palm Springs, Florida, USA. This larger-than-life pianist had no major chart hits – but had an indefinable charm and talent that gave delight to multitudes of fans across the globe. Of Polish-Italian extraction, he was raised in a household where there was always music – particularly from father Salvatore who played French horn in both John Philip Sousa's Concert Band and the Milwaukee Symphony Orchestra. George and the younger Wladziu were, likewise, both eager to become professional players. Wladziu's piano skills were praised by no less than Paderewski, and he won a place at Wisconsin College of Music at the age of seven.

During his 17-year scholarship – the longest ever awarded by the academy – he made his concert debut as a soloist at the age of 11 and was fronting renowned symphony orchestras while still an adolescent. A fulfilling career of classical recitals and university master classes might have beckoned but for the artist's innate sense of humour and flair for self-promotion. In 1934, he had elocution lessons to dilute his Polish accent. After service in an overseas entertainments unit during World War II, he played and sang in club dance bands and it was during a residency at the Wunderbar in Warsaw, Wisconsin, that he was first introduced as 'Liberace'. At New York's Persian Rooms, an experiment whereby he performed counterpoints to records – including his own one-shot single for the Signature label – played on the venue's sound system, was curtailed by a Musicians Union ban. A happier season in a Californian hotel resulted in a Decca Records contract, for which he was visualized as a second Frankie Carle. However, wishing to develop a more personal style, he moved to Columbia Records where, supervised by Mitch Miller, he recorded a flamboyant version of 'September Song' which, supplemented by an in-concert album, brought Liberace to the attention of a national audience.

By the early 50s, his repertoire embraced George Gershwin favourites, cocktail jazz, film themes ('Unchained Melody'), boogie-woogie and self-composed pieces ('Rhapsody By Candlelight'), as well as adaptations of light classics such as 'The Story Of Three Loves' – borrowed from a Rachmaninov variation on a tune by Paganini. Nevertheless, Liberace struck the most popular chord with his encores, in which doggerel such as 'Maizy Doats' or 'Three Little Fishies' were dressed in arrangements littered with twee arpeggios and trills. He also started garbing himself from a wardrobe that stretched to rhinestone, white mink, sequins, gold lamé and similar razzle-dazzle. Crowned with a carefully waved coiffeur, he oozed charm and extravagant gesture, with a candelabra-lit piano as the focal point of the epic vulgarity that was *The Liberace Show*, televised coast-to-coast from Los Angeles; the show established a public image that he later tried in vain to modify. His fame was such that he was name-checked in 'Mr. Sandman', a 1954 million-seller by the Chordettes, and a year later, starred (as a deaf concert pianist) in a film, *Sincerely Yours*, with brother George (future administrator of the Liberace Museum in Las Vegas) as musical director. Another spin-off was the publication of a Liberace cookbook.

Following the celebration of his quarter century in showbusiness with a Hollywood Bowl spectacular in 1956, Liberace crossed to England (where a vocal outing, 'I Don't Care', was lodged in the Top 30) for the first of three Royal Command Performances. While in the UK, he instigated a High Court action, successfully suing the *Daily Mirror*, whose waspish columnist Cassandra had written an article on the star laced with sexual innuendo. During the next decade, a cameo in the film satire *The Loved One* was reviewed not unfavourably, as was one of his early albums for RCA Records in which he aimed more directly at the contemporary market. This, however, was a rare excursion, as his work generally maintained a certain steady consistency – or 'squareness', in the words of his detractors – that deviated little from the commercial blueprint wrought in the 50s. Nonetheless, Liberace's mode of presentation left its mark on stars such as Gary Glitter, Elton John and Queen. Although attendant publicity boosted box office takings on a world tour, embarrassing tabloid newspaper allegations by a former employee placed his career in a darker perspective. When the singer died on 4 February 1987 at his Palm Springs mansion, the words 'kidney complaint' were assumed to be a euphemism for an AIDS-related illness. For a 75th Birthday Celebration in 1994, fans from all over America gathered to pay their respects at Liberace Plaza in Las Vegas.

● ALBUMS: *Piano* (Advance 1951) ★★★, *Liberace At the Piano* (Columbia 1952) ★★★, *An Evening With Liberace* (Columbia 1953) ★★★★, *Liberace By Candlelight* (Columbia 1953) ★★★, *Concertos For You* (Columbia 1953) ★★★, *Concertos For You Volume 2* (Columbia 1954) ★★★, *Plays Chopin* (Columbia 1954) ★★★, *Plays Chopin Volume 2* (Columbia 1954) ★★★, *Sincerely Yours* film soundtrack (Columbia 1953) ★★★, *Piano Reverie* (Columbia 1955) ★★★, *Kiddin' On The Keys* (Columbia 1956) ★★★, *My Inspiration* (Coral 1960) ★★★, *Liberace At The Palladium* (Coral 1961) ★★★, *My Parade Of Golden Favourites* (Coral 1961) ★★★, *As Time Goes By* (Coral 1962) ★★★, *Rhapsody By Candlelight* (Coral 1962) ★★★, *Mr. Showmanship* (Coral 1963) ★★★, *Christmas* (Coral 1963) ★★, *My Most Requested* (Coral 1964) ★★★, *Liberace At The American* (Coral 1964) ★★★, *Golden Hits Of Hollywood* (Coral 1965) ★★★,

Liberace Now (Coral 1967) ★★★, *A Brand New Me* (Warners 1970) ★★, *Candlelight Classics* (Ember 1973) ★★★, *Piano Gems* (Pye 1976) ★★★, *Mr. Showmanship – Live* (Pye 1978) ★★★, *New Sounds* (Dot 1979) ★★★.
● COMPILATIONS: *Just For You* (PRT 1976) ★★★, *Best Of Liberace* (MCA 1983) ★★★, *The Collection* (Castle 1988) ★★★, *The Very Best Of Liberace* (Half Moon 1998) ★★★.
● VIDEOS: *Liberace In Las Vegas* (Virgin Vision 1988), *Liberace Live* (Vestron Music 1988).
● FURTHER READING: *Liberace*, Liberace. *Liberace: The True Story*, B. Thomas.

LIGGINS, JOE

b. 9 July 1916, Guthrie, Oklahoma, USA, d. 26 July 1987, Los Angeles, California, USA. After attempting to learn various brass instruments, Joe Liggins settled down to study musical composition and piano arrangement. After moving to California, he began writing for and playing with local bands, graduating in the 40s to the respected units of Cee Pee Johnson and Sammy Franklin; he was working with the latter when, in 1945, he left to form his own group, the Honeydrippers. Joe Liggins And His Honeydrippers first recorded for Exclusive, with whom they had 10 hits between 1945 and 1949 – including the huge crossover hits 'The Honeydripper' and 'I've Got A Right To Cry'; he followed his brother Jimmy to Specialty Records in 1950 where the hits continued with 'Rag Mop' and the hugely successful 'Pink Champagne' (*Billboard*'s number 1 blues record of the year). Leaving Specialty in 1954, Liggins went briefly to Mercury (1954) and Aladdin Records (1956) before returning to Mercury to record an album in 1962. Later singles appeared on tiny independents such as his own Honeydripper label and Jimmy Liggins' Duplex Records, and he was enjoying something of a renaissance at the time of his death in 1987.
● ALBUMS: *Honeydripper* (Mercury 1962) ★★★★, *Great R&B Oldies* (1972) ★★★, with Jimmy Liggins *Saturday Night Boogie Woogie Man* (Sonet 1974) ★★★.
● COMPILATIONS: *Darktown Strutters' Ball* (Jukebox Lil 1981) ★★★, *The Honeydripper* (Jukebox Lil 1988) ★★★, *Joe Liggins & The Honeydrippers* (Ace 1989) ★★★★, *Vol. 2: Drippers Boogie* (Ace 1993) ★★★★.

LIGHT, ENOCH

b. Enoch Henry Light, 18 August 1905, Canton, Ohio, USA, d. 31 July 1978, New York City, New York, USA. Tagged Enoch Light And His Light Brigade, Light's dance band recorded a number of original compositions for Bluebird Records, Vocalion Records and RCA Records during their lifetime. These included 'Rio Junction', 'The Daddy Of Them All', 'Big Band Bossa', 'Private Eye Suite', 'Cinderella' and 'Daniel Boone', as well as their theme tune, 'You Are My Lucky Star'. Many of these were novelty affairs themed after popular characters and occupations of the day, but all were performed with skill and verve. Light had originally attended Johns Hopkins University

before establishing the band in the late-20s, with the intention of playing the hotel and ballroom circuit with their sweet, highly commercial music. In the early 30s the band toured Europe, before returning to the US for dates at the Taft Hotel in New York. Light also enjoyed enormous popularity on radio during this period. The early 40s saw the Light Brigade switch direction to swing, shortly before their leader retired from bandleading to concentrate on a career as a manager.
In the early 50s Light made a career move which, ultimately, would lead to him being remembered in the history of popular music as more than just a purveyor of sweet danceband music. In 1954 he became president of Waldorf Music Hall Records, a label which issued cheap 10-inch albums for sale through the Woolworths store. Two years later Light set up Grand Award, many of whose recordings were stereo sound recordings of staples of the big band era engineered and performed by a personnel list including Light, arranger Lew Davies, trombonist Bobby Byrne, and pianist Dick Hyman, the latter often under the alias Knuckles O'Toole. In 1959 Light inaugurated Command Records, with the aim of pursuing his interest in the burgeoning market for stereo sound. Though he employed top-notch musicians such as Hyman and guitarist Tony Mottola, Light's own production work on the label's pop percussion albums was the instrumental factor in popularising left-right channelization. Command's releases were precisely engineered masterpieces that never resorted to the cheap audio effects employed by other studios.
The label's debut release, 1959's *Persuasive Percussion*, remains one of the biggest-selling albums in the history of the US charts, remaining in the number 1 position for 13 weeks. The album also set the style for future releases – a bold abstract design by artist Josef Albers, and a gatefold sleeve containing verbose liner notes by Light himself. Light continued to experiment in the studio, recording 1961's *Stereo 35/MM* on 35mm film instead of tape, dramatically reducing sound distortion in the process. The album was another huge success, topping the US album chart for seven weeks. Light sold Command to ABC Records in 1965, and instantly disassociated himself from the cost cutting antics of the new major label owners. He set up Project 3 Records with many of his loyal staff from Command and continued to oversee the release of beautifully designed and recorded easy listening albums until his retirement in 1974.
● ALBUMS: *Roaring 20s* (Grand Award 1958) ★★, *Flirty 30s* (Grand Award 1958) ★★, *Waltzes For Dancing* (Grand Award 1958) ★★, *Tommy Dorsey's Song Hits* (Grand Award 1958) ★★, *Glenn Miller's Song Hits* (Grand Award 1958) ★★, *Roaring 20s Volume 2* (Grand Award 1958) ★★★, *Viennese Waltzes* (Grand Award 1958) ★★, *Torchy 30s* (Grand Award 1958) ★★, *I Want To Be Happy Cha Chas* (Grand Award 1958) ★★, *Roaring 20s Volume 3* (Grand Award 1959) ★★, *Happy Cha Chas Volume 2* (Grand Award 1959) ★★, *Persuasive Percussion* (Command 1959) ★★★★, *Provocative*

Percussion (Command 1959) ★★★, *Persuasive Percussion Volume 2* (Command 1960) ★★★, *Provocative Percussion Volume 2* (Command 1960) ★★★, *Pertinent Percussive Cha Chas* (Command 1960) ★★, *Persuasive Percussion Volume 3* (Command 1960) ★★★, *Big Bold And Brassy: Percussion In Brass* (Command 1960) ★★, *Reeds And Percussion* (Command 1961) ★★, *Provocative Percussion Vol. III* (Command 1961) ★★★, *Far Away Places* (Command 1961) ★★★, *Stereo 35/MM* (Command 1961) ★★★★, *Persuasive Percussion Volume 4* (Command 1961) ★★★, *Stereo 35/MM Volume Two* (Command 1961) ★★★, *Vibrations* (Command 1962) ★★★, *Provocative Percussion Volume 4* (Command 1962) ★★★, *Great Themes From Hit Films* (Command 1962) ★★★, *Enoch Light And His Orchestra At Carnegie Hall Play Irving Berlin* (Command 1962) ★★, *Big Band Bossa Nova: The New Beat From Brazil* (Command 1962) ★★★, *Musical Coloring Book* (Command 1963) ★★, *Far Away Places Volume 2* (Command 1963) ★★★★, *Let's Dance The Bossa Nova* (Command 1963) ★★★, *1963 – The Year's Most Popular Themes* (Command 1963) ★★★, *Popular Music Of Leonard Bernstein* (Command 1963) ★★★, *Rome 35/MM – Roman Pops Promenade* (Command 1964) ★★★, *Dimension '3'* (Command 1964) ★★★★, *Great Themes From Hit Films* (Command 1964) ★★, *Discotheque Dance ... Dance ... Dance* (Command 1964) ★★★, *A New Concept Of Great Cole Porter Songs* (Command 1964) ★★, *Discotheque Volume 2* (Command 1965) ★★, *Magnificent Movie Themes* (Command 1965) ★★, *Discotheque* (Command 1966) ★★★, *Persuasive Percussion 1966* (Command 1966) ★★, *Rock Island* (Project 3 1966) ★★, *Spanish Strings* (Project 3 1966) ★★, *Film On Film – Great Movie Themes* (Project 3 1966) ★★, *Film Fame* (Project 3 1966) ★★, *The Best Of Hollywood '68, '69* (Project 3 1969) ★★, *Enoch Light And The Brass Menagerie* (Project 3 1969) ★★★, *Glittering Guitars* (Project 3 1969) ★★, *Enoch Light And The Brass Menagerie Volume 2* (Project 3 1969) ★★, *Spaced Out* (Project 3 1969) ★★★, *The Best Of The 1970 Movie Themes* (Project 3 1970) ★★, *Permissive Polyphonics* (Project 3 1970) ★★, *Big Band Hits Of The 30's* (Project 3 1970) ★★, *Big Band Hits Of The 30's & 40's* (Project 3 1970) ★★, *Big 'Hit Movie' Themes* (Project 3 1970) ★★, *Big Hits Of The 20's* (Project 3 1971) ★★, *Movie Hits!* (Project 3 1972) ★★, *Charge!* (Project 3 1972) ★★, *Brass Menagerie 1973* (Project 3 1973) ★★, *The Big Band Hits Of The 40's & 50's* (Project 3 1973) ★★★, *Future Sound Shock* (Project 3 1973) ★★, *Beatles Classics* (Project 3 1974) ★★.
● COMPILATIONS: *Command Performances* (Command 1964) ★★★★, *Command Performances Volume 2* (Command 1967) ★★★, *The Original Persuasive Percussion And Other Catalytic Sounds* (Command 1973) ★★★★, *The Best Of Enoch Light* (Project 3 1978) ★★★.

LIGHTNIN' SLIM

b. Otis Hicks, 13 March 1913, St. Louis, Missouri, USA, d. 27 July 1974, Detroit, Michigan, USA. It is as a Louisiana blues stylist that Hicks is best known, having settled in that state in his early teens. He learned guitar from his father and his brother, and made a name for himself on the Baton Rouge blues circuit during the 40s. In 1954, he recorded for Jay Miller's Feature label, and began that producer's long and fruitful relationship with the blues. These early recordings had a tough, spare sound that helps to place them alongside the very finest down-home blues of the 50s, and the quality was largely maintained over much of the next decade, with many singles leased to Excello Records. His partnership with harmonica player Lazy Lester was particularly effective and releases such as 'Mean Old Lonesome Train', 'Hoodoo Blues' and, especially, 'Rooster Blues', provided him with commercial success and kept him in demand for tours both locally and further afield. Many of his releases demonstrate his particular facility for taking raw material from the work of other popular bluesmen, such as Muddy Waters and Lightnin' Hopkins, and turning it into something entirely his own. The relationship with Miller finally came to an end in 1965, but within a few years, Slim found a wider forum for his music when he became a regular visitor to Europe.
● ALBUMS: *Rooster Blues* (Excello 1960) ★★★★, *Lightnin' Slim's Bell Ringer* (Excello 1965) ★★★★, *High And Lowdown* (Excello 1971) ★★★, *Over Easy* (Excello 1971) ★★.
● COMPILATIONS: *The Early Years* (1976) ★★★, *London Gumbo* (Sonet 1978) ★★, *The Feature Sides* (Flyright 1981) ★★★, *We Gotta Rock Tonight* (Flyright 1986) ★★★, *Blue Lightnin'* (Indigo 1992) ★★★, *King Of The Swamp Blues* 1954 recording (Flyright 1992) ★★★, *It's Mighty Crazy* 1954-58 recordings (Ace 1995) ★★★★, *Nothing But The Devil* (Ace 1996) ★★★★, *Winter Time Blues* (Ace 1998) ★★★★.

LITTLE RICHARD

b. Richard Wayne Penniman, 5 December 1935, Macon, Georgia, USA. The wildest and arguably the greatest and most influential of the 50s rock 'n' roll singers and songwriters. He first recorded in late 1951 in Atlanta for RCA Records, cutting eight urban blues tracks with his mentor Billy Wright's Orchestra, 'Taxi Blues' being the first of four unsuccessful single releases on the label. He moved to Houston, Texas, in 1953, and with the Tempo Toppers (vocals) and the Duces Of Rhythm (backing), he recorded four R&B tracks including 'Ain't That Good News'. Eight months later he recorded another four with Johnny Otis' Orchestra but none of these were released at the time. In February 1955, at the suggestion of Lloyd Price, he sent a demo to Specialty Records who realized his potential, and in September, under the guidance of producer Robert 'Bumps' Blackwell, recorded a dozen tracks in New Orleans. The classic 'Tutti Frutti', which was among them, gave him his first R&B and pop hit in the USA. The follow-up, 'Long Tall Sally', topped the R&B chart and was the first of his three US Top 10 hits, despite being covered by Pat Boone, whose previous record, a cover version of 'Tutti Frutti', was still charting. Richard's string of Top 20 hits continued with the double-sider 'Rip It Up'/'Ready Teddy', the former being his first UK release and chart entry in late 1956. Richard's frantic, unrestrained performance of his first two hits, 'Long Tall Sally' and 'Tutti Frutti', in the film *Don't Knock The Rock*, undoubtedly helped to push his subsequent UK single, which coupled the tracks, into the Top 3.

His next film and single was *The Girl Can't Help It*, the title song of which missed the US Top 40 but together with its b-side, 'She's Got It' (a reworking of his earlier track 'I Got It'), gave him two more UK Top 20 hits. The remainder of 1957 saw him notch up three more huge transatlantic hits with the rock 'n' roll classics 'Lucille', 'Keep A Knockin'' (he featured both in the movie *Mr. Rock & Roll*) and 'Jenny Jenny' and a Top 20 album with *Here's Little Richard*. At the very height of his career, the man with the highest pompadour in the business shocked the rock world by announcing, during an Australian tour, that he was quitting music to go into a theological college. In 1958, previously recorded material such as the transatlantic Top 10 hit 'Good Golly Miss Molly' kept his name on the chart, and a year later he had his biggest UK hit with a 1956 recording of the oldie 'Baby Face', which reached number 2. Between 1958 and 1962 Richard recorded only gospel music for Gone, Mercury Records (with producer Quincy Jones) and Atlantic Records. In late 1962, Richard toured the UK for the first time and the now short-haired wild man who pounded pianos and pierced eardrums with his manic falsetto was a huge success. In 1963, he worked in Europe with the Beatles and the Rolling Stones, who were both great admirers of his music.

His first rock recordings in the 60s were made back at Specialty and resulted in the UK Top 20 hit 'Bama Lama Bama Loo'. In 1964, he signed with Vee Jay Records where he re-recorded all his hits, revived a few oldies and cut some new rockers – but the sales were unimpressive. In the mid-60s, soul music was taking hold worldwide and Richard's soulful Vee Jay tracks, 'I Don't Know What You've Got But It's Got Me' (which featured Jimi Hendrix on guitar) and 'Without Love', although not pop hits, were among the best recordings of the genre. For the rest of the 60s he continued to draw the crowds, singing his old hits, and in the studios he mixed 50s rock and 60s soul for Modern Records in 1965, OKeh Records a year later and Brunswick Records in 1967. The best of these were his OKeh tracks, which included 'Poor Dog', 'Hurry Sundown' and the UK-recorded 'Get Down With It' (which gave Slade their first hit in the 70s).

Reprise Records, whom he joined in 1970, tried very hard to return him to the top, and under the expertise of producer Richard Perry he managed minor US hits 'Freedom Blues' and 'Greenwood, Mississippi', but his three albums sold poorly. The rest of the 70s was spent jumping from label to label, recording in supergroup-type projects and playing oldies shows. When he desired, he could still 'out-rock' anyone, but there was often too much Las Vegas glitter, excessive posturing and an element of self-parody. In 1976, he rejoined the church and for the next decade preached throughout America. In 1986, Richard was one of the first artists inducted into the Rock And Roll Hall of Fame and he successfully acted in the movie *Down And Out In Beverly Hills*, which included the rocking 'Great Gosh A'Mighty', which narrowly missed the US Top 40. Renewed interest spurred WEA Records to sign him and release *Lifetime Friend*, which included the chart record 'Operator'. Since the mid-80s he has become a frequent visitor on chat shows, an in-demand guest on other artist's records and a familiar face in videos (by acts ranging from Hank Williams Jnr. to Living Colour to Cinderella). He even has his own star on the Hollywood Walk of Fame and a boulevard named after him in his home town. Nowadays a regular presenter of music awards, he has also been the star of Jive Bunny hits. The leader of rebellious 50s rock 'n' roll, and the man who shook up the music business and the parents of the period, is now a much-loved personality accepted by all age groups.

● ALBUMS: *Little Richard* (Camden 1956) ★★★, *Here's Little Richard* (Specialty 1957) ★★★★★, *Little Richard Volume 2* (Specialty 1957) ★★★★★, *The Fabulous Little Richard* (Specialty 1958) ★★★★★, *Sings Gospel* (20th Century 1959) ★★, *It's Real* (Mercury 1961) ★★, *Little Richard Sings Freedom Songs* (Crown 1963) ★★, *Coming Home* (Coral 1963) ★★, *King Of The Gospel Singers* (Wing 1964) ★, *Little Richard Is Back* (Vee Jay 1965) ★★, *The Explosive Little Richard* (Columbia 1967) ★★★, *Good Golly Miss Molly* (Specialty 1969) ★★★, *The Little Richard Story* (Joy 1970) ★★★, *Well Alright* (Specialty 1970) ★★★, *Rock Hard Rock Heavy* (Specialty 1970) ★★, *You Can't Keep A Good Man Down* (Union Pacific 1970) ★★, *The Rill Thing* (Reprise 1970) ★★, *Mr Big* (Joy 1971) ★★, *Cast A Long Shadow* (Epic 1971) ★★, *King Of Rock 'n' Roll* (Reprise 1971) ★★★, *The Original Little Richard* (Specialty 1972) ★★★, *The Second Coming* (Warners 1973) ★★★, *Rip It Up* (Joy 1973) ★★, *Slippin' And Slidin'* (Joy 1973) ★★, *Good Golly Miss Molly* (Hallmark 1974) ★★★, *Greatest Hits Recorded Live* (Embassy 1974) ★★★, *Keep A Knockin'* (Rhapsody 1975) ★★, *Dollars Dollars* (Charly 1975) ★★, *The Great Ones* (MFP 1976) ★★, *Little Richard And Jimi Hendrix Together* (Ember 1977) ★, *Whole Lotta Shakin' Goin' On* (DJM 1977) ★★★, *Little Richard Now* (Creole 1977) ★★, *The Georgia Peach* (Charly 1980) ★★★, *Little Richard And His Band* (Specialty 1980) ★★, *Ooh! My Soul* (Charly 1982) ★★★, *Whole Lotta Shakin'* (Bulldog 1982) ★★★, *Get Down With It* (Edsel 1982) ★★, *The Real Thing* (Magnum Force 1983) ★★★, *Little Richard* (Cambra 1983) ★★★, *He's Got It* (Topline 1984) ★★, *Lifetime Friend* (Warners 1986) ★★★, *Black Diamond: Live In Boston – 1970* (Fireball 1998) ★★.

● COMPILATIONS: *His Biggest Hits* (Specialty 1963) ★★★★, *Little Richard's Greatest Hits* (Vee Jay 1965) ★★★★, *Little Richard's Greatest Hits* (OKeh 1967) ★★★★, *Little Richard's Greatest Hits* (Joy 1968) ★★★, *Little Richard's Grooviest 17 Original Hits* (Specialty 1968) ★★★★, *20 Original Greatest Hits* (Specialty 1976) ★★★★, *The*

Essential Little Richard (Specialty 1985) ★★★★, *18 Greatest Hits* (Rhino 1985) ★★★★, *20 Classic Cuts* (Ace 1986) ★★★★, *Shut Up! A Collection Of Rare Tracks (1951 – 1964)* (Rhino 1988) ★★★, *The Collection* (Castle 1989) ★★★★, *The Specialty Sessions* 6-CD box set (Specialty 1990) ★★★★★, *The Formative Years, 1951-53* (Bear Family 1989) ★★★, *The EP Collection* (See For Miles 1993) ★★★★★, *King Of Rock 'N' Roll* (ABM 1999) ★★★, *Talkin' Bout Soul* (RPM 2001) ★★.
● FURTHER READING: *The Life And Times Of Little Richard: The Quasar Of Rock*, Charles White.
● FILMS: *The Girl Can't Help It* (1956), *Don't Knock The Rock* (1956), *Catalina Caper* (1967).

LITTLE WALTER
b. Marion Walter Jacobs, 1 May 1930, Marksville, Louisiana, USA, d. 15 February 1968, Chicago, Illinois, USA. A major figure of post-war blues, Little Walter is credited for bringing the harmonica, or 'French harp', out from its rural setting and into an urban context. His career began at the age of 12 when he left home for New Orleans, but by 1946 Jacobs was working in Chicago's famed Maxwell Street. Early recordings for the Ora Nelle label were the prelude to his joining the Muddy Waters band, where he helped to forge what became the definitive electric Chicago blues group. The harmonica player emerged as a performer in his own right in 1952 when 'Juke', an instrumental recorded at the end of a Waters session, topped the R&B chart, where it remained for eight consecutive weeks. Little Walter And The Night Caps – David Myers (guitar), Louis Myers (guitar) and Fred Below (drums) – enjoyed further success when 'Sad Hours' and 'Mean Old World' reached the Top 10 in the same chart. The group then became known as Little Walter And The Jukes and, although obliged to fulfil recording agreements with Waters, Jacobs actively pursued his own career. He enjoyed further R&B hits with 'Blues With A Feeling' (1953), 'Last Night' (1954) and the infectious 'My Babe' (1955). The last song, patterned on a spiritual tune, 'This Train', was a second number 1 single and became much covered during later years.

Other notable releases included 'Mellow Down Easy' and 'Boom Boom (Out Go The Lights)' which were later recorded, respectively, by Paul Butterfield and the Blues Band. A haunting version of 'Key To The Highway' (1958), previously recorded by Big Bill Broonzy, gave Walter his final Top 10 entry. He nonetheless remained a pivotal figure, undertaking several tours, including one of Britain in 1964. His career, however, was undermined by personal problems. A pugnacious man with a quick temper and a reputation for heavy drinking, he died on 15 February 1968 as a result of injuries sustained in a street brawl. This ignominious end should not detract from Little Walter's status as an innovative figure. The first musician to amplify the harmonica, his heavy, swooping style became the linchpin for all who followed him, including Norton Buffalo, Butterfield and

Charlie Musselwhite.
● ALBUMS: *The Best Of Little Walter* (Checker 1958) ★★★★, *Little Walter* (Pye International 1964) ★★★★, *Hate To See You Go* (Chess 1969) ★★★, *Thunderbird* (Syndicate Chapter 1971) ★★★, *On The Road Again* (Xtra 1979) ★★★, *Quarter To Twelve* (Red Lightnin' 1982) ★★★.
● COMPILATIONS: *Chess Masters* (Charly 1983) ★★★★, *Boss Blues Harmonica* (Vogue 1986) ★★★★★, *Confessin' The Blues* (Chess 1986) ★★★★, *Windy City Blues* (Blue Moon 1986) ★★★, *Collection: Little Walter 20 Blues Greats* (Deja Vu 1987) ★★★, *The Blues World Of Little Walter* (Delmark 1988) ★★★★, *The Best Of Little Walter Volume 2* (Chess 1989) ★★★, *The Chess Years 1952 – '63* 4-CD box set (Chess 1993) ★★★★, *Blues With A Feeling* (MCA/Chess 1995) ★★★★.

LLOYD, A.L.
b. Albert Lancaster Lloyd, February 1908, London, England, d. 29 September 1982. Bert Lloyd was one of the prime movers of the 50s folk song revival in Britain. He had collected some 500 songs by 1935 and was determined to study and conduct research into folk music. In 1937, he sailed to Antarctica with a whaling fleet, adding further songs to his repertoire. On his return he joined BBC Radio as a scriptwriter. During the 40s he wrote *The Singing Englishman*, the first general book on folk song since Cecil Sharp's in 1909. He also compiled the *Penguin Book Of English Folk Song* with the composer Ralph Vaughan Williams. By the 50s, Lloyd was a full-time folklorist, making several field trips to record material in Bulgaria and Albania as well as publishing a selection of coalfield ballads, which provided repertoire for young singers in the growing number of folk song clubs. At this time he met Ewan MacColl, with whom he made his own first recordings, as part of the *Radio Ballads* series. During the 60s he made a series of solo albums for Topic Records, with accompanists including singers Anne Briggs and Frankie Armstrong, Alf Edwards (accordion), Martin Carthy (guitar, mandolin), Dave Swarbrick (fiddle) and actor and singer Harry H. Corbett. They covered drinking songs, industrial songs and selections from his sheep-shearing and whaling exploits. Lloyd also arranged compilation albums of sea shanties, industrial songs (*The Iron Muse*) and recordings from the Balkan field trips.
● ALBUMS: *Selections From The Penguin Book Of English Folk Songs* (Topic 1960) ★★★, *English Drinking Songs* (Topic 1962) ★★★, *The Iron Muse* (Topic 1963) ★★★, with Ewan MacColl *English And Scottish Popular Ballads* (Topic 1964) ★★★★, *All For Me Grog* (Topic 1964) ★★★, *The Bird In The Bush* (Topic 1964) ★★★, *First Person* (Topic 1966) ★★★, *Leviathan! Ballads & Songs Of The Whaling Trade* (Topic 1967) ★★★, *The Great Australian Legend* (Topic 1969) ★★★.
● COMPILATIONS: *Classic A.L. Lloyd* (Fellside 1995) ★★★★.
● FURTHER READING: *The Singing Englishman*, A.L. Lloyd.

LOCK UP YOUR DAUGHTERS

This show was the first to be presented at the new Mermaid Theatre in the City of London, on 28 May 1959, and was, appropriately enough, the brainchild of the Mermaid's founder, Bernard (later, Sir Bernard) Miles. His adaptation of Henry Fielding's *Rape Upon Rape* was an extremely bawdy tale in which a gentle maiden, Hilaret (Stephanie Voss), and her would-be rapist, Ramble (Frederick Jaeger), appear before the lecherous Justice Squeezum (Richard Wordsworth). Squeezum's efforts to inflict his own individual brand of custodial sentence on Hilaret lead to highly complicated manoeuvres that involve the far-from-innocent Mrs Squeezum (Hy Hazell), and result in the Justice himself going to prison. The object of his affections is then reunited with her true love, Captain Constant (Terence Cooper). The score, by two young newcomers, composer Laurie Johnson and lyricist Lionel Bart (Bart's *Fings Ain't Wot They Used T'Be* was just starting out at the Theatre Royal Stratford), complemented perfectly the lusty outrages of the story, in songs such as 'Lock Up Your Daughters' ('Here comes a rake!'), 'When Does The Ravishing Begin?', 'Red Wine And A Wench' and 'I'll Be There'. Hilaret *almost* seduces Squeezum in 'On A Sunny Sunday Morning', and the other delights included 'Lovely Lover', 'Kind Fate', 'A Proper Man', 'It Must Be True', ''Tis Plain To See' and 'Mr. Jones'. The show ran for 330 performances, and subsequently had its US premiere in New Haven in April 1960. *Lock Up Your Daughters* returned to the Mermaid two years later before transferring to the Her Majesty's theatre in the West End for a stay of some 16 months; it returned to the Mermaid in 1969 for a brief stay. Another American production, with 50s film star Carleton Carpenter as Squeezum, was presented at the Goodspeed Opera House in 1982.

LOCKYER, MALCOLM

b. Malcolm Neville Lockyer, 5 October 1923, Greenwich, London, England, d. 28 June 1976, England. Trained as an architect, Lockyer's interest in dance music dated from the age of 12, and he played semi-professionally until called up for war service as a musician in the Royal Air Force at the age of 19. He played with Sid Phillips And His Quintet, and in 1944 he joined the Buddy Featherstonhaugh Sextet and recorded with them for Radion and HMV. After leaving the RAF, Lockyer worked as pianist with Ambrose, Cyril Stapleton and Robert Farnon. He started with BBC radio in 1945, and during his career he worked on almost 6,000 broadcasts. He formed his own orchestra in 1951. A prolific composer (often under the pseudonym Howard Shaw), his biggest successes were 'Friends And Neighbours' (for the 1954 BBC television series), 'Fiddler's Boogie' and 'The Big Guitar' (for the BBC television series *Stranger Than Fiction* – 1955). Lockyer scored over 30 feature films and also the television series *The Pursuers* and *The Pathfinders*. Together with Reg Owen he made a collection of albums for Top Rank with the Knightsbridge Strings and the Cambridge Strings. He succeeded Harry Rabinowitz as conductor of the BBC Revue Orchestra in 1960, and was associated with many radio shows, among them *Mid-day Music Hall*, *Take It From Here* and *Beyond Our Ken*. When the Revue and Variety orchestras were amalgamated in 1966 to form the new Radio Orchestra, Lockyer became associate conductor. His connection with Glenn Miller began in 1944, when he was stationed in Bedford at the same time as the famous American band leader. He was able to study at first-hand how that unmistakable sound was achieved. Shortly before his death in 1976 he conducted the Million Airs Orchestra in 26 highly-successful Glenn Miller Tribute Concerts.

LOESSER, FRANK

b. Frank Henry Loesser, 29 June 1910, New York City, New York, USA, d. 28 July 1969. A leading songwriter for the stage, films and Tin Pan Alley from the 30s through to the 60s. Initially, he only wrote lyrics, but later in his career he provided both words and music, and sometimes co-produced through his Frank Productions. Born into a musical family (his father was a music teacher, and his brother a music critic and pianist), Loesser rejected a formal musical education, and trained himself. During the Depression years of the early 30s, following a brief spell at City College, New York, Loesser worked in a variety of jobs including city editor for a local newspaper, jewellery salesman and waiter. His first published song, written with William Schuman in 1931, was 'In Love With A Memory Of You'. Loesser also wrote for vaudeville performers and played piano in nightclubs around New York's 52nd Street.

In 1936, he contributed some lyrics to *The Illustrators Show*, with music by Irving Actman, including 'Bang-The Bell Rang!' and 'If You Didn't Love Me', but the show closed after only five Broadway performances. In 1937, Loesser went to Hollywood and spent the next few years writing lyrics for movies such as *Cocoanut Grove* ('Says My Heart'), *College Swing* ('Moments Like This' and 'How'dja Like To Make Love To Me?'), *Sing You Sinners* (Bing Crosby singing 'Small Fry'), *Thanks For The Memory* (Bob Hope and Shirley Ross singing 'Two Sleepy People'), *The Hurricane* (Dorothy Lamour singing 'Moon Of Manakoora'), *Man About Town* ('Fidgety Joe' and 'Strange Enchantment'), *Some Like It Hot* (1939 film starring Bob Hope and Shirley Ross singing 'The Lady's In Love With You'), *Destry Rides Again* (Marlene Dietrich with a memorable version of 'See What The Boys In The Back Room Will Have'), *Dancing On A Dime* ('I Hear Music'), *Las Vegas Nights* ('Dolores'), *Kiss The Boys Goodbye* ('I'll Never Let A Day Pass By', 'Sand In My Shoes' and the title song), *Sweater Girl* ('I Don't Want To Walk Without You' and 'I Said No'), *Forest Rangers* ('Jingle, Jangle, Jingle'), *Happy-Go-Lucky* ('Let's Get Lost' and "Murder" She Says'), *Seven Days Leave* ('Can't Get Out Of This Mood') and *Thank Your Lucky Stars* ('They're Either Too Young Or Too Old', sung by Bette Davis, and featuring one of Loesser's most amusing lyrics, including the couplet: 'I either get a fossil, or an adolescent pup/I either have to hold him off, or have to hold him up!'). These songs were written in collaboration with composers Burton Lane, Hoagy Carmichael, Alfred Newman, Matty Malneck, Frederick Hollander, Louis Alter, Victor Schertzinger, Jule Styne, Joseph Lilley, Jimmy McHugh and Arthur Schwartz.

The first song for which Loesser wrote both music and lyrics is said to be 'Praise The Lord And Pass The Ammunition', and when he left Hollywood for military service during World War II he added some more service songs to his catalogue, including 'First Class Private Mary Brown', 'The Ballad Of Roger Young', 'What Do You Do In The Infantry?' and 'Salute To The Army Service Forces'. He also continued to write for films such as *Christmas Holiday* (1944, 'Spring Will Be A Little Late This Year') and *The Perils Of Pauline* (1947), the biopic of silent-movie queen Pearl White, with Loesser's songs 'Poppa Don't Preach To Me' and 'I Wish I Didn't Love You So', the latter of which was nominated for an Academy Award. Loesser finally received his Oscar in 1949 for 'Baby It's Cold Outside', from the Esther Williams/Red Skelton movie *Neptune's Daughter*. In 1948, Loesser wrote 'On A Slow Boat To China', which became a hit for several US artists including Kay Kyser, Freddy Martin, Eddy Howard and Benny Goodman. In the same year he again turned his attention to the Broadway stage, writing the score for a musical adaptation of Brandon Thomas' classic English farce, *Charley's Aunt*. *Where's Charley?*, starring Ray Bolger, included the songs 'My Darling, My Darling', 'Once In Love With Amy', 'New Ashmoleon Marching Society And Student Conservatory Band' and 'Make A Miracle'. The show ran for a creditable 792 performances.

Far more successful, two years later, was *Guys And Dolls*, a musical setting of a Damon Runyon fable, starring Robert Alda, Vivian Blaine, Sam Levene, Isabel Bigley and Stubby Kaye. It ran for 1,200 performances, and is generally considered to be Loesser's masterpiece. As with *Where's Charley?*, he was now writing both music and lyrics, and the show is such a legend that it is worth listing the principal songs: 'Fugue For Tinhorns', 'The Oldest Established', 'I'll Know', 'A Bushel And A Peck', 'Adelaide's Lament', 'Guys And Dolls', 'If I Were A Bell', 'My Time Of Day', 'I've Never Been In Love Before', 'Take Back Your Mink', 'More I Cannot Wish You', 'Luck Be A Lady', 'Sue Me', 'Sit Down, You're Rockin' The Boat' and 'Marry The Man Today'. The original cast album is still available in the 90s, and among the other associated issues was an all-black cast album, released on the Motown label, and *Guys And Dolls: The Kirby Stone Four*. A film adaptation of *Guys And Dolls* was released in 1955, starring Frank Sinatra, Marlon Brando, Jean Simmons and Vivian Blaine. The movie version left out some of the original songs, and Loesser replaced them with 'A Woman In Love' and 'Adelaide'. In 1952, *Where's Charley?* was released as a film version,

and the same year saw a movie of *Hans Christian Andersen*, starring Danny Kaye in the title role, and featuring a Loesser score that included 'Wonderful Copenhagen', 'No Two People', 'Anywhere I Wander', 'Inchworm' and 'Thumbelina'.

Loesser's next Broadway project was *The Most Happy Fella*, for which he also wrote the libretto. The show was adapted from the original story *They Knew What They Wanted*, by Sidney Howard, which told the tale of an elderly Italian wine grower living in California, who falls in love at first sight with a waitress. Loesser created what has been called 'one of the most ambitiously operatic works ever written for the Broadway musical theatre'. Arias such as 'Rosabella' and 'My Heart Is So Full Of You' contrast with more familiar Broadway fare such as 'Standing On the Corner', 'Big D' and 'Happy To Make Your Acquaintance'. The show ran for 676 performances, far more than Loesser's 1960 production of the folksy *Greenwillow*, which closed after less than three months. It starred Anthony Perkins in his first musical, and contained a religious hymn, the baptism of a cow, and wistful ballads such as 'Faraway Boy' and 'Walking Away Whistling', along with 'Never Will I Marry' and 'Summertime Love', both sung by Perkins. A three-album set was issued, containing the complete score. In terms of number of performances (1,417), Loesser's last Broadway show, which opened in 1961, was his most successful. *How To Succeed In Business Without Really Trying* was a satire on big business that starred Robert Morse as the aspiring executive J. Pierpont Finch, and Rudy Vallee as his stuffy boss, J.B. Biggley. The songs, which most critics agreed, fitted the plot neatly, included 'The Company Way', 'A Secretary Is Not A Toy', 'Grand Old Ivy', 'Been A Long Day', 'I Believe In You' and 'Brotherhood Of Man'. The show became one of the select band of American musicals to be awarded a Pulitzer Prize; a film version was released in 1967.

Loesser died of lung cancer on 28 July 1969, with a pack of cigarettes by his side. A lifelong smoker, with a contentious, volatile temperament, he is regarded as one of the most original, innovative men of the musical theatre. In the early 90s *The Most Happy Fella*, *Guys And Dolls* and *How To Succeed In Business Without Really Trying*, were all revived on Broadway, and Loesser's second wife, Jo Sullivan, and one of his daughters, Emily Loesser, appeared in a provincial production of *Where's Charley?* In 1993, the two ladies also featured on the album *An Evening With Frank Loesser*, singing medleys of songs from his shows. Of even more interest, in the same year a fascinating album consisting of demo recordings by Loesser himself was released.

● ALBUMS: *An Evening With Frank Loesser* (DRG 1993) ★★★, *Loesser By Loesser* (DRG 1993) ★★★★.

● FURTHER READING: *A Most Remarkable Fella*, Susan Loesser.

LOEWE, FREDERICK

b. 10 June 1901, Vienna, Austria, d. 14 February 1988, Palm Springs, Florida, USA. A distinguished composer for the musical theatre, Loewe was born into a musical family (his father was a professional singer). He studied piano as a child, appearing with the Berlin Symphony Orchestra in 1917. In 1924, he visited the USA, but was unable to find work in a classical environment. Instead, he eked out a living playing piano in restaurants and bars, then roamed throughout the USA, tackling a variety of jobs, including boxing, prospecting and cowpunching. As a young teenager he had written songs and he resumed this activity in New York in the early 30s. Later in the decade he contributed to various musical shows, and in 1942 began to collaborate with lyricist Alan Jay Lerner. Their first Broadway score was for *What's Up?* in 1943, which was followed two year later with *The Day Before Spring*. From that point onwards, they wrote the music and lyrics (Lerner also contributed the librettos) for some of the most memorable productions in the history of the American musical theatre. They had their first hit in 1947 with *Brigadoon*, from which came 'The Heather On The Hill', 'From This Day On' and 'Almost Like Being In Love', and the association was renewed in 1951 with *Paint Your Wagon*, containing such lovely songs as 'They Call The Wind Maria', 'I Talk To The Trees' and 'Wand'rin' Star'.

In 1956, the team had a major triumph with the legendary *My Fair Lady*, which ran on Broadway for 2,717 performances. The score included such lasting favourites as 'On The Street Where You Live', 'Get Me To The Church On Time', 'With A Little Bit Of Luck', 'Wouldn't It Be Lovely?', 'The Rain In Spain', 'Why Can't The English?', 'I'm An Ordinary Man' and 'I Could Have Danced All Night'. After the huge success of *My Fair Lady*, Lerner and Loewe were invited to write the script, music and lyrics for a musical film, and while Lerner was enthusiastic about the idea, Loewe was somewhat reluctant. Eventually he agreed, and together they created the incomparable *Gigi* (1958), one of the final flourishes of the old-style Hollywood musical. The magnificent score included 'Thank Heaven For Little Girls', 'I'm Glad I'm Not Young Anymore', 'I Remember It Well', 'The Night They Invented Champagne', and the charming title song. After being hospitalized with serious heart trouble, Loewe collaborated with Lerner on *Camelot*, which opened in 1960, and ran for over two years. Although the show's pre-production was marred with problems, the result was another success, with such outstanding songs as 'If Ever I Would Leave You' and 'How To Handle A Woman'. Afterwards, Loewe decided to retire, emerging briefly in the early 70s to work with Lerner on two unsuccessful projects – a stage adaptation of *Gigi* and the film *The Little Prince*.

LONDON, JULIE

b. Julie Peck, 26 September 1926, Santa Rosa, California, USA, d. 18 October 2000, Encino, California, USA. Actress-singer London was inextricably linked to the sultry Andy Hamilton song 'Cry Me A River', which gave the artist her sole million-seller in 1955. Her memorable performance of the song in the movie *The Girl Can't Help It*, showcased a lachrymose delivery best exemplified on her debut album *Julie Is Her Name*, which also featured the talent of jazz guitarist Barney Kessel. London continued to record prodigiously throughout the late 50s to the mid-60s, but this aspect of her career vied with her movie roles, notably *The Great Man* and *A Question Of Adultery*. She later appeared in several television series, often alongside her second husband and long-time producer and songwriter Bobby Troup. In 1972, she starred as nurse Dixie McCall in the popular series *Emergency!*. The series was produced by her first husband, Jack Webb, and also starred Troup. Her popularity underwent a revival in the UK in the early 80s after Mari Wilson gained a hit with London's classic lament. London's looks were stunning, she oozed style, but unfortunately she did not possess the vocal range or expression to make her a truly great singer.

● ALBUMS: *Julie Is Her Name* (Liberty 1956) ★★★, *Lonely Girl* (Liberty 1956) ★★★, *Calendar Girl* (Liberty 1956) ★★★, *About The Blues* (Liberty 1957) ★★, *Make Love To Me* (Liberty 1957) ★★★, *Julie* (Liberty 1957) ★★, *Julie Is Her Name ii* (Liberty 1958) ★★, *London By Night* (Liberty 1958) ★★, *Swing Me An Old Song* (Liberty 1959) ★★, *Your Number Please ...* (Liberty 1959) ★★, *Julie ... At Home* (Liberty 1960) ★★, *Around Midnight* (Liberty 1960) ★★, *Send For Me* (Liberty 1961) ★★, *Whatever Julie Wants* (Liberty 1961) ★★, *Sophisticated Lady* (Liberty 1962) ★★, *Love Letters* (Liberty 1962) ★★, *Love On The Rocks* (Liberty 1963) ★★, *Latin In A Satin Mood* (Liberty 1963) ★★, *The End Of The World* (Liberty 1963) ★★, *The Wonderful World Of* (Liberty 1963) ★★, *Julie London* (Liberty 1964) ★★, *In Person: Julie London At The Americana* (Liberty 1964) ★★, *Our Fair Lady* (Liberty 1965) ★★, *Feelin' Good* (Liberty 1965) ★★, *All Through The Night: Julie London Sings The Choicest Of Cole Porter* (Liberty 1965) ★★, *For The Night People* (Liberty 1966) ★★, *Nice Girls Don't Stay For Breakfast* (Liberty 1967) ★★, *The Incomparable Miss Julie London: With Body And Soul* (Liberty 1967) ★★, *Easy Does It* (Liberty 1968) ★★, *Yummy, Yummy, Yummy* (Liberty 1969) ★★, *By Myself* (Liberty 1969) ★★.

● COMPILATIONS: *The Best Of Julie* (Liberty 1962) ★★★, *Great Performances* (Liberty 1968) ★★★, *The Best Of Julie London* (United Artists 1984) ★★★, *The Best Of Julie London: The Liberty Years* (United Artists 1988) ★★★★, *Time For Love: The Best Of Julie London* (Rhino) ★★★★, *Swing Me An Old Song* (Marginal 1996) ★★★, *Sophisticated Lady* (MFP 1998) ★★★, *Wild, Cool & Swingin'* (Capitol 1999) ★★★.

● FILMS: *Nabonga* aka *The Jungle Woman* (1944), *On Stage Everybody* (1945), *Diamond Horseshoe* aka *Billy Rose's Diamond Horseshoe* (1945), *A Night In Paradise* (1946), *The Red House* aka *No Trespassing* (1947), *Tap Roots* (1948), *Task Force* (1949), *Return Of The Frontiersman* (1950), *The Fat Man* (1951), *The Fighting Chance* (1955), *The Great*

Man (1956), *The Girl Can't Help It* (1956), *Crime Against Joe* (1956), *Drango* (1957), *Voice In The Mirror* (1958), *Saddle In The Wind* (1958), *Man Of The West* (1958), *The Wonderful Country* (1959), *A Question Of Adultery* aka *The Case Of Mrs. Loring* (1959), *Night Of The Quarter Moon* aka *Flesh And Flame* (1959), *The Third Voice* (1960), *The George Raft Story* aka *Spin Of A Coin* (1961).

LONDON, LAURIE

b. 19 January 1944, London, England. At the age of 13, this pop singer, who had the confidence and showmanship of a veteran, appeared in a closed circuit transmission of *6.5 Special* at the BBC stand at the 1958 Radio Show. He so impressed producer John Warrinton that he was invited back every day and thereby came to the attention of EMI Records, who put him in the studio with producer Norman Newell. The result was a Geoff Love-arranged revival of the spiritual 'He's Got The Whole World In His Hands'. The record climbed to number 12 in the UK and went on to become the most successful record by a British male in the 50s in the USA, topping the *Billboard* chart. Fame forced London to leave school and his father Will gave up his sales management job to manage him, but he refused the chance of a US tour in 1958 for the 14-year-old. London recorded a handful of other pop/gospel singles including 'Joshua', 'The Gospel Train' and 'I Gotta Robe', but the adolescent, who for all too brief a time had the whole world in his hands, never charted again. He released one album for Capitol Records. He was later reported to be successfully working in the clothing industry in London.
● ALBUMS: *Laurie London* (Parlophone 1958) ★★.
● COMPILATIONS: *He's Got The Whole World In His Hands* (Bear Family 1984) ★★.

LORD KITCHENER

b. Aldwyn Roberts, 18 April 1922, Arima, Trinidad, West Indies, d. 11 February 2000, Port Of Spain, Trinidad, West Indies. The self-styled 'grand master of calypso', Lord Kitchener was, alongside the Mighty Sparrow, the greatest exponent of Trinidad's native musical style. Dubbed 'the people's newspaper', calypso's lilting African and Latin American rhythms provide the perfect vehicle for the analysis of topical events, and often slyly humorous social and political commentary. Roberts, the son of a blacksmith, was brought up in the eastern Trinidad town of Arima. He attended the local government school before being forced by the death of his parents to give up education at the age of 14. Known as 'Bean' because of his height he was already writing calypso tunes, and first performed live in 1936 serenading the employees of the local water works. He enjoyed his first local hit in 1939 with 'Shops Close Too Early'. By the time Roberts moved to Port Of Spain three years later he had overcome any reservations about a speech defect (a slight stammer which stayed with him all his life) to set out on the road

to becoming a leading calypso singer. To this end he joined the Roving Brigade of young calypso singers, singing to partisan audiences in local cinema houses.

His breakthrough came with an appearance at the Victory Calypso tent singing one of his best-known songs, 'Green Fig', on a bill which included giants of calypso such as Growling Tiger, Attila The Hun, and the Roaring Lion. The former became his patron and named him Lord Kitchener. Under his new moniker he established himself with a string of hits, including 'Lai Fung Lee (Chinee Never Had A VJ Day)', 'Tie Tongue Mopsy', and 'I Am A Worrier', and by the mid-40s was headlining his own tent and leading the new wave of calypso artists. He moved to Jamaica for six months before sailing to England on the *Empire Windrush*, landing at Tilbury docks on 21 June 1948. Kitchener was to prove highly popular on the London nightclub circuit alongside fellow calypso immigrants such as Lord Beginner, and also broke into the lucrative music hall and variety shows. The duo recorded several sessions for EMI Records, later issued on the Melodisc label, providing a highly topical commentary on immigrant life in post-war Britain. Kitchener moved to Manchester in 1958, marrying an English woman and opening his own nightclub while continuing to pour out hit calypsos such as 'Ah, Bernice!' and 'Nora'. Kitchener also remembered to send songs back to Trinidad for entry in the annual carnival, and in 1962, the year of his country's independence, he returned home. He retained his status as the country's leading calypso performer and songwriter, and in the subsequent decades managed to win the Road March King title (awarded to the calypso performed most often in the streets during the annual carnival) a record 10 times.

Since the early 40s Kitchener had established himself as a leading composer of the pan music played by steel bands, with the winner of the annual Panorama steel band competition more often than not performing a Kitchener composition. His Calypso Revue tent show, established in the early 60s, helped foster the careers of new calypso artists and encourage new developments such as soca. Instead of taking up a reactionary stance, Kitchener adapted to the challenge of the new music and, in 1978, enjoyed international success with the soca hit 'Sugar Bum Bum'. Kitchener continued performing well into the 90s although he was forced to abdicate the stage in the year before his death, which was the result of a severe infection brought on by a blood disorder and organ failure.
● ALBUMS: *Kitch '67* (RCA 1967) ★★★, *Longevity* (JW 1993) ★★★.
● COMPILATIONS: with Mighty Sparrow *16 Carnival Hits* (Ice 1991) ★★★, *Klassic Kitchener Volume One* (Ice 1994) ★★★★, *Klassic Kitchener Volume Two* (Ice 1994) ★★★★, *Klassic Kitchener Volume Three* (Ice 1994) ★★★.

LORD ROCKINGHAM'S XI

Scottish bandleader Harry Robinson and his band assumed the pseudonym of Lord Rockingham's XI (after a genuine historical character) to appear on the Jack Good UK television pop programme *Oh Boy*, playing 'novelty' rock instrumentals. Other key members were Chery Wainer (organ), and Red Price (saxophone) as well as renowned British rock 'n' roll drummer Rory Blackwell, the former two of which would feature in their own spots on *Oh Boy*. The first release was 'Fried Onions' in May 1958, but in September Decca released the Robinson-penned 'Hoots Mon', complete with Scottish cries of 'Hoots mon, there's a moose in the hoose!'. It was a UK number 1 hit but the follow-up, 'Wee Tom', only made number 16. They featured on an *Oh Boy* EP but after a further attempt to have a hit with 'Ra Ra Rockingham' failed, Robinson reverted to more straightforward orchestra names such as Harry Robinson's XV and the Robinson Crew. He later revived the Lord Rockingham moniker in an attempt to cash in on the 1962 Twist phenomenon with 'Newcastle Twist'/'Rockingham Twist'. Benny Green played tenor sax with Rockingham before he realized he could make more money writing and talking about jazz than performing. He is now a respected author and broadcaster, but still plays saxophone semi-professionally. Robinson was later involved with another UK number 1 when he provided the musical accompaniment to Millie's 'My Boy Lollipop'.

LOSS, JOE

b. Joshua Alexander Loss, 22 June 1909, Spitalfields, London, England, d. 6 June 1990, London, England. One of the most popular bandleaders in the UK over a period of many years, Loss was taught to play the violin with a view to pursuing a classical career. He won a scholarship to the Trinity College of Music, and later studied at the London School of Music before forming his own band at the age of 16, playing local halls and accompanying silent movies. In 1930 he moved into London's Astoria Ballroom, and played at the Kit-Kat Club a year later. His band made its broadcasting debut in 1933, and, early in 1934, topped the variety bill at the Holborn Empire. Later that year, he returned to the Astoria for a long residency, and while there adopted 'Let's Dance At The Make Believe Ballroom' as his first proper signature tune. Also in 1934, he started recording for the Regal-Zonophone Records label, later part of EMI Records, and stayed with the company for over 50 years. A large part of the Loss band's popularity during the 30s was due to the many featured vocalists including Paula Greene, Betty Dale, Adelaide Hall, Shirley Lenner, Elizabeth Batey, Marjorie Kingsley, Monte Rey (with his big hit 'The Donkey Serenade') and especially Chick Henderson, later killed while in the Royal Navy, who recorded the very popular 'Begin The Beguine'.

Some of the band's other successes were 'Wood-chopper's Ball' and 'Honky Tonk Train Blues'. Loss also gave Vera Lynn her first broadcasting opportunity in 1935, when she sang 'Red Sails In The Sunset'. In 1940, Loss left the Astoria and went to France to play for the British Expeditionary Forces before returning to the UK, and spending the rest of World War II successfully touring the UK's ballrooms. After the war he was resident at the Hammersmith Palais, and later, during the 50s, survived the onslaught of rock 'n' roll. By this time, he also had a successful band agency. In the early 60s he had chart hits with 'Wheels Cha Cha', 'Sucu Sucu', 'The Maigret Theme', 'Must Be Madison', 'The March Of The Mods', and many bestselling albums. During the war Loss had adopted the Glenn Miller favourite 'In The Mood' as his theme tune, and it was his recording that featured on the Jive Bunny And The Mastermixers novelty single in 1989. His series of *World Championship Ballroom Dances* albums reflected his many appearances on BBC Television's *Come Dancing*, and the 14 Carl Alan Awards presented by the industry. During one of his annual working holidays on the QE2 in 1978, he became the first dance bandleader to play in communist China.

His post-war singers included Howard Jones (the vocalist on the 1948 Loss US hit 'A Tree In A Meadow'), Larry Gretton, Rose Brennan (who stayed with the band for over 15 years) and Ross McManus (father of Elvis Costello). (McManus and Costello sang together for the first time on stage in a charity tribute to Joe Loss that was presented at the Barbican Theatre in London in 1994.) Loss played at many royal functions, including the Queen's 50th birthday celebrations and the Queen Mother's 80th birthday. The most energetic and mobile of bandleaders officially retired in 1989 after 60 years at the top. Among his many awards were an OBE in 1978, Her Majesty's Silver Medal in 1977 and a Lieutenancy in the Royal Victorian Order in 1984.

● ALBUMS: *Dancing Time For Dancers, Number 11* (HMV 1957) ★★★, *Dancing Time For Dancers, Number 12* (HMV 1957) ★★★, *Dancing Time For Dancers, Number 13* (HMV 1958) ★★★, *Dancing Time For Dancers, Number 14* (HMV 1958) ★★★, *36 All-Time Hits* (HMV 1960) ★★★, *Come Dancing* (HMV 1960) ★★★, *Party Dance Time – Another 36 All-Time Hits* (HMV 1961) ★★★, *Dancing Party* (HMV 1962) ★★★, *Must Be Madison – Must Be Twist* (HMV 1963) ★★★★, *Go Latin With Loss* (HMV 1964) ★★★, *Latin À La Loss* (Columbia 1968) ★★★, *Joe Loss Plays Glenn Miller* (MFP 1969) ★★★, *Latin Like Loss* (Columbia 1970) ★★★, *Play It Latin* (Starline 1971) ★★★, *All-Time Party Hits* (MFP 1971) ★★★, *The Loss Concertium* (1972) ★★★, *Dances For The World Ballroom Championship* (Columbia 1972) ★★★, *Non-Stop Latin Lovelies* (EMI 1973) ★★★, *Joe Loss Hits The Road To Songland* (EMI 1974) ★★★, *Dance At Your Party* (Columbia 1975) ★★★, *Top Pop Party Time* (Columbia 1975) ★★★, *Jitterbug And Jive With Joe Loss* (EMI 1976) ★★★, *Swing Is The Thing* (MFP 1976) ★★★, *World Ballroom Championship Dances* (Note 1977) ★★★, *Championship Dances For The World Ballroom* (Columbia 1978) ★★★, *New World*

Championship Ballroom Dances (Columbia 1979) ★★★.
● COMPILATIONS: *The Very Best Of Joe Loss And His Big Band* (Studio 2 1976) ★★★, *Let's Dance At The Make-Believe Ballroom 1934-40* (Retrospect 1977) ★★★, *50 Fabulous Years* (Note 1980) ★★★, *The Golden Age Of Joe Loss* (Golden Age 1985) ★★★, *Isn't It Heavenly* (Happy Days 1986) ★★★, *In A Romantic Mood* (EMI 1987) ★★★, *The Joe Loss Story* (EMI 1990) ★★★.

LOTIS, DENNIS
b. 8 March 1925, Johannesburg, South Africa. An extremely popular singer in the UK, particularly in the 50s, with a sophisticated style that was particularly attractive to the young female population. Lotis trained for four years as a boy soprano, and won several cups and medals. He made his first stage appearance at the age of seven, and his first broadcast when he was nine. After leaving school, he worked as a bus conductor and electrician, and sang in cinemas and nightclubs in Johannesburg. When he moved to the UK in the early 50s, he carried with him a letter of introduction to Ted Heath from the former London saxophonist and bandleader Don Barrigo. Following a couple of broadcasts with Henry Hall, Lotis joined the Heath band, and, together with the other resident vocalists Lita Roza and Dickie Valentine, became one of the most popular singers on the circuit. Lotis' vocal talents were evident on such records as 'Sam's Song', 'Goodnight Irene', 'Nevertheless' and 'She's A Lady' (with Roza and Valentine). After enjoying a hit with 'Cuddle Me', he went solo, and during the late 50s toured the UK variety circuit, appeared in his first Royal Command Performances, and rejoined the Heath band for a tour of the USA, including an appearance at Carnegie Hall. He was also voted Top Male Singer in the 1957 *Melody Maker* poll. In 1956 he appeared in a touring production of the stage musical *Harmony Close* and, two years later, starred in John Osborne's *The World Of Paul Slickey*, a 'musical comedy of manners' that was poorly received in Britain. Lotis also made several films, a mixture of drama, comedy, musicals and horror, including *The Extra Day*, *It's A Wonderful World*, *City Of The Dead* and *She'll Have To Go*. Among his other stage roles was an appearance as Lucio in John Neville's Playhouse Production of Shakespeare's *Measure For Measure*. Adversely affected by the changing face of popular music, he played the working men's clubs, and ran his own antiques and restaurant businesses for a time. Eventually, in the 80s and 90s, he returned to the theatres, singing in nostalgia shows with contemporaries such as Joan Regan and Russ Conway.
● ALBUMS: *How About You?* (1958) ★★★, *Bidin' My Time* (1959) ★★★, *Night And Day* (1983) ★★, *Get Happy* (1994) ★★★.

LOUVIN BROTHERS
Brothers Lonnie Ira Loudermilk (b. 21 April 1924, d. 20 June 1965) and Charlie Elzer Loudermilk (b. 7 July 1927) were both born in Rainesville,

Alabama, USA. They were raised on a 40-acre farm in Henegar, Alabama, but only half of it could be cultivated. Despite their poverty, their parents sang gospel songs and encouraged their sons' musical talents. Ira took up the mandolin and Charlie the guitar, and they created perfect harmonies for country and gospel music, inspired, in particular, by the Blue Sky Boys. In 1943, after winning a talent contest in Chattanooga, they began broadcasting regularly, leading to three shows a day for WMPS in Memphis. They recorded for Decca Records, MGM Records and Capitol Records, but they found it hard to make ends meet and worked night shifts in the Post Office. Some radio broadcasts to promote a songbook, *Songs That Tell A Story*, have been released and show the Louvin Brothers at their best, with no additional instruments. Their career was also interrupted by Charlie's military service in Korea (their 'Weapon Of Prayer' was an emotional plea for peace). They performed as the Louvin Brothers because the family name was considered too long for stage work, although their cousin, John D. Loudermilk, was to have no such qualms. Capitol re-signed the brothers as gospel artists but a tobacco company sponsoring a portion of the *Grand Ole Opry* told them to sing secular songs as 'you can't sell tobacco with gospel music'. They crossed over to the country market with their own composition 'When I Stop Dreaming', which is now a standard. Their secular US country hits included 'I Don't Believe You've Met My Baby' (their only number 1), 'Hoping That You're Hoping', 'You're Running Wild' and 'My Baby's Gone', but Charlie says, 'I don't think we ever did a show without some gospel music. Our mother would have thrashed us if we hadn't done that!'
By the late 50s, their sound was old-fashioned and their songs too melodramatic for the rock 'n' roll era. The Everly Brothers, who acknowledged their debt to the Louvins, may also have contributed unwittingly to their downfall. Charlie says, 'Ken Nelson told Ira, in 1958, that the mandolin was hindering the sales of our music, so my brother lost total interest in the mandolin and never picked another note on it on a record. He had put 25 years of his life into mastering that instrument, and it messed his head to hear a good friend whose opinion he respected say, "You're the problem, you've got to throw that thing away".' Ira's drink problem worsened, their own relationship deteriorated and their last success together was, ironically, 'Must You Throw Dirt In My Face?'. Charlie broke up the partnership on 18 August 1963: '*He* had said a lot of times he was going to quit, but it was the first time *I* had ever said it.' Charlie went on to have solo hits with 'I Don't Love You Anymore' and 'See The Big Man Cry'. Ira started his solo career with 'Yodel Sweet Molly' but he was shot and badly injured by his wife, Faye, whom he then divorced. He then married Florence, who sang on his shows as Anne Young, but soon afterwards they both perished in a car crash in Jefferson City, Missouri, USA, on 20 June 1965. Ira and Bill Monroe had pledged that

whoever lived the longest would sing at the other's funeral, and Monroe sang 'Where No One Stands Alone'. Gram Parsons introduced their songs to a new audience, recording 'The Christian Life' with the Byrds, and 'Cash On The Barrelhead' and 'The Angels Rejoiced In Heaven Last Night' with Emmylou Harris. After Parsons' death, Harris continued recording their songs: 'If I Could Only Win Your Love', 'When I Stop Dreaming', 'You're Learning' and, with Don Everly, 'Everytime You Leave'. Charlie Louvin had a country hit with 'You're My Wife, She's My Woman' and made two successful albums with Melba Montgomery. A single, 'Love Don't Care' with Emmylou Harris, made the US country charts.

● ALBUMS: *Tragic Songs Of Life* (Capitol 1956) ★★★★, *Nearer My God To Thee* (Capitol 1957) ★★★, *The Louvin Brothers* (MGM 1957) ★★★★, *Ira And Charlie* (Capitol 1958) ★★★, *The Family Who Prays* (Capitol 1958) ★★★★, *Country Love Ballads* (Capitol 1959) ★★★, *Satan Is Real* (Capitol 1960) ★★★, *Those Louvin Brothers Sing The Songs Of The Delmores* (Capitol 1960) ★★★, *My Baby's Gone* (Capitol 1960) ★★★, *Encore* (Capitol 1961) ★★★, *Country Christmas With The Louvin Brothers* (Capitol 1961) ★★★, *Weapon Of Prayer* (Capitol 1962) ★★★, *Keep Your Eyes On Jesus* (Capitol 1963) ★★★, *The Louvin Brothers Sing And Play Their Current Hits* (Capitol 1964) ★★★, *Thank God For My Christian Home* (Capitol 1965) ★★★, *Two Different Worlds* (Capitol 1966) ★★★, *The Louvin Brothers Sing The Great Roy Acuff Songs* (Capitol 1967) ★★★, *Country Heart And Soul* (Tower 1968) ★★★, *Live At The New River Ranch* 1956 recording (Copper Creek 1989) ★★★. Solo: Ira Louvin *The Unforgettable Ira Louvin* (Capitol 1965) ★★★.

● COMPILATIONS: *The Great Gospel Singing Of The Louvin Brothers* (1973) ★★★, *Songs That Tell A Story* (Rounder 1981) ★★★, *Radio Favorites 1951-1957* (CMF 1987) ★★★, *Close Harmony* 8-CD box set (Bear Family 1992) ★★★★, *Capitol Country Music Classics* (1993) ★★★, *When I Stop Dreaming: The Best Of The Louvin Brothers* (Razor & Tie 1995) ★★★★.

LOVE IS THE THING – NAT 'KING' COLE
Released in the days when albums were not promoted by extracting individual tracks and issuing them as singles, this was the first opportunity that young record-buyers had of hearing Nat 'King' Cole sing 'When I Fall In Love' and 'Stardust', songs with which he would forever be identified. Composer Hoagy Carmichael, who wrote 'Stardust' with Mitchell Parish, always maintained that this version, complete with the lovely verse, was his personal favourite. Of all the singer's varied albums – jazz, 'soft' country, easy listening – *Love Is The Thing*, which spent 55 weeks in the US Top 40, was the only one that went to number 1, where it stayed for eight weeks.

● Tracks: *When I Fall In Love; The End Of A Love Affair; Stardust; Stay As Sweet As You Are; Where Can I Go Without You; Maybe It's Because I Love

You Too Much; Love Letters; Ain't Misbehavin'; I Thought About Marie; At Last; It's All In The Game; When Sunny Gets Blue; Love Is The Thing*.
● First released 1957
● UK peak chart position: did not chart
● USA peak chart position: 1

LOVE ME TENDER
Elvis Presley's first feature, released in 1956, cast the singer as one of three brothers who rob a bank. Strife over a share of the spoils is compounded by conflicting love interests, culminating with the Presley character's slaying, although he appears as a wraith in the final reel. Although cast as a miscreant, the singer had opted for a more conservatively styled film, a western, rather than embracing contemporary teen subcultures in the manner of *Rebel Without A Cause*. Indeed, he did not enjoy top billing – Richard Egan was the star – but interest naturally focused on Presley's performance. Critics were generally impressed, citing great potential, something tossed to the wind by much of the singer's subsequent film output. Although not a musical, the film's mournful title track gave the singer his third US chart-topper and *Love Me Tender* also featured 'Let Me', 'Poor Boy' and 'We're Gonna Move'. Again, by avoiding any 'controversial' musical content, the Presley industry showed that, even at this early stage, a wider audience was being courted.

LOVING YOU
Similarly titled to his debut movie, *Loving You* introduced a regular guy Deke Rivers (Elvis), as a humble delivery boy who has a great natural ability as a rock 'n' roll singer. He is hired as the singer in the band he gate crashes, and like Elvis' career, the rest is history. Wendell Corey plays a convincing Tex Warner and the girl who Elvis gets this time is Lizabeth Scot (Glenda). The Hal B. Wallis production did contain a number of great songs, and in view of the way Elvis movies soon deteriorated with some truly appalling songs, this must be regarded as a classic. The stellar tracklist includes 'Lets Have A Party', Teddy Bear', 'Mean Woman Blues', You Got A Lot Of Livin To Do' and the title track. Brief cameos were made by Ma and Pa Presley, as both Vernon and Gladys can be spotted as members of the audience in the theatre scene.

LYMAN, ARTHUR, GROUP
b. 1936, Kauai, Hawaii, USA. Lyman popularized a jazzy style of Hawaiian music during the 50s, and gathered a following as a purveyor of so-called exotic music. As a child, Lyman moved to the large Hawaiian city of Honolulu, where he became interested in the music of Benny Goodman and Lionel Hampton. He learned to play along with their records on a toy marimba. At the age of 14, he joined a jazz group and by his early 20s was performing with 'mood music' king Martin Denny. Lyman was signed to the Hi-Fi record label in 1957 and released his debut, *Taboo*, the following year. It ultimately reached

number 6 in the USA and remained on the chart for over a year. Lyman led a quartet, with himself on four-mallet vibes, guitar and percussion, John Kramer (bass, ukulele, guitar, flute, clarinet, percussion), Alan Soares (piano, celeste, guitar, glockenspiel, chimes, clavinet, percussion) and Harold Chang (percussion). Because of its superior production – all of their music was recorded at the Henry J. Kaiser Aluminum Dome in Hawaii – and the unusual orchestral sounds created by the group, the record was particularly popular among consumers purchasing the then-new stereo equipment. In 1961, Lyman's single 'Yellow Bird' reached number 4 in the USA, one of the most uncharacteristic hits of the era. The album of the same name reached number 10. Lyman's last charting album in 1963 was *I Wish You Love*.

● ALBUMS: *Taboo* (Hi-Fi 1958) ★★★, *Bahia* (Hi-Fi 1959) ★★★, *Leis Of Jazz* (Hi-Fi 1959) ★★, *On Broadway* (Hi-Fi 1960) ★★★, *Yellow Bird* (Hi-Fi 1961) ★★, *Many Moods Of Arthur Lyman* (Hi-Fi 1962) ★★★★, *The Colourful Percussions Of Arthur Lyman* (Hi-Fi 1962) ★★★, *I Wish You Love* (Hi-Fi 1963) ★★★, *Blowin' In The Wind* (Hi-Fi 1963) ★★, *Merry Christmas* (Hi-Fi 1963) ★★, *Midnight Sun* (Hi-Fi 1964) ★★, *Cast Your Fate* (GNP Crescendo 1988) ★★★, *Pearly Shells* (GNP Crescendo 1988) ★★★, *Puka Shells* (GNP Crescendo 1988) ★★★.

● COMPILATIONS: *The Exotic Sound Of The Arthur Lyman Group* (1991) ★★★★, *The Best Of The Arthur Lyman Group* (DCC 1996) ★★★★, *More Of The Best Of The Arthur Lyman Group* (DCC 1996) ★★★, *Sonic Sixties* (Tradition 1997) ★★★.

LYMON, FRANKIE, AND THE TEENAGERS

b. 30 September 1942, Washington Heights, New York, USA, d. 28 February 1968, New York City, New York, USA. Often billed as the 'boy wonder', Lymon first entered the music business after teaming up with a local all-vocal quartet, the Premiers. The latter comprised Jimmy Merchant (b. 10 February 1940, New York, USA), Sherman Garnes (b. 8 June 1940, New York, USA, d. 26 February 1977), Herman Santiago (b. 18 February 1941, New York, USA) and Joe Negroni (b. 9 September 1940, New York, USA, d. 5 September 1978). Lymon joined them in 1954 and soon afterwards they were signed to the Gee label as the Teenagers. Their debut, the startling 'Why Do Fools Fall In Love?', was issued on 1 January 1956 and soon climbed into the US Top 10, alongside the early recordings of Elvis Presley and Carl Perkins. The song went on to reach number 1 in the UK and sold two million copies. Lymon soon left school and the group toured extensively. For their second single, 'I Want You To Be My Girl', the 13-year-old boy wonder was given superior billing to the group.

With their use of high tenor, deep bass and soprano, and teen-orientated lyrics, the Teenagers boasted one of the most distinctive sounds in 50s pop. After registering chart entries in the USA with 'I Promise To Remember' and 'The ABCs Of Love', they found greater acclaim in England. The

soaring 'I'm Not A Juvenile Delinquent' (from the movie *Rock Rock Rock*) hit the UK Top 12 and Lymon was afforded the honour of appearing at the London Palladium. So strong was his appeal at this point that the single's b-side, 'Baby Baby', received separate promotion and outshone the a-side by climbing to number 4. During his celebrated UK tour, Lymon recorded as a soloist with producer Norrie Paramor and the resulting 'Goody Goody' reached the Top 30 on both sides of the Atlantic. By the summer of 1957, he had split from the Teenagers, and thereafter, his career prospects plummeted. He enjoyed the excesses of stardom, smoking cigars, drinking heavily and enjoying underage sex with women old enough to be his mother.

Despite recording a strong album, his novelty appeal waned when his voice broke. By 1961, the teenager was a heroin addict and entered Manhattan General Hospital on a drug rehabilitation programme. Although he tried to reconstruct his career with the help of Dizzy Gillespie and even took dancing lessons and studied as a jazz drummer, his drug habit endured. In 1964, he was convicted of possessing narcotics and his finances were in a mess. His private life was equally chaotic and was punctuated by three marriages. In February 1968, he was discovered dead on the bathroom floor of his grandmother's New York apartment with a syringe by his side. The Teenager who never grew up was dead at the tragically young age of 25. His former group continued to record sporadically and in the 80s, surviving members Santiago and Merchant formed a new Teenagers and Pearl McKinnon took Lymon's part. They were inducted into the Rock And Roll Hall Of Fame in 1993.

● ALBUMS: *The Teenagers Featuring Frankie Lymon* (Gee 1957) ★★★, *The Teenagers At The London Palladium* (Roulette 1958) ★★, *Rock 'N' Roll Party With Frankie Lymon* (Guest 1959) ★★★.

● COMPILATIONS: *Frankie Lymon And The Teenagers* 61-track set (Murray Hill 1987) ★★★, *The Best Of Frankie Lymon And The Teenagers* (Roulette 1990) ★★★, *Not Too Young To Dream: Undiscovered Rarities* (Fireball 1998) ★★★, *The Very Best Of* (Rhino 1998) ★★★.

LYTTELTON, HUMPHREY

b. 23 May 1921, Eton, Buckinghamshire, England. Raised in an academic atmosphere (his father was a housemaster at Eton College), he taught himself to play a variety of instruments including the banjolele. His prodigious talent was spotted early and he was given formal lessons on piano and, a little later, in military band drumming. Eventually, his education took him back to Eton College, this time as a pupil. He joined the school orchestra as a timpanist but after a while drifted away from the orchestra and the instrument. At the age of 15 he discovered jazz, thanks to records by trumpeters Nat Gonella and, decisively, Louis Armstrong. By this time Lyttelton had switched to playing the mouth-organ, but, realizing the instrument's limitations, he acquired a trumpet, which he taught himself to play. Forming his own small jazz band at the college, he developed his playing ability and his consuming interest in jazz. With the outbreak of World War II he joined the Grenadier Guards, continuing to play whenever possible.

After the war he resumed playing, this time professionally, and in 1947 became a member of George Webb's Dixielanders. The following year he formed his own band and quickly became an important figure in the British revivalist movement. In the late 40s and through to the mid-50s Lyttelton's stature in British jazz increased. Significantly, his deep interest in virtually all aspects of jazz meant that he was constantly listening to other musicians, many of whom played different forms of the music. Although he was never to lose his admiration for Armstrong, he refused to remain rooted in the revivalist tradition. His acceptance and absorption of music from the jazz mainstream ensured that when the trad boom fizzled out, Lyttelton continued to find an audience. In the mid-50s he added alto saxophonist Bruce Turner to his band, outraging some reactionary elements in British jazz circles, and a few years later added Tony Coe, Joe Temperley and other outstanding and forward-thinking musicians.

In the early 60s Lyttelton's reputation spread far beyond the UK and he also developed another important and long-term admiration for a trumpet player, this time, Buck Clayton. By this time, however, Lyttelton's personal style had matured and he was very much his own man. He was also heavily involved in many areas outside the performance of music. In 1954, he had published his first autobiographical volume and in the 60s he began to spread his writing wings as an essayist, journalist and critic. He also broadcast on radio and television, sometimes as a performer but also as a speaker and presenter. These multiple activities continued throughout the next two decades, his UK BBC Radio 2 series, The Best Of Jazz, running for many years. His writings included further autobiographical work and his ready wit found outlets in seemingly unlikely settings, such as his role as quiz master on the long-running radio comedy-panel series, I'm Sorry I Haven't A Clue. During this time he continued to lead a band, employing first-rate musicians with whom he toured and made numerous records.

Among the sidemen of the 70s and 80s were Dave Green, Mick Pyne, John Surman, John Barnes, Roy Williams and Adrian Macintosh. He also toured and recorded with singers Helen Shapiro, Carol Kidd and Lillian Boutté. Back in the late 40s Lyttelton had recorded with Sidney Bechet and in the 70s and 80s he occasionally made albums with other American jazz stars, including Buddy Tate on Kansas City Woman, and Kenny Davern on Scatterbrains and This Old Gang Of Ours. In the early 80s Lyttelton formed his own recording company, Calligraph, and by the end of the decade numerous new albums were available. In addition to these came others, mostly on the

Dormouse label, which reissued his earlier recordings and were eagerly snapped up by fans of all ages. Although he has chosen to spend most of his career in the UK, Lyttelton's reputation elsewhere is extremely high and thoroughly deserved. As a trumpet player and bandleader, and occasional clarinettist, he has ranged from echoing early jazz to near-domination of the British mainstream. In the early 90s, touring with Kathy Stobart, he showed no signs of letting up and barely acknowledged the fact that he had sailed past his 70th birthday. In 2001, his 80th year, he sessioned on Radiohead's Amnesiac and received an award at the BBC Jazz Awards. For more than 50 years he has succeeded in maintaining the highest musical standards, all the time conducting himself with dignity, charm and good humour. With the start of the new century, and his 80th birthday in view, Lyttelton continued to perform with undiminished flair and enthusiasm.

● ALBUMS: Jazz Concert (Parlophone 1953) ★★★★, Humph At The Conway (Parlophone 1954) ★★★★, Jazz At The Royal Festival Hall (Parlophone 1955) ★★★★, Jazz Session With Humph (Parlophone 1956) ★★★★, Humph Swings Out (Parlophone 1956) ★★★★, Here's Humph (Parlophone 1957) ★★★★, I Play As I Please (Decca 1958) ★★★★, with Kathy Stobart Kath Meets Humph (Parlophone 1958) ★★★★, Humph In Perspective (Parlophone 1958) ★★★, Triple Exposure (Parlophone 1959) ★★★, Back To The 60s 1960-63 recordings (Philips 60s) ★★★, Humph Plays Standards (1960) ★★★★, Buck Clayton With Humphrey Lyttelton And His Band (Harlequin 1965) ★★★, 21 Years On (1969) ★★★, South Bank Swing Session (1973) ★★★, with Buddy Tate Kansas City Woman (Black Lion 1974) ★★★, Spreadin' Joy (Black Lion 1978) ★★★, One Day I Met An African (Black Lion 1980) ★★★, In Canada (Sackville 1980) ★★★, It Seems Like Yesterday (Calligraph 1983) ★★★, Movin' And Groovin' (Black Lion 1983) ★★★, with Kenny Davern Scatterbrains (Stomp Off 1984) ★★★, Humph At The Bull's Head (Calligraph 1985) ★★★★, with Davern This Old Gang Of Ours ... (Calligraph 1985) ★★★, with Helen Shapiro Echoes Of The Duke (Calligraph 1985) ★★★★, Gonna Call My Children Home: The World Of Buddy Bolden (Calligraph 1986) ★★★, Gigs (Calligraph 1987) ★★★, Doggin' Around (Wam 1987) ★★★, The Dazzling Lillian Boutté (1988) ★★★, The Beano Boogie (Calligraph 1989) ★★★, with Shapiro I Can't Get Started (Calligraph 1990) ★★★★, Rock Me Gently (Calligraph 1991) ★★★, Hook Line And Sinker (Angel 1991) ★★★, At Sundown (Calligraph 1992) ★★★, Rent Party (Stomp Off 1992) ★★★, Movin' And Groovin' (1993) ★★★, Hear Me Talkin' To Ya (Calligraph 1994) ★★★★, Three In The Morning (Calligraph 1995) ★★★★, Lay 'Em Straight (Calligraph 1997) ★★★, Between Friends (Calligraph 2000) ★★★.

● COMPILATIONS: Delving Back And Forth With Humph 1948-86 recordings (Esquire 1979) ★★★, Bad Penny Blues: The Best Of Humph 1949-56 recordings (Cube 1983) ★★★★, Tribute To Humph

Vols 1-8 1949-56 recordings (Dormouse 1984-88) ★★★, *The Parlophone Years* 1949-56 recordings (Dormouse 1989) ★★★★, *Jazz At The Royal Festival Hall & Jazz At The Conway Hall* 1951-54 recordings (Dormouse 1991) ★★★★, *Dixie Gold* 1960-63 recordings (1991) ★★★, *The Parlophones, Volume 1* 1949-50 recordings (Calligraph 1998) ★★★, *The Parlophones, Volume 2* 1951-52 recordings (Calligraph 1998) ★★★, *The Parlophones, Volume 3* 1953-55 recordings (Calligraph 1999) ★★★, *The Parlophones, Volume 4* 1955-59 recordings (Calligraph 1999) ★★★.

● FURTHER READING: *I Play As I Please*, Humphrey Lyttelton. *Second Chorus*, Humphrey Lyttelton. *Take It From The Top*, Humphrey Lyttelton. *Humph*, Julian Purser.

MABON, WILLIE

b. 24 October 1925, Hollywood, Tennessee, USA, d. 19 April 1986, Paris, France. Accompanying himself on piano and secondly on harmonica, Mabon sang in an urbane blues style similar to Charles Brown. He moved from Memphis, Tennessee, to Chicago in 1942 and was first recorded in 1949 as a member of the Blues Rockers group. After military service he became a popular entertainer in Chicago's Black Belt, and by the early 50s, was well established as an R&B singer with a number of successful records to his credit. Signed as a solo artist to Chess Records in 1951, Mabon immediately hit with a novelty blues, 'I Don't Know' (R&B number 1, 1952), a remake of a Cripple Clarence Lofton record from 1938. Mabon had other hits with 'I'm Mad' (R&B number 1, 1953), 'Poison Ivy' (R&B Top 10, 1954) and 'Seventh Son' (1955). After leaving Chess in 1956, he continued to record on various small labels, achieving success on Formal in 1962 with 'Got To Have Some'. During the 70s and 80s, Mabon would flit back and forth between Chicago and Europe, making occasional albums for German and French labels, most of which were poorly received. He found a wider audience in Europe, playing the Montreux Jazz Festival and festivals in Berlin and Holland. A polished performer, with a measure of glossy sophistication to his singing, Mabon retained a strong affinity with the earthier aspects of the blues and was an influence upon Mose Allison.

● ALBUMS: *Funky* (1972) ★★, *Cold Chilly Woman* (1973) ★★★, *Come Back* (1973) ★★★, *Live And Well* (1974) ★★★, *Shake That Thing* (1975) ★★, *Sings 'I Don't Know' And Other Chicago Blues Hits* (1977) ★★★, *Chicago Blues Session* (Evidence 1980) ★★★.

● COMPILATIONS: *Chicago 1963* (1974) ★★★, *I'm The Fixer: Original USA Recordings 1963-64* (Flyright 1986) ★★★, *The Seventh Son* (Crown Prince 1987) ★★★, *Blues Roots Volume 16* (Chess 1988) ★★★, *I Don't Know* (Wolf 1995) ★★★.

MacCOLL, EWAN

b. Jimmie Miller, 25 January 1915, Salford, Manchester, England, d. 22 October 1989. The singing talents of his parents enabled MacColl to learn many of their songs while he was still young. He subsequently wrote many classic and regularly covered songs of his own, including 'Dirty Old Town', which was inspired by his home-town of Salford. The song was later made popular by the Pogues and the Dubliners, among others. Having left school at the age of 14, MacColl joined the Salford Clarion Players, and by the age of 16 he was already actively involved in street theatre. His lifelong allegiance to the Communist Party was influenced by his first-hand experiences during the Depression years, and by seeing the effects of the era on his own father and others around him. As a result of his early involvement in political theatre, MacColl, as playwright, actor, director and singer, co-founded the Theatre Workshop at Stratford, London, with Joan Littlewood, who became his first wife. A meeting with folklorist and collector Alan Lomax in the 50s persuaded MacColl to become involved in the revival of British folk songs, which at the time took a back seat to the wealth of American folk material that had arrived via the skiffle boom.

The Critics Group was formed by MacColl in 1964, in an effort to analyse folk song and folk-singing technique. This had its critics, who felt that MacColl and the group were setting themselves up as an élitist authority on folk music. It was in the Critics Group that he met Jean Newlove, who became his second wife. They had two children, Hamish and Kirsty MacColl. In 1965, a series of programmes called *The Song Carriers* was broadcast on Midlands Radio. Later, the innovative *Radio Ballads* was formulated, combining the voice of the ordinary working man with songs and music relevant to their work. The first series, *The Ballad Of John Axon*, was broadcast in 1958. This brought together Peggy Seeger and radio producer Charles Parker. Despite the success of these programmes, no more were commissioned by the BBC on the grounds of expense. It is more likely, however, that the views and opinions expressed in the series did not conform to prevailing ideas on what was suitable for broadcast. Unlike many, MacColl believed that it was not sufficient to perform only old songs, but that new material should be aired, and 'The Travelling People' emerged from these ideas. Both Seeger and MacColl continued to perform professionally throughout the 70s and 80s, having married following the break-up of MacColl's second marriage. Together they set up Blackthorne Records. They were particularly noticeable during the UK miners' strike of 1984, recording and appearing at benefits.

Outside folk music circles, MacColl is probably best remembered for the beautiful 'The First Time Ever I Saw Your Face', which he wrote in 1957 for Seeger. Roberta Flack reached the top of the US charts with the song in 1972, as well as the UK Top 20. MacColl received an Ivor Novello Award for the song in 1973. He died in October 1989, having only recently completed an autobiography. In addition to the three children born to him and Seeger, songs such as 'My Old Man' and 'The Joy Of Living', and a pride in British traditional song, are just part of the considerable legacy he left behind.

● ALBUMS: with Peggy Seeger *Bad Lads And Hard Cases* (Riverside 1956) ★★★, with Seeger *Matching Songs Of Britain And America* (Riverside 1957) ★★★, with Seeger *Bless 'Em All* (Riverside 1957) ★★★, with Seeger, A.L. Lloyd *Thar She Blows* (Riverside 1957) ★★★, with Seeger *Shuttle And Cage* (Topic 1957) ★★★, with Seeger *Barrack Room Ballads* 10-inch album (Topic 1958) ★★★★, with Seeger, Isla Cameron *Still I Love Him* (Topic 1958)

★★★, with Seeger *Steam Whistle Ballads* (Topic 1958) ★★★, with Seeger *Second Shift* (Topic 1958) ★★★, with Dominic Behan *Streets Of Song* (1959) ★★★★, with Seeger *Songs Of Robert Burns* (Folkways 1959) ★★★, with Seeger *The Jacobite Rebellions* (Topic 1960) ★★★, with Seeger *New Briton Gazette I* (Folkways 1960) ★★★, with Seeger *Popular Scottish Songs* (Folkways 1960) ★★★, with Seeger *Songs Of Two Rebellions* (Folkways 1960) ★★★, with Seeger *Two Way Trip* (Folkways 1961) ★★★, with Seeger *Chorus From The Gallows* (Topic 1961) ★★★★, with Seeger *Merry Muses Of Caledonia* (Dionysius 1961) ★★★, with Seeger *Bothy Ballads Of Scotland* (Folkways 1961) ★★★, with Seeger *British Industrial Ballads* (Vanguard 1961) ★★★, with Seeger *Broadside Ballads 1600-1700, Volume 1* (Folkways 1962) ★★★★, with Seeger *Broadside Ballads 1600-1700, Volume 2* (Folkways 1962) ★★★★, *Haul On The Bowlin'* (1962) ★★★, with Seeger *Jacobite Songs* (Topic 1962) ★★★★, with Seeger *New Briton Gazette II* (Folkways 1963) ★★★, *Off To Sea Once More* (1963) ★★★★, *Fourpence A Day-British Industrial Folk Songs* (1963) ★★★, with Lloyd *English And Scottish Folk Ballads* (Topic 1964) ★★★★, with Seeger *Traditional Songs And Ballads* (Folkways 1964) ★★★, *The Ballad Of John Axon* (1965) ★★★, with Seeger *Bundook Ballads* (Topic 1965) ★★★★, with Seeger *The Long Harvest, Vol. 1* (Argo 1966) ★★★, with Seeger *The Long Harvest, Vol. 2* (Argo 1966) ★★★, with Seeger *The Long Harvest, Vol. 3* (Argo 1966) ★★★, with Seeger *The Long Harvest, Vol. 4* (Argo 1966) ★★★, *A Sailor's Garland* (1966) ★★★, with Seeger *Manchester Angel* (Topic 1966) ★★★★, with Seeger *The Long Harvest, Vol. 5* (Argo 1967) ★★★, with Seeger *The Long Harvest, Vol. 6* (Argo 1967) ★★★, with Seeger *The Long Harvest, Vol. 7* (Argo 1967) ★★★, with Seeger *The Long Harvest, Vol. 8* (Argo 1967) ★★★, *Blow Boys Blow* (1967) ★★★, *Singing The Fishing* (1967) ★★★, *The Big Hewer* (1967) ★★★, *The Fight Game* (1967) ★★, with Seeger *The Long Harvest, Vol. 9* (Argo 1968) ★★★, with Seeger *The Long Harvest, Vol. 10* (Argo 1968) ★★★, with Seeger *The Wanton Muse* (Argo 1968) ★★★, with Seeger *The Amorous Muse* (Argo 1968) ★★★, with Seeger *The Angry Muse* (Argo 1968) ★★★, with Seeger *Paper Stage, Vol. 1* (Argo 1968) ★★★, with Seeger *Paper Stage, Vol. 2* (Argo 1968) ★★★, *The Travelling People* (1969) ★★★, *On The Edge* (1970) ★★★, with Seeger *Solo Flight* (Topic 1972) ★★★, with Seeger *At The Present Moment* (Rounder 1973) ★★★, with Seeger *Saturday Night At The Bull And Mouth* (Blackthorne 1977) ★★★, with Seeger *Cold Snap* (Blackthorne 1977) ★★★, with Seeger *Hot Blast* (Blackthorne 1978) ★★★, with Seeger *Blood And Roses* (Blackthorne 1979) ★★★★, with Seeger *Kilroy Was Here* (Blackthorne 1980) ★★★, with Seeger *Blood And Roses, Vol. 2* (Blackthorne 1981) ★★★, with Seeger *Blood And Roses, Vol. 3* (Blackthorne 1982) ★★★, with Seeger *Freeborn Man* (Blackthorne 1983) ★★★, with Seeger *Daddy, What Did You Do In The Strike?* (Blackthorne 1984) ★★★★, with Seeger *White Wind, Black Tide* (Blackthorne 1986) ★★★, with Seeger *Blood And Roses, Vol. 4* (Blackthorne 1986) ★★★, with Seeger *Blood And*

Roses, Vol. 5 (Blackthorne 1986) ★★★, with Seeger Items Of News (Blackthorne 1986) ★★★, with Seeger Naming Of Names (Cooking Vinyl 1990) ★★★.

● COMPILATIONS: with Seeger The Best Of Ewan MacColl (Prestige 1961) ★★★★, The World Of Ewan MacColl And Peggy Seeger (Argo 1969) ★★★★, The World Of Ewan MacColl And Peggy Seeger, Vol. 2 (Argo 1971) ★★★★, with Seeger No Tyme Like The Present (EMI 1976) ★★★, with Seeger Black And White: The Definitive Collection (Cooking Vinyl 1990) ★★★★, with Seeger The Real MacColl (Topic 1993) ★★★★, Solo Flight (Topic 2000) ★★★★.

● FURTHER READING: Journeyman, Ewan MacColl. Traveller's Songs From England And Scotland, Ewan MacColl and Peggy Seeger.

MACKINTOSH, KEN

b. 4 September 1919, Liversedge, West Yorkshire, England. Mackintosh began playing alto saxophone as a child and worked with various bands in Yorkshire in his teens. In 1939, he joined the army and towards the end of the war was playing in military bands. He formed his own unit in 1948 and enjoyed a measure of local popularity in dancehalls and on regional radio. In 1950, his band was booked to open the Wimbledon Palais in London and met with immediate success. The band broadcast regularly and won a recording contract with HMV. The Wimbledon engagement lasted three years. During the last year, Mackintosh had a record hit with 'The Creep', his own composition, and this led to a bill-topping tour of the UK. Throughout the 50s the band toured, recorded, broadcast extensively on radio and television, where it headlined its own show, Flying Standards, and was featured in the film An Alligator Named Daisy (1955). Mackintosh was able to give an early career boost to Frankie Vaughan and Alma Cogan, making records with both artists. Among the band's record successes of the 50s were 'Harlem Nocturne' and 'Raunchy', which reached number 8 in 1958. In 1963, Mackintosh was hired to open the new Empire Ballroom in London's Leicester Square, at the time billed as the world's greatest and most expensive ballroom. This engagement lasted for seven years, after which the band moved to the Hammersmith Palais for a further seven-year stint. Late in the 70s, Mackintosh took his band on the road where he frequently backed touring singers, including Matt Monro, Pat Boone, Tom Jones and Shirley Bassey. Throughout the 80s and into the 90s, Mackintosh continued on the road with his band, playing dances at which he acknowledged contemporary sounds while nostalgically recreating the best popular dance music of earlier years. His son is Andy Mackintosh.

● ALBUMS: Skyliner (1980) ★★, The Very Thought Of You (President 1985) ★★★, Blue Skies (1990) ★★★.

MACRAE, GORDON

b. 12 March 1921, East Orange, New Jersey, USA, d. 24 January 1986, Lincoln, Nebraska, USA. A popular singer on record, radio and in films during the 50s, MacRae was the son of local radio celebrity Wee Willie MacRae, and often worked on radio as a child actor before joining the Millpond Playhouse in New York. There he met actress Sheila Stephens who became his first wife in 1941. After winning an amateur singing contest at the 1939/40 New York World's Fair, he sang for two weeks with the Harry James and Les Brown bands. While working as a pageboy at NBC Radio, he was heard by bandleader Horace Heidt who signed him for two years, during which time he appeared with Heidt, James Stewart and Paulette Goddard in a movie about Heidt's radio giveaway show, Pot O' Gold. After serving in the US Army Air Force Corps in World War II, MacRae returned to New York to take a singing role in the 1946 Broadway revue Three To Make Ready, starring Ray Bolger. In 1947, he signed to Capitol Records and had a string of hits up to 1954, including 'I Still Get Jealous', 'At The Candlelight Cafe', 'It's Magic', 'Hair Of Gold, Eyes Of Blue', 'So In Love', 'Mule Train'/'Dear Hearts And Gentle People' and 'Rambling Rose'. After a four-year gap, he entered the US charts again in 1958 with 'The Secret'. MacRae also made a series of successful singles with ex-Tommy Dorsey singer Jo Stafford. These included 'Say Something Sweet To Your Sweetheart', 'Bluebird Of Happiness', 'My Darling, My Darling' (a US number 1), 'A-You're Adorable', 'Need You', 'Whispering Hope', 'Bibbidi-Bobbidi-Boo' and 'Dearie'. MacRae's film career, mostly for Warner Brothers, started in 1948 with a non-singing role in The Big Punch. This was followed by a series of musicals that included Look For The Silver Lining (1949) and The Daughter Of Rosie O'Grady (1950), both co-starring June Haver, and four films in which he was partnered by Doris Day: Tea For Two (1950), West Point Story (1950), On Moonlight Bay (1951) and By The Light Of The Silvery Moon (1953). Among his other screen appearances were roles in The Desert Song (1953), co-starring Kathryn Grayson, and Three Sailors And A Girl (1953), with Jane Powell. In 1955 and 1956 he had the two most satisfying film parts of his career, when he played opposite Shirley Jones in highly successful adaptations of the Broadway shows Oklahoma! and Carousel. Also in 1956, MacRae appeared in his last film musical as Buddy De Sylva in The Best Things In Life Are Free, a biopic of the 20s/30s songwriting team of De Sylva, Brown And Henderson. In 1979, he made one final film appearance, in a dramatic role in The Pilot. In the mid-50s, MacRae was also popular on US television as the singing host of The Railroad Hour, The Colgate Comedy Hour, and his own Gordon MacRae Show. After divorcing his first wife, he was remarried in 1967 to Elizabeth Lambert Schrafft. In the same year, he made his first Broadway musical appearance since 1946, replacing Robert Preston in I Do! I Do! In the 70s he struggled with alcoholism and, in the early 80s, claimed that he had won the battle. He died from cancer of the mouth and jaw in January 1986.

● ALBUMS: with Jo Stafford Songs Of Faith 10-inch album (Capitol 1950) ★★, Prisoner Of Love film

soundtrack (MGM 1952) ★★★, with various artists *Roberta* 10-inch album (Capitol 1952) ★★★, with various artists *Merry Widow* 10-inch album (Capitol 1952) ★★★, with Lucille Norman *New Moon/Vagabond King* film soundtrack (Capitol 1952) ★★★, with Stafford *Sunday Evening Songs* 10-inch album (Capitol 1953) ★★★, with various artists *The Desert Song* (Capitol 1953) ★★★★, with various artists *Student Prince* 10-inch album (Capitol 1953) ★★★, *By The Light Of The Silvery Moon* film soundtrack (Capitol 1953) ★★, *The Red Mill* film soundtrack (Capitol 1954) ★★★, with Stafford *Memory Songs* (Capitol 1954) ★★★, *Romantic Ballads* (Capitol 1955) ★★★, *Oklahoma!* film soundtrack (Capitol 1955) ★★★★★, *Carousel* film soundtrack (Capitol 1956) ★★★★★, *Operetta Favourites* (Capitol 1956) ★★★★, *The Best Things In Life Are Free* (Capitol 1956) ★★★, *Motion Picture Soundstage* (Capitol 1957) ★★★, *Cowboy's Lament* (Capitol 1957) ★★★, *Gordon MacRae In Concert* (Capitol 1958) ★★, *This Is Gordon MacRae* (Capitol 1958) ★★★★, *Seasons Of Love* (Capitol 1959) ★★★, with Stafford *Whispering Hope* (Capitol 1962) ★★★, with Stafford *Peace In The Valley* (Capitol 1963) ★★, with Stafford *Old Rugged Cross* (Capitol 1963) ★★★.
● COMPILATIONS: *Best Of The Capitol Years* (Capitol 1990) ★★★★, *Gordon McRae Collection* (HMV Easy 2001) ★★★★.
● FURTHER READING: *Hollywood Mother Of The Year: Sheila MacRae's Own Story*, Sheila MacRae with Paul Jeffers.

MALTBY, RICHARD

b. 26 June 1914, Chicago, Illinois, USA, d. 19 August 1991, Santa Monica, California, USA. Maltby started playing cornet in his school band, going on to Northwest University Music School, before his first professional experience with 'Little' Jack Little and his band. He was musical director for CBS radio in Chicago (1940-45), and during this period he wrote 'Six Flats Unfurnished' for the Benny Goodman band, and then spent 10 years working as musical associate for Paul Whiteman at ABC radio in New York. During 1950-65, Maltby was also musical director for SESAC Jazz Classics, recording radio transcriptions with a big band which he took on the road from 1955, encouraged by the success of his 'St Louis Blues Mambo' which had charted the previous year, followed in 1956 by 'The Man With The Golden Arm'. The band recorded prolifically for various RCA labels and Columbia during the 50s, and Maltby was active on many different labels, directing backings for artists Peggy Lee, Giselle Mackenzie, Sarah Vaughan, Gordon MacRae, Johnnie Ray, Vic Damone and Ethel Merman. *Downbeat* voted his unit 'Best New Swing Band', but, the swing era having long since passed, he found more financial reward, if less musical satisfaction, as Lawrence Welk's arranger and conductor on records and television. Maltby's original compositions (mostly for the SESAC transcriptions) for his own orchestra and big band must number in the hundreds, although few measured up to the commercial success of his first

Goodman hit and its successor, 'Five Flats Unfurnished', for Sy Oliver. Maltby's only venture into 'serious music' was his threnody 'Requiem For John Fitzgerald Kennedy'. He suffered from ill health in the 80s, enduring five bouts of open-heart surgery before his death in 1991. His son, Richard Maltby Jnr., is a Broadway director and lyricist.
● ALBUMS: *Manhattan Bandstand* (Viking 50s) ★★, *Hello, Young Lovers* (Columbia 1959) ★★★★, *A Bow To The Big Name Bands* (Camden 1959) ★★★, *Swings For Dancers* (Roulette 50s) ★★★, *Mr Lucky* (Camden 1960) ★★★, *Swingin' Down The Lane* (Columbia 1961) ★★★★, *Swings Folk Songs* (Roulette 1961) ★★★, *Most Requested* (1962) ★★★, *Music From Mr. Lucky* (Camden 60s) ★★★.

MANNE, SHELLY

b. Sheldon Manne, 11 June 1920, New York City, New York, USA, d. 26 September 1984, Los Angeles, California, USA. After switching to drums from saxophone, Manne worked with a number of dance and swing bands of the late 30s and early 40s, including Joe Marsala's big band. He was also active in small groups in New York, accompanying Coleman Hawkins as well as some of the up-and-coming bebop artists. He first attracted widespread attention in 1946, the year he joined Stan Kenton. On and off, he was with Kenton until 1952, finding time in between stints to work in bands led by George Shearing, Woody Herman and others. From the early 50s, he was resident in Los Angeles, working in the studios by day and gradually becoming one of the most important musicians in the rising west coast school of jazz. In 1951, he had recorded with Shorty Rogers and become a member of the house band at Howard Rumsey's Lighthouse Cafe at Hermosa Beach. During the next few years he took part in many fine record sessions, notably for Contemporary, with Teddy Edwards, Jimmy Giuffre, Art Pepper, Lennie Niehaus, Bud Shank, Bob Cooper, Maynard Ferguson, Hampton Hawes and most of the other west coast stars. Among the most successful of these recordings were those made with Rogers in 1951 and 1955/6, a set he recorded with Russ Freeman and Chet Baker, and an album of tunes from the Broadway Show, *My Fair Lady*, which he recorded with Leroy Vinnegar and André Previn. This set, the first ever complete album of jazz versions of tunes from a single show, was particularly successful. Almost as popular was another album made by the same trio with visiting guest Sonny Rollins. Although recording with many different musicians, Manne retained a fairly constant personnel for his regular working band, and towards the end of 1959 was booked into the Blackhawk in San Francisco. The band comprised trumpeter Joe Gordon, Richie Kamuca, Monty Budwig, who had recently taken over from Vinnegar, and Freeman's replacement, Vic Feldman. It was immediately apparent to Manne that the band he had assembled for this two-week engagement was something special, and he persuaded Les Koenig of Contemporary to travel to San Francisco to record them. The resulting four albums became some of the most successful in Contemporary's catalogue and an outstanding example of the west coast's so-called 'cool' sounds at their smokiest. In 1960, Manne opened his own nightclub, Shelly's Manne-Hole, which remained in existence until the middle of the following decade. In the 60s he recorded with Bill Evans and in 1974 joined Shank, Ray Brown and Laurindo Almeida in the L.A. 4, although he was later replaced by Jeff Hamilton. By the late 70s Manne was a familiar figure on the international jazz festival circuit, appearing at the 1980 Aurex festival in Japan with Benny Carter's Gentlemen Of Swing. Although deeply rooted in the swinging tradition of drumming, Manne's sensitive, explorative playing made him an ideal accompanist in almost any setting and one of the finest drummers of the post-war period.

● ALBUMS: with Shorty Rogers *Modern Sounds* (1951) ★★★, *Here's That Manne* (DeeGee 1952) ★★★, with Rogers *Cool And Crazy* (1953) ★★★, *The Three And The Two* (Contemporary 1954) ★★★, with Lennie Niehaus *The Quintet* (1954) ★★★, *The Shelly Manne-Russ Freeman Duo* (1954) ★★★, with Rogers *The Swinging Mr Rogers* (1955) ★★★, *And His Men Volume 1* (Contemporary 1955) ★★★★, *Shelly Manne And His Men Volume 2* (Contemporary 1955) ★★★★, *Concerto For Clarinet And Combo* (Contemporary 1955) ★★★, *The West Coast Sound* (Contemporary 1955) ★★★, with Rogers *Martians Come Back!* (1955) ★★★, with Rogers *Big Band Express/Blues Express* (1956) ★★★, *Swinging Sounds Volume 4* (Contemporary 1956) ★★★, *Quartet: Russ Freeman And Chet Baker* (1956) ★★★, *Shelly Manne And His Friends* (Contemporary 1956) ★★★★, *More Swinging Sounds Volume 5* (Contemporary 1956) ★★★, *My Fair Lady* (Contemporary 1957) ★★★, *Lil' Abner* (Contemporary 1957) ★★★, *The Gambit* (Contemporary 1957) ★★★, with Sonny Rollins *Way Out West* (1957) ★★★★, *The Bells Are Ringing* (Contemporary 1958) ★★★, *Shelly Manne And His Men Play Peter Gunn* (Contemporary 1959) ★★★, *Son Of Gunn* (Contemporary 1959) ★★★, *Shelly Manne And His Men At The Blackhawk Volumes 1-4* (Contemporary 1959) ★★★★, *Swinging Sounds In Stereo* (Contemporary 1959) ★★★★, *The Proper Time* (Contemporary 1960) ★★★, *West Coast Jazz In England* (1960) ★★★, *Shelly Manne And His Men Live At The Manne-Hole Volumes 1 and 2* (Contemporary 1961) ★★★★, *Checkmate* (Contemporary 1961) ★★★, *Sounds Unheard Of* (Contemporary 1962) ★★★, *2,3,4* (Impulse! 1962) ★★★, with Bill Evans *Empathy* (1962) ★★★, *My Son, The Jazz Drummer* (Contemporary 1962) ★★★, with Art Pepper *Pepper/Manne* (Charlie Parker 1963) ★★★, *Shelly Manne And His Orchestra* i (1964) ★★★★, *My Fair Lady With Un-Original Cast* (Capitol 1964) ★★★, *Shelly Manne And His Orchestra* ii (1965) ★★★, *Manne – That's Gershwin!* (Capitol 1965) ★★★★, *Shelly Manne Sounds* (Capitol 1966) ★★★, *Perk Up* (1967) ★★★, *Shelly Manne And His Orchestra* iii (1967) ★★★, *Boss Sounds* (Atlantic 1967) ★★★, *Jazz Gun* (Atlantic 1968) ★★★, *Daktari* (Atlantic 1968) ★★, *Outside* (Contemporary 1968) ★★★, *Alive In*

London (Contemporary 1970) ★★★, *A Night On The Coast* (Moon 1970) ★★★, *Mannekind* (Original Master Recordings 1972) ★★★, with The L.A. 4 *The L.A. Four Scores!* (Concord Jazz 1974) ★★★, *Hot Coles* (1975) ★★★, with The L.A. 4 *Concierto De Aranjuez* (Concord Jazz 1976) ★★★, *Rex – Shelly Manne Plays Richard Rodgers* (1976) ★★★, *Essence* (Galaxy 1977) ★★, *French Concert* (1977) ★★★, *Jazz Crystallizations* (PAUSA 1978) ★★, *The Manne We Love* (1978) ★★, *Interpretations Of Bach And Mozart* (Trend 1980) ★★★, *In Concert At Carmelo's/Double Piano Jazz Quartet Volume 1* (Trend 1980) ★★★, *Double Piano Jazz Quartet Volume 2* (Trend 1980) ★★★, with Benny Carter *The Gentlemen Of Swing* (1980) ★★★, *Hollywood Jam* (1981) ★★★, *Fingering* (1981) ★★★, *Remember* (1984) ★★★, *In Concert At Carmelo's Volumes 1 & 2* (Trend 1986) ★★★.

MANTOVANI

b. Annunzio Paolo Mantovani, 15 November 1905, Venice, Italy, d. 30 March 1980, Tunbridge Wells, Kent, England. A violinist, pianist, musical director, conductor, composer and arranger, Mantovani was one of the most successful orchestra leaders and album sellers in the history of popular music. His father was principal violinist at La Scala, Milan, under Arturo Toscanini, and also served under Mascagni, Richter and Saint-Saens, and subsequently, led the Covent Garden Orchestra. It is said that Mantovani received encouragement to become a professional musician from his mother, rather than his father. He began his musical training on the piano, and later learned to play the violin. After the family moved to England in 1912, he made his professional debut at the age of 16, playing the Bruch Violin Concerto Number 1. Four years later he had installed his own orchestra at London's Hotel Metropole, and began his broadcasting career. In the early 30s he formed the Tipica Orchestra and began a series of lunchtime broadcasts from the famous Monseigneur Restaurant in Piccadilly, London, and started recording for Regal Zonophone. He had two US hits in 1935-36, with 'Red Sails In The Sunset' and 'Serenade In The Night'. In the 40s, Mantovani served as musical director for several London West End shows, including *Lady Behave*, *Twenty To One*, *Meet Me Victoria*, *And So To Bed*, *Bob's Your Uncle* and *La-Di-Da-Di-Da*. He was also involved in Noël Coward's *Pacific 1860* and *Ace Of Clubs*; conducting from the theatre pit for artists such as Lupino Lane, Pat Kirkwood, Mary Martin, Sally Gray, Leslie Henson and many others.

His records for UK Decca Records included 'The Green Cockatoo', 'Hear My Song, Violetta' and 'Tell Me, Marianne' (vocal by Val Merrall). Experimenting with various arrangements with which to target the lucrative US market, he came up with what has been variously called the 'cascading strings', 'cascading violins', or 'tumbling strings' effect, said to be an original idea of arranger Ronnie Binge. It became the Orchestra's trademark and was first used to great effect in 1951, on Mantovani's recording of

'Charmaine', a song originally written to promote the 1926 silent film classic *What Price Glory?*. The Mantovani recording was the first of several million-selling singles for his orchestra, which included 'Wyoming', (another 20s number), 'Greensleeves', 'Song From Moulin Rouge' (a UK number 1), 'Swedish Rhapsody' and 'Lonely Ballerina'. Mantovani's own compositions included 'Serenata d'Amore', 'A Poem To The Moon', 'Royal Blue Waltz', 'Dance Of The Eighth Veil', 'Toy Shop Ballet' (Ivor Novello Award 1956), 'Red Petticoats', 'Brass Buttons', 'Tango In the Night' and 'Cara Mia', written with UK record producer/manager Bunny Lewis. David Whitfield's 1954 recording of 'Cara Mia', with Mantovani's orchestra accompaniment, sold over a million copies, and stayed at number 1 in the UK charts for a record (at the time) 10 weeks. It also made Whitfield one of the earliest UK artists to break into the US Top 10. Mantovani issued an instrumental version of the number, featuring himself on piano. This was most unusual in that the instrument was rarely a part of his 40-piece orchestral set-up.

Singles apart, it was as an album artist that Mantovani excelled around the world, and especially in the USA. He is said to have been the first to sell over a million stereo units, aided in no small measure by the superb quality of sound obtained by Decca. Between 1955 and 1966 he had 28 albums in the US Top 30. Although he toured many countries of the world, including Russia, his popularity in the USA, where his style of orchestral offerings were often referred to as 'the beautiful music', was unique. An indication of the US audience's devotion can be gained from a claim by George Elrick, Mantovani's manager of 21 years, that at the beginning of one tour of the USA, the maestro was taken ill and a few concerts had to be cancelled; the prospective capacity audience at one of them, the University of Minnesota and Minneapolis, refused to claim refunds, preferring to retain their tickets for the following year. Mantovani continued to perform throughout the ever-changing musical climate of the 60s and 70s. He was awarded a special Ivor Novello Award in 1956 for services to popular music.

● ALBUMS: *Mantovani Plays Tangos* (Decca/London 1953) ★★★, *Strauss Waltzes* (Decca/London 1953) ★★★, *Christmas Carols* (Decca/London 1953) ★★★, *The Music Of Rudolph Friml* (Decca/London 1955) ★★★, *Waltz Time* (Decca/London 1955) ★★★, *Song Hits From Theatreland* (Decca/London 1955) ★★★, *Ballet Memories* (Decca/London 1956) ★★★, *Waltzes Of Irving Berlin* (Decca/London 1956) ★★★, *Film Encores* (Decca/London 1957) ★★★, *Gems Forever* (Decca/London 1958) ★★★, *Continental Encores* (Decca/London 1959) ★★★, *Film Encores, Volume 2* (Decca/London 1959) ★★★, *The American Scene* (Decca/London 1960) ★★★, *Songs To Remember* (Decca/London 1960) ★★★, *Mantovani Plays Music From Exodus And Other Great Themes* (Decca/London 1960) ★★★, *Concert Spectacular* (Decca/London 1961) ★★★, *Operetta Memories* (Decca/London 1961) ★★★, *Italia Mia* (Decca/London 1961) ★★★, *Themes From Broadway* (Decca/London 1961) ★★★, *Songs Of Praise* (Decca/London 1961) ★★★, *American Waltzes* (Decca/London 1962) ★★★, *Moon River And Other Great Film Themes* (Decca/London 1962) ★★★, *Stop The World – I Want To Get Off/Oliver!* (Decca/London 1962) ★★★, *Latin Rendezvous* (Decca/London 1963) ★★★, *Classical Encores* (Decca/London 1963) ★★★, *Mantovani/Manhattan* (Decca/London 1963) ★★★, *Christmas Greetings From Mantovani* (Decca/London 1963) ★★, *Kismet* (Decca/London 1964) ★★★, *Folk Songs Around The World* (Decca/London 1964) ★★★, *The Incomparable Mantovani* (Decca/London 1964) ★★★, *The Mantovani Sound – Big Hits From Broadway And Hollywood* (Decca/London 1965) ★★★★, *Mantovani Olé* (Decca/London 1965) ★★★, *Mantovani Magic* (Decca/London 1966) ★★★, *Mr. Music … Mantovani* (Decca/London 1966) ★★★, *Mantovani Hollywood* (Decca/London 1967) ★★★, *Old And New Fangled Tangos* (Decca/London 1967) ★★★, *The Mantovani Touch* (Decca/London 1968) ★★★, *Mantovani/Tango* (Decca/London 1968) ★★★, *Mantovani Memories* (Decca/London 1968) ★★★, *The Mantovani Scene* (Decca/London 1969) ★★★, *Mantovani Today* (Decca/London 1970) ★★★, *Mantovani Presents His Concert Successes* (Decca/London 1970) ★★★, *To Lovers Everywhere USA* (Decca/London 1971) ★★★, *From Monty With Love* (Decca/London 1971) ★★★, *Annunzio Paolo Mantovani* (Decca/London 1972) ★★★, *Cascade Of Praise* (Word 1985) ★★★.

● COMPILATIONS: *Mantovani Stereo Showcase* (Decca/London 1959) ★★★, *All-American Showcase* (Decca/London 1959) ★★★, *Mantovani's Golden Hits* (Decca/London 1967) ★★★, *The World Of Mantovani* (Decca/London 1969) ★★★, *The World Of Mantovani, Volume 2* (Decca/London 1969) ★★★, *Focus On Mantovani* (Decca 1975) ★★★, *Twenty Golden Greats* (Warwick 1979) ★★★, *A Lifetime Of Music* (Decca 1980) ★★★, *The Golden Age Of The Young Mantovani 1935-1939* (Retrospect 1980) ★★★, *The Unforgettable Sounds Of Mantovani* (Decca 1984) ★★★, *Mantovani Magic* (Telstar 1985) ★★★, *Love Themes* (Horatio Nelson 1985) ★★★, *Sixteen Golden Classics* (Unforgettable 1986) ★★★, *The Incomparable Mantovani* (K-Tel 1987) ★★★, *Collection: Mantovani* (Castle 1987) ★★★, *Golden Hits* (Decca 1988) ★★★, *The Love Album* (Platinum 1988) ★★★, *Film Themes* (Horatio Nelson 1989) ★★★, *The Golden Age Of Mantovani* (Horatio Nelson 1995) ★★★, *Candlelight Romance – 20 Great Love Songs* (Spectrum 1998) ★★★.

MANUEL AND THE MUSIC OF THE MOUNTAINS

Orchestra leader Geoff Love (b. 4 September 1917, Todmorden, Yorkshire, England, d. 8 July 1991, London, England) initially used the above name pseudonymously. The British-born son of a black American dancer, he took to music at an early age and by the late 50s/early 60s joined Joe Loss and Ted Heath as one of the country's leading bandleaders. Love's Manuel appellation allowed him an artistic freedom to draw influence from South American music and, although early releases did not reveal its creator's identity (Love was 'unmasked' during a cameo appearance on BBC television's *Juke Box Jury*), such recordings later became the natural outlet for his talents. A prodigious output, notably for EMI's prestigious Studio 2 stereo series, ensured that the band remained one of Britain's most popular light orchestral attractions throughout the 60s and 70s.

● ALBUMS: *Manuel And His Music Of The Mountains* (Columbia 1960) ★★★★, *Mountain Carnival* (c.60s) ★★★★, *Ecstasy* (c.60s) ★★★, *Mountain Fiesta* (c.60s) ★★★, *Blue Waters* (1966) ★★★, *Reflections* (Studio 2 1969) ★★★, *This Is Manuel* (Studio 2 1971) ★★★★, *Carnival* (Studio 2 1971) ★★★★, *Mardi Gras* (1972) ★★★, *Shangri-La* (1973) ★★★, *Sun, Sea And Sky* (1973) ★★★, *Y Viva Espana* (1974) ★★★★, *You, The Night And Music* (1975) ★★★, *El Bimbo* (1975) ★★, *Manuel And The Voices Of Mountains* (1975) ★★★, *Masquerade* (1976) ★★★, *Mountain Fire* (1977) ★★★, *Blue Tangos* (Note 1977) ★★, *Bossa Nova* (1978) ★★, *Cha Cha* (1978) ★★★, *Music Of Manuel* (1978) ★★★★, *Supernatural* (EMI 1979) ★★★, *Viva Manuel* (1979) ★★★★, *Manuel Movie Hits* (Note 1979) ★★, *Fiesta* (EMI 1980) ★★★★, *Digital Spectacular* (EMI 1981) ★★★★.

● COMPILATIONS: *The Very Best Of Manuel* (Columbia 1976) ★★★★, *Bolero* (MFP 1984) ★★★, *Magic Of Manuel And The Music Of The Mountains* (MFP 1986) ★★★, *Latin Hits* (EMI 1988) ★★★.

MARTIN, DEAN

b. Dino Paul Crocetti, 7 June 1917, Steubenville, Ohio, USA, d. 25 December 1995, Beverly Hills, California, USA. An extremely popular ballad singer and light comedian with a relaxed and easy style, who developed into an accomplished dramatic actor. After leaving school in the tenth grade, he worked as a shoe-shine boy and a gas station attendant before becoming an 'amateur' welterweight boxer, 'Kid Crochet', earning 10 dollars a fight. When he retired from the boxing arena, he became a croupier at a local casino. His first singing job is said to have been with the Sammy Watkins band in 1941, when he was initially billed as Dino Martini, but the name was soon changed to Dean Martin. His earliest recordings were for the Diamond label, and included 'Which Way Did My Heart Go'/'All Of Me' and 'I Got the Sun In The Morning'/'The Sweetheart Of Sigma Chi'. He also recorded some tracks for the Apollo label, well known for its impressive roster of black talent. The Martin recordings included 'Walkin' My Baby Back Home', 'Oh Marie', 'Santa Lucia', 'Hold Me', 'Memory Lane' and 'Louise'. In 1946, Martin first worked with comedian Jerry Lewis at the 500 Club in Atlantic City. Together they developed an ad-libbing song and comedy act that became very popular on US television and radio in the late 40s. In 1949, they appeared in supporting roles in the film *My Friend Irma*, and in the sequel, *My Friend Irma Goes West*, the following year. The team then starred in another 14 popular

comedies, with Martin providing the songs and romantic interest, and Lewis contributing the zany fun. These films included *At War With The Army* (1950), *Jumping Jacks* (1952), *Sailor, Beware!*, *The Stooge*, *Scared Stiff* (1953), *The Caddy* (1953), *Living It Up* (1954), *Pardners* (1956) and *Hollywood Or Bust* (1956). Their parting was somewhat acrimonious, and it was widely felt that Martin would be the one to suffer most from the split. In fact, they both did well. After a shaky start in the comedy movie *Ten Thousand Bedrooms* (1957), Martin blossomed as a dramatic actor in *The Young Lions* (1958), *Some Came Running* (1958), *Rio Bravo* (1959), *Ada* (1961), *Toys In The Attic* (1963), *The Sons Of Katie Elder* (1965) and *Airport* (1970). He still retained his comic touch in *Who Was That Lady?* (1960) and *What A Way To Go* (1964), but made surprisingly few musicals. The most notable were *Bells Are Ringing* (1960), with Judy Holliday, and *Robin And The Seven Hoods* (1964).

Meanwhile, Martin had signed to Capitol Records in 1948, and for the next 10 years had a series of US Top 30 chart entries, including 'That Certain Party' (duet with Jerry Lewis), 'Powder Your Face With Sunshine', 'I'll Always Love You', 'If', 'You Belong To Me', 'Love Me, Love Me', 'That's Amore', 'I'd Cry Like A Baby', 'Sway', 'Money Burns A Hole In My Pocket, 'Memories Are Made Of This' (number 1), 'Innamorata', 'Standing On The Corner', 'Return To Me', 'Angel Baby' and 'Volare' ('Nel Blu Dipinto Di Blu'). Martin's version of 'That's Amore' resurfaced when it was featured in the 1987 hit movie *Moonstruck*.

Although Martin was still a big attraction on film and in nightclubs, his records found difficulty in making the singles charts during the early part of the 60s. In 1961, Frank Sinatra, who had also been with Capitol Records, started his own Reprise Records. Martin, who was a member of Sinatra's 'Clan', or 'Ratpack', was one of the first recruits to the new label. In 1964, Martin returned to the US singles charts with a bang. His recording of 'Everybody Loves Somebody', produced by Jimmy Bowen, had a commercial country 'feel' to it, and knocked the Beatles' 'A Hard Day's Night' off the top of the chart. Martin's subsequent Top 30 entries were all in the same vein – records such as 'The Door Is Still Open To My Heart', 'You're Nobody 'Til Somebody Loves You', 'Send Me The Pillow You Dream On', 'Houston', 'In The Chapel In The Moonlight' and 'Little Ole Wine Drinker, Me'. The latter number was a fitting selection for an artist whose stage persona was that of a man more than slightly inebriated. 'Everybody Loves Somebody' became the theme song for *The Dean Martin Show* on NBC TV which started in 1964, ran for nine seasons and was syndicated worldwide. As well being a showcase for Martin's singing talents, the show gave him the opportunity to display his improvisational skills in comedy. He continued to be a big draw in clubs, especially in Las Vegas, and played the London Palladium in the summer of 1987 to favourable reviews. Later that year, he joined ex-Rat Pack colleagues Sinatra and Sammy Davis Jnr.

in the 'Together Again' tour, involving 40 performances in 29 cities, but had to withdraw at an early stage because of a kidney ailment. In the autumn of 1993 it was reported that Martin had lung cancer and he died on Christmas Day 1995.

● ALBUMS: *Capitol Presents Dean Martin* (Capitol 1953) ★★★, *Swingin' Down Yonder* (Capitol 1955) ★★★, *Dean Martin Sings, Nicolini Lucchesi Plays* (Britone 1956) ★★, *The Stooge* film soundtrack (Capitol 1956) ★★, *Pretty Baby* (Capitol 1957) ★★★, *This Is Dean Martin* (Capitol 1958) ★★★, *Sleep Warm* (Capitol 1959) ★★★, *Winter Romance* (Capitol 1959) ★★★, *Bells Are Ringing* film soundtrack (Capitol 1960) ★★★, *This Time I'm Swingin'* (Capitol 1961) ★★★, *Dino Goes Dixie* (Encore 1961) ★★, *Dean Martin* (Capitol 1961) ★★★, *Dino – Italian Love Songs* (Capitol 1962) ★★★, *French Style* (Reprise 1962) ★★★, *Cha Cha De Amor* (Capitol 1962) ★★★, *Dino Latino* (Reprise 1963) ★★★, *Dean Martin Country Style* (Reprise 1963) ★★, *Dean 'Tex' Martin Rides Again* (Reprise 1963) ★★, *Everybody Loves Somebody* (Reprise 1964) ★★★, *Hey Brother, Pour The Wine* (Reprise 1964) ★★★, *Dream With Dean* (Reprise 1964) ★★★, *The Door Is Still Open To My Heart* (Reprise 1964) ★★★, *Dean Martin Hits Again* (Reprise 1965) ★★★, *Dean Martin Sings, Sinatra Conducts* (Reprise 1965) ★★★, *Southern Style* (Reprise 1965) ★★★, *Dean Martin Month* (Reprise 1965) ★★★, *Holiday Cheer* (Reprise 1965) ★★★, *I'm Yours* (Sears 1965) ★★★, *(Remember Me) I'm The One Who Loves You* (Reprise 1965) ★★★, *Houston* (Reprise 1965) ★★★, *Somewhere There's A Someone* (Reprise 1966) ★★★, *Relaxin'* (Reprise 1966) ★★★, *Happy In Love* (Reprise 1966) ★★★, *Sings Songs From The Silencers* (Reprise 1966) ★★★, *The Hit Sound Of Dean Martin* (Reprise 1966) ★★★, *The Dean Martin TV Show* (Reprise 1966) ★★★, *The Dean Martin Christmas Album* (Reprise 1966) ★★★, *At Ease With Dean* (Reprise 1967) ★★★, *Happiness Is Dean Martin* (Reprise 1967) ★★★, *Love Is A Career* (Stateside 1967) ★★★, *Welcome To My World* (Reprise 1967) ★★★, *Gentle On My Mind* (Reprise 1969) ★★★, *I Take A Lot Of Pride In What I Am* (Reprise 1969) ★★★, *My Woman, My Wife* (Reprise 1970) ★★★, *For The Good Times* (Reprise 1971) ★★★, *Dino* (Reprise 1972) ★★★, *Sittin' On Top Of The World* (Reprise 1973) ★★★, *You're The Best Thing That Ever Happened To Me* (Reprise 1974) ★★★, *Once In A While* (Reprise 1978) ★★★, *The Nashville Sessions* (Warners 1983) ★★.

● COMPILATIONS: *The Best Of Dean Martin* (Capitol 1966) ★★★, *Deluxe Set* 3-LP box set (Capitol 1967) ★★★, *Dean Of Music* (MFP 1967) ★★★, *Dean Martin's Greatest Hits! Volume 1* (Reprise 1968) ★★★, *Dean Martin's Greatest Hits! Volume 2* (Reprise 1968) ★★★, *The Best Of Dean Martin* (Capitol 1969) ★★★, *The Best Of Dean Martin, Volume 2* (Capitol 1970) ★★★, *One More Time* (World Record Club 1970) ★★★, *20 Original Dean Martin Hits* (Reprise 1976) ★★★, *The Classic Dino* (Capitol 1979) ★★★, *Dean Martin* 4-LP box set (World Record Club 1981) ★★★, *The Very Best Of Dean Martin* (Capitol 1983) ★★★, *20 Love Songs* (Black Tulip 1988) ★★★, *The Dean Martin Collection* (Deja Vu 1989) ★★★, *The Collection* (Castle 1988) ★★★, *That's Amore* (Entertainers 1988) ★★★, *The Best Of The Capitol Years* (Capitol 1989) ★★★, *Capitol Collectors Series* (Capitol 1990) ★★★, *Singles* (1994) ★★★, *The Capitol Years* (Capitol 1996) ★★★, *Memories Are Made Of This* 8-CD box set (Bear Family 1997) ★★★, *The Very Best Of Dean Martin: The Capitol & Reprise Years* (Capitol 1998) ★★★★, *The Very Best Of Dean Martin, Volume 2* (Capitol 2000) ★★★.

● FURTHER READING: *Everybody Loves Somebody*, Arthur Marx. *Dino: Living High In The Dirty Business Of Dreams*, Nick Tosches.

● FILMS: *My Friend Irma* (1949), *My Friend Irma Goes West* (1950), *At War With The Army* (1950), *That's My Boy* (1951), *Sailor Beware* (1951), *The Stooge* (1952), *Road To Bali* (1952), *Jumping Jacks* (1952), *Money From Home* (1953), *Scared Stiff* (1953), *The Caddy* (1953), *Living It Up* (1954), *Three Ring Circus* (1954), *You're Never Too Young* (1955), *Artists And Models* (1955), *Hollywood Or Bust* (1956), *Pardners* (1956), *Ten Thousand Bedrooms* (1957), *Some Came Running* (1958), *The Young Lions* (1958), *Career* (1959), *Rio Bravo* (1960), cameo *Pepe* (1960), *Who Was That Lady?* (1960), *Bells Are Ringing* (1960), *Ocean's Eleven* (1960), *All In A Night's Work* (1961), *Ada* (1961), *Who's Got The Action?* (1962), *Sergeants 3* (1962), guest star *The Road To Hong Kong* (1962), *Who's Been Sleeping In My Bed?* (1963), *Toys In The Attic* (1963), *Canzoni Nel Mondo* (1963), *Come Blow Your Horn* (1963), *4 For Texas* (1963), *Kiss Me, Stupid* (1964), *What A Way To Go!* (1964), *Robin And The 7 Hoods* (1964), *Marriage On The Rocks* (1965), *The Sons Of Katie Elder* (1965), *Murders' Row* (1966), *The Silencers* (1966), *Texas Across The River* (1966), *Rough Night In Jericho* (1967), *Rowan & Martin At The Movies* (1968), *How To Save A Marriage (And Ruin Your Life)* (1968), *The Ambushers* (1968), *Bandolero!* (1968), *5 Card Stud* (1968), *The Wrecking Crew* (1969), *Airport* (1970), *Something Big* (1971), *Showdown* (1973), *Mr. Ricco* (1975), *The Cannonball Run* (1981), *L.A. Is My Lady* (1984), *Cannonball Run II* (1984).

MARTIN, RAY

b. Raymond Stuart Martin, 11 October 1918, Vienna, Austria, d. February 1988, South Africa. A composer, arranger, musical director and author, after studying violin, composition and orchestration at the State Academy for Music and Fine Arts in Vienna, Martin moved to Britain in 1937. He joined the *Carroll Levis Discoveries* show as a solo violin act, touring the UK variety circuit, and was then chosen as the 'New Voice' in the popular BBC radio series *Bandwaggon*, which starred Arthur Askey and Richard Murdoch. After appearing in several editions of *Sidney Torch's Half Hour*, he enlisted in the British Army in 1940 and worked in the Intelligence Corps, aided by his fluency in German, French and English. Later, he became musical director of the Variety Department for the British Forces Network in Hamburg, Germany. He started broadcasting his *Melody From The Sky* programme from there, with a German string orchestra culled from the

Hamburg Philharmonic Orchestra, and transferred the show to the BBC in December 1946, where it ran for over 500 broadcasts. Martin was also instrumental in founding the BBC Northern Variety Orchestra, and, from 1949-51, conducted at least six shows a week. He started recording for Columbia Records in 1949 with his own Concert Orchestra accompanying other artists including Julie Andrews, Steve Conway and Jimmy Young. Eventually he became the company's recording manager. His 50s instrumental hits included Leroy Anderson's 'Blue Tango', 'Swedish Rhapsody' and 'Carousel Waltz'. Some of his many compositions and film scores are difficult to locate because, besides his own name, he wrote under several pseudonyms, such as Tony Simmonds, Buddy Cadbury, Lester Powell and Marshall Ross. In 1956 he wrote the background score, and served as musical director, for a British musical film called *It's Great To Be Young*, starring John Mills. In addition to the title track, written under his own name, the film contained Martin's (as Marshall Ross) 1952 composition 'Marching Strings'; and his (as Lester Powell) romantic ballad 'You Are My First Love' (in collaboration with Paddy Roberts). Martin's other compositions included 'Melody From The Sky', 'Once Upon A Winter Time', 'Muriella', 'Begorra', 'Parlour Game', 'Blue Violins' (a US hit for Hugo Winterhalter's Orchestra), 'Any Old Time', 'Waltzing Bugle Boy', 'Airborne', 'Ballet Of The Bells', 'Tango Of The Bells', 'Big Ben Blues', 'Never Too Young' and 'Sounds Out Of Sight'. He composed the incidental music for over 20 BBC Sound cartoons, and wrote the scores for several films, including *Yield To The Night*, a prison melodrama in which ex-'glamour girl' Diana Dors gave a highly acclaimed dramatic performance, and the 1956 version of *My Wife's Father*. In 1957 Martin moved to America to work in New York and Hollywood. His US film scores included *The Young Graduates* and *The Hoax*. In 1972 he returned to work in the UK and, in 1980, appeared as himself in *The Baltimore Bullit*. During the 80s he settled in South Africa, and died there in 1988.

● ALBUMS: *Music In The Ray Martin Manner* (Columbia 1953) ★★★★, *Music In The Ray Martin Manner Volume 2* (Columbia 1954) ★★★★, *Lehar, Strauss And Novello Melodies* (Columbia 1956) ★★★, *High Barbaree-12 Famous Sea Shanties* (Columbia 1957) ★★, *Olives, Almonds And Raisins* (Columbia 1958) ★★★, *Million Dollar Melodies* (Columbia 1959) ★★★, *Melodies D'Amour* (Columbia 1961) ★★★, *Boots And Saddles* (Columbia 1961) ★★, *I Could Have Danced All Night* (1961) ★★★, *Dynamica* (RCA 1961) ★★★, *We* (1962) ★★★, *Spotlight On Strings* (1962) ★★★, *Sounds Out Of Sight* (1963) ★★★, *The Sound Of Sight* (Phase 4 1964) ★★★, *London Under The Stars* (1966) ★★★, *Favourite TV Themes* (Decca 1973) ★★★, *Favourite TV Themes, Volume 2* (Decca 1975) ★★★, *Viva Mariachi* (Gold Star 1975) ★★★, *Welcome Home* (Goldstar 1975) ★★★.

MARTINO, AL

b. Alfred Cini, 7 October 1927, Philadelphia, Pennsylvania, USA. The son of Italian immigrants, a fact that was evident in his style and manner, Martino worked as bricklayer in his father's construction business before being encouraged to become a singer by his friend Mario Lanza. After singing in local clubs, and winning Arthur Godfrey's *Talent Scouts*, he recorded 'Here In My Heart' for the small BBS record label. It shot to number 1 in the US chart, and reputedly sold over a million copies. This disc was also the first ever record to top the *New Musical Express* UK listings, inaugurated in 1952. Martino's success led to a contract with Capitol Records, and more hits in 1953 with 'Take My Heart', 'Rachel' and 'When You're Mine'. For several years after that, the US record buyers apparently tired of Martino's soulful ballads, although he remained popular in Europe for a time – particularly in the UK, where he made the Top 20 with 'Now', 'Wanted', 'The Story Of Tina' and 'The Man From Laramie'. After some telling performances on US television, he made his recording comeback in 1963 with country singer Leon Payne's 'I Love You Because', followed by 'Painted, Tainted Rose', 'Living A Lie', 'I Love You More And More Every Day', 'Tears And Roses', 'Always Together', 'Think I'll Go And Cry Myself To Sleep' and 'Mary In The Morning'.

His second million-seller, 'Spanish Eyes' (1965), was originally an instrumental piece, 'Moon Over Naples', written by the popular German orchestra leader, Bert Kaempfert. With lyrics by Charles Singleton and Eddy Snyder, Martino's version became, particularly in Europe, a dreamy dance favourite to rival Charles Aznavour's 'Dance In The Old Fashioned Way'. In 1964, Martino sang the title song for the Bette Davis/Olivia De Havilland film *Hush ... Hush Sweet Charlotte*, and this led to his playing singer Johnny Fontane in the smash hit movie *The Godfather* (1972). In the film, Martino sang the Italian number 'O Marenariello' ('I Have But One Heart'). He also recorded the film's love theme, 'Speak Softly Love', and had chart success with further Italian songs, 'To The Door Of The Sun' ('Alle Porte Del Sole') and the old Dean Martin hit, Domenico Modugno's 'Volare'. In vogue once more, Martino played top nightclubs and theatres, and continued to record with Capitol who have reissued many of his early albums on CD. In 1992 he played some UK dates, mixing selections from *Cats* and *The Phantom Of The Opera* with much requested favourites such as 'Granada'. Martino returned to recording after a long break in 2000 with *Smile*, a sparkling album of danceband classics. Like Martin, Martino's vocals are seeped in understatement and relaxed confidence.

● ALBUMS: *Al Martino* (20th Century 1959) ★★★, *Sing Along With Al Martino* (20th Century 1959) ★★★, *Al Martino Sings* (20th Century 1962) ★★★, *The Exciting Voice Of Al Martino* (Capitol 1962) ★★★, *The Italian Voice Of Al Martino* (Capitol 1963) ★★★, *Love Notes* (20th Century 1963) ★★★, *I Love You Because* (Capitol 1963) ★★★★, *Painted, Tainted Rose* (Capitol 1963) ★★★★, *Living A Lie*

(Capitol 1964) ★★★, *I Love You More And More Every Day/Tears And Roses* (Capitol 1964) ★★★, *We Could* (Capitol 1965) ★★★, *Somebody Else Is Taking My Place* (Capitol 1965) ★★★, *My Cherie* (Capitol 1965) ★★★★, *Spanish Eyes* (Capitol 1966) ★★★★, *Think I'll Go Somewhere And Cry Myself To Sleep* (Capitol 1966) ★★★, *This Is Love* (Capitol 1966) ★★★, *This Love For You* (Capitol 1967) ★★★, *Daddy's Little Girl* (Capitol 1967) ★★★, *Mary In The Morning* (Capitol 1967) ★★★, *This Is Al Martino* (Capitol 1968) ★★★, *Love Is Blue* (Capitol 1968) ★★★, *Sausalito* (Capitol 1969) ★★★, *Jean* (Capitol 1969) ★★★, *Can't Help Falling In Love* (Capitol 1970) ★★★, *My Heart Sings* (Capitol 1970) ★★★, *Love Theme From 'The Godfather'* (Capitol 1972) ★★, *Country Style* (Capitol 1974) ★, *To The Door Of The Sun* (Capitol 1975) ★★, *Sing My Love Songs* (Capitol 1977) ★★★, *The Next Hundred Years* (Capitol 1978) ★★★, *Smile* (Fuel 2000) ★★★★.

● COMPILATIONS: *The Best Of Al Martino* (Capitol 1968) ★★★, *The Very Best Of Al Martino* (Capitol 1974) ★★★, *Love Songs: Al Martino* (MFP 1983) ★★★, *The Hits Of Al Martino* (MFP 1985) ★★★, *Greatest Hits* (Prism 1991) ★★★, *Capitol Collectors Series: Al Martino* (Capitol 1992) ★★★, *The Al Martino Collection: I Love You Because ...* (Razor & Tie 1999) ★★★.

MARVIN AND JOHNNY

From Los Angeles, California, USA, Marvin Phillips (b. 23 October 1931, Guthrie, Oklahoma, USA) and Emory 'Johnny' Perry (b. 1 March 1928, Sherman, Texas, USA) made a brief impact on the rock 'n' roll scene when Los Angeles was a major centre of the R&B recording scene during the late 40s and early 50s. Phillips and Perry had known each other since 1949, when they both played saxophones in the Richard Lewis Band. When Phillips formed the Marvin Phillips And His Men From Mars combo, Perry joined him. Phillips had gained his first success in the recording business when he teamed with Jesse Belvin in a duo called Marvin And Jesse, reaching the charts with the dreamy ballad 'Dream Girl' (number 2 R&B) in 1952 for Specialty Records. After Belvin was drafted into the army in 1953, Phillips, at the behest of Specialty, recruited a new partner, his old friend Perry, to form Marvin And Johnny. The duo immediately had a hit with 'Baby Doll' (number 9 R&B) in 1953. They moved to Modern in 1954 and released 'Tick Tock' (number 9 R&B). However, they are best remembered for 'Cherry Pie', the b-side to 'Tick Tock', which, although not making any national charts, possibly achieved more radio airplay. The song was revived by Skip And Flip in 1960, putting it high on the pop charts.

● ALBUMS: *Marvin And Johnny* (Crown 1963) ★★★.

● COMPILATIONS: *Flipped Out* (Specialty 1992) ★★★.

MASTERS, VALERIE

b. 24 April 1940, London, England. This red-headed pop singer from London's East End sang during her childhood in the local underground station during air raids and later became the private secretary to the Mayor of Stepney. She received her big musical break when she replaced Marion Ryan in the popular Ray Ellington Quartet. Masters made her first recording, 'Ding Dong', for Fontana in 1958 and was first seen on television on the *Hughie Green Show*. She was given her own series on Radio Luxembourg in 1959, which ran for over two years. Her only chart success came in 1960 with her sixth single on Fontana, a version of the European song 'Banjo Boy'. This was the same song that gave much-loved singer/comedian George Formby his last chart hit. Masters represented Britain in the European (not Eurovision) Song Contest in Belgium in 1960, and this led to her working in Scandinavia, Germany and the Netherlands. She recorded for HMV in 1963, Columbia in 1964, Polydor in 1966 and once more on Columbia in 1969 but has not graced the chart since.

MATHIS, JOHNNY

b. John Royce Mathis, 30 September 1935, San Francisco, California, USA. In 1956, the 19-year-old Mathis was signed to Columbia Records where he began his career with a jazz-tinged album. A US Top 20 hit with 'Wonderful! Wonderful!' saw him move adroitly towards the balladeer market, and before long he was a major concert attraction, with regular appearances on highly rated American television shows. In 1957, together with his first hit, Mathis was barely absent from the US bestseller lists, and that year had a further five hits, including the number 1 'Chances Are', 'The Twelfth Of Never' and 'It's Not For Me To Say'. Mathis had become a phenomenon; his popularity at that time ranked alongside that of Frank Sinatra. By May 1958, he was scraping the UK charts with 'Teacher, Teacher', and soon established himself with major hits such as 'A Certain Smile', 'Winter Wonderland', 'Someone', 'Misty' and 'My Love For You'. His appeal to the adult market ensured spectacular album success, and *Johnny's Greatest Hits* stayed a record 490 weeks in the US chart.

With the beat boom and 60s pop explosion making it more difficult for visiting American balladeers to infiltrate the singles chart, Mathis concentrated increasingly on releasing albums. Indeed, he seemed willing to tackle a variety of concepts presented by his various producers and arrangers. *Away From Home*, produced by Norman Newell, saw the singer concentrating on the songs of European composers; *Olé*, the Latin-American outing, was sung in Portuguese and Spanish; *Wonderful World Of Make Believe* consisted entirely of songs based on fairytales; and there were tribute albums to such composers as Burt Bacharach and Bert Kaempfert. Meanwhile, Mathis was suffering from serious drug addiction, but fortunately he managed to kick the habit. By the late 60s, Mathis seemed equally adept at tackling MOR standards and John Lennon/Paul McCartney songs, as well as hoping to update his image. He returned to the UK singles chart in 1974 for the first time in a decade with 'I'm Stone In

Love With You' and, two years later, secured the Christmas number 1 with 'When A Child Is Born'. Back in the USA, he was still searching for new ideas and in April 1978, collaborated with Deniece Williams on 'Too Much, Too Little, Too Late'. This, his first duet, became a surprise number 1, his first US chart-topper since 1957. Since then, Mathis has duetted incessantly with a list that includes Gladys Knight, Paulette McWilliams, Stephanie Lawrence, Jane Oliver, Dionne Warwick, Angela Bofill, Natalie Cole, Barbara Dickson and Nana Mouskouri. What has been overlooked is Mathis' incredible commercial success: he is one of the most successful recording artists of all time, although behind Sinatra and Elvis Presley. His remarkable durability and unfailing professionalism demand admiration, quite apart from his incredibly distinctive voice.

● ALBUMS: *Johnny Mathis* (Columbia 1957) ★★★, *Wonderful! Wonderful!* (Columbia 1957) ★★★, *Warm* (Columbia 1957) ★★★, *Wild Is The Night* film soundtrack (Columbia 1957) ★★, *Good Night, Dear Lord* (Columbia 1958) ★★, *Swing Softly* (Columbia 1958) ★★★, *Merry Christmas* (Columbia 1958) ★★★★, *A Certain Smile* film soundtrack (Columbia 1958) ★★★, with Al Caiola *Open Fire, Two Guitars* (Columbia 1959) ★★★, *Heavenly* (Columbia 1959) ★★★★, *Faithfully* (Columbia 1960) ★★★★, *Ride On A Rainbow* (Columbia 1960) ★★★, *Johnny's Mood* (Columbia 1960) ★★★★, *The Rhythms And Ballads Of Broadway* (Columbia 1960) ★★★, *I'll Buy You A Star* (Columbia 1961) ★★★, *Portrait Of Johnny* (Columbia 1961) ★★★★, *Live It Up!* (Columbia 1962) ★★★, *Rapture* (Columbia 1962) ★★★★, *Johnny* (Columbia 1963) ★★★, *Romantically* (Columbia 1963) ★★★, *Tender Is The Night* (Mercury 1964) ★★★★, *I'll Search My Heart And Other Great Hits* (Columbia 1964) ★★★, *The Wonderful World Of Make Believe* (Mercury 1964) ★★★, *The Great Years* (Columbia 1964) ★★★, *This Is Love* (Mercury 1964) ★★★, *Sounds Of Christmas* (Columbia 1964) ★★★, *Love Is Everything* (Mercury 1965) ★★★, *The Sweetheart Tree* (Mercury 1965) ★★★, *Away From Home* (Columbia 1965) ★★★, *Olé* (Columbia 1965) ★★★, *The Shadow Of Your Smile* (Mercury 1966) ★★★, *So Nice* (Mercury 1966) ★★★, *Johnny Mathis Sings* (Mercury 1967) ★★★, *Up, Up And Away* (Columbia 1967) ★★★, *Love Is Blue* (Columbia 1968) ★★★, *Those Were The Days* (Columbia 1968) ★★★, *The Impossible Dream* (Columbia 1969) ★★★★, *People* (Columbia 1969) ★★★, *Love Theme From 'Romeo And Juliet'* (Columbia 1969) ★★★, *Johnny Mathis Sings The Music Of Bert Kaempfert* (Columbia 1969) ★★★, *Raindrops Keep Fallin' On My Head* (Columbia 1970) ★★★★, *The Long And Winding Road* (Columbia 1970) ★★★, *Close To You* (Columbia 1970) ★★★, *Johnny Mathis Sings The Music Of Bacharach And Kaempfert* (Columbia 1971) ★★★, *Love Story* (Columbia 1971) ★★★, *You've Got A Friend* (Columbia 1971) ★★★, *Christmas With Johnny Mathis* (Columbia 1972) ★★★, *Johnny Mathis In Person* (Columbia 1972) ★★★, *The First Time Ever (I Saw Your Face)* (Columbia 1972)

★★★★, *Make It Easy On Yourself* (Columbia 1972) ★★★, *Song Sung Blue* (Columbia 1972) ★★★, *Me And Mrs Jones* (Columbia 1973) ★★★, *Killing Me Softly With Her Song* (Columbia 1973) ★★★, *I'm Coming Home* (Columbia 1973) ★★★, *Johnny Mathis Sings The Great Songs* (Columbia 1974) ★★★, *The Heart Of A Woman* (Columbia 1974) ★★★, *When Will I See You Again* (Columbia 1975) ★★★, *Feelings* (Columbia 1975) ★★★, *I Only Have Eyes For You* (Columbia 1976) ★★★, *Sweet Surrender* (Columbia 1977) ★★★, *Mathis Is ...* (Columbia 1977) ★★★, *You Light Up My Life* (Columbia 1978) ★★★★, with Deniece Williams *That's What Friends Are For* (Columbia 1978) ★★★, *When A Child Is Born* (Columbia 1978) ★★★, *The Best Days Of My Life* (Columbia 1979) ★★★, *Mathis Magic* (Columbia 1979) ★★★, *Tears And Laughters* (Columbia 1980) ★★★, *All For You* (Columbia 1980) ★★★, *Different Kinda Different* (Columbia 1980) ★★, *Friends In Love* (Columbia 1982) ★★★, *A Special Part Of Me* (Columbia 1984) ★★★, *Johnny Mathis Live* (Columbia 1985) ★★★, *Right From The Heart* (Columbia 1985) ★★★, with Henry Mancini *The Hollywood Musicals* (Columbia 1987) ★★★, *In A Sentimental Mood: Mathis Sings Ellington* (Columbia 1990) ★★★, *Better Together – The Duet Album* (Columbia 1992) ★★★, *How Do You Keep The Music Playing?* (Columbia 1993) ★★★, *The Christmas Music Of Johnny Mathis – A Personal Collection* (Legacy 1993) ★★★, *All About Love* (Columbia 1996) ★★★, *Mathis On Broadway* (Columbia 2000) ★★★★.

● COMPILATIONS: *Johnny's Greatest Hits* (Columbia 1958) ★★★★, *More Of Johnny's Greatest Hits* (Columbia 1959) ★★★★, *Johnny's Newest Hits* (Columbia 1963) ★★★★, *Johnny Mathis' All-Time Greatest Hits* (Columbia 1972) ★★★★, *The Best Of Johnny Mathis 1975-1980* (Columbia 1980) ★★★, *The First 25 Years – The Silver Anniversary Album* (Columbia 1981) ★★★★, *16 Most Requested Songs* (Columbia/Legacy 1994) ★★★★, *The Love Songs* (Columbia 1997) ★★★, *The Global Masters* (Legacy 1997) ★★★, *The Ultimate Hits Collection* (Columbia/Legacy 1998) ★★★.

● VIDEOS: *Johnny Mathis In Concert* (Video Collection 1987), *Home For Christmas* (CMV Enterprises 1990), *Chances Are* (Sony Music Video 1991)

● FURTHER READING: *Johnny: The Authorized Biography Of Johnny Mathis*, Tony Jasper.

MAY, BILLY

b. 10 November 1916, Pittsburgh, Pennsylvania, USA. May's first impact on the big band scene came in 1938, when he joined the trumpet section of the Charlie Barnet Band and, most notably, began contributing arrangements. Among his best-known charts was Barnet's hit record of the old Ray Noble song 'Cherokee'. In 1939, he joined Glenn Miller, bringing a previously absent vitality to the trumpet section and more fine arrangements. In 1942, he also wrote arrangements for Les Brown and Alvino Rey. The early 40s found him in great demand in radio and film studios, but he continued to write for popular bands of the day. When Capitol Records was formed, with a policy that called for the highest standards of musicianship, May was employed to write and direct for many major singing stars, including Frank Sinatra, Peggy Lee and Nat 'King' Cole. During the 50s, May also began making big band albums, on which he gave full rein to his highly distinctive arranging style. Although adept at all kinds of big band music, he had a particular fondness for voicing the reed section in thirds, creating a so-called 'slurping' saxophone sound. Among his band's successes were arrangements of 'All Of Me', 'Lulu's Back In Town', 'Charmaine', 'When My Sugar Walks Down The Street', 'Lean Baby' and 'Fat Man Boogie' (the last two also his own compositions). His recording of the movie theme 'The Man With The Golden Arm' made the UK Top 10 in 1956. For his studio band, May called upon such reliable sidemen as Murray McEachern, Ted Nash Snr. and Alvin Stoller. He also wrote for television, lending musical quality to series such as *Naked City* and to the occasional commercial. He was also musical director on the recording dates on which swing era music was recreated for a series of albums issued by *Time-Life*.

● ALBUMS: *A Band Is Born* (1951) ★★★, *Capitol Presents Billy May And His Orchestra* (Capitol 1953) ★★★★, *Big Band Bash* (Capitol 1953) ★★★★, *Sorta May* (Capitol 1954) ★★★★, *Bacchanalia* (Capitol 1954) ★★★, *Naughty Operetta* (Capitol 1954) ★★★, *Sorta Dixie* (Capitol 1955) ★★, *Billy May And His Orchestra* i (Capitol 1956) ★★★★, *The Great Jimmie Lunceford* (1957) ★★★, *Billy May And His Orchestra* ii (1958) ★★★, *The Girls And Boys On Broadway* (1958) ★★★, *Billy May And His Orchestra* iii (1963) ★★★, *Billy May And His Orchestra* iv (1966) ★★★, *I Believe In You* (1975) ★★★, *You May Swing* (Intersound 1980) ★★★.

● COMPILATIONS: *20 Golden Pieces* (Bulldog 1981) ★★★, *Best Of Billy May And His Orchestra* (MFP 1983) ★★★, *The Capitol Years* (Capitol 1987) ★★★★.

McDEVITT, CHAS

b. 1935, Glasgow, Scotland. McDevitt was the banjo player with the Crane River Jazz Band in 1955, before forming a skiffle group that won a talent contest organized by Radio Luxembourg. Another contestant, vocalist Nancy Whiskey joined the McDevitt group, which included guitarists Tony Kohn and Bill Branwell (from the Cotton Pickers skiffle group), Marc Sharratt (d. May 1991; washboard) and Lennie Hanson (bass). The group appeared in the film *The Tommy Steele Story* in 1957, performing 'Freight Train', a song introduced to Britain by Peggy Seeger who had learned it from its composer, black American folk singer Elizabeth 'Libba' Cotten. Issued by Oriole, the McDevitt/Whiskey version was a Top 5 hit in the UK and reached the US charts, although McDevitt was the object of a US lawsuit over the ownership of the copyright. After the release of a version of 'Greenback Dollar' and an EP as follow-ups, Whiskey left the group. With a studio group, the Skifflers, she made a series of singles for Oriole from 1957-59, including 'He's Solid Gone' and the folk song 'I Know Where I'm Going' and

also released *The Intoxicating Miss Whiskey*. Having opened a Freight Train coffee bar in London, McDevitt continued to perform and record with new vocalist Shirley Douglas (b. 1936, Belfast, Northern Ireland), whom he later married. He briefly followed the rock 'n' roll trend with a conspicuous lack of success, and later performed duets with Douglas after the manner of Nina And Frederick. Among his later efforts were 'It Takes A Worried Man' (Oriole 1957), 'Teenage Letter' (1959) and 'One Love' (HMV 1961). Both McDevitt and Douglas recorded for Joy Records in the 70s enlisting session support from Joe Brown and Wizz Jones.

● ALBUMS: with Nancy Whiskey *Chas And Nancy* (Oriole 1957) ★★★, with Whiskey *The Intoxicating Miss Whiskey* (Oriole 1957) ★★★, *The Six-Five Special* (50s) ★★★★, *Sing Something Old, New, Borrowed & Blue* (1972) ★★, *Takes Ya Back Don't It* (Joy 1976) ★★.

● FURTHER READING: *Skiffle: The Definitive Inside Story*, Chas McDevitt.

McGUIRE SISTERS

This close-harmony vocal group, popular in the 50s and early 60s, consisted of three sisters, Christine (b. 30 July 1929, Middletown, Ohio, USA), Dorothy (b. 13 February 1930, Middletown, Ohio, USA) and Phyllis (b. 14 February 1931, Middletown, Ohio, USA). While in their teens the sisters sang with church choirs, and won an amateur talent contest at their local cinema for three consecutive weeks. After singing on their local radio station, the McGuires had their first big break, entertaining at army camps and hospitals during a nine-month tour in 1950/1. They then played club and radio dates in Cincinnati before moving to New York in 1952, and successfully auditioning for the *Arthur Godfrey Talent Scouts* contest. They subsequently became regulars on the show, and also appeared for eight weeks on singer Kate Smith's top-rated radio programme. Signed to the Coral label, they had their first minor hit in 1954 with 'Pine Tree, Pine Over Me', in collaboration with Johnny Desmond and Eileen Barton. During the rest of that year they had further successes with their version of the Spaniels' R&B hit 'Goodnight Sweetheart, Goodnight', followed by 'Muskrat Ramble', 'Lonesome Polecat' and 'Christmas Alphabet'. In 1955 the sisters had their first million-seller with another cover version, 'Sincerely', originally recorded by the Moonglows. The McGuires' version stayed at number 1 in the USA for 10 weeks, and accelerated their breakthrough into the big time in clubs, theatres and on television. They sang on the *Red Skelton Show* and the *Phil Silvers Show* and appeared at the Waldorf Astoria, the Desert Inn, Las Vegas and the Coconut Grove in Los Angeles. They made their first visit to London in 1961, and played a season at the Talk Of The Town. Their other hits, up until 1961, included 'No More', 'It May Sound Silly', 'Something's Gotta Give', 'He', 'Moonglow And Theme From *Picnic*', 'Delilah Jones'; 'Weary Blues' (with Lawrence Welk), 'Every Day Of My Life',

'Goodnight My Love, Pleasant Dreams', 'Sugartime', 'Ding Dong', 'May You Always' and 'Just For Old Time's Sake'. When the McGuires' sweet style was overtaken by the harder sounds of the Crystals, Shirelles and Supremes during the 60s, they turned to cabaret, and eventually disbanded. Phyllis continued solo, appearing regularly in Las Vegas and other cities. In 1985 the McGuire Sisters re-formed and, in the following year, undertook a national tour, stopping off at Bally's Reno to headline in Donn Arden's lavish revue *Hello, Hollywood, Hello*. Their well-received act continued into the 90s, leaning heavily on their old catalogue, along with more contemporary material from *Cats* and *Les Misérables*, and an a cappella version of 'Danny Boy'. In January 1986, Murray Kane, their personal manager and arranger since 1952, died in Las Vegas. He was responsible for writing the arrangements that won the sisters a spot on the *Arthur Godfrey Show*, their first break in New York. Prior to that, Kane had worked with Fred Waring, and had been a member of the Crew Chiefs, Glenn Miller's vocal group during World War II.

● ALBUMS: *By Request* (Coral 1955) ★★★★, *Children's Holiday* (Coral 1956) ★★★, *Do You Remember When?* (Coral 1956) ★★★, *He* (Coral 1956) ★★★, *Sincerely* (Coral 1956) ★★★, *Teenage Party* (Coral 1957) ★★★, *When The Lights Are Low* (Coral 1958) *Musical Magic* (Coral 1957) ★★★, *Sugartime* (Coral 1958) ★★★★, *Greetings From The McGuire Sisters* (Coral 1958) ★★★, *May You Always* (Coral 1959) ★★★, *In Harmony With Him* (Coral 1959) ★★★, *His And Her's* (Coral 1960) ★★★, *Just For Old Time's Sake* (Coral 1961) ★★★, *Our Golden Favourites* (Coral 1961) ★★★, *Subways Are For Sleeping* (Coral 1962) ★★★, *Songs Everybody Knows* (1962) ★★★, *Showcase* (1963) ★★★, *The McGuire Sisters Today* (1966) ★★★.

● COMPILATIONS: *The Best Of The McGuire Sisters* (MCA 1982) ★★★, *Greatest Hits* (MCA 1989) ★★★.

MCPHATTER, CLYDE

b. Clyde Lensley McPhatter, 15 November 1932, Durham, North Carolina, USA, d. 13 June 1972, New York City, New York, USA. For three years, McPhatter was the lead singer in the seminal R&B vocal group Billy Ward And His Dominoes. He left in 1953 to form the Drifters, whose early releases were enhanced by the singer's emotional, gospel-drenched delivery. In 1954 McPhatter was drafted into the US Army, where he entertained fellow servicemen. Such work prompted a solo career, and the vibrant 'Seven Days' (1956) was followed by several other superb performances, many of which, including 'Treasure Of Love', 'Without Love (There Is Nothing)' and 'A Lover's Question', became R&B standards. A hugely influential figure, McPhatter inspired a generation of singers. His work was covered by Elvis Presley, Ry Cooder and Otis Redding, but his departure from the Atlantic Records label to MGM Records in 1959 precipitated an artistic decline. He had several minor hits on Mercury Records during the early 60s, and arguably his finest work was the US Top 10 single 'Lover Please' in 1962. The follow-up,

'Little Bitty Pretty One', became standard fodder for many UK beat groups in the early 60s (it was recorded by the Paramounts). The singer became increasingly overshadowed by new performers and his career started to wane in the mid-60s. Beset by personal problems, he came to Britain in 1968, but left two years later without an appreciable change in his fortunes. A 1970 album on Decca Records, *Welcome Home*, was his last recording. McPhatter, one of R&B's finest voices, died from a heart attack as a result of alcohol abuse in 1972. He was inducted into the Rock And Roll Hall Of Fame in 1987.

● ALBUMS: *Clyde McPhatter And The Drifters* (Atlantic 1958) ★★★★, *Love Ballads* (Atlantic 1958) ★★★★, *Clyde* (Atlantic 1959) ★★★, *Let's Start Over Again* (MGM 1959) ★★★, *Ta Ta* (Mercury 1960) ★★★, *Golden Blues Hits* (Mercury 1962) ★★★, *Lover Please* (Mercury 1962) ★★★★, *May I Sing For You?* (Wing 1962) ★★★, *Rhythm And Soul* (Mercury 1963) ★★★, *Songs Of The Big City* (Mercury 1964) ★★, *Live At The Apollo* (Mercury 1964) ★★, *Welcome Home* (Decca 1970) ★★.

● COMPILATIONS: *Greatest Hits* (MGM 1960) ★★★, *The Best Of Clyde McPhatter* (Atlantic 1963) ★★★, *Rock And Cry* (Charly 1984) ★★★, *Rhythm And Soul* 8-LP box set of MGM/Mercury recordings (Bear Family 1987) ★★★★, *Deep Sea Ball: The Best Of Clyde McPhatter* (Atlantic 1991) ★★★★, *The Mercury Sessions Featuring Live & Studio Recordings* (Collectables 1996) ★★★.

MCRAE, CARMEN

b. 8 April 1920, New York City, New York, USA, d. 10 November 1994, Beverly Hills, California, USA. One of the best American jazz singers, McRae was also an accomplished pianist and songwriter. Early in her career she sang with bands led by Benny Carter, Mercer Ellington, Charlie Barnet and Count Basie (sometimes under the name of Carmen Clarke, from her brief marriage to Kenny Clarke). Although a familiar figure on the New York jazz club scene, including a spell in the early 50s as intermission pianist at Minton's Playhouse, her reputation did not spread far outside the jazz community. In the 60s and 70s she toured internationally and continued to record – usually accompanied by a small group – but she was joined on one occasion by the Clarke-Boland Big Band. By the 80s, she was one of only a tiny handful of major jazz singers whose work had not been diluted by commercial pressures. One of her early songs, 'Dream Of Life', written when she was just 16 years old, was recorded in 1939 by Billie Holiday. Although very much her own woman, McRae occasionally demonstrated the influence of Holiday through her ability to project a lyric with bittersweet intimacy. She also sang with remarkable rhythmic ease and her deft turns-of-phrase helped to conceal a relatively limited range, while her ballad singing revealed enormous emotional depths. Her repertoire included many popular items from the Great American Songbook, but her jazz background ensured that she rarely strayed outside the idiom. Relaxed and unpretentious in performance and dedicated to her craft, McRae secured a place of honour in the history of jazz singing.

● ALBUMS: *Carmen McRae* i 10-inch album (Bethlehem 1954) ★★★, *By Special Request* (Decca 1955) ★★★, *Torchy!* (Decca 1956) ★★★, *Blue Moon* (Decca 1956) ★★★, *After Glow* (Decca 1957) ★★★, *Carmen For Cool Ones* (Decca 1957) ★★★★, *Mad About The Man* (Decca 1957) ★★★★, with Sammy Davis Jnr. *Boy Meets Girl* (Epic 1957) ★★★, *Book Of Ballads* (Kapp 1958) ★★★★, *Birds Of A Feather* (Decca 1958) ★★★, *When You're Away* (Kapp 1958) ★★★, *Something To Swing About* (Kapp 1959) ★★★★, *Carmen McRae Live At Sugar Hill* (Time 1960) ★★★, *Carmen McRae Sings Lover Man And Other Billie Holiday Classics* (Columbia 1961) ★★★★, *Carmen McRae* ii (Vocalion 1962) ★★★, *Something Wonderful* (Columbia 1962) ★★★, *Carmen McRae* iii (Vocalion 1963) ★★★, *Bittersweet* (Focus 1964) ★★★, *Take Five* (Columbia 1965) ★★★, *Woman Talk: Carmen McRae Live At The Village Gate* (Mainstream 1965) ★★★★, *Second To None* (Mainstream 1965) ★★★, *Haven't We Met?* (Mainstream 1965) ★★★, *Alfie* (Mainstream 1966) ★★★, *Portrait Of Carmen* (Atlantic 1967) ★★★, *This Is Carmen McRae* (Kapp 1967) ★★★★, *For Once In My Life* (Atlantic 1967) ★★★, *Yesterday* (Harmony 1968) ★★★, *Just A Little Lovin'* (Atlantic 1970) ★★★, *The Great American Songbook* (Atlantic 1972) ★★★★, *It Takes A Whole Lot Of Human Feeling* (Groove 1973) ★★★, *I Am Music* (Blue Note 1975) ★★★, *Can't Hide Love* (Blue Note 1976) ★★, *Carmen McRae At The Great American Music Hall* (Blue Note 1976) ★★★, *Ronnie Scott Presents Carmen McRae 'Live'* (Pye/Ronnie Scott 1977) ★★★, *I'm Coming Home Again* (1978) ★★★, with George Shearing *Two For The Road* (Concord Jazz 1980) ★★★, *Recorded Live At Bubba's* (Who's Who In Jazz 1981) ★★★, with Cal Tjader *Heat Wave* (Concord Jazz 1982) ★★★, *You're Lookin' At Me (A Collection Of Nat 'King' Cole Songs)* (Concord Jazz 1983) ★★★★, *For Lady Day* (Novus 1984) ★★★★, *Any Old Time* (Denon 1986) ★★★, *Carmen McRae/Betty Carter Duets* (Great American Music Hall 1987) ★★★, *Fine And Mellow: Live At Birdland West* (Concord Jazz 1988) ★★★★, *Velvet Soul* 1973 recording (Denon 1988) ★★★, *Carmen Sings Monk* (Novus 1989) ★★★★, *Sarah: Dedicated To You* (Novus 1991) ★★★, *Dream Of Life* 1989 recording (Qwest 1998) ★★★★.

● COMPILATIONS: *The Ultimate Carmen McRae* (Mainstream 1991) ★★★★, *Sings Great American Songwriters* 1955-59 recordings (GRP 1994) ★★★★★, *Song Time* 1963-69 recordings (Hindsight 1995) ★★★, *The Best Of Carmen McRae* (Blue Note 1995) ★★★★, *Some Of The Best* (Delta 1996) ★★★, *More Of The Best* (Delta 1996) ★★★, *The Greatest Of Carmen McRae* 1955-59 recordings (MCA 1997) ★★★, *Priceless Jazz Collection* (GRP 1998) ★★★, *Here To Stay* 1955-59 recordings (GRP/Decca 1998) ★★★, *The Collected Carmen McRae* (RCA 1998) ★★★.

● VIDEOS: *Live* (Verve Video 1990), *Saying It With Jazz* (Merrill Video 1996), *Ralph Gleason's Jazz Casual: Carmen McRae* (Rhino Home Video 1999).

MELACHRINO, GEORGE

b. George Militiades, 1 May 1909, London, England, d. 18 June 1965, London, England. An orchestra leader, composer, arranger, multi-instrumentalist and singer, Melachrino was the son of Greek parents. He learned to play a miniature violin, and wrote his first composition when he was five years old. He was already an accomplished musician by the age of 14 when he enrolled at the Trinity College Of Music, where he specialized in chamber music and the use of strings. At the age of 16, he wrote a string sextet that was performed in London. He resolved to learn to play every instrument in the orchestra, and succeeded, with the exception of the harp and piano. In 1927, he began his broadcasting career, playing and singing from the BBC studio at Savoy Hill. He strayed further and further away from his initial ambition to be a classical musician, playing jazz instead, and working in dance bands for leaders such as Bert Firman, Harry Hudson, Ambrose and Carroll Gibbons' Savoy Hotel Orchestra. In 1939, Melachrino formed his own dance band to play at the prestigious London venue the Café de Paris, until 1940. During the period of the 'Battle of Britain', he joined the British Army as a military policeman, eventually becoming a Regimental Sergeant-Major. He later toured in the *Stars Of Battledress* and was musical director of the Army Radio Unit, as well as the leader of the British Band of the Allied Expeditionary Forces. He also led the 50-piece 'Orchestra in Khaki', recruited from professional musicians serving in the ranks, who were much amused when he was introduced on broadcasts as 'the Sentimental Sergeant-Major'. The unit held its own against the American band led by Glenn Miller and the Canadian combination led by Robert Farnon, with both of whom Melachrino guested as vocalist on occasions during the war years.

While in the forces, he experimented with large string sounds, and after the war he ran two outfits, the Melachrino Strings and the George Melachrino Orchestra, both purveying the sentimental mood music so popular in the 50s, especially in the USA. The full orchestra consisted of 30 strings, 10 reeds, seven brass, two percussion, a harp and a piano. He formed the Melachrino Music Organization, creating work in concerts, broadcasting, recordings and film music. His film scores included *Woman To Woman* (1946), *Code Of Scotland Yard* (1948), *No Orchids For Miss Blandish* (1948), *Story Of Shirley Yorke* (1948), *Dark Secret* (1949), *The Gamma People* (1956) and *Odongo* (1956). In 1947, he contributed the music, with book and lyrics by Eric Maschwitz and Matt Brooks, to the revue *Starlight Roof*, which starred Fred Emney, Pat Kirkwood and Vic Oliver, and introduced Julie Andrews to London audiences. He also wrote the music for the ill-fated *Lucky Boy*, with lyrics by Ian Douglas. His other compositions included 'First Rhapsody' (his theme tune), 'Winter Sunshine', 'Vision D'Amour', 'Woodland Revel' and 'Portrait Of A Lady'. He had a UK chart entry in 1956 with the Italian melody 'Autumn Concerto', but, like Mantovani, who also specialized in lush string arrangements, his albums sold more in the USA than in the UK. His US hits included *Christmas In High Fidelity*, *Under Western Skies* and *Immortal Ladies*, a set of standards with girls' names as their titles, such as 'Laura', 'Dolores', 'Chloe' and 'Dinah'. Also popular was his series of mood records designed for various times of the day, such as *Music For Daydreaming*, *Music For Relaxation*, *Music For Two People Alone*, *Music For Dining*, *Music for Reading*, *Music To Help You Sleep*, and others. He died in 1965 following an accident at his home in Kensington, London. The Melachrino Strings and Orchestra continued to record into the 80s, conducted by Robert Mandell.

● ALBUMS: *Soft Lights And Sweet Music* (1954) ★★★★, *Christmas In High Fidelity* (RCA 1954) ★★, *Music For The Nostalgic Traveller* (1956) ★★★, *Famous Themes For Piano And Orchestra* (1957) ★★★★, *Moonlight Concerto* (1958) ★★★★, *Great Show Tunes – Medleys* (1958) ★★★, *Under Western Skies* (RCA 1959) ★★★, *The World's Greatest Melodies* (1962) ★★★★, *The World Of George Melachrino* (1969) ★★★★, *The World Of George Melachrino, Volume Two* (1972) ★★★, *Strauss Waltzes* (1973) ★★★, *The Immortal Melodies Of Victor Herbert And Sigmund Romberg* (1974) ★★★, *Great British Light Orchestras George Melachrino* (EMI 1993) ★★★★.

MELLO-KINGS

The Mello-Kings were responsible for one of the most durable doo-wop hits of the 50s. Despite the fact that their only hit, 'Tonite Tonite', never climbed higher than number 77 in the US charts, the single is still considered one of the most popular group harmony recordings of the era, more than three decades after its initial release. The group consisted of brothers Jerry and Bob Scholl, Eddie Quinn, Neil Arena and Larry Esposito. The quintet was formed in 1956 at a high school in Mount Vernon, New York, USA, under the guidance of manager Dick Levister. Originally named the Mellotones, the group was signed to the Herald label. 'Tonite Tonite' was written by Billy Myles, a staff composer for the label. The group was forced to change its name after the single's release, as another group had already claimed Mellotones. The record lasted only 10 weeks in the US charts, and the group was never able to repeat this success, although 'Tonite Tonite' returned in 1961, reaching number 95, due to a resurgence of interest in the doo-wop sound, and has been consistently voted among the top five doo-wop records of all time in radio polls, particularly in the New York area. A new Mello-Kings led by Jerry Scholl, whose brother Bob died on 27 August 1975, was still touring the rock 'n' roll revival circuit in the early 90s.

● ALBUMS: *Tonight – Tonight* (Herald 1960) ★★★.
● COMPILATIONS: *Tonite, Tonite* (Relic 1991) ★★★, *Greatest Hits* (Collectables 1992) ★★★.

MEMORIAL ALBUM – HANK WILLIAMS

Hank Williams died on the road, on his way to a gig in Canton, Ohio, on New Year's Day 1953. The *Grand Ole Opry* had discredited him as a drunk and he was the first rock star, living a squalid life of amphetamine and alcohol addiction and describing family quarrels in his songs. This album, the first to cash in on a musician's death, was issued in 10-inch and 12-inch formats with eight and 12 songs, respectively. Country music does not come any better and Hank Williams' influence is immense: Elvis Presley, Buddy Holly and Bob Dylan all owe him a debt. Play 'Move It On Over' next to 'Rock Around The Clock' and you will discover Bill Haley's listening habits.

● Tracks: *You Win Again; Cold Cold Heart; I Could Never Be Ashamed Of You; Settin' The Woods On Fire; Hey, Good Lookin'; Kaw-Liga; Half As Much*.
● First released 1953
● UK peak chart position: did not chart
● USA peak chart position: did not chart

MERCER, JOHNNY

b. John Herndon Mercer, 18 November 1909, Savannah, Georgia, USA, d. 25 June 1976, Los Angeles, California, USA. A distinguished lyricist, composer and singer, Mercer was an important link with the first generation of composers of indigenous American popular music such as Jerome Kern and Harry Warren, through to post-World War II writers like Henry Mancini. Along the way, he collaborated with several others, including Harold Arlen, Hoagy Carmichael, Gene De Paul, Rube Bloom, Richard Whiting, Victor Schertzinger, Gordon Jenkins, Jimmy Van Heusen, Duke Ellington, Billy Strayhorn, Arthur Schwartz and Matty Malneck. Most of the time, Mercer wrote the literate and witty lyrics, but occasionally the melody as well.

Mercer moved to New York in the late 20s and worked in a variety of jobs before placing one of his first songs, 'Out Of Breath And Scared To Death Of You', (written with Everett Miller), in *The Garrick Gaieties Of 1930*. During the 30s, Mercer contributed the lyrics to several movie songs, including 'If You Were Mine' from *To Beat The Band*, a record hit for Billie Holiday with Teddy Wilson, 'I'm An Old Cowhand' (words and music) (*Rhythm On The Range*), 'Too Marvelous For Words' (co-written with Richard Whiting for *Ready, Willing And Able*), 'Have You Got Any Castles, Baby?' (*Varsity Show*), 'Hooray For Hollywood' (*Hollywood Hotel*), 'Jeepers Creepers' (*Going Places*) and 'Love Is Where You Find It' (*Garden Of The Moon*). Mercer's other songs during the decade included 'Fare-Thee-Well To Harlem', 'Moon Country', 'When A Woman Loves A Man' (with Gordon Jenkins and Bernard Hanighan), 'P.S. I Love You', 'Goody Goody', 'You Must Have Been A Beautiful Baby', 'And The Angels Sing', 'Cuckoo In The Clock', 'Day In-Day Out' and 'I Thought About You'. In the 30s he appeared frequently on radio, as MC and singer with Paul Whiteman, Benny Goodman and Bob Crosby. With his southern drawl and warm, good-natured style, he was a natural for the medium, and, in the early 40s, had his own show, *Johnny Mercer's Music Shop*. During this period, Mercer became a director of the songwriter's copyright organization, ASCAP. Also, in 1942, he combined with songwriter-turned-film-producer, Buddy De Sylva, and businessman, Glen Wallichs, to form Capitol Records, which was, in its original form, dedicated to musical excellence, a policy which reflected Mercer's approach to all his work.

He had previously had record hits with other writers' songs, such as 'Mr Gallagher And Mr Sheen' and 'Small Fry', along with his own 'Mr. Meadowlark' (a duet with Bing Crosby), and 'Strip Polka'. For Capitol, he continued to register in the US Hit Parade with popular favourites such as 'Personality', 'Candy'; and some of his own numbers such as 'G.I. Jive', 'Ac-Cent-Tchu-Ate The Positive', 'Glow Worm'; and 'On The Atchison, Topeka, And The Santa Fe', which was also sung by Judy Garland in *The Harvey Girls* (1946), and gained Mercer his first Academy Award. His other 40s song successes, many of them from movies, included 'The Waiter And The Porter And The Upstairs Maid' (from *Birth Of The Blues*); 'Blues In The Night' and 'This Time's The Dream's On Me' (*Blues In The Night*); 'Tangerine', 'I Remember You' and 'Arthur Murray Taught Me Dancing In A Hurry' (*The Fleet's In*), 'Dearly Beloved' and 'I'm Old Fashioned' (*You Were Never Lovelier*) (Kern), 'Hit The Road To Dreamland' and 'That Old Black Magic', Billy Daniels' identity song, (*Star Spangled Rhythm*), 'My Shining Hour' (*The Sky's The Limit*) and 'Come Rain Or Come Shine', 'Legalize My Name' and 'Any Place I Hang My Hat Is Home', from the stage show *St. Louis Woman* (Arlen).

Two particularly attractive compositions were 'Fools Rush In' (with Rube Bloom), which was a big hit for Glenn Miller (and later Ricky Nelson), and the movie title song 'Laura', with Mercer's lyric complementing a haunting tune by David Raksin. Mercer's collaboration with Hoagy Carmichael produced some of his most memorable songs, such as 'Lazybones', 'The Old Music Master', 'Skylark', 'How Little We Know' and the Oscar-winning 'In The Cool, Cool, Cool Of The Evening', sung by Bing Crosby and Jane Wyman in *Here Comes The Groom* (1951). In the same year, Mercer provided both the music and lyrics for the Broadway show, *Top Banana*, a 'burlesque musical' starring Phil Silvers and a host of mature funny men. The entertaining score included the witty 'A Word A Day'.

The 50s were extremely productive years for Mercer, with songs such as 'Here's To My Lady', 'I Wanna Be Around' (later successful for Tony Bennett), and yet more movie songs, including 'I Want To Be A Dancing Man', 'The Bachelor Dinner Song' and 'Seeing's Believing', sung by Fred Astaire in *The Belle Of New York*; 'I Like Men' (covered by Peggy Lee), 'I Got Out Of Bed On The Right Side' and 'Ain't Nature Grand' from *Dangerous When Wet*; and 'Something's Gotta Give' and 'Sluefoot' (words and music by Mercer) from another Fred Astaire showcase, *Daddy Long Legs*. Mercer also provided additional lyrics to 'When The World Was Young' ('Ah, The Apple Trees'), 'Midnight Sun', 'Early Autumn' and 'Autumn Leaves'. The highlight of the decade was, perhaps, *Seven Brides For Seven Brothers* (1954).

Starring Howard Keel and Jane Powell, Mercer and Gene De Paul's 'pip of a score' included 'Spring, Spring, Spring', 'Bless Your Beautiful Hide', 'Sobbin' Women', 'When You're In Love', and 'Goin' Courtin', amongst others. Two years later Mercer and De Paul got together again for the stage show *Li'l Abner*, starring Stubby Kaye, and including such songs as 'Namely You', 'Jubilation T. Cornpone' and 'The Country's In The Very Best Of Hands'. It ran on Broadway for nearly 700 performances and was filmed in 1959. The early 60s brought Mercer two further Academy Awards; one for 'Moon River' from *Breakfast At Tiffany's* (1961), and the other, the title song to *The Days Of Wine And Roses* (1962). 'Moon River' was the song in which Mercer first coined the now-famous phrase, 'my huckleberry friend'. Danny Williams took the former song to the UK number 1 slot in 1961, while namesake Andy Williams and Mercer's co-composer Henry Mancini both scored US Top 40 hits with the latter in 1963. Mancini also wrote other movie songs with Mercer, such as 'Charade', 'The Sweetheart Tree' (from *The Great Race*) and 'Whistling Away The Dark' (*Darling Lili*). In the early 70s, Mercer spent a great deal of time in Britain, and, in 1974, wrote the score, with André Previn, for the West End musical *The Good Companions*. He died, two years later, in 1976.

Several of his 1,000-plus songs became an integral part of many a singer's repertoire. In 1992, Frank Sinatra was still using 'One For My Baby' (music by Harold Arlen), 'the greatest saloon song ever written', as a moving set-piece in his concert performances. 'Dream' (words and music by Mercer), closed Sinatra's radio and television shows for many years, and the singer also made impressive recordings of lesser-known Mercer items, such as 'Talk To Me, Baby' and 'The Summer Wind'. Memories of his rapport with Bing Crosby in their early days were revived in 1961, when Mercer recorded *Two Of A Kind* with Bobby Darin, full of spontaneous asides, and featuring Mercer numbers such as 'Bob White' and 'If I Had My Druthers', plus other humorous oldies, like 'Who Takes Care Of The Caretaker's Daughter' and 'My Cutey's Due At Two-To-Two Today'. Several artists, such as Marlene VerPlanck, Susannah McCorkle, and Nancy LaMott, have devoted complete albums to his work, and in 1992 Capitol Records celebrated its 50th anniversary by issuing *Too Marvelous For Words: Capitol Sings Johnny Mercer*, which consisted of some of the label's most eminent artists singing their co-founder's popular song lyrics. Five years later, the soundtrack of the movie *Midnight In The Garden Of Good And Evil*, starring Clint Eastwood and Kevin Spacey, featured a host of Johnny Mercer songs. In February 1999, Michael Feinstein hosted a concert 'celebrating Johnny Mercer and his legacy' at New York's Carnegie Hall.

● ALBUMS: *Capitol Presents Johnny Mercer* (Capitol 1953) ★★★, *Capitol Presents Johnny Mercer Volume 2* (Capitol 1954) ★★★, *Capitol Presents Johnny Mercer Volume 3* (Capitol 1954) ★★★, *Capitol Presents Johnny Mercer Volume 4*

(Capitol 1954) ★★★, with Bobby Darin *Two Of A Kind* (Atco 1961) ★★★, *Johnny Mercer Sings Johnny Mercer* (Capitol 1972) ★★★, *Ac-Cent-Tchu-Ate The Positive*, *Johnny Mercer's Music Shop*, *My Huckleberry Friend* (Pye 1974) ★★★, *An Evening With Johnny Mercer* (Laureate 1977) ★★★.

● COMPILATIONS: various artists *Too Marvelous For Words: Capitol Sings Johnny Mercer* (Capitol 1992) ★★★★, *The Complete Johnny Mercer Songbooks* 3-CD box set (Verve 1999) ★★★★.

● FURTHER READING: *Our Huckleberry Friend: The Life, Times And Song Lyrics Of Johnny Mercer*, B. Back and G. Mercer.

MERRICK, DAVID

b. David Margulois, 27 November 1911, St. Louis, Missouri, USA, d. 25 April 2000, London, England. One of the most colourful and controversial theatrical producers and impresarios in the post-World War II years, Merrick is said to have believed that his life began on 4 November 1954, the night a musical called *Fanny* opened at New York's Majestic Theatre. After an early, insecure life as the son of a weak father and mentally disturbed mother, Merrick changed his name and trained as a lawyer before moving into the world of theatre as an associate producer in the late 40s. His production of *Fanny* ran for 888 performances on Broadway, and was followed by a series of successful shows, including the musicals *Jamaica*, *Destry Rides Again*, *Take Me Along*, *Vintage '60*, *Irma La Douce*, *Do Re Mi*, *Carnival*, *I Can Get It For You Wholesale*, *Stop The World – I Want To Get Off*, *110 In The Shade*, *The Roar Of The Greasepaint – The Smell Of The Crowd*, *How Now, Dow Jones*, *The Happy Time*, *Sugar*, *Mack And Mabel* and *Very Good Eddie* (1975 revival). Among his greatest triumphs were *Gypsy* (1959), *Oliver!*, *Hello, Dolly!* (1964), *I Do! I Do!* (1966), *Promises, Promises* (1968) and *42nd Street* (1980). The latter ran for 3,486 performances, his most enduring Broadway production to date. Along the way, there were several failures, such as *Oh, What A Lovely War!* (1964), *Foxy* (1964) and *Pickwick* (1965). In addition, *Breakfast At Tiffany's* (1966) folded during previews, while *Mata Hari* (1967) and *The Baker's Wife* (1976) closed out of town. However, with his sheer determination and flair for publicity, Merrick managed to wring every ounce of possibility out of even the most ailing shows. One of his most famous stunts came in 1961 during the run of the disappointing *Subways Are For Sleeping*. A member of his staff arranged for seven members of the public, with the same names as the leading New York drama critics, to be quoted in newspaper advertisements for the show ('7 Out Of 7 Are Ecstatically Unanimous About *Subways Are For Sleeping*', ran the copy). When it was published, each of these 'namesakes' appeared opposite a rave quote that the Merrick organization had apparently culled from real reviews of some of Broadway's greatest hits. Such outrageous, but immensely profitable, behaviour came to a temporary halt in February 1983, when Merrick suffered a debilitating stroke that seriously impaired his powers of speech. After

initially handing over the reins to others, in 1985 he regained control of his affairs, and subsequently presented an all-black revival of *Oh, Kay!* (1990), and a stage adaptation of the popular movie *State Fair* (1996). The last of the great American showmen, throughout his career Merrick was admired, feared, detested and respected – but never ignored. His several Tony Awards and nominations included one for *Hello, Dolly!*, and special Tonys in 1961 and 1968 'in recognition of his fabulous production record'. On his 87th birthday Merrick retired as a producer, and was replaced at the head of his company by Natalie Lloyd, the only Asian-born American producer working on Broadway. Lloyd became Merrick's sixth wife shortly before his death in April 2000.

● FURTHER READING: *The Abominable Showman*, Howard Kissell.

MERRILL, BOB

b. Henry Robert Merrill Levan, 17 May 1920, Atlantic City, New Jersey, USA, d. 17 February 1998, Beverly Hills, California, USA. A popular songwriter for Tin Pan Alley, a screenwriter, and a distinguished composer, lyricist and librettist for the musical theatre. Merrill grew up in Philadelphia, and was educated at Temple University. Having enjoyed his first taste of the theatre when he took a temporary job at the Buck's County Playhouse, Merrill moved to New York in 1942, and performed as a comedian and mimic in nightclubs and vaudeville. While serving in the US Army during World War II, he wrote and produced troop shows, and subsequently moved to Hollywood to work as a scriptwriter for NBC Television and Columbia Pictures. He also spent some time as a dialogue coach and casting director, and acted in a few movies. In the late 40s, encouraged by the country-style comedienne Dorothy Shay, who asked him to write some songs for her, Merrill collaborated on 'Lover's Gold' (music: Morty Nevins), 'The Chicken Song' (with Terry Shand) and 'Fool's Paradise' (words and music: Merrill). In 1950, he had his first success with the lively 'If I Knew You Were Comin', I'd Have Baked A Cake' (Al Hoffman and Clem Watts), which was a hit in the USA for Eileen Barton, Georgia Gibbs, Benny Strong, Ethel Merman with Ray Bolger, and Art Mooney. Merrill teamed again with Hoffman on 'Where Will The Dimple Be?', but he provided his own words and music to Guy Mitchell novelty hits such as 'Sparrow In The Tree Top', 'My Truly, Truly Fair', 'Belle, Belle, My Liberty Belle', 'Pittsburgh, Pennsylvania', 'Feet Up (Pat Him On The Po-Po)', 'She Wears Red Feathers', 'Look At That Girl', 'Chicka Boom' and 'Cuff Of My Shirt'. Several other artists, both in the USA and UK, had chart successes with Merrill numbers, including the Caravelles ('You Don't Have To Be A Baby To Cry'), Lita Roza and Patti Page (('How Much Is That) Doggie In The Window?' – UK and US number 1), Rosemary Clooney ('Mambo Italiano'), Dickie Valentine ('All The Time And Everywhere'), Sarah Vaughan ('Make Yourself

Comfortable'), Teresa Brewer ('A Sweet Old-Fashioned Girl'), Sammy Kaye And His Orchestra ('Walkin' To Missouri'), Arthur Godfrey, Mindy Carson ('Candy And Cake'), and more.

Progressing from pop songs to the musical theatre was difficult, and Merrill's first Broadway show, *New Girl In Town*, began as a projected film. When MGM decided against his musical adaptation of Eugene O'Neill's play, *Anna Christie*, Merrill took it to the distinguished author and director, George Abbott. He wrote the book, and with Merrill's sprightly score ('Flings', 'If That Was Love', 'Yer My Friend Aintcha?', 'Did You Close Your Eyes?'), *New Girl In Town* opened on Broadway in May 1957. Producer David Merrick was more than impressed, and some two years later he was at the helm when Merrill and librettists Joseph Stein and Robert Russell musicalized another O'Neill play, *Ah, Wilderness*. *Take Me Along* (1959) had a charming, nostalgic score, including 'But Yours', 'Little Green Snake', 'We're Home' and 'Promise Me A Rose'. Like *New Girl In Town*, it ran for more than 400 performances, but Merrill's next show, *Carnival* (1961), did even better, residing in New York for 719 performances. Based on a Paul Gallico story, which was turned into the 1953 hit film *Lili*, starring Leslie Caron, Merrill and book writer Michael Stewart created a magical musical comedy containing a delightful variety of songs, such as 'Yes, My Heart', 'Her Face', 'Yum-Ticky-Tum-Tum', and the gently swaying 'Love Makes The World Go Round'. In 1964, Merrill contributed 'Elegance' and 'Motherhood March' to Jerry Herman's Carol Channing vehicle, *Hello, Dolly!*, before collaborating with composer Jule Styne on the score for the smash hit *Funny Girl* ('People', 'Don't Rain On My Parade', 'You Are Woman, I Am Man', 'The Music That Makes Me Dance'). Ironically, *Funny Girl* lost out to *Hello, Dolly!* in the Tony Awards, but the show elevated Barbra Streisand to stardom, and the cast album won Grammy awards for Merrill and Styne. Although the pair wrote the music and lyrics for the animated television special *Mr. Magoo's Christmas Carol* (1963) and a television musical starring Liza Minnelli, *The Dangerous Christmas Of Red Riding Hood* (1965), Merrill's later stage projects proved disappointing. *Breakfast At Tiffany's* (1966) closed during previews, *Henry, Sweet Henry* (1967) folded after only 80 performances, and *Prettybelle* (1971, with Styne) failed to reach Broadway. However, *Sugar* (1972, Styne), based on the highly successful Billy Wilder film *Some Like It Hot*, ran for 505 performances, and in a production that reverted to the title of the movie, became a short-lived showcase for the popular UK entertainer Tommy Steele in 1992. Completing the sad sequence, *The Prince Of Grand Street* (1978), starring Robert Preston, closed during its pre-Broadway try-out and *Hannah ... 1939*, in which Julie Wilson gave a thrilling performance as a dressmaker in Nazi-occupied Czechoslovakia, had a brief stay off-Broadway in 1990. Three years later Merrill teamed with Styne once more (under the pseudonym of Paul Stryker) to provide extra lyrics for *The Red Shoes*, which lasted for just three days. Failures these later shows certainly were, but there was always a song or two in each of them that bore the Merrill stamp of style and humour. In 1984, 37 selections from his prolific output were assembled in a four-character off-Broadway musical entitled *We're Home*. In between the forays to Broadway, Merrill continued to be associated with the film world, co-writing screenplays such as *Mahogany* (1975), starring Diana Ross, and *W.C. Fields And Me* (1976) with Rod Steiger. He also wrote the songs for *The Wonderful World Of The Brothers Grimm* (1962). Despite suffering from a chronic illness, Merrill was still working through the 90s until his death from 'self inflicted gunshot wounds while sitting in a car outside his Los Angeles home'.

MERRILL, HELEN

b. Jelena Ana Milcetic, 21 June 1929, New York City, New York, USA. Merrill's early career found her singing in exalted bebop company. Among the major artists with whom she sang in the late 40s were Charlie Parker, Miles Davis and Bud Powell. She spent part of the 50s outside music, but continued to make a few records with notable figures such as Clifford Brown; by the end of the decade, she was resident in Italy and a familiar figure at European festivals. In the early 60s, she returned to the USA but had difficulty in attracting the attention of either radio and television networks or the major record companies. She did make a handful of records backed by leading musicians such as Thad Jones, Ron Carter, Richard Davis, Elvin Jones and Jim Hall. By the late 60s, Merrill was again resident outside the USA, this time in Japan, where her talents were much appreciated. Back in the USA in the mid-70s, she was still largely overlooked but was periodically recorded, again with excellent jazz backing from the likes of Teddy Wilson, John Lewis and Pepper Adams. In November 1994, Merrill reappeared on the scene, promoting a new album and planning a UK and European tour for 1995. One of the most musical of singers, Merrill customarily explores the emotional depths of the lyrics of songs, imbuing them with great passion.

● ALBUMS: *Helen Merrill Featuring Clifford Brown* (EmArcy 1954) ★★★★★, *Helen Merrill With Hal Mooney And His Orchestra* i (1955) ★★★, *Helen Merrill With Gil Evans And His Orchestra* (1956) ★★★★, *Dream Of You* (EmArcy 1956) ★★★, *Helen Merrill With Hal Mooney And His Orchestra* ii (1957) ★★★, *Merrill At Midnight* (EmArcy 1957) ★★★★, *Helen Merrill* i (Philips 1957) ★★★, *The Nearness Of You* (EmArcy 1958) ★★★★, *You've Got A Date With The Blues* (Metrojazz 1958) ★★★, *American Country Songs* (Atco 1959) ★★, *Helen Merrill* ii (1959) ★★★, *Helen Merrill With Quincy Jones And His Orchestra* (1959) ★★★★, *Helen Merrill In Italy* (Liuto 1959-62 recordings) ★★, *Helen Merrill* iii (1964) ★★★, *The Artistry Of Helen Merrill* (Mainstream 1965) ★★★★, *Something Special* (Inner City 1967) ★★★, *Autumn Love*

(1967) ★★★, *The Feeling Is Mutual* (Milestone 1967) ★★★★, *A Shade Of Difference* (Spotlite 1968) ★★★, *Helen Merrill In Tokyo* (1969) ★★, with Teddy Wilson *Helen Sings, Teddy Swings* (1970) ★★★, *Sposin'* (Storyville 1971), *Helen Merrill/John Lewis* (Mercury 1977) ★★★, *Chasin' The Bird* (EmArcy 1979) ★★★, *Case Forte* (EmArcy 1980) ★★, *The Rodgers & Hammerstein Album* (DRG 1982) ★★★, with Gordon Beck *No Tears ... No Goodbyes* (Owl 1984) ★★★, with Gordon Beck, Stéphane Grappelli, Steve Lacy *Music Makers* (Owl 1986) ★★★, *Irving Berlin Album* (Victor 1988) ★★★, with Ron Carter *Duets* (EmArcy 1988) ★★★, with Gil Evans *Helen Merrill/Gil Evans: Collaboration* (EmArcy 1988) ★★★★, *This Is My Night To Cry* (EmArcy 1989) ★★★, *Just Friends* (EmArcy 1989) ★★★★, *Dream Of You* 1956 recording (EmArcy 1993) ★★, *Clear Out Of This World* (EmArcy 1992) ★★★, *Brownie: Homage To Clifford Brown* (Verve 1994) ★★★, *You And The Night And The Music* (Verve 1996) ★★★★, *Carousel* (Finlandia 1996) ★★★, *Jelena Ana Milcetic a.k.a. Helen Merrill* (Verve 1999) ★★★.
● COMPILATIONS: *Helen Merrill On Mercury* 4-LP box set 1954-58 recordings (Mercury 1958) ★★★, *Blossom Of Stars* 1954-92 recordings (EmArcy 1993) ★★★★.

MICKEY AND SYLVIA

McHouston 'Mickey' Baker (b. 15 October 1925, Louisville, Kentucky, USA) and Sylvia Vanderpool (b. 6 March 1936, New York City, New York, USA). This popular duo began recording together in 1956 and enjoyed an US R&B chart-topper that year with 'Love Is Strange', which peaked at number 11 in the US pop chart the following year. This enduring call-and-response song is rightly regarded as a classic of its genre, and later became a minor UK hit when recorded by the Everly Brothers. Mickey and Sylvia had further success with 'There Oughta Be A Law' (1957) and, after a brief hiatus as a duo, 'Baby You're So Fine' (1961), but their career together was undermined by commitments elsewhere. Prolific session work for Atlantic Records, Savoy, King and Aladdin earned the former the epithet Mickey 'Guitar' Baker, while the latter had made her recording debut with jazz trumpeter Oran 'Hot Lips' Page as early as 1950. In 1973, she began recording as Sylvia, and later achieved notable success as an entrepreneur through her ownership of Sugar Hill Records, early champions of the rap/hip-hop scene.
● ALBUMS: *New Sounds* (Vix 1957) ★★, *Love Is Strange* (Camden 1965) ★★.
● COMPILATIONS: *Love Is Strange And Other Hits* (RCA 1989) ★★★, *The Willow Sessions* (Sequel 1996) ★★★.

MIGHTY SPARROW

b. Francisco Slinger, Grenada. Having moved to Trinidad as a child, calypso singer Mighty Sparrow first rose to domestic prominence in the 50s. He earned his underwhelming nickname (most calypso singers dealt in more self-aggrandizing names such as Executor and Lion) by virtue of his stage performances, which involved him moving around rapidly while most other singers were stationary. He was rewarded with the Calypso Crown of 1956 for his song 'Jean And Dinah', which protested about the fallout from Americans who had left Trinidad's military bases. At the same time he lent his support to Eric Williams' People's National Movement, writing many calypso songs in praise of the nationalist leader. His anthem 'Cricket Lovely Cricket' was a particularly painful reminder to UK cricket fans after the humiliating drubbing West Indian star batsman Garfield Sobers gave to the English team in the early 50s. In politics, however, he subsequently revised his position in the 60s as the initial optimism of the PNP soured into disillusionment. Despite his earlier recordings, calypso was ironically just beginning to secure a large following in the USA. His popularity was such that in the 50s and 60s he was capable of filling a venue such as New York's Madison Square Gardens. With the development of soca, Sparrow became a willing convert, although he faced some opposition from calypso purists who despised the new hybrid.
● ALBUMS: *The Slave* (Island 1963) ★★★, *Sparrow Come Back* (RCA 1966) ★★★, *Hotter Than Ever* (Trojan 1972) ★★★★, *Only A Fool* (Trojan 1981) ★★★, *Peace & Love* (Trojan 1981) ★★★, *King Of The World* (Dynamic 1986) ★★★, *Calypso Carnival* (La Records 1990) ★★★, with Lord Kitchener *Carnival Hits* (Ice 1991) ★★★.
● COMPILATIONS: *Party Classics Volume 1 And 2* (Charlie 1987) ★★★.

MILBURN, AMOS

b. 1 April 1927, Houston, Texas, USA, d. 3 January 1980, Houston, Texas, USA. After service in the US Navy in World War II, Milburn formed his own blues and R&B band in Houston in which he played piano and sang, and in 1946 he was offered a contract by the Aladdin label. Between November 1948 and February 1954 he and his band, the Aladdin Chicken Shackers, had an extraordinary run of 19 consecutive Top 10 hits on the *Billboard* R&B chart, including four number 1s ('Chicken Shack Boogie', 'A&M Blues', 'Roomin' House Boogie' and 'Bad, Bad Whiskey'). His romping boogies about drinking and partying were hugely popular and for two years (1949 and 1950) he was voted Top R&B Artist by *Billboard*. Following the break-up of his band in 1954 he never achieved the same level of success, and he left Aladdin in 1956. He then recorded as part of a duo with Charles Brown for the Ace label, and in 1963 recorded an album for Motown Records. In the 60s he played clubs around Cincinnati and Cleveland, Ohio, drawing heavily on his catalogue of old hits, but did not have any more hit records. In 1970 he suffered the first of a series of strokes. In 1972 he retired and returned to his home-town of Houston where he died eight years later.
● ALBUMS: with Wynonie Harris *Party After Hours* (Aladdin 1955) ★★★, *Rockin' The Boogie* (Aladdin 1955) ★★★, *Let's Have A Party* (Score 1957) ★★★, *Amos Milburn Sings The Blues* (Score 1958) ★★★, *Return Of The Blues Boss* (Motown 1963) ★★★, *13 Unreleased Masters* (Pathé-Marconi 1984) ★★.

● COMPILATIONS: *Million Sellers* (Imperial 1962) ★★★★, *Greatest Hits* Aladdin recordings (Official Records 1988) ★★★★, *Blues & Boogie: His Greatest Hits* (Sequel 1991) ★★★★, *Down The Road Apiece: The Best Of Amos Milbur* (EMI 1994) ★★★★, *The Complete Aladdin Recordings Of Amos Milburn* (Mosaic 1995) ★★★★, *The Motown Sessions, 1962-1964* (Motown 1996) ★★★, *Blues, Barrelhouse & Boogie Woogie, 1946-1955* (Capitol 1996) ★★★★.

MILLER, GARY

b. Neville Williams, 1924, Blackpool, Lancashire, England, d. 15 June 1968, London, England. Miller was a popular singer in the UK during the 50s and early 60s, with a smooth and polished style. As a young man, Miller was a talented soccer player and played for Blackpool Football Club as an amateur. During World War II, he served as a lieutenant in the Royal Navy Volunteer Reserve and, on release, enrolled as a student at London University with the intention of becoming a teacher of languages. After performing in college concerts, and with the experience of singing at a Welsh Eisteddfod festival as a schoolboy, Miller embarked on the learning process of small-time cabaret and concert tours, and made his first radio broadcast on *Beginners, Please*. As well as singing, he also included dancing in his act, and was involved in negotiations for a small part in the Ray Bolger movie *Where's Charley?*, when it was being made in England, but nothing materialized. His first real break came when he was discovered by record executive and songwriter Norman Newell during a Variety appearance at Northampton, which led to him making a few tracks for Columbia. He also made regular appearances, singing and dancing, on television in *Shop Window*, and appeared on the fortnightly *Kaleidoscope* series. By 1954, he was headlining in variety on the Moss Empires circuit. After a spell with Newell at the newly formed Philips Records in 1953, during which he released mostly romantic ballads, Miller switched to another new label, Pye Nixa, and started recording more up-tempo material. His first hit, 'The Yellow Rose Of Texas', in 1955, was overtaken by the US Mitch Miller version, but 'Robin Hood' made the Top 10 despite opposition from Dick James, who benefited by having his version played over the titles during the weekly television show. During that era it was commonplace for several versions of the same song to jostle each other in the singles chart. This was the case with Miller's 'Garden Of Eden', which lost out to Frankie Vaughan. There was also strong competition on 'Wonderful! Wonderful!' from Ronnie Hilton, and on 'The Story Of My Life' from Michael Holliday. Miller's record of the latter song is said to have suffered in popularity because he was touring North Africa at the time of its release. Perhaps in an effort to avoid the competition, Miller reached back to 1945 for his final chart entry, 'I've Heard That Song Before' (1961); it proved to be one of his best vocal performances. His first album, *Meet Mister Miller*, contained standards such as 'Manhattan', 'April Showers' and 'Stella By Starlight'. This was followed by *Gary On The Ball*, with the Kenny Ball Jazz Band. In 1964, Miller appeared in the West End production of *She Loves Me*, Jerry Bock and Sheldon Harnick's musical based on the Hungarian play *Perfumerie*. He returned to the London stage in 1966 to play the role of the crooning Agent VO3 in Bryan Blackburn's comedy musical, *Come Spy With Me*, starring female impersonator Danny La Rue, at London's 'home of farce', the Whitehall Theatre. Two years later he died of a heart attack at his south London home.

● ALBUMS: *Meet Mister Miller* (Nixa 1957) ★★★, with Kenny Ball *Gary On The Ball* (Pye 1961) ★★★★.

MILLER, GLENN

b. 1 March 1905, Clarinda, Iowa, USA, d. 15 December 1944. Miller was the first artist to be credited with a million-selling disc (for 'Chattanooga Choo Choo'), and was the toast of North American popular music during World War II for his uniformed orchestra's fusion of sober virtuosity, infectious dance rhythms and varied intonation of brass and woodwind. In Miller's hands, close harmony vocals – often wordless – were almost incidental in a slick repertoire that embraced Tin Pan Alley standards ('April In Paris', Hoagy Carmichael's 'The Nearness Of You'), jump blues ('St. Louis Blues', Jelly Roll Morton's 'King Porter Stomp'), western swing ('Blueberry Hill', once sung by Gene Autry) and orthodox swing ('Jersey Bounce', 'Tuxedo Junction'), also exemplified by the 'hotter' big bands of Artie Shaw and Jimmy Dorsey.

After his family moved to North Platts, Nebraska, Miller's trombone skills earned him places in bands operational within his Fort Morgan high school, and afterwards at the University of Colorado. On becoming a professional musician, he found work on the west coast and in New York as both a player and arranger – notably for Victor Young, whose Los Angeles studio orchestra accompanied Judy Garland and Bing Crosby. Other prestigious feathers in Miller's cap were his supervision of Britain's Ray Noble And The New Mayfair Orchestra's first USA tour and a scoring commission for Columbia Records. His earnings were ploughed back into the organization and rehearsal of his own band which, despite setbacks such as his wife's long illness in 1938, built up a huge following in New York, through dogged rounds of one-night-stands and record-breaking residencies in venues such as Pompton Turnpike roadhouse and the celebrated Glen Island Casino. Signed to RCA Records in 1939, Miller proved a sound investment with immediate consecutive bestsellers in evocative classics such as 'Little Brown Jug' (written in 1869), 'In The Mood' and 'Sunrise Serenade'. The latter was coupled with 'Moonlight Serenade' – a strikingly effective extrapolation of a trombone exercise that became Miller's signature tune. As synonymous with him, too, was 1940's 'Chattanooga Choo Choo' with a vocal chorus (by Tex Beneke, Marion Hutton and the Modernaires) atypically to the fore. This novelty was also among highlights of *Sun Valley Serenade* (1941), the orchestra's first movie (co-starring Norwegian ice-skating champion, Sonja Henie). Other Miller classics included the irresistible 'Pennsylvania 6-5000' and the haunting 'Tuxedo Junction'. At Miller's commercial peak the next year, *Orchestra Wives* (1942, with Ann Rutherford and Cesar Romero), enveloped a similarly vacuous plot with musical interludes that included another smash in '(I've Got A Gal In) Kalamazoo'. The enduring lyric brilliantly used the alphabet; 'a b c d e f g h I got a gal in Kalamazoo'. That same year also brought both Miller's lively hit arrangement of 'American Patrol' and his enlistment into the US Army. Even though he was too old for combat he still volunteered out of patriotism, was elevated to the rank of captain and sent out to entertain the Allied forces. He was promoted to major in August 1944. Following a visit to Britain, his aircraft disappeared over the English Channel on 15 December 1944 (it was probably downed by Allied aircraft dumping excess bombs after a mission). Miller's death was an assumption that some devotees found too grievous to bear, and rumours of his survival persisted as his commercial star rose during the following decade and his orchestra lived on – even if the economics of staying on the road, combined with the rise of rock 'n' roll, finished off lesser rivals. Universal Pictures produced the immensely successful 1954 biopic, *The Glenn Miller Story* (with James Stewart in the title role). An Oscar-nominated soundtrack album (directed by Henry Mancini) was released, and a reissued 'Moonlight Serenade' reached number 12 in the UK singles charts. Miller's habit of preserving many of his radio broadcasts on private discs enabled the issue of another album, *Marvellous Miller Moods*. Also reaching the US chart in the late 50s was a 1939 Carnegie Hall concert recording and *The New Glenn Miller Orchestra In Hi-Fi*.

Miller's original arrangements were regarded as definitive by those multitudes who continued to put repackagings such as *The Real Glenn Miller And His Orchestra* high into the international charts as late as 1977. The sound was recreated so precisely by the Syd Lawrence Orchestra that it was employed in a 1969 television documentary of the late bandleader whose UK fan club booked Lawrence regularly for its annual tribute shows. Among the best tributes paid were those by Manhattan Transfer in a 1976 version of 'Tuxedo Junction', and Jive Bunny And The Mastermixers, whose 1989 medley, 'Swing The Mood' – a UK number 1 – was sandwiched between excerpts of 'In The Mood', sampled from Miller's 1938 recording. The arranging style perfected by Miller's staff arrangers, notably Jerry Gray, continued to influence several middle-of-the-road writers and bandleaders during the next two or three decades. Curiously enough, for a musician whose work is now preserved eternally in its 40s style, Miller was always eager to move on. Shortly before his death he remarked to Ray McKinley that the style that had made him famous was no

longer of interest to him, 'I've gone as far as I can go with the saxophone sound. I've got to have something new'. The enduring quality of Miller's work is most forcibly underlined by the realization that his tunes have become part of the instant musical vocabulary of listeners young and old. In 1995, just over 50 years after Miller's death, a set of recordings made by the American Band of the AEF at the Abbey Road studios in London late in 1944, was released as a two-CD set.

● COMPILATIONS: *Glenn Miller Concert Vol. 1* (RCA Victor 1951) ★★★★, *Glenn Miller Concert Vol. 2* (RCA Victor 1951) ★★★★, *Glenn Miller* (RCA Victor 1951) ★★★, *Glenn Miller Concert Vol. 3* (RCA Victor 1951) ★★★★, *This Is Glenn Miller* (RCA Victor 1951) ★★★, *This Is Glenn Miller Vol 2* (RCA Victor 1951) ★★★, *Sunrise Serenade* (RCA Victor 1951) ★★★, *The Glenn Miller Story* (1954) ★★★★, *Marvelous Miller Moods* (RCA Victor 1957) ★★★, *The Glenn Miller Carnegie Hall Concert* (RCA Victor 1957) ★★★, *Something Old, New, Borrowed And Blue* (RCA Victor 1958) ★★★, *The Miller Sound* (RCA Victor 1959) ★★★, *Marvelous Miller Medleys* (RCA Victor 1959) ★★★, *The Great Dance Bands Of The 30s And 40s* (RCA Victor 1959) ★★★, *Dance Anyone?* (RCA Victor 1960) ★★★, *Glenn Miller Time* (RCA Victor 1961) ★★★, *Echoes Of Glenn Miller* (RCA Victor 1962) ★★★, *On The Air* 3-LP box set (RCA Victor 1963) ★★★, *The Best Of Glenn Miller Vols. 1-3* (RCA Victor 1963) ★★★★, *Blue Moonlight* (RCA Victor 1966) ★★★, *In The Mood* (RCA Victor 1967) ★★★, *The Chesterfield Broadcasts Vol 1* (RCA Victor 1967) ★★★, *The Chesterfield Broadcasts Vol. 2* (RCA Victor 1968) ★★★, *The Nearness Of You* (1969) ★★★, *The Real Glenn Miller And His Orchestra Play The Original Music From The Film 'The Glenn Miller Story' And Other Hits* (1971) ★★★, *A Legendary Performer* (1975) ★★★, *A Legendary Performer Vol. 2* (1976) ★★★, *The Unforgettable Glenn Miller* (1977) ★★★, *Glenn Miller Army Air Force Band (1943-44)* (1981) ★★★, *Chesterfield Shows 1941-42* (1984) ★★★, *Chesterfield Shows – Chicago 1940* (1984) ★★★, *Chesterfield Shows – New York City 1940* (1984) ★★★, *Glenn Miller Airforce Orchestra, June 10, 1944* (1984) ★★★, *April 3, 1940 Chesterfield Show* (1989) ★★★, *The Glenn Miller Gold Collection* (1993) ★★★★, *The Ultimate Glenn Miller* (RCA Bluebird 1993) ★★★★, *Live At The Café Rouge* (1994) ★★★, *The Lost Recordings* 2-CD set (RCA Victor 1995) ★★★, *The Secret Broadcasts* 3-CD set (RCA Victor 1996) ★★★, *Candlelight Miller* (BMG 1998) ★★★, *The Very Best Of Glenn Miller* (Camden 1997) ★★★, *The Unforgettable* (RCA 1998) ★★★★, *Falling In Love With Glenn Miller* (RCE Victor 2000) ★★★★, *Forever Gold* (St Clair 2000) ★★★.

● FURTHER READING: *Next To A Letter From Home: Major Glenn Miller's Wartime Band*, Geoffrey Butcher. *Glenn Miller & His Orchestra*, George Thomas Simon.

MILLER, MITCH

b. Mitchell William Miller, 4 July 1911, Rochester, New York, USA. An oboist, record producer, arranger and one of the most commercially successful recording artists of the 50s and early

60s. Miller learned to play the piano at the age of six, and began studying the oboe when he was 12, and later attended Rochester's Eastman School of Music. After graduating in 1932, Miller played oboe with symphony orchestras in the area, before joining CBS Radio in 1932. For the next 11 years he was a soloist with the CBS Symphony, and played with André Kostelanetz, Percy Faith, the Saidenburg Little Symphony and the Budapest String Quartet. In the late 40s he became director of Mercury Records' 'pop' division, and then in 1950, was appointed head of A&R at Columbia Records. While at Mercury, Miller was responsible for producing several big hits, including Frankie Laine's 'That Lucky Old Sun', 'Mule Train' and 'The Cry Of The Wild Goose'. Miller also conducted the orchestra on Laine's 'Jezebel' and 'Rose, Rose, I Love You'. Shortly after he left the label, Patti Page released 'The Tennessee Waltz', which became one of the biggest-selling singles ever. The original was by R&B singer Erskine Hawkins, and the Page disc is sometimes credited as being the first really successful example of 'crossover' from country to pop, although Miller had already fashioned Hank Williams' 'Hey, Good Lookin'' into a minor hit for Frankie Laine and Jo Stafford. Miller developed this policy when he moved to Columbia, and recorded Guy Mitchell ('Singing The Blues' and 'Knee Deep In The Blues'), Tony Bennett ('Cold, Cold Heart'), Rosemary Clooney ('Half As Much'), Jo Stafford ('Jambalaya') and the little-known Joan Weber ('Let Me Go Lover'). Miller's roster at Columbia also included Johnnie Ray ('Cry', 'The Little White Cloud That Cried', 'Just Crying In The Rain') and Frank Sinatra.

There was little empathy between Miller and Sinatra, and the singer rejected several songs that eventually became successful for Guy Mitchell. After he left Columbia, Sinatra sent telegrams to judiciary and senate committees, accusing Miller of presenting him with inferior songs, and of accepting money from writers whose songs he (Miller) had used. Certainly, Sinatra recorded some unsuitable material under Miller's auspices during his final years with the label, although 'American Beauty Rose' and 'Goodnight, Irene', both with Miller's accompaniment, and 'Bim Bam Baby', paled in comparison with perhaps the most bizarre item of all, 'Mama Will Bark', on which Sinatra made barking and growling noises, and duetted with Miller's latest signing, a female named Dagmar.

Miller's own hit recordings, mostly credited to 'Mitch Miller And His Gang', began in 1950 with his adaptation of the Israeli folk song 'Tzena, Tzena, Tzena', complete with a happy vocal chorus that would typify his later work. After 'Meet Mr. Callaghan', 'Without My Lover', 'Under Paris Skies' and 'Napoleon' in the early 50s, he spent six weeks at number 1 with the million-selling 'The Yellow Rose Of Texas', one of the great marching songs from the American Civil War. This was followed by three instrumentals: 'Lisbon Antigua', 'Song For A Summer Night (Parts 1 & 2)' and 'March From The River Kwai

And Colonel Bogey'. There was also the novelty 'The Children's Marching Song' from the 1959 movie *The Inn Of The Sixth Happiness*. The previous year, Miller had started his series of *Sing Along With Mitch* albums, which featured an all-male chorus singing old favourites, many from before the turn of the century. Nineteen variations on the theme made the US Top 40 between 1958 and 1962, of which seven titles achieved million-selling status.

The phenomenally successful *Sing Along* formula was developed as a popular television series which ran from 1961-66, and featured several solo singers such as Victor Griffin, Leslie Uggams and Louise O'Brien. Despite the obvious financial gain to Columbia from his record sales, Miller was constantly criticized for his negative attitude towards rock 'n' roll. He turned down Buddy Holly, among others, and was blamed for his company's relatively small market share in the rapidly changing music scene during his tenure as an influential executive, yet his promotion of the artists already mentioned, plus Doris Day ('Whatever Will Be, Will Be (Que Sera, Sera)'), Johnny Mathis, Percy Faith, and many more, substantially aided Columbia. Out of place in the 'swinging 60s', he emerged occasionally to conduct the orchestra on various light and classical music recordings.

● ALBUMS: *Sing Along With Mitch* (Columbia 1958) ★★★★, *More Sing Along ...* (Columbia 1958) ★★★, *Christmas Sing Along ...* (Columbia 1958) ★★★★, *Still More! Sing Along ...* (Columbia 1959) ★★★, *Folk Songs Sing Along ...* (Columbia 1959) ★★★, *Party Sing Along ...* (Columbia 1959) ★★★, *Fireside Sing Along ...* (Columbia 1959) ★★★, *Saturday Night Sing Along ...* (Columbia 1960) ★★★, *Sentimental Sing Along ...* (Columbia 1960) ★★★, *March Along ...* (Columbia 1960) ★★★, *Memories Sing Along ...* (Columbia 1960) ★★★★, *Happy Times! Sing Along ...* (Columbia 1961) ★★★, *TV Sing Along ...* (Columbia 1961) ★★★, *Your Request Sing Along ...* (Columbia 1961) ★★★, *Holiday Sing Along ...* (Columbia 1961) ★★★★, *Rhythm Sing Along ...* (Columbia 1962) ★★★, *Family Sing Along ...* (Columbia 1962) ★★★.
● COMPILATIONS: *Mitch's Greatest Hits* (Columbia 1961) ★★★★.

MILLER, NED

b. Henry Ned Miller, 12 April 1925, Raines, Utah, USA. When Miller was a small child, the family moved to Salt Lake City, Utah where, after completing his education, he worked as a pipe fitter. He became interested in songwriting and country music and learned to play the guitar, but had no real inclination to be a performer. In the mid-50s, he married and moved to California, where he hoped to sell some of his songs, and joined the Fabor label as a writer and/or performer. Early in 1957, a deal between Fabor and Dot Records, which gave the latter label first choice of all Fabor masters, saw two of his songs, 'Dark Moon' and 'A Fallen Star', both become US country and pop hits for Bonnie Guitar and Jimmy C. Newman, respectively. Miller himself played guitar on the former recording, which also was a number 4 US pop hit for Gale Storm. The song became a UK Top 20 pop hit for Tony Brent and was also recorded by the Kaye Sisters and Joe Loss And His Orchestra. In July 1957, Miller's most famous song appeared when, as a result of a game of patience, he wrote 'From A Jack To A King'. Both his own version and a pop one by Jim Lowe were released by Dot, but created no major impression.

From the start, Miller had little interest in a career as a singer and detested touring; he suffered constantly with stage fright and shyness, and was always a most reluctant performer. Stories are told of him on occasions actually sending a friend to perform as Ned Miller in his place. Although he made some further recordings, including 'Lights In The Street' and 'Turn Back', he achieved no chart success and concentrated on his writing. Between 1959 and 1961, he recorded briefly for Jackpot and Capitol. In 1962, he persuaded Fabor Robison to reissue his recording of 'From A Jack To A King' and this time, despite Miller's reluctance to tour and publicize the song, it became a number 2 country and number 6 pop hit. Released in the UK on the London label, it also soon reached number 2 in the UK pop charts. 'From A Jack To A King', an old-fashioned, traditional-sounding country song, was hardly a record that was ahead of its time, but it became an extraordinary success in Britain, where, in April 1963, it held the number 2 position for four weeks – in spite of the fact that there was no promotion from either the artist or label, and it went against the grain of songs that were hits at the time. It obviously says much for the quality of the song. Further Fabor recordings followed and Miller had Top 20 US country and pop hits with 'Invisible Tears' (1964) and 'Do What You Do Do Well' (1965). He returned to Capitol in 1965, and had five minor hits before being dropped by the label, again due to his unwillingness to tour. He moved to Republic where, in 1970, he achieved his last chart entry with 'The Lover's Song'. He then gave up recording and after moving to Prescott, Arizona, finally wrote his last song in the mid-70s. After eight years at Prescott, he settled in Las Vegas where he completely withdrew from all public appearances and gave up songwriting. In 1991, the German Bear Family label released a 31-track CD of his work, which included some previously unissued material.

● ALBUMS: *From A Jack To A King* i (Fabor 1963) ★★★★, *Ned Miller (Sings The Songs Of Ned Miller)* (Capitol 1965) ★★★, *Teardrop Lane* (Capitol 1967) ★★★, *In The Name Of Love* (Capitol 1968) ★★, *Ned Miller's Back* (Republic 1970) ★★.

● COMPILATIONS: *The Best Of Ned Miller* (Capitol 1966) ★★★, *From A Jack To A King* ii (Bear Family 1991) ★★★★.

MILLS BROTHERS

The three permanent members of this vocal group were Herbert Mills (b. 2 April 1912, d. 12 April 1989, Las Vegas, Nevada, USA), Harry Mills (b. 19 August 1913, d. 28 June 1982, Los Angeles,

California, USA) and Donald Mills (b. 29 April 1915, d. 18 November 1999, Los Angeles, California, USA). John Mills Jnr. (b. 11 February 1911, d. 24 January 1936, Bellefontaine, Ohio, USA), added vocal notes in string bass form and played guitar. All the brothers were born in Piqua, Ohio, USA, sons of a barber who had been a successful concert singer. By the mid-20s, they were singing in sweet, close harmony in local vaudeville, providing their own backing by accurately imitating saxophones, trumpets, trombones and bass. With the main trio still teenagers, they had their own show on Cincinnati radio before moving to New York in 1930.

The brothers signed to Brunswick Records and had a hit in 1931 with their first disc, 'Tiger Rag', which they also sang in the following year's movie *The Big Broadcast*, featuring Bing Crosby and many other stars of US radio. They appeared in several other musical montage movies such as *Twenty Million Sweethearts* (1934), *Broadway Gondolier* (1935) and *Reveille With Beverly* (1943), *Rhythm Parade* (1943), *Cowboy Canteen* (1944) and *When You're Smiling* (1950). In the early 30s, Crosby featured on several of the brothers' record hits, including 'Dinah'/'Can't We Talk It Over', 'Shine' and 'Gems From George White's Scandals', which also included the Boswell Sisters. On later tracks, the Mills Brothers were also joined by Louis Armstrong, Ella Fitzgerald and Cab Calloway. Their early records were labelled: 'No musical instruments or mechanical devices used on this recording other than one guitar'. Other 30s hits included 'You Rascal, You', 'I Heard', 'Good-Bye, Blues', 'Rockin' Chair', 'St. Louis Blues', 'Sweet Sue', 'Bugle Call Rag', 'It Don't Mean A Thing (If It Ain't Got That Swing)', 'Swing It Sister', 'Sleepy Head' and 'Sixty Seconds Together'. In 1935, John Mills died suddenly and the brothers' father, John Snr. (b. 11 February 1882, Bellafonte, Pennsylvania, USA, d. 8 December 1967, Bellafontaine, Ohio, USA), took over as bass singer, and ex-bandleader Bernard Addison joined the group on guitar. During the late 30s, the Mills Brothers toured the USA and abroad, appearing in two UK Royal Command Performances. Their popularity peaked in 1943 with the record 'Paper Doll', which sold over six million copies. They had consistent chart success throughout the 40s with titles on the Decca Records label such as 'You Always Hurt The One You Love', 'Til Then', 'I Wish', 'I Don't Know Enough About You', 'Across The Alley From The Alamo', 'I Love You So Much It Hurts', 'I've Got My Love To Keep Me Warm', 'Someday (You'll Want Me To Want You)' and 'Put Another Chair At The Table'.

By 1950, the instrumental impressions having generally been discarded, the brothers were accompanied by ex-Tommy Dorsey arranger Sy Oliver's orchestra on their hit 'Nevertheless (I'm In Love With You)' and again in 1952 on 'Be My Life's Companion'. That same year, 'Glow Worm', gave them another blockbuster. This was a 1908 song from the German operetta *Lysistrata*, with a new lyric by Johnny Mercer. Other 50s favourites from the brothers included Sy Oliver's own composition 'Opus Number One', 'Say Si Si', 'Lazy River' and 'Smack Dab In The Middle'. In 1956, John Snr. retired, and the brothers continued as a trio. Their last hit on Decca was 'Queen Of The Senior Prom' in 1957. The switch to the Dot Records label gave them two US Top 30 entries, 'Get A Job' and their final chart success, 'Cab Driver', in 1968. After Harry Mills' death in 1982, Herbert and Donald continued to perform their brand of highly polished, humorous entertainment with a substitute singer. However, when Herbert died seven years later, Donald, now walking with a cane, gained excellent reviews and favourable audience reaction when he played nightclubs with his son John, using mainly the old Mills Brothers catalogue, but with additional new material.

● ALBUMS: *Barber Shop Ballads* 10-inch album (Decca 1950) ★★★★, *Souvenir Album* 10-inch album (Decca 1950) ★★★, *Wonderful Words* 10-inch album (Decca 1951) ★★★, *Meet The Mills Brothers* 10-inch album (Decca 1954) ★★★★, *Louis Armstrong And The Mills Brothers* 10-inch album (Decca 1954) ★★★★, *Four Boys And A Guitar* 10-inch album (Decca 1954) ★★★, *Singin' And Swingin'* (Decca 1956) ★★★, *Memory Lane* (Decca 1956) ★★★★, *One Dozen Roses* (Decca 1957) ★★★, *The Mills Brothers In Hi-Fi* (Decca 1958) ★★★★, *Mmmm, The Mills Brothers* (Dot 1958) ★★★, *Glow With The Mills Brothers* (Decca 1959) ★★★, *Barbershop Harmony* (Decca 1959) ★★★, *Harmonizin' With The Mills Brothers* (Decca 1959) ★★★, *Great Barbershop Hits* (Dot 1959) ★★★, *Merry Christmas* (Dot 1959) ★★★, *The Mills Brothers Sing* (Dot 1960) ★★★, *Yellow Bird* (Dot 1961) ★★★, *Great Hawaiian Hits* (Dot 1961) ★★, *The Beer Barrel Polka And Other Hits* (Dot 1962) ★★, *Sing 'The End Of The World' & Other Great Hits* (Dot 1963) ★★, *Hymns We Love* (Dot 1964) ★★, *Say Si Si, And Other Great Latin Hits* (Dot 1964) ★★, *The Mills Brothers Sing For You* (Hamilton 1964) ★★★, *These Are The Mills Brothers* (Dot 1966) ★★★, *That Country Feelin'* (Dot 1966) ★★, *The Mills Brothers Live* (Dot 1967) ★★, *Fortuosity* (Dot 1968) ★★★, with Count Basie *The Board Of Directors* (Dot 1968) ★★★, *My Shy Violet* (Dot 1968) ★★★, *Dream* (Dot 1969) ★★★.

● COMPILATIONS: *The Mills Brothers Great Hits* (Dot 1958) ★★★, *Ten Years Of Hits 1954-1964* (Dot 1965) ★★★, *Greatest Hits* (MCA 1987) ★★★, *Early Transcripts And Rare Recordings 1931-45* recordings (Broadway Intermission 1988) ★★★, *The Best Of The Decca Years* (Decca 1990) ★★★★, *Mills Brothers: The Anthology (1931-1968)* (MCA 1994) ★★★★, *The Very Best Of The Mills Brothers* (Half Moon 1998) ★★★, *Chronological, Volumes 1-6 1932-39* recordings (JSP 1998) ★★★★, in addition, there are a great many compilations available.

● FILMS: *I Ain't Got Nobody* (1932), *Dinah* (1933), *When Yuba Plays The Rumba On The Tuba* (1933), *Strictly Dynamite* (1934), *Broadway Gondolier* (1935), *Lawless Valley* (1939), *Rhythm Parade* (1943), *Chatterbox* (1943), *The Big Beat* (1957).

MILLS, GARRY

b. 13 October 1941, West Wickham, Kent, England. Mills was the nephew of jazz band leader Nat Gonella. Like many other UK pop singers of the late 50s, he started at London's 2 I's coffee bar and this led to his signing with Dick Rowe at Top Rank. He covered major US hits such as 'Running Bear', 'Teen Angel', 'Hey, Baby', 'Seven Little Girls' and 'Footsteps' before charting with the b-side of the last single. The song 'Look For A Star' had been written for the Norman Wisdom film *Follow A Star* but was actually used in the Hammer movie *Circus Of Horrors*. In America, Gary's (he dropped one 'r' for the USA) original soundtrack version was joined on the charts by three local cover versions, and, although he made the Top 40 in 1960, the biggest hit was by his near namesake Garry Miles (aka Buzz Cason). The record was not only Mills' biggest success, it was also the first hit for composer Mark Anthony, better known as Tony Hatch. Mills, who was backed on the road by the Flee-Rekkers, had two smaller UK hits with the follow-up 'Top Teen Baby' and 'I'll Step Down' on Decca in 1961, and also appeared in the long-forgotten films *London Nights* and *Treasure Island W.C.2*.

MINEO, SAL

b. Salvatore Mineo, 10 January 1939, New York City, New York, USA, d. 12 February 1976. After a difficult childhood, Mineo studied dancing and made his Broadway debut in *The Rose Tattoo*. He followed this with an appearance in *The King And I* in 1952. In the mid-50s he went to Hollywood and began making films, usually appearing as a troubled teenager. Among his best-known films were *Rebel Without A Cause* (1955), for which he was nominated for an Oscar as Best Supporting Actor, *Somebody Up There Likes Me* and *Giant* (both 1956), and *Exodus* (1960), another unsuccessful Oscar nomination. He also played the title role in *The Gene Krupa Story* (1959). In the late 50s, Mineo made a number of records, including 'Love Affair', 'Start Movin' (In My Direction)', 'Lasting Love' and 'You Shouldn't Do That'. He continued making films during the 60s and also returned to stage work. He directed and starred in *Fortune And Men's Eyes*, a play that reflected Mineo's own homosexuality. He was returning home from the theatre when he was stabbed to death in a Hollywood street.

● ALBUMS: *Sal* (Epic 1958) ★★.

● COMPILATIONS: *The Secret Doorway: The Ultimate Collection* (Fireball 1998) ★★.

MINNELLI, VINCENTE

b. 28 February 1903, Chicago, Illinois, USA, d. 25 July 1986, Los Angeles, California, USA. A distinguished film director with a sophisticated style and flair, particularly in the use of colour and the innovative filming of the most exquisite dance sequences. Minnelli is credited, in collaboration with Gene Kelly, with being the main influence on the classic MGM musicals of the 50s. As a young child Minnelli appeared in plays produced by the family Minnelli Bros. Tent Theatre, which toured the American Midwest. After leaving school at 16 he studied at the Art Institute of Chicago, and worked as a window and costume designer before moving to New York to design the scenery and costumes for two 1932 Broadway shows, the *Earl Carroll Vanities* and *The DuBarry*. From 1933-35 Minnelli was art director at the Radio City Music Hall where he staged a series of ballets and musicals. In 1935 he directed as well as designed the Beatrice Lillie musical *At Home Abroad*, and throughout the 30s worked successfully on productions such as *Ziegfeld Follies*, *The Show Is On*, *Hooray For What!* and *Very Warm For May* (1939). From 1940-42, under the aegis of MGM producer Arthur Freed, Minnelli trained in various aspects of Hollywood film techniques and supervised speciality numbers in a number of films including *Strike Up The Band*, *Babes On Broadway* and *Panama Hattie*. He made his debut as a director in 1943 with the all-black musical *Cabin In The Sky*, which was followed by *I Dood It* a year later. Then came *Meet Me In St. Louis* (1944), a delightful piece of nostalgic Americana that became one of the most beloved musicals of all time. Minnelli married its star, Judy Garland, in 1945 (divorced 1951), and in the following year their daughter, Liza Minnelli, was born. Over the next 25 years Minnelli directed a number of musicals that met with varying degrees of success. *Yolande And The Thief* (1945), which starred Fred Astaire, was followed by the all-star spectacular *Ziegfeld Follies* (1946), and two films with Gene Kelly, the underrated *The Pirate* (1948), and *An American In Paris* (1951), which is often considered to be Minnelli's masterpiece. However, many would argue that another of the director's collaborations with Fred Astaire, *The Band Wagon* (1953), or the delightful *Gigi* (1958), were equally important events in the director's distinguished career. Certainly, whatever their merits – and they were not inconsiderable – few would suggest *Brigadoon* (1954), *Kismet* (1955), *Bells Are Ringing* (1960) or *On A Clear Day You Can See Forever* (1970) as being prime examples of Vincente Minnelli's art. The latter film was made for Paramount after he had ended an association with MGM that had lasted for more than 25 years. However, the majority of Minnelli's films were not musicals. Over the years he made many other pictures in a wide variety of styles and moods, and finally achieved his ambition to work with daughter Liza Minnelli in 1976 on his last film, *A Matter Of Time*. By then, Minnelli's style of films – particularly musicals – were anachronistic, and he lived quietly in retirement until his death at his home in Beverly Hills in 1986. The year of his birth has always been the subject of speculation. The one cited above is that which was printed in the excellent obituary notice in *Variety*. In 1993 the young cabaret entertainer Jeff Harnar presented his solo revue *Dancing In The Dark – Vincente Minnelli's Hollywood* in New York.

● FURTHER READING: *I Remember It Well*, Vincente Minnelli.
● FILMS: as director *I Dood It* (1943), *Cabin In*

The Sky (1943), *Meet Me In St. Louis* (1944), *Yolande And The Thief* (1945), *The Clock* (1945), *Till The Clouds Roll By (Judy Garland's sequences only)* (1946), *Ziegfeld Follies* (1946), *Undercurrent* (1946), *The Pirate* (1948), *Madame Bovary* (1949), *Father Of The Bride* (1950), *An American In Paris* (1951), *Father's Little Dividend* (1951), *The Story Of Three Loves (Mademoiselle Sequence)* (1952), *The Bad And The Beautiful* (1952), *The Band Wagon* (1953), *Brigadoon* (1954), *The Long Long Trailer* (1954), *The Cobweb* (1955), *Kismet* (1955), *Lust For Life* (1956), *Tea And Sympathy* (1956), *Designing Woman* (1957), *Some Came Running* (1958), *The Reluctant Debutante* (1958), *Gigi* (1958), *Bells Are Ringing* (1960), *Home From The Hill* (1960), *Two Weeks In Another Town* (1962), *The Four Horsemen Of The Apocalypse* (1962), *The Courtship Of Eddie's Father* (1963), *Goodbye Charlie* (1964), *The Sandpiper* (1965), *On A Clear Day You Can See Forever* (1970), *A Matter Of Time* (1976).

MITCHELL, GUY

b. Albert Cernick, 22 February 1927, Detroit, Michigan, USA, d. 2 July 1999, Las Vegas, Nevada, USA. Mitchell was an enormously popular singer in the USA and especially the UK, particularly during the 50s, with a straightforward style, rich voice and affable personality. Although his birthplace is often given as Yugoslavia, his parents' homeland, Mitchell confirmed in a 1988 UK interview that he was born in Detroit, and was brought up there until the family moved to Colorado, and then to Los Angeles, California, when he was 11 years old. In Los Angeles, he successfully auditioned for Warner Brothers Records and, for the next few years, was groomed for a possible movie career as a child star, in addition to singing on the Hollywood radio station KFWB. The possibility of the world having another Mickey Rooney was averted when the family moved again, this time to San Francisco. Mitchell became an apprentice saddle-maker, and worked on ranches and in rodeos in the San Joaquin Valley, and also sang on cowboy singer Dude Martin's radio show. His affection for country music stayed with him for the remainder of his career. After a spell in the US Navy, Mitchell joined pianist Carmen Cavallaro, and made his first records with the band, including 'I Go In When The Moon Comes Out' and 'Ah, But It Happens'. He then spent some time in New York, making demonstration records, and also won first place on the *Arthur Godfrey Talent Show*. In 1949, he recorded a few tracks for King Records, which were subsequently reissued on *Sincerely Yours* when Mitchell became successful. In 1950, he was signed to Columbia Records by Mitch Miller, who is said to have been responsible for changing Cernick to Mitchell, Miller's full given name. Their first success came in 1950, with 'My Heart Cries For You' and 'The Roving Kind', which were followed by a string of hits throughout the decade, mostly jaunty novelty numbers, usually with Miller arrangements that used French horns to considerable effect. Several of the songs were written by Bob Merrill, including 'Sparrow In The Tree Top', 'Pittsburgh, Pennsylvania', 'My Truly, Truly Fair', 'Feet Up (Pat Him On The Po-Po)', 'Belle, Belle, My Liberty Belle' and 'She Wears Red Feathers', which contained the immortal Merrill couplet: 'An elephant brought her in, placed her by my side/While six baboons got out bassoons, and played 'Here Comes The Bride'!' Other US Top 30 entries during this period included 'You're Just In Love', a duet with another Miller protégée, Rosemary Clooney, 'Christopher Columbus', 'Unless' (a 30s Tolchard Evans number), 'Sweetheart Of Yesterday', 'There's Always Room At Our House', 'I Can't Help It', 'Day Of Jubilo', ''Cause I Love You, That's A-Why', 'Tell Us Where The Good Times Are' (the latter two duets with Mindy Carson) and 'Ninety-Nine Years (Dead Or Alive)'. 'Singing The Blues' (with Ray Conniff And His Orchestra) became his most successful record, staying at number 1 in the US charts for 10 weeks in 1956. In the UK, Tommy Steele had a hit with his cover version, but Mitchell also succeeded by reaching number 1.

Further infectious hits followed: 'Knee Deep In The Blues', the irritatingly catchy 'Rock-A-Billy' ('rock-a-billy, rock-a-billy, rock-a-billy rock, rock-a-billy rock-a-billy, ooh rock rock'), and his last US chart entry in 1959, 'Heartaches By The Number' (number 1). Of the aforementioned singles, six sold over a million copies. Most of Mitchell's US hits were also successful in the UK, where he was highly popular, touring regularly, appearing at the London Palladium for the first time in 1952, and performing at the 1954 Royal Variety Performance. Additional chart entries in the UK included 'Pretty Little Black-Eyed Susie', 'Look At That Girl' (number 1), 'Cloud Lucky Seven', 'Cuff Of My Shirt', 'A Dime And A Dollar' and 'Chicka Boom'. The latter was featured in Mitchell's first movie, a 3-D musical entitled *Those Redheads From Seattle* (1953), with Rhonda Fleming, Gene Barry and Teresa Brewer. Brewer and Mitchell proved a pleasant combination on the Johnny Mercer/Hoagy Carmichael song 'I Guess It Was You All The Time'. In 1954, Mitchell appeared with Gene Barry again, in the spoof western movie *Red Garters*, which also starred Rosemary Clooney, and contained another Mitchell 'special', 'A Dime And A Dollar'. In contrast to the somewhat perky style, so effective on his singles, some of Mitchell's albums revealed him to be an excellent ballad singer, particularly *A Guy In Love*, with Glenn Osser And His Orchestra, which contained standards such as 'The Moon Got In My Eyes', 'Allegheny Moon', 'East Of The Sun' and 'East Side Of Heaven'. *Sunshine Guitar*, with its guitar choir, was 'carefree and breezy, full of innocent gaiety', with a country 'feel' on several of the numbers.

With the 60s beat boom imminent, Mitchell's contract with Columbia ended in 1962, and he released some singles on the Joy and Reprise Records labels. In 1967, he signed for the Nashville-based Starday label, but shortly after his *Traveling Shoes* and *Singin' Up A Storm* were released, the company went out of business.

During some periods of the 60s and 70s, Mitchell ceased performing. He issued only a few tracks on his own GMI label – partly because of poor health and serious alcohol problems. In 1979, he toured Australia, and started to play nightclubs in the USA. In the 80s he made several appearances in the UK, and released the old Elvis Presley favourite 'Always On My Mind', backed with 'The Wind Beneath My Wings' from the Bette Midler hit movie *Beaches*. This was followed by *A Garden In The Rain*, a set of UK numbers that included 'My Kind Of Girl', 'Yesterday', 'I Hadn't Anyone Till You' and Noël Coward's theme tune, 'I'll See You Again'. In the 90s, the old hits were still being repackaged and sold to a younger audience following Mitchell's appearance in John Byrne's UK television drama *Your Cheatin' Heart*, in 1990. During the filming in the UK he took the opportunity to play a number of country festival gigs.

In 1991, during a tour of Australia he had a horse-riding accident that resulted in serious internal injuries. He spent some time in intensive care but made a complete recovery. In 1997, he was diagnosed as having leukemia and started a course of treatment. Complications from the treatment resulted in a fatal blood clot causing gangrene in the stomach. He had a loyal following in the UK (where arguably he was more popular); these devotees of 50s nostalgia subscribe to a regular magazine *Mitchell Music* – it is remarkable that their enthusiasm remains as strong nearly 50 years after his heyday. Mitchell typified 50s pop more than any other performer, and his catalogue of hits remains formidable. His work is destined to endure way beyond his death in 1999.

● ALBUMS: *Songs Of The Open Spaces* 10-inch album (Columbia 1952) ★★★ UK title *Guy Mitchell Sings* (Columbia 1954) ★★★, *Red Garters* film soundtrack (Columbia 1954) ★★★, *The Voice Of Your Choice* 10-inch album (Philips 1955) ★★★, *A Guy In Love* (Columbia/Philips 1958) ★★★★, as Al Grant *Sincerely Yours* (King 1959) ★★★, *Sunshine Guitar* (Columbia/Philips 1960) ★★★★, *Traveling Shoes* (Starday/London 1967) ★★★, *Singin' Up A Storm* (Starday 1969) ★★★, *The Roving Kind* (Encore 1981) ★★★, *A Garden In The Rain* (President 1985) ★★★, *Dusty The Magic Elf* Australia only (1996) ★.
● COMPILATIONS: *Guy Mitchell's Greatest Hits* (Columbia 1958) ★★★★, *Showcase Of Hits* (Philips 1958) ★★★★, *The Best Of Guy Mitchell* (CBS 1966) ★★★, *American Legend – 16 Greatest Hits* (Embassy 1977) ★★★★, *The Hit Singles 1950-1960* (CBS 1980) ★★★★, *20 Golden Pieces Of Guy Mitchell* (Bulldog 1984) ★★★★, *Guy's Greatest Hits* (Cameo 1984) ★★★★, *Singing The Blues* (Castle 1986) ★★★★, *Portrait Of A Song Stylist* (Masterpiece 1989) ★★★, *Sweep Your Blues Away* (Top Hat 1989) ★★★, *Heartaches By The Number* (Bear Family 1990) ★★★★, *20 All Time Hits* (MFP 1991) ★★★★, *16 Most Requested Songs* (Columbia/Legacy 1992) ★★★★, *The Essential Collection* (Columbia/Legacy 1993) ★★★★.
● FURTHER READING: *Mitchell Music*, privately published UK fanzine.

● FILMS: *Those Redheads From Seattle* (1953), *Red Garters* (1954), *The Wild Westerners* (1962).

MODERN JAZZ QUARTET

Often described as the greatest small group in jazz. In 1951, four musicians who had previously played together in the Dizzy Gillespie big band formed a small recording group. Known as the Milt Jackson Quartet, the group consisted of Jackson (b. 1 January 1923, Detroit, Michigan, USA, d. 9 October 1999, New York City, New York, USA; vibraphone), John Lewis (b. John Aaron Lewis, 3 May 1920, LaGrange, Illinois, USA, d. 29 March 2001, New York, USA; piano), Ray Brown (b. 13 October 1926, Pittsburgh, Pennsylvania, USA; bass), and Kenny Clarke (b. 9 January 1914, Pittsburgh, Pennsylvania, USA, d. 26 January 1985, Paris, France; drums). Brown's place was soon taken by Percy Heath (b. 30 April 1923, Wilmington, North Carolina, USA), and by the following year, the group had adopted the name Modern Jazz Quartet. Although initially only a recording group, they then began playing concert engagements. In 1955, Clarke dropped out to be replaced by Connie Kay (b. Conrad Henry Kirnon, 27 April 1927, Tuckahoe, New York, USA, d. 30 November 1994, New York City, New York, USA). The new line-up of Jackson, Lewis, Heath and Kay continued performing as a full-time ensemble for the next few years, later reducing their collective commitments to several months each year. Seen as both a black response to the intellectualism of the Dave Brubeck quartet and New York's answer to west coast cool jazz, the MJQ were both very popular and very controversial, their detractors claiming that their music was too delicate and too cerebral. Whatever the case, there was certainly no denying that the group brought the dignity and professionalism of a classical quartet to their jazz performances. In 1974, the MJQ was disbanded, but re-formed once more in 1981 for a concert tour of Japan. The success of this comeback convinced the members to reunite on a semi-permanent basis, which they did in the following year. Since 1982 they have continued to play concert and festival dates. Among the most sophisticated of all bop ensembles, the MJQ's directing influence has always been Lewis, whose sober performing and composing style was never more apparent than in this context. Lewis' interest in classical music has been influential in MJQ performances, thus placing the group occasionally, and possibly misleadingly, on the fringes of third-stream jazz. The playing of Heath and Kay in this, as in most other settings in which they work, is distinguished by its subtle swing. Of the four, Jackson was the most musically volatile, and the restraints placed upon him in the MJQ created intriguing formal tensions which were, in jazz terms, one of the most exciting aspects of the group's immaculately played, quietly serious music.

● ALBUMS: *Modern Jazz Quartet With Milt Jackson* (Prestige 1953) ★★★★, *Modern Jazz Quartet Vol 2* (Prestige 1953) ★★★, *Django* (Pres 1954) ★★★★, *Concorde* (Prestige 1955) ★★★★, *Modern Jazz Quartet* (Savoy 1955) ★★★, *The Artistry Of* (Prestige 1956) ★★★★, *The MJQ At Music Inn* (Atlantic 1956) ★★★, *Django* (Prestige 1956) ★★★★, *Fontessa* (Atlantic 1956) ★★★★, *Live* (Jazz Anthology 1956) ★★★, *One Never Knows* (1957) ★★★, *MJQ* (Atlantic 1957) ★★★★, *Live At The Lighthouse* (Atlantic 1957) ★★★★, *At Music Inn: Vol 2* (Atlantic 1958) ★★★, *Odds Against Tomorrow* (1959) ★★★, *Longing For The Continent* (LRC 1959) ★★★, *European Concert* (Atlantic 1960) ★★★, *Patterns* (United Artists 1960) ★★★, *Third Stream Music: MJQ And Guests* (Atlantic 1960) ★★★, *Pyramid* (Atlantic 1960) ★★★★, *MJQ And Orchestra* (Atlantic 1961) ★★, *Lonely Woman* (Atlantic 1962) ★★★, *The Comedy* (Atlantic 1962) ★★★, *The Sheriff* (Atlantic 1964) ★★★, with Laurindo Almeida *Collaboration* (Atlantic 1964) ★★★, *A Quartet Is A Quartet Is A Quartet* (Atlantic 1964) ★★★, *Plays Gershwin's Porgy And Bess* (Atlantic 1965) ★★★, *Play For Lovers* (Prestige 1966) ★★★, *Plays Jazz Classics* (Prestige 1966) ★★★, *Jazz Dialogue* (Atlantic 1966) ★★★, *Blues At Carnegie Hall* (Atlantic 1967) ★★★, *Under The Jasmine Tree* (Apple 1968) ★★, *Space* (Apple 1969) ★★, *Plastic Dreams* (Atlantic 1971) ★★, *The Legendary Profile* (Atlantic 1972) ★★★, *Blues On Bach* (Atlantic 1974) ★★★★, *The Complete Last Concert* (Atlantic 1974) ★★★★, *In Memoriam* (1977) ★★★, *Together Again!* (Pablo 1982) ★★★, *Together Again!: Echoes* (Pablo 1984) ★★★, *Three Windows* (Atlantic 1987) ★★★, *For Ellington* (East West 1988) ★★★, *MJQ & Friends* (Atlantic 1994) ★★★, *A Celebration* (Atlantic 1994) ★★★, *In A Crowd* 1963 live recording (Douglas Music 1998) ★★★.

● COMPILATIONS: *MJQ 40* 4-CD box set (Atlantic 1992) ★★★★.

● VIDEOS: *40 Years Of MJQ* (View Video 1995).

MODUGNO, DOMENICO

b. 9 January 1928, Polignano a Mare, Italy, d. 6 August 1994, Lampeduso. Modugno disappointed his father, a civic dignitary, by rejecting higher education to seek a career as a film actor in Rome. However, although he passed an entrance examination to drama college, National Service postponed entry for two years. Among the parts he gained on graduation was that of a balladeer in 1955's *Il Mantello Rosso*. More conspicuous than expected in this role, he was contracted by both national radio and Fonit Records as a vocalist, with accompaniment that varied from his own lone guitar or accordion to full orchestra. In a developing repertoire were self-composed pieces such as 'Ninna Nanna' (a lullaby penned in 1943), 'Lu Piscispada' and – recorded by many other Latinate artists – 'La Donna Riccia'. While he was runner-up in 1957's Neapolitan Song Festival with 'Lazzarella', 'Nel Blu Dipinto Di Blu' (written with Franco Migliacci) was placed first at the more prestigious San Remo event the following year, and thus flung Modugno into a lucrative round of appearances in venues beyond Italy – including North America. With English lyrics by Mitchell Parish, the opus became better known as 'Volare', a Grammy-earning US chart-topper that also reached the UK Top 10 – despite cover versions by Charlie Drake, Marino Marini and Dean Martin. 1959's 'Piove' – another San Remo winner – was an international smash, too – if overtaken in Britain by a version from Marini – when translated by Parish (as 'Ciao Ciao Bambino'). This and lesser triumphs, such as 'Addio Addio' and 1966's 'Dio Come Ti Amo', blessed Modugno with the dubious title of 'genius', though many claim that his most enduring work was his earliest, as demonstrated by periodic revivals of 'Volare', from Bobby Rydell in 1960 to David Bowie in 1986's *Absolute Beginners* movie.

MONOTONES

Formed in 1955 in Newark, New Jersey, USA, the Monotones recorded one of the most memorable doo-wop novelty songs of the 50s, 'Book Of Love'. The group was a sextet, Warren Davis, George Malone, Charles Patrick, Frank Smith, and John and Warren Ryanes. They had sung in the same church choir as Dionne Warwick and Cissy Houston before forming their own group. In 1956, they appeared on the *Ted Mack's Amateur Hour* television programme, singing the Cadillacs' 'Zoom'. They won first prize and began to think more seriously about a career in music. Inspired by a television commercial for toothpaste ('You'll wonder where the yellow went when you brush your teeth with Pepsodent'), Patrick, Malone and Davis wrote 'Book Of Love' to a similar melody. They recorded it at Bell Studio in New York and it was released on the small Mascot label, a subsidiary of Hull Records. It was then picked up by Argo Records for national distribution and ultimately reached number 5 in the USA. The group was touring when their record entered the charts, and months passed before they had a chance to record a follow-up. A single called 'Tom Foolery' was released but failed to chart; the third, 'The Legend Of Sleepy Hollow', was a fine record and is still played on doo-wop radio programmes today, but it also failed to chart in its own time. After a few more singles, the Monotones gave up, although some of the original members performed under that name in the 90s. John Ryanes died on 30 May 1972.
● COMPILATIONS: *Who Wrote The Book Of Love?* (Collectables 1992) ★★★.

MONROE, BILL

b. William Smith Monroe, 13 September 1911, on a farm near Rosine, Ohio County, Kentucky, USA, d. 9 September 1996, Springfield, Tennessee, USA. The Monroes were a musical family; his father, known affectionately as Buck, was a noted step-dancer, his mother played fiddle, accordion and harmonica, and was respected locally as a singer of old-time songs. Among the siblings, elder brothers Harry and Birch both played fiddle, and brother Charlie and sister Bertha played guitar. They were all influenced by their uncle, Pendleton Vanderver, who was a fiddler of considerable talent, and noted for his playing at local events. (Monroe later immortalized him in

one of his best-known numbers, 'Uncle Pen', with tribute lines such as 'Late in the evening about sundown; high on the hill above the town, Uncle Pen played the fiddle, oh, how it would ring. You can hear it talk, you can hear it sing').

At the age of nine, Monroe began to concentrate on the mandolin; his first choice had been the guitar or fiddle, but his brothers pointed out that no family member played mandolin, and as the baby, he was given little choice, although he still kept up his guitar playing. His mother died when he was 10, followed soon after by his father. He moved in to live with Uncle Pen and they were soon playing guitar together at local dances. Monroe also played with a black blues musician, Arnold Schultz, who was to become a major influence on his future music. After the death of his father, most of the family moved away in their search for work. Birch and Charlie headed north, working for a time in the car industry in Detroit, before moving to Whiting and East Chicago, Indiana, where they were employed in the oil refineries. When he was 18, Bill joined them, and for four years worked at the Sinclair refinery. At one time, during the Depression, Bill was the only one with work, and the three began to play for local dances to raise money.

In 1932, the three Monroe brothers and their girlfriends became part of a team of dancers and toured with a show organized by WLS Chicago, the radio station responsible for the *National Barn Dance* programme. They also played on local radio stations, including WAE Hammond and WJKS Gary, Indiana. In 1934, Bill, finding the touring conflicted with his work, decided to become a full-time musician. Soon afterwards, they received an offer to tour for Texas Crystals (the makers of a patent purgative medicine), which sponsored radio programmes in several states. Birch, back in employment at Sinclair and also looking after a sister, decided against a musical career. Bill married in 1935, and between then and 1936, he and Charlie (appearing as the Monroe Brothers) had stays at various stations, including Shenandoah, Columbia, Greenville and Charlotte. In 1936, they moved to the rival and much larger Crazy Water Crystals and, until 1938, they worked on the noted *Crazy Barn Dance* at WBT Charlotte for that company. They became a very popular act and sang mainly traditional material, often with a blues influence. Charlie always provided the lead vocal, and Bill added tenor harmonies.

In February 1936, they made their first recordings on the Bluebird Records label, which proved popular. Further sessions followed, and in total they cut some 60 tracks for the label. Early in 1938, the brothers decided that they should follow their own careers. Charlie kept the recording contract and formed his own band, the Kentucky Pardners. Since he had always handled all lead vocals, he found things easier and soon established himself in his own right. Prior to the split, Bill had never recorded an instrumental or a vocal solo, but he had ideas that he wished to put into practice. He moved to KARK Little Rock, where he formed his first band, the Kentuckians. This failed to satisfy him, and he soon moved to Atlanta, where he worked on the noted *Crossroad Follies*; at this point, he formed the first of the bands he would call the Blue Grass Boys. In 1939, he made his first appearance on the *Grand Ole Opry*, singing his version of 'New Muleskinner Blues', after which George D. Hay (the Solemn Old Judge) told him, 'Bill, if you ever leave the Opry, it'll be because you fire yourself' (over 50 years later, he was still there).

During the early 40s, Monroe's band was similar to other string bands such as Mainer's Mountaineers, but by the middle of the decade, the leading influence of Monroe's driving mandolin and his high (some would say shrill) tenor singing became the dominant factor, and set the Blue Grass Boys of Bill Monroe apart from the other bands. This period gave birth to a new genre of music, and led to Monroe becoming affectionately known as the Father of Bluegrass Music. He began to tour with the *Grand Ole Opry* roadshows, and his weekly network WSM radio work soon made him a national name. In 1940 and 1941, he recorded a variety of material for RCA-Victor Records, including gospel songs, old-time numbers and instrumentals such as the 'Orange Blossom Special' (the second known recording of the number). Wartime restrictions prevented him from recording between 1941 and early 1945, but later that year, he cut tracks for Columbia Records. In 1946, he gained his first hits when his own song, 'Kentucky Waltz', reached number 3, and his now-immortal recording of 'Footprints In The Snow' reached number 5 in the US country charts. By 1945, several fiddle players had made their impact on the band's overall sound, including Chubby Wise, Art Wooten, Tommy Magness, Howdy Forrester and in 1945, guitarist/vocalist Lester Flatt and banjo player Earl Scruggs joined. Stringbean had provided the comedy and the banjo playing since 1942, although it was generally reckoned later that his playing contributed little to the overall sound that Monroe sought. Scruggs' style of playing was very different, and it quickly became responsible for not only establishing his own name as one of the greatest exponents of the instrument, but also for making bluegrass music an internationally identifiable sound. It was while Flatt and Scruggs were with the band that Monroe first recorded his now-immortal song 'Blue Moon Of Kentucky'. By 1948, other bands such as the Stanley Brothers were beginning to reflect the influence of Monroe, and bluegrass music was firmly established.

During the 40s, Monroe toured with his tent show, which included his famous baseball team (the reason for Stringbean's first connections with Monroe), which played against local teams as an attraction before the musical show began. In 1951, he bought some land at Bean Blossom, Brown County, Indiana, and established a country park, which became the home for bluegrass music shows. He was involved in a very serious car accident in January 1953, and was unable to perform for several months. In 1954, Elvis Presley recorded Monroe's 'Blue Moon Of Kentucky' in a 4/4 rock tempo and sang it at his solitary appearance on the *Grand Ole Opry*. A dejected Presley found the performance made no impact with the *Opry* audience, but the song became a hit. It also led to Monroe re-recording it in a style that, like the original, started as a waltz, but after a verse and chorus featuring three fiddles, it changed to 4/4 tempo; Monroe repeated the vocal in the new style. (N.B. Paul McCartney's 1991 *Unplugged* album features a version in both styles).

Monroe toured extensively throughout the 50s, and had chart success in 1958 with his own instrumental number, 'Scotland'. He used the twin fiddles of Kenny Baker and Bobby Hicks to produce the sound of bagpipes behind his own mandolin – no doubt his tribute to his family's Scottish ancestry. By the end of the decade, the impact of rock 'n' roll was affecting his record sales and music generally. By this time, Flatt and Scruggs were firmly established with their own band and finding success on television and at folk festivals. Monroe was a strong-willed person and it was not always easy for those who worked with him, or for him, to achieve the perfect arrangement. He had stubborn ideas, and in 1959, he refused to play a major concert in Carnegie Hall, because he believed that Alan Lomax, the organizer, was a communist. He was also suspicious of the press and rarely, if ever, gave interviews. In 1962, however, he became friendly with Ralph Rinzler, a writer and member of the Greenbriar Boys, who became his manager. In 1963, Monroe played his first folk festival at the University of Chicago. He soon created a great interest among students generally and, with Rinzler's planning, he was soon busily connected with festivals devoted solely to bluegrass music. In 1965, he was involved with the major Roanoke festival in Virginia, and in 1967, he started his own at Bean Blossom. During the 60s, many young musicians benefited from their time as a member of Monroe's band, including Bill Keith, Peter Rowan, Byron Berline, Roland White and Del McCoury.

In 1969, he was made an honorary Kentucky Colonel, and in 1970, was elected to the Country Music Hall Of Fame in Nashville. The plaque stated: 'The Father of Bluegrass Music. Bill Monroe developed and perfected this music form and taught it to a great many names in the industry'. Some of the biggest names in country music started as members of Monroe's band before progressing to their own careers. In addition to the names already mentioned, these included Clyde Moody, Jim Eanes, Mac Wiseman, Jimmy Martin, Vassar Clements, Carter Stanley, Sonny Osborne, and his own son James Monroe. Monroe wrote many songs, including 'Memories Of Mother And Dad', 'When The Golden Leaves Begin To Fall', 'My Little Georgia Rose', 'Blue Moon Of Kentucky' and countless others. Many were written using pseudonyms such as Albert Price, James B. Smith and James W. Smith. In 1971, his talent as a songwriter saw him elected to the Nashville Songwriters' Association International Hall Of Fame. Amazingly, bearing in mind his popularity, Monroe's last chart entry was 'Gotta Travel On', a Top 20 country hit in March 1959.

Monroe kept up a hectic touring schedule throughout the 70s, but in 1981, he was diagnosed with cancer. He survived after treatment and, during the 80s, maintained a schedule that would have daunted much younger men. In 1984, he recorded the album *Bill Monroe And Friends*, which contains some of his songs sung as duets with other artists, including the Oak Ridge Boys ('Blue Moon Of Kentucky'), Emmylou Harris ('Kentucky Waltz'), Barbara Mandrell ('My Rose Of Old Kentucky'), Ricky Skaggs ('My Sweet Darling') and Willie Nelson ('The Sunset Trail'). Johnny Cash, who also appeared on the album, presumably did not know any Monroe songs because they sang Cash's own 'I Still Miss Someone'. Monroe continued to play the *Grand Ole Opry*, and in 1989, he celebrated his 50th year as a member, the occasion being marked by MCA recording a live concert from the stage. The subsequent album became his first ever release on the new CD format. He underwent surgery for a double coronary bypass on 9 August 1991, but by October, he was back performing and once again hosting his normal *Grand Ole Opry* show. His records continued to be collected, with the German Bear Family Records label releasing box sets on compact disc of his Decca Records recordings. (Between 1950, when he first recorded for Decca and 1969, he made almost 250 recordings for the label.) The acknowledged 'father of bluegrass music' died a few days before his 85th birthday in 1996.

● ALBUMS: *Knee Deep In Bluegrass* (Decca 1958) ★★★, *I Saw The Light* (Decca 1959) ★★★, *Mr. Bluegrass* (Decca 1960) ★★★, *The Great Bill Monroe & The Blue Grass Boys* (Harmony 1961) ★★★, *Bluegrass Ramble* (Decca 1962) ★★★, with Rose Maddox *Rose Maddox Sings Bluegrass* (Decca 1962) ★★★, *The Father Of Bluegrass Music* (Decca 1962) ★★★, *My All-Time Country Favorites* (Decca 1962) ★★★, as the Monroe Brothers *Early Bluegrass Music* (Camden 1963) ★★★, *Bluegrass Special* (Decca 1963) ★★★★, *Bill Monroe Sings Country Songs* (Decca 1964) ★★★, *I'll Meet You In Church Sunday Morning* (Decca 1964) ★★★, *Original Bluegrass Sound* (Harmony 1965) ★★★, *Bluegrass Instrumentals* (Decca 1965) ★★★, *The High Lonesome Sound Of Bill Monroe* (Decca 1966) ★★★, *Bluegrass Time* (Decca 1967) ★★★, as the Monroe Brothers *The Monroe Brothers, Bill & Charlie* (Decca 1969) ★★★, *I Saw The Light* (Decca 1969) ★★★, *A Voice From On High* (Decca 1969) ★★★, *Bluegrass Style* (Vocalion 1970) ★★★, *Kentucky Bluegrass* (Decca 1970) ★★★, *Bill Monroe's Country Hall Of Fame* (Decca 1971) ★★★★, *Uncle Pen* (Decca 1972) ★★★, *Bean Blossom* (Decca 1973) ★★★, with James Monroe *Father And Son* (Decca 1973) ★★★, *The Road Of Life* (Decca 1974) ★★★, with Birch Monroe *Brother Birch Monroe Plays Old-Time Fiddle Favorites* (Decca 1975) ★★★, with Doc Watson *Bill*

& Doc Sing Country Songs (FBN 1975) ★★★, as the Monroe Brothers *Feast Here Tonight* (Bluebird 1975) ★★★, with Kenny Baker *Kenny Baker Plays Bill Monroe* (Decca 1976) ★★★, *Weary Traveller* (Decca 1976) ★★★, *Sings Bluegrass, Body And Soul* (Decca 1977) ★★★, *Bluegrass Memories* (Decca 1977) ★★★, with James Monroe *Together Again* (Decca 1978) ★★★, *Bill Monroe With Lester Flatt & Earl Scruggs: The Original Bluegrass Band* (Rounder 1979) ★★★★, *Bluegrass Classic (Radio Shows 1946-1948)* (MCA 1980) ★★★, *Bean Blossom 1979* (MCA 1980) ★★★, *Orange Blossom Special (Recorded Live At Melody Ranch)* (MCA 1981) ★★, *Master Of Bluegrass* (MCA 1981) ★★★, *Bill Monroe & Friends* (MCA 1984) ★★★, *Bluegrass '87* (MCA 1987) ★★★, *Southern Flavor* (MCA 1988) ★★★, *Live At The Opry: Celebrating 50 Years On The Grand Ole Opry* (MCA 1989) ★★★, *Muleskinner Blues* 1940-41 recordings (RCA 1991) ★★★.

● COMPILATIONS: *Bill Monroe & His Blue Grass Boys (16 Hits)* (Columbia 1970) ★★★, *The Classic Bluegrass Recordings Volume 1* (County 1980) ★★★, *The Classic Bluegrass Recordings Volume 2* (County 1980) ★★★, *MCA Singles Collection Volumes 1, 2 & 3* (MCA 1983) ★★★, *Columbia Historic Edition* (Columbia 1987) ★★★, *Bill Monroe Bluegrass 1950-1958* 4-CD box set (Bear Family 1989) ★★★★, *Country Music Hall Of Fame* (MCA 1991) ★★★★, *Bill Monroe Bluegrass 1959-1969* 4-CD box set (Bear Family 1991) ★★★★, *The Essential Bill Monroe 1945-1949* (Columbia/Legacy 1992) ★★★★, with the Blue Grass Boys *Live Recordings 1956-1969: Off The Record Volume 1* (Smithsonian/Folkways 1993) ★★★, with Doc Watson *Live Duet Recordings 1963-80* (Smithsonian/Folkways 1993) ★★★, *The Music Of Bill Monroe* 4-CD box set (MCA 1994) ★★★★, *Bluegrass (1970-1979)* 4-CD box set (Bear Family 1995) ★★★★, *16 Gems* (Columbia/Legacy 1996) ★★★★, *The Essential Bill Monroe And Monroe Brothers* (RCA 1997) ★★★★, *The Early Years* (Vanguard 1998) ★★★.

● FURTHER READING: *Bossmen: Bill Monroe And Muddy Waters*, J. Rooney. *Bill Monroe And His Blue Grass Boys*, Neil V. Rosenberg. *Can't You Hear Me Callin': The Life Of Bill Monroe*, Richard D. Smith.

MONROE, MARILYN
b. Norma Jean Mortenson, 1 June 1926, Los Angeles, California, USA, d. 5 August 1962, Brentwood, California, USA. As well as being a talented comedienne and the number 1 sex symbol in movies during the 50s, Monroe proved to be an appealing interpreter of flirtatious ballads in several of her most popular films. As one of the *Ladies Of The Chorus* (1948), she made a promising start with Lester Lee and Allan Roberts' 'Every Baby Needs A Da-Da-Daddy', which, with its reference to 'Tiffany's', was a precursor to one of her most celebrated performances a few years later, when the same New York store cropped up in 'Diamonds Are A Girl's Best Friend', from Jule Styne and Leo Robin's score for *Gentlemen Prefer Blondes* (1953). In that film Monroe duetted with another of Hollywood's top glamour girls, Jane Russell, on 'Two Little Girls From Little Rock', 'Bye Bye, Baby' and a Hoagy Carmichael/Harold

Adamson number, 'When Loves Goes Wrong'. Co-starring with Robert Mitchum in *River Of No Return* (1954), Monroe's role as a saloon singer conveniently gave her the opportunity to perform the title song and 'I'm Gonna File My Claim', among others, and, in the same year, she registered strongly with a bundle of Irving Berlin numbers in *There's No Business Like Show Business*. These included 'A Man Chases A Girl (Until She Catches Him)' (with Donald O'Connor), 'After You Get What You Want You Don't Want It', 'Heatwave', 'Lazy' and 'You'd Be Surprised'. In 1959 she made what became her most commercially successful film – and arguably the highlight of her career. The classic *Some Like It Hot*, with Tony Curtis, Jack Lemmon and Joe E. ('nobody's perfect') Brown, featured some of Monroe's most effective vocal performances, such as 'I'm Through With Love', 'I Wanna Be Loved By You' and 'Running Wild'. She sang for the last time on screen in *Let's Make Love* (1960). Apart from contributing the film's high spot, a compelling version of 'My Heart Belongs To Daddy', Monroe duetted with two European heart-throbs, Yves Montand and Frankie Vaughan, on Sammy Cahn and Jimmy Van Heusen's 'Specialization', 'Incurably Romantic' and the title song. Her final performance, a sultry rendering of 'Happy Birthday Mr. President' and 'Thanks For The Memory', was given in May 1962 for President Kennedy's birthday celebrations in Madison Square Garden. Just over two months later she died as the result of an overdose of barbiturates, at the age of 36 (Monroe's death has since been the subject of numerous conspiracy theories, most of which concern her alleged affair with John F. Kennedy). One of the musical selections chosen for her funeral service was a recording of 'Over The Rainbow' sung by Judy Garland, another showbusiness legend who met a tragic end. Since her death, it has been estimated that over 100 Monroe biographies have been published. She was also the subject of several songs, the most famous being Elton John's 'Candle In the Wind'. Others included James Cunningham's 'Norma Jean Wants To Be A Movie Star' and 'Elvis And Marilyn' by Leon Russell.

● COMPILATIONS: *Marilyn* (20th Century Fox 1962) ★★★, *Collection: 20 Golden Greats* (Deja Vu 1985) ★★★★, *Marilyn Monroe: The Complete Recordings* (Rare 1988) ★★★, *The Marilyn Monroe Story* (Deja Vu 1989) ★★★, *The Very Best Of* (Stardust 2000) ★★★.

● VIDEOS: *Marilyn And The Kennedys (Say Goodbye To The President)* (Weinerworld 1998).

● FURTHER READING: *Marilyn*, Norman Mailer. *Marilyn Monroe: The Biography*, Donald Spoto. *Goddess: Secret Lives Of Marilyn Monroe*, Anthony Summers. *The Complete Films Of Marilyn Monroe*, Mark Ricci and Michael Conway, *Young Marilyn Becoming The Legend* James Haspiel. *Marilyn Monroe*, Barbara Leaming.

● FILMS: *Dangerous Years* (1948), *Ladies Of The Chorus* (1948), *Love Happy* (1950), *A Ticket To Tomahawk* (1950), *The Asphalt Jungle* (1950), *All About Eve* (1950), *The Fireball* (1950), *Right Cross* (1950), *Home Town Story* (1951), *As Young As You Feel* (1951), *Love Nest* (1951), *Let's Make It Legal* (1951), *We're Not Married* (1952), *Clash By Night* (1952), *Full House* (1952), *Monkey Business* (1952), *Don't Bother To Knock* (1952), *Niagara* (1952), *Gentlemen Prefer Blondes* (1953), *How To Marry A Millionaire* (1953), *River Of No Return* (1954), *There's No Business Like Show Business* (1954), *The Seven-Year Itch* (1955), *Bus Stop* (1956), *The Prince And The Showgirl* (1957), *Some Like It Hot* (1959), *Let's Make Love* (1960), *The Misfits* (1960).

MONTGOMERY, BOB

b. 1936, Lambasas, Texas, USA. While attending Lubbock's Hutchinson High School, this rhythm guitarist was partnered by Buddy Holly as a 'Singer of Western and Bop' when entertaining at parents' evenings, parties and, indeed, 'anywhere we could get to a microphone'. Sometimes augmented by the younger Larry Welborn on double bass, they were heard regularly on local radio with Montgomery as main vocalist in a repertoire that embraced his (and Holly's) own compositions. Among these were 'Flower Of My Heart' and other items taped as demos in the mid-50s. With superimposed backing, these would be released after Holly's death gave them historical importance, as it was Buddy who was singled out by Decca Records in 1956 as the most commercial talent. However, not begrudging him his luck, Montgomery continued to write songs with his friend, among them 'Wishing', 'Love's Made A Fool Of You' and other Holly hits. After serving as engineer in Norman Petty's Clovis studio, Montgomery moved to Nashville in 1959 where, as a songwriter, he provided Wilma Burgess with 'Misty Blue' (revived in 1976 by Dorothy Moore), 'Two Of A Kind' (written with Earl Sinks) for Sue Thompson and Roy Orbison, and 1965's 'Wind Me Up' for Cliff Richard. Among other recipients of Montgomery pieces were Bob Luman and Mel Tillis. In 1966, he became a United Artists staff producer. His most enduring labours in this sphere were for Bobby Goldsboro (including 'Honey' and 'Summer (The First Time)') but other ventures into what was to be named 'country-pop' included records by Bill Dees, Johnny Darrell, Buddy Knox, Del Reeves and Earl Richards. In the early 70s, Montgomery founded House Of Gold, one of Nashville's most respected music publishing concerns.

MOONDOG

b. Louis Thomas Hardin, 26 May 1916, Marysville, Kansas, USA, d. 8 September 1999, Münster, Germany. This idiosyncratic composer lost his sight at the age of 16 following an accident with a dynamite cap. He was introduced to classical music at the Iowa School for the Blind, studying violin, viola and piano. Hardin moved to New York in 1943, attending rehearsals of the New York Philharmonic at Carnegie Hall, but by the mid-40s he had opted for a life as a 'street musician'. He took the name Moondog in 1947 and established a pitch on the city's fabled Times Square. Such was his fame, Hardin successfully retained this sobriquet after issuing legal proceedings against disc jockey Alan Freed, who had claimed the 'Moondog' name for his radio show. In a manner similar to fellow maverick Harry Partch, Moondog constructed his own instruments, claiming conventional scales could not reproduce the sounds heard in his head. This was immediately apparent on his first release, *On The Streets Of New York* (1953), a 45 rpm EP issued by Epic and London/American.

Percussive devices, named the 'oo' and 'trimba', were at the fore of albums recorded for the Prestige Records label, notably *More Moondog* and *The Story Of Moondog*, although a distinctive jazz influence could also be detected. Further releases ensued, including *Moondog And His Honking Geese*, which the composer financed and distributed. Hardin also arranged an album of Mother Goose songs for singer Julie Andrews. During the 60s Moondog continued to perform and beg on the city's streets, but his unconventional lifestyle and appearance – he wrapped himself in army surplus blankets and wore a Viking-styled helmet – found succour in the emergent counter-culture. He performed with anti-establishment comedian Lenny Bruce and eccentric singer Tiny Tim, while several groups, including Big Brother And the Holding Company and the Insect Trust, recorded his distinctive musical rounds. In 1969, Jim Guercio, producer of the highly successful band Chicago, introduced Moondog to CBS Records. Buoyed by a full orchestra, *Moondog* encapsulated 20 years of compositions, showing musical references to such diverse figures as Stravinsky and Charlie Parker, the latter of whom often conversed with Moondog. One particular selection, 'The Witch Of Endor', is now regarded as one of his finest pieces. *Moondog 2* was a collection of rounds, inspired by the recognition afforded the composer by the hip cognoscenti. In 1974 Moondog undertook a tour of Germany where he opted to settle. 'I am a European at heart', he later stated. A further series of albums maintained his unique musical vision. Although he ceased recording for over 20 years, interest in this fascinating individual continued to flourish, and he performed at London's Meltdown festival in 1995. Two years later Atlantic Records released an album recorded with nine saxophonists and a stellar cast of British musicians, including Danny Thompson and Peter Hammill.

● ALBUMS: *Moondog And His Friends* 10-inch album (Epic 1954) ★★★, *Moondog* i (Prestige 1956) ★★★★, *More Moondog* (Prestige 1956) ★★★, *The Story Of Moondog* (Prestige 1957) ★★★, *Moondog* ii (Columbia 1969) ★★★★, *Moondog 2* (Columbia 1971) ★★★, *Moondog In Europe* (Kopf 1978) ★★★, *H'Art Songs* (Kopf 1979) ★★★, *A New Sound Of An Old Instrument* (Kopf 1980) ★★★, with the London Saxophonic *Sax Pax For A Sax* (Atlantic 1997) ★★★.

MOONGLOWS

This R&B vocal group was formed in Cleveland, Ohio, USA, in 1952. If there were any group that best signalled the birth of rock 'n' roll – by which R&B emerged out of its black subculture into mainstream teen culture – it was the Moonglows. The group's career paralleled that of their mentor, legendary disc jockey Alan Freed, who during his rise in rock 'n' roll made the Moonglows the mainstays of his radio programmes, motion pictures and stage shows. He was also responsible for naming the group, who originally performed as the Crazy Sounds. Their membership comprised lead singer Bobby Lester (b. 13 January 1930, Louisville, Kentucky, USA, d. 15 October 1980), Harvey Fuqua (b. 27 July 1929, Louisville, Kentucky, USA; his uncle was Charlie Fuqua of the Ink Spots), Alexander 'Pete' Graves (b. 17 April 1930, Cleveland, Ohio, USA), and Prentiss Barnes (b. 12 April 1925, Magnolia, Mississippi, USA). After recording for Freed's Champagne label in 1953, the group signed with Chicago-based Chance Records, where they managed to secure a few regional hits, most notably a cover version of Doris Day's 'Secret Love' in 1954.

Freed used his connections to sign the Moonglows to a stronger Chicago label, the fast-rising Chess Records, and the group enjoyed a major hit with 'Sincerely' (number 1 R&B/number 20 pop, 1954). Joining the group at this time was guitarist Billy Johnson (b. 1924, Hartford, Connecticut, USA, d. 1987). Using a novel technique they called 'blow harmony', other great hits followed: 'Most Of All' (number 5 R&B, 1955), 'We Go Together' (number 9 R&B, 1956), 'See Saw' (number 6 R&B/number 25 pop, 1956), all of which featured Lester on lead; and a remake of Percy Mayfield's 'Please Send Me Someone To Love' (number 5 R&B/number 73 pop, 1957). The original Moonglows disbanded in 1958, and Fuqua put together a new group called Harvey And The Moonglows that included a young Marvin Gaye. Featuring Fuqua on lead, 'Ten Commandments Of Love' (number 9 R&B/number 22 pop, 1958) was the last of the group's major hits. In 1960 Fuqua disbanded this group and he and Gaye went to Detroit to work in the city's burgeoning music industry. Fuqua worked with Berry Gordy's sister, Gwen Gordy, on the Anna label and Gaye joined Berry Gordy's Motown Records operation. Fuqua carved out a very successful career as a producer and record executive, working with Motown artists in the 60s and a stable of Louisville artists in the 70s on the RCA Records label. Fuqua, Lester and Graves reunited in 1972, with new members Doc Williams and Chuck Lewis.

● ALBUMS: *Look! It's The Moonglows* (Chess 1959) ★★★, *The Return Of The Moonglows* (RCA Victor 1972) ★★★, *The Moonglows On Stage* (Relic 1992) ★★.

● COMPILATIONS: *The Best Of Bobby Lester And The Moonglows* (Chess 1962) ★★★, *The Moonglows* (Constellation 1964) ★★★, *Moonglows* (Chess 1976) ★★★, *Their Greatest Sides* (Chess 1984) ★★★, *Blue Velvet: The Ultimate Collection* (MCA/Chess 1993) ★★★★, *The Flamingos Meet the Moonglows: 'On The Dusty Road Of Hits': The Complete 25 Chance Sides* (Vee Jay 1993) ★★★, *Their Greatest Hits* (MCA 1997) ★★★.

MOORE, MARILYN

b. 16 June 1931, Oklahoma City, Oklahoma, USA, d. March 1992, Florida, USA. Born into a showbusiness family, Moore began performing at the age of three, singing and dancing in the finale of her family's vaudeville act. As a teenager, she decided to concentrate on singing and soon turned to jazz, working in clubs in Oklahoma City and Chicago. In 1949 she sang with Woody Herman, then with Charlie Ventura and by the early 50s had settled in New York. She sang with various groups, including those led by Ray McKinley, Boyd Raeburn and Al Cohn, whom she married in 1953. They had two children, Lisa and Joe Cohn (now a leading jazz guitarist), and Moore's life became focused upon her home and family. In 1957, however, she was invited to record for Bethlehem and the resulting album, on which she is backed by Cohn, Joe Wilder, Don Abney, Barry Galbraith and other leading jazzmen, attracted a great deal of interest. The following year, she was cast in a jazz show, *Oh Captain!*, recorded by MGM Records in which Coleman Hawkins, Art Farmer, Oscar Pettiford and Harry 'Sweets' Edison also appeared. Soon afterwards, Moore and Cohn were divorced and once again she was tied to home-making and family-raising. Despite a deep desire to go back to professional singing and make more records, she never returned. A warm and sensitive voice marked Moore's work and in her phrasing and overall style there is evidence of her affinity for Billie Holiday. Overlooked and under-recorded (the MGM album was swiftly deleted and never reissued), the quality of Moore's singing on her first album, reissued on CD in 1990, marks her out as one of the great losses to the world of jazz.
● ALBUMS: *Moody Marilyn Moore* (Affinity 1957) ★★★, with others *Oh Captain!* (MGM 1958) ★★.

MOORE, SCOTTY

b. Winfield Scott Moore, 27 December 1931, Gadsden, Tennessee, USA. Guitarist Moore started playing at the age of eight and formed his first band while in the US Navy in 1948. After he left the service he joined the Memphis group Doug Poindexter And His Starlite Wranglers who also included bass player Bill Black. The band recorded Moore's 'My Kind Of Carryin' On' for Sam Phillips' Sun Records label and both Moore and Black played on several other Sun artists' recordings. In June 1954 Phillips invited a young singer he was trying out to Moore's apartment to rehearse some songs: that man was Elvis Presley. A week later, Moore, Presley and Black went into Sun studios to record together for the first time. As a trio (later a quartet with drummer D.J. Fontana) they cut some of Elvis' finest records. When Presley was sold to RCA Records for a 'king's ransom', Moore and Black were taken on as his sidemen on a relatively meagre salary.
Moore had acted as a kind of unpaid manager before Bob Neal and then 'Colonel' Tom Parker took over the role. While Presley was busy filming *Loving You*, Moore and Black headed for the Dallas State Fair where they performed as Scotty

And Bill, Elvis' Original Backing Group. Moore also went to work for the small Memphis label Fernwood Records, whose most successful record was Thomas Wayne's 'Tragedy'. Moore himself released a solo single called 'Have Guitar Will Travel'. During the same period he also played on some sessions for Dale Hawkins at Chess Records. Unlike Black, Moore returned to play with Presley when he came out of the army in 1960, but not for long. Over the next few years he recorded infrequently with Presley and went back to Sun as production manager. Later in the 60s he went to Nashville to start his own studio. Presley invited him back for the 1968 television special, which was the last time Moore played with, or even saw, him. By the 70s Moore had virtually retired from playing to concentrate on production (most notably engineering Ringo Starr's *Beaucoups Of Blues*).
He was enticed out of retirement by Billy Swan to play on his self-titled 1976 album and later played on Ral Donner's Elvis tribute album. By the 80s Moore had established a successful tape copying service in Nashville and rarely picked up his guitar. In 1997, however, Moore recorded a Presley tribute album with Fontana.
● ALBUMS: *The Guitar That Changed The World!* (Epic 1964) ★★★, with Carl Perkins *706 Reunion – A Sentimental Journey* cassette only (Belle Meade 1993) ★★★, with D.J. Fontana *All The King's Men* (Sweetfish/Polydor 1997) ★★★.
● VIDEOS: *Scotty Moore & D.J. Fontana Live In Concert* (1993).
● FURTHER READING: *That's Alright Elvis*, Scotty Moore and James Dickerson.

MORLEY, ANGELA

b. 1924, Sheffield, England. In the 50s, 60s and into the 70s, Wally Stott was a highly respected conductor, arranger and composer on the UK music scene. In the early 70s he underwent a sex-change operation, and was subsequently known professionally as Angela Morley. Stott attended the same Mexboro school as Tony Mercer, who went on to become one of the principal singers with the *Black And White Minstrel Show*. Mercer sang and played the piano accordion, while Stott concentrated on the saxophone. On leaving school, they each spent some time with Archie's Juveniles and Oscar Rabin's Band. Stott's route to Rabin was via the bands of Billy Merrin and Bram Martin. By 1944, after some years with the Rabin Band, Stott was leading the saxophone section on alto, and had become the band's sole arranger: a great future was already being forecast for him. Stott's next move was to Geraldo, with whom he stayed for about four years, leaving in late 1948 to 'pursue arranging and film music work, which he is to make his future career'. He still managed to find the time to play the saxophone for outfits such as Jack Nathan's Coconut Grove Orchestra. In the early 50s Stott joined Philips Records, and soon became one of their key arrangers, along with Peter Knight and Ivor Raymonde. During the next 20 years he arranged and conducted for some of the UK's most popular artists, such as

Frankie Vaughan ('Green Door', 'The Garden Of Eden' and 'The Heart Of A Man'), Anne Shelton ('Lay Down Your Arms' and *My Heart Sings*), Harry Secombe ('This Is My Song'), the Beverley Sisters ('Somebody Bad Stole De Wedding Bell' and 'Happy Wanderer'), Roy Castle (*Newcomer*), Ronnie Carroll ('Say Wonderful Things' and *Carroll Calling*), the Kaye Sisters ('Paper Roses'), Shirley Bassey ('Banana Boat Song' and 'As I Love You'), Muriel Smith ('Hold Me, Thrill Me, Kiss Me'), the Polka Dots (*Nice Work & You Can Buy It*) and many more, plus a few 'foreigners', too, as on *Mel Tormé Meets The British* (1959). Stott also made several of his own instrumental albums, sometimes augmented by a vocal chorus. He began writing music early in his career, and his first significant piece came to light in November 1954, when *Hancock's Half Hour* began. It proved to be one of BBC Radio's most popular programmes, later moving to television, and its opening theme, played on a tuba over Tony Hancock's stuttering introduction, was composed by Stott. He also wrote and arranged the show's instrumental links, and conducted the orchestra for many other radio programmes, including *The Last Goon Show Of All*. Stott composed numerous pieces of mood music for London publishers, especially Chappell's, which included 'A Canadian In Mayfair' (dedicated to Robert Farnon, who gave Stott valuable advice on arranging and composition), 'Mock Turtles', 'Quiz', 'Travelling Along', 'Miss Universe', 'Flight By Jet', 'Casbah', 'Commonwealth March', 'Practice Makes Perfect', 'China', 'Focus On Fashion' and 'Skylight'. In the late 60s and early 70s, Stott wrote the music for several films, including *The Looking Glass War*, *Captain Nemo And The Underwater City* and *When Eight Bells Toll*, and for television productions such as *Hugh And I*, and *The Maladjusted Busker*. Around that time, credits began to be given in the name of Angela Morley, and these include two Academy Award nominations, for her arrangements of Alan Jay Lerner and Frederick Loewe's score for *The Little Prince* (1974), and Richard M. and Robert B. Shermans' score for *The Slipper And The Rose* (1977). Morley also composed for the animated feature *Watership Down*, the Italian production *La Colina Dei Comali*, and for television films such as *Friendships, Secrets And Lies*, *Madame X*, *Summer Girl*, *Two Marriages* and *Threesome* (1984). Most of this work has been completed in the USA, where Morley is reported to have been living for most of the last 20 years.

● ALBUMS: *Wally Stott Tribute To George Gershwin* (Parlophone 1955) ★★★★, *Tribute To Irving Berlin* (Parlophone 1956) ★★★, *Tribute To Jerome Kern* (Parlophone 1957) ★★★★, *London Pride* (1959) ★★★, *Chorale In Concert* (1967) ★★, *Christmas By The Fireside* (1969) ★★.

MOROSS, JEROME

b. 1 August 1913, Brooklyn, New York, USA, d. 25 July 1983, Miami, Florida, USA. A highly regarded composer who wrote symphonic works as well as scores for films and Broadway shows. After graduating from New York University at the age of

18, Moross contributed some incidental music to the theatre, and then composed most of the score for the short-lived Broadway revue *Parade* in 1935. Later in that same year he was engaged by George Gershwin as assistant conductor and pianist for the last few weeks of the New York run of *Porgy And Bess*, and subsequently for the west coast production. Moross moved to Hollywood in 1940 and spent the next decade orchestrating scores for a great many films, including *Our Town*, *Action In The North Atlantic* and *Conflict*. He also worked on Hugo Friedhofer's Oscar-winning score for *The Best Years Of Our Lives* (1946). In 1948 he was given the opportunity to compose his own original score for *Close-Up*, which was followed during the 50s and 60s by others such as *When I Grow Up*, *Captive City*, *The Sharkfighters*, *Hans Christian Andersen* (ballet music only), *Seven Wonders Of The World* (with David Raksin and Sol Kaplan), *The Proud Rebel*, *The Jayhawkers*, *The Adventures Of Huckleberry Finn* (1960), *The Mountain Road*, *Five Finger Exercise*, *The Cardinal*, *The War Lord*, *Rachel Rachel*, *Valley Of The Gwang!* and *Hail, Hero!* (1969). His most acclaimed work during that time was undoubtedly for William Wyler's dramatic western, *The Big Country* (1958), for which he was nominated for an Academy Award. The music, and particularly its electrifying main theme, is considered to be among the most memorable in the history of the cinema. His work was also heard regularly on television in such popular programmes as *Lancer* and *Wagon Train*. On Broadway, Moross collaborated twice with the author and librettist John Latouche, firstly in 1948 for *Ballet Ballads*, a musical adaptation of three one-act plays, and again in 1954, for the innovative *The Golden Apple*, which, although it folded after only 127 performances, won the New York Drama Critics Circle Award for best musical, and has since become a cult piece. One of its songs, the ballad 'Lazy Afternoon', has been recorded by several artists, including Tony Bennett. During his long and distinguished career, Moross also won two Guggenheim fellowship awards, in 1947 and 1948. He brought his own individual brand of folksy homespun Americana to his music for ballets such as *American Patterns*, *The Last Judgement* and *Frankie And Johnny*, along with numerous orchestral works which included 'Biguine', 'A Tall Story', 'Paeans', 'Those Everlasting Blues' and 'First Symphony'. His last completed work was a one-act opera, *Sorry, Wrong Number!*

MOST HAPPY FELLA, THE

Any show that opened in the same season as *My Fair Lady* was bound to be somewhat overshadowed by Alan Jay Lerner and Frederick Loewe's masterpiece, which was destined to be a smash hit. However, *The Most Happy Fella* was, in some ways, a more ambitious work than its female counterpart, and enjoyed a satisfactory run of 676 performances on Broadway. The show opened on 3 May 1956 at the Imperial Theatre, and immediately confused many of the critics: was it an opera? A play with music, perhaps? Frank

Loesser, who wrote the music, lyrics, and libretto, settled on 'an extended musical comedy'. His adaptation of Sidney Howard's 1924 Pulitzer Prize-winning play, *They Knew What They Wanted*, was set in Napa Valley, California, and tells of an Italian vintner, Tony (Robert Weede, a former opera singer, making his Broadway debut), who is maturing rather more quickly than the grapes in his vineyard. He longs for a wife, and proposes by post to Rosabella (Jo Sullivan, who later became Loesser's wife), a waitress he has noticed in a San Francisco restaurant. To increase his chances of success, he includes a photograph of his handsome young foreman, Joey (Art Lund), and she hurried there to meet him. Even though he has deceived her, she still marries Tony – but tarries with Joey. When she discovers that she is pregnant with Joey's child she is determined to leave, but Tony forgives her and adopts the child as his own. With spoken dialogue at a minimum, *The Most Happy Fella* is a virtually sung-through show, and Loesser's score has moments of high emotion in songs such as 'Somebody Somewhere', My Heart Is Full Of You', and 'Joey, Joey'. Rosabella's friend Cleo (Susan Johnson), who follows her out from San Francisco, becomes fairly friendly herself with one of the ranch hands, Herman (Shorty Long), and leads the company in a hymn to Dallas, the rousing 'Big D'. The show's big hit song was 'Standing On The Corner', which became popular in the USA for Dean Martin, and the Four Lads who repeated their success in the UK, in competition with the King Brothers. Another of the show's lighter numbers, 'Happy To Make Your Acquaintance', also entered the UK chart in a version by Sammy Davis Jnr. and Carmen McRae. The rest of Loesser's highly distinguished score, which contained well over 30 songs in a wide variety of musical styles such as arias and choral pieces, included 'Ooh! My Feet', 'Mama, Mama', 'Warm All Over', 'I Like Everybody', 'Song Of A Summer Night', 'Sposalizio', 'How Beautiful The Days', 'Rosabella', 'The Most Happy Fella' and 'Abbondanza'. *The Most Happy Fella* was not everybody's idea of what a Broadway musical should be, but during a 20-month stay on Broadway, it won the New York Drama Critics Award for best musical, and subsequently ran for 288 performances at the London Coliseum. Lund reprised his role in the West End, during which time he became a favourite of audiences there, and returned with Richard Rogers' *No Strings* in 1963. *The Most Happy Fella* was revived on Broadway in 1979, and presented by the New York City Opera in 1991, with Giorgio Tozzi in the lead. In the following year the show was back on Broadway again, via the Goodspeed Opera House and Los Angeles, this time with just a two-piano orchestration, which Loesser himself had commissioned some years previously. Although critically acclaimed, the production ran for only 229 performances and lost most of its $1.4 million investment. It was nominated for four Tony Awards, but won just one – Scott Waara for best featured actor – being pipped at the post for 'best revival' by *Guys And Dolls*, which is, of course,

another Frank Loesser show. Unusually, the Original Cast album was recorded in 'real time' – in two long takes – just as the show was performed in the theatre. Even with part-retakes, the recording took only one day to complete, in comparison with the 1956 three-album set which needed a week of session time. In 1993, a concert performance of *The Most Happy Fella* became 'the first of its kind to be broadcast on BBC radio in England'.

MUDDY WATERS

b. McKinley Morganfield, 4 April 1915, Rolling Fork, Mississippi, USA, d. 30 April 1983, Chicago, Illinois, USA. One of the dominant figures of post-war blues, Muddy Waters was raised in the rural Mississippi town of Clarksdale, in whose juke-joints he came into contact with the legendary Son House. Having already mastered the rudiments of the guitar, Waters began performing and this early, country blues period was later documented by Alan Lomax. Touring the south making field recordings for the Library Of Congress, this renowned archivist taped Waters on three occasions between 1941-42. The following year Waters moved to Chicago where he befriended 'Big' Bill Broonzy, whose influence and help proved vital to the younger performer. Waters soon began using amplified, electric instruments and by 1948 had signed a recording contract with the newly founded Aristocrat label, the name of which was later changed to Chess Records. Waters' second release, 'I Feel Like Goin' Home'/'I Can't Be Satisfied', was a minor R&B hit and its understated accompaniment from bass player Big Crawford set a pattern for several further singles, including 'Rollin' And Tumblin'', 'Rollin' Stone' and 'Walkin' Blues'.

By 1951 the guitarist was using a full backing band and among the musicians who passed through its ranks were Otis Spann (piano), Jimmy Rogers (guitar), Little Walter, Walter 'Shakey' Horton and James Cotton (all harmonica). This pool of talent ensured that the Muddy Waters Band was Chicago's most influential unit and a score of seminal recordings, including 'Hoochie Coochie Man', 'I've Got My Mojo Working', 'Mannish Boy', 'You Need Love' and 'I'm Ready', established the leader's abrasive guitar style and impassioned singing. Waters' international stature was secured in 1958 when he toured Britain at the behest of jazz trombonist Chris Barber. Although criticized in some quarters for his use of amplification, Waters' effect on a new generation of white enthusiasts was incalculable. Cyril Davies and Alexis Korner abandoned skiffle in his wake and their subsequent combo, Blues Incorporated, was the catalyst for the Rolling Stones, the Graham Bond Organisation, Long John Baldry and indeed British R&B itself. Paradoxically, while such groups enjoyed commercial success, Waters struggled against indifference.

Deemed 'old-fashioned' in the wake of soul music, he was obliged to update his sound and repertoire, resulting in such misjudged releases as *Electric Mud*, which featured a reading of the Rolling

Stones' 'Let's Spend The Night Together', the ultimate artistic volte-face. The artist did complete a more sympathetic project in *Fathers And Sons* on which he was joined by Paul Butterfield and Mike Bloomfield, but his work during the 60s was generally disappointing. *The London Sessions* kept Waters in the public eye, as did his appearance at the Band's *The Last Waltz* concert, but it was an inspired series of collaborations with guitarist Johnny Winter that signalled a dramatic rebirth. This pupil produced and arranged four excellent albums that recaptured the fire and purpose of Muddy's early releases and bestowed a sense of dignity to this musical giant's legacy. Waters died of heart failure in 1983, his status as one of the world's most influential musicians secured.

● ALBUMS: *Muddy Waters Sings Big Bill Broonzy* (Chess 1960) ★★★, *Muddy Waters At Newport, 1960* (Chess 1963) ★★★★, *Muddy Waters, Folk Singer* (Chess 1964) ★★★★, *Muddy, Brass And The Blues* (Chess 1965) ★★, *Down On Stovall's Plantation* (Testament 1966) ★★★, *Blues From Big Bill's Copacabana* (Chess 1968) ★★★, *Electric Mud* (Cadet 1968) ★★, *Fathers And Sons* (Chess 1969) ★★★, *After The Rain* (Cadet 1969) ★★, *Sail On* (Chess 1969) ★★★, *The London Sessions* (Chess 1971) ★★★, *Live At Mister Kelly's* (1971) ★★★, *Experiment In Blues* (1972) ★★★, *Can't Get No Grindin'* (Chess 1973) ★★★, *Mud In Your Ear* (Musicor 1973) ★★★, *London Revisited* (Chess 1974) ★★, *The Muddy Waters Woodstock Album* (Chess 1975) ★★, *Unk In Funk* (Chess 1977) ★★, *Hard Again* (Blue Sky 1977) ★★★, *I'm Ready* (Blue Sky 1978) ★★★, *Muddy Mississippi Waters Live* (Blue Sky 1979) ★★★, *King Bee* (Blue Sky 1981) ★★★, *Paris 1972* (Pablo 1997) ★★★, *Goin' Way Back* 1967 recording (Just A Memory 1998) ★★★.

● COMPILATIONS: *The Best Of Muddy Waters* (Chess 1957) ★★★★★, *The Real Folk Blues Of Muddy Waters* (Chess 1966) ★★★★, *More Real Folk Blues* (Chess 1967) ★★★★, *Vintage Mud* (Sunnyland 1970) ★★★, *They Call Me Muddy Waters* (Chess 1970) ★★★, *McKinley Morganfield aka Muddy Waters* (Chess 1971) ★★★★, *Back In The Early Days* (Red Lightnin' 1977) ★★★, *Chess Masters* 3 volumes (Chess 1981-83) ★★★★, *Rolling Stone* (Chess 1982) ★★★, *Rare And Unissued* (Chess 1984) ★★★, *Trouble No More: Singles 1955-1959* (Chess/MCA 1989) ★★★, *Muddy Waters* 6-LP box set (Chess 1989) ★★★★★, *The Chess Box 1947-67* 9-CD box set (Chess/MCA 1990) ★★★★★, *Blues Sky* (Columbia/Legacy 1992) ★★★★, *The Complete Plantation Recordings* (Chess/MCA 1993) ★★★★, *The King Of Chicago Blues* (Charly 1995) ★★★★, *His Best: 1947 To 1955* (Chess/MCA 1997) ★★★★, *His Best: 1956 To 1964* (Chess/MCA 1997) ★★★★, *King Of The Electric Blues* (Columbia/Legacy 1999) ★★★, *The Lost Tapes* (Blind Pig 1999) ★★★★, *Best Of Muddy Waters: 20th Century Masters* (MCA 1999) ★★★★, *Mojo: The Live Collection* (MCI 2000) ★★★, *The Best Of Muddy Waters: The Millennium Collection* (MCA 2000) ★★★★, *Rollin' Stone: The Golden Anniversary Collection* (MCA 2000) ★★★★.

● VIDEOS: *Messin' With The Blues* (BMG 1991), *Live* (BMG 1993), *Got My Mojo Working: Rare Performances 1968-1978* (Yazoo 2000).

● FURTHER READING: *The Complete Muddy Waters Discography*, Phil Wight and Fred Rothwell. *Muddy Waters Biographie*, Francis Hofstein. *Muddy Waters: Mojo Man*, Sandra B. Tooze.

MUDLARKS

Soprano Mary Mudd, baritone Fred Mudd and tenor Jeff Mudd were the Mudlarks: a clean-cut family pop trio from Bedford, Bedfordshire, England. They started singing in public as the Mudd Trio in 1951 when they were just 12, 14 and 16 years old. Discovered by disc jockey David Jacobs and produced on Columbia Records by Norrie Paramor, they had a hit in 1958 with their second single, 'Lollipop', a cover version of the Chordettes' US hit. Their follow-up, 'Book Of Love', originally by the Monotones, also made the UK Top 10. They were often seen on the pioneering UK television series *6.5 Special*, and won the *New Musical Express* poll award as Top British Vocal Group for both 1958 and 1959. Jeff was called up by the army in early 1959 and David Lane replaced him until his return two years later. One of the few UK pop groups in the 50s, they recorded several more cover versions of US hits without further chart success.

MULLIGAN, GERRY

b. Gerald Joseph Mulligan, 6 April 1927, New York City, New York, USA, d. 19 January 1996, Darien, Connecticut, USA. Raised in Philadelphia, Mulligan started out on piano before concentrating on arranging. He also took up the saxophone, first the alto and a few years later the baritone. Among the name bands that used his arrangements were those led by Gene Krupa and Claude Thornhill and he occasionally played in their reed sections. While writing for Thornhill he met and began a musical association with fellow arranger Gil Evans. In New York in 1948 Mulligan joined Evans and Miles Davis, for whom he wrote and played, by now almost exclusively on baritone. It is important to point out that Mulligan wrote seven tracks on the pivotal *Birth Of The Cool* recordings. In the early 50s Mulligan led his own groups but continued to arrange on a freelance basis. In this capacity his work was performed by Stan Kenton (these charts also being performed in the UK by Vic Lewis).

In 1952 Mulligan began a musical association that not only attracted critical acclaim but also brought him widespread popularity with audiences. His performance of 'My Funny Valentine' around this time was usually stunning. This came about through the formation with Chet Baker of a quartet that was unusual for the absence of a piano. When Baker quit in 1953, Mulligan subsequently led other quartets, notably with Bob Brookmeyer in the mid-50s. He became a doyen of the California 'cool jazz' movement. Although the quartet format dominated Mulligan's work during this part of his career he occasionally formed larger groups and early in the 60s formed his Concert Jazz Band. This band was periodically revived during the decade and beyond. He interspersed this with periods of leading groups of various sizes, working and recording with other leaders, including Dave Brubeck, in frequently rewarding partnerships with musicians such as Paul Desmond, Stan Getz, Johnny Hodges, Zoot Sims and Thelonious Monk, and writing arrangements on a freelance basis. In the early 70s Mulligan led big bands, some of which used the name Age Of Steam, and small groups for worldwide concert tours, recording sessions and radio and television appearances. The 80s and early 90s saw him following a similar pattern, sometimes expanding the size of the big band, sometimes content to work in the intimate setting of a quartet or quintet.

As an arranger, Mulligan was among the first to attempt to adapt the language of bop for big band and achieved a measure of success with both Krupa (who recalled for George T. Simon that Mulligan was 'a kind of temperamental guy who wanted to expound a lot of his ideas'), and Thornhill. For all the variety of his later work, in many ways his music, as writer and performer, retains the colours and effects of his 50s quartets. In these groups Mulligan explored the possibilities of scoring and improvising jazz in a low-key, seemingly subdued manner. In fact, he thoroughly exploited the possibilities of creating interesting and complex lines that always retained a rich, melodic approach. His classic compositions from the 50s, including 'Night At The Turntable', 'Walkin' Shoes', 'Venus De Milo', 'Soft Shoe' and 'Jeru', and his superb arrangements for 'Bernie's Tune', 'Godchild' and others, helped to establish the sound and style of the so-called 'cool school'. The intimate styling favoured in such settings was retained in his big-band work and his concert band recordings from the 60s retained interest not only for their own sake, but also for the manner in which they contrasted with most other big-band writing of the same and other periods. By the late 70s and early 80s he was reluctant to perform and found greater solace in working on arrangements from his home, much like a solitary writer. In the 80s he made something of a comeback when he signed to GRP Records. *Little Big Horn* and *Re-Birth Of The Cool* were both satisfying and commercially successful records, as was *Dragonfly* for Telarc Records in 1995.

As a player, the beautiful lightness of touch Mulligan used in his writing was uniquely brought to the baritone saxophone, an instrument that in other, not always lesser, hands sometimes overpowers the fragility of some areas of jazz. It is hard to see in Mulligan's work, whether as writer, arranger or performer he had a clearly discernible influence. Similarly, despite the enormous popularity he enjoyed over more than five decades, few, if any, writers or players seem to have adopted him as a role model. Maybe it is because the baritone saxophone has never become a popular instrument, in favour of tenor and alto. This seems both perplexing and unfair, as whatever skill he exerted, he succeeded with artistic success and seemingly effortless grace. At the least, this must be something to regret and maybe in time his contribution to jazz, especially in the pioneering decade of the 50s will be seen as 'great' and important.

● ALBUMS: *Gerry Mulligan* 10-inch album (Prestige 1951) ★★★★, *Mulligan Plays Mulligan* (Prestige 1951) ★★★★, *Jazz Superstars* (1952) ★★★, *The Gerry Mulligan Quartet With Chet Baker* (Pacific 1952-53) ★★★★, with Lee Konitz *Konitz Meets Mulligan* 10-inch album (Pacific Jazz 1953) ★★★★, *Gerry Mulligan And His Ten-tette* 10-inch album (Capitol 1953) ★★★, *The Fabulous Gerry Mulligan Quartet: Paris Concert 1954* (Vogue 1954) ★★★★, *Gerry Mulligan And His Quartet, Featuring Guests Zoot Sims And Bob Brookmeyer: California Concerts* (World Pacific 1954) ★★★, *California Concerts Vols 1 & 2* (Pacific Jazz 1955) ★★★, *Presenting The Gerry Mulligan Sextet* (EmArcy 1955) ★★★★, *Gerry Mulligan Live In Stockholm* (1955) ★★★, *The Original Gerry Mulligan Quartet* (Pacific Jazz 1955) ★★★★, *Mainstream Of Jazz* (EmArcy 1955) ★★★, *The Vibes Are On* (Chazzer 1955) ★★★, *Paris Concert* (Pacific Jazz 1956) ★★★★, *Recorded Live In Boston At Storyville* (Pacific Jazz 1956) ★★★, *Lee Konitz With The Gerry Mulligan Quartet* (Pacific Jazz 1956) ★★★★, *Gerry Mulligan Quartet/Paul Desmond Quintet* (Fantasy 1956) ★★★★, *Gerry Mulligan, The Arranger* (Columbia 1957) ★★★, *Quartet Live In Stockholm* (Moon 1957) ★★★, *The Mulligan Songbook* (World Pacific 1957) ★★★, with Desmond *Blues In Time* (Fantasy 1957) ★★★★, with Thelonious Monk *Mulligan Meets Monk* (Riverside 1957) ★★★★, with Monk *Alternate Takes* (1957) ★★★, *Gerry Mulligan With Vinnie Burke's String Jazz Quartet* (Pacific Jazz 1957) ★★★, *At Storyville* (Pacific Jazz 1957) ★★★★, with Chet Baker *Reunion With Baker* (Pacific Jazz 1957) ★★★, *The Teddy Wilson Trio And The Gerry Mulligan Quartet At Newport* (Verve 1958) ★★★★, *I Want To Live* (United Artists 1958) ★★★, *The Gerry Mulligan-Paul Desmond Quartet* (Verve 1958) ★★★★, *Annie Ross Sings A Song With Mulligan!* (World Pacific 1958) ★★★, with Stan Getz *Getz Meets Gerry Mulligan In Hi-Fi* (Verve 1958) ★★★★, *What Is There To Say?* (Columbia 1959) ★★★★★, *Gerry Mulligan Meets Ben Webster* (Verve 1959) ★★★★★, *A Profile Of Gerry Mulligan* (Mercury 1959) ★★★, *The Subterraneans: Original Soundtrack* (MGM 1959) ★★★, *Gerry Mulligan And The Concert Band On Tour* (1960) ★★★, *New York-December 1960* (Jazz Anthology 1960) ★★★, *Gerry Mulligan And The Concert Jazz Band* (Verve 1960) ★★★, *Nightwatch* (United Artists 1960) ★★★, *Mulligan* (Columbia 1960) ★★★, *Gerry Mulligan Meets Johnny Hodges* (Verve 1960) ★★★, *Gerry Mulligan Presents A Concert In Jazz* (Verve 1961) ★★★, *Gerry Mulligan And The Concert Jazz Band Live At The Village Vanguard* (Verve 1961) ★★★★, *The Gerry Mulligan Quartet* (Verve 1962) ★★★, *Jeru* (Columbia 1962) ★★★★, *Gerry Mulligan And The Concert Jazz Band Presents A Concert In Jazz* (Verve 1962) ★★★, with Desmond *Two Of A Mind* (RCA Victor 1962) ★★★★★, *Gerry Mulligan And The Concert Jazz Band On Tour With Guest Soloist Zoot Sims* (Verve 1962) ★★★★, *Blues In Time*

(Verve 1962) ★★★, *Historically Speaking* (Prestige 1963) ★★★, *Timeless* (Pacific Jazz 1963) ★★★, *Gerry Mulligan '63-The Concert Jazz Band* (Verve 1963) ★★★, *Spring Is Sprung* (Philips 1963) ★★★, *Night Lights* (Philips 1963) ★★★, *The Essential Gerry Mulligan* (Verve 1964) ★★★, *Butterfly With Hiccups* (Limelight 1964) ★★★, *If You Can't Beat 'Em, Join Em'* (Limelight 1965) ★★★, with Red Rodney, Kai Winding *Broadway* (Status 1965) ★★★, *Feelin' Good* (Limelight 1965) ★★★, *Gerry's Time* (Verve 1966) ★★★, *Something Borrowed Something Blue* (Limelight 1966) ★★★, *Concert Days* (Sunset 1966) ★★★, *Live In New Orleans* (Scotti Bros 1969) ★★★, *The Age Of Steam* (A&M 1970) ★★★★, *The Shadow Of Your Smile* (Moon 1971) ★★★★, *Astor Piazzolla Summit Tango Nuevo* (Atlantic 1974) ★★★, *Carnegie Hall Concert* (CTI 1974) ★★★, *Gerry Mulligan Meets Enrico Intra* (Pausa 1975) ★★★, *Idle Gossip* (Chiaroscuro 1976) ★★★, *Lionel Hampton Presents Gerry Mulligan* (Who's Who 1977) ★★★, *Mulligan* (LRC 1977) ★★★, *Benny Carter/Gerry Mulligan* (LRC 1977) ★★★, with Judy Holliday *Holliday With Mulligan* 1961 recording (DRG 1980) ★★★, *Walk On The Water* (DRG 1980) ★★★, *LA Menace* film soundtrack (DRG 1982) ★★★, *Little Big Horn* (GRP 1983) ★★★★, with Scott Hamilton *Soft Lights & Sweet Music* (Concord 1986) ★★★, *Symphonic Dream* (Sion 1988) ★★★, *Lonesome Boulevard* (A&M 1990) ★★★★, *Re-Birth Of The Cool* (GRP 1992) ★★★, *Dream A Little Dream* (Telarc 1995) ★★★, *Dragonfly* (Telarc 1995) ★★★★, *Symphonic Dreams* (Sion 1997) ★★★, *The Gerry Mulligan Quartets In Concert* (Pablo 2001) ★★★.

● COMPILATIONS: *Gerry Mulligan And Chet Baker* 1951-65 recordings (GNP Crescendo 1988) ★★★★, *The Best Of The Gerry Mulligan Quartet With Chet Baker* 1952-57 recordings (Pacific Jazz 1991) ★★★★, *The Complete Pacific Jazz Recordings Of The Gerry Mulligan Quartet With Chet Baker* 4-CD box set (Pacific Jazz 1996) ★★★★, *Legacy* (N-coded Jazz 1997) ★★★★, *Jazz Profile* (Blue Note 1997) ★★★★.

● VIDEOS: *A Master Class On Jazz And Its Legendary Players* (1996), *Ralph Gleason's Jazz Casual: Gerry Mulligan* (Rhino Home 2000).

● FURTHER READING: *Gerry Mulligan's Ark*, Raymond Horricks. *Listen: Gerry Mulligan: An Aural Narrative In Jazz*, Jerome Klinkowitz.

● FILMS: *The Subterraneans* (1959), *The Fortune Cookie* (1966).

MURRAY, RUBY

b. 29 March 1935, Belfast, Northern Ireland, d. 17 December 1996. One of the most popular singers in the UK during the 50s, Murray toured Ulster as a child singer in various variety shows, and, after being spotted by producer Richard Afton, made her television debut at the age of 12. Stringent Irish laws regarding child performers held her back for two years, and she returned to school in Belfast until she was 14. In 1954 she travelled to London in comedian Tommy Morgan's touring revue, *Mrs. Mulligan's Hotel*, and was again seen by Afton, at the famous Metropolitan Theatre, Edgware Road. He offered her a position as resident singer on BBC Television's *Quite Contrary*, replacing Joan Regan who was about to leave. Signed to Columbia Records by recording manager and musical director Ray Martin, Murray's first release, 'Heartbeat', made the UK Top 5 in 1954, and was followed by 'Softly, Softly'. The latter reached number 1 in 1955, and became an ideal theme song, reflecting her shy image.

In the early part of 1955 Murray had five singles in the Top 20 at the same time, an extraordinary record that lasted until the emergence of Madonna in the 80s. Murray's hits included 'Happy Days And Lonely Nights', 'Let Me Go Lover', 'If Anyone Finds This, I Love You' (with Anne Warren), 'Evermore', 'I'll Come When You Call', 'You Are My First Love', 'Real Love' and 'Goodbye Jimmy, Goodbye'. She sang 'You Are My First Love' over the opening titles of the film musical *It's Great To Be Young*. Murray's own film appearances included the comedy, *A Touch Of The Sun*, with Frankie Howerd and Dennis Price. During a hectic period in the mid-50s, she had her own television show, starred at the London Palladium in *Painting The Town* with Norman Wisdom, appeared in a Royal Command Performance, and toured the USA, Malta and North Africa. In 1957, while appearing in a summer season at Blackpool, she met Bernie Burgess, a member of the vocal group the Jones Boys. They married in secret 10 days later. Burgess became her personal manager and, during the early 60s, they toured as a double act. In 1970 Murray had some success with 'Change Your Mind', and released an album with the same title, which included contemporary songs such as 'Raindrops Keep Fallin' On My Head', and revamped some of her hits. In 1989 *Ruby Murray's EMI Years* included other songs regularly featured in her act such as 'Mr. Wonderful', 'Scarlet Ribbons (For Her Hair)' and 'It's The Irish In Me'. In the 90s, based in Torquay, Devon, with her second husband, impresario Ray Lamar, she was still performing in cabaret and in nostalgia shows with other stars of the 50s right up to her death in 1996. Her memory will be kept alive as the subject of a popular cockney rhyming slang. Most people who use the term 'fancy going for a Ruby' (Murray), meaning 'a curry', have no idea as to who it alludes to.

● ALBUMS: *When Irish Eyes Are Smiling* (Columbia 1955) ★★★, *Endearing Young Charms* (Columbia 1958) ★★★, *Ruby* (Columbia 1960) ★★★, *Ruby Murray Successes* (Columbia 1962) ★★★, *Irish – And Proud Of It* (1962) ★★★, *Your Favourite Colleen* (1965) ★★★, *The Spinning Wheel* (1967) ★★★, *This Is Ireland* (1968) ★★★, *Change Your Mind* (1970) ★★★.

● COMPILATIONS: *Best Of Ruby Murray* (EMI 1975) ★★★, *Very Best Of Ruby Murray* (MFP 1984) ★★★, *Ruby Murray's EMI Years* (EMI 1989) ★★★.

MUSIC MAN, THE

Not many people have been brave (or foolish?) enough to write the book, music, and lyrics for a stage musical, but two major exponents, one from either side of the Atlantic, come to mind.

However, the advantage that Meredith Willson had over Frank Loesser and Noël Coward when he created *The Music Man* (from a story by Willson and Franklin Lacey), was that in many ways the piece was autobiographical. So for this show, which opened at the Majestic Theatre in New York on 19 December 1957, Willson's hometown of Mason City, Iowa, becomes River City, Iowa (population 2,212). It is there, that the Music Man – or rather, 'con-man' – descends from the Rock Island steam train in search of suckers just in time for the 4 July celebrations. The name is Professor Harold Hill (Robert Preston), a smooth operator who convinces the good citizens of various (preferably small and remote) townships to cough up the cash for musical instruments, uniforms, and instruction books, he will teach their kids to play. Further, he will form these budding prodigies into a band with himself as leader. Problem is, as one of his fellow-salesman puts it: 'He don't know one note from another. He can't tell a bass drum from a pipe organ.' However, things work out differently than usual during the Professor's visit to River City. After meeting up with former sidekick Marcellus Washburn (Iggie Wolfington), he charms Eulalie Shinn (Helen Raymond), wife of the highly suspicious Mayor Shinn (David Burns), and her fellow members of the Ladies' Auxiliary for the Classic Dance. He also endears himself to Mrs. Paroo (Pert Kelton), her young son, Winthrop (Eddie Hodges), and – after some kind of struggle – her daughter, the music teacher and local librarian Marian Paroo (Barbara Cook). A happy ending then, but not before the Professor has warned the residents of River City of the moral danger of introducing a pool table into the community ('That game with the fifteen numbered balls is the Devil's tool') in 'Ya Got Trouble'. That was the highlight of a score which was chock-full of engaging old-fashioned charm, such as the Buffalo Bills' barbershop-style 'Sincere' ('How can there be any sin in sincere?/Where is the good in goodbye?'), along with 'Overture And Iowa Stubborn', 'Piano Lesson', 'Goodnight My Someone', 'Seventy-Six Trombones', 'The Sadder-But-Wiser Girl', 'Pick-A-Little, Talk-A-Little', 'Goodnight Ladies', 'Marian The Librarian', 'My White Knight', 'Wells Fargo Wagon', 'It's You', 'Shipoopi', 'Lida Rose', 'Will I Ever Tell You?', 'Gary, Indiana', and 'Till There Was You'. The producers took a big chance casting Robert Preston, a film actor who was more familiar with roping cattle, than singing and dancing on Broadway, but he made his way delightfully through a minefield of counter melodies, rhythmic dialogue and strutting dance routines. Onna White was the choreographer for those dances, the period costumes were by Raoul Péne du Bois, and the entire production was staged by Morton Da Costa. *The Music Man* proved to be a copper-bottomed hit, and ran for 1,375 performances, winning Tony Awards for best musical, actor (Preston), featured actress (Cook), featured actor (Burns), author (Willson/Lacey), composer-lyricist (Willson), the show's producers, and conductor-musical director (Herbert Greene).

The 1961 London production, with Van Johnson (Hill), Patricia Lambert (Marian), C. Denier Warren (Mayor), Ruth Kettlewell (Mrs. Paroo), Bernard Spear (Marcellus), Nan Munro (Eualalie), and the Iowa Four singing quartet, only lasted for 395 performances. Winthrop was played by Dennis Waterman, later renowned for his parts in UK television shows such as *The Sweeney* and *Minder*. Subsequent major revivals have been rare, but included one at New York's City Center in 1980, which was headed by Dick Van Dyke (Hill), Meg Bussert (Marian), and Christian Slater (Winthrop). Marriott's Lincolnshire Theatre in Chicago also staged a production in 1993, with Kurt Johns, Pamela Harden, Ross Lehman, Alene Robertson, and Don Forston. Two years later, at the attractive Open Air Theatre in London's Regent's Park, Brian Cox's Harold Hill was still tangling with Liz Robertson's Marian. In the same year, a BBC Radio 2 presentation was led by Jim Dale (Hill) and Claire Moore (Marian). In April 2000, *The Music Man* returned in triumph to Broadway with a cast led by the virtually unknown Craig Bierko (Hill) along with Rebecca Luker (Marian), Max Casella (Marcellus), Paul Benedict (Shinn), Ruth Williamson (Eulalie), Katherine McGrath (Mrs Paroo), and Michael Phelan (Winthrop). Robert Preston reprised his marvellous performance for the 1962 film version, with Shirley Jones as Marian.

MY FAIR LADY

One of the most successful shows in the history of the American musical theatre, *My Fair Lady* opened to rave reviews at the Mark Hellinger Theatre in New York on 15 March 1956. Alan Jay Lerner's book is based on *Pygmalion* by George Bernard Shaw, and deals with the attempts of Professor Henry Higgins (Rex Harrison) to transform a Cockney flower girl, Eliza Doolittle (Julie Andrews), into a society lady simply by teaching her to speak correctly. In the course of the story Higgins and Eliza fall in love and all ends happily, if a little differently from the way Shaw intended. In the strong supporting cast were Stanley Holloway (Alfred P. Doolittle, Eliza's father), Robert Coote (Colonel Pickering, friend of Higgins), Michael King (Freddie Eynsford-Hill, Eliza's would-be suitor), and Cathleen Nesbitt (Mrs. Higgins, mother of the Professor). Alan Jay Lerner and Frederick Loewe's score was full of marvellous songs which included 'Why Can't The English?', 'I'm An Ordinary Man', 'A Hymn To Him', and 'I've Grown Accustomed To Her Face', which found Higgins, in turns, exasperated, defensive, perplexed, and (perish the thought) in love; Eliza's dreamy 'Wouldn't It Be Lovely?', defiant 'Just You Wait' and 'Without You', demanding 'Show Me' (in answer to Freddie's wet, but enchanting, 'On The Street Where You Live'), and exuberant 'I Could Have Danced All Night'. That number came towards the end of Act One, well before Eliza had convinced everyone at the Embassy Ball, including the dreaded Zoltan Karpathy (Christopher Hewett), that she was the genuine high-born article. Even her father, dustman Doolittle, does not recognize her ('Blimey, it's Eliza.'), when he calls in at 27a Wimpole Street and admits to Higgins that he is one of the undeserving poor, although: 'I don't need less than a deserving man, I need more. I don't eat less hearty than he does, and I drink a lot more.' Poor or (eventually) rich, Doolittle certainly has two terrific songs, 'With A Little Bit Of Luck', and 'I'm Getting Married In The Morning', in a score which also included 'Ascot Gavotte' (the famous sequence in which Eliza urges her chosen horse Dover on with the immortal words: 'Move your bloomin' arse!'). In those early shows, Harrison and Andrews, in particular, were both superb. Their delight and joy as they, and Pickering, realised that Eliza had finally 'got it' – celebrating their triumph with 'The Rain In Spain' – remains a magical and endearing theatrical moment equal to that in Richard Rodgers and Oscar Hammerstein's *The King And I*, when the King of Siam and Anna take the floor for 'Shall We Dance?'. *My Fair Lady* ran on Broadway for six-and-a-half years, a total of 2,717 performances, and won Tony Awards for best musical, actor (Harrison), director (Moss Hart), musical director (Franz Allers), Oliver Smith (scenic design) and Cecil Beaton (costumes). Numerous road companies toured the show across the USA and it was subsequently presented in many other countries around the world. Four of the principals, Harrison, Andrews, Holloway and Coote, recreated their roles for the London production (with Zena Dare as Mrs. Higgins, and Leonard Wier playing Freddie) which stayed at the Drury Lane Theatre Royal for five and a half years. The Broadway cast album spent nearly 300 weeks in the US chart, 15 of them at number 1. It was also inducted into the NARAS (Grammy) Hall of Fame in 1977. New York City Center brought the show back to New York a couple of times, before Broadway audiences saw a 20th anniversary staging in 1976 with Ian Richardson as Higgins and Christine Andreas as Eliza. There was a West End revival three years later, starring Tony Britton (Higgins), Liz Robertson (Eliza) and the much-loved Anna Neagle as Mrs. Higgins. The 1981 revival with 73-year-old Harrison, and Cathleen Nesbitt who by then was 92, toured the USA before spending nearly four months in New York. By all accounts it attempted to stay true to the original version, which is more than can be said for some of the later efforts. A 1991 UK provincial production, with a cast headed by Edward Fox (Higgins) and Helen Hobson (Eliza), was described by its director Simon Callow, as 'a politically correct' version, and the 1993 Broadway revival, directed by Howard Davies, with Richard Chamberlain (Higgins), Melissa Errico (Eliza), and Stanley Holloway's son Julian as Doolittle, was 'stripped almost entirely of its romanticism and honed to a provocative post-modern edge', according to the *Variety* theatre critic. He went on: 'The famous 'Ascot Gavotte' scene is recreated as a living Magritte canvas, the actors in colourful finery descending from the flies to hover above the action against a field of brilliant blue'. In March 2001, a more traditional, although updated production was staged at London's Royal National Theatre, with a cast headed by Martine McCutcheon (Eliza), Jonathan Pryce (Higgins), Dennis Waterman (Doolittle), Mark Umbers (Freddy), and Nicholas le Prevost (Pickering).

The 1964 film version was also reasonably faithful to the original stage show, and starred Harrison, Holloway, and – somewhat controversially – Audrey Hepburn as Eliza. As well as the various cast albums, in 1987 Decca Records issued a studio recording with Kiri Te Kanawa (Eliza), Jeremy Irons (Higgins), John Gielgud (Pickering), Jerry Hadley (Freddie), the London Voices, and the London Symphony Orchestra conducted by John Mauceri.

MYSTICS

This rock 'n' roll vocal ensemble came from Brooklyn, New York, USA. The members were brothers Phil (lead) and Albee Cracolici (baritone), Bob Ferrante (first tenor), George Galfo (second tenor), and Allie Contrera (bass). The Mystics helped popularize the Italian-American doo-wop sound that came out of New York City in the early 60s, but like many such groups they did it with only one hit, 'Hushabye' (US pop Top 20, 1959). The song was written by the great songwriting team of Doc Pomus and Mort Shuman and has become a staple of US oldie stations. A follow-up, 'Don't Take The Stars', scraped the bottom of the charts later in 1959. Failing to get another hit record, the Mystics broke up in the early 60s. They reunited in the 80s to perform at oldies shows and that led to a critically well-received album for a revival label, Ambient Sound, in 1982. By this time, however, the audience for doo-wop was limited to a passionate few on the Eastern seaboard and the album remained obscure.

● COMPILATIONS: with the Passions *The Mystics And The Passions* (1979) ★★★, *Crazy For You* (1982), *The Complete Mystics* (1985), *Golden Classics* (1987), with the Jarmels *The Mystics Meet The Jarmels* (Ace 1990) ★★★.

N

NELSON, OZZIE

b. 20 March 1906, Jersey City, New Jersey, USA, d.
3 June 1975. While studying for a career in the
legal profession, Nelson ran a dance band as a
hobby, but it was so successful that he abandoned
law for music. He played many of the east coast's
more prestigious venues, including Glen Island
Casino and the New Yorker Hotel. Nelson's
extremely relaxed singing style proved remarkably
popular, as did the work of the band's female
singer, Harriet Hilliard (b. 1909, d. 1994). Ozzie
and Harriet married in 1935 and their romantic
duets, coupled with their real-life romance, gave
fans something to coo over. In the early 40s Nelson
and the band appeared in a number of movies, and
he made a great impact with a US radio series, *The
Adventures Of Ozzie And Harriet*, which began in
1944. In 1952, the show transferred to television
and ran until 1966. Nelson's interests expanded
into other areas of showbusiness; he worked on
the stage and also produced and directed on
television. Also in the cast of the television show,
when they were old enough, were Ozzie and
Harriet's sons, David and Ricky Nelson. After the
show's run finished, Ozzie Nelson continued to
work in many different facets of showbusiness.
● COMPILATIONS: *Young America's Favorite*
(Aircheck 1986) ★★★, *Ozzie Nelson (1940-42)*
(Hindsight 1988) ★★★, *Ozzie Nelson 1937* (Circle
1988) ★★★, *Satan Takes A Holiday 1936-41*
(Bandstand 1988) ★★★, with Harriet *The Nelson
Touch* (ASV 1996) ★★★.
● FURTHER READING: *Ozzie*, Ozzie Nelson.

NERVOUS NORVUS

b. Jimmy Drake, 1912, d. 1968. The California-
based ex-truck driver's first record was the country
ballad 'Gambling Fury', which he recorded as
Singing Jimmy Drake on the Indiana label
Claudra. He joined Dot Records in 1956 and had
two of the biggest novelty hits of that year. His first
hit, 'Transfusion', concerned the thoughts of a
drink-driver who is in need of a blood transfusion
after a car crash. Despite the sick subject matter, it
was hilarious, though the British public were
spared it when London Records refused its release.
The follow-up to this US Top 10 hit was 'Ape Call',
a tale about cavemen recorded in hip language,
with jungle calls courtesy of Red Blanchard. After
his few months in the spotlight he returned to
obscurity, despite later unsuccessful recordings on
Big Ben and Embee.
● COMPILATIONS: *Transfusion* (1985) ★★.

NEW LOST CITY RAMBLERS

Mike Seeger (b. 15 August 1933, New York City,
New York, USA), John Cohen (b. 1932, New York,

USA) and Tom Paley (b. 19 March 1928, New York,
USA) formed this influential old-time string band
in 1958. Rather than ape their immediate
predecessors who popularized the style, the trio
preferred to invoke the music's original
proponents, including the Skillet Lickers and the
Carolina Tar Heels. Seeger undertook numerous
field recordings to preserve authenticity and while
their adherence to traditional values made
commercial acceptance difficult, the group
enjoyed the admiration of their peers and was
crucial in the development of the urban folk
revival.
The original line-up remained together until 1962,
when Paley left to resume his teaching career.
Replacement Tracy Schwartz (b. 1938, New York,
USA) primarily played fiddle, but his arrival
coincided with a broadening of the Ramblers'
repertoire. They began to incorporate
unaccompanied ballads and modern bluegrass
music but although the trio remained a popular
attraction on the college and coffee-house circuit,
they began to drift apart during the latter half of
the 60s. *Remembrance Of Things To Come* included
British traditional, riverboat songs and even some
early bluegrass. *American Moonshine And
Prohibition* was more light-hearted, but certainly
not lightweight in its criticism of the government
legislation on prohibition. Cohen initially pursued
his interest in photography before producing a
series of excellent documentary films. Schwartz
and Seeger, meanwhile, performed with different
musicians and together formed the short-lived
Strange Creek Singers. John Cohen, Mike Seeger
and Tracy Schwartz reunited in 1997 for *There Ain't
No Way Out*.
● ALBUMS: *New Lost City Ramblers* (Folkways
1958) ★★★★, *New Lost City Ramblers Vol. 2*
(Folkways 1959) ★★★, *Songs From The Depression*
(Folkways 1959) ★★★★, *Old Timey Songs For
Children* (Folkways 1959) ★★, *New Lost City
Ramblers Vol. 3* (Folkways 1961) ★★★, *New Lost
City Ramblers Vol. 4* (Folkways 1961) ★★, *American
Moonshine And Prohibition* (Folkways 1962)
★★★★, *New Lost City Ramblers Vol. 5* (Folkways
1963) ★★★, *Gone To The Country* (Folkways 1963)
★★★, *String Band Instrumentals* (Folkways 1964)
★★★, *Old Timey Music* (1964) ★★, *Rural Delivery
No. 1* (Folkways 1965) ★★★, *Remembrance Of
Things To Come* (Folkways 1966) ★★★★, *Modern
Times-Rural Songs From An Industrial Society*
(Folkways 1968) ★★★, *On The Great Divide*
(Folkways 1973) ★★★, *20 Years-Concert
Performances 1958-1977* (Flying Fish 1978) ★★,
20th Anniversary Concert, Carnegie Hall (Flying
Fish 1978) ★★, *There Ain't No Way Out*
(Smithsonian Recordings 1997) ★★★.
● COMPILATIONS: *Tom Paley, John Cohen And
Mike Seeger Sing Songs Of The New Lost City
Ramblers* (Folkways 1961) ★★★, *Twenty Years*
(1979) ★★★, *The Early Years 1958-62* (1991)
★★★★.

NEWELL, NORMAN

b. England. As a young man, Newell worked in a
music shop in London, England, and discovered

an aptitude for writing song lyrics. He was hired by EMI Records in 1949 as head of Artists and Repertory for the Columbia Records label. He also talked his way into a job as staff producer: 'I knew nothing about recording and nobody at the time taught me anything,' he comments now. His first record was with an adolescent Petula Clark and he secured his first success with 'The Jimmy Brown Song' ('Les Trois Cloches') for Champagnons De La Chanson in 1950. He had success with Steve Conway, including 'My Thanks To You' and 'My Foolish Heart'. Conway died in 1952 and by way of tribute, Newell used his surname to rename the pianist, Trevor Stanford, as Russ Conway. He encouraged Joyce Grenfell and Norman Wisdom to combine their talents on the hilarious 'Narcissus' (1952), and he placed the gospel song, 'He's Got The Whole World In His Hands', with a 14-year old boy, Laurie London, which became an international hit in 1957. Newell also recorded Alma Cogan, writing 'Cowboy Jimmy Joe' and 'With You In Mind' for her, but he is primarily associated with Shirley Bassey. 'She is so wonderful and I am so dedicated to her,' says Newell, 'When she sings, you feel that she is so much in love or that she has lost someone, and her body language becomes a part of the songs.' Newell's early work as a songwriter included 'Nice To Know You Care' (1948) with the pianist Leslie Baguley, which was recorded by Leslie 'Hutch' Hutchinson and Tommy Dorsey, but his work is often uncredited because he used pseudonyms – 'I had to use pseudonyms because otherwise a record producer might think, "If it's such a good song, why doesn't Norman Newell record it himself?"' His greatest success, however, was his own production of 'Portrait Of My Love' for Matt Monro. This song, co-written with Cyril Ornadel, won an Ivor Novello for Best Song Of The Year in 1960. 'I used the name of David West for that and Matt didn't know it was my song at first. I didn't think it would be a hit as I thought the lyric was too sophisticated with its reference to Michelangelo. I couldn't imagine anyone singing it in a pub, but I was wrong.' Newell wrote the English lyrics for many continental hits including 'More Than Ever (Come Prima)' (Malcolm Vaughan, 1958), 'This Is My Life (La Vida)' (Shirley Bassey, 1968) and 'Go (Before You Break My Heart)' (Gigliola Cinquetti, 1974), but the major one being 'Sailor' in 1961. 'I said I would write the English lyric over the weekend,' Newell recalls, 'but I forgot about it. A messenger boy called on Monday morning so I sent him to the canteen and while he had a coffee, I wrote the lyrics. If you do something that quickly, you wonder if it can any good, but it was a tremendous hit for Petula Clark, Anne Shelton and the Andrews Sisters.' As well as producing Russ Conway's many hits, he and Conway wrote 'Jeannie', a hit song for Danny Williams in 1962. Williams recorded the first vocal version of 'More', Newell's lyric to a theme in the movie, Mondo Cane, which now has over 1,000 different recordings. Newell also produced John Barry and Geoff Love, often as Manuel And The Music Of The Mountains.

Newell was uncomfortable with the beat boom of the 60s but still had hits by producing Peter And Gordon with a John Lennon and Paul McCartney song, 'A World Without Love'. Newell produced several albums of show tunes and he became the first UK producer to record a Broadway show, On Your Toes. Newell enjoys his retirement but still writes songs, sometimes with Les Reed: 'I would much prefer people to remember me as a songwriter rather than as a producer. Producing a record is something you have helped create, but the songs belong to you.'

NEWMAN, DAVID 'FATHEAD'

b. 24 February 1933, Dallas, Texas, USA. Newman is a tenor/baritone/soprano saxophone player and flautist, whose work contains elements of both jazz and R&B. In the early 50s he toured with Texan blues guitarist 'T-Bone' Walker and recorded the classic 'Reconsider Baby' with Lowell Fulson in 1954. For the next 10 years Newman was part of Ray Charles's orchestra, appearing on landmark recordings such as 'I Got A Woman', 'What'd I Say' and 'Lonely Avenue'. Other tenures have included the saxophone position in Herbie Mann's Family Of Mann (1972-74). He has recorded some two dozen albums as a leader since 1958, most tending towards mainstream and post-bop jazz with a funk edge, and has worked extensively as an accompanist in the blues, rock and jazz fields. He worked on Natalie Cole's bestselling Unforgettable (1990), and enjoyed much acclaim for his involvement in the Bluesiana Triangle benefit projects in aid of the homeless. Blue Greens And Beans was a collection of bop standards also featuring another Texan player, Marchel Ivery.

● ALBUMS: Ray Charles Presents David 'Fathead' Newman (Atlantic 1959) ★★★★, Straight Ahead (Atlantic 1961) ★★★★, Fathead Comes On (Atlantic 1962) ★★★, House Of David (Atlantic 1968) ★★, with Brother Jack McDuff Double Barrelled Soul (Atlantic 1968) ★★★, Lonely Avenue (1971) ★★★, Mr. Fathead (1976) ★★★, Fire! Live At the Village Vanguard (Atlantic 1989) ★★★, Blue Greens And Beans (Timeless 1991) ★★★, Blue Head (Candid 1991) ★★★, with Art Blakey, Dr. John Bluesiana Triangle (1990) ★★★, Return To The Wide Open Spaces (Meteor 1993) ★★★, Chillin' (HighNote 2000) ★★, Keep The Spirits Singing (HighNote 2001) ★★★.

● COMPILATIONS: Back To Basics (1990) ★★★.

NEWMAN, LIONEL

b. 4 January 1916, New Haven, Connecticut, USA. d. 3 February 1989, California, USA. A distinguished composer, musical director, conductor and arranger for movies for more than 30 years, Newman was a talented pianist as a child, and while in his teens started as a rehearsal pianist for Earl Carroll's Vanities, graduating to the position of musical director. He toured with other shows, played piano for Mae West for a while, and performed the same function at 20th Century-Fox when he joined them in 1943. Earlier in 1938, he had composed the title song (lyric by Arthur

Quenzer) for the movie *The Cowboy And The Lady*, which had a score by his elder brother, Alfred Newman. In the late 40s Newman's songs included 'As If I Didn't Have Enough On My Mind' (with Harry James), sung by Dick Haymes in *Do You Love Me?*, as well as 'The Morning Glory Road', 'Ramblin' Around' and 'Sentimental Souvenirs'. He had a smash hit in 1948 with the romantic ballad 'Again' (lyric by Dorcas Cochrane), from the film *Road House*. It was successful at the time for Doris Day, Gordon Jenkins and Vic Damone, among others. Another of his numbers, *Never* (lyric by Eliot Daniel), sung by Dennis Day in *Golden Girl* (1951), was nominated for an Oscar. In his career as a musical director, Newman worked on such films as *Cheaper By The Dozen* (1950), *Mother Didn't Tell Me* (1950), *I'll Get By* (1950), *Dangerous Crossing* (1953), *Love Me Tender* (1956, Elvis Presley's first film), *The Best Things In Life Are Free* (1956), *Mardi Gras* (1958), *Doctor Dolittle* (1967), *The Great White Hope* (1970) and *The Saltzburg Connection* (1972). He supervised all Marilyn Monroe's movies for 20th Century-Fox, such as *Gentlemen Prefer Blondes* (1953), *River Of No Return* (1954) and *There's No Business Like Show Business* (1954). As the studio's general music director, and senior vice-president in 1982, he was a powerful influence on the Fox output. His original music scores included *Don't Bother To Knock* (1952), *The Proud Ones* (1956), *A Kiss Before Dying* (1956), *Compulsion* (1959), *North To Alaska* (1960), *Move Over Darling* (1963), *The Pleasure Seekers* (1964, with Alexander Courage) and *Do Not Disturb* (1965). He was nominated for 11 Academy Awards, and won the Oscar, with Lennie Hayton, in 1969 for his adaptation of Jerry Herman's score for the film version of *Hello, Dolly!*. During the early 80s he conducted the Boston Pops Orchestra in the USA, and performed at London's Royal Albert Hall. He retired in 1985, but was persuaded by MGM to return to the business in 1987. He died two years later.

NEWPORT JAZZ FESTIVAL

Newport, Rhode Island, USA is not the kind of venue normally associated with music that began as low-life entertainment, but the jazz festival, begun in 1954, blended comfortably into Newport's somewhat refined surroundings with considerable ease. The nature of the event, which was founded by two of Newport's top set, Louis and Elaine Lorillard and directed by George Wein, was exposed to the world at large thanks to a marvellous, if occasionally visually overwrought, evocation of the 1958 festival filmed by Bert Stern and released in 1960 under the title *Jazz On A Summer's Day*. The artists at Newport that year included Louis Armstrong, Gerry Mulligan, Dinah Washington, Thelonious Monk, gospel singer Mahalia Jackson and, perhaps the most visually arresting sight of the festival, Anita O'Day in hip-hugging dress, gloves and cartwheel hat. Following crowd trouble in 1960, the 1961 festival was cancelled, but it was back the following year. However, more unsavoury events in 1971 caused it be moved permanently to New York City. Still

under Wein's benignly autocratic direction, the festival gained in strength and has never lost its early importance. New York is where it remains, with events taking place over 10 days in June in venues ranging from Carnegie Hall to small intimate clubs, and even onto the streets of the city. Over the years the festival's name has changed slightly to accommodate different sponsors but most recently, in deference to the Japanese Victor Corporation, it has been known as the JVC Jazz Festival New York. Since 1984 Newport has once again had its own festival, with George Wein presenting a two-day show in August at Fort Adams State Park, again under the patronage of JVC.

NORTH, ALEX

b. 4 December 1910, Chester, Pennsylvania, USA, d. 8 September 1991, Pacific Palisades, California, USA. An important composer for films, theatre, television, ballet and classical music, whose career stretched from the late 30s through to the 80s. After studying at Juilliard with the distinguished composer Aaron Copland, as well as at the Moscow Conservatory (1933-35), North composed for the Federal Theatre Project in the late 30s. During those years, through to 1950, he wrote the scores for government documentary and information films, and served in the US Army in World War II. In 1948 he composed the incidental score for Arthur Miller's landmark play *Death Of A Salesman*, on Broadway, and repeated the role for the film version in 1951. For that, and for his innovative jazz-tinged score to *A Streetcar Named Desire* (1951), he gained the first two of his 15 Academy Award nominations. Other early 50s film music included *The 13th Letter*, *Viva Zapata!* (considered an early milestone in his career), *Les Miserables*, the ballet music for Fred Astaire and Leslie Caron in *Daddy Long Legs*, and *Unchained* (1955). The latter featured 'Unchained Melody' (lyric by Hy Zaret), a ballad of yearning that was nominated for an Academy Award, and became popular at the time for Les Baxter (US number 1), Al Hibbler and Jimmy Young (UK number 1), among others, and through the years was constantly remembered and revived. The Righteous Brothers' 1965 smash-hit version accompanied an erotic scene in the popular 1990 movie *Ghost*, and in 1995 the song topped the UK chart once again in a version by Robson Green and Jerome Flynn, two actors from the popular television series *Soldier, Soldier*. North's other 50s scores included *The Man With The Gun* (1955), *I'll Cry Tomorrow* (1955), *The Rose Tattoo* (1955), *The Bad Seed* (1956), *The Rainmaker* (1956), *Four Girls In Town* (1956), *The King And Four Queens* (1956), *The Bachelor Party* (1957), *The Long Hot Summer* (1958), *Stage Struck* (1958), *Hot Spell* (1958), *The Sound And The Fury* (1959) and *The Wonderful Country* (1959). Early in the 60s North began an association with director John Huston that lasted until Huston's death in 1987. Together they worked on such films as *The Misfits* (1961), *Wise Blood* (1979), *Under The Volcano* (1984), *Prizzi's Honor* (1985) and *The Dead* (1987), Huston's swansong. North's 60s film work began with the epic *Spartacus* ('magnificent score, staggering battle scenes'), followed, in complete contrast, by *The Children's Hour*. His other scores of the decade included another epic, *Cleopatra*, John Ford's *Cheyenne Autumn*, *The Agony And The Ecstasy*, *Who's Afraid Of Virginia Woolf?*, *The Shoes Of The Fisherman*, *Hard Contract* and *A Dream Of Kings*. In the 70s, as his style of spectacular, dramatic scores went out of fashion, North worked less for the big screen. However, in later years he composed the music for movies such as *Pocket Money*, *Once Upon A Scoundrel*, *Bite The Bullet* and *Somebody Killed Her Husband*. In the 80s, besides his collaborations with Huston, North was still being critically acclaimed for scores such as *Carny*, *Dragonslayer*, *Under The Volcano*, *Good Morning Vietnam*, and his final film, *The Penitent* (1988). In 1986 he became the first composer to receive an honorary Academy Award 'in recognition of his brilliant artistry in the creation of memorable music for a host of distinguished motion pictures'. He died, five years later, in 1991. As well as films, his occasional television work included the feature documentary *Africa* (1967), music for the mini-series *The Word*, which was nominated for an Emmy, and *Rich Man, Poor Man*, which won two, the television feature *Death Of A Salesman* (again), and music for other programmes, such as *Your Show Of Shows*, *77 Sunset Strip*, *Playhouse 90* and *The F.D.R. Story*. Many of North's scores were made available on albums, and several individual items, such as the title themes from *I'll Cry Tomorrow* and *The Long Hot Summer*, and 'Unchained Melody', of course, endure.

NUDIE

b. Nudie Cohen, 1902, Kiev, Russia, d. May 1984. The surname has also been given as Cohn but he is usually referred to as just 'Nudie'. His father was a bootmaker in the Russian army and as a boy he began to learn the trade of a tailor. Around 1911, because of anti-Jewish purges in Russia, he and an elder brother emigrated to the USA, where they initially settled in Brooklyn. Around 1920, he began travelling around the USA, struggling to make a living. He had a brief and financially unrewarding career as a flyweight boxer, appeared as a Hollywood film extra and did tailoring work in the costume department of Warner Brothers. In New York, he even worked on costumes for striptease acts. In the early 40s, in Los Angeles, he became friendly with country singer Tex Williams, and persuaded Williams that he could make stage costumes for him and his band that would attract attention. Williams was delighted with the result, ordered further costumes and widely advertised their designer. The popularity of his suits quickly spread and soon other West Coast artists, especially singing cowboys such as Gene Autry, Roy Rogers and Rex Allen were wearing brightly coloured, rhinestone-studded Nudie creations. Nudie designed a 'free' suit, whose pattern included wagon wheels and cacti, for Porter Wagoner, then a struggling young hopeful. It was

a very shrewd investment on Nudie's part. Wagoner, who continued to wear Nudie suits on the *Grand Ole Opry* for a great many years, became Nudie's best and longest-running advert. The attraction soon passed on to other country singers and during the 40s and 50s, most of Nashville's major stars were dressed by Nudie. His first cowboy designs were mainly elaborately decorated western wear, but for the country stars, he designed the clothes for the individual, as he had done with the wagon wheels for Wagoner. Hawkshaw Hawkins' jacket had a large hawk on the back, Ferlin Husky had husky dogs and Jimmy C. Newman had alligators (after his hit 'Alligator Man'). Hank Williams regularly wore Nudie-designed drape suits and was actually buried in one. Nudie also designed the stage costumes of Bill Anderson and his band, and Hank Snow, another long-time flamboyant dresser, regularly wore his rhinestone-studded creations. It was Nudie who created the $10,000 gold lamé tuxedo worn by Elvis Presley and later the flashy suits worn by the Flying Burrito Brothers, which had marijuana leaves embroidered on them, and stage costumes for the Rolling Stones. However, not all of his creations were so brightly coloured, since it was Nudie who was responsible for Johnny Cash's Man in Black image. Nudie inevitably became a wealthy man and his own suits usually attracted considerable interest, as did his penchant for jewellery, which often saw him wearing $25,000 worth of gold (he was once described as 'a caricature of an American cowboy drawn by an enraged Russian cartoonist'). He was also noted for his famous white Pontiac convertible. The hood had giant Texas longhorn horn ornaments, while the interior contained patterned hand tool leather, with a silver saddle between the rear seats. There were 14 guns mounted in varying positions, which included Colt revolvers that worked as arm rests and door handles, gear lever and direction indicators and three rifles on the rear boot lid. The interior was decorated with hundreds of silver dollars, the front bumper had chrome quarter horses and the tape player could blast out a recording of a cattle stampede, while the horn played Dale Evans singing 'Happy Trails'. It seems that when they were going out together, Nudie's wife, not surprisingly, used to suggest that they took her car. Naturally, the car was at one point stolen, but the police appear to have had little trouble finding it again. Later there were several other Nudie-designed cars, which over the years have had several owners, including Webb Pierce and Hank Williams Jnr. Nudie died from natural causes in May 1984 but his wife continued to operate their store. Nudie, who was once quoted as saying, 'If Tom Mix got out of his grave and saw my clothes, he'd get back in again', was always proud of his achievements but never forgot the early days of struggle. A reminder was the photograph sent to him by famous American strip artist Lili St. Cyr, and autographed with: 'If I ever wear clothes, they'll be yours', which he proudly displayed in his store. For many years, clothes bearing a label that said 'Nudie's Rodeo Tailors, North Hollywood, California', were very much a status symbol to country artists. Nudie also played mandolin and apparently recorded an album featuring himself on that instrument, but recording data is seemingly not readily available. (In 1974, Manual Cuevas, who had started to work for Nudie in the late 50s, formed his own Manual's Western Wear in North Hollywood, from which he carried on the traditions of dressing stars, including Dolly Parton, Marty Stuart and Dwight Yoakam, in styles he had learned while with Nudie.)

NUTMEGS

The Nutmegs comprised lead Leroy Griffin, first tenor James 'Sonny' Griffin, second tenor James Tyson, baritone Billy Emery and bass Leroy McNeil. The group was formed in New Haven, Connecticut, USA, in 1954. The Nutmegs are famed for just two records, 'Story Untold' (number 2 R&B) and the follow-up, 'Ship Of Love' (number 13 R&B), both from 1955. The songs, with their exotic warbling, are a working definition of 'rockaballad', a valuable term of the era that anticipated the rock 'n' roll revolution. Most notable among the lesser songs are 'Whispering Sorrows', 'My Story', and the west coast-sounding 'My Sweet Dream'. Surviving less well in the Nutmegs' canon were the rock 'n' roll jumps, which were mostly routine. After several years of declining fortunes and many personnel changes, the group broke up in 1962. The Nutmegs were one of the cult groups of the east coast collecting scene, and during the early 60s, a cappella practice versions of their songs launched a craze for a cappella doo-wop recordings. The group, without lead Leroy Griffin (who died years earlier), worked the doo-wop revival circuit on the east coast during the 70s.

● COMPILATIONS: *The Nutmegs Featuring Leroy Griffin* (Relic 1971) ★★★, *Story Untold* (Relic 1993) ★★★.

O'DAY, ANITA

b. Anita Belle Colton, 18 October 1919, Kansas City, Missouri, USA. As Anita Colton, in her early teens she scraped a living as a professional Walkathon contestant (marathon dancer). During this period she changed her surname to O'Day. By her late teens she had switched to singing and was told by Gene Krupa, who heard her at a Chicago club, that if he ever had a slot for her he would call. In the meantime, she failed an audition with Benny Goodman, who complained that she did not stick to the melody, and upset Raymond Scott, who disliked her scatting – actually, she had momentarily forgotten the words of the song. Eventually Krupa called and O'Day joined the band early in 1941, just a few weeks before Roy Eldridge was also hired. The combination of Krupa, Eldridge and O'Day was potent and the band, already popular, quickly became one of the best of the later swing era. O'Day helped to give the band some of its hit records, notably 'Let Me Off Uptown' (also a feature for Eldridge), 'Alreet', 'Kick It' and 'Bolero At The Savoy'. After Krupa folded in 1943, O'Day went with Stan Kenton, recording hits with 'And Her Tears Flowed Like Wine' and 'The Lady In Red'.

In 1945 she was back with the re-formed Krupa band for more hit records, including 'Opus No. 1'. In 1946 she went solo and thereafter remained a headliner. She made a number of fine albums in the 50s, including a set with Ralph Burns in 1952, and made a memorable appearance at the 1958 Newport Jazz Festival. This performance, at which she sang 'Tea For Two' and 'Sweet Georgia Brown', resplendent in cartwheel hat, gloves, and stoned out of her mind, was captured on film in *Jazz On A Summer's Day* (1960). Drug addiction severely damaged O'Day's life for many years, although she continued to turn out excellent albums, including *Cool Heat* with Jimmy Giuffre, *Trav'lin' Light* with Johnny Mandel and Barney Kessel and *Time For Two* with Cal Tjader. Extensive touring, high living and a punishing lifestyle (not to mention a dozen years of heroin addiction) eventually brought collapse, and she almost died in 1966. Eventually clear of drugs, O'Day continued to tour, playing clubs, concerts and festivals around the world. She recorded less frequently, but thanks to forming her own record company, Emily, in the early 70s, many of the albums that she did make were entirely under her control. In 1985 she played Carnegie Hall in celebration of 50 years in the business, and towards the end of the decade appeared in the UK at Ronnie Scott's club and at the Leeds Castle Jazz Festival in Kent.

O'Day's singing voice is throaty and she sings with great rhythmic drive. Her scat singing and the liberties she takes on songs, especially when singing up-tempo, result in some remarkable vocal creations. In her hey-days her diction was exceptional and even at the fastest tempos she articulated clearly and precisely. On ballads she is assured and distinctive, and although very much her own woman, her phrasing suggests the influence of Billie Holiday. Late in her career some of her performances were marred by problems of pitch but, live at least, she compensated for such difficulties through the sheer force of her personality.

● ALBUMS: *Anita O'Day Specials* reissued as *Singin' And Swingin'* (Advance/Coral 1951) ★★★★, *Anita O'Day Collates* reissued as *Anita O'Day* and *The Lady Is A Tramp* (Clef/Norgran/Verve 1953) ★★★, *Songs By Anita O'Day* reissued as *An Evening With Anita O'Day* (Norgran 1954) ★★★★, *Anita* reissued as *This Is Anita* (Verve 1956) ★★★★, *Pick Yourself Up With Anita O'Day* (Verve 1957) ★★★, *For Oscar* (American Recording Society 1957) ★★★, *Anita O'Day At Mr. Kelly's* (Verve 1958) ★★★, *Anita Sings The Most* (Verve 1958) ★★★★, *Anita O'Day Sings The Winners* (Verve 1958) ★★★★, with Jimmy Giuffre *Cool Heat – Anita O'Day Sings Jimmy Giuffre Arrangements* (Verve 1959) ★★★★, *Anita O'Day Swings Cole Porter* (Verve 1959) ★★★★, *Anita O'Day And Billy May Swing Rodgers And Hart* (Verve 1960) ★★★★, *Waiter, Make Mine Blues* (Verve 1960) ★★★, *Trav'lin' Light* (Verve 1960) ★★★★, *All The Sad Young Men* (Verve 1962) ★★★★, with Cal Tjader *Time For Two* (Verve 1962) ★★★★, with the Three Sounds *Anita O'Day & The Three Sounds* (Verve 1963) ★★★, *Incomparable! Anita O'Day* (Verve 1964) ★★★★, *Recorded Live At The Berlin Jazz Festival* (MPS 1970) ★★★, *I Get A Kick Out Of You* (Emily 1975) ★★★, *My Ship* (Emily 1975) ★★★, *Live At Mingo's* (Emily 1976) ★★★, *Once Upon A Summertime* 1963-1976 recordings (Glendale 1976) ★★★, *Angel Eyes* (Emily 1978) ★★★, *Mello' Day* (GNP 1979) ★★★, *Live At The City* (Emily 1979) ★★, *A Song For You* (Emily 1984) ★★★, *In A Mellow Tone* (DRG 1989) ★★★, *At Vine St.: Live* (DRG 1992) ★★, *Anita O'Day Live* 1976 recording (Star Line 1993) ★★★, *Rules Of The Road* (Pablo 1994) ★★.

● COMPILATIONS: with Roy Eldridge, Gene Krupa *Uptown* 1941-42 recordings (Columbia) ★★★★, *Hi Ho Trailus Boot Whip* 1947 recordings (Flying Dutchman) ★★★, *Anita O'Day 1949-1950* (Tono) ★★★★, *Verve Jazz Masters 49* (PolyGram 1995) ★★★★★, *The Complete Anita O'Day Verve/Clef Sessions* 9-CD box set (Mosaic 1999) ★★★★, *Young Anita* 4-CD set (Proper 2001) ★★★.

● FURTHER READING: *High Times Hard Times*, Anita O'Day with George Eells.

ODETTA

b. Odetta Holmes, 31 December 1930, Birmingham, Alabama, USA. This legendary folk singer moved to Los Angeles when she was six, adopting the surname of her new stepfather, Felious. A classically trained vocalist, Odetta sang in the chorus of the 1947 Broadway production of *Finian's Rainbow*, before opting for a career in folk music. Successful residencies in San Francisco clubs, the Hungry i and Tin Angel, inspired interest in New York circles although her early releases revealed a still maturing talent. She had been brought up in

the blues tradition, but moved increasingly towards folk during the late 50s (she sung jazz and blues for the RCA Records and Riverside Records labels, and, only occasionally, folk for the Tradition Records label). Her blues was sung in the Bessie Smith tradition, but without the same level of emotion. Nevertheless, she recorded standards including 'House Of The Rising Sun' and 'Make Me A Pallet On The Floor'. In 1960, she took to the solo acoustic guitar and moved to Vanguard Records where her career flourished. The singer was championed by Pete Seeger and Harry Belafonte, the latter of whom Odetta accompanied on a 1961 UK hit, 'Hole In The Bucket'. Eventually Odetta fell foul of changing trends and fashions in music, and much was forgotten of her early work from the 50s and 60s. She continues to tour and is a fixture at political benefit concerts. In the late 90s she appeared to great effect on Nanci Griffith's *Other Voices Too (A Trip Back To Bountiful)*. Possessed of a powerful voice, her style embraces gospel, jazz and blues. The emotional mixture of spiritual, ethnic and jazz styles is best captured in person, and, therefore, *Odetta At Town Hall* and *Odetta At Carnegie Hall* remain her most representative sets.

● ALBUMS: *Odetta And Larry* 10-inch album (Fantasy 1955) ★★★, *Odetta Sings Ballads And Blues* (Tradition 1956) ★★★, *Odetta At The Gate Of Horn* (Tradition 1957) ★★★, *My Eyes Have Seen* (Vanguard 1960) ★★★, *Odetta Sings The Ballad For Americans* (Vanguard 1960) ★★★, *Odetta At Carnegie Hall* (Vanguard 1961) ★★★★, *Christmas Spirituals* (Vanguard 1961) ★★★, *Odetta And The Blues* (Riverside 1962) ★★★, *Sometimes I Feel Like Crying* (RCA Victor 1962) ★★★, *Odetta At Town Hall* (Vanguard 1962) ★★★★, *Odetta Sings Folk Songs* (RCA Victor 1963) ★★★★, *One Grain Of Sand* (Vanguard 1963) ★★★, *It's A Mighty World* (RCA Victor 1964) ★★★, *Odetta Sings Of Many Things* (RCA Victor 1964) ★★★, *Odetta Sings Dylan* (RCA Victor 1965) ★★★, *Odetta In Japan* (RCA Victor 1965) ★★★★, *Odetta Sings The Blues* (RCA Victor 1968) ★★★, *Odetta Sings* (Polydor 1971) ★★★, *It's Impossible* (Four Leaf Clover 1978) ★★★, *Movin' It On* (Rose Quartz 1987) ★★★, *Christmas Spirituals* (Alcazar 1988) ★★★, *To Ella* 1996 recording (Silverwolf 1998) ★★★, *Blues Everywhere I Go* (M.C. 1999) ★★★, *Livin' With The Blues* (Vanguard 2000) ★★★, *Lookin' For A Home* (M.C. 2001) ★★★.

● COMPILATIONS: *The Best Of Odetta* (Tradition 1967) ★★★, *The Essential Odetta* (Vanguard 1989) ★★★★, *Best Of The Vanguard Years* (Vanguard 1999) ★★★★.

● VIDEOS: *Exploring Life, Music And Song* (Homespun Video 2000).

OKLAHOMA!

The show that opened on Broadway in 1943, and is credited with being a significant turning point in the history of the musical theatre, was transferred to the screen in the less than glorious Todd-AO widescreen process in 1955. The skilful integration of Richard Rodgers and Oscar Hammerstein II's wonderful songs into the sentimental but sincere story for which the stage production was so rightly admired, was equally impressive in this celluloid version. The action takes place just after the turn of the century, on and around a ranch in the Oklahoma Territory, where Laurey (Shirley Jones) lives with her Aunt Eller (Charlotte Greenwood). The handsome and decent Curly (Gordon MacRae) and the evil-looking and devious Jud (Rod Steiger) both want to take Laurey to the 'box social'. Her decision to spite Curly (with whom she actually wants to go) by accepting Jud's invitation, sets off a train of events that culminates in Jud's death, for which Curly is immediately blamed, but just as swiftly exonerated. Jones and MacRae were perfect together, and the supporting cast was exceptionally fine, with Gene Nelson as Will Parker and Gloria Grahame as his girlfriend Ado Annie, who 'just cain't say no'. Eddie Albert played a travelling peddler-man, Ali Akim, whose indiscriminate use of a kissing technique known in his native country as 'A Persian Goodbye', results in a shotgun wedding. Other parts were taken by James Whitmore, Marc Platt, Barbara Lawrence and Roy Barcroft. Dancers James Mitchell and Bambi Lynn were stunning in the ballet sequence to the music of 'Out Of My Dreams'. Most of the rest of Rodgers and Hammerstein's rich and varied score was retained, and included all the favourites such as 'Oh, What A Beautiful Mornin'', 'The Surrey With The Fringe On Top', 'Kansas City', 'I Cain't Say No', 'Many A New Day', 'People Will Say We're In Love', 'Poor Jud Is Dead', 'The Farmer And The Cowman', 'All Er Nothin'', and the rousing 'Oklahoma'. Choreographer Agnes de Mille and musical arranger Robert Russell Bennett adapted their original stage work for the film, and Russell Bennett, together with Jay Blackton and Adolph Deutsch, won Oscars for 'scoring of a musical picture'. It was photographed in Technicolor and produced for Magna by Arthur Hornblow Jnr. The director was Fred Zinnemann. Sonya Levian and William Ludwig's screenplay was adapted from the original libretto by Oscar Hammerstein II, which was based on Lynn Riggs' play *Green Grow The Lilacs*.

ORNADEL, CYRIL

b. 2 December 1924, London, England. A composer, arranger and conductor for the theatre and films, Ornadel studied piano, double bass, and composition at the Royal College of Music. He was with ENSA for a while, and later toured Europe with the popular singer Dorothy Carless. He led his own all-female band at Murray's Club in London, and later worked as a concert party pianist. After providing some musical and vocal arrangements for the Players' Theatre, he was appointed musical director of the touring show *Hello Beautiful*, which led to his first London assignment as the conductor of a pantomime at the People's Palace in the Mile End Road. In 1950, he became the West End's youngest pit conductor when he took over the baton for the musical revue *Take It From Us* at the Adelphi Theatre. During the remainder of the 50s he conducted for the London productions of several successful American musicals, such as *Kiss Me, Kate*, *Call Me Madam*, *Paint Your Wagon*, *Wish You Were Here*, *Pal Joey*, *Wonderful Town*, *Kismet*, *Plain And Fancy*, and *My Fair Lady*. Ornadel also

collaborated with David Croft on the scores for regional productions of *Star Maker*, *The Pied Piper*, and the London Palladium's 1956 pantomime, *The Wonderful Lamp* (with Phil Park). For much of the 50s he was the resident musical director for the top-rated television programme, *Sunday Night At The London Palladium*. In 1960, he and lyricist Norman Newell won Ivor Novello Awards for their delightful ballad, 'Portrait Of My Love', which gave Matt Monro his first UK chart hit. Ornadel's other 'Ivors' (to date) came in 1963 for 'If I Ruled The World' (lyric by Leslie Bricusse), the hit song from his score for the immensely successful musical, *Pickwick*, starring Harry Secombe; and the scores for two 'Best British Musicals', *Treasure Island* (1973) and *Great Expectations* (1975), both with Hal Shaper. After playing its initial UK dates and in several Canadian cities, Ornadel and Shaper rewrote the score for *Great Expectations*, and the revised version was presented at the Liverpool Playhouse (1989) and in Sydney, Australia (1991). Ornadel's other stage musicals have included *Ann Veronica* (1969, with Croft), *Once More, Darling* (1978, with Newell), *Winnie* (1988, additional songs with Arnold Sundgaard), *Cyrano: The Musical* (with Shaper), and *The Last Flower On Earth* (1991, with Kelvin Reynolds). Over the years, Ornadel has also conducted and/or composed and orchestrated the music for numerous radio, film and television productions, including *Some May Live*, *Subterfuge*, *The Waitors*, *I Can't, I Can't*, *Wedding Night*, *Man Of Violence*, *Europa Express*, *Cool It Carol*, *Die Screaming Marianne*, *Yesterday*, *The Flesh And The Blood Show*, *The Strauss Family* (series), *Edward VII* (series), *Christina*, *Brief Encounter* (1974 remake), and many more. His albums, especially those on which his Starlight Symphony Orchestra celebrated the great popular composers, have been extremely successful, especially in America. He also composed a series of children's records for EMI, and was the musical supervisor for the *Living Bible* records with Sir Laurence Olivier, and created the 'Stereoaction Orchestra' for RCA Records. A genial, and much-liked man, in the early 90s Cyril Ornadel was living and working in Israel. His many albums include: *Musical World Of Lerner And Loewe*, *Opening Night-Broadway Overtures*, *Bewitched*, *Camelot*, *Carnival*, *Dearly Beloved*, *Enchanted Evening*, *Gone With The Wind*, *Musical World Of Jerome Kern*, *Musical World Of Cole Porter*, *Musical World Of Rodgers And Hammerstein*, *So Nice To Come Home To*, and *The Music Man* .

OSSER, GLENN

b. 28 August 1914, Munising, Michigan, USA. The son of Russian immigrants, Osser has had a successful career arranging and conducting for many leading bands and singers. He has also achieved a distinctive string sound through his clever scoring, which he describes as 'voicing register, and composition of the counterpoint'. In his early career Osser concentrated on arranging, and his scores were accepted by Bob Crosby, Charlie Barnet, Bunny Berigan, Paul Whiteman, Les Brown and Red Nichols. During the 50s, while still regularly working with Whiteman (who was

Musical Director of the ABC Network at that time), Osser was in demand to back many singers for albums, including Georgia Gibbs, Vic Damone, Jack Jones, Frankie Laine, John Raitt, Maurice Chevalier and Guy Mitchell. Osser was also recording his own instrumental albums, notably some with Bobby Hackett and Joe Bushkin. Further albums found Osser backing Johnny Mathis, Jerry Vale, Tony Bennett, Robert Goulet and Leslie Uggams. Leaving US Columbia and moving to RCA, Osser worked with Della Reese and Sam Cooke. Until 1987 he was Music Director and arranger for the *Miss America Beauty Pageant* on television, with Osser and his wife contributing various original songs including 'Miss America, You're Beautiful' and 'Look At Her'. He has also written many works for concert bands that are still regularly performed by many high school and college bands in the USA.

● ALBUMS: as Glenn Osser Orchestra *But Beautiful* (Kapp 1956) ★★★, with Joe Bushkin *Midnight Rhapsody* (Capitol 1957) ★★★, *March Along Sing Along (Marching Band And Chorus)* (United Artists 1960) ★★★, *Be There At Five* (Mercury 1960) ★★★. As accompanist: Marian McPartland *With You In Mind* (Capitol 1957) ★★★, Georgia Gibbs *Swingin' With Her Nibs* (Mercury 1957) ★★★, Vivian Blaine *Songs From Ziegfeld Follies* (Mercury 1957) ★★★★, Jerry Vale *I Remember Buddy* (Columbia 1958) ★★, Red Buttons, Barbara Cook *Hansel And Gretel* (MGM 1958) ★★★, Maurice Chevalier *Maurice Chevalier Sings Songs Of Yesterday/Today* (MGM 1958) ★★★, Guy Mitchell *A Guy In Love* (Columbia/Philips 1959) ★★★, Vic Damone *Angela Mia* (Columbia 1959) ★★★, Johnny Mathis *Heavenly* (Columbia 1959) ★★★★, Leslie Uggams *The Eyes Of God* (Columbia 1959) ★★★, Della Reese *Della By Starlight* (RCA 1960) ★★★★, Sam Cooke *Cooke's Tour* (RCA 1960) ★★★, Tony Bennett *Tony Bennett Sings A String Of Harold Arlen* (Columbia 1960) ★★★, Diana Trask *Diana Trask* (Columbia 1961) ★★★★, Dona Jacoby *Swinging Big Sound* (Decca 1962) ★★★, Bobby Hackett *The Most Beautiful Horn In The World* (Columbia 1962) ★★★, Jack Jones *Gift Of Love* (Kapp 1962) ★★★, George Maharis *Portrait In Music* (Epic 1962) ★★★, Robert Goulet *Two Of Us* (Columbia 1962) ★★★, Jerry Vale *Arrivederci Roma* (Columbia 1963) ★★★★, Barbara Carroll *Fresh From Broadway* (Warners 1964) ★★★, Brook Benton *That Old Feeling* (RCA 1966) ★★★, Jerry Vale *The Impossible Dream* (Columbia 1967) ★★★, Johnny Mathis *Up Up And Away* (Columbia 1967) ★★★, Bob Thiele *Those Were The Days* (Flying Dutchman 1972) ★★★.

OTIS, JOHNNY

b. 28 December 1921, Vallejo, California, USA. Born into a family of Greek immigrants, Otis was raised in a largely black neighbourhood where he thoroughly absorbed the prevailing culture and lifestyle. He began playing drums in his mid-teens and worked for a time with some of the locally based jazz bands, including, in 1941, Lloyd Hunter's orchestra. In 1943 he gained his first name-band experience when he joined Harlan Leonard for a short spell. Some sources suggest that, during the difficult days when the draft was pulling musicians

out of bands all across the USA, Otis then replaced another ex-Leonard drummer, Jesse Price, in the Stan Kenton band. In the mid-40s Otis also recorded with several jazz groups, including Illinois Jacquet's all-star band and a septet led by Lester Young, which also featured Howard McGhee and Willie Smith. In 1945 Otis formed his own big band in Los Angeles. In an early edition assembled for a recording session, he leaned strongly towards a blues-based jazz repertoire and hired such musicians as Eli Robinson, Paul Quinichette, Teddy Buckner, Bill Doggett, Curtis Counce and singer Jimmy Rushing. This particular date produced a major success in 'Harlem Nocturne'.

He also led a small band, including McGhee and Teddy Edwards, on a record date backing Wynonie Harris. However, Otis was aware of audience interest in R&B and began to angle his repertoire accordingly. Alert to the possibilities of the music and with a keen ear for new talent, he quickly became one of the leading figures in the R&B boom of the late 40s and early 50s. Otis also enjoyed credit for writing several songs, although, in some cases, this was an area fraught with confusion and litigation. Among his songs was 'Every Beat Of My Heart', which was a minor hit for Jackie Wilson in 1951 and a massive hit a decade later for Gladys Knight. Otis was instrumental in the discovery of Etta James and Willie Mae 'Big Mama' Thornton. A highly complex case of song co-authorship came to light with 'Hound Dog', which was recorded by Thornton. Otis, who had set up the date, was listed first as composer, then as co-composer with its originators, Leiber And Stoller. After the song was turned into a multi-million dollar hit by Elvis Presley, other names appeared on the credits and the lawyers stepped in. Otis had a hit record in the UK with an updated version of 'Ma, He's Making Eyes At Me' in 1957. During the 50s Otis broadcast daily in the USA as a radio disc jockey, and had a weekly television show with his band and also formed several recording companies, all of which helped to make him a widely recognized force in west coast R&B. During the 60s and 70s, Otis continued to appear on radio and television, touring with his well-packaged R&B-based show. His son, Johnny 'Shuggie' Otis Jnr., appeared with the show and at the age of 13 had a hit with 'Country Girl'. In addition to his busy musical career, Otis also found time to write a book, *Listen To The Lambs*, written in the aftermath of the Watts riots of the late 60s.

● ALBUMS: *Rock 'N' Roll Parade, Volume 1* (Dig 1957) ★★★, *The Johnny Otis Show* (Capitol 1958) ★★★★, *Cold Shot* (Kent 1969) ★★★★, *Cuttin' Up* (Epic 1970) ★★, *Live At Monterey* (Epic 1971) ★★, *The New Johnny Otis Show* (Alligator 1981) ★★, *Spirit Of The Black Territory Bands* (Arhoolie 1992) ★★.

● COMPILATIONS: *The Original Johnny Otis Show* (Savoy 1985) ★★★★, *The Capitol Years* (Capitol 1989) ★★★★, *Creepin' With The Cats: The Legendary Dig Masters Volume One* (Ace 1991) ★★★, *The Greatest Johnny Otis Show* (Ace 1998) ★★★, *The Complete Savoy Recordings* 3-CD set (Savoy 2000) ★★★★, *Watts Funky?* (Ace 2001) ★★★.

● FURTHER READING: *Upside Your Head! Rhythm And Blues On Central Avenue*, Johnny Otis.

P

PAGE, PATTI

b. Clara Ann Fowler, 8 November 1927, Tulsa, Oklahoma, USA. A popular singer who is said to have sold more records during the 50s than any other female artist, Page's total sales (singles and albums) are claimed to be in excess of 60 million. One of eight girls in a family of 11, Clara Fowler started her career singing country songs on radio station KTUL in Tulsa, and played weekend gigs with Art Klauser And His Oklahomans. She successfully auditioned for KTUL's *Meet Patti Page* show, sponsored by the Page Milk Company, and took the name with her when she left. Jack Rael, who was road manager and played baritone saxophone for the Jimmy Joy band, heard her on the radio and engaged her to sing with them; he later became her manager for over 40 years. In 1948 Page appeared on the top-rated *Breakfast Club* on Chicago radio, and sang with the Benny Goodman Septet. In the same year she had her first hit record, 'Confess', on which, in the cause of economy, she overdubbed her own voice to create the effect of a vocal group. In 1949, she used that revolutionary technique again on her first million-seller, 'With My Eyes Wide Open I'm Dreaming'. The song was re-released 10 years later with a more modern orchestral backing.

Throughout the 50s, the hits continued to flow: 'I Don't Care If The Sun Don't Shine', 'All My Love' (US number 1), 'Tennessee Waltz' (said to be the first real 'crossover' hit from country music to pop, and one of the biggest record hits of all time), 'Would I Love You (Love You, Love You)', 'Mockin' Bird Hill' (a cover version of the record made by Les Paul And Mary Ford, who took multi-tracking to the extreme in the 50s), 'Mister And Mississippi', 'Detour' (recorded for her first country music album), 'I Went To Your Wedding', 'Once In A While', 'You Belong To Me', 'Why Don't You Believe Me', '(How Much Is) That Doggie In The Window', written by novelty song specialist Bob Merrill, and recorded by Page for a children's album, 'Changing Partners', 'Cross Over The Bridge', 'Steam Heat', 'Let Me Go, Lover', 'Go On With The Wedding', 'Allegheny Moon', 'Old Cape Cod', 'Mama From The Train' (sung in a Pennsylvanian Dutch dialect), 'Left Right Out Of Your Heart', and many more. Her records continued to sell well into the 60s, and she had her last US Top 10 entry in 1965 with the title song from the Bette Davis-Olivia De Havilland movie *Hush, Hush, Sweet Charlotte*. Page also appeared extensively on US television during the 50s, on shows such as the *Scott Music Hall*, the *Big Record* variety show, and her own shows for NBC and CBS. She also made several films, including *Elmer Gantry* (1960), *Dondi* (1961, a comedy-drama, in

which she co-starred with David Janssen) and *Boys Night Out* (1962). In the 70s, she recorded mainly country material, and in the 80s, after many successful years with Mercury Records and Columbia Records, signed for the Nashville-based company Plantation Records, a move that reunited her with top record producer Shelby Singleton. In 1988, Page gained excellent reviews when she played the Ballroom in New York, her first appearance in that city for nearly 20 years. More than 10 years later she won a Grammy Award in the Traditional Pop Vocal Performance category for her album *Live At Carnegie Hall – The 50th Anniversary Concert*.

● ALBUMS: *Songs* (Mercury 1950) ★★★, *Folksong Favorites* 10-inch album (Mercury 1951) ★★★, *Christmas* (Mercury 1951) ★★★, *Tennessee Waltz* 10-inch album (Mercury 1952) ★★★, *Patti Sings For Romance* (Mercury 1954) ★★★, *Song Souvenirs* (Mercury 1954) ★★★, *Just Patti* (Mercury 1954) ★★★, *Patti's Songs* (Mercury 1954) ★★★, *And I Thought About You* (Mercury 1954) ★★★, *So Many Memories* (Mercury 1954) ★★★, *Romance On The Range* (Mercury 1955) ★★★, *Page I* (Mercury 1956) ★★★, *Page II* (Mercury 1956) ★★★, *Page III* (Mercury 1956) ★★★, *You Go To My Head* (Mercury 1956) ★★★★, *In The Land Of Hi-Fi* (EmArcy 1956) ★★★★, *Music For Two In Love* (Mercury 1956) ★★★, *The Voices Of Patti Page* (Mercury 1956) ★★★, *Page IV* (Mercury 1956) ★★★, *Let's Get Away From It All* (Mercury 1956) ★★★, *I've Heard That Song Before* (Mercury 1956) ★★★, *The East Side* (EmArcy 1956) ★★★, *Manhattan Tower* (Mercury 1956) ★★★, *The Waltz Queen* (Mercury 1957) ★★★, *The West Side* (EmArcy 1958) ★★★, *Patti Page On Camera* (Mercury 1959) ★★★, *I'll Remember April* (Mercury 1959) ★★★, *Indiscretion* (Mercury 1959) ★★★, *Sings And Stars In 'Elmer Gantry'* (Mercury 1960) ★★★, *Three Little Words* (Mercury 1960) ★★★, *Just A Closer Walk With Thee* (Mercury 1960) ★★, *Country And Western Golden Hits* (Mercury 1961) ★★, *Go On Home* (Mercury 1962) ★★★, *Golden Hit Of The Boys* (Mercury 1962) ★★★, *Patti Page On Stage* (Mercury 1963) ★★★, *Say Wonderful Things* (Columbia 1963) ★★, *Blue Dream Street* (Mercury 1964) ★★, *The Nearness Of You* (Mercury 1964) ★★★, *Hush, Hush, Sweet Charlotte* (Columbia 1965) ★★★, *Gentle On My Mind* (Columbia 1968) ★★, *Patti Page With Lou Stein's Music, 1949* (Hindsight 1988) ★★★, *Live At Carnegie Hall – The 50th Anniversary Concert* (DRG 1998) ★★★★, *Brand New Tennessee Waltz* (C.A.F./Gold 2000) ★★★.

● COMPILATIONS: *Patti Page's Golden Hits* (Mercury 1960) ★★★, *Patti Page's Golden Hits, Volume 2* (Mercury 1963) ★★★, *The Best Of Patti Page* (Creole 1984) ★★★, *The Mercury Years, Vol. 1* (Mercury 1991) ★★★★, *The Mercury Years, Vol. 2* (Mercury 1991) ★★★★, *Golden Celebration* 4-CD boxed set (PolyGram 1997) ★★★.

● VIDEOS: *The Patti Page Video Songbook* (View 1994), *The Singing Rage* (PBS 2000).

● FILMS: *Stazione Termini* aka *Indiscretion* (1953), *Elmer Gantry* (1960), *Dondi* (1961), *Boys' Night Out* (1962).

PAICH, MARTY

b. Marty Louis Paich, 23 January 1925, Oakland, California, USA, d. 12 August 1995, Hidden Hills, California, USA. While still undergoing a long and thorough academic training, Paich began writing arrangements. After military service, during which he was able to continue his musical career, he returned to his studies and by the end of the 40s had gained numerous qualifications. In the early 50s he worked with a number of dance bands and also with Shelly Manne and Shorty Rogers, with whom he appeared on the successful and influential album *Cool And Crazy*. Also in the early 50s he was, for a while, pianist and arranger for Peggy Lee and wrote arrangements for Mel Tormé. He also wrote charts for another highly successful west coast album, *Art Pepper Plus Eleven*. An inventive and inquiring mind was clearly at work in all Paich's writing, whether as arranger or composer, and he proved particularly adept at creating material for small to medium-sized groups that allows the bands to sound as though they involve many more musicians. His work with such singers as Ella Fitzgerald, Ray Charles, Anita O'Day, Sammy Davis Jnr., Lena Horne and Sarah Vaughan, whether as arranger or musical director and conductor, demonstrated an acute appreciation of the particular needs of interpreters of the Great American Songbook. Paich also composed for films and television but the late 80s saw him back on the road with Tormé and some of his former Dek-tette sidemen, reunions that updated past glories with no hint of repetition and resulted in some remarkable record albums. He died of cancer of the colon in 1995.

● ALBUMS: *Marty Paich Octet* (GNP 1956) ★★★, *Mel Tormé With The Marty Paich Dek-tette* (Bethlehem 1956) ★★★★, *What's New?* (1957) ★★★, *Jazz For Relaxation* (Tampa 1957) ★★★, *Marty Paich Quintet Featuring Art Pepper* (Tampa 1958) ★★★, *The Picasso Of Big Band Jazz* (Candid 1958) ★★★, *I Get A Boot Out Of You* (Warners 1959) ★★★, *The Broadway Bit* (Warners 1959) ★★★, *Piano Quartet* (RCA Victor 1960) ★★★, with Mel Tormé *Reunion* (Concord Jazz 1988) ★★★★, *Hot Piano* (VSOP 1988), with Tormé *In Concert Tokyo* (Concord Jazz 1989) ★★★★, *Moanin'* (1993) ★★★★.

PAINT YOUR WAGON

This musical morality play, set in the goldfields of North California around the mid-1800s, opened at the Shubert Theatre in New York on 12 November 1951. The central characters in Alan Jay Lerner's book are Ben Rumson (James Barton) and his daughter Jennifer. (Olga San Juan). After they accidentally discover gold, a heap of hard-bitten characters flock to Rumson Town from miles around. As the only female around, this makes life difficult for Jennifer – and anyway she has become far too fond of the Mexican dreamer Julio Valvera (Tony Bavaar). So she is sent back east to school, although sadly not before she has witnessed her father bidding successfully for a Mormon's spare wife. On her return, she finds a ghost town. The gold has dwindled to nothing, and

the fevered prospectors have moved on. Ben's wife has gone too, but when Julio turns up, having finally discovered there is no pot at the end of that mythical rainbow, he and Jennifer can at last settle down and begin to build a life together. Frederick Loewe (music) and Lerner (lyrics) came up with a perfect score for this lively, rumbustious, but often poignant scenario, which included 'Another Autumn', 'I Still See Elisa', 'I'm On My Way', 'Wand'rin' Star', 'Hand Me Down That Can O' Beans', 'What's Goin' On?', 'Whoop-Ti-Ay', 'How Can I Wait?', 'Carino Mio', 'There's A Coach Comin' In', and 'All For Him'. Two of the numbers, 'They Call The Wind Maria' and 'I Talk To The Trees', quickly became popular, but the show, which was directed by Daniel Mann, had a disappointing run of only 289 performances. Choreographer Agnes De Mille was in her element with all those prancing miners, and there were the inevitable ballet sequences. From 11 February 1953, London audiences at Her Majesty's Theatre liked it much better, and it played there 477 times, with an initial cast led by Bobby Howes and his real-life daughter Sally Ann Howes, with Ken Cantril as Julio. There was a spirited revival in 1992 at the Goodspeed Opera House, Connecticut, starring George Ball (Ben), Maria Schaffel (Jennifer). and David Bedella (Julio). Four years later, in the rather appropriate setting of the Open Air Theatre, Regent's Park, Tony Selby (Ben), Claire Carrie (Jennifer), Chook Sibtain (Julio), and the remainder of a splendid cast, gloried in what has finally come to be regarded as a marvellous score. The Californian characters were still searching for that elusive rainbow, but at least Lerner and Loewe found their own pot of gold some four years and a few months after the show first opened on Broadway. It was called *My Fair Lady*. A film version of *Paint Your Wagon* was released in 1969, with Lee Marvin, Clint Eastwood, Jean Seberg, and Harve Presnell.

PAJAMA GAME, THE

The new songwriting team of Richard Adler and Jerry Ross joined with Bob Fosse, who was making his Broadway debut as a choreographer, and veteran George Abbott, to help create this immensely enjoyable musical which opened at the St. James Theatre in New York on 13 May 1954. Abbott and Richard Bissell's book, which was based on Bissell's novel *Seven And A Half Cents*, deals with a dispute between workers and management in the Sleep Tite Pajama Factory in Cedar Rapids, Iowa. New factory superintendent Sid Sorokin (John Raitt) gets on well with the head of the Grievance Committee, Babe Williams (Janis Paige), but is forced to dismiss her – although their non-industrial relations are progressing quite nicely – when she sabotages the production line. Sid sorts out her, and everyone else's grievances, when he discovers that the big bad boss has been including the requested seven and a half cent rise in his costings for ages – even though the workers have not been receiving it. Now, everyone is delighted – even time and motion man Hines (Eddie Foy Jnr.), who is constantly consulting

Mabel (Reta Shaw) about the (imagined) unfaithfulness of his girlfriend Gladys (Carol Haney), and union freak Prez (Stanley Prager), who would be unfaithful with any of the female staff if only they would let him. Adler and Ross's sparkling score included 'The Pajama Game; Racing With The Clock', 'A New Town Is A Blue Town', 'I'm Not At All In Love', 'I'll Never Be Jealous Again', 'Her Is', 'Once-A-Year-Day', 'Small Talk', 'There Once Was A Man', 'Think Of The Time I Save', and 'Seven-And-A-Half Cents'. Raitt had a neat scene in which he duetted with his own voice on a dictation machine for 'Hey There', and Haney made a great impression with the sensual 'Steam Heat' and the dimly-lit 'Hernando's Hideaway'. George Abbott and Jerome Robbins directed this smash hit production which ran for 1,063 performances, and won Tony Awards for best musical, featured musical actress (Haney), producers (more Broadway newcomers, Frederick Brisson, Robert E. Griffith and Harold Prince), authors, composer and lyricist, and choreographer. Joy Nichols (Babe), Edmund Hockridge (Sid), Max Wall (Hines), Elizabeth Seal (Gladys), Joan Emney (Mabel), and Frank Lawless (Prez) led the 1955 London show which played 588 times at the Coliseum and is remembered with a great deal of affection. Hockridge had considerable success with his recording of 'Hey There', and it became one of his signature songs. Richard Adler's 1973 Broadway revival introduced a little racial romanticism into the piece, with a black Babe (Barbara McNair) and white Sid (Hal Linden), along with Sharron Miller (Gladys), Cab Calloway (Hines), and Mary Jo Catlett (Mabel). In 1958, the musical *Say, Darling*, allegedly based on Richard Bissell's experiences with *The Pajama Game*, opened on Broadway and ran for 332 performances. The cast was headed by Vivian Blaine, David Wayne, and Johnny Desmond sang and danced to the music and lyrics of Jule Styne, Betty Comden and Adolph Green. The 1985 Leicester Haymarket production toured the UK regions with Paul Jones and Fiona Hendley, and Adler wrote Hendley a new song, a reflective little waltz called 'If You Win, You Lose'. A different number, but with the same title, featured in the 1998 Goodspeed Opera House revival, which had Sean McDermott (Sid), Colleen Fitzpatrick (Babe), Bob Walton (Hines), Valerie Wright (Gladys), Nora Mae Lyng (Mabel), and Casey Nicholaw (Prez). In April 1999, British director Simon Callow 'put a contemporary spin' on a Birmingham Repertory Theatre revival, assisted by ballet director David Bintley (choreography), American abstract artist Frank Stella (sets), and classical saxophone virtuoso John Harle (music supervision). Heading the cast were Graham Bickley (Sid), Ulrika Johnsson (Babe), John Hegley (Hines), Alison Limerick (Gladys), Anita Dobson (Mabel), and Jonathan D. Ellis (Prez). The vocal demands of the role proved too much for Johnsson, and she was replaced by *Crazy For You*'s Camilla Scott during the brief Toronto run. Leslie Ash was in the lead when *The Pajama Game* opened in the West End on the 4 October 1999. John Raitt, Carol

Haney, and Eddie Foy Jnr. were among members of the original Broadway stage cast who recreated their roles for the 1957 film version, which also starred Doris Day.

PAL JOEY

This somewhat sanitized version of the 1940 Broadway show and John O'Hara's witty essays on which it was based, came to the screen in 1957. Frank Sinatra proved to be the ideal choice for the role of 'the heel of all-time', Joey Evans, the nightclub singer and compere, whose apparent mission in life is to seduce each 'mouse' in the chorus with the offer of 'shrimp cocktail, a steak, french fries, a little wine – the whole mish-mosh', so that he can 'help her with her arrangements'. The ingenuous Linda English (Kim Novak) accepts his offer, and, after the usual complications, and to the surprise of many who had read O'Hara's original short stories, goes off with him into the sunset. The musical high spot comes when Joey sings an electrifying version of 'The Lady Is A Tramp' to the wealthy widow Vera Simpson (Rita Hayworth), who had been known as 'Vanessa The Undresser' in her former life as a stripper. London film critics at the time thought it slightly ridiculous when some of their number actually applauded a piece of celluloid, but it was that kind of performance. Hank Henry, as the grumpy owner of the Barbary Coast nightspot where Joey 'operates', and Bobby Sherwood as the leader of its orchestra, headed a supporting cast that also included Barbara Nicholls and Elizabeth Patterson. The majority of Richard Rodgers and Lorenz Hart's fine stage score was retained, with four additional songs from their other shows. Sinatra was in great voice on 'I Could Write A Book', 'There's a Small Hotel' and 'What Do I Care For A Dame?', while Hayworth shimmied her way through 'Zip' and 'Bewitched' (vocals dubbed by Jo Ann Greer). Trudy Erwin's voice was behind Novak's sultry rendering of 'My Funny Valentine' and 'That Terrific Rainbow'. Hermes Pan was the choreographer, and Dorothy Kingsley's screenplay was adequate – O'Hara's version of events would never have been acceptable even in the late 50s – and this entertaining film grossed nearly $5 million in US rentals alone. It was produced in Technicolor for Columbia by Fred Kohlmar. The director was George Sidney.

PARAMOR, NORRIE

b. 1913, London, England, d. 9 September 1979. The most prolific producer of UK pop chart-toppers was a mild, bespectacled gentleman who had studied piano and worked as an accompanist, prior to playing and arranging with a number of London dance bands, among them Maurice Winnick's Orchestra. During his time in the RAF during World War II, Paramor entertained servicemen in the company of artists such as Sidney Torch and Max Wall, served as a musical director for Ralph Reader's Gang Shows, and scored music for Noël Coward, Mantovani and Jack Buchanan. After the war he was the featured pianist with Harry Gold And His Pieces Of Eight, and toured with the lively Dixieland unit for five years. In 1950 he recorded some sides for the Oriole label with Australian singer Marie Benson, and two years later, joined Columbia Records, an EMI Records subsidiary, as arranger and A&R manager. In 1954, he produced the first of two UK number 1 hits for Eddie Calvert, and another for Ruby Murray the following year. Although quoted as believing that rock 'n' roll was 'an American phenomenon – and they do it best', he still provided Columbia with such an act in Tony Crombie's Rockets, but had better luck with the mainstream efforts of Michael Holliday and the Mudlarks – both backed by the Ken Jones Orchestra.

Then, in 1958, a demo tape by Cliff Richard And The Drifters arrived on his desk. With no rock 'n' roller currently on his books, he contracted Richard, intending to play it safe with a US cover version with the Jones band, until he was persuaded to stick with the Drifters (soon renamed the Shadows) and push a group original ('Move It') as the a-side. Partly through newspaper publicity engineered by Paramor, 'Move It' was a huge hit, and a subsequent policy was instigated of Richard recording singles of untried numbers – among them, at Paramor's insistence, Lionel Bart's 'Living Doll'. Columbia was also successful with the Shadows – even though Paramor initially wished to issue 'Apache' – their first smash – as a b-side. Later, he offended Shadows purists by augmenting the quartet on disc with horn sections and his trademark lush string arrangements.

Other Paramor signings were not allowed to develop to the same idiosyncratic extent as Richard and his associates. Ricky Valance achieved his sole chart-topper with a cover version of Ray Peterson's US hit 'Tell Laura I Love Her', while Helen Shapiro was visualized as a vague 'answer' to Brenda Lee; Paramor even booked and supervised some Shapiro sessions in Nashville in 1963. His greatest success during this period, however, was with Frank Ifield, who dominated the early 60s' UK pop scene with three formidable number 1 hits. Even as late as 1968, Paramor notched up another number 1 with Scaffold's 'Lily The Pink'.

Throughout his career, Paramor wrote, and co-wrote, many hit songs, several of them for films, such as *Expresso Bongo* ('A Voice In The Wilderness', Cliff Richard), *The Young Ones* ('The Savage') and *The Frightened City* (title song), both performed by the Shadows, *Play It Cool* ('Once Upon A Dream', Billy Fury), *It's Trad, Dad!* ('Let's Talk About Love', Helen Shapiro) and *Band Of Thieves* ('Lonely', Acker Bilk). He also composed several complete movie scores, and some light orchestral works such as 'The Zodiac' and 'Emotions', which he recorded with his Concert Orchestra, and released several 'mood' albums in the USA, including *London After Dark*, *Amore, Amore!*, *Autumn* and *In London, In Love*, which made the US Top 20. In complete contrast, the Big Ben Banjo, and Big Ben Hawaiian Bands, along with similar 'happy-go-lucky' 'trad jazz' line-ups, were originally formed in 1955 purely as recording units, utilizing the cream of UK session musicians.

Paramor was in charge of them all, and their popularity was such that 'live' performances had to be organized. The Big Ben Banjo Band appeared at the Royal Variety Performance in 1958, and were resident on BBC Radio's *Everybody Step* programme, as well as having their own Radio Luxembourg series. Two of the band's 'Let's Get Together' singles, and *More Minstrel Melodies*, reached the UK Top 20. One of the highlights of Paramor's career came in 1960 when he arranged and conducted for Judy Garland's British recording sessions, and was her musical director at the London Palladium and subsequent dates in Europe. In the same year, with his Orchestra, he made the UK singles chart with 'Theme From A Summer Place' and in 1962, registered again with 'Theme From Z Cars'. From 1972-78 Paramor was the Director of the BBC Midland Radio Orchestra, but he continued to dabble in independent production for acts such as the Excaliburs, and his publishing company was still finding material for Cliff in the 70s. Paramor remains one of the most underrated figures in the history of UK pop and a posthumous reappraisal of his work is overdue.

● ALBUMS: *Just We Two* (Columbia 1955) ★★★, *In London, In Love ...* (Columbia 1956) ★★★, *The Zodiac* (Columbia 1957) ★★★, *New York Impressions* (Columbia 1957) ★★★, *Emotions* (Columbia 1958) ★★★, *Dreams And Desires* (Columbia 1958) ★★★, *The Wonderful Waltz* (Columbia 1958) ★★★, *My Fair Lady* (Columbia 1959) ★★★, *Paramor In Paris* (Columbia 1959) ★★★, *Jet Flight* (Columbia 1959) ★★★, *Lovers In Latin* (Columbia 1959) ★★★, *Staged For Stereo* (Columbia 1961) ★★★, *Autumn* (Columbia 1961) ★★★, *The Golden Waltz* (Columbia 1961) ★★★, *Lovers In London* (Columbia 1964) ★★★, with Patricia Clark *Lovers In Tokyo* (1964) ★★, *Warm And Willing* (1965) ★★★, *Shadows In Latin* (Studio 2 1966) ★★★, *Norrie Paramor Plays The Hits Of Cliff Richard* (Studio 2 1967) ★★★, *Soul Coaxing* (1968) ★★★, *BBC Top Tunes* (BBC 1974) ★★★, *Radio 2 Top Tunes, Volume 1* (BBC 1974) ★★★, *Radio 2 Top Tunes, Volume 2* (BBC 1975) ★★★, *Radio 2 Top Tunes, Volume 3* (BBC 1975) ★★★, *Love* (Pye 1975) ★★★, *My Personal Choice* (BBC 1976) ★★★, *Norrie Paramor Remembers ... 40 Years Of TV Themes* (BBC 1976) ★★★, *Silver Serenade* (BBC 1977) ★★★, *By Request* (BBC 1978) ★★★, *Temptation* (Pye 1978) ★★★, *Rags And Tatters* aka *Ragtime* (Pye 1978) ★★, *Classical Rhythm* (Pye 1979) ★★, *Thank You For The Music* (BBC 1979) ★★★.

● COMPILATIONS: *Paramagic Pianos* (Golden Hour 1977) ★★★, *The Best Of Norrie Paramor* (BBC 1984) ★★★.

PARKER, 'COLONEL' TOM

b. Andreas Cornelius van Kuijk, 26 June 1909, Breda, The Netherlands, d. 21 January 1997. Since his death, there still remains bitter division about Parker. Was he Sam Katzman's 'biggest con artist in the world' or merely an unsophisticated fairground barker sucked into a vortex of circumstances he was unwilling to resist? Arguments supporting either view might be construed from the icy ruthlessness formidable to those accustomed to Tin Pan Alley's glib bonhomie, and his blunt stance in negotiation on behalf of Elvis Presley, his most famous managerial client. 'Don't criticize what you can't understand, son', Presley said in the Colonel's defence. 'You never walked in that man's shoes.' Parker was an illegal immigrant, without passport or papers, who settled into carnival life in the 20s. Over the next decade, he evolved into a cigar-chewing huckster of spectacular amorality – exemplified by his practice of snaring sparrows, painting them yellow and selling them as canaries. With duties that included palm reading, he served the Royal American, the Union's top travelling show, for a while before a seemingly steady job as promoter for a charity organization in Tampa, Florida. Extremely potent fund raisers, he discovered, were shows headlined by a popular C&W artist – and so it was that Parker came to commit himself full-time to the genre by moving to Nashville, where he became Eddy Arnold's personal manager. Once, when this vocalist was indisposed, an unruffled Parker allegedly offered a substitute attraction of two unhappy 'dancing chickens' who high-stepped around a cage to ease feet scorched by an electric hot plate hidden under their straw.

After Arnold left him, the Colonel (an honorary title conferred by the Tennessee Militia in 1953) took on Hank Snow – and it was in a support spot on a Snow tour of the deep south that 19-year-old Presley was noticed by his future svengali. Via connections nurtured during proceedings concerning Arnold and Snow, Parker persuaded RCA Records to contract his new find. A few months later in March 1956, the boy committed himself formally to Parker for life – and beyond. From that month, 'Elvis has required every minute of my time, and I think he would have suffered had I signed anyone else'. While facilitating Presley's captivation of a global 'youth market', the Colonel's instinct for the commercial and economic machinations of the record industry obliged RCA to accede to his every desire, such as the pressing of one million copies of every Elvis release, regardless of positioning research. Moreover, to the team fell an average of eight per cent of approved merchandise associated with Presley – and, when the time came for the King to act in films, producer Hal Wallis grew to 'rather try and close a deal with the Devil' than Parker. To publicize one Presley movie, Parker was not above hiring dwarfs to parade through Hollywood as 'The Elvis Presley Midget Fan Club'. He was also behind the taming of Presley via the stressing of a cheerful diligence while on national service; the post-army chart potboilers; the overall projection of Presley as an 'all-round entertainer', and, arguably, the moulding of his reactionary leanings. Nor did Parker object to Katzman dashing off a Presley vehicle in less than a month, each one a quasi-musical of cheery unreality usually more vacuous and streamlined than the one before. This was almost all fans saw of the myth-shrouded Elvis until his impatient return to the stage in 1968, whether the Colonel liked it or not.

After Presley's death in 1977, there were rumours that Parker would be devoting himself professionally to Rick Nelson, but only Presley's posthumous career interrupted a virtual retirement in Palm Springs. Parker was a consummate showman and media manipulator, who clearly enjoyed turning down million of dollars whenever his charge was asked to headline some grand concert package. His handling of merchandising rights during the early part of Presley's career has been compared favourably to the business dealings of later star makers such as Brian Epstein. The obsession with commerce and disavowal of artistry dominated the Colonel's thinking, however, which mainly explains the singer's appalling film-related output during the early/mid-60s. After Presley's death, Parker's business empire was threatened by the star's estate – in the form of Elvis' ex-wife Priscilla and daughter Lisa Marie. Parker fought tenaciously to protect his empire before settling in June 1983. Thereafter, he surrendered claims to all future Elvis income, but received two million dollars from RCA, and 50 per cent of all Presley's record royalties prior to September 1982. In January 1993, Parker made one of his rare public appearances, signing autographs to promote the newly issued Elvis Presley postage stamp. He spent the last years of his life in his beloved Las Vegas, where he could feed his gambling addiction.

● FURTHER READING: *Elvis*, Albert Grossman. *Elvis And The Colonel*, Dirk Vallenga and Mick Farren. *Colonel Tom Parker: The Curious Life Of Elvis Presley's Eccentric Manager*, James L. Dickerson.

PARKER, FESS

b. 16 August 1925, Fort Worth, Texas, USA. An actor and singer, Parker did some stage work before making his film debut in 1952 in *Untamed Frontier*, a western starring Joseph Cotton and Shelley Winters. Two years later he appeared as the famous Indian scout-legislator-Alamo defender Davy Crockett, in three episodes of the television series *Disneyland*. The shows were extremely popular, and the theme, 'The Ballad Of Davy Crockett', written by scriptwriter Tom Blackburn and George Bruns, became a US number 1 hit for Bill Hayes, well known on television himself for *Show Of Shows*. Subsequently, Parker's own version of the song made the US Top 10. When the big screen version, *Davy Crockett, King Of The Wild Frontier!*, was made in 1955, coonskin caps abounded, nationwide and beyond; the inevitable sequel, *Davy Crockett And The River Pirates*, was released in 1956. In the same year, Parker starred in Walt Disney's *Westward Ho, The Wagons!*, which featured five new songs, including 'Wringle Wrangle', Parker's second, and last, chart success. His other movies, through to the 60s, included *The Great Locomotive Chase* (1956), *Old Yeller* (1957 – the first of the many Disney films about a boy and his dog), *The Hangman* (1959) and *Hell Is For Heroes* (1962), an exciting World War II drama, with Steve McQueen and Bobby Darin. Parker was also prominent on US television; in 1962 he co-starred with country singer Red Foley in a series based on Lewis R. Foster's classic, *Mr. Smith Goes To Washington*. Two years later he returned to the backwoods and portrayed yet another legendary American pioneer in *Daniel Boone*, which ran until 1968. In 1972 he played a tough sheriff in the US television movie *Climb An Angry Mountain*. After he retired from showbusiness, Parker moved to Santa Barbara, California, and initially concentrated on a career in real estate. Since then, as the owner of Santa Barbara's Red Lion Resort and Parker Winery, he has become something of a tycoon, and by the early 90s his products were selling in over 30 states.

● ALBUMS: with Marion Marlowe *TV Sweethearts* (Columbia 1955) ★★, *The Adventures Of Davy Crockett* (Columbia 1955) ★★★, *Yarns And Songs* (Disneyland 1959) ★★, *Cowboy And Indian Songs* (Disneyland 1960) ★★, *Fess Parker Sings About Daniel Boone, Davy Crockett And Abe Lincoln* (RCA Victor 1964) ★.

PARNES, LARRY

b. Laurence Maurice Parnes, 1930, Willesden, London, England, d. 4 August 1989, London, England. Parnes, 'Mr Parnes shillings and pence' was the most famous UK pop manager and impresario of the 50s, and one of the greatest of all time. After briefly working in the family clothing business, he took over a bar in London's West End called La Caverne. The establishment was frequented by many theatrical agents and producers and, before long, Parnes was inveigled into investing in a play entitled *Women Of The Streets*. One night at a coffee bar he met publicist John Kennedy, who was then overseeing the affairs of singer Tommy Hicks. After seeing the boy perform at Lionel Bart's suggestion Parnes was impressed and went into partnership with Kennedy. Hicks was rechristened Tommy Steele and became the UK's first rock 'n' roll celebrity. He later emerged as an all-round entertainer and star of several musicals. Parnes specialized in discovering young boys, who would be systematically groomed, launched on the rock 'n' roll circuit, and finally assimilated into traditional showbusiness areas. The technique was habitual. Parnes played the part of the svengali, carefully renaming his acts with some exotically powerful surname that suggested power, virility or glamour. His second discovery proved another winner. Reg Smith was quickly snapped up by the starmaker, rechristened Marty Wilde and soon enjoyed a string of UK hits, before 'retiring' from rock 'n' roll at the close of the 50s.

By this time, Parnes had a network of contacts, including A&R managers like Hugh Mendl, Dick Rowe and Jack Baverstock, who would always take notice of a Parnes act. The bombastic television producer Jack Good also realized that supporting Parnes ensured a steady flow of teenage talent. Finally, there were the songwriters like Lionel Bart, who could provide original material, although cover versions of US hits were always popular. Parnes' third great discovery of the 50s was Billy Fury, one of the most important figures

to emerge from British rock 'n' roll. Significantly, Parnes remained with the star for a considerable time and was still handling his business affairs during the late 60s. The irrepressible Joe Brown was another major find for Parnes, although their association was often stormy. Brown was an exceptional guitarist and was frequently used to back other Parnes acts. For every star he unearthed, however, there were a series of lesser talents or unlucky singers who failed to find chart success. Among the famous Parnes 'stable of stars' were Dickie Pride, Duffy Power, Johnny Gentle, Terry Dene, Nelson Keene, Sally Kelly, and Peter Wynne. Larry was also briefly associated with Georgie Fame and the Tornados. Beyond his management interests, Parnes was a great provider of package shows with grandiloquent titles such as 'The Big New Rock 'n' Roll Trad Show' and the 'Star Spangled Nights'.

Parnes' influence effectively ended during the early to mid-60s when new managers and entrepreneurs such as Brian Epstein and Andrew Loog Oldham took centre stage. Ironically, Parnes had two chances to sign the Beatles but passed up the opportunity. Like his stars, he seemed intent on abdicating his position in rock 'n' roll and increasingly moved into more conservative areas of British showbusiness and theatre. During the 60s, he was involved in musicals such as *Charlie Girl*. During the 70s, he returned to management in a different sphere, administering the business affairs of ice-skater John Currie. He subsequently fell ill with meningitis and effectively retired. His public image remained contradictory and subject to caricature. As the prototype British pop svengali, he was used as the inspiration for the vapid, camp starmaker in Julien Temple's 1986 movie *Absolute Beginners*. Ever self-protective and litigious, his wrath descended upon the BBC, among others, when he won a substantial out-of-court settlement for an alleged libel by Paul McCartney on a most unlikely programme, *Desert Island Discs*.

● FURTHER READING: *Starmakers & Svengalis: The History Of British Pop Management*, Johnny Rogan.

PATTERSON, OTTILIE

b. Anna-Ottilie Patterson, 31 January 1932, Comber, Co. Down, Northern Ireland. Patterson is perhaps best known for her long-time association with Chris Barber, then her husband, in the 50s and 60s. With Barber she sang jazz and blues but she was also an accomplished folk-singer. Ranging outside popular fields, she has also composed music to accompany poetry. For some years she was obliged through ill health to abandon her singing career, but later returned to the stage to the delight of her many fans. An engaging singer, with a strong, earthy delivery that lends itself well to the blues and some aspects of the jazz songbook, for her folk-singing she was always able to adjust to a more pensive approach. A bright and bubbling personality, she is at her best in live performances and has been captured in splendid form on a number of live albums by the Barber band.

● ALBUMS: with Chris Barber *Chris Barber At The London Palladium* (Columbia 1961) ★★★★.
● COMPILATIONS: with Barber *40 Years Jubilee Volumes 1* and *2* (Timeless 1990) ★★★★.

PAUL, LES

b. 9 June 1915, Wankesha, Wisconsin, USA. Paul began playing guitar and other instruments while still a child. In the early 30s he broadcast on the radio and in 1936 was leading his own trio. In the late 30s and early 40s he worked in New York, where he was featured on Fred Waring's radio show. He made records accompanying singers such as Bing Crosby and the Andrews Sisters. Although his work was in the popular vein, with a strong country leaning, Paul was highly adaptable and frequently sat in with jazz musicians. One of his favourites was Nat 'King' Cole, whom he knew in Los Angeles, and the two men appeared together at a Jazz At The Philharmonic concert in 1944, on which Paul played some especially fine blues. Dissatisfied with the sound of the guitars he played, Paul developed his own design for a solid-bodied instrument, which he had made at his own expense. Indeed, the company, Gibson, were so cool towards the concept that they insisted their name should not appear on the instruments they made for him. In later years, when it seemed that half the guitarists in the world were playing Les Paul-style Gibson guitars, the company's attitude was understandably a little different.

Paul's dissatisfaction with existing techniques extended beyond the instrument and into the recording studios. Eager to experiment with a multi-tracking concept, he built a primitive studio in his own home. He produced a succession of superb recordings on which he played multi-track guitar, among them 'Lover', 'Nola', 'Brazil' and 'Whispering'. During the 50s Paul continued his experimentation with other, similar recordings, while his wife, Mary Ford (b. 7 July 1928, d. 30 September 1977), sang multiple vocal lines. Other major record successes were 'The World Is Waiting For The Sunrise', 'How High The Moon', which reached number 1, and 'Vaya Con Dios', another US number 1 hit. By the early 60s Paul had tired of the recording business and retired. He and Ford were divorced in 1963 and he spent his time inventing and helping to promote Gibson guitars. In the late 70s he returned to the studios for two successful albums of duets with Chet Atkins, but by the end of the decade he had retired again. A television documentary in 1980, *The Wizard Of Wankesha*, charted his life and revived interest in his career. In 1984 he made a comeback to performing and continued to make sporadic appearances throughout the rest of the decade. He was even performing at the guitar festival in Seville, Spain, in 1992. A remarkably gifted and far-sighted guitarist, Paul's contribution to popular music must inevitably centre upon his pioneering work on multi-tracking and his creation of the solid-bodied guitar. It would be sad, however, if his efforts in these directions wholly concealed his considerable abilities as a performer.

● ALBUMS: with Mary Ford *Hawaiian Paradise* (Decca 1949) ★★, *Galloping Guitars* (Decca 1952) ★★★, with Ford *New Sound, Volume 1 & 2* (Capitol 1950) ★★★, *Bye, Bye Blues* (Capitol 1952) ★★★★, with Ford *The Hitmakers* (Capitol 1955) ★★★, *Les And Mary* (Capitol 1955) ★★★★, with Ford *Time To Dream* (Capitol 1957) ★★★, *More Of Les* (Decca 1958) ★★★, with Ford *Lover's Luau* (Columbia 1959) ★★★, with Ford *Warm And Wonderful* (Columbia 1962) ★★★, with Ford *Bouquet Of Roses* (Columbia 1962) ★★★, with Ford *Swingin' South* (Columbia 1963) ★★★, *Les Paul Now* (Decca 1968) ★★★, with Chet Atkins *Chester & Lester* (RCA Victor 1975) ★★★, with Atkins *Guitar Monsters* (RCA Victor 1978) ★★★.
● COMPILATIONS: *The Hits Of Les And Mary* (Capitol 1960) ★★★★, *The Fabulous Les Paul And Mary Ford* (Columbia 1965) ★★★, *The Very Best Of Les Paul And Mary Ford* (1974) ★★★★, with Ford *The Capitol Years* (Capitol 1989) ★★★★, *The Legend And The Legacy* 4-CD box set (Capitol 1991) ★★★★, with Ford *Blowing The Smoke Away From A Trail Of Hits* (Jasmine 2000) ★★, with Ford *The Collection ... Plus* (See For Miles 2001) ★★★.
● VIDEOS: *He Changed The Music* (Excalibur 1990), *Living Legend Of The Electric Guitar* (BMG 1995).
● FURTHER READING: *Les Paul: An American Original*, Mary Alice Shaughnessy. *Gibson Les Paul Book: A Complete History Of Les Paul Guitars*, Tony Bacon and Paul Day.

PENGUINS

Formed in 1954 in Fremont High School, Los Angeles, California, USA, the Penguins were one of the most important R&B vocal groups from the west coast in the early 50s. Their hit ballad 'Earth Angel' remains one of the most fondly recalled 'doo-wop' recordings. The group consisted of lead vocalist Cleveland 'Cleve' Duncan (b. 23 July 1935, Los Angeles, California, USA), Bruce Tate (baritone), Curtis Williams (first tenor) and Dexter Tisby (second tenor). Williams learned 'Earth Angel' from Los Angeles R&B singer Jesse Belvin, and passed it on to his group. Some sources give co-writing credit to Williams, Belvin and Gaynel Hodge, a member of vocal group the Turks. Hodge won a 1956 lawsuit recognizing his role in the writing of the song. However, most reissues of 'Earth Angel' still list only either Belvin, Williams or both. The Penguins, who took their name from a penguin on a cigarette packet, signed with the local DooTone Records, owned by Dootsie Williams. Their first recording date was as a backing group for a blues singer, Willie Headon. They next recorded 'Hey Senorita', an up-tempo number. 'Earth Angel' was chosen as their first single's b-side but when both sides were played on LA radio station KGJF, listeners called in to request that 'Earth Angel' be played again. It ultimately reached number 1 in the US *Billboard* R&B chart. It also reached the pop Top 10, but was eclipsed by a cover version by the white group the Crew-Cuts. The song has also charted by Gloria Mann (1955), Johnny Tillotson (1960), the Vogues (1969) and New Edition (1986). The Penguins

continued to record other singles for DooTone (plus one album for the related Dooto label) and then Mercury Records, before disbanding in 1959. Members Williams and Tate have since died, Tisby retired from music, and Duncan later formed new bands under the name Penguins.
● COMPILATIONS: *The Cool, Cool Penguins* (Dooto 1959) ★★★, side 1 only *The Best Vocal Groups: Rhythm And Blues* (Dooto 1959) ★★★, *Big Jay McNeely Meets The Penguins* (Ace 1984) ★★★, *Earth Angel* (Ace 1988) ★★★, *The Authentic Golden Hits Of The Penguins* (Juke Box 1993) ★★★.

PEPPER, ART
b. 1 September 1925, Gardena, Los Angeles, California, USA, d. 15 June 1982, Panorama City, California, USA. Pepper started out on clarinet at the age of nine, switching to alto saxophone four years later. After appearing in school groups, he first played professionally with Gus Arnheim's band. During his mid-teens he developed his jazz style sitting in with otherwise all-black bands along Los Angeles' Central Avenue. After leaving Arnheim he worked with Dexter Gordon in Lee Young's band at the Club Alabam. He then joined Benny Carter, playing alongside artists such as Gerald Wilson, Freddie Webster and J.J. Johnson. In 1943 Pepper joined Stan Kenton but soon afterwards was drafted into the US Army, spending most of his wartime service in England. In 1946 he rejoined Kenton, staying with the band until 1951. That year he also recorded with Shorty Rogers, playing a marvellous version of 'Over The Rainbow', a tune he would regularly play over the years. Later, he appeared on Rogers' *Cool And Crazy* album. Pepper subsequently freelanced around Los Angeles, performing many record dates, some under his own name, and usually playing extremely well. Nevertheless, his career in the 50s and 60s was marred by his drug addiction and interrupted by several prison sentences. At the end of the 60s Pepper began a slow, uphill fight against his addiction, a struggle that was eventually successful and heralded his re-emergence in the mid-70s as a major figure on the international jazz scene. In the last years of his life, he produced a rich crop of recordings, including *Winter Moon*, an album with strings (a long-held ambition of Pepper's), the three-album set *Live At The Village Vanguard* (a fourth volume appeared posthumously) and two records recorded live in London under the name of pianist Milcho Leviev, *Blues For The Fisherman* and *True Blues*.
Early in his career Pepper played with a light airy tone, through which burned a rare intensity of emotion that reflected his admiration for Charlie Parker and the lessons he learned playing with Carter. After his rehabilitation and a period playing tenor saxophone, on which instrument he showed both the influence of Lester Young and an awareness of John Coltrane, Pepper developed a strong, bop-rooted alto style that retained much of the richly melodic elements of his earlier playing. Pepper's life story was memorably recounted in his candid autobiography and a subsequent film, *Art Pepper: Notes From A Jazz Survivor*, which offered a potent and harshly unsentimental lesson for any young musician contemplating the use of addictive drugs.
● ALBUMS: *Art Pepper Quartet* 10-inch album (Discovery 1952) ★★★, *Art Pepper Quintet* reissued as *Surf Ride* (Discovery/Savoy 1954) ★★★★, with Richie Kamuca, Bill Perkins *Just Friends* (Pacific Jazz 1956) ★★★, *The Return Of Art Pepper* (Jazz: West 1956) ★★★, *The Route* (Pacific Jazz 1956) ★★★, with Joe Morello, Red Norvo *Joe Morello Sextet* reissued as *The Art Pepper-Red Norvo Sextet* (Intro/Score 1957) ★★★★, with Chet Baker *Playboys* reissued as *Picture Of Health* (Pacific Jazz 1957) ★★★, *The Artistry Of Pepper* (Pacific 1957) ★★★★, *Modern Art* (Intro 1957) ★★★★, *The Art Of Pepper* (Blue Note 1957) ★★★★, *Art Pepper Meets The Rhythm Section* (Contemporary 1957) ★★★★★, *The Art Pepper Quartet* (Tampa 1958) ★★★, *Art Pepper + Eleven: Modern Jazz Classics* (Contemporary 1959) ★★★★★, with Sonny Red *Two Altos* reissued as *Art Pepper-Sonny Redd* (Regent/Savoy 1959) ★★★, *Gettin' Together!* (Contemporary 1960) ★★★★, *Smack Up!* (Contemporary 1961) ★★★★, *Intensity* 1960 recording (Contemporary 1963) ★★★★, with Shelly Manne *Pepper/Manne* (Charlie Parker 1963) ★★★, *The Art Pepper Quartet In San Francisco* (Fresh Sound 1964) ★★★, *The Way It Was!* (Contemporary 1966) ★★★★, *I'll Remember April: Live At Foothill College* (Storyville 1975) ★★★, *Living Legend* (Storyville 1976) ★★★★, *The Trip* (Storyville 1977) ★★★, *A Night In Tunisia* (Storyville 1977) ★★★, *No Limit* (Storyville 1978) ★★★★, *Among Friends* (Discovery 1978) ★★★, *Live In Japan, Vol. 1* (Storyville 1978) ★★★, *Live In Japan, Vol. 2* (Storyville 1978) ★★★, *Art Pepper Today* (Galaxy 1979) ★★★, *Landscape* (Galaxy 1979) ★★★, *Straight Life* (Galaxy 1979) ★★★★, *Omega Alpha* 1957 recording (Blue Note 1980) ★★★, *So In Love* (Artists House 1980) ★★★, *Thursday Night At The Village Vanguard* 1977 recording (Contemporary 1981) ★★★★, *Friday Night At The Village Vanguard* 1977 recording (Contemporary 1981) ★★★★, *Saturday Night At The Village Vanguard* 1977 recording (Contemporary 1981) ★★★★, *More For Less* 1977 recording (Contemporary 1981) ★★★★, *Winter Moon* (Galaxy 1981) ★★★, *Besame Mucho* 1979 recording (1981) ★★★, *One September Afternoon* (Galaxy 1981) ★★★, *Road Game* (Galaxy 1982) ★★★, *Darn That Dream* (Galaxy 1982) ★★★, *Goin' Home* (Galaxy 1982) ★★★, *Art Lives* 1981 recording (Galaxy 1983) ★★★, *Art Works* 1979 recording (Galaxy 1984) ★★★, *Tokyo Debut* 1977 recording (Galaxy 1995) ★★★★, with Zoot Sims *Art 'N' Zoot* 1981 recording (Pablo 1995) ★★★★.
● COMPILATIONS: *Early Art* 1956/1957 recordings (Blue Note 1976) ★★★★, *Discoveries* 1952-1954 recordings (Muse 1985) ★★★★, *Rediscoveries* 1952-1954 recordings (Muse 1986) ★★★★, *Artistry In Jazz* (JVC 1987) ★★★, *The Complete Galaxy Recordings* 16-CD box set (Galaxy 1989) ★★★★, *Memorial Collection Vols. 1-4* (Storyville 1990) ★★★, *The Best Of Art Pepper*

(Blue Note 1993) ★★★★, *The Complete Village Vanguard Sessions* 9-CD box set (Contemporary 1995) ★★★★, *Laurie's Choice* 1978-1981 recordings (Laserlight) ★★★, *The Complete Pacific Jazz Small Group Recordings Of Art Pepper* 3-LP box set (Mosaic) ★★★★, *The Return Of Art Pepper: The Complete Art Pepper Aladdin Recordings* 1956/1957 recordings (Blue Note) ★★★, *The Art Of The Ballad* (Prestige 1998) ★★★★, *The Discovery Sessions* (Savoy 2000) ★★★, *The Hollywood All-Star Sessions* 5-CD box set (Fantasy 2001) ★★★★.
● FURTHER READING: *Straight Life: The Story Of Art Pepper*, Art and Laurie Pepper. *The Art Pepper Companion: Writings On A Jazz Original*, Todd Selbert (ed.).
● FILMS: *Art Pepper: Notes From A Jazz Survivor* (1982).

PERKINS, CARL

b. Carl Lee Perkins, 9 April 1932, Ridgely, Tennessee, USA (his birth certificate misspelled the last name as Perkings), d. 19 January 1998, Nashville, Tennessee, USA. Carl Perkins was one of the most renowned rockabilly artists recording for Sun Records in the 50s and the author of the classic song 'Blue Suede Shoes'. As a guitarist, he influenced many of the next generation of rock 'n' rollers, most prominently George Harrison and Dave Edmunds. His parents, Fonie 'Buck' and Louise Brantley Perkins, were sharecroppers during the Depression and the family was thus very poor. As a child Perkins listened to the *Grand Ole Opry* on the radio, exposing him to C&W (or hillbilly) music, and he listened to the blues being sung by a black sharecropper named John Westbrook across the field from where he worked. After World War II the Perkins family relocated to Bemis, Tennessee, where he and his brothers picked cotton; by that time his father was unable to work due to a lung infection. Having taught himself rudimentary guitar from listening to such players as Butterball Page and Arthur Smith, Perkins bought an electric guitar and learned to play it more competently.
In 1953 Carl, his brothers Jay (rhythm guitar) and Clayton (upright bass), and drummer W.S. 'Fluke' Holland formed a band that worked up a repertoire of hillbilly songs performing at local honky tonks, primarily in the Jackson, Tennessee area, where Carl settled with his wife Valda Crider in 1954. His borrowing of some techniques from the black musicians he had studied set Perkins apart from the many other country guitarists in that region at that time; his style of playing lead guitar fills around his own vocals was similar to that used in the blues. Encouraged by his wife, and by hearing a record by Elvis Presley on the radio, Perkins decided in 1954 to pursue a musical career. That October the Perkins brothers travelled to Memphis to audition for Sam Phillips at Sun Records. Phillips was not overly impressed, but agreed that the group had potential. In February 1955 he issued two songs from that first Perkins session, 'Movie Magg' and 'Turn Around', on his new Flip label. Pure country in nature, these did not make a dent in the market. Perkins'

next single was issued in August, this time on Sun itself. One track, 'Let The Jukebox Keep On Playing', was again country, but the other song, 'Gone! Gone! Gone!' was pure rockabilly. Again, it was not a hit. That November, after Phillips sold Presley's Sun contract to RCA Records, Phillips decided to push the next Perkins single, an original called 'Blue Suede Shoes'. The song had its origins when Johnny Cash, another Sun artist, suggested to Perkins that he write a song based on the phrase 'Don't step on my blue suede shoes'. It was recorded at Sun on 19 December 1955, along with three other songs, among them the b-side 'Honey Don't', later to be covered by the Beatles. 'Blue Suede Shoes' entered the US *Billboard* chart on 3 March 1956 (the same day Presley's first single entered the chart), by which time several cover versions had been recorded, by a range of artists from Presley to Lawrence Welk. Perkins' version quickly became a huge hit and was also the first country record to appear on both the R&B chart and the pop chart, in addition to the country chart.
Just as Perkins was beginning to enjoy the fruits of his labour, the car in which he and his band were driving to New York was involved in a severe accident near Dover, Delaware, when their manager, Stuart Pinkham, fell asleep at the wheel. Perkins and his brother Clayton suffered broken bones; brother Jay suffered a fractured neck; and the driver of the truck they hit, Thomas Phillips, was killed. 'Blue Suede Shoes' ultimately reached number 2 on the pop chart, a number 1 country hit and an R&B number 2. Owing to the accident, Perkins was unable to promote the record, the momentum was lost, and none of his four future chart singles would climb nearly as high. In the UK, 'Blue Suede Shoes' became Perkins' only chart single, and was upstaged commercially by the Presley cover version. Perkins continued to record for Sun until mid-1958, but the label's newcomers, Johnny Cash and Jerry Lee Lewis, occupied most of Sam Phillips' attention. Perkins' follow-up to 'Blue Suede Shoes', 'Boppin' The Blues', only reached number 70, and 'Your True Love' number 67. While still at Sun, Perkins did record numerous tracks that would later be revered by rockabilly fans, among them 'Everybody's Trying To Be My Baby' and 'Matchbox', both of which were also covered by the Beatles. On 4 December 1956, Perkins was joined by Lewis and a visiting Presley at Sun in an impromptu jam session which was recorded and released two decades later under the title 'The Million Dollar Quartet'. (Johnny Cash, despite having his photograph taken with Presley, Lewis and Carl, did not take part in the 'million dollar session' – he went shopping instead.) One of Perkins' last acts while at Sun was to appear in the film *Jamboree*, singing a song called 'Glad All Over'. In January 1958, Perkins signed with Columbia Records, where Cash would soon follow. Although some of the songs he recorded for that label were very good, only two, 'Pink Pedal Pushers' and 'Pointed Toe Shoes', both obvious attempts to recapture the success of his first footwear-oriented hit, had a

minor impression on the charts. Later that year Jay Perkins died of a brain tumour, causing Carl to turn alcoholic, an affliction from which he would not recover until the late 60s.

In 1963 Perkins signed with Decca Records, for whom there were no successful releases. He also toured outside of the USA in 1963-64; while in Britain, he met the Beatles, and watched as they recorded his songs. Perkins, who, ironically, was becoming something of a legend in Europe (as were many early rockers), returned to England for a second tour in October 1964. By 1966 he had left Decca for the small Dollie Records, a country label. In 1967 he joined Johnny Cash's band as guitarist and was allotted a guest singing spot during each of Cash's concerts and television shows. In 1969, Cash recorded Perkins' song 'Daddy Sang Bass', a minor hit in the USA. By 1970, Perkins was back on Columbia, this time recording an album together with new rock revival group NRBQ. In 1974 he signed with Mercury Records. Late that year his brother Clayton committed suicide and their father died. Perkins left Cash in 1976 and went on the road with a band consisting of Perkins' two sons, with whom he was still performing in the 90s. A tribute single to the late Presley, 'The EP Express', came in 1977 and a new album, now for the Jet label, was released in 1978. By the 80s Perkins' reputation as one of rock's pioneers had grown. He recorded an album with Cash and Lewis, *The Survivors* (another similar project, with Cash, Lewis and Roy Orbison, *Class Of '55*, followed in 1986). Perkins spent much of the 80s touring and working with younger musicians who were influenced by him, among them Paul McCartney and the Stray Cats. In 1985 he starred in a television special to mark the 30th anniversary of 'Blue Suede Shoes'. It co-starred Harrison, Ringo Starr, Dave Edmunds, two members of the Stray Cats, Rosanne Cash and Eric Clapton. In 1987 Perkins was elected to the Rock And Roll Hall of Fame. He signed to the Universal label in 1989 and released *Born To Rock*. His early work has been anthologized many times in several countries. He was unwell for much of the 90s and suffered from a heart condition that took its toll in January 1998.
● ALBUMS: *The Dance Album Of Carl Perkins* (Sun 1957) ★★★★, *Whole Lotta Shakin'* (Columbia 1958) ★★★, *Country Boy's Dream* (Dollie 1967) ★★★, *Blue Suede Shoes* (Sun 1969) ★★★, *Carl Perkins On Top* (Columbia 1969) ★★★, with the NRBQ *Boppin' The Blues* (Columbia 1970) ★★★, *My Kind Of Country* (Mercury 1973) ★★★, *The Carl Perkins Show* (Suede 1976) ★★★, *Ol' Blue Suede's Back* (Jet 1978) ★★, *Rock 'N' Gospel* (Koala 1979) ★★, *Sing A Song With Me* (Koala 1979) ★★, *Country Soul* (Koala 1979) ★★, *Cane Creek Glory Church* (Koala 1979) ★★, *Live At Austin City Limits* (Suede 1981) ★★★, with Jerry Lee Lewis, Johnny Cash *The Survivors* (Columbia 1982) ★★★, *Carl Perkins* (Dot 1985) ★★★, *Turn Around* Decca demos (Culture Press 1985) ★★★, with Jerry Lee Lewis, Johnny Cash, Roy Orbison *Class Of '55* (America 1986) ★★★, *Interviews From The Class Of '55 Recording Sessions* (America 1986) ★★, *Born To Rock*

(Universal/MCA 1989) ★★★, with Elvis Presley and Jerry Lee Lewis *The Million Dollar Quartet* (RCA 1990) ★★★, *Friends, Family & Legends* (Platinum 1992) ★★★, with Scotty Moore *706 Reunion – A Sentimental Journey* cassette only (Belle Meade 1993) ★★★, *Hound Dog* (Muskateer 1995) ★★★, with various artists *Go Cat Go!* (Dinosaur 1996) ★★★, *Live At Gilley's* (Connoisseur Collection 2000) ★★★★★.
● COMPILATIONS: *King Of Rock* (Columbia 1968) ★★★, *Carl Perkins' Greatest Hits* re-recorded Sun material (Columbia 1969) ★★, *Original Golden Hits* (Sun 1970) ★★★, *Blue Suede Shoes* (Sun 1971) ★★★, *Carl Perkins* (Harmony 1970) ★★★, *The Sun Years* 3-LP box set (Sun 1982) ★★★★, *Carl Perkins* (Cambra 1983) ★★★, *The Heart And Soul Of Carl Perkins* (Allegiance 1984) ★★★, *Dixie Fried* (Charly 1986) ★★★, *Up Through The Years, 1954-1957* (Bear Family 1986) ★★★★, *Original Sun Greatest Hits* (Rhino 1986) ★★★★, *The Country Store Collection* (Country Store 1988) ★★, *Honky Tonk Gal: Rare And Unissued Sun Masters* (Rounder 1989) ★★, *Matchbox* (Tring 1990) ★★, *Jive After Five: Best Of Carl Perkins (1958-1978)* (Rhino 1990) ★★★, *The Classic Carl Perkins* 5-CD box set (Bear Family 1990) ★★★★, *Restless: The Columbia Recordings* (Columbia 1992) ★★★, *Country Boy's Dream: The Dollie Masters* (Bear Family 1994) ★★★, *Best Of Carl Perkins* (Castle 1995) ★★★, *Boppin' Blue Suede Shoes* (Charly 1995) ★★★, *The Rockabilly King* (Charly 1995) ★★★, *The Unissued Carl Perkins* (Charly 1995) ★★, *The Masters* (Eagle 1997) ★★★, *The Definitive Collection* (Charly 1998) ★★★, *Back On Top* 4-CD box set (Bear Family 2000) ★★★.
● VIDEOS: *Rockabilly Session* (Virgin Vision 1986), *Carl Perkins & Jerry Lee Lewis Live* (BBC Video 1987), *This Country's Rockin'* (1993).
● FURTHER READING: *Disciple In Blue Suede Shoes*, Carl Perkins. *Go, Cat, Go: Life And Times Of Carl Perkins The King Of Rockability*, Carl Perkins with David McGee.
● FILMS: *Jamboree* aka *Disc Jockey Jamboree* (1957).

PERKINS, PINETOP

b. Joe Willie Perkins, 7 July 1913, Belzoni, Mississippi, USA. A barrelhouse blues pianist who has been playing piano since the age of 12, prior to that he played guitar. Perkins travelled through Mississippi and Arkansas, and north to St. Louis and Chicago, playing piano, and sometimes guitar, behind Big Joe Williams, Robert Nighthawk, John Lee 'Sonny Boy' Williamson and others. In the late 40s he was stabbed in the arm and has been unable to play guitar ever since, although clearly this injury has not impaired his playing. He recorded for Sun Records in 1953, although only 'Pinetop's Boogie Woogie' was issued, many years later. He also accompanied Earl Hooker and Boyd Gilmore on Sun, and Nighthawk on Aristocrat. From the early 60s, he settled in Chicago. In 1969, Perkins replaced Otis Spann in the Muddy Waters Band, with which he toured up to and after the leader's death, also working as a solo act. He was still performing and recording regularly in the 90s.

● ALBUMS: *Chicago Boogie Blues Piano Man* (JSP 1986) ★★★, *Boogie Woogie King* (Black & Blue 1986) ★★★, *Chicago Blues Session, Volume 12* (1989) ★★★, *The Ultimate Sun Blues Collection* (1991) ★★★, *With Chicago Beau And The Blue Ice Band* (Earwig 1992) ★★, *Solitare* (Lunacy 1995) ★★, *Big City Blues* (Antones 1995) ★★★, *Live Top 1982 recording* (Deluge 1995) ★★★, *On Top* (Deluge 1996) ★★★, *Born In The Delta* (Telarc 1997) ★★★, *Down In Mississippi* (HMG/HighTone 1998) ★★★★, *Sweet Black Angel* (Verve/Gitanes 1998) ★★, with Hubert Sumlin *Legends* (Telarc 1998) ★★★★, *Eye To Eye* (Telarc 1999) ★★★, with Michael Parrish *One Heart* (Geographic 1999) ★★, *Back On Top* (Telarc 2000) ★★★, *Live At Antones Vol 1* (Antones 2000) ★★★.

PETER PAN

A musical adaptation of J.M. Barrie's classic story was presented in New York as early as 1905 when Maude Adams and Ernest Lawford starred in a Charles Frohman production. It was revived in 1924, with Marilyn Miller in the leading role, and included two Jerome Kern songs, 'The Sweetest Thing In Life' and 'Just Because You're You'. The 1950 version, which ran for 321 performances, starred Jean Arthur and Boris Karloff. Leonard Bernstein wrote the music and lyrics for several songs, such as 'Who Am I?', 'Never-Land', 'Peter, Peter' and 'My House', and Alec Wilder also provided some incidental music. In the fourth interpretation, which opened at the Winter Garden in New York on 20 October 1954, Mary Martin, returning to Broadway for the first time since her triumph in South Pacific, played a spirited, high-flying Peter, to Cyril Ritchard's amusingly degenerate Captain Hook. The initial score, which was written by Mark 'Moose' Charlap and Carolyn Leigh, contained songs such as 'Tender Shepherd', 'I've Got To Crow', 'I'm Flying', and 'I Won't Grow Up'. Before the show reached Broadway, director and choreographer Jerome Robbins asked Jule Styne, Betty Comden and Adolph Green to provide the music and lyrics for several additional numbers, including 'Captain Hook's Waltz', 'Wendy', 'Mysterious Lady', and the lovely 'Never Never Land', which is still sung occasionally, and received a sensitive reading from Lena Horne on her *Lena At The Sands*. Mary Martin received the Tony Award for best actress, and this version ran for 152 performances before it was taped and shown on US television, giving non theatre-going audiences a rare opportunity to see a Broadway show. A 1979 New York revival, starring Sandy Duncan and George Rose, beat all the previous versions and lasted for 551 performances. Six years later, the same production played London's West End, with Joss Ackland, Judith Bruce and Bonnie Langford. In 1990, Cathy Rigby and Stephen Hanan were Peter and Hook/Darling when *Peter Pan* looked in on Broadway again for a limited six-week engagement as part of its nationwide tour. Later in the 90s Cathy Rigby (by now a mother of four) was back on the road again with a new production (Paul Schoeffler as Hook/Darling) which spent

Christmas 1998 in New York at the Marquis Theatre. Earlier that year the much acclaimed *Peter And Wendy*, Liza Lorwin's adaptation of the Barrie fantasy, was presented at New York's Victory Theatre by the Mabou Mines troupe. It 'melded movement, theatre, imagery and music into a rich theatrical tapestry', and featured an extraordinary performance by Karen Kandel. She narrated the action and provided the voices for all the characters, including Peter Pan, Captain Hook, and Mr. and Mrs. Darling, which were represented by Bunraku puppets. Johnny Cunningham's Celtic music score enhanced this delightful show perfectly, and Karen Kandel won a Village Voice Obie Award for outstanding work. Numerous other, quite different adaptations of J.M. Barrie's *Peter Pan* have been presented in the UK, including two major London productions: one with music and lyrics by Stephen Oliver at the Barbican Theatre in 1982; and another, *Peter Pan: The British Musical*, with a score by Piers Chater-Robinson, which starred Ron Moody (Hook) and Nicola Stapleton (Peter), and played at the Cambridge Theatre in 1994. In 1997, John Caird directed a Royal National Theatre revival of their 1982 version of *Peter Pan*, with Ian McKellen's Hook sparring with a male Peter, Daniel Evans. In 1996, Varèse Sarabande released *The Musical Adventures Of Peter Pan*, which featured 'Great songs from Mary Martin's *Peter Pan*, Walt Disney's *Peter Pan*, Leonard Bernstein's *Peter Pan*, Anthony Newley and Leslie Bricusse's *Peter Pan*, *Hook* by John Williams, and more!' Several classic numbers were included, plus rare cut items by Broadway singers such as Susan Egan, Liz Larsen, Christa Moore, and Jonathan Freeman.

● FURTHER READING: *The Peter Pan Chronicles*, Bruce K. Hanson.

PETERSON, RAY

b. 23 April 1939, Denton, Texas, USA. Peterson entertained other patients with his singing during lengthy treatment for polio in the Texas Warm Springs Foundation Hospital. On discharge, he performed in local clubs before moving to Los Angeles where he was spotted by manager Stan Shulman who procured an RCA-Victor Records recording contract. 'Let's Try Romance' (1958) paved the way for further failures in 'Tail Light', a cover of the Little Willie John hit 'Fever' and the uptempo 'Shirley Purley'. However, Peterson came up trumps with 'The Wonder Of You' (later a million-seller for Elvis Presley) in the US and UK Top 30 charts in 1959 and had a minor UK hit a year later with 'Answer Me'. In 1960, he swept into the US Top 10 with the original version of car crash epic 'Tell Laura I Love Her' – which financed the foundation of Dunes, Peterson's own record company. Its flagship acts were Curtis Lee – and Peterson himself who was successful with the traditional 'Corinne Corinna', 'Missing You' (a Gerry Goffin/Carole King ballad), and 'I Could Have Loved You So Well' (1961). On transferring to MGM Records, he attempted to rise anew as a C&W star after a pop chart swansong in 1963 with 'Give Us Your Blessing'.

● ALBUMS: *Tell Laura I Love Her* (Victor 1960) ★★★, *The Other Side Of Ray Peterson* (MGM 1965) ★★★, *Goodnight My Love, Pleasant Dreams* (RCA 1967) ★★, *Ray Peterson Country* (Decca 1971) ★★.
● COMPILATIONS: *The Very Best Of Ray Peterson* (MGM 1964) ★★★, *Missing You: The Best Of Ray Peterson* (Uni 1969) ★★★, *Roy Orbison/Ray Peterson* (1993) ★★.

PETTY, NORMAN

b. 1927, Clovis, New Mexico, USA, d. 15 August 1984, Lubbock, Texas, USA. Petty studied piano during his youth but became a recording engineer on local radio in Texas until his Norman Petty Trio – with wife Violet (organ) and Jack Vaughn (guitar) – achieved moderate record success in 1954 with an arrangement of Duke Ellington's 'Mood Indigo'. In similar cocktail lounge-style were smaller sellers, notably 'On The Alamo' and 1957's self-composed 'Almost Paradise' (revived in the 70s by Roger Whittaker). More immediate proceeds from these discs enabled him to build a private studio, NorVaJak, in Clovis for the sole use of the Trio, until Petty realized that he was unwittingly the owner of the only such facility in New Mexico and West Texas. Confident in his own technical abilities as both engineer and producer, he went public in 1955 – with Roy Orbison's Teen Kings among early customers. Petty was amenable to working at a paper loss in exchange for first refusal on publishing rights (for the Trio's own Nor Vi Jak Music) on items recorded. With a foot in various doors via 'Mood Indigo' *et al.*, he next tried to interest labels in those tracks he considered marketable. Through a leasing agreement with Roulette Records, the studio's first million-seller was Buddy Knox's 'Party Doll', but the most famous of its clients was Buddy Holly, who, with his Crickets, showed sufficient promise for Petty to offer to manage them. Furthermore, he (and Violet) received writing and arranging credits for certain Holly smashes – including 'That'll Be The Day' – and, until their sale to Paul McCartney in 1973, Petty retained rights to all items recorded by Holly. Indeed, in the years after Holly's fatal aircraft accident in 1958, Petty felt entitled to overdub fuller backings onto often sketchy material for commercial release. Although after Holly's death, Petty continued to record the Crickets, further hits were sporadic. In 1961 he secured an international chartbuster in the String-A-Longs' 'Wheels', while Jimmy Gilmer And The Fireballs topped Billboard's Hot 100 in 1963 with 'Sugar Shack'. In the mid-60s, Petty assisted on two of Brian Poole And The Tremeloes' UK chart entries. He maintained a practical interest in his increasingly more splendid studio until his death from leukaemia in August 1984 in Lubbock, Texas, home-town of Buddy Holly – with whom Petty's name will always be synonymous.
● COMPILATIONS: *15 Classic Memories* (Ace 1994) ★★★.

PHILLIPS, DON

b. 18 December 1913, d. 24 February 1994. A popular figure in the worlds of both theatre and music, Phillips made his reputation in the 50s and 60s as a musical arranger for Shirley Bassey, Joan Regan, Donald Peers, Anne Shelton, Dickie Valentine, Alan Jones and others. He also played piano on stage for the Marx Brothers, and toured Cyprus with Harry Secombe to entertain troops. Phillips left school at the age of 14 with no musical training, but by the following year had begun his career playing the piano in London pubs. Almost immediately he was spotted by music publisher Lawrence Wright, who bought his songs. Among his many noteworthy compositions were 'Old Pianna Rag', 'Skyscraper Fantasy', 'Concerto In Jazz' and 'A Live Show Is The Best Show', which became the theme tune to literally thousands of summer-season seaside shows. He was granted a Royal Command Performance in 1954. 'Melody Of The Sea' brought him an Ivor Novello award in 1958, while many of his songs were entered in the Eurovision Song Contest, the best-known pair being 'Love Is The Same Everywhere' (Matt Monro) and 'Girl With The Curl' (Ronnie Carroll). He went on to become musical director of several travelling shows and pantomimes, maintaining an office in Denmark Street ('Tin Pan Alley') until he became ill with Parkinson's Disease in the late 80s.

PHILLIPS, SAM

b. 1923, Florence, Alabama, USA. Although harbouring ambitions as a criminal lawyer, Phillips was obliged to drop out of high school to support his family. In 1942 he took up a post as disc jockey at station WLAY in Muscle Shoals, before moving to WREC in Memphis as an announcer four years later. In 1950 he opened Sam's Memphis Recording Studio at 706 Union Avenue and although initial work largely consisted of chronicling weddings and social gatherings, Phillips' main ambition was to record local blues acts and license the resultant masters. Howlin' Wolf, Bobby Bland, Ike Turner, B.B. King and Roscoe Gordon were among the many acts Phillips produced for independent outlets Chess Records, Duke and RPM. Their success inspired the founding of Sun Records in February 1952, a venture which flourished the following year when Rufus Thomas scored a notable R&B hit with 'Bear Cat'. Success was maintained by 'Little' Junior Parker and Billy 'The Kid' Emerson, while Phillips looked to expand the label's horizons by recording country acts. His wish to find a white singer comfortable with R&B was answered in 1954 with the arrival of Elvis Presley. The singer's five singles recorded with Phillips rank among pop's greatest achievements, and although criticized for allowing his protégé to sign for RCA Records, the producer used the settlement fee to further the careers of Carl Perkins, Johnny Cash and, later, Jerry Lee Lewis. Phillips' simple recording technique – single track, rhythmic string bass and judicious echo – defined classic rockabilly and for a brief period the label was in the ascendant. The style, however, proved too inflexible and by the beginning of the 60s new Memphis-based studios, Stax Records and Hi Records, challenged Sun's pre-eminent position. Phillips also became increasingly distracted by other ventures, including mining concerns, radio stations and, more crucially, his share of the giant Holiday Inn hotel chain. In 1969 he sold the entire Sun empire to country entrepreneur Shelby Singleton, thus effectively ending an era. Sam Phillips is nonetheless still revered as one of the leading catalysts in post-war American music and, if nothing else, for launching the career of Elvis Presley.

PHILLIPS, SID

b. 14 June 1902, London, England, d. 23 May 1973, Chertsey, Surrey, England. Deeply involved in the music business from childhood, Phillips played clarinet in various bands, including one led by his brothers, and also worked in music publishing and for record companies. In the early 30s he was staff arranger for the popular band led by Bert Ambrose and later became a member of the band. He also began leading his own small group in the 30s, but it was the bands he led from 1949 onwards that built his reputation. Broadcasting regularly on the radio, Phillips also recorded, and his band became one of the best-known Dixieland groups in the UK. Among the many fine musicians he employed at one time or another were George Shearing, Kenny Ball and Tommy Whittle. A gutsy, full-toned clarinettist, Phillips was also a skilful arranger and composed jazz-orientated dance tunes and several classical works. Changes in popular taste meant that from the 60s onwards his music was not in great demand, but he continued working until his death in 1973.

● ALBUMS: *Sid Phillips And His Band* i (1960) ★★★★, *Stardust* (60s) ★★★, *Sid Phillips And His Band* ii (1962) ★★★★, *Sid Phillips And His Band* iii (1964) ★★★, *Rhythm Is Our Business* (1970) ★★★, *Clarinet Marmalade* (Rediffusion 1975) ★★★, *Sid Phillips And His Great Band Play Stomps, Rags And Blues* (Rediffusion 1975) ★★★, *Sid Phillips Plays Barrelhouse Piano* (Rediffusion 1975) ★★★.

● COMPILATIONS: *Golden Hour Presents Sid Phillips H'ors D'Ouvres* (Golden Hour 1976) ★★★, *Anthology, Volume 1 – Chicago* (Gold Star 1976) ★★★★, *Anthology, Volume 2 – Lonesome Road* (Gold Star 1977) ★★★, *Anthology, Volume 3 – Way Down Yonder In New Orleans* (Gold Star 1978) ★★★, *The Best Of Sid Phillips* (EMI 1977) ★★★★.

PIAF, EDITH

b. Edith Giovanna Gassion, 19 December 1915, Paris, France, d. 11 October 1963. Born into desperate poverty, Piaf survived desertion by her mother and temporary childhood blindness, to eke out a living singing on the streets of Paris. After a brief period living in the country she sang in the streets with her father, an impoverished entertainer. The owner of Cerny's cabaret, Louis Leplée, heard the little girl and not only encouraged her but, struck by her diminutive stature, nicknamed her 'piaf', Parisian argot for 'little sparrow'. Piaf's dramatic singing style and her anguished voice appealed to French audiences and by the outbreak of World War II she had become a star. She proved her capacity for survival when she maintained her popularity despite being held as a material witness to Leplée's murder and facing accusations of collaboration with the German occupying forces. After the war Piaf's reputation spread internationally and she appeared in New York, singing at Carnegie Hall. In her private life Piaf was as tormented as the heroines of her songs and she had many relationships, most causing her severe emotional damage. She collapsed in 1959 but came back to sing with renewed vigour, even though her physical condition was visibly deteriorating. Among her many hits were several songs that she made her own, 'Les Trois Cloches', 'Milord', 'La Vie En Rose' and, above all others, if only because the sentiment expressed in the title and lyric so eloquently expressed her attitude to life, 'Non, Je Ne Regrette Rien'.

● ALBUMS: *Chansons De Cafe De Paris* (Decca 1951) ★★★, *Chansons* (Columbia 1951) ★★★, *La Vie En Rose* (Columbia 1956) ★★★, *Sincerely* (Columbia 1960) ★★★, *Piaf At The Paris Olympia* (Columbia 1961) ★★★, *C'est La Piaf* (1962) ★★★, *La Reine De La Chanson* (1963) ★★★, *Ses Plus Belles Chansons* (Contour 1969) ★★★, *I Regret Nothing* (Columbia 1971) ★★★, *Her Legendary Live Recordings* (Columbia 1979) ★★★, *De L'Accordeoniste A Milord* (EMI 1983) ★★★, *De L'Accordeoniste A Milord (Volume 2)* (EMI 1986) ★★★, *Heart And Soul* (Stylus 1987) ★★★.

● COMPILATIONS: *Deluxe Set* 3-LP box set (Capitol 1968) ★★★, *Edith Piaf, Volumes 1-4* (EMI 1986) ★★★, *The Best Of Edith Piaf, Volumes 1 & 2* (Philips 1986) ★★★, *Collection: Edith Piaf (20 Golden Greats)* (Deja Vu 1986) ★★★, *25th Anniversaire, Volumes 1 & 2* (EMI 1988) ★★★, *30eme Anniversaire* (1993) ★★★, *Edith Piaf 1946-1963* 10-CD box set (1993) ★★★, *L'Immortelle* (1994) ★★★, various artists *Edith Piaf Tribute* (D# Records 1994) ★★★, *The Rare Piaf* (DRG 1998) ★★★, *Legends Of The 20th Century* (EMI 1999) ★★★.

● FURTHER READING: *The Wheel Of Fortune: The Autobiography Of Edith Piaf*, Edith Piaf. *Piaf*, Monique Lange. *The Piaf Legend*, David Bret. *Piaf*, Margaret Crosland. *Piaf*, Simone Berteaut. *Edith Piaf: My Life*, Edith Piaf and Jean Noli. *Piaf: A Passionate Life*, David Bret.

PIERCE, NAT

b. 16 July 1925, Somerville, Massachusetts, USA, d. 10 June 1992, Los Angeles, California, USA. After studying and playing in local bands in his home state, Pierce worked with a handful of name bands, including Larry Clinton's, then briefly led his own band in 1949-51, instigating what is commonly regarded among fellow musicians as being the birth of the so-called 'rehearsal band' concept. In 1951 he joined Woody Herman, in whose band he played piano, arranged, and acted as straw boss until 1955.

Thereafter, he arranged for several bands and singers, including Count Basie and Ella Fitzgerald. In great demand as a session musician, he made countless record dates, on which he played with almost everyone who was anyone in the upper echelons of jazz. In 1957 he appeared in the television programme *The Sound Of Jazz*, on which he was responsible for several of the arrangements, including the classic performance of 'Dickie's Dream' that featured Basie, Roy Eldridge, Coleman Hawkins, Ben Webster, Joe Newman, Vic Dickenson and Gerry Mulligan among others. In the late 50s he led a band that included Buck Clayton and that had the dubious honour of being the last band to play at Harlem's 'Home of Happy Feet', the Savoy Ballroom, before it closed forever. Also in the late 50s he worked with Pee Wee Russell, Quincy Jones, Fitzgerald, Hawkins and others. In 1960, he returned to Herman for a brief spell as road manager and was back again the following year, this time in his former capacities, remaining until 1966. In the early 70s Pierce relocated to the west coast where he played in several bands, including those led by Louie Bellson and Bill Berry. In 1975 he joined Frank Capp as co-leader of a big band that mostly played his arrangements, many of which were in the Basie/Kansas City tradition. This band, which became known as Juggernaut, continued to play through the 80s and on into the 90s. Pierce also continued to write for other musicians and to appear on record dates. He toured extensively, appearing in the UK and Europe with several Basie-alumni bands and other concert packages. A superb pianist in his own right, Pierce's eclecticism was such that at various times he appeared at the piano as substitute for three of the best-known piano-playing bandleaders in big band history: Basie, Duke Ellington and Stan Kenton. In small groups he proved the lynchpin of the rhythm section, swinging with unflagging enthusiasm. As an arranger, especially for big bands, Pierce made an invaluable contribution to jazz, effortlessly creating swinging charts that underscored the 60s success stories of both Herman and Basie. Apart from his performing and arranging, Pierce was also a major source of information on many aspects of jazz history, a history that, through his personal dedication and extensive contributions, he helped to create.

● ALBUMS: *The Nat Pierce-Dick Collins Nonet* 10-inch album (Fantasy 1954) ★★★, *Nat Pierce Bandstand* 10-inch album (Vanguard 1955) ★★★, *Kansas City Memories* (Coral 1956) ★★★, *The Nat Pierce Octet And Tentette* (Keynote 1957) ★★★, *The Nat Pierce Big Band At The Savoy Ballroom* (RCA Victor 1957) ★★★, *The Ballad Of Jazz Street* (Hep 1961) ★★★★, *Juggernaut* (Concord 1977) ★★★★, *Juggernaut Live At Century Plaza* (Concord 1978) ★★, with Mary Ann McCall *5400 North ... In Concert With Mary Ann McCall* (Hep 1978) ★★★, *Juggernaut Strikes Again* (Concord 1981) ★★★, *Boston Bustout* (Hep Jazz 1981) ★★★, *Juggernaut Live At The Alleycat* (Concord 1986) ★★★★, with various artists *The Legendary Sound Of Jazz*

Telecast 1957 soundtrack recording (Bandstand 1990) ★★★★★.

PILGRIM TRAVELERS

Primarily known today as one of soul singer Lou Rawls' first groups, the close-harmony group the Pilgrim Travelers was formed in 1936 in Houston, Texas, USA, as an offshoot of the Pleasantgrove Baptist Church. The founder-members were Joe Johnson, Kylo Turner, Keith Barber and Rayfield Taylor. They won a talent contest in 1944, the prize for which was a national tour with the Soul Stirrers. After the tour the group moved to Los Angeles, California, and added J.W. Alexander as tenor, and Jessie Whitaker as baritone. After brief spells with Big Town and Swing Time, the Pilgrim Travelers moved to Specialty Records in the late 40s. In addition to gospel standards such as 'The Old Rugged Cross', their most fondly remembered track from this period was 'Jesus Met The Woman At The Well'. When Rayfield Taylor departed in the 50s he was replaced by George McCurn. By 1957 Kylo Turner and Keith Barber had also left, and they were replaced by Ernest Booker and Lou Rawls (ex-Teenage Kings Of Harmony and Holy Wonders). With Rawls, Whitaker and Booker alternating leads the group released a string of singles for Andex Records in the 50s, with Sam Cooke guesting on recording sessions and some touring dates. However, after Booker left in 1957 the group abbreviated their name to simply the Travelers and recorded more secular material for a time. The group ground to a halt two years later, with Rawls going on to a successful R&B career and Alexander partnering Sam Cooke in the formation of Sar Records.

PITTMAN, BARBARA

b. Memphis, Tennessee, USA. Pittman was one of the few women who recorded for the legendary Sun Records. She heard blues music on Beale Street in Memphis as a child and began performing in Memphis clubs such as the Eagle's Nest, where a young Elvis Presley, whom Pittman dated, also honed his act during the mid-50s. In 1955 she went on the road as a singer with cowboy movie star Lash LaRue's travelling show. In 1956 she signed with Sun; although she released a number of singles on the label, none were hits. During the 60s Pittman moved to California where she sang on soundtracks for such 'motorcycle movies' as *Wild Angels*, *Wild On Wheels* and *Hells Angels*, under the name Barbara And The Visitors. She also recorded for Del-Fi Records but nothing was ever released. Pittman never recorded an album under her own name.

PLAIN AND FANCY

Rock 'n' roll music had begun to take a hold in America by the mid-50s, but the 1954/5 Broadway season was full of more traditional fare, such as *The Boy Friend*, *Peter Pan*, *Silk Stockings*, and *Damn Yankees*, amongst others. One of the others was *Plain And Fancy*, which opened at the Mark Hellinger Theatre on 27 January 1955. Joseph Stein and Will Glickman's book was set in Bird-in-

Hand, Pennsylvania, the home territory of the Amish people, members of a fundamentalist religious sect who have no time or use for even the most basic modern aids. Don King (Richard Derr) has inherited a farm in the area, and he travels there from New York with Ruth Winters (Shirl Conway) to try to sell it to an Amish farmer, Papa Yoder (Stefan Schnabel). Yoder's daughter, Katie (Gloria Marlowe), is about to go through with an arranged marriage to Ezra Reber (Douglas Fletcher Rodgers), but she is still in love with an old flame, Ezra's brother, Peter (David Daniels). Peter has left the Amish community, and, when he returns just before the wedding, he is shunned by the traditionalists. Matters resolve themselves when Peter's bravery in a crisis gains him the respect of Katie's father, and the young people are allowed to marry. Don and Ruth make it a double wedding. The score, by composer Albert Hague – whose first full Broadway score this was – and lyricist Arnold Horwitt, contained a ballad that many feel to be one of the loveliest of all popular songs, 'Young And Foolish'. It was introduced by Daniels and Marlowe, and they also had 'Follow Your Heart' with Barbara Cook, who made a favourable impression in the role of Hilda Miller. Cook sang 'This Is All Very New To Me', 'I'll Show Him', and 'Take Your Time And Take Your Pick' (with Richard Kerr and Shirl Conway). The remainder of the delightful and romantic score included 'You Can't Miss It', 'It Wonders Me', 'Plenty Of Pennsylvania', 'Why Not Katie?', 'It's A Helluva Way To Run A Love Affair', 'Plain We Live', 'How Do You Raise A Barn?' (a spectacular scene to open Act II), 'Follow Your Heart', and 'City Mouse, Country Mouse'. Sophisticated New York audiences obviously loved this folksy view of their country cousins, and *Plain And Fancy* had a decent run of 461 performances. Barbara Cook went on to become Broadway's favourite ingénue during the 50s in shows such as Candide, The Music Man, The Gay Life and She Loves Me.

PLATER, BOBBY

b. Robert Plater, 13 May 1914, Newark, New Jersey, USA, d. 20 November 1982, Lake Tahoe, Nevada, USA. Plater began playing alto saxophone while still a child and in his early teens was talented enough to work with several noted musicians, including Donald Lambert. He became a full-time professional musician in the late 30s, working with Tiny Bradshaw and others. After military service during World War II, he returned to gigging but then joined Lionel Hampton in 1946 where he remained until 1964. With Hampton, Plater played lead alto and was also an important soloist. He also wrote arrangements for the band, showing a special aptitude for writing for singers, notably Sonny Parker. He had also taken the time to teach some basic principles to Dinah Washington during her first major professional engagement with Hampton. After leaving Hampton, Plater moved into the Count Basie band, becoming lead alto there, too, and musical director of the band. A highly skilled instrumentalist with a wide musical knowledge,

Plater's sound was rich and creamy, suggesting an influence of Johnny Hodges but overlaid with a slightly acerbic touch that gave his solos added poignancy. He was co-composer of 'Jersey Bounce', a 40s hit.

● ALBUMS: with Lionel Hampton *Lionel Hampton And His Orchestra: Apollo Hall Concert* (Epic 1954) ★★★★, with Count Basie *Basie Big Band* (Pablo 1975) ★★★, with Basie *Farmer's Market Barbecue* (Pablo 1982) ★★★.

PLATTERS

One of the leading R&B vocal groups of the 50s, they were the first black group to be accepted as a major chart act and, for a short time, were the most successful vocal group in the world. The Platters were formed in Los Angeles in 1953 by entrepreneur/songwriter Buck Ram (b. 21 November 1907, Chicago, Illinois, USA, d. 1 January 1991). Through his ownership of the Platters' name, Ram was able to control the group throughout their career, and his talent for composing and arranging enabled the Platters to make a lasting impression upon popular music. Their original line-up, Tony Williams (b. 5 April 1928, Elizabeth, New Jersey, USA, d. 14 August 1992, New York, USA; lead tenor), David Lynch (b. 1929, St. Louis, Missouri, USA, d. 2 January 1981; tenor), Alex Hodge (baritone) and Herb Reed (b. 1931, Kansas City, Missouri, USA; bass), recorded unsuccessfully in 1954, precipitating the arrival of two new members, Paul Robi (b. 1931, New Orleans, Louisiana, USA, d. 2 January 1989), who replaced Hodge, and Zola Taylor (b. 1934; contralto). Signed to Mercury Records, the Platters secured their first hit in 1955 when 'Only You' reached the US Top 5, an effortlessly light performance that set the pattern for subsequent releases, including 'The Great Pretender', 'My Prayer' and 'Twilight Time', each of which reached number 1 in the US charts. 'Smoke Gets In Your Eyes' (previously a hit for Paul Whiteman in 1934), which was an international number 1 hit single in 1958-59, highlighted their smooth delivery and arguably remains the group's best-loved release.

Lead singer Williams left for a solo career in 1961, taking with him much of the Platters' distinctive style. His departure led to further changes, with Sandra Dawn and Nate Nelson replacing Taylor and Robi. With Sonny Turner as the featured voice, the group began embracing a more contemporary direction, evidenced in such occasional pop hits as 'I Love You 1000 Times' (1966) and 'With This Ring' (1967). During the late 60s and for a long time afterwards, personnel changes brought much confusion as to who were the legitimate Platters. Sonny Turner and Herb Reed formed their own version, while Tony Williams did likewise. The Platters' legacy has since been undermined by the myriad of line-ups performing under that name, some of which had no tangible links to the actual group. This should not detract from those seminal recordings that bridged the gap between the harmonies of the Mills Brothers and the Ink Spots and the sweet soul of the ensuing decade. In the late 80s, Buck Ram continued to keep an eagle eye on the Platters' sold-out appearances at Las Vegas and other US cities. The group were inducted into the Rock And Roll Hall Of Fame in 1990, but Ram died the following year.

● ALBUMS: *The Platters* (Federal 1955) ★★★★ also released on King as *Only You* and Mercury labels, *The Platters, Volume 2* (Mercury 1956) ★★★★, *The Flying Platters* (Mercury 1957) ★★★, *The Platters On Parade* (Mercury 1959) ★★★, *Flying Platters Around The World* (Mercury 1959) ★★★, *Remember When* (Mercury 1959) ★★★, *Reflections* (Mercury 1960) ★★★, *Encore Of Golden Hits* (Mercury 1960) ★★★, *More Encore Of Golden Hits* (Mercury 1960) ★★★, *The Platters* (Mercury 1960) ★★★, *Life Is Just A Bowl Of Cherries* (Mercury 1961) ★★★, *The Platters Sing For The Lonely* (Mercury 1962) ★★★, *Encore Of The Golden Hits Of The Groups* (Mercury 1962) ★★★, *Moonlight Memories* (Mercury 1963) ★★★, *Platters Sing All The Movie Hits* (Mercury 1963) ★★, *Platters Sing Latino* (Mercury 1963) ★★, *Christmas With The Platters* (Mercury 1963) ★★★, *New Soul Campus Style Of The Platters* (Mercury 1965) ★★, *I Love You 1000 Times* (Musicor 1966) ★★, *Going Back To Detroit* (Musicor 1967) ★★★, *I Get The Sweetest Feeling* (Musicor 1968) ★★★, *Sweet Sweet Lovin'* (Musicor 1968) ★★, *Our Way* (Pye International 1971) ★★★, *Encore Of Broadway Golden Hits* (1972) ★★★, *Live* (Contour 1974) ★★.

● COMPILATIONS: *The Original Platters – 20 Classic Hits* (Mercury 1978) ★★★, *Platterama* (Mercury 1982) ★★★, *Smoke Gets In Your Eyes* (Charly 1991) ★★★, *The Magic Touch: An Anthology* (Mercury 1992) ★★★★, *The Very Best Of The Platters 1966-1969* (Varèse 1997) ★★★★, *Enchanted: The Best Of The Platters* (Rhino 1998) ★★★★.

● FILMS: *Carnival Rock* (1957), *Girl's Town* aka *The Innocent And The Damned* (1959).

PLATZ, DAVID

b. 13 January 1929, Hanover, Germany, d. 20 May 1994, London, England. Born of Jewish stock in the volatile political climate of Germany, Platz was exiled, with his sister, Gina, to Neasden, in Middlesex, in the 30s. Placed in publishing by his guardian, Platz was initially disappointed to discover it was in music rather than literature. At age 14 he became an office boy for Southern Music in Denmark Street, London. Graduating from copyright to manager of an office specialising in Latin-American recordings, he eventually left to set up his own company, Essex Music. That company, with Platz at the helm, became arguably the leading publishing agency by the late 50s, with the Rolling Stones its first major coup. They were soon joined by major talents like the Moody Blues, Who, Procol Harum, Ralph McTell, David Bowie and Marc Bolan. The *modus operandi* with each such major songwriter was to form a separate division of the company, overlooked by Essex, so that artists maintained a financial and business incentive in their affairs. In addition he inaugurated two record labels, Fly and

Cube. Platz also went on to help finance and publish songs from the world of stage musicals, including *Stop The World – I Want To Get Off*, *The Roar Of The Greasepaint – The Smell Of The Crowd* and Lionel Bart's *Oliver.* Between 1973 and 1986 he was publishing director of the Performing Rights Society, but his entrepreneurial activities were finally curtailed by the onset of motor neurone disease in his mid-60s.

PLAYMATES

This humorous US pop trio comprised Donny Conn (b. 29 March 1930), Morey Carr (b. 31 July 1932) and Chic Hetti (b. 26 February 1930), all from Waterbury, Connecticut, USA. They formed the comedy and music trio the Nitwits while studying at the University of Connecticut and started touring in 1952 with an act that relied more on humour than singing ability. Renamed the Playmates, they made their first record, 'I Only Have Myself To Blame', on Rainbow in 1956. They moved to Roulette Records in 1957 and their third single on that label, 'Jo-Ann', a cover version of the Twin Tones' record, hit the US Top 20 in 1958. Over the next four years the clean-cut vocal group chalked up another nine US chart entries including the Top 20 hits 'What Is Love?' and 'Beep Beep', which reached number 4 in the USA. They later recorded on ABC-Paramount, Colpix, Congress and Bell but their sound proved too dated to sell in the 60s.

POMEROY, HERB

b. Irving Herbert Pomeroy III, 15 April 1930, Gloucester, Massachusetts, USA. After extensive studies at what later became known as the Berklee College Of Music in Boston, Massachusetts, Pomeroy joined the faculty to become one of the most respected teachers of the trumpet in jazz. His experience as a performer included work with the big bands of Lionel Hampton and Stan Kenton and, although he also played in small groups with Charlie Parker and others, it is in a big band context that he has made his greatest mark. Numerous contemporary jazz stars have graduated from Berklee, many of them paying tribute to Pomeroy's contribution to their musical education. His big bands, usually formed from college students and graduates, maintain an enviably high standard of musicianship. Unlike many of the college and university bands, Pomeroy's are not merely showcases for exceptional musical ability but also display an awareness of the underlying emotional qualities of jazz. The fact that his students demonstrate a greater involvement in the music they play is a tribute to his dedication to pursuing aims that transcend the simple imparting of knowledge. Pomeroy has also taught at the Massachusetts Institute of Technology, the Lenox School of Jazz and was, in 1962, employed by the US State Department to direct the house orchestra at Radio Malaya.

● ALBUMS: *Jazz In A Stable* (Transition 1955) ★★★, *Life Is A Many Splendoured Gig* (Roulette 1957) ★★, *Band In Boston* (United Artists 1958)

★★★, *Pramlatta's Hips: Live At The El Morocco* (Shiah 1980) ★★★, with Billy Novick *This Is Always* (Daring 1996) ★★★, with Donna Byrne *Walking On Air* (Arbors 1997) ★★★, *Live At Cafe Beaujolais* (Amaral 2000) ★★★★.

PONI-TAILS

A US female trio known for the 1958 Top 10 hit 'Born Too Late', the Poni-Tails – who, naturally, sported that hairstyle – were lead vocalist Toni Cistone, Patti McCabe (d. 1989; low harmony – replacing original member Karen Topinka) and LaVerne Novak (high harmony). The group met at their high school in Lyndhurst, Ohio, USA, in 1957. They first recorded for Point Records, an RKO Pictures division, but their two singles for that label were not successful. The members were then signed to ABC-Paramount Records, and their first single for that company fared badly. The next one, 'Born Too Late', an innocent ballad about being passed over by an older boy, catapulted to number 7 in the US chart the following year. Two further singles for ABC reached the charts but did not approach hit status and the group disbanded, each member retiring from the music business.
● COMPILATIONS: *Born Too Late* (South Bay 1994) ★★.

PORGY AND BESS

The last film of producer Sam Goldwyn's illustrious career, released by Columbia in 1959, proved to be an expensive and troubled affair. After various disputes with his first choice director, Rouben Mamoulian (who had staged the original 1935 Broadway production), Goldwyn replaced him with Otto Preminger, whose work on this occasion was considered to be somewhat laboured and uninspired. For some reason, the well-known story of the crippled beggar Porgy (Sidney Poitier), who lives in the Catfish Row slum area and loves the tempestuous Bess (Dorothy Dandridge), did not transfer successfully to the big screen. The supporting cast was excellent, with Sammy Davis Jnr. (Sportin' Life), Pearl Bailey (Maria), Brock Peters (Crown), Diahann Carroll (Clara) and Ruth Attaway (Serena) all turning in outstanding performances. Other roles were taken by Leslie Scott, Clarence Muse and Joel Fluellen. Because of the extremely demanding operatic score by composer George Gershwin and lyricists DuBose Heyward and Ira Gershwin, several of the principals were dubbed, including Poitier (Robert McFerrin), Dandridge (Adele Addison), Carroll (Loulie Jean Norman), and Attaway (Inez Matthews). Even so, there were some reservations regarding the vocal quality of the production, but these were swept aside by the sheer magnificence of the songs, which included 'Summertime', 'Bess, You Is My Woman Now', 'There's A Boat Dat's Leavin' Soon For New York', 'I Loves You Porgy', 'A Woman Is A Sometimes Thing', 'I Got Plenty O' Nuttin'', 'It Ain't Necessarily So', 'My Man's Gone Now' and 'Oh Bess, Oh Where's My Bess'. André Previn and Ken Darby both won Oscars for 'scoring a dramatic picture', and Leo Shamroy was nominated for his superb photography in Technicolor and Panavision. Hermes Pan, who had been associated with many top musical films in his long career including the Fred Astaire and Ginger Rogers RKO series, staged the dances. The screenplay, by N. Richard Nash, was based on the original Broadway libretto and novel by Heyward, and his and Dorothy Heyward's play *Porgy*. In the early 90s, this film remained one of the few major musicals not to have been released on video. Cinema distribution has also been curtailed; the Gershwin estate has had this film firmly under lock and key for some years now.
● FURTHER READING: *DuBose Heyward – The Man Who Wrote 'Porgy'*, Frank Durham. *The Life And Times Of Porgy And Bess*, H. Alpert.

POWELL, BUD

b. Earl Rudolph Powell, 27 September 1924, Harlem, New York City, New York, USA, d. 31 July 1966, New York City, New York, USA. After learning to play the piano in the classical tradition while still a child, Powell began working around New York's Coney Island, where he played in a band featuring Valaida Snow around 1940. During the next couple of years he became a regular visitor to Minton's Playhouse, where he heard the first stirrings of bebop. In particular, he was influenced by Thelonious Monk's harmonic innovations but quickly developed his own style. Despite his leanings towards the new music, he was hired by Cootie Williams for his big band. During his stay with Williams he was arrested in Philadelphia and reportedly badly beaten by police officers, an event usually cited as the beginning of the mental problems that were to dog him for the rest of his life. He retained his links with events on 52nd Street and was soon one of the most striking of the bebop pianists. By 1945, however, he was displaying the first overt signs of acute mental instability and was hospitalized – the first of many incarcerations in mental hospitals, during some of which he was given electro-convulsive therapy. Throughout the 50s he worked regularly, appearing with all the leading figures of bebop, including Charlie Parker, Charles Mingus, Dizzy Gillespie and Max Roach as part of 'The Quintet'. During this same period his mental instability increased, the sudden death in 1956 of his brother Richie Powell adding to his problems. Additionally, his mental and physical health were being gravely damaged by his growing dependence on narcotics and alcohol. At the end of the decade he left New York for Paris, where he spent three years of popular success but was still plagued by his mental and addiction troubles. Back in New York in 1964, his performances became fewer and were frequently fraught with emotional and technical breakdowns. He died in July 1966.
At his performing peak, Powell's playing style displayed a startling brilliance, with remarkable ideas being executed with absolute technical mastery and his dominant right hand playing at extraordinary speeds. By the late 50s his personal problems were such that he rarely played at his

best, although the flow of ideas continued, as can be deduced from some of his compositions from these years. He was a major figure in bebop and an influence, both directly and indirectly, upon most pianists in jazz since the 50s.

● ALBUMS: *Bud Powell Trio* 10-inch album (Roost 1950) ★★★, *Bud Powell Piano* 10-inch album (Mercury 1950) ★★★, *Piano Solos* 10-inch album (Mercury 1951) ★★★★, *Piano Solos, No. 2* 10-inch album (Mercury 1951) ★★★, *Bud Powell Trio ii* (Roost 1953) ★★★, *Jazz At Massey Hall, Volume 2* 10-inch album (Debut 1953) ★★★★, *Bud Powell's Moods* (Mercury 1953) ★★★, with The Quintet *Jazz At Massey Hall* 10-inch album (Debut 1953) ★★★★, *Jazz Original* (Norgran 1955) ★★★, *The Lonely One* (Verve 1956) ★★★, *Blues In The Closet* (Verve 1956) ★★★, *Strictly Powell* (RCA 1956) ★★★, *Swingin' With Bud* (RCA 1957) ★★★, *Bud!* (Blue Note 1957) ★★★★, *The Time Waits* (Blue Note 1959) ★★★★, *The Scene Changes* (Blue Note 1959) ★★★★, *Bud Powell In Paris i* (Xanadu 1960) ★★★, *A Portrait Of Thelonious* (CBS 1961) ★★★, *Bouncing With Bud* (Delmark 1962) ★★★, *Bud Powell In Paris ii* (Reprise 1963) ★★★, *Blues For Bouffemont* (Black Lion 1964) ★★★, *The Invisible Cage* (Black Lion 1964) ★★★, *Salt Peanuts* (Black Lion 1964) ★★★, *Ups 'N' Downs* (Mainstream 1965) ★★★, *The Return Of Bud Powell* (Roulette 1965) ★★★, with Don Byas *A Tribute To Cannonball* 1961 recording (Columbia 1979) ★★★★, *Round Midnight At The Blue Note Cafe* 1962 recording (Dreyfus 1981) ★★★, *Inner Fires* 1953 recording (Elektra 1982) ★★★, *The Complete Essen Jazz Festival Concert* 1960 recording (Black Lion 1988) ★★★, *Writin' For Duke* 1963 recording (Mythic Sound 1989) ★★★, *Holidays In Edenville* 1964 recording (Mythic Sound 1989) ★★★, *Award At Birdland* 1964 recording (Mythic Sound 1989) ★★★, *At The Golden Circle* 1962 recording (SteepleChase 1995) ★★★, *At The Golden Circle, Vol. 2* 1962 recording (SteepleChase 1995) ★★★, *At The Golden Circle, Vol. 3* 1962 recording (SteepleChase 1995) ★★★, *At The Golden Circle, Vol. 4* 1962 recording (SteepleChase 1995) ★★★, *At The Golden Circle, Vol. 5* 1962 recording (SteepleChase 1995) ★★★, *Bud Plays Bird* 1957/1958 recordings (Roulette 1996) ★★★.

● COMPILATIONS: *The Amazing Bud Powell, Vol. 1* (Blue Note 1982) ★★★★, *The Amazing Bud Powell, Vol. 2* (Blue Note 1982) ★★★★, *The Amazing Bud Powell, Vol. 3* (Blue Note 1984) ★★★★, *The Best Of Bud Powell* (Blue Note 1989) ★★★★, *Early Years Of A Genius (1944-1948)* (Mythic Sound 1989) ★★★, *Burning In The USA (1953-1955)* (Mythic Sound 1989) ★★★, *Cookin' At Saint Germain (1957-1959)* (Mythic Sound 1989) ★★★, *Relaxin' At Home (1961-1964)* (Mythic Sound 1989) ★★★, *Groovin' At The Blue Note (1959-1961)* (Mythic Sound 1989) ★★★, *Complete Bud Powell On Verve* 5-CD box set (Verve 1992) ★★★★, *Summer Broadcasts 1953* (ESP 1993) ★★★, *Winter Broadcasts 1953* (ESP 1993) ★★★, *Compact Jazz* (Verve 1993) ★★★★, *The Complete Bud Powell Blue Note Recordings (1949-1958)* 4-CD box set (Mosaic 1994) ★★★★, *Jazz Profile* (Blue Note 1997) ★★★★, *Ultimate Bud Powell* (Verve 1998) ★★★★, *Jazz Giant* (Verve 2001) ★★★★,

Tempus Fugue-It 4-CD box set (Proper 2001) ★★★★.

● FURTHER READING: *The Glass Enclosure: The Life Of Bud Powell*, Alan Groves with Alyn Shipton. *Bud Powell*, Clifford Jay Safane (ed.). *Bouncing With Bud: All The Recordings Of Bud Powell*, Carl Smith. *Dance Of The Infidels: A Portrait Of Bud Powell*, Francis Paudras.

POWELL, JANE

b. Suzanne Burce, 1 April 1929, Portland, Oregon, USA. A petite, vivacious, actress and singer with a thrilling soprano voice who excelled in several popular MGM musicals of the 50s. After singing a mixture of classical and popular songs on local radio, she won a film contract with MGM when she was just 15 years old. Her debut in *Song Of The Open Road* was followed in the 40s and early 50s by *Delightfully Dangerous*, *Holiday In Mexico*, *Three Daring Daughters*, *A Date With Judy*, *Luxury Liner*, *Nancy Goes To Rio*, *Two Weeks With Love*, *Rich, Young And Pretty*, *Small Town Girl* and *Three Sailors And A Girl* (1953). In 1951 she co-starred with Fred Astaire in *Royal Wedding*, and they duetted on one of the longest song titles ever – 'How Could You Believe Me When I Said I Loved You When You Know I've Been A Liar All My Life?'. Their recording became a million-seller. Later, in 1956, Powell made the US Top 20 on her own with 'True Love' from High Society. Her best film role was in 1954 when she joined Howard Keel in the marvellous Seven Brides For Seven Brothers, and she continued to appear on the screen into the late 50s, in musicals such as *Athena*, *Deep In My Heart*, *Hit The Deck* and *The Girl Most Likely* (1957). The golden era of movie musicals was drawing to a close by then, and Powell turned to provincial theatre and nightclubs. In the 70s she was active on US television in programmes such as *Murdoch*, *The Letters* and *Mayday At 40,000 Feet*. She also succeeded Debbie Reynolds in the leading role of the 1973 Broadway revival of Irene. In 1988 Powell married her fifth husband, Dick Moore, who was a child star himself, and is an authority on the genre, having written a book entitled *Twinkle, Twinkle Little Star (But Don't Have Sex Or Take The Car)*. In the same year she appeared in concert at Carnegie Hall with Skitch Henderson and the New York Pops. In the mid-90s, she co-hosted *Cabaret Sings The Movies* at the Cabaret Convention at New York's Town Hall. This special evening featured Frank Loesser's widow, Jo Sullivan, singing his Oscar-winning 'Baby, It's Cold Outside' from *Neptune's Daughter* (1949), and David Staller recreating 'Isn't It Romantic' from *Love Me Tonight* (1932), amongst other good things. Powell also hosted the television special *Nelson And Jeanette* (1992) and appeared as herself in *The Making Of Seven Brides For Seven Brothers* (1997).

● ALBUMS: *Romance* 10-inch album (Columbia 1949) ★★★, *A Date With Jane Powell* 10-inch album (Columbia 1949) ★★★, *Alice In Wonderland* (Columbia 1950) ★★, *Nancy Goes To Rio* film soundtrack (MGM 1950) ★★, *Two Weeks With Love* film soundtrack (MGM 1950) ★★★, *Royal Wedding* film soundtrack (MGM 1951) ★★★, *Rich, Young And Pretty* film soundtrack (MGM 1951) ★★★, *Three Sailors And A Girl* film soundtrack (MGM 1953) ★★★, *Seven Brides For Seven Brothers* film soundtrack (MGM 1954) ★★★, *Athena* film soundtrack (Mercury 1954) ★★, *Can't We Be Friends?* (Verve 1956) ★★★, *Something Wonderful* (MGM 1957) ★★★.

● COMPILATIONS: *Songs From Her Films* (1989) ★★★★.

● FILMS: *Song Of The Open Road* (1944), *Delightfully Dangerous* (1945), *Holiday In Mexico* (1946), *Luxury Liner* (1948), *Three Daring Daughters* (1948), *A Date With Judy* (1948), *Two Weeks With Love* (1948), *Nancy Goes To Rio* (1950), *Rich, Young And Pretty* (1951), *Royal Wedding* (1951), *Three Sailors And A Girl* (1953), *Small Town Girl* (1953), *Seven Brides For Seven Brothers* (1954), *Athena* (1954), *Deep In My Heart* guest star (1954), *Hit The Deck* (1955), *The Female Animal* (1957), *The Girl Most Likely* (1957), *Enchanted Island* (1958), *Marie* (1985).

PRADO, PÉREZ

b. Damaso Pérez Prado, 11 December 1916, Mantanzas, Cuba, d. 14 September 1989, Mexico City, Mexico. Prado played organ and piano in cinemas and clubs before becoming an arranger for mambo-style local bands in 1942. He formed his own unit in 1948 in Mexico when the mambo beat was becoming very popular. Prado was 'King of the Mambo' in Latin America with his scorching brass and persuasive percussion, exemplified in his 1950 recording of 'Mambo Jambo'. He had some modest US success in 1953/4 with the title theme from the Italian movie *Anne*, and a South African song, 'Skokiaan'. Strong indications that the mambo craze was beginning to catch on in the USA came in 1954, when Perry Como with 'Papa Loves Mambo', and 'Mambo Italiano' by Rosemary Clooney, both reached the Top 10. Prado made his worldwide breakthrough in 1955 when RCA Records released 'Cherry Pink And Apple Blossom White', with an exciting trumpet solo by Billy Regis. It stayed at number 1 in the US charts for 10 weeks and was featured in the Jane Russell/Richard Egan movie *Underwater!* (1955). In Britain, Eddie Calvert and the Ted Heath orchestra had their own bestselling versions. Prado's follow-up in 1958 was another instrumental, his own composition, 'Patricia'. Another chart-topper, it contained more than a hint of the current burgeoning pop sounds with its heavy bass and rocking organ rhythms, along with the cha-cha-cha beat, and was used by Federico Fellini as the theme song for the movie *La Dolce Vita* in 1960. By then Prado was out of the limelight, but in 1981 he featured in a musical revue entitled *Sun*, which enjoyed a long run in Mexico City. Persistent ill health led to the amputation of one leg, and he eventually died from a stroke in 1989. Six years later, he narrowly failed to reach the top of the UK chart with the exciting 'Guaglione', following its use in a television commercial for Guinness. He enjoyed further posthumous chart action in 1999 when Lou Bega's reworking of 'Mambo No. 5' and

Shaft's 'Mucho Mambo (Sway)', a reworking of 'Quien Sera (Sway)', enjoyed huge chart success throughout Europe.

● ALBUMS: *Mambo By The King* 10-inch album (RCA Victor 1953) ★★★, *Mambo Mania* (RCA Victor 1955) ★★★, *Voodoo Suite (And Six All Time Greats)* (RCA Victor 1955) ★★★, *Havana 3 am* (RCA Victor 1956) ★★★, *Latin Satin* (RCA Victor 1957) ★★★, *Prez* (RCA Victor 1958) ★★★★, *Dilo Ugh!* (RCA Victor 1958) ★★★, *Pops And Prado* (RCA Victor 1959) ★★★, *Big Hits By Prado* (RCA Victor 1959) ★★★, *A Touch Of Tabasco* (RCA Victor 1960) ★★★, *Rockambo* (RCA Victor 1961) ★★★, *The New Dance La Chunga* (RCA Victor 1961) ★★★, *The Twist Goes Latin* (RCA Victor 1962) ★★★, *Exotic Suite* (RCA Victor 1962) ★★★, *Our Man In Latin America* (RCA Victor 1963) ★★★, *A Cat In Latin* (RCA Victor 1964) ★★★.

● COMPILATIONS: *Pérez Prado* (Bright Orange 1979) ★★★, *Pérez Prado And Orchestra* (Joker 1988) ★★★, *Guantanamera* (W.S. Latino 1989) ★★★, *King Of Mambo* (RCA 1991) ★★★★, *Go Go Mambo* (1993) ★★★★, *Mondo Mambo: The Best Of ...* (Rhino 1995) ★★★★, *Pérez Prado: Our Man In Havana* (Camden 1998) ★★★★, *Mambo By The King* (Blue Moon 1999) ★★★.

PRESLEY, ELVIS

b. Elvis Aaron Presley, 8 January 1935, Tupelo, Mississippi, USA, d. 16 August 1977, Memphis, Tennessee, USA. The most celebrated popular music phenomenon of his era and, for many, the purest embodiment of rock 'n' roll, Elvis Presley's life and career have become part of rock legend. The elder of twins, his younger brother, Jesse Garon, was stillborn, a tragedy that partly contributed to the maternal solicitude dominating his childhood and teenage years. Presley's first significant step towards a musical career took place at the age of eight when he won $5 in a local song contest performing the lachrymose Red Foley ballad, 'Old Shep'. His earliest musical influence came from attending the Pentecostal Church and listening to the psalms and gospel songs. He also had a strong grounding in country and blues and it was the combination of these different styles that was to provide his unique musical identity. By the age of 13, Presley had moved with his family to Memphis, and during his later school years began cultivating an outsider image, with long hair, spidery sideburns and ostentatious clothes. After leaving school he took a job as a truck driver, a role in keeping with his unconventional appearance. In spite of his rebel posturing, Presley remained studiously polite to his elders and was devoted to his mother. Indeed, it was his filial affection that first prompted him to visit Sun Records, whose studios offered the sophisticated equivalent of a fairground recording booth service. As a birthday present to his mother, Gladys, Presley cut a version of the Ink Spots' 'My Happiness', backed with the Raskin/Brown/Fisher standard 'That's When Your Heartaches Begin'. The studio manager, Marion Keisker, noted Presley's unusual but distinctive vocal style and informed Sun's owner/producer Sam Phillips of his potential. Phillips nurtured the boy for almost a year before putting him together with country guitarist Scotty Moore and bass player Bill Black. Their early sessions showed considerable promise, especially when Presley began alternating his unorthodox low-key delivery with a high-pitched whine. The amplified guitars of Moore and Black contributed strongly to the effect and convinced Phillips that the singer was startlingly original. In Presley, Phillips saw something that he had long dreamed and spoken of discovering; a white boy who sang like a Negro.

Presley's debut disc on Sun was the extraordinary 'That's All Right (Mama)', a showcase for his rich, multi-textured vocal dexterity, with sharp, solid backing from his compatriots. The b-side, 'Blue Moon Of Kentucky', was a country song, but the arrangement showed that Presley was threatening to slip into an entirely different genre, closer to R&B. Local response to these strange-sounding performances was encouraging and Phillips eventually shifted 20,000 copies of the disc. For his second single, Presley recorded Roy Brown's 'Good Rockin' Tonight' backed by the zingy 'I Don't Care If The Sun Don't Shine'. The more roots-influenced 'Milk Cow Blues Boogie' followed, while the b-side, 'You're A Heartbreaker', had some strong tempo changes that neatly complemented Presley's quirky vocal. 'Baby Let's Play House'/'I'm Left, You're Right, She's Gone' continued the momentum and led to Presley performing on *The Grand Old Opry* and *Louisiana Hayride* radio programmes. A series of live dates commenced in 1955 with drummer D.J. Fontana added to the ranks. Presley toured clubs in Arkansas, Louisiana and Texas billed as 'The King Of Western Bop' and 'The Hillbilly Cat'. Audience reaction verged on the fanatical, which was hardly surprising given Presley's semi-erotic performances. His hip-swivelling routine, in which he cascaded across the stage and plunged to his knees at dramatic moments in a song, was remarkable for the period and prompted near-riotous fan mania. The final Sun single, a cover version of Junior Parker's 'Mystery Train', was later acclaimed by many as the definitive rock 'n' roll single, with its chugging rhythm, soaring vocal and enticing lead guitar breaks.

It established Presley as an artist worthy of national attention and ushered in the next phase of his career, which was dominated by the imposing figure of Colonel Tom Parker. The Colonel was a former fairground huckster who managed several country artists including Hank Snow and Eddy Arnold. After relieving disc jockey Bob Neal of Presley's managership, Parker persuaded Sam Phillips that his financial interests would be better served by releasing the boy to a major label. RCA Records had already noted the commercial potential of the phenomenon under offer and agreed to pay Sun Records a release fee of $35,000, an incredible sum for the period. The sheer diversity of Presley's musical heritage and his remarkable ability as a vocalist and interpreter of material enabled him to escape the cultural parochialism of his R&B-influenced predecessors.

The attendant rock 'n' roll explosion, in which Presley was both a creator and participant, ensured that he could reach a mass audience, many of them newly affluent teenagers.

It was on 10 January 1956, a mere two days after his 21st birthday, that Presley entered RCA's studios in Nashville to record his first tracks for a major label. His debut session produced the epochal 'Heartbreak Hotel', one of the most striking pop records ever released. Co-composed by Hoyt Axton's mother Mae, the song evoked nothing less than a vision of absolute funereal despair. There was nothing in the pop charts of the period that even hinted at the degree of desolation described in the song. Presley's reading was extraordinarily mature and moving, with a determined avoidance of any histrionics in favour of a pained and resigned acceptance of loneliness as death. The economical yet acutely emphatic piano work of Floyd Cramer enhanced the stark mood of the piece, which was frozen in a suitably minimalist production. The startling originality and intensity of 'Heartbreak Hotel' entranced the American public and pushed the single to number 1 for an astonishing eight weeks. Whatever else he achieved, Presley was already assured a place in pop history for one of the greatest major label debut records ever released. During the same month that 'Heartbreak Hotel' was recorded, Presley made his national television debut displaying his sexually enticing gyrations before a bewildered adult audience whose alleged outrage subsequently persuaded producers to film the star exclusively from the waist upwards. Having outsold his former Sun colleague Carl Perkins with 'Blue Suede Shoes', Presley released a debut album that contained several of the songs he had previously recorded with Sam Phillips, including Little Richard's 'Tutti Frutti', the R&B classic 'I Got A Woman' and an eerie, wailing version of Richard Rodgers/Lorenz Hart's 'Blue Moon', which emphasized his remarkable vocal range.

Since hitting number 2 in the UK lists with 'Heartbreak Hotel', Presley had been virtually guaranteed European success and his profile was increased via a regular series of releases as RCA took full advantage of their bulging back catalogue. Although there was a danger of overkill, Presley's talent, reputation and immensely strong fanbase vindicated the intense release schedule and the quality of the material ensured that the public was not disappointed. After hitting number 1 for the second time with the slight ballad 'I Want You, I Need You, I Love You', Presley released what was to become the most commercially successful double-sided single in pop history, 'Hound Dog'/'Don't Be Cruel'. The former was composed by the immortal rock 'n' roll songwriting team of Leiber And Stoller, and presented Presley at his upbeat best with a novel lyric, complete with a striking guitar solo and spirited hand clapping from his backing group the Jordanaires. Otis Blackwell's 'Don't Be Cruel' was equally effective with a striking melody line and some clever and amusing vocal gymnastics from the hiccuping

King of Western Bop, who also received a co-writing credit. The single remained at number 1 in the USA for a staggering 11 weeks and both sides of the record were massive hits in the UK.

Celluloid fame for Presley next beckoned with *Love Me Tender*, produced by David Weisbert, who had previously worked on James Dean's *Rebel Without A Cause*. Presley's movie debut received mixed reviews but was a box-office smash, while the smouldering, perfectly enunciated title track topped the US charts for five weeks. The spate of Presley singles continued in earnest through 1957 and one of the biggest was another Otis Blackwell composition, 'All Shook Up', which the singer used as a cheekily oblique comment on his by now legendary dance movements. By late 1956 it was rumoured that Presley would be drafted into the US Army and, as if to compensate for that irksome eventuality, RCA, Twentieth Century Fox and the Colonel stepped up the work-rate and release schedules. Incredibly, three major films were completed in the next two-and-a-half years. *Loving You* boasted a quasi-autobiographical script with Presley playing a truck driver who becomes a pop star. The title track became the b-side of '(Let Me Be Your) Teddy Bear' which reigned at number 1 for seven weeks. The third movie, *Jailhouse Rock*, was Presley's most successful to date with an excellent soundtrack and some inspired choreography. The Leiber and Stoller title track was an instant classic that again topped the US charts for seven weeks and made pop history by entering the UK listings at number 1.

The fourth celluloid outing, *King Creole* (adapted from the Harold Robbins novel, *A Stone For Danny Fisher*), is regarded by many as Presley's finest film and a firm indicator of his sadly unfulfilled potential as a serious actor. Once more the soundtrack album featured some surprisingly strong material such as the haunting 'Crawfish' and the vibrant 'Dixieland Rock'. By the time *King Creole* was released in 1958, Elvis had already been inducted into the US Forces. A publicity photograph of the singer having his hair shorn symbolically commented on his approaching musical emasculation. Although rock 'n' roll purists mourned the passing of the old Elvis, it seemed inevitable in the context of the 50s that he would move towards a broader base appeal and tone down his rebellious image. From 1958-60, Presley served in the US Armed Forces, spending much of his time in Germany where he was regarded as a model soldier. It was during this period that he first met 14-year-old Priscilla Beaulieu, whom he later married in 1967. Back in America, the Colonel kept his absent star's reputation intact via a series of films, record releases and extensive merchandising. Hits such as 'Wear My Ring Around Your Neck', 'Hard Headed Woman', 'One Night', 'I Got Stung', 'A Fool Such As I' and 'A Big Hunk O' Love' filled the long, two-year gap and by the time Presley reappeared, he was ready to assume the mantle of all-round entertainer. The change was immediately evident in the series of number 1 hits that he enjoyed in the early 60s. The enormously successful 'It's Now

Or Never', based on the Italian melody 'O Sole Mio', revealed the King as an operatic crooner, far removed from his earlier raucous recordings. 'Are You Lonesome Tonight?', originally recorded by Al Jolson as early as 1927, allowed Presley to quote some Shakespeare in the spoken-word middle section as well as showing his ham-acting ability with an overwrought vocal.

The new clean-cut Presley was presented on celluloid in *GI Blues*. The movie played upon his recent army exploits and saw him serenading a puppet on the charming chart-topper 'Wooden Heart', which also allowed Elvis to show off his knowledge of German. The grandiose 'Surrender' completed this phase of big ballads in the old-fashioned style. For the next few years Presley concentrated on an undemanding spree of films, including *Flaming Star, Wild In The Country, Blue Hawaii, Kid Galahad, Girls! Girls! Girls!, Follow That Dream, Fun In Acapulco, It Happened At The World's Fair, Kissin' Cousins, Viva Las Vegas, Roustabout, Girl Happy, Tickle Me, Harem Scarum, Frankie And Johnny, Paradise – Hawaiian Style* and *Spinout*. Not surprisingly, most of his album recordings were hastily completed soundtracks with unadventurous commissioned songs. For his singles he relied increasingly on the formidable Doc Pomus/Mort Shuman team who composed such hits as 'Mess Of Blues', 'Little Sister' and 'His Latest Flame'. More and more, however, the hits were adapted from films and their chart positions suffered accordingly. After the 1963 number 1 'Devil In Disguise', a bleak period followed in which such minor songs as 'Bossa Nova Baby', 'Kiss Me Quick', 'Ain't That Lovin' You Baby' and 'Blue Christmas' became the rule rather than the exception. Significantly, his biggest success of the mid-60s, 'Crying In The Chapel', had been recorded five years earlier, and part of its appeal came from the realization that it represented something ineffably lost.

In the wake of the Beatles' rise to fame and the beat boom explosion, Presley seemed a figure out of time. Nevertheless, in spite of the dated nature of many of his recordings, he could still invest power and emotion into classic songs. The sassy 'Frankie And Johnny' was expertly sung by Presley, as was his moving reading of Ketty Lester's 'Love Letters'. His other significant 1966 release, 'If Everyday Was Like Christmas', was a beautiful festive song unlike anything else in the charts of the period. By 1967, however, it was clear to critics and even a large proportion of his devoted following that Presley had seriously lost his way. He continued to grind out pointless movies such as *Double Trouble, Speedway, Clambake* and *Live A Little, Love A Little*, even though the box office returns were increasingly poor. His capacity to register instant hits, irrespective of the material was also wearing thin, as such lowly placed singles as 'You Gotta Stop' and 'Long Legged Woman' demonstrated all too alarmingly. However, just as Elvis' career had reached its all-time nadir he seemed to wake up, take stock, and break free from the artistic malaise in which he found himself. Two songs written by country guitarist Jerry Reed,

'Guitar Man' and 'US Male', proved a spectacular return to form for Elvis in 1968, such was Presley's conviction that the compositions almost seemed to be written specifically for him. During the same year, Colonel Tom Parker had approached NBC-TV about the possibility of recording a Presley Christmas special in which the singer would perform a selection of religious songs similar in feel to his early 60s album *His Hand In Mine*. However, the executive producers of the show vetoed that concept in favour of a one-hour spectacular designed to capture Elvis at his rock 'n' rollin' best. It was a remarkable challenge for the singer, seemingly at the autumn of his career, and he responded to the idea with unexpected enthusiasm.

The *Elvis TV Special* was broadcast in America on 3 December 1968 and has since become legendary as one of the most celebrated moments in pop broadcasting history. The show was not merely good but an absolute revelation, with the King emerging as if he had been frozen in time for 10 years. His determination to recapture past glories oozed from every movement and was discernible in every aside. With his leather jacket and acoustic guitar strung casually round his neck, he resembled nothing less than the consummate pop idol of the 50s who had entranced a generation. To add authenticity to the proceedings he was accompanied by his old sidekicks Scotty Moore and D.J. Fontana. There was no sense of self-parody in the show as Presley joked about his famous surly curled-lip movement and even heaped passing ridicule on his endless stream of bad movies. The music concentrated heavily on his 50s classics but, significantly, there was a startling finale courtesy of the passionate 'If I Can Dream' in which he seemed to sum up the frustration of a decade in a few short lines. The critical plaudits heaped upon Elvis in the wake of his television special prompted the singer to undertake his most significant recordings in years. With producer Chips Moman overseeing the sessions in January 1969, Presley recorded enough material to cover two highly praised albums, *From Elvis In Memphis* and *From Memphis To Vegas/From Vegas To Memphis*. The former was particularly strong with such distinctive tracks as the eerie 'Long Black Limousine' and the engagingly melodic 'Any Day Now'. On the singles front, Presley was back in top form and finally coming to terms with contemporary issues, most notably on the socially aware 'In The Ghetto', which hit number 2 in the UK and number 3 in the USA. The glorious 'Suspicious Minds', a wonderful song of marital jealousy, with cascading tempo changes and an exceptional vocal arrangement, gave him his first US chart-topper since 'Good Luck Charm' back in 1962. Subsequent hits such as the maudlin 'Don't Cry Daddy', which dealt with the death of a marriage, ably demonstrated Presley's ability to read a song. Even his final few films seemed less disastrous than expected.

In 1969's *Charro*, he grew a beard for the first time in his portrayal of a moody cowboy, while *A Change Of Habit* dealt with more serious subject matter than usual. More importantly, Presley returned as a live performer at Las Vegas, with a strong backing group including guitarist James Burton and pianist Glen D. Hardin. In common with John Lennon, who also returned to the stage that same year with the Plastic Ono Band, Presley opened his set with Carl Perkins' 'Blue Suede Shoes'. His comeback was well received and one of the live songs, 'The Wonder Of You', stayed at number 1 in Britain for six weeks during the summer of 1970. There was also a revealing documentary film of the tour – *That's The Way It Is* – and a companion album that included contemporary cover versions, such as Tony Joe White's 'Polk Salad Annie', Creedence Clearwater Revival's 'Proud Mary' and Neil Diamond's 'Sweet Caroline'.

During the early 70s Presley continued his live performances, but soon fell victim to the same artistic atrophy that had bedevilled his celluloid career. Rather than re-entering the studio to record fresh material he relied on a slew of patchy live albums that saturated the marketplace. What had been innovative and exciting in 1969 swiftly became a tedious routine and an exercise in misdirected potential. The backdrop to Presley's final years was a sordid slump into drug dependency, reinforced by the pervasive unreality of a pampered lifestyle in his fantasy home, Gracelands. The dissolution of his marriage in 1973 coincided with a further decline and an alarming tendency to put on weight. Remarkably, he continued to undertake live appearances, covering up his bloated frame with brightly coloured jump suits and an enormous, ostentatiously jewelled belt. He collapsed onstage on a couple of occasions and finally on 16 August 1977 his tired body expired. The official cause of death was a heart attack, undoubtedly brought on by barbiturate usage over a long period. In the weeks following his demise, his record sales predictably rocketed and 'Way Down' proved a fittingly final UK number 1.

The importance of Presley in the history of rock 'n' roll and popular music remains incalculable. In spite of his iconographic status, the Elvis image was never captured in a single moment of time like that of Bill Haley, Buddy Holly or even Chuck Berry. Presley, in spite of his apparent creative inertia, was not a one-dimensional artist clinging to history but a multi-faceted performer whose career spanned several decades and phases. For purists and rockabilly enthusiasts it is the early Presley that remains of greatest importance and there is no doubting that his personal fusion of black and white musical influences, incorporating R&B and country, produced some of the finest and most durable recordings of the century. Beyond Elvis 'The Hillbilly Cat', however, there was the face that launched a thousand imitators, that black-haired, smiling or smouldering presence who stared from the front covers of numerous EPs, albums and film posters of the late 50s and early 60s. It was that well-groomed, immaculate pop star who inspired a generation of performers and second-rate imitators in the 60s. There was also

Elvis the Las Vegas performer, vibrant and vulgar, yet still distant and increasingly appealing to a later generation brought up on the excesses of 70s rock and glam ephemera. Finally, there was the bloated Presley who bestrode the stage in the last months of his career. For many, he has come to symbolize the decadence and loss of dignity that is all too often heir to pop idolatry. It is no wonder that Presley's remarkable career so sharply divides those who testify to his ultimate greatness and those who bemoan the gifts that he seemingly squandered along the way. Twenty years after his death, in August 1997, there was no waning of his power and appeal. Television, radio, newspapers and magazines all over the world still found that, whatever was happening elsewhere, little could compare to this anniversary.

● ALBUMS: *Elvis Presley* (RCA Victor 1956) ★★★★, *Elvis* (RCA Victor 1956) ★★★★★, *Rock 'N' Roll* UK release (HMV 1956) ★★★★, *Rock 'N' Roll No. 2* UK release (HMV 1957) ★★★★, *Loving You* film soundtrack (RCA Victor 1957) ★★★★, *Elvis' Christmas Album* (RCA Victor 1957) ★★★, *King Creole* film soundtrack (RCA Victor 1958) ★★★★, *For LP Fans Only* (RCA Victor 1959) ★★★★, *A Date With Elvis* (RCA Victor 1959) ★★★★, *Elvis Is Back!* (RCA Victor 1960) ★★★★, *G.I. Blues* film soundtrack (RCA Victor 1960) ★★★, *His Hand In Mine* (RCA Victor 1961) ★★★, *Something For Everybody* (RCA Victor 1961) ★★★, *Blue Hawaii* (RCA Victor 1961) ★★★, *Pot Luck* (RCA Victor 1962) ★★★, *Girls! Girls! Girls!* film soundtrack (RCA Victor 1963) ★★★, *It Happened At The World's Fair* film soundtrack (RCA Victor 1963) ★★, *Fun In Acapulco* film soundtrack (RCA Victor 1963) ★★, *Kissin' Cousins* film soundtrack (RCA Victor 1964) ★★, *Roustabout* film soundtrack (RCA Victor 1964) ★★, *Girl Happy* film soundtrack (RCA Victor 1965) ★★, *Harem Scarum* film soundtrack (RCA Victor 1965) ★★, *Frankie And Johnny* film soundtrack (RCA Victor 1966) ★★, *Paradise, Hawaiian Style* film soundtrack (RCA Victor 1966) ★★, *Spinout* film soundtrack (RCA Victor 1966) ★★, *How Great Thou Art* (RCA Victor 1967) ★★★, *Double Trouble* film soundtrack (RCA Victor 1967) ★★, *Clambake* film soundtrack (RCA Victor 1967) ★★, *Speedway* film soundtrack (RCA Victor 1968) ★★, *Elvis – TV Special* (RCA Victor 1968) ★★★, *From Elvis In Memphis* (RCA Victor 1969) ★★★★, *From Memphis To Vegas/From Vegas To Memphis* (RCA Victor 1969) ★★★, *On Stage February 1970* (RCA Victor 1970) ★★★★, *Elvis Back In Memphis* (RCA Victor 1970) ★★★, *That's The Way It Is* (RCA 1970) ★★★, *Elvis Country (I'm 10,000 Years Old)* (RCA 1971) ★★★, *Love Letters From Elvis* (RCA 1971) ★★★, *Elvis Sings The Wonderful World Of Christmas* (RCA 1971) ★★★, *Elvis Now* (RCA 1972) ★★★, *He Touched Me* (RCA 1972) ★★★, *Elvis As Recorded At Madison Square Garden* (RCA 1972) ★★★, *Aloha From Hawaii Via Satellite* (RCA 1973) ★★★, *Elvis* (RCA 1973) ★★★, *Raised On Rock/For Ol' Times Sake* (RCA 1973) ★★★, *Good Times* (RCA 1974) ★★★, *Elvis Recorded Live On Stage In Memphis* (RCA 1974) ★★★★, *Having Fun With Elvis On Stage* (RCA 1974) ★, *Promised Land* (RCA 1975) ★★★, *Elvis Today* (RCA 1975) ★★★, *From Elvis Presley Boulevard,*

Memphis, Tennessee (RCA 1976) ★★★, *Welcome To My World* (RCA 1977) ★★★, *Moody Blue* (RCA 1977) ★★★, *Guitar Man* (RCA 1980) ★★★, *The Ultimate Performance* (RCA 1981) ★★★, *The Sound Of Your Cry* (RCA 1982) ★★★, *The First Year* (Sun 1983) ★★★, *Jailhouse Rock/Love In Las Vegas* (RCA 1983) ★★★, *Elvis: The First Live Recordings* (Music Works 1984) ★★★, *The Elvis Presley Interview Record: An Audio Self-Portrait* (RCA 1984) ★★, with Carl Perkins and Jerry Lee Lewis *The Million Dollar Quartet* (RCA 1990) ★★★, *The Lost Album* (RCA 1991) ★★★, *If Every Day Was Like Christmas* (RCA 1994) ★★★, *Elvis Presley '56* (RCA 1996) ★★★★★, *Essential Elvis, Volume 4: A Hundred Years From Now* (RCA 1996) ★★★, *Essential Elvis, Volume 5: Rhythm And Country* (RCA 1998) ★★★, *Tiger Man* 1968 recording (RCA 1998) ★★★★, *Essential Elvis, Volume 6: Such A Night* (RCA 2000) ★★★.

● COMPILATIONS: *The Best Of Elvis* UK release (HMV 1957) ★★★★, *Elvis' Golden Records* (RCA Victor 1958) ★★★★★, *50,000,000 Elvis Fans Can't Be Wrong: Golden Records, Volume 2* (RCA Victor 1960) ★★★★★, *Elvis' Golden Records, Volume 3* (RCA Victor 1963) ★★★★, *Elvis For Everyone!* (RCA Victor 1965) ★★★, *Elvis' Golden Records, Volume 4* (RCA Victor 1968) ★★★★, *Elvis Sings 'Flaming Star' And Other Hits From His Movies* (RCA Camden 1969) ★★, *Let's Be Friends* (RCA Camden 1970) ★★★★, *Almost In Love* (RCA Camden 1970) ★★, *Worldwide 50 Gold Award Hits, Volume 1 – A Touch Of Gold* 4-LP box set (RCA Victor 1970) ★★★★★, *You'll Never Walk Alone* (RCA Camden 1971) ★★★, *C'mon Everybody* (RCA Camden 1971) ★★★, *The Other Sides – Worldwide 50 Gold Award Hits, Volume 2* 4-LP box set (RCA Victor 1971) ★★★★, *I Got Lucky* (RCA Camden 1971) ★★★, *Elvis Sings Hits From His Movies, Volume 1* (RCA Camden 1972) ★★★, *Burning Love And Hits From His Movies, Volume 2* (RCA Camden 1972) ★★★, *Separate Ways* (RCA Camden 1973) ★★★, *Elvis – A Legendary Performer, Volume 1* (RCA 1974) ★★★★, *Hits Of The 70s* (RCA 1974) ★★★, *Pure Gold* (RCA 1975) ★★★, *Easy Come Easy Go* (RCA Camden 1975) ★★★, *The U.S. Male* (RCA Camden 1975) ★★★, *Elvis Presley's Greatest Hits* 7-LP box set (Readers Digest 1975) ★★★, *Pictures Of Elvis* (RCA Starcall 1975) ★★, *Elvis – A Legendary Performer, Volume 2* (RCA 1976) ★★★★, *Sun Sessions* (RCA 1976) ★★★★★, *Elvis In Demand* (RCA 1977) ★★★, *The Elvis Tapes* interview disc (Redwood 1977) ★★, *He Walks Beside Me* (RCA 1978) ★★★, *Elvis Sings For Children And Grownups Too!* (RCA 1978) ★★★, *Elvis – A Canadian Tribute* (RCA 1978) ★★★, *The '56 Sessions, Volume 1* (RCA 1978) ★★★★, *Elvis' 40 Greatest* (RCA 1978) ★★★★★, *Elvis – A Legendary Performer, Volume 3* (RCA 1979) ★★★★, *Our Memories Of Elvis* (RCA 1979) ★★★, *Our Memories Of Elvis Volume 2* (RCA 1979) ★★★, *The '56 Sessions, Volume 2* (RCA 1979) ★★★★, *Elvis Presley Sings Leiber And Stoller* (RCA 1979) ★★★★, *Elvis – A Legendary Performer, Volume 4* (RCA 1980) ★★★★, *Elvis Aaron Presley* 8-LP box set (RCA 1980) ★★★, *This Is Elvis* (RCA 1981) ★★★, *Elvis – Greatest Hits, Volume 1* (RCA 1981) ★★, *The Elvis Medley* (RCA 1982) ★★★, *I Was The One* (RCA 1983) ★★★★, *Elvis' Golden Records, Volume 5* (RCA 1984) ★★★★,

Elvis: A Golden Celebration 6-LP box set (RCA 1984) ★★★, *Rocker* (RCA 1984) ★★★★, *Reconsider Baby* (RCA 1985) ★★★★, *A Valentine Gift For You* (RCA 1985) ★★★, *Always On My Mind* (RCA 1985) ★★★★, *Return Of The Rocker* (RCA 1986) ★★★, *The Number One Hits* (RCA 1987) ★★★★★, *The Top Ten Hits* (RCA 1987) ★★★★, *The Complete Sun Sessions* (RCA 1987) ★★★★★, *Essential Elvis* (RCA 1988) ★★★★, *Stereo '57 (Essential Elvis Volume 2)* (RCA 1988) ★★★★, *Known Only To Him: Elvis Gospel: 1957-1971* (RCA 1989) ★★★★, *Hits Like Never Before: Essential Elvis, Volume 3* (RCA 1990) ★★★, *Collector's Gold* (RCA 1991) ★★★★, *The King Of Rock 'n' Roll: The Complete '50s Masters* 5-CD box set (RCA 1992) ★★★★★, *From Nashville To Memphis: The Essential '60s Masters* 5-CD box set (RCA 1993) ★★★★★, *Amazing Grace: His Greatest Sacred Songs* (RCA 1994) ★★★★, *Heart And Soul* (RCA 1995) ★★, *Walk A Mile In My Shoes: The Essential '70s Masters* 5-CD box set (RCA 1995) ★★★★, *Presley – The All Time Greats* (RCA 1996) ★★★★, *Great Country Songs* (RCA 1997) ★★★, *Platinum: A Life In Music* 4-CD box set (RCA 1997) ★★★★, *Love Songs* (Camden 1999) ★★★★, *Sunrise* (RCA 1999) ★★★★, *Suspicious Minds: The Memphis 1969 Anthology* (RCA 1999) ★★★★, *The Home Recordings* (RCA 1999) ★★, *Artist Of The Century* 3-CD set (RCA 1999) ★★★★★, *Can't Help Falling In Love: The Hollywood Hits* (RCA 1999) ★★★, *The Legend Begins* (Manifest 2000) ★★★, *Peace In The Valley* 3-CD box set (RCA 2000) ★★★★, *The 50 Greatest Hits* (RCA 2000) ★★★★★, *The Live Greatest Hits* (RCA 2001) ★★★★, *Elvis: Live In Las Vegas* 4-CD box set (RCA 2001) ★★★★.

● VIDEOS: *Elvis On Tour* (MGM/UA 1984), *Elvis Presley In Concert* (Mountain Films 1986), *68 Comeback Special* (Virgin Vision 1986), *One Night With You* (Virgin Vision 1986), *Aloha From Hawaii* (Virgin Vision 1986), *'56 In the Beginning* (Virgin Vision 1987), *Memories* (Vestron Music Video 1987), *This Is Elvis* (Warner Home Video 1988), *Graceland* (Video Gems 1988), *Great Performances Volume 1* (Buena Vista 1990), *Great Performances Volume 2* (Buena Vista 1990), *Young Elvis* (Channel 5 1990), *Sun Days With Elvis* (MMG Video 1991), *Elvis: A Portrait By His Friends* (Qube Pictures 1991), *The Lost Performances* (BMG 1992), *Private Elvis* (1993), *Elvis In Hollywood* (1993), *The Alternate Aloha Concert* (Lightyear 1996), *Elvis 56 – The Video* (BMG 1996), *Elvis – That's The Way It Is* (1996), *Private Moments* (Telstar 1997), *The Great Performances* (Wienerworld 1997), *The Legend Lives On* (Real Entertainment 1997), *Collapse Of The Kingdom* (Real Entertainment 1997), *The King Comes Back* (Real Entertainment 1997), *Wild In Hollywood* (Real Entertainment 1997), *Rocket Ride To Stardom* (Real Entertainment 1997), *Elvis: All The Kings Men* (Real Entertainment 1997), *NBC T.V. Special* (Lightyear 1997).

● FURTHER READING: To begin to wade through the list of books about Elvis is daunting. Many are appalling, some are excellent. In reality you only need two, and both were written in recent years by Peter Guralnick. *Last Train To Memphis* and *Careless Love* are historically accurate, objective and beautifully written.

I Called Him Babe: Elvis Presley's Nurse Remembers, Marian J. Cocke. *The Three Loves Of Elvis Presley: The True Story Of The Presley Legend*, Robert Holmes. *A Century Of Elvis*, Albert Hand. *The Elvis They Dig*, Albert Hand. *Operation Elvis*, Alan Levy. *The Elvis Presley Pocket Handbook*, Albert Hand. *All Elvis: An Unofficial Biography Of The 'King Of Discs'*, Philip Buckle. *The Elvis Presley Encyclopedia*, Roy Barlow. *Elvis: A Biography*, Jerry Hopkins. *Meet Elvis Presley*, Favius Friedman *Elvis Presley*, Paula Taylor. *Elvis*, Jerry Hopkins. *The Elvis Presley Scrapbook 1935-1977*, James Robert Paris. *Elvis And The Colonel*, May Mann. *Recording Sessions 1954-1974*, Ernst Jorgensen and Erik Rasmussen. *Elvis Presley: An Illustrated Biography*, W.A. Harbinson. *Elvis: The Films And Career Of Elvis Presley*, Steven Zmijewsky and Boris Zmijewsky. *Presley Nation*, Spencer Leigh. *Elvis*, Peter Jones. *Presley: Entertainer Of The Century*, Antony James. *Elvis And His Secret*, Maria Gripe. *On Stage, Elvis Presley*, Kathleen Bowman. *The Elvis Presley American Discography*, Ron Barry. *Elvis: What Happened*, Red West, Sonny West and Dave Hebler. *Elvis: Tribute To The King Of Rock*, Dick Tatham. *Elvis Presley*, Todd Slaughter. *Elvis: Recording Sessions*, Ernst Jorgensen, Erick Rasmussen and Johnny Mikkelsen. *The Life And Death Of Elvis Presley*, W.A. Harbinson. *Elvis: Lonely Star At The Top*, David Hanna. *Elvis In His Own Words*, Mick Farren and Pearce Marchbank. *Twenty Years Of Elvis: The Session File*, Colin Escott and Martin Hawkins. *Starring Elvis*, James W. Bowser. *My Life With Elvis*, Becky Yancey and Cliff Lindecker. *The Real Elvis: A Good Old Boy*, Vince Staten. *The Elvis Presley Trivia Quiz Book*, Helen Rosenbaum. *A Presley Speaks*, Vester Presley. *The Graceland Gates*, Harold Lloyd. *The Boy Who Dared To Rock: The Definitive Elvis*, Paul Lichter. *Eine Illustrierte Dokumentation*, Bernd King and Heinz Plehn. *Elvis Presley Speaks*, Hans Holzer. *Elvis: The Legend Lives! One Year Later*, Martin A. Grove. *Private Elvis*, Diego Cortez. *Bill Adler's Love Letters To Elvis*, Bill Adler. *Elvis: His Life And Times In Poetry And Lines*, Joan Buchanan West. *Elvis '56: In The Beginning*, Alfred Wertheimer. *Elvis Presley: An Illustrated Biography*, Rainer Wallraf and Heinz Plehn. *Even Elvis*, Mary Ann Thornton. *Elvis: Images & Fancies*, Jac L. Tharpe. *Elvis In Concert*, John Reggero. *Elvis Presley: A Study In Music*, Robert Matthew-Walker. *Elvis; Portrait Of A Friend*, Marty Lacker, Patsy Lacker and Leslie E. Smith. *Elvis Is That You?*, Holly Hatcher. *Elvis: Newly Discovered Drawings Of Elvis Presley*, Betty Harper. *Trying To Get To You: The Story Of Elvis Presley*, Valerie Harms. *Love Of Elvis*, Bruce Hamilton and Michael L. Liben. *To Elvis With Love*, Lena Canada. *The Truth About Elvis*, Jess Stearn. *Elvis: We Love You Tender*, Dee Presley, David Rick and Billy Stanley. *Presleyana*, Jerry Osborne and Bruce Hamilton. *Elvis: The Final Years*, Jerry Hopkins. *When Elvis Died*, Nancy Gregory and Joseph. *All About Elvis*, Fred L. Worth and Steve D. Tamerius. *Elvis Presley: A Reference Guide And Discography*, John A. Whisle. *The Illustrated Discography*, Martin Hawkins and Colin Escott. *Elvis: Legend Of Love*, Marie Greenfield. *Elvis Presley: King Of Rock 'N'*

Roll, Richard Wooton. *The Complete Elvis*, Martin Torgoff. *Elvis Special 1982*, Todd Slaughter. *Elvis*, Dave Marsh. *Up And Down With Elvis Presley*, Marge Crumbaker with Gabe Tucker. *Elvis For The Record*, Maureen Covey. *Elvis: The Complete Illustrated Record*, Roy Carr and Mick Farren. *Elvis Collectables*, Rosalind Cranor. *Jailhouse Rock: The Bootleg Records Of Elvis Presley 1970*, Lee Cotten and Howard A. DeWitt. *Elvis The Soldier*, Rex and Elisabeth Mansfield. *All Shook Up: Elvis Day-By-Day, 1954-1977*, Lee Cotten. *Elvis*, John Townson, Gordon Minto and George Richardson. *Priscilla, Elvis & Me*, Michael Edwards. *Elvis On The Road To Stardom: 1955-1956*, Jim Black. *Return To Sender*, Howard F. Banney. *Elvis: His Life From A To Z*, Fred L. Worth and Steve D. Tamerius. *Elvis And The Colonel*, Dirk Vallenga with Mick Farren. *Elvis: My Brother*, Bill Stanley with George Erikson. *Long Lonely Highway: 1950's Elvis Scrapbook*, Ger J. Rijff. *Elvis In Hollywood*, Gerry McLafferty. *Reconsider Baby: Definitive Elvis Sessionography*, E. Jorgensen. *Elvis '69, The Return*, Joseph A. Tunzi. *The Death Of Elvis: What Really Happened*, Charles C. Thompson and James P. Cole. *Elvis For Beginners*, Jill Pearlman. *Elvis, The Cool King*, Bob Morel and Jan Van Gestel. *The Elvis Presley Scrapbooks 1955-1965*, Peter Haining (ed.). *The Boy Who Would Be King. An Intimate Portrait Of Elvis Presley By His Cousin*, Earl Greenwood and Kathleen Tracy. *Elvis: The Last 24 Hours*, Albert Goldman. *The Elvis Files*, Gail Brewer-Giorgio. *Elvis, My Dad*, David Adler and Ernest Andrews. *The Elvis Reader: Texts And Sources On The King Of Rock 'n' Roll*, Kevin Quain (ed.). *Elvis Bootlegs Buyer's Guide, Pts 1 & 2*, Tommy Robinson. *Elvis: The Music Lives On – The Recording Sessions 1954-1976*, Richard Peters. *The King Forever*, no author listed. *Dead Elvis: A Chronicle Of A Cultural Obsession*, Greil Marcus. *Elvis People: Cult Of The King*, Ted Harrison. *In Search Of The King*, Craig Gelfand, Lynn Blocker-Krantz and Rogerio Noguera. *Aren Med Elvis*, Roger Ersson and Lennart Svedberg. *Elvis And Gladys*, Elaine Dundy. *King And I: Little Gallery of Elvis Impersonators*, Kent Barker and Karin Pritikin. *Elvis Sessions: The Recorded Music Of Elvis Aaron Presley 1953-1977*, Joseph A. Tunzi. *Elvis: The Sun Years*, Howard A. DeWitt. *Elvis In Germany: The Missing Years*, Andreas Schroer. *Graceland: The Living Legend Of Elvis Presley*, Chet Flippo. *Elvis: The Secret Files*, John Parker. *The Life And Cuisine Of Elvis Presley*, David Adler. *Last Train To Memphis: The Rise Of Elvis Presley*, Peter Guralnick. *In His Own Words*, Mick Farren. *Elvis: Murdered By The Mob*, John Parker. *The Complete Guide To The Music Of ...*, John Robertson. *Elvis' Man Friday*, Gene Smith. *The Hitchhiker's Guide To Elvis*, Mick Farren. *Elvis, The Lost Photographs 1948-1969*, Joseph Tunzi and O'Neal. *Elvis Aaron Presley: Revelations From The Memphis Mafia*, Alanna Nash. *The Elvis Encyclopaedia*, David E. Stanley. *E: Reflections On The Birth Of The Elvis Faith*, John E. Strausbaugh. *Elvis Meets The Beatles: The Untold Story Of Their Entangled Lives*, Chris Hutchins and Peter Thompson. *Elvis, Highway 51 South, Memphis, Tennessee*, Joseph A. Tunzi. *Elvis In The Army*, William J. Taylor Jnr. *Everything Elvis*, Pauline Bartel. *Elvis In Wonderland*, Bob Jope. *Elvis: Memories And Memorabilia*, Richard Bushkin. *Elvis Sessions II: The Recorded Music Of Elvis Aaron Presley 1953-1977*, Joseph A. Tunzi. *The Ultimate Album Cover Book*, Paul Dowling. *The King Of The Road*, Robert Gordon. *That's Alright, Elvis*, Scotty Moore and James Dickerson. *Raised On Rock: Growing Up At Graceland*, David A. Stanley and Mark Bego. *Elvis: In The Twilight Of Memory*, June Juanico. *The Rise And Fall And Rise Of Elvis*, Aubrey Dillon-Malone. *In Search Of Elvis: Music, Race, Art, Religion*, Vernon Chadwick (editor). *The Complete Idiot's Guide To Elvis*, Frank Coffey. *The Elvis Encyclopedia: An Impartial Guide To The Films Of Elvis*, Eric Braun. *Essential Elvis*, Peter Silverton. *Talking Elvis*, Trevor Cajiao. *A Life In Music: The Complete Recording Sessions*, Ernst Jorgensen. *Careless Love: The Unmaking Of Elvis Presley*, Peter Guralnick. *Elvis For CD Fans Only*, Dale Hampton. *Double Trouble: Bill Clinton And Elvis Presley In The Land Of No Alternatives*, Greil Marcus. *A Life In Music: The Complete Recording Sessions*, Ernst Jorgensen. *Elvis Day By Day: The Definitive Record Of His Life And Music*, Peter Guralnick and Ernst Jorgensen. *Elvis: The King On Film*, Chutley Chops (ed.). *Colonel Tom Parker: The Curious Life Of Elvis Presley's Eccentric Manager*, James L. Dickerson.

● FILMS: *Love Me Tender* (1956), *Loving You* (1957), *Jailhouse Rock* (1957), *King Creole* (1958), *G.I. Blues* (1960), *Flaming Star* (1960), *Wild In The Country* (1961), *Blue Hawaii* (1961), *Kid Galahad* (1962), *Girls Girls Girls* (1962), *Follow That Dream* (1962), *It Happened At The World's Fair* (1963), *Fun In Acapulco* (1963), *Roustabout* (1964), *Viva Las Vegas* (1964), *Kissin' Cousins* (1964), *Tickle Me* (1965), *Harem Scarum* aka *Harem Holiday* (1965), *Girl Happy* (1965), *Spinout* (1966), *Paradise Hawaiian Style* (1966), *Frankie And Johnny* (1966), *Easy Come Easy Go* (1967), *Clambake* (1967), *Live A Little Love A Little* (1968), *Speedway* (1968), *Stay Away Joe* (1968), *Double Trouble* (1968), *The Trouble With Girls* (1969), *Charro!* (1969), *Change Of Habit* (1969), *This Is Elvis* compilation (1981).

PRESTON, ROBERT

b. Robert Preston Meservey, 8 June 1918, Newton Highlands, Massachusetts, USA, d. 21 March 1987, Santa Barbara, California, USA. An actor and singer, Preston had already enjoyed a busy, but undistinguished career in Hollywood for nearly 20 years when he landed the role of a lifetime on Broadway in *The Music Man* (1957). He grew up in Hollywood, and spent several of his teenage years in the theatre before signing for Paramount and making his first movie, *King Of Alcatraz*, in 1938. From then, until 1942, he made some 15 films, including *Union Pacific*, *Beau Geste*, *Typhoon*, *Moon Over Burma*, *Northwest Mounted Police*, and *This Gun For Hire* (1942). After serving in the US Army Air Force during World War II, Preston resumed his film career in features such as *The Macomber Affair*, *Tulsa* and *When I Grow Up*, until 1951 when he moved to New York. He appeared on Broadway in a number of straight plays including *Twentieth*

Century, The Tender Trap and Janus, and was out of town in Philadelphia with Boy Meets Girl when he was asked to audition for The Music Man. His portrayal of the likeable con man, Harold Hill, who travels to small US towns such as Iowa, selling band instruments (which never materialize) to parents for their children to play, made Preston a gilt-edged Broadway star. Meredith Willson's fine score featured numbers such as 'Seventy-Six Trombones', 'Till There Was You', and Preston's tour de force, 'Ya Got Trouble'. He won the Tony Award for best actor in a musical, and stayed with the show for over two years. After being virtually ignored during initial casting, he recreated the part in the 1962 film version. Cary Grant was one of the actors to whom the role was offered, and he reportedly said: 'Not only won't I play it, but unless Robert Preston plays it, I won't even go see it.' After appearing in several more straight parts, Preston returned to the musical stage in 1964 with Ben Franklin In Paris, but, unlike the large onstage floating balloon in which Preston rode, the show did not really take off. Much more satisfying was I Do! I Do!, a two-hander with Mary Martin for which Preston won another Tony. His final Broadway musical appearance came in 1974 with Mack And Mabel, which, despite a splendid Jerry Herman score, only lasted for six weeks. During the 50s and 60s he had continued to make films, and in the 70s and early 80s he appeared in several more, including the musical Mame (1973), with Lucille Ball, and S.O.B. and Victor/Victoria (1982), both with Julie Andrews. He also starred in several television movies, including the highly regarded Finnegan Begin Again, a poignant story of the love of an older man for a young woman played by Mary Tyler Moore. Preston died of lung cancer in 1987, and in the same year was awarded a special posthumous Tony, the Lawrence Langner Memorial Award for Distinguished Lifetime Achievement in the American Theatre.

PRICE, LLOYD

b. 9 March 1933, Kenner, Louisiana, USA. Price, who launched his career in the early 50s performing rocking R&B, New Orleans-style, was – like his Crescent City compatriot Fats Domino – made for the rock 'n' roll era. He did not have to modify his approach at all to become a rock 'n' roll hit-maker in the late 50s. Price formed his own band in New Orleans in 1949 and in 1952 was signed with the Los Angeles-based Specialty Records, who made a practice of recording New Orleans artists. His first hit, 'Lawdy Miss Clawdy' (US R&B number 1, 1952), established his career in the R&B field and he followed with four more Top 10 hits. Military service intervened and took Price out of action from 1954-56. On returning to civilian life he settled in Washington, DC, and set up a record company with Harold Logan. Price regained his place on the chart in 1957 with 'Just Because' (US R&B number 3 and pop Top 30). Signed to ABC-Paramount Records, the company transformed their R&B veteran into a rock 'n' roll hit-maker for the new teen market. He and Logan

revamped an old blues, 'Stack-O-Lee', that had been a hit for Ma Rainey in the 20s, and made it one of his biggest successes (US R&B and pop number 1, 1959). In the UK, it entered the Top 10. Price's chart career peaked in 1959, with such hits as 'Where Were You (On Our Wedding Day)' (US R&B number 4 and pop Top 30), 'Personality' (US R&B number 1 and pop number 2) and 'I'm Gonna Get Married' (US R&B number 1 and pop number 3), all of which were similarly successful in the UK. The hits continued, to a lesser extent, the following year with 'Lady Luck' (US R&B number 3 and pop Top 20) and 'Question' (US R&B number 5 and number 19 pop). Three years later Price resurfaced on the Double-L label (owned by Price and Logan), briefly making an impact on the emerging soul market with his reworking of jazz standards 'Misty' (US R&B number 11 and pop Top 30) and 'Bill Bailey' (US R&B Top 40 and pop Top 100 as 'Billy Baby'). Double-L also released Wilson Pickett's first solo sides, and in the late 60s Price began another label called Turntable for which Howard Tate, among others, recorded. Price's last chart record was in 1976 on the LPG label, a label he formed in partnership with the notorious boxing promoter Don King.

● ALBUMS: Lloyd Price (Specialty 1959) ★★★★, The Exciting Lloyd Price (ABC-Paramount 1959) ★★★★, Mr. Personality (ABC-Paramount 1959) ★★★★, Mr. Personality Sings The Blues (ABC-Paramount 1960) ★★★★, The Fantastic Lloyd Price (ABC-Paramount 1960) ★★★, Lloyd Price Sings The Million Sellers (ABC-Paramount 1961) ★★★, Cookin' With Lloyd Price (ABC-Paramount 1961) ★★, The Lloyd Price Orchestra (Double-L 1963) ★★, Misty (Double-L 1963) ★★, Lloyd Swings For Sammy (Monument 1965) ★★, Lloyd Price Now (Jad 1969) ★★, To The Roots And Back (1972) ★★, The Nominee (1978) ★★.

● COMPILATIONS: Mr. Personality's Big 15 (ABC-Paramount 1960) ★★★★, The Best Of Lloyd Price (1970) ★★★★, Lloyd Price's 16 Greatest Hits (ABC 1972) ★★★★, Original Hits (1972) ★★★, The ABC Collection (ABC 1976) ★★★★, Mr. Personality Revisited (Charly 1983) ★★★, Lloyd Price (Specialty 1986) ★★★, Personality Plus (Specialty 1986) ★★★, Walkin' The Track (Specialty 1986) ★★, Lawdy! (Specialty 1991) ★★★, Stagger Lee & All His Other Greatest Hits (1993) ★★★★, Greatest Hits (MCA 1995) ★★★★.

PRICE, RAY

b. Ray Noble Price, 12 January 1926, on a farm near Perryville, Cherokee County, Texas, USA. Price grew up on a farm and by the time he left high school, was already singing and playing guitar locally. In 1942, while studying veterinary medicine at Abilene's North Texas Agricultural College, he was drafted into the Marines. He returned to his studies in 1946, but also began performing at local clubs, and as the Cherokee Cowboy, he appeared on KRBC. He still had thoughts of a career as a rancher but in 1949, the opportunity to join the Big D Jamboree in Dallas finally convinced him that his future lay in country music. He first recorded for a minor label, Bullet, and had some success in Texas with 'Jealous Lies', but in 1952 he joined Columbia Records and had immediate US country Top 10 hits with 'Talk To Your Heart' and 'Don't Let The Stars Get In Your Eyes'. Price moved to Nashville, where he became a member of the *Grand Ole Opry*. He was also befriended by Hank Williams, with whom he lived for a time and on occasions worked with the Drifting Cowboys on shows that Hank missed. When he later formed his own band, the Cherokee Cowboys, quite apart from appearances by members of the old Hank Williams band, it was occasionally to include Willie Nelson, Johnny Paycheck, Johnny Bush, Buddy Emmons and Roger Miller. Price's vocals and the excellence of the Cherokee Cowboys represented some of the finest honky-tonk country music of all time. The immense popularity Price gained may be judged by his chart successes. In the 20 years between 1954 and 1974 he amassed a total of 64 US country chart hits, only 11 of which failed to make the Top 20 and 13 also crossed over to the pop charts. He registered 7 country number 1 hits including 'Crazy Arms' (his first million-seller), 'My Shoes Keep Walking Back To You', 'City Lights' (his second million-seller, which also launched Bill Anderson's songwriting career) and 'For The Good Times', a third million-seller which first introduced the songwriting talent of a young Nashville janitor called Kris Kristofferson. He also recorded what is probably the most popular country version of 'Release Me', a song that 13 years later became a UK pop chart number 1 for Engelbert Humperdinck. In 1967, Price moved from honky-tonk music to a more pop-orientated approach. His backings began to feature strong orchestral accompaniment, far removed from the traditional fiddle and steel guitar influence of his mentor, Hank Williams. Price maintained that most of his songs were ballads and that the strings provided the soul. In concert, he often used up to ten violins in his backing but for his records there were often many more; when he recorded his version of 'Danny Boy', the backing was by an orchestra that consisted of forty-seven musicians. He also dispensed with his western-style dress and took to appearing in smart evening suits; the Cherokee Cowboy was dead. He toured extensively and appeared on all major network radio and television shows. By 1973, Price had grown rather tired of the touring and semi-retired to his ranch near Dallas to breed horses. Five years later, he found that he missed the musical life and once more was to be found back on the circuit. From the mid-70s through to the late 80s, he recorded for Myrrh, ABC, Monument, Dimension, Warner Brothers, Viva and Step One, and although there were few Top 20 hits after 1974, he continued regularly to register country chart entries. In 1980, in an effort to boost his somewhat flagging chart successes, he asked Willie Nelson to record an album with him. Nelson obliged his old boss and their duet of 'Faded Love', from the album *San Antonio Rose*, charted at

number 3. A feud had existed for many years between Price and Nelson dating back to when they were neighbours. Nelson had shot and eaten one of Price's fighting roosters for killing some of his hens and Price swore he would never record another Nelson song (the reason why Price kept fighting roosters is open to conjecture). He eventually overcame his anger, but Nelson had no real reason to agree to the request to record the album since Price had not recorded any of his songs for a long time. Price also appeared in the Clint Eastwood film *Honkytonk Man*. From the mid-80s, some of his recordings were of dubious country content, such as his versions of the Frank Sinatra pop hit 'All The Way' and the 1931 Gene Austin hit 'Please Don't Talk About Me When I'm Gone', but on others he tended to revert more to the simple country backings of his early days. When 'I'd Do It All Over Again' charted in December 1988, it took his tally of country hits to 108 and in the statistics produced by Joel Whitburn for his *Record Research*, based on country music chart success from 1944-88, Price stands at number 6 in the Top 200 country artists of all time. He currently performs at his own theatre in Branson, Missouri. In 1996, he was inducted into the Country Music Hall Of Fame. An all-new album appeared in 2000 on which he recorded cover versions of the Beatles' 'In My Life' and the classic Johnny Green, Edward Heyman, Robert Sour, Frank Eyton collaboration 'Body And Soul'.

● ALBUMS: *Ray Price Sings Heart Songs* (Columbia 1957) ★★★, *Talk To Your Heart* (Columbia 1958) ★★★★, with orchestra and chorus *Faith* (Columbia 1960) ★★★, *Sings San Antonio Rose (A Tribute To The Great Bob Wills)* (Columbia 1962) ★★★★, *Night Life* (Columbia 1963) ★★★, *Love Life* (Columbia 1964) ★★★, *Burning Memories* (Columbia 1965) ★★★, *Western Strings* (Columbia 1965) ★★★, *The Other Woman* (Columbia 1965) ★★★, *Another Bridge To Burn* (Columbia 1966) ★★★, *Touch My Heart* (Columbia 1967) ★★★, *Born To Lose* (Harmony 1967) ★★★, *Danny Boy* (Columbia 1967) ★★, *She Wears My Ring* (Columbia 1968) ★★★, *Take Me As I Am* (Columbia 1968) ★★★, *I Fall To Pieces* (Harmony 1969) ★★★, *Ray Price's Christmas Album* (Columbia 1969) ★★, *Sweetheart Of The Year* (Columbia 1969) ★★★, *For The Good Times* (Columbia 1970) ★★★, *The World Of Ray Price* (Columbia 1970) ★★★, *You Wouldn't Know Love* (Columbia 1970) ★★★, *Make The World Go Away* (Harmony 1970) ★★★, *I Won't Mention It Again* (Columbia 1971) ★★★, *Release Me* (Columbia 1971) ★★★, *The Lonesomest Lonesome* (Columbia 1972) ★★★, *She's Got To Be A Saint* (Columbia 1973) ★★★, *Like Old Times Again* (Columbia 1974) ★★★, *This Time Lord* (Myrrh 1974) ★★★, *You're The Best Thing That Ever Happened To Me* (Myrrh 1974) ★★★, *If You Ever Change Your Mind* (ABC 1975) ★★★, *Say I Do* (ABC 1975) ★★, *Hank 'N' Me* (ABC 1976) ★★★, *Rainbows And Tears* (ABC 1976) ★★★, *Help Me* (Columbia 1977) ★★★, *How Great Thou Art* (1977) ★★★, *Reunited – Ray Price And The Cherokee Cowboys* (ABC 1977) ★★★, *Precious*

Memories (ABC 1977) ★★★, *There's Always Me* (Monument 1979) ★★★, with Willie Nelson *San Antonio Rose* (Columbia 1980) ★★★, *Ray Price* (Dimension 1981) ★★★, *Town And Country* (Dimension 1981) ★★★, *Tribute To Willie & Kris* (Dimension 1981) ★★★, *Diamonds In The Stars* (Dimension 1981) ★★★, *Loving You* (Dimension 1982) ★★★, *Somewhere In Texas* (Dimension 1982) ★★★, *Master Of The Art* (Viva 1983) ★★★, *Portrait Of A Singer* (1985) ★★★, *Welcome To The Country* (1985) ★★★, *A Revival Of Old Time Singing* (Step One 1987) ★★★, *The Heart Of Country Music* (Step One 1987) ★★★, *A Christmas Gift For You* (Step One 1987) ★★, *Just Enough Love* (Step One 1988) ★★, *Sometimes A Rose* (1992) ★★★, with Faron Young *Memories That Last* (1992) ★★★, *Prisoner Of Love* (Buddha/Justice 2000) ★★★.
● COMPILATIONS: *Ray Price's Greatest Hits* (Columbia 1961) ★★★, *Ray Price – Collector's Choice* (Harmony 1966) ★★★, *Ray Price's Greatest Hits, Volume 2* (Columbia 1967) ★★★, *Welcome To My World* (1971) ★★★, *Ray Price's All-Time Greatest Hits* (1972) ★★★, *The Best Of Ray Price* (Columbia 1976) ★★★, *Happens To Be The Best* (Pair 1983) ★★★, *Greatest Hits, Volume 1, 2 & 3* (1986) ★★★, *By Request – Greatest Hits, Volume 4* (1988) ★★★, *American Originals* (Columbia 1989) ★★★, *The Essential Ray Price (1951-1962)* (Columbia 1991) ★★★★, *Ray Price And The Cherokee Cowboys: The Honky Tonk Years (1950-1966)* 10-CD box set (Bear Family 1995) ★★★★, *In A Honky Tonk Mood* (Jasmine 2000) ★★★.

PRICE, RONNIE

b. Ronald Frederick Price, 9 August 1923, Lancashire, England, d. 25 June 1996. Price began piano studies at the age of eight, then won several talent contests. However, he entered industry as an apprentice draughtsman but also formed a small band, playing dance dates in and around Manchester. He became a full-time professional musician in 1947, playing piano with Teddy Foster and his popular dance band. A few years later Price joined the Tito Burns Sextet, in which his brother, Derek Price, played drums for a while. He then played in several leading London bands, including Sydney Lipton's and was then prompted to extend his knowledge of music with extensive formal studies. He studied arranging at the Harrow School of Music and was soon one of the most sought-after session musicians playing in London. He worked on countless radio and television shows, played on numerous motion-picture soundtracks, and backed many famous recording artists including Sammy Davis Jnr., Andy Williams and Bing Crosby. Price also played in West End theatre pit bands and for many years was Anne Shelton's musical director. His immensely varied repertoire allowed him to turn readily from jazz to popular and light classical music, performing solos with the BBC Concert Orchestra on radio's *Friday Night Is Music Night* and also with Don Lusher's big band. Famously, if anonymously, his hands were featured on television's game show, *Name That Tune*. A superb and conscientious craftsman, Price's careful studies and dedication to music rightly brought him a reputation as one of the UK's best and most reliable session musicians.

PRIDE, DICKIE

b. Richard Knellar, Thornton Heath, England. Pride, a former Royal College of Church Music chorister and trainee stonemason, was 'discovered' in 1958 singing rock 'n' roll in a London pub by Russ Conway who recommended him to both EMI producer Norrie Paramor and pop svengali Larry Parnes. Groomed and given a *nom de théâtre*, the diminutive youth's voice rather than his face was his fortune – though his onstage convulsions earned him the nickname 'The Sheik Of Shake'. The first that Britain at large saw of him was on ITV's *Oh Boy!*, promoting his 1959 cover version of Little Richard's 'Slippin' And Slidin''. While his third single, 'Primrose Lane', touched the Top 30, the failure of later singles contradicted any claims that Pride was realistically a potential rival to Cliff Richard. Nevertheless, he was still impressing audiences in 1960 when he recorded a creditable album of Tin Pan Alley chestnuts with Ted Heath's orchestra. This ploy might have set him on the road of the 'all round entertainer' had not his dabbling with amphetamines alienated him from Parnes, and precipitated a fall from grace that found him delivering coal and nursing debilities related to the drug abuse that sent him to an early grave.
● ALBUMS: *Pride Without Prejudice* (Columbia 1960) ★★.

PRIMA, LOUIS

b. 7 December 1911, New Orleans, Louisiana, USA, d. 24 August 1978, New Orleans, Louisiana, USA. A trumpeter, bandleader, singer and composer, Prima was the son of Italian immigrant parents. He was educated at Jesuit High School, and studied the violin for several years under Hemmersback, before switching to the trumpet. At the age of 17, inspired by jazz greats such as Louis Armstrong and King Oliver, he gained his first job as a singer/trumpeter in a New Orleans theatre – his elder brother, Leon, also played trumpet at a local nightspot. For a time in the early 30s Prima worked with Red Nichols, before forming his own seven-piece New Orleans Gang, with its signature tune, 'Way Down Yonder In New Orleans', who recorded more than 70 titles in New York for various labels from 1934-39. Several of them made the US Hit Parade, including 'The Lady In Red', 'In A Little Gypsy Tea Room' and 'The Goose Hangs High'. His sidemen during this period included Georg Brunis (trombone), Claude Thornhill (piano), George Van Eps (guitar), Artie Shapiro (bass), Eddie Miller (reeds), Ray Bauduc (drums), Sidney Arodin (clarinet), Frank Pinero (piano), Frank Frederico (guitar), Oscar Bradley (drums), and Pee Wee Russell (clarinet). By this stage, Prima was also composing songs, and one of them, 'Sing, Sing, Sing', when developed by Benny Goodman, became a smash hit for the 'King Of Swing', and remains a Swing Era classic.
Over the years, Prima wrote or co-wrote many

other numbers, including 'Robin Hood', which was successful for Les Brown in 1945, and the 1947 Jo Stafford hit, 'A Sunday Kind Of Love', along with 'Alone', 'Little Boy Blew His Top', 'Marguerita', 'New Aulins', 'Angelina', 'Where Have We Met Before?', 'Brooklyn Boogie', 'Boogie In The Bronx', 'Bridget O'Brien', 'Boogie In Chicago', 'It's The Rhythm In Me', 'Sing A Spell', 'It's A Southern Holiday' and 'Rhythm On The Radio'. His collaborators included Jack Loman, Dave Franklin, Milton Kabak, Bob Miketta, Barbara Belle, Anita Leonard, and Stan Rhodes. After making an good impression on his feature film debut in the Bing Crosby movie musical *Rhythm On The Range* (1936), Prima continued to have relatively small, but telling roles in a number of other movies, notably *Rose Of Washington Square* (1939), in which he enhanced Alice Faye's rendering of 'I'm Just Wild About Harry' with his ebullient and exciting trumpet accompaniment. By this time he had his own big band which he fronted with great showmanship and panache. It had 40s hits with 'Angelina', 'Bell-Bottom Trousers' (vocal: Lily Ann Carol), and 'Civilization (Bongo, Bongo, Bongo)', an amusing novelty from the 1947 Broadway revue *Angel In The Wings*. In 1948, Prima began working with the poker-faced singer Keely Smith, and, after having a US hit in 1950 with their joint composition, 'Oh, Babe!', they were married two years later.

During the next decade they were recognized as one of the hottest nightclub acts in the USA, and became known as 'The Wildest Show In Las Vegas'. Prima's inspired clowning and zany vocals delivered in a fractured Italian dialect, coupled with Smith's cool image and classy singing, were augmented by tenor saxophonist Sam Butera and his group, the Witnesses. A typical performance was filmed at Lake Tahoe in 1957, and released under the title of *The Wildest*, and they reassembled in 1959 for the feature *Hey Boy! Hey Girl!* Prima and Smith were awarded Grammys in 1958 for their inimitable reading of the Harold Arlen-Johnny Mercer standard, 'That Old Black Magic'. In 1958 Prima was briefly in the UK Top 30 with Carl Sigman and Peter de Rose's likeable 'Buona Sera', and two years later made the US singles and albums charts with the instrumental 'Wonderland By Night'. Other Top 40 albums included *Las Vegas-Prima Style* and *Hey Boy!, Hey Girl!* In 1961, while still at the height of their fame – and having recently signed a multi-million dollar contract with the Desert Inn, Las Vegas – the couple were divorced. Prima and Butera subsequently attempted to cash in on the then-popular dance fad by appearing in the movie *Twist All Night*, which sank without a trace, in spite (or because) of items such as 'When The Saints Go Twistin' In'. Far more lasting was Prima's contribution in 1967 to *The Jungle Book*, the Walt Disney Studio's first cartoon feature for four years, which went on to gross around $26 million. Prima provided the voice of hip orang-utan King Louie, and sang the film's hit song, 'I Wanna Be Like You'. In later years he mostly confined himself to performing with a small group at venues such as the Sands Hotel, Las Vegas, and in 1975 underwent surgery for the removal of a brain tumour. He never recovered from the operation, and remained in a coma until his death nearly three years later in a New Orleans nursing home.

● ALBUMS: *Louis Prima At Frank Dailey's Terrace Room* (Mercury 1953) ★★, *Swings* (Capitol 1955) ★★★, *The Wildest* (Capitol 1956) ★★★, *Call Of The Wildest* (Capitol 1957) ★★★, *The Wildest Show At Tahoe* (Capitol 1957) ★★★, with Keely Smith *Las Vegas-Prima Style* (Capitol 1958) ★★★★, *Jump, Jive An' Wail* (Capitol 1958) ★★★, with Smith *Hey Boy! Hey Girl!* film soundtrack (Capitol 1959) ★★★★, with Smith *Louis And Keely!* (Dot 1959) ★★★, *Strictly Prima* (Capitol 1959) ★★★, with Smith *Senior Prom* (1959) ★★★, with Sam Butera *The Continental Twist* (Capitol 60s) ★★★, with Smith *Together* (Dot 1960) ★★★, *Plays Pretty Music Prima Style* (Dot 1960) ★★★, with Smith *On Stage* (Dot 1960) ★★★, *Wonderland By Night* (Dot 1961) ★★★★, *Blue Moon* (Dot 1961) ★★★, with Smith *Return Of The Wildest* (Dot 1961) ★★★, *The Wildest Comes Home* (Capitol 1962) ★★★, *Doin' The Twist* (Dot 1962) ★★★, *Lake Tahoe Prima Style* (Capitol 1963) ★★★, *Plays Pretty For The People* (1964) ★★★, *Plays And Sings* (Hamilton 1965) ★★★, *On Broadway* (United Artists 1967) ★★, with Jimmie Lunceford *Lunceford And Prima – 1945* (Aircheck 1979) ★★★, *Live From Las Vegas* (Jazz Band 1988) ★★, *Angelina* (Big Band Era 1989) ★★★.

● COMPILATIONS: *His Greatest Hits* (Dot 1960) ★★★★, with Keely Smith *Hits* (Capitol 1961) ★★★★, *Best Of Louis Prima* (MFP 1985) ★★★, *Just A Gigolo 1945-50* (Bandstand 1988) ★★★, *Capitol Collectors Series* (Capitol 1991) ★★★★, with Keely Smith *Ultra Lounge: Wild, Cool & Swingin'* (Capitol 1999) ★★★★.

● FILMS: *Rhythm On The Range* (1936), *The Star Reporter In Hollywood* (1936), *Swing It* (1936), *Vitaphone Variété* (1936), *You Can't Have Everything* (1937), *Manhattan Merry-Go-Round* (1937), *Start Cheering* (1938), *Swing Cat's Jamboree* (1938), *Rose Of Washington Square* (1939), *New Orleans Blues* (1943), *Rhythm Masters* (1948), *The Wildest* (1957), *Senior Prom* (1958), *Hey Boy! Hey Girl!* (1959), *Twist All Night* (1961), voice only *The Man Called Flintstone* (1966), voice only *The Jungle Book* (1967), *Rafferty And The Gold Dust Twins* (1974).

PRIMES

Formed in Birmingham, Alabama, in 1958, the Primes comprised Eddie Kendricks (b. 17 December 1939, Union Springs, Alabama, USA, d. 5 October 1992, Alabama, USA), Paul Williams and Kel Osborn. Unable to secure a recording contract for their R&B-styled vocal group material in Alabama, the group moved to Detroit in 1959, where they became established in the black neighbourhood housing projects. They encouraged a group of female friends to form a sister group called the Primettes; however, the Primes disbanded in 1961 when Kendricks and Williams joined three members of another Detroit group, the Distants, to form the Temptations.

PRISONAIRES

As their name suggests, this doo-wop group were formed in 1940 while each member was in the State Penitentiary, Tennessee, USA. The founding member was second tenor Ed Thurman, and he took on Johnny Bragg (lead), John Drue (first tenor), William Stuart (baritone and guitar) and Marcell Sanders (bass). The group was paraded around a variety of receptions and civic functions as demonstration of the jail's enlightened rehabilitation programme, where they played a mix of blues, gospel and pop songs under armed guard. Edwards then arranged for two talent scouts from Sam Phillips' Sun Records to see the group. They were subsequently driven down to Memphis in June 1953 to record a song written by Bragg and fellow inmate Robert Riley, 'Just Walkin' In The Rain'. The record took hold first on radio and then became a major seller, moving over 250,000 copies, despite a competing version from Johnny Ray that sold eight times that amount. Still, the Prisonaires had arrived, and found themselves in demand for a series of television and concert appearances. They gradually became high-status figures in Tennessee, and never betrayed the trust placed in them by trying to escape their guards on their numerous forays outside the prison. A second single followed in August 1953, the highly spiritual 'My God Is Real', followed by 'I Know' and its autobiographical b-side, 'A Prisoner's Prayer'. While recording it they made the acquaintance of Elvis Presley, who later visited them in prison. By now some of his colleagues had become eligible for parole, so Bragg formed a new version of the band titled the Sunbeams with Hal Hebb, Willy Wilson, Al Brooks and Henry 'Dishrag' Jones. This group lasted only until 1955, when the group was retitled the Marigolds and had a number 8 R&B chart success with 'Rollin' Stone'. However, by 1956 Bragg had been released and he recorded a series of singles under his own name for Decca Records. He was then arrested for 'parole violation' in 1960 when found in the back seat of a car with a white woman (his wife). His penalty was to return to prison for an incredible six and a half years. Despite this second injustice, Bragg put together another version of the Prisonaires with new inmates, but they never recorded again. On release, he worked in a cemetery.

● COMPILATIONS: *Five Beats Behind Bars* (Charly 1978) ★★★.

PRYOR, SNOOKY

b. James Edward Pryor, 15 September 1921, Lambert, Mississippi, USA. As a child he became drawn to the harmonica after watching an albino player, John Blissett, together with his friend Jimmy Rogers. When he was 13 he saw Rice Miller (Sonny Boy Williamson number 2) play. After settling in Chicago in 1945 after US Army service, Pryor joined the Maxwell Street group of blues singers which included Johnny Young, Floyd Jones and Moody Jones, with whom he recorded in 1948. Their records were harbingers of the amplified down-home sound of post-war Chicago

blues, although at this time Pryor's singing and harmonica were heavily influenced by John Lee 'Sonny Boy' Williamson. Pryor made his first record, 'Telephone Blues', with guitarist Moody Jones in 1949. There were later singles for J.O.B. ('Boogy Fool', 1950), Parrot (1953), Blue Lake (1954) and Vee Jay Records ('Someone To Love Me', 1956). During the 50s Pryor also frequently toured the south. After making the dance novelty 'Boogie Twist', Pryor left the music business in 1963 but returned in the early 70s, touring and recording in Europe in 1973. A 1974 album was made with a New Orleans rhythm section including guitarist Justin Adams. In recent years he has benefited from the revived interest in blues, recording his 1992 album for Texas label Antone's, which has to date resulted in regular new albums, notably his 1997 release *Mind Your Own Business, Can't Stop Blowing* and *Shake My Hand* recorded on Blind Pig. He has a long-standing and fruitful musical partnership with guitarist Mel Brown, in addition to his own projects.

● ALBUMS: *Snooky Pryor* (Flyright 1969) ★★, *Snooky Pryor And The Country Blues* (1973) ★★★, *Do It If You Want To* (1973) ★★★, *Homesick James And Snooky Pryor* (Caroline 1974) ★★★, *Shake Your Boogie* (Big Bear 1979) ★★★, *Too Cool To Move* (Antone's 1992) ★★, with Johnny Shines *Back To The Country* (Black Pig 1993) ★★★, *In This Mess Up To My Chest* (Antone's 1994) ★★★, *Mind Your Own Business* (Antone's 1997) ★★★★, *Can't Stop Blowing* (Electro 1998) ★★★★, *Shake My Hand* (Blind Pig 1999) ★★★★, with Mel Brown *Double Shot* (Electro 2000) ★★★, with Carey Bell, Lazy Lester, Raful Neal *Superharps II* (Telarc 2001) ★★★★.

● COMPILATIONS: *Snooky Pryor – 1947 To 1960s* (Flyright 1990) ★★★, *Pitch A Boogie Woogie If It Takes Me All Night Long* (Westlife 2001) ★★★.

PRYSOCK, RED

b. Wilbert Prysock, 2 February 1926, Greensboro, North Carolina, USA, d. 19 February 1993, Chicago, Illinois, USA. After attempting to learn piano, organ, clarinet and trumpet, Prysock received a tenor saxophone from his sister for his seventeenth birthday. He learned to play the instrument during his military service in World War II. Prysock turned professional upon his demobilization in 1947 and joined Tiny Grimes' Rocking Highlanders, with whom he recorded for the fledgling Atlantic Records. He left them in 1950 to join Roy Milton's Solid Senders before finding fame with Tiny Bradshaw's band and such recordings as 'Soft', 'Off And On' and 'Free For All' (which became known as 'Go, Red, Go') on King Records. Prysock formed his own band in 1953, after experimenting with three releases on Bobby Robinson's Red Robin label, and was signed by Mercury Records the following year, for whom he notched up many big sellers, among them 'Hand Clappin'', 'Jump, Red, Jump' and 'Finger Tips'. He played with the Alan Freed Big Band, backing all the top rock 'n' roll artists of the 50s, and was able to switch styles with the advent of soul music in the 60s, recording for King and Chess and supporting many of the era's big names. In 1971, Red teamed up with his famous elder brother, Arthur Prysock, and toured and performed together – the saxophone and the voice.

● ALBUMS: *Rock 'N' Roll* (Mercury 1956) ★★★★, *Cryin' My Heart Out* (1983) ★★★, *Rock 'n' Roll: The Best Of Red Prysock* (Avi 1996) ★★★★.

PUENTE, TITO

b. Ernesto Antonio Puente Jnr., 20 April 1923, Harlem Hospital, New York City, New York, USA, d. 31 May 2000, New York City, New York, USA. Born of Puerto Rican parentage, Puente began piano lessons when he was seven years old and around the age of 10 started tuition in drums and percussion, which became his forte. Around 1936, Puente commenced his professional career as a drummer with the orchestra of Noro Morales. In 1941, he played with the Machito band which provided valuable lessons in the fusion of Latin rhythms and modern jazz. World War II intervened and Puente was drafted into the US Navy for three years' service. After his discharge he took composition and piano courses at New York's Juilliard School of Music and did stints with the bands of José Curbelo and Fernando Alvarez between 1946 and 1947. With Curbelo, Puente performed alongside Tito Rodríguez, who later became his arch-rival. Puente's reputation as a sizzling arranger quickly grew and led to numerous assignments from prominent bandleaders. Even Rodríguez hired him to write the charts for four numbers he recorded with his Mambo Devils on Gabriel Oller's SMC (Spanish Music Center) label. In the late 40s, while Tito was performing the roles of contractor, arranger and timbales player with Pupi Campo's orchestra, he organized a group that promoter Federico Pagani dubbed the Picadilly Boys ('Picadillo' meaning beef or pork hash) after being impressed by their performance of the Latin jam style (descarga). With them, Puente recorded a number of sides for SMC. Shortly afterwards, he renamed his aggregation Tito Puente And His Orchestra. He used two lead vocalists, Angel Rosa and then Paquito Sosa, before settling for Cuban Vicentico Valdés as his resident lead singer.

In late 1949, Puente organized a line-up of four trumpets, three trombones, four saxophones and a full rhythm section for a recording session for Tico Records. One recording from this session, leaving out the trombones and saxophones, resulted in a fiery version of 'Abaniquito'. With the help of an English translation by disc jockey Dick 'Ricardo' Sugar, the song became one of the first crossover mambo hits. Between the late 40s and mid-50s, Puente issued recordings on Tico. During a suspension of recording by the company in 1950 – due to a wrangle between the co-founders, George Goldner and Art 'Pancho' Raymond – Puente recorded for the Seeco, Verne and RCA Records labels. Along with Tito Rodríguez and Machito, Puente became one of the kings of the 50s mambo era. His consistent top billing at New York's Palladium Ballroom, the famed 'Home of

the Mambo', became one of the areas of friction between himself and Rodríguez. Puente switched to RCA Victor Records and between 1956 and 1960 he released a string of albums on the label, including the notable *Cuban Carnival* and the bestselling *Dance Mania*. The album marked the debut of Santos Colón (b. 1 November, Mayagüez, Puerto Rico) as Puente's new lead singer. Colón arrived in New York in 1950 and performed with the bands of Jorge Lopés, Tony Novos and José Curbelo before joining Puente. He remained with him until 1970, when he departed to pursue a solo career and released a series of albums on Fania Records.

Several of Puente's Tico and RCA Victor releases between the mid- to late 50s were entirely devoted to the cha cha chá rhythm, which was enjoying considerable popularity at the time. At the beginning of the 60s, the pachanga style took over. One of the prime-movers of the dance craze was Afro-Cuban singer Rolando La Serie's 1960 smash hit recording of 'La Pachanga' with the Bebo Valdés band. The following year, while the fad was still raging at full force, Puente teamed up with La Serie to make *Pachanga In New York* for Gema Records. In 1960, Tito And His Orchestra journeyed to the west coast of America to record *The Exciting Tito Puente Band In Hollywood* (aka *Puente Now!*) for GNP Records. Upon his arrival, Puente contacted Los Angeles-based flautist Rolando Lozano (b. José Calazan Lozano, 27 August 1931, Cienfuegos, Santa Clara Province, Cuba), an alumnus of Orquesta Aragón, Orquesta América, Orquesta Nuevo Ritmo, Mongo Santamaría and Cal Tjader. Puente rejoined Tico Records (and remained with them until the mid-80s) to make *Pachanga Con Puente*, which yielded the big hit 'Caramelos'. *El Rey Bravo* was essentially a descarga set: an untypical Puente album, it stands as one of his strongest recordings. The disc featured Cuban violinist/flautist Félix 'Pupi' Legarreta and spawned the original version of Puente's perennial classic 'Oye Como Va', which was given a hit Latin-rock treatment by Santana in 1970.

Puente linked up with Alegre Records for *Y Parece Bobo*, which was produced by the label's founder, Al Santiago, and featured Chivirico Dávila on lead vocals. Santiago also co-produced *Cuba Y Puerto Rico Son ...* on Tico, Puente's first in a series of collaborations with the 'Queen of Salsa' Celia Cruz. Puente also recorded a string of successful albums with La Lupe between 1965 and 1967, and made a couple of albums with Beny Moré's widow, Noraida, at the beginning of the 70s. On his late 60s releases, *20th Anniversary* and *El Rey Tito Puente*, he was obliged to bow to the overwhelming popularity of the R&B/Latin fusion form called boogaloo. 'The Boogaloo meant nothing to me. It stunk', he said forthrightly in 1977. 'It hurt the established bandleaders. It was a dance Eddie Palmieri, I and other bandleaders didn't want to record but had to in order to keep up with the times' (quote from *Latin Times*).

Panamanian vocalist Meñique Barcasnegras, who worked previously with Kako and Willie Rosario, did a brief stint with Puente's band in the early 70s. After performing on *Pa'Lante! (Straight!)* and *Para Los Rumberos*, Barcasnegras departed to work as a solo artist (Puente arranged and directed his 1972 solo debut *Meñique*) and with Santos Colón, Charlie Palmieri, Charanga Sensación De Rolando Valdés and Conjunto Chaney. In 1977, Puente and Santos Colón reunited on *The Legend*, the title track of which was written by Rubén Blades. The album, which was nominated for a Grammy Award, was produced by Louie Ramírez. The following year, Puente's first tribute album to Beny Moré (in a series of three volumes) won a Grammy Award. The trio of albums featured a galaxy of vocalists from the Fania Records stable, including Cruz, Colón, Cheo Feliciano, Ismael 'Pat' Quintana, Adalberto Santiago, Héctor Lavoe, Pete 'El Conde' Rodríguez, Ismael Miranda and Justo Betancourt. In 1979 and 1980, Puente toured Europe and recorded with the Latin Percussion Jazz Ensemble (LPJE), members of which included Argentinian pianist Jorge Dalto, violinist Alfredo De La Fé and conga player Carlos 'Patato' Valdez. This group was a precursor of his own Latin jazz outfit, which debuted on the Concord Picante label in 1983 with *Tito Puente And His Latin Ensemble On Broadway*. He garnered another Grammy Award for the album. Puente released a further seven albums with his Latin Ensemble on Concord Picante between 1984 and 1991, two of which – *Mambo Diablo* and *Goza Mí Timbal* – received Grammys. However, his work with his Latin Ensemble woefully sank into tired recycling of his earlier material. At concerts Puente and his high-calibre musicians often appeared just to be 'going through the motions'.

For 1991's *The Mambo King: 100th LP* on RMM Records, Puente returned to a full big band line-up to back an assortment of the label's vocalists (including Oscar D'León, Tito Nieves, Tony Vega, José 'El Canario' Alberto and Domingo Quiñones) plus Santos Colón and Celia Cruz. Although the album was purported to be his 100th, the actual total of his recordings by 1992 exceeded that figure. He carried on recording throughout the 90s, winning a final Grammy for 1999's *Mambo Birdland*. In addition to those artists mentioned, Puente recorded with an array of Latin music and jazz names, including the Tico All-Stars, Fania All Stars, Bobby Capó, Ray Barretto, Camilo Azuquita, Gilberto Monroig, Sophy, Myrta Silva, Manny Roman, Doc Severinsen, Woody Herman, Buddy Morrow, Cal Tjader, Terry Gibbs, George Shearing, Phil Woods, Pete Escovedo and Sheila E. (Escovedo's daughter). Shortly before his death in May 2000, of complications following open-heart surgery, Puente was bestowed the honour of 'Living Legend' by the United States Library Of Congress.

● ALBUMS: *Mambos, Vol. 1* 10-inch album (Tico 1949) ★★★, *Mambos, Vol. 2* 10-inch album (Tico) ★★★, *Mambos, Vol. 3* 10-inch album (Tico), *Mambos, Vol. 4* 10-inch album (Tico) ★★★, *Mambos, Vol. 5* 10-inch album (Tico) ★★★, *King Of The Mambo* 10-inch album (Tico) ★★★★, *At The Vibes* 10-inch album (Tico) ★★★, *Cha Cha Cha,*

Vol. 1 10-inch album (Tico) ★★★★, *Cha Cha Cha, Vol. 2* 10-inch album (Tico) ★★★, *Mambos, Vol. 8* 10-inch album (Tico) ★★★, *Instrumental Mambos* 10-inch album (Tico) ★★★, *Cha Cha Cha, Vol. 3* 10-inch album (Tico) ★★★, *Mambo On Broadway* 10-inch album (RCA Victor) ★★★★, *Mamborama* (Tico) ★★★, *Mambo With Me* (Tico) ★★★, *Cha Cha Chas For Lovers* (Tico 1954) ★★★★, *Dance The Cha Cha Cha* (Tico 1955) ★★★★, *Puente In Percussion* (Tico), with Pete Terrace *Basic Cha Cha Chas* (Tico) ★★★, *Cuban Carnival* (RCA Victor 1955) ★★★★, *Puente Goes Jazz* (RCA Victor 1956) ★★★, *Mambo On Broadway* (RCA Victor 1957) ★★★, *Let's Cha-Cha With Puente* (RCA Victor 1957) ★★★, *Night Beat* (RCA Victor 1957) ★★★★, *Mucho Puente* (RCA Victor 1957) ★★★★, *Top Percussion* (RCA Victor 1958) ★★★, *Dance Mania* (RCA Victor 1958) ★★★★, with Vicentico Valdés *Tito Puente Swings, Vicentico Valdés Sings* (Tico 1958) ★★★, with Woody Herman *Herman's Heat, Puente's Beat* (Everest 1958) ★★★, *Puente In Love* (Tico 1959) ★★★, *Dancing Under Latin Skies* (RCA Victor 1959) ★★★, *Mucho Cha-Cha* (RCA Victor 1959) ★★★, *Cha Cha At Grossinger's* (RCA Victor 1960) ★★, *Tambó* (RCA Victor 1960) ★★★★, with Rolando La Serie *Pachanga In New York* (Gema 1961) ★★★, *The Exciting Tito Puente Band In Hollywood* aka *Puente Now!* (GNP 1961) ★★★, *Pachanga Con Puente* (Tico 1961) ★★★★, *Vaya Puente* (Tico 1961) ★★★, *El Rey Bravo* (Tico 1962) ★★★★, *Bossa Nova By Puente* (Roulette/Tico 1962) ★★★, *In Puerto Rico* (Tico 1963) ★★★, *Tito Puente Bailables* (Tico 1963) ★★★, *Exitante Ritmo* (Tico 1963) ★★★, *More Dance Mania* 1959 recording (RCA Victor 1963) ★★★, *Tito Puente Y Parece Bobo* (Alegre 1963) ★★★, with Gilbert Monroig *The Perfect Combination* (Alegre) ★★★, *Mucho Puente* (Tico 1964) ★★★, with Santos Colón *De Mi Para Ti (From Me To You)* (Tico 1964) ★★★, *My Fair Lady Goes Latin* (Roulette/Tico 1964) ★★, with La Lupe *Tito Puente Swings, The Exciting Lupe Sings* (Tico 1965) ★★★, with La Lupe *Tu Y Yo (You And I)* (Tico 1965) ★★★, with Santos Colón *Carnaval En Harlem* (Tico 1965) ★★★, with La Lupe *Homenaje A Rafael Hernández* (Tico 1966) ★★★, with Celia Cruz *Cuba Y Puerto Rico Son ...* (Tico 1966) ★★★★, *20th Anniversary* (Tico 1967) ★★★★, with La Lupe *El Rey Y Yo/The King And I* (Tico 1967) ★★★, with Shawn Elliot *What Now My Love* (Tico) ★★★, *El Rey Tito Puente (The King)* (Tico 1968) ★★★, *En El Puente/On The Bridge* (Tico 1969) ★★★, with Cruz *Quimbo Quimbumbia* (Tico 1969) ★★★, with Sophy *Tito Puente Con Orgullo* (Tico) ★★★, *La Lloroncita: El Sol Brilla Para Todos* (Tico) ★★★, with Cruz *Etc., Etc., Etc.* (Tico 1970) ★★★, *Pa'Lante! (Straight!)* (Tico 1971) ★★★, with Cruz *Alma Con Alma (The Heart And Soul Of)* (Tico 1971) ★★★★, with Cruz *Celia Cruz Y Tito Puente En España* (Tico 1971) ★★★★, *Para Los Rumberos* (Tico 1972) ★★★★, with Cruz *Algo Especial Para Recordar* (Tico 1972) ★★★, *Tito Puente And His Concert Orchestra* (Tico 1973) ★★★, *Tito Unlimited* (Tico 1974) ★★★, with Santos Colón *Los Originales* (Tico 1976) ★★★, *The Legend* (Tico 1977) ★★★, with La Lupe *La Pareja* (Tico 1979) ★★★, *Dance Mania 80's* (Tico 1980) ★★★, with

Camilo Azuquita *Ce' Magnifique* (Tico 1981) ★★★, *Tito Puente And His Latin Ensemble On Broadway* (Concord Picante 1983) ★★★, *El Rey* (Concord Picante 1984) ★★★, *Mambo Diablo* (Concord Picante 1985) ★★★, *Sensación* (Concord Picante 1986) ★★★, *Un Poco Loco* (Concord Picante 1987) ★★★, *Salsa Meets Jazz* (Concord Picante 1988) ★★★, *Goza Mí Timbal* (Concord Picante 1989) ★★★, *Out Of This World* (Concord Picante 1991) ★★★, *The Mambo King: 100th LP* (RMM 1991) ★★★, *Royal 'T'* (Concord Jazz 1993) ★★★, *Master Timabelero* (Concord Picante 1994) ★★★, *In Session* (Bellaphon 1994) ★★★, *Tito's Idea* (Tropijazz 1995) ★★★, with the Count Basie Orchestra, India *Jazzin'* (RMM/Tropijazz 1996) ★★★, *Special Delivery* (Concord Picante 1997) ★★★★, with TropiJazz All Stars *TropiJazz All Stars* (RMM TropiJazz 1997) ★★★, *Dancemania '99: Live At Birdland* (RMM Tropijazz 1998) ★★★, *Mambo Birdland* (RMM Tropijazz 1999) ★★★★, with Eddie Palmieri *Masterpiece/Obra Maestra* (RMM 2000) ★★★★.

● COMPILATIONS: *El Mundo Latino De (The Latin World Of)* (Tico 1964) ★★★★, *The Best Of Gilbert Monroig & Tito Puente* (Tico 1964) ★★★★, *The Best Of Tito Puente* (RCA Victor 1965) ★★★★, *Ti Mon Bo* (RCA 1969) ★★★★, *Lo Mejor De (The Best Of)* (Tico) ★★★★, with Santos Colón *No Hay Mejor (There Is No Better)* (Tico 1975) ★★★★, *The Best Of Tito Puente Volume 1* (RCA 1990) ★★★★, *Mambo Macoco* (Tumbao 1992) ★★★★, *Cuando Suenan Los Tambores* (BMG 1992) ★★★★, *The Best Of The Sixties* (Charly 1994) ★★★, *The King Of Cha-Cha Mambo* (Caney 1995) ★★★, *Yambeque: The Progressive Side Of Tito Puente Vol. 2* (RCA 1995) ★★★, *Oyo Como Va! The Dance Collection* (Concord Picante 1996) ★★★★, *50 Years Of Swing* 3-CD box set (RMM/Tropijazz 1997) ★★★★, *El Rey Del Timba! The Best Of Tito Puente* (Rhino 1997) ★★★★, *The Best Of The Concord Years* (Concord Jazz 2000) ★★★★, *The Complete RCA Recordings* 6-CD box set (BMG 2000) ★★★★, *RCA Recordings 49-60* (Camden 2001) ★★★.

● FILMS: *Armed And Dangerous* (1986), *Radio Days* (1987), *Salsa* (1988), *The Mambo Kings* (1992).

QUARRY MEN

This skiffle outfit were John Lennon's first group. They were formed in March 1957, taking their name from the Quarry Bank High School in Liverpool. The initial line-up comprised Lennon (guitar, vocals), Eric Griffiths (guitar), Rod Davis (banjo), Colin Hanton (drums), Pete Shotton (washboard) and Bill Smith (tea-chest bass), who was soon replaced by Len Garry. Their repertoire included skiffle favourites, 'Lost John' and 'Cumberland Gap', and a few rock 'n' roll songs. Lennon was introduced to Paul McCartney by a common friend, Ivan Vaughan, at St. Peter's church fête in Woolton on 6 July 1957. McCartney told Lennon the correct words to 'Come Go With Me' and became a member. McCartney brought George Harrison into the group and in June 1958, the three future Beatles, Colin Hanton and pianist John Duff Lowe recorded 'That'll Be The Day' and 'In Spite Of All The Danger' at Percy Phillips' recording studio in Kensington, Liverpool. The tracks were released on the Beatles' *Anthology 1* along with some rehearsal tapes from 1960. Although the Quarry Men did not play many bookings, they had a residency at the Casbah, the club owned by Mona Best, Pete's mother. In October 1959, the Quarry Men disbanded over an argument about fees, but Lennon, McCartney and Harrison stayed together, becoming Johnny And The Moondogs, then the Beatals, the Silver Beatles and, of course, the Beatles. In recent years, former Quarry Men have appeared at Beatles Conventions and Pete Shotton, a long-standing friend of John Lennon, has written a memoir, *John Lennon: In My Life*. Pianist John Duff Lowe, now a member of the Four Pennies, used the group as the nucleus for *Open For Engagements*, which also included Rod Davis. Five former Quarry Men were together at the celebrations for the 40th anniversary of the Cavern Club in January 1997.

● ALBUMS: *Open For Engagements* (Kewbank 1994) ★★.

● FURTHER READING: *The Quarrymen*, Hunter Davies.

QUIN-TONES

Formed in 1957 in Philadelphia, Pennsylvania, USA, the Quin-Tones were a doo-wop sextet (five vocalists and a pianist) with one Top 20 single to its name, 1958's 'Down The Aisle Of Love'. The group consisted of lead singer Roberta Haymon and back-up vocalists Phyllis Carr, Jeannie Crist, Carolyn Holmes and Kenny Sexton, plus piano player Ronnie Scott, who also arranged their material. Originally called the Quinteros, they were taken under the wing of disc jockey Paul Landersman, who secured the group a recording contract under their new name Quin-Tones (the hyphen was to avoid confusion with another Quintones group), with Chess Records. Their first single, 1958's 'Ding Dong', did not attract attention, and neither did the follow-up, the ballad 'Down The Aisle Of Love', on Red Top. However, after Dick Clark aired the song on *American Bandstand* and agreed to purchase the song's publishing rights, it was re-released on Hunt Records. This time it sold, giving the group its one taste of success. Subsequent recordings failed and the group disbanded in 1960.

● COMPILATIONS: *There's Gonna Be Joy* (1993) ★★★.

RABINOWITZ, HARRY

b. 26 March 1916, Johannesburg, South Africa. Trained as a classical pianist, Rabinowitz was educated at Athlone High School and Witwatersrand University and made his first radio broadcast in 1933. After service with the South African Army, he studied composition and conducting, and moved to London in 1946 to continue his studies at the Guildhall School of Music. He played the piano on several popular BBC radio programmes, including *Variety Bandbox*, and spent some time as house pianist at EMI Records. His first conducting jobs were with the show *Golden City* (1950), followed by four ice spectaculars at London's Empress Hall, and as musical director for Alan Jay Lerner and Frederick Loewe's 1953 hit, *Paint Your Wagon*. In the same year he joined the BBC staff and was conductor of the BBC Revue Orchestra until 1960, working on programmes such as *Take It From Here, Henry Hall's Guest Night, Variety Playhouse* and *Just Fancy*. He also featured as a pianist on *Piano Playtime, Rendezvous* and *Midday Music Hall*. In 1960, he moved to BBC Television as Head Of Music for Light Entertainment, and was responsible for programmes such as the *Val Doonican Show, Michael Bentine Show, Billy Cotton Band Show* and *Not Only But Also*, featuring Peter Cook and Dudley Moore. Rabinowitz moved to the rival London Weekend Television as Head of Music in 1968, and during the next nine years his projects included *Black Beauty, Upstairs, Downstairs* and several David Frost programmes. He also composed many themes to successful television programmes such *The Agatha Christie Hour* and *Love For Lydia*, which was nominated for an Ivor Novello Award in 1977. In the same year he won the Television And Radio Industries Council Celebrity Award for 'Best Television Theme Music Of The Year' for his music to *Reilly, Ace Of Spies*. Since returning to freelance work in 1977, Rabinowitz has been musical director for many feature films, such as *The Greek Tycoon* (1978), *Mon Oncle D'Amerique* (1980), *Chariots Of Fire* (1981), *Time Bandits* (1981), *Heat And Dust* (1982), *Maurice* (1987), *Queen Of Hearts* (1989), *Music Box* (1989), *Lord Of The Flies* (1990) and *The Ballad Of The Sad Cafe* (1990). In the early 80s, he conducted the first six weeks of the London runs of Andrew Lloyd Webber's *Cats* and *Song And Dance*, and travelled to the USA to conduct the Los Angeles Philharmonic Orchestra in concerts at the Hollywood Bowl. In the UK, he frequently conducts the Royal Philharmonic, the London Symphony, and the London Concert Orchestras at venues such as London's Barbican Centre and the Royal Festival Hall. In 1977, he was awarded an MBE for services to music.

RAINBOWS

This R&B vocal group was formed in the early 50s in Washington, DC, USA, by John Berry (lead and second tenor), Ronald 'Poosie' Miles (lead and second tenor), Henry 'Shorty' Womble (first tenor; ex-Serenaders), James 'Sally' Nolan (baritone) and Frank 'Jake' Hardy (bass; also ex-Serenaders). They were signed by Bobby Robinson of Red Robin Records in 1955 after unsuccessfully auditioning a year earlier. 'Mary Lee', their debut, followed in June, and proved popular both in New York and Boston (where it was licensed to Pilgrim Records). After a young Marvin Gaye and soul star Billy Stewart had sung with the group, Henry Womble's impending college career meant the group had a vacancy; it was filled by two new members, Don Covay and Chester Simmons. However, only two further Rainbows singles emerged. 'Shirley' and 'Minnie' continued their use of female names as titles. By 1957 the group had broken up, allowing Nolan and Simmons to join with Gaye and Reese Palmer to form the Marquees before becoming the new Moonglows. A new Rainbows was formed in 1961 with Miles now joined by Duval Potter (tenor), Joe Walls (tenor), Layton McDonald (baritone) and Victor English (bass). Two singles were released in 1963, 'I Know' and 'It Wouldn't Be Right'. Neither charted and the group folded once more with members scattering in various directions. Covay became a major songwriting talent. Simmons worked for the Reflection Sound studio before joining Reese in 70s group Choice Of Color. The other members retired from the music industry.

RAINWATER, MARVIN

b. Marvin Karlton Percy, 2 July 1925, Wichita, Kansas, USA. A big-voiced, rockabilly singer-songwriter, who is a quarter Cherokee Indian (using his mother's maiden name on stage), Percy became a regular on Red Foley's Ozark Mountain Jubilee in the early 50s. After being spotted on Arthur Godfrey's Talent Scouts television show in the mid-50s, he was signed to Coral. The first of his two singles for them, 'I Gotta Go Get My Baby', became a hit for the label when their top act Teresa Brewer covered his record. Rainwater then joined MGM Records and his second release, the self-composed 'Gonna Find Me A Bluebird' in 1957, gave him his only US Top 40 hit. Later that year a duet with Connie Francis (before her string of hits), 'Majesty Of Love', graced the US Top 100. In 1958, another of his songs, 'Whole Lotta Woman', which only reached number 60 in his homeland, topped the UK chart, and his UK-recorded follow-up, 'I Dig You Baby', also entered the British Top 20. He later recorded without success for Warwick, Warner Brothers, United Artists, Wesco, his own label Brave, as well as UK labels Philips, Sonet and Westwood. In subsequent years, the man who performed in full American Indian regalia has continued to play the rockabilly and country circuits on both sides of the Atlantic.

● ALBUMS: Songs By Marvin Rainwater (MGM 1957) ★★★, Marvin Rainwater Sings With A Beat (MGM 1958) ★★★★, Gonna Find Me A Bluebird (MGM 1962) ★★★, Marvin Rainwater (Crown 1974) ★★★, Marvin Rainwater & Mike Cowdery (Hoky 1981) ★★.

● COMPILATIONS: Rockin' Rollin' Rainwater (Bear Family 1982) ★★★, Classic Recordings (Bear Family 1992) ★★★★, Whole Lotta Woman (Bear Family 1994) ★★★★, Rock Me: The Westwood Recordings (Bear Family 2001) ★★★.

RAITT, JOHN

b. John Emmett Raitt, 19 January 1917, Santa Ana, California, USA. An actor and singer with a fine baritone voice, Raitt sang in light opera and concerts before playing the lead in a Chicago production of Oklahoma! (1944). In the following year he made his Broadway debut, playing Billy Bigelow, and introducing immortal songs such as 'If I Loved You' and 'Soliloquy', in Richard Rodgers and Oscar Hammerstein II's magnificent Carousel. Three years later, he appeared on Broadway again in the short-lived and 'unconventional' Magdelana. This was followed in 1952 by the 'whimsical' Three Wishes For Jamie, which was 'too treacly' to run for long. Carnival In Flanders (1953), despite a score by Johnny Burke and Jimmy Van Heusen that contained 'Here's That Rainy Day', provided less than a week's employment, but his next job, as the factory superintendent in The Pajama Game (1954), lasted nearly two and a half years. Raitt's spirited and sensitive renditions of Richard Adler and Jerry Ross' 'There Once Was A Man' and 'Small Talk' (both with Janis Paige), plus 'Hey There', a duet with a Dictaphone machine, made sufficient impact in Hollywood for him to be cast opposite Doris Day in the 1957 film version, despite his being a complete newcomer to the big screen.

In the 50s and 60s Raitt appeared frequently on US television, and in 1960 toured with the satirical musical Destry Rides Again. In the spring of 1966 he recreated his original role in a New York Music Theater revival of Carousel and, later in the year, dwelt for a brief spell amid the 'newly created folk songs' of A Joyful Noise. Thereafter, Raitt devoted much of his time to touring, and in 1975 was back on Broadway, along with Patricia Munsell, Tammy Grimes, Larry Kert, Lillian Gish and Cyril Ritchard, in A Musical Jubilee, a 'potpourri' claiming to demonstrate the development of the American musical. By that time, his daughter, Bonnie Raitt, was gaining recognition as one of the best female singer/guitarists of the 70s and 80s. John Raitt himself continued to be active, and in 1992 he received an Ovation Award in Hollywood for services to the Los Angeles theatre scene. A year later he was inducted into New York's Theater Hall Of Fame, and celebrated the 50th anniversary of Oklahoma! by singing the show's title song on the stage of the St. James Theatre in New York (the theatre in which Oklahoma! first opened in 1943) prior to a performance of a very different kind of musical – The Who's Tommy. In 1998, Raitt appeared in a London concert, and received a Lifetime achievement award from the Los Angeles Critics Circle.

● ALBUMS: Highlights Of Broadway (Capitol 1955)

★★★★, *Mediterranean Magic* (Capitol 1956) ★★★, *Under Open Skies* (Capitol 1958) ★★★, *Songs The Kids Brought Home* (Capitol 1959) ★★★, with Bonnie Raitt *Broadway Legend* (Angel 1995) ★★★★, and many Original Cast recordings.

RANDALL, FREDDY

b. 6 May 1921, London, England, d. 18 May 1999, Teignmouth, Devon, England. Randall began playing trumpet in the late 30s and by 1939 was leading his own small band. His involvement in the war ended when he was invalided out of the rifle brigade in 1943. He gained attention playing with Freddy Mirfield's Garbage Men, with whom he recorded for Decca Records in 1944. By the mid-40s he was one of the most respected dixieland trumpeters in the UK, appearing on radio and at clubs and concerts. His band included saxophonist Bruce Turner and trombonist Eddie Harvey, and their Cooks Ferry Inn sessions (run for the Cleveland Rhythm Club by Randall's brother, Harry) have passed into British jazz lore. Randall was well placed to take advantage of the trad boom that swept the UK from the late 40s and on through the 50s, and his band became one of the most popular of the era. They toured the USA in 1956, and backed singers such as Pearl Carr, Diana Coupland and Billy Banks. Ill health forced Randall's retirement in the late 50s and he concentrated on running a hotel in Brighton. He returned to jazz, part-time, in 1963, and thereafter continued to make occasional and usually unscheduled appearances at London clubs and pubs. These gigs found him playing as well as ever and delighting an army of fans that seemed to grow stronger and more numerous as the years passed. A band he formed in the early 70s in collaboration with Dave Shepherd (the clarinettist who had persuaded Randall to return to jazz in 1963) played at international festivals to great acclaim. Other shortlived comebacks included a 1982 session with American saxophonist Benny Waters. Reissues of Randall's earlier records confirmed that his qualities were not the result of nostalgic glow. Randall played hard-driving Chicago-style jazz with verve and great skill, and the many fine musicians who played in his band at one time or another responded to his enthusiastic lead.

● ALBUMS: *His Great Sixteen* (1951-56) ★★★, with Wild Bill Davison *Wild Bill Davison With Freddie Randall And His Band* (Black Lion 1965) ★★★, with Dave Shepherd *Freddy Randall/Dave Shepherd All Stars 'Live' At Montreux Jazz Festival* (1973) ★★★, *Something Borrowed, Something Blue* 50s recordings (Alamo 1978) ★★★, *Freddie Randall And His Band* (Dormouse 1986) ★★★.

RASPBERRY, RAYMOND

b. 1930, USA, d. 20 October 1995, Los Angeles, California, USA. After working as a pianist with several of the most prominent gospel stars, including Mahalia Jackson, Wynona Carr and the Clara Ward Singers, in 1954 Raspberry formed his own group, the Raspberry Singers. One of the first all-male gospel choirs, they frequently recorded in Spanish. They eventually disbanded in 1966 when Raspberry moved to New York, where he worked as a songwriter. His compositions include staples of the gospel repertoire including 'I'll Let Nothing Separate Me From The Love Of God', 'Touch Somebody's Life' and 'I Want To Be More Like Jesus'. In 1971 he moved to Los Angeles where he founded a new Raspberry Singers with an all-female line up. He died in 1995 while receiving dialysis treatment.

RAVENS

An African-American vocal group from New York City, New York, USA. Formed in 1945, the Ravens are considered the first of the 'bird groups' and their success was highly influential in ushering in an avalanche of vocal groups in the post-World War II R&B revolution. The original members were Ollie Jones (tenor), Leonard Puzey (tenor), Warren Suttles (baritone) and Jimmy Ricks (bass). After Maithe Marshall replaced Jones in 1946, the Ravens featured two leads, Ricks, who used his outstanding bass with terrific rhythmic bounce on the mid-tempo tunes, and Marshall, whose soaring falsetto tenor lent great poignancy to the ballads. The group also used with great effectiveness the switchover lead between Marshall and Ricks, which gave the Ravens a unique sound until it was widely imitated by other vocal ensembles. The Ravens first recorded for the Hub label in 1946, but only after they signed with National did they reach the charts, with the Ricks-led 'Write Me A Letter' (number 5 R&B) in 1948. Memorable recordings by the group at this time also included the Marshall-led songs 'September Song' and 'Searching For Love'. Their 1948 hit versions of 'Silent Night' (number 8 R&B) and 'White Christmas' (number 9 R&B) paved the way for later R&B vocal groups to interpret Christmas standards with an R&B flavour (the Ravens' vocal arrangement of 'White Christmas' was lifted for Clyde McPhatter And The Drifters' version from 1955). The Ravens' last chart record was in 1952 on Mercury with 'Rock Me All Night Long' (number 4 R&B). The group's last notable recording was 'Give Me A Simple Pray' in 1955 on the Argo label. With Ricks' departure for a solo career in 1956 the group faded from the scene.

● COMPILATIONS: *The Ravens* (Harlem Hit Parade 1973) ★★★, *The Greatest Group Of Them All* (Savoy 1978) ★★★★, *Old Man River* (Savoy Jazz 1985) ★★★, *Be I Bumble Bee Or Not* (Indigo 2000) ★★★.

RAY, JOHNNIE

b. 10 January 1927, Dallas, Oregon, USA, d. 24 February 1990, Los Angeles, California, USA. Known at various times in his career as the Prince of Wails, the Nabob of Sob and the Howling Success because of his highly emotional singing and apparent ability to cry at will, Ray is rated an important influence in the development of 50s and early 60s popular music. Of North American Indian origin, he became deaf in his right ear at the age of 12, which caused him to wear a hearing-aid throughout his career. He was heavily influenced by gospel and R&B music and performed in bars and clubs around Detroit in the late 40s, singing to his own piano accompaniment. Signed by Columbia Records in 1951, his first two releases were on their small OKeh Records label, usually reserved for black artists. His first record, 'Whiskey And Gin', was followed by 'Cry'. Unsophisticated, full of anguish, despair and a good deal of sobbing, it shocked a pop world accustomed to male singers crooning in front of big bands, and streaked to the top of the US charts, complete with Ray's own composition, 'The Little White Cloud That Cried', on the b-side. 'Cry' became his 'identity' song, and a multi-million-seller.

Ray was then transferred to the Columbia label, and during the next couple of years, he had several massive US hits including 'Please Mr Sun', 'Here Am I – Broken Hearted', 'Walkin' My Baby Back Home' and 'Somebody Stole My Gal'. His stage performances, with their overt sexuality and hysterical audience reaction, made him *persona non grata* to parents of teenagers worldwide. For a few years during the 50s, he enjoyed phenomenal success, revolutionizing popular music and symbolizing teenagers' frustrations and desires. Always acknowledging his gospel roots, Ray recorded several tracks associated with black artists, including the Drifters' R&B hit 'Such a Night' (1954), which was banned on several US radio stations, and 'Just Walkin'' In the Rain' (1956), which climbed to number 2 in the US charts, and was originally recorded by the Prisonaires. By contrast, in 1954, he played a young singer who decides to become a priest in Irving Berlin's musical film *There's No Business Like Show Business*. Ray sang the gospel-styled 'If You Believe' and 'Alexander's Ragtime Band'. During the late 50s in the USA, rumours were rife concerning his possible homosexuality and drug-taking, and as a result he became more popular abroad than at home. In the UK, in person and on record, he had been a favourite since 1952. Three of his US hits reached UK number 1, including 'Yes Tonight Josephine' (1957).

Other UK successes included 'Faith Can Move Mountains', 'Hey There' and 'Look Homeward Angel'. Ray also duetted with Doris Day ('Ma Says Pa Says', 'Full Time Job', 'Let's Walk That A-Way') and Frankie Laine ('Good Evening Friends'). In the early 60s, suffering from financial problems and alcoholism, and left behind as the musical climate rapidly changed, he turned to cabaret in the USA. During the 70s he began to revive his career, leaning heavily on his old material for its nostalgic appeal. Always in demand in the UK, he was headlining there until the late 80s. His last performance is said to have been in his home-town on 7 October 1989, and he died of liver failure a few months later in Los Angeles. As to his influence and legacy, one writer concluded: 'Ray was the link between Frank Sinatra and Elvis Presley, re-creating the bobby-sox mayhem that elevated "The Voice" while anticipating the sexual chaos that accompanied Presley.'

● ALBUMS: *Johnnie Ray* 10-inch album (Columbia 1952) ★★★, *At The London Palladium* 10-inch album (Philips 1954) ★★★, *I Cry For You* 10-inch album (Columbia 1955) ★★★, *Johnnie Ray* 10-inch album (Epic 1955) ★★★, *The Voice Of Your Choice* 10-inch album (Philips 1955) ★★★, *Sings The Big Beat* (Columbia/Philips 1957) ★★★★, *At The Desert Inn In Las Vegas* (Columbia/Philips 1958) ★★★, *Showcase Of Hits* (Philips 1958) ★★★★, *A Sinner Am I* (Philips 1959) ★★, *'Til Morning* (Columbia 1959) ★★, *On The Trail* (Columbia/Philips 1959) ★★, *Johnnie Ray* (Liberty 1962) ★★, *Yesterday, Today And Tomorrow* (Celebrity 1980) ★★.

● COMPILATIONS: *Johnnie Ray's Greatest Hits* (Columbia 1959) ★★★★, *The Best Of Johnnie Ray* (Realm 1966) ★★★★, *An American Legend* (Columbia 1978) ★★★★, *Portrait Of A Song Stylist* (Masterpiece 1989) ★★★★, *Greatest Hits* (Pickwick 1991) ★★★, *Cry* 5-CD box set (Bear Family 1998) ★★★★, *Yes Tonight Josephine* 5-CD box set (Bear Family 1999) ★★★★.

● FURTHER READING: *The Johnnie Ray Story*, Ray Sonin.

RAYBURN, MARGIE

b. Madera, California, USA, d. 2000, Oceanside, California, USA. Rayburn's first significant professional experience was as vocalist for the Ray Anthony Orchestra. She later sang with Gene Autry and as a member of the Sunnysiders, on their sole Top 20 hit, 'Hey, Mr. Banjo', in 1955. Going solo after the Sunnysiders' fortunes dimmed, Rayburn released 'I'm Available', written by Dave Burgess later of the Champs. This Liberty Records single eventually peaked at number 9 in the *Billboard* pop charts in October 1957. She was unable to follow the single with another hit and gave up her recording career by the mid-60s.

RAYS

This R&B group consisted of Harold Miller (b. 17 January 1931), tenor Walter Ford (b. 5 September 1931), second tenor Davey Jones (b. 1931) and baritone Harry James (b. 1932). It was formed in New York in 1955, when two refugees from the Four Fellows (of 'Soldier Boy' fame), Miller and Jones, teamed up with James and Ford. They first recorded for Chess with no success, then moved to the Philadelphia-based Cameo label in 1957 and achieved lasting fame, albeit as one-hit-wonders, with 'Silhouettes.' The song went to number 3 both R&B and pop in late 1957. The flip-side, the rousing jump led by Ford, 'Daddy Cool', received solid play and briefly charted. These songs are much better known than the Rays, having been remade innumerable times. Herman's Hermits in 1965 and Cliff Richard in 1990 both took 'Silhouettes' up the charts, while British revivalist band Darts, in 1977, and Boney M in 1976, each took 'Daddy Cool' into the UK Top 10.

REECE, DIZZY

b. Alphonso Son Reece, 5 January 1931, Kingston, Jamaica, West Indies. After playing in Jamaica as a young teenager, trumpeter Reece moved to the UK in 1948. Over the next few years he established a reputation in the UK and throughout Europe, working mostly with bop musicians like Kenny Graham, Victor Feldman and Tubby Hayes. Reece also occasionally played with leading swing era figures such as Don Byas. At the end of the 50s, an especially active period of creative work, Reece settled in the USA. There he played with Duke Jordan, Philly Joe Jones and others, and made occasional and usually well-spaced return trips to Europe with bands such as that led by Dizzy Gillespie and the Paris Reunion Band. A technically gifted player with an eclectic yet distinctive playing style, Reece has not been recorded as frequently or as well as his talent deserves.

● ALBUMS: *Progress Report* (Jasmine 1956) ★★★, *Victor Feldman In London* (Tempo 1956) ★★★, *Blues In Trinity* (Blue Note 1958) ★★★★, *Star Bright* (Blue Note 1959) ★★★, *Soundin' Off* (Blue Note 1960) ★★★, *Asia Minor* (Original Jazz Classics 1962) ★★★★, *From In To Out* (1970) ★, *Possession, Exorcism, Peace* (Honeydew 1972) ★★, *Manhattan Project* (Bee Hive 1978) ★★★, *Moose The Mooche* (Discovery 1978) ★★★, *Blowin' Away* (Interplay 1979) ★★★.

REED, JIMMY

b. Mathis James Reed, 6 September 1925, Leland, Mississippi, USA, d. 29 August 1976, Oakland, California, USA. Jimmy Reed was a true original: he sang in a lazy mush-mouthed ramble, played limited, if instantly recognizable, harmonica, and even more minimal guitar. He produced a series of hits in the 50s that made him the most successful blues singer of the era. He was born into a large sharecropping family and spent his early years on Mr. Johnny Collier's plantation situated near Dunleith, Mississippi. Here, he formed a childhood friendship with Eddie Taylor which was to have a marked effect on his later career. Reed sang in church and learned rudimentary guitar along with Taylor, but while the latter progressed Reed never became more than basically competent on the instrument. He left school in 1939 and found work farming around Duncan and Meltonia, Mississippi. Around 1943-44 he left the south to find work in Chicago where opportunities abounded due to the war effort. He was drafted in 1944 and served out his time in the US Navy. Discharged in 1945 he returned briefly to Mississippi before gravitating north once more to the Chicago area. Working in the steel mills, Reed gigged around in his leisure time with a friend named Willie Joe Duncan, who played a one-string guitar, or Diddley-bow. He also re-established contact with Eddie Taylor who had similarly moved north to try his luck. This led to Reed's becoming known on the local club scene and after appearances with John and Grace Brim, he secured a recording contract with Vee Jay Records in 1953.

His initial sessions, though highly regarded by collectors, produced no hits and Vee Jay were considering dropping him from their roster when in 1955 'You Don't Have To Go' took off. From then on, his success was phenomenal as a string of hits

such as 'Ain't That Lovin' You Baby', 'You've Got Me Dizzy', 'Bright Lights Big City', 'I'm Gonna Get My Baby' and 'Honest I Do' carried him through to the close of the decade. Many of these timeless blues numbers were adopted by every white R&B beat group during the early 60s. Two of his songs are now standards and are often used as rousing encores by name bands; 'Baby What You Want Me To Do' closed the Byrds' and Closer Than Most's live performances for many years and 'Big Boss Man' is arguably the most performed song of its kind – sung by the Merseybeats, Pretty Things, Grateful Dead and countless blues artists. Much of the credit for this success must be attributed to his friend Eddie Taylor, who played on most of Reed's sessions, and his wife, Mama Reed, who wrote many of his songs and even sat behind him in the studio reciting the lyrics into his forgetful ear as he sang. On some recordings her participation is audible. Reed's songs had little to do with the traditional blues, but they were eminently danceable and despite employing the basic blues line-up of harmonica, guitars and drums were generally classed as R&B. His hits were 'crossovers', appealing to whites as well as blacks. Perhaps this contributed to his continuing success as the blues entered its post-rock 'n' roll hard times. In his later days at Vee Jay, various gimmicks were tried, such as dubbing an album's worth of 12-string guitar solos over his backing tracks, faking live performances and introducing a commentary between album cuts; none were too successful in reviving his flagging sales.

To counter the positive elements in his life, Reed was continually undermined by his own unreliability, illness (he was an epileptic) and a propensity towards the bottle. He visited Europe in the early 60s, by which time it was obvious that all was not well with him. He was supremely unreliable and prone to appear on stage drunk. By the mid-60s his career was in the hands of the controversial Al Smith and his recordings were appearing on the Bluesway label. Inactive much of the time due to illness, Reed seemed on the road to recovery and further success, having gained control over his drink problem. Ironically, he died soon afterwards of respiratory failure, and was buried in Chicago. Reed is an important figure who has influenced countless artists through his songs. Steve Miller recorded *Living In The 20th Century* with a segment of Reed songs and dedicated the album to him. The Rolling Stones, Pretty Things and the Grateful Dead also acknowledge a considerable debt to him.

● ALBUMS: *I'm Jimmy Reed* (Vee Jay 1958) ★★★★, *Rockin' With Reed* (Vee Jay 1959) ★★★★, *Found Love* (Vee Jay 1960) ★★★★, *Now Appearing* (Vee Jay 1960) ★★★★, *At Carnegie Hall* (Vee Jay 1961) ★★★, *Just Jimmy Reed* (Vee Jay 1962) ★★★★, *T'ain't No Big Thing ... But He Is!* (Vee Jay 1963) ★★★, *The Best Of The Blues* (Vee Jay 1963) ★★★, *The 12-String Guitar Blues* (Vee Jay 1963) ★★★★, *Jimmy Reed At Soul City* (Vee Jay 1964) ★★★, *The Legend, The Man* (Vee Jay 1965) ★★★, *The New Jimmy Reed Album* (Bluesway 1967) ★★★, *Soulin'* (Bluesway 1967) ★★★, *Big Boss Man*

(Bluesway 1968) ★★★, *Down In Virginia* (Bluesway 1969) ★★★, *As Jimmy Is* (Roker 1970) ★★★, *Let The Bossman Speak!* (Blues On Blues 1971) ★★★.
● COMPILATIONS: *The Best Of Jimmy Reed* (Vee Jay 1962) ★★★★, *More Of The Best Of Jimmy Reed* (Vee Jay 1964) ★★★★, *The Soulful Sound Of Jimmy Reed* (Upfront 1970) ★★★, *I Ain't From Chicago* (Bluesway 1973) ★★★, *The Ultimate Jimmy Reed* (Bluesway 1973) ★★★★, *Cold Chills* (Antilles 1976) ★★★, *Jimmy Reed Is Back* (Roots 1980) ★★★, *Hard Walkin' Hanna* (Versatile 1980) ★★★, *Greatest Hits* (Hollywood 1992) ★★★, *Speak The Lyrics To Me, Mama Reed* (Vee Jay 1993) ★★★, *Cry Before I Go* (Drive Archive 1995) ★★★, *The Classic Recordings Volumes 1-3* (Tomato/Rhino 1995) ★★★★, *Big Legged Woman* (Collectables 1996) ★★★★, *All Night Boogie* (Javelin 1996) ★★.

REGAN, JOAN

b. 19 January 1928, Romford, Essex, England. A popular singer in the UK during the 50s and early 60s, with a particularly glamorous image, it was after working at various jobs, including one as a photographer's re-toucher, that Regan first made an impression on the music scene in 1953. Her private recordings of 'Too Young' and 'I'll Walk Alone' gained her a contract with Decca Records, partly because she was thought to have a 'Vera Lynn sound'. Her first releases, 'Till I Waltz Again With You' and 'I'll Always Be Thinking Of You', were followed by 'Ricochet', on which she was backed by Ronnie Aldrich's Squadronaires. It made the UK Top 10, and led to the nationwide fame she achieved when she became the resident singer on producer Richard Afton's television series *Quite Contrary*, followed later by four series of her own *Be My Guest* programmes. After being knocked out by a descending safety curtain during her first appearance in variety, she developed her act to include effective impressions of artists such as Gracie Fields, Judy Garland, and actress Anna Neagle, to whom Regan bore a remarkable facial resemblance. During the late 50s and early 60s, Regan appeared in several shows at the London Palladium, including *We're Having A Ball* with Max Bygraves; *Stars In Your Eyes* with Russ Conway, Cliff Richard, Edmund Hockridge and Billy Dainty; in pantomime with Frankie Vaughan and Jimmy Edwards; and several Royal Command Performances. Her other record hits, through to 1961, included 'Someone Else's Roses', 'If I Give My Heart To You', 'Prize Of Gold', 'Open Up Your Heart', 'May You Always', 'Happy Anniversary', 'Papa Loves Mama', 'One Of The Lucky Ones', 'Must Be Santa' and 'Wait For Me' (with the Johnston Brothers). She also recorded several duets, such as 'Seven And A Half Cents'/'Good Evening Friends' with Max Bygraves, 'Cleo And Me-O' with Dickie Valentine, and 'Open Up Your Heart' with her son, Rusty.
In July 1957 Regan married Harry Claff, the joint general manager and box office manager of the London Palladium. In November, the *Daily Herald* reported that she was to have a baby in February of the following year – seven months after the

wedding. After receiving 'abusive and wounding letters from people who were personally unknown to her', Regan successfully sued the newspaper for libel, and her daughter was born in April. In 1963, she was involved in a far more serious court case, when her husband was sentenced to five years' imprisonment for 'frauds on his employers involving £62,000'. Regan, who had known nothing about the deceptions, suffered a nervous breakdown, and divorced him later on the grounds of adultery. She resumed work later, and in 1968 married a doctor, Martin Cowan, eventually settling in Florida, USA. In 1984 she slipped in the shower, hit her head on the tiles, and suffered a brain haemorrhage. After an emergency operation she was left paralyzed and speechless. Her recovery, which entailed much physical and speech therapy, was aided by her miming to her old records. In 1987, some of those tracks, together with others by various 'Stars Of The Fifties', including Dickie Valentine, Lita Roza and Jimmy Young, were issued on the double album *Unchained Melodies*. In the same year, while on holiday in the UK, Regan was invited by her old accompanist, Russ Conway, to sing on stage again. Such was the response, that she has become a familiar figure in UK shows in the 90s.
● ALBUMS: *The Girl Next Door* (Decca 1955) ★★★, *Just Joan* (Decca 1957) ★★★★, with Edmund Hockridge *Joan And Ted* (Pye-Nixa 1961) ★★.
● COMPILATIONS: *The World Of Joan Regan* (Decca 1976) ★★★★, *Joan Regan Collection* (Nectar 1989) ★★★★.

RENDELL, DON

b. 4 March 1926, Plymouth, Devon, England. Rendell began playing alto saxophone as a child but later switched to tenor. He played in a number of dance bands during the late 40s, and in 1950 became a member of John Dankworth's septet. After leaving Dankworth in 1953 he formed his own small group but also worked with bands led by Tony Crombie, Ted Heath and others. In 1956 he joined Stan Kenton for a European tour, appearing on *Live At The Albert Hall*. In the late 50s he played with Woody Herman. During the 60s Rendell was again leading his own bands, featuring musicians such as Graham Bond, Michael Garrick and Ian Carr, with whom he was co-leader of a successful band. Rendell has also recorded with Stan Tracey (*The Latin American Caper*), and Neil Ardley (*Greek Variations*). A fluent improviser, with hints of post-bop styling overlaying a deep admiration for the earlier work of Lester Young, Rendell has long been one of the most admired of British jazz artists. For many years he has been tireless in the promotion of jazz through his activities as a sought-after teacher.
● ALBUMS: *Meet Don Rendell* (Tempo 1955) ★★★, *Recontre A Paris* (Vogue 1955) ★★★★, *Presents The Jazz Six* (Nixa 1957) ★★★, *Playtime* (Decca 1958) ★★★, *Roarin'* (Jazzland 1962) ★★★, with Ian Carr *Shades Of Blue* (Columbia 1964) ★★★★, with Carr *Phase III* (Columbia 1968) ★★★, with Carr *Live* (Columbia 1968) ★★★, with Carr *Change Is 1*

(Columbia 1969) ★★★, with Carr *Dusk Fire* (Columbia 1970) ★★★, *Space Walk* (Columbia 1972) ★★★, *Live At The Avgarde Gallery, Manchester* (1973) ★★★, *Just Music* (1974) ★★★, *Earth Music* (1979) ★★★.

REYNOLDS, DEBBIE

b. Mary Frances Reynolds, 1 April 1932, El Paso, Texas, USA. A popular actress and singer, particularly in movies. After moving to California in 1940 she became a majorette and played French horn with the Burbank Youth Orchestra. It was there she was spotted by talent scouts at a Miss Burbank competition in 1948. She quickly became a leading light in film musicals such as *The Daughter Of Rosie O'Grady* (1950), *Three Little Words* (as 'Boop-Boop-A-Doop' girl Helen Kane), *Two Weeks With Love*, *Singin' In The Rain* (perhaps her most memorable role), *Skirts Ahoy!*, *I Love Melvin*, *The Affairs Of Dobie Gillis*, *Give A Girl A Break*, *Hit The Deck*, *The Tender Trap* (comedy with music), *Bundle Of Joy*, *Meet Me In Las Vegas*, *Say One For Me*, *Pepe* and *The Unsinkable Molly Brown* (1964, Oscar nomination). In 1951 she recorded her first million-selling single, 'Abba Daba Honeymoon' (from the film *Two Weeks With Love*), on which she duetted with Carleton Carpenter. She also went to the top of the US charts in 1957 with the million-selling 'Tammy' (from *Tammy And The Bachelor*). She married the singer and actor Eddie Fisher in September 1955, and their daughter Carrie has since become an established actress and writer. They divorced in 1959 when Fisher married Elizabeth Taylor. In 1966 Reynolds appeared in *The Singing Nun* (a fictionalized story about Soeur Sourire), and three years later starred in her own television series, *Debbie*. As her film career declined, she made an acclaimed Broadway debut in the 1973 revival of the much-loved American musical *Irene*, and appeared in her own nightclub revue. In later years, she survived severe financial problems when her second husband's business failed, and she and Carrie were estranged after Carrie's hard-hitting novel, *Postcards From The Edge*, which was supposedly based on their lives together, was filmed in 1990. Always the trouper, she bounced right back, launching two keep-fit videos, and headlining at venues such as Harrah's in Reno, and Caesar's Palace in Las Vegas, often in the company of her former film co-stars, such as Donald O'Connor (*Singin' In The Rain*) and Harve Presnell (*The Unsinkable Molly Brown*). In 1993 she opened the Debbie Reynolds Hotel on the fringe of the Las Vegas Strip, where she presents her two-hour autobiographical one-woman show, which contains often bawdy impressions of Zsa Zsa Gabor, Mae West and Barbra Streisand. The complex also houses Reynolds' museum of Hollywood memorabilia. After struggling for nearly five years to make it a success, Reynolds filed for bankruptcy, two months after an agreement to sell the hotel for $10 million fell through. In 1997 she unveiled her second star on the Hollywood Walk of Fame. This latest one honours her stage revivals of *Woman Of The Year*, *Annie Get Your Gun*, and *The Unsinkable Molly Brown*. She received her first star in 1960 for film roles such as *Singin' In The Rain*.

● ALBUMS: *Debbie Reynolds* (Dot 1959) ★★★, *Am I That Easy To Forget* (Dot 1960) ★★★ *Fine & Dandy* (Dot 1960) ★★, *From Debbie With Love* (Dot 1960) ★★, *Tammy* (Dot 1963) ★★★, *Raising A Ruckus* (Metro 1965) ★★★, *Debbie* (Jasmine 1985) ★★, and film soundtrack recordings.

● FURTHER READING: *Debbie – My Life*, Debbie Reynolds with David Patrick Columba.

● FILMS: *June Bride* (1948), *Three Little Words* (1950), *Two Weeks With Love* (1950), *The Daughter Of Rosie O'Grady* (1950), *Mr. Imperium* (1951), *Singin' In The Rain* (1952), *Skirts Ahoy!* (1952), *Give A Girl A Break* (1953), *The Affairs Of Dobie Gillis* (1953), *I Love Melvin* (1953), *Susan Slept Here* (1954), *Athena* (1954), *The Tender Trap* (1955), *Hit The Deck* (1955), *Bundle Of Joy* (1956), *The Catered Affair* (1956), *Meet Me In Las Vegas* (1956), *Tammy And The Bachelor* (1957), *This Happy Feeling* (1958), *It Started With A Kiss* (1959), *The Mating Game* (1959), *Say One For Me* (1959), *Pepe* (1960), *The Rat Race* (1960), *The Gazebo* (1960), *The Pleasure Of His Company* (1961), *The Second Time Around* (1961), *How The West Was Won* (1962), *My Six Loves* (1963), *Mary, Mary* (1963), *The Unsinkable Molly Brown* (1964), *Goodbye Charlie* (1964), *The Singing Nun* (1966), *Divorce American Style* (1967), *How Sweet It Is* (1968), *What's The Matter With Helen?* (1971), *Charlottes's Web* (1973), *That's Entertainment!* (1974), *The Bodyguard* (1992), *Heaven And Earth* (1993), *That's Entertainment! III* (1994), *Wedding Bell Blues* (1996), *Mother* (1996), *In And Out* (1997), *Fear And Loathing In Las Vegas* voice only (1998), *Zack And Reba* (1998).

REYNOLDS, JODY

b. 3 December 1938, Denver, Colorado, USA. Reynolds grew up in Oklahoma and formed his first band, the Storms, in 1952. He played guitar in the group and worked various jobs until he could make a living playing music. In 1958 the band went to Los Angeles, where they were signed to the new Demon label. The label did not use the Storms but did record Reynolds, backed with a number of professional session musicians on his 1958 single 'Endless Sleep' (covered in the UK by Marty Wilde), a song Reynolds had written with George Brown (credited under the pseudonym Delores Nance). The song reached number 5 and became one of the first of the so-called 'death rock' hits of the 50s and 60s (others in that category included 'Tell Laura I Love Her', 'Terry', 'Teen Angel' and 'Leader Of The Pack'). Reynolds made the charts once more with 'Fire Of Love' (also in 1958), but none of his subsequent recordings for Demon, Smash or other labels charted. Reynolds continued to perform with the Storms for much of the 60s, but by the 70s had retired to a non-musical career. His only album was a 1978 set on the Tru-Gems label including a remake of his only hit.

● ALBUMS: *Endless Sleep* (Tru-Gems 1978) ★★.

RHODES, TODD WASHINGTON

b. 31 August 1900, Hopkinsville, Kentucky, USA, d. 4. June 1965, Detroit, Michigan, USA. Pianist Rhodes first came to prominence in the late 20s as a founder-member of McKinney's Cotton Pickers, recording several dozen tracks for RCA Victor between 1928 and 1931. Leaving the Cotton Pickers in 1934, Rhodes became a popular act on the Detroit jazz scene and formed his own band in the early 40s, recording for the local Sensation label between 1947 and 1950. He hit the R&B charts with 'Bell Boy Boogie', and gave Alan Freed his famous signature tune 'Blues For The Red Boy'. Rhodes' material was leased to Vitacoustic in Chicago and King in Cincinnati. In 1951, Todd Rhodes And His Toddlers began recording for King Records proper, and for the following three years produced some of the best R&B of the 50s, both alone and as backing band for artists including Wynonie Harris and Dave Bartholomew. Rhodes was also instrumental in giving R&B singer LaVern Baker her big break. Rhodes disbanded his group in 1957, although he continued to play as a solo act until his death in 1965. Many of his sidemen and associates progressed to become respected jazz musicians or session players for the mighty Motown empire.

● ALBUMS: *Your Daddy's Doggin' Around* (Jukebox Lil 1985) ★★★, *Dance Music That Hits The Spot* (Swingtime 1988) ★★★.

RICH, BUDDY

b. Bernard Rich, 30 September 1917, New York City, New York, USA, d. 2 April 1987, Los Angeles, California, USA. In showbusiness from the age of two, Rich achieved considerable fame as a drummer and tap dancer, performing on Broadway when he was four years old as a member of his parents' act. Two years later he was touring as a solo artist, playing the US vaudeville circuit and also visiting Australia. At the age of 11 he formed his own band and within a few more years was attracting attention sitting in with bands in New York clubs. In 1937 he was hired by Joe Marsala and soon thereafter began to rise in critical estimation and public popularity. In quick succession he played in several important bands of the swing era, including those of Bunny Berigan, Harry James, Artie Shaw and Tommy Dorsey. After military service he again played with Dorsey, then formed his own big band which survived for a few years in the late 40s. He next worked with Les Brown and also became a regular with Jazz At The Philharmonic. In the early 50s he led his own briefly re-formed big band and also became a member of the Big Four, led by Charlie Ventura. He also recorded extensively for Norman Granz, not only with the impresario's JATP but also with Art Tatum, Lionel Hampton, Ray Brown, Oscar Peterson, Flip Phillips, Dizzy Gillespie, Roy Eldridge, Louis Armstrong, Lester Young, Gene Krupa and many others.

Return stints with James and Dorsey followed, but by the late 50s, despite a heart attack, he was appearing as a singer and leading his own small bands. He continued to make records with, amongst others, Max Roach. In the early 60s, Rich was once more with James, but by 1966 had decided to try again with his own big band. He continued to lead a big band for the next dozen years, spent a while leading a small group, then re-formed a big band in the 80s, continuing to lead this band for the rest of his life. His later bands frequently featured young, recently graduated musicians, towards whom he displayed an attitude that resembled that of a feudal lord. Nevertheless, whether through awareness of these musicians' interests or the demands of audiences, the repertoire of many of Rich's 60s and 70s bands contained elements of rock without ever becoming a true fusion band. Rich's playing was characterized by his phenomenal speed and astonishing technical dexterity. His precision and clarity were legendary even if, at times, the band's charts were specifically designed to display his remarkable skills. During his bandleading years, Rich continued to make records in many settings; in these he would usually revert to the drummer's traditional role of supporting player. In such contexts Rich was a subtle accompanist, adept with brushes but always swinging and propulsive. Early in his career Rich was notorious for his short temper, and during his stint with Dorsey frequently clashed with the band's singer, Frank Sinatra, a similarly short-fused artist. A caustically witty man, later in his life Rich became popular on television chat shows, where his put-downs of ill-equipped pop singers often bordered upon the slanderous. In person he was particularly unpleasant to Dusty Springfield, although she returned the abuse. Rich came back frequently from illness and accident (once playing one-handed when his other arm was in a sling, without any noticeable diminution of his ability) but was finally diagnosed as having a brain tumour. Even during his final illness, his wit did not desert him. When a nurse preparing him for surgery asked if there was anything to which he was allergic, he told her, 'Only country music.'

● ALBUMS: with Nat 'King' Cole, Lester Young *The Lester Young Trio* 10-inch album (Mercury 1951) ★★★★, with Cole, Young *The Lester Young Trio ii* (Clef 1953) ★★★★, *Buddy Rich Swinging* 10-inch album (Norgran 1954) ★★★★, *Sing And Swing With Buddy Rich* (Norgran 1955) ★★★★, with Harry 'Sweets' Edison *Buddy And Sweets* (Norgran 1955) ★★★, with Lionel Hampton, Art Tatum *The Hampton-Tatum-Rich Trio* (Clef 1956) ★★★, with Gene Krupa *Krupa And Rich* (Clef 1956) ★★★★, *Lester Young-Nat 'King' Cole-Buddy Rich Trio* (Norgran 1956) ★★★★, *Buddy Rich Sings Johnny Mercer* (Verve 1956) ★★, *The Wailing Buddy Rich* (Norgran 1956) ★★★, *This One's For Basie* reissued as *Big Band Shout* (Norgran 1956) ★★★★, *Buddy Just Sings* (Verve 1957) ★, *The Buddy Rich Quartet In Miami* (Verve 1957) ★★★, with Max Roach *Rich Versus Roach* (Mercury 1959) ★★★★, *Richcraft* (Mercury 1959) ★★★, *The Voice Is Rich* (Mercury 1959) ★★, *Playtime* (Argo 1961) ★★, *Blues Caravan* (Verve 1962) ★★★★, with Gene Krupa *Burnin' Beat* (Verve 1962) ★★★★, *Swingin' New Big Band* (Pacific Jazz 1966) ★★★,

Big Swing Face (Pacific Jazz 1967) ★★★★, *The New One!* (Pacific Jazz 1967) ★★★★, *Mercy, Mercy* (World Pacific 1968) ★★★★, *Buddy & Soul* (World Pacific 1969) ★★★★, *Rich A La Rakha* (World Pacific 1969) ★★★, *Super Rich* (Verve 1969) ★★★, *Keep The Customer Satisfied* (Liberty 1970) ★★★, *A Different Drummer* (RCA 1971) ★★★, *Rich In London* (RCA 1971) ★★★, *Time Being* (RCA 1972) ★★★, *Stick It* (RCA 1972) ★★★, *The Roar Of '74* (Groove Merchant 1973) ★★★, *Buddy Rich And His Orchestra* (Laserlight 1973) ★★★, *Ease On Down The Road* (LRC 1974) ★★★, *The Last Blues Album Vol. 1* (Groove 1974) ★★★, *Speak No Evil* (RCA 1976) ★★★, *Buddy Rich Plays And Plays And Plays* (RCA 1977) ★★★, *Class Of '78* (RCA 1977) ★★★, *Lionel Hampton Presents Buddy Rich* (Kingdom Gate 1977) ★★★, *The Man From Planet Jazz* (1980) ★★★, *The Legendary Buddy Rich* (1982) ★★★, *The Magic Of Buddy Rich* (1984) ★★★, *Tuff Dude* (LRC 1984) ★★★, *Live At King Street Cafe* (Pacific Jazz 1985) ★★★, *The Cinch* (1985) ★★★.
● COMPILATIONS: *Buddy Rich And His Greatest Band 1946-47* recordings (First Heard 1977) ★★★, *Rich Riot* (First Heard 1979) ★★★, *Illusion* 3-CD set (Sequel) ★★★★, *One Night Stand 1946* recording (Bandstand *c.*1980) ★★★, *Buddy Rich And His Legendary '47-'48 Orchestra 1945-48* recordings (Hep *c.*1980) ★★★, *No Jive* (Novus 1992) ★★★, *The Collection* (Beat Goes On 1998) ★★★.
● VIDEOS: *The Making Of Burning For Buddy, Parts One And Two* (DCI 1997), *Buddy Rich At The Top* (Hudson Music 2000).
● FURTHER READING: *Improvising*, Whitney Balliett.

RICHARD, CLIFF
b. Harry Roger Webb, 14 October 1940, Lucknow, India. One of the most popular and enduring talents in the history of UK showbusiness, Webb began his career as a rock 'n' roll performer in 1957. His fascination for Elvis Presley encouraged him to join the Dick Teague Skiffle Group and several months later he teamed up with drummer Terry Smart and guitarist Norman Mitham to form the Drifters. They played at various clubs in the Cheshunt/Hoddesdon area of Hertfordshire before descending on the famous 2I's coffee bar in London's Soho. There, they were approached by lead guitarist Ian Samwell and developed their act as a quartet. In 1958, they secured their big break in the unlikely setting of a Saturday morning talent show at the Gaumont cinema in Shepherd's Bush. It was there that the senatorial theatrical agent George Ganyou recognized Webb's sexual appeal and singing abilities and duly financed the recording of a demonstration tape of 'Breathless' and 'Lawdy Miss Clawdy'. A copy reached the hands of EMI Records producer Norrie Paramor who was impressed enough to grant the ensemble an audition. Initially, he intended to record the newly christened Cliff Richard as a solo artist backed by an orchestra, but the persuasive performer insisted upon retaining his own backing group.

With the assistance of a couple of session musicians, the unit recorded the American teen ballad 'Schoolboy Crush' as a projected first single. An acetate of the recording was paraded around Tin Pan Alley and came to the attention of the influential television producer Jack Good. It was not the juvenile 'Schoolboy Crush' that captured his attention, however, but the Ian Samwell b-side 'Move It'. Good reacted with characteristically manic enthusiasm when he heard the disc, rightly recognizing that it sounded like nothing else in the history of UK pop. The distinctive riff and unaffected vocal seemed authentically American, completely at odds with the mannered material that usually emanated from British recording studios. With Good's ceaseless promotion, which included a full-page review in the music paper *Disc*, Richard's debut was eagerly anticipated and swiftly rose to number 2 in the UK charts. Meanwhile, the star made his debut on Good's television showcase *Oh Boy!*, and rapidly replaced Marty Wilde as Britain's premier rock 'n' roll talent. The low-key role offered to the Drifters persuaded Samwell to leave the group to become a professional songwriter and producer, and by the end of 1958 a new line-up emerged featuring Hank B. Marvin and Bruce Welch. Before long, they changed their name to the Shadows, in order to avoid confusion with the black American R&B group, the Drifters. Meanwhile, Richard consolidated his position in the rock 'n' roll pantheon, even outraging critics in true Elvis Presley fashion. The *New Musical Express* denounced his 'violent, hip-swinging' and 'crude exhibitionism' and pontificated: 'Tommy Steele became Britain's teenage idol without resorting to this form of indecent, short-sighted vulgarity'. Critical mortification had little effect on the screaming female fans who responded to the singer's boyish sexuality with increasing intensity.

1959 was a decisive year for Richard and a firm indicator of his longevity as a performer. With management shake-ups, shifts in national musical taste and some distinctly average singles his career could easily have been curtailed, but instead he matured and transcended his Presley-like beginnings. A recording of Lionel Bart's 'Living Doll' provided him with a massive UK number 1 and three months later he returned to the top with the plaintive 'Travellin' Light'. He also starred in two films, within 12 months. *Serious Charge*, a non-musical drama, was banned in some areas as it dealt with the controversial subject of homosexual blackmail. The Wolf Mankowitz-directed *Expresso Bongo*, in which Richard played the delightfully named Bongo Herbert, was a cinematic pop landmark, brilliantly evoking the rapacious world of Tin Pan Alley. It remains one of the most revealing and humorous films ever made on the music business and proved an interesting vehicle for Richard's varied talents. From 1960 onwards Richard's career progressed along more traditional lines leading to acceptance as a middle-of-the-road entertainer. Varied hits such as the breezy, chart-topping 'Please Don't Tease', the rock 'n' rolling 'Nine Times Out Of Ten' and reflective 'Theme For A Dream' demonstrated his range, and in 1962 he hit a new peak with 'The Young Ones'. A glorious pop anthem to youth, with some striking guitar work from Hank Marvin, the song proved one of his most memorable number 1 hits.

The film of the same name was a charming period piece, with a strong cast and fine score. It broke box office records and spawned a series of similar movies from its star, who was clearly following Elvis Presley's cinematic excursions as a means of extending his audience. Unlike the King, however, Richard supplemented his frequent movie commitments with tours, summer seasons, regular television slots and even pantomime appearances. The run of UK Top 10 hits continued uninterrupted until as late as mid-1965. Although the showbiz glitz had brought a certain aural homogeneity to the material, the catchiness of songs such as 'Bachelor Boy', 'Summer Holiday', 'On The Beach' and 'I Could Easily Fall' was undeniable. These were neatly, if predictably, complemented by ballad releases such as 'Constantly', 'The Twelfth Of Never' and 'The Minute You're Gone'. The formula looked likely to be rendered redundant by the British beat boom, but Richard expertly rode that wave, even improving his selection of material along the way. He bravely, although relatively unsuccessfully, covered a Rolling Stones song, 'Blue Turns To Grey', before again hitting top form with the beautifully melodic 'Visions'. During 1966, he had almost retired after converting to fundamentalist Christianity, but elected to use his singing career as a positive expression of his faith. The sparkling 'In The Country' and gorgeously evocative 'The Day I Met Marie' displayed the old strengths to the full, but in the swiftly changing cultural climate of the late 60s, Richard's hold on the pop charts could no longer be guaranteed.

The 1968 Eurovision Song Contest offered him a chance of further glory, but the jury placed him a close second with the 'oom-pah-pah'-sounding 'Congratulations'. The song was nevertheless a consummate Eurovision performance and proved one of the biggest UK number 1s of the year. Immediately thereafter, Richard's chart progress declined and his choice of material proved at best desultory. Although there were a couple of solid entries, Raymond Froggatt's 'Big Ship' and a superb duet with Hank Marvin, 'Throw Down A Line', Richard seemed a likely contender for Variety as the decade closed.

The first half of the 70s saw him in a musical rut. The chirpy but insubstantial 'Goodbye Sam, Hello Samantha' was a Top 10 hit in 1970 and heralded a notable decline. A second shot at the Eurovision Song Contest with 'Power To All Our Friends' brought his only other Top 10 success of the period and it was widely assumed that his chart career was over. However, in 1976 there was a surprise resurgence in his career when Bruce Welch of the Shadows was assigned to produce his colleague. The sessions resulted in the bestselling album *I'm Nearly Famous*, which included two major hits,

'Miss You Nights' and 'Devil Woman'. The latter was notable for its decidedly un-Christian imagery and the fact that it gave Richard a rare US chart success. Although Welch remained at the controls for two more albums, time again looked as although it would kill off Richard's perennial chart success. A string of meagre singles culminated in the dull 'Green Light', which stalled at number 57, his lowest chart placing since he started singing. Coincidentally, his backing musicians, Terry Britten and Alan Tarney, had moved into songwriting and production at this point and encouraged him to adopt a more contemporary sound on the album *Rock 'N' Roll Juvenile*. The most startling breakthrough, however, was the attendant single 'We Don't Talk Anymore', written by Tarney and produced by Welch. An exceptional pop record, the song gave Richard his first UK number 1 hit in over a decade and also reached the Top 10 in the USA.

The 'new' Richard sound, so refreshing after some of his staid offerings in the late 70s, brought further well-arranged hits, such as 'Carrie' and 'Wired For Sound', and ensured that he was a chart regular throughout the 80s. Although he resisted the temptation to try anything radical, there were subtle changes in his musical approach. One feature of his talent that emerged during the 80s was a remarkable facility as a duettist. Collaborations with Olivia Newton-John, Phil Everly, Sarah Brightman, Sheila Walsh, Elton John and Van Morrison added a completely new dimension to his career. It was something of a belated shock to realize that Richard may be one of the finest harmony singers working in the field of popular music. His perfectly enunciated vocals and the smooth texture of his voice have the power to complement work that he might not usually tackle alone. The possibility of his collaborating with an artist even further from his sphere than Van Morrison remains a tantalizing challenge.

Throughout his six decades in the pop charts, Richard has displayed a valiant longevity. He parodied one of his earliest hits with comedy quartet the Young Ones and registered yet another number 1, while still singing religious songs on gospel tours. He appeared in *Time* and in John Farrar and Tim Rice's hugely successful *Heathcliff* (his own *Songs From Heathcliff* was drawn from the show). He sued the *New Musical Express* for an appallingly libellous review, far more vicious than their acerbic comments back in 1958. He celebrated his 50th birthday with a move into social commentary with the anti-war hit 'From A Distance'. He was nominated to perform at the celebrations for VE day in 1995, appearing with Vera Lynn, and has now been adopted as her male equivalent. It was no surprise, therefore, to learn that he was to be knighted for his services to popular music in May 1995. Richard's long-held belief that most UK pop radio stations have an official veto on his tracks seemed to be proven in September 1998, when he distributed a heavily remixed promo of his soon-to-be-released single, 'Can't Keep This Feeling In', under the pseudonym Blacknight. It was instantly playlisted by youth-orientated stations all over the country, and went to number 10 in the singles chart the following month. The singer was further angered when DJ Chris Evans, owner of Virgin Radio, announced that he wanted the station's entire stock of Richard's records 'thrown out'. In an unprecedented move, BBC Radio 1 responded by clearing its morning schedules for a four-hour tribute 'Stand Up For Cliff Day' hosted by Jill Dando. Such was the demand for tickets to his November/December 1998 Royal Albert Hall concerts celebrating 40 years in showbusiness, that a further 12 performances were scheduled for March 1999. At the end of the year he was criticised for being opportunistic when he combined the 'Lord's Prayer' and 'Auld Lang Syne' into 'The Millennium Prayer'. Tacky though it was it still reached number 1 in the UK. So he goes on – Sir Cliff Richard has outlasted every musical trend of the past four decades with a sincerity and commitment that may well be unmatched in his field. He is British pop's most celebrated survivor.

● ALBUMS: *Cliff* (Columbia 1959) ★★★, *Cliff Sings* (Columbia 1959) ★★★★, *Me And My Shadows* (Columbia 1960) ★★★★, *Listen To Cliff* (Columbia 1961) ★★★, *21 Today* (Columbia 1961) ★★★, *The Young Ones* (Columbia 1961) ★★★, *32 Minutes And 17 Seconds With Cliff Richard* (Columbia 1962) ★★★★, *Summer Holiday* (Columbia 1963) ★★★, *Cliff's Hit Album* (Columbia 1963) ★★★★, *When In Spain* (Columbia 1963) ★★★, *Wonderful Life* (Columbia 1964) ★★★, *Aladdin And His Wonderful Lamp* (Columbia 1964) ★★★, *Cliff Richard* (Columbia 1965) ★★★, *More Hits By Cliff* (Columbia 1965) ★★★, *When In Rome* (Columbia 1965) ★★, *Love Is Forever* (Columbia 1965) ★★★, *Kinda Latin* (Columbia 1966) ★★★, *Finders Keepers* (Columbia 1966) ★★, *Cinderella* (Columbia 1967) ★★, *Don't Stop Me Now* (Columbia 1967) ★★★, *Good News* (Columbia 1967) ★★★, *Cliff In Japan* (Columbia 1968) ★★★, *Two A Penny* (Columbia 1968) ★★★, *Established 1958* (Columbia 1968) ★★★, *Sincerely Cliff* (Columbia 1969) ★★★, *It'll Be Me* (Regal Starline 1969) ★★★, *Cliff 'Live' At The Talk Of The Town* (Regal Starline 1970) ★★★, *All My Love* (MFP 1970) ★★★, *About That Man* (Columbia 1970) ★★★, *Tracks 'N' Grooves* (Columbia 1970) ★★★, *His Land* (Columbia 1970) ★★★, *Cliff's Hit Album* stereo reissue of 1963 album (EMI 1971) ★★★★, *Take Me High* (EMI 1973) ★★★, *Help It Along* (EMI 1974) ★★★, *The 31st Of February Street* (EMI 1974) ★★★, *Everybody Needs Someone* (MFP 1975) ★★★, *I'm Nearly Famous* (EMI 1976) ★★★, *Cliff Live* (MFP 1976) ★★★, *Every Face Tells A Story* (EMI 1977) ★★★, *Small Corners* (EMI 1977) ★★★, *Green Light* (EMI 1978) ★★★, *Thank You Very Much* (EMI 1979) ★★★, *Rock 'N' Roll Juvenile* (EMI 1979) ★★★, *Rock On With Cliff* (MFP 1980) ★★★, *Listen To Cliff* (MFP 1980) ★★★, *I'm No Hero* (EMI 1980) ★★★, *Love Songs* (EMI 1981) ★★★, *Wired For Sound* (EMI 1981) ★★★, *Now You See Me, Now You Don't* (EMI 1982) ★★★, *Dressed For The Occasion* (EMI 1983) ★★★, *Silver* (EMI 1983) ★★★, *Cliff In The 60s* (MFP 1984) ★★★, *Cliff And The Shadows* (EMI 1984) ★★★, *Thank You Very Much* (MFP 1984) ★★★, *The Rock Connection* (EMI 1984) ★★★, *Walking In The Light* (Myrrh 1985) ★★★, *Time* (EMI 1986) ★★★, *Hymns And Inspirational Songs* (Word 1986) ★★★, *Always Guaranteed* (EMI 1987) ★★★, *Stronger* (EMI 1989) ★★★, *From A Distance ... The Event* (EMI 1990) ★★★, *Together With Cliff* (EMI 1991) ★★★, *The Album* (EMI 1993) ★★★, *Songs From Heathcliff* (EMI 1995) ★★★, *Real As I Wanna Be* (EMI 1998) ★★★, *Wanted* (Papillon 2001) ★★★.

● COMPILATIONS: *The Best Of Cliff* (Columbia 1969) ★★★★, *The Best Of Cliff Volume 2* (Columbia 1972) ★★★★, *The Cliff Richard Story* 6-LP box set (WRC 1972) ★★★, *40 Golden Greats* (EMI 1979) ★★★★, *The Cliff Richard Songbook* 6-LP box set (WRC 1980) ★★★★, *Private Collection 1979-1988* (EMI 1988) ★★★, *20 Original Greats* (EMI 1989) ★★★, *The Hit List* (EMI 1994) ★★★★, *At The Movies 1959-1974* (EMI 1996) ★★★, *The Rock 'N' Roll Years 1958-1963* 4-CD box set (EMI 1997) ★★★, *On The Continent* 5-CD box set (Bear Family 1998) ★★★, *1960s* (EMI 1998) ★★★, *1970s* (EMI 1998) ★★★, *1980s* (EMI 1998) ★★★, *The Whole Story: His Greatest Hits* (EMI 2000) ★★★★.

● VIDEOS: *Two A Penny* (1978), *The Video Connection* (PMI 1984), *Together* (PMI 1984), *Thank You Very Much* (Thorn-EMI 1984), *Rock In Australia* (PMI 1986), *We Don't Talk Anymore* (Gold Rushes 1987), *Video EP* (PMI 1988), *The Young Ones* (1988), *Summer Holiday* (1988), *Wonderful Life* (1988), *Take Me High* (Warner Home Video 1988), *Private Collection* (PMI 1988), *Always Guaranteed* (PMI 1988), *Live And Guaranteed* (PMI 1989), *From A Distance ... The Event Volumes 1 and 2* (PMI 1990), *Together With Cliff Richard* (PMI 1991), *Expresso Bongo* (1992), *Cliff – When The Music Stops* (1993), *Access All Areas* (1993), *The Story So Far* (1993), *The Hit List* (PMI 1995), *The Hit List Live* (PMI 1995), *Finders Keepers* (1996), *Cliff At The Movies* (PolyGram Music Video 1996), *The 40th Anniversary Concert* (VCI 1998, *An Audience With* (VCI 2000).

● FURTHER READING: *Driftin' With Cliff Richard: The Inside Story Of What Really Happens On Tour*, Jet Harris and Royston Ellis. *Cliff, The Baron Of Beat*, Jack Sutter. *It's Great To Be Young*, Cliff Richard. *Me And My Shadows*, Cliff Richard. *Top Pops*, Cliff Richard. *Cliff Around The Clock*, Bob Ferrier. *The Wonderful World Of Cliff Richard*, Bob Ferrier. *Questions: Cliff Answering Reader And Fan Queries*, Cliff Richard. *The Way I See It*, Cliff Richard. *The Cliff Richard Story*, George Tremlett. *New Singer, New Song: The Cliff Richard Story*, David Winter. *Which One's Cliff?*, Cliff Richard with Bill Latham. *Happy Christmas From Cliff*, Cliff Richard. *Cliff In His Own Words*, Kevin St. John. *Cliff*, Patrick Doncaster and Tony Jasper. *Cliff Richard*, John Tobler. *Silver Cliff: A 25 Year Journal 1958-1983*, Tony Jasper. *Cliff Richard, Single-Minded*, no author listed. *Cliff Richard: The Complete Recording Sessions, 1958-1990*, Peter Lewry and Nigel Goodall. *Cliff: A Biography*, Tony Jasper. *Cliff Richard, The Complete Chronicle*, Mike Read, Nigel Goodall and Peter Lewry. *Cliff Richard: The Autobiography*, Steve Turner. *Ultimate Cliff*, Peter Lewry and Nigel

Goodall. *A Celebration: The Official Story Of 40 Years In Show Business*, André Deutsch.

● FILMS: *Serious Charge* (1959), *Expresso Bongo* (1960), *The Young Ones* (1961), *Summer Holiday* (1962), *Wonderful Life* (1964), *Thunderbirds Are Go!* (1966), *Finders Keepers* (1966), *Two A Penny* (1968), *Take Me High* (1973).

RICHARDS, JOHNNY

b. John Cascales, 2 November 1911, Queretaro State, Mexico, d. 7 October 1968, New York City, New York, USA. This most progressive of modern jazz arrangers began his musical career at the age of 10 playing trumpet, violin and banjo in a vaudeville act called The Seven Wonders Of The World. Taking up the saxophone when 17 years old, he was in London in 1931 working in films, then went to Hollywood as an arranger. Forming a big band in the 40s, he had trouble finding musicians who could cope with his involved scores, so he gave it up to write for Boyd Raeburn's forward-looking band. Oddly enough, considering the reputations of both men, Richards' contributions to the Raeburn library were pretty, romantic, woodwind scores for *inter alia*, 'Prelude To The Dawn', 'Love Tales' and 'Man With The Horn'. He scored and conducted the first *Dizzy Gillespie With Strings* album, and in a more commercial vein wrote (with Carolyn Leigh) 'Young At Heart' for the Frank Sinatra film (1954). He later joined the Stan Kenton arranging staff, which gave scope for his progressive writing (e.g., 1957's *Cuban Fire!* album). That year he formed a new band for recording, resulting in several albums for Capitol Records, Roulette Records, Coral Records and Bethlehem Records. Hardly a commercial success, Richards was nevertheless a musical, if sometimes misused asset to any employer.

● ALBUMS: *Dizzy Gillespie Plays/Johnny Richards Conducts* 10-inch album (Discovery 1950) ★★★, *Something Else By Johnny Richards* (Bethlehem 1957) ★★★, *Wide Range* (Capitol 1957) ★★★, *I'm Shooting High* (Capitol 1957) ★★★, *Experiments In Sound* (Capitol 1958) ★★★, *The Rites Of Diablo* (Roulette 1958) ★★★, *Walk Softly/Run Wild* (Coral 1959) ★★★, *My Fair Lady* (Roulette 1964) ★★★.

RIDDLE, NELSON

b. Nelson Smock Riddle, 1 June 1921, Oradell, New Jersey, USA, d. 6 October 1985, Los Angeles, California, USA. After studying piano, Riddle took up the trombone when in his early teens, and in the late 30s played in a number of big bands, including those led by Jerry Wald, Charlie Spivak, Tommy Dorsey and Bob Crosby. After a stint in the army, he settled in California and studied arranging with Mario Castelnuovo-Tedesco and conducting with Victor Bay. In the late 40s Riddle joined NBC, but was lured to Capitol Records and registered immediately with a driving arrangement of 'Blacksmith Blues' for Ella Mae Morse. He confirmed his outstanding ability when he began to arrange and conduct for recordings by Nat 'King' Cole and Frank Sinatra. Among these were some of Cole's most engaging and

memorable sides, such as 'Unforgettable', 'Somewhere Along The Way' and 'Ballerina', along with a good many of his bestselling albums. Riddle also worked with Sinatra on his important early Capitol albums, such as *Songs For Young Lovers*, *Swing Easy!*, *Songs For Swingin' Lovers!*, *In The Wee Small Hours*, and many other later ones. In addition, he served as musical director on most of the singer's popular television specials.

To a considerable extent, Riddle's easy swinging charts, with their echoes of the big band music of an earlier era (and the distinctive solos of George Roberts on trombone and Harry 'Sweets' Edison on trumpet), were of considerable importance in re-establishing Sinatra as a major star of popular music. Riddle also worked extensively with Ella Fitzgerald on *Ella Swings Brightly With Nelson*, and the highly acclaimed *Songbook* series. Other artists to benefit from the distinctive Riddle touch were Judy Garland (*Judy*), Rosemary Clooney (*Rosie Solves The Swinging Riddle*), Sammy Davis Jnr. (*That's Entertainment*), Eddie Fisher (*Games That Lovers Play*), Jack Jones (*There's Love*), Peggy Lee (*Jump For Joy*), Dean Martin (*This Time I'm Swinging*), Johnny Mathis (*I'll Buy You A Star*), Antonio Jobim (*The Brazilian Mood*), Shirley Bassey (*Let's Face The Music*), Dinah Shore (*Yes Indeed*) and many more. In 1954, Riddle had some success with 'Brother John', adapted from the French song 'Frère Jacques', and in the following year, his instrumental version of 'Lisbon Antigua' topped the US chart. He also made some fine, non-vocal albums, which contrasted the lush ballads of *The Tender Touch* and *The Joy Of Living* with the up-tempo exuberance of *Hey ... Let Yourself Go* and *C'mon ... Get Happy*.

Although under contract to Capitol at the time, he is usually credited with conducting and arranging another label's *Phil Silvers Swings Bugle Calls For Big Band*, which contained Riddle compositions (with US Army/Sgt. Bilko connotations) such as 'Chow, A Can Of Cow And Thou' and 'The Eagle Screams'. Another unusual record item was *Sing A Song With Riddle*, a set of genuine Riddle arrangements, complete with sheet music, and an invitation to the listener to become the featured vocalist. From the mid-50s Riddle was also active in television and feature films: he wrote the theme for the long-running series *Route 66*, and received Oscar nominations for his background scores for the movies *Li'l Abner*, *Can-Can*, *Robin And The Seven Hoods* and *Paint Your Wagon*, and won an Academy Award in 1974 for his music for *The Great Gatsby*. Among his other film credits were *The Pajama Game*, *St. Louis Blues*, *Merry Andrew* and several Sinatra movies such as *The Joker Is Wild* and *Pal Joey*. After attempting retirement, Riddle made an unexpected and hugely successful comeback in the early 80s, when he recorded three albums with Linda Ronstadt: *What's New*, *Lush Life* and *For Sentimental Reasons*. A gentle, self-effacing man, he was in poor heath for some years before he died. Riddle was probably the finest arranger/leader of modern times, always having the edge and always guaranteeing quality with whoever he worked, especially his magnificent work with Sinatra.

● ALBUMS: *Oklahoma!* (Capitol 1955) ★★★, *Moonglow* (Capitol 1955) ★★★, *Lisbon Antigua* (Capitol 1956) ★★★, *Hey ... Let Yourself Go!* (Capitol 1957) ★★★, *The Tender Touch* (Capitol 1957) ★★★, *Conducts Johnny Concho* (Capitol 1957) ★★★, *C'mon ... Get Happy!* (Capitol 1958) ★★★, *Gold Record* (Capitol 1958) ★★★, *Pal Joey* film soundtrack (Capitol 1958) ★★★, *Sea Of Dreams* (Capitol 1958) ★★★, *The Girl Most Likely* film soundtrack (Capitol 1958) ★★★, *Merry Andrew* film soundtrack (Capitol 1959) ★★★, *Sing A Song With Riddle* (Capitol 1959) ★★★, *The Joy Of Living* (Capitol 1959) ★★★, *Can-Can* film soundtrack (Capitol 1960) ★★★, *Love Tide* (Capitol 1961) ★★★, *The Gay Life* (Capitol 1961) ★★★, *Tenderloin* (Capitol 1961) ★★★, *Magic Moments* (Capitol 1962) ★★★, *Route 66 And Other Great TV Themes* (Capitol 1962) ★★★, *Love Is Just A Game Of Poker* (Capitol 1962) ★★★, *Come Blow Your Horn* film soundtrack (1962) ★★★, *Lolita* film soundtrack (MCA 1962) ★★★, *British Columbia Suite* (1963) ★★★, *Paris When It Sizzles* film soundtrack (Reprise 1963) ★★★, *Robin And the Seven Hoods* film soundtrack (Reprise 1964) ★★★, *Hits Of 1964* (Reprise 1964) ★★★, *A Rage To Live* film soundtrack (United Artists 1965) ★★★, *Harlow* film soundtrack (Warners 1965) ★★★, *Great Music, Great Films, Great Sounds* (Reprise 1965) ★★★, *Batman* film soundtrack (20th Century-Fox 1966) ★★★, *Music For Wives And Lovers* (United Artists 1967) ★★★, *El Dorado* film soundtrack (Columbia 1967) ★★★, *How To Succeed In Business Without Really Trying* film soundtrack (United Artists 1967) ★★★, *Bright And The Beautiful* (1967) ★★★, *Riddle Of Today* (1968) ★★★, *The Today Sound Of Nelson Riddle* (Sunset 1969) ★★★, *Nat – An Orchestral Portrait* (Columbia 1969) ★★★, *The Look Of Love* (Bulldog 1970) ★★★, *On A Clear Day You Can See Forever* film soundtrack (Columbia 1970) ★★★, *Nelson Riddle Conducts The 101 Strings* (Marble Arch 1970) ★★★, *Communication* (MPS 1972) ★★★, *Changing Colours* (MPS 1972) ★★★, *Vivé Legrand!* (Daybreak 1973) ★★★, *The Great Gatsby* (Paramount 1974) ★★★, *Romance Fire And Fancy* (Intersound 1983) ★★★.

● COMPILATIONS: *The Silver Collection* (Polydor 1985) ★★★, *The Capitol Years* (Capitol 1993) ★★★.

RITCHIE, JEAN

b. 8 December 1922, Viper, Kentucky, USA. Ritchie was the youngest of 14 children from a well-known family of traditional singers. Her parents, Balis and Abigail Ritchie were of Scottish-Irish descent, and it was her father who taught her to play the mountain dulcimer (Ritchie's book, *Singing Family Of The Cumberlands*, recounts the history of her family growing up in the Cumberland mountains.) The family were visited by Cecil Sharp in 1917 during one of his song-collecting expeditions to the Appalachian Mountains. Ritchie graduated with a bachelor's degree in social work from the University Of Kentucky in 1946 and moved to New York City.

She was first recorded two years later when she was heard by Mitch Miller as she demonstrated a dulcimer in a store. Miller was impressed enough to produce her debut, *Round And Roundelays*. She was later introduced to Alan Lomax, the well-known, and equally well-respected, folklorist. Lomax recorded Ritchie's songs, both for his own collection and for the Library Of Congress Folksong Archives.

In 1952 Ritchie travelled to the UK after winning a Fulbright scholarship, giving her the chance to trace the origins of her family's songs. While in the UK she appeared at the Royal Albert Hall and Cecil Sharp House, the headquarters of the English Folk Dance And Song Society. Ritchie's 1952 release, *Singing The Traditional Songs Of Her Kentucky Mountain Family*, was the first folk recording to be issued on the Elektra Records label. In 1953 she attended the International Conference of Folk Music held in Biaritz-Pamplona, and appeared at many folk seminars countrywide.

Numerous television and radio appearances, and a wealth of recorded material have ensured her place in her country's folk heritage. Her light voice and simple arrangements have gained the appeal of a wide audience, and she has performed all over the USA and given recitals at universities and colleges. Many folk song collectors have sought the Ritchie family as a source of traditional tunes and songs, and Jean's own composition 'My Dear Companion' was recorded by Linda Ronstadt, Emmylou Harris and Dolly Parton on their 1987 release *Trio*. Ritchie's sister Edna also recorded on Jean's own Greenhays label, which was set up in 1979 by the singer and her husband George Pickow in order to assure the availability of her own recordings.

● ALBUMS: *Round And Roundelays* (1948) ★★★, *Singing The Traditional Songs Of Her Kentucky Mountain Family* (Elektra 1952) ★★★★, with Oscar Brand *Courting Songs* 10-inch album (Elektra 1954) ★★★, *Kentucky Mountain Songs* 10-inch album (Elektra 1954) ★★★, with Brand *Shivaree!* (Esoteric 1955) ★★★, *Saturday Night And Sunday Too* (Riverside 1956) ★★★, *Carols For All Seasons* (Tradition 1959) ★★★, *Field Trip – England* (Folkways 1960) ★★★★, *As I Roved Out – Field Trip Ireland* (Folkways 1960) ★★★★, *Child Ballads Of The Southern Mountains Volume 1* (Folkways 1961) ★★★, *Child Ballads Of The Southern Mountains Volume 2* (Folkways 1961) ★★★, *Come On In, We're Pickin' And Singin'* (Folkways 1962) ★★★, with Doc Watson *Jean & Doc At Folk City* (Folkways 1963) ★★★, *The Appalachian Dulcimer* (Folkways 1963) ★★★★, *Marching Across The Green Grass And Other American Children's Game Songs* (Folkways 1968) ★★★, *None But One* (Sire 1977) ★★★, *Mountain Born: Jean RItchie & Sons Sing* (Greenhays 1996) ★★★, *Kentucky Christmas Old And New* (Greenhays 1997) ★★★.

● COMPILATIONS: *Songs Of Her Kentucky Mountain Family* (Elektra 1957) ★★★★.

● VIDEOS: *Mountain Born: The Jean Ritchie Story* (KET 1997).

● FURTHER READING: *Garland Of Mountain Songs*, Jean Ritchie. *Singing Family Of The*

Cumberlands, Jean Ritchie. *The Dulcimer Book*, Jean Ritchie. *The Swapping Song Book*, Jean Ritchie. *Folk Songs Of The Southern Appalachians As Sung By Jean Ritchie*, Jean Ritchie. *Apple Seeds And Soda Straws: Love Charms And Legends Written Down For Young And Old*, Jean Ritchie. *From Fair To Fair*, Jean Ritchie. *Celebration Of Life*, Jean Ritchie. *Jean Ritchie's Dulcimer People*, Jean Ritchie. *Traditional Mountain Dulcimer*, Jean Ritchie.

RIVERA, CHITA

b. Dolores Conchita Figueroa del Rivero, 23 January 1933, Washington, DC, USA. A vivacious singer, dancer, and actress – an exciting and explosive performer – Rivera was born to Puerto Rican parents and grew up in the Bronx. She started dancing when she was seven, and from the age of 11, trained for a career in classical ballet. After studying at the New York City Ballet via a scholarship from choreographer George Balanchine, in 1952 she turned from classical dance and joined the chorus of *Call Me Madam* on Broadway. Further chorus work in *Guys And Dolls* and *Can-Can* was followed by appearances in *Shoestring Revue*, *Seventh Heaven*, and *Mr. Wonderful* (1956). She rocketed to stardom in 1957 as Anita in *West Side Story*, and stopped the show nightly by singing and dancing herself into a frenzy to the whooping rhythms of 'America'. She caused even more of a sensation when *West Side Story* opened in London on 12 December 1958; it is still regarded by many as the most exciting first night of the post-war years. Two years later she was back on Broadway as Dick Van Dyke's secretary Rose, in the first successful rock 'n' roll musical, *Bye Bye Birdie*, and she recreated her role in London in the following year. A musical adaptation of *The Prisoner Of Zenda* (1963), in which she starred with Alfred Drake, folded before it reached New York, but a year later, Rivera was acclaimed for her role as a gypsy princess in *Bajour* on Broadway. In the late 60s she toured in various productions including *Sweet Charity*, and also appeared in the 1969 film version with Shirley MacLaine. After more national tours in the early 70s in musicals such as *Jacques Brel Is Alive And Well And Living In Paris* and *Kiss, Me Kate*, in addition to several straight roles, she co-starred with Gwen Verdon in the 'sinfully seductive' *Chicago* (1975). John Kander and Fred Ebb wrote the score, and they also devised and developed Chita Rivera's cabaret act, which included a number called 'Losing', a reference to the number of Tony Award nominations she had received. She gained one more nomination for her performance in *Bring Back Birdie* (1981), which closed after only four nights, and *Merlin* (1983) was also unsuccessful. Rivera was finally awarded the coveted Tony – and a Drama Desk Award – when she co-starred with Liza Minnelli in *The Rink* (1984), another of Kander and Ebb's projects. Shortly afterwards, she was involved in a serious car accident which 'mangled my leg from the knee down'. After having 12 bolts inserted in the bones, she was back on Broadway, along with

Leslie Uggams, Dorothy Loudon, and others, in *Jerry's Girls*, a tribute to the composer Jerry Herman. During the rest of the 80s, she performed in cabaret and continued to tour in America and other countries including the UK. In 1988/9, she joined the Radio City Music Hall Rockettes in a national tour of *Can-Can* that lasted for over a year. In 1991, she was inducted into New York's Theatre Hall Of Fame, along with Kander and Ebb. She was subsequently widely applauded – and won London *Evening Standard* and Tony Awards – for her outstanding dual performance as the movie star Aurora and the Spider Woman in Kander and Ebb's musical *Kiss Of the Spider Woman*. After 749 performances in Toronto, London and New York, in November 1994 she set out on the show's two-year road tour of North America. Her outstanding contribution to the musical theatre was recognized in the early 90s by the Drama Desk's Annual Achievement Award, and the first annual Bandai Musical Award for Excellence in Broadway Theatre. While in Washington D.C. during 1996 with *The Kiss Of The Spider Woman*, she was presented with an honorary Gold Record by the Recording Industry Association of America for her contribution to American sound recording. In the late 90s, Rivera co-starred with Carol Channing on stage in *Broadway Legends* ('Together At Last!') and toured her own revue, *Chita & All That Jazz*, through the US regions. In June 1998, she also appeared in a unique reunion of Sweet Charity at the Avery Fisher Hall at New York's Lincoln Center, and in the following year starred as Roxie Hart in the Las Vegas production of *Chicago*. She left that show after three months in order to play the same role in the hit West End version. Her subsequent work early in the new millennium included the part of the proverbial hooker with the heart of gold in Arthur Laurents' new play, *Venecia*, and a US tour of the family musical, *Casper*. In February 2001, Rivera was honoured by the Drama League in New York.

ROBBINS, JEROME

b. Jerome Rabinowitz, 11 October 1918, New York City, New York, USA, d. 29 July 1998, New York City, New York, USA. An important director, choreographer and dancer, Robbins began his career with the celebrated Ballet Theatre in New York, and subsequently appeared as a dancer on Broadway in shows such as *Great Lady*, *The Straw Hat Revue* and *Stars In Your Eyes*. In 1944, he and composer Leonard Bernstein conceived a short ballet, *Fancy Free*, which, with the participation of Betty Comden and Adolph Green, evolved into the musical *On The Town*. During the 40s and early 50s he was constantly acclaimed for his stylish and original choreography for shows such as *Billion Dollar Baby* (1945), *High Button Shoes* (1947, Tony Award), *Look Ma, I'm Dancing* (1948), *Miss Liberty* (1949), *Call Me Madam* (1950), *The King And I* (1951) and *Two's Company* (1952). From then on, he also served as the director on series of notable productions: *The Pajama Game* (1954), *Peter Pan* (1954), *Bells Are Ringing* (1956), *West Side*

Story (1957; Tony Award), *Gypsy* (1959), *A Funny Thing Happened On The Way To The Forum* (1962), *Funny Girl* (1964) and *Fiddler On The Roof* (1964). For the last-named show, one of his greatest achievements, he won Tony Awards as choreographer and director. He and Robert Wise were also awarded Oscars when they co-directed the film version of *West Side Story* in 1961. After working on the London productions of *Funny Girl* and *Fiddler On The Roof* in 1966 and 1967, Robbins turned away from the Broadway musical theatre and announced that he was devoting his life to ballet. He had worked with the New York City Ballet since 1948 as dancer, choreographer and associate artistic director, and in 1958 briefly formed his own chamber-sized company Ballets: USA. He returned to the popular field in February 1989 to direct a celebratory revue of his work entitled *Jerome Robbins' Broadway*. In a season that was so bereft of original musicals that *Kenny Loggins On Broadway* and *Barry Manilow At The Gershwin* were categorized as such, this reminder of Broadway's glory days was greeted with relief and rejoicing (and six Tony Awards). It featured extended sequences from *West Side Story* and *Fiddler On The Roof*, along with other delights such as the gloriously incongruous 'You Gotta Have A Gimmick' from *Gypsy*, and the famous Keystone Cops chase from *High Button Shoes*, all sandwiched between excerpts from Robbins' first hit, *On The Town*, which opened and closed the show. An enormously expensive investment at $8 million, the show reportedly lost around half of that, even though it ran for 538 performances. Robbins continued to work on ballets until his death in July 1998.

ROBBINS, MARTY

b. Martin David Robinson, with twin sister Mamie, 26 September 1925, near Glendale, Arizona, USA, d. 8 December 1982, Nashville, Tennessee, USA. He later maintained that his father hated him and that his early childhood was unhappy. Reports indicate that John Robinson (originally a Polish immigrant named Mazinski) suffered from a drink problem that led to him abusing his family before eventually leaving his wife, Emma, to cope alone with their seven children plus the two from her previous marriage. At one time they lived in a tent in the desert, but in 1937 his parents divorced and Emma and the children moved to a shack in Glendale, where she took in laundry to support the family. In his early teens, Marty spent some time with an elder brother breaking wild horses on a ranch near Phoenix. Consequently his education suffered; he attended high school in Glendale but never graduated, and by the early 40s he was becoming involved in a life of petty crime.

He left home to live the life of a hobo until he joined the US Navy in May 1943. It was during his three years in the service, where he saw action in the Pacific, that he learned to play the guitar and first started songwriting and singing. He also acquired a love of Hawaiian music that would surface several times during his career. After discharge in February 1946, he returned to Glendale, where he tried many jobs before starting to sing around the clubs and on local radio under the names of either Martin or Jack Robinson (his mother strongly disapproved of him singing in clubs and he used the name 'Jack' to try to prevent her finding out). By 1950, he had built a local reputation and was regularly appearing on KTYL Mesa and on both radio and in his own television show, *Western Caravan*, on KPHO Phoenix. He married Marizona Baldwin on 27 September 1948, a marriage that lasted until Marty's death. A son, Ronald Carson Robinson, was born in 1949 and 10 years later, their daughter Janet was born (Ronald eventually became a singer, performing both as Ronnie Robbins and as Marty Robbins Jnr.).

Through the assistance of Little Jimmy Dickens, and by now known as Marty Robbins, he was signed by Columbia Records, for whom he first recorded in November 1951. In December 1952, 'I'll Go On Alone' became his first US country hit. It charted for 18 weeks, two of which were spent at number 1 (Marty wrote the song because initially his wife disliked his showbusiness life). He moved to Nashville in January 1953 and became a member of the *Grand Ole Opry*. Early in his career, he acquired the nickname of 'Mr Teardrop' and later wrote and recorded a song with that title. In 1955, his career, which by the end of 1954 appeared somewhat becalmed, received a welcome boost with the success of his recordings of rockabilly numbers, 'That's All Right' (originally written and recorded by Arthur 'Big Boy' Crudup in 1947 but more recently a hit for Elvis Presley) and 'Maybellene' both became Top 10 country hits.

He had always realized that it would be advantageous to record in differing styles and accordingly his recordings varied from country to pop, from Hawaiian to gospel, and even some with his own guitar providing the sole accompaniment. In 1956, he achieved another country number 1 with his version of Melvin Endsley's 'Singing The Blues'. The song also made number 17 in the US pop charts, where Guy Mitchell's version was number 1. The following year, Marty turned Endsley's song 'Knee Deep In The Blues' into a number 3 country hit but again lost out in the pop charts to Mitchell, who had immediately covered Robbins' recording. Somewhat frustrated, Robbins made his next recordings in New York with Ray Conniff and his orchestra and during 1957/8, with what may be best termed teenage love songs, he registered three more country number 1s with his own song, 'A White Sports Coat (And A Pink Carnation)' (a million-seller), the Hal David-Burt Bacharach song, 'The Story Of My Life' and 'Stairway Of Love'. The first two were also major US pop hits for him (in the UK, the former was a hit for the King Brothers and Terry Dene, while Michael Holliday had Top 3 successes with the latter two). During the late 50s, he formed a talent and booking agency and launched his own record label. Robbins had always had a love of the Old

West. He always considered the cowboy state of Arizona to be his home (his maternal grandfather had once been a Texas Ranger), and in the late 50s he appeared in three B-movie westerns, *Raiders Of Old California*, *Badge Of Marshal Brennan* and *Buffalo Gun*. The first two were straight acting roles but the latter co-starred Webb Pierce and Carl Smith and included several songs. It was also at this time that he began to record the material that would see release on albums such as his now legendary *Gunfighter Ballads And Trail Songs* (he actually recorded the whole album in one day). In 1959, he wrote and charted the title track of the film *The Hanging Tree*, which starred Gary Cooper, before his classic 'El Paso' became a number 1 country and pop hit. It gave him a second million-seller and was also the first country music song to be awarded a Grammy. The success of this song established Robbins once and for all and songs such as 'Big Iron' and 'Running Gun' became firm favourites with audiences the world over.

During the 60s, he registered 31 US country hits, 13 of which also found success in the pop charts. The country number 1s included 'Don't Worry' (which has the distinction of being the first song to include the 'fuzz' sound on the recording: a fuse had blown in the control room channel carrying Grady Martin's lead guitar, with the result that it sounded fuzzy – Robbins liked the effect and left it in), 'Devil Woman' (a UK Top 5 pop hit for him), 'Ruby Ann', 'Ribbon Of Darkness', 'Tonight Carmen' and 'I Walk Alone'. In 1964, Robbins supported Barry Goldwater in his bid for President and also wrote 'Ain't I Right' and 'My Own Native Land', two protest songs against communism and anti-American war protesters. He felt the first would be a hit but Columbia, fearing racial repercussions, would not let him release them. However, his guitarist and backing vocalist Bobby Sykes' recordings of the songs were released on the Sims label. He used the pseudonym Johnny Freedom, but sounded so much like his boss that for years many people have believed the recordings were by Robbins himself (Robbins' own recordings were later released by Bear Family on the album *Pieces Of Your Heart*).

In 1969, Frankie Laine enjoyed a pop hit with Robbins' semi-autobiographical song 'You Gave Me A Mountain', while Johnny Bush released a country version. Surprisingly, Robbins' own recording was never released as a single. He also had a great interest in stock-car racing and during the 60s he began driving at the Nashville Speedway, an occupation that later saw him fortunate to survive several serious crashes. During the 60s, he also filmed a television series called *The Drifter*, appeared in eight films, including *Hell On Wheels*, *The Nashville Story*, *Ballad Of A Gunfighter*, *Road To Nashville* and *From Nashville With Music*, and wrote a Western novel, *The Small Man*. In August 1969, he suffered a heart attack on his tour bus near Cleveland and in January 1970 he underwent bypass surgery. He soon returned to his punishing schedules and in April he was starring in Las Vegas. The same year his moving ballad 'My Woman, My Woman, My

Wife' became his second Grammy winner and the *Academy Of Country Music* voted him The Man of the Decade (originally, it had been intended that Frankie Laine should have the song but Robbins' wife told him to keep it for himself). He left Columbia for Decca Records in 1972 but returned in December 1975 and immediately registered two number 1 country hits with 'El Paso City' (a look back at his previous hit) and the old pop ballad 'Among My Souvenirs'. He had previously returned to El Paso with the nine-minute long 'Feleena (From El Paso)'. During the 70s, he had a further 30 country hits, made film appearances in *Country Music*, *Guns Of A Stranger*, *Country Hits* and *Atoka* as well as starring in his network television series *Marty Robbins Spotlight*.

His songwriting talents saw him elected to the Nashville Songwriters' International Hall Of Fame in 1975. His extensive touring schedules included crowd-pleasing appearances at the 1975 and 1976 Wembley Festivals in London. He continued with these punishing schedules into the 80s but was again hospitalized following a second heart attack in January 1981. He returned to London for the April 1982 Festival, before making a tour in Canada. 'Some Memories Just Won't Die' became his biggest hit since 1978 and on 11 October 1982 he was inducted into the Country Music Hall Of Fame in Nashville. He toured on the west coast but in Cincinnati, on 1 December 1982, he played what turned out to be his last concert. The following day he suffered his third heart attack. He underwent major surgery but died of cardiac arrest on 8 December and was buried in Nashville three days later. A few days after his funeral, his recording of 'Honky Tonk Man', the title track of a Clint Eastwood film in which he had made a cameo appearance, entered the charts, eventually peaking at number 10. A quiet and withdrawn man offstage, Robbins possessed an onstage ability to communicate with and hold his audience, and his clever use of in-jokes, asides and sheer personality made him one of the finest entertainers to grace any genre of music. His tally of 94 *Billboard* country chart hits places him in eighth position in the list of most-charted country artists. He charted at least one song every year from 1952 (when he first recorded) to 1983 and during this period he also registered 31 pop hits.

● ALBUMS: *Rock 'N' Rollin' Robbins* 10-inch album (Columbia 1956) ★★★, *The Song Of Robbins* (Columbia 1957) ★★★, *Song Of The Islands* (Columbia 1957) ★★★, *Marty Robbins* (Columbia 1958) ★★★, *Gunfighter Ballads And Trail Songs* (Columbia 1959) ★★★★, *More Gunfighter Ballads And Trail Songs* (Columbia 1960) ★★★★, *The Alamo* film soundtrack (Columbia 1961) ★★★, *Just A Little Sentimental* (Columbia 1961) ★★★, *Devil Woman* (Columbia 1962) ★★★★, *Marty After Midnight* (Columbia 1962) ★★★, *Portrait Of Marty* (Columbia 1962) ★★★, *Hawaii's Calling Me* (Columbia 1963) ★★, *Return Of The Gunfighter* (Columbia 1963) ★★★, *R.F.D. Marty Robbins* (Columbia 1964) ★★★, *Island Woman* (Columbia 1964) ★★, *Turn The Lights Down Low* (Columbia 1965) ★★★★, *What God Has Done* (Columbia

1965) ★★, *Saddle Tramp* (Columbia 1966) ★★★, *The Drifter* (Columbia 1966) ★★★, *Christmas With Marty Robbins* (Columbia 1967) ★★, *My Kind Of Country* (Columbia 1967) ★★★, *Tonight Carmen* (Columbia 1967) ★★★, *By The Time I Get To Phoenix* (Columbia 1968) ★★, *Bend In The River* (Columbia 1968) ★★★, *I Walk Alone* (Columbia 1968) ★★★, *Heart Of Marty Robbins* (Columbia 1969) ★★★, *It's A Sin* (Columbia 1969) ★★★, *Singing The Blues* (Columbia 1969) ★★★, *My Woman, My Woman, My Wife* (Columbia 1970) ★★★, *The Story Of My Life* (Columbia 1970) ★★★, *From The Heart* (Columbia 1971) ★★★, *Today* (Columbia 1971) ★★★, *Marty Robbins Favorites* (Columbia 1972) ★★★, with his Friends *Joy Of Christmas* (Columbia 1972) ★★, *This Much A Man* (Decca 1972) ★★★, *I've Got A Woman's Love* (Columbia 1972) ★★★, *Bound For Old Mexico (Great Hits From South Of The Border)* (Columbia 1973) ★★★, *Marty Robbins* (MCA 1973) ★★★, *Good 'N' Country* (MCA 1974) ★★★, *Have I Told You Lately That I Love You* (Columbia 1974) ★★★, *No Sign Of Loneliness Here* (Columbia 1976) ★★★, *El Paso City* (Columbia 1976) ★★★, *Two Gun Daddy* (Columbia 1976) ★★★, *Adios Amigo* (Columbia 1977) ★★★, *Don't Let Me Touch You* (Columbia 1977) ★★★, *All Around Cowboy* (Columbia 1979) ★★★, *The Performer* (Columbia 1979) ★★★, *With Love* (Columbia 1980) ★★★, *Encore* (Columbia 1981) ★★★, *Everything I've Always Wanted* (Columbia 1981) ★★★, *The Legend* (Columbia 1981) ★★★, *Come Back To Me* (Columbia 1982) ★★★, *Some Memories Just Won't Die* (Columbia 1982) ★★★, *Sincerely* (Columbia 1983) ★★★, *Forever Yours* (Columbia 1983) ★★★, *Twentieth Century Drifter* (Columbia 1983) ★★★★, *Just Me And My Guitar* (Columbia 1983) ★★★, *Hawaii's Calling Me* (Columbia 1983) ★★★, *Pieces Of Your Heart* (Columbia 1985) ★★★.
● COMPILATIONS: *Marty's Greatest Hits* (Columbia 1959) ★★★, *More Greatest Hits* (Columbia 1961) ★★★, *Marty Robbins' Greatest Hits, Volume 3* (Columbia 1971) ★★★, *All Time Greatest Hits* (Columbia 1972) ★★★★, *Marty Robbins' Greatest Hits, Volume 4* (Columbia 1978) ★★★, *Biggest Hits* (Columbia 1982) ★★★, *Rockin' Rollin' Robbins Volumes 1-3* (Bear Family 1985) ★★★★, *The Essential Marty Robbins: 1951-1982* (Columbia 1991) ★★★★, *Marty Robbins Country 1951-58* 5-CD box set (Bear Family 1991) ★★★, *Lost And Found* (Columbia 1994) ★★★, *Country 1960-1966* 4-CD box set (Bear Family 1995) ★★★★, *Under Western Skies* 4-CD box set (Bear Family 1995) ★★★★, *The Story Of My Life: The Best Of Marty Robbins* (Columbia/Legacy 1996) ★★★★.
● VIDEOS: *The Best Of The Marty Robbins Show Vol. 1 & 2* (1993), *The Best Of The Marty Robbins Show Vol. 3 & 4* (1993).
● FURTHER READING: *Marty Robbins: Fast Cars And Country Music*, Barbara J. Pruett.

ROBERTS, PADDY

b. 1910, South Africa, d. September 1975, England. A songwriter, pianist and singer, Roberts' early education took place in England. He subsequently attended university in South Africa before joining a law practice. Intent on becoming a songwriter, he returned to the UK where he had some success in the late 30s with songs such as 'Angel Of The Great White Way' (written with Elton Box, Desmond Cox and Don Pelosi), and 'Horsey, Horsey' (with Box, Cox and Ralph Butler) which became popular for Jack Jackson, Billy Cotton and Henry Hall. During World War II Roberts flew with the RAF, and when peace came he became an airline captain on BOAC Constellations. Subsequently, he returned to songwriting, and during the 50s, had several UK chart hits, including 'The Book' (David Whitfield), 'Heart Of A Man' (Frankie Vaughan), 'Lay Down Your Arms' (Anne Shelton), 'Meet Me On The Corner' (Max Bygraves), 'Pickin' A Chicken' (Eve Boswell); and 'Evermore', 'Softly, Softly' (number 1) and 'You Are My First Love' (the last three sung by Ruby Murray). The latter song was featured in the British musical film *It's Great To Be Young*, and Roberts wrote several other movie songs, including 'In Love For The Very First Time' (for *An Alligator Named Daisy*, starring Diana Dors) and the title number to *The Good Companions*. His other 50s compositions included 'Johnny Is The Boy For Me', 'It's A Boy', 'That Dear Old Gentleman', 'Send For Me' and 'The Three Galleons (Las Tres Carabelas)'. Most of the aforementioned songs were written in collaboration with others, such as Hans Gottwald, C.A. Rossi, Geoffrey Parsons, Peggy Cochran, Jack Woodman, Gerry Levine, Ake Gerhard, Leon Land, Peter Hart, Garfield De Mortimer, Derek Bernfield, Augusto Alguego, G. Moreu and Lester Powell. However, towards the end of the decade, he was beginning to write unaided more and more frequently, and during the 60s he included several of his own, often wry, witty and sophisticated numbers in an accomplished cabaret act. Probably the best-known of these is 'The Ballad Of Bethnal Green', which enjoyed a good deal of airplay, but there were many others too, including 'The Belle Of Barking Creek', 'The Big Dee-Jay', 'Follow Me', 'Country Girl', 'I Love Mary', 'The Tattooed Lady', 'What's All This Fuss About Love?', 'The Lavender Cowboy' and 'Don't Upset The Little Kiddywinks'. Roberts won several Ivor Novello Awards, and held high office in the Performing Right Society and the Song Writers Guild.
● ALBUMS: *Paddy Roberts At The Blue Angel* (Decca 1961) ★★.
● COMPILATIONS: *Best Of Paddy Roberts* (MFP 1968) ★★★.

ROBERTSON, JEANNIE

b. Regina Christina Robertson, 1908, Aberdeen, Scotland, d. March 1975. This Scottish traditional singer was the youngest of five children of Donald Robertson and Maria Stewart. Her parents were both from tinker families, who would travel in caravans, selling goods from house to house during the summer, and then spend the winter living in Aberdeen. It was from her mother that Jeannie learned much of her repertoire. Robertson was 'discovered' in Aberdeen by Hamish Henderson in 1953, when it was apparent that she possessed an outstanding voice and capacity for story-telling. Riverside Records in the USA, were the first to offer a recording contact to Robertson. The recordings were made by Bill Leader, in April 1956, and featured a guitar accompaniment by the late Josh MacRae. *Songs Of A Scots Tinker Lady* was re-released in the UK in 1965 by Topic Records and retitled *Jeannie Robertson*. They also removed the accompanying guitar tracks. A series of EPs were issued in 1959 by Collector Records that included *The Gallowa' Hills*, *The Twa Brothers*, *I Know Where I'm Going* and *Jeannie's Merry Muse*. Robertson was awarded the MBE in 1968 for her services to traditional music, and continued singing up to her death in 1975.

● ALBUMS: *Songs Of A Scots Tinker Lady* (Riverside 1956) ★★★, *Lord Donald* (1959) ★★★★, *The Cuckoo's Nest* (1960) ★★★ *Jeannie Robertson, The World's Greatest Folksinger* (Prestige International 1961) ★★★, *Scotch Folk Songs* (Prestige International 1963) ★★★.

● COMPILATIONS: *The Queen Among The Heather* (Rounder 1998) ★★★★.

ROBEY, DON

b. 1 November 1903, Houston, Texas, USA, d. 16 June 1975, Houston, Texas, USA. Houston businessman and impresario Don Robey bought his nightclub, the Bronze Peacock, in 1945, and it soon became a centre for developing local talent as well as bringing in big names from across the country. Soon afterwards, he opened a record shop, which eventually became the base of operations for his Peacock Records, one of the first ever labels in the USA to have a black owner. Peacock developed as one of the most important R&B and gospel labels, featuring artists such as Clarence 'Gatemouth' Brown, Johnny Ace and Big Mama Thornton, as well as the Dixie Hummingbirds and Five Blind Boys. Robey then bought the Duke label from Memphis, which became another major outlet, especially for Bobby Bland and Junior Parker. Another label, Songbird, also issued gospel records for many years.

ROBINS

This Los Angeles, California, USA-based vocal group was formed in 1947. 'Ty' Terrell Leonard (b. 1930, Jackson, Mississippi, USA) and twins Billy (b. William Gene Richards, 11 November 1933, USA) and Roy Richards (b. 11 November 1933, USA, d. 18 October 1975, Orange City, California, USA) had originally sung together as the A-Sharp Trio, but changed their name to the Four Bluebirds with the addition of Bobby Nunn (b. Ulysses B. Nunn, 20 September 1925, Birmingham, Alabama, USA, d. 5 November 1986, Los Angeles, California, USA). This act hooked up with bandleader Johnny Otis, when they won second place at a talent contest at his club, The Barrelhouse. After recording a track with Otis and his orchestra for Excelsior Records, they changed their name to the Robins for an Aladdin Records session. Their first chart record, in 1950 for Savoy Records, was the mid-tempo 'If It's So, Baby' (number 10 R&B),

recorded with the Johnny Otis Orchestra. Its excellent ballad b-side, 'If I Didn't Love You So', received much more airplay in many areas. Otis also used the Robins to back his young prodigy, Little Esther, on the hit 'Double Crossing Blues' in 1950. The Savoy recordings were made in a bluesy modulated style of the period and did nothing to set apart the Robins from other groups. During 1950-52 the group recorded for Modern Records, RPM (as the Nic Nacs, with Mickey Champion as female lead vocalist), and Recorded In Hollywood without notable success. In 1953 the Robins, with the addition of tenor lead Grady Chapman, were signed to RCA Records and came under the production aegis of the up-and-coming songwriting team of Leiber And Stoller. Jerry Leiber and Mike Stoller began radically to transform the Robins into a proto-rock 'n' roll group with an exuberant beat-infected sound. No hits resulted on RCA, but in 1954, with a move to Leiber and Stoller's own Spark label, and with Carl Gardner (b. Carl Edward Gardner, 29 April 1928, Tyler, Texas, USA) having replaced the temporarily indisposed Grady Chapman, the Robins found success with 'Riot In Cell Block #9'. The song, which used the menacing bass of Richard Berry and machine-gun sound-effects, was one of the most controversial records of 1954. It sold well in California and a few other locales but failed to chart nationally because of poor distribution. The group successfully followed it with another regional hit, 'Framed' (1954), and in 1955 hit with 'Smokey Joe's Cafe'. Fast-rising independent Atlantic Records took notice of sales in California and assumed distribution, making it a national hit (number 10 R&B) on their Atco Records subsidiary. The Robins, however, split up, with Gardner and Nunn joining with Billy Guy and Leon Hughes to form the Coasters to record for Atlantic. Under the aegis of producers Leiber And Stoller, the Coasters flourished. The Robins, with newcomer and producer H.B. Barnum and Grady Chapman once more installed as main lead vocalist, continued to record, on Whippet and other labels, albeit unsuccessfully, until breaking up some time in the early 60s.

● ALBUMS: *Rock 'N' Roll With The Robins* (Whippet 1958) ★★★.

● COMPILATIONS: *The Roots Of Rock 'N Roll* collects their Savoy recordings (Savoy Jazz 1987) ★★★, *Cherry Lips* 1956-1961 recordings (Famous Grooves 1997) ★★★.

ROBINSON, BOBBY

Robinson opened a record shop in Harlem, New York City, USA, shortly after World War II, and became an authority on the music scene. His advice was sought by many independent labels. In November 1951 he formed his first record company, Robin Records – which swiftly became Red Robin Records when a southern independent of the same name threatened legal action. He began producing and releasing records by such artists as Morris Lane, Tiny Grimes and Wilbert 'Red' Prysock, but found greater success with the birth of the New York doo-wop groups, and such acts as the Mello Moods, Vocaleers and the Du Droppers. Red Robin was dissolved in 1956, but many more labels were to follow through to the 60s – Whirlin Disc, Fury, Fire, Fling, Enjoy and Everlast – mainly issuing classic vocal group numbers by acts such as the Channels, Velvets, Scarlets, Teenchords, the Delfonics and Gladys Knight And the Pips. These labels occasionally achieved success with single R&B stars such as Wilbert Harrison ('Kansas City'), Buster Brown ('Fannie Mae'), Bobby Marchan ('There Is Something On Your Mind'), Lee Dorsey ('Ya Ya'), Lightnin' Hopkins, Elmore James and King Curtis. In the early 70s Bobby Robinson started a new label, Front Page Records, and reactivated his Enjoy label.

ROBINSON, JESSIE MAE

b. Jessie Mae Booker, 1 October 1919, Call, Texas, USA, d. 26 October 1966. A songwriter whose compositions were recorded by the major R&B artists of the post-World War II era, Robinson was one of the few black songwriters to break the colour barrier, and wrote a number of hits for major pop stars of the 50s. She was raised in Los Angeles and there married Leonard Robinson. Among the many R&B hits composed by Jessie Mae Robinson were 'Old Maid Boogie' (Eddie Vinson, 1947), 'Blue Light Boogie' (Louis Jordan, 1950), 'Double Crossing Blues' (Little Esther And Johnny Otis, 1950), 'Black Night' (Charles Brown, 1951), 'Roomin' House Boogie' (Amos Milburn, 1949) and 'Sneakin' Around' (B.B. King, 1955). Robinson's most successful song, 'I Went To Your Wedding' (1952), launched her career in the pop market. The song was first recorded by Damita Jo And The Red Caps, and then Patti Page made it a number 1 pop hit. Other pop success came with Jo Stafford ('Keep It A Secret', 1952), Frankie Laine ('I'm Just A Poor Bachelor', 1953), and both Wanda Jackson and Elvis Presley ('Let's Have A Party', 1957). In the early 60s Robinson formed a couple of small record labels with notable lack of success.

ROCK 'N ROLL STAGE SHOW – BILL HALEY AND HIS COMETS

Although this album features studio recordings, it gives you an idea of what Bill Haley And His Comets sounded like on stage. Haley led a showband who just happened to find fame with rock 'n' roll. When they had success, he wanted the Comets to show their versatility and he did not mind if he was not the centre of attraction. There are instrumentals, notably 'Rudy's Rock', featuring Rudy Pompilli's sax, 'Goofin' Around' featuring Franny Beecher's lead guitar, and an old-style vocal number, 'Hey Then, There Now', with the Comets, who shortly afterwards left for the Jodimars. Accordionist Johnny Grande takes the lead vocal on 'A Rockin' Little Tune' and steel guitarist Billy Williamson takes lead vocals on 'Tonight's The Night' and 'Hide And Seek'. It all gives the impression that Bill Haley is making a guest appearance on his own record.
● Tracks: Calling All Comets; Rockin' Through The Rye; A Rockin' Little Tune; Hide And Seek; Hey Then, There Now; Goofin' Around; Hook, Line And Sinker; Rudy's Rock; Choo Choo Ch'boogie; Blue Comet Blues; Hot Dog, Buddy Buddy; Tonight's The Night.
● First released 1956
● UK peak chart position: did not chart
● USA peak chart position: 18

ROCK 'N' ROLL REVUE

Jazz and R&B performers were at the fore of this 1956 film, despite its grossly misleading title. Also known as Harlem Rock 'n' Roll, it was shot at New York's fabled Apollo Theatre. Lionel Hampton, Duke Ellington and Nat 'King' Cole headed a star-studded cast that also featured the Clovers, Joe Turner and Ruth Brown. Shot in sepia-inspired yellow and brown – known as Wondercolour – the film captures several performers at their peak and provides a fascinating insight into several acts inspiring, although not recording, rock 'n' roll. Curiously, the portion featuring Dinah Washington was cut from the UK print, but Rock 'n' Roll Revue remains a highly interesting feature.

ROCK AROUND THE CLOCK

Fred Sears directed this 1956 second feature, inspired by the reaction generated by Bill Haley And The Comets' contribution to The Blackboard Jungle. Although not seen on-screen, the group's recording of 'Rock Around The Clock' had been heard over the opening credits, provoking riots in cinemas. The same occurred when this film was screened, prompting several local authorities to ban it from municipal screens. The first feature wholly devoted to rock 'n' roll music, Rock Around The Clock cast Haley's group as a small-town act that a bank manager tries to turn into a national attraction, despite the efforts of a booking agent to sabotage his plans. The Comets naturally provide the lion's share of the material, including 'Rock-A-Beatin' Boogie', 'See You Later Alligator' and the title track. The Platters, Little Richard and Freddie Bell And His Bellboys are among the other acts included, as is disc jockey Alan Freed in the first of a string of roles in rock 'n' roll films. Although hardly innovatory in terms of plot or acting, for better or worse, Rock Around The Clock opened the doors for celluloid pop.

ROCK AROUND THE CLOCK – BILL HALEY AND HIS COMETS

Bill Haley was not an overnight success: he had been working as a country performer since the 40s and 'Rock Around The Clock' was his 28th single. He had even recorded rock 'n' roll before, but it was 'Rock Around The Clock', used in the film The Blackboard Jungle, that became the international teenage anthem. The only thing Haley dropped was his yodel – somewhat reluctantly, as he had been a champion yodeller in Indiana. 'Shake, Rattle And Roll' was an expurgated version of a R&B hit by 'Big' Joe Turner. Haley's perception of his audience can also be gleaned from 'Rock-a-beatin' Boogie', which, like many of his songs, seems intent on teaching his audience to spell.

● Tracks: *Rock Around The Clock; Shake, Rattle And Roll; ABC Boogie; Thirteen Women; Razzle-dazzle; Two Hound Dogs; Dim, Dim The Lights; Happy Baby; Birth Of The Boogie; Mambo Rock; Burn That Candle; Rock-a-beatin' Boogie.*
● First released 1956
● UK peak chart position: 34
● USA peak chart position: 12

ROCK ROCK ROCK
Manifestly another formula 'quickie' made to cash in on rock 'n' roll, *Rock Rock Rock* nonetheless contains several points of interest to pop historians. This 1957 film, reportedly shot in two weeks, starred Tuesday Weld as the girlfriend of an aspiring entrepreneur who organizes a concert. Famed disc jockey Alan Freed makes an obligatory appearance – herein leading an 18-piece band – but *Rock Rock Rock* is notable for the acts it enshrines. Frankie Lymon And The Teenagers offer the memorable 'I'm Not A Juvenile Delinquent', while doo-wop acts the Flamingos and Moonglows perform 'Would I Be Crying' and 'Over And Over Again', respectively. Chuck Berry makes his celluloid debut with 'You Can't Catch Me' and vibrant rockabilly act the Johnny Burnette Trio roar through 'Lonesome Train' in what was their only appearance on film. LaVern Baker, the Three Chuckles and the Bowties are among the others on offer. Ms. Weld contributes 'I Never Had A Sweetheart' and 'Little Blue Wren', but her 'voice' was provided by the then-unknown Connie Francis. Much of the material aired in *Rock Rock Rock* was released by the Chess label, who advertised the set as the first rock soundtrack album. Although failing to break new ground as far as plot and style were concerned, the film showcases several seminal acts at the height of their creative powers.

ROCK-A-BYE BABY
Frank Tashlin, who directed the seminal rock film *The Girl Can't Help It*, took charge of this 1958 feature. It starred comedian Jerry Lewis, former partner of Dean Martin, who excelled in zany, 'misfit' roles, notably *The Nutty Professor*. In *Rock-A-Bye Baby* he plays a nanny, responsible for a film star's triplets, who finds time to satirize rock 'n' roll and US television. The film is largely forgettable, although Lewis does perform a duet, 'In The Land Of La La La', with his 12-year-old son, Gary. In the following decade, Gary Lewis became a pop star in his own right as leader of Gary Lewis And The Playboys, who enjoyed a number 1 US hit with 'This Diamond Ring', following it with six further Top 10 entries.

ROCKABILLY
The derivation of the term rockabilly comes from the classification US trade papers employed to identify rock 'n' roll music that originated in rural (hillbilly) areas. Only later in the 50s did it come to symbolize a specific type of music – generally, basic rock 'n' roll mixed with country and bluegrass roots, with an emphasis on acoustic instruments. Elvis Presley is widely cited as its main popularizer, but Dale Hawkins, Sonny Burgess and Carl Perkins are better examples of artists who remained within the tradition. Country artists such as Roy Orbison and Johnny Cash also flourished from a starting point in rockabilly, but many of the 'true' rockabilly stars remained largely anonymous, except to their devotees in the USA and UK. The Beatles recorded Perkins' 'Matchbox' and 'Honey Don't', but rockabilly never truly escaped its public perception of being 'backward' music. Chart success was rare – though Hank Mizell's 'Jungle Rock' did reach number 3 in the UK charts in 1976. Typically, this came many years after its initial recording, and its popularity was largely prompted by the proliferation of 'Teddy Boy' rocker cults during the period. Ironically, the Teds' sworn enemies, punk rockers, would flock to see the Clash perform updated rockabilly material such as 'Brand New Cadillac', while in America the Cramps created a similar hybrid. It took New York trio the Stray Cats to bring about a popular revival of the form in the early 80s, accompanied by UK bands Matchbox and the Polecats. By the late 80s and early 90s, labels such as Ace Records had begun to repackage rare 45s from the golden era of rockabilly as further evidence of the form's overlooked musical vitality. UK broadcaster Mark Lamarr has also done much to keep this overlooked music alive on his late night radio programme on BBC Radio 2, especially by playing some lesser known material.

ROCKETONES
The Rocketones were an R&B group started at Junior High School in Brooklyn, New York, USA. Bill Witt (lead), Allen Days (first tenor), Ronald Johnson (second tenor), Harold Chapman (baritone) and Arthur Blackman (bass) originally titled themselves the Avalons, and practised hard to perfect their vocal blend. After numerous attempts the group finally found a sympathetic hearing at Melba Records, who signed the band in 1956. However, it took some time before their sole single, 'Mexico'/'Dee I', was released, and when it was they discovered Melba Records' boss Marty Croft had credited the band as the Rocketones. With its distinctive bull-fighting intro, 'Mexico' proved popular on New York radio, but was never followed up. Both Days and Johnson were later drafted while Witt joined the Paragons. The Rocketones' solitary recording is now something of a legend in doo-wop nostalgia circles.

RODGERS, JIMMIE
b. James Frederick Rodgers, 18 September 1933, Camus, Washington, USA. After being taught by his mother, the young Rodgers successfully auditioned for the Arthur Godfrey talent show and impressed Luigi Creatore and Hugo Peretti who signed him to their recently formed Roulette Records. Rodgers' creamy, effortless voice and blend of folk-tinged pop appealed to a post-war middle America, and over the next decade he

made the *Billboard* singles chart 25 times. He never, however, topped his debut, 'Honeycomb', which stayed at number 1 for four weeks in 1957 (number 30 in the UK). His early successes included 'Kisses Sweeter Than Wine' a Top 3 hit in 1957 which vied with Frankie Vaughan in the UK for the best position (Rodgers number 7, Vaughan number 8).

One of Rodgers' most memorable songs was the innocent but catchy 'English Country Garden', which, although it became his biggest UK hit (reaching the Top 5 in 1962), did not appear to warrant an American release, possibly because of its parochial title. Rodgers was the victim of a serious mugging in 1967 that left him with a fractured skull. Although he eventually returned to performing full-time, his career had lost its momentum. He was still singing professionally in the late 80s.

● ALBUMS: *Jimmie Rodgers* (Roulette 1957) ★★★★, *The Long Hot Summer* film soundtrack (Roulette 1958) ★★, *Number One Ballads* (Roulette 1958) ★★★, *Sings Folk Songs* (Roulette 1958) ★★★★, *His Golden Year* (Roulette 1959) ★★★, *TV Favorites* (Roulette 1959) ★★★, *Twilight On The Trail* (Roulette 1959) ★★★, *It's Christmas Once Again* (Roulette 1959) ★★★, *When The Spirit Moves You* (Roulette 1960) ★★★, *At Home With Jimmie Rodgers* (Roulette 1960) ★★★, *The Folk Song World Of Jimmie Rodgers* (Roulette 1961) ★★★★, *15 Million Sellers* (Roulette 1962) ★★★, *Folk Songs* (Roulette 1963) ★★★★, *Its Over* (Dot 1966) ★★★, *Child Of Clay* (A&M 1968) ★★, *Windmills Of Your Mind* (A&M 1969) ★★, *This Is Jimmie Rodgers* (1987) ★★.

● COMPILATIONS: *The Best Of Jimmie Rodgers Folk Songs* (Roulette 1961) ★★★, *Best Of Jimmie Rodgers* (MCA 1988) ★★★, *Kisses Sweeter Than Wine* (Pickwick 1988) ★★★, *The Very Best Of 1957-1962* (Westside 1998) ★★★.

RODGERS, RICHARD

b. 28 June 1902, Hammells Station, Arverne, Long Island, New York, USA, d. 30 December 1979, New York, USA. One of the all-time great composers for the musical theatre, Rodgers was raised in a comfortable middle-class family and developed an early love of music. Encouraged by his parents, he was able to pick out a tune on the piano at the age of four, and wrote his first songs, 'Campfire Days' and 'Auto Show Girl' (lyric: David Dyrenforth), when he was 14. Many years later, when he was asked what he had done before he began composing music, he is supposed to have said: 'I was a baby.' In 1919, Rodgers was introduced to the lyricist Lorenz Hart, and they collaborated on the scores for two well-received Columbia University Varsity shows, *Fly With Me* and *You'll Never Know*, and on songs for other productions, such as the Broadway musicals *A Lonely Romeo* (1919, 'Any Old Place With You') and *Poor Little Ritz Girl* (1920). The early 20s presented few further opportunities, and a frustrated Rodgers was contemplating taking a job as a wholesaler in the baby-wear business, when, in 1925, he and Hart were asked to write the score for a benefit show in aid of the Theatre Guild, the prestigious theatrical production organization. The resulting revue, *The Garrick Gaieties*, was so successful that it began a commercial run that lasted for 211 performances. Rodgers and Hart's lively and amusing score included the charming 'Sentimental Me' as well as one of their most enduring standards, 'Manhattan'.

A second edition of the *Gaieties* in 1926, featured another of the songwriters' brightest and inventive numbers, 'Mountain Greenery', which was associated in later years with the distinguished jazz singer Mel Tormé. From this point, Rodgers and Hart were off and running, and during the next few years, wrote some of their most romantic and innovative songs for a series of musical shows that met with varying degrees of success. They included *Dearest Enemy* (1925, 'Here In My Arms'), *The Girl Friend* (1926, 'The Blue Room', 'The Girl Friend'), *Lido Lady* (London 1926, 'Try Again Tomorrow'), *Peggy-Ann* (1926, 'Where's That Rainbow?', 'A Tree In The Park'), *Betsy* (a 39 performance flop in 1926, 'This Funny World'), *One Dam Thing After Another* (London 1927, 'My Heart Stood Still'), *A Connecticut Yankee* (1927, 'Thou Swell', 'On A Desert Island With Thee!', 'Nothing's Wrong'), *She's My Baby* (1928, 'You're What I Need'), *Present Arms!* (1928, 'You Took Advantage Of Me', 'A Kiss For Cinderella'), *Chee-Chee* (a 31-performance flop in 1928, 'Better Be Good to Me'), *Lady Fingers* (1929, 'I Love You More Than Yesterday'), *Spring Is Here* (1929, 'With A Song In My Heart', 'Why Can't I?', 'Baby's Awake Now'), *Heads Up!* (1929, 'A Ship Without A Sail'), *Simple Simon* ('Ten Cents A Dance', 'He Was Too Good To Me'), and *Ever Green* (London 1930, 'Dancing On The Ceiling', 'No Place But Home', 'The Colour Of Her Eyes'). When the team wrote the optimistic 'I've Got Five Dollars' for Ann Sothern and Jack Whiting to sing in *America's Sweetheart* in 1931, the USA was in the middle of the Depression.

Although more than 20 new musicals were being produced each season on Broadway, Rodgers and Hart's previous five shows had been relatively unsuccessful, and they spent much of the early 30s in Hollywood writing some memorable songs for early film musicals such as *The Hot Heiress* (1931, 'You're The Cats'), *Love Me Tonight* (1932, 'Isn't It Romantic?', 'Mimi', 'Lover'), *The Phantom President* (1932, 'Give Her A Kiss'), *Hallelujah, I'm A Bum* (1933, 'You Are Too Beautiful'), *Hollywood Party* (1934, 'Hello'), *Nana* (1934, 'That's Love'), and *Mississippi* (1935, 'It's Easy To Remember', 'Soon', 'Down By The River'). They also contributed a song called 'The Bad In Every Man' (previously known as 'Prayer') to the Oscar-winning screen thriller *Manhattan Melodrama*. After Hart wrote a new lyric, it was retitled 'Blue Moon', and became one of their biggest hits. That song, alongside many of their other successful numbers, was featured in the 1948 biopic *Words And Music*, in which Rodgers was played by Tom Drake and Hart by Mickey Rooney.

Rodgers and Hart returned to New York in 1935, and embarked on a body of work that surpassed even their previous achievements. *Jumbo* (1935), with a score containing three outstanding numbers, 'My Romance', 'Little Girl Blue' and 'The Most Beautiful Girl In The World', was followed by the splendid *On Your Toes* (1936, 'Glad To Be Unhappy', 'There's A Small Hotel', 'Too Good For The Average Man', 'Slaughter On Tenth Avenue'), *Babes In Arms* (1937, 'I Wish I Were In Love Again', 'The Lady Is A Tramp', 'My Funny Valentine', 'Where Or When', 'Johnny One Note'), *I'd Rather Be Right* (1937, 'Have You Met Miss Jones?'), *I Married An Angel* (1938, 'Spring Is Here', 'I Married An Angel', 'At The Roxy Music Hall'), *The Boys From Syracuse* (1938, 'Falling In Love With Love', 'This Can't Be Love', 'Sing For Your Supper', 'You Have Cast Your Shadow On The Sea'), *Too Many Girls* (1939, 'I Didn't Know What Time It Was', 'Give It Back To The Indians', 'I Like To Recognize The Tune', 'You're Nearer'), *Higher And Higher* (1940, 'It Never Entered My Mind'), *Pal Joey* ('Bewitched', 'I Could Write A Book', 'Den Of Iniquity') and *By Jupiter* (1942, 'Wait Till You See Her', 'Nobody's Heart', 'Careless Rhapsody'). *Pal Joey*, in particular, was regarded as a landmark in Broadway history, partly because it was the first musical in which the leading character, played by Gene Kelly, was a villain – an anti-hero. Rodgers and Hart's final work together was probably on the songs for a revised production of their 1927 hit, *A Connecticut Yankee*, which contained the witty 'To Keep My Love Alive'. By the time that show opened on 3 November 1943, Hart's physical condition, which had been worsening for several years, had deteriorated to such an extent that he was unable to work, and he died some two weeks later.

In the previous year, Rodgers had been asked by the Theatre Guild to write the score for what eventually became *Oklahoma!* (1943). With Hart unavailable, he began a collaboration with Oscar Hammerstein II that produced some of the biggest blockbusters in the (pre-Andrew Lloyd Webber) history of the musical theatre. Marvellous songs such as 'Oh, What A Beautiful Mornin'', 'People Will Say We're In Love', 'The Surrey With The Fringe On Top', and the rousing title number, were cleverly integrated into the story, and *Oklahoma!* won a special Pulitzer Prize, and ran for 2,212 performances in New York. Next came the magnificent *Carousel* (1945, 'If I Loved You', 'June Is Bustin' Out All Over', 'What's The Use Of Wond'rin'', 'You'll Never Walk Alone', 'Soliloquy'), which is often regarded as Rodgers and Hammerstein's best score. Also in 1945, the partners wrote their only original film score for the highly popular *State Fair*, which featured the exuberant 'It's A Grand Night For Singing' and the lovely ballad 'It Might As Well Be Spring'. Back on Broadway, the uncharacteristic *Allegro* (1947, 'A Fellow Needs A Girl', 'The Gentleman Is A Dope'), complete with its Greek chorus, was a disappointment. However, there were more triumphs just around the corner in the shape of *South Pacific* (1949, 'I'm Gonna Wash That Man

Right Outa My Hair', 'Bali Ha'i', 'Some Enchanted Evening', 'This Nearly Was Mine', 'There Is Nothing Like A Dame'), which ran for nearly five years and won the Pulitzer Prize for Drama, and *The King And I* (1951, 'Hello, Young Lovers', 'I Have Dreamed', 'Shall We Dance?', 'We Kiss In A Shadow', 'Getting To Know You').

In 1952, Richard Rodgers wrote the music for the NBC documentary television series *Victory At Sea*, for which he was awarded the US Navy's Distinguished Public Service Medal. A musical theme from one of the episodes entitled 'Beyond The Southern Cross', attracted a great deal of interest, and Rodgers used it, with a lyric by Hammerstein, as a part of the score for their next Broadway show, *Me And Juliet* (1953). The song was called 'No Other Love', and featured again in television and stage versions of *Cinderella*. Neither *Me And Juliet*, or Rodgers and Hammerstein's Broadway follow-up, *Pipe Dream* (1955, 'All At Once You Love Her', 'The Next Time It Happens'), are considered to be among their best work. Nor, for that matter, is *Flower Drum Song* ('I Enjoy Being A Girl', 'Sunday', 'Love, Look Away'), but the show did endure for 602 performances, and was still running when the final Rodgers and Hammerstein smash hit, *The Sound Of Music* ('Climb Ev'ry Mountain', 'Edelweiss', 'Do-Re-Mi', 'My Favourite Things', 'The Sound Of Music') opened in November 1959 and ran for nearly three and a half years in New York, and more than five and a half in London. The film versions of this and several other Rodgers and Hammerstein shows were among the highest-grossing movie musicals of the 50s and 60s. Less than a year after *The Sound Of Music* opened, Hammerstein was dead. Rodgers subsequently contributed five new songs (music and lyrics) to the 1962 remake of *State Fair*, and wrote the complete score for the Broadway musical *No Strings* ('The Sweetest Sounds'), which ran for 580 performances. For his work on that show he won a Tony Award for Outstanding Composer, and a Grammy for the Original Cast album.

From then on, apart from providing both words and music for a US television adaptation of *Androcles And The Lion* (1967), starring Noël Coward and Norman Wisdom, for the remainder of his career Rodgers worked with established lyricists. These included Stephen Sondheim (in 1965 for *Do I Hear A Waltz?*, 'We're Gonna Be All Right', 'Do I Hear A Waltz'), Martin Charnin (in 1970 for *Two By Two*, 'I Do Not Know A Day I Did Not Love You'), Sheldon Harnick (in 1976 for *Rex*), and Martin Charnin (in 1979 for *I Remember Mama*). When he was working on the last two shows, which were both dismal failures at the box office, Rodgers was a sick man, and he died in December 1979. The emotionally uplifting and often witty and sophisticated melodies he left behind – written in collaboration with two supremely gifted, but temperamentally opposite partners – played an important part in the development of American's own indigenous popular music, and in the acceptance of the musical as an important and respected art form. His honours included special Tonys in 1962 and 1972, a Trustee Grammy Award, and the 1979 Lawrence Langner Award for Distinguished Lifetime Achievement in the Theatre. In 1993, on the 50th anniversary of the birth of his second momentous partnership, a celebratory revue entitled *A Grand Night For Singing*, which was crammed with Rodgers and Hammerstein's songs, was presented in New York.

Richard Rodgers' elder daughter, Mary Rodgers (b. 11 January 1931, New York, USA), enjoyed substantial success in the musical theatre with her music for *Once Upon A Mattress* (1959). Earlier, she had studied harmony and counterpoint and written numerous songs for children's records. Rodgers collaborated with lyricist and librettist Marshall Barer on *Once Upon A Mattress*, which was based on the fairytale *The Princess And The Pea*. It ran for 216 performances off-Broadway, and a further 244 at Broadway's Alvin Theatre. Her next effort on Broadway was a musical about the Peace Corps, *Hot Spot* (1963), which had lyrics by Martin Charnin. It folded rapidly, in spite of the presence in the cast of Judy Holliday. Rodgers worked with Barer again in 1966 on *The Mad Show*, which was inspired by the immensely popular *Mad* magazine. The *Mad Show* stayed at the New Theatre, off-Broadway, for 871 performances, and included one song that Rodgers wrote with Stephen Sondheim, entitled 'The Boy From', which mocked the worldwide bossa nova hit, 'The Girl From Ipanema'. In 1978 Rodgers contributed material to the New York musical *Working*, along with others such as Stephen Schwartz, and has also been involved with several projects that were not developed. One that was developed, however, was *The Griffin And The Minor Canon*, which was described as 'a folk tale about the bonding friendship between the last griffin on earth and a minor church official in a small French village.' It had a book by Wendy Kesselman and lyrics by Ellen Fitzhugh, and was presented at Stockbridge, Massachusetts, in August 1988. Over the years, Rodgers has also written several children's books, including the classic teen novel *Freaky Friday*. She later adapted it into a movie and a children's musical.

In 1993, the revue *Hey, Love: The Songs Of Mary Rodgers*, played at Eighty-Eight's in New York. The show, named after a song from *Hot Spot*, was conceived and directed by Richard Maltby Jnr. It contained some of his lyrics, and those of Martin Charnin, Marshall Barer, John Forster, Stephen Sondheim and William Shakespeare.

● ALBUMS: *Mary Martin Sings Richard Rodgers Plays* (1958) ★★★.

● FURTHER READING: *Musical Stages: His Autobiog-raphy*, Richard Rodgers. *Rodgers & Hart: Bewitched, Bothered And Bedevilled*, Samuel Marx and Jay Clayton. *With A Song In His Heart*, David Ewen. *The Rodgers And Hammerstein Story*, Stanley Green. *The Sound Of Their Music: The Story Of Rodgers And Hammerstein*, Frederick Nolan. *Richard Rodgers*, William G. Hyland.

ROGER, ROGER

b. 5 August 1911, Rouen, France, d. 12 June 1995. One of the most prolific composer/conductors to contribute scores to numerous French radio, television and film productions. Roger calculated that he had made over 2,000 recordings, half of which were his own compositions. He also claimed to have worked on 500 French films, many shown overseas. Roger's father, Edmond Roger (who gave his son the same christian name as his surname to satisfy a personal whim) was a well-known conductor of opera, and a friend of Claude Debussy. He encouraged his son into the music profession, and arranged for him to conduct his first five-man orchestra at the age of 18 in a small French music hall. This encouraged him to work with singers, and develop his arranging skills. Roger contributed works to many mood music publishers, notably Chappells of London, for whom he wrote 'New Town', 'Paris Fashions', 'The Toy Shop Window', 'Holiday Party', 'Clowneries', 'Along The Avenue', and 'City Movement' (used in the 60s BBC television soap *Compact*). His style of background music made it particularly suitable for situations such as television test card transmissions.

● ALBUMS: *Musique Aux 4 Vents* (Pacific) ★★★, *Tourbillon de Paris* (Mode/Vogue) ★★, *American Flavour* (Pacific) ★★★, *Varietes Pour Tous* (Vega) ★★★, *Roger Roger* (MGM) ★★★.

ROGERS, JIMMY

b. James A. Lane, 3 June 1924, Ruleville, Mississippi, USA, d. 19 December 1997, Chicago, Illinois, USA. Self-taught on both harmonica and guitar, Rogers began working at local house parties in his early teens. He then followed an itinerant path, performing in Mississippi and St. Louis, before moving to Chicago in 1939. Rogers frequently took work outside of music, but having played for tips on the city's famed Maxwell Street, began appearing in several clubs and bars. Although he worked as an accompanist with pianist Sunnyland Slim, Rogers established his reputation with the Muddy Waters Band, with whom he remained until 1960. The guitarist contributed to many of urban blues' finest performances, including 'Hoochie Coochie Man', 'I Got My Mojo Workin'' and the seminal *Muddy Waters At Newport*. Rogers also enjoyed a moderately successful career in his own right. 'That's All Right' (1950), credited to Jimmy Rogers And His Trio, featured Waters, Little Walter (harmonica) and Big Crawford (bass), and its popularity around the Chicago area engendered a new group, Jimmy Rogers And His Rocking Four.

Several more sessions ensued over the subsequent decade, but the guitarist only enjoyed one national R&B hit when 'Walking By Myself' reached number 14 in 1957. By the 60s Rogers found himself eclipsed by a new generation of guitarists, including Buddy Guy and Magic Sam. Despite enjoying work supporting John Lee 'Sonny Boy' Williamson and Howlin' Wolf, he spent much of the decade in seclusion and only re-emerged during the blues revival of the early

70s. He was signed to Leon Russell's Shelter Records label for whom he completed *Gold Tailed Bird*, a low-key but highly satisfying set. It inspired a period of frenetic live activity which saw Rogers tour Europe on two occasions, with the American Folk Blues Festival (1972) and the Chicago Blues Festival (1973). Appearances in the USA were also well received, but the artist retired from music during the middle of the decade to work as the manager of an apartment building. However, Rogers rejoined Muddy Waters on *I'm Ready* (1978), one of the excellent selections recorded under the aegis of Johnny Winter. These releases brought Waters new dignity towards the end of his career and invested Rogers with a new found confidence. He continued to perform on the contemporary blues circuit and his 1990 release, *Ludella*, named after the artist's guitar, was produced by Kim Wilson from the Fabulous Thunderbirds. *Blue Bird* was a raw Chicago blues album featuring Carey Bell on harmonica, his son, Jimmy D. Lane, on lead guitar and Johnnie Johnson (piano). Following his death the excellent *Blues Blues Blues* was released.

● ALBUMS: *Gold Tailed Bird* (Shelter 1971) ★★★★, *That's All Right* i (1974) ★★★, *Live: Jimmy Rogers* (JSP 1982) ★★★, *Feelin' Good* (Blind Pig 1985) ★★★, *Dirty Dozens* (JSP 1985) ★★★, *Ludella* (Bedrock 1990) ★★★, *Blue Bird* (Analogue Productions 1994) ★★★★, with Rod Piazza *Feelin' Good* (Blind Pig 1995) ★★★, various artists as the Jimmy Rogers All-Stars *Blues Blues Blues* (Atlantic 1999) ★★★★.

● COMPILATIONS: *Chicago Bound*, *Golden Years* (Vogue 1976) ★★★, *Chess Masters* (Chess 1982) ★★★★, *Chicago Blues* (JSP 1982) ★★★, *That's All Right* ii (Charly 1989) ★★★, *Jimmy Rogers Sings The Blues* (Sequel 1990) ★★★, *Hard Working Man* (Charly 1992) ★★★★, *Chicago Blues Masters* (Capitol 1996) ★★★, *Chicago Blues Masters, Volume 2* (Capitol 1996) ★★★★, *The Complete Chess Recordings* (Chess/MCA 1997) ★★★★.

ROLAND, GENE

b. 15 September 1921, Dallas, Texas, USA, d. 11 August 1982, New York City, New York, USA. In the early 40s many of Roland's arrangements played an important part in establishing the success of the Stan Kenton band. Among his arrangements was the June Christy hit, 'Tampico'. During this period he sometimes played trumpet in the band, later switching to trombone. Generally credited with Jimmy Giuffre as co-creator of the 'Four Brothers' sound of the Woody Herman band, Roland arranged for and played piano with Stan Getz, Giuffre (with whom he had studied at North Texas State Teachers' College, forerunner of NTSU), Herbie Steward and Zoot Sims in a small group that was heard by Herman in 1947. Later in the 40s Roland played in the bands of Georgie Auld, Count Basie, Charlie Barnet and Lucky Millinder, sometimes on trumpet, at other times on trombone. He tried his hand at bandleading in 1950 with an adventurous but ill-fated bebop big band which featured Charlie Parker, Don Fagerquist, Red Rodney, Jimmy

Knepper, Sims and Al Cohn. In the 50s he again wrote for Kenton and Herman, helping to create the former's 'mellophonium band'. During the 60s Roland worked in Scandinavia, writing and directing a radio orchestra, and in the 70s, back in the USA, he continued to write challenging big band charts and to play on a variety of instruments.

● ALBUMS: *Jazzville – Volume 4* (Dawn 1958) ★★★, *Swingin' Friends* (Brunswick 1963) ★★★.

ROME, HAROLD

b. 27 May 1908, Hartford, Connecticut, USA, d. 26 October 1993, New York, USA. While still attending school Rome played piano in local dance bands and was already writing music. Despite this early interest in music, he went on to study architecture and law at Yale. In 1934 he practised as an architect in New York City, but studied piano and composition in his spare time. This was a fortunate decision because by the following year, with work opportunities diminishing with the Depression, he was obliged to turn more and more to his second string activity for support. Much of the music Rome was writing at this time was socially conscious and was thus of little interest to Tin Pan Alley. Nevertheless, he was engaged to write a revue for the International Garment Workers' Union. To everyone's surprise, the revue, *Pins And Needles* (1937), staged for members of the union, became a popular success and one song, 'Sunday In The Park', established a life outside of the show. Rome was now much sought-after, although his next show displayed similarly political concerns. This was *Sing Out The News* (1939) and, once again, there was a universally accepted hit song, 'F.D.R. Jones'. In the early 40s Rome wrote songs for several revues and shows, but it was not until after the end of World War II that he had his first major success. This was *Call Me Mister* (1946), from which came 'South America, Take It Away'. More revues followed until his first fully fledged musical show, *Wish You Were Here*, in 1952. Two years later he wrote *Fanny*, his most popular Broadway show, which included 'Love Is A Very Light Thing'. This was followed by *Destry Rides Again* (1959) and *I Can Get It For You Wholesale* (1962), in which Barbra Streisand made her Broadway debut. In the mid-60s Rome showed that the social conscience that had marked his early work was still intact when he wrote *The Zulu And The Zayda* (1965), which dealt with racial and religious intolerance. In 1970 he wrote *Scarlett*, based upon the novel *Gone With The Wind*, for a Japanese production in Tokyo. More than with any other American composer in the field of mainstream popular music, Rome's work consistently demonstrated an awareness of social issues, often to the extent that it kept him from the massive successes enjoyed by many of his contemporaries. He was also a gifted painter and a dedicated art collector.

RONALD AND RUBY

Ronald was teenage singer Ronald Gumby and Ruby was Beverly Ross (b. 1939, New Jersey,

USA), his singing partner. Ross, who had already penned a hit for Bill Haley And His Comets ('Dim, Dim The Lights'), wrote a song in 1958 called 'Lollipop' and the pair, renamed Ronald and Ruby by their manager, recorded it for RCA-Victor. The irritating repeated lyric 'lollipop, lollipop ooh lolly lolly lolly' was hummed by millions over the next few months. The Chordettes immediately covered the song for Cadence Records, and that group's version outsold Ronald And Ruby's; the pair's rendition reached number 20 in the US charts while the Chordettes' made it to number 2 (in the UK the Mudlarks took it to number 2). Ross went on to become a successful songwriter; among her credits were Roy Orbison's 'Candy Man', Lesley Gore's 'Judy's Turn To Cry' and the Earls' 'Remember Then'. Ronald And Ruby never recorded an album and the act disintegrated after their initial hit.

ROS, EDMUNDO

b. 7 December 1910, Port of Spain, Trinidad. The leader of one of the most popular – if not the most popular – Latin American band in the UK for many years, spent his early life in Venezuela, before attending the Military Academy at Caracas, where, via the Academy's band, he became interested in music and learned to play the euphonium or 'bombardin'. Despite harbouring ambitions to study criminal law, he travelled to the UK in 1937 and studied composition and harmony at the Royal Academy of Music. Although he recorded with jazzman Fats Waller in 1938, Ros mainly sang and served as a percussionist with various Latin-styled bands, including one led by pianist Don Marino Barretto. He formed his own five-piece unit, Rumba With Ros, in 1940, and for the next 35 years, played and recorded with groups such as Ros' Rumba Romeos, his Rumba Band, and Edmundo Ros and his Orchestra. After making his London debut at the New Cosmos Club and St. Regis Hotel, he played all the smartest nightspots, including the Bagatelle, before opening his own Edmundo Ros Club, on the site of the Coconut Grove, in 1949.

By then, with his gently rhythmic style and engaging vocals, he was enormously popular with the public generally, and a favourite of London's high society and some members of the Royal Family. Earlier in his career, he had decided that the best way to introduce complex Latin rhythms to his audiences would be to apply them to popular and familiar songs, and throughout the 40s and 50s, on radio and records, he had great success with numbers such as 'Enjoy Yourself', 'Melodie D'Amour', 'Tico Tico', 'I Got The Sun In The Morning', 'South America, Take It Away', ' I'm Crazy For You', 'Her Bathing Suit Never Got Wet', 'The Coffee Song', 'No Can Do', 'The Maharajah Of Magador', his theme, 'The Cuban Love Song', and especially 'The Wedding Samba', which was also a hit in the USA in 1949, although he was not allowed to perform there because of Musicians' Union regulations. His music was in demand in many other parts of the world too, particularly in Japan.

In the early 60s, he collaborated on an album with Ted Heath that exploited the relatively new stereo recording process. The shift in musical tastes during the decade affected Ros' standing but he played on into the 70s. Disillusioned with the business, he disbanded in 1975, and, so he says, destroyed most of the bands' arrangements, keeping just one set in case he received an offer he could not refuse. He retired to Spain, emerging occasionally for events such as his 80th birthday celebrations in 1990, and to introduce a series of record programmes for BBC Radio in 1992. Two years later, he joined another veteran musical personality, Stanley Black, in a 'Latin Reunion' at London's Royal Festival Hall. Often the butt of jokes by the musical élite, he was gently satirized by the Bonzo Dog Doo-Dah Band in 'Look Out There's A Monster Coming'.

● ALBUMS: *Calypsos* (Decca 1956) ★★★, *Mambos* (Decca 1956) ★★★, *Rhythms Of The South* (Decca 1957) ★★★, *Calypso Man* (Decca 1958) ★★★, *Perfect For Dancing* (Decca 1958) ★★★, *Ros On Broadway* (Decca 1959) ★★★, *Hollywood Cha Cha Cha* (Decca 1959) ★★★, *Bongos From The South* (Decca 1961) ★★★, *Dance Again* (Decca 1962) ★★★, *Sing And Dance With Edmundo Ros* (Decca 1963) ★★★, with Ted Heath *Heath Versus Ros* (Phase 4 1964) ★★★, with Heath *Heath Versus Ros, Round Two* (Phase 4 1967) ★★, *This Is My World* (Decca 1972) ★★★, *Ros Remembers* (Decca 1974) ★★★, *Edmundo Ros Today* (Decca 1978) ★★★, *Latin Favourites* (Gold Crown 1979) ★★★, *Latin Song And Dance Men* (Pye 1980) ★★★, *Music For The Millions* (Decca 1983) ★★★, *Strings Latino* (London 1985) ★★★, *Cuban Love Song* (1985) ★★★, *Latin Magic* (London 1987) ★★★, *Edmundo Ros & His Rumba Band, 1939-1941* (1992) ★★★, *That Latin Sound* (Pulse 1997) ★★★.

ROSE, DAVID

b. 15 June 1910, London, England, d. 23 August, 1990, Burbank, California, USA. A distinguished orchestra leader, composer, and arranger in the 40s and 50s, Rose was taken to the USA when he was just four-years-old. After graduating from the Chicago College of Music at the age of 16, he joined Ted Fio Rito's dance band, and three years later became a pianist/arranger/conductor for NBC Radio. In 1936 he provided the arrangement for Benny Goodman's big hit 'It's Been So Long', before moving to Hollywood, where he formed his own orchestra in 1938 for the Mutual Broadcasting System, and featured on the programme *California Melodies*. In the same year Rose married comedienne/singer Martha Raye and backed her on her hit record 'Melancholy Mood'. The marriage was later dissolved, and, after meeting Judy Garland when she was appearing on Bob Hope's radio show, he became the first of her five husbands from 1941 until 1945. During military service in World War II Rose was composer/conductor for the Army/Air Force morale-boosting stage musical *Winged Victory*, which was filmed in 1944. In 1943 he had a big hit with his own composition 'Holiday For Strings' and, a year later, with 'Poinciana (Song Of The Tree)'. By the late 40s he was a regular on Red Skelton's radio show, moving with him into television. He later wrote scores and themes for over 20 television series and won Emmy awards for his 14 year stint on *Bonanza*, 10 years with *Little House On The Prairie* and his work on three much-acclaimed Fred Astaire specials, beginning with *An Evening With Fred Astaire* in 1959.

Rose began working in movies in 1941, and is credited with scoring 36 films through to the 60s including *Texas Carnival* (1951), *Rich, Young And Pretty* (1951), *Everything I Have Is Yours* (1952), *Operation Petticoat* (1959), *Please Don't Eat The Daisies* (1960) and *Never Too Late* (1965). He received an Oscar nomination for his song 'So In Love', with a lyric by Leo Robin, which was featured in the 1944 Danny Kaye movie *Wonder Man*. His other compositions included 'Our Waltz' (which he is said to have written for Judy Garland), 'Dance Of The Spanish Onion', 'Manhattan Square Dance', 'Deserted City', 'Holiday For Trombones', 'Rose Of Bel-Air', 'Holiday For Flutes', 'Four Twenty AM', 'Waltz Of The Bubbles', 'Like Young', 'Taco Holiday', 'The Tiny Ballerina', 'Gay Spirits', 'Parade Of The Clowns', 'The Christmas Tree' (familiar to millions of Americans through its traditional use each Yuletide on *The Red Skelton Show*), and a collection of 32 piano solos entitled *Music For Moderns*. After chart success with 'Calypso Melody' in 1957 and his accompaniment for the Connie Francis 1959 hit 'My Happiness', Rose had a worldwide smash hit in 1962 with another of his own tunes, a humorous and satirical piece called 'The Stripper', which was written for a television show called *Burlesque*, starring Dan Dailey. Naturally, it was included on *The Stripper And Other Fun Songs For The Family*, which reached number 3 in the US album chart in 1962. Among Rose's other reported 50 or so albums, were the best-selling *Like Young* and *Like Blue*, recorded with André Previn. Apart from his record, film and television work, Rose was guest conductor with several symphony orchestras. His 'Concerto For Flute And Orchestra' was first played by the Los Angeles Philharmonic Orchestra and later by the Boston Pops.

● ALBUMS: *Autumn Leaves* (MGM 1957) ★★★★, *Gigi* (1958) ★★★, *Jamaica* (1958) ★★★, *Reflections In The Water* (MGM 1958) ★★, *Songs Of The Fabulous 30s* (MGM 1958) ★★★, *Great Waltzes* (MGM 1958) ★★★, *Holiday For Strings* (MGM 1959) ★★★, *Fiddlin' For Fun* (MGM 50s) ★★, *Let's Fall In Love* (MGM 50s) ★★, *Love Walked In* (MGM 50s) ★★, *Music From Motion Pictures* (MGM 50s) ★★★★, *Sentimental Journey* (MGM 50s) ★★★, *Concert With A Beat* (1960) ★★★, *Bonanza* (MGM 1961) ★★★, *Spectacular Strings* (MGM 1961) ★★★, *Box-Office Blockbusters* (MGM 1961) ★★★★, *Cimarron And Others* (MGM 1961) ★★★, *21 Channel Sound* (1962) ★★, *The Stripper And Other Fun Songs For The Family* (MGM 1962) ★★★★, *Velvet Beat* (MGM 1965) ★★★, *Like Young, Like Blue* (1974) ★★★, *In The Still Of The Night* (1976) ★★★, *Melody Fair* (1977) ★★★, *Great Orchestras Of The World* (1978) ★★, *Very Thought Of You* (1984) ★★★.

● COMPILATIONS: *16 Original Hits* (1984) ★★★★.

ROSE, WESLEY

b. 11 February 1918, Chicago, Illinois, USA, d. 26 April 1990, Nashville, Tennessee, USA. The son of Fred Rose, he lived with his mother when his parents divorced and after completing college, worked as an accountant in the Chicago offices of Standard Life. (He married Margaret Erdelyan on 16 November 1940 and they had one daughter, Scarlett.) In April 1945, while visiting an aunt in St. Louis, he was persuaded to call on his father. They had not seen each other since 1933 and he did not recognize Fred, nor, apparently, did the short-sighted Fred recognize his son. After this first reunion, Fred saw Wesley on his regular business trips to Chicago and tried to persuade him to work for the mighty Acuff-Rose publishing company, established by himself and Roy Acuff on 13 October 1942 as Nashville's first publishing house. At the time, Wesley Rose had no interest at all in country music and certainly no desire to live in Nashville. After considerable discussions and much hesitation on Wesley's part, he finally accepted his father's offer of the post of general manager with responsibility for all business decisions. From December 1945, Wesley Rose became a most important part of the family business and his undoubted business skills and accountancy training freed his father to concentrate more on handling the music side of the business – not least of all the emerging talent of Hank Williams. Although Wesley had no love for country music in his early days, he had no hesitation in believing that a good country song such as those written by Hank could be a hit in popular music. He soon proved his point and made the initial breakthrough when, under his careful guidance, 'Cold Cold Heart' became a million-seller for Tony Bennett in 1951. Other crossover hits followed, including 'Jambalaya' for Jo Stafford and 'Hey Good Lookin'' for Frankie Laine. When Fred Rose died in 1954, Roy Acuff immediately recognized Wesley as the natural successor and placed him in full charge of all the company's business. Under his guidance the successes are too numerous to mention, but the company's list of talented songwriters included the Everly Brothers (whom he also managed for seven years), Don Gibson, Marty Robbins, the Louvin Brothers and Roy Orbison. In spite of his work as the head of the organization, Rose still became very active in record production of artists, including Bob Luman and others, on the company's Hickory Label, which he had founded. Exactly when Rose's opinion of country music changed is not clear, but in later years, he was certainly a staunch supporter of traditional country singers such as Boxcar Willie and, while he had no objections or qualms about using a country song for a crossover hit, he had a considerable abhorrence for rock 'n' roll. Several journalists have related the story of his statement that radio stations should not play a particular Elvis Presley recording because he always maintained that Presley was not a country singer. It was a dedicated belief, particularly when one takes into consideration that Acuff-Rose would have benefited by Presley's record sales, since the song concerned was on their own roster. Over the years, some of his dealings caused animosity and problems. In September 1982, Roy Orbison filed a $50 million suit accusing Wesley Rose of mismanagement and fraud; Rose had been his manager since 1958. It was settled out of court for around $3 million and then the law firm sued Orbison for non-payment of fees. The Everlys also had a disagreement with him. In the early 60s, they began to record songs that were not Acuff-Rose and dropped Rose as manager. He sued them for lack of earnings and refused to let Felice and Boudleaux Bryant give them any more songs. Don Everly took to writing songs under a pseudonym so that Rose could not seize them. Over the years, Rose became connected with many aspects of the industry and also served on various boards, including the Nashville Chamber Of Commerce, Vanderbilt Medical Centre, First American National Bank and Boy Scouts Of America. He was the first southern publisher elected to the board of ASCAP and also served as National President of NARAS. He was a founder-member of the Country Music Association, being chairman of the organization on three different occasions, and he also served on the board of the Country Music Foundation. In 1986, he was elected to the Country Music Hall Of Fame, thus joining his father, who had been one of the first three entrants (with Jimmie Rodgers and Hank Williams) when the award was first created in 1961. He remained active with Acuff-Rose until the company was sold to Opryland USA in 1985. Wesley Rose, a highly respected gentleman, who was once the most powerful man in Nashville's music industry, died in April 1990 in the Edgefield Hospital, Nashville, following a long illness. Mrs. Margaret Rose died in Nashville in late December 1990.

ROSENMAN, LEONARD

b. 7 September 1924, Brooklyn, New York, USA. A composer and arranger for films and television, who only studied music seriously after serving in the US Air Force during World War II. His first film score, *East Of Eden* (1955), was followed in the same year by another James Dean vehicle, *Rebel Without A Cause*. Rosenman's other 50s scores included dramas such as *Bombers B-52*, *Edge Of The City*, *The Young Stranger*, *Lafayett Escadrille*, *Pork Chop Hill* and *The Savage Eye*. After providing music for more in the same genre in the 60s, such as *The Rise And Fall Of Legs Diamond*, *The Bramble Bush*, *The Chapman Report*, *A Covenant With Death* and *Hellfighters*, plus essays into science-fiction with *Countdown* and *Fantastic Voyage*, Rosenman received much critical acclaim for his score to *A Man Called Horse* and *Beneath The Planet Of The Apes* (1970). He also scored two 'Apes' sequels. During the 70s Rosenman received two Academy Awards for his adaptation of the scores to *Barry Lyndon* (1975) and *Bound For Glory* (1976). Rosenman's original background scores around that time included *Birch Interval*, *The Car*, *Race With The Devil*, *Prophecy*, *Promises In The Dark* and the animated feature *The Lord Of The Rings*. In the 80s and early 90s, apart from the occasional feature film such as *Hide In Plain Sight*, *Making Love*, *Cross Creek* (Oscar nomination), *Robocop 2*, *Heart Of The Stag* and *Ambition* (1992), Rosenman wrote more and more for television, although he still managed to score the occasional big feature, such as *The Jazz Singer* and *Star Trek IV: The Voyage Home*. Rosenman's music for television included *Stranger On The Run*, *Shadow Over Elveron*, *Any Second Now*, *Banyon*, *Vanished*, *In Broad Daylight*, *The Bravos*, *The Cat Creature*, *The Phantom Of Hollywood*, *Nakia*, *Lanigan's Rabbi*, *Kingston: The Power Play*, *The Possessed*, *Friendly Fire*, *City In Fear*, *The Wall*, *Murder In Texas*, *Celebrity* (mini-series), *Heartsounds*, *First Steps*, *Promised A Miracle*, *Where Pigeons Go To Die*, the popular series *The Defenders*, *Marcus Welby MD*, its sequel, *The Return Of Marcus Welby MD* and the television film *Keeper Of The City* (1991). He also composed several classical works.

ROSOLINO, FRANK

b. 20 August 1926, Detroit, Michigan, USA, d. 26 November 1978, Los Angeles, California, USA. After dabbling with guitar, Rosolino took up the trombone while in his teens. After military service during World War II he played in a succession of big bands, including those of Bob Chester and Glen Gray. In 1948 he was one of several bebop-influenced musicians playing in Gene Krupa's big band (contributing the scat vocalizing on the band's hit record of 'Lemon Drop'). After playing in several other dance bands he briefly led his own group before joining Stan Kenton in 1952. Two years later he left the band and settled in California, where he divided his time between studio and jazz work. He recorded with Dexter Gordon, Stan Levey, Conte Candoli and many of the musicians who frequented the Lighthouse. In the mid-70s Rosolino again worked with Candoli, visiting Europe, and he also played several times with Benny Carter, who was one of the trombonist's greatest admirers. Also in the 70s he played in Med Flory's band, Supersax, and with Quincy Jones. A brilliant technician with a precisely articulated attacking style, Rosolino was one of the finest trombonists of his time and one of few practitioners on the instrument to adapt fully to bebop. His later work showed him to be a consummate section player whether in big bands or small groups. He died in 1978 in acutely tragic circumstances, shooting both of his children (one of whom survived) before shooting himself.

● ALBUMS: with Stan Kenton *New Concepts Of Artistry In Rhythm* (Capitol 1952) ★★★★, one side only *The Trombone Album/Swing Not Spring* (1952) ★, *Stan Kenton Presents: Frank Rosolino Sextet* (1954) ★★★, *Frankly Speaking* (Affinity 1955) ★★★, with Stan Levey *This Time The Drum's On Me* (1955) ★★★, with Levey *Grand Stan* (Bethlehem 1956) ★★★, *I Play Trombone* (1956) ★★, with Lighthouse All Stars *Double Or Nothin'* (1957) ★★★, *The Most Happy Fella* (1957) ★★★, with Benny Carter *Aspects* (1959) ★★★, *Turn Me Loose!* (1961) ★★★, *Conversations* (1975) ★★★, *Just Friends* (1975) ★★★, *Thinking About You* (Sackville 1976) ★★★, *In Denmark* (1978) ★★.

● COMPILATIONS: *Fond Memories Of ...* 1973, 1975 recordings (Double-Time 1997) ★★★.

ROUSE, CHARLIE

b. 6 April 1924, Washington, DC, USA, d. 30 November 1988, Seattle, Washington, USA. After learning to play clarinet, Rouse took up the tenor saxophone; by the end of his teens he was proficient enough to be hired by Billy Eckstine for his bebop-orientated big band. Thereafter, Rouse played with Dizzy Gillespie, Tadd Dameron and Fats Navarro. At the end of the 40s he worked in an R&B band but also subbed with Duke Ellington and Count Basie. In the early 50s he played and recorded with a number of important small groups, including those led by Clifford Brown, Art Farmer, Paul Quinichette and Oscar Pettiford. In the second half of the decade he co-led Les Jazz Modes with Julius Watkins, was briefly with Buddy Rich and the Gerry Mulligan Concert Band and then, at the end of 1958, began a long and fruitful association with Thelonious Monk that lasted until 1970. During this period he made records with others, including Donald Byrd and Benny Carter, appearing on the latter's fine *Further Definitions*. Throughout the 70s and 80s he freelanced, touring as a single or playing as accompanist. In 1982 he formed the Monk tribute group Sphere alongside Kenny Barron, Ben Riley and Buster Williams. A distinctively quirky player, Rouse's long musical partnership with Monk had the advantage of bringing his work to a very wide audience, and the disadvantages of linking him with an often overpowering personality, and enclosing him in a very specific, fairly limited area of bop.

● ALBUMS: with Les Jazz Modes *Jazzville* (Dawn 1956) ★★★, with Les Jazz Modes *Les Jazz Modes* (Dawn 1956) ★★★, with Les Jazz Modes *Mood In Scarlet* reissued as *Smart Jazz For The Smart Set* (Dawn 1957) ★★★, with Les Jazz Modes *The Most Happy Fella* (Atlantic 1958) ★★★, with Paul Quinichette *The Chase Is On* (Bethlehem 1958) ★★★, *Takin' Care Of Business* (Jazzland 1960) ★★★★, *We Paid Our Dues* (Epic 1961) ★★★, *Yeah!* (Epic 1960) ★★★, *Bossa Nova Bacchanal* (Blue Note 1962) ★★★, *Two Is One* (Strata-East 1974) ★★★★, *Cinnamon Flower* (Rykodisc 1976) ★★★, *Moment's Notice* (Storyville 1977) ★★★, with Howard McGhee *Jazzbrothers* (Storyville 1977) ★★★, *The Upper Manhattan Jazz Society* (Enja 1981) ★★★, with Sphere *Four In One* (Elektra Musician 1982) ★★★★, with Sphere *Flight Path* (Elektra Musician 1983) ★★★, *Social Call* (Uptown 1984) ★★★, with Sphere *Sphere On Tour* (Red 1985) ★★★, with Sphere *Four For All* (Verve 1987) ★★★, *Epistrophy* (Landmark 1988) ★★★, with Les Jazz Modes *Les Jazz Modes* 1956 recordings (Biograph) ★★★★, *Unsung Hero* 1960/1961 recordings (Columbia) ★★★.

ROYAL TEENS

Formed in 1956 in Bergen County, New Jersey, USA, the Royal Teens are remembered primarily for the 1958 rock 'n' roll novelty number 'Short Shorts'. Originally a quartet called the Royal Tones, the line-up included pianist Bob Gaudio (b. 17 December 1942, Bronx, New York, USA), saxophonist Bill Crandall, bassist Billy Dalton and drummer Tom Austin. Influenced by black music, they worked as back-up band to travelling R&B artists. Gaudio and Austin had written an instrumental dance song as a warm-up for their stage show. Adding the lyrics, 'Who wears short shorts? We wear short shorts', the song was heard by an executive of ABC-Paramount Records, who signed them to the label; the single hit number 3 in the USA. At that time Crandall was replaced by Larry Quagliano and Dalton also left, to be replaced by Al Kooper. Joe Villa, formerly of the doo-wop outfit the Three Friends, was added as vocalist, making the band a quintet. They scored one further chart single for ABC and one for Capitol Records before starting to disintegrate in 1960. Although some members continued with the unit until 1965, recording for such labels as Mighty, All New, Jubilee, Blue Jay and Swan, there was no further success. Gaudio went on to become a member of the Four Seasons and a top producer. Kooper later formed the Blues Project and Blood, Sweat And Tears. The Royal Teens never recorded an album.

ROYAL WEDDING

Inspired by the wedding of Princess Elizabeth to Philip Mountbatten in 1947, this film, which was released by MGM four years later in 1951, was also loosely based on the experiences of one of its stars, Fred Astaire. In 1928, he and his sister Adele appeared in the London production of the stage musical *Funny Face*. They were fêted by the city's fashionable high society, and, eventually, Adele broke up their double act and married Lord Charles Cavendish in 1932. Alan Jay Lerner's screenplay for *Royal Wedding* also concerns a brother and sister dance team, Tom and Ellen Bowen (Astaire and Jane Powell) who take their hit Broadway show, *Every Night At Seven*, to the British capital where Ellen marries Lord John Brindale (Peter Lawford) and gives up her showbusiness career. Tom also finds happiness in London with a music hall performer (played by Sarah Churchill, daughter of Britain's new Prime Minister in 1951), and all three couples (including Elizabeth and Philip) are married on the same November day. Burton Lane (music) and Alan Jay Lerner (lyrics) wrote the score which contained one of the longest song titles ever: 'How Could You Believe Me When I Said I Loved You When You Know I've Been A Liar All My Life?' That number provided a humorous, no-punches-pulled, knockabout duet for Astaire and Powell, a young and up-and-coming singer-actress who surprised many people with her all-round versatility in this film. She also had the tender 'Too Late Now' and 'Open Your Eyes', while Fred, amazingly innovative as usual, danced with a hat stand in 'Sunday Jumps', and appeared to dance on the floor, walls and ceiling of a room filled with furniture, accompanied by 'You're All The World To Me'. Illustrated lectures have since been given as to how that last feat was accomplished. Nick Castle (with uncredited assistance from Astaire) was responsible for the choreography. The rest of the score included 'I Left My Hat In Haiti', 'Open Your Eyes', 'Ev'ry Night At Seven', 'The Happiest Day Of My Life' and 'What A Lovely Day For A Wedding'. Stanley Donen directed the film, which was photographed in Technicolor and retitled *Wedding Bells* when it was released in the UK.

ROYALTONES

This rock 'n' roll instrumental band came from Dearborn, Michigan, USA. With its honking saxophone-dominated records, the Royaltones typified the sound of rock 'n' roll bands of the late 50s, before the guitar sound had become dominant. The band was formed in 1957 as the Paragons, and comprised George Katsakis on tenor saxophone, Karl Kay on guitar, and two brothers, Mike Popoff on piano and Greg Popoff on drums. 'Bad Boy' was a US Top 20 hit in 1958. 'Flamingo Express' went to number 82 in 1961. The Royaltones broke up in the mid-60s long after their sound had become passé.

ROZA, LITA

b. 1926, Liverpool, England. A popular singer, particularly during the 50s, whose name is forever associated with the renowned Ted Heath Orchestra. At the age of 12 she appeared in a Christmas pantomime in Norwich, and when she was 15, took part in the revue *Black Velvet*, which starred top UK comedian Ted Ray. After working outside showbusiness for a while, she became the resident vocalist at the New York restaurant in the northern seaside resort of Southport. By the time she was 17, she had joined Harry Roy's Band for a tour of the Middle East, and then sang with Art Thompson's group at London's Embassy Club. Later, she toured with Edmundo Ros before moving to the USA, where she stayed until 1950. On her return to the UK, Roza successfully auditioned for Ted Heath by singing on one of his popular London Palladium Swing Concerts, and was allocated the middle stool, between Dickie Valentine and Dennis Lotis. During her stay of over four years with Heath, she recorded both with his band and in her own right. In 1951 she had a big hit with Irving Gordon's 'Allentown Jail', followed by other successful sides, such as 'High Noon', 'Half As Much', 'Walkin' To Missouri', 'I Went To Your Wedding', 'Why Don't You Believe Me' and 'Hi-Lili, Hi-Lo'. In 1953 she topped the UK chart with Bob Merrill's novelty '(How Much Is) That Doggie In The Window', a cover version of Patti Page's enormous US hit. Her other chart entries included 'Hey There', the big ballad from *The Pajama Game*, which was also successful in the UK for Rosemary Clooney, Sammy Davis Jnr. and Johnnie Ray, and, finally, 'Jimmy Unknown'. She also sang 'A Tear Fell' on *All Star Hit Parade*, a single record that also featured songs by Joan Regan, David Whitfield, Dennis Lotis, Winifred Atwell and Dave King. When Roza left Heath, she toured the UK variety

circuit and appeared extensively on radio and television in shows such as *Off The Record*, *The Jack Jackson Show*, *Saturday Spectacular*, *Music Shop* and the top pop music programmes, *6.5 Special* and *Oh Boy!*; she also featured in the ITV series *The Ted Heath Story*. She recorded several albums, including one entitled *Drinka Lita Roza Day* (presumably a play on the television advertising slogan 'Drinka Pinta Milka Day'), but eventually became yet another victim of the rapidly changing musical climate. In later years she has made television and concert appearances with her contemporaries, celebrating the good times of years gone by, and was one of the 'Four Stars Of The 50s', along with Jimmy Young, Dickie Valentine and Joan Regan, on the double album *Unchained Melodies*.
● ALBUMS: *Presenting Lita Roza* (Decca 1954) ★★★, *Love Is The Answer* (Decca 1957) ★★★★★, *The Night Is Young* (Decca 1957) ★★★, *Between The Devil And The Deep Blue Sea* (Decca 1958) ★★★, *Me On A Carousel* (Pye 1959) ★★★, *Drinka Lita Roza Day* (Pye 1960) ★★, *Love Songs For Night People* (Ember 1964) ★★, *You're Driving Me Crazy* (President 1983) ★★, *Somewhere, Somehow, Someday* (C5 1990) ★★.
● COMPILATIONS: includes performances with Dennis Lotis and the Ted Heath Orchestra *Lita Roza* (1977) ★★★.

ROZSA, MIKLOS

b. 18 April 1907, Budapest, Hungary, d. 27 July 1995. An important composer for films from the early 30s until the early 80s, who had an equally distinguished career in the world of classical music, Rozsa began to play the piano at the age of five and soon added the violin to his studies. He gave his first public performance when he was seven, playing a movement from a Mozart violin concerto and conducting a children's orchestra in Haydn's 'Toy Symphony'. In his teens Rozsa attended Leipzig University and, during his four years there, completed his first serious compositions. His big breakthrough came in 1934 with his 'Theme, Variations, And Finale (Opus 13)'. A year later he moved to London to write a ballet, and was invited to compose the music for Alexandra Korda's film *Knight Without Armour*, starring Robert Donat and Marlene Dietrich. The successful outcome marked the beginning of Rozsa's five-year association with Korda, which, in the late 30s, produced *The Squeaker*, *The Divorce Of Lady X*, *The Spy In Black* and *The Four Feathers*.
In 1940, Rozsa went to Hollywood to finish work on *The Thief Of Baghdad* and then scored *Sundown* and *The Jungle Book*. All three films gained him Oscar nominations, and together with *The Four Feathers*, were designated as his 'Oriental' period. Rozsa was nominated again, for *Lydia*, before Korda shut down London Films for the duration of World War II. Rozsa moved to Paramount where he provided the 'stark, powerful, dissonant score' for 'the archetypal film noir of the 40s', Billy Wilder's *Double Indemnity* (1944), followed by other Wilder movies such as

Five Graves To Cairo and *The Lost Weekend* (1945). In the latter, Rozsa introduced a new instrument, the theremin, 'an ideal accompaniment to torture'. It was one of around 10 'psychological' movies with which Rozsa was involved during his career. Another, in the same year, was Alfred Hitchcock's *Spellbound*, for which Rozsa won his first Academy Award for a 'bleak and exciting' score. In the late 40s, besides Paramount, Rozsa worked mostly for United Artists and Universal on films such as *Because Of Him*, *The Strange Love Of Martha Ivers*, *The Killers* (Burt Lancaster's first movie), *The Red House*, *The Macomber Affair*, *Brute Force*, *The Naked City* (with Frank Skinner) and *A Double Life* (1947), for which he won another Oscar.

At the end of the decade Rozsa began to work for MGM, and embarked on his 'religious and historical epic' period, with monumental scores for *Quo Vadis*, *Ivanhoe*, *Julius Caesar*, *Knights Of The Round Table*, *Valley Of The Kings* and *Ben Hur* (1959 – his third Academy Award, and his last major assignment for MGM). Rozsa pursued the epic into the 60s with the blockbusters *King Of Kings* and *El Cid* (1961), both of which were made in Spain. By no means all of Rozsa's scores in the 50s and 60s were of such gigantic proportions; he also provided the music for movies with a wide variety of subjects, such as *The Asphalt Jungle*, *Crisis*, *The Story Of Three Loves*, *Moonfleet*, *Tribute To A Bad Man*, *Bhowani Junction*, *Lust For Life*, *Something Of Value*, *The World*, *The Flesh And The Devil*, *The V.I.P's*, *The Power*, *The Green Berets*, and many more. In 1970 Rozsa made his last film with Billy Wilder, *The Private Life Of Sherlock Holmes*, and played a cameo role as a ballet conductor. His other 70s film music included *The Golden Voyage Of Sinbad*, *The Secret Files Of J. Edgar Hoover*, *Fedora*, *The Last Embrace*, *Time After Time* and *Providence*, described as his 'most inspiring project for years'.

Somewhat ironically, during the 70s and 80s, when the demand for elaborate orchestral movie scores had declined, to be replaced by a montage of pop records, renewed interest in Rozsa's earlier classic film works caused record companies to make new recordings of his scores. In 1981, Rozsa's music for *Eye Of The Needle*, suggested, for some, shades of Korda's *The Spy In Black* over 40 years earlier, and *Dead Men Don't Wear Plaid* (1982), a parody of the 40s film noir which included footage from classics of the genre, found Rozsa writing music for scenes that he had originally scored many years previously. Even though he was partially paralyzed by a stroke in 1982, he continued to compose classical works and, on his 80th birthday, was presented with a Golden Soundtrack Award by ASCAP. The anniversary was declared 'Miklos Rozsa Day' in Los Angeles, and the composer was presented with greetings from President Reagan, Queen Elizabeth, and other luminaries such as Margaret Thatcher and Pope John Paul II. Later in 1987 Rozsa was the guest of honour at a gala charity concert of his music given by the Royal Philharmonic Orchestra at London's Royal Festival Hall.

● ALBUMS: *Miklos Rozsa Conducts His Great Film Music* (Polydor 1975) ★★★★, *Spellbound-The Classic Film Scores Of Miklos Rozsa* (RCA 1975) ★★★★, *Miklos Rozsa Conducting The Royal Philharmonic Orchestra* (Polydor 1976) ★★★.

● FURTHER READING: *Miklos Rozsa: A Sketch Of His Life And Work*, C. Palmer. *Double Life: The Autobiography Of Miklos Rozsa*, Miklos Rozsa.

RUSSO, BILL

b. William Joseph Russo Jnr., 25 June 1928, Chicago, Illinois, USA. After extensive studies in arranging, Russo wrote for Lennie Tristano and also occasionally played trombone. One of the earliest musicians to lead a rehearsal band, his experimental style came to the attention of Stan Kenton in the early 50s. In the mid-50s he concentrated on performing with a small group but by the end of the decade was again deeply involved in writing for larger jazz ensembles. He was also active as a teacher and this combination of work continued on throughout the 60s and early 70s. After spending some time in film and television work he returned to teaching in the 80s. He remains one of the more interesting writers for the large modern jazz orchestra.

● ALBUMS: *A Recital In New American Music* 10-inch album (Dee Gee 1952) ★★, with Shelly Manne *Deep People* (Savoy 1955) ★★★, *Bill Russo Plus The Hans Koller Ensemble* (1955) ★★, *Bill Russo And The New Jazz Group, Hanover* (1955) ★★★★, *The World Of Alcina* (Atlantic 1956) ★★★, with Lee Konitz *An Image – Lee Konitz With Strings* (Verve 1958) ★★★, *School Of Rebellion* (Roulette 1960) ★★★, *The Seven Deadly Sins* (Roulette 1960) ★★, *Suite No. 1 Opus 5 & Suite No. 2 Opus 8* (1962) ★★★, *Bill Russo On The Air In London* (1963) ★★★, *Bill Russo And The London Jazz Orchestra* (1964) ★★★.

RYAN, MARION

b. Marion Sapherson, 4 February 1931, Middlesborough, Yorkshire, England, d. 15 January 1999, Boca Raton, Florida, USA. This popular singer, with a vivacious style, was successful in the UK on records, radio and television in the 50s and early 60s. In one sense Marion Ryan's contribution to the UK charts began in 1948 when she gave birth to twins, Paul And Barry Ryan, who had hits of their own in the late 60s. Barry's 'Eloise' went to number 2, which was three places higher than his mother's best effort. Marion Ryan first appeared on the UK music scene in 1953 after a spell singing with Edmundo Ros, and became a favourite on UK television with programmes such as *Off The Record*, *Music Shop*, *Festival Of British Song*, *Jack Jackson's Record Roundup*, *Gerry's Inn*, *Sunday Night At Blackpool*, *6.5 Special*, *Oh Boy* and *Two's Company*. She also starred in four series of *Spot The Tune* with Canadian vocalist-comedian Jackie Rae. She sang regularly with the Ray Ellington Quartet, and appeared with them in the 1956 movie *Eric Winstone's Stagecoach*. In the late 50s, Ryan covered several big hits, including

Perry Como's 'Hot Diggity (Dog Ziggity Boom)', Peggy Lee's 'Mr Wonderful' and Rosemary Clooney's 'Mangos'. In 1958 she had chart success with 'Love Me Forever', which beat the Eydie Gorme version and rose to number 5. She also released some EPs, including *That Ryan Gal* and *Hit Parade*. In 1963 she featured in the Tommy Steele movie *It's All Happening*, with Russ Conway, Danny Williams, John Barry and Shane Fenton. Ryan retired from singing after marrying impresario Harold Davison in the late 60s, and they subsequently moved to Florida where she died following a heart attack.

● ALBUMS: *A Lady Loves* (Pye-Nixa 1960) ★★★.
● COMPILATIONS: *At Her Best* (C5 1994) ★★★, *Love Me Forever* (Sequel 1998) ★★.
● FILMS: *It's All Happening* (1963).

RYDELL, BOBBY

b. Robert Ridarelli, 26 April 1942, Philadelphia, Pennsylvania, USA. Probably the most musically talented of the late 50s Philadelphia school of clean-cut teen-idols, Rydell first performed in public as a drummer at the age of seven. At nine he debuted on Paul Whiteman's *Teen Club* amateur television show and was the show's regular drummer for three years. He attended the same boys club as Fabian and Frankie Avalon, formed a duo with Avalon in 1954 and shortly afterwards, they both joined local group Rocco And The Saints. After several rejections from labels, he recorded his first solo single 'Fatty Fatty' for his manager's Veko label. In 1958 he joined Cameo-Parkway and his fourth release for that label, 'Kissin' Time' (which owed something to 'Sweet Little Sixteen'), became the first of his 18 US Top 40 hits over the next four years. The photogenic pop/rock singer's best-known transatlantic hits are 'Wild One', 'Sway' and 'Volare' (only two years after the song first topped the charts) all in 1960 and 'Forget Him', a song written and produced in Britain by Tony Hatch in 1963. Rydell, whose ambition was always to be an all-round entertainer, starred in the movie *Bye Bye Birdie* and quickly, and initially successfully, moved into the cabaret circuit. The arrival of the British groups in 1964 was the final nail in his chart coffin. He later recorded without success for Capitol, Reprise, RCA, Perception and Pickwick International. Rydell has continued to work the club and oldies circuit and had some recognition for his role in rock when the high school in the hit 70s musical *Grease* was named after him. He returned to the studio in 1995 to re-record all his greatest hits as *The Best Of Bobby Rydell*.

● ALBUMS: *We Got Love* (Cameo 1959) ★★★, *Bobby Sings* (Cameo 1960) ★★, *Bobby Rydell Salutes The Great Ones* (Cameo 1961) ★★, *Rydell At The Copa* (Cameo 1961) ★★, *Bobby Rydell/Chubby Checker* (Cameo-Parkway 1961) ★★★, *Bye Bye Birdie* (Cameo 1963) ★★, *Wild Wood Days* (Cameo 1963) ★★, *The Top Hits Of 1963* (Cameo 1964) ★★, *Forget Him* (Cameo 1964) ★★.
● COMPILATIONS: *Bobby's Biggest Hits* (Cameo 1961) ★★★, *All The Hits* (Cameo 1962) ★★★, *Biggest Hits, Volume 2* (Cameo 1962) ★★, *16 Golden Hits* (Cameo 1965) ★★, *Greatest Hits* (1993) ★★, *Best Of Bobby Rydell* (K-Tel 1995) ★★.
● FILMS: *Because They're Young* (1960).

S

SAMWELL, IAN

b. Ian Ralph Samwell, England. A musician, songwriter and record producer, Ian 'Sammy' Samwell was present at the beginning of the UK's rock 'n' roll movement, and wrote Cliff Richard's first hit song, 'Move It'. After playing in the Ash Valley Skiffle group, Samwell joined Richard and the Drifters following a gig they played at the 2 I's coffee bar in London's Soho district. He is also credited with changing the singer's name from Richards to Richard, pointing out that if people were corrected when they said it wrongly, they would remember it all the more. At first Samwell played lead guitar, but later switched to bass. 'Move It' was originally released on the b-side of a cover version of Bobby Helms' 'Schoolboy Crush', but captured the fans imagination immediately, and soon rose to number 2 in the UK chart in 1958. Samwell composed or co-composed several other numbers for Richard over the years, notably 'High Class Baby', 'Mean Streak', 'My Feet Hit The Ground', 'Dynamite', 'Never Mind', 'Steady With You', 'Gee Whiz It's You', 'I Cannot Find A True Love', and 'Fall In Love With You'. It was when Norman Mitham quit the Drifters that Samwell took up the bass, but he was eventually relegated to a songwriting and, for a time, management role with the arrival of Jet Harris. In 1961, Samwell was hired to play records in between performances by live dance bands at the Lyceum in London, and built up quite a following for his brand of American R&B music. He subsequently became one of Britain's first independent record producers, being among the first to record artists such as Georgie Fame, Elkie Brooks, Aynsley Dunbar, John Mayall, Linda Lewis, Isaac Guillory, Prelude and Hummingbird. In 1965, he wrote and produced 'Whatcha Gonna Do About It' for the Small Faces, one of the best singles to come out of the British 'Mod' movement. In the late 60s Samwell joined Warner Brothers Records UK, and when Steve Marriott left the Small Faces, he recorded the new Faces whose personnel included the future superstar, Rod Stewart. During the 70s Samwell discovered and recorded the highly successful America, produced the Original Cast album of the musical John, Paul, George, Ringo ... & Bert, and produced and managed Hummingbird. Samwell relocated to California in 1980, where he worked with the bands Uncle Rainbow and Bourgeois Tagg. His career was put on hold in the early 90s by the serious illness idiopathic cardiomyopathy, necessitating a life-saving heart transplant. In 1995, Samwell wrote a second verse to 'Move It', which had been selected by the Rock And Roll Hall Of Fame as one of the 500 songs that shaped rock 'n' roll. The updated number was

recorded by Richard and Hank B. Marvin and included on the album Hank Plays Cliff. Two years later, nine Samwell songs, plus six previously unreleased recordings from 1958 on which Samwell played lead guitar with the Drifters, were included on the 4-CD box set, The Rock 'N' Roll Years 1958-1963.

SANDS, TOMMY

b. 27 August 1937, Chicago, Illinois, USA. Tommy Sands' father was a pianist, and his mother was Grace Lou Dixon, a singer with the Art Keassel Band. He sang in a local folk music television series, Lady Of The Mountain, when he was only five years old, and made his first recording, 'Love Pains', on Freedom in 1949, when aged only 12. In 1952, with help from his new manager, Colonel Tom Parker, he joined RCA Records as a country artist. In the early and mid-50s Sands played many country shows including some with Hank Williams, Elvis Presley and Johnny Cash. His big break came when he secured the role of a rock 'n' roll star in NBC's The Singing Idol, a part that was originally offered to Elvis Presley. The show was a smash hit, and its main song, 'Teen-Age Crush', attracted over half a million advance orders and shot to number 2 in the US charts. The television show was snapped up by Hollywood and was adapted to become Sands' first film, Sing, Boy, Sing (1958). The first of his five albums on Capitol Records, Steady Date With Tommy Sands, and Sing Boy Sing both made the US Top 20, and he was tipped by some as likely to replace Presley. However, of his other eight singles that charted, only 'Goin' Steady' made the US Top 40 in 1957. That same year in the UK he was the subject of BBC Television's This Is Your Life. He made a string of films including Mardi Gras with Pat Boone, Love In A Goldfish Bowl with Fabian, Babes In Toyland with Annette, the star-studded The Longest Day, and None But The Brave with his father-in-law Frank Sinatra (he was married to Nancy Sinatra from 1960-65). Together with his group the Raiders (aka the Sharks), which included the future top session drummer Hal Blaine, he later recorded on ABC Records, Paramount, Imperial Records and Liberty Records without further chart success. In the late 60s he moved to Hawaii and opened a club. He tried to make a comeback between 1974 and 1979, and again in 1987. He played his first UK dates in 1990.
● ALBUMS: Steady Date With Tommy Sands (Capitol 1957) ★★★, Sing, Boy, Sing film soundtrack (Capitol 1958) ★★, Sands Storm (Capitol 1959) ★★★, Teenage Rock (1959) ★★★, This Thing Called Love (Capitol 1959) ★★★, When I'm Thinking Of You (Capitol 1960) ★★★, Sands At The Sands (Capitol 1960) ★★★, Dream Of Me (Capitol 1961) ★★★, The Parent Trap film soundtrack (1961) ★★, Babes In Toyland film soundtrack (1961) ★★, Blue Ribbon Baby (Revival 1987) ★★, Down By Bendy's Lane (Green Linnet 1988) ★★, Beyond The Shadows (1992) ★★.
● COMPILATIONS: The Worryin' Kind (Bear Family 1992) ★★★.
● FILMS: Sing, Boy, Sing (1958), Mardi Gras (1958),

Babes In Toyland (1961), *Love In A Goldfish Bowl* (1961), *The Longest Day* (1962), *Ensign Pulver* (1964), *None But The Brave* (1965), *The Violent Ones* (1967).

SATCHMO THE GREAT

Made for television by Ed Murrow, this 1956 film follows Louis Armstrong on a tour of Europe and Africa. Intercut with scenes of live performance by Armstrong And His All Stars, and their reception, often by tens of thousands of well-wishers, at airports, are interviews with Armstrong. Although one of the finest and most respected journalists of his, or any other, era, Murrow's questions are sometimes a shade naïve, but Armstrong takes it all in his stride. The film ends with a New York concert performance of 'St Louis Blues' in which Armstrong and his men are joined by Leonard Bernstein and the New York Philharmonic to play to a capacity audience that includes W.C. Handy. One moving moment shows Handy, then over 80, removing his hat to take his handkerchief from his head to mop a tear from his blind eyes. The All Stars featured are Trummy Young, Edmond Hall, Billy Kyle, Jack Lesberg and Barrett Deems with singer Velma Middleton.

SATINTONES

An R&B vocal group from Detroit, Michigan, USA. The Satintones are known not so much for their recordings but for their early association with the famed Motown Records organization, and for producing future talents in the Detroit recording scene. The original members were Robert Bateman, Chico Laverett, James Ellis and Sonny Sanders, who came together in 1957. They were the first group signed to one of Berry Gordy's labels, when 'Going To The Hop' was issued on Tamla in 1959, followed by the first single on Motown Records, 'Sugar Daddy'. After three further singles for Motown, all in the R&B vocal group style of the late 50s, the group disbanded, with Robert Bateman becoming a producer for the label. He worked on the Marvelettes' hit single 'Please Mr. Postman' in 1962, before leaving Motown and setting up as an independent producer in Detroit. In 1967, Bateman produced the solo recordings by the former Supreme, Florence Ballard. Sonny Sanders had the most impressive post-Satintones career, working as an arranger, producer and bandleader in Detroit and later Chicago. In Detroit, he arranged and produced several big hits, notably Edwin Starr's 'Stop Her On Sight (S.O.S.)' and the Reflections' '(Just Like) Romeo And Juliet'. In Chicago, working under producer Carl Davis, he arranged such hits as Mary Wells' 'Dear Lover', the Artistics' 'I'm Gonna Miss You', Barbara Acklin's 'Love Makes A Woman', and Gene Chandler's 'The Girl Don't Care'. Sanders was one of the key backroom talents in the success of the Brunswick Records label during the late 60s and early 70s.

SAUTER, EDDIE

b. Edward Ernest Sauter, 2 December 1914, New York City, New York, USA, d. 21 April 1981, Nyjack, New York, USA. After studying arranging and composition at the Juilliard School of Music, Sauter became staff arranger for Red Norvo. In 1939, after four years with Norvo, he freelanced, writing charts for several prominent big bands, including Artie Shaw's, Woody Herman's and Tommy Dorsey's. He made his greatest impact with Benny Goodman, for whom he wrote 'Clarinet A La King' in the early 40s. He later worked for Ray McKinley where, unusually for an arranger at that time (or any other), he was given prominent billing. While hospitalized with tuberculosis Sauter began corresponding with Bill Finegan and in 1952 the two arrangers formed their own orchestra. The resulting 21-piece band was conceived as a studio band, but its records, which included the joyous 'The Doodletown Fifers' and the irresistible 'Midnight Sleigh Ride', were so popular that they took it on the road. In 1957, Sauter became musical director of the South-West German Radio Big Band in Baden-Baden. He later worked with Stan Getz, the New York Saxophone Quartet and in films and television.

● ALBUMS: all by Sauter-Finegan Orchestra *New Directions In Music* 10-inch album (RCA Victor 1953) ★★★★, *Inside Sauter-Finegan* (RCA Victor 1954) ★★★, *The Sound Of Sauter-Finegen* (RCA Victor 1954) ★★★, *Sons Of Sauter-Finegan* (RCA Victor 1955) ★★★, *Concert Jazz* (RCA Victor 1955) ★★★, *New Directions In Music* (RCA Victor 1956) ★★★★★, *Adventure In Time* (RCA Victor 1956) ★★★, *Under Analysis* (RCA Victor 1957) ★★★★, *One Night Stand With The Sauter-Finegan Orchestra* (RCA Victor 1957) ★★★, *Straight Down The Middle* (RCA Victor 1957) ★★★, *Inside Sauter-Finegan Revisited* (RCA Victor 1961) ★★★, *Sleigh Ride* (RCA Victor 1961) ★★★★, *The Return Of The Doodletown Fifers* (Capitol 1985) ★★★.

SCHOOLBOYS

An R&B vocal group from Harlem, New York City, New York, USA. With a remarkable series of pleading ballads in 1957, the Schoolboys typified the east coast pre-teen soprano sound, but like most such groups their career was short-lived. The group members were Leslie Martin (lead), Roger Hayes (tenor), James McKay (baritone) and Renaldo Gamble (bass), and their entry into the recording business was facilitated by famed New York disc jockey Tommy 'Dr. Jive' Smalls, who was introduced to the group at the behest of their manager. Smalls then arranged for the group to be signed to OKeh Records. The Schoolboys' first success was a double-sided hit, 'Please Say You Want Me' (number 13 R&B)/'Shirley' (number 15 R&B), in early 1957. The group broke up soon afterwards, but 'Carol' made a strong impression later in the year on the east coast, even though it failed to make the national charts. The Schoolboys' last record on OKeh, 'Pearl', featured Martin in the lead, who was supported by some members of the Cadillacs. Gamble had gone to join the Kodaks (another pre-teen group) and Hayes joined the Collegians of 'Zoom Zoom Zoom' fame. The Schoolboys made one more record, for Juanita, 'Angel Of Love', in 1958, before ending their career.

● COMPILATIONS: *Little Joe And The Thrillers Meet The Schoolboys* contains six tracks by the Schoolboys (Collectables 1991) ★★★.

SCHULLER, GUNTHER

b. Gunther Alexander Schuller, 22 November 1925, New York City, New York, USA. The son of a violinist with the New York Philharmonic Orchestra, Schuller studied flute and French horn together with arranging, composition and music theory. Schuller played the French horn in several symphony orchestras before turning to jazz, recording with Miles Davis in the late 40s and early 50s, including the groundbreaking *Birth Of The Cool* sessions. Schuller subsequently became a prime mover in what he referred to, in a 1957 lecture, as 'Third Stream' music, a form that sought to blend jazz with appropriate aspects of western classical music He founded the Jazz And Classical Music Society with John Lewis in 1955. Schuller continued to combine his interests in classical music and jazz in his playing, composing and teaching career. Among the jazz musicians for whom he has written special pieces, and in some cases has recorded with, are Ornette Coleman, Eric Dolphy, Bill Evans, John Lewis and Joe Lovano. His teaching has included spells at the Lenox School Of Jazz, of which he was a co-founder with Lewis, and the New England Conservatory in Boston. He became the president of the latter in 1967, establishing a four-year BA degree in jazz during his 10 years in office. Around this time, Schuller inaugurated the New England Conservatory Jazz Repertory Orchestra and Ragtime Ensemble. Their performances of Scott Joplin numbers helped revive interest in ragtime in the early 70s, leading indirectly to the extensive use of Joplin's rags in the hit movie *The Sting*. In the classical field, Schuller won the Pulitzer Prize for music in 1994 with his symphonic piece *Of Reminiscences And Reflections*. He was also made an inaugural member of the American Classical Music Hall Of Fame.

Schuller has also been active in music publishing and recording, forming his own companies in both fields (Margun Music and GunMar Music and GM Records). He has also written extensively on jazz and, apart from numerous magazine articles, he is the author of an important trilogy tracing the history of jazz, of which the first two volumes are *Early Jazz: Its Roots And Musical Development* (1968) and *The Swing Era: The Development Of Jazz, 1930-1945* (1989).

He has two jazz musician sons, Ed Schuller (b. 11 January 1955, New York City, New York, USA), who plays bass, and George Schuller (b. 29 December 1958, New York City, New York, USA), who is a drummer.

● ALBUMS: *Jazz Abstractions* (Atlantic 1960) ★★★★, with the New England Conservatory Ragtime Ensemble *The Red Back Book* (Angel 1973) ★★★★, with Orange Then Blue *Jumpin' In The Future* (GM 1988) ★★★★, with the New England Ragtime Ensemble *The Art Of The Rag* (GM 1989) ★★★★, with Joe Lovano *Rush Hour* (Blue Note 1995) ★★★★.

● FURTHER READING: *Early Jazz: Its Roots And Musical Development*, Gunther Schuller. *Gunther Schuller: A Bio-Bibliography*, Norbert Carnovale. *The Swing Era: The Development Of Jazz 1930-1945*, Gunther Schuller. *The Compleat Conductor*, Gunther Schuller. *Musings: The Musical Worlds Of Gunther Schuller – A Collection Of His Writings*, Gunther Schuller.

SCOTT, BOBBY

b. 29 January 1937, New York City, New York, USA, d. 5 November 1990, New York City, New York, USA. Scott was a pianist, singer, composer, arranger, teacher and record producer. He also played several other instruments such as cello, bass, vibes, accordion and clarinet, but was mainly known for his jazz piano work and vocals. He attended Dorothea Anderson Follette's School of Music, and then in 1949 studied composition with Edward Moritz, a former pupil of Claude Debussy. Despite his early classical training, Scott turned to jazz in his teens, and played with small bands led by the likes of Louis Prima, Tony Scott and Gene Krupa, with whom he cut some sides for Verve Records. From 1954, he recorded under his own name for labels such as Bethlehem, Savoy, Atlantic and ABC, and in 1956 had a US Top 20 hit with 'Chain Gang', written by Sol Quasha and Hank Yakus (not the Sam Cooke song). In 1960, Scott wrote the title theme for Shelagh Delaney's play *A Taste Of Honey*, which became popular for pianist Martin Denny and, when Ric Marlow added a lyric, for Tony Bennett. It was also included on the Beatles' first album (UK). The song won a Grammy in 1962, and three more when Herb Alpert took it into the US Top 10 in 1965. In the early 60s Scott was the musical director for Dick Haymes for a time, and, as a pianist, arranger and record producer for Mercury Records, also maintained a close working relationship with Quincy Jones. Scott played piano on most of Jones's Mercury albums, and accompanied Tania Vega and John Lee Hooker on Jones's soundtrack music for the film *The Color Purple* (1986). As a producer, Scott supervised sessions for important artists such as Aretha Franklin, Marvin Gaye, Bobby Darin, Harry Belafonte and Sarah Vaughan. He discovered and recorded guitarist/vocalist Perry Miller, who changed his name to Jesse Colin Young, and he is also credited with taking singer Bobby Hebb back to Mercury, although Scott left the label before Hebb released his biggest hit, 'Sunny', in 1966. Scott's compositions included 'He Ain't Heavy, He's My Brother' (written with Bob Russell), a hit for Neil Diamond in 1970 and a UK number 1 for the Hollies that same year and later in 1988, when it featured impressively in a UK television commercial for Miller Lite Lager; 'Where Are You Going?' (with Danny Meehan), sung by Joe Butler in the film *Joe* (1970); and 'Slaves (Don't You Know My Name?)', performed by Dionne Warwick in the movie *Slaves* (1969). Scott also composed incidental music for the play *Dinny And The Witches*, and several pieces for harp and string trios, including 'The Giacometti Variations', so-called because it was part-used as a radio advertisement for the Giacometti Exhibition held at the New York Museum of Modern Art. His compositions for guitar included 'Solitude Book' and 'The Book Of Hours', the latter recorded with Brazilian guitarist Carlos Barbosa-Lima. *For Sentimental Reasons* displayed Scott simply as an accomplished pianist, who also sang. He died of lung cancer in the year of its release.

● ALBUMS: *The Jazz Keyboard Of Bobby Scott* (1953) ★★★, *Great Scott* 10-inch album (Bethlehem 1954) ★★★, *The Compositions Of Bobby Scott, Volume 1* 10-inch album (Bethlehem 1954) ★★, *The Compositions Of Bobby Scott, Volume 2* 10-inch album (Bethlehem 1954) ★★, *The Compositions Of Bobby Scott* (Bethlehem 1955) ★★, *Scott Free* (ABC-Paramount 1956) ★★★, *Bobby Scott And Two Horns* (ABC-Paramount 1957) ★★★, *Bobby Scott Sings The Best Of Lerner And Loewe* (Verve 1958) ★★★, *Serenade – Bobby Scott, Pianist* (Verve 1959) ★★★, *Bobby Scott Plays The Music Of Leonard Bernstein* (Verve 1959) ★★★, *Bobby Scott With Friends* (1960) ★★★, *The Complete Musician* (Atlantic 1960) ★★★, *A Taste Of Honey* (Atlantic 1960) ★★, *Joyful Noises* (Mercury 1962) ★★★, *When The Feeling Hits You* (Mercury 1963) ★★★, *108 Pounds Of Heartache* (Mercury 1963) ★★, *I Had A Ball* (Mercury 1964) ★★★, *For Sentimental Reasons* (Music Masters 1990) ★★★.

SCOTT, JACK

b. Giovanni Dominico Scafone Jnr., 24 January 1936, Windsor, Ontario, Canada. This distinctive, deep-voiced rock 'n' roll and ballad singer-songwriter moved to Detroit at the age of 10, and began performing regularly with his sister Linda on the WEXL radio station. After changing his name to Jack Scott, he formed the country and western outfit Southern Drifters in 1954. Playing at local dances, the band began to introduce rock 'n' roll numbers into their act. Scott signed to ABC Records in 1957 and his first release was the rocker 'Baby She's Gone'. Scott joined the recently formed Carlton label in 1958 and had a transatlantic Top 10 hit with his double-sided debut for the label, 'My True Love'/'Leroy'. Always backed on records by session vocal group the Chantones, he had a further seven US Top 40 successes over the next two years, including the Top 10 hits 'Goodbye Baby' in 1958, 'What In The World's Come Over You' (a UK Top 20 hit) and 'Burning Bridges', both in 1960 (the latter two released on Top Rank). He achieved a couple of minor hits on Capitol Records in 1961 and later recorded on various labels including Groove, RCA-Victor Records, Jubilee, GRT, Dot Records (where he notched up a country hit in 1974) and Ponie. He remains a top-drawing act on the rock 'n' roll club circuit around the world.

● ALBUMS: *Jack Scott* (Carlton 1958) ★★★, *What Am I Living For* (Carlton 1959) ★★★, *I Remember Hank Williams* (Top Rank 1960) ★★★, *What In The World's Come Over You?* (Top Rank 1960) ★★★, *The Spirit Moves Me* (Top Rank 1961) ★★★, *Burning Bridges* (Capitol 1964) ★★, *Greaseball* (Bison Bop 1985) ★★.

● COMPILATIONS: *Scott On Groove* (Bear Family 1980) ★★, *Grizzily Bear* (Charly 1986) ★★★, *Capitol Collectors Series* (Capitol 1991) ★★★, *The Way I Walk: The Original Carlton Recordings 1958-1960* (Rollercoaster) ★★★★, *Classic Scott* 5-CD box set (Bear Family) ★★★.

SCOTT, LITTLE JIMMY

b. James Victor Scott, 17 July 1925, Cleveland, Ohio, USA. An influential figure to popular singers as stylistically diverse as Nancy Wilson, Ray Charles, and Frankie Valli, the highly acclaimed balladeer 'Little' Jimmy Scott nevertheless found it extremely difficult to transcend his enduring cult status. Revered by only the most knowledgeable of jazz aficionados, it was not until quite recently that Scott was able to mount a successful comeback after suffering decades of undeserved obscurity. His wavering, ethereal contralto vocal range, much closer in pitch to that of a woman than a man, was a result of a rare hereditary condition called Kallmann's Syndrome, which restricted Scott's height to 4 feet 11 inches until he was in his mid-thirties (when he suddenly grew to 5 feet 7 inches), blocked his sexual development, and stopped his voice from lowering into a conventional masculine register – thereby creating one of the most unusual and stunning vocal deliveries in post-war music history. He was one of 10 children, all of whom sang along heartily to their mother Justine's spirited piano playing at Hagar's Universal Spiritual Church in Cleveland. After her death (she was struck down while pushing her daughter out of the way of a speeding car), Scott was raised in various foster homes from the age of 13.

While in his teens, he ushered at Cleveland's Metropolitan Theater, where he heard the bands of Buddy Johnson, Erskine Hawkins and Lucky Millinder. He received his first chance to sing in front of an audience in Meadsville, Pennsylvania, in the mid-40s, backed by jazz saxophone legends Ben Webster and Lester Young. Scott toured from 1945-49 with shake dancer Estelle 'Caledonia' Young. Comedian Redd Foxx, actor Ralph Cooper, and heavyweight boxing champion Joe Louis helped the promising young singer to gain a job in 1948 at the Baby Grand nightclub on 125th Street in New York City. Scott joined Lionel Hampton's band the next year, with whom he made his debut recordings. In 1950, he sang the hit 'Everybody's Somebody's Fool' on Decca Records as Hampton's featured vocalist (the song reached number 6 on *Billboard*'s R&B charts). Scott was also spotlighted vocally on 'I Wish I Knew', a popular but non-charting 1950 Decca side credited to the Lionel Hampton Quintet that featured Doug Duke's organ accompaniment, and 'I've Been A Fool'. Scott soon left Hampton's band to join forces with New Orleans R&B mainstay Paul Gayten's band (which also featured vocalist Annie Laurie) in 1951. Scott made some live recordings for Fred Mendelsohn's Regal label that year with Gayten's band (trumpeter John Hunt, tenor saxophonist Ray Abrams, baritone saxophonist Pee Wee Numa-Moore, pianist Teddy Brannon, bass player

Thomas Legange, and drummer Wesley Landis) that were captured for posterity at Rip's Playhouse, a New Orleans nightspot.

Those long-buried tapes belatedly saw the light of day in 1991 on a Specialty Records disc. Mendelsohn sold Scott's contract to Teddy Reig and Jack Hook's Roost Records, where he recorded 16 further tracks under his own name (including his first classic rendition of 'The Masquerade Is Over') before signing with Herman Lubinsky's larger Savoy label in 1955. Four ballad-heavy sessions were held that year for Savoy, surrounding Scott with top-notch bandsmen including pianist/arranger Howard Biggs, saxophonist Budd Johnson, guitarists Mundell Lowe, George Barnes, and Everett Barksdale, bass player Charles Mingus, and drummer Kenny Clarke. Scott was unhappy with the skimpy financial rewards he received while under contract to the Newark, New Jersey-based Savoy (more dates ensued in 1956 and 1958). Nevertheless, under Mendelsohn's astute supervision, Scott did manage to create numerous classic ballads for the company despite the fiscal discord. 'When Did You Leave Heaven', 'Imagination', and the bluesy 'Don't Cry Baby' are among Scott's finest performances for Savoy. Although his early years were artistically enriching, Scott's offstage existence was apparently another matter. The singer endured multiple divorces and suffered from a reported drinking problem.

Scott temporarily switched over to Sydney Nathan's King Records in 1957 for a dozen sides supervised by Henry Glover before returning to Savoy in 1960 for one more session. Finally, in 1962, Scott received what appeared to be his big break: a contract with Ray Charles' fledgling Tangerine label. With Marty Paich and Gerald Wilson supplying lush arrangements and Charles himself deftly handling the keyboards, the resulting album, *Falling in Love is Wonderful*, would have most likely boosted Scott's national profile considerably. Unfortunately, Lubinsky quashed the set's distribution shortly after its release, claiming that Scott remained under contract to Savoy. In 1969, Atlantic Records producer Joel Dorn recorded an album with Scott, *The Source*, with arrangements by Arif Mardin and sporting a varied set that included 'Day By Day', 'This Love Of Mine', and 'Exodus', but it failed to further Scott's fortunes. He returned to Savoy one last time in 1975 for a Mendelsohn-produced album that made little impact. For a lengthy period prior to his triumphant return to live performance in 1985 (which was spurred by the urging of his fourth wife, Earlene), Scott toiled as a shipping clerk at Cleveland's Sheraton Hotel, forgotten by all but his most loyal fans. Scott has engineered quite an amazing comeback in the years since. In 1992, his Blue Horizon album *All The Way* (listed as being by Jimmy Scott, with no reference to his height) found him backed by an all-star jazz aggregation that included saxophonist David 'Fathead' Newman, pianist Kenny Barron, bass player Ron Carter, and drummer Grady Tate and string arrangements by Johnny Mandel. Scott

followed it in 1994 with another set for Sire/Blue Horizon, *Dream*, and ended the 90s with the excellent *Holding Back The Years*. Jimmy Scott's reputation as a unique vocal master is assured, but his status definitely has not come easily.

● ALBUMS: *Very Truly Yours* (Savoy 1955) ★★★, *The Fabulous Little Jimmy Scott* reissued as *The Fabulous Songs Of Jimmy Scott* (Savoy 1959) ★★★★, *Falling In Love Is Wonderful* (Tangerine 1962) ★★★★, *If You Only Knew* (Savoy 1963) ★★★, *The Source* (Atlantic 1970) ★★, *Can't We Begin Again* (Savoy 1975) ★★, *Little Jimmy Scott* (Savoy Jazz 1984) ★★★, *All Over Again* (Savoy Jazz 1985) ★★★, *Regal Records: Live In New Orleans!* (Specialty 1991) ★★★, *All The Way* (Blue Horizon 1992) ★★★, *Lost And Found* (Rhino/Atlantic 1993) ★★★, *Dream* (Sire/Blue Horizon 1994) ★★★, *All Over Again* (Denon/Savoy Jazz 1994) ★★★, *Heaven* (Warners 1996) ★★★, *Holding Back The Years* (Artists Only! 1998) ★★★★, *Over The Rainbow* (Fantasy 2001) ★★★.
● COMPILATIONS: *Everybody's Somebody's Fool* (GRP 1999) ★★★★, *The Savoy Years And More* (Savoy 2000) ★★★.

SCOTT, RAYMOND

b. Harry Warnow, 10 September 1908, Brooklyn, New York, USA, d. 8 February 1994, North Hills, California, USA. After extensive studies, Scott became popular on radio as pianist, composer and leader of a small band. Playing mostly dance music and popular songs of the day, plus a smattering of novelty numbers, many of which were his own compositions, his radio exposure had made him one of the best-known names in the USA by the end of the 30s. Although most of his radio work had been with a polished sextet, he decided to exploit his popularity by forming a big band. After some limited touring he was persuaded back into the studios, where he formed one of the first mixed-race bands to be heard regularly on American radio. Several hundred of his tunes, including the perennial 'Powerhouse', were licensed to Warner Bros. in 1943, ensuring that his music became indelibly linked to the golden age of cartoons, providing the background to the antics of immortal characters such as Bugs Bunny, Porky Pig and Daffy Duck. From the mid-40s onwards he worked in many areas of music; arranging, composing and directing orchestras on radio and television, and running recording companies. For several years in the 50s, he led the orchestra on NBC's *Your Hit Parade*.

From the mid-40s onwards Scott had become increasingly involved in the pioneering of electronic music. Setting up his state of the art Manhattan Research studio, the intensely secretive Scott invented electronic musical instruments such as the Karloff, the Electronium, the Clavivox, the Circle Machine, and the Videola. Scott's use of sequencers and electronic oscillators to produce sounds is an often unacknowledged influence on the work of pioneering minimalist and ambient composers such as Philip Glass and Brian Eno. In the 70s Scott worked as the head of electronic research and development for Motown

Records before retiring to California. His work is commemorated in the superb *Manhattan Research Inc.* compilation, which includes a 144-page hardcover book.

● ALBUMS: *The Raymond Scott Quintet ... And His New Orchestra* 10-inch album (Columbia 1950) ★★★, *Raymond Scott And His Orchestra Play* 10-inch album (MGM 1953) ★★★, *Rock 'N Roll Symphony* (Everest 1958) ★★★, *The Unexpected* (Top Rank 1960) ★★★, *Soothing Sounds For Baby Volume 1: 1 To 6 Months* (Epic 1963) ★★★, *Soothing Sounds For Baby Volume 2: 6 To 12 Months* (Epic 1963) ★★★, *Soothing Sounds For Baby Volume 3: 12 To 18 Months* (Epic 1963) ★★★.

● COMPILATIONS: *Business Man's Bounce (1939-40)* (Golden Era 1982) ★★★, *The Uncollected Raymond Scott And His Orchestra* (Hindsight 1983) ★★★, *Popular Music* (Swing House 1984) ★★★, *The Uncollected Raymond Scott And His Orchestra: Vol. 2* (Hindsight 1985) ★★★, *Raymond Scott And His Orchestra (1944)* (Hindsight 1988) ★★★, *The Raymond Scott Project, Powerhouse Vol. 1* (Stash 1991) ★★★, *The Music Of Raymond Scott: Reckless Nights And Turkish Twilights* (Columbia 1992) ★★★★, *RSO On The Perry Como Show* (Intermusic 1996) ★★★, *Manhattan Research Inc.* (Basta 2000) ★★★★.

SCOTT, TONY

b. Anthony Sciacca, 17 June 1921, Morristown, New Jersey, USA. Scott learned to play clarinet as a child, later studying formally at the Juilliard School of Music in Manhattan. During the late 40s and beyond, he made his living playing in big bands and as a sideman in mainstream groups, sometimes playing tenor saxophone. Fascinated by the new jazz sounds emerging from Minton's Playhouse and other New York venues, he became a strongly committed bop musician. Unfortunately for the development of his career, bop and the clarinet were uneasy bedfellows, although Scott was one of the tiny number of clarinettists to achieve some recognition, building a reputation through the 50s as one of the best new players on his instrument. He was also active as an arranger and musical director for several singers, including Harry Belafonte, Billie Holiday and Sarah Vaughan. In 1959 he recorded the remarkably forward-looking *Sung Heroes*, with Bill Evans, Scott La Faro and Paul Motian, but the same year left America, tired of music business racism and despairing of the fact that so many of his close friends – Oran 'Hot Lips' Page, Charlie Parker, Art Tatum, Sid Catlett, Lester Young, Billie Holiday – had recently died. Scott spent six years travelling, both in Europe and (mostly) the Far East, and began to incorporate into his repertoire elements of ethnic music, especially from India and the Orient, creating a personal precedent for world music long before the genre was acknowledged. The records he made in the mid-60s as aids to meditation proved to be popular and consistent sellers – 'a godsend' he said of them in 1988, claiming that their royalties were still his main source of income. In the early 70s Scott settled in Italy, playing at festivals and touring, often to the

Far East, making occasional records and as often as not anticipating trends and fashions in music – even if, as so often happens with pioneers, his work has been overshadowed by that of other less talented musicians. One recent project was a double album consisting entirely of different versions of Billy Strayhorn's standard, 'Lush Life'. 'No one has sung it right yet', Scott told *Wire* magazine in 1988, 'including Nat 'King' Cole, Sarah Vaughan, everybody – they all goof it'.

● ALBUMS: *Music After Midnight* 10-inch album (Brunswick 1953) ★★★, *Tony Scott Quartet* 10-inch album (Brunswick 1954) ★★★, *Jazz For GI's* 10-inch album (Brunswick 1954) ★★★, *Scott's Fling* (RCA-Victor 1955) ★★★, *The Touch Of Tony Scott* (RCA-Victor 1956) ★★★★, *Tony Scott In Hi Fi* (Brunswick 1957) ★★★, *Tony Scott Quartet* (Brunswick 1957) ★★★, *The Complete Tony Scott* (RCA-Victor 1957) ★★★★, *A Day In New York* (Fresh Sound 1958) ★★★, *52nd Street Scene* (Coral 1958) ★★★, *South Pacific Jazz* (ABC-Paramount 1958) ★★, *Gypsy* (Signature 1959) ★★★, *The Modern Art Of Jazz* (Seeco 1959) ★★★★, *Hi Fi Land Of Jazz* (Seeco 1959) ★★★, with Jimmy Knepper *Free Blown Jazz* (Carlton 1959) ★★★, *Sung Heroes* (Sunnyside 1959) ★★★, *My Kind Of Jazz* (Perfect 1960) ★★★, with Herman 'Trigger' Alpert, Al Cohn, Zoot Sims *East Coast Sounds* (Jazzland 1960) ★★★, *Music For Zen Meditation* (Verve 1965) ★★★, *Music For Yoga Meditation & Other Joys* (Verve 1967) ★★★, *Homage To Lord Krishna* (Verve 1969) ★★, *Prism* (1977) ★★, *Boomerang* (1977) ★★, *African Bird: Come Back! Mother Africa* (Soul Note 1984) ★★★, *Lush Life Vols. 1 & 2* (Core 1989) ★★★, *Astral Meditation: Voyage Into A Black Hole 1-3* (Core 1989) ★★★, *The Clarinet Album* (Philology 1993) ★★★, *At Last* 1959 recordings (32 Jazz 2000) ★★★.

SEAL, ELIZABETH

b. Elizabeth Anne Seal, 28 August 1933, Genoa, Italy. A dynamic, vivacious dancer, singer, and actress, Elizabeth Seal won a scholarship to the Royal Academy of Dancing at the age of five. As a teenager she was in the chorus of several shows, including *Gay's The Word* in the West End, and in the mid-50s made a big impression in two US musicals at the London Coliseum – *The Pajama Game* (Gladys) and *Damn Yankees* (Lola). In the latter she took over from Belita shortly after the opening. However, she enjoyed her greatest success in the English adaptation of *Irma La Douce* (1958), and reprised her role in New York, winning the 1961 best actress Tony Award in the face of competition from Julie Andrews, Carol Channing, and Nancy Walker. Out of the limelight for some years after that triumph, she was set to make her West End comeback as Cassie in *A Chorus Line* (1976), but was 'sacked' during rehearsals by Michael Bennett, the show's director. The appearance on the scene of Bennett's wife, Donna McKechnie, who had played Cassie on Broadway, sparked off furious protests within the profession. They resulted in McKechnie's withdrawal, and radical rule changes by Equity, the actor's union. Ironically, three years after Seal appeared in the

1976 revival of *Salad Days*, she was involved in another Equity dispute. Having taken over the role of Roxie Hart in *Chicago* at the Cambridge Theatre, she and other members of the cast were threatened with blacklisting after they offered to take wage cuts in an attempt to keep the show running. The outcome was that Equity invested its own funds in an effort to keep their members in work. Thereafter she devoted much of her time to teaching and directing, but continued to make occasional appearances in regional theatre, including one in *Stepping Out* (1991), which she also choreographed. In 1996, to the delight of those attending the celebrations for composer David Heneker's 90th birthday, Elizabeth Seal reunited with her *Irma La Douce* co-star Keith Michell in the show's big ballad, 'Our Language Of Love'. In the following year, Seal played the role of Solange in a special concert performance of *Follies* at London's Theatre Royal, Drury Lane.
● FILMS: *Radio Cab Murder* (1954), *Town On Trial* (1956), *Cone Of Silence* (1961), *Vampire Circus* (1971), *Philby, Burgess And Maclean* for television (1977), *Mack The Knife* (1989).

SEARS, ZENAS
b. *c.*1914, d. 4 October 1989, Atlanta, Georgia, USA. A respected white Atlanta jazz and pop disc jockey, 'Daddy' Sears began programming jump blues and R&B records in January 1946. Two years later he took a job at the state-owned radio station WGST, on the condition that he would be allowed a nightly blues show, *The Blues Caravan*. Owing to his success with this format, he was able to expand the show to include talent shows, which he broadcast live from Atlanta theatres such as Decatur Street's 81 Theatre. Here he discovered local singers such as Tommy Brown, Billy Wright, Chuck Willis (whom he managed in the early to mid-50s, and secured him his first recording contract with OKeh Records) and Little Richard. These artists were invariably backed by the Blues Caravan All Stars, a group of local musicians that included John Peek and Roy Mays. In 1954, Georgia's new governor banned Sears' programme from the WGST, and Sears formed WAOK. He continued with his policy to play the best of black music – in 1959 he recorded Ray Charles's set at the WAOK 5th Anniversary Party which Atlantic issued as the bestselling *Ray Charles In Person*. In the late 50s and 60s, Sears became involved with Dr Martin Luther King and the SCLC, and his position with the radio station allowed him to spread his views on integration and equal rights.

SEEGER, PETE
b. 3 May 1919, New York City, New York, USA. Educated at Harvard University, he is the brother of Peggy Seeger and half-brother of Mike Seeger. Pete Seeger's mother was a violin teacher, and his father a renowned musicologist. While still young, Pete Seeger learned to play banjo and ukulele, and shortly afterwards he developed his interest in American folk music. Seeger took his banjo round the country, playing and learning songs from the workers and farmers. He served in the US Army during World War II. In addition to being a member of the Weavers from 1949-58, he had earlier been in a group called the Almanac Singers. The group included Woody Guthrie, Lee Hays and Millard Lampell. The Almanac Singers had frequently given free performances to union meetings and strikers' demonstrations. Despite such apparent diversions, Seeger maintained a successfully high profile in his own solo career. The era of McCarthyism put a blight on many live performances, owing to the right-wing political paranoia that existed at the time. It was in 1948 that Seeger was blacklisted and had to appear before the House of Un-American Activities Committee for his alleged communist sympathies. This did not stop Seeger from performing sell-out concerts abroad and speaking out on a wide range of civil rights and environmental issues. He became known for popularizing songs such as 'Little Boxes', 'Where Have All The Flowers Gone' and 'We Shall Overcome'. He has released in excess of 200 albums, several of which are instructional records for banjo playing. In addition to these albums Seeger has appeared on the work of many other artists providing either vocal or instrumental back-up. The 1993 release *Live At Newport* consisted of previously unreleased recordings made at the Newport Folk Festival between 1963 and 1965. After a gap of 14 years in releasing a new album Seeger was aided and produced by Paul Winter on 1996's *Pete*, which won the following year's Grammy award for Best Traditional Folk Album.

Seeger's most prominent environmental work was on the Clearwater Sloop project on the Hudson River, attempting to publicize the threat of pollution. He has always worked and campaigned for civil rights, peace and equality, and has never compromised his ideals, remaining one of the most important figures in the development of free speech and humanitarian causes through folk music.
● ALBUMS: *Songs For John Doe* (Almanac 1941) ★★★, *Talking Union And Other Union Songs* (Folkways 1941) ★★★, *The Soil And The Sea* (Fontana 1941) ★★★, *Dear Mr. President* (Folkways 1942) ★★★, *America's Favorite Songs* (Asch 1944) ★★★, *Songs For Victory* (Stinson/Asch 1944) ★★★, *Songs For Political Action* (CIO-Political Action Committee 1946) ★★★, *Bawdy Ballads And Real Sad Songs* (Charter 1947) ★★★, *Darling Corey* (Folkways 1950) ★★★★, *Lonesome Valley* (Folkways 1951) ★★★, *Songs To Grow On* (Folkways 1952) ★★★, *Lincoln Bridge* (Stinson 1953) ★★★, *A Pete Seeger Concert* (Stinson 1953) ★★★, *American Folk Songs For Children* (Folkways 1953) ★★★, *Pete Seeger Sampler* (Folkways 1954) ★★★, *Goofing-Off Suite* (Folkways 1954) ★★★, *How To Play The Five String Banjo* (Folkways 1954) ★, *Frontier Ballads, Volume 1* (Folkways 1954) ★★★★, *Frontier Ballads, Volume 2* (Folkways 1954) ★★★★, *Birds, Beasts, Bugs And Little Fishes* (Folkways 1954) ★★★, *The Folksinger's Guitar Guide* (Folkways 1955) ★★, *Bantu Choral Folk Songs* (Folkways 1955) ★★★★,

Folk Songs Of Four Continents (Folkways 1955) ★★★, With Voices Together We Sing (Folkways 1956) ★★★, American Industrial Ballads (Folkways 1956) ★★★, Love Songs For Friends And Foes (Folkways 1956) ★★★, American Ballads (Folkways 1957) ★★★★, American Favorite Ballads, (Folkways 1957) ★★★★, Gazette With Pete Seeger, Volume 1 (Folkways 1958) ★★★, Sleep Time (Folkways 1958) ★★★, Song And Play Time With Pete Seeger (Folkways 1958) ★★★, American Favorite Ballads, Volume 2 (Folkways 1959) ★★★★, Hootenanny At Carnegie Hall (Folkways 1959) ★★★, American Playparties (Folkways 1959) ★★★, Folk Songs For Young People (Folkways 1959) ★★★, American Favorite Ballads, Volume 3 (Folkways 1959) ★★★, Nonesuch (Folkways 1959) ★★★, Folk Festival At Newport, Volume 1 (Vanguard 1959) ★★★, The Unfortunate Rake (Folkways 1960) ★★★, Highlights Of Pete Seeger At The Village Gate With Memphis Slim And Willie Dixon, Vol. 1 (Folkways 1960) ★★★★, At The Village Gate, Volume 2 (Folkways 1960) ★★★★, Songs Of The Civil War (Folkways 1960) ★★★★, American History In Ballad And Song (Folkways 1960) ★★★, Champlain Valley Songs (Folkways 1960) ★★★, The Rainbow Quest (Folkways 1960) ★★★, Bill McAdoo Sings (Folkways 1960) ★★★, Old Time Fiddle Tunes (Folkways 1960) ★★★, American Favorite Ballads, Volume 4 (Folkways 1961) ★★★, Gazette, Volume 2 (Folkways 1961) ★★★, Pete Seeger: Story Songs (Columbia 1961) ★★★, American Favorite Ballads, Volume 5 (Folkways 1962) ★★★, American Game And Activity Songs For Children (Folkways 1962) ★★★, The 12 String Guitar As Played By Leadbelly (Folkways 1962) ★★★, The Bitter And The Sweet (Columbia 1962) ★★★, Hootenanny (Prestige 1962) ★★★, Children's Concert At Town Hall (Columbia 1963) ★★★, Broadside Ballads, Volume 1 (Folkways 1963) ★★★, We Shall Overcome (Columbia 1963) ★★★, Newport Broadside (Vanguard 1963) ★★★, The Nativity (Folkways 1963) ★★★, Broadside Ballads, Volume 2 (Folkways 1963) ★★★, Little Boxes And Other Broadsides (Verve/Folkways 1964) ★★★, Songs Of Struggle And Protest 1930 – 1950 (Folkways 1964) ★★★, Strangers And Cousins (Columbia 1964) ★★★, WNEW's Story Of The Sea (Folkways 1965) ★★★, Pete Seeger On Campus (Verve/Folkways 1965) ★★★, I Can See A New Day (Columbia 1966) ★★★, God Bless The Grass (Columbia 1966) ★★★★, Dangerous Songs!? (Columbia 1966) ★★★, Pete Seeger Sings Woody Guthrie (Folkways 1967) ★★★★, Waist Deep In The Big Muddy (Columbia 1967) ★★★, Traditional Christmas Carols (Folkways 1967) ★★, Pete Seeger Sings Leadbelly (Folkways 1968) ★★★, Pete Seeger Sings And Answers Questions At The Ford Hall Forum In Boston (Broadside 1968) ★★★, Pete Seeger Now (Columbia 1968) ★★★, Young Vs. Old (Columbia 1971) ★★★, Rainbow Race (Columbia 1973) ★★★, Banks Of Marble (Folkways 1974) ★★★, Pete Seeger And Brother Kirk Visit Sesame Street (Childrens Records Of America 1974) ★, with Arlo Guthrie Together In Concert (Warners 1975) ★★, Canto Obrero (Americanto 1975) ★★, Fifty Sail On Newburgh Bay (Folkways 1976) ★★★, Circles And Seasons (Warners 1979) ★★★, with Arlo Guthrie Precious Friend (Warners 1982) ★★★, We Shall Overcome: The Complete Carnegie Hall Concert (Columbia 1989) ★★★, Pete Seeger Singalong: Sanders Theater, 1980 (Smithsonian/Folkways/Rounder 1991) ★★★, Pete (Living Music 1996) ★★★, In Prague 1964 (Flyright 2001) ★★★.

● COMPILATIONS: Pete Seeger's Greatest Hits (Columbia 1967) ★★★★, The World Of Pete Seeger (Columbia 1974) ★★★, The Essential Pete Seeger (Vanguard 1978) ★★★, Greatest Hits (Ember 1984) ★★★, Live At The Royal Festival Hall (Greenwich Village 1985) ★★★, Can't You See This System's Rotten Through And Through (Greenwich Village 1985) ★★★, Live At Newport (Vanguard 1993) ★★★, A Link In The Chain (Columbia/Legacy 1998) ★★★★, various artists Where Have All The Flowers Gone: The Songs Of Pete Seeger (Appleseed 1998) ★★★, Headlines & Footnotes: A Collection Of Topical Songs (Smithsonian/Folkways 1999) ★★★★.

● FURTHER READING: How Can I Keep From Singing, David King Dunaway. The Foolish Frog, Pete Seeger. How Can I Keep From Singing?, David King Dunaway. Everybody Says Freedom, Bob Reiser. Carry It On!: History In Song And Pictures Of The Working Men & Women Of America, Pete Seeger and Bob Reiser. Where Have All The Flowers Gone?, Pete Seeger. Incompleat Folksinger, Jo Metcalf Schwartz.

● FILMS: Alice's Restaurant (1969).

SELLERS, BROTHER JOHN

b. 27 May 1924, Clarksdale, Mississippi, USA, d. 27 March 1999, New York, USA. Raised by his godmother after his family broke up in the aftermath of a terrible flood, Sellers moved to Chicago in the 30s, and began his professional music career in gospel. He subsequently toured with Mahalia Jackson in the 40s. His religious convictions did not prohibit him from singing blues music, and he recorded in both genres from 1945. He was quick to see the growing market among whites for black music, and was working festivals and white clubs by the early 50s. In 1957 he went to Europe with 'Big' Bill Broonzy. After Broonzy's death his star began to wane as research uncovered more intuitive blues singers, whose approaches were regarded as more 'authentic' than Sellers' stagey and rather inflexible singing. He continued to make solo appearances, and was with the Alvin Ailey Dance Company (as a musician) from the early 60s.

● ALBUMS: Brother John Sellers Sings Blues And Folk Songs (1954) ★★★, In London (1957) ★★★, Big Boat Up The River (1959) ★★★, Baptist Shouts And Gospel Songs (1959) ★★★.

SENSATIONS

This Philadelphia R&B ensemble featured the warm, chirpy lead of Yvonne Mills Baker (b. Philadelphia, Pennsylvania, USA). The group was formed in 1954, and in 1956 they had two minor ballad hits, a remake of the old standard 'Yes Sir, That's My Baby' (US R&B number 15) and 'Please

Mr. Disc Jockey' (US R&B number 13) for the Atlantic subsidiary label Atco. The group included lead Baker, alternate lead Tommy Wicks and bass Alphonso Howell. The Sensations failed to register further hits and disbanded. In 1961 Howell persuaded Baker to re-form the group and they added Richard Curtain (tenor) and Sam Armstrong (baritone). Through their mentor and producer, Philadelphia disc jockey Kae Williams, the Sensations won a contract with the Chess subsidiary label Argo. Singing with greater robustness and at a faster pace, the group had success first with a remake of Teresa Brewer's, 'Music! Music! Music!' (US R&B number 12 in 1961). The following year they struck gold with 'Let Me In' (US R&B number 2, pop number 4). The last chart record for the Sensations was a remake of the Frankie Laine hit 'That's My Desire' (US pop Top 75 in 1962). The group disbanded around 1964 and Baker continued making records for a few more years in the soul idiom.

● ALBUMS: *Let Me In* (Argo 1963) ★★★.

SEVEN BRIDES FOR SEVEN BROTHERS

Adapted from Stephen Vincent Benet's short story *The Sobbin' Women*, which was 'inspired' by Plutach's *Rape Of The Sabine Women*, this film was released by MGM in 1954 and, somewhat surprisingly, went on to become one of the most successful screen musicals of the decade. Frances Goodrich, Albert Hackett, and Dorothy Kingsley wrote the screenplay, which told of Adam Pontipee (Howard Keel), who leaves his six scruffy brothers to the squalor of their farmhouse in Oregon (c.1850s) to go in search of a hard-working wife. He finds her in the shape of Milly (Jane Powell), and their subsequent life together, during which Milly successfully advises the slovenly sextet on how to live and love, makes for an endearing and entertaining film. Her first 'lesson' is 'Goin' Co'tin'', just one of the many musical highlights in Gene De Paul and Johnny Mercer's spirited and exuberant score. Others included the optimistic 'Bless Your Beautiful Hide' (Keel), 'Wonderful, Wonderful Day' (Powell), 'When You're In Love' (Powell-Keel), 'Sobbin' Women' (Keel-brothers), 'June Bride' (Powell-brides), and 'Spring, Spring, Spring' (Powell-brothers-brides). The six virile brothers, named by their god-fearing mother as Benjamin, Caleb, Daniel, Ephram, Frankincense and Gideon, were played by Russ Tamblyn, Tommy Rall, Marc Platt, Jeff Richards, Matt Mattox and Jacques d'Amboise. In the end, they all find their brides (Virginia Gibson, Julie Newmeyer, Betty Carr, Nancy Kilgas, Norma Doggett and Rita Kilmonis) by somewhat unconventional methods, after displaying exceptionally brilliant dancing skills in the contrasting languorous 'Lonesome Polecat' and spectacular 'barn-raising' scenes. The choreography for those, and the rest of the innovative dance numbers, was designed by Michael Kidd. Saul Chaplin and Adolph Deutsch won Academy Awards for 'scoring of a musical picture'. Stanley Donen directed with style and vigour. George Folsey was responsible for the breathtakingly beautiful photography in Amsco and CinemaScope. This film is considered by many to be among the all-time great musicals, but a 1982 stage version was not welcomed in New York and folded after five performances. Four years later, a West End production fared a little better.

SEVILLE, DAVID

b. Ross Bagdasarian, 27 January 1919, Fresno, California, USA, d. 16 January 1972. This singer-songwriter, conductor and actor is best remembered as the creator of the Chipmunks. He first appeared on Broadway in the late 30s and was drafted to Britain during the war. His first musical success came in 1951 when a song he had co-written a decade earlier, 'Come On-A My House', topped the chart in a version by Rosemary Clooney. He recorded on Coral Records in 1951 and joined Mercury Records two years later. Seville made the UK Top 20 in 1956 under the name Alfi And Harry with 'The Trouble With Harry' (inspired by the film of the same name, in which he appeared), and he was successful again later that year with 'Armen's Theme' (inspired not by his Armenian descent but by his wife, singer Kay Armen). His biggest 'solo' hit came in 1958 with the transatlantic novelty smash 'Witch Doctor', which topped the US chart. He extended the idea of a speeded-up voice (as used on that hit) to produce a trio that he called the Chipmunks. They sold millions of records and had a top-rated cartoon television show before he retired them in 1967. After his death in 1972, his son Ross Jnr. brought back the Chipmunks and they have since enjoyed more success on both sides of the Atlantic.

● ALBUMS: *The Music Of David Seville* (Liberty 1957) ★★★, *The Witch Doctor* (Liberty 1958) ★★★.

SHAD, BOB

b. 12 February 1920, New York City, New York, USA, d. 13 March 1985, Los Angeles, California, USA. Shad entered record production in the 40s, producing jazz (including Charlie Parker) and blues and R&B (including Dusty Fletcher) for Savoy, National and other companies. In 1948 he founded Sittin' In With, initially recording jazz, but concluded that there was a bigger market for blues, which the majors were neglecting. He cut material by Lightnin' Hopkins, Sonny Terry and Brownie McGhee, and the last sides by Curley Weaver. On field trips to the south, Shad recorded Smokey Hogg and Peppermint Harris (including his hit 'Rainin' In My Heart') on portable equipment. In 1951, he joined Mercury Records as A&R director, producing Patti Page, Vic Damone and the Platters as well as blues sessions by Hopkins, Big Bill Broonzy and others, and launching the jazz marque EmArcy, for which he made important sessions with Sarah Vaughan, Maynard Ferguson, Dinah Washington (her first with strings) and many others. After leaving Mercury, Shad founded Mainstream, which issued, besides his Sittin' In With material, jazz by such as Shelly Manne and Dizzy Gillespie, and Sarah Vaughan's collaborations with Michel Legrand. Shad also produced rock artists, making the first recordings of Janis Joplin and Ted Nugent, and remained active with Mainstream through the 70s.

SHAKE, RATTLE AND ROLL

Taking its title from a bestselling single by Bill Haley And The Comets, this 1956 'B' film attempted to capitalize on rock 'n' roll. In a plot that would quickly become overused, conservative adults attempt to ban the new music, but are challenged to a television trial by teenagers. R&B singer Joe Turner performs 'Lipstick, Powder And Paint' and 'Feelin' Happy', and Fats Domino adds 'Ain't That A Shame', 'Honey Chile' and 'I'm In Love Again'; otherwise, Shake, Rattle And Roll is largely forgettable. Clumsily scripted hip parlance – 'dig', 'dad', 'man' and 'the most' – renders the youths' arguments laughable, while the use of subtitles as translation verges on spiteful. It is difficult to imagine the motives behind director Edward Cahn's ideas, but the final sensation is of a film desperate to exploit a genre while apparently at the same time belittling it and its adherents.

SHAND, JIMMY

b. James Shand, 28 January 1908, East Wemyss, Fife, Scotland, d. 23 December 2000, Perth, Scotland. The leading exponent of Scottish country dance music, accordionist and band leader Shand's remarkable career stretched over a period of 60 years. Shand was one of nine children of a coal miner, and followed his father down the pit at the age of 14. More importantly, he also learnt how to play melodeon, becoming a fluent exponent of a wide-ranging repertoire of traditional jigs, reels and polkas. Shand left the mining industry following the General Strike of 1926, taking up employment with the Fife Power Company until 1933 when he was hired as an accordion salesman and demonstrator by the J.T. Forbes Music Shop in Dundee. He made his first button accordion recording for Regal Zonophone Records the same year, and shortly afterwards gave his first performance on the wireless. A productive recording relationship with the Beltona label ensued, but it was not until the end of World War II that Shand elected to become a full-time musician. He formed the Jimmy Shand Band, comprising Shand, George McKelvey (accordion), Dave Ireland (fiddle), Owney McCabe (drums) and Johnny Knight (piano), and signed an exclusive recording contract with Parlophone Records. The band soon became an institution on the Saturday evening broadcasts of the BBC Scottish Home Service, and in 1955 enjoyed a Top 20 hit with 'Bluebell Polka' although the musicians' only reward was a £12 session fee. During the subsequent decade Shand became a regular on the nation's television screens, appearing on the BBC shows The White Heather Club and Top Of The Pops. He also attracted a 20,000 strong audience to an open-air concert in

Aberdeen. Shand retired in 1972, retreating to his beloved home village in Auchtermuchty, Fife. In 1978 he was the subject of the popular UK television programme This Is Your Life. He enjoyed an unexpected revival in 1994 when the music video Dancing With The Shands, featuring a 1990 live performance by Shand and his son Jimmy Jnr. at Letham village hall in Angus, broke into the Top 10 of the UK video charts. Five years later Shand was knighted by the Prince of Wales for services to Scottish culture. Previous awards had included an MBE in 1962, the Freedom of Fife, and an honorary degree from Dundee University.

● ALBUMS: Awa Frae Home (Parlophone 1963) ★★★, Happy Hours With Jimmy Shand (Parlophone) ★★★, Waltzing Thru' Scotland (Parlophone) ★★★, Whistle With Jimmy Shand (Parlophone) ★★★★, A Swirl Of The Kilt (Parlophone) ★★★, Jimmy's Fancy (Parlophone) ★★★, 20 Golden Tracks By The One And Only Jimmy Shand (Parlophone) ★★★, The Auchtermuchty Ceilidh (Ross) ★★★, Fifty Years On With Jimmy Shand (Ross 1983) ★★★, Echoes In The Glen (Ross) ★★★, At The End Of A Perfect Day (Ross 1987) ★★★, Dancing With The Shands (Rel 1994) ★★★.

● COMPILATIONS: The Last Ten Years (Ross) ★★★, The King Of The Melodeon Men (EMI 1992) ★★★★, The Legendary Jimmy Shand (Rel 1995) ★★★.

● VIDEOS: Dancing With The Shands (Rel 1994).
● FURTHER READING: The Jimmy Shand Story, Ian Cameron.

SHANK, BUD

b. Clifford Everett Shank Jnr., 27 May 1926, Dayton, Ohio, USA. After studying and gigging on most of the reed instruments, Shank concentrated on alto saxophone, later doubling on flute and baritone saxophone. From 1947 he was resident on the west coast, playing in the big bands of Charlie Barnet, Alvino Rey, Art Mooney and Stan Kenton but making his greatest impact in small groups. With Shorty Rogers, Milt Bernhardt, Bob Cooper, Art Pepper and Shelly Manne, he was one of the tightly knit group of Los Angeles-based musicians who formed the nucleus of the white west coast jazz scene of the 50s. As a member of the Lighthouse All-Stars and groups recording under the names of one or another of the leaders of the movement, Shank built a substantial reputation. He also recorded with Laurindo Almeida, beginning an association that was renewed several years later with the formation of the L.A. 4 (also featuring Ray Brown and Jeff Hamilton). Although active in the film and television studios during the 50s and 60s, Shank continued to make jazz dates, and with increasing frequency. In 1974 he was a founder-member of the LA Four. In the early 80s, by then wholly engaged in jazz, he toured as a single and also with Rogers, appearing in the UK with the Vic Lewis big band and recording with the Royal Philharmonic Orchestra. Shank's extensive recorded output over four decades allows an interesting examination of his development as a musician. His early alto playing was derivative of Charlie Parker and Art Pepper, while his flute playing, taken up during his stint with Kenton, was highly original and greatly advanced the use of the instrument in bebop settings. In later years his alto style became highly personalized and no longer showed influences outside of his own creative impulse. Indeed, by the mid-80s he had abandoned his other instruments in order to concentrate fully on alto.

● ALBUMS: *Compositions Of Shorty Rogers* 10-inch album (Nocturne 1954) ★★★, *Bud Shank And Three Trombones* 10-inch album (Pacific Jazz 1954) ★★, *The Laurindo Almeida Quartet Featuring Bud Shank* aka *Brazilliance, Volume 1* (Pacific Jazz 1955) ★★★, *Bud Shank And Bob Brookmeyer* 10-inch album (Pacific Jazz 1955) ★★★, with Bob Cooper *Jazz At Cal-Tech* (Pacific Jazz 1956) ★★★, with Cooper *Flute 'N Oboe* (Pacific Jazz 1957) ★★★, with Claude Williamson *The Bud Shank Quartet* (Pacific Jazz 1957) ★★★, with Cooper *The Swing's To TV* (Pacific Jazz 1957) ★★, *I'll Take Romance* (World Pacific 1958) ★★★, *Misty Eyes* (West Wind 1958) ★★, *Holiday In Brazil* (World Pacific 1959) ★★★, *Latin Contrasts* (World Pacific 1959) ★★★, *Flute 'N Alto* (World Pacific 1960) ★★★, *Koto 'N Flute* (World Pacific 1960) ★★★, *Bud Shank Plays Tenor* (Pacific Jazz 1960) ★★★, *New Groove* (Pacific Jazz 1961) ★★★, *Improvisations* (World Pacific 1962) ★★★, with Laurindo Almeida *Brazilliance, Volume 2* (World Pacific 1962) ★★★, with Almeida *Brazilliance, Volume 3* 1953 recordings (World Pacific 1962) ★★★, *Bossa Nova Jazz Samba* (Pacific Jazz 1962) ★★★, *Brasamba Bossa Nova* (Pacific Jazz 1963) ★★★, *Bud Shank And His Brazilian Friends* (Pacific Jazz 1965) ★★, *Bud Shank And The Sax Section* (Pacific Jazz 1966) ★★★, *Folk 'N Flute* (World Pacific 1966) ★★★, *Flute, Oboe And Strings* (World Pacific 1966) ★★★, with Chet Baker *Michelle* (World Pacific 1966) ★★★, *California Dreaming* (World Pacific 1966) ★★★, *Girl In Love* (World Pacific 1967) ★★★, *Brazil! Brazil! Brazil!* (World Pacific 1967) ★★★, *A Spoonful Of Jazz* (World Pacific 1967) ★★★, *Magical Mystery* (World Pacific 1967) ★★★, *The Windmills Of Your Mind* (1969) ★★, *Bud Shank And The Bob Alcivar Singers* (1970) ★★, with The L.A. 4 *The L.A. Four Scores!* (Concord Jazz 1974) ★★★, with The L.A. 4 *Concierto De Aranjuez* (Concord Jazz 1976) ★★★, *Sunshine Express* (Concord 1976) ★★★, *Heritage* (1977) ★★★, with The L.A. 4 *Watch What Happens* (Concord Jazz 1978) ★★★, with The L.A. 4 *Just Friends* (Concord Jazz 1978) ★★★, *Crystal Comments* (Concord 1979) ★★★, *Explorations 1980* (Concord 1979) ★★★, with The L.A. 4 *LA Live At Montreux Summer 1979* (Concord Jazz 1979) ★★★, with The L.A. 4 *Zaca* (Concord Jazz 1980) ★★★, *Shades Of Dring* (1981) ★★, with The L.A. 4 *Montage* (Concord Jazz 1981) ★★★, with The L.A. 4 *Executive Suite* (Concord Jazz 1982) ★★★, with Almeida *Selected Classical Works For Guitar And Flute* (1982) ★★★, with Rogers *Yesterday, Today, And Forever* (1983) ★★★, with Rogers, Vic Lewis *Back Again* (1984) ★★★, *This Bud's For You* (Muse 1984) ★★★★, *California Concert* (1985) ★★★, *That Old Feeling*

(Contemporary 1986) ★★★, *Concert For Alto Saxophone And Symphony Orchestra* (1987) ★★★, *Serious Swingers* (Contemporary 1987) ★★★, *Tomorrow's Rainbow* (Contemporary 1987) ★★★, *At Jazz Alley* (Contemporary 1987) ★★★, *Tales Of The Pilot* (1989) ★★★, *Lost In The Stars* (Fresh Sound 1991) ★★★, *The Doctor Is In* (Candid 1992) ★★★, with Almeida *Baa-Too-Kee* (1993) ★★★, *I Told You So* (Candid 1994) ★★★, *New Gold!* (Candid 1995) ★★★, *Plays Harold Arlen* (1996) ★★★★, *By Request* (Milestone 1998) ★★★, *After You, Jeru* (Fresh Sound 1999) ★★★★, *Silver Storm* (Raw 2001) ★★★.

● COMPILATIONS: with The L.A. 4 *The Concord Jazz Heritage Series* (Concord Jazz 1998) ★★★★, *The Pacific Jazz Bud Shank Studio Sessions* 5-CD/7-LP box set (Mosaic 1998) ★★★★.

SHARON, RALPH

b. 17 September 1923, London, England. Sharon came to prominence as pianist with the Ted Heath band in the years immediately following World War II. He also played, and sometimes recorded, with British bop musicians of the late 40s, including Ronnie Scott and Victor Feldman. In the early 50s he moved to the USA, became an American citizen, and continued to play piano in a variety of settings, frequently in distinguished company. He also established a reputation as a sympathetic accompanist to singers, notably Tony Bennett and Chris Connor. On one of his albums with Bennett, Sharon wrote arrangements for the Count Basie band, playing piano on most tracks, while on another album, three decades later, he arranged songs by Irving Berlin for his own small group, with added guests who included George Benson, Dexter Gordon and Dizzy Gillespie. Sharon's habitual diffidence has kept him hidden from the spotlight he clearly deserves. Among his early American recordings were some with his wife, the singer Sue Ryan. In the mid-90s he was regularly on the world's stages accompanying Tony Bennett.

● ALBUMS: *The Ralph Sharon Sextet i* (1955) ★★★, *The Ralph Sharon Trio* (Bethlehem 1956) ★★★, *Mr & Mrs Jazz* (Fresh Sounds 1956) ★★, *The Ralph Sharon Sextet ii* (1957) ★★★, *The Ralph Sharon Quartet* (1958) ★★★, *Ralph Sharon With The Rolena Carter Chorale* (1962) ★★★, *Do I Hear A Waltz* (Columbia 1965) ★★★, *The Magic Of George Gershwin* (Horatio Nelson 1988) ★★★★, *The Magic Of Irving Berlin* (Horatio Nelson 1989) ★★★★, *The Magic Of Cole Porter* (Horatio Nelson 1989) ★★★★, *Portrait Of Harold* (DRG 1996) ★★★, *Plays The Frank Loesser Songbook* (DRG 2000) ★★.

SHELDON, JACK

b. 30 November 1931, Jacksonville, Florida, USA. After studying trumpet as a child, Sheldon played professionally while still in his early teens. In the late 40s, now relocated in the Los Angeles area, he played with many leading west coast musicians, including Art Pepper, Dexter Gordon and Wardell Gray. He was also closely associated with comedian Lenny Bruce. In 1955 he was one of the first of the west coast school to record for the Pacific Jazz label. In the mid-50s he recorded with the Curtis Counce group, which included Harold Land, and later in the decade with Dave Pell and Pepper. He also toured with Gray, Stan Kenton and Benny Goodman. In the 60s Sheldon's natural wit brought him work as a stand-up comedian and he also took up acting, playing the lead in a US television series, *What Makes Sammy Run?* In the 70s he worked with various bands, big and small, including Goodman's, Woody Herman's and Bill Berry's, and also led his own small bands for club and record dates. Sheldon's trumpet playing is deeply rooted in bebop but he ably adapts it to the mainstream settings in which he often works. His live appearances always include examples of his engaging singing style and his sparkling, frequently abrasive wit. Much less well known internationally than his talent deserves, Sheldon has survived many problems, including drug addiction and alcoholism, that would have ended the careers of less durable men.

● ALBUMS: *Get Out Of Town* 10-inch album (Jazz: West 1955) ★★★, *The Jack Sheldon Quintet* 10-inch album (Jazz: West 1955) ★★★, *Jack's Groove* (Gene Norman 1961) ★★★, *A Jazz Profile Of Ray Charles* (Reprise 1961) ★★★, *Out!* (Capitol 1963) ★★★, *Play Buddy, Play!* (Capitol 1966) ★★★, *Jack Sheldon With Orchestra Conducted By Don Sebesky* (1968) ★★, *Singular* (1980) ★★★, *Angel Wings* (1980) ★★★, *Playin' It Straight* (1980) ★★★, *Stand By For The Jack Sheldon Quartet* (Concord Jazz 1983) ★★★★, *Blues In The Night* (Phontastic 1984) ★★, *Hollywood Heroes* (Concord Jazz 1988) ★★, with Ross Tomkins *On My Own* (Concord Jazz 1992) ★★★, *Jack Sheldon Sings* (Butterfly 1996) ★★★, *Jack Is Back!* (Butterfly 1996) ★★★, with Tompkins *Class Act* (Butterfly 1997) ★★★.

● VIDEOS: *In New Orleans* (Hendring Music Video 1990).

SHELTON, ANNE

b. Patricia Sibley, 10 November 1923, Dulwich, London, England, d. 31 July 1994, East Sussex, England. One of the most important and admired of UK popular singers, Anne Shelton came to prominence as the 'Forces sweetheart' during World War II and remained a fondly regarded figure thereafter. She made her first BBC radio broadcast on 30 May 1940 in *Monday Night At Eight*, in which she sang 'Let The Curtain Come Down'. Her performance was heard by top UK bandleader Bert Ambrose, who signed her to sing with his band, and with whom she appeared on radio in *School Uniform*. Her own radio show, *Introducing Anne*, aimed mainly at British troops in the North African Desert, ran for four years, and she co-hosted *Calling Malta* with comedy actor Ronald Shiner; the programme was the only link with British troops on the island during the air bombardment and siege during the early months of 1942. In that same year, Shelton started her recording career, and in 1944 had an enormous hit with her signature tune, 'Lili Marlene', a German song that was equally popular with the armed forces of 'both sides', and to which UK songwriter

Tommie Connor added an English lyric. Also in 1944, she was one of the UK 'guest' vocalists who sang in concerts and on broadcasts with the American Band of the Supreme Allied Command and the American Band of the Allied Expeditionary Force, directed by Glenn Miller. Shelton also worked on radio with Bing Crosby.

She appeared in several films, a mixture of musicals and comedies, including *Miss London Ltd.*, *Bees In Paradise*, and *King Arthur Was A Gentleman* (each starring diminutive comedian Arthur Askey) and *Come Dance With Me* (with comedians Derek Roy and Max Wall). After the war, she toured the UK variety circuit, and in 1949 updated her wartime hit by recording 'The Wedding Of Lilli Marlene'. In the same year she had two US hits with 'Be Mine' and 'Galway Bay', and in 1951, became the first British artist to tour the USA coast to coast, staying there for almost a year. In the UK she appeared extensively on radio and television during the 50s, and had several successful records, including 'I Remember The Cornfields', 'My Yiddishe Momma', 'Once In A While', 'I'm Praying To St. Christopher', 'Arrivederci Darling', 'Seven Days', 'Lay Down Your Arms' (a Swedish song with an English lyric by Paddy Roberts, which spent several weeks at the top of the UK chart), and 'The Village Of St. Bernadette'. Her last chart entry, in 1961, was 'Sailor', a song of Austrian origin, which was a UK number 1 for Petula Clark. Albums around this time included *The Shelton Sound*, which contained impressive readings of standards such as 'Happiness Is Just A Thing Called Joe', 'Tangerine' and 'I'll Never Smile Again'. Throughout her career she worked with the cream of musical directors, including Percy Faith, Wally Stott, Stanley Black, George Melachrino, Frank Cordell, Ken Mackintosh, Robert Farnon, Reg Owen, David Rose, Jerry Gray and many more.

In later years Shelton continued to feature on television and tour various parts of the world, including the UK, Europe, USA and Hong Kong. In 1978 she appeared in cabaret when 1,200 US veterans revisited the D-Day Normandy beaches, and in the following year, performed one of her most popular 40s songs, 'I'll Be Seeing You', in John Schlesinger's movie *Yanks*, which starred Richard Gere. In 1980 she sang 'You'll Never Know' for the Queen Mother on the occasion of her 80th birthday, and during the rest of the decade took part in charity and reunion affairs in aid of the British Legion and British Services organizations. These included occasions such as the 40th anniversary of D-Day, when she sang on UK television with a contemporary 'Glenn Miller' Band, and the 50th anniversary of the start of World War II. Anne Shelton also held the important post of Entertainments Officer for the Not Forgotten Association, which looks after disabled ex-servicemen and women from as far back as World War I. In 1990 she was awarded the OBE for services to the Association, and in the same year, her husband, Lieutenant Commander David Reid, died. They had met when she was only 17 years of age.

● ALBUMS: *Favourites Volumes 1 & 2* (Decca 1952) ★★★★, *The Shelton Sound* (Philips 1958) ★★★, *Songs From Her Heart* (Philips 1959) ★★★, *Anne Shelton Showcase* (Philips 1961) ★★★, *Anne* (Ace Of Clubs 1962) ★★★, *Captivating Anne* (Encore 1962) ★★★, *A Souvenir Of Ireland* (Philips 1962) ★★★, *My Heart Sings* (Wing 1967) ★★★, *Irish Singalong* (Fontana 1968) ★★, *The World Of Anne Shelton* (Decca 1971) ★★★★, *I'll Be Seeing You* (Decca 1977) ★★★★, *I'll Be There* (Decca 1977) ★★★, *Anne Shelton's Sentimental Journey* (President 1982) ★★★, *Sing It Again, Anne* (President 1983) ★★, *Anne Shelton Sings With Ambrose And His Orchestra* (Recollections 1984) ★★★, *Wartime Memories* (EMI 1993) ★★★★, *Lili Marlene* (ASV Living Era 1995) ★★★.
● COMPILATIONS: *The Anne Shelton Collection* (Encore 1979) ★★★, *The Magic Of Anne Shelton* (MFP 1984) ★★★, *EMI Years* (Capitol 1990) ★★★★.

SHEP AND THE LIMELITES

This R&B vocal group came from New York City, New York, USA. James Sheppard (b. *c.*1936, Queens, New York, USA, d. 24 January 1970, Long Island, New York, USA) was lead and songwriter successively for two R&B groups, the Heartbeats and Shep And The Limelites. He created the first 'song cycle' (i.e., a string of songs constituting a musical and literary unit) in rock 'n' roll. With the Limelites he attained his only Top 10 pop success with 'Daddy's Home', making him a one-hit-wonder. However, that song was part of a long cycle of songs, among the most distinctive being 'A Thousand Miles Away' (US R&B number 5 and pop Top 60 in 1956), '500 Miles To Go' (1957), recorded with the Heartbeats, 'Daddy's Home' (US R&B number 4 and pop number 2 in 1961), 'Ready For Your Love' (US pop Top 50 in 1961), 'Three Steps From The Altar' (US pop Top 60 in 1961), 'Our Anniversary' (US R&B number 7 in 1962) and 'What Did Daddy Do' (1962). The song-cycle first emerged in the nineteenth century as part of the German *lied* tradition, and many critics have thought that the Beatles, with Sgt. Pepper's Lonely Heart's Club Band in 1967, had created the first rock 'n' roll song cycle. The Heartbeats were formed in New York City in 1954, and first recorded the following year. Members on the first record were James Sheppard (tenor/baritone lead), Albert Crump (first tenor), Vernon Seavers (baritone), Robby Tatum (baritone) and Wally Roker (bass). The group distinguished itself with smooth tight harmony and a knack for creating great nonsense vocal riffs. Their sound was the ultimate in romantic doo-wop balladry. In 1960 the group broke up, and the following year Sheppard formed a new group, Shep And The Limelites, with two veterans of the New York doo-wop scene, first tenor Clarence Bassett and second tenor Charles Baskerville. A rarity among doo-wop groups, using no bass and relying on two-part harmony, Shep and the Limelites magnificently continued the great smooth romantic sound of the Heartbeats, albeit with less flavourful harmonies. The group broke up in 1966. Sheppard was shot dead on 24 January 1970. Bassett continued singing, firstly in the Flamingos, and later in Creative Funk. Wally Roker became a successful executive in the music business.
● ALBUMS: *Our Anniversary* (Hull 1962) ★★★.
● COMPILATIONS: *Echoes Of The Rock Era* (1972) ★★★, with the Heartbeats *The Best Of The Heartbeats Including Shep & The Limelites* (Rhino 1990) ★★★★, *Daddy's Home To Stay: The Complete Shep & The Limelites* (Westside 1999) ★★★★.

SHEPARD, JEAN

b. Imogene Shepard, 21 November 1933, Pauls Valley, Oklahoma, USA. Shepard was one of 11 children in her family, who moved to Visalia, California, in 1946. Shepard learned to sing by listening to Jimmie Rodgers records on a wind-up Victrola. She joined the Melody Ranch Girls, in which she played string bass and sang, and recorded for Capitol Records while still at school. The record was not successful but she subsequently played on the same bill as Hank Thompson, who assured Capitol of her talent. In 1953 a single for the Korean war, 'Dear John Letter', with a narration from Ferlin Husky, topped the US country charts for 23 weeks. However, because she was under 21, she could not legally leave the state on her own to tour to promote the song. Shepard followed 'Dear John' with 'Forgive Me John,' while the original was satirized by Stan Freberg. Shepard had further country hits with 'A Satisfied Mind' and 'Beautiful Lies' and she has been a regular member of the *Grand Ole Opry* since 1955. She worked with Red Foley from 1955-57 on his television show The Ozark Jubilee. Her 1956 *Songs Of A Love Affair* was a concept album, one side from the single woman's view, the other from the wife's. She was married to Hawkshaw Hawkins, who was killed in 1963 in the plane crash that also took the lives of Patsy Cline and Cowboy Copas. At the time, Shepard was eight months pregnant with their second child. She returned to country music in 1964 with 'Second Fiddle To An Old Guitar' and she named her road band The Second Fiddles. She also had success with 'Happy Hangovers To You', 'If Teardrops Were Silver', and two duets with Ray Pillow, 'I'll Take The Dog' and 'Mr. Do It Yourself. Shepard was one of the first artists to be produced by crossover producer Larry Butler. In the 70s, she did well on the US country charts with Bill Anderson's songs 'Slippin' Away', 'At The Time', 'The Tips Of My Fingers' and 'Mercy', and recorded an album of his songs, *Poor Sweet Baby*. In 1975 she recorded a tribute to Hawkshaw Hawkins, 'Two Little Boys', which was written by their sons. Shepard was one of the objectors to Olivia Newton-John's award from the Country Music Association and she helped to found the Association Of Country Music Entertainers to 'keep it country'. To the public, it looked like sour grapes, especially as she had recorded 'Let Me Be There' and several pop hits. In recent years, Shepard has recorded duets with Gerry Ford, and plays live accompanied by her guitarist/husband, Benny Birchfield.

● ALBUMS: *Songs Of A Love Affair* (Capitol 1956) ★★, *Lonesome Love* (Capitol 1959) ★★★, *This Is Jean Shepard* (Capitol 1959) ★★★, *Got You On My Mind* (Capitol 1961) ★★★★, *Heartaches And Tears* (Capitol 1962) ★★★, *Lighthearted And Blue* (Capitol 1964) ★★★, *It's A Man Every Time* (Capitol 1965) ★★★, *Many Happy Hangovers* (Capitol 1966) ★★★, with Ray Pillow *I'll Take The Dog* (Capitol 1966) ★★, *Hello Old Broken Heart* (Capitol 1967) ★★★, *Heart, We Did All That We Could* (Capitol 1967) ★★★, *Your Forevers Don't Last Very Long* (Capitol 1967) ★★★, *A Real Good Woman* (Capitol 1968) ★★★, *Heart To Heart* (Capitol 1968) ★★★, *Seven Lonely Days* (Capitol 1969) ★★★, *I'll Fly Away* (Capitol 1969) ★★★, *A Woman's Hand* (Capitol 1970) ★★★, *Declassified Jean Shepard* (Mercury 1971) ★★, *Here And Now* (Capitol 1971) ★★★, *Just As Soon As I Get Over Loving You* (Capitol 1972) ★★★, *Just Like Walking In The Sunshine* (Capitol 1972) ★★, *Slippin' Away* (United Artists 1973) ★★★, *Poor Sweet Baby And Ten More Bill Anderson Songs* (United Artists 1975) ★★★, *For The Good Times* (United Artists 1975) ★★, *I'm A Believer* (United Artists 1975) ★★★, *Mercy, Ain't Love Good* (United Artists 1976) ★★★, *I'll Do Anything It Takes* (Scorpion 1978) ★★★.
● COMPILATIONS: *The Best Of Jean Shepard* (Capitol 1963) ★★★, *Greatest Hits* (United Artists 1976) ★★★, *Honky Tonk Heroine: Classic Capitol Recordings, 1952-1962* (CMF 1995) ★★★★, *The Melody Ranch Girl* 5-CD box set (Bear Family 1997) ★★★★.

SHEPHERD SISTERS

A quartet consisting of sisters Martha, Mary Lou, Gayle and Judy Shepherd, this group is best remembered for the 1957 Top 20 hit 'Alone (Why Must I Be Alone)'. Hailing from Middletown, Ohio, USA, the girls sang in four-part harmony and were originally called the La-La Quartet when a booking agent discovered them. They were signed to the small Melba Records with no success. The label's owner, Morty Craft, next gave the sisters a song he had written, 'Alone', which he placed on his Lance label. The single, an upbeat, if melancholy, number, reached number 18 in the US chart and number 14 in the UK. The Shepherd Sisters recorded further singles for such labels as MGM Records and United Artists Records without any luck. 'Alone' was later covered by the Four Seasons, who had a moderate hit with it in the 60s.

SHIELDS

This R&B vocal group came from Los Angeles, California, USA. The Shields were an *ad hoc* group formed in 1958 by producer George Motola to record a cover version of the Slades' 'You Cheated'. The membership has always been conjectural, but it is generally accepted to have comprised lead Frankie Ervin (b. 27 March 1926, Blythe, California, USA), falsetto Jesse Belvin (b. 15 December 1932, San Antonio, Texas, USA, d. 6 February 1960), Johnny 'Guitar' Watson (b. 3 February 1935, Houston, Texas, USA, d. 17 May 1996, Yokohama, Japan), Mel Williams and Buster

Williams. 'You Cheated', which went to number 11 R&B and number 12 pop in 1958, was the group's only hit, and the song remains one of the most enduring legacies of the age of doo-wop.

SHIRLEY AND LEE

New Orleans-based duo Shirley Goodman (b. 19 June 1936, New Orleans, Louisiana, USA) and Leonard Lee (b. 29 June 1936, d. 23 October 1976) began recording together in 1952. Billed as 'The Sweethearts Of The Blues', they enjoyed a series of US R&B hits, including 'I'm Gone' (1952) and 'Feel So Good' (1955), marked by the juxtaposition between Shirley's shrill, childlike intonation and Lee's bluesy counterpoint. In 1956 they crossed over into the US pop Top 20 with 'Let The Good Times Roll', a charming, infectious performance, written and arranged by Lee. The song became the first million-seller for the Aladdin label and is now regarded as an R&B standard. Shirley And Lee enjoyed minor hits with 'I Feel Good' (1956) and 'When I Saw You' (1957), before parting company in 1963. Shirley moved to the west coast, where she appeared on sessions for producer Harold Battiste and Dr. John, while Lee pursued a low-key solo career. His death in 1976 paradoxically coincided with Goodman's new-found popularity as leader of Shirley And Company.
● ALBUMS: *Let The Good Times Roll* (Aladdin 1956) ★★★, *Let The Good Times Roll* (Imperial 1962) ★★★.
● COMPILATIONS: *Legendary Masters Shirley & Lee* (EMI 1974) ★★★, *Happy Days* (Manhattan 1980) ★★, *Respectfully Yours* (Manhattan 1980) ★★, *The Best Of Shirley & Lee* (Ace 1982) ★★★.

SHORE, DINAH

b. Frances Rose Shore, 1 March 1917, Winchester, Tennessee, USA, d. 24 February 1994, Los Angeles, California, USA. One of her country's most enduring all-round entertainers, Shore staked her first claim to fame while still at school, on Nashville radio. Further broadcasting and theatre engagements in New York soon followed. She recorded with Xaviar Cugat and Ben Bernie, and sang on some of Cugat's early 40s hits, such as 'The Breeze And I', 'Whatever Happened To You?', 'The Rhumba-Cardi' and 'Quiereme Mucho', initially under the name Dinah Shaw. Shore was one of the first vocalists to break free from the big bands (she had been rejected at auditions for Benny Goodman and Tommy Dorsey) and become a star in her own right. She became extremely popular on radio, and made her solo recording debut in 1939. Her smoky, low-pitched voice was especially attractive on slow ballads, and from 1940-57 she had a string of some 80 US chart hits, including 'Yes, My Darling Daughter', 'Jim', 'Blues In The Night', 'Skylark', 'You'd Be So Nice To Come Home To', 'Murder, He Says', 'Candy', 'Laughing On The Outside (Crying On The Inside)', 'All That Glitters Is Not Gold', 'Doin' What Comes Natur'lly', 'You Keep Coming Back Like A Song', 'I Wish I Didn't Love You So', 'You Do', 'Baby, It's Cold Outside' (with Buddy

Clark), 'Dear Hearts And Gentle People', 'My Heart Cries For You', 'A Penny A Kiss', 'Sweet Violets', and number 1s with 'I'll Walk Alone', 'The Gypsy', 'Anniversary Song' and 'Buttons And Bows'.

She made a number of film appearances, including *Thank Your Lucky Stars* (1943), *Up In Arms* (1944), *Follow The Boys* (1944), *Belle Of The Yukon* (1945), *Till The Clouds Roll By* (1946) and *Aaron Slick From Punkin Crick* (1952). She also lent her voice to two Walt Disney animated features, *Make Mine Music* (1946) and *Fun And Fancy Free* (1957), and was last seen on the big screen in the George Burns comedy *Oh God!* (1977), and Robert Altman's quirky political satire *H.E.A.L.T.H.* (1979). In 1951 Shore began appearing regularly on television, making several spectaculars. Later, it was her continuing success on the small screen that brought about a career change when she became host on a highly rated daytime talk show, a role she maintained into the 80s. Her popularity on television barely declined throughout this period, and she won no less than 10 Emmys in all. The late 80s saw her performing on stage once more, though she returned to the television format for *Conversation With Dinah*, which ran from 1989-91. Shore succumbed to cancer in 1994.
● ALBUMS: *Dinah Shore Sings* 10-inch album (Columbia 1949) ★★★, *Reminiscing* 10-inch album (Columbia 1949) ★★★, *Bongo/Land Of The Lost* (Columbia 1950) ★★, *Call Me Madam* 10-inch album (RCA Victor 1950) ★★★, *The King And I* 10-inch album (RCA Victor 1951) ★★★, *Two Tickets To Broadway* 10-inch album (RCA Victor 1951) ★★★, *Aaron Slick From Punkin Crick* film soundtrack (RCA Victor 1952) ★★, *Dinah Shore Sings The Blues* 10-inch album (RCA Victor 1953) ★★★, *The Dinah Shore TV Show* 10-inch album (RCA Victor 1954) ★★, *Holding Hands At Midnight* (RCA Victor 1955) ★★★, *Bouquet Of Blues* (RCA Victor 1956) ★★★, *Moments Like These* (RCA Victor 1957) ★★★, *Buttons And Bows* (Capitol 1959) ★★★★, *Dinah, Yes Indeed!* (Capitol 1959) ★★★, with André Previn *Dinah Sings, Previn Plays* (Capitol 1960) ★★★, *Lavender Blue* (Capitol 1960) ★★★, with Red Norvo *Dinah Sings Some Blues With Red* (Capitol 1960) ★★★★, *Dinah, Down Home!* (Capitol 1962) ★★★, *Fabulous Hits Newly Recorded* (Capitol 1962) ★★★, *Lower Basin St. Revisited* (Project 3 1965) ★★★, *Songs For Sometimes Losers* (Project 3 1966) ★★, *Make The World Go Away* (MCA 1987) ★★★, *Oh Lonesome Me* (MCA 1988) ★★★.
● COMPILATIONS: *Best Of Dinah Shore* (RCA 1981) ★★★, *'Deed I Do (1942-1952)* (Hep Jazz 1988) ★★★, *Dinah Shore's Greatest Hits* (Capitol 1988) ★★★★, *The Capitol Years* (Capitol 1989) ★★★★.
● FURTHER READING: *Dinah!*, B. Cassidy.
● FILMS: *Thank Your Lucky Stars* (1943), *Up In Arms* (1944), *Follow The Boys* (1944), *Belle Of The Yukon* (1945), *Till The Clouds Roll By* (1946), *Make Mine Music* (1946), *Aaron Slick From Punkin Crick* (1952), *Fun And Fancy Free* (1957), *Oh God!* (1977), *H.E.A.L.T.H.* (1979).

SHORT, BOBBY

b. Robert Waltrip, 15 September 1926, Danville, Illinois, USA. A self-taught pianist, Short worked in vaudeville as a child and sang in clubs and on radio in Chicago. In mid-1937 he went to New York where he played and sang for audiences unprepared for smart-suited sophistication from a pre-teenager. Short went back to school, but, influenced by the stylish performances of such nightclub artists as Hildegarde, he continued to hone his act. When he returned to showbusiness he toured extensively, eventually spending some time on the west coast. By the early 50s he had matured into a sophisticated singer-pianist. Whether in Los Angeles, New York or Paris, he played the most exclusive nightclubs, establishing a reputation as a witty purveyor of songs. His vocal range is limited, and accordingly he sings with engaging restraint. His club appearances over the years at such places as the Café Carlyle and 21 have earned him a loyal following.
● ALBUMS: *Bobby Short Loves Cole Porter* (Atlantic 1952) ★★★, *Songs By Bobby Short* (Atlantic 1955) ★★★, *Bobby Short* (Atlantic 1956) ★★★, *Speaking Of Love* (Atlantic 1958) ★★★, *Sing Me A Swing Song* (Atlantic 1958) ★★★, *The Mad Twenties* (Atlantic 1959) ★★, *On The East Side* (Atlantic 1960) ★★, *Songs Of New York Live At The Cafe Carlyle* (Telarc 1995) ★★★★, *Celebrating 40 Years At The Café Carlyle* (Telarc 1997) ★★★, *You're The Top: Love Songs Of Cole Porter* (Telarc 1999) ★★★, *How's Your Romance?* (Telarc 1999) ★★.
● FURTHER READING: *Black And White Baby*, Bobby Short. *The Life And Times Of A Saloon Slinger*, Bobby Short with Robert Mackintosh.

SIGNATURES

Formed in 1954 at the Servicemen's Center in Seattle, Washington, USA, the Signatures featured Cathi Hayes (lead), Lee Humes (tenor), Ruth Alcivar (alto), Jerry Hayes (baritone) and Bob Alcivar (bass). Their style, as well as being made notable by the presence of two female singers, was distinguished by a pronounced lean towards jazz as well as doo-wop. They were also proficient on several instruments: Cathi Hayes (vibes), Ruth Alcivar (drums), Humes (bass), Bob Alcivar (piano) and Jerry Hayes (guitar). Their first major performance came in front of a big-band jazz ensemble created by local disc jockey Norm Bobrow, and thereafter, they continued to feature prominently on the jazz circuit. After a year of such pursuits the Hayes siblings were replaced by Bunny Phillips on lead, and multi-instrumentalist and former Four Freshmen member Hal Kratzsch as bass singer. Their recording debut came in July 1956, when an album was recorded for Whippet Records. The resulting collection sold steadily, as did the accompanying single 'Julie Is Her Name'. Engagements at prestigious New York jazz nightclubs followed, where Count Basie became a fan. He encouraged Morris Levy of Roulette Records to sign the still young band, but they stayed instead with an earlier mentor, Stan

Kenton, who brought them to Warner Brothers Records. A second album attracted further good notices, and was used as the launch pad for coast-to-coast tours playing with prestigious jazz artists including Dizzy Gillespie. Phillips was replaced on lead by Dottie Dunn just as the album was released, and Don Purdy also stepped in for Humes. Their next project was a tribute album to Duke Ellington and Billy Strayhorn, but this was never completed. Instead, they issued *Prepared To Flip* before appearing at the Playboy Jazz Festival in Chicago. However, the advent of rock 'n' roll in the 60s proved to be their nemesis, and after several more tours they finally folded. Most of the ex-members retired to day jobs, though Cathi Hayes recorded a solo jazz album. Bob Alcivar and his wife Ruth moved to Los Angeles where he still works as a film composer and she as a painter.

● ALBUMS: *The Signatures, Their Voices And Instruments* (Whippet 1956) ★★★, *The Signatures Sign In* (Warners 1959) ★★★, *The Signatures – Prepared To Flip* (Warners 1959) ★★★.

SILHOUETTES

Formed in 1956 in Philadelphia, Pennsylvania, USA, the Silhouettes recorded one of the classics of the doo-wop era, 'Get A Job'. The song was written by tenor Rick Lewis (b. 23 September 1933) while he was in the US Army, stationed in Germany. Upon returning home, Lewis joined a singing group called the Parakeets. He left them to front a band called the Gospel Tornadoes, comprising lead singer Bill Horton (b. 25 December 1929, d. 23 December 1995), bass singer Raymond Edwards (b. 22 September 1922) and baritone Earl Beal (b. 18 July 1924). When the gospel group changed to secular music, it took on a new name, the Thunderbirds. A disc jockey, Kae Williams, signed the group to his own Junior Records in 1958 and 'Get A Job' was recorded as the b-side to the ballad 'I Am Lonely'. The group's name was changed to the Silhouettes (after a 1957 hit by the Rays) and the record was released on the larger Herald-Ember label. 'Get A Job' received more attention than the ballad side and ultimately found its way to number 1 in the USA, becoming, in time, one of the best-known up-tempo doo-wop records. The nonsense phrase 'sha-na-na-na', part of its lyric, was borrowed in the late 60s by the rock 'n' roll revival group Sha Na Na. The Silhouettes recorded a number of follow-ups but never again returned to the charts. With numerous personnel changes, the group managed to stay afloat until 1968, latterly as the New Silhouettes. The four original members reunited in 1980 and carried on working the revival circuit until Horton's death in 1995.

● ALBUMS: *The Original And New Silhouettes – '58-'68 Get A Job* (Goodway 1968) ★★★.

SILK STOCKINGS (FILM MUSICAL)

Two years after Silk Stockings began its successful run on Broadway, MGM released this screen version which reunited Fred Astaire with one of his most thrilling dancing partners, Cyd Charisse.

Leonard Gershe and Leonard Spigelgass's screenplay was adapted from the show's libretto, which itself was based on the 1939 Greta Garbo movie *Ninotchka* and a story by Melchior Lengyel. The plot concerns a beautiful Russian emissary, Nina (Ninotchka), played by Charisse, who eventually falls for an American businessman (Astaire) after being sent to the USA in an effort to discover why three previous 'comrades' have failed to retrieve a Russian composer who is believed to be contemplating defection to the West. However, by then, the trio of messengers, Jules Munshin, Peter Lorre and Joseph Buloff, are themselves well on the way to capitulating to the capitalist way of life. Most of Cole Porter's songs from the stage show were retained and two new ones, 'Fated To Be Mated' and 'The Ritz Roll And Rock', added. The dancing, predictably, was 'out of this world', and Astaire was his usual charming vocal self on numbers such as 'All Of You', 'Paris Loves Lovers' and 'It's A Chemical Reaction, That's All' (with Charisse, dubbed by Carol Richards), and 'Stereophonic Sound' (with Janis Paige). Other numbers included 'Too Bad', 'Silk Stockings', 'Satin And Silk', 'Without Love', 'Josephine' and 'The Red Blues'. After helping themselves to generous portions of Western liquid hospitality, the three reluctant Reds, Munshin, Lorre and Buloff, are hilarious as they muse – musically – on the subject of 'Siberia'. *Silk Stockings*, which turned out to be Fred Astaire's last musical film (apart from the generally unsatisfactory Finian's Rainbow, made when he was nearly 70), was a fine affair. The choreographers were Hermes Pan and Eugene Loring (with Astaire, as usual, uncredited) and the director was Rouben Mamoulian. The musical director was André Previn, and the film was photographed in Metrocolor and Cinemascope.

SILK STOCKINGS (STAGE MUSICAL)

Cole Porter's final Broadway show was based on the 1939 film *Ninotchka*, which starred Greta Garbo. During the out-of-town try-outs, Abe Burrows' name was added to those of librettists George S. Kaufman and Leueen McGrath, and Kaufman was replaced as director by Cy Feur. *Silk Stockings* opened at the Imperial Theatre in New York on 24 February 1955. In this musical version of the by now familiar story, Ninotchka (Hildegarde Neff) is seduced by a glib Hollywood talent agent, Steve Canfield (Don Ameche), who is trying to persuade a famous Russian composer, Peter Ilyich Boroff (Philip Sterling), to expand his 'Ode To A Tractor' into the score for a ritzy movie version of *War And Peace*. The score was not top-drawer Porter by any means, but there were some worthwhile numbers, especially the gorgeous ballad 'All Of You', the amusing and contemporary 'Stereophonic Sound', and several more varied and entertaining items including 'Paris Loves Lovers', 'Without Love', 'It's A Chemical Reaction, That's All', 'Too Bad', 'Silk Stockings', 'The Red Blues', 'As On The Seasons We Sail', 'Satin And Silk', 'Josephine' and 'Siberia'. The show enjoyed a run of 478 performances and was filmed in 1957 with Fred Astaire and Cyd Charisse.

SIMEONE, HARRY, CHORALE

b. 9 May 1911, Newark, New Jersey, USA. An arranger, conductor and composer, Simeone studied at the Juilliard School of Music, before working for CBS, where he was spotted by bandleader Fred Waring. He took him onto his staff as an arranger in 1939, and from there Simeone moved to Hollywood and worked for Paramount with the legendary composer-conductor Victor Young on several Bing Crosby movies, including *Here Come The Waves* and the 'Road' series with Hope and Lamour. In 1945 he rejoined Waring and became the editor of Waring's *Shawnee Press*. From 1952-59 he served as the conductor and chorale arranger for the popular weekly *Firestone Hour* on television.

In 1958 Simeone released the chorale album *Sing We Now Of Christmas*, a collection of sacred songs and carols. It also contained 'The Little Drummer Boy', written by Simeone with Henry Onorati and Katherine Davis. The tune was taken from the Spanish song 'Tabolilleros'. Issued as a single, the Harry Simeone Chorale version entered the US charts each December for five consecutive years, from 1958-62. In the UK Top 20 there were additional versions by the Beverley Sisters and Michael Flanders in 1959, and in 1972 the songs was again successful in Britain in a version by the Pipes And Drums And Military Band Of The Royal Scots Guards. In 1970, estimated sales from some 150 versions were in the order of 25 million. The original *Sing We Now Of Christmas* was retitled *The Little Drummer Boy* in 1963, and remained in catalogues throughout the 80s.

● ALBUMS: *Sing We Now Of Christmas* aka *The Little Drummer Boy* (20th Century Fox 1958) ★★★.

SIMS, FRANKIE LEE

b. 30 April 1917, New Orleans, Louisiana, USA, d. 10 May 1970. Despite his birthplace, Sims' music is very much in the blues vein of Texas, where he lived in childhood. On his earliest records in 1947-48, for the Blue Bonnet label, he played a traditional finger-style guitar, but later developed an electric style of his own, riffing behind the vocals and filling the breaks with exciting, often distorted, flashes of lead. His best-known song was 'Lucy Mae', which he recorded several times, most successfully with Specialty in 1953. Later recordings on Ace and Vin developed his rocking style still further with a small band, but they marked the end of his brief period of success. A New York session in 1960 remained unissued until well after his death.

● COMPILATIONS: *Lucy Mae Blues* (1970) ★★★, *Walking With Frankie* (Krazy Kat 1985) ★★★.

SINATRA, FRANK

b. Francis Albert Sinatra, 12 December 1915, Hoboken, New Jersey, USA, d. 15 May 1998, Los Angeles, California, USA. After working for a time in the office of a local newspaper, *The Jersey Observer*, Frank Sinatra decided to pursue a career as a singer. Already an admirer of Bing Crosby, he was impelled to pursue this course after attending a 1933 Crosby concert, and sang whenever and wherever he could, working locally in clubs and bars. Then, in 1935 he entered a popular US radio talent show, *Major Bowes Amateur Hour*. Also on the show was a singing trio, and the four young men found themselves teamed together by the no-nonsense promoter. The ad-hoc teaming worked, and the group, renamed 'The Hoboken Four', won first prize. Resulting from this came a succession of concert dates with the Major Bowes travelling show, along with club and occasional radio dates. By 1938 Sinatra was singing on several shows on each of a half-dozen radio stations, sometimes for expenses – often for nothing. The experience and, especially, the exposure were vital if he was to be recognized. Among the bands with which he performed was one led by songwriter Harold Arlen but in 1939, shortly after he married his childhood sweetheart, Nancy Barbato, he was heard and hired by Harry James, who had only recently formed his own big band. James recognized Sinatra's talent from the beginning and also identified the source of his determination to succeed, his massive self-confidence and powerful ego. During their brief association, James remarked to an interviewer, 'His name is Sinatra, and he considers himself the greatest vocalist in the business. Get that! No one's even heard of him! He's never had a hit record, and he looks like a wet rag, but he says he's the greatest.' In 1939 and early 1940 Sinatra made a number of records with James and began to develop a small following. His records with James included 'My Buddy' and 'All Or Nothing At All'.

In 1940 Sinatra was approached with an offer by Tommy Dorsey, then leading one of the most popular swing era bands. Only some six months had expired on Sinatra's two-year contract with James, who must have realized he was parting with a potential goldmine, but he was a generous-spirited man and let the singer go. Sinatra had many successful records with Dorsey including 'Polka Dots And Moonbeams', 'Imagination', 'Fools Rush In', 'I'll Never Smile Again', 'The One I Love', 'Violets For Your Furs', 'How About You?' and 'In The Blue Of Evening', some of which became fixtures in his repertoire. One record from this period became a major hit a few years later when the USA entered World War II. This song, recorded at Sinatra's second session with Dorsey in February 1940, was 'I'll Be Seeing You', and its lyric gained a special significance for servicemen, and the women they had left behind. Sinatra's popularity with the young female population, achieved despite, or perhaps because of, his gangling, unheroic and rather vulnerable appearance, prompted him to leave Dorsey and begin a solo career. In spite of the tough line taken by Dorsey over the remaining half of his five-year contract (Dorsey allegedly settled for 43% of the singer's gross over the next 10 years), Sinatra quit. Within months his decision proved to be right. He had become the idol of hordes of teenage girls, his public appearances were sell-outs and his records jostled with one another for hit status. In the early 40s he had appeared in a handful of films as Dorsey's vocalist, but by the middle of the decade he began appearing in feature films as an actor-singer. These included lightweight if enjoyable fare such as *Higher And Higher* (1944), *Anchors Aweigh* (1945), *It Happened In Brooklyn* (1947), *The Kissing Bandit* (1948) and *Double Dynamite* (1951). By the 50s, however, Sinatra's career was in trouble; both as a singer and actor, he appeared to have reached the end of the road. His acting had suffered in part from the quality of material he was offered, and had accepted. Nevertheless, it was his film career that was the first to recover when he landed the role of Angelo Maggio in *From Here To Eternity* (1953) for which he won an Academy Award as Best Supporting Actor. Thereafter, he was taken seriously as an actor even if he was rarely given the same standard of role or achieved the same quality of performance. He continued to make films, usually in straight acting roles, but occasionally in musicals. Among the former were *The Man With The Golden Arm* (1955), one of the roles that matched his breakthrough performance as Maggio, *Johnny Concho* (1956), *Kings Go Forth* (1958), *A Hole In The Head* (1959), *The Manchurian Candidate* (1962), *Von Ryan's Express* (1965), *Assault On A Queen* (1966), *Tony Rome* (1967) and *The Detective* (1968). His musicals included *Guys And Dolls* (1955), *High Society* (1956), *Pal Joey* (1957), *The Joker Is Wild* (1957), *Can-Can* (1960) and *Robin And The 7 Hoods* (1964). Later, he appeared in an above average television movie, *Contract On Cherry Street* (1977), and *The First Deadly Sin* (1980).

Soon after his Oscar-winning appearance in *From Here To Eternity*, Sinatra made a comeback as a recording artist. He had been recording for Columbia, where he fell out of step when changes were made to the company's musical policy, and in 1953 he was signed by Capitol Records. Sinatra's first session at Capitol was arranged and conducted by Axel Stordahl whom Sinatra had known in the Dorsey band. For the next session, however, he was teamed with Nelson Riddle. Sinatra had heard the results of earlier recording sessions made by Nat 'King' Cole at Capitol on which Riddle had collaborated. Sinatra was deeply impressed by the results and some sources suggest that on joining Capitol he had asked for Riddle. The results of this partnership set Sinatra's singing career firmly in the spotlight. Over the next few years classic albums such as *Songs For Young Lovers*, *This Is Sinatra*, *A Swingin' Affair*, *Come Fly With Me*, *Swing Easy!*, *In The Wee Small Hours* and the exceptional *Songs For Swingin' Lovers* set standards for popular singers that have rarely been equalled and almost never surpassed. The two men were intensely aware of one another's talents and although critics were unanimous in their praise of Riddle, the arranger was unassumingly diffident, declaring that it was the singer's 'great talent that put him back on top'. For all Riddle's modesty, there can be little doubt that the arranger encouraged Sinatra's latent feeling for jazz, which helped to create the relaxed yet superbly swinging atmosphere that epitomized their work together. On his albums for Capitol, his own label Reprise Records, and other labels, sometimes with Riddle, other times with Robert Farnon, Neal Hefti, Gordon Jenkins, Quincy Jones, Billy May or Stordahl, Sinatra built upon his penchant for the best in American popular song, displaying a deep understanding of the wishes of composer and lyricist.

Fans old and new bought his albums in their tens of thousands and several reached the top in the *Billboard* charts. The 1955 album *In The Wee Small Hours* was in the charts for 29 weeks, reaching number 2; the following year's *Songs For Swingin' Lovers* charted for 66 weeks, also reaching the second spot. *Come Fly With Me*, from 1958, spent 71 weeks in the charts, reaching number 1, and other top positions were attained by 1958's *Only The Lonely* (120 weeks), 1960's *Nice 'N' Easy* (86 weeks), and in 1966, *Strangers In The Night* (73 weeks). The title song from this latter album also made number 1 in *Billboard*'s singles charts, as did the following year's million-selling 'Something Stupid' on which he duetted with his daughter, Nancy Sinatra. At a time in popular music's history when ballads were not the most appealing form, and singers were usually in groups and getting younger by the minute, these represented no mean achievements for a middle-aged solo singer making a comeback. The secret of this late success lay in Sinatra's superior technical ability, his wealth of experience, his abiding love for the material with which he worked and the invariably high standards of professionalism he brought to his recordings and public performances.

During his stint with Dorsey, the singer had taken a marked professional interest in the bandleader's trombone playing. He consciously learned breath control, in particular circular breathing, and the use of dynamics from Dorsey. Additionally, he employed Dorsey's legato style, which aided the smooth phrasing of his best ballad work. Complementing this, Sinatra's enjoyment of jazz and the company of jazz musicians prompted him to adopt jazz phrasing, which greatly enhanced his rhythmic style. More than any other popular singer of his or previous generations, Sinatra learned the value of delayed phrasing and singing behind the beat, and he and his arrangers invariably found exactly the right tempo. His relaxed rhythmic style contrasted strikingly with the stiffer-sounding singers who preceded him. Even Crosby, whose popularity Sinatra eventually surpassed, later accommodated some of Sinatra's stylistic devices. (Crosby's habitual lazy-sounding style was of a different order from Sinatra's and until late in his career he never fully shook off his 2/4 style, while Sinatra, almost from the start, was completely comfortable with the 4/4 beat of swing.)

Sinatra's revived career brought him more attention even than in his heyday as the bobby-soxers' idol. Much of the interest was intrusive and led to frequently acrimonious and sometimes violent clashes with reporters. With much of what is written about him stemming from a decidedly ambivalent view, the picture of the man behind the voice is often confused. Undoubtedly, his private persona is multi-faceted. He has been described by acquaintances as quick-tempered, pugnacious, sometimes vicious and capable of extreme verbal cruelty, and he has often displayed serious lack of judgement in the company he has kept. In marked contrast, others have categorically declared him to be enormously generous to friends in need and to individuals and organizations he believes can benefit from his personal or financial support. His political stance has changed dramatically over the years and here again his judgement seems to be flawed. At first a Democrat, he supported Roosevelt and later Kennedy with enormous enthusiasm. His ties with the Kennedy clan were close, and not always for the best of reasons. Sinatra was unceremoniously dropped by the Kennedys following allegations that he had introduced to John Kennedy a woman who became simultaneously the mistress of the President of the United States and a leading figure in the Mafia. Sinatra then became a Republican and lent his support as fund-raiser and campaigner to Richard Nixon and Ronald Reagan, apparently oblivious to their serious flaws.

An immensely rich man, with interests in industry, real estate, recording companies, and film and television production, Sinatra chose to continue working, making frequent comebacks and presenting a never-ending succession of 'farewell' concerts, which, as time passed, became less like concerts and more like major events in contemporary popular culture. He continued to attract adoring audiences and in the late 80s and early 90s, despite being in his mid- to late seventies, could command staggering fees for personal appearances. In 1992, a two-part television biography, *Sinatra*, was transmitted in the USA, produced by Tina Sinatra, and starring Philip Casnoff in the leading role. Almost inevitably, it topped the weekly ratings. In 1993 Capitol Records re-signed Sinatra after 30 years with Reprise Records and announced a new album as 'the recording event of the decade'. *Duets* was a brilliant piece of marketing: it had Sinatra teamed with a varied all-star cast, including Aretha Franklin, Carly Simon, Barbra Streisand, Tony Bennett, Natalie Cole, Kenny G. and U2's Bono. A subsequent volume, *Duets II*, featuring artists such as Stevie Wonder, Antonio Jobim, Chrissie Hynde, Willie Nelson, Lena Horne, Gladys Knight and Patti LaBelle, was released in 1994. However, rumours of ill health persisted through 1996 and 1997, and although it was not confirmed, Alzheimer's disease was cited as the most likely condition. The voice of the century was finally silenced on 15 May 1998. There were countless tributes from fans, world leaders and musicians.

When an assessment has to be made of his life, it is not the money or the worship of his fans that matters; neither is it the mixed quality of his film career and the uncertainties surrounding his personal characteristics and shortcomings. What really matters is that in his treatment of the classics from the Great American Songbook, Sinatra made a unique contribution to twentieth-century popular music. Despite an occasional lapse, when carefully crafted lyrics were replaced with his own inimitable (yet all too often badly imitated) phrases, over several decades he fashioned countless timeless performances. There are some songs that, however many singers may have recorded them before or since Sinatra, or will record them in the future, have become inextricably linked with his name: 'I'll Walk Alone', 'It Could Happen To You', 'I'll Never Smile Again', 'Violets For Your Furs', 'How About You?', 'Jeepers Creepers', 'All Of Me', 'Taking A Chance On Love', 'Just One Of Those Things', 'My Funny Valentine', 'They Can't Take That Away From Me', 'I Get A Kick Out Of You', 'You Make Me Feel So Young', 'Old Devil Moon', 'The Girl Next Door', 'My One And Only Love', 'Three Coins In The Fountain', 'Love And Marriage', 'Swingin' Down The Lane', 'Come Fly With Me', 'Fly Me To The Moon', 'The Tender Trap', 'Chicago', 'New York, New York', 'Let Me Try Again', 'Night And Day', 'Here's That Rainy Day', 'Strangers In The Night', 'I Thought About You', 'Lady Is A Tramp', 'Anything Goes', 'All The Way', 'One For My Baby' and 'I've Got You Under My Skin'.

Not all these songs are major examples of the songwriters' art, yet even on lesser material, of which 'My Way' is a notable example, he provided a patina of quality the songs and their writers may not have deserved and that no one else could have supplied. Since the 70s Sinatra's voice showed serious signs of decay. The pleasing baritone had given way to a worn and slightly rusting replica of what it once had been. Nevertheless, he sang on, adjusting to the changes in his voice and, as often as not, still creating exemplary performances of many of his favourite songs. In these twilight years he was especially effective in the easy-swinging mid-tempo he had always preferred and that concealed the inevitable vocal deterioration wrought by time.

In assessing Sinatra's place in popular music it is very easy to slip into hyperbole. After all, through dedication to his craft and his indisputable love for the songs he sang, Sinatra became the greatest exponent of a form of music that he helped to turn into an art form. In so doing, he became an icon of popular culture, a huge achievement for a skinny kid from Hoboken. Writing in the *Observer*, when Sinatra's retirement was thought, mistakenly, to be imminent, music critic Benny Green observed: 'What few people, apart from musicians, have never seemed to grasp is that he is not simply the best popular singer of his generation . . . but the culminating point in an evolutionary process which has refined the art of interpreting words set to music. Nor is there even the remotest possibility that he will have a successor. Sinatra was the result of a fusing of a set of historical circumstances which can never be repeated.' Sinatra himself never publicly spoke of his work in such glowing terms, choosing instead to describe himself simply as a 'saloon singer'.

Deep in his heart, however, Sinatra must have known that Green's judgement was the more accurate and it is one that will long be echoed by countless millions of fans all around the world. Musically at least, it is a world better for the care that Frank Sinatra lavished upon its popular songs. On his death the newspapers were ready to bring up his dark side, although fortunately the music, and his gigantic contribution to it, was acknowledged. Sinatra was the greatest interpreter of the popular song the world has known. As Gore Vidal remarked in 1998, it was likely that 50% of the current population of North America was conceived while Frank Sinatra was singing in the background. He was quite possibly right.

● ALBUMS: *The Voice Of Frank Sinatra* 10-inch album (Columbia 1949) ★★★, *Christmas Songs By Frank Sinatra* 10-inch album (Columbia 1950) ★★★, *Frankly Sentimental* 10-inch album (Columbia 1951) ★★★, *Songs By Sinatra, Volume 1* 10-inch album (Columbia 1951) ★★★★, *Dedicated To You* 10-inch album (Columbia 1952) ★★★, *Sing And Dance With Frank Sinatra* 10-inch album (Columbia 1953) ★★★, *I've Got A Crush On You* 10-inch album (Columbia 1954) ★★★, *Songs For Young Lovers* 10-inch album (Capitol 1954) ★★★★, *Swing Easy* 10-inch album (Capitol 1954) ★★★★★, *In The Wee Small Hours* (Capitol 1955) ★★★★★, *Songs For Swingin' Lovers!* (Capitol 1956) ★★★★★, *High Society* film soundtrack (Capitol 1956) ★★★★, *Frank Sinatra Conducts Tone Poems Of Colour* (Capitol 1956) ★★★, *Close To You* (Capitol 1957) ★★★★, *A Swingin' Affair!* (Capitol 1957) ★★★★★, *Where Are You?* (Capitol 1957) ★★★★, *Pal Joey* film soundtrack (Capitol 1957) ★★★, *A Jolly Christmas From Frank Sinatra* (Capitol 1957) ★★★, *Come Fly With Me* (Capitol 1958) ★★★★★, *Frank Sinatra Sings For Only The Lonely* (Capitol 1958) ★★★★★, *Come Dance With Me!* (Capitol 1959) ★★★★★, *No One Cares* (Capitol 1959) ★★★★, *Can-Can* film soundtrack (Capitol 1960) ★★, *Nice 'N' Easy* (Capitol 1960) ★★★★★, *Sinatra's Swinging Session!!!* (Capitol 1961) ★★★★, *Ring-A-Ding Ding!* (Reprise 1961) ★★★★★, *Sinatra Swings* (Reprise 1961) ★★★★, *Come Swing With Me!* (Capitol 1961) ★★★★, *I Remember Tommie ...* (Reprise 1961) ★★★, *Sinatra And Strings* (Reprise 1962) ★★★★, *Point Of No Return* (Capitol 1962) ★★★★, *Sinatra And Swingin' Brass* (Reprise 1962) ★★★★★, *All Alone* (Reprise 1962) ★★★★★, with Count Basie *Sinatra-Basie* (Reprise 1963) ★★★, *The Concert Sinatra* (Reprise 1963) ★★★★★, *Sinatra's Sinatra* (Reprise 1963) ★★★, *Days Of Wine And Roses, Moon River, And Other Academy Award Winners* (Reprise 1964) ★★★, with Bing Crosby, Fred Waring *America I Hear You Singing* (Reprise 1964) ★★, with Count Basie *It Might As Well Be Swing* (Reprise 1964) ★★★, *Softly As I Leave You* (Reprise 1964) ★★★, *Sinatra '65* (Reprise 1965) ★★★, *September Of My Years* (Reprise 1965) ★★★★★, *My Kind Of Broadway* (Reprise 1965) ★★★, *Moonlight Sinatra* (Reprise 1965) ★★★★, *A Man And His Music* (Reprise 1965) ★★★★, *Strangers In The Night* (Reprise 1966) ★★★, with Count Basie *Sinatra At The Sands*

(Reprise 1966) ★★★★, *That's Life* (Reprise 1966) ★★★, with Antonio Jobim *Francis Albert Sinatra And Antonio Carlos Jobim* (Reprise 1967) ★★★★, *Frank Sinatra (The World We Knew)* (Reprise 1967) ★★, with Duke Ellington *Francis A. And Edward K.* (Reprise 1968) ★★★, *Cycles* (Reprise 1968) ★★★, *The Sinatra Family Wish You A Merry Christmas* (Reprise 1968) ★★, *My Way* (Reprise 1969) ★★★, *A Man Alone And Other Songs By Rod McKuen* (Reprise 1969) ★★, *Watertown* (Reprise 1970) ★★, with Antonio Jobim *Sinatra And Company* (Reprise 1971) ★★★, *Ol' Blue Eyes Is Back* (Reprise 1973) ★★★, *Some Nice Things I've Missed* (Reprise 1974) ★★, *Sinatra – The Main Event Live* (Reprise 1974) ★★★, *Trilogy: Past, Present, Future* (Reprise 1980) ★★★, *She Shot Me Down* (Reprise 1981) ★★, *LA Is My Lady* (Qwest 1984) ★★, *Duets* (Capitol 1993) ★★, *Sinatra And Sextet: Live In Paris* (Reprise 1994) ★★★, *Duets II* (Capitol 1994) ★★, with Red Norvo *Live In Australia, 1959* (Blue Note 1997) ★★★.

● COMPILATIONS: *Frankie* (Columbia 1955) ★★★, *That Old Feeling* (Columbia 1956) ★★★, *This Is Sinatra!* (Capitol 1957) ★★★★, *Adventures Of The Heart* (Columbia 1957) ★★★, *This Is Sinatra, Volume 2* (Capitol 1958) ★★★★, *The Frank Sinatra Story In Music* (Columbia 1958) ★★★★, *Look To Your Heart* (Capitol 1958) ★★★, *Put Your Dreams Away* (Columbia 1958) ★★★, *Love Is A Kick* (Columbia 1958) ★★★, *The Broadway Kick* (Columbia 1959) ★★★, *Come Back To Sorrento* (Columbia 1959) ★★★, *Reflections* (Columbia 1959) ★★★, *All The Way* (Capitol 1961) ★★★★, *Sinatra Sings ... Of Love And Things* (Capitol 1962) ★★★★, *Tell Her You Love Her* (Capitol 1963) ★★★, *Sinatra: A Man And His Music (1960-65)* (Reprise 1965) ★★★★★★, *The Essential Frank Sinatra, Volumes 1-3* (Columbia 1966) ★★★★, *The Movie Songs (1954-60)* (Capitol 1967) ★★★, *Greatest Hits – The Early Years* (Columbia 1967) ★★★, *Frank Sinatra In Hollywood 1943-1949* (Columbia 1968) ★★★, *Frank Sinatra's Greatest Hits!* (Reprise 1968) ★★★★, *Frank Sinatra's Greatest Hits, Vol. 2* (Reprise 1972) ★★★★, *The Dorsey/Sinatra Sessions, 1940-42* (RCA 1972) ★★★★, *Round # 1* (Capitol 1974) ★★★, *The Best Of Ol' Blue Eyes* (Reprise 1975) ★★★★, *Classics* (Columbia 1977) ★★★★, *Portrait Of Sinatra (400 Songs From The Life Of A Man)* (Reprise 1977) ★★★★, *20 Golden Greats* (Capitol 1978) ★★★★, *The Rare Sinatra* (Capitol 1978) ★★★, *Screen Sinatra* (Capitol 1980) ★★★, *20 Classic Tracks* (MFP 1981) ★★★★, with Tommy Dorsey *The Dorsey/Sinatra Radio Years* (RCA 1983) ★★★★, *Lena Horne And Frank Sinatra* (Astan 1984) ★★★, *The Capitol Years* 20-LP box set (Capitol 1985) ★★★★, *Collection* (Castle 1986) ★★★, *Now Is The Hour* (Castle 1986) ★★★, *All-Time Classics* (Pair 1986) ★★★★, *The Voice: The Columbia Years (1943-1952)* 6-LP box set (Columbia 1986) ★★★★, *Sinatra: The Radio Years 1939 – 1955* (Meteor 1987) ★★★, *Hello Young Lovers* (Columbia 1987) ★★★, with Tommy Dorsey *Tommy Dorsey/Frank Sinatra All-Time Greatest Hits, Volumes 1-4* (RCA 1988-90) ★★★★, *Sinatra Rarities* (Columbia 1988) ★★★, *Rare Recordings 1935-70* (Sandy Hook 1989) ★★★, *Capitol Collectors Series*

(Capitol 1990) ★★★★, *The Capitol Years* 3-CD box set (Capitol 1990) ★★★★, *The Reprise Collection* 4-CD box set (Reprise 1990) ★★★★, *Sinatra Reprise – The Very Good Years* (Reprise 1991) ★★★★, with Tommy Dorsey *The Song Is You* 5-CD box set (Columbia 1994) ★★★★, *The Soundtrack Sessions* (Bravura 1994) ★★★, *Two From Sinatra* (Capitol 1995) ★★★, *The Columbia Years* (Sony 1995) ★★★★, *Sinatra 80th: Live In Concert* (EMI 1995) ★★★, *All The Best* 2-CD (EMI 1995) ★★★★, *Swing And Dance With Frank Sinatra* (Legacy 1996) ★★★★, *Sinatra Sings Rodgers And Hammerstein* (Legacy 1996) ★★★, *The Complete Capitol Singles Collection* 4-CD box set (Capitol 1996) ★★★★★, with Tommy Dorsey *Love Songs* (RCA 1997) ★★★★, *My Way: The Best Of Frank Sinatra* (Reprise 1997) ★★★, *Sinatra Swings* 3-CD set (Delta 1997) ★★★, *The Frank Sinatra Story* (Carlton 1998) ★★, *The Capitol Years* 21-CD box set (Capitol 1998) ★★★★★, *Classic Sinatra: His Great Performances 1953-1960* (Capitol 2000) ★★★★, *The Very Best Of The Radio Years* (Castle 2001) ★★★.

● VIDEOS: *Old Blue Eyes* (World Of Video 1988), *A Man And His Music (1965)* (Braveworld 1990), *A Man And His Music Part II (1966)* (Braveworld 1990), *A Man And His Music + Ella + Jobim (1967)* (Braveworld 1990), *Francis Albert Sinatra Does His Thing (1968)* (Braveworld 1990), *Sinatra (1969)* (Braveworld 1990), *Sinatra In Concert: Royal Festival Hall (1970)* (Braveworld 1990), *Ol' Blue Eyes Is Back (1973)* (Braveworld 1990), *The Main Event: Madison Square Garden (1974)* (Braveworld 1990), *Sinatra And Friends (1977)* (Braveworld 1990), *Sinatra: The First 40 Years (1979)* (Braveworld 1990), *Sinatra: The Man And His Music (1981)* (Braveworld 1990), *Concert For The Americas (1982)* (Braveworld 1990), *Sinatra In Japan (1985)* (Braveworld 1990), *His Way* (PolyGram 1995), *My Way – Sinatra's Greatest Ever Performances* (VCI 1997), *Sinatra: The Best Is Yet To Come* (Orion Home Video 1999).

● FURTHER READING: *The Voice: The Story Of An American Phenomenon*, E.J. Kahn. *Sinatra And His Rat Pack: A Biography*, Richard Gehman. *Sinatra*, Robin Douglas-Home. *Sinatra: Retreat Of The Romantic*, Arnold Shaw. *The Films Of Frank Sinatra*, Gene Ringold. *Sinatra And The Great Song Stylists*, Ken Barnes. *Songs By Sinatra, 1939-1970*, Brian Hainsworth. *Frank Sinatra*, Paula Taylor. *On Stage: Frank Sinatra*, Harriet Lake. *Frank Sinatra*, Anthony Scaduto. *The Sinatra File: Part One*, John Ridgway. *Sinatra: An Unauthorized Biography*, Earl Wilson. *The Sinatra File: Part Two*, John Ridgway. *Sinatra*, Alan Frank. *The Revised Complete Sinatra: Discography, Filmography And Television Appearances*, Albert I. Lonstein. *Frank Sinatra*, John Howlett. *Sinatra In His Own Words*, Frank Sinatra. *The Frank Sinatra Scrapbook: His Life And Times In Words And Pictures*, Richard Peters. *Frank Sinatra: My Father*, Nancy Sinatra. *His Way: The Unauthorized Biography Of Frank Sinatra*, Kitty Kelley. *Frank Sinatra*, Jessica Hodge. *Frank Sinatra: A Complete Recording History*, Richard W. Ackelson. *The Recording Artistry Of Francis Albert Sinatra 1939-1992* , Ed O'Brien and Scott P. Sayers.

Frank Sinatra Reader: Seven Decades Of American Popular Music, Steven Petkov and Leonard Mustazza (eds.). *Sinatra! The Song Is You: A Singer's Art*, Will Friedwald. *Sinatra: His Life And Times*, Fred Dellar. *Why Sinatra Matters*, Pete Hamill.

● FILMS: *Major Bowes' Amateur Theatre Of The Air* (1935), *Las Vegas Nights* (1941), *Ship Ahoy* (1942), *Reveille With Beverley* (1943), *Higher And Higher* (1943), *Step Lively* (1944), *The Road To Victory* (1944), *The House I Live In* (1945), *Anchors Aweigh* (1945), *The All Star Bond Rally* (1945), *Till The Clouds Roll By* (1946), *It Happened In Brooklyn* (1947), *The Miracle Of The Bells* (1948), *The Kissing Bandit* (1948), *Take Me Out To The Ball Game* (1949), *On The Town* (1949), *Double Dynamite* (1951), *Meet Danny Wilson* (1952), *From Here To Eternity* (1953), *Suddenly* (1954), *Young At Heart* (1955), *Not As A Stranger* (1955), *The Tender Trap* (1955), *Guys And Dolls* (1955), *The Man With The Golden Arm* (1955), *Meet Me In Las Vegas* cameo (1956), *Johnny Concho* (1956), *High Society* (1956), *Around The World In 80 Days* cameo (1956), *The Pride And The Passion* (1957), *The Joker Is Wild* (1957), *Pal Joey* (1957), *Kings Go Forth* (1958), *Some Came Running* (1958), *A Hole In The Head* (1959), *Invitation To Monte Carlo* travelogue (1959), *Never So Few* (1959), *Can-Can* (1960), *Ocean's Eleven* (1960), *Pepe* cameo (1960), *The Devil At 4 O'Clock* (1961), *Sergeants 3* (1962), *The Road To Hong Kong* cameo (1962), *The Manchurian Candidate* (1962), *Sinatra In Israel* (1962), *The List Of Adrian Messenger* (1963), *Come Blow Your Horn* (1963), *4 For Texas* (1963), *Robin And The 7 Hoods* (1964), *None But The Brave* (1965), *Von Ryan's Express* (1965), *Marriage On The Rocks* (1965), *The Oscar* cameo (1966), *Cast A Giant Shadow* (1966), *Assault On A Queen* (1966), *The Naked Runner* (1967), *Tony Rome* (1967), *The Detective* (1968), *Lady In Cement* (1968), *Dirty Dingus Magee* (1970), *That's Entertainment!* narrator (1974), *Contract On Cherry Street* (1977), *The First Deadly Sin* (1980), *Cannonball Run II* (1984), *Who Framed Roger Rabbit?* voice of Singing Sword (1988), *Listen Up: The Lives Of Quincy Jones* (1990).

SINGERS UNLIMITED

This vocal quartet originally started life as an extension of jazz band the Hi-Lo's. From that prominent 50s band came Don Shelton, who decided to form Singers Unlimited after the Hi-Lo's broke up in 1964. After retreating to Chicago, Illinois, USA, where he worked on a series of television commercials, he enlisted fellow Hi-Lo's veteran Gene Puerling to join him in the city in 1967. The group was formed with the addition of Len Dresslar (ex-J's) and Bonnie Herman, with the express intention of recording commercials in the doo-wop/vocal group idiom. Shelton's connections in the industry ensured the group was able to exploit the market successfully, and lucrative work rolled in. However, the 30-second snatches of songs hardly satisfied their artistic ambitions, and when they found themselves with studio time left over after one session they recorded a take on the Beatles' 'The Fool On The

Hill'. Through visiting jazz pianist Oscar Peterson, the demo of the a cappella recording was passed to MPS Records. As a consequence the Singers Unlimited, as the group had christened themselves, found themselves with their own recording contract. An album of standards followed in 1972, with more John Lennon/Paul McCartney compositions, plus material plucked from Joni Mitchell's back catalogue, all performed in a technically precise but spirited doo-wop/a cappella idiom. While it hardly set the pop charts alight, the collection did receive one notable accolade, the German Record Grand Prix of 1973. A steady stream of albums has continued to be issued ever since to a loyal following, the best of which were on Verve Records in the mid-80s.
● ALBUMS: *A Cappella* (MPS 1972) ★★★, *Eventide* (MPS 1978) ★★★.
● COMPILATIONS: *A Cappella 1* (PolyGram 1991) ★★★.

SINGIN' IN THE RAIN

Regarded by many as the most entertaining film musical of all time, this MGM classic was released in 1952. Betty Comden and Adolph Green's witty screenplay parodies that momentous and painful period in Hollywood movie history when talkies took over from silent pictures. Don Lockwood (Gene Kelly) and Lina Lamont (Jean Hagen) are Monumental Studio's brightest silent stars. Lockwood, encouraged by his ex-dancing partner Cosmo Brown (Donald O'Connor), has no problem making the transition, while Lina's voice is so squeaky and sharp it could break glass. Luckily, aspiring actress Kathy Selden (Debbie Reynolds) pops out of a giant cake and provides a dubbing service – and Kelly's love interest. The team's first attempt at a sound film is a total disaster, but Kelly and O'Connor turn it into a musical, and, at the triumphant premiere, Reynolds is revealed as the hidden starlet, while Hagen is hilariously disgraced. *Singin' In The Rain* is indeed one of the greatest film musicals of all time, and its comedy exists apart from, and within, the musical numbers. The scenes poking fun at the changeover to sound are very effective, particularly when irate director Roscoe Dexter (Douglas Fowley) is attempting to place Hagen's microphone in a strategic position, desperate to find a place on the set ('It's in the bush!') or on her person where a consistent level of sound can be obtained. Most of the score consisted of a collection of songs written by Arthur Freed and Nacio Herb Brown for early MGM musicals, and every one of them is performed brilliantly. O'Connor is marvellously athletic and funny on 'Make 'Em Laugh' (most critics noted the similarities with Cole Porter's 'Be A Clown'), and on two duets with Kelly, 'Fit As A Fiddle' (Al Goodhart-Al Hoffman) and 'Moses Supposes' (Roger Edens-Comden-Green). Reynolds joins both of them for the uplifting 'Good Morning', and then, just with Kelly, milks the lovely 'You Were Meant For Me' for all its worth. Other highlights include the spectacular 'Broadway Ballet' which is presented as part of the film within a film

featuring Cyd Charisse and Kelly, and 'All I Do Is Dream Of You', 'Beautiful Girl', 'I've Got A Feelin' You're Foolin'', 'Should I' and 'Would You?'. However, the moment from the film people always remember, and the clip that most frequently crops up in nostalgia programmes, is the one in which Kelly splashes around in the teeming rain, viewed by a rather bemused and soaking-wet policeman, creating a truly memorable moment from a memorable film. The film was photographed in Technicolor by Harold Rosson and produced by Arthur Freed's MGM unit; the director-choreographers were Gene Kelly and Stanley Donen.
In 1983 Comden and Green adapted the film into a stage musical that ran at the London Palladium for over three years, breaking all theatre records. It starred Tommy Steele (who also directed), Roy Castle, Sarah Payne and Danielle Carson, and featured several additional songs. A 1985 Broadway production failed to recover its costs. Ten years later, Steele directed a highly successful UK revival tour, with Paul Nicholas in the leading role.

6.5 SPECIAL

BBC Television's *6.5 Special*, so-called after the time it was screened, was one of the first British attempts at a pop-based television show. The opening 'train' credits are fixed in the mind of a generation of rock music aficionados. Producer Jack Good used informal camera angles and unconventional methods to invest the show with a sense of spontaneity and movement, and although staid in comparison with its immediate successors, *Oh Boy* and *Boy Meets Girl*, *6.5 Special* began to link music's aural excitement with complementary visual effects. The show's success inspired this 1957 feature, which simply repeated the formula for the big screen. In keeping with its television counterpart, the film contained many acts of questionable quality, including MOR-styled singers Dickie Valentine, Petula Clark and Joan Regan. Comperes Pete Murray and Josephine Douglas did introduce a handful of home-grown, but polite, rock 'n' roll acts, Jim Dale, the King Brothers and the kilt-wearing Jackie Dennis, but their contributions were overtly sanitized. One of the brightest moments was provided by skiffle king Lonnie Donegan, while studio house band Don Lang And His Frantic Five injected a measure of pulse into the proceedings. Better still were the superb John Barry Seven, but *6.5 Special* is recalled for the doors it opened, rather than this film. It does, however, document the sterile nature of British 50s pop and helps to explain why Good later left for the USA.

SIX TEENS

An R&B vocal group from Los Angeles, California, USA. In the wake of the success of Frankie Lymon And The Teenagers, many east coast groups emerged with a pre-teen lead sound. The Six Teens diverged slightly from the pattern by virtue of their west coast origin and the use of a female

to sing the 'adolescent teen boy' part. The members were Trudy Williams (lead), Ed Wells (lead), Richard Owens, Darryl Lewis, Beverly Pecot and Louise Williams. Their one hit was the fetching 'A Casual Look' (number 7 R&B, number 25 pop), from 1956, on which Williams' youth was most telling and appealing. The group's follow-up, 'Send Me Flowers', was a regional hit in Hawaii, and 'Only Jim' and 'Arrow Of Love' likewise achieved regional sales. The group's last recordings were made in 1958, and Owens became a member of the Vibrations.
● COMPILATIONS: *A Casual Look* (Official 1989) ★★★.

SKEAT, LEN

b. 9 February 1937, London, England. After playing bass with the Ted Heath band, Skeat began widening his musical foundation by working in numerous contexts. Among the artists with whom he has worked are singers Tom Jones and Peggy Lee, tenor saxophonists Al Cohn, Spike Robinson and Tommy Whittle, the Pizza Express All Stars, trumpeters Ruby Braff and Digby Fairweather and violinist Stéphane Grappelli. A master technician, Skeat exemplifies the great tradition of mainstream bass-playing and the invariably high quality of his performances ranks with the best. His heavy workload throughout the 70s and 80s led to ill health but, after a major operation in 1990, he was back at work, effortlessly providing the immaculate timekeeping and rhythmic pulse for which he is known.
● ALBUMS: *The Pizza Express All Star Jazz Band* (1988) ★★★.

SKIP AND FLIP

This US pop duo, Skip Battin (b. Clyde Battin, 2 February 1934, Galipolis, Ohio, USA) and Flip (b. Gary S. Paxton, Mesa, Arizona, USA), met while attending the University of Arizona in the late 50s. Once known as the Rockabillies, they recorded on Rev as the Pledges and then as Gary & Clyde. Time Records picked up their Rev master, 'Why Not Confess'/'Johnny Risk', and then moved them to its Brent label, with the more distinctive name Skip And Flip. Their recording of Paxton's song 'It Was I' entered the US Top 20 in 1959 and the follow-up, 'Fancy Nancy', also charted. Their next release, a revival of Marvin And Johnny's R&B hit 'Cherry Pie' made the Top 20 but proved to be their last chart entry together. Paxton went on to record under several names (including the Hollywood Argyles, who topped the charts in 1960 with the novelty number 'Alley-Oop') for many labels. He has also had hits as a producer and label owner, including the two-time charter 'Monster Mash', by Bobby 'Boris' Pickett. Paxton went into country music in the 70s and is now a noted personality in the gospel music world. Battin recorded on Indigo, May, Groove, Audicon and Signpost and played in the Byrds, New Riders Of The Purple Sage and the Flying Burrito Brothers.
● COMPILATIONS: *It Was I* (Collectables 1998) ★★★.

SKYLARKS

This vocal group was formed in 1942 when four army servicemen in Panama started touring together. The group consisted of Bob Sprague (first tenor), Harry Gedicke (second tenor), Harry Shuman (baritone) and George Becker (lead). When the war ended the group returned to Detroit, Michigan, where Gilda Maiken joined as lead singer. Band leader Woody Herman invited the group to join his orchestra and they made their debut recording with Herman in 1946 with 'Stars Fell On Alabama'. While in New York the Herman Orchestra broke up, but the Skylarks then met Bing Crosby, with whom they recorded two singles, 'Ko Ko Mo Indiana' and 'Chaperone'. Afterwards they joined Jimmy Dorsey's orchestra and made several recordings for MGM before that orchestra broke up too. Undeterred, they moved to California where they were hired by the bandleader and trumpet player Harry James. With trombonist Russ Morgan, the Skylarks had two number 1 singles with 'Cruisin' Down The River' and 'Forever And Ever'. Following this they played live with Frank Sinatra, Danny Kaye, Dinah Shore, Dean Martin and others, although by this time only Maiken and Becker remained of the original formation. The replacements for Gedicke, Shuman and Sprague were Joe Hamilton, Earl Brown and Jackie Gershwin. In the 50s the Skylarks signed a new contract with RCA Records and reached number 28 with 'I Had The Craziest Dream', taken from the film *Springtime In The Rockies*. Jackie Gershwin replaced Carol Lombard as lead. From the 50s television shows of Danny Kaye and Dinah Shore they progressed to Sonny And Cher's 60s shows. The band finally broke up in 1979 with a farewell appearance at the Hollywood Palladium.

SKYLINERS

This white vocal doo-wop quintet comprised of members drawn from two Pittsburgh, USA groups. Jimmy Beaumont (lead vocals), Wally Lester (tenor) and Jackie Taylor (bass) had sung with the Crescents, while Janet Vogel and Joe VerScharen (baritone) were formerly of the El Rios. The new act reached number 12 in the US charts in 1959 with the poignant 'Since I Don't Have You', a much-covered classic marked by Beaumont's superb, sweeping delivery. The Skyliners later enjoyed two Top 30 entries with 'This I Swear' (1959) and 'Pennies From Heaven' (1960), but were quickly overtaken by newer, more contemporary acts. Beaumont branched out as a solo singer in 1961. They did enjoy minor success in 1965 with 'The Loser', but the Skyliners became increasingly confined to the nostalgia circuit. Although Vogel retained a professional self-confidence, she was latterly beset by personal problems and committed suicide on 21 February 1980.
● ALBUMS: *The Skyliners* (Calico 1959) ★★★, *Since I Don't Have You* (Original Sound 1963) ★★★, *Once Upon A Time* (1971) ★★★.
● COMPILATIONS: *Since I Don't Have You* (1991) ★★★.

SLADE, JULIAN

b. 28 May 1930, London, England. A composer, lyricist, librettist and pianist, Slade began to write when he was at Cambridge University, and his first two musicals, *The Meringue* and *Lady May*, were presented by the Cambridge Amateur Dramatic Club. He then went to the Bristol Old Vic Theatre School, and in 1952 was invited by Denis Carey to join the company as a minor role actor and musical director. In the same year he composed the music for a highly successful version of Sheridan's *The Duenna*, and it was at Bristol that he met Dorothy Reynolds, a leading actress, who collaborated with him on libretto and lyrics. Their long association began with *Christmas In King Street* and *The Merry Gentlemen*, written for the Theatre Royal, Bristol, and then, in 1954, *Salad Days*, which transferred to the Vaudeville Theatre in London. It continued to delight audiences until 1960, becoming the longest-running British musical of its era. Slade played the piano in the pit for the first 18 months, while onstage, a magic piano in a London park caused passers-by to dance uncontrollably. The piece was typical Slade – a simple plot and inconsequential humour, accompanied by charming, hummable songs, such as 'We Said We Wouldn't Look Back', 'I Sit In The Sun', 'It's Easy To Sing', 'The Time Of My Life' and 'Cleopatra'. In 1956, *The Comedy Of Errors*, a comic operetta adapted from Shakespeare's play, for which Slade wrote the music, played a season at the Arts Theatre. It had originally been performed on BBC Television two years earlier. In 1957, Slade and Reynolds wrote *Free As Air*, which lasted for over a year. This was succeeded by *Follow That Girl*, *Hooray For Daisy* and *Wildest Dreams*, which even contained a 'rock' number. However, these shows seemed out of place in the theatre of the 'angry young men'. 'Our shows went well out of town, but London didn't seem to want them', Slade recalled. *Vanity Fair*, with lyrics by Roger Miller, faded after 70 performances at the Queen's Theatre, and Slade's first solo effort, *Nutmeg And Ginger* (1963), based on Francis Beaumont's 1609 comedy, *The Knight Of The Burning Pestle*, did not play the West End. Neither did some of the others, such as *The Pursuit Of Love* and *Out Of Bounds* (1973), although *Trelawney* (1972) stayed at the Prince of Wales Theatre for over six months. Slade received his warmest reviews for that show, the last time London saw his work until 1991, when a revival of his *Nutmeg And Ginger* opened to enthusiastic reviews on the Fringe, at the Orange Tree Theatre in Richmond, Surrey, England.

SLIM DUSTY

b. David Gordon Kirkpatrick, 13 June 1927, Kempsey, New South Wales, Australia. Kirkpatrick grew up on his parents' farm on Nulla Nulla Creek. His first introduction to music came through listening to renditions by his father, who was known throughout the area as Noisy Dan, owing to his overly loud vocal performances, only matched by his old-time fiddle playing. He listened avidly to the radio, being initially attracted by the recordings he heard of such singers as Jimmie Rodgers and Wilf Carter, and later, the first recordings of Australian artists Tex Morton and Buddy Williams. He was particularly attracted to cowboy songs and wrote his first song, 'The Way The Cowboy Dies', at the age of 10. At school, he became very friendly with Edwin Haberfield who lived on the next farm. The two boys spent many hours learning to play the guitar and to sing and yodel like Rodgers and Carter. They began performing as a duo around their local area. After searching for suitable names (and quickly discarding Buddy Bluebird and Buddy Blackbird), they finally became Slim Dusty and Shorty Ranger. In the early 40s, they appeared regularly on *Request Hour* on 2KM Kempsey. In 1942, impressed by his son's talent, Noisy Dan arranged an audition with Columbia Records in Sydney and afterwards paid £25 for the boy to record two self-penned songs, 'Song For The Aussies' and 'My Final Song'. Copies were sent to radio stations but they failed to make any impact, as did further similarly made recordings the following year.

However, Dusty slowly built some reputation through his radio appearances and during the war years, with Shorty Ranger, he made various trips further afield. They played with travelling tent shows, but none lasted for long and they usually arrived back home broke. When Noisy Dan died suddenly in May 1945, Dusty had to spend more time looking after the farm. In 1946, perhaps because of a growing reputation, he was invited by Regal Zonophone Records to record six songs. He was offered only a £10 fee (with no royalties) but on 19 November, he made the recordings. The first was a Dusty original called 'When The Rain Tumbles Down In July'. It was released in 1947 and proved a hit for him. It has since become an Australian country standard and is rated by some followers of Australian country as the first real bush ballad (Dusty was always saddened that Noisy Dan, who had pushed so hard for his son's success, did not live to see his initial recording breakthrough). Although a hit, because of the royalty waiver, Dusty received no financial benefit and consequently, he spent much of the next two years working on the farm. He made some appearances with Shorty Ranger, including playing the agricultural show circuit at Armidale and the touring magic show of the Great Dante, until the lack of promised wages saw them quit and head for their farms. In 1948, a visit to Sydney failed and the following year a trip to Adelaide also, owing to a polio epidemic threat there, which, naturally, did not encourage people to visit theatres. However, a further trip to Sydney eventually led to them finding employment with Tim McNamara's 2SM radio show. Here they worked with Gordon Parsons and the McKean Sisters and were employed by the Foster Family to tour with their celebrated circus.

In 1951, Dusty married Joy McKean and from that point his association with Shorty Ranger ended, although their friendship continued and Dusty later recorded many of his friend's songs. Between

1948 and 1953, Dusty made almost 30 more recordings, including his sad 'Rusty It's Goodbye', and the follow-up to his initial hit called 'The Rain Still Tumbles Down'. He and his wife had worked wherever they could find employment; at times he had even been employed as a plasterer and they now had their daughter Anne (b. 4 July 1952, Sydney, New South Wales, Australia) to consider. In 1954, he decided to set up his own travelling show. At the time, they decided it was for a three-month trial period, little realizing that it would still be in operation four decades later. Apart from Slim and his wife, the show initially featured Bob McKean (Joy's brother), rope-spinner Malcolm Mason and yodeller/comedian Barry Thornton. Thornton, with his alter ego character of Mulga Dan, stayed for 19 years and is rated by many as the most influential Australian country music guitarist through his development of Dusty's bush ballad style, instigated initially by providing amplification to his acoustic guitar. The Slim Dusty Show toured extensively and further recordings were made for the next three years without incident.

Things began to change when Dusty asked his friend, Gordon Parsons, for permission to record a song he had written about a pub that ran out of beer (those who knew of Parsons' fondness for beer later jokingly said that he not only wrote the song, he actually caused such an event). Parsons readily agreed and on 1 April 1957, Dusty duly recorded the song, 'A Pub With No Beer', merely to make up the number of songs scheduled for the session. After initial airplay on 2UE Sydney, it sold 30,000 copies; when other stations added it to their play-lists, it became a smash hit that stayed in the Australian charts for six months. The song went on to become a number 1 in Ireland and when, in January 1959, it entered the UK pop charts to peak at number 3, it made the name of Slim Dusty known to audiences far beyond his native land. (There has been some contention over the years regarding the actual authorship of the song. It seems that Parsons had once been given some lines of verse and from them, he had written the song. It was later found that a poem by Dan Sheahan called 'A Pub Without Beer', which contained many similarities in the wording, had been printed in a 1944 newspaper. Dusty, who later became Sheahan's friend and recorded several of his songs, has always maintained that Parsons had believed the lines that he had been given were from some anonymous work.) The next year, Dusty recorded follow-ups called 'The Answer To A Pub With No Beer' and 'The Sequel To A Pub With No Beer'. He later agreed that he was being overly optimistic when, in 1959, he recorded a number called 'The Pub Rock', which failed dismally. It was also in 1957 that Dusty recorded his now classic version of Shorty Ranger's song 'Winter Winds'.

Following his success with 'The Pub' (as he calls the song), Dusty and his travelling family show joined with Frank Foster's touring extravaganza. This included everything from boxers to strippers, and for six years, Dusty toured the length and breadth of Australia singing his country music to any audience that was attracted to the show. When television began to affect the audiences at such shows, Dusty decided to aim for places not covered by television transmissions. In 1964, he made his first Round Australia Slim Dusty Tour. It lasted 10 months and covered 30,000 miles, during which time he played in halls in some of the most remote areas in Australia. Since then he has repeated the process many times. He made a very successful tour to New Zealand in 1969 and the following year, on a visit to New Guinea and the Solomon Islands, he attracted thousands of fans to the concerts. During the 70s, he cut down on the length of the tours in order to meet his recording commitments.

At regular sessions, he recorded a great many of his own songs and some by noted writers such as Stan Coster. His first album, *Slim Dusty Sings*, was released in 1960 and has been followed by 87 others by the mid-90s. In 1970, he became the first Australian country music entertainer to be awarded the MBE. In 1973, Radio 2TM began the Australian Country Music Awards, and over the next 10 years, the Dusty family collected no less than 27 of them. Since 1973, he has collected 25 Golden Guitars for his songs at the Tamworth Country Music Awards. His wife Joy also won awards for her songs 'Lights On The Hill' (one of Dusty's biggest hits), 'Biggest Disappointment' and 'Indian Pacific' and in 1978, daughter Anne took the best female vocal award for her recording of 'Grievous Angel'. Dusty had some throat problems in 1974 but was soon back performing. Apart from Anne, the Dusty Family show has also included son David Kirkpatrick (b. 1958, Rockampton, Queensland, Australia), and over the years various Australian artists launched their careers as part of the show. In 1977, Dusty and country comedian Chad Morgan headed the first ever country music show to be held at the Sydney Opera House. His life story, *Walk A Country Mile*, was published in 1979 and the same year, he became only the fourth person (after Australian pioneers Tex Morton, Buddy Williams and Smoky Dawson), to be elected to the Country Music Roll Of Renown (Australia's equivalent to Nashville's Country Music Hall Of Fame). In 1983, Joy and sister Heather were reunited on stage together for the first time in 25 years and also elected to the Roll of Renown. Further awards followed, and in 1984, the film *The Slim Dusty Story* was released.

His appearances outside of his native Australia have been very limited. He visited the UK during a world trip in 1990 that also saw him visit the USA. In Nashville, he professed interest in the Ryman Auditorium and the Country Music Hall Of Fame but was highly critical of some other places. He is reported to have said of Twitty City, 'If you put that up in Australia, they'd throw bricks through the window'. Unlike many country singers, he had no desire to perform in Nashville, not even on the *Grand Ole Opry*, which seemingly failed to impress him. It has been stated that when he arrived back on Australian soil, he knelt down to kiss the tarmac. He accepted the brilliance of the American musicians but the Nashville sound was far removed from his bush ballads and consequently held little interest for him. At times he has fuelled controversy as with the occasion when he would not remove his hat for the Queen at an Australian Royal Variety Performance. He reputedly stated, 'I don't take my hat off for anyone', but photographs of a bareheaded Dusty do exist. In 1981, his Australian hit 'Duncan' received much airplay on BBC Radio and almost made the UK pop charts. Slim Dusty recorded an album with his daughter Anne Kirkpatrick (by then a popular artist in her own right) in 1990. He was still busily entertaining in the 90s, and in 1997 released an album covering pop hits from the pre-war era. Arguably, Slim Dusty may well be Australia's most recorded artist, with sales over the years that compare favourably with those of Kylie Minogue and Jason Donovan.

● ALBUMS: *Slim Dusty Sings* (EMI 1960) ★★★, *Songs For Rolling Stones* (EMI 1961) ★★★, *Along The Road Of Song* (EMI 1962) ★★★, *Aussie Sing Song* (EMI 1962) ★★★, *Songs In The Saddle* (EMI 1963) ★★★, *Another Aussie Sing Song* (EMI 1963) ★★★, *Songs Of Australia* (EMI 1964) ★★★, *People And Places* (EMI 1964) ★★★, *Australian Bush Ballads & Old Time Songs* (EMI 1965) ★★★, *The Nature Of Man* (EMI 1966) ★★★, with Joy McKern *An Evening With Slim And Joy* (EMI 1966) ★★, *Essentially Australian* (EMI 1967) ★★★, *Songs My Father Sang To Me* (EMI 1967) ★★★, *Songs From The Cattle Camps* (EMI 1968) ★★★, *Sing Along With Dad* (EMI 1968) ★★★, *Cattle Camp Crooner* (EMI 1969) ★★★, *Slim Dusty Encores* (EMI 1969) ★★★, *Sing A Happy Song* (EMI 1970) ★★★, *Songs From The Land I Love* (EMI 1971) ★★★, *Glory Bound Train* (EMI 1971) ★★★, *Live At Wagga Wagga* (EMI 1972) ★★★, *Me And My Guitar* (EMI 1972) ★★★, *Foolin' Around* (EMI 1973) ★★★, *Live At Tamworth* (EMI 1973) ★★, *Dusty Tracks* (EMI 1973) ★★★, *Tall Stories And Sad Songs* (EMI 1973) ★★★, *Australiana* (EMI 1974) ★★★, *Dinki Di Aussies* (EMI 1974) ★★★, *Lights On The Hill* (EMI 1975) ★★★, *Way Out There* (EMI 1975) ★★★, *Things I See Around Me* (EMI 1976) ★★★, *Give Me The Road* (EMI 1976) ★★★, *Slim Dusty – This Is Your Life* (EMI 1976) ★★★, *Songs From Down Under* (EMI 1976) ★★★, *Just Slim And Old Friends* (EMI 1977) ★★, *On The Move* (EMI 1977) ★★★, *Travellin' Country Man* (EMI 1977) ★★★, *To Whom It May Concern* (EMI 1978) ★★★, *The Entertainer – Live At The Sidney Opera House* (EMI 1978) ★★★, *Spirit Of Australia* (EMI 1979) ★★★★, *Slim Dusty Rarities* (EMI 1979) ★★, *Rodeo Riders* (EMI 1979) ★★★, *Walk A Country Mile* (EMI 1980) ★★★, *The Man Who Steadies The Lead* (EMI 1980) ★★★, *Slim Dusty No: 50 The Anniversary Album* (EMI 1981) ★★★★, *Where Country Is* (EMI 1981) ★★★, *The Slim Dusty Family Album* (EMI 1981) ★★★, *Vintage Album Volume 1* (EMI 1982) ★★★, *Who's Riding Old Harlequin Now* (EMI 1982) ★★★, *Vintage Album Volume 2* (EMI 1983) ★★★, *On The Wallaby* (EMI 1983) ★★★, *I Haven't Changed A Bit* (EMI 1983) ★★★, *Trucks On The Track* (EMI 1984) ★★★★, *The Slim Dusty Movie* double album soundtrack (EMI 1984) ★★★★, *I'll Take Mine*

Country Style (EMI 1985) ★★★, *Vintage Album Volume 3* (EMI 1985) ★★★, *Singer From Down Under* (EMI 1985) ★★★, *To A Mate (Mack Cormack)* cassette only (FA 1985) ★★★, *Live Across Australia* (EMI 1986) ★★★, *Stories I Wanted To Tell* (EMI 1986) ★★★, *Beer Drinking Songs Of Australia* (EMI 1986) ★★, *Neon City* (EMI 1987) ★★★, *Slim Dusty Family* (EMI 1987) ★★★, *Sings Joy McKean* (EMI 1987) ★★★, *Country Livin'* (EMI 1988) ★★★, *Cattlemen From The High Plains* (EMI 1988) ★★★, *G'Day, G'Day* (EMI 1988) ★★★, *Sings Stan Coster* cassette only (FA 1988) ★★★, *King Of Kalgoorlie* (EMI 1989) ★★★, *Vintage Album Volume 4* (EMI 1989) ★★★, *Henry Lawson & Banjo Patterson* cassette only (TP 1989) ★★★, *Travellin' Guitar* (EMI 80s) ★★★, *That's The Song We're Singing* (EMI 80s) ★★★, *Vintage Album Volume 5* (EMI 1990) ★★★, *Live Into The 90s* (EMI 1990) ★★★, with Anne Kirkpatrick *Two Singers One Song* (EMI 1990) ★★★, *Coming Home* (EMI 1991) ★★★, *Ringer From The Top End* (EMI 1994) ★★★★, *Natural High* (EMI 1994) ★★★, *Country Way Of Life* (EMI 1995) ★★★, *The Slim Dusty Show Live At Townsville 1956* (EMI 1996) ★★★, *91 Over 50* (EMI 1997) ★★★★, *A Time To Remember* (EMI 1997) ★★★, *Makin' A Mile* (EMI 1998) ★★★★, *Looking Forward Looking Back* (EMI 2000) ★★★★.

● COMPILATIONS: *The Best Of Slim Dusty* 6-LP box set (Reader's Digest 1984) ★★★, *Australia Is His Name* 4-LP box set (EMI 1985) ★★★★, *Regal Zonophone Collection* 3-CD box set (EMI 1996) ★★★★, various artists *Not So Dusty: A Tribute To Slim Dusty* (EMI 1998) ★★★.

● VIDEOS: *Into The 90s* (EMI), *Across Australia* (EMI).

● FURTHER READING: *Slim Dusty Around Australia*, Peter Phillips. *Slim Dusty: Walk A Country Mile*, Slim Dusty and John Japsley. *Slim Dusty: Another Day, Another Town*, Slim Dusty and Joy McKean.

SMITH, ARTHUR 'GUITAR BOOGIE'

b. 1 April 1921, Clinton, South Carolina, USA. After the Smith family moved to Kershaw when Arthur was four years old, his father ran the town band and his son played trumpet with it. A few years later, by now playing guitar, mandolin and banjo, he formed a country band with two of his brothers. He graduated with honours in the late 30s but turned down lucrative employment, deciding instead to form a dixieland jazz band, the Crackerjacks, which played on WSPA Spartanburg. After his brothers were drafted, he worked on WBT Charlotte before joining the navy in 1944. He played in the navy band, wrote songs and on his return to civilian life, organized variety shows featuring country and gospel music on WBT and WBT-TV; in 1947, he also gave bible classes. In 1948, he achieved Top 10 US country chart success with his MGM Records recordings of 'Guitar Boogie' and 'Banjo Boogie', with the former crossing over to the US pop chart, introducing many people to the potential of the electric guitar (in 1959, 'Guitar Boogie' was a US and UK pop hit for the Virtues and the same year became British guitarist Bert Weedon's first UK pop hit, although both recorded it as 'Guitar Boogie Shuffle') – *Billboard* initially seemed unsure in which chart to place the recording. Fender began to produce his 'Broadcaster' model, soon changing the name to 'Telecaster', the beginning of that instrument's popularity. The following year 'Boomerang', another guitar instrumental, became a country hit. *The Arthur Smith Show* on television started in the 50s and became so popular that by the mid-70s, it was still networked to most of the USA; artists from all fields were eager guests. Smith and the Crackerjacks (no longer a jazz band) recorded regularly over the years for various labels, with gospel music always prominent. Smith later became a deacon in a Baptist church. By the 70s, he had extended his business interests to include record, show and commercial productions and was also a director of a large insurance company. For a time in the mid-70s, he even ran a chain of supermarkets and formed the Arthur Smith Inns Corporation. In 1973, he and banjoist Don Reno instigated legal action against Warner Brothers Records over the use of 'Duelin' Banjos' as the theme music for the movie *Deliverance*. They claimed that the music was based on a tune called 'Feudin' Banjos', written by Smith and recorded by them in 1955. After approximately two years of legal wrangling they won the case, received damages and legal rulings about future royalties. 'Duelin' Banjos' was named Best Country Music Song Of The Year in 1973. The following year George Hamilton IV recorded his *Bluegrass Gospel* album at Smith's recording studio in Charlotte, North Carolina. Smith has copyrighted more than 500 songs, only one of which, 'Our Pilot Knows The Sea', is co-authored. In 1991, he published his first book, *Apply It To Life*. It includes the words and music to 10 of his best-known hymns, which have also been released as an album with vocals by Johnny Cash, George Beverly Shea, George Hamilton IV and Smith himself with the Crossroads Quartet. This artist should not be confused with Fiddlin' Arthur Smith or with Arthur Q. Smith (real name James Arthur Pritchett), a Knoxville songwriter, who sometimes co-wrote songs with Jim Eanes.

● ALBUMS: *Foolish Questions* 10-inch album (MGM 1955) ★★★, *Specials* (MGM 1955) ★★★, *Fingers On Fire* (MGM 1957) ★★★★, *Mr Guitar* (Starday 1962) ★★★, *Arthur Smith And The Crossroads Quartet* (Starday 1962) ★★★, *Arthur 'Guitar Boogie' Smith Goes To Town* (Starday 1963) ★★★, *In Person* (Starday 1963) ★★, *The Arthur Smith Show* (Hamilton 1964) ★★, *Original Guitar Boogie* (Dot 1964) ★★★★, *Down Home With Arthur 'Guitar Boogie' Smith* (Starday 1964) ★★★, *Great Country & Western Hits* (Dot 1965) ★★★, *Arthur Smith & Son* (1966) ★★★, *Presents A Tribute To Jim Reeves* (Dot 1966) ★★★, *Arthur 'Guitar' Smith And Voices* (ABC-Paramount 1968) ★★, *Guitar Boogie* (Nashville 1968) ★★★, *The Guitars Of Arthur 'Guitar Boogie' Smith* (Starday 1968) ★★★, *Arthur Smith* (1970) ★★★, *Battling Banjos* (Monument 1973) ★★★★, with George Hamilton IV *Singing On The Mountain* (1973) ★★, *Guitars Galore* (1975) ★★★, with Don Reno *Feudin' Again* (1979) ★★★,

Jumpin' Guitar (1987) ★★★, with Johnny Cash, George Beverly Shea, George Hamilton IV *Apply It To Life* (1991) ★★★.

● COMPILATIONS: *Here Comes The Boogie Man: The Original Recordings* (Jasmine 2000) ★★★★.

● FURTHER READING: *Apply It To Life*, Arthur Smith.

SMITH, BETTY

b. 6 July 1929, Sileby, Lincolnshire, England. After studying piano and tenor saxophone as a child, Smith concentrated on the latter instrument at the start of her professional career. In the early 50s she played in Freddy Randall's popular traditional band, but her real forte was in the mainstream. From the late 50s she regularly led her own small group and also played and sang with the Ted Heath band. Her solo career continued through the next two decades and in the 70s she was one of the highlights of the touring package 'The Best Of British Jazz'. In the 80s she was still active and playing as well as ever. An outstanding performer, Smith is one of only a few women of her generation to overcome successfully the offensive yet seemingly immovable prejudice against women instrumentalists in jazz. The quality of her playing and the high standards she has set herself reveal the absurdity of such prejudices.

● ALBUMS: with others *The Best Of British Jazz* (1981) ★★, with others *The Very Best Of British Jazz* (1984) ★★.

SMITH, CARL

b. 15 March 1927, Maynardsville, Tennessee, USA. The legendary Roy Acuff also came from Maynardsville and was Smith's hero. Smith sold seeds to pay for his first guitar and then cut grass to pay for lessons. He became a regular on a Knoxville country radio station, served in the navy in World War II, and was discovered by the 40s country singer Molly O'Day, which led to a recording contract with Columbia Records. In 1951 he made his US country chart debut with 'Let's Live A Little', had a double-sided success with 'If Teardrops Were Pennies'/'Mr. Moon' and followed it with a number 1, 'Let Old Mother Nature Have Her Way'. His impressive tally of 41 chart records during the 50s included four more chart-toppers, 'Don't Just Stand There', 'Are You Teasing Me?' (both 1952), 'Hey, Joe' (1953) and 'Loose Talk' (1955) as well as having success with 'This Orchid Means Goodbye', 'Cut Across Shorty' and 'Ten Thousand Drums'. Smith was a ballad singer with a rich, mature voice and, as he preferred steel guitars and fiddles to modern instrumentation, he did not cross over to the pop market. Known as the Tall Gentleman, he was a natural for television and for several years he hosted a highly successful country series in Canada, *Carl Smith's Country Music Hall*. He also appeared in the westerns *The Badge Of Marshal Brennan* (1957) and *Buffalo Gun* (1961), the latter with Webb Pierce and Marty Robbins. Smith had a tempestuous marriage to June Carter from the Carter Family; their daughter, Carlene Carter, is also a recording artist. After their divorce, in 1957 Smith married Goldie

Hill, who had had her own number 1 country single with 'I Let The Stars Get In My Eyes' (1953). Although Smith rarely made the US country Top 10 after the 50s, he had hits until well into the 70s and his total of 93 has rarely been surpassed. In the 80s, Carl re-recorded his hits for new albums, but it was only a half-hearted comeback. His main interest is in his prize-winning quarter-horses, which he raises on a 500-acre ranch outside Nashville.

● ALBUMS: *Carl Smith* 10-inch album (Columbia 1956) ★★★★, with the Carter Sisters *Softly And Tenderly* 10-inch album (Columbia 1956) ★★★★, *Sentimental Songs* 10-inch album (Columbia 1956) ★★★, *Smith's The Name* (Columbia 1957) ★★★, *Sunday Down South* (Columbia 1957) ★★★★, *Let's Live A Little* (Columbia 1958) ★★★★, *The Carl Smith Touch* (Columbia 1960) ★★★, *Easy To Please* (Columbia 1962), *The Tall, Tall Gentleman* (Columbia 1963) ★★★, *There Stands The Glass* (Columbia 1964) ★★, *I Want To Live And Love* (Columbia 1965) ★★★, *Kisses Don't Lie* (Columbia 1965) ★★★ *Man With A Plan* (Columbia 1966) ★★★, *Satisfaction Guaranteed* (Harmony 1967) ★★★, *The Country Gentleman* (Columbia 1967) ★★★, *The Country Gentleman Sings His Favourites* (Columbia 1967) ★★, *Country On My Mind* (Columbia 1968) ★★★, *Deep Water* (Columbia 1968) ★★★, *Gentleman In Love* (Harmony 1968) ★★★, *Take It Like A Man* (Harmony 1969) ★★, *Carl Smith Sings A Tribute To Roy Acuff* (Columbia 1969) ★★, *Faded Love And Winter Roses* (Columbia 1969) ★★★, *Carl Smith And The Tunesmiths* (Columbia 1970) ★★★, *I Love You Because* (Columbia 1970) ★★★, *Knee Deep In The Blues* (Columbia 1971) ★★, *Carl Smith Sings Bluegrass* (Columbia 1971) ★★★, *Don't Say You're Mine* (Columbia 1972) ★★★, *The Great Speckled Bird* (Columbia 1972) ★★★★, *If This Is Goodbye* (Columbia 1972) ★★★, *The Girl I Love* (1975) ★★, *The Way I Lose My Mind* (Hickory/MGM 1975) ★★★, *This Lady Loving Me* (1977) ★★, *Silver Tongued Cowboy* (1978) ★★, *Greatest Hits, Volume 1* (1980) ★★★, *Legendary* (1981) ★★, *Old Lonesome Times* (Rounder 1988) ★★.

● COMPILATIONS: *Carl Smith's Greatest Hits* (Columbia 1962) ★★★, *Carl Smith's Greatest Hits, Volume 2* (Columbia 1969) ★★★, *The Carl Smith Anniversary Album/20 Years Of Hits* (Columbia 1970) ★★★, *The Essential Carl Smith (1950-1956)* (Columbia/Legacy 1991) ★★★★, *Satisfaction Guaranteed* 5-CD set (Bear Family 1996) ★★★★.

SMITH, CARSON

b. Carson Raymond Smith, 9 January 1931, San Francisco, California, USA, d. 2 November 1997, Las Vegas, Nevada USA. Smith's family moved to Los Angeles while he was still a child, but, after completing his schooling, he first tried working in the New York area. Although he was a good bass player, work was scarce and in 1952 he returned to Los Angeles, where he promptly found work in Gerry Mulligan's legendary quartet alongside Chet Baker. Mulligan not only used his playing abilities but also recorded some of his compositions, and later acknowledged that some

of Smith's ideas helped to shape the sound and style of the group. The absence of a piano, in particular, made his bass a central part of the quartet's sound. The band broke up in 1953 soon after 'My Funny Valentine' had provided them with a big hit, and during the remainder of the 50s Smith worked in small bands led by Russ Freeman and Chico Hamilton; he also worked with Charlie Parker, Clifford Brown, Billie Holiday and Dick Twardzik. At the end of the decade he was briefly with Stan Kenton before relocating to Las Vegas, where he continued to work in jazz groups, including Charlie Teagarden's band, Buddy Rich, Georgie Auld, with whom he toured Japan, Lew Tabackin, Zoot Sims and many others, including a Los Angeles reunion concert with Mulligan. Dizzy Gillespie remarked of Smith in the 80s that he had not heard a bass player like him since Oscar Pettiford. Smith's brother, Putter Smith, is also a well-known west coast-based bass player.

SMITH, GEORGE

b. 22 April 1924, Helena, Arkansas, USA, d. 2 October 1983, Los Angeles, USA. A master of amplified and chromatic blues harmonica, Smith made a stunning debut in 1954 with 'Telephone Blues'/'Blues In The Dark', but failed to capture the audience that elevated Little Walter to stardom. This may have been because his west coast record label tended to back him with saxophones rather than the guitar-based sound of Chicago. Smith had worked in Chicago and Kansas City, but resided in Los Angeles from 1955, where he worked as a name act and accompanied Big Mama Thornton for many years. He continued to make recordings of variable quality, and was briefly a member of the Muddy Waters band. He toured Europe during the 70s, and was a member with J.D. Nicholson of the mainly white blues band Bacon Fat.

● ALBUMS: *Blues With A Feeling* (1969) ★★★, *Arkansas Trap* (1970) ★★★, *No Time For Jive* (1970) ★★★, *Blowin' The Blues* (1979) ★★★, *Boogiein' With George* (Murray Brothers 1983) ★★★, *Harmonica Ace* (1991) ★★★.

● COMPILATIONS: *"Now You Can Talk About Me"* (Blind Pig 1998) ★★.

SMITH, HUEY 'PIANO'

b. 26 January 1934, New Orleans, Louisiana, USA. Pianist Smith drew his pulsating style from a variety of musical sources, including the boogie-woogie of Albert Ammons and jazz of Jelly Roll Morton. Having served in bands led by Earl King and Eddie 'Guitar Slim' Jones, Smith became a respected session musician before embarking on an independent recording career. Leading his own group, the Clowns, which at its peak included Gerry Hall, Eugene Francis, Billy Roosevelt and vocalist Bobby Marchan, he achieved two million-selling singles in 1957 with 'Rockin' Pneumonia And The Boogie Woogie Flu' and 'Don't You Just Know It'. Both releases showcased classic New Orleans rhythms as well as the leader's vibrant, percussive technique. The pianist was also featured on 'Sea Cruise', a 1959 smash for Frankie Ford, whose speeded-up vocal was overdubbed onto an existing Clowns tape. However, despite other excellent releases, Huey Smith did not enjoy another substantial hit and, having become a Jehovah's Witness, forsook music in favour of preaching.

● ALBUMS: *Having A Good Time* (Imperial 1959) ★★★★, *For Dancing* (Imperial 1961) ★★, *T'was The Night Before Christmas* (Imperial 1962) ★★, *Rock 'N' Roll Revival* (Imperial 1963) ★★★.

● COMPILATIONS: *Rockin' Pneumonia And The Boogie Woogie Flu* (1965) ★★★, *Huey 'Piano' Smith's Rock And Roll Revival* (1974) ★★★, *Rockin' Pneumonia And The Boogie Woogie Flu* (Ace 1979) ★★★, *Rockin' And Jivin'* (Charly 1981) ★★★, *The Imperial Sides 1960/1961* (Pathe Marconi 1984) ★★★, *Somewhere There's Honey For The Grizzly* (Ace 1984) ★★★, *Serious Clownin' – The History Of Huey 'Piano' Smith And The Clowns* (Rhino 1986) ★★★★, *Pitta Pattin'* (Charly 1987) ★★★, *That'll Get It (Even More Of The Best)* (Westside 1999) ★★★.

SMITH, JOHNNY

b. John Henry Smith Jnr., 25 June 1922, Birmingham, Alabama, USA. After first playing trumpet and violin, Smith took up the guitar, on which he became best known, although he continued to play trumpet in later years. In New York in the 40s Smith maintained steady employment as a studio musician, but also took part in after-hours bop sessions. In the early 50s a recording under his own name of 'Moonlight In Vermont', with Stan Getz, was greeted with great popular and critical acclaim. He also recorded with Bennie Green, Kenny Clarke and others on *Jazz Studio*, using the pseudonym Sir Jonathan Gasser, and made albums under his own name. In the 60s Smith moved west, remaining active in music as a teacher and occasional performer.

● ALBUMS: *A Three Dimension Sound Recording Of Jazz At NBC With The Johnny Smith Quintet* 10-inch album (Roost 1953) ★★★★, *Johnny Smith Quintet* 10-inch album (Roost 1953) ★★★★, *In A Mellow Mood* reissued as *Moods* (Roost 1954) ★★★, *In A Sentimental Mood* 10-inch album (Roost 1954) ★★★, *Annotations Of The Muses* 10-inch album (Legende 1955) ★★★, *Johnny Smith Plays Jimmy Van Heusen* (Roost 1955) ★★★, *Johnny Smith Quartet* (Roost 1955) ★★★, *Moonlight In Vermont* (Roost 1956) ★★★★, *New Quartet* (Roost 1956) ★★★★, *Johnny Smith Foursome, Volume 1* (Roost 1956) ★★★, *Johnny Smith Foursome, Volume 2* (Roost 1956) ★★★, *Flower Drum Song* (Roost 1958) ★★★, with Jeri Southern *Jeri Southern Meets Jimmy Smith* (Roulette 1958) ★★★, *Easy Listening* (Roost 1959) ★★★, *Favorites* (Roost 1959) ★★★, *Designed For You* (Roost 1960) ★★★, *Dear Little Sweetheart* (Roost 1960) ★★★, *Guitar And Strings* (Roost 1960) ★★★, *Johnny Smith Plus The Trio* (Roost 1960) ★★★, *The Sound Of The Johnny Smith Guitar* (Roost 1961) ★★★, *Man With The Blue Guitar* (Roost 1962) ★★★.

SMITH, KEELY

b. Dorothy Jaqueline Keely Smith, 9 March 1932, Norfolk, Virginia, USA. A jazzy singer most famous for her work with her husband, bandleader Louis Prima. Smith made her professional debut with Prima in 1949, and the couple were married in July 1953. As well as her solo spots with the big band, she frequently duetted with Prima on stylized versions of well-known songs. In 1958, one of these, Johnny Mercer and Harold Arlen's 'That Ol' Black Magic' became a surprise US Top 20 hit. The duo followed up with the minor successes 'I've Got You Under My Skin' and 'Bei Mir Bist Du Schoen', a revival of the 1937 Andrews Sisters hit. Smith appeared with Prima in the 1959 movie *Hey Boy! Hey Girl!*, singing 'Fever', and also appeared in and sang on the soundtrack of the previous year's *Thunder Road*. In 1961, Smith separated from Prima and signed to Reprise Records, where her musical director was Nelson Riddle. In 1965, she had Top 20 hits in the UK with an album of Beatles compositions and a version of 'You're Breaking My Heart'. After marrying producer Jimmy Bowen, Smith retired from music to concentrate on raising her children. She made a well-received comeback in 1985 with *I'm In Love Again*. Fifteen years later, at the age of 68, and following the leap in popularity of her late husband's work, Smith recorded a new album which proved to be one of the best of her career.

● ALBUMS: *I Wish You Love* (Capitol 1957) ★★, with Louis Prima *Las Vegas-Prima Style* (Capitol 1958) ★★★★, *Politely!* (Capitol 1958) ★★★★, with Prima *Hey Boy! Hey Girl!* film soundtrack (Capitol 1959) ★★★★, with Prima *Louis And Keely!* (Dot 1959) ★★★, *Swingin' Pretty* (Capitol 1959) ★★★, with Prima *Together* (Dot 1960) ★★★, with Prima *On Stage* (Dot 1960) ★★★, *Be My Love* (Dot 1960) ★★★, *Swing, You Lovers* (Dot 1960) ★★★, with Prima *Return Of The Wildest* (Dot 1961) ★★★, *Dearly Beloved* (Dot 1961) ★★★, *A Keely Christmas* (Dot 1961) ★★, *Twist With Keely Smith* (Dot 1962) ★★, *Because You're Mine* (Dot 1962) ★★★, *Cherokeely Swings* (Dot 1962) ★★, *What Kind Of Fool Am I* (Dot 1962) ★★★, *Little Girl Blue, Little Girl New* (Reprise 1963) ★★★, *The Lennon-McCartney Songbook* (Reprise 1964) ★★, *The Intimate Keely Smith* (Reprise 1964) ★★★, *That Old Black Magic* (Reprise 1965) ★★★, *I'm In Love Again* (Fantasy 1985) ★★★, *Swing, Swing, Swing* (Concord Jazz 2000) ★★★★, *Keely Sings Sinatra* (Concord Jazz 2001) ★★★.

● COMPILATIONS: with Louis Prima *Hits* (Capitol 1961) ★★★★, *Spotlight On Keely Smith* (Capitol 1994) ★★★★, with Prima *Ultra Lounge: Wild, Cool & Swingin'* (Capitol 1999) ★★★★.

● FILMS: *Thunder Road* (1958), *Senior Prom* (1958), *Hey Boy! Hey Girl!* (1959).

SMITH, ROBERT CURTIS

b. *c.*1930, Mississippi, USA. This accomplished guitarist was influenced by Big Bill Broonzy. A wistful but committed blues singer, Smith was discovered by chance in Wade Walton's barber shop. Smith worked as a farm labourer, and raised a large family in considerable poverty. He was recorded again in 1962, but failed to achieve success with the new white audience. In 1969 he was reported to have joined the church and abandoned the blues.

● ALBUMS: *The Blues Of Robert Curtis Smith* (1963) ★★★, *I Have To Paint My Face* (1969) ★★★.

SMITH, STUFF

b. Hezekiah Leroy Gordon Smith, 14 August 1909, Portsmouth, Ohio, USA, d. 25 September 1967, Munich, Germany. Smith began playing violin as a child; he had some formal tuition but left home at the age of 15 to make his way as a professional musician. In 1926, he became a member of the popular Alphonso Trent band, where he remained, with side trips to other bands, for four years. In 1930, he settled in Buffalo, where he formed his own group, and in 1936 he went to New York for a long and highly successful residency at the Onyx Club. This band, which included Jonah Jones and Cozy Cole, established Smith's reputation as a forceful, hard-swinging jazzman with an anarchic sense of humour (he performed wearing a battered top hat and with a stuffed parrot on his shoulder). Offstage he was an aggressive and disorganized individual, and in the late 30s he was forced to disband because of trouble with his sidemen, bookers, club owners and the union. Following Fats Waller's death in 1943, Smith took over the band but this too was a short-lived affair. By the late 40s his career was in decline, but a series of recordings for Norman Granz in the late 50s, in which he was teamed, improbably but successfully, with Dizzy Gillespie, brought him back into the spotlight. He began to tour, especially in Europe where he was extremely popular, settled in Denmark and continued to record. Perhaps the most exciting and dynamic of all the jazz fiddlers, Smith concentrated on swinging, attacking his instrument with wild fervour and producing a rough-edged, almost violent sound. His performance of 'Bugle Call Rag' at a New York Town Hall concert in 1945 vividly demonstrates his all-stops-out approach to jazz and is a remarkable bravura display. Despite his swing era roots, Smith's recordings with Gillespie are filled with interesting explorations and he never seems ill at ease. A hard-drinker, Smith's later years were beset by hospitalizations, during which parts of his stomach and liver were removed. A visit to a Paris hospital resulted in his being declared a 'medical museum' and he was placed on the critical list, but within a few days he was back on the concert platform.

● ALBUMS: *Soft Winds* (Verve 1957) ★★★, with Stéphane Grappelli *Violins No End* (Verve 1957) ★★★, *Stuff Smith* (Verve 1958) ★★★★, *Dizzy Gillespie And Stuff Smith* (Verve 1958) ★★★★, *Have Violin, Will Swing* (Verve 1958) ★★★, *Cat On A Hot Fiddle* (Verve 1959) ★★★, *Herb Ellis & 'Stuff' Smith Together* (Epic 1963) ★★★, *Blues In G* (1965) ★★★, with Grappelli, Svend Asmussen, Jean-Luc Ponty *Violin Summit* (MPS 1966) ★★★★, *Black Violin* (1967) ★★★, *Live At The Monmartre* 1965 recording (Storyville 1999) ★★★, with Asmussen,

Poul Olsen *Hot Violins* 1965 recording (Storyville 1999) ★★★.

● COMPILATIONS: *Stuff Smith (1936-1939)* (Classics 1990) ★★★, *The Complete Verve Stuff Smith Sessions* 4-CD box set (Mosaic 1999) ★★★.

● FURTHER READING: *Stuff Smith: Pure At Heart*, Anthony Barnett and Evan Logager. *Desert Sands: The Recordings And Performances Of Stuff Smith*, Anthony Barnett.

SNOW, HANK

b. Clarence Eugene Snow, 9 May 1914, Brooklyn, near Liverpool, Nova Scotia, Canada, d. 20 December 1999, Madison, Tennessee, USA. After his parents divorced when he was eight years old, Snow spent four unhappy years with his grandmother, finally running away to rejoin his mother when she remarried. However, he was cruelly mistreated by his stepfather, which prompted him to abscond again. Snow stated 'I took so many beatings from him I still carry scars across my body that were left by his ham-like hands'. Though only 12 years old, he went to sea and spent the next four years working on fishing boats in the Atlantic where, on several occasions, he almost lost his life. An early interest in music, gained from his mother who had been a pianist for silent films, led him to sing for fellow crew members. On his return home, he worked wherever he could but at the same time seeking a singing career. He gained great inspiration listening to his mother's recordings of Jimmie Rodgers, and, acquiring a cheap guitar, he practised Rodgers' blue yodel, guitar playing and delivery, and set out to emulate his idol. He began to sing locally and eventually, through the help of Cecil Landry, the station announcer and chief engineer, he obtained a weekly unpaid spot on CHNS Halifax on a programme called *Down On The Farm*, where he became known as Clarence Snow And His Guitar and The Cowboy Blue Yodeller. It was Landry who, in 1934, first suggested the name of Hank, since he thought the boy needed a good western name.

Snow became a talented guitarist and in the following years always played lead guitar for his own recordings. He met and married his wife Minnie in 1936 and the couple struggled to overcome financial hardship; eventually through sponsorship, he was given a programme on the network *Canadian Farm Hour*. In October 1936, by now known as 'Hank the Yodelling Ranger', he persuaded Hugh Joseph of RCA-Victor Records, Montreal, to allow him to record two of his own songs, 'Lonesome Blue Yodel' and 'The Prisoned Cowboy'. This marked the start of a recording career destined to become the longest that any one country artist ever spent with the same record company. Rodgers' influence remained with him and when Snow's only son was born in 1937, he was named Jimmie Rodgers Snow. In 1944, after further recordings and regular work in Canada, and having become 'Hank The Singing Ranger' (due to the fact that as his voice deepened he found he could no longer yodel), he extended his career to the USA. He played various venues, including the *Wheeling Jamboree*, and worked in Hollywood, usually appearing with his performing horse, Shawnee. However, the anticipated breakthrough did not materialize; RCA, New York informed him that they could not record him until he was known in America, but eventually they relented and in 1949 his recording of 'Brand On My Heart' brought him success in Texas. In December 1949, he achieved his first minor country chart hit with 'Marriage Vow'.

At the recommendation of fellow Jimmie Rodgers devotee Ernest Tubb, he made his debut on the *Grand Ole Opry* in January 1950; he did not make a great impression and seriously considered abandoning thoughts of a career in the USA. This idea was forgotten when his self-penned million-seller, 'I'm Moving On', established him for all time. It spent 44 weeks on the US country charts, 21 at number 1 and even reached number 27 on the US pop charts. In the late 40s, Snow worked on tours with Hank Williams, later stating, 'I found Hank to be a fine person but the stories about him have been blown completely out of proportion. Take it from me, Hank Williams was okay'. Williams can be heard introducing Snow on 1977's *A Tribute To Hank Williams*. Snow formed a booking agency with Colonel Tom Parker and in 1954, they were responsible for Elvis Presley's only *Grand Ole Opry* performance. Presley sang 'Blue Moon Of Kentucky', but failed to make any impression on the audience that night. Parker, to Snow's chagrin, took over Presley's management, but Presley recorded material associated with Snow, including 'A Fool Such As I', 'Old Shep' and later, 'I'm Movin' On'. 'I don't mean to brag but Elvis was a big fan of mine and he was always sitting around singing my songs', says Snow. After his initial breakthrough, Snow became an internationally famous star whose records sold in their millions, and between 1950 and 1980, he amassed 85 country chart hits. Further number 1 records were 'The Golden Rocket', 'I Don't Hurt Anymore', 'Let Me Go, Lover', 'Hello Love' and the tongue-twisting 'I've Been Everywhere'. The last, which gave him his second million-seller, was an Australian song originally naming Australian towns, but Snow requested that the writer change it to appeal to Americans. He was later proud to state he recorded it on the sixth take, in spite of the fact that there were 93 place names to memorize.

Snow's penchant for wearing a toupee that did not always appear to fit correctly at times caused mirth, and many people believed he deliberately emphasized it. Legend has it that, as a joke for the audience, one night on stage his fiddler player removed it with his bow and, understandably, received instant dismissal from his boss. Some album sleeves clearly show the toupee; others, such as *My Nova Scotia Home*, are most beautiful designs, while the noose on *Songs Of Tragedy* easily makes it one of the most remembered. It is generally assumed that the character played by Henry Gibson in Robert Altman's controversial 1975 movie *Nashville* was modelled on Snow.

Over the years his melodic voice, perfect diction and distinctive guitar playing made his recordings immediately identifiable, and his band, the Rainbow Ranch Boys, always contained some of country music's finest musicians. His songwriting gained him election to the Nashville Songwriters' International Hall Of Fame in 1978 and the following year he was inducted into the Country Music Hall Of Fame, the plaque rightly proclaiming him as one of country music's most influential entertainers. In 1981, after a 45-year association, he parted company from RCA, stating it was 'because I would not record the type of things that are going today'.

Snow did not record another solo album, feeling that 'I have done everything in the recording line that was possible'. He resisted over-commercializing country music during his long career and said of the modern scene that '80% of today's would be country music is a joke and not fit to listen to – suggestive material and a lot of it you can't even understand the words, just a lot of loud music'. Snow played in many countries all over the world, being a particular favourite in the UK. An ability to handle all types of material led to him being classed as one of the most versatile country artists in the music's history. In memory of his own unhappy childhood, he set up a foundation in Nashville to help abused children. In his last years he rarely toured, but maintained his regular *Grand Ole Opry* appearances. He was still readily recognizable by his flamboyant stage costumes, which were his hallmark over the years. With well over 800 recordings over the years and sales approaching 70 million, Snow was not only influential, but hugely successful in commercial terms. A gigantic figure in the history of country music.

● ALBUMS: *Hank Snow Sings* 10-inch album (RCA Victor 1952) ★★★★, *Country Classics* 10-inch album (RCA Victor 1952) ★★★★, *Hank Snow Salutes Jimmie Rodgers* 10-inch album (RCA Victor 1953) ★★★★, *Country Guitar* 10-inch album (RCA Victor 1954) ★★★, *Just Keep A-Moving* (RCA Victor 1955) ★★★★, *Old Doc Brown & Other Narrations* (RCA Victor 1955) ★★★, *Country & Western Jamboree* (RCA Victor 1957) ★★★, *Hank Snow Sings Sacred Songs* (RCA Victor 1958) ★★, *The Hank Snow E-Z Method Of Spanish Guitar* (School Of Music 1958) ★, *When Tragedy Struck* (RCA Victor 1958) ★★★, *Hank Snow Sings Jimmie Rodgers Songs* (RCA Victor 1959) ★★★★, *The Singing Ranger* (RCA Victor 1959) ★★★, *Hank Snow's Souvenirs* (RCA Victor 1961) ★★★, *Big Country Hits (Songs I Hadn't Recorded Till Now)* (RCA Victor 1961) ★★★, *The Southern Cannonball* (RCA Victor 1961) ★★★★, *One & Only Hank Snow* (RCA Camden 1962) ★★★, with Anita Carter *Together Again* (RCA Victor 1962) ★★★, *Railroad Man* (RCA Victor 1963) ★★★★, *I've Been Everywhere* (RCA Victor 1963) ★★★★, *The Last Ride* (RCA Camden 1963) ★★★, *More Hank Snow Souvenirs* (RCA Victor 1964) ★★★, *Old & Great Songs by Hank Snow* (RCA Camden 1964) ★★★, *Songs Of Tragedy* (RCA Victor 1964) ★★★★, with Chet Atkins *Reminiscing* (RCA Victor 1964) ★★★,

Gloryland March (RCA Victor 1965) ★★★, Heartbreak Trail – A Tribute To The Sons Of The Pioneers (RCA Victor 1965) ★★★, The Highest Bidder And Other Favorites (RCA Camden 1965) ★★★, Your Favorite Country Hits (RCA Victor 1965) ★★★, Gospel Train (RCA Victor 1966) ★★★, The Guitar Stylings Of Hank Snow (RCA Victor 1966) ★★, This Is My Story (RCA Victor 1966) ★★★, Gospel Stylings (RCA Victor 1966) ★★, Travelin' Blues (RCA Camden 1966) ★★★, Spanish Fireball (RCA Victor 1967) ★★, My Early Country Favorites (RCA Camden 1967) ★★★★, Snow In Hawaii (RCA Victor 1967) ★★★, Christmas With Hank Snow (RCA Victor 1967) ★★★, My Nova Scotia Home i (RCA Victor 1967) ★★★, My Nova Scotia Home ii (RCA Victor 1968) ★★★, Lonely And Heartsick (RCA Victor 1968) ★★★, Somewhere Along Life's Highway (RCA Victor 1968) ★★★, Tales of The Yukon (RCA Victor 1968) ★★★, I Went To Your Wedding (RCA Victor 1969) ★★★, Snow In All Seasons (RCA Victor 1969) ★★★, Hits Covered By Snow (RCA Victor 1969) ★★★, with Chet Atkins C.B. Atkins And C.E. Snow By Special Request (RCA Victor 1969) ★★★, Cure For The Blues (RCA Victor 1970) ★★★, Hank Snow Sings In Memory Of Jimmie Rodgers (RCA Victor 1970) ★★★★, Memories Are Made Of This (RCA Victor 1970) ★★★, Wreck Of The Old 97 (RCA Camden 1971) ★★★, Award Winners (RCA Victor 1971) ★★★, Tracks & Trains (RCA Victor 1971) ★★★, Lonesome Whistle (RCA Victor 1972) ★★★, The Jimmie Rodgers Story (RCA Victor 1972) ★★★★, Legend Of Old Doc Brown (RCA Victor 1972) ★★★, Snowbird (RCA Victor 1973) ★★★, When My Blue Moon Turns To Gold Again (RCA Victor 1973) ★★★, Grand Ole Opry Favorites (RCA Victor 1973) ★★★, Hello Love (RCA Victor 1974) ★★★, I'm Moving On (RCA Victor 1974) ★★★, Now Is The Hour – For Me To Sing To My Friends In New Zealand (RCA Victor 1974) ★★★, That's You And Me (RCA Victor 1974) ★★★, You're Easy To Love (RCA Victor 1975) ★★★, All About Trains one side Jimmie Rodgers (RCA Victor 1975) ★★★★, #104 – Still Movin' On (RCA Victor 1977) ★★★, Living Legend (RCA Victor 1978) ★★★, Mysterious Lady (RCA Victor 1979) ★★★, Instrumentally Yours (RCA Victor 1979) ★★★, with Kelly Foxton Lovingly Yours (RCA Victor 1980) ★★★, By Request (RCA Victor 1981) ★★★, with Kelly Foxton Win Some, Lose Some, Lonesome (RCA Victor 1981) ★★★, with Willie Nelson Brand On My Heart (Columbia 1985) ★★★★.
● COMPILATIONS: The Best Of Hank Snow (RCA Victor 1966) ★★★, Hits, Hits & More Hits (RCA Victor 1968) ★★★★, Hank Snow, The Singing Ranger Volume 1 (1949-1953) box set (Bear Family 1989) ★★★★, Hank Snow, The Singing Ranger Volume 2 (1953-1958) 4-CD box set (Bear Family 1990) ★★★★, Hank Snow, The Thesaurus Transcriptions (1950-1956) 5-CD box set (Bear Family 1991) ★★★★, Hank Snow, The Singing Ranger Volume 3 (1958-1969) 12-CD box set (Bear Family 1992) ★★★★, The Yodelling Ranger 1936-47 5-CD box set (Bear Family 1993) ★★★★, The Singing Ranger Volume 4 9-CD box set (Bear Family 1994) ★★★★, My Early Country Favorites (RCA

Camden 1996) ★★★, The Essential Hank Snow (RCA 1997) ★★★★.
● FURTHER READING: The Hank Snow Story, Hank Snow with Jack Ownby and Bob Burris.

SOLITAIRES

From Harlem, New York, USA, the Solitaires, like no other vocal group of the 50s, sang lushly harmonized doo-wop with a dreamy romantic feeling, and rank as one of the great groups of the 50s. Formed in 1953, the group originally comprised veterans of the doo-wop scene and consisted of lead Herman Curtis (ex-Vocaleers), tenor Buzzy Willis and bass Pat Gaston (both ex-Crows), tenor/guitarist Monte Owens and baritone Bobby Baylor (both of whom had recorded with the Mellomoods), and pianist Bobby Williams. They signed with Hy Weiss' Old Town label in 1954, and with Curtis' haunting falsetto on 'Wonder Why', 'Blue Valentine', 'Please Remember My Heart' and 'I Don't Stand A Ghost Of A Chance', the group quickly established themselves locally, if not nationally. Their deep, yet crisp and clean, R&B sound set a standard for other groups. Curtis left in 1955 and, with the wonderfully flavourful tenor of new recruit Milton Love, the group entered their most commercially successful period. With such great records as 'The Wedding' (1955), 'The Angels Sang' (1956), 'You've Sin' (1956) and 'Walking Along' (1957), the latter covered by the Diamonds, they became a rock 'n' roll phenomenon. By the time the Solitaires left Old Town in 1960, however, they had metamorphosed into a Coasters-sounding group, and by the time of their last recording in 1964 personnel changes had left little that was recognizable from the classic group. In the following decades, various ensembles of the Solitaires would appear on revival shows.
● COMPILATIONS: Walking Along With (Ace 1992) ★★★.

SONGS FOR SWINGIN' LOVERS! – FRANK SINATRA

The most familiar Frank Sinatra album and one that captured a generation of music lovers in the 50s; it is unquestionably his most perfect work. No album could begin to encapsulate quality lounge pop more than this. Quite apart from his graceful vocals, the orchestral arrangements are immaculate and crisp 40 years later. The band, conducted by Nelson Riddle, gave Sinatra such space and freedom that he was able to make already established songs his own. The 15 songs contained on this record should serve to educate elitists that pop music has to swing before it rocks. Nobody should be too proud to have this indispensable record in their collection.
● Tracks: You Make Me Feel So Young; It Happened In Monterey; You're Getting To Be A Habit With Me; You Brought A New Kind of Love To Me; Too Marvellous For Words; Old Devil Moon; Pennies From Heaven; Love Is Here To Stay; I've Got You Under My Skin; I Thought About You; We'll Be Together Again; Makin' Whoopee; Swingin' Down

The Lane; Anything Goes; How About You.
- First released 1958
- UK peak chart position: 8
- USA peak chart position: 2

SONGS OUR DADDY TAUGHT US – THE EVERLY BROTHERS

Don and Phil Everly walked right back to the songs of their youth for a delightful set of 12 plaintive, old-time melodies. They had been regular performers on their parents' radio show and this tribute to their father, Ike, was performed with warmth and affection. The only accompaniment came from Don's guitar and Floyd Chance's stand-up bass: Chance remarked, 'Damn. You would put me on an album where every one of my notes can be heard.' Their hit single, 'Take A Message To Mary', continued the mood of the album and to this day, the Everlys perform the same songs, usually 'Long Time Gone' and 'Barbara Allen'.
- Tracks: *Roving Gambler; Down In The Willow Green; Long Time Gone; Lightning Express; That Silver Haired Daddy Of Mine; Who's Gonna Shoe Your Pretty Little Feet?; Barbara Allen; Oh So Many Years; I'm Here To Get My Baby Out Of Jail; Rockin' Alone In My Old Rockin' Chair; Kentucky; Put My Little Shoes Away.*
- First released 1958
- UK peak chart position: did not chart
- USA peak chart position: did not chart

SOUL STIRRERS

One of gospel's renowned vocal groups, the Soul Stirrers first performed in the early 30s, but their ascendancy began the following decade under the leadership of Rebert H. Harris (b. 1926, Trinity, Texas, USA, d. 3 September 2000). The group was formed by Silas Roy Crain (b. 1911, Texas, USA, d. 14 September 1996), who was joined in the classic early line-up by Harris, Jesse J. Farley (bass), T.L. Bruster (baritone) and James Medlock (second lead). The latter was soon replaced by Paul Foster (d. 20 August 1995). The group earned their reputation on the road, and by the 40s the Soul Stirrers had established themselves as one of America's leading vocal groups. Eschewing the accustomed quartet format, Harris introduced the notion of a fifth member, a featured vocalist, thus infusing a greater flexibility without undermining traditional four-part harmonies.

The group recorded several sides for Specialty Records in 1950, but Harris left the same year, tiring of what he perceived as non-spiritual influences. His replacement was Sam Cooke, late of the Highway QCs. Cooke's silky delivery brought the group an even wider appeal, while his compositions, including 'Nearer To Thee' and 'Touch The Hem Of His Garment', anticipated the styles he would follow on embracing secular music in 1956. Further line-up changes saw guitarist and baritone Bob King replacing Bruster in 1953, and Julius Cheeks briefly joining the ranks. Cooke's replacement, Johnnie Taylor, was also drawn from the ranks of the Highway QCs. The newcomer bore an obvious debt to the former singer as the group's work on Cooke's Sar label attested. Taylor also embarked on a solo career, but the Stirrers continued to record throughout the 60s with Willie Rogers, Martin Jacox and Richard Miles assuming the lead role in turn. Like the Staple Singers before them, the veteran group latterly began to include material regarded as inspirational (for example 'Let It Be'), as opposed to strictly religious. In the late 80s and early 90s UK Ace released a series of fine CD reissues of Specialty material, chiefly featuring Sam Cooke as lead singer. *Lotto Man* was an original album featuring long-time vocalist Leroy Crume.
- ALBUMS: *The Soul Stirrers Featuring Sam Cooke* (Specialty 1959) ★★★★, *Jesus Be A Fence Around Me* (Sar 1961) ★★★, *Gospel Pearls* (Sar 1962) ★★★, *Encore* (Sar 1964) ★★★, *Lotto Man* (Gospel Jubilee 1998) ★★★★, *Traveling On ...* (Gospel Jubilee 1999) ★★★.
- COMPILATIONS: *Going Back To The Lord Again* (Specialty 1972) ★★★, *A Tribute To Sam Cooke* (Chess/MCA 1984) ★★★, *Resting Easy* (Chess/MCA 1984) ★★★, *In The Beginning* (Ace 1991) ★★★, *Sam Cooke With The Soul Stirrers* (Specialty 1992) ★★★★, *The Soul Stirrers Featuring R.H. Harris Shine On Me* (Ace 1992) ★★★, *Jesus Gave Me Water* (Ace 1993) ★★★, *Heaven Is My Home* (Ace 1993) ★★★, *The Last Mile Of The Way* (Ace 1994) ★★.

SOUND OF JAZZ, THE

An outstanding achievement in the presentation of jazz on US television, this 1957 film was conceived and produced by Robert Herridge with the advice of jazz writers Nat Hentoff and Whitney Balliett. Directed by Jack Smight, the film shows the musicians playing in an atmosphere of complete relaxation and achieving an exceptionally high standard of performance. Regardless of who the musicians might have been, the concept and format would have been commendable. The fact that the musicians on display are some of the greatest figures in the history of jazz make this an hour of continuous joy. The all-star bands led by Count Basie and Red Allen feature Doc Cheatham, Freddie Green, Coleman Hawkins, Jo Jones, Roy Eldridge, Joe Newman, Gerry Mulligan, Rex Stewart, Earle Warren, Dicky Wells, Ben Webster, Lester Young, singer Jimmy Rushing, Vic Dickenson, Danny Barker, Milt Hinton, Nat Pierce (who also contributed the arrangements played by the Basie-led band) and Pee Wee Russell. Also on hand is the Jimmy Giuffre trio with Jim Hall and Jim Atlas playing 'The Train And The River', and Thelonious Monk plays 'Blue Monk' accompanied by Ahmed Abdul-Malik and Osie Johnson. If all this were not enough there is Billie Holiday accompanied by Mal Waldron. She sings her own composition, 'Fine And Mellow', in what must be this song's definitive performance, backed by many of the listed musicians, with Lester Young contributing a poignant solo. Four decades after its making, this film remains a high-water mark in jazz and its standards remain those to which all other film-makers aspire.

SOUND OF MILES DAVIS, THE

Produced and directed by the same team responsible for *The Sound Of Jazz* (Robert Herridge and Jack Smight), this 1959 film was originally entitled *Theater For A Song*. Davis is presented with his quintet (John Coltrane, Wynton Kelly, Paul Chambers and Jimmy Cobb) and also with Gil Evans And His Orchestra. The performance captures Davis in eloquent form and the contributions from the other musicians on hand help to make this an important filmed record of one of the music's most important figures.

SOUND OF MUSIC, THE

Even before its Broadway opening at the Lunt-Fontanne Theatre on 16 November 1959, *The Sound Of Music* was set to become a financial success. Advance sales exceeded three million dollars and with numerous touring versions, bestselling albums and a blockbuster film, it made a fortune for its composers, Richard Rodgers and Oscar Hammerstein II. The show had a strong narrative book, by Howard Lindsey and Russel Crouse, that was based upon the real-life story of Maria Rainer, her marriage to George von Trapp and her relationship with his family of singing youngsters. The family's evasion of capture by the Nazis during World War II gave the story a tense dramatic core and the fact that the family became professional singers meant that music and song blended well into the narrative, even if, at times, there seemed to be rather more sentiment than reality would have allowed. Starring Mary Martin as Maria, Theodore Bikel (Von Trapp), Marion Marlowe (Elsa Schraeder), Kurt Kasznar (Max Detweiler), and Patricia Neway (Mother Abbess), the show was filled with marvellous songs, including the title song, 'Do-Re-Mi', 'My Favorite Things', 'Edelweiss', 'So Long, Farewell', 'Sixteen Going On Seventeen', 'How Can Love Survive?', 'Maria', 'The Lonely Goatherd', and 'Climb Ev'ry Mountain'. Sentimental or not, it is hard to imagine that at the time he was working on this show, Hammerstein was a sick man; less than a year after the Broadway opening he was dead. *The Sound Of Music* played for 1,443 performances, and won Tony Awards for best musical (tied with *Fiorello!*), actress (Martin), featured actress (Neway), musical director (Frederick Dvonch), and scenic design (Oliver Smith). Jean Bayliss and Roger Dann headed the cast of the 1961 London production, which surpassed the original and ran for 2,385 performances. New York revivals included one in 1967 at the City Centre, and another in 1990, presented by the New York City Opera, in which the ex-chart-topper Debby Boone played Maria. London audiences saw the show again in 1992 when it was presented at Sadlers Wells, with Liz Robertson and Christopher Cazenove. Paul Kerryson's 1997 Leicester Haymarket production had Kathryn Evans as Maria and Richard Willis as Von Trapp, while the cast of the 1998 Broadway revival, directed by Susan H. Schulman, was headed by Rebecca Luker and the classy British actor Michael Siberry.

The 1965 film version, which starred Julie Andrews, won three Oscars and spawned one of the bestselling soundtrack albums of all time.

SOUTH PACIFIC

This immensely successful screen version of Richard Rodgers and Oscar Hammerstein's 1949 Broadway hit musical was released by 20th Century-Fox in 1958. Paul Osborn's screenplay, which was adapted from the stage production and James A. Michener's *Tales Of The South Pacific*, told the story of life on a South Sea island that is temporarily occupied by American troops during World War II. Two love stories run in parallel: that between the mature, sophisticated French planter, Emile de Becque (Rossano Brazzi), and a young nurse, Nellie Forbush (Mitzi Gaynor); and the other, which involves Lt. Joe Cable (John Kerr) and Liat (France Nuyen), the Polynesian daughter of Bloody Mary (Juanita Hall). Some felt that Oscar Hammerstein and Joshua Logan, who wrote the original libretto, fudged the 'racial issue' by allowing Cable to be killed in action so that he could not marry Liat. On the other hand, Nellie, after much personal torment and heart-searching, found herself able to accept de Becque's ethnic children from a previous marriage. The supporting cast was excellent, with Ray Walston outstanding as Luther Billis. Early on in the film he led a group of fellow marines in the rousing, but poignant, 'There Is Nothing Like A Dame', one of the songs in Rodgers and Hammerstein's marvellous score that came from Broadway intact – with the addition of one other number, 'My Girl Back Home', which had been written, but not used, for the 1949 show. The remainder of the film's much-loved songs were 'Dites-moi', 'A Cockeyed Optimist', 'Twin Soliloquies', 'Some Enchanted Evening', 'Bloody Mary', 'Bali Ha'i', 'I'm Gonna Wash That Man Right Outa My Hair', 'A Wonderful Guy', 'Younger Than Springtime', 'Happy Talk', 'Honey Bun', 'Carefully Taught' and 'This Nearly Was Mine'. The singing voices of Rossano Brazzi, John Kerr, and Juanita Hall were dubbed by Giorgio Tozzi, Bill Lee, and Muriel Smith, respectively. The choreographer was LeRoy Prinz, and Joshua Logan directed, as he had done on Broadway. *South Pacific* was photographed by Leon Shamroy in Technicolor and the Todd-AO wide-screen process. There was a good deal of adverse criticism regarding the use of colour filters in the various musical sequences. The soundtrack album proved to be one of the bestsellers of all time, spending an unprecedented (to date) total of 115 weeks at the top of the UK chart, and 31 weeks at number 1 in the USA.

SOUTHERN, JERI

b. Genevieve Hering, 5 August 1926, Royal, Nebraska, USA, d. 4 August 1991, Los Angeles, California, USA. A warm, 'smokey' voiced, jazz-influenced singer/pianist, Southern studied at the Notre Dame Academy, Omaha, and later played piano at the local Blackstone Hotel. After touring with a US Navy recruiting show, where she began singing, she worked at several venues in Chicago in the late 40s. These included the Hi Note Club, where she supported stars such as Anita O'Day. After obtaining a nightly spot on television, Southern was signed to Decca Records and had US Top 30 hits with 'You Better Go Now' (1951) and 'Joey' (1954). Her wistful version of 'When I Fall In Love' established her as a favourite in the UK, where she also had a Top 30 hit with 'Fire Down Below' (1957). She then switched to the Capitol label and made the highly acclaimed *Jeri Southern Meets Cole Porter*, which featured a set of humorous arrangements by Billy May, including a 20s setting of 'Don't Look At Me That Way'. One of her many album releases, *When I Fall In Love*, which was released by MCA Records in 1984, contained several numbers closely identified with Southern including 'An Occasional Man'. She retired from performing in the mid-60s to become a vocal and piano coach for professional artists. She subsequently moved to Hollywood, and worked on arrangements with the film music composer Hugo Wilhelm Friedhofer, and later, cared for him. She also published a book, *Interpreting Popular Music At The Keyboard*. In 1991, her last public performance was at the Vine Street Bar And Grill in Los Angeles, where she was persuaded by Anita O'Day to emerge from the audience and play a medley of Jerome Kern songs. She died of pneumonia six months later.

● ALBUMS: *Intimate Songs* 10-inch album (Decca 1954) ★★★, *Southern Style* (Decca 1955) ★★★, *You Better Go Now* (Decca 1956) ★★★, *When Your Heart's On Fire* (Decca 1956) ★★★, *Jeri Southern Gently Jumps* (Decca 1957) ★★★, *Prelude To A Kiss* (Decca 1958) ★★★, *Southern Breeze* (Roulette 1958) ★★★, *Southern Hospitality* (Decca 1958) ★★★, with Johnny Smith *Jeri Southern Meets Johnny Smith* (Roulette 1959) ★★★, *Jeri Southern Meets Cole Porter* (Capitol 1959) ★★★★, *Coffee, Cigarettes And Memories* (Capitol 1959) ★★★, *At The Crescendo* (Capitol 1960) ★★, *You Better Go Now* (Official 1989) ★★★.

● COMPILATIONS: *When I Fall In Love* (MCA 1984) ★★★, *The Very Thought Of You: The Decca Years, 1951-1957* (GRP 1999) ★★★★.

● FURTHER READING: *Interpreting Popular Music At The Keyboard*, Jeri Southern.

SOVINE, RED

b. Woodrow Wilson Sovine, 17 July 1918, Charleston, West Virginia, USA, d. 4 April 1980, Nashville, Tennessee, USA. Sovine was taught the guitar by his mother and was working professionally by the time he was 17 on WCHS Charleston with Johnny Bailes, and then as part of Jim Pike And His Carolina Tarheels. In 1948 Sovine formed his own band, The Echo Valley Boys, and became a regular on *Louisiana Hayride*. Sovine acquired the nickname of 'The Old Syrup Sopper' following the sponsorship by Johnny Fair Syrup of some radio shows, and the title is apt for such narrations as 'Daddy's Girl'. Sovine recorded for US Decca Records and first made the country charts with 'Are You Mine?', a duet with Goldie Hill. Later that year, a further duet, this time with Webb Pierce, 'Why Baby Why', made number 1 on

the US country charts. They followed this with the tear-jerking narration 'Little Rosa', which became a mainstay of Sovine's act. From 1954 Sovine was a regular at the *Grand Ole Opry* and, in all, he had 31 US country chart entries. He was particularly successful with maudlin narrations about truck-drivers and his hits include 'Giddyup Go' (a US country number 1 about a truck-driver being reunited with his son), 'Phantom 309' (a truck-driving ghost story!) and his million-selling saga of a crippled boy and his CB radio, 'Teddy Bear' (1976). Sequels and parodies of 'Teddy Bear' abound; Sovine refused to record 'Teddy Bear's Last Ride', which became a US country hit for Diana Williams. He retaliated with 'Little Joe' to indicate that Teddy Bear was not dead after all. Among his own compositions are 'I Didn't Jump The Fence' and 'Missing You', which was a UK hit for Jim Reeves. Sovine recorded 'The Hero' as a tribute to John Wayne, and his son, Roger Wayne Sovine, was named in his honour. The young Sovine was briefly a country singer, making the lower end of the US country charts with 'Culman, Alabam' and 'Little Bitty Nitty Gritty Dirt Town'. Red Sovine's country music owed nothing to contemporary trends but his sentimentality was popular in UK clubs. He had no big-time image and, while touring the UK, he made a point of visiting specialist country music shops. In 1980 Sovine died of a heart attack at the wheel of his car in Nashville. The following year, as CB radio finally hit the UK, a reissue of 'Teddy Bear' reached number 5, his first UK chart entry.

● ALBUMS: *Red Sovine* (MGM 1957) ★★★★, *The One And Only Red Sovine* (Starday 1961) ★★★★, *Golden Country Ballads Of The 60's* (Somerset 1962) ★★★, *Red Sovine* (Decca 1964) ★★★★, *Red Sovine – Fine* (1964) ★★★, *Little Rosa* (1965) ★★★, *Town And Country Action* (Starday 1965) ★★★, *Country Music Time* (Decca 1966) ★★★, *Giddyup Go* (Starday 1966) ★★★, *I Didn't Jump The Fence* (Starday 1967) ★★★, *Farewell So Long Goodbye* (Metro 1967) ★★★, *The Nashville Sound Of Red Sovine* (Starday 1967) ★★★, *Phantom 309* (Starday 1967) ★★★, *Sunday With Sovine* (Starday 1968) ★★★, *Tell Maude I Slipped* (Starday 1968) ★★★, *The Country Way* (Vocalion 1968) ★★★, *Classic Narrations* (1969) ★★, *Closing Time 'Til Dawn* (1969) ★★★, *Who Am I?* (Starday 1969) ★★, *I Know You're Married* (1970) ★★★, *Ruby, Don't Take Your Love To Town* (1970) ★★★, *The Greatest Grand Ole Opry* (Chart 1972) ★★★, *It'll Come Back* (Chart 1974) ★★★, *Teddy Bear* (Starday 1976) ★★★, *Woodrow Wilson Sovine* (Gusto/Starday 1977) ★★★, *16 New Gospel Songs* (1980) ★★.

● COMPILATIONS: *Red Sovine's 16 Greatest Hits* (Gusto/Starday 1977) ★★★★.

SPANIELS

This vocal ensemble was formed in 1952 in Gary, Indiana, USA. The Spaniels were universally recognized as one of the great R&B vocal harmony groups of the 50s, whose magnificent body of work was not truly reflected in their moderate chart success. The group originally

consisted of Roosevelt High students James 'Pookie' Hudson (lead), Ernest Warren (first tenor), Opal Courtney (baritone), Willis C. Jackson (baritone) and Gerald Gregory (b. 1934, Gary, Indiana, USA, d. 12 February 1999, Gary, Indiana, USA; bass). In 1953 the quintet enjoyed an R&B Top 10 hit with 'Baby, It's You', but the following year achieved their biggest success when 'Goodnite Sweetheart, Goodnite' reached the US pop Top 30 despite competition from an opportunistic pop-style version by the McGuire Sisters. The Spaniels' delicate doo-wop harmonies turned this ballad into one of the era's best-loved performances, with the song's emotional pull outweighing its intrinsic simplicity. The Spaniels in 1955 followed with two fine regional hits, 'Let's Make Up' and 'You Painted Pictures'. The Spaniels reorganized in 1956, Hudson and Gregory joined by James Cochran (baritone), Carl Rainge (tenor) and Don Porter (second tenor). Top recordings by this group included 'You Gave Me Peace Of Mind' (1956), 'Everyone's Laughing' (number 13 R&B, 1957) and 'I Lost You' (1958). Another reorganization in 1960, in which Hudson and Gregory brought in Andy McGruder, Billy Cary and Ernest Warren, yielded the group's last hit featuring the classic Spaniels sound, 'I Know' (US R&B number 23 in 1960). Hudson went solo in 1961, but formed a soul-styled Spaniels group in 1969 that brought 'Fairy Tales' to the charts in 1970.
● ALBUMS: *Goodnite, It's Time To Go* (Vee Jay 1958) ★★★, *The Spaniels* (Vee Jay 1960) ★★★, *Spaniels* (Calla 1968) ★★★.
● COMPILATIONS: *Hits Of The Spaniels* (1971) ★★★, *Great Googley Moo!* (Charly 1981) ★★★, *16 Soulful Serenades* (1984) ★★★, *Stormy Weather* (Charly 1986) ★★★, *Play It Cool* (Charly 1990) ★★★★, *40th Anniversary 1953-1993* (1993) ★★★.

SPANN, LES
b. Leslie L. Spann Jnr., 23 May 1932, Pine Bluff, Arkansas, USA. Playing both guitar and flute, Spann was already becoming an accomplished performer when he began studying at Tennessee State University. In the late 50s, now concentrating on guitar, he played professionally with Phineas Newborn and Dizzy Gillespie, recording on the 1959 Verve Records session for *The Ebullient Mr. Gillespie*. In contrast, he also recorded with artists from different spheres, including Katie Bell Nubin on *Soul Searching* (Verve 1960), a set that had in the backing band Nubin's mother, Sister Rosetta Tharpe, bowing to Spann and playing piano instead of her usual guitar. He made several tours of the USA and Europe, recording there with Quincy Jones, and he appeared on a number of recording dates with artists such as Ben Webster, Johnny Hodges and Duke Ellington, playing on the latter pair's 1959 Verve session *Back To Back*, Benny Bailey, Randy Weston, Charlie Shavers, Charles Mingus and Sonny Stitt among many. He also occasionally led small bands of his own. Adept equally in mainstream and hard bop settings, Spann's guitar playing demonstrates an affinity with the blues

and a sound technique.
● ALBUMS: *Gemini* (Jazzland 1961) ★★★.

SPECIALTY RECORDS
Formed in 1946 in Los Angeles, California, USA, by Art Rupe, originally from Pittsburgh, Pennsylvania, Specialty Records gave rise to some of the most powerful early R&B and rock 'n' roll performers, particularly Little Richard. Rupe had briefly run the small-time label Jukebox Records, and with money earned there from singles such as Roy Milton's 'R.M. Blues', launched Specialty. Among the label's first signings were blues singers Percy Mayfield ('Please Send Me Someone To Love') and Joe Liggins. He also signed gospel artists including the Soul Stirrers. In 1952 Rupe expanded his artist roster beyond the west coast and signed New Orleans R&B singer Lloyd Price, who was the label's greatest success up to that time with his number 1 R&B hit 'Lawdy Miss Clawdy'. Other New Orleans acts on Specialty included Art Neville and Ernie K-Doe. In 1955, Rupe signed Little Richard (Penniman), who became the label's greatest success and one of the pioneers of early rock 'n' roll. All of Little Richard's hits, including 'Tutti Frutti', 'Good Golly Miss Molly' and 'Lucille', were on the Specialty label. Other Specialty rock 'n' roll/R&B artists included Larry Williams and Don And Dewey. The label was wound down during the 60s, but later revived in the 80s by Beverly Rupe, daughter of Art, who launched a reissue campaign making much of the classic Specialty material available once more.
● COMPILATIONS: *The Specialty Story* 5-CD box set (Specialty 1994) ★★★★, *The Story Of Specialty Records* 2-CD set (Ace 1998) ★★★.

SPIDERS
The members of this vocal group from New Orleans, Louisiana, USA, were lead Hayward 'Chuck' Carbo, first tenor Joe Maxon, baritone Matthew 'Mac' West, bass Oliver Howard and bass/alternate lead Leonard 'Chick' Carbo (d. 1999). The Spiders purveyed an original bluesy sound and added the lilting swing of their New Orleans heritage to create a unique style of 50s vocal harmony. The group began in the mid-40s singing gospel as the Zion Harmonizers. In 1953 they were still singing gospel when they were discovered by recording studio owner Cosimo Matassa. Under his encouragement they revamped themselves as a R&B group under the name Spiders. The group had three sizeable R&B hits on the charts during their first year, 1954, namely the syncopated 'I Didn't Want To Do It' (number 3 R&B), the bluesy 'You're The One' (number 8 R&B), and the swinging 'I'm Slippin' In' (number 6 R&B). Maxon and West had both left by 1955, and were replaced with new members, tenor Bill Moore and baritone Issacher Gordon. The new line-up hit the charts with 'Twenty One' (number 9 R&B) and one of their most superb records, the bouncy 'Witchcraft' (number 5 R&B). The group split in 1956, and the Carbo brothers worked to establish solo careers.

Chuck Carbo was the more successful brother, recording many singles and albums including *Life's Ups And Downs* (504 1989) and *Drawers Trouble* (Rounder 1993).

● COMPILATIONS: *I Didn't Want To Do It* (Imperial 1961) ★★★, *The Imperial Sessions* (Bear Family 1992) ★★★.

SQUIRES, DOROTHY

b. Edna May Squires, 25 March 1918, Llanelli, Dyfed, Wales, d. 14 April 1998, Llwynpia, Mid Glamorgan, Wales. A dynamic, dramatic and highly emotional singer, who retained an army of fans throughout a career spanning over 50 years. At her 'live' performances, especially during the 70s, the audience were there not just to be entertained, but also to pay homage. At the age of 18 she moved to London to become a singer, and worked at the Burlington Club, where she was discovered by American pianist and bandleader Charlie Kunz. She sang with his band at the Casani Club, and made her first radio broadcast from there. In 1938 she joined songwriter Billy Reid and his Orchestra, beginning a professional and personal partnership that lasted until 1951, when she left to concentrate on a solo career. In between, she recorded many of Reid's songs, such as 'The Gypsy', 'It's A Pity To Say Goodnight', 'A Tree In A Meadow' and 'When China Boy Meets China Girl'. During the 40s Reid and Squires teamed up to become one of the most successful double acts on the UK variety circuit, and she made frequent appearances on BBC Radio's *Melody Lane*, *Band Parade*, *Variety Fanfare* and *Henry Hall's Guest Night*.

In 1953 Squires had a UK chart hit with one of Reid's biggest hit songs, 'I'm Walking Behind You' and, in the same year, married the young British actor Roger Moore. They settled in California for most of the 50s, sometimes playing cabaret engagements. After the couple's acrimonious split in 1961, Squires made the UK Top 30 in collaboration with personality pianist Russ Conway, with her own composition 'Say It With Flowers'. She also became the first British artist to play London's Talk Of The Town. In 1968, after several unfruitful years, she financed her own album, *Say It With Flowers*, for President Records. This was followed by a version of the Stevie Wonder hit 'For Once In My Life', along with 'Till' and 'My Way' (an anthem which fitted her as perfectly as it did Frank Sinatra). During 1970, her version spent nearly six months in the UK chart, and inspired her to hire the London Palladium for a sell-out comeback concert, which she played to an ecstatic reception; a double album was released on Decca. In the 70s Squires was headlining again throughout the UK, in concerts and cabaret, and also returned to the USA to play New York's Carnegie Hall. She hired the Palladium again in 1974 for a concert in memory of Billy Reid, and in 1979 released another double album, *With All My Heart*. During the 80s she became semi-retired, giving a few concerts, one of which became *We Clowns – Live At The Dominion* (1984), on her own Esban label;

she also released *Three Beautiful Words Of Love* on Conifer.

Squires' career was bathed in controversy and she became one of the most notoriously prolific libel litigants in showbusiness history, before eventually being instructed by a weary judge that she could no longer enter any further litigation without High Court consent. In 1989 she was evicted from her 17-bedroom Thames-side mansion that had once belonged to the celebrated actress Lily Langtry, and in 1995 her home was reportedly under threat once again. During the early 90s, Squires was still performing occasionally and in 1991 she released *The Best Of The EMI Years*, a 20-track compilation of her work with Billy Reid, some of her own compositions, and several of the other recordings she made for Columbia during the early 60s. After she was diagnosed with cancer, Squires auctioned the final items of her jewellery, and Roger Moore is said to have contributed to the cost of the treatment which failed to prevent her death in April 1998.

● ALBUMS: *Dorothy Squires Sings Billy Reid* (Nixa 1958) ★★★, *Say It With Flowers* (President 1968) ★★★, *This Is My Life* (Ace Of Clubs 1967) ★★★, *Reflections* (Marble Arch 1968) ★★★, *Seasons Of Dorothy Squires* (President 1969) ★★★, with Dennis Lotis *Cheese And Wine* (Pye 1973) ★★★, *London Palladium* (Decca 1973) ★★★, *Live At The Theatre Royal Drury Lane* (Pye 1974) ★★★, *Rain, Rain Go Away* (Decca 1977) ★★★, *Golden Hour Presents Dorothy Squires* (Golden Hour 1977) ★★★, *With All My Heart* (Decca 1979) ★★★, *We Clowns – Live At The Dominion* (Esban 1984) ★★★, *Three Beautiful Words Of Love* (Conifer 1988) ★★★, *Live At The London Palladium* (Sterndale 1997) ★★★.

● COMPILATIONS: *The Best Of The EMI Years* (EMI 1991) ★★★.

STAFFORD, JO

b. 12 November 1920, Coalinga, near Fresno, California, USA. Although the birth date above is the one that has been accepted for some time, the alternative year of 1917 is given in the booklet accompanying the 1991 CD in the Capitol Records *Collectors Series*. One of the most popular female singers of the 40s and 50s, while still at high school Stafford studied serious music with the intention of pursuing a career as a classical soprano. After five years of intensive work, she abandoned the idea and joined her two older sisters in their country music act, but later left to freelance on radio with the seven-man vocal group the Pied Pipers. In 1939, after appearing on radio with Tommy Dorsey, they reduced the group to a quartet and joined Dorsey permanently. A large part of their appeal was Stafford's pure, almost academic tone, her distinctive vocal timbre and the complete lack of vibrato, which provided a rock-steady lead. While with Dorsey she had solo success with 'Little Man With A Candy Cigar', 'Manhattan Serenade' and a 12-inch disc of 'For You'. She also duetted with Dorsey arranger Sy Oliver on his own composition, 'Yes Indeed'.

When the Pipers left Dorsey in 1942 and started recording for Capitol Records, Stafford was soon out on her own as one of the top stars of the 40s. She stayed with the label until 1950, having hits such as 'Candy' (with Johnny Mercer), 'That's For Me', 'Serenade Of The Bells', 'Some Enchanted Evening' and 'Tennessee Waltz'. There were also several duets with Gordon MacRae, including 'My Darling, My Darling' from the Broadway musical *Where's Charley?*, and 'Whispering Hope', an old religious song also recorded by Pat Boone. In 1950 she switched to Columbia Records, immediately having further success with 'Make Love To Me', 'Shrimp Boats', 'Keep It A Secret', 'Jambalaya' and her biggest seller, 'You Belong To Me'. Just as important as the singles were a series of high-class albums of standards scored by her husband, ex-Dorsey arranger Paul Weston, who had become her musical alter ego. Her reputation in some quarters as being a purely academic singer was given the lie on two notable occasions. The first was when she recorded pseudonymously as the lunatic Cinderella G. Stump on Red Ingle and the Natural Seven's 1947 comedy hit 'Temptation'; and the second was a decade later when, with her husband, she made a series of albums as 'Jonathan And Darlene Edwards', in which they wickedly sent up amateur pianists and singers. In 1959 Stafford retired from public performing, but recorded until the mid-60s, sometimes for Frank Sinatra's Reprise Records. Dissatisfied with their former recording companies' neglect of their output, Stafford and Weston acquired the rights themselves and released them on their own Corinthian label.

● ALBUMS: *American Folk Songs* 10-inch album (Capitol 1950) ★★, with Gordon MacRae *Songs Of Faith* 10-inch album (Capitol 1950) ★★, *Autumn In New York* 10-inch album (Capitol 1950) ★★, *As You Desire Me* 10-inch album (Columbia 1952) ★★★, with MacRae *Sunday Evening Songs* 10-inch album (Capitol 1953) ★★★, *Broadways Best* 10-inch album (Columbia 1953) ★★★, *Starring Jo Stafford* 10-inch album (Capitol 1953) ★★★, with MacRae *Memory Songs* (Capitol 1954) ★★★, with Frankie Laine *Musical Portrait Of New Orleans* (Columbia 1954) ★★, *Garden Of Prayers* 10-inch album (Columbia 1954) ★★, *My Heart's In The Highlands* 10-inch album (Columbia 1954) ★, *Soft And Sentimental* 10-inch album (Columbia 1955) ★★★, *A Gal Named Jo* (Columbia 1956) ★★★, *Happy Holiday* (Columbia 1956) ★★, *Ski Trails* (Columbia 1956) ★★★★, *Once Over Lightly* (Columbia 1957) ★★★, *Songs Of Scotland* (Columbia 1957) ★★, *Swingin' Down Broadway* (Columbia 1958) ★★★, *I'll Be Seeing You* (Columbia 1959) ★★★, *Ballad Of The Blues* (Columbia 1959) ★★★, *Jo + Jazz* (Columbia 1960) ★★★, *Jo + Blues* (Columbia 1961) ★★★, *Jo + Broadway* (Columbia 1961) ★★★, *Songs Of Faith Hope And Love* (Columbia 1961) ★★★, with MacRae *Whispering Hope* (Capitol 1962) ★★★, with MacRae *Peace In The Valley* (Capitol 1963) ★★, with MacRae *Old Rugged Cross* (Capitol 1963) ★★★, *Getting Sentimental Over Tommy Dorsey* (Reprise 1964) ★★★, *Do I*

Hear A Waltz? (Dot 1965) ★★★, *This Is Jo Stafford* (Dot 1966) ★★★, *G.I. Joe – Songs Of World War II* (Corinthian 1979) ★★★, *Broadway Revisited – Romantic Ballads From The Theater* (Corinthian 1983) ★★★, *Fan Favorites Through The Years* (Corinthian 1984) ★★★, *International Hits* (Corinthian 1988) ★★★.

As Jonathan And Darlene Edwards *Sing Along With Jonathan And Darlene Edwards – Only The Chorus Is For Real* (Columbia 1959) ★★★, *Jonathan And Darlene's Original Masterpiece* (Columbia 1960) ★★★, *Jonathan And Darlene Edwards In Paris* (Columbia 1960) ★★★.

● COMPILATIONS: *Jo Stafford's Greatest Hits* (Columbia 1959) ★★★★, *Jo Stafford Showcase* (Columbia 1960) ★★★★, *The Hits Of Jo Stafford* (Columbia 1963) ★★★★, *Jo Stafford's Greatest Hits – Best On Columbia* (Columbia 1977) ★★★★, *Hits Of Jo Stafford* (MFP 1984) ★★★★, *Stars Of The 50s* (EMI 1984) ★★★★, *Introducing Jo Stafford* (Capitol 1987) ★★★, *Capitol Collectors Series* (Capitol 1991) ★★★★, *The Very Best Of Jo Stafford* (Parade 1995) ★★, *The Jo Stafford Story* (Jasmine 1997) ★★★★.

STANLEY BROTHERS

Carter Glen Stanley (b. 27 August 1925, McClure, Dickenson County, Virginia, USA, d. 1 December 1966, Bristol, Virginia, USA) and his brother Ralph Edmond Stanley (b. 25 February 1927, Big Spraddle Creek, near Stratton, Dickenson County, Virginia, USA). Their father Lee Stanley was a noted singer and their mother played banjo. They learned many old-time songs as children and soon began to sing at church and family functions. In 1941, with two schoolfriends, they formed the Lazy Ramblers and played some local venues. In 1942, with Carter playing guitar and Ralph the banjo, they appeared as a duo on WJHL Johnson City, Tennessee. After graduation, Ralph spent eighteen months in the army, mainly serving in Germany. In 1946, after a brief spell with Roy Sykes' Blue Ridge Mountain Boys, they formed their own Clinch Mountain Boys and began playing on WNVA Norton. Soon afterwards they moved to WCYB Bristol, Tennessee, to appear regularly on *Farm And Fun Time*. Their intricate harmony vocal work (Carter sang lead to Ralph's tenor harmony) and their variety of music, with styles varying from the old-time to bluegrass, then being popularized by Bill Monroe, proved a great success. In 1947, they made their first recordings for the Rich-R-Tone label and later moved to WPTF Raleigh, North Carolina. With their standard five instrument line-up, they became one of the most renowned bluegrass bands and were much in demand for concert appearances.

Between 1949 and 1952 they made some recordings for Columbia Records which are now rated as classic bluegrass. These included many of Carter's own compositions, such as 'The White Dove', 'Too Late To Cry', 'We'll Be Sweethearts In Heaven' and 'The Fields Have Turned Brown'. They disbanded for a short time in 1951. Ralph briefly played banjo with Bill Monroe before being injured in a car crash. During this time, Carter played guitar and recorded with Bill Monroe.

However, they soon re-formed their band and returned to *Farm And Fun Time* on WCYB. After leaving Columbia, they first recorded a great many sides for Mercury Records. The material included more self-penned numbers, honky-tonk songs, instrumentals and numerous gospel songs recorded with quartet vocal harmonies. Ralph Stanley has always maintained that this period produced their best recordings and experts have rated the mid-50s as the Stanley Brothers' 'Golden Era'. Later recordings were issued on Starday, King, Wango, Rimrock and Cabin Creek. (Over the years Copper Creek records have released a series taken from radio shows, which at the time of writing already totals 10 albums.) Their only US country chart success came in 1960; a Top 20 hit for the novelty number 'How Far To Little Rock'. The mandolin/guitarist Bill Napier (b. William Napier, 17 December 1935, near Grundy, Wize County, Virginia, USA, d. 3 May 2000), was a member of the band from 1957 to 1961.

Through the 50s and up to the mid-60s, they played at venues and festivals all over the USA and made overseas tours. It was during a European tour in March 1966 that they appeared in concert in London. The hectic schedules caused Carter to develop a drink problem; his health was badly affected and he died in hospital in Bristol, Virginia, on 1 December 1966. After his brother's death, Ralph Stanley re-formed the Clinch Mountain Boys, hiring Roy Lee Centers (b. 8 November 1944, Jackson, Kentucky, USA, d. 2 May 1974, Breathitt County, Kentucky, USA) as lead vocalist, and continued to play and record bluegrass music. In 1970, he started the annual Bluegrass Festival (named after his brother), an event that attracted large numbers of musicians and bluegrass fans. Over the years, his style of banjo playing has been copied by many young musicians and he has become respected (like Monroe) as one of the most important artists in the popularization of bluegrass music. During the 70s and 80s, the Clinch Mountain Boys included within their ranks such country artists as Ricky Skaggs, Keith Whitley and Larry Sparks, and others, including John Conlee and Emmylou Harris, have recorded Stanley Brothers songs. UK bluegrass followers were delighted to see Ralph Stanley live at the 1991 Edale Festival. He was later featured in the movie *O Brother, Where Art Thou?* singing an *a cappella* rendition of 'O Death'.

● ALBUMS: *Country Pickin' & Singin'* (Mercury 1958) ★★★★, *The Stanley Brothers* (King 1959) ★★★★, *Mountain Song Favorites* (Starday 1959) ★★★★, *Sing Everybody's Country Favorites* (King 1959) ★★, *Hymns & Sacred Songs* (King 1959) ★★, *Sacred Songs Of The Hills* (Starday 1960) ★★★, *For The Good People* (King 1960) ★★★, *Old Time Camp Meeting* (King 1961) ★★★★, *The Stanley Brothers* (Harmony 1961) ★★★, *The Stanleys In Person* (King 1961) ★★, *The Stanley Brothers And The Clinch Mountain Boys Sing The Songs They Like The Best* (King 1961) ★★★, *Stanley Brothers Live At Antioch College-1960* (Vintage 1961) ★★, *Award Winners At The Folk Song Festival* (King 1962) ★★, *The Mountain Music Sound* (Starday 1962) ★★★,

Good Old Camp Meeting Songs (King 1962) ★★★★, *Five String Banjo Hootenanny* (1963) ★★★, *The World's Finest Five String Banjo* (King 1963) ★★★, *Just Because (Folk Concert)* (King 1963) ★★, *Hard Times* (Mercury 1963) ★★★★, *Country-Folk Music Spotlight* (King 1963) ★★★, *Old Country Church* (1963) ★★★, *Sing Bluegrass Songs For You* (King 1964) ★★★, *Hymns Of The Cross* (King 1964) ★★, *The Stanley Brothers – Their Original Recordings* (1965) ★★★, *The Angels Are Singing* (Harmony 1966) ★★★, *Jacob's Vision* (Starday 1966) ★★★, *Bluegrass Gospel Favorites* (Cabin Creek 1966) ★★, *The Greatest Country & Western Show On Earth* (King 1966) ★★, *A Collection Of Original Gospel & Sacred Songs* (1966) ★★★, *The Stanley Brothers Go To Europe* (1966) ★★, *An Empty Mansion* (1967) ★★★, *Memorial Album* (1967) ★★★★, *The Best Loved Songs Of The Carter Family* (King 1967) ★★★, *The Legendary Stanley Brothers Recorded Live, Volume 1* (1968) ★★★, *The Legendary Stanley Brothers Recorded Live, Volume 2* (1969) ★★, *On Stage* (1969) ★★, *How Far To Little Rock* (1969) ★★★, *Deluxe Album* (1970) ★★★, *Together For The Last Time* (1971) ★★★, *Rank Strangers* (1973) ★★★, *The Stanley Brothers* (1974) ★★★, *The Stanley Brothers On The Air* (1976) ★★★★, *A Beautiful Life* (1978) ★★★, *I Saw The Light* (1980) ★★★, *Stanley Brothers On Radio, Volume 1* (1984) ★★★★, *Stanley Brothers On Radio, Volume 2* (1984) ★★★★, *The Starday Sessions* (1984) ★★★★, *On WCYB Bristol Farm & Fun Time* (1988) ★★★, *Gospel Songs From Cabin Creek* (1990) ★★★.

Albums issued on Wango in early 60s as John's Gospel Quartet: *John's Gospel Quartet* (reissued 1973 as *The Stanley Brothers of Virginia Volume 1*) ★★★, *John's Country Quartet* (reissued 1973 as *The Long Journey Home*) ★★★, *John's Gospel Quartet Volume 2* (reissued 1973 as *The Stanley Brothers Volume 4*) ★★★, *John's Gospel Quartet Songs Of Mother & Home* (reissued 1973 as *The Little Old Country Church House*) ★★★.

● COMPILATIONS: *The Columbia Sessions, Volume 1* (Rounder 1981) ★★★★, *Shadows Of The Past* (1981) ★★★★, *The Columbia Sessions, Volume 2* (Rounder 1982) ★★★★, *The Stanley Series 11-volume set* (Copper Creek 80s) ★★★★, *Early Years 1958-1961* 4-CD box set (King 1994) ★★★★, *The Stanley Brothers And The Clinch Mountain Boys* (Bear Family 1994) ★★★★, *Angel Band: The Classic Mercury Recordings* (Mercury Nashville 1995) ★★★★, *Complete Columbia Recordings* (Columbia/Legacy 1996) ★★★★, *Earliest Recordings* (Revenant 1998) ★★★★, *Riding That Midnight Train: The Starday-King Years 1958-61* (West Side 1999) ★★★★, *Man Of Constant Sorrow* (Rebel 2000) ★★★★, *Too Late To Go* (Catfish 2001) ★★★.

STAPLETON, CYRIL

b. 31 December 1914, Nottingham, England, d. 25 February 1974, England. Stapleton played the violin at the age of 11, and served in pit orchestras for silent movies before joining Henry Hall as a violinist in the early 30s. By 1939, and the outbreak of World War II, he had moved on to working under Billy Ternent, via Jack Payne, and married impressionist Beryl Orde. He joined the Royal Air Force, initially as an air-gunner, later conducting the RAF Symphony Orchestra at the Potsdam Summit Conference. At the end of the war he formed a band to play at Fisher's Restaurant in London's New Bond Street. In the late 40s, the band, plus strings, was featured on BBC radio programmes such as *Hit Parade* and *Golden Slipper*.

In the 50s he became known as the UK's 'Mr. Music' when he became the leader of the all-star BBC Show Band which made its first broadcast on the Light Programme on 2 October 1952, and was featured three nights a week thereafter. He led the band for five years, playing host to star US artists such as Frank Sinatra and Nat 'King' Cole, along with residents Janie Marlow and the Stargazers vocal group. With his own band he had a string of UK chart hits for Decca Records from 1955-57, including 'Elephant Tango', 'Blue Star' (theme from the US television series *The Medics*), 'The Italian Theme', 'The Happy Whistler' and 'Forgotten Dreams'. In the USA Stapleton made the Top 30 with 'The Children's Marching Song' (from the film *The Inn Of The Sixth Happiness*) which, along with 'Blue Star', sold a million copies.

In the early 60s Stapleton was resident band leader at the Lyceum Ballroom in the Strand, London. One of his early protégés was a 14-year-old dancer by the name of Jeff Dexter, who achieved notoriety as a disc jockey and compere of numerous rock festivals and concerts in the 60s and 70s, and became the manager of the 70s soft rock band America. In 1966 the Stapleton band moved to Pye Records, where Stapleton later became A&R controller and an independent producer, masterminding the multi-million-selling *Singalong* series of albums by Max Bygraves. In the last few years of his life Stapleton began to tour with a big band, attempting to recreate the sounds of his heyday.

● ALBUMS: *Songs Of The Golden West* (Decca 1958) ★★★, *Music For Dancing In The Dark* (Decca 1958) ★★★, *Just For You* (Decca 1959) ★★★, *Italy After Dark* (Decca 1959) ★★★, *New York After Dark* (Decca 1959) ★★★★, *Come 'N' Get It* (Decca 1959) ★★★, *Big Hits From Broadway* (Decca 1960) ★★★, with Don Rendell *All-Time Big Band Hits* (Decca 1960) ★★★, with his Concert Orchestra *'Congress Dances'* (Decca 1960) ★★★, with Brian Johnson, Ray Merrell, Joy Worth *'Gigi' And 'South Pacific'* (Decca 1960) ★★★, *Great Movie Hits* (Decca 1960) ★★★★, *Great Movie Hits, Volume 2* (Decca 1961) ★★★, *Top Pop Instrumentals* (Decca 1961) ★★★, *Songs You Won't Forget* (Decca 1962) ★★★, *My Fair Lady/King And I* (Eclipse 1969) ★★★.

● COMPILATIONS: *The Big Band's Back* (Golden Hour 1974) ★★★, *Golden Hour Of Strict Tempo* (Golden Hour 1974) ★★★.

STAPP, JACK

b. 8 December 1912, Nashville, Tennessee, USA, d. 20 December 1980. The family relocated to Atlanta in 1921, where Stapp was educated. He attended Georgia Tech, who had their own radio station, and became Programme Controller when WGST went commercial. He then relocated to New York, where he became a senior CBS Records executive and a friend of Phil Carlin, the Production Manager of NBC. Stapp's abilities came to the attention of WSM in Nashville and in 1939, they appointed him Programme Manager. He created new shows on WSM and he used his friendship with Carlin to gain some of the programmes, including the *Prince Albert* segment of the *Grand Ole Opry*, network exposure. He has also been credited for ending the predominance of string bands on the *Opry*, by promoting Roy Acuff and later Pee Wee King and Ernest Tubb. During World War II, Stapp was involved in the study of psychological warfare in New York but spent some time working on the preparation of propaganda in London. He returned to WSM and although he had no initial interest in country music, he was appointed manager of the *Opry* and in that capacity instigated many continuing WSM events such as the annual DJ Convention. In 1951, with his partner providing the money and Stapp providing the know-how, he and Lou Cowan launched Tree Publishing. He hired Buddy Killen to review songs and, in 1954, the first Tree-published song, 'By The Law of My Heart', was recorded by Benny Martin. In 1955, two of Tree's writers, Mae Boren Axton and Tommy Durden (with the assistance of Elvis Presley), came up with 'Heartbreak Hotel', which firmly established the company when Presley's recording topped the US country and pop charts. In 1957, Stapp left WSM to become head of WKDA, a rock station and when Cowan left Tree, Killen was made a partner. In 1964, when Stapp left WKDA to devote all his time to Tree, he made Killen his vice-president. In 1975, Stapp became chairman of the Tree Board. A founder-member of the Country Music Association, he held top posts in other organizations, including NARAS. He died in 1980, but in 1989, he received acknowledgement of his services to country music by his induction to the Country Music Hall Of Fame. Tree Publishing, now part of the Japanese Sony company, has been rated by *Billboard* as the most successful publishing company in country music.

STAR IS BORN, A

Over the years, several films have attempted to strip the veneer of glamour from Hollywood, the film capital of the world, and expose the sadness and bitterness that sometimes lay beneath. *Sunset Boulevard* (1950) is, perhaps, the prime example of the genre, and, more recently, *The Player* (1992) dwelt on the greed and double-dealing inherent in the movie business. Adela Rogers St. John's original story, which eventually evolved into the 1954 Warner Brothers musical picture *A Star Is Born*, first came to the screen in 1932 under the title of *What Price Hollywood?*. Five years later, it was adapted for an Academy Award-winning dramatic film entitled *A Star Is Born*, which had a story by William A. Wellman, a screenplay by Dorothy Parker, Alan Campbell and Robert Carson, and starred Janet Gaynor and Fredric

March. Moss Hart's superbly crafted screenplay for the 1954 musical version, which stayed fairly close to the plot of the previous film, tells of Norman Maine (James Mason), a has-been movie actor, whose temperamental and brutish behaviour results in him being ostracized from Hollywood studios and society. While taking solace in the bottle, he is forced to become dependent on his wife, Esther Blodgett (professional name Vicki Lester), played by Judy Garland. Mainly through his influence (and her talent), she becomes a big star herself. Eventually, unable to cope with life at the bottom of the barrel, he drowns himself. Garland was outstanding throughout – this was probably her greatest film role – and Mason, who is said to have been the fifth choice for the part, was wonderful, too. Charles Bickford, as the studio head who is reluctant to let Maine go, and Jack Carson, in the role of the studio's publicity chief who is only too glad to be rid of him, featured in a fine supporting cast, along with Lucy Marlow, Grady Sutton, Tommy Noonan, Amanda Blake, Irving Bacon and James Brown. Harold Arlen and Ira Gershwin wrote most of the songs, including the compelling 'The Man That Got Away', 'Gotta Have Me Go With You', 'Someone At Last (Somewhere There's A Someone)', 'It's A New World' and two that were cut because of the film's excessive length, 'Lose That Long Face' and 'Here's What I'm Here For'. The remainder were 'Swanee' (George Gershwin – Irving Caesar), and 'Born In A Trunk' (Leonard Gershe – Roger Edens) which effectively topped and tailed a medley of old songs. The choreographer was Richard Barstow, and the film was produced by Sidney Luft (at that time Garland's husband), directed by George Cukor, and photographed in Technicolor and CinemaScope. One of the all-time great film musicals, A Star Is Born was re-released in the 80s complete with the two songs that were cut from the original print, and with some other scenes restored. In the 1976 remake of A Star Is Born, starring Barbra Streisand and Kris Kristofferson, screenwriters John Gregory Dunne, Frank Pierson and Joan Didion set their new plot in the world of rock music, with an appropriate score that included such numbers as 'Lost Inside Of You' (Streisand – Leon Russell), 'I Believe In Love' (Kenny Loggins – Alan And Marilyn Bergman), 'Queen Bee' (Rupert Holmes) and 'The Woman In The Moon' (Paul Williams – Kenny Ascher). Streisand and Williams also collaborated on 'Love Theme (Evergreen)', which won an Academy Award and topped the US chart. The film was released by Warner Brothers and photographed in Metrocolor and Panavision. The director was Frank Pierson, and A Star Is Born (Mark III) was a smash hit, grossing nearly $40 million in the USA and Canada alone.

● FURTHER READING: *The Making Of The 1954 Movie And Its 1983 Reconstruction*, Ronald Haver.

STARGAZERS

Formed in 1949, the Stargazers developed into Britain's most popular vocal group in the early 50s. The original line-up comprised Dick James, Cliff Adams, Marie Benson, Fred Datchler and Ronnie Milne. They first attracted attention on radio programmes such as *The Derek Roy Show* and *The Family Hour*, later moving to *Top Score*, the *Goon Show* and *Take It From Here*. The Stargazers began recording towards the end of 1949, working for a variety of labels, including Decca Records, HMV Records, Columbia Records and Polygon, backing artists such as Steve Conway and Benny Lee, and later, Dennis Lotis and Jimmy Young. Their own releases included 'Me And My Imagination', 'Red Silken Stockings', 'A-Round The Corner' and 'Sugarbush'. In April 1953, they became the first British act to reach number 1 in the infant *New Musical Express* chart, with 'Broken Wings'. Almost a year later, they hit the top spot again, with Meredith Willson's 'I See The Moon'. They continued to record into the late 50s, and made the UK chart with 'The Happy Wanderer', 'Somebody', 'The Finger Of Suspicion' (with Dickie Valentine), 'The Crazy Otto Rag', 'Close The Door', 'Twenty Tiny Fingers' and 'Hot Diggity (Dog Ziggity Boom)'.

They worked constantly in radio, and their own series, *The Stargazers' Music Shop*, opened for business on Radio Luxembourg in 1952, crossing to the BBC nearly five years later. The group also had a regular radio slot on the BBC's *Show Band Show* with Cyril Stapleton, and toured the UK variety circuit. Their first permanent personnel change came in 1953, when David Carey replaced Ronnie Milne. Milne emigrated to Canada and took up a post in the Canadian Army, training young musicians. Two years later, the group appeared in the Royal Variety Performance, and, in the same year, Eula Parker took over from her fellow Australian, Marie Benson, who embarked on a solo career, armed with a two-year contract with Philips Records. Parker herself was later succeeded by June Marlow. After being replaced by Bob Brown, Dick James, the Stargazers' original leader, had solo hits with 'Robin Hood' and 'Garden Of Eden' before becoming a successful music publisher and the proprietor of DJM Records. Cliff Adams went on to devise the radio programme *Sing Something Simple* in 1959, and he and his Singers have remained with the show ever since. Fred Datchler became a member of the Polka Dots, a vocal group bearing some resemblance to the Hi-Lo's. Datchler's son, Clark, was a member of the 80s pop band Johnny Hates Jazz. These Stargazers are not associated with the 80s vocal group the of the same name, who recorded *Back In Orbit!* on Ace Records in 1991.

● ALBUMS: *Make It Soon* (Decca 1955) ★★, *South Of The Border* (Decca 1960) ★★★.

STARR, KAY

b. Katherine LaVerne Starks, 21 July 1922, Dougherty, Oklahoma, USA. While she was still a child, Starr's family moved to Dallas, Texas, where she made her professional debut on local radio before she had left school. In 1939 she was hired briefly by Glenn Miller when his regular singer, Marion Hutton, was sick. Starr made records with

Miller, but was soon on the move. She spent brief spells with the bands of Bob Crosby and Joe Venuti, and attracted most attention during her mid-40s stint with Charlie Barnet. Among the records she made with Barnet was 'Share Croppin' Blues', which was modestly successful. However, the record sold well enough to interest Capitol Records, and, from 1948-54, she had a string of hits with the label, including 'So Tired', 'Hoop-Dee-Doo', 'Bonaparte's Retreat', 'I'll Never Be Free', 'Oh, Babe!', 'Come On-Aa My House', 'Wheel Of Fortune' (US number 1 1952), 'Comes A-Long A-Love' (UK number 1 1952), 'Side By Side', 'Half A Photograph', 'Allez-Vous-En', 'Changing Partners', 'The Man Upstairs', 'If You Love Me (Really Love Me)' and 'Am I A Toy Or A Treasure?'. In 1955 she switched to RCA Records, and went straight to the top of the charts in the USA and UK with 'Rock And Roll Waltz'. Her last singles hit to date was 'My Heart Reminds Me' (1957). Starr sang with controlled power and a strong emotional undertow, which made her an appealing live performer. In the 60s she became a regular attraction at venues such as Harrah's, Reno, and, as recently as the late 80s, she returned there, and also played New York clubs as a solo attraction and as part of nostalgia packages such as 3 Girls 3 (with Helen O'Connell and Margaret Whiting), and 4 Girls 4 (then joined by Kaye Ballard). In the spring of 1993, she joined Pat Boone, another popular 50s survivor, on The April Love Tour of the UK. She continues to perform in the USA on the supper club circuit, her voice still in fine form.
● ALBUMS: Songs By Starr 10-inch album (Capitol 1950) ★★, Kay Starr Style 10-inch album (Capitol 1953) ★★★, The Hits Of Kay Starr 10-inch album (Capitol 1953) ★★★, In A Blue Mood (Capitol 1955) ★★★, The One And Only Kay Starr (RCA Victor 1955) ★★★, Swingin' With The Starr (Liberty 1956) ★★★, with Erroll Garner Singin' Kay Starr, Swingin' Erroll Garner (Modern 1956) ★★★, Blue Starr (RCA Victor 1957) ★★★, Them There Eyes (Rondo-lette 1958) ★★★, Movin' (Capitol 1959) ★★★, Rockin' With Kay (RCA Victor 1959) ★★, I Hear The Word (RCA Victor 1959) ★★★, Losers Weepers (Capitol 1960) ★★★, One More Time (Capitol 1960) ★★★, Movin' On Broadway (Capitol 1960) ★★★, Jazz Singer (Capitol 1960) ★★★, I Cry By Night (Capitol 1962) ★★★, Fabulous Favorites (Capitol 1964) ★★★, Tears And Heartaches (Capitol 1966) ★★, When The Lights Go On Again (ABC 1968) ★★, with Count Basie How About This (Paramount 1969) ★★, Live At Freddy's 1986 (Baldwin Street Music 1999) ★★.
● COMPILATIONS: All Starr Hits (Capitol 1961) ★★★, Pure Gold (RCA 1981) ★★★, with Bob Crosby Suddenly It's 1939 (Giants Of Jazz 1985) ★★★, 1947: Kay Starr (Hindsight 1986) ★★★, Wheel Of Fortune And Other Hits (Capitol 1989) ★★★, Capitol Collectors Series (Capitol 1991) ★★★, I've Got To Sing, 1944-1948 (Hep 1998) ★★★, The Complete Lamplighter Recordings 1945-46 (Baldwin Street Music 1999) ★★★.

STATON, DAKOTA
b. Aliyah Rabia, 3 June 1931, Pittsburgh, Pennsylvania, USA. After singing in clubs in a style modelled on that of such diverse artists as Dinah Washington and Sarah Vaughan, Staton began to attract wider attention in the mid-50s. She extended her repertoire to include popular songs, R&B, soul and gospel and made a number of successful record albums. In the mid-60s she took up residence in the UK and Europe, but was back in the USA early in the following decade. She is at her best with mainstream jazz accompaniment, whether a big band, such as Manny Albam's or Kurt Edelhagen's, or a small group, such as those led by George Shearing and Jonah Jones. Staton's R&B material is less attractive, often performed at feverish tempos and with a deliberate coarsening of her powerful voice.
● ALBUMS: The Late, Late Show (Capitol 1957) ★★★★, In The Night (Capitol 1958) ★★★, Dynamic! (Capitol 1958) ★★★, Crazy He Calls Me (Capitol 1959) ★★★, Time To Swing (Capitol 1959) ★★★, More Than The Most (Capitol 1959) ★★★, Ballads And The Blues (Capitol 1960) ★★★, Softly (Capitol 1960) ★★★, Round Midnight (Capitol 1961) ★★★, Dakota Staton At Storyville (Capitol 1961) ★★★, From Dakota With Love (United Artists 1963) ★★★, Live And Swinging (United Artists 1963) ★★★★, Dakota Staton With Strings (United Artists 1964) ★★★, with Richard 'Groove' Holmes Let Me Off Uptown (1972) ★★★, Dakota Staton With The Manny Albam Big Band (1973) ★★★, Darling, Please Save Your Love (1992) ★★★, A Packet Of Love Letters (High Note 1999) ★★★.

STEELE, TOMMY
b. Thomas Hicks, 17 December 1936, Bermondsey, London, England. After serving as a merchant seaman, Hicks formed a skiffle trio called the Cavemen, with Lionel Bart and Mike Pratt, before being discovered by entrepreneur John Kennedy in the 2I's coffee bar in Soho, London. A name change to Tommy Steele followed, and after an appearance at London's Condor Club, the boy was introduced to manager Larry Parnes. From that point, his rise to stardom was meteoric. Using the old 'working-class boy makes good' angle, Kennedy launched the chirpy cockney in the unlikely setting of a debutante's ball. Class-conscious Fleet Street lapped up the idea of Steele as the 'deb's delight' and took him to their hearts. His debut single, 'Rock With The Caveman', was an immediate Top 20 hit and although the follow-up, 'Doomsday Rock'/ 'Elevator Rock', failed to chart, the management was unfazed. Their confidence was rewarded when Steele hit number 1 in the UK charts with a cover version of Guy Mitchell's 'Singing The Blues' in January 1957. By this point, he was briefly Britain's first and premier rock 'n' roll singer and, without resorting to sexual suggestiveness, provoked mass teenage hysteria unseen since the days of Johnnie Ray. At one stage, he had four songs in the Top 30, although he never restricted himself to pure rock 'n' roll. A minor role in the film Kill Me Tomorrow led to an autobiographical

musical, *The Tommy Steele Story*, which also spawned a book of the same title. For a time, Steele combined the twin roles of rock 'n' roller and family entertainer, but his original persona faded towards the end of the 50s. Further movie success in *The Duke Wore Jeans* (1958) and *Tommy The Toreador* (1959) effectively redefined his image. His rocking days closed with cover versions of Ritchie Valens' 'Come On Let's Go' and Freddy Cannon's 'Tallahassee Lassie'. The decade ended with the novelty 'Little White Bull', after which it was farewell to rock 'n' roll.

After appearing on several variety bills during the late 50s, Steele sampled the 'legit' side of showbusiness in 1960 when he played Tony Lumpkin in *She Stoops To Conquer* at the Old Vic, and he was back in straight theatre again in 1969, in the role of Truffaldino in *The Servant Of Two Masters* at the Queen's Theatre. In the years between those two plays, he experienced some of the highlights of his career. In 1963, he starred as Arthur Kipps in the stage musical *Half A Sixpence*, which ran for 18 months in the West End before transferring to Broadway in 1965. Steele recreated the role in the 1967 film version. A year later, he appeared in another major musical movie, *Finian's Rainbow*, with Fred Astaire and Petula Clark. His other films included *Touch It Light*, *It's All Happening*, *The Happiest Millionaire* and *Where's Jack?*. In 1974, Steele made one of his rare television appearances in the autobiographical *My Life, My Song*, and appeared at the London Palladium in the musical *Hans Andersen*. He also starred in the revival three years later. In 1979/80 his one-man show was resident at London's Prince of Wales Theatre for a record 60 weeks – the Variety Club Of Great Britain made him their Entertainer Of The Year. He was also awarded the OBE.

Steele was back at the Palladium again in 1983 and 1989, heading the cast of the highly popular *Singin' In The Rain*, which he also directed. In the latter capacity he tried – too late as it transpired – to save impresario Harold Fielding's *Ziegfeld* (1988) from becoming a spectacular flop. Fielding had originally cast Steele in *Half A Sixpence* some 25 years earlier. Off-stage in the 80s, Steele published a thriller called *The Final Run*, had one of his paintings exhibited at the Royal Academy, was commissioned by Liverpool City Council to fashion a bronze statue of 'Eleanor Rigby' as a tribute to the Beatles, and composed two musical pieces, 'A Portrait Of Pablo' and 'Rock Suite – An Elderly Person's Guide To Rock'. After *Hans Andersen* and *Singin' In The Rain*, the third, and least successful of Steele's stage adaptations of memorable musical movies, was *Some Like It Hot* (1992). A hybrid of Billy Wilder's classic film, and the Broadway stage musical *Sugar* (1972), it received derisory reviews ('The show's hero is Mr Steele's dentist'), and staggered along for three months in the West End on the strength of its star's undoubted box-office appeal. In 1993, Steele was presented with the Hans Andersen Award at the Danish Embassy in London, and two years later he received the Bernard Delfont Award from the Variety Club of Great Britain for his 'outstanding contribution to showbusiness'. By that time, Tommy Steele was back on the road again with 'A Dazzling New Song & Dance Spectacular' entitled *What A Show!*.

● ALBUMS: *The Tommy Steele Stage Show* 10-inch album (Decca 1957) ★★★, *The Tommy Steele Story* 10-inch album (Decca 1957) ★★★★, *Stars Of 6.05* (Decca 1958) ★★★, *Get Happy With Tommy* (Decca 1960) ★★★, *It's All Happening* (Decca 1962) ★★★, *My Life My Song* (Buena Vista 1974) ★★★.

● COMPILATIONS: *The Happy World Of Tommy Steele* (Decca 1969) ★★★, *The World Of Tommy Steele, Volume 2* (Decca 1971) ★★★, *Focus On Tommy Steele* (Decca 1977) ★★★, *The Family Album* (Ronco 1979) ★★★★, *The Tommy Steele Story* (Decca 1981) ★★★, *20 Greatest Hits* (Spot 1983) ★★★, *Tommy Steele And The Steelmen – The Rock 'N' Roll Years* (See For Miles 1988) ★★★, *Very Best Of Tommy Steele* (Pickwick 1991) ★★★, *The EP Collection* (See For Miles 1992) ★★★.

● FURTHER READING: *Tommy Steele: The Facts About A Teenage Idol And An Inside Picture Of Show Business*, John Kennedy.

● FILMS: *Kill Me Tomorrow* (1955), *The Tommy Steele Story* (1957), *The Duke Wore Jeans* (1959), *Light Up The Sky* (1959), *Tommy The Toreador* (1960), *It's All Happening* (1962), *The Happiest Millionaire* (1967), *Half A Sixpence* (1967), *Finian's Rainbow* (1968), *Where's Jack?* (1969).

STEWART, WYNN

b. Wynnford Lindsey Stewart, 7 June 1934, on a farm near Morrisville, Missouri, USA, d. 17 July 1985, Hendersonville, Tennessee, USA. Stewart's uncle was a major league pitcher, which inspired hopes of a baseball career, until he was told that he would never be big enough. He became interested in songwriting, learned to play the guitar, and at the age of 13, he appeared regularly on KWTO Springfield. A year later the family moved to California, where Stewart became friendly and for a time ran a band with Ralph Mooney, the now legendary steel guitarist. Stewart first recorded for Intro in 1954 and local success with his own song, 'Strolling', led to him signing for Capitol Records. In 1956, his recording of 'Waltz Of The Angels' became his first hit, further minor ones followed but it was not until 1959, after he moved to the Challenge label, that he achieved major success with 'Wishful Thinking' and also recorded with Jan Howard. In the late 50s, he moved to Las Vegas, where he opened the Nashville Nevada Club and hosted his own television series on KTOO. In 1959, Miki And Griff had a UK pop chart hit with Stewart's song 'Hold Back Tomorrow'. Competition for places in his band was fierce and in 1962, Stewart gave Merle Haggard the job of playing bass and singing the odd song during his own breaks. A year later he provided Haggard with 'Sing A Sad Song', which became his first chart hit. He returned to California in the mid-60s, toured with his band the Tourists and also rejoined Capitol, where between 1965 and 1971, he had 17 country chart hits, including 'It's Such A Pretty World Today', his only number 1. He moved to RCA Records in 1972, but achieved his next Top 20 hits in 1976 with 'After The Storm' and his own version of 'Sing A Sad Song', after moving to Playboy Records. Stewart's reputation became somewhat marred by problems; his private life suffered (he was married three times) and at times drinking caused him to miss bookings. He eventually moved to Nashville, where he believed he could achieve another breakthrough with a special comeback tour. At 6 pm on 17 July 1985, the evening the tour was due to start, he suffered a heart attack and died. Stewart was a fine singer, who should have been a bigger star, for, as John Morthland later wrote, 'He may not have been as consistent as Haggard or Buck Owens but at his best, he was their equal as a writer'.

● ALBUMS: with Jan Howard *Sweethearts Of Country Music* (Challenge 1961) ★★★, *Wynn Stewart* (Wrangler 1962) ★★★, *The Songs Of Wynn Stewart* (Capitol 1965) ★★★, *Above And Beyond* (1967) ★★★, *It's Such A Pretty World Today* (Capitol 1967) ★★★, with Howard *Wynn Stewart And Jan Howard Sing Their Hits* (Starday 1968) ★★★★, *In Love* (Capitol 1968) ★★★, *Love's Gonna Happen To Me* (Capitol 1968) ★★★, *Something Pretty* (Capitol 1968) ★★★, *Let The Whole World Sing With Me* (Capitol 1969) ★★, *Yours Forever* (Capitol 1969) ★★★, *You Don't Care What Happens To Me* (Capitol 1970) ★★★, *It's A Beautiful Day* (Capitol 1970) ★★★, *Baby It's Yours* (Capitol 1971) ★★★, *After The Storm* (Playboy 1976) ★★★.

● COMPILATIONS: *Wishful Thinking (The Challenge Years 1958-1963)* (1988) ★★★★, *California Country: The Best Of The Challenge Masters* (AVI 1995) ★★★, *Wishful Thinking* 10-CD box set (Bear Family 2000) ★★★★.

STITT, SONNY

b. Edward Boatner Stitt, 2 February 1924, Boston, Massachusetts, USA, d. 22 July 1982, Washington, DC, USA. Starting out on alto saxophone, Stitt gained his early experience playing in the big bands led by Tiny Bradshaw and Billy Eckstine. Influenced by Charlie Parker and by the many fine young beboppers he encountered on the Eckstine band, Stitt quickly developed into a formidable player. He played with Dizzy Gillespie, Kenny Clarke and others but by the late 40s was concerned that he should develop a more personal style. In pursuit of this he switched to tenor saxophone and formed the first of many bands he was to lead and co-lead over the years. Among his early collaborators was Gene Ammons, whom he had met during the Eckstine stint. In the late 50s he was with Jazz At The Philharmonic and in 1960 was briefly with Miles Davis. Throughout the 60s and 70s Stitt maintained a high level of performances at home and abroad, despite periodic bouts of ill health generated by his drug addictions. In the early 60s he recorded with Paul Gonsalves, *Salt And Pepper*, and in the early 70s toured with Gillespie as a member of the Giants Of Jazz, continuing to make many fine record albums. His early 80s albums

included *Sonny, Sweets And Jaws*, with Harry Edison and Eddie 'Lockjaw' Davis, and a fine set made just weeks before his death. Although his early career was overshadowed by Parker, Stitt was never a copyist. Indeed, his was a highly original musical mind, as became apparent after he switched to tenor and forged a new and appreciative audience for his work. In later years he played alto saxophone as often as he played tenor, by which time it was plain to see that the comparisons to Parker were largely the result of critical pigeonholing.

● ALBUMS: *Sonny Stitt And Bud Powell* 10-inch album aka as *Sonny Stitt With Bud Powell & J.J. Johnson* (New Jazz 1950) ★★★★, *Sonny Stitt And Bud Powell* 10-inch album (Prestige 1951) ★★★★, with Gene Ammons *Battle Of The Saxes: Ammons Vs. Stitt* 10-inch album (Prestige 1951) ★★★★, *Mr Saxophone* 10-inch album (Prestige 1951) ★★★, *Super Stitt, Volume 1 – Favorites* 10-inch album aka *Stitt's Bits* (Prestige 1952) ★★★★, *Super Stitt, Volume 2 – Tenor Sax* 10-inch album (Prestige 1953) ★★★, *All Star Series: Sonny Stitt* 10-inch album (Savoy 1952) ★★★, *New Trends Of Jazz* 10-inch album (Savoy 1952) ★★★★, *New Sounds In Modern Music* 10-inch album (Savoy 1952) ★★★★, *Sonny Stitt Plays Arrangements From The Pen Of Johnny Richards* 10-inch album (Roost 1953) ★★★, *Jazz At The Hi-Hat* 10-inch album (Roost 1954) ★★★★, with Eddie Davis *Battle Of Birdland* (Roost 1955) ★★★, *Early Modern* (Jazztone 1956) ★★★★, *Sonny Stitt* (Roost 1956) ★★★★, *Sonny Stitt Plays Arrangements Of Quincy Jones* (Roost 1956) ★★★, *37 Minutes And 48 Seconds* (Roost 1957) ★★★, *Kaleidoscope* (Prestige 1957) ★★★, *Sonny Stitt With The New Yorkers* (Roost 1957) ★★★, with Dizzy Gillespie, Sonny Rollins *Duets* reissued as *Dizzy, Rollins & Stitt* (Verve 1958) ★★★★, *New York Jazz* (Verve 1958) ★★★★★, *Only The Blues* (Verve 1958) ★★★★, *Sonny Side Up* (Verve 1958) ★★★★, *Sonny Stitt* (Argo 1958) ★★★, *Burnin'* (Argo 1958) ★★★, *The Hard Swing* (Verve 1959) ★★★, *Sonny Stitt Plays Jimmy Giuffre Arrangements* (Verve 1959) ★★★, *Personal Appearances* (Verve 1959) ★★, *The Saxophone Of Sonny Stitt* (Roost 1959) ★★★, *Little Bit Of Stitt* (Roost 1959) ★★★, *Sonny Stitt Sits In With The Oscar Peterson Trio* (Verve 1959) ★★, *Sonny Stitt Blows The Blues* (Verve 1960) ★★★, *Saxophone Supremacy* (Verve 1960) ★★★, *Sonny Stitt Swings The Most* (Verve 1960) ★★★, *Sonny Side Of Stitt* (Roost 1960) ★★, *Stittsville* (Roost 1960) ★★★, *Sonny Stitt At The D.J. Lounge* (Argo 1961) ★★, *Sonny Stitt And The Top Brass* (Atlantic 1962) ★★★, *Rearin' Back* (Argo 1962) ★★★, *Low Flame* (Jazzland 1962) ★★★, *The Sensual Sound Of Sonny Stitt* (Verve 1962) ★★★, *Feelin's* (Roost 1962) ★★★, *Autumn In New York* (1962-67) ★★★, with Jack McDuff *Sonny Stitt Meets Brother Jack* aka *Nuther Fu'ther* (Prestige 1962) ★★, with Ammons *Boss Tenors* (Verve 1962) ★★★, with Ammons, Brother Jack McDuff *Soul Summit* (Prestige 1962) ★★★, with Ammons *Boss Tenors In Orbit* (Verve 1962) ★★★, *Sonny Stitt In Orbit* (Roost 1963) ★★★, *Sonny Stitt Goes Latin* (Roost 1963) ★, *My Mother's Eyes* (Pacific Jazz 1963) ★★★, *Sonny Stitt*

Now! (Impulse! 1963) ★★★, *Salt And Pepper* (Impulse! 1963) ★★★, *Sonny Stitt Plays Bird* (Atlantic 1964) ★★★★, *Move On Over* (Argo 1964) ★★★, with McDuff *Soul Shack* (Prestige 1964) ★★, *Primitivo Soul!* (Prestige 1964) ★★★, *Broadway Soul* (Colpix 1964) ★★★, *My Main Man* (Argo 1965) ★★★, *Soul People* (Prestige 1965) ★★, *Interaction* (Cadet 1965) ★★, *Soul In The Night* (Cadet 1965) ★★★, *The Matadors Meet The Bull* (Roulette 1965) ★★★, *What's New!!! Sonny Stitt Plays The Varitone* (Roulette 1966) ★★★, *I Keep Comin' Back* (Roulette 1966) ★★★, with Don Patterson *Night Crawler* (Prestige 1967) ★★★★, with Ammons *Jug And Sonny* (Cadet 1967) ★★★★, *Sonny Stitt ... Pow!* (Prestige 1967) ★★★, *Autumn In New York* (Black Lion 1968) ★★★, *Little Green Apples* (Solid State 1969) ★★, *Come Together* (Solid State 1969) ★★, *Night Letter* (1969) ★★★, with Ammons *We'll Be Together Again* (Prestige 1969) ★★★★, *Soul Electricity* (Prestige 1969) ★★★, *Black Vibrations* (1971) ★★★, with Ammons *You Talk That Talk* (Prestige 1971) ★★★★, *So Doggone Good* (1972) ★★★, *Constellation* (Muse 1972) ★★★, *Tune Up!* (Muse 1972) ★★★★, *The Champ* (Muse 1973) ★★★★, with Ammons *Together Again For The Last Time* (1973) ★★★★, *Satan* (1974) ★★★, *In Walked Sonny* (Sonet 1975) ★★★, *I Remember Bird* (Catalyst 1976) ★★, *Moonlight In Vermont* (Denon 1977) ★★★, *Back To My Old Home Town* (Black And Blue 1979) ★★★, *Groovin' High* (1980) ★★★, *Sonny, Sweets And Jaws* (1981) ★★★, *At Last* (1982) ★★★, *The Last Stitt Sessions* (Muse 1982) ★★★, *Made For Each Other* (Delmark 1997) ★★★, with Ronnie Scott *The Night Has A Thousand Eyes* (Jazz House 1998) ★★★★, *Just In Case You Forgot How Bad He Really Was* 1981 recording (32 Jazz 1998) ★★★, *Live At Ronnie Scott's* (DCC 2000) ★, *Just The Way It Was* 1971 recording (Label M 2000) ★★.

● COMPILATIONS: *The Best Of Sonny Stitt With Brother Jack McDuff* (Prestige 1969) ★★★, *Soul Classics* (Prestige 1988) ★★★★.

STONE, JESSE

b. 16 November 1901, Atchison, Kansas, USA, d. 1 April 1999, Altamonte Springs, Florida, USA. Stone's earliest musical experience was performing with his family's minstrel show. After moving to Kansas City, he played piano with several territory bands throughout the south-west during the 20s and additionally led his own band. Although little known and not recorded, the band was home for a while to musicians who later made their names in the wider world of jazz, among them Coleman Hawkins, Budd Johnson and Alton Moore. In addition to working with his own bands, Stone also became arranger and musical director with other territory bands. These included the bands of Terrence Holder, whom Stone helped form the Clouds Of Joy in 1929; George E. Lee, recording with this band and its singer, Julia Lee, also in 1929; Thamon Hayes' Kansas City Rockets, for which he was co-director from 1931; and this band's successor, Harlan Leonard's Rockets, from 1934. Stone was also responsible for coaching and rehearsing these bands into ever more polished units. He returned to band leading in the mid-30s, playing several prestigious venues in Chicago and New York City. His bands included, at one time or another, the Blue Serenaders and the Cyclones, while the Coquettes was a white all-female band. He continued to write arrangements for others and to compose. Among his best known compositions are 'Sorghum Switch', a big seller for Jimmy Dorsey, 'Smack Dab In The Middle', and 'Idaho', a song that was recorded by many artists including Benny Goodman and Guy Lombardo, the latter's version selling three million copies. For two years in the early 40s, Stone worked as arranger and musical director with the International Sweethearts Of Rhythm. He also helped develop their stage presence, giving them the polish that became a byword of excellence. He was also partly responsible for introducing to the original band several experienced musicians, including Tiny Davis and Vi Burnside. It was at this time that he first met the Sweethearts' singer, Evelyn McGee, whom he married several decades later. By the late 40s, Stone's reputation was such that he was hired in 1947 by Ahmet Ertegun for his fledgling Atlantic Records. Here, Stone's talents flourished and he worked as composer (sometimes using the name Charles Calhoun), arranger, producer and A&R man. He even found time to make some records, as Charlie Calhound And His Orchestra and also as Chuck Calhoun And His Atlantic All-Stars. Among songs composed by Stone during his time with Atlantic were 'Money Honey', recorded by the Clyde McPhatter-fronted Drifters (11 weeks at number 1 in the R&B charts in 1953), and 'Soul On Fire', for LaVern Baker. Stone played piano on both of these dates and he was also involved in hit-making sessions by Ruth Brown, the Clovers and the Cardinals. Among other significant activities at this time, he also arranged 'Big' Joe Turner's groundbreaking 1954 hit, 'Shake, Rattle And Roll'. During these years, Stone's influence inside the music business was profound, leading Ertegun to declare that he had done 'more to develop the basic rock 'n' roll sound than anybody else'. By the 60s, as tastes in pop music shifted, Stone transferred his activities into management, continuing to work throughout the 70s. He also played piano, for a time working in a duo with McGee whom he had re-encountered. The couple married in 1975 and in the early 80s Stone eventually retired. Even then, he maintained an interest in music and in the mid-90s played piano on his wife's *Jump Back*. She later reported that at the time of his admission to hospital, four days before his death at the age of 97, her husband was working on a new song, appositely entitled, 'That's It'. Perhaps because Stone made few recordings he is often unjustly regarded as one of the lesser figures in the development of Kansas City Jazz. In reality, his arrangements and expertise as a musical director made him an honourable member of a small nucleus of important, if not indeed crucial, arrangers who helped fashion the propulsive swing that marked this important transitional style in the development of jazz. Add to this his immensely influential activities in the world of R&B during the pre-rock era, and his overall role in the history of popular music is clearly one of considerable importance.

● COMPILATIONS: included on *Jazz In St. Louis 1924-1927* (Timeless 1997) ★★★, *Jesse Stone – Alias Charles 'Chuck' Calhoun 1947-1956* recordings (Bear Family 1997) ★★★.

STONE, KIRBY, FOUR

This vocal quartet comprised Kirby Stone (b. 27 April 1918, New York, New York, USA), Eddie Hall, Larry Foster and Mike Gardner. They had a hip brand of humour and a distinctive, upbeat, swinging style. Originally an instrumental quintet, the group became a vocal foursome before making a name for themselves in nightclubs and local television shows. They came to prominence in 1958 with an appearance on the *Ed Sullivan Show*, which led to a contract with Columbia Records, and the release of *Man, I Flipped . . . When I Heard The Kirby Stone Four*. It was a mixture of standards, such as 'S'Wonderful' and 'It Could Happen To You', and special material written by Stone and Gardner. Their programme included 'Juke Box Dream', a vehicle for Foster's uncanny vocal impressions. In the same year they also had a Top 30 single with their extremely original version of 'Baubles, Bangles And Beads', from the 1953 Broadway musical *Kismet*. The accompanying album reached the US Top 20. Among their other album releases, *Guys And Dolls (Like Today)* (1962) included a 'liberetto-ture' (a combination of libretto and overture) by Kirby Stone and the group's frequent arranger and conductor, Dick Hyman, as an attempt to present the Abe Burrows/Jo Swerling/Frank Loesser masterpiece as a 'show for the ear alone'. Stone added some extra lyrics for his 'guys', who were augmented by the 'dolls' – a female vocal chorus – plus a 25-piece orchestra that included such luminaries as Alvino Rey, Shelly Manne and Al Klink. Subsequently, the Kirby Stone Four continued to flourish, and went forward, armed with this common credo: 'A pox on all harmonica players, nightclub owners named Rocky, and juveniles who win contests by playing "Lady Of Spain" on white accordions.'

● ALBUMS: *Man, I Flipped...When I Heard The Kirby Stone Four* (Columbia 1958) ★★★★, *Baubles, Bangles And Beads* (Columbia 1958) ★★★★, *The "Go" Sound Of The Kirby Stone Four* (Columbia 1959) ★★★, *The Kirby Stone Touch* (Columbia 1959) ★★★, *The Kirby Stone Four At The Playboy Club* (Columbia 1960) ★★★, *Guys And Dolls (Like Today)* (Columbia 1962) ★★★.

STORDAHL, AXEL

b. 8 August 1913, Staten Island, New York, USA, d. 30 August 1963, Encino, California, USA. An accomplished arranger-conductor, and sometime composer, whose name is indelibly linked with Frank Sinatra's Columbia recordings of the 40s. Early in his career, Stordahl played trumpet and arranged for the Bert Block Orchestra, before being hired by Tommy Dorsey in the mid-30s.

When Sinatra left Dorsey to go solo in 1943, Stordahl's arrangements played an important role, mainly on the singer's ballad records through to 1949. He also worked with Sinatra on his many radio broadcasts, including the immensely popular *Your Hit Parade*. After Sinatra moved to Capitol Records, and the backings of Nelson Riddle, Gordon Jenkins, Billy May, *et al.*, Stordahl served as arranger-conductor for vocalists such as Giselle Mackenzie, Doris Day, Eddie Fisher, Nanette Fabray, Bing Crosby, Dean Martin, and Stordahl's wife, June Hutton, and was continuously in demand for various television programmes. Stordahl's catalogue of songs and instrumental works included two outstanding romantic ballads, 'I Should Care' and 'Day By Day' (both written with Paul Weston and Sammy Cahn), as well as others such as the pleasant 'Ain'tcha Ever Comin' Back?', 'Neiani', 'Talking To Myself About You', 'Night After Night', 'Return To The Magic Islands', 'Recollections', 'Jasmine And Jade' and 'Ride Off'.

● ALBUMS: *The Strings Of Stordahl* (Capitol 50s) ★★★★, *Lure* (Decca 1959) ★★★, *Jasmine And Jade* (Dot 1960) ★★★, *Magic Islands Revisited* (Decca 1961) ★★, *Axel Stordahl* (Decca 1963) ★★★.

STORM, GALE

b. Josephine Cottle, 5 April 1922, Bloomington, Texas, USA. A dynamic singer who came to fame mainly through covering the hits of others, Storm arrived in Hollywood in 1939 after winning a 'Gateway To Hollywood' contest in her home state. She was soon working for the Universal and RKO studios, though she ultimately achieved popularity playing Margie Albright in *My Little Margie* (1952-54), a television series, credited as being the first of its kind to be screened five days a week. By 1955, she was recording for Randy Wood's Dot label, reaching the US Top 5 with her cover version of Smiley Lewis' 'I Hear You Knocking', followed by 'Teen Age Prayer', Memories Are Made Of This' (both 1955), 'Why Do Fools Fall In Love?', 'Ivory Tower' (both 1956) and 'Dark Moon' (1957). During 1956-59, she had her own 125-segment television series which was considered a precursor for *Love Boat*. By the late 70s, Storm was living in the San Fernando Valley, but still working with local theatre companies. In 1987 Storm was appearing on the west coast with two other veterans, Betty Garrett and Sheree North, in Terry Kingsley-Smith's comedy *Breaking Up The Act*.

● ALBUMS: *Gale Storm* (Dot 1956) ★★★, *Sentimental Me* (Dot 1956) ★★★, *Softly And Tenderly* (Dot 1959) ★★★, *Gale Storm Sings* (Dot 1959) ★★★.

● COMPILATIONS: *Gale Storm Hits* (Dot 1958) ★★★, *Dark Moon: The Best Of ...* (Varèse Sarabande 1995) ★★★.

STRINGBEAN

b. David Akeman, 17 June 1914, Annville, Jackson County, Kentucky, USA, d. 10 November 1973. Akeman was raised on a farm and received his first banjo by trading a pair of his prized bantams.

Between 1935 and 1939 he worked with several bands including that of local celebrity Asa Martin, who, because of his gangling appearance, first gave him the nickname of String Beans. Akeman's baseball pitching attracted the attention of Bill Monroe, who signed him for his private team, not knowing that he was also a banjo player. During his time with Monroe, Akeman also worked with Willie Egbert Westbrooks as String Beans and Cousin Wilbur. In 1945 he left Monroe, being replaced by Earl Scruggs and for three years worked with Lew Childre, the two becoming a popular *Grand Ole Opry* act. Akemen, now known as Stringbean, also adopted a strange stage attire, probably based on an outfit worn by old-time comedian Slim Miller, which gave the effect of a tall man with very short legs. He married Estelle Stanfill in 1945, who shared his love of the outdoor life and acted as his chauffeur (Akemen had two cars but never learned to drive). In 1946, he formed a lasting friendship with Grandpa Jones and by 1950 was an established solo star of the *Opry*, which he remained to his death. Akeman recorded for Starday in the 60s, achieving success with songs such as 'Chewing Gum', 'I Wonder Where Wanda Went' and 'I'm Going To The Grand Ole Opry And Make Myself A Name'. In 1969, along with Jones, he also became a regular on the network television show *Hee-Haw*. His love of the quiet country life and his distrust of banks had fatal consequences when, on returning to their farm at Goodlettsville after his *Opry* performance on 10 November 1973, the Akemans surprised two intruders. Stringbean was shot on entering the house and his wife, then parking the car, was pursued and shot down on the lawn. The killers fled with $250 leaving the bodies to be discovered early next morning by Grandpa Jones. John and Douglas Brown were arrested, charged with murder and in spite of the public outcry for the death penalty, were sentenced to life imprisonment.

● ALBUMS: *Old Time Pickin' & Singin' With Stringbean* (Starday 1961) ★★★, *Stringbean* (Starday 1962) ★★★★, *Kentucky Wonder* (1962) ★★★, *A Salute To Uncle Dave Macon* (Starday 1963) ★★★, *Old Time Banjo Picking And Singing* (1964) ★★★, *Way Back In The Hills Of Old Kentucky* (Starday 1964) ★★★, *Hee-Haw Cornshucker* (Nashville 1971) ★★★, *Me & Old Crow (Got A Good Thing Goin')* (Nugget 1972) ★★★, *Stringbean Goin' To The Grand Ole Opry* (Ovation 1977) ★★.

STRIP, THE

A would-be jazz drummer, Mickey Rooney, fresh out of the army, tangles with criminals. Directed by Leslie Kardos in 1951, all is very predictable but the pleasures in this film centre upon the band he joins, no less than Louis Armstrong And His All Stars. To meet some Hollywood executive's misconceived ideas on racial integration, apart from Rooney, another white face appears on-screen in the band, behind the string bass. However, part of what you see and all of what you hear is the real All Stars back in the days when

Armstrong's group truly merited the term: Jack Teagarden, Barney Bigard, Earl Hines, Arvell Shaw and William 'Cozy' Cole (the last two dubbing for their on-screen counterparts). Armstrong recorded one of the film's songs, 'A Kiss To Build A Dream On', which became a minor hit for him. He also sings 'Shadrack' and the band plays a handful of other 'good old good ones' including 'Ole Miss'/'Bugle Call Rag' which is a feature for Rooney/Cole. In some scenes without the band Rooney may have played drums himself, something at which he was rather good, although he was no Cozy Cole.

STRITCH, ELAINE

b. 2 February 1925, Detroit, Michigan, USA. An inimitable actress and singer with a magnetic appeal, who has combined a career in the musical theatre with another in drama, films and on television. Stritch has been called caustic, sardonic, witty, tough, and much else besides. She is said to have sung for the first time on stage in the Long Island revue *The Shape Of Things!*, in June 1947, and a few months later introduced 'Civilization (Bongo, Bongo, Bongo)' on Broadway in another revue, *Angels In The Wings*. Stritch subsequently understudied Ethel Merman in Irving Berlin's hit musical *Call Me Madam*, and played Merman's role of ambassador Sally Adams in the 1952/3 US tour. Also in 1952, she was Melba Snyder in a revival of *Pal Joey* at the Broadhurst Theatre, and gave a memorable reading of the amusing 'Zip'. During the remainder of the 50s, Stritch appeared on Broadway in the 1954 revival of *On Your Toes* (rendering a 'drop dead' version of the interpolated 'You Took Advantage Of Me') and with Don Ameche and Russell Nype in *Goldilocks* (1958). In 1961, she sang 'Why Do The Wrong People Travel?', amongst other songs, in Noël Coward's *Sail Away*, and in the following year went with the show to London. Although she starred as Vera Charles in the US tour of *Mame*, and appeared in a US television version of the legendary revue *Pins And Needles*, Stritch did not appear on Broadway again until *Company* (1970), the show which gave her cult status. The television programme documenting the agonies involved in recording its Original Cast album, particularly the sequence in which a weary Stritch struggles to lay down a Stephen Sondheim-pleasing version of 'The Ladies Who Lunch', proved to be riveting viewing, and was eventually released on videotape and laserdisc. After reprising her role for the 1972 London production of *Company*, Stritch lived in England for about 10 years, appearing in various plays, and co-starring with Donald Sinden in the top-rated television series *Two's Company*. In 1985, she returned in triumph to New York for the two-performance *Follies In Concert* at the Lincoln Center. She played Hattie, and very nearly stopped the show with her 'sensational' rendering of 'Broadway Baby'. In the early 90s, she was back at the Lincoln Center with the original cast of *Company* for benefit concerts, made her cabaret debut at New York's Rainbow & Stars, and played the role of Parthy in the 1994

Tony Award-winning revival of *Show Boat* on Broadway. Stritch was inducted into The Theatre Hall of Fame in 1995, and two years later made a rare working trip to London in order to join a host of stars celebrating Barbara Cook's 70th birthday at the Royal Albert Hall. In May 1998 she withdrew from the cast of Bob Kingdom's play *Elsa Edgar* at the Bay Street Theatre, Long Island, just a few hours before its scheduled opening. Stritch was to portray socialite Elsa Maxwell in the first act, and FBI director J. Edgar Hoover in the second.

● ALBUMS: *Stritch* re-released 1995 (Dolphin 1955) ★★★, Original and Studio Cast recordings, and Painted Smiles *Revisited* albums.

● FILMS: *The Scarlet Hour* (1956), *Three Violent People* (1956), *A Farewell To Arms* (1957), *The Perfect Furlough* (1958), *Kiss Her Goodbye* (1958), *Who Killed Teddy Bear?* (1965), *Too Many Thieves* (1966), *Pigeons* (1971), *Providence* (1977), *September* (1987), *Cocoon: The Return* (1988), *Cadillac Man* (1990), *Out To Sea* (1997), *Krippendorf's Tribe* (1998).

STUDENT PRINCE, THE

Mario Lanza walked out on MGM producer Joe Pasternak before filming had even started on Sigmund Romberg and Dorothy Donnelly's epic operetta, which eventually reached the screen in 1954. Fortunately for all concerned, Lanza had recorded all the songs before he left, so it was simply a matter of matching his voice to the performing style of Edmund Purdom, the British actor chosen to co-star with Ann Blyth in this tale located in old Heidelberg. Set in the late 1800s, Sonia Levien and William Ludwig's screenplay, which was based on Donnelly's Broadway libretto and Wilhelm Meyer-Forster's play, told the familiar story of the brief romance between the Student Prince, Karl Franz (Purdom), and the waitress, Kathy (Blyth), to the accompaniment of immortal songs from the 1924 hit stage production, such as 'Serenade', 'Deep In My Heart, Dear', 'Drinking Song', 'Come Boys, Let's All Be Gay Boys' and 'Golden Days'. To these were added three new ones by Nicholas Brodszky and Paul Francis Webster, 'I Walk With God', 'Summertime In Heidelberg' and 'Beloved'. Louis Calhern, S.Z. Sakall, Edmund Gwenn, John Williams, Evelyn Vardon, Richard Anderson and John Hoyt were among those taking part in this lavish production which was expertly photographed in Ansco Color and CinemaScope by Paul Vogel and directed by Richard Thorpe. An earlier, silent film of *The Student Prince*, directed by Ernst Lubitsch and starring Ramon Navarro and Norma Shearer, was released in 1927.

STYNE, JULE

b. Julius Kerwin Stein, 31 December 1905, London, England, d. 20 September 1994, New York, USA. A highly distinguished composer for the musical theatre, films and Tin Pan Alley, Styne spent his early life in Bethnal Green, east London, where his father ran a butter and eggs store. He used to do Harry Lauder impressions, and when he was five, he was taken by his parents to see the great entertainer at the London Hippodrome. He climbed up on stage, and Lauder lent him his crook and encouraged him to sing 'She's My Daisy'. Something of a child prodigy, he was a competent pianist even before he emigrated with his family to the USA at the age of eight. They settled in Chicago, and Styne studied harmony and composition, and played with the Chicago Symphony Orchestra, but had to abandon a classical career because 'my hands were too small – my span was inadequate'. While he was still at high school, Styne played the piano at burlesque houses, and composed his first two songs, 'The Guy In the Polka-Dot Tie' and 'The Moth And The Flame'. After graduating, he worked in nightclubs and for various pick-up groups, and in 1927, had a hit with the catchy 'Sunday' (written with Ned Miller, Chester Conn and Bennie Kreuger).

In the late 20s, Styne was a member of Ben Pollack's big-time Chicago Band, which at various times included legendary names such as Benny Goodman, Glenn Miller and Charlie Spivak. By 1932, he had formed his own band, which played at the nightclubs and speakeasies in Chicago. During the 30s he moved to Hollywood, via New York, and worked as a vocal coach at 20th Century Fox ('I taught Shirley Temple and Alice Faye how to sing!'), and wrote some songs for low-budget movies such as *Hold That Co-Ed* (1938, 'Limpy Dimp' with Sidney Clare and Nick Castle). He transferred to Republic Studios, the home of Gene Autry and Roy Rogers, and continued to contribute to shoestring productions such as *Hit Parade Of 1941* ('Who Am I?', with Walter Bullock), *Melody Ranch*, *Rookies On Parade* and *Angels With Broken Wings*. On loan to Paramount, Styne teamed with Frank Loesser for 'I Don't Want To Walk Without You' and 'I Said No', which were featured in the Eddie Bracken movie *Sweater Girl* (1942). The former number was an enormous wartime hit, particularly for Harry James and his Orchestra, with a vocal by Helen Forrest. While at Republic, Styne met lyricist Sammy Cahn, and during the 40s they collaborated on numerous appealing songs, mostly for films, including 'I've Heard That Song Before', 'Five Minutes More', 'Victory Polka', 'Poor Little Rhode Island', 'Saturday Night (Is The Loneliest Night Of The Week)', 'Zuyder Zee', 'Guess I'll Hang My Tears Out To Dry' (from the 1944 flop musical *Glad To See You*), 'Anywhere', 'Can't You Read Between The Lines?', 'When The One You Love (Simply Won't Come Back)', 'I've Never Forgotten', 'The Things We Did Last Summer', 'Let It Snow! Let It Snow! Let It Snow!', 'I Gotta Gal I Love In North And South Dakota', 'It's Been A Long, Long Time', 'Ev'ry Day I Love You (Just A Little Bit More)', 'I'm In Love', 'It's Magic', 'It's You Or No One', 'Put 'Em In A Box, Tie It With A Ribbon' (the last three were from Doris Day's first movie, *Romance On The High Seas*), 'Give Me A Song With A Beautiful Melody' and 'It's A Great Feeling' (1949).

During that period, Styne also collaborated with others, including Herb Magidson ('Barrelhouse Bessie From Basin Street' and 'Conchita, Marquita,

Lolita, Pepita, Rosita, Juanita Lopez') and Walter Bishop ('Bop! Goes My Heart'). Many of those songs were immensely successful for Frank Sinatra, and Styne and Cahn wrote the scores for three of the singer's most successful films of the 40s, *Step Lively* ('As Long As There's Music', 'Come Out, Wherever You Are', 'Some Other Time'), *Anchors Aweigh* ('The Charm Of You', 'I Fall In Love Too Easily', 'I Begged Her'), and *It Happened In Brooklyn* ('It's The Same Old Dream', 'Time After Time', 'I Believe', 'The Brooklyn Bridge'). Sinatra also introduced Styne and Cahn's Oscar-winning 'Three Coins In The Fountain' in 1954. Some years before that, Styne and Cahn had moved to New York to work on the score for the stage musical *High Button Shoes* ('Papa, Won't You Dance With Me', 'I Still Get Jealous', 'Can't You Just See Yourself?'). It starred Phil Silvers and Nanette Fabray, and ran for 727 performances. After returning briefly to Hollywood, at the age of 44 Styne embarked on an illustrious Broadway career, composing the music for a string of mostly highly successful shows, including *Gentlemen Prefer Blondes* (1949, 'Diamonds Are A Girl's Best Friend', 'Bye, Bye, Baby'), *Two On The Aisle* (1951, 'Hold Me-Hold Me-Hold Me', 'If You Hadn't But You Did'), *Hazel Flagg* (1953, 'Ev'ry Street's A Boulevard (In Old New York)', 'How do You Speak To An Angel?'), *Peter Pan* (1954, 'Never Never Land', 'Distant Melody'), *Wake Up Darling* (1956, a five-performance flop, 'L'il Ol' You And L'il Ol' Me'), *Bells Are Ringing* (1956, 'Just In Time', 'The Party's Over', 'Long Before I Knew You'), *Say, Darling* (1958, 'Dance Only With Me'), *Gypsy* (1959, 'Small World', 'Everything's Coming Up Roses', 'Rose's Turn', 'All I Need Is The Girl'), *Do Re Mi* (1960, 'Make Someone Happy', 'Fireworks'), *Subways Are For Sleeping* (1961, 'I Just Can't Wait', 'Comes Once In A Lifetime', 'Be A Santa'), *Funny Girl* (1964, 'The Music That Makes Me Dance', 'Sadie, Sadie', 'People', 'Don't Rain On My Parade'), *Fade Out-Fade In* (1964, 'You Mustn't Feel Discouraged'), *Hallelujah, Baby!* (1967, 'My Own Morning', 'Now's The Time'), *Darling Of The Day* (1968, 'Let's See What Happens', 'That Something Extra Special'), *Look To The Lilies* (1970, 'I! Yes, Me! That's Who!'), *Prettybelle* (1971, closed out of town), *Sugar* (1972, 'It's Always Love', 'We Could Be Close' [revised for London as *Some Like It Hot* in 1992]), *Lorelei* (1974, a revised version of *Gentlemen Prefer Blondes*), *Hellzapoppin'!* (1976, closed out of town, 'Only One To A Customer'), *Bar Mitzvah Boy* (London 1978, 'You Wouldn't Be You', 'The Sun Shines Out Of Your Eyes', 'Where The Music Is Coming From'), *One Night Stand* (1980, closed during previews, 'Too Old To Be So Young', 'Long Way From Home'), *Pieces Of Eight* (1985, closed during regional try-out in Canada), and *The Red Shoes* (1993, closed after three days). Styne's chief collaborators for Broadway were Betty Comden and Adolph Green, and he also worked with Leo Robin, E.Y 'Yip' Harburg, Sammy Cahn and Bob Hilliard, among others. His two longest-running (and legendary) shows were written with Bob Merrill (*Funny Girl*) and Stephen Sondheim (*Gypsy*). Styne also co-produced several musicals, and composed the

scores for television specials, and films such as *West Point Story*, *Two Tickets To Broadway* and *My Sister Eileen*.
One of the most talented, and prolific ('I believe in perspiration – not inspiration') all-round songwriters in the history of American popular music, Styne won many awards and honours, and was inducted into the Songwriters Hall of Fame and the Theatre Hall of Fame. Several artists have devoted complete albums to his songs, and in 1995, *Everything's Coming Up Roses – The Overtures Of Jule Styne*, played by the National Symphony Orchestra conducted by Jack Everly, was released. ASCAP's memorial tribute to Styne in February of that year included a Stephen Sondheim lyric that ran: 'Jule/You never took things coolly/Your syntax was unduly/Unruly/ But Jule/I love you truly.'
● ALBUMS: *My Name Is Jule* (United Artists 1958) ★★, with Michael Feinstein *Michael Feinstein Sings The Jule Styne Songbook* (Elektra Nonesuch 1991) ★★★.
● FURTHER READING: *Jule*, Theodore Taylor.

SUGAR

Based on the enormously popular 1959 film, *Some Like It Hot*, this musical, which had a score by the *Funny Girl* team of Jule Styne and Bob Merrill, opened at the Majestic Theatre in New York on 9 April 1972. Peter Stone's book stayed closely to the original story of two musicians who, having accidentally witnessed the notorious St. Valentine's Day Massacre in Chicago, flee to Miami disguised as members of an all-female orchestra. Robert Morse and Tony Roberts played the roles that were taken in the film by Jack Lemmon and Tony Curtis, Cyril Ritchard was the eccentric millionaire who found himself completely beguiled by Morse in drag, and Elaine Joyce did her best to make people forget the unforgettable Marilyn Monroe. The score was suitably 20s in style, and included numbers such as 'When You Meet A Man In Chicago', '(Doing It For) Sugar', 'Sun On My Face', 'What Do You Give To A Man Who's Had Everything?', 'Beautiful Through And Through', 'We Could Be Close', 'It's Always Love', 'Hey, Why Not!', and 'Penniless Bums'. Gower Champion contributed some slick choreography, and *Sugar* stayed around for 505 performances. Twenty years later a revised edition with the original film title, *Some Like It Hot*, reached London's West End. The emphasis was switched from the character of Sugar to the show's star, Tommy Steele, and when he had to leave the cast for a time following an on-stage accident, the production went rapidly downhill and closed after a run of three months with losses estimated at around £2 million.

SULTANS

The Sultans trace their origins to Omaha, Nebraska, USA gospel group the Echoes Of Joy, formed by 11-year-old Eugene McDaniels in 1946. This troupe then became the Five Echoes with the addition of brothers Willie and Gene Barnes (both on lead), James Farmer (baritone), Rosenwald Alexander (tenor) and Jimmy Mims (bass). The latter pair were soon replaced by Wesley Devereaux and Richard Beasley, respectively. Devereaux was actually the son of blues singer Wynonie Harris. Farmer's uncle owned a local record shop and the Showcase nightclub, which became the Five Echoes' semi-official home. This was 1953, at which time the group changed name to the Sultans and upped their tempo from gospel to R&B. Their first recordings took place shortly thereafter, for the Houston-based Duke Records label. Released in June, 'Good Thing Baby' was backed by a cover version of Rudy Vallee's 1932 hit 'How Deep Is The Ocean', but failed to make any impression. Johnny Otis, who had brought the Sultans to Duke, then took them on tour, before the release of their second single, 'I Cried My Heart Out'. Like 1954's 'Boppin' With The Mambo', it floundered. Dissatisfied with their label's promotion, the group found a new contract with King Records in Cincinnati, but were forced to change their name to the Admirals to break out of their existing contract. The Admirals debuted with 'Oh Yes', before a cover version of the Five Keys' 'Close Your Eyes'. It was to be their final single, though they did back other New York artists, including Robert 'Bubber' Johnson and Kathy Ryan, on record. The Admirals retreated to Omaha and back to their old name, the Sultans. Two singles for original home Duke Records followed, 'If I Could Tell' and 'My Love Is So High'. However, when Farmer enlisted there seemed little point in continuing the group. Willie Barnes went on to record solo for United Artists Records as Bobby Barnes. His brother, Gene (as Eugene Barnes was now called), also worked solo, finding significant early 60s success with Liberty Records ('A Hundred Pounds Of Clay' reaching number 3 in the *Billboard* charts). He also wrote a number 1 single for Roberta Flack ('Feel Like Makin' Love'). The Sultans then re-formed for a well-received appearance at Ronnie I's Collectors Group Concert Volume 3.

SUMAC, YMA

b. Emperatriz Chavarri, 10 September 1927, Ichocan, Peru. A flamboyant singer, of striking appearance, who was the subject of a series of publicity campaigns designed to shroud her origins in mystery: was she an Inca princess, one of the chosen 'Golden Virgins'? Or a Brooklyn housewife named Amy Camus (Yma Sumac spelt backwards)? Whatever the doubts as to her heritage, what was abundantly genuine was her four octave range, ascending from 'female baritone', through lyric soprano, to high coloratura'. Reportedly, she was the sixth child of an Indian mother and a mixed Indian and Spanish father, and was raised a Quechuan. After performing in local Indian festivals, she moved with her family to Lima, and joined the Compania Peruana de Arte, a group of 46 Indian dancers, singers and musicians. In 1942, Sumac married the Compania's leader, musician and composer Moises Vivanco, and four years later, travelled to New York with him and her cousin, Cholita Rivero, as the Inca Taqui Trio. In the late 40s the

Trio played nightclubs such as New York's Blue Angel, and appeared on radio programmes and Arthur Godfrey's television show. Other work included an eight-week tour of the Borscht Circuit in the Catskill mountains. Signed for Capitol Records, her first album, *Voice Of Xtabay*, was released in 1950. It featured Sumac 'imitating birds and kettledrums, and singing a selection of strangely compelling songs, such as "Chant Of The Chosen Maidens" and "Virgin Of The Sun God", which were written for her by Moises Vivanco, and based on ancient Peruvian folk music'. With only the advantage of minimum publicity (at first), and the notorious 'phoney biography', the 10-inch album sold half a million copies 'overnight'. It was followed by several more in the same vein, and led to an enormously successful concert appearance at the Hollywood Bowl. In 1951, Sumac made her Broadway debut in the short-lived musical *Flahooley*, singing three songs written for her by Vivanco 'with no lyrics and no real relevance to the story'. During the 50s she continued to be popular, playing Carnegie Hall, the Roxy Theatre with Danny Kaye, Las Vegas nightclubs and concert tours of South America and Europe. She also appeared in the film *Secret Of The Incas* (1954), with Charlton Heston and Robert Young. By the end of the decade she was beginning to be regarded by some as *passé*, and, eventually, as a 'nostalgic camp icon'. She retired in the early 60s, but is reported to have performed in 1975 at the Chateau Madrid club in Manhattan. In 1987 she hit the comeback trail with a three-week engagement at New York's Ballroom, and a year later, gained favourable reviews in Los Angeles for 'charming and frequently breathtaking performance'. In her set she featured well-known Latin songs such as 'La Molina' as well as the ethereal material 'that I recorded for Capitol 2,000 years ago!'. In 1992, a German documentary film, *Yma Sumac: Hollywood's Inca Princess*, mapped out her exotic career, and attempted to examine her remarkable range with the aid of computer technology. The lady herself declined to co-operate with the venture, thereby leaving the mystery, and the legend, intact.

● ALBUMS: *Voice Of Xtabay* 10-inch album (Capitol 1950) ★★★, with various artists *Flahooley* 10-inch album (Capitol 1951), *Legend Of The Sun Virgin* 10-inch album (Capitol 1951) ★★★, *Presenting Yma Sumac/Early Recordings* 10-inch album (Coral 1952) ★★★, *Inca Taqui* 10-inch album (Capitol 1953) ★★, *Mambo!* 10-inch album (Capitol 1954) ★★★★, *Legend Of The Jivaro* (Capitol 1957) ★★★, *Feugo Del Andes* (Capitol 1959) ★★★ *Live In Concert* (1961) ★★, *Miracles* (London 1972) ★★★.
● FILMS: *Secret Of The Incas* (1954).

SUMLIN, HUBERT

b. 16 November 1931, Greenwood, Mississippi, USA. One of 11 children, Sumlin's Mother saved hard to buy him an $8 guitar when he was a child. Renowned for his guitar work, particularly in support of his mentor Howlin' Wolf, Hubert

Sumlin began his career in the Mississippi juke-joints. He joined Jimmy Cotton and first met Wolf when he was 19 in Memphis where he worked with him briefly before following him to Chicago in 1954. His occasionally stormy relationship with Wolf lasted until the latter's death, although on Wolf's obsequies he is listed as a son. He was in Europe with Wolf on the AFBF of 1964 and later worked with other bluesmen including Eddie Taylor and Muddy Waters.

Sumlin was devastated when Wolf died in 1967 and since then he has pursued his career under his own name, often working with alumni of Wolf's band. Never a strong singer, he has relied on his guitar-playing prowess to see him through, but his work has been patchy and some feel that he has yet to regain his original stature. It is significant that much of the sound created on Wolf's records was due in no small part to Sumlin's tremendous guitar playing. He can be heard on dozens of Chess Records sides throughout the 50s and 60s. Sumlin was back in the recording studio in 2000 with an impressive line up of supporting musicians including; Eric Clapton, Keith Richards and Levon Helm.

● ALBUMS: *Blues Party* (Demon 1987) ★★, *Healing Feeling* (Black Top 1990) ★★, *Blues Guitar Boss* (JSP 1991) ★★, *My Guitar And Me* (Evidence 1994) ★★, *Blues Anytime* 60s recording (Bellaphon 1994) ★★★, with Pinetop Perkins *Legends* (Telarc 1998) ★★★★, *Wake Up Call* (Blues Planet 1998) ★★, *I Know You* (Acoustic Sounds 1999) ★★★.

SUMMER STOCK

Of the three films in which Judy Garland and Gene Kelly starred together, their final project, *Summer Stock*, is the least impressive. Yet this 1950 MGM release still remains a favourite for many, and has some genuinely charming moments. It tells the tale of the two Falbury sisters – Jane (Garland) has remained at home in New England to run the farm, while Abigail (Gloria DeHaven), has left the roost to pursue a showbiz career. To her sister's horror, Abigail brings the people, props and paraphernalia of a whole new show, written and organised by Joe D. Ross (Kelly), to rehearse on the farm. Jane insists that if the whole gang is going to live there and use the barn for rehearsals, they had better earn their keep. This results in some amusing shenanigans, with cows, chickens and an accident with a brand new tractor – disasters which Phil Silvers normally has something to do with. When Abigail suddenly leaves the production, Jane steps into her place, and does so with a hard working attitude and passion that her sister never displayed. When Abigail returns to apologise half way through the opening night of the show, she not only finds that Jane's performance has been a triumph, but that Jane and Joe have fallen in love. Jane's fiancé, Orville (Eddie Bracken), is left out in the cold, but it looks like Abigail is going to help him recover from the blow. George Wells and Sy Gomberg's screenplay is a happy bundle of clichés – let's put a show on in a barn . . . you've

only got a few days to learn the part etc. Not that anyone cared much, because *Summer Stock*, directed by Charles Walters and produced by Joe Pasternak, was good fun, and several of the sequences are still quite memorable. Garland's singing and dancing in 'Get Happy' (Harold Arlen/Ted Koehler) combine to create one of her all-time best and sophisticated performances. During the rest of the film she was obviously overweight, but 'Get Happy' was shot two months after filming had officially ended, and by then she was back in fine condition. Whatever her physical problems, Garland's voice did not seem to be affected on the uplifting 'If You Feel Like Singing, Sing' and the poignant 'Friendly Star'. They were both written by Harry Warren and Mack Gordon, who also contributed 'Happy Harvest', 'Blue Jean Polka', 'Dig-Dig-Dig For Your Dinner' and Mem'ry Island'. Garland and Kelly were perfect together, and Kelly and Silvers also had a great time with the more comical material, as they did in *Cover Girl* six years earlier. Kelly's own personal mark of genius showed itself in the sequence when, while walking on the stage, he stepped on a squeaky floorboard. Simply by using this, a sheet of newspaper and the accompaniment of 'You, Wonderful You' (Warren-Jack Brooks-Saul Chaplin), he devised one of the film's most enchanting dances. Nick Castle handled the rest of the choreography, and the film was shot in Technicolor by Robert Planck. For UK audiences the title was changed to *If You Feel Like Singing*.

SUN RECORDS

The Sun Record Company was founded in Memphis, Tennessee, in February 1952. It evolved out of the Memphis Recording Service, a small studio installed two years earlier by Sam Phillips, a former disc jockey on stations WMSL and WREC. Although early work often consisted of social occasions, Phillips' ambitions focused on an untapped local blues market. Completed masters were leased to a variety of independent outlets, including Chess Records, Duke and RPM, in the process launching the careers of B.B. King, Howlin' Wolf and Bobby Bland. The Sun label was the natural extension of this success and its early reputation for superior R&B was established with hits by Rufus Thomas ('Bear Cat') and 'Little' Junior Parker ('Feelin' Good'). In 1954 Phillips began recording country music, and the confluence of these two styles resulted in rockabilly. Its most vocal proponent was Elvis Presley, signed by Phillips that year, who completed five exceptional singles for the label before joining RCA-Victor Records. Presley's recordings, which included 'That's Alright Mama', 'Good Rockin' Tonight' and 'Mystery Train', featured Scotty Moore on guitar and Bill Black on bass, whose sparse, economical support enhanced the singer's unfettered delivery.

The crisp production defined Sun rockabilly, a sound the singer was unable to recapture following his move to a major label. Although many commentators questioned Phillips' decision, he retorted that he could now develop the careers of Carl Perkins and Johnny Cash. The former's exemplary releases included 'Blue Suede Shoes' (Sun's first national pop hit), 'Matchbox' and 'Boppin' The Blues', but a near-fatal car crash undermined his progress. His mantle was taken up by other rockabilly singers – Warren Smith, Sonny Burgess and Billy Lee Riley – but these lesser acts failed to establish a consistent career. Roy Orbison and Charlie Rich enjoyed limited success on Sun, but found greater acclaim elsewhere. The aforementioned Cash then became Sun's most commercial property and he enjoyed several hits, including 'I Walk The Line' (1957), 'Ballad Of A Teenage Queen' and 'Guess Things Happen That Way' (both 1958), thus emphasizing the label's country heritage. Four million-sellers – 'Whole Lotta Shakin' Goin' On', 'Great Balls Of Fire', 'Breathless' and 'High School Confidential' – by the exuberant Jerry Lee Lewis, closed a highly productive decade, but the same singer's rapid fall from grace, coupled with the loss of Cash and Perkins, proved hard to surmount.

Sun's simple, rhythmic sound – the only device used to enhance a performance was echo – now proved anachronistic, yet a move to new, larger premises in 1960 paradoxically meant it was lost forever. The label was never Phillips' sole business investment; radio stations, mining and the Holiday Inn Hotel chain vied for his attention, while new record companies, Hi Records and Stax Records, seemed better able to capture the changing Memphis music scene. Paradoxically, this allowed Sun's achievements to remain untarnished and thus its legend is still undiminished. On 1 July 1969, Sam Phillips sold the entire company to country music entrepreneur Shelby Singleton who, with the able assistance of British licensees Charly Records, have completed a series of judicious repackages.

● COMPILATIONS: *The Roots Of Rock Volumes 1-13* (Sun 1977) ★★★, *Sun Golden Hits* (Sun 1981) ★★★, *The Sun Box* (1982) ★★★★, *Sun: The Blues 9-LP box set* (Sun 1985) ★★★, *The Sun Country Years 11-LP box set* (Bear Family 1987) ★★★★, *Sun: The Rocking Years 12-LP box set* (Charly 1987) ★★★★, *The Sound Of Sun* (Sun 1988) ★★★, *The Sun Story Volumes 1 & 2* (Sun 1991) ★★★★, *The Very Best Of Sun Rock 'N' Roll* (Sun 1991) ★★★, *The Sun Singles Collection Volume 1 4-CD box set* (Bear Family 1995) ★★★.

● FURTHER READING: *Sun Records*, Colin Escott and Martin Hawkins.

SUNNYLAND SLIM

b. Albert Luandrew, 5 September 1907, Vance, Mississippi, USA, d. 17 March 1995, Chicago, Illinois, USA. A seminal figure in the development of the post-war Chicago blues, Sunnyland Slim taught himself piano and organ as a child in Mississippi and spent many years playing around the south, before settling in Chicago in 1942. There he established his reputation with older musicians such as Lonnie Johnson, Tampa Red and Peter J. Clayton (some of his earliest records were issued under the pseudonym Doctor

Clayton's Buddy), but more importantly with the new breed of blues singers and musicians that included figures such as Muddy Waters and Little Walter. In the company of artists such as these, his powerful piano work was to set the standard for underpinning the hard, electric sound associated with Chicago blues in the 50s. He recorded extensively under his own name for many important labels of the period, such as Chess Records, Vee Jay Records and Cobra Records, as well as smaller labels, producing such classic Chicago blues sides as 'Johnson Machine Gun', 'Going Back To Memphis' and 'Highway 51'. He was also to be heard accompanying many other important artists of the time, including Robert Lockwood, Floyd Jones and J.B. Lenoir, as well as those already mentioned. He is often credited as having helped younger musicians to get their careers started. Throughout the 60s and 70s, he recorded prolifically and toured widely both in the USA and overseas. In the 80s, although in ill health, he produced albums on his own Airway label, and lent assistance to young players such as Professor Eddie Lusk and Lurrie Bell. He died in 1995 of complications from kidney failure which prompted an immediate reappraisal and a series of reissued albums.

● ALBUMS: *Slim's Shout* (Bluesville 1961) ★★★★, *Midnight Jump* (Blue Horizon 1969) ★★★, *Give Me Time* (Delmark 1984) ★★★, *Devil Is A Busy Man* (Charly 1989) ★★★★, *Be Careful How You Vote* (Airway 1989) ★★★, *Slim's Got His Thing* (BMG 1992) ★★★, *Sunnyland Train* (Evidence 1995) ★★★, *Chicago Jump* (Evidence 1995) ★★★, *Live At The D.C. Blues Society* (Mapleshade 1995) ★★.

● COMPILATIONS: *Legacy Of The Blues Volume Eleven* (Sonet 1975) ★★★★, *She Got A Thing Goin' On* (Earwig 1998) ★★★.

SUNNYSIDERS

Freddy Morgan (b. 7 November 1910, New York City, New York, USA, d. 1970), formed the Sunnysiders in the mid-50s with Margie Rayburn (b. Madera, California, USA, d. 2000, Oceanside, California, USA), Norman Milkin and Jad Paul. Morgan was a banjoist and songwriter and a member of Spike Jones's City Slickers between 1947 and 1958. The group signed with Kapp Records and their first single, 'Hey, Mr. Banjo', penned by Morgan and Milkin, reached number 12 in the US in May 1955. They followed it up with other banjo-related songs, including 'The Lonesome Banjo' and 'Banjo Picker's Ball', but were unable to return to the charts. Rayburn (who married Milkin) did have her own US Top 10 single in 1957 with 'I'm Available'.

● COMPILATIONS: *Motor City Bluegrass* (1970) ★★★.

SUNSHINE, MONTY

b. 8 April 1928, London, England. After teaching himself to play clarinet, Sunshine became involved in the UK trad jazz scene of the late 40s. He was a founder-member of the Crane River Jazz Band and later teamed up with Chris Barber to form a co-operative group. For a while this band was under the nominal leadership of Ken Colyer, but later reverted to its original democratic status. Sunshine was featured on several records, notably the major hit for Barber's band 'Petite Fleur', and helped the band to establish a reputation as one of the best of the UK trad outfits. In 1960 he left Barber to form his own band which, while retaining a high level of popularity for a number of years, never equalled the success of the Barber/Sunshine band. However, Sunshine established a name in Europe, especially in Germany. In the 70s he had occasional reunions with the re-formed Crane River Jazz Band and with Barber. Although a proponent of New Orleans jazz, Sunshine's playing style has always favoured the full, romantic sound of musicians such as Sidney Bechet and Barney Bigard. In the 80s and 90s he was often on tour, still popular with the audience he had known from his earliest days in the business.

● ALBUMS: *A Taste Of Sunshine* (DJM 1976) ★★★, *Magic Is The Moonlight* (Telefunken 1978) ★★★, *Sunshine In London* (Black Lion 1979) ★★★, *On Sunday* (Wam 1987) ★★★, *Just A Little While To Stay Here* (Lake 1990) ★★, *Gotta Travel On* (Timeless 1992) ★★★, *South* (Timeless) ★★, *Live At The Worker's Museum Copenhagen* (Music Mecca 1997) ★★★★.

● COMPILATIONS: *Monty Sunshine And The Crane River Jazz Band, 1950-53* (Dormouse 1988) ★★★.

SWALLOWS

This vocal group from Baltimore, Maryland, USA, comprised Eddie Rich (lead), Irving Turner (tenor/baritone), Earl Hurley (tenor), Herman 'Junior' Denby (second tenor/baritone), Frederick 'Money' Johnson (baritone) and Norris 'Bunky' Mack (bass). The Swallows were one of the most sophisticated of the early 50s vocal harmony groups, recording sleepy ballads much in the style of their Baltimore counterparts the Orioles, but also recording outstanding jump and bluesy tunes in the style of Charles Brown. The group was formed in 1946 and signed with King Records in 1951. Their first recordings were largely Rich-led sweet ballads, best exemplified by their first hit 'Will You Be Mine' (number 9 R&B), from 1951. The Swallows developed some notoriety for a 1952 song, the risqué 'It Ain't The Meat (It's The Motion)', an up-tempo number led by their bass Mack in the same style of the Dominoes' 'Sixty Minute Man'. Another 1952 song set a new style for the group, 'Beside You' (number 8 R&B), in which lead Denby captured perfectly the sound of the urbane blues singer Charles Brown. Much of the Swallows' subsequent material was in this style, but by 1953 it had come to sound dated next to up-and-coming groups such as the Drifters and Clovers. The Swallows left King and made one more recording, for the After Hours label in 1954, and then began to fall apart. Rich kept a group together with new members until he disbanded the Swallows in 1956. In 1958 a new Swallows group consisting of three original members – Rich, Hurley and Johnson – plus new recruits Buddy

Bailey and Calvin Kollette assembled. They signed with King Records' Federal subsidiary and recorded mostly up-tempo songs. When their excellent recording of 'Itchy Twitchy Feeling' failed to compete with Bobby Hendricks' hit version, they disbanded.

● COMPILATIONS: *Dearest* (Charly 1991) ★★★.

SWAN SILVERTONES

This vocal quartet was formed in 1938 in West Virginia, USA, by four coalminers, Claude Jeter (lead), Eddie Boroughas, John Myles and Leroy Watkins. The Swan in their name refers to their early sponsors, the Swan Bakery. Their first sessions were recorded for King Records in Cincinnati in 1946. At this time Henry Brossard (bass) and Soloman Womack (joint lead) joined. The line-up changed frequently throughout the late 40s, with Reverend Percell Perkins, Reverend Robert Crenshaw and Roosevelt Payne all joining at various points. Paul Owens, formerly of the Nightingales and Dixie Hummingbirds, also joined the group. Although their recording career (for Specialty Records) was sparser than more celebrated gospel/R&B groups, the Silvertones continued to tour and appear on radio. William Connor of the Trumpeteers replaced Brossard in 1955, though by the time the group moved to Vee Jay Records in 1959, Louis Johnson had joined as third lead. Claude Jeter became a minister in 1963, after which the group lost much of its momentum. Various singers flitted in and out of the group, and the only remaining original member, John Miles, retired in 1978. The same year former members reunited to play a one-off concert in Chicago.

SWANN, DONALD

b. Donald Ibrahim Swann, 30 September 1923, Llanelli, Wales, d. 23 March 1994, London, England. Swann was the progeny of a union between a Russian doctor and Turkoman nurse who fled St. Petersburg, Russia, during the Revolution. He attended school at Westminster where he proved a popular member of the revue team alongside Michael Flanders (see Flanders And Swann) and stage manager and future UK MP Tony Benn, before beginning studies at Oxford University. While working with the Friends' Ambulance Unit he visited Greece, whose serenity and sense of community, alongside his Russian heritage, greatly influenced his music. However, he soon returned to London to contribute material to West End revues, linking again with Michael Flanders. Both were soon buoyed by the success of ventures such as *Penny Plain* (1951), *Airs On A Shoestring* (1953) and *Fresh Airs* (1956). However, it was their own two-man show, *At The Drop Of A Hat*, that propelled them to nationwide fame after it opened on New Year's Eve in 1956. A massive hit, the show ran for over two years in London, before playing on Broadway and touring the USA and Canada. It was followed in 1963 by *At The Drop Of Another Hat*. However, Swann grew discontented with the endless cycle of engagements and touring that followed, leading to the dissolution of his first marriage. He remained in his house in Battersea, collaborating with Flanders on an album of animal songs for children, and scoring adaptations of the works of his friends C.S. Lewis and J.R.R. Tolkien. He also composed music as a backdrop to his favourite poet, Emily Dickinson, and formed less successful partnerships with John Amis, Frank Topping, Ian Wallace and Lili Malandraki, following the death of Flanders in 1975. Fortunately, he was able to complete his autobiography with the help of second wife Alison Smith before he succumbed to cancer at the age of 70. At that time he was also working on material for a new revue, *Swann Amongst The Sirens*, based on his wartime experiences in Greece (to have been staged by the Cherub Theatre Company).

● FURTHER READING: *Swann's Way: A Life In Song*.

SWEET BEAT

This low-budget 1959 British film was produced by Jeff Kruger who co-owned London's fabled Flamingo nightclub and subsequently operated the Ember label. It starred Julie Amber as a beauty queen-turned-singer who is offered a lucrative spot in a New York venue by a promoter seeking sexual favours in return. The title song was performed by Tony Crombie who, as leader of Tony Crombie And His Rockets, was one of the first UK musicians to embrace nascent rock 'n' roll earlier in the decade. Fred Parris And His Satins, Cindy Mann, Jeri Lee and Lee Allen And His Band were among the other acts featured in a film that promptly sank with little trace.

SWINGIN' AFFAIR! – FRANK SINATRA

A further sequence of immaculate songs, chosen with an uncanny knowledge that they could be adapted for 'swingability'. This set features four songs by Cole Porter, including 'Night And Day' and 'You'd Be So Nice To Come Home To', and further gems from Richard Rodgers and Lorenz Hart ('I Wish I Was In Love Again'), the Gershwin brothers and Duke Ellington's glorious 'I Got It Bad And That Ain't Good'. The CD release includes the bonus of 'The Lady Is A Tramp'. All 15 tracks are once again beautifully arranged by Nelson Riddle, giving space for the strings, trumpets and bassoons. For swingin' romantics only.

● Tracks: *Night And Day; I Wish I Was In Love Again; I Got Plenty O' Nuttin'; I Guess I'll Have To Change My Plan; Nice Work If You Can Get it; Stars Fell On Alabama; No One Ever Tells You; I Won't Dance; Lonesome Road; At Long Last Love; You'd Be So Nice To Come Home To; I Got It Bad And That Ain't Good; From This Moment On; If I Had You; Oh Look At Me Now.*

● First released 1957
● UK peak chart position: did not chart
● USA peak chart position: 2

SYMS, SYLVIA

b. Sylvia Blagman, 2 December 1917, Brooklyn, USA, d. 10 May 1992, New York City, New York,

USA. One of America's most distinguished cabaret and jazz singers with a profound appreciation of lyrics, Sylvia Syms overcame polio as a child, and in her teens discovered the delights of jazz in the clubs of New York's 52nd Street. Inspired and informally trained by Billie Holiday, she made her singing debut in 1941 at Kelly's Stable, and in 1948 was spotted while performing at the Cinderella Club in Greenwich Village by Mae West, who gave her the part of Flo the Shoplifter in a revival of *Diamond Lil*. She subsequently appeared in the regional theatre on many occasions as Bloody Mary in *South Pacific* and as Dolly Levi in *Hello, Dolly!*, and also acted in straight roles. Signed to Decca Records, she had a million-selling record in 1956 with an up-tempo version of 'I Could Have Danced All Night' from *My Fair Lady*, and enjoyed further success with 'English Muffins And Irish Stew' and 'It's Good To Be Alive'. Frank Sinatra called her the 'Buddha' on account of her short 'beer barrel' stature, but he was one of her greatest admirers, hailing her as 'the best saloon singer in the world'. He also produced her 1982 album *Syms By Sinatra*. In the late 80s and early 90s, Syms still performed occasionally at intimate venues such as Eighty Eight's, Michael's Pub, and Freddy's in New York, where sensitive audiences thrilled to her tasteful selections, which included such delights as 'Skylark', 'You Are Not My First Love', 'I Want To Be Yours', 'Fun To Be Fooled', 'I Guess I'll Hang My Tears Out To Dry', 'It Amazes Me', and 'Pink Taffeta'. She died of a heart attack while performing a tribute programme to Frank Sinatra in the Oak Room of the Algonquin Hotel in Manhattan.

● ALBUMS: *Songs By Sylvia Syms* 10-inch album (Atlantic 1952) ★★★★, *After Dark* 10-inch album (Version 1955) ★★★, *Sylvia Syms Sings* (Decca 1955) ★★★★, *Songs Of Love* (Decca 1958) ★★★, *Torch Songs* (Columbia 1960) ★★★★, *That Man – Love Songs To Frank Sinatra* (Kapp 1961) ★★★★, *The Fabulous Sylvia Syms* (20th Century Fox 1963) ★★★, *Sylvia Is!* (Prestige 1967) ★★★, *For Once In My Life* (Prestige 1967) ★★★, *Syms By Sinatra* (Reprise 1982) ★★★, *Along Came Bill* (80s) ★★★, *You Must Believe In Spring* (Cabaret 1992) ★★★, *A Jazz Portrait Of Johnny Mercer* 1984 recording (Koch 1995) ★★.

TAKE ME ALONG

Bob Merrill, the composer and lyricist for a host of pop hits during the 50s, wrote his first Broadway score in 1957 for *New Girl In Town*, a musical adaptation of Eugene O'Neill's classic drama *Anna Christie*. Two years later, for *Take Me Along*, he tackled another of the playwright's works, but one with a much lighter theme – *Ah, Wilderness!* It opened at the Shubert Theatre in New York on 22 October 1959 with a strong cast that was headed by a legendary Hollywood leading man of the 30s and 40s, Walter Pidgeon, and Jackie Gleason, whose main claim to fame at that time was as a comedian on US television. Joseph Stein and Robert Russell wrote the book, which was set in the homely town of Centerville, Connecticut, in 1910. Pidgeon plays Ned Miller, the publisher of the local newspaper, and the father of Richard, whose adolescent problems with his girlfriend, Muriel Macomber (Susan Luckey), and the devil drink, are resolved when he enters the hallowed halls of Yale University. The sub-plot concerns Sid Davis (Jackie Gleason), a far more serious drinker, who would like to settle down with Ned's sister, Lily (Eileen Herlie), but has to sober up before she will accept him. Pidgeon and Gleason duetted on the lively 'Take Me Along', and the rest of Merrill's score, which has been described as 'wistful and enchanting', included 'I Would Die', 'Staying Young', 'I Get Embarrassed', 'Sid Ol' Kid', 'We're Home', 'Promise Me A Rose', 'Nine O'Clock' and 'But Yours'. Pidgeon and Gleason were both nominated for the Tony Award for best actor, and Gleason won for the most satisfying stage role of his career. He was succeeded during the show's run of 448 performances by William Bendix, a movie tough-guy with a heart of gold. *Take Me Along* returned to Broadway during the 1984/5 season, which, according to experienced Broadway watchers, was one of the worst in living memory. The climate was not right for the show's warm and charming approach, and it closed after only one performance.

TAN TAN

b. Edward Thornton, *c.*1934, Jamaica, West Indies. Tan Tan is acknowledged as one of Jamaica's leading trumpeters, having played with a number of notable performers. From humble beginnings playing over a comb wrapped in paper, by the mid-50s Tan Tan was playing trumpet alongside Don Drummond on trombone in the Roy Coulton band, performing at the Glass Bucket and Silver Slipper clubs. The band were also the first combo to play live on Jamaican radio and were later employed to accompany jazz legends on world tours. While touring, Tan Tan decided to settle in

Europe and Drummond returned to Jamaica. Tan Tan played in a number of bands in Europe before settling with Georgie Fame And The Blue Flames in 1963. The band enjoyed a string of hits featuring Tan Tan's accomplished trumpet playing, which led to his being invited to perform on the Beatles hit 'Got To Get You Into My Life'. Although Tan Tan remained with Georgie Fame, he was also enrolled to perform alongside Boney M. Despite Tan Tan having been involved on the Jamaican music scene from its earliest years, it was not until he performed with Aswad that he made a significant impression within the reggae community. He played in the band's dextrous horn section, featuring Michael 'Bammi' Rose and Vin Gordon. Classic tunes include 'African Children', 'Love Fire' (which provided the rhythm for Dennis Brown's 'Promised Land'), a version of the Maytals' '54-46 That's My Number', as well as the dancehall anthems 'Pull Up' and 'Bubbling'. The horn section also provided the musical foundation for other Grove Music performers, including King Sounds and the Sons Of Jah.

● ALBUMS: *Misty* (Third World 1981) ★★★, with Aswad *A New Chapter Of Dub* (Mango/Island 1982) ★★★, *Musical Nostalgia For Today* (Macabees 1985) ★★★, with Ossie Scott *At Their Best* (Shelley 1996) ★★★.

TARHEEL SLIM

b. Alden Bunn, 24 September 1924, Bailey, North Carolina, USA, d. 21 August 1977. Tarheel Slim was a blues, gospel and doo-wop singer and guitarist who took his sobriquet from the popular nickname of North Carolina – Tarheel State. Bunn learned guitar at the age of 12 and sang in church by the age of 20. He began working with the Gospel Four following World War II and then joined the Selah Jubilee Singers, with whom he first recorded, in the late 40s. As the gospel group could not record secular music, they also worked under the names the Four Barons and the Larks, recording the R&B hits 'Eyesight To The Blind' and 'Little Side Car' for Apollo Records in 1951. Bunn recorded under his real name for Apollo and also with the group the Wheels in 1956 on Premium Records. That was followed by a partnership with his wife as the Lovers for Lamp Records in 1958. They then recorded for the Fire label as Tarheel Slim And Little Ann, a name they kept until 1962. After a spell outside the music business, Slim returned in 1970, when he recorded for Trix Records, an association that lasted until his death.

● ALBUMS: *Lock Me In Your Heart* (1989) ★★★, *No Time At All* (Trix 1994) ★★★.

TARRIERS

Formed in 1954, the Tarriers are remembered for two primary reasons: their 1956 US Top 5 recording of 'The Banana Boat Song' and the fact that one of the group members was Alan Arkin, who went on to become a highly successful actor. The folk group was put together by Erik Darling (b. 25 September 1933, Baltimore, Maryland, USA), who was influenced by the folk revivalists of the day. After performing briefly with a large troupe of vocalists, Darling hooked up with Arkin (b. 26 March 1934, Brooklyn, New York) and Bob Carey as the Tunetellers. The group changed its name to the Tarriers and wrote and recorded 'The Banana Boat Song' to capitalize on the calypso music craze then sweeping the USA. Simultaneously, they recorded a similar song called 'Cindy, Oh Cindy' with singer Vince Martin. Both singles were released on Glory Records, 'Cindy' reaching number 9 and 'The Banana Boat Song' number 4. The Tarriers never again made the charts, however, and the original trio dissolved two years later. Darling joined the Weavers and later went on to form the Rooftop Singers; Arkin began his acting career and Carey kept a Tarriers group in existence until 1964.

● ALBUMS: *The Tarriers* (Glory 1958) ★★★, *Hard Travelin'* (United Artists 1959) ★★★★, *Tell The World About This* (Atlantic 1960) ★★★, *The Tarriers* (Decca 1962) ★★★, *The Original Tarriers* (Kapp 1963) ★★★, *Gather 'Round* (Decca 1964) ★★.

TATUM, ART

b. 13 October 1909, Toledo, Ohio, USA, d. 5 November 1956, Los Angeles, California, USA. Born into a musical family, Tatum was handicapped from birth by impaired sight. Blind in one eye and only partially sighted in the other, he nevertheless studied piano formally and learned to read music. By his mid-teens he was playing professionally in Toledo. He played briefly in the Speed Webb band, but was mostly active as a soloist or in small groups working in clubs and playing on radio. He was heard by singer Adelaide Hall, who took him on the road as her accompanist. With Hall he travelled to New York in 1932 and the following year made his first recordings. He spent the next few years playing clubs in Cleveland and Chicago, but in 1937 was back in New York, where his playing in clubs, on radio and on record established his reputation as a major figure in jazz circles.

He toured the USA and also played in the UK. In the early 40s he formed a trio with bass player Slam Stewart and guitarist Tiny Grimes that became extremely popular. For the next decade Tatum toured extensively, performing throughout North America. In the early 50s he was signed by Norman Granz who recorded him in a series of remarkable performances, both as soloist (*The Solo Masterpieces*) and in a small group context with Benny Carter, Buddy De Franco, Roy Eldridge, Lionel Hampton, Ben Webster and others (*The Group Masterpieces*). A matchless virtuoso performer, Tatum's impact on the New York jazz scene in the early 30s had extensive repercussions. Even Fats Waller, an acknowledged master and someone to whom Tatum had listened on record in his own formative years, was aware of the phenomenal talent of the newcomer, reputedly declaring onstage – when he spotted Tatum in the audience – 'God is in the house tonight'.

Tatum's dazzling extemporizations on themes from jazz and the classics, but mostly from the popular songbook, became bywords and set standards few of his successors matched and none surpassed. Capable of breathtaking runs, interspersed with striking single notes and sometimes unexpected chords, he developed a unique solo style. His powerful left-hand figures tipped a hat in the direction of stride while he simultaneously explored the limits of an orthodox keyboard like no other pianist in jazz (and few elsewhere). A playful habit of quoting from other melodies, a technique that in unskilled hands can be merely irritating, was developed into a singular stylistic device. Unlike some virtuoso performers, Tatum never sacrificed feeling and swing for effect. Although he continued to develop throughout his career, it is hard to discover any recorded evidence that he was never poised and polished.

His prodigious talent allowed him to achieve extraordinary recording successes: his solo sessions for Granz were mostly completed in two days – 69 tracks, all but three needing only one take. Ray Spencer, whose studies of the artist are extensive, has commented that Tatum achieved such a remarkable work rate through constant 'refining and honing down after each performance until an ideal version remained needing no further adjustments'. While this is clearly the case, Tatum's performances never suggest a man merely going through the motions. Everything he did sounded fresh and vital, as if minted especially for the occasion in hand. Although he remains a major figure in jazz piano, Tatum is often overlooked in the cataloguing of those who affected the course of the music. He appears to stand to one side of the developing thrust of jazz, yet his creativity and the manner in which he explored harmonic complexities and unusual chord sequences influenced many musicians, including Bud Powell and Herbie Hancock, and especially non-pianists, among whom can be listed Charlie Parker and John Coltrane. The word genius is often used carelessly but, in assessing Tatum and the manner in which he transformed ideas and the imagined limitations of the piano in jazz, any other word would be inadequate.

● ALBUMS: *Art Tatum Trio* i 10-inch album (Dial 1950) ★★★★, *Art Tatum* i 10-inch album (Asch 1950) ★★★★, *Art Tatum Trio* ii 10-inch album (Stinson 1950) ★★★★, *Art Tatum Trio* iii 10-inch album (Brunswick 1950) ★★★★, *Art Tatum Piano Solos* (Brunswick 1950) ★★★★, *Tatum Piano* 10-inch album (Remington 1950) ★★★★, *Art Tatum Encores* 10-inch album (Capitol 1951) ★★★★, *Art Tatum Trio* iv 10-inch album (Folkways 1951) ★★★★, *Gene Norman Concert At Shrine Auditorium, May 1949* 10-inch album (Columbia 1952) ★★★★, *Art Tatum Trio* v 10-inch album (Capitol 1953) ★★★★, *Here's Art Tatum* (Brunswick 1954) ★★★★, *An Art Tatum Concert* reissued as *The Tatum Touch* (Columbia 1954) ★★★★, *Art Tatum* ii (Capitol 1955) ★★★, *The Art Tatum-Roy Eldridge-Alvin Stoller-John Simmons Quartet* (Clef 1955) ★★★, with Louis Bellson, Benny Carter *Tatum-Carter-Bellson* reissued as *The*

Three Giants (Clef 1955) ★★★, with Lionel Hampton, Buddy Rich *The Hampton-Tatum-Rich Trio* (Clef 1956) ★★★, *The Art Tatum-Buddy De Franco Quartet* (American Recording Society 1956) ★★★, with Erroll Garner *Giants Of The Piano* (Roost 1956) ★★★, with Mary Lou Williams *The King And Queen* (Jazztone 1958) ★★★, with Bellson, Carter *Makin' Whoopee* (Verve 1958) ★★★, *The Art Tatum-Ben Webster Quartet* (Verve 1958) ★★★★, *Presenting The Art Tatum Trio* (Verve 1961) ★★★★.

● COMPILATIONS: *Classic Early Solos (1934-1937)* (GRP) ★★★★, *Classic Piano Solos (1934-1939)* (GRP) ★★★★, *Art Tatum Standards* 1938-39 recordings (Black Lion) ★★★, *The Genius Of Art Tatum Volumes 1-11* (Clef/Verve 1954-57) ★★★★, *The Greatest Piano Hits Of Them All* (Verve 1959) ★★★★, *The Incomparable Music Of Art Tatum* (Verve 1959) ★★★★, *More Of The Greatest Piano Of Them All* (Verve 1959) ★★★★, *Still More Of The Greatest Piano Of Them All* (Verve 1960) ★★★★, *The Essential Art Tatum* 1953-56 recordings (Verve 1962) ★★★★, *God Is In The House* 1940-41 recordings (Onyx 1973) ★★★★, *The Complete Pablo Solo Masterpieces Volumes 1-12* 1953-55 recordings (Pablo 1978) ★★★★★, *The Tatum Group Masterpieces Volumes 1-9* 1954-56 recordings (Pablo 1978) ★★★★★, *Art Tatum On The Air* (Aircheck 1978) ★★★★, *Masterpieces* 1934-37 recordings (MCA 1979) ★★★★, *20th Century Piano Genius* (EmArcy 1987) ★★★★, *The Complete Capitol Recordings, Volume One* 1949-52 recordings (Capitol 1989) ★★★★, *The Complete Capitol Recordings, Volume Two* 1949-52 recordings (Capitol 1989) ★★★★, *Complete Art Tatum Volumes 1 & 2* (Capitol 1990) ★★★★, *The Best Of Art Tatum* (Pablo 1990) ★★★★, *The V Discs* 1944-46 recordings (Black Lion 1990) ★★★★★, *Art Tatum Standards* (Pablo 1991) ★★★★★, *Piano Starts Here* 1933 and 1949 recordings (Columbia/Legacy 1991) ★★★★, *The Complete Pablo Solo Masterpieces* 7-CD box set 1953-55 recordings (Pablo 1991) ★★★★★, *The Complete Pablo Group Masterpieces* 6-CD box set 1954-56 recordings (Pablo 1992) ★★★★★, *20th Century Piano Genius* recorded 1955 (Verve 1992) ★★★★, *Complete Brunswick And Decca Sessions 1932-41* (Affinity 1993) ★★★★, *Art Tatum 1932-1934* (Classics 1995) ★★★, *Art Tatum 1934-1940* (Classics 1995) ★★★★, *Art Tatum 1940-1944* (Classics 1995) ★★★, *Art Tatum 1944* (Classics 1995) ★★★, *20th Century Piano Genius* (Verve 1996) ★★★★, *His Best Recordings 1933-1944* (Best Of Jazz 1996) ★★★, *The Complete Capitol Recordings* 1949-52 recordings (Blue Note 1997) ★★★★, *Standards* 1935-43 recordings (Black Lion 1998) ★★★, *The Standard Transcriptions 1935-45* recordings (Music & Arts 1998) ★★★, *The Standard Transcriptions 1935-1945* (Storyville 1998) ★★★, *Art Tatum 1945-1947* (Classics 1998) ★★★, *On The Sunny Side Of The Street* 1944-45 recordings (Topaz 1999) ★★★, *The Art Of Tatum* 1932-44 recordings (ASV 1999) ★★★.

● FURTHER READING: *Art Tatum, A Guide To His Recorded Music*, Arnold Laubich. *Too Marvellous For Words: The Life And Genius Of*, James Lester.
● FILMS: *The Fabulous Dorseys* (1947).

TAYLOR, ART

b. 6 April 1929, New York City, New York, USA, d. 6 February 1995, New York City, New York, USA. As a teenager Taylor played drums with Sonny Rollins, Howard McGhee and other young bop musicians in New York. In the early 50s he was also to be heard in mainstream groups, playing with Buddy De Franco and Coleman Hawkins. He continued to play with leading beboppers, including Bud Powell, and later in the decade was with Miles Davis and John Coltrane. From time to time he led his own bands, and toured the USA and Europe with several groups. He became resident in Europe in the early 60s, playing with visiting fellow Americans including Dexter Gordon and Johnny Griffin. During this period, Taylor began recording interviews with musicians, the results of which, often acutely angled towards the racial and political circumstances surrounding jazz, were first published in 1977 under the title *Notes And Tones*. In the mid-80s Taylor returned to the USA and hosted a radio show. His last studio session was with Jimmy Smith in 1995 for the excellent *Damn!*, and the album was dedicated to his memory.

● ALBUMS: *Taylor's Wailers* (Prestige 1957) ★★★★, *Taylor's Tenors* (New Jazz 1959) ★★★★, *A.T.'s Delight* (Blue Note 1960) ★★★, shared with Art Farmer *Hard Cookin'* (Prestige 1964) ★★★★, with Dexter Gordon *A Day In Copenhagen* (1969) ★★★, *Mr A. T.* (Enja 1992) ★★★, *Wailin' At The Vanguard* (Verve 1993) ★★★★, with Jimmy Smith *Damn!* (Verve 1995) ★★★★, with Steve Grossman, Tyler Mitchell *Bouncing With Mr A.T.* (Dreyfus 1996) ★★★.
● FURTHER READING: *Notes And Tones*, Arthur Taylor.

TAYLOR, BILLY

b. 24 July 1921, Greenville, North Carolina, USA. After extensive formal studies, Taylor began playing piano with numerous leading jazzmen of the late swing era/early bebop period. These included Ben Webster, Dizzy Gillespie, Stuff Smith and Charlie Parker. By the early 50s Taylor's high reputation led to his being hired as house pianist at Birdland. His main contribution to jazz in the 50s was as leader of a trio, usually in New York, which continued more or less non-stop for the next three decades. He also appeared regularly on radio and television as both a performer and a presenter of programmes, including a successful regular slot on CBS' *Sunday Morning* programme. Taylor also developed an abiding interest in jazz education, writing piano tutors and, in 1965, forming Jazzmobile, the Harlem-based concert group. In 1969 he became band director for *The David Frost Show*, the first black musician to achieve this role on a network television series. Taylor has frequently played and composed music that fuses jazz with the classical form. Among these works are his 'Suite For Jazz Piano And Orchestra', composed in 1973, and 'Homage', a chamber music piece first performed by the Billy Taylor Trio and the Juilliard String Quartet in 1990. An inventive and technically facile player,

Taylor's dedication to the development of interest in jazz in the community has sometimes led the wider audience to overlook his undoubted skills. One of the most popular jazz classics of recent years is 'I Wish I Knew (How It Would Feel To Be Free)', a handclapping happy-go-lucky song in the style of Ramsey Lewis' 'Wade In The Water'. Taylor's song is better known as the long-running theme to UK film critic Barry Norman's television programme – a sad fact, that outside the jazz circle, his song is better known than he is. (This artist should not be confused with either Billy Taylor Snr. or Billy Taylor Jnr., father-and-son bass players.)

● ALBUMS: *Piano Panorama* reissued as *The Billy Taylor Touch* (Atlantic 1951) ★★★, *Jazz At Storyville* 10-inch album (Roost 1952) ★★★, *Taylor Made Jazz* 10-inch album (Roost 1952) ★★★, *Billy Taylor Piano* 10-inch album (Savoy 1953) ★★★, *Billy Taylor Trio, Volume 1* 10-inch album (Prestige 1953) ★★★, *Billy Taylor Trio, Volume 2* 10-inch album (Prestige 1953) ★★★, *Billy Taylor Trio, Volume 3* 10-inch album (Prestige 1953) ★★★, *Billy Taylor Trio* reissued as *Cross Section* (Prestige 1954) ★★★★, *Billy Taylor Trio* reissued as *The Billy Taylor Trio With Candido* (Prestige 1954) ★★★★, *Billy Taylor Trio In Concert At Town Hall, December 17, 1954* 10-inch album (Prestige 1955) ★★★, *A Touch Of Taylor* (Prestige 1955) ★★★, *Evergreens* (ABC-Paramount 1956) ★★★, *Billy Taylor At The London House* (ABC-Paramount 1956) ★★★, *Billy Taylor Introduces Ira Sullivan* (ABC-Paramount 1957) ★★★, *My Fair Lady Loves Jazz* (ABC-Paramount 1957) ★★★, *The New Trio* (ABC-Paramount 1958) ★★★, *Taylor Made Flute* (Argo 1959) ★★★, *Custom Taylored* (SeSac 1959) ★★★, *Billy Taylor With Four Flutes* (Riverside 1959) ★★★★, *One For Fun* (Atlantic 1960) ★★★, *Billy Taylor Trio Uptown* (Riverside 1960) ★★★, *Warming Up* (Riverside 1960) ★★★, *Interlude* (Moodsville 1961) ★★★, *Impromptu* (Mercury 1962) ★★★, *Right Here, Right Now* (Capitol 1963) ★★★, *Midnight Piano* (Capitol 1965) ★★★, *Easy Life* (Surrey 1966) ★★★, *I Wish I Knew How It Would Feel To Be Free* (Tower 1968) ★★★, *Billy Taylor Today/A Sleeping Bee* (MPS 1969) ★★★, *OK Billy* (Bell 1970) ★★★, *Jazz Alive* (Monmouth Evergreen 1977) ★★★, *Live At Storyville* (West 54 1977) ★★★★, with Joe Kennedy *Where've You Been?* (Concord Jazz 1981) ★★★★, *White Nights And Jazz In Leningrad* (Taylor Made 1988) ★★★, *You Tempt Me* 1985 recording (Taylor Made 1989) ★★★, *Solo* (Taylor Made 1989) ★★★, *Billy Taylor And The Jazzmobile All Stars* (Taylor Made 1989) ★★★, *Dr. T* (GRP 1993) ★★★★, *It's A Matter Of Pride* (GRP 1993) ★★★, *Homage* (GRP 1995) ★★★, *Music Keeps Us Young* (Arkadia 1997) ★★★★, *Ten Fingers, One Voice* (Arkadia 1999) ★★★, *Urban Griot* (Soundpost 2001) ★★★.

● FURTHER READING: *The History And Development Of Jazz Piano*, Billy Taylor.

TAYLOR, CECIL

b. 15 March 1929, New York City, New York, USA. A towering figure in post-war *avant garde* jazz, Taylor has been hailed as the greatest piano virtuoso of the twentieth century because of the phenomenal power, speed and intensity of his playing. 'We in black music think of the piano as a percussive instrument,' he told writer John Litweiler, 'we beat the keyboard, we get inside the instrument. . . the physical force going into the making of black music – if that is misunderstood, it leads to screaming'. Taylor grew up in Long Island, studying piano from the age of five and percussion (with a classical tutor) soon afterwards. He attended the New York College of Music and the New England Conservatory in Boston, though he later claimed he had learned more by listening to Duke Ellington records. Despite an early interest in European classical composers, especially Stravinsky, Taylor's major influences come from the jazz tradition, notably big band leaders such as Ellington, drummers Sonny Greer and Chick Webb and a lineage of pianists that runs through Fats Waller, Erroll Garner, Thelonious Monk and Horace Silver. Although his first gigs were with swing era veterans Hot Lips Page, Johnny Hodges and Lawrence Brown, by the mid-50s Taylor was leading his own small groups and laying the basis for a musical revolution that is still in progress. His early associates included Buell Neidlinger, Dennis Charles, Steve Lacy and Archie Shepp (plus a fairly disastrous one-off encounter with John Coltrane) and his first recordings still bore a discernible, if carefully distanced, relationship to the jazz mainstream. By the early 60s, working with Sunny Murray, Alan Silva and his longest-serving colleague, Jimmy Lyons, Taylor's music had shed all direct reference to tonality and regular time-keeping and sounded almost purely abstract. However, the arrival of Ornette Coleman in New York in 1959, playing his own version of 'free jazz', rather overshadowed all other innovators and Taylor's more radical and complex music was largely ignored by the press and public, although a handful of fellow pioneers – the best-known of whom was Albert Ayler – embraced it enthusiastically. (Another admirer was Gil Evans, whose *Into The Hot* actually comprised one side of music by Taylor and one side by Johnny Carisi: Evans himself is not on the album!) Taylor lived in poverty for much of the 60s, even working as a dishwasher on occasion; but gradually his influence began to permeate the scene, particularly after Blue Note Records released two outstanding 1966 sessions. Both featured his regular partners Lyons, Silva, Andrew Cyrille and Henry Grimes; in addition, *Unit Structures* had Ken McIntyre and trumpeter Eddie Gale Stevens and *Conquistador!* had Bill Dixon (with whom Taylor had worked in the Jazz Composers' Guild). In 1968 Taylor made an album with the Jazz Composers Orchestra and a 1969 concert with a new group of Lyons, Cyrille and Sam Rivers was released on the French label Shandar; but recording opportunities remained scarce. In the early 70s he became involved in education, teaching at Wisconsin University and colleges in Ohio and New Jersey; in 1973 he briefly ran his own label, Unit Core, releasing *Indents (Mysteries)* and *Spring Of Two Blue-Js.*

Finally, the trickle of other releases – on Trio in Japan, on Arista's Freedom label in the USA, on Enja in Europe – began to gather momentum and by the early 80s Taylor was recording regularly for the European Soul Note and Hat Hut labels, while later in the decade Leo Records and FMP also championed his work. During this period his ensembles included Lyons (always), Cyrille (often), Silva (occasionally) plus players such as Sirone, Ronald Shannon Jackson, violinist Ramsey Ameer, trumpeter Raphé Malik, Jerome Cooper, William Parker and percussionist Rashid Bak. Their characteristic sound was a torrential flood of full-tilt, densely textured, swirling, churning, flying improvisation that could and usually did last for two to three hours without pause.

Taylor also recorded a series of stunning solo albums, notably *Fly! Fly! Fly! Fly! Fly!* and the live double-set *Garden*, which showed he was one of the most dazzling, dynamic pianists in jazz history, and released two memorable duo albums – *Embraced*, with Mary Lou Williams, and *Historic Concerts*, with Max Roach – that further enhanced his reputation. In 1985 the first recording of Taylor's big band music, *Winged Serpent (Sliding Quadrants)*, was released by Soul Note. In 1986 Jimmy Lyons died of lung cancer; Taylor lost both a close friend and his most dedicated musical collaborator. In 1987 he toured with a new Unit (Parker, Carlos Ward, Leroy Jenkins, Thurman Barker – three of their concerts were released by Leo the following year) but since then has worked mostly in a trio format, usually with Parker and Tony Oxley (sometimes calling themselves the Feel Trio). In 1988, FMP brought 20 European improvisers to Berlin for a month-long festival of concerts and workshops that featured Taylor. Several of these were later released in the lavishly packaged, 11-CD box-set *Cecil Taylor In Berlin '88*, which comprised two discs of Taylor's big band music, one of a big band workshop, one solo concert, one trio set with Tristan Honsinger and Evan Parker, a duo with Derek Bailey and five discs of duos with drummers – Oxley, Günter Sommer, Paul Lovens, Han Bennink and Louis Moholo. The set was released to worldwide acclaim in the music press and sealed Taylor's standing as one of the four or five leading innovators in post-bebop jazz. Although he has few direct imitators, he has proved an inspiration to free players everywhere and in particular to many jazz pianists, from Alex Von Schlippenbach to Marilyn Crispell.

The tremendous energy and sweep of his music has fooled many listeners into believing it has no structural underpinning, but Ekkehard Jost, both in his book *Free Jazz* and in one of the several essays in the booklet that accompanies the FMP box-set, has identified certain formal elements that recur in Taylor's work. (There are also useful chapters on his music in John Litweiler's *The Freedom Principle* and Valerie Wilmer's *As Serious As Your Life*, plus a detailed account of his early career in A.B. Spellman's *Four Lives In The Bebop Business*. Taylor himself has always stressed the spiritual and mystical nature of African American

music: 'It's about magic and capturing spirits.') A devotee of dance from Baby Lawrence to contemporary ballet (he once remarked 'I try to imitate on the piano the leaps in space a dancer makes'), Taylor has worked extensively in this field, for example on projects with choreographers/dancers Dianne McIntyre and Mikhail Baryshnikov. A poet too, whose writings often adorn his album sleeves, Taylor's *Chinampus* had him half-reciting, half-chanting a selection of sound-poetry and accompanying himself on various percussion instruments. For many years he has been working on a book about 'methodological concepts of black music', to be entitled *Mysteries*.

● ALBUMS: *Jazz Advance* (Advance 1956) ★★★★, *Hard Driving Jazz* reissued as John Coltrane's *Coltrane Time* (United Artists 1959) ★★★, *Stereo Drive* (United Artists 1959) ★★★, *Love For Sale* (United Artists 1959) ★★★★, *Looking Ahead!* (United Artists 1959) ★★★★, *The World Of Cecil Taylor* (Candid 1960) ★★★★, *Live At The Cafe Montmartre* (Fantasy 1964) ★★★★, *Unit Structures* (Blue Note 1966) ★★★★, *Conquistador* (Blue Note 1967) ★★★★, *Student Studies* (Affinity 1967) ★★★, *Great Paris Concert* 3-LP set (Prestige 1969) ★★★★, *J For Jazz Broadcasts Present Cecil Taylor* (1971) ★★★, with Buell Neidlinger *New York City R&B* 1961 recording (Barnaby 1971) ★★★★, *Indent (Mysteries)* (Unit Core/Arista Freedom 1973) ★★★, *Akisakila* (Konnex 1973) ★★★, *Spring Of Two Blue-Js* (1974) ★★★, *Silent Tongues* (Arista Freedom 1975) ★★★★, *Dark Unto Themselves* (Enja 1976) ★★★, *Air Above Mountains (Buildings Within)* (Enja 1977) ★★★★, with Neidlinger *Cecil Taylor All Stars Featuring Buell Neidlinger* 1961 recording (Candid/Victor 1977) ★★★★, with Mary Lou Williams *Embraced* (Pablo 1977) ★★, *The Cecil Taylor Unit* (New World 1978) ★★★★, *Three Phasis* (New World 1979) ★★★★, *One Too Many Salty Swifty And Not Goodbye* 1978 recordings (hatART 1980) ★★★★, *Spots Circles And Fantasy* (FMP 1979) ★★★★, *It Is In The Brewing Luminous* (hatART 1981) ★★★★, *Fly! Fly! Fly! Fly! Fly!* (MPS 1981) ★★★, *Garden Part One* (hatART 1982) ★★★★, *Garden Part Two* (hatART 1982) ★★★★, *Praxis* 1968 recording (1982) ★★★, *Live In Willisau '83* (1983) ★★★, *Calling It The 8th* (hatART 1983) ★★★★, with Max Roach *Historic Concerts* 1979 recording (Soul Note 1984) ★★★★, *Winged Serpent (Sliding Quadrants)* (Soul Note 1985) ★★★★, *The Eighth* 1981 recording (1986) ★★★★, *For Olim* (Soul Note 1987) ★★★, with Neidlinger *Jumpin' Punkins* 1961 recordings (Candid 1987) ★★★★, *Live In Bologna* (Leo 1988) ★★★, *Live In Vienna* (Leo 1988) ★★★★, *Chinampus* (Leo 1988) ★★★★, *Alms/Tiergarten (Spree)* (FMP 1988) ★★★★, *Tzotzil Mummers Tzotzil* (1989) ★★★, *Cecil Taylor In Berlin '88* 11-CD box set (1989) ★★★, *Erzulie Maketh Scent* (FMP 1989) ★★★★, with Derek Bailey *Pleistozaen Mit Wasser* (FMP 1989) ★★★, with Evan Parker, Tristan Honsinger *The Hearth* (FMP 1989) ★★★★, *Leaf Palm Hand* (FMP 1989) ★★★★, *Regalia* (FMP 1989) ★★★, *Remembrance* (FMP 1989) ★★★★, *Riobec* (FMP 1989) ★★★★, *The Hearth* (FMP 1989)

★★★★, *Legba Crossing* (FMP 1989) ★★★★, with Günter Sommer *In East Berlin* (1989) ★★★, *Looking (The Feel Trio)*, (FMP 1990) ★★★★, *In Florescence* (1990) ★★★★, with Tony Oxley, William Parker *Looking (Berlin Version) The Feel Trio* (1990) ★★★★, *Looking (Berlin Version) Corona* (1991) ★★★★, *Looking (Berlin Version) Solo* (1991) ★★★★, with Oxley, Parker *Celebrated Blazons* (FMP 1991) ★★★, *Double Holy House* (FMP 1991) ★★★, with Art Ensemble Of Chicago *Thelonious Sphere Monk* (DIW 1991) ★★★, with Neidlinger *Cecil* 1961 recordings (Maestri Del Jazz 1991) ★★★★, *Olu Iwa* 1986 recording (Soul Note 1994) ★★★★, *Iwontunwonsi: Live At Sweet Basil* 1986 recording (Sound Hills 1996) ★★★, *Nefertiti, The Beautiful One Has Come* 1962 recording (Revenant 1997) ★★★★, *The Tree Of Life* 1991 recording (FMP 1998) ★★★, *Always A Pleasure* 1993 recording (FMP 1998) ★★★, *Qu'a: Live At The Iridium Vol 1* (Cadence 1998) ★★★★, with Dewey Redman, Elvin Jones *Momentum Space* (Verve 1999) ★★★, *Qu'a Yuba Live At The Iridium Vol 2* (Cadence 1999) ★★★, *Melancholy* 1990 recording (FMP 2000) ★★★.
● COMPILATIONS: *In Transition* 1955-1959 recordings (1975) ★★★★, with others *Masters Of The Modern Piano* 1957 recordings (1976) ★★★, *The Complete Candid Recordings Of Cecil Taylor And Buell Neidlinger* 6-LP/4-CD box set (Mosaic 1989) ★★★★.
● FURTHER READING: *Black Music: Four Lives*, A.B. Spellman. *The Freedom Principle: Jazz After 1958*, John Litweiler.

TAYLOR, EARL

b. 17 June 1929, Rose Hill, Lee County, Virginia, USA, d. 28 January 1984. In the late 30s, Taylor was attracted to the music of the Monroe Brothers and learned to play mandolin (on which he later specialized), guitar and harmonica. In 1946, he relocated to Michigan where he played with the Mountaineers, before forming his own Stoney Mountain Boys. In 1948, broke and disenchanted, he disbanded his group and returned to Virginia before moving to Maryland, where he worked outside of music until 1953. He became friendly with teenagers Charlie Waller (later of Country Gentlemen fame), Sam Hutchins and Louie Profitt and the quartet began playing bluegrass music. With some changes, they played their local area until 1955, when Taylor joined Jimmy Martin in Detroit. He also recorded with Martin, before returning to Maryland in 1957, where he formed a new version of the Stoney Mountain Boys and worked the club circuit in the Baltimore area. In April 1959, Taylor and his group had the distinction of being the first bluegrass band to play in Carnegie Hall. Soon afterwards, he relocated to Cincinnati and played various venues and did television and radio work until 1965. During this time, he recorded for Rebel, United Artists and Capitol Records. He disbanded to work with Jimmy Martin until 1966, when he spent 18 months touring and recording with Flatt And Scruggs. He later returned to Cincinnati and, after re-forming his band, he not only worked the local area but also spent some time in California. In the early 70s, he continued to play the Cincinnati and Columbus area with bands that saw various personnel changes, and made further recordings for Rural Rhythm (listed as Earl Taylor And Jim McCall) and Vetco. In 1975, his own ill health and the tragic death of his young son saw him withdraw from public appearances for some time. He returned in the early 80s, before declining health severely limited his playing and finally led to his death in 1984. Experts on the genre maintain that over the years, Taylor's various line-ups of Stoney Mountain Boys played some of the finest bluegrass music, yet it would appear that writers on the music have sadly neglected to afford him the credit he deserved.
● ALBUMS: *Folk Songs From The Bluegrass* (United Artists 1959) ★★★, *Bluegrass Taylor-Made* UK reissue by Stetson 1988 (Capitol 1963) ★★★, *Bluegrass Favorites* (Rural Rhythm 1968) ★★★★, *Bluegrass Favorites Volume 2* (Rural Rhythm 1971) ★★★, *Bluegrass Favorites Volume 3* (Rural Rhythm 1971) ★★★, *The Bluegrass Touch* covers 1969 (Vetco 1974) ★★★, *Body & Soul* (Vetco 1976) ★★★.

TAYLOR, EDDIE

b. 29 January 1923, Benoit, Mississippi, USA, d. 1985. A self-taught musician, Eddie 'Playboy' Taylor found early inspiration in the work of Charley Patton, Son House and Robert Johnson. His formative years were spent playing guitar at local social gatherings and clubs but in 1948 he travelled to Chicago to pursue a full-time career. Taylor's combo became a popular attraction and in 1953 he auditioned for the city's Vee Jay label. Paradoxically, the company preferred the style of back-up guitarist Jimmy Reed and their roles were consequently reversed. Taylor appeared on the majority of masters Reed recorded between 1953 and 1964, including 'You Don't Have To Go' (1955), 'Ain't That Lovin' You Baby' (1956) and 'Honest I Do' (1957), each of which reached the R&B Top 10. Taylor's sessions as a leader commenced in 1955 and he later achieved a local hit with 'Big Town Playboy'. Despite such success, further recordings were sporadic, and only six more titles were issued, the last of those in 1964. Taylor, meanwhile, sought employment as an accompanist with other Vee Jay acts, including John Lee Hooker and Sunnyland Slim. In 1968 he joined Hooker and Reed on a successful European tour, but positive reviews did not engender a new recording deal. The guitarist continued sporadic studio work until 1972 when he completed *I Feel So Bad* for a west coast independent label. This in turn inspired a second transatlantic tour, during which Taylor recorded *Ready For Eddie* for the Birmingham-based Big Bear company. He then endured a further low-key period, but a collection of masters from the Vee Jay era, released in 1981, rekindled interest in this accomplished, yet underrated, bluesman's career. Eddie Taylor was never a self-promoter and he has probably sold more records since his death in 1985 than while he was alive. His son Edward released a tribute album in 1998.

● ALBUMS: *I Feel So Bad* (1972) ★★★, *Ready For Eddie* (Big Bear 1972) ★★★, *My Heart Is Bleeding* (L&R 1988) ★★★, *Still Not Ready For Eddie* (Antone's 1988) ★★★, *Stormy Monday* (Blues Beacon 1994) ★★★, with Floyd Jones *Masters Of Modern Blues* (Testament 1994) ★★★, *Long Way From Home* (Blind Pig 1995) ★★★.
● COMPILATIONS: *Big Town Playboy* (Charly 1981) ★★★, *Bad Boy* (Wolf 1993) ★★★.

TAYLOR, VINCE

b. Brian Holden, 1940, London, England, d. August 1991. One of the first and most authentic British rock 'n' rollers, Taylor was virtually ignored by his native Britons but managed to make a decent living in France, where he spent most of his life. He started out in 1958 backed by his Playboys, who comprised Tony Harvey (guitar), Tony Sheridan (guitar, vocals), Brian 'Licorice' Locking (bass) and Brian Bennett (drums). They appeared regularly on the pioneering UK television rock show *Oh Boy!* and released a cover version of a Charlie Rich song, 'Right Behind You Baby', on Parlophone Records. A second single in 1959, 'Brand New Cadillac', penned by Taylor, ranks alongside Ian Samwell's 'Move It' as one of *the* authentic British rock records. The Clash would later contribute a version that restored it to the UK rock tradition. The band split in early 1959 (Locking and Bennett moved to various bands, including the Shadows, and Sheridan went to Hamburg where he worked with the fledgling Beatles) and Taylor assembled a new backing band with Harvey plus Alan LeClaire on piano, Johnny Vance on bass, and Bobby Woodman on drums. This line-up of the Playboys also backed Screaming Lord Sutch in 1960. Taylor toured with Sutch, Keith Kelly and Lance Fortune on a '2 I's (coffee bar)' package tour. Around the summer of 1961 Harvey joined Nero And The Gladiators, the rest of the Playboys went to France to back Johnny Hallyday, and Taylor followed their trail, becoming a minor celebrity in the process. He continued to record throughout the 60s, 70s and 80s, mostly doing cover versions of rock 'n' roll classics, before succumbing to cancer in 1991.
● ALBUMS: *Le Rock C'est Ça!* (1961) ★★★, *Vince* (1965) ★★★, *Alive, Well & Rocking In Paris* (1972) ★★, *Cadillac* (1975) ★★, *Live 1977* (1979) ★★, *Luv* (1980) ★★★, *Bien Compris* (1987) ★★★, *Black Leather Rebel* (1993) ★★★, *Vince Taylor Live At The Olympia* 10-inch album (Big Beat 1997) ★★.
● COMPILATIONS: *The Early Sides* 10-inch album (Big Beat 1997) ★★★.

TEDDY BEARS

Were it not for the fact that Phil Spector began as a member of the Teddy Bears, this one-hit-wonder trio would most likely be a minor footnote in the history of rock. Spector moved to the USA with his family at the age of nine following the suicide of his father, whose tombstone bore the legend 'To know him is to love him'. While in high school in Los Angeles, Spector sang at talent shows and assembled a group called the Sleepwalkers. He formed the Teddy Bears with singers Marshall Leib, Annette Kleinbard and Harvey Goldstein (who left the group shortly after its formation), after graduating from high school in June 1958. The group recorded a demo of Spector's composition 'Don't You Worry, My Little Pet', which Dore Records released. For the b-side, Spector's 'To Know Him Is To Love Him' was recorded and it was that side which caught the ear of the public, rising to number 1 in the US charts in late 1958. Following that success, the group signed with the larger Imperial Records and recorded an album (which is very rare and valuable today) as well as further singles. No more were hits and the group disbanded after Kleinbard was seriously injured in a 1960 car accident. The striking 'To Know Him, Is To Love Him' became a standard, and was later successfully revived by Peter And Gordon in 1965. The later career of Spector has been well documented. Kleinbard, after her recovery, changed her name to Carol Connors and became a successful songwriter ('Hey Little Cobra' for the Rip Chords, Vicki Lawrence's 'The Night The Lights Went Out In Georgia', and music for numerous films including two of the *Rocky* series). Marshall Leib joined the group the Hollywood Argyles, played guitar on some Duane Eddy records and produced records by the Everly Brothers and others.
● ALBUMS: *The Teddy Bears Sing!* (Imperial 1959) ★★.

TEEN QUEENS

This R&B duo of Betty (b. 1939, USA, d. 1971) and Rosie Collins (b. 1941, USA, d. 1968) came from Los Angeles, California, USA. Their entry into the recording business and signing to RPM Records in 1955 was facilitated by their older brother, Aaron Collins of the Jacks/Cadets, who recorded for the same company. The youthful amateurishness of the singing on their one hit, 'Eddie My Love' (number 2 R&B and number 14 pop), probably helped to make the record a hit in 1956. It was one of the first records specifically to direct its appeal to teenagers. It was the era of the cover record, and both the Fontane Sisters and the Chordettes also took the song high on the pop charts, but it is the Teen Queens' version that endures. The duo could not follow up with a hit, and the second single 'So All Alone'/'Baby Mine' flopped miserably. Despite recording some excellent material over the years including 'Two Loves And Two Lives' and 'Dear Tommy' they had no further chart action. Moves to RCA Records in 1958, Antler in 1960 and Crown Records did not help, and the duo broke up in 1961. The final tragic ending was when Rosie took her own life in 1968, and Betty died in 1971 after falling a victim to drugs.
● ALBUMS: *Eddie My Love* (RPM 1956) ★★★, *The Teen Queens* (Crown 1963) ★★★.
● COMPILATIONS: *Rock Everybody* (Ace 1986) ★★★, *Eddie My Love* (Ace 1995) ★★★.

TERRY, CLARK

b. 14 December 1920, St. Louis, Missouri, USA. Terry gained invaluable experience playing trumpet in local bands, but developed his remarkable technique while in the US Navy. As he recalled for jazz writer Steve Voce, he practised using a clarinet book, preferring the more fluid sound this generated in his playing. After his military service he joined Charlie Barnet, then became a mainstay of the Count Basie band for three years until 1951, when he joined Duke Ellington for an eight-year stint. At the end of the 50s he went into studio work in New York City, becoming one of the first black musicians regularly to be employed in this way. For a dozen years he was featured in the Doc Severinsen band, which played on the Johnny Carson *Tonight Show*. During this time he continued to play in jazz groups for club and record dates, working with Bob Brookmeyer, J.J. Johnson and others, and also leading his own 'Big B-A-D Band', which featured many leading New York session men. In the early 70s Terry became a member of Norman Granz's Pablo edition of Jazz At The Philharmonic, and began playing flügelhorn, eventually making this his principal instrument. The 70s and 80s found him touring extensively, playing concerts, clubs and festivals around the world, usually as leader but ably blending in with almost any background from late swing style to post-bop. Terry's remarkable technical accomplishment has never overwhelmed the depth of emotion that imbues his playing, and neither of these characteristics has ever dampened his infectious humour. This quality is most readily apparent on his singing of 'Mumbles', for which he created a unique variation on scat. His duets with himself, during which he plays flügelhorn and trumpet, are remarkable displays of his astonishing skills yet never degenerate into mere bravura exercises. Terry remained a major figure in the history of jazz trumpet into the beginning of the new century, after a lifetime as one of the music's most respected and widely admired ambassadors.

● ALBUMS: *Introducing Clark Terry* (EmArcy 1955) ★★★, The *Jazz School* (Wing 1955) ★★, *Out On A Limb* (Argo 1957) ★★, *Serenade To A Bus Seat* (Riverside 1957) ★★★★, *Duke With A Difference* (Riverside 1957) ★★★★, with Thelonious Monk *In Orbit* reissued as *C.T. Meets Monk* (Riverside 1958) ★★★★, *In Orbit* (Riverside 1958) ★★★★, *Top And Bottom Brass* (Riverside 1959) ★★★★, *Color Changes* (Candid 1960) ★★★, *Everything's Mellow* (Moodsville 1961) ★★★, *The Jazz Version Of 'All American'* (Moodsville 1962) ★★★, *What Makes Sammy Swing!* (20th Century Fox 1963) ★★★, with Coleman Hawkins *Eddie Costa Memorial Concert* (Colpix 1963) ★★★, shared with Gary Burton, Sonny Rollins *3 In Jazz* (RCA Victor 1963) ★★★, *More* (Cameo 1964) ★★★, *Tread Ye Lightly* (Cameo 1964) ★★★★, *The Happy Horn Of Clark Terry* (Impulse! 1964) ★★★★, with Bob Brookmeyer *Clark Terry Tonight* (Mainstream 1965) ★★★, *The Power Of Positive Swinging* (Mainstream 1965) ★★★, *Mumbles* (Mainstream 1966) ★★★, *Spanish Rice* (Impulse! 1966) ★★★, with Brookmeyer *Gingerbread Men* (Mainstream 1966) ★★★, *It's What's Happenin'* (Impulse! 1968) ★★★, *Clark Terry At The Montreux*

Jazz Festival (1969) ★★★★, *Big B-A-D-Band Live On 57th Street* (1970) ★★★, *Big B-A-D-Band Live At The Wichita Jazz Festival* (Vanguard 1974) ★★★, *Clark Terry And His Jolly Giants* (Vanguard 1975) ★★★, *Ain't Misbehavin'* (Pablo 1976) ★★★★, *Wham! Live At The Lighthouse* (1976) ★★★, *Big B-A-D-Band Live At Buddy's Place* (Vanguard 1976) ★★★, *The Globetrotter* (Vanguard 1977) ★★★, *Clark After Dark* (MPS 1978) ★★★, *Out Of Nowhere* (Bingow 1978) ★★★, *Funk Dumplin's* (Matrix 1978) ★★★, *Clark Terry's Big Band In Warsaw* (1978) ★★★, *Brahms Lullaby* (1978) ★★★, *Mother...! Mother...!* (Pablo 1979) ★★★, *Clark Terry At Buffalo State* (1979) ★★★, *Memories Of Duke* (Pablo 1980) ★★★★, *Yes, The Blues* (1981) ★★★, with Red Mitchell *To Duke And Basie* (Rhino 1986) ★★★★, *Take Double* (1986) ★★★, with Mitchell *Jive At Five* (Enja 1988) ★★★★, *Portraits* (Chesky 1988) ★★★★, *The Clark Terry Spacemen* (1989) ★★★, with Oliver Jones *Just Friends* (1989) ★★★, *Second Set* (Chesky 1990) ★★★, *Live From The Village Gate* (Chesky 1990) ★★★★, with George Robert *Live At The Q-4 Rheinfelden* (TCB 1990) ★★★, *Youngbloods* (Mons 1992) ★★★, *Having Fun* (Delos 1991) ★★★, *Remember The Time* (Mons 1994) ★★★, *Shades Of Blue* (Challenge 1994) ★★★, *Reunion With Pee Wee Claybrook & Swing Fever* (D'Note 1995) ★★★, *Top And Bottom Brass* (Chiaroscuro 1995) ★★★, and the De Paul University Big Band *Clark Terry Express* (Reference 1996) ★★★, with Robert 1993 recording *The Good Things In Life* (Mons 1996) ★★★, with Frank Wess and the De Paul Jazz Ensemble *Big Band Basie* (Reference 1996) ★★★, with Phil Woods *Lucerne 1978* (TCOB 1997) ★★★, *What A Wonderful World: For Louis* 1993 recording (Red Baron 1997) ★★★★, with Carol Sloane *The Songs Ella & Louis Sang* (Concord Jazz 1998) ★★, *One On One* (Chesky 2000) ★★★, *Herr Ober* (Nagel-Heyer 2001) ★★★★.

TESTER, SCAN

b. Lewis Tester, 1887, Chelwood Common, Sussex, England, d. 1972. Tester showed a penchant for music from a very young age, progressing quickly from tambourine to melodeon, concertina and fiddle. In addition to his early days busking in Brighton, Sussex, Scan played for dances in a number of local inns. After World War I, he continued playing for dances and formed Tester's Imperial Band which featured, in addition to Tester, his second wife Sarah on drums, and daughter Daisy on piano. Occasionally, Tester's brother Will would play on bandoneon. The band survived until 1931, after which Scan played at a pub called the Stone Quarry, until he died in 1972. In his lifetime, he had built an extensive repertoire of dance material. It was thanks to a collector, Mervyn Plunkett, that Tester's music, and the music of Sussex, came to the attention of a much wider audience in 1957. Plunkett recorded Tester and his music; *I Never Played Too Many Posh Dances*, is a double album featuring recordings from 1957-68.

● ALBUMS: *The Man In The Moon* (1975) ★★★, *I Never Played Too Many Posh Dances* (1990) ★★★; with other artists *Music Of The Sussex Weald* (1966)

★★, *Boscastle Breakdown* (1974) ★★★, *Sussex Harvest* (1975) ★★★.
● FURTHER READING: *I Never Played Too Many Posh Dances*, Reg Hall.

THERE'S NO BUSINESS LIKE SHOW BUSINESS

Incongruous is perhaps an appropriate word to describe the casting of the 'Nabob of Sob', pop singer Johnnie Ray, in this film, which was one of the last of the truly lavish screen musicals and was released by 20th Century-Fox in 1955. Ray plays one of the Donahues, a vaudeville act consisting of his brother and sister (Mitzi Gaynor and Donald O'Connor) and their parents (Dan Dailey and Ethel Merman). Ray even manages to induce a few of his trademark tears, although in this instance they swell up in the eyes of his proud old Mom and Dad after he has announced his decision to become a priest. That scene, and his strangulated version of 'If You Believe', one of the two new songs in Irving Berlin's otherwise entertaining score, should surely have won someone a bad-taste Oscar. Instead, the only whiff of an Academy Award was the nomination for Lamar Trotti's story (adapted for the screen by Henry and Phoebe Ephron). It deals with the triumphs and crises experienced by the family group, and O'Connor's initially ill-fated love affair with a cabaret singer played by Marilyn Monroe. After spending some time in the US Navy 'growing up', O'Connor joins the rest of the clan for the finale and a rousing version of the title song. Before going away to sea, he has some of the best numbers, singing and dancing delightfully in 'A Man Chases A Girl (Until She Catches Him)' and (with Gaynor and Monroe) 'Lazy'. He also adopted a Scottish accent for his part in a spectacular setting of 'Alexander's Ragtime Band'. Gaynor gave the number a touch of the Parisian, Merman was gamely Germanic, and Johnnie Ray . . . well, his intended articulation was unclear. Other highlights of the film were Monroe's sizzling versions of 'Heat Wave' and 'After You Get What You Want You Don't Want It', and Merman and Dailey's 'Play A Simple Melody', 'A Pretty Girl Is Like A Melody', 'Let's Have Another Cup Of Coffee' and 'You'd Be Surprised'. Jack Cole, who had worked with Monroe on *Gentlemen Prefer Blondes* two years earlier, staged her dances, and the remainder of the film's spirited routines were choreographed by Robert Alton. Sol C. Siegel was the producer, and it was directed by Walter Lang. The impressive DeLuxe Color and CinemaScope photography was by Leon Shamroy.

THINK

New York songwriter Lou Stallman was the man behind many novelty hits including the unusual one by Think. Stallman, who had recorded on Rainbow in 1956, wrote 50s hits like Clyde McPhatter's 'Treasure Of Love', Perry Como's US number 1 'Round And Round' and Linda Laurie's novelty 'Ambrose'. In the 60s his novelty song 'Yogi' hit the Top 10 by the Ivy Three (who included Charles Koppelman – the 'K' of SBK Records) and the Royalettes scored with his 'It's

Gonna Take a Miracle' (a Top 10 hit for Deniece Williams in 1982). In 1971, together with Bobby Susser, he recorded 'Once You Understand', which was a dialogue between children and parents, highlighting the problems caused by the generation gap. It ended with a father being told his son had died of an overdose and dad (played by Stallman) sobbing his heart out! Despite being banned in half the country, the record hit the US Top 40 and three years later returned to the chart when the ban was dropped. Think (as the act was called) released a follow-up, 'It's Not The World – It's The People', but it did nothing. Their hit resurfaced in 1990 when sampled on the dance record 'Mr. Kirk's Nightmare' by 4 Hero.

THOMAS, KID

b. Louis Thomas Watts, 20 June 1934, Sturgis, Mississippi, USA, d. 13 April 1970, Beverly Hills, California, USA. Watts was also known as Tommy Lewis/Louis. Chicago-based from 1941, he played harmonica and sang blues from the end of the 40s, recording for Federal in 1955, and seeing occasional releases on small labels until the end of his life. This came shortly after his location by a music researcher in California, where Thomas had settled in 1960. He had killed a child in a road accident and was shot by the boy's father after manslaughter charges were dismissed. The strong feelings this aroused among blues enthusiasts should not be allowed to mask the fact that Thomas was a minor and derivative performer, albeit an impressively energetic one, especially when imitating Little Richard.
● ALBUMS: *Rockin' This Joint Tonite* (1979) ★★★, *Here's My Story* (1991) ★★★.

THOMPSON, EDDIE

b. Edgar Charles Thompson, 31 May 1925, London, England, d. 6 November 1986, London, England. Born blind, Thompson learned to play piano as a child. In the late 40s he was active in London clubs, playing with Carlo Krahmer, Vic Feldman and others. In the 50s he played on radio, in studio bands, made records under his own name and with Tony Crombie, Tommy Whittle, Freddy Randall and others and by the end of the decade was house pianist at Ronnie Scott's club. In the early 60s he went to the USA to live, playing regularly at the Hickory House in New York. Back in the UK in the early 70s, he led a trio that toured extensively and frequently backed visiting American jazzmen, including Buddy Tate, Ruby Braff and Spike Robinson. A dazzlingly inventive player in his early days, Thompson sometimes delivered bravura performances at the expense of feeling but in his maturity he made many memorable appearances at concerts around the UK. He had an enormous repertoire and when in musical sympathy with a guest he could be the best of accompanists. His solo playing was long overlooked by record companies but Alastair Robertson of Hep Records compensated for this with some excellent sessions in the early 80s. Thompson's death at the age of 61 came when he was at the height of his powers.

● ALBUMS: *I Hear Music* (Dormouse 1956) ★★★, *By Myself* (77 1970) ★★★, *Some Strings, Some Skins And A Bunch Of Keys* (1975) ★★★, *Dutch Treat* (1976) ★★, *Ain't She Sweet* (1978) ★★★★, *When Lights Are Low* (1980) ★★★★, *Memories Of You* (Hep Jazz 1983) ★★★★, with Roy Williams *When Lights Are Low* (Hep Jazz 1988) ★★.

THOMPSON, HANK
b. Henry William Thompson, 3 September 1925, Waco, Texas, USA. Thompson, as a young boy, was fond of records by Jimmie Rodgers and the Carter Family. He first learned the harmonica and then his parents gave him a guitar for his tenth birthday. He also played Hawaiian guitar, learned conjuring tricks and had a ventriloquist's doll. With his range of talents, he was a popular performer at Saturday morning stage shows in Waco. In 1942, he began his own local radio series, *Hank – The Hired Hand*. From 1943 Thompson served three years in the US Navy. He worked as an electrical engineer and, in his spare time, he entertained his shipmates. He says, 'The navy enhanced my career as it gave the opportunity to perform all the time. When I was overseas, I knew the guys were getting tired of hearing the same songs and so I started writing.' In 1946, he returned to Waco, formed the Brazos Valley Boys (named after the river running through Waco), and began performing at dances throughout Texas. His own song, 'Whoa Sailor', was a regional hit on Globe Records. It was followed by 'A Lonely Heart Knows' on Bluebonnet. Country star Tex Ritter heard Thompson and recommended him to his label, Capitol Records. Almost immediately, Thompson had a number 2 country hit with '(I've Got A) Humpty Dumpty Heart'. In 1949 he had another country hit with a re-recorded 'Whoa Sailor'. Thompson was a tall, upright performer with a resonant voice not unlike Ritter's, who dressed himself and his band in expensive Nudie suits. Applying his engineering knowledge, he gave the band a powerful live sound and lighting, and soon had the most successful western swing band in the USA. In 1951 Thompson began a 13-year partnership with the Hollywood record producer Ken Nelson and recorded his most successful single, 'The Wild Side Of Life', in one take (ironically 'Crying In The Deep Blue Sea' was the original a-side). 'The Wild Side Of Life' stayed at the top of the US country charts for 15 weeks and won Thompson a gold record. Kitty Wells recorded an answer version, 'It Wasn't God Who Made Honky Tonk Angels', while Thompson himself answered 'Goodnight, Irene' with 'Wake Up, Irene'. Defying convention, Thompson was permitted to repeat its snare drum sound on the *Grand Ole Opry*. Thompson had further country hits with 'Waiting In The Lobby Of Your Heart', 'Rub-A-Dub-Dub', 'Breakin' The Rules', 'Honky Tonk Girl', 'The Blackboard Of My Heart', and 'Breakin' In Another Heart', which was co-written with his wife Dorothy. In 1957 Thompson parodied rock 'n' roll in 'Rockin' In The Congo' and became a successful performer in Las Vegas.

He heard 'Squaws Along The Yukon' on a hunting trip in Alaska with Merle Travis and together they arranged and updated the song. In 1959 he became the first country artist to record in stereo via the bestselling *Songs For Rounders*, and the first to record an 'in concert' album, *Live At The Golden Nugget*. He heard a band in a club in Holbrook, Arizona, and was most impressed with their original song, 'A Six Pack To Go'. Thompson turned the song into a country standard, later reviving it in duet with George Strait, and had further country hits with 'She's Just A Whole Lot Like You' and 'Oklahoma Hills'. Since Thompson left Capitol in 1964, he has recorded for several labels and his country hits have included 'Smokey The Bar', 'Where Is The Circus?', 'The Older The Violin, The Sweeter The Music' and, appropriately, 'Mr. Honky Tonk, The King Of Western Swing'. He has recorded tribute albums to the Mills Brothers (*Cab Driver*) and Nat 'King' Cole. In 1973 Thompson opened a school of country music in Claremore, Oklahoma, where he taught. He was elected to the Country Music Hall Of Fame in 1989, and still tours throughout the world, wearing his sequinned jackets: 'The public is entitled to something that is colourful and flashy. We're in showbusiness and there's nothing colourful about a T-shirt and ragged jeans.' His excellent 1997 album included duets with Tanya Tucker, Kitty Wells and Junior Brown.
● ALBUMS: *Songs Of The Brazos Valley* (Capitol 1953/1956) ★★★, *North Of The Rio Grande* (Capitol 1953/1956) ★★★★, *New Recordings Of Hank's All Time Hits* (Capitol 1953/1956) ★★★, *Hank Thompson Favorites* (Capitol 1953/1957) ★★★★, *Hank!* (Capitol 1957) ★★★★, *Hank Thompson's Dance Ranch* (Capitol 1958) ★★★, *Favorite Waltzes By Hank Thompson* (Capitol 1959) ★★★, *Songs For Rounders* (Capitol 1959) ★★★★, *Most Of All* (Capitol 1960) ★★★, *This Broken Heart Of Mine* (Capitol 1960) ★★★, *An Old Love Affair* (Capitol 1961) ★★★, *At The Golden Nugget* (Capitol 1961) ★★★★, *The No. 1 Country And Western Band* (Capitol 1962) ★★★, *Live At The Cherokee Frontier Days Rodeo In Wyoming* (Capitol 1962) ★★★, *Live At The State Fair Of Texas* (Capitol 1963) ★★★, *It's Christmas Time With Hank* (Capitol 1964) ★★, *Breakin' In Another Heart* (Capitol 1965) ★★★, *The Luckiest Heartache In Town* (Capitol 1965) ★★★, *A Six Pack To Go* (Capitol 1966) ★★★★, *Breakin' The Rules* (Capitol 1966) ★★★, *Just An Old Flame* (Capitol 1967) ★★★, *The Countrypolitan Sound Of Hank's Brazos Boys* (Warners 1967) ★★★, *Country Blues* (Tower 1968) ★★★, *On Tap, In The Can Or In The Bottle* (Dot 1968) ★★★, *Smokey The Bar* (Dot 1969) ★★★, *Hank Thompson Salutes Oklahoma* (Dot 1969) ★★★, *The Instrumental Sound Of Hank Thompson's Brazos Valley Boys* (1970) ★★★, *Next Time I Fall In Love (I Won't)* (Dot 1971) ★★★, *Cab Driver – A Salute To The Mills Brothers* (Dot 1972) ★★★, *1000 And One Nighters* (1973) ★★★, *Kindly Keep It Country* (Dot 1973) ★★★, *Movin' On* (ABC 1974) ★★★, *Hank Thompson Sings The Hits Of Nat 'King' Cole* (Dot 1975) ★★★, *Back In The Swing Of Things* (ABC/Dot 1976) ★★★, *The Thompson*

Touch (ABC 1977) ★★★, with Roy Clark, Freddy Fender, Don Williams *Country Comes To Carnegie Hall* (ABC/Dot 1977) ★★★★, *Doin' My Thing* (1977) ★★★, *Brand New Hank* (1978) ★★★, *Take Me Back To Texas* (1980) ★★★, *Here's To Country Music* (1988) ★★★, *Hank Thompson And Friends* (Curb 1997) ★★★★, *Seven Decades* (Hightone 2000) ★★★.

● COMPILATIONS: *The Best Of Hank Thompson* (Capitol 1963) ★★★, *Golden Country Hits* (Capitol 1964) ★★★★, *Where Is The Circus (And Other Heart Breakin' Hits)* (Warners 1966) ★★★★, *The Best Of Hank Thompson, Volume 2* (Capitol 1967) ★★★, *The Gold Standard Collection Of Hank Thompson* (Warners 1967) ★★★★, *Hank Thompson's 25th Anniversary Album* (Dot 1971) ★★★★, *Hank Thompson's Greatest Hits, Volume 1* (Dot 1973) ★★★, *Best Of The Best Of Hank Thompson* (Gusto 1980) ★★★, *Hank Thompson* (MCA 1987) ★★★, *Capitol Collector's Series* (Capitol 1989) ★★★★, *All-Time Greatest Hits* (Curb 1990) ★★★, *Country Music Hall Of Fame Series* (MCA 1992) ★★★, *Vintage* (Capitol 1996) ★★★★, *Hank Thompson And His Brazos Valley Boys (1946-1964)* 12-CD box set (Bear Family 1996) ★★★★, *The Best Of Hank Thompson 1966-1979* (Varèse Sarabande 1997) ★★★★, *World Masters (1951-1953)* (Bronco Buster 1998) ★★★.

THOMPSON, HAYDEN

b. 5 March 1938, Booneville, Mississippi, USA. Rockabilly and country performer Thompson was brought up on a typical southern radio diet of Hank Snow and Bob Wills, although later he also discovered B.B. King and Howlin' Wolf courtesy of Memphis' KWEM station. Both his parents were musical, his father playing the guitar and his mother the harmonica. He formed his first band, the Southern Melody Boys, while still at high school. Their sole recording resulted from a radio session in 1954 in Hamilton, Alabama. Released on Von, 'I Feel The Blues Coming On' and 'Act Like You Love Me' were unassuming country blues offerings featuring Hayden's rich, emotive vocals. The group lasted for a further year, making their debut on *The Louisiana Hayride* radio show, before Thompson joined the Dixie Jazzlanders, who toured Mississippi in support of the theatrical release of *Rock Around The Clock*. A brief spell with the Slim Rhodes band followed before Thompson moved to Memphis, keen to monitor developments at Sun Records in the wake of Elvis Presley's success. He recorded his first sessions there in the summer of 1956, although nothing was released. He returned a few months later, recording a strong version of Junior Parker's 'Love My Baby', backed by session men including, a then unknown, Jerry Lee Lewis. Sun Records' owner Sam Phillips again passed over the song, before finally releasing a new version of 'Love My Baby' on Phillips International, Sun's sister label, in September 1957. Thompson toured in support of it, alongside Sonny Burgess and Billy Lee Riley. In 1958, he relocated to Chicago, Illinois, taking a residency at the Tally Ho Club. After further singles for B.E.A.T. Records ('Tom Thumb') and

Profile Records ('Whatcha Gonna Do') before Thompson earned a slot on the WGN Barn Dance. Following 1962's 'Queen Bee' on Arlen Records Thompson was contracted to play in the house band at Chicago's new country venue, the Rivoli Ballroom. In an attempt to woo a mainstream country audience Thompson recorded '$16.88' for Kapp Records. It was successful enough to win him the offer of a debut album, released in 1966. In the early 70s Thompson recorded several singles for the Nashville North label but eventually quit the music business to work full-time as a limo driver. It was only in the late 70s that interest in his catalogue, triggered by the inclusion of 'Love My Baby' on samplers such as *Put Your Cat Clothes On*, brought him out of semi-retirement. By the mid-80s he was a regular on rockabilly revival tours, one of which was recorded by Charly Records for release in 1985. *The Time Is Now*, a return to his country roots, followed for Swedish label Sunjay in 1991.

● ALBUMS: *Here's Hayden Thompson* (Kapp 1966) ★★★, *Booneville Mississippi* (Charly 1985) ★★★, *The Time Is Now* (Sunjay 1991) ★★★.

THORNTON, BIG MAMA

b. 11 December 1926, Montgomery, Alabama, USA, d. 25 July 1984, Los Angeles, California, USA. Willie Mae Thornton was the daughter of a minister and learned drums and harmonica as a child. By the late 40s she was singing and dancing in Sammy Green's Hot Harlem Revue throughout the southern states. Basing herself in Texas, she made her first records as Big Mama Thornton for Peacock in 1951. Two years later she topped the R&B charts with the original version of 'Hound Dog', the Leiber And Stoller song that Elvis Presley would later make world famous. The backing was by Johnny Otis' band with Pete Lewis contributing a memorable guitar solo. Thornton toured with Otis and recorded less successfully for Peacock until 1957 when she moved to California. There she made records for Bay-Tone (1961), Sotoplay (1963) and Kent (1964). Her career took a new turn when she joined the 1965 Folk Blues Festival troupe and entranced audiences in Europe. The next year, Arhoolie Records recorded her in Chicago with Muddy Waters, James Cotton and Otis Spann. A 1968 live album for the same label included 'Ball And Chain' which inspired Janis Joplin's notable version of the song. She sang some pop standards on her 1969 Mercury Records release, and in the 70s she recorded for Backbeat, Vanguard Records and Crazy Cajun. On 1975's *Jail*, recorded before prison audiences, she performed new versions of 'Hound Dog' and 'Ball And Chain'. Thornton died in Los Angeles in July 1984.

● ALBUMS: *In Europe* (Arhoolie 1965) ★★★, *Big Mama Thornton, Vol. 2* (Arhoolie 1966) ★★★, *With Chicago Blues* (Arhoolie 1967) ★★★, *Ball & Chain* (Arhoolie 1968) ★★★, *Stronger Than Dirt* (Mercury 1969) ★★★, *The Way It Is* (Mercury 1970) ★★★, *Maybe* (Roulette 1970) ★★★, *She's Back* (Backbeat 1970) ★★★, *Saved* (Pentagram 1973) ★★★, *Jail* (Vanguard 1975) ★★★★, *Sassy*

Mama! (Vanguard 1975) ★★★, *Mama's Pride* (Vanguard 1978) ★★★.
● COMPILATIONS: *The Original Hound Dog* (Ace 1990) ★★★, *Hound Dog: The Peacock Recordings* (MCA 1992) ★★★, *The Rising Sun Collection* (Just A Memory 1994) ★★★, *The Complete Vanguard Recordings* (Vanguard 2000) ★★★★.

THREE CHUCKLES

Formed in Brooklyn, New York, USA, vocal/instrumental doo-wop group the Three Chuckles took their name from the fact that they began life as a comedy troupe. Tommy Romano (tenor and guitar) and Russ Gilberto (lead vocals and bass guitar) met while playing baseball, and soon added accordion player Phil Benti. After lengthy touring, Benti departed, and they took on 15-year-old Teddy Randazzo as replacement. After further local concerts the group were spotted at a bowling alley in Detroit in 1953 by Ray Gayhan. Through him they secured a recording contract with Great Lakes Records' subsidiary, Boulevard Records. Two songs were recorded, 'At Last You Understand' and 'Runaround', the latter written for them by Cirino Colacrais. It was this side that caused all the interest, and significant local airplay led to the band being snapped up for wider distribution by RCA Records. 'Runaround' subsequently peaked at number 20 in the *Billboard* charts, going on to sell over a million copies. The Three Chuckles used this exposure to secure prestigious television slots on shows hosted by Perry Como, Steve Allen and others, before being recruited by disc jockey Alan Freed for his 1955 movie, *Rock, Rock, Rock*, in which Romano played the male lead. A second celluloid appearance came in 1958 with *The Girl Can't Help It*, before the group retired to the studio to complete their first album. This was a steady seller, but their success on the singles front had now declined, with only 'Times Two, I Love You' and 'And The Angels Sing', the latter part of a new contract with Vik Records, making the charts. Randazzo then left for a solo career (subsequently writing hits for Little Anthony And The Imperials), and although he was replaced by Jackie Farrell, no further Three Chuckles recordings were issued.
● ALBUMS: *The Three Chuckles* (RCA 1958) ★★.

THREEPENNY OPERA, THE

A dramatic play with music by Kurt Weill, and a book and lyrics by Bertolt Brecht, this three-act production was first presented at the Theatre am Schiffbauerdam in Berlin on 31 August 1928 under the title of *Die Dreigroschenoper*. That was 200 years after the show on which it was based, *The Beggar's Opera* by John Gay, was first seen in London. *The Threepenny Opera* had its first English language production on Broadway in 1933, and then returned to New York in 1954. This revised version, with an English book and lyrics by Marc Blitzstein, opened off-Broadway at the Theatre de Lys on 10 March, and ran for just three months. Public demand caused it to return in September 1955, and this time it stayed for an incredible 2,706 performances. The cynical and satirical tale of morality that had seemed so appropriate, yet futile, in the Germany of the 20s, remained the same, with its familiar characters including the outlaw Macheath, otherwise known as Mack the Knife (Scott Merrill), his wife Polly Peachum (Jo Sullivan), the police chief's daughter Lucy Brown (Beatrice Arthur), and Jenny Diver, the whore, played by Lotte Lenya (Weill's widow), the actress who had created the role in Germany. The score included 'The Ballad Of Mack The Knife', 'Love Song', 'Army Song', 'Pirate Jenny', 'Tango-Ballad', 'Useless Song', 'Ballad Of The Easy Life', 'Barbara Song', 'Solomon Song' and 'Instead-Of-Song'. During the show's extremely long run, many well-known actors and actresses took part, including Charlotte Rae, James Mitchell, Jerry Orbach, Carole Cook, Nancy Andrews, and Edward Asner. The English actress Georgia Brown played Lucy for a time, and she recreated her role, along with Bill Owen, Daphne Anderson, Lisa Lee, Eric Pohlmann and Warren Mitchell for the 1956 London production, which ran for 140 performances. Thirty years later in March 1986, a UK National Theatre production starred Tim Curry. A new adaptation of the piece, by Ralph Manheim and John Willett, spent 10 months on Broadway in 1976, and yet another version, billed as *3 Penny Opera* and translated by Michael Feingold, gave 65 performances at the Lunt-Fontanne Theatre in November 1989. Perhaps in an attempt to attract a different kind of audience, the cast for that production included rock star Sting as Macheath, along with popular singers Maureen McGovern and Kim Criswell. A 1994 London revival at the Donmar Warehouse, starring Tom Hollander and Sharon Small as Macheath and Polly Peachum, was set in the year 2001. Several film versions have been released, notably in 1931 with Lotte Lenya, and in 1964 with Hildegarde Neff and Curt Jurgens. The show is best remembered by many people for one song – 'Mack The Knife' (originally entitled 'Moritat'). It was introduced by Lotte Lenya in the tinkly Victorian-style of most of the show's music, and became successful in 1956 in the USA for several artists including the Dick Hyman Trio, Richard Hayman with Jan August, Lawrence Welk, Louis Armstrong and Billy Vaughn. Three years later the song became a massive number 1 hit on both sides of the Atlantic in a superb swinging version by Bobby Darin. Shortly afterwards, Ella Fitzgerald made a popular recording, and in 1984, yet another version, by the vocal-instrumental group King Kurt, entered the UK chart.

TINSLEY, JOHN

b. 10 February 1920, Chestnut Mountain, Virginia, USA. Tinsley learned guitar when he was 11, and from the age of 18 played at social events. He acquired much of his repertoire from, and was stylistically influenced by, the records of Blind Boy Fuller and Buddy Moss. He also composed personal blues, including one arising from a 1949 incident when he shot and wounded his stepfather. In 1952 Tinsley recorded a 78 with

Fred Holland for a local label, but its failure to sell induced him to stop playing blues by 1955. In 1977, he resumed playing with the encouragement of blues music researchers, made some likeable recordings and visited Europe a couple of times, despite a dispute with a Danish promoter on the first occasion.

● ALBUMS: *Country Blues Roots Revived* (1978) ★★★, *Home Again Blues* (1980) ★★★, *Sunrise Blues* (1982) ★★★.

TIOMKIN, DIMITRI

b. 10 May 1894, St. Petersburg, Russia, d. 11 November 1979, London, England. An important composer of film music from the 30s through to the 60s. After being coached in music by his mother as a small child, Tiomkin later studied at the St. Petersburg Conservatory. He worked as a professional musician, playing on the concert platform and as a pianist in silent-movie theatres, before moving to Berlin in 1921 to continue his studies. He gave numerous concert performances in Europe as a soloist, and duetting with another pianist. In 1925 he made his first visit to the USA, and returned in 1930 when his wife, a ballet dancer and choreographer, was hired to work on some Hollywood films. Tiomkin was also engaged to write music for films, and was soon in great demand. His first major film score was for *Alice In Wonderland* (1933). By now an American citizen, Tiomkin quickly became one of the most successful and prolific film composers, writing scores and incidental music in the late 30s, 40s and 50s for films such *Lost Horizon, The Great Waltz, You Can't Take It With You, Lucky Partners, The Westerner, Meet John Doe, The Corsican Brothers, Twin Beds, A Gentleman After Dark, The Moon And Sixpence, Unknown Guest, The Bridge Of San Luis Rey, The Imposter, Forever Yours, Dillinger, Pardon My Past, Duel In The Sun, The Dark Mirror, Whistle Stop, The Long Night, It's A Wonderful Life, Red River, So This Is New York, Champion, Home Of The Brave, Cyrano De Bergerac, Champagne For Caesar, Strangers On A Train, Bugles In The Afternoon, High Noon* (1952, Oscars for best score and title song with lyric by Ned Washington), *The Big Sky, The Four Poster, Angel Face, The Steel Trap, Return To Paradise, The High And The Mighty* (1954, another Oscar), *Dial M For Murder, Blowing In the Wind, Take The High Ground, Land Of The Pharaohs, Giant, Friendly Persuasion, Wild Is The Wind, Search For Paradise, Gun Fight At The O.K Corral, The Old Man And The Sea* (1958, his fourth Oscar) and *Rio Bravo* (1959). In the late 50s Tiomkin composed the theme music for the popular television series *Rawhide*, and throughout the 60s provided scores for some of the most popular and spectacular movies of the decade, including *The Alamo, The Sundowners, The Unforgiven, The Guns Of Navarone, Town Without Pity, 55 Days At Peking, The Fall Of The Roman Empire, Circus World, 36 Hours, The War Wagon* and *Great Catherine*. Among the songs that came from these and other films were 'Friendly Persuasion (Thee I Love)' and The Green Leaves Of Summer' (both with

lyrics by Paul Francis Webster) and 'Wild Is The Wind' and 'Strange Are The Ways Of Love' (with Washington). He also worked as executive producer on the Russian film *Tchaikovsky* (1970), arranging the music of the film's subject. After moving to London in the 70s, Tiomkin died there in 1979.

● COMPILATIONS: *Lost Horizon-The Classic Film Scores Of Dimitri Tiomkin* (RCA 1976) ★★★★.

TJADER, CAL

b. Callen Radcliffe Tjader, 16 July 1925, St. Louis, Missouri, USA, d. 5 May 1982, Manila, Philippines. After studying formally, Tjader played drums with various bands on the west coast before joining Dave Brubeck in 1949. In the early 50s he played with Alvino Rey and also led his own small bands. By 1953, the year he joined George Shearing, he had added vibraphone and various other percussion instruments to his roster. In 1954, he again formed a band of his own, concentrating on Latin American music and making numerous records on the Fantasy Records and Verve Records labels. He hired his sidemen with care, employing over the years distinguished musicians such as Lalo Schifrin, Willie Bobo, Donald Byrd and Kenny Burrell, while later musical associates included Hank Jones and Scott Hamilton. For all his undoubted skills as an instrumentalist, much of Tjader's solo recorded output lacks urgency and vitality, often slipping gently into well-played but undemanding background music. At his best, however, Tjader performed Latin music with the verve it demands and enjoyed a secure and lasting respect among his peers.

● ALBUMS: *The Cal Tjader Trio* 10-inch album (Fantasy 1953) ★★★, *Cal Tjader – Vibist* 10-inch album (Savoy 1954) ★★★, *Ritmo Caliente* 10-inch album (Fantasy 1954) ★★★, *Mambo With Tjader* (Fantasy 1955) ★★★, *Tjader Plays Tjazz* (Fantasy 1956) ★★★, *Tjader Plays Mambo* (Fantasy 1956) ★★★, *Cal Tjader Quartet* i (Fantasy 1956) ★★★, *The Cal Tjader Quintet* (Fantasy 1956) ★★★, *Jazz At The Blackhawk* (Fantasy 1957) ★★★, *Latin Kick* (Fantasy 1957) ★★★, *Mass Ritmo Caliente* (Fantasy 1957) ★★★, with Stan Getz *Cal Tjader-Stan Getz Sextet* (Fantasy 1958) ★★★, *San Francisco Moods* (Fantasy 1958) ★★★, *Latin Concert* (Fantasy 1958) ★★★, *Latin For Lovers* (Fantasy 1958) ★★, *Jazz At Blackhawk* (Fantasy 1959) ★★★, *Tjader Goes Latin* (Fantasy 1959) ★★, *Concert By The Sea* (Fantasy 1959) ★★★, *Concert On The Campus* (Fantasy 1960) ★★★, *Cal Tjader Quartet* ii (Fantasy 1960) ★★★, *Demasado Caliente* (Fantasy 1960) ★★★, *West Side Story* (Fantasy 1960) ★★★, *Cal Tjader* (Fantasy 1961) ★★★, *Cal Tjader Live And Direct* (Fantasy 1961) ★★, *Cal Tjader Plays Harold Arlen* (Fantasy 1961) ★★★, *Concert By The Sea, Volume 2* (Fantasy 1961) ★★★, *In A Latin Bag* (Verve 1961) ★★★, *Latino* (Fantasy 1962) ★★★, *Saturday Night-Sunday Night At The Blackhawk* (Verve 1962) ★★★, *The Contemporary Music Of Mexico & Brazil* (Verve 1962) ★★★, *Several Shades Of Jade* (Verve 1963) ★★★, *Sona Libre* (Verve 1963) ★★★, *Breeze*

From The East (Verve 1964) ★★, Warm Wave (Verve 1964) ★★, Soul Sauce (Verve 1965) ★★★, Soul Bird/Whiffenpoof (Verve 1965) ★★, Soul Burst (Verve 1965) ★★, Latin For Dancers (Fantasy 1966) ★★, with Eddie Palmieri El Sonid Nuevo – The New Soul Sound (Verve 1966) ★★★★, Along Comes Cal (Verve 1966) ★★★, Hip Vibrations (Verve 1967) ★★★, with Palmieri Bamboleate (Verve 1967) ★★★, Solar Heat (Rhapsody 1968) ★★, Cal Tjader Sounds Out Burt Bacharach (Skye 1968) ★, The Prophet (Verve 1969) ★, Primo (Fantasy 1971) ★★★, Agua Dulce (Fantasy 1972) ★★★, Concert At Hermosa Beach (Fantasy 1973) ★★, with Charlie Byrd Tambu (Fantasy 1974) ★★★, Amazonas (Fantasy 1975) ★★★, Cal Tjader At Grace Cathedral (Fantasy 1976) ★★, Guarabe (Fantasy 1976) ★★★, Here (Fantasy 1977) ★★★, Breathe Easy (Fantasy 1977) ★★★, La Onda Va Bien (Concord Picante 1979) ★★★, Gozame! Pero Ya (Concord Picante 1980) ★★★, The Shining Sea (Concord Picante 1981) ★★★, A Fuego Vivo (Concord Picante 1981) ★★, with Carmen McRae Heat Wave (Concord Jazz 1982) ★★★, Good Vibes (Concord Jazz 1984) ★★★.
● COMPILATIONS: Cal Tjader's Greatest Hits (Fantasy 1965) ★★★, The Best Of Cal Tjader (Verve 1967) ★★★, Talkin' Verve (Verve 1997) ★★★.

TODD, ART AND DOTTY
Husband and wife act Art (b. 11 March 1920, Elizabeth, New Jersey, USA) and Dotty Todd (b. 22 June 1923, Elizabeth, New Jersey, USA, d. 12 December 2000, Los Angeles, California, USA) had one fling at fame when their recording of a song by Wayne Shanklin, 'Chanson D'Amour (Songs Of Love)', reached the US Top 10 in 1958. The couple met accidentally in 1941 in Baltimore when they were booked into the same hotel room. They discovered a mutual interest in singing, and first formed the duo and were married within a year. After relocating to Los Angeles, they began recording for RCA-Victor Records and had some success in Europe. Art found the Shanklin song and worked it into a soft shuffle in the style of Les Paul and Mary Ford. It was issued on Era Records and became the couple's only chart hit in the USA. They continued to perform together on radio and in Las Vegas cabaret, before retiring to Honolulu in 1980.
● ALBUMS: Chanson D'Amour (Dot 1966) ★★.

TODD, NICK
b. Nicholas Boone, 1 June 1935, Jacksonville, Florida, USA. Todd's brief career from 1957-60 was built during the era when record companies were flooding the market with teen idol types who could sing a poppish unthreatening style of rock 'n' roll. As the younger brother of the king of poppish rock 'n' roll, Pat Boone, Todd was quickly snapped up. After one release on Deb, he was signed to Dot Records (which gave the singer his name by reversing the company's name). Todd's 'Plaything', which entered the US Top 50 in 1957, brought the singer to the public's attention, and, that same year, a cover of Danny And The

Juniors' 'At The Hop' (number 21) cemented a relationship with his teenage fans. There then followed a spate of television appearances and fan magazine profiles, but it did not last and Todd left the music business to pursue a career in social work.

TOMLINSON, ERNEST
b. 19 September 1924, Rawtenstall, Lancashire, England. A prolific writer with boundless energy, Tomlinson has been one of the major figures in British light music during the second half of the twentieth century. Delayed by war service in the RAF, his musical career began as a staff arranger for a London publisher after graduating in 1947 with a degree of Bachelor of Music for composition. Tomlinson was soon in demand for radio, television, stage and recording commitments, providing numerous arrangements as well as, occasionally, his own compositions – the first was broadcast in 1949. Many of his own works were first heard with his Ernest Tomlinson Light Orchestra (formed in 1955), and his 'Little Serenade' (1955) was destined to become a light music standard. Later the same year his work for the radio play The Story Of Cinderella finally allowed him to become a full-time freelance composer. His north country roots explain Tomlinson's love of brass bands and choirs, and he has been active in both these areas. 'An English Overture' was originally conceived for brass band, but it transferred well to full orchestra. Of special importance have been his suites of 'English Folk-Songs' – the first was in 1949 (receiving the first performance at the English Folk-Dance and Song Society's New Year Festival at London's Royal Albert Hall in January 1950), and the second suite followed in 1977. Many of the individual movements have become recognized in their own right, with wonderful titles such as 'Dick's Maggot', 'Jenny Pluck Pears', 'Woodicock' and 'Love-in-a-Mist'. Other popular works include 'Concert Jig' (from the 'Silverthorn Suite'), 'Kielder Water', 'Comedy Overture', 'Mediterranean Suite', 'English Pageant Suite', the 'Light Music Suite' (1971) and 'Passepied'. Tomlinson has been a tireless worker for his profession, serving in various capacities with the Light Music Society, the Composers' Guild of Great Britain and the Performing Rights Society. He is the recipient of the Composers' Guild Award (1965) and two Ivor Novello Awards (1970 and 1975). In 1984 he founded The Library Of Light Orchestral Music which is housed in a huge barn at his farmhouse in Lancashire, and contains over 10,000 scores, many of which would have been otherwise lost.
● ALBUMS: British Light Music – Ernest Tomlinson Volume 1 (Marco Polo 1992) ★★★★, British Light Music – Ernest Tomlinson Volume 2 (Marco Polo 1994) ★★★★.

TOMMY STEELE STORY, THE
Former merchant seaman Tommy Hicks was discovered while performing in Soho's legendary 2 I's coffee bar. Renamed by manager Larry Parnes,

Tommy Steele became Britain's first bona fide rock 'n' roll star with two 1956 hit singles, 'Rock With The Caveman' and 'Singing The Blues', the latter of which was a chart-topper. Although touted as the antidote to Elvis Presley, it was quickly clear that Steele lacked sex appeal or sultry menace, offering instead a clean-cut, boy-next-door image, ripe for his subsequent mutation into all-round entertainer. For many years he remained a peculiarly British institution; indeed, the film was retitled Rock Around The World for the USA. Steele was an unknown quantity there and his name had little significance.

Released in 1957, The Tommy Steele Story retold the artist's rise from rags to riches, while offering a glimpse of music popular in the UK during this transitional period. The influence of jazz on rock 'n' roll was acknowledged by an appearance by Humphrey Lyttelton's band, while the concurrent skiffle craze allowed for the inclusion of Chas McDevitt's Skiffle Group, who, with Nancy Whiskey, were high in the UK charts with the memorable 'Freight Train'. Chris O'Brien's Caribbeans and Tommy Etie's Calypso Band reflected London's nascent interest in West Indian music, yet the film's lacklustre style and pace meant that its symbolism was greater than the audio/visual experience. Indeed, its star's appeal was already undergoing a transformation by the time The Tommy Steele Story reached the cinema. His last rock 'n' roll hit, 'Tallahassie Lassie', was succeeded by 'Little White Bull' from the singer's 1959 feature, Tommy The Toreador. His mutation into a peculiarly adult attraction was all but complete, and was finally accomplished with Steele's subsequent role in Half A Sixpence.

TOPIC RECORDS

Topic Records evolved out of a UK organization called the Worker's Music Association, or WMA, during the 40s. The WMA was founded in 1936 by a group of leading personalities from the musical side of the working-class movement. A number of these groups had taken part in the Pageant of Labour in the mid-30s, and a committee was formed to co-ordinate members' musical activity. The subsequent conference saw the Worker's Music Association set up. Topic was essentially the recording section of the WMA. Those involved included A.L. Lloyd, Michael Tippett, and the current president of the WMA Alan Bush. The organization evolved, until the current Topic label started in 1958. This was at a time when skiffle was all the rage, influenced by the growing interest in folk music, and encouraged by Ewan MacColl and A.L. Lloyd. With a new generation of British folk performers looking for an outlet, Topic were able to give the Spinners and the Ian Campbell Folk Group a platform. They followed up with releases by such folk artists as the McPeakes (now Clan McPeake) and Jeannie Robertson. The label released a number of sampler albums, featuring a variety of topics, from the mid-60s. The Folksongs Of Britain series was originally released on the American Caedmon label in 1961. Managing Director Tony Engle, took

over from the late Gerry Sharp in 1973. Topic has grown over the years, and now includes subsidiary labels such as String and Special Delivery, as well as distributing for other labels, both at home and in the USA. The impressive 20-CD anthology Voice Of The People, anthologised several hundred traditional songs and dances of the British Isles.

● COMPILATIONS: The Folksongs Of Britain series volumes 1-10: Songs Of Courtship (Topic 1968) ★★★, Songs Of Seduction (Topic 1968) ★★★★, Jack Of All Trades (Topic 1968) ★★, The Child Ballads 1 (Topic 1969) ★★, The Child Ballads 2 (Topic 1969) ★★, Sailormen And Serving Maids (Topic 1970) ★★★★, Fair Game And Foul (Topic 1970) ★★★, A Soldier's Life For Me (Topic 1971) ★★★, Songs Of Christmas (Topic 1971) ★★, Songs Of Animals And Other Marvels (Topic 1971) ★★★; Topic Sampler series volumes 1-8: Folk Songs 1 (Topic 1964) ★★★, Folk Songs 2 (Topic 1966) ★★★, Men At Work (Topic 1966) ★★★★, From Erin's Green Shore (Topic 1966) ★★★, A Prospect Of Scotland (Topic 1967) ★★★, Folk Songs: A Collection Of Ballads And Broadsides (Topic 1967) ★★★, Sea Songs And Shanties (Topic 1967) ★★★★, English Garland (Topic 1972), ★★★ The Good Old Way – The Best Of British Folk (Topic 1980) ★★★, Ancient Celtic Roots (Topic 1996) ★★★, The Voice Of Folk (Topic 1996) ★★★, The Voice Of The People 20-CD box set (Topic 1998) ★★★★.

TORMÉ, MEL

b. Melvin Howard Torme, 13 September 1925, Chicago, Illinois, USA, d. 5 June 1999, Beverly Hill, California, USA. A child prodigy, Tormé first sang on radio as a toddler and while still in his teens he was performing as a singer, pianist, drummer and dancer. He was also composing songs at an early age and wrote arrangements for the band led by Chico Marx, and composed 'Lament To Love' for Harry James. He also acted on radio and in films and in addition to singing solo, led his own vocal group, the Mel-Tones. In this last capacity he recorded with Artie Shaw, enjoying a hit with 'Sunny Side Of The Street'. By the 50s he was established as one of the leading song stylists, performing the great standards and often working with a jazz backing, notably with the Marty Paich Dek-tette on albums such as Lulu's Back In Town. He headlined concert packages across the USA and in Europe, appeared on television, often producing his own shows, and always delivering performances of impeccable professionalism. Tormé continued in such a vein throughout the 60s and 70s, making many fine albums of superior popular music, on several of which he was accompanied by jazzmen. Among these were Shorty Rogers ('Round Midnight), Al Porcino (Live At The Maisonette), Buddy Rich (Together Again – For The First Time), Gerry Mulligan (Mel Tormé And Friends) and Rob McConnell (Mel Tormé With Rob McConnell And The Boss Brass).

Of all his musical collaborations, however, the best and most satisfying was a long series of concerts and radio and television shows, many of which were issued on record, with George Shearing. Among these albums were *An Evening At Charlie's*, *An Elegant Evening*, *A Vintage Year* and *Mel And George "Do" World War II*. In the early 90s Tormé was still drawing rave reviews for records and personal appearances, with Shearing, at festivals in California and the Channel Islands, and with Bill Berry's big band at the Hollywood Bowl. As a songwriter Tormé had several hundred compositions to his credit, of which the best known by far was 'The Christmas Song' (written with Robert Wells), first recorded by Nat 'King' Cole and covered by dozens of top popular song artists. As a performer, Tormé often featured himself on drums – for many years he used a drum kit that was formerly the property of Gene Krupa – and he played with unforced swing. As a singer, Tormé's work was touched with elegant charm. His voice, with the characteristic huskiness that earned him the sobriquet 'The Velvet Fog', deepened over the years and by the early 90s still retained all the qualities of his youth, not least, remarkable pitch and vocal control. In his choice of material he never showed anything other than perfect taste and his repertoire was an object lesson in musical quality. The fact that he also wrote almost all the arrangements of the songs he sang added to his status as a major figure in the history of American popular song. Tormé suffered a stroke in 1996, curtailing a magnificent career which was recognized in 1999 with a Grammy Lifetime Achievement Award. He died later that year leaving a great legacy of recorded music and two very fine literary autobiographical works.

● ALBUMS: *California Suite* 10-inch album (Capitol 1950) ★★★, *Songs* 10-inch album (MGM 1952) ★★★, *Musical Sounds Are The Best Songs* (Coral 1955) ★★★, *It's A Blue World* (Bethlehem 1955) ★★★★, with Marty Paich *Mel Tormé With The Marty Paich Dek-tette* (Bethlehem 1956) ★★★★, *Gene Norman Presents Mel Tormé Live At The Crescendo* (Coral 1956) ★★★★, *Lulu's Back In Town* (1957) ★★★, *Mel Tormé Sings Astaire* (Bethlehem 1957) ★★★, *'Round Midnight* i (1957) ★★★, with Paich *Tormé* (Verve 1958) ★★★, with Paich *Prelude To A Kiss* (Tops 1958) ★★★, *Songs For Any Taste* (Bethlehem 1959) ★★★, *Olé Tormé – Mel Tormé Goes South Of The Border With Billy May* (Verve 1959) ★★★★, with Paich *Back In Town* (Verve 1959) ★★★, with Paich *Mel Tormé Swings Schubert Alley* (Verve 1960) ★★★★★, *Swingin' On The Moon* (Verve 1960) ★★★★, *I Dig The Duke, I Dig The Count* (Verve 1960) ★★★★, *Mel Tormé Sings* (Strand 1960) ★★★, with Margaret Whiting *Broadway Right Now!* (Verve 1961) ★★★, *'Round Midnight* ii (1961) ★★★, *Mel Tormé At The Red Hill Inn* (Atlantic 1962) ★★★, *Comin' Home Baby* (Atlantic 1962) ★★★★, *Sunday In New York* (Atlantic 1963) ★★★★, *I Wished On The Moon* (Metro 1965) ★★★, *That's All; A Lush Romantic Album* (Columbia 1965) ★★★, *Mel Tormé Right Now* (Columbia 1966) ★★★, *A Day In The Life Of Bonnie And Clyde* (Liberty 1968) ★★★, *Live At The Maisonette* (1974) ★★★, *London Sessions* aka *Mel's London Mood* (Sandstone/Parade

1977) ★★★, *Tormé A New Album* (Paddlewheel 1978) ★★★★, with Buddy Rich *Together Again – For The First Time* (RCA 1978) ★★★, *Mel Tormé And Friends* (Finesse 1981) ★★★, *Encore At Marty's, New York* (1982) ★★★, with George Shearing *An Evening At Charlie's* (Concord Jazz 1983) ★★★, with Shearing *An Elegant Evening* (Concord Jazz 1985) ★★★, *Mel Tormé With Rob McConnell And The Boss Brass* (Concord Jazz 1986) ★★★, with Shearing *A Vintage Year* (Concord Jazz 1987) ★★★, with Paich *Reunion* (Concord Jazz 1988) ★★★★, with Paich *In Concert Tokyo* (Concord Jazz 1989) ★★★★, *Night At The Concord Pavilion* (Concord Jazz 1990) ★★★★, with Shearing *Mel And George 'Do' World War II* (Concord Jazz 1991) ★★★, *In Hollywood* 1954 recording (1992) ★★★, *Live At Fujitsu – Concord Jazz Festival 1992* (1992) ★★★, *Christmas Songs* (Telarc 1992) ★★, with Cleo Laine *Nothing Without You* (1993) ★★★★, *A Tribute To Bing Crosby* (Concord 1994) ★★★★, *Velvet & Brass* (Concord 1995) ★★★★, *A&E: An Evening With Mel Tormé* (Concord Jazz 1996) ★★★★, *My Night To Dream* (Concord Jazz 1997) ★★★.

● COMPILATIONS: *Verve's Choice The Best Of Mel Tormé* (Verve 1964) ★★★, *Walkman Jazz* 1958-61 recordings (Verve 1990) ★★★, *Capitol Years* (Capitol 1992) ★★★, *The Magic Of Mel Tormé* (Music Club 1995) ★★★, *The Mel Tormé Collection: 1944-1985* 4-CD box set (Rhino 1996) ★★★★, *Mel Tormé: The Best Of The Concord Years* (Concord Jazz 2000) ★★★★, *In The Lounge With* (Columbia 2001) ★★★, *Mel Tormé's Finest Hour* (Verve 2001) ★★★.

● FURTHER READING: *The Other Side Of The Rainbow: With Judy Garland On The Dawn Patrol*, Mel Tormé. *It Wasn't All Velvet: An Autobiography*, Mel Tormé. *My Singing Teachers*, Mel Tormé.

● FILMS: *Girl's Town* aka *The Innocent And The Damned* (1959).

TOROK, MITCHELL

b. 28 October 1929, Houston, Texas, USA. A singer-songwriter, Torok played guitar at the age of 12. In 1953, while Torok was still at college, he saw Jim Reeves' Abbott recording of a song he had written, called 'Mexican Joe', become a smash hit number 1 on all charts (Torok, who at the time did not know anything about Jim Reeves, had hoped that Hank Snow would be given the song – his wish came true the following year when his song 'My Arabian Baby' appeared as the b-side of Snow's hit 'I Don't Hurt Anymore'). Torok was himself signed to the Abbott label and later that year, he had a number 1 in both the *Billboard* country and juke-box charts with his song 'Caribbean'. The song, which remained in the country charts for 24 weeks, also became a Top 5 hit in both the Best Sellers and Jockey charts. He became a member of the *Louisiana Hayride* on KWKH Shreveport. In 1954, Torok gained a number 9 country hit with the ridiculous-sounding 'Hootchy Kootchy Henry (From Hawaii)', and in 1956/7, he even had success in the UK pop charts with his songs 'When Mexico Gave Up The Rhumba' and 'Red Light, Green Light'. This success led to him touring in

the UK in 1957. Torok made further recordings for Mercury, RCA, and Starday, and his last US chart entry was 'Instant Love', for the Reprise label in 1967. He continued to write songs, usually working in partnership with his wife (she has used both Gayle Jones and Ramona Redd as pseudonyms), and some have been recorded by top artists including Skeeter Davis, Kitty Wells, Glen Campbell and even Dean Martin. Hank Snow recorded 'The Mysterious Lady From Martinique' on one of his last RCA albums and 'Redneck' was a Top 20 hit for Vernon Oxford in 1976. Torok joined Cedarwood Music in the late 70s and worked on a recording project telling the history of Nashville from 1780 to 1980. He is also a talented painter and painted a mural on display in the Elvis Presley Museum in Nashville.
● ALBUMS: *Caribbean* (Guyden 1960) ★★★, *Guitar Course (Instant Fun)* (Reprise 1966) ★.
● COMPILATIONS: *Mexican Joe In The Caribbean* 4-CD box set (Bear Family 1996) ★★★★.

TOSCANO, ELI
b. Elias P. Toscano. Toscano was of Mexican and Italian descent and lived on the near west side of Chicago. He began his career in the music business operating a television repair and record shop, which he expanded into a one-stop distributorship and then a record company. He ran three important record labels, issuing blues and R&B in Chicago in the 50s. The first was Abco, on which, with co-owner Joe Brown, he issued eight releases, most notably by Arbee Stidham and Louis Myers. Then he began his Cobra label, which issued more than 30 discs including classic tracks by Otis Rush, Ike Turner, Harold Burrage and Magic Sam. A subsidiary label was Artistic, whose five issues included two by Buddy Guy and another by Turner. Toscano reportedly died in a boating accident in the early 60s, but rumours continued for decades afterwards that it was a gangland slaying, reputedly over an unpaid gambling debt.

TOWN HALL PARTY
This popular programme first began in 1951 as a Barn Dance on KFI Compton, California, USA. In 1953, as a one-hour show, it was moved to KFI television and networked by NBC, and filmed for use overseas by the Armed Forces Network television service. The show had its regular stars, which included well-known west coast performers such as Rex Allen, Johnny Bond (who usually wrote the show), Eddie Dean, Wayne Raney, Tex Ritter, Merle Travis, Tex Williams and special guest stars that once included Lefty Frizzell. It also helped to start the careers of Freddie Hart and Buck Owens. The show, which included comedy and even non-country performers at times, was directed by Wesley Tuttle and proved popular enough to run until 1960, when it was dropped by the station. During its existence, Screen Gems filmed 39 half-hour segments, which were syndicated to stations all over the world, in some areas being shown long after the show had ended.

TOWNSEND, ED
b. 16 April 1929, Fayetteville, Tennessee, USA. Townsend was an R&B balladeer who placed one lasting single on the US charts, 'For Your Love', in 1958. Townsend, whose father was a minister, sang in his church choir but received his first real performing experience while serving in the US Marine Corps in Korea, where he joined a troupe of travelling minstrels. Upon his return to civilian life, he hosted a television programme in Los Angeles and wrote songs which were recorded by Nat 'King' Cole, Etta James and others. In 1958 he signed to Capitol Records and recorded his composition 'For Your Love' (no relation to the later Yardbirds song). A lush ballad sung in a vocal style reminiscent of Jerry Butler, it reached the US Top 20. None of Townsend's follow-up recordings for Capitol, Liberty, Tru-Glo or Warner Brothers Records sold appreciably and he switched over to the production and writing side of the business. Among his credits were 'Let's Get It On' (Marvin Gaye), 'Finally Got Myself Together (I'm A Changed Man)' (the Impressions), and 'You Don't Want To Believe It (My Man)' (Joe Simon). Townsend also released a 1975 solo album for the Curtom Records label.
● ALBUMS: *New In Town* (Capitol 1959) ★★★, *Glad To Be Here* (Capitol 1959) ★★★, *Now* (Curtom 1975) ★★★.
● COMPILATIONS: *For Your Love: A Golden Classics Edition* (Collectables 1974) ★★★.

TRADITION RECORDS
Before the emergence of Tradition Records in the 50s, American folk and blues had often been poorly recorded and packaged. Tradition changed all that, establishing a catalogue of fine recordings that also engaged with flamenco, Irish and jazz music. Arguably the most pivotal release on the label was Odetta's *Sings Ballads & Blues*, which was later cited by Bob Dylan as 'the first thing that turned me on to folk singing'. Lightnin' Hopkins released two groundbreaking live albums, *Autobiography In Blues* and *Country Blues*, for the label, drawn from a Houston, Texas performance in 1959. 'Big' Bill Broonzy's *Treat Me Right* was also recorded live in Paris in 1951, and the label was additionally responsible for the first release of Lead Belly sessions conducted in New York between 1943 and 1944. Irish folk legends Liam Clancy and Tommy Makem (from Clancy Brothers And Tommy Makem) also recorded their first album, *The Lark In The Morning*, for Tradition. Other artists on the roster included Carlos Montoya, Erroll Garner, Woody Herman and Coleman Hawkins. A series of reissues in 1996 on the Rykodisc Records label helped to reinstate Tradition's role in the emergence of popular music.
● COMPILATIONS: *The Best Of The Blues Tradition, Vol. One* 3-CD box set (Tradition 1998) ★★★★.

TRAVIS AND BOB
A duo consisting of Travis Pritchett (b. 1939, Jackson, Alabama, USA) and Bob Weaver (b. 1939,

Jackson, Alabama, USA), Travis and Bob left their tiny mark on the pop world in 1959 with their Top 10 single 'Tell Him No'. The Everly Brothers-style country-rock tune was written by Pritchett and released on the small Sandy label. The larger Dot Records picked up distribution and the single peaked at number 9. A few subsequent singles failed to chart and although Travis and Bob continued to record, first for Big Top and then for Mercury Records, their hit recording career was never revitalized.

TRAVIS, MERLE
b. Merle Robert Travis, 29 November 1917, Rosewood, Kentucky, USA, d. 20 October 1983, Tahlequah, Oklahoma, USA. Travis was the son of a tobacco farmer but by the time he was four years old, the family had moved to Ebenezer, Kentucky, and his father was working down the mines. Travis' father often remarked, 'Another day older and deeper in debt', a phrase his son used in 'Sixteen Tons'. His father played the banjo, but Travis preferred the guitar. He befriended two coal miners, Mose Reger and Ike Everly, the father of the Everly Brothers, who demonstrated how to use the thumb for the bass strings while playing the melody on treble strings. Travis hitched around the country, busking where he could, and in 1935, he joined the Tennessee Tomcats and from there, went to a better-known country group, Clayton McMichen's Georgia Wildcats. In 1937 he became a member of the Drifting Pioneers, who performed on WLW Cincinnati. In 1943 he recorded for the local King Records label, recording a solo as Bob McCarthy and a duet with Grandpa Jones as the Shepherd Brothers. He and Jones did many radio shows together and many years later, recreated that atmosphere for an album. Travis, Jones and the Delmore Brothers also worked as a gospel quartet, the Browns Ferry Four.
After brief war service in the marines, Travis settled in California. Here he played with several bands, becoming one of the first to appreciate that a guitar could be a lead instrument. His arrangement of 'Muskrat' for Tex Ritter was later developed into a hit single for the Everly Brothers. Travis enjoyed success as a solo artist for the newly formed Capitol Records with 'Cincinnati Lou', 'No Vacancy', 'Missouri' and two US country number ones, 'Divorce Me C.O.D.' and 'So Round, So Firm, So Fully Packed'. He co-wrote Capitol's first million-seller, 'Smoke! Smoke! Smoke! (That Cigarette)' with Tex Williams, who recorded it. Burl Ives and Josh White were spearheading a craze for folk music, so Capitol producer Lee Gillette asked Travis for a 78 rpm album set of Kentucky folk songs. His eight-song debut, Folk Songs Of Our Hills, included 'Nine Pound Hammer' (a rewritten folk song), 'Dark As A Dungeon' and 'Sixteen Tons', with spoken introductions about the coal mining locale. Although Travis maintained that 'Sixteen Tons' was a 'fun song', it dealt with the exploitation of miners in the company store. It

won a gold record for Tennessee Ernie Ford in 1955 and was parodied by Spike Jones as 'Sixteen Tacos' and by Max Bygraves as 'Seventeen Tons'. Travis himself was also enjoying a country hit with a revival of 'Wildwood Flower' with Hank Thompson, and he won acclaim for his portrayal of a young GI in the 1954 movie From Here To Eternity, in which he sang 'Re-enlistment Blues'. In 1948 Travis devised a solid-body electric guitar, which was built for him by Paul Bigsby and developed by Leo Fender. 'I got the idea from a steel guitar,' he said, 'I wanted the same sustainability of notes, and I came up with a solid-body electric guitar with the keys all on one side.' Travis had an entertaining stage act in which he would mimic animals on his guitars, but his 1960 collection Walkin' The Strings is a highly regarded album of acoustic guitar solos. His style influenced Doc Watson, who named his son after him, and Chet Atkins, who did the same with his daughter. Travis was also a good cartoonist and he worked as a scriptwriter on Johnny Cash's television shows. He was less active during the 70s, but took part in the Nitty Gritty Dirt Band's tribute to country music, Will The Circle Be Unbroken?, received a Grammy for his acclaimed collaboration with Chet Atkins, and recorded several albums for CMH Records. Travis was elected to the Country Music Hall Of Fame in 1977 but his drug addiction and alcoholism made him unreliable and wrecked his private life. Says Tennessee Ernie Ford, 'Merle Travis was one of the most talented men I ever met. He could write songs that would knock your hat off, but he was a chronic alcoholic and when those binges would come, there was nothing we could do about it.' Travis died in October 1983, a year after appearing as one of the Texas Playboys in the Clint Eastwood movie Honkytonk Man. A posthumous album of blues songs played on 12-string guitar, Rough, Rowdy And Blue, included a tune from his mentor, Mose Reger, 'Merry Christmas, Pretty Baby'. His friend and fellow guitarist Joe Maphis wrote a tribute, 'Me And Ol' Merle', which concluded, 'We liked good whiskey and we loved the pretty girls, And we loved them guitars – Me and Ol' Merle.'
● ALBUMS: Folk Songs Of The Hills 10-inch album (Capitol 1947) ★★★, The Merle Travis Guitar (Capitol 1956) ★★★, Back Home expanded reissue of Folk Songs Of The Hills (Capitol 1957) ★★★, Walkin' The Strings (Capitol 1960) ★★★★, Travis! (Capitol 1962) ★★★, Songs Of The Coal Mines (Capitol 1963) ★★★, with Joe Maphis Two Guitar Greats (Capitol 1964) ★★★, with Johnny Bond Great Songs Of The Delmore Brothers (Capitol 1969) ★★★, Strictly Guitar (Capitol 1969) ★★★★, with Chet Atkins The Atkins-Travis Traveling Show (RCA Victor 1974) ★★★, with Maphis Country Guitar Giants (CMH 1979) ★★★, Light Singin' And Heavy Pickin' (CMH 1980) ★★★, Guitar Standards (CMH 1980) ★★★, Travis Pickin' (CMH 1981) ★★★, with Mac Wiseman The Clayton McMichen Story (CHM 1982) ★★★, with Grandpa Jones Merle And Grandpa's Farm And Home Hour (1985) ★★★, Rough, Rowdy And Blue

(CMH 1985) ★★★.
● COMPILATIONS: *The Best Of Merle Travis* (Capitol 1967) ★★★, *The Merle Travis Story* (CMH 1979) ★★★★, *The Best Of Merle Travis* (Rhino 1990) ★★★, *The Radio Shows 1944-1949* (Country Routes 1991) ★★★, *Capitol Country Music Classics* (Capitol 1993) ★★★, *Guitar Retrospective* (CMH 1995) ★★★, *Turn Your Radio On: Merle Travis 1944-1965* (Country Routes 1998) ★★★, *The Best Of Merle Travis: Sweet Temptation 1946-1953* (Razor & Tie 2000) ★★★★.
● VIDEOS: *Sixteen Tons: Rare Recordings 1946-1981* (Vestapol 1996).
● FURTHER READING: *In Search Of My Father*, Pat Travis Eatherly.
● FILMS: *The Old Texas Trail* aka *Stagecoach Line* (1944), *Lone Star Moonlight* (1946), *Cyclone Fury* (1951), *From Here To Eternity* (1953), *Door-To-Door Maniac* aka *Five Minutes To Live* (1961), *Night Rider* (1962), *That Tennessee Beat* (1966), *Honkytonk Man* (1982).

TREE GROWS IN BROOKLYN, A

With a book by George Abbott and Betty Smith which was adapted from Smith's best-selling novel of the same name, this sentimental story of an ordinary, working-class Brooklyn family opened at the Alvin Theatre in New York on 19 April 1951. Set in the early 1900s, the story follows the fortunes of the hard-drinking Johnny Nolan (Johnny Johnston), a singing waiter, who meets and marries Katie (Marcia Van Dyke). She has a sister named Cissy who 'collects' husbands and calls them all Harry. Eventually, her current spouse becomes so used to the name that he objects to being called by his real name of Oscar. Meanwhile, Johnny and Katie have a daughter, Francie (Nomi Mitty), but Johnny's drinking is getting worse. He loses his job and leaves home to find other work, only to get killed in the process. However, he has left sufficient money to enable Francie to finish her education, and the curtain falls on the celebrations following her graduation. In Smith's original book, and in the 1945 film, the story focused on the daughter Francie, but for this musical treatment the authors shifted the emphasis on to the older players, particularly Shirley Booth who gave a wonderfully humorous performance, particularly when reflecting on her 'late' Harry in 'He Had Refinement' ('One time he said: "May I suggest/You call a lady's chest, a chest/Instead of her points of interest?"/Dainty, ain't he?'). The remainder of Dorothy Fields and Arthur Schwartz's warmly romantic and sometimes lively score, included the lovely 'Make The Man Love Me', 'Look Who's Dancing', 'Love Is The Reason', 'I'm Like A New Broom', 'Growing Pains', 'Mine Till Monday', 'Don't Be Afraid', and 'If You Haven't Got A Sweetheart'. One of the other numbers, 'I'll Buy You A Star', was sung by Johnny Mathis on his 1961 album of the same title. *A Tree Grows In Brooklyn* had a decent run of 270 performances, but is rarely revived.

TRENET, CHARLES

b. 18 May 1913, Narbonne, France, d. 19 February 2001, Paris, France. One of the leading exponents of the French chanson, Trenet's mixture of light-hearted comedy and nostalgic romanticism continued to endear him to his countrymen long after most of his contemporaries had passed away. After studying art at the Académie des Arts Décoratives in Paris, Trenet formed a songwriting partnership with pianist Johnny Hess. The two performed in cabaret as Charles et Johnny, and issued their first recordings in January 1934. The partnership was ended by military service in 1936, but Trenet was by now establishing a substantial reputation as a songwriter in his homeland. His commissions included songs for Maurice Chevalier ('Y'a De La Joie') and Jean Sablon ('Vous Qui Passez Sans Me Voir'), while Yves Montand made his debut in 1937 with Trenet's 'C'est La Vie Qui Va'). During this period Trenet also inaugurated a solo career marked by his dapper stage dress (blue suit topped by a narrow-brimmed Fedora) and beguiling light baritone.

During the second world war Trenet remained in Paris, performing his regular shows at the Folies Bergère and Gaieté Parisienne. His career expanded after World War II, his songs being taken up by internationally known artists. One of the first songs to gain wide acceptance was 'La Mer', with Trenet's recording being extremely popular in the UK. In 1960 the song (with English words by Jack Lawrence) became a hit all over again for, Bobby Darin, under the title of 'Beyond The Sea'. Trenet made his name through such songs as 'Le Soleil A Des Rayons De Pluie', 'Il Y Avait Des Arbres', 'Printemps A Rio', 'Bonsoir Jolie Madame', 'Boum!', and 'At Last, At Last', but it was the massive success of 'Que Reste-T-Il De Nos Amours' ('I Wish You Love') that had the greatest impact. This song, recorded by numerous singers (often with the English lyric by Lee Wilson), confirmed his reputation as one of France's finest songwriters. Trenet continued to perform into the 70s, when he gave a series of 'farewell' concerts in France. He was then persuaded to travel to Canada in order to deliver a farewell concert there, and was so successful that he returned to regular performing both in Canada and in Europe, with triumphant concerts in Paris. He was still going strong in 1993, when Paris staged a three-day celebration of his music and BBC Radio presented *Je Chante: Charles Trenet At 80*. Two years later he released a CD containing 12 new tracks. His death in February 2001 was a source of national grieving in France.
● ALBUMS: *Fais Ta Vie* (1995) ★★★.
● COMPILATIONS: *Les Disques D'Or* (1983) ★★★, *Chansons* (1988) ★★★, *Top Sixteen* (1988) ★★★, *The Very Best Of Charles Trenet: The Extraordinary Garden* (1990) ★★★★.
● FILMS: *La Route Enchantée* (1938), *Je Chante* (1938), *Romance de Paris* (1941), *Frédérica* (1942), *La Cavalcade Des Heures* (1943), *Adieu Léonard* (1943), *Bouquet De Joie* (1952), *Printemps À Paris* (1957), *C'est Arrivé À 36 Chandelles* (1957), *L'Or Du Duc* (1965).

TRENIER TWINS

b. 14 July 1919, Mobile, Alabama, USA. Cliff (d. 2 March 1983) and Claude Trenier formed their first band, the Alabama State Collegians, in college during the 30s and took it on the road after graduating in 1941. Claude left in 1943 to replace Dan Grissom as ballad singer with Jimmie Lunceford's Orchestra, and Cliff joined him the following year. Claude also sang on sessions headed by Barney Bigard and Charles Mingus in 1946. After going solo in 1947 with their own small group, which included Don Hill on alto saxophone and Gene Gilbeaux on piano, they began recording for Mercury Records, going on to record for Chord (1949), London (1950), OKeh/Epic (1951-55), RCA's Vik subsidiary (1956), Brunswick (1957) and Dot (1958). After becoming the visual act of the early rock 'n' roll era and inspiring clones such as the Comets and the Bellboys, the Treniers appeared in several major rock 'n' roll movies (notably *Don't Knock The Rock* and *The Girl Can't Help It*) and visited Europe in 1958, where they were the support act on the ill-fated Jerry Lee Lewis tour. Increasingly becoming a supper-club act in the 60s, they made albums for Hermitage, TT and their own Mobile Records. Cliff died in 1983, but Claude is still active and continues to lead the Treniers with older brother Buddy, nephew Skip and Don Hill on alto saxophone.

● ALBUMS: *Go! Go! Go! The Treniers On TV* (OKeh/Epic 1955) ★★, *The Treniers Souvenir Album* (Dot 1958) ★★★, *After Hours With The Fabulous Treniers* (Hermitage 1962) ★★★, *The Treniers By The Sea* (1962) ★★, *Popcorn Man* (60s) ★★★, *Live And Wild At The Flamingo* (70s) ★★, *The Fabulous Treniers* (70s) ★★, *Those Crazy Treniers* (70s) ★★★, *Rockin' Is Our Bizness* (Edsel 1983) ★★★, *You're Killin' Me* (Mr R&B 1985) ★★★, *Hey Sister Lucy* (Bear Family 1988) ★★★, *Cool It Baby* (Bear Family 1988) ★★★.

TRENT, BRUCE

b. William Butters, 21 August 1912, St. Helier, Jersey, d. 19 November 1995, Burgh Heath, Surrey, England. An actor and singer with a fine, baritone voice and matinée idol good looks, Trent was one of the British theatre's most popular romantic leading men in the 40s and 50s. After singing with local dance groups, in the late 30s he spent two years touring the UK with Jack Hylton's famous show band, before joining Jack Payne's new BBC orchestra in 1940. He left Payne in 1942 in order to co-star with Frances Day, Arthur Riscoe, Jackie Hunter and Bud Flanagan in Cole Porter's musical *Du Barry Was A Lady* at His Majesty's Theatre in London. Trent subsequently returned to the West End, and then toured, in *The Student Prince*, before joining the army and entertaining the troops in the company of the Stars In Battledress. He was also a guest artist, along with Dorothy Carless, on a BBC broadcast with Glenn Miller's Band of the AEF. After the war, Trent took over the leading roles in *Carissima* (1948) and *Brigadoon* (1950), as well as starring in London in *Rainbow Square* (1951), *Wish*

You Were Here (1953) and *The Burning Boat* (1955, Royal Court Theatre). He also toured in various other productions, including *Lilac Time*, *Good-Night Vienna* and *The Desert Song*. In 1958, Trent joined the all-star cast of Tommy Steele, Jimmy Edwards, Yana, and Ted Durante, in Richard Rodgers and Oscar Hammerstein II's lavish *Cinderella* at the Coliseum. As the dashing Prince, he sang the show's big ballad, 'No Other Love', and duetted with Yana on the equally splendid 'Do I Love You (Because You're Beautiful)'. In later years he continued to tour in numerous revivals, both at home and abroad, notably as Arthur in *Camelot* in 1966. He also participated in re-recordings of favourite musicals, and was a regular broadcaster on BBC light music programmes. After retiring in the 70s, he worked tirelessly for the Grand Order of Water Rats charity.

TRIBBLE, THOMAS E., 'TNT'

b. 5 August 1921, Ferrel, Pennsylvania, USA. Tribble took up the drums upon moving to Washington, DC in the late 30s and carried his musical studies through his army service until his demobilization in 1946, when he joined his brother Floyd's band, the Treble Clefs, and later formed his own group. In 1949, Tribble joined Frank Motley's Motley Crew who were signed to the local DC label as 'name' act and houseband. Their session tapes were then leased or sold to other record companies, and releases resulted on Gotham and other independent labels. Tribble had records on Gotham both in his own right and as singer/drummer with the Motley Crew, as well as separate sessions recorded for RCA Victor in 1951. In 1952 he split from Motley and DC and became an exclusive Gotham artist until 1955 when he embarked upon a lengthy tour of the eastern seaboard and Cuba, recording for Miami's Chart label in 1957, Atlantic's East-West subsidiary in 1960, and the tiny Frandy label in 1961. He has managed to eke out a fairly satisfying living as a live act since the late 50s and continues to lead a rock 'n' roll and soul revival revue in Washington, DC.

● ALBUMS: *T.N.T. Tribble* (1987) ★★★, *T.N.T. Tribble Vol. 2: Red Hot Boogie* (1988) ★★, with Frank Motley *The Best Of Washington, D.C. R 'N' B* (1991) ★★★.

TRISTANO, LENNIE

b. Leonard Joseph Tristano, 19 March 1919, Chicago, Illinois, USA, d. 18 November 1978, New York City, New York, USA. Encouraged by his mother, Tristano learned piano and various reed instruments while still a very small child, despite steadily deteriorating eyesight (he was born during a measles epidemic). By the age of 11 he was completely blind but, overcoming this handicap, he studied formally at the American Conservatory in Chicago, graduating in 1943. Before graduation he had already established a reputation as a session musician and teacher, including among his pupils outstanding talents such as Lee Konitz and Bill Russo. He also made a handful of records with Earl Swope. Based in New York from 1946, he worked with Charlie Parker and other leading bop musicians and attracted considerable attention within the jazz community, even if his work was little known outside (his first recordings were not released until many years later). In New York Tristano continued to teach; Warne Marsh was one of his important pupils from this period. The extent of his teaching increased so much that by the early 50s he had founded the first important jazz school in New York, a development that kept him still further away from the wider public. By the mid-50s he had returned to private teaching and although he made a few recordings and some public appearances, including a mid-60s tour of Europe, he lived out the remaining years of his life in undeserved, but presumably intentional obscurity. An exceptionally original thinker, Tristano's work follows a path that, while related to the development of bop, traces different concepts. He was an early experimenter in playing jazz free from traditional notions of time signatures, but the results were very different from the later free jazz movement developed by Ornette Coleman and others. Among the lessons Tristano imparted to his pupils were those of strict precision in ensemble playing, complete command of the instrument and the ability to play complex shifts of time signature within a piece. He also lay particular stress upon listening – 'ear training'. In his own playing he preferred a pure sound and line, devoid of emotional content, and persuaded his pupils to follow this example so that, in Brian Priestley's words, their performances would 'stand or fall on the quality of their construction and not on emotional coloration'. Despite this almost puritanical attitude towards jazz, Tristano's teaching encouraged detailed study of solos by emotional players such as Louis Armstrong, Roy Eldridge and Charlie Parker. Clearly, Tristano was a powerful influence upon the many musicians he taught and through them upon countless more, especially through the work of such pupils as Peter Ind and Konitz, himself an important teacher.

● ALBUMS: *Live In Toronto* (Jazz Records 1952) ★★★, *Lines* (1955), *Lennie Tristano* (Atlantic 1955) ★★★, *New York Improvisations* (1956) ★★★, *The New Tristano* (Rhino 1962) ★★★★, *Manhattan Studio* (Elektra 1983) ★★★★.

● COMPILATIONS: *Live At Birdland 1949* (Jazz Records 1945-49) ★★★, *The Lost Session* (1946) ★★★, *The Rarest Trio/Quartet Sessions 1946/7* (1946-47) ★★★★, *Cool In Jam* (1947) ★★★, *Crosscurrents* (1949) ★★★, *Wow* (Jazz Records 1950 recording) ★★★★, *Descent Into The Maelstrom* (1951-66) ★★★★, *Note To Note* (Jazz Records 1997) ★★★★, *The Complete Atlantic Recordings Of Lennie Tristano, Lee Konitz & Warne Marsh* 6-CD box set (Mosaic 1997) ★★★★.

TROUP, BOBBY

b. Robert William Troup, 18 October 1918, Harrisburg, Pennsylvania, USA, d. 7 February 1999, Sherman Oaks, California, USA. After studying extensively, including a degree in economics, Troup turned to songwriting and singing to his own piano accompaniment. In 1941 he was hired by Tommy Dorsey, but was drafted the same year. After five years in the US Navy, where he wrote scores for several shows, he settled in Los Angeles. He played nightclubs, married Julie London and formed a jazz trio. Troup also began making films, gaining small acting roles and sometimes playing piano and singing. Among these films were *The Duchess Of Idaho* (1950), *The Five Pennies* (1959) and *The Gene Krupa Story* (1959). He wrote scores for several films, including *The Girl Can't Help It* (1956), for which he also contributed the title song, and *Man Of The West* (1958). Among his other songs are 'Daddy', the standard '(Get Your Kicks On) Route 66', 'Baby, Baby, All The Time', both of which were recorded by Nat 'King' Cole, and 'The Meaning Of The Blues'; he also wrote the lyrics for 'Free And Easy' and 'Girl Talk'.

By the early 60s Troup's acting career was in good shape; he had leading roles in several movies and also appeared on television in *Acapulco*, for which he wrote the background music. In the 60s and on through the 70s he took leading roles in such television movies as *Dragnet* and *Benny And Barney: Las Vegas Undercover*. He also acted in 1972's *Emergency!* and its spin-off series, in which Julie London appeared. Not surprisingly, given the number of acting roles he was offered over the years, this area of Troup's work tended to overshadow his music. In some respects this was a pity because, although an eclectic piano player, Troup sang with an engaging simplicity, and a dedication to the intentions of the lyricist seldom displayed by many more famous performers.

● ALBUMS: *Bobby* 10-inch album (Capitol 1953) ★★★, *Bobby Troup* 10-inch album (Capitol 1955) ★★★, *The Distinctive Style Of Bobby Troup* (Bethlehem 1955) ★★★, *Bobby Troup With Bob Enevoldsen And His Orchestra* (Liberty 1955) ★★, *Bobby Troup Sings Johnny Mercer* (Bethlehem 1955) ★★★, *Do Re Mi* (Liberty 1957) ★★, *Bobby Swings Tenderly* (Mode 1957) ★★★, *In A Class Beyond Compare* (1957) ★★★, *Here's To My Lady* (Liberty 1958) ★★, *Bobby Troup And His Jazz All-Stars* (RCA Victor 1959) ★★.

● COMPILATIONS: *The Feeling Of Jazz* 1955, 1967 recordings (Starline 1998) ★★★.

● FILMS: *Mr. Imperium* (1951), *Bop Girl Goes Calypso* aka *Bop Girl* (1957), *The High Cost Of Loving* (1958), *The Gene Krupa Story* aka *Drum Crazy* (1959), *The Five Pennies* (1959), *First To Fight* (1967), *Number One* (1969), *M*A*S*H* (1970).

TUBB, ERNEST

b. Ernest Dale Tubb, 9 February 1914, near Crisp, Ellis County, Texas, USA, d. 6 September 1984, Nashville, Tennessee, USA. Ernest was the youngest of five children of Calvin Tubb, the foreman of a 300-acre cotton farm, and his wife Sarah. In 1920 the family relocated to Benjamin, and then moved again, to Kemp, in 1925. The following year, his parents divorced and initially he stayed with his mother when she moved to her brother's farm near Lively. His mother, a very religious woman who was one-quarter Cherokee, played the piano and organ and sang hymns around the farms and at the local church. Ernest's education suffered and he later related that he only went to school when he could not find work. In 1928 he heard a recording of Jimmie Rodgers singing one of his blue yodels. He was immediately fascinated and quickly decided that he wanted to be a singer; he began to learn Rodgers' songs and whenever he had the money, he bought his records.

In 1930 after his mother remarried, he travelled around, working on various tasks and living at different times with married siblings or his remarried father. Early in 1933, while working on the roads near Benjamin, he became friendly with a young guitarist called Merwyn 'Buff' Buffington, who liked Tubb's singing but suggested he should learn to play guitar. He bought his first guitar from a pawnshop in Abilene and Buffington taught him his first chords. In May 1933 Tubb was greatly distressed by the death of Rodgers, although the event served to strengthen his resolve to emulate his idol. He moved to San Antonio, where he lived with his brother Calvin Jnr. He also renewed his acquaintance with Buffington, who at the time was playing guitar with the Castleman Brothers (Joe and Jim) on Radio KONO. He persuaded Tubb to make some appearances as guest vocalist with them, which led to him being offered his own twice-weekly early morning show. On 26 May 1934 he married Lois Elaine Cook. Still very much the Rodgers imitator, he decided to contact Jimmie Rodgers' widow; Carrie Rodgers was impressed with Tubb and not only gave him a picture, but also showed him many of her late husband's possessions and agreed to listen to his radio show. She also offered to help him with his career, and in 1936 she loaned him one of Jimmie's C.F. Martin guitars.

In October of that year, mainly due to her influence with her late husband's label, Tubb made his first recordings for RCA Records (she later gave him the guitar, which, after using it for many years, Tubb eventually donated to the Country Music Hall Of Fame Museum). The first two of the six songs recorded were tribute songs written by Elsie McWilliams, Rodgers' sister-in-law; the others were self-penned numbers. RCA released the first but sales were poor. A further session in March 1937 saw another single released but again sales were poor. These two singles are so scarce that they represent the most collectable recordings of Tubb's entire career (the other RCA tracks were not released until 1942, by which time Tubb was a known artist). He played countless small venues and appeared on various radio stations as he struggled to keep his family, which by now comprised Justin (b. 1935) and Violet Elaine (b. 1939). (His son Roger Dale (b. 1938) had died in a car crash when only seven weeks old.)

In spite of Carrie Rodgers' help, it was not until April 1940 that Tubb recorded again, this time for Decca Records. By now his style and sound had changed, due to the fact that late in 1939 his tonsils had been removed, taking with them his ability to yodel. This effectively stopped him being a Rodgers clone and he began to develop his own identity (in later years, he recalled the event with his song 'He Took 50 Dollars And My Yodel, When He Took My Tonsils Out'). Decca were impressed enough to record further sessions. He was sponsored by a flour company and began touring and appearing on KGKO Fort Worth as the Gold Chain Troubadour. Tubb continued to write songs and in April 1941, this time using a backing that included the electric guitar of KGKO's staff guitarist Fay 'Smitty Smith', he recorded six more numbers. After some argument with Decca over which song to release first, Tubb's choice of 'Walking The Floor Over You' was accepted. In the first year it sold 400,000 copies and went on to become a million-selling record and Tubb's greatest hit. In 1941 he sang it and three more songs in the Charles Starrett film *Fighting Buckeroos*, and in 1942 he appeared with Starrett again in *Ridin' West*.

That same year, his popularity secured him a release from his Gold Chain contract and he moved to Nashville. By January 1943 the *Grand Ole Opry* had a new honky-tonk singer who dared to use an electric lead guitar on that sacred stage. When a union strike stopped recordings in 1942 and 1943, he toured extensively on various shows, including tours with Pee Wee King, but he was soon fronting his own band, the Texas Troubadours. In 1944 he appeared in the film *Jamboree* and the same year, making his first recordings with his own band, he gained his first US country chart number 1 and a pop chart number 16 with 'Soldier's Last Letter'. In February 1946 he was probably only the second modern country artist ever to record in Nashville, Decca having recorded Red Foley the previous year. In 1947, he opened the now world-famous Ernest Tubb Record Shop in Nashville and started his *Midnight Jamboree*, initially on the *Opry*, but before long the show was being broadcast direct from the actual record shop itself. He also headlined the first ever country music show held in New York's Carnegie Hall, telling the audience: 'This place could sure hold a lot of hay'. He continued to tour and record and by the end of 1948 he had amassed 16 country Top 5s, including two more number 1s with 'It's Been So Long, Darling' and 'Rainbow At Midnight', and four songs had made the pop charts. His popularity was increased even further in 1949, when he tallied 12 chart entries (11 Top 10 hits) including number 1 hits with 'Slippin' Around' and 'Blue Christmas', and duet hits with Red Foley ('Tennessee Border No. 2') and the Andrews Sisters ('I'm Biting My Fingernails And Thinking Of You'). Bing Crosby even asked to record with him but the session never materialized (Bing did record 'Walking The Floor Over You' and in 1960 it also became a UK pop hit for Pat Boone).

In 1948 Tubb's first marriage ended in divorce but in June 1949, he married Olene Adams Carter (this marriage lasted 26 years and produced five children). Tubb was always ready to offer a helping hand and in 1950 he helped fellow Rodgers admirer Hank Snow to appear on the *Grand Ole Opry*. He had befriended Hank Williams when he first broke into country music and in 1953, he sang 'Beyond The Sunset' at Williams' funeral. During the 50s he maintained a rigorous touring and recording schedule. By the end of the decade, although only achieving one number 1 with his duet with Red Foley of 'Goodnight, Irene', he totalled 34 hits, the majority being Top 10s. Major hits included 'I Love You Because', 'Driftwood On The River' and 'Missing In Action'. In 1953 he and Hank Snow, Danny Dill and Lew Childre were the first country acts to tour a live war zone when they played about 40 shows in Korea, many in the open air and within range of enemy guns. Tubb had been advised not to go – on his return his health suffered and for a time he was unable to perform. By the mid-50s, his eldest son Justin Tubb, then establishing himself as an artist and songwriter, became involved with the business organization.

The hits slowed in the 60s but Tubb's popularity did not, and in spite of his health problems, he kept up a rigorous touring schedule and hosted his network television show. His hits at this time included 'Thanks A Lot', 'Pass The Booze', his nostalgic 'Waltz Across Texas' and a duet with Loretta Lynn titled 'Mr. & Mrs. Used To Be'. In 1965, in recognition of his important contribution to the music, he became the sixth member of the Country Music Hall Of Fame. The many songs that he had written and successfully recorded also led to him being one of the first writers elected to the Nashville Songwriters' International Hall Of Fame when it was founded in 1970. During the 70s he played the *Grand Ole Opry*, hosted the *Midnight Jamboree* and in spite of the worsening effects of the emphysema that had first developed in 1965, he still kept up a touring schedule that would have taxed younger men.

He finally parted company with Decca and in 1979, to mark his 65th birthday, Pete Drake masterminded a tribute on First Generation Records called *The Legend And The Legacy*, on which various stars overdubbed vocal contributions on Tubb's recordings (Tubb was not informed until the project was completed). The album became a bestseller and singles of a Tubb and Willie Nelson duet of 'Waltz Across Texas' and a joint Merle Haggard, Chet Atkins, Charlie Daniels and Tubb version of 'Walking The Floor Over You' both charted. It was initially released as a double album but ran foul of various claims of conflicting contractual details or unauthorized performances. It was subsequently withdrawn and copies supposedly destroyed. Record One of the original issue soon reappeared as a single album on Cachet, minus only a single track – the Nelson/Tubb duet. By 1982 his failing health forced him to retire. In the last year of touring, he had to rest on his bed in his customized touring bus and take oxygen between and during shows

(ironically similar to the latter days of the career of his idol, Jimmie Rodgers, almost 50 years earlier). He made one of his last recordings in 1982, when he spoke a line on the Waylon Jennings and Hank Williams Jnr. song 'Leave Them Boys Alone'.

Ernest Tubb died in September 1984 of emphysema and related complications in Nashville's Baptist Hospital. He was buried on 10 September in Nashville's Hermitage Memorial Gardens. Over the years the Texas Troubadours included some of country music's finest musicians, such as Jimmie Short, Leon Rhodes, Billy Byrd, Jerry Byrd and Red Herron. Two others, Jack Greene and Cal Smith, went on to successful solo careers. Ernest Tubb registered in total 91 country chart hits, of which only 17 failed to reach the Top 20. His distinctive growling vocals, in a voice that deepened but softened as the years went by, usually began somewhat off-key, and by some unique means, he managed to use this flatness to emphasize and convey the songs, whether they were happy or sad. After starting out as a blatant imitator, no one could deny that he became a completely original and unique artist.

● ALBUMS: *Ernest Tubb Favorites* 10-inch album (Decca 1951) ★★★★, *Jimmie Rodgers Songs Sung By Ernest Tubb* 10-inch album (Decca 1951) ★★★, *Old Rugged Cross* 10-inch album (Decca 1951) ★★★, *Sing A Song Of Christmas* 10-inch album (Decca 1952) ★★★, *Ernest Tubb Favourites* (Decca 1956) ★★★★, *The Daddy Of 'Em All* (Decca 1956) ★★★, *Ernest Tubb & The Wilburn Brothers* (Decca 1959) ★★★★, *The Importance Of Being Ernest* (Decca 1959) ★★★★, *Ernest Tubb & His Texas Troubadours* (Vocalion 1960) ★★★★, *Ernest Tubb Record Shop* (Decca 1960) ★★★★, with guests *Midnight Jamboree* (Decca 1960) ★★★, *All Time Hits* (Decca 1961) ★★★, *On Tour* (Decca 1962) ★★, *Just Call Me Lonesome* (Decca 1963) ★★★, *The Family Bible* (Decca 1963) ★★★, *Presents The Texas Troubadours* (Decca 1964) ★★★★, *Thanks A Lot* (Decca 1964) ★★★, *Blue Christmas* (Decca 1964) ★★★, *Country Dance Time* (Decca 1965) ★★★★, *Hittin' The Road* (Decca 1965) ★★★, with Loretta Lynn *Mr. & Mrs. Used To Be* (Decca 1965) ★★★★, *My Pick Of The Hits* (Decca 1965) ★★★, *Ernest Tubb's Fabulous Texas Troubadours* (Decca 1966) ★★★★, *By Request* (Decca 1966) ★★★, *Ernest Tubb Sings Country Hits Old & New* (Decca 1966) ★★★, *Another Story* (Decca 1967) ★★★, *Stand By Me* (Vocalion 1967) ★★★, *Ernest Tubb & Loretta Lynn Singin' Again* (Decca 1967) ★★★★, *The Terrific Texas Troubadours* (Decca 1968) ★★★, *Country Hit Time* (Decca 1968) ★★★, *Ernest Tubb Sings Hank Williams* (Decca 1968) ★★★, with Lynn *If We Put Our Heads Together* (Decca 1969) ★★★★, *Let's Turn Back The Years* (Decca 1969) ★★★, *Saturday Satan, Sunday Saint* (Decca 1969) ★★★, *Great Country* (Vocalion 1969) ★★★, *A Good Year For The Wine* (Decca 1970) ★★★, *One Sweet Hello* (Decca 1971) ★★★, *Baby, It's So Hard To Be Good* (Decca 1972) ★★★, *Say Something Nice To Sarah* (Decca 1972) ★★★, *I've Got All The Heartaches I Can Handle* (Decca 1973) ★★★, *Ernest*

Tubb (MCA 1975) ★★★, *Rare Recordings* (1983) ★★★★, *Live, 1965* (Rhino 1990) ★★★★, *New Year's Eve Live 1979* (Lost Gold 1999) ★★★.

● COMPILATIONS: *The Ernest Tubb Story* contains re-recorded material (Decca 1958) ★★★★, *Ernest Tubb's Golden Favorites* (Decca 1961) ★★★, *Ernest Tubb's Greatest Hits* contains re-recorded material (Decca 1968) ★★, *Ernest Tubb's Greatest Hits Volume 2* contains re-recorded material(Decca 1970) ★★★, *The Ernest Tubb/Loretta Lynn Story* (MCA 1973) ★★★★, *Ernest Tubb: Country Music Hall Of Fame* (Coral 1979) ★★★, with various artists *The Legend And The Legacy* (First Generation/Cachet 1979) ★★★★, *Honky Tonk Classics* (Rounder 1982) ★★★, *Country Music Hall Of Fame* (MCA 1987) ★★★★, *Let's Say Goodbye Like We Say Hello* 5-CD box set (Bear Family 1991) ★★★★, *Yellow Rose Of Texas* 5-CD box set (Bear Family 1993) ★★★★, *Walking The Floor Over You* 8-CD box set (Bear Family 1996) ★★★★, *The Best Of Ernest Tubb* (Curb 1996) ★★★★, *The Legend And The Legacy* (Edsel 1997) ★★★, *The Very Best Of Ernest Tubb* (Half Moon 1997) ★★★★, *Ernest Tubb & The Texas Troubadours: Waltz Across Texas* 6-CD box set (Bear Family 1998) ★★★★.

● FURTHER READING: *Ernest Tubb: The Original E.T.*, Norma Barthel. *The Texas Troubadour*, Ronnie Pugh.

TUBB, JUSTIN

b. Justin Wayne Tubb, 20 August 1935, San Antonio, Texas, USA, d. 24 January 1998, Nashville, Texas, USA. The eldest son of country music legend Ernest Tubb, he attended Castle Heights Military School, Lebanon, from 1944-48. He was naturally attracted to his father's music and when school holidays permitted, he toured with his father and regularly appeared on his WSM radio programme. He made his debut on the *Grand Ole Opry* at the age of nine. He began to write songs and by the time he left Brackenridge High School, San Antonio, he was an accomplished guitarist and singer. In 1952, tiring of being told he was going to be just like his father, he entered the University of Texas at Austin with thoughts of a career in journalism. The following year he wrote a tribute song to Hank Williams that his father recorded. He left university when he was offered a job as a disc jockey on WHIN Gallatin. This gave him the chance to sing some of his own songs to his listeners and also led to a Decca Records contract. He gained his first US country chart hit in 1954 when 'Looking Back To See', a duet with Goldie Hill, reached number 4. In 1955 he became the youngest ever regular member of the *Grand Ole Opry*. He always resisted any attempt to capitalize on his father's name and for some time he deliberately avoided appearing on the same shows. In the 60s when Ernest's health worsened, he began to combine his career with assisting his father in his business ventures and later became manager of the *Ernest Tubb Midnight Jamboree* radio show and record shops, as well as forming his own publishing company. He had solo Top 10s with 'I Gotta Go Get My Baby' and 'Take A Letter Miss Gray', and further duet successes with Lorene

Mann with 'Hurry, Mr Peters' (the answer song to the Roy Drusky-Priscilla Mitchell hit 'Yes, Mr Peters') and 'We've Gone Too Far Again'. Many of his songs became hits for others, including 'Keeping Up With The Joneses' (Faron Young-Margie Singleton), 'Love Is No Excuse' (Jim Reeves-Dottie West) and 'Lonesome 7-7203' (Hawkshaw Hawkins). Over the years, he recorded for several labels, including Starday, Challenge and RCA Records. He toured all over the USA, Canada, Europe, even to Vietnam, and he also appeared on most major US television shows. Like his father, Tubb was a strict traditionalist, and during the 70s his career faltered. He registered his personal feelings about attempts to change country music in his song 'What's Wrong With The Way That We're Doing It Now', which won him five standing ovations for encores on the first occasion that he sang it on the *Grand Ole Opry*. He continued making *Opry* appearances right up to his death and was regularly expected to sing that song and his tribute to his late father, 'Thanks Troubadour, Thanks'.

● ALBUMS: *Country Boy In Love* (Decca 1957) ★★★, *The Modern Country Sound Of Justin Tubb* (Starday 1962) ★★★, *Star Of The Grand Ole Opry* (Starday 1962) ★★★, *Justin Tubb* (Vocalion 1965) ★★★, *Where You're Concerned* (RCA Victor 1965) ★★★, with Lorene Mann *Together And Alone* (RCA Victor 1966) ★★★, *That Country Style* (1967) ★★★, *Things I Still Remember Very Well* (Dot 1969) ★★★, *New Country Heard From* (1974) ★★★, *Justin Tubb* (1979) ★★.

● COMPILATIONS: *The Best Of Justin Tubb* (Starday 1965) ★★★.

TUCKER, LUTHER

b. 20 January 1936, Memphis, Tennessee, USA, d. 17 June 1993, San Rafael, California, USA. Tucker moved to Chicago, Illinois, at the age of nine and was probably best known as one of Little Walter's backing guitarists both on stage and on record in the 50s. He was heavily influenced by his mother who played piano and guitar, but Tucker started playing guitar himself after hearing Robert Lockwood Jnr. Lockwood became his mentor, together with his mother. He also worked with other musicians such as J.T. Brown, Junior Wells, Muddy Waters and Sonny Boy 'Rice Miller' Williamson in the same decade. Tucker remained an in-demand backing guitarist and recorded with numerous blues artists, including James Cotton, Otis Rush and John Lee Hooker. He settled in California in 1969 and occasionally led a group under his own name. He was known for the speed of his playing and recorded in his own right for Messaround and Paris Albums. He lived in the Netherlands for some years but later returned to live in California. Tucker died in 1993 from a heart attack.

● COMPILATIONS: *Blue Bay* three tracks only (1976) ★★, *San Francisco Blues Festival European Sessions* three tracks only (1980) ★★, *Sad Hours* (Antone's 1994) ★★★, with the Ford Blues Band *Luther Tucker And The Ford Blues Band* (Cross Cut 1995) ★★★.

TUNE WEAVERS

This R&B vocal ensemble came from Woburn, Massachusetts, USA, and comprised lead Margo Sylvia (b. 4 April 1936), her husband and bass Johnny Sylvia (b. 8 September 1935), her brother and tenor Gilbert J. Lopez (b. 4 July 1934), and her cousin and obligato Charlotte Davis (b. 12 November 1936). The group got together in 1956 and within six months were recording for one-time big bandleader Frank Paul. He put out on his Casa Grande label a song Margo and Gilbert had written way back in 1952, and the result was a slice of classic rock 'n' roll balladry, 'Happy, Happy Birthday Baby'. With Chicago-based Chess Records picking up the record, it went to number 4 R&B and number 5 pop in 1957. Paul had a real find in Margo Sylvia, whose warm seductive voice was utterly beguiling, and he put it to good use on a number of follow-ups. Sadly, he was unable to get the Tuneweavers to chart again and the group broke up in 1961.
● ALBUMS: *Happy Happy Birthday Baby* (1973) ★★★.

TURBANS

This Philadelphia R&B group consisted of Al Banks (b. Andrew Banks, 26 July 1937, d. 1977; lead), Matthew Pratt (tenor), Charles Williams (baritone) and Andrew 'Chet' Jones (bass). The Turbans have gone down in rock 'n' roll history as proverbial one-hit-wonders for their Mambo beat classic, 'When You Dance' (US R&B number 3 and pop number 33 in 1955). It achieved a historic mystique by being one of the first rock 'n' roll tunes (as an early cross-over hit) and one of the selections on Art Laboe's *Oldies But Goodies* from 1960. No other records by the Turbans ever charted, but their 'Congratulations' (1957), is a highly esteemed example of doo-wop balladry in which Banks' falsetto voice comes to the forefront. Following their last release in 1962, the Turbans broke up.
● COMPILATIONS: *Turbans Greatest Hits* (1973) ★★, *Best Of The Turbans* (1985) ★★.

TURNER, BRUCE

b. 5 July 1922, Saltburn, Yorkshire, England, d. 28 November 1993, Newport Pagnell, Buckingham-shire, England. A self-taught clarinettist, Turner took up alto saxophone during military service in World War II. In the immediate post-war years, Turner showed himself to be a thoroughly eclectic and accommodating musician, playing both bebop and dixieland with equal aplomb and ability. Significantly, he also played these diverse forms of jazz with considerable integrity. At the start of the 50s he joined a current trend among British musicians and played aboard transatlantic liners in order to visit New York. While there he studied with Lee Konitz (this at a time when Konitz was himself studying with Lennie Tristano). Despite this exposure to contemporary thought in jazz, on his return to the UK Turner joined Freddy Randall, with whom he had played in the late 40s, and then began a long association with Humphrey Lyttelton. His tenure with Lyttelton was marked at its outset by one of the more extreme examples of the division in loyalties among UK jazz audiences of the era; a banner bearing the words 'Go home, dirty bopper' was waved at a concert and the phrase entered the vocabulary even if, subsequently, it was not always used with defamatory intent. In 1957 Turner formed his own 'jump' band, a move that appears to have given him the most suitable setting for his quirky, driving playing style, which reflects the work of predecessors such as Pete Brown while remaining distinctively personal. With this band, Turner toured extensively, often accompanying visiting American jazzmen such as Ben Webster, Ray Nance, Bill Coleman and Don Byas. Some of these tours brought personality clashes and led to Turner's decision to fold the jump band. In the mid-60s Turner then returned to a more traditional setting with Acker Bilk. In the early 70s his relationship with Lyttelton was resumed, although Turner continued to lead his own small bands and to work in a richly varied selection of bands, from the traditional, with Keith Smith, to the modern, with Dave Green (notably in the group Fingers). Late in his career Turner also took up soprano saxophone, displaying an effective command of the instrument. One of the outstanding British musicians of his generation, Turner's eclecticism might well have limited the spread of his reputation. Certainly, this enormously talented and well-liked figure deserved to be better represented on records and on the international festival and club circuits.
● ALBUMS: with Humphrey Lyttelton *Live At The Royal Festival Hall* (Parlophone 1954) ★★★★, *Accent On Swing* i (1959) ★★★, *Jumping At The NFT* (1961) ★★★, *Accent On Swing* ii (1962) ★★★, *Going Places* (1962) ★★, *Bruce Turner-John Barnes: Jazz Masters* (1975) ★★★, with Keith Smith *Up Jumped The Blues* (1978) ★★★, *The Dirty Bopper* (Calligraph 1985) ★★★, *New Orleans* (Metronome 1990) ★★★, *Fishmouth* (Decca 1991) ★★★, *Shiek Of Araby* (Decca 1991) ★★★.
● COMPILATIONS: *That's The Blues, Dad* 50s recordings (Lake 1998) ★★★.
● FURTHER READING: *Hot Air, Cool Music*, Bruce Turner.

TURNER, DANNY

b. James Daniel Turner, 8 March 1920, Farrell, Pennsylvania, USA, d. 14 April 1995. Raised in upstate New York, he studied music, then began playing alto saxophone while living in Philadelphia in the late 40s; he associated with many distinguished jazzmen including John Coltrane and Philly Joe Jones. He occasionally led his own small groups and also worked with other leaders including Johnny Lynch and the Four Kings And A Queen vocal group. In 1950 he was a member of the Gerald Wilson big band that accompanied Billie Holiday on a disastrous tour of southern states. He was a member of the Milt Buckner small group for four years in the 50s and also played and recorded with Dakota Staton, Jimmy McGriff, Ray Charles and others throughout the 60s, sometimes playing alto, sometimes tenor saxophone. He spent some time with Machito and then, in the early 70s, became an on-call substitute with Count Basie. From the mid-70s he was permanently with Basie, usually playing alto and eventually becoming section leader. A fluid, elegant soloist, Turner's style always charmed and often sparked with boppish fire. After Basie died, Turner continued to play in alumni bands and was a member of the continuing Count Basie Orchestra until shortly before his death.

● ALBUMS: with Milt Buckner *Rockin' With Milt* (Capitol 1955) ★★, *First Time Out* (Hemisphere 1983) ★★★.

TURNER, IKE

b. Izear Luster Turner Jnr., 5 November 1931, Clarksdale, Mississippi, USA. R&B stalwart Ike Turner is a music business legend for the best and worst of reasons. As the undisputed leader of the Ike And Tina Turner Revue he helped to revolutionize the world of R&B and live performance in the 60s. As a husband to Tina Turner (b. Annie Mae Bullock, 26 November 1939, Brownsville, Tennessee, USA), he was given to numerous bouts of alleged cruelty and violence, and also spent periods of his later career as a self-pitying prison inmate. Enfeebled by cocaine abuse and his own deluded view of his importance in the subsequent rise of Turner's career, he cut a sad figure. However, rejuvenated by his marriage to new wife Jeanette (allegedly his thirteenth marriage), and a drug and alcohol-free lifestyle, by the mid-90s Turner seemed to have finally straightened himself out.

Ike Turner first learned to play piano in the 40s, inspired by the Clarksdale performances of Pinetop Perkins. With a clutch of local musicians he formed his first band, the Kings Of Rhythm. Turner made his first record, 'Rocket 88', at Sam Phillips' studio in Memphis in March 1951. It went to number 1 on the R&B charts, but the singer featured on it, Jackie Brenston, chose to carve out a solo career on the back of its success. In the meantime, Turner played the piano parts on Howling Wolf's first record, 'How Many More Years'. In the mid-50s, having set up his own studio in Clarksdale and taken up the guitar as his primary instrument, he released a number of singles credited either to himself or Lover Boy. Then, accused of 'fraternising with whites', Turner was run out of town, choosing St. Louis as his next destination. There, recording once again under the moniker Kings Of Rhythm, he had further success with efforts such as 'I'm Tore Up'. The band enjoyed further success, and Turner also made records with Otis Rush and Buddy Guy.

By 1960 band member Annie Mae Bullock had become Tina Turner. The Ike And Tina Turner Revue was adopted as the band's name, and they achieved an immediate hit with the release of 'A Fool In Love' on Sue Records. After over a decade of success, Tina Turner finally opted to leave Ike and the band in 1976. Ike never recovered

mentally from the shock, and he ultimately reached rock bottom by spending time in prison after narcotic offences. He attempted to regain some sense of personal dignity in the 90s with only cult success. An embarrassing 'I Like Ike' campaign was undertaken by the UK purist fanzine *Juke Blues*, which failed to convince the outside world that he still had anything to offer musically. In 1999 he published *Takin' Back My Name*, a typically flamboyant account of his life in music and his relationship with Tina, which attempted to fight the accusations made by his former wife in her 1985 autobiography, *I, Tina*. Whatever his personal failings, Ike Turner is one of the musical legends of the period, and some of his background work in the 60s should be seen as crucial to the development of R&B.

● COMPILATIONS: *Blues Roots* (United Artists 1972) ★★, *Bad Dreams* (United Artists 1973) ★★, *Funky Mule* (DJM 1975) ★★, *I'm Tore Up* (Red Lightnin' 1978) ★★, *All The Blues All The Time* (Ember 1980) ★★, *Hey Hey* (Red Lightnin' 1984) ★★★, *Rockin' Blues* (Stateside 1986) ★★★, *Ike Turner And His Kings Of Rhythm Volumes 1 & 2* (Ace 1988) ★★★, *My Confessions* (Starforce 1988) ★★★, *Talent Scout Blues* (Ace 1988) ★★★, *Rhythm Rockin' Blues* (Ace 1995) ★★★, *Without Love I Have Nothing* (Juke Blues 1996) ★★, *My Blues Country* (Mystic 1997) ★★, *Ike's Instrumentals* (Ace 2000) ★★★, *Here And Now* (Koch 2001) ★★★, *The Sun Sessions* (Varèse Sarabande 2001) ★★★.

● FURTHER READING: *Takin' Back My Name: The Confessions Of Ike Turner*, Ike Turner with Nigel Cawthorne.

TURNER, JESSE LEE

b. c. late 30s, Bowling, Texas, USA. Turner was an Elvis Presley look-alike and sound-alike who placed one single, 'The Little Space Girl', in the US Top 20 in 1959 before fading from the national spotlight. He first recorded for Fraternity Records with no success. The novelty song that brought him his only brush with fame was a period piece on Carlton Records about visiting space aliens, recorded with a speeded-up voice similar to the then-popular Chipmunks recordings. Turner's follow-up recordings, including 'Thinkin'' and 'Baby Please Don't Tease' (on one record), and 'Do I Worry (Yes I Do)' on Top Rank Records, did not follow the one hit into the charts. He later recorded for the Sudden and GNP labels, again without success.

TURNER, SAMMY

b. Samuel Black, 2 June 1932, Paterson, New Jersey, USA. Turner briefly achieved fame in the late 50s as a rock 'n' roll balladeer, whose speciality was recycled pop songs of the past, particularly those by Guy Lombardo. His most notable record was a remake of a Sammy Kaye hit from 1949, 'Lavender Blue' (number 14 R&B/ number 3 pop), in 1959. Three follow-ups were similarly remakes of old pop hits: 'Always' (number 2 R&B/number 20 pop), a frequently recorded pop song, and a notable hit for Vincent

Lopez in 1926 and Guy Lombardo in 1945; 'Symphony' (number 82 pop), a hit for Freddy Martin, Guy Lombardo, and others in 1946; and 'Paradise' (number 13 R&B/number 46 pop), a Guy Lombardo hit from 1932. Turner's only success in the UK was with 'Always', which went to number 26. Although essentially a pop performer, because of his African-American heritage Turner also garnered considerable success on the R&B charts. However, he was unable to make the transition into the soul era, and rapidly faded as a recording artist after 1960.
● ALBUMS: *Lavender Blue Moods* (Big Top 1962) ★★.

TURNER, TITUS

b. Georgia, USA. A singer and songwriter, Turner made his first records for OKeh Records in 1951, but his first big success came in 1955 when Little Willie John had a Top 10 R&B hit with the Turner composition 'All Around The World'. The song was revived as 'Grits Ain't Groceries' by Little Milton in 1969. Turner made other singles for Wing and Atlantic Records before he had his first hits in 1959 with a pair of 'answer' songs to current bestsellers by Lloyd Price, a singer with a similar style to Turner's. 'The Return Of Stag-O-Lee' (King Records) was a follow-up to 'Stagger Lee' while Turner's 'We Told You Not To Marry' (Glover Records), was a riposte to 'I'm Gonna Get Married'. In 1961, Turner had a minor pop hit with a revival of 'Sound Off', produced by Al Gallico on Jamie, but this was overshadowed by Ray Charles' success with 'Sticks And Stones', the powerful gospel blues that is Turner's best-known composition. During the 60s, Turner discovered blues singer Tommy Tucker and worked with producer Herb Abramson. He continued to record a range of blues, soul, novelty and disco material for such companies as Josie, Atco Records, Philips Records and Mala.
● ALBUMS: *Sound Off* (Jamie 1961) ★★★.

TWARDZIK, DICK

b. Richard Twardzik, 30 April 1931, Boston, Massachusetts, USA, d. 1955, Paris, France. Twardzik was an original pianist and composer whose promising career was cut short by his untimely death. His meagre discography suggests that, had he survived, he would have flourished in the young *avant garde* movement of the late 50s. Twardzik started playing when he was nine years old. He pursued an education in classical music at the Longy School of Music in Cambridge, Massachusetts, and the New England Conservatory, but from the age of 14 he played professionally with many of the great names of swing and bop, including Charlie Parker, Lionel Hampton, Chet Baker and Serge Chaloff. He recorded with Chaloff and Baker in 1954/5, contributing compositions to the former, and in no small way ensuring the classic status of both discs. Twardzik recorded only once under his own name, a trio session including the composition 'Albuquerque Social Swim' which in its

extraordinary percussive attack and bizarre creativity emphasizes the pianist's originality. Twardzik summed up his approach: 'Development is not my primary consideration. The ability to project ever-changing emotions or moods, plus rhythmic freedom, is far more important to me'.
● ALBUMS: *Trio: Russ Freeman/Richard Twardzik* (Pacific Jazz 1956) ★★★, *The Last Set* (Pacific Jazz 1962) ★★★, *1954 Improvisations* 1954 recordings (New Artists 1998) ★★★.

U

V

Uncle Cyp And Aunt Sap

A popular husband-and-wife comedy duo, Uncle Cyp (b. Laurence Lemarr Brasfield, 1 March 1888, Smithville, Mississippi, USA, d. 6 September 1966, Raymondsville, Texas, USA) and Aunt Sap (b. Neva Inez Fisher Greevi, 14 March 1889, Luther, Michigan, USA, d. 19 March 1980, Raymondsville, Texas, USA) married *circa* 1906 and put together a comedy act that featured a rustic couple. Brasfield initially played a country hayseed character known as Boob, which became Cyprus, and eventually they adopted the names of Uncle Cyp and Aunt Sap. They first worked on various tent and vaudeville shows, including the Bisbee Comedians, all over the USA, before they became regulars on the original *Ozark Jubilee*, when it was formed. They were the only act to play on the show from its beginning until it closed in 1961, whereupon they retired from showbusiness. Brasfield, who died of lung cancer in 1966, was an elder brother of *Grand Ole Opry* comedian Rod Brasfield, who at one time worked with him on the vaudeville circuit.

Vale, Jerry

b. Genaro Louis Vitaliano, 8 July 1932, Bronx, New York, USA. A popular singer, especially of ballads, with several chart hits to his credit during the 50s and 60s, Vale had studied piano and worked as a shoeshine boy while still at school. Later, he was employed in an electrical component factory, and sang in his spare time. After winning a talent contest at the Club del Rio, he stayed there for over a year, and then, while performing at the Enchanted Room in New York, he was spotted by Guy Mitchell, who recommended him to Columbia Records' A&R manager, Mitch Miller. His first chart entry for the label, 'You Can Never Give Me Back My Heart' (1953), on which he was accompanied by Percy Faith And His Orchestra, was followed by 'Two Purple Shadows', 'I Live Each Day', 'Innamorata' and 'You Don't Know Me' (1956). Despite the 60s beat boom, Vale registered in the bestsellers lists with singles such as 'Have You Looked Into Your Heart?' (1964), and entered the US Top 40 album chart six times between 1963 and 1966. He continued to be popular in clubs and on television during the 70s and 80s, and, in 1988, was the guest of honour at a Friars Club dinner, held to celebrate his long and successful career. Vale wound up the proceedings by singing a few favourites, including his signature tune, 'Al Di La', the winner of the San Remo Song Festival in 1961.

● ALBUMS: *I Remember Buddy* (Columbia 1958) ★★, *I Remember Russ* (1958) ★★, *Same Old Moon* (1959) ★★, *I Have But One Heart* (Columbia 1962) ★★★, *Arrivederci Roma* (Columbia 1963) ★★★★, *Language Of Love* (Columbia 1963) ★★★, *Till The End Of Time* (Columbia 1964) ★★★★, *Be My Love* (Columbia 1964) ★★★★, *Moonlight Becomes You* (Columbia 1965) ★★★, *Have You Looked Into Your Heart* (Columbia 1965) ★★★, *Standing Ovations* (Columbia 1965) ★★★, *There Goes My Heart* (Columbia 1965) ★★★, *Everybody Loves Somebody* (Columbia 1966) ★★★, *Great Moments On Broadway* (Columbia 1966) ★★★, *It's Magic* (Columbia 1966) ★★★, *The Impossible Dream* (Columbia 1967) ★★★, *Time Alone Will Tell* (Columbia 1967) ★★★, *You Don't Have To Say You Love Me* (Columbia 1968) ★★★, *This Guy's In Love With You* (Columbia 1968) ★★★, *Till* (Columbia 1969) ★★★, *Where's The Playground Susie?* (Columbia 1969) ★★, *With Love Jerry Vale* (Columbia 1969) ★★, *Jerry Vale Sings 16 Greatest Hits Of The 60s* (Columbia 1970) ★★, *Let It Be* (Columbia 1970) ★★, *Jerry Vale Sings The Great Hits Of Nat King Cole* (Columbia 1972) ★★.

● COMPILATIONS: *Greatest Hits* (Columbia 1960) ★★★, *More Greatest Hits* (Columbia 1967) ★★★.

VALENS, RITCHIE

b. Richard Steve Valenzuela, 13 May 1941, Pacoima, Los Angeles, California, USA, d. 3 February 1959, Iowa, USA. Valens was the first major Hispanic-American rock star, the artist who popularized the classic 50s hit 'La Bamba'. He grew up in the city of Pacoima, California, and was raised in poverty. His parents separated when he was a child and Valens lived with his father until the latter's death in 1951. Afterwards he lived with his mother and brothers and sisters, but occasionally they stayed with other relatives who introduced him to traditional Mexican music. He also enjoyed cowboy songs by Roy Rogers and Gene Autry and began playing in junior high school. It was while attending school that Valens was first exposed to R&B music and rock 'n' roll. In 1956 he joined the Silhouettes (not the group that recorded 'Get A Job'), who performed at record hops in the San Fernando Valley area. Valens also performed solo and was heard by Bob Keane of Del-Fi Records, who took him into Gold Star Studios to record several songs. (Keane also shortened the singer's name from Valenzuela to Valens and added the 't' to Richie.)

A session band including Earl Palmer (drums), Carol Kaye (guitar), Red Collendar (stand-up bass), Ernie Freeman (piano) and Rene Hall (guitar) played behind Valens (who also played guitar). Their first single, the Valens original 'Come On, Let's Go', reached number 42 in the USA, and following its release the singer went on an 11-city US tour. In October 1958 the single 'Donna'/'La Bamba' was issued. Contrary to popular belief it was actually the ballad 'Donna', written by Valens about his high school friend Donna Ludwig, that was the bigger hit, reaching number 2. 'La Bamba', the b-side, only reached number 22 in the USA but has proved to be the more fondly remembered song. 'La Bamba' was a traditional huapango song from the Vera Cruz region of eastern Mexico, performed as early as World War II, and sung at weddings. (A huapango is a Mexican song consisting of nonsense verses, the meaning of the lyrics often known only to the composer.) Valens was reportedly reluctant to record the song, fearing its Spanish lyrics would not catch on with American record buyers. Following the record's release, Valens again went on tour, performing in California, Hawaii and on the *American Bandstand* show in Philadelphia.

It was during the winter part of the tour that Valens and his fellow performers met their fate, choosing to charter a small aeroplane rather than ride to the next concert site in a bus whose heater had broken. It was on 3 February 1959 when he, Buddy Holly and the Big Bopper were killed in an aeroplane crash following a concert in Clear Lake, Iowa. In the wake of Valens' death, several further singles were issued, only two of which – 'That's My Little Suzie' and 'Little Girl' – were minor chart hits. Three albums – *Ritchie Valens, Ritchie* and *Ritchie Valens In Concert At Pacoima Junior High* – were released from sessions recorded for Del-Fi and at a performance for Valens' classmates. Valens' status grew in the years following his death, culminating in the 1987 film *La Bamba,* a dramatized version of Valens' brief life and stardom. His songs have been covered by several artists, including the Hispanic-American group Los Lobos, who supervised the film's music and recorded 'La Bamba'. Their version, ironically, went to number 1 in 1987, outperforming Valens' original chart position.

● ALBUMS: *Ritchie Valens* (Del Fi 1959) ★★★★, *Ritchie* (Del Fi 1959) ★★★★, *Ritchie Valens In Concert At Pacoima Junior High* (Del Fi 1960) ★★★.

● COMPILATIONS: *His Greatest Hits* (Del Fi 1963) ★★★★, *His Greatest Hits Volume 2* (Del Fi 1965) ★★, *I Remember Ritchie Valens* (President 1967) ★★★, *The Best Of Ritchie Valens* (Rhino 1987) ★★★, *The Best Of Ritchie Valens* (Ace 1992) ★★★★, *The Ritchie Valens Story* (Ace 1993) ★★★★, *The Very Best Of Ritchie Valens* (Music Club 1995) ★★★, *Come On Let's Go!* 3-CD box set (Del-Fi 1998) ★★★★.

● FURTHER READING: *Ritchie Valens: The First Latino Rocker*, Beverly Mendheim. *Ritchie Valens 1941-1959: 30th Anniversary Memorial Series No. 2*, Alan Clark.

● FILMS: *Go Johnny Go* (1958).

VALENTINE, DICKIE

b. Richard Brice, 4 November 1929, London, England, d. 6 May 1971, Wales. An extremely popular singer in the UK during the 50s. At the age of three, Valentine appeared in the Jack Hulbert/Cicely Courtneidge comedy film *Jack's The Boy*. Later, as a backstage assistant at Her Majesty's Theatre in London, he became the protégé of Canadian stage star Bill O'Connor, who sent him for singing tuition. After playing the club circuit as a singer/impressionist he made his debut with the successful Ted Heath band in a broadcast from Aeolian Hall. Initially, Heath featured him as a straight ballad vocalist, but later allowed him to display his range of impressions, including those of Mario Lanza, Nat 'King' Cole, Billy Daniels and an accurate parody of Johnnie Ray. Good-looking, with dark, curly hair and a rich melodic voice, Valentine became Britain's number one band singer, a heart-throb who set the teenagers screaming.

In 1952 he recorded 'Never' (from the Mitzi Gaynor movie *Golden Girl*) and 'Lorelei' for Melodisc Records. In the following year he signed for Decca Records, and throughout the 50s produced a string of Top 20 hits, including 'Broken Wings', 'Endless', 'Mr Sandman', 'A Blossom Fell', 'I Wonder', 'Old Pianna Rag', 'Christmas Island', 'Venus', and two number 1 hits, 'The Finger Of Suspicion' (with the Stargazers) and 'Christmas Alphabet'. In 1959 he again made the Top 20 with 'One More Sunrise (Morgen)' for Pye Records, but groups rather than solo singers soon came to dominate the charts, and Valentine described his own 'Rock 'N' Roll Party' as 'the biggest clanger I have dropped'. At the height of his career he appeared on American television with a performance on the *Ed Sullivan Show*, and headlined at theatres where he had once been employed backstage. After the record hits dried up, he remained a firm favourite on the British club circuit, and while returning from one such engagement in Wales, died in a car crash in 1971.

● ALBUMS: *Presenting* (Decca 1954) ★★★, *Here Is Dickie Valentine* (Decca 1955) ★★★, *Over My Shoulder* (Decca 1956) ★★★★, *With Vocal Refrain By* (Decca 1958) ★★★, *Dickie* (Ace Of Clubs 1961) ★★★, *At The Talk Of The Town* (Philips 1967) ★★★, *My Favourite Songs* (1993) ★★★, with Lita Roza, Dennis Lotis, Joan Regan *Dickie Valentine & Friends* (1993) ★★★.

● COMPILATIONS: *The World Of Dickie Valentine* (Decca 1981) ★★★, *The Very Best Of Dickie Valentine* (Decca 1984) ★★★, *The Voice* (President 1989) ★★★, *The Best Of ...* (Soundwaves 1994) ★★★.

VALENTINES
From Harlem, New York, USA, the original members of this vocal group were lead Richard Barrett, tenor Raymond Briggs, second tenor Carl Hogan, baritone Mickey Francis and bass Ronnie Bright. (Hogan was replaced by Donald Razor in 1954, who in turn was replaced by Eddie Edgehill in 1955, who, in full circle, was replaced by Hogan in 1957.) The Valentines typified the New York City doo-wop sound. The group's first record, 'Tonight Kathleen' (1954), recorded for Hy Weiss' Old Town label, established the group locally. The following year the Valentines joined George Goldner's Rama label where they achieved a string of hits. The group had success with the up-tempo 'Lily Maebelle', followed by their biggest hit, 'The Woo Woo Train' (1956). Also recorded that year was the splendid ballad 'Nature's Creation'. The Valentines made their last record in 1957. Barrett was becoming more involved in the backroom aspect of the recording industry, having discovered and brought Frankie Lymon And The Teenagers to Goldner and also having begun regular production duties with the Chantels. Bright later joined the Cadillacs and the Coasters, and was the bass player on Johnny Cymbal's 'Mr. Bassman'.

● COMPILATIONS: *The Best Of The Valentines* (Collectables 1991) ★★★.

VALINO, JOE
b. 9 March 1929, Philadelphia, Pennsylvania, USA. A pop-jazz vocalist in the mode of Frank Sinatra, Valino belongs to a breed of pop singers who were generally swept away in the late 50s with the advent of rock 'n' roll. His one hit, 'Garden Of Eden', was a pop confection, but it had enough teen-appeal to reach many of the same buyers of rock 'n' roll in 1956. He had minor success in the UK as well with the song, which went to number 23. As a youngster, Valino was proficient at piano and guitar as well as at singing, and by the age of 13 was on the road touring. He sang in several bands, notably those of Charlie Ventura and Woody Herman, before beginning his recording career in 1950 on the Philadelphia-based Gotham label. He was thwarted in gaining his first hit with 'Learnin' The Blues' in 1955 when it was covered

by Frank Sinatra. He moved to Los Angeles in the 60s and acted in several motion pictures, notably *The Commitment* (1976).

● ALBUMS: *Sinner Or Saint* (1967) ★★, *Atlantic City To MacArthur Park* (1968) ★★★.

VALMOUTH
A British cult musical that shocked some, is fondly remembered by many, and – so the story goes – is understood by relatively few. *Valmouth* opened on 2 October 1958 at the Lyric Theatre, Hammersmith, which is located a few miles away from the glamorous West End. It was adapted from the 'scandalous' works of Ronald Firbank by Sandy Wilson, whose smash-hit *The Boy Friend* was coming to the end of its five-year run at Wyndhams Theatre. Many wise and learned beings have attempted unsuccessfully to fathom the mysteries of this show, but what seems to be clear is that Valmouth is one of those essentially English spa towns, where life-enhancing benefits of a somewhat bizarre kind can be had by visitors and residents alike. In the case of Valmouth, the residents are mostly centenarians, and the main benefits involve an abnormally long and active sex life. The inhabitants include Mrs. Yajnavalka (Bertice Reading), the black masseuse with the 'magic fingers', who provides a variety of advice and services to Grannie Took (Doris Hare) and her granddaughter Thetis (Patsy Rowlands). Thetis imagines she is to be the bride of Captain Dick Thoroughfare (Alan Edwards), heir to Mrs Hurstpierpoint (Barbara Couper), the Catholic châtelaine of Hare Hatch House ('the former favourite of a King, but for just a few minutes'). In actual fact, Captain Dick has already married Mrs. Yajnavalka's niece, Niri-Esther (Maxine Daniels). It's that complicated. Another familiar figure in the area is Lady Parvula de Panzoust (Fenella Fielding), an ageing nymphomaniac – but she is just visiting.

The song mostly associated with the show is 'My Big Best Shoes', joyously performed by Bertice Reading, but there were other memorable moments too in Wilson's wonderfully witty score. These included 'Just Once More' and 'Only A Passing Phase' (both Fielding), 'Magic Fingers', 'Mustapha', 'The Cry Of The Peacock', 'Little Girl Baby' (all Reading), 'I Will Miss You' (Hare and Reading), and 'I Loved A Man', 'What Then Can Make Him Come So Slow', 'All The Girls Were Pretty', 'Lady Of The Manor', 'What Do I Want With Love', 'Where The Trees Are Green With Parrots', and 'My Talking Day'. *Valmouth* ran for 84 performances at the Lyric, but by the time the show transferred to the Saville Theatre in the West End on 27 January 1959, Bertice Reading had returned to America, to be replaced by the young up-and-coming jazz singer Cleo Laine. A further run of 102 performances to frequently puzzled and offended audiences, was followed by complete rejection in New York where the show was withdrawn after less than two weeks. Over 20 years later in May 1982, *Valmouth* was revived at the Chichester Festival Theatre with several of the original cast, including Bertice Reading and

Fenella Fielding, who were joined by pop-star-turned-actor Mark Wynter as Captain Dick. The production was highly acclaimed, and although it is inconceivable that audiences would be even slightly outraged by this show nowadays, no impresario has so far stepped forward to present it in London.

VAN HEUSEN, JIMMY

b. Edward Chester Babcock, 26 January 1913, Syracuse, New York, USA, d. 6 February 1990, Rancho Mirage, California, USA. Van Heusen was an extremely popular and prolific composer from the late 30s through to the 60s, particularly for movies. He was an affable, high-living, fun-loving character. His main collaborators were lyricists Johnny Burke and Sammy Cahn. While still at high school, Van Heusen worked at a local radio station, playing piano and singing. He changed his name to Van Heusen, after the famous shirt manufacturer. In the early 30s he studied piano and composition at Syracuse University, and met Jerry Arlen, son of composer Harold Arlen. Arlen Snr. gave Van Heusen the opportunity to write for Harlem's Cotton Club Revues. His big break came in 1938 when bandleader Jimmy Dorsey wrote a lyric to Van Heusen's tune for 'It's The Dreamer In Me'. Ironically, the song was a big hit for rival bandleader Harry James. In the same year Van Heusen started working with lyricist Eddie DeLange.

Their songs included 'Deep In A Dream', 'All This And Heaven Too', 'Heaven Can Wait' (a number 1 hit for Glen Gray), 'This Is Madness' and 'Shake Down The Stars' (a hit for Glenn Miller). In 1939 they wrote the score for the Broadway musical Swingin' The Dream, a jazzy treatment of Shakespeare's A Midsummer Night's Dream. Despite the presence in the cast of the all-star Benny Goodman Sextet, Louis Armstrong, Maxine Sullivan, and the Deep River Boys, plus the song 'Darn That Dream', the show folded after only 13 performances. In 1940 Van Heusen was placed under contract to Paramount Pictures, and began his association with Johnny Burke. Their first songs together included 'Polka Dots And Moonbeams' and 'Imagination', both hits for the Tommy Dorsey Orchestra, with vocals by Frank Sinatra, who was to have an enormous effect on Van Heusen's later career. After contributing to the Fred Allen-Jack Benny comedy film Love Thy Neighbor (1940), Van Heusen and Burke supplied songs for 16 Bing Crosby films through to 1953, including 'It's Always You' (Road To Zanzibar), 'Road To Morocco', 'Moonlight Becomes You' (Road To Morocco), 'Sunday, Monday, Or Always' (Dixie), 'Swinging On A Star' (which won the 1944 Academy Award, from the film Going My Way), 'Aren't You Glad You're You?' (The Bells Of St Mary's), 'Personality' (Road To Utopia), 'But Beautiful', 'You Don't Have To Know The Language', 'Experience' (Road To Rio), 'If You Stub Your Toe On the Moon', 'Busy Doing Nothing' (A Connecticut Yankee In King Arthur's Court) and 'Sunshine Cake' (Riding High).

Besides working on other films, Van Heusen and

Burke also wrote the score for the 1953 Broadway musical Carnival In Flanders, which contained the songs 'Here's That Rainy Day' and 'It's An Old Spanish Custom'. Other Van Heusen songs during this period include 'Oh, You Crazy Moon', 'Suddenly It's Spring' and 'Like Someone In Love' (all with Burke). The last song received a memorable delivery from Frank Sinatra on his first album, Songs For Young Lovers, in 1953, as did 'I Thought About You', on Sinatra's Songs For Swinging Lovers. Van Heusen also wrote, along with comedian Phil Silvers, one of Sinatra's special songs, dedicated to his daughter, 'Nancy (With The Laughing Face)'.

When Burke became seriously ill in 1954 and was unable to work for two years, Van Heusen began a collaboration with Sammy Cahn. Cahn had recently ended his partnership with Jule Styne in style by winning an Oscar for their title song to the film Three Coins In The Fountain (1954). The new team had immediate success with another title song, for the 1955 Sinatra comedy, The Tender Trap, and then won Academy Awards for their songs in two more Sinatra films: 'All The Way' (from the Joe E. Lewis biopic, The Joker Is Wild) in 1957, and 'High Hopes' (from A Hole In The Head) in 1959. They also contributed songs to several other Sinatra movies, including 'Ain't That A Kick In The Head' (Ocean's 11), 'My Kind Of Town', 'Style' (Robin And The Seven Hoods), the title songs to A Pocketful Of Miracles, Come Blow Your Horn and several of Sinatra's bestselling albums, such as Come Fly With Me, Only The Lonely, Come Dance With Me, No One Cares, Ring-A-Ding-Ding and September Of My Years. Van Heusen and Cahn also produced his successful Timex television series (1959-60).

They won their third Academy Award in 1963 for 'Call Me Irresponsible', from the film Papa's Delicate Condition, and contributed songs to many other movies, including 'The Second Time Around' (High Time), and the title songs for Say One For Me, Where Love Has Gone, Thoroughly Modern Millie and Star!. The duo also supplied the songs for a musical version of Thornton Wilder's classic play Our Town, which included 'Love And Marriage' and 'The Impatient Years'. They wrote the scores for two Broadway musicals, Skyscraper in 1965 ('Everybody Has The Right To Be Wrong', 'I'll Only Miss Her When I Think Of Her') and Walking Happy in 1966, starring Norman Wisdom. From then on, Van Heusen concentrated on his other interests such as music publishing (he had formed a company with Johnny Burke in 1944), photography, flying his own aeroplanes, and collecting rare manuscripts by classical composers. He also continued to make television appearances, especially on tribute shows for composers. He died in 1990, after a long illness.

VAN WALLS, HARRY

b. Harold Eugene Vann Walls, 24 August 1918, Millersboro, Kentucky, USA. Van Walls was raised in Charleston, West Virginia, by his music teacher mother, and learned to play piano at a very early age, accompanying the local church choir. His

attention switched to blues and jazz in his teens with Jay McShann becoming a particularly potent influence. Soon he began playing dates locally, both with bands and as a solo pianist and vocalist. In 1949 Van Walls and his band travelled to New York to back tenor saxophonist Frank 'Floorshow' Culley at his debut session for the fledgling Atlantic label, and there he remained to provide the distinctive piano part to the famed Atlantic R&B Sound on the records of Granville 'Stick' McGhee, Ruth Brown, Joseph 'Joe' Morris, the Drifters, the Clovers and Big Joe Turner. In 1954 Van Walls eased up on the session work to join a band, the Nite Riders, who had a solid career recording for Grand, Apollo (for whom they recorded the classic 'Women And Cadillacs'), Teen/Sound and a host of other licensees. In 1963 Van Walls left the group to settle in Canada, but was rediscovered by *Whiskey, Women And Song* magazine in 1987 and was persuaded to record again.
● ALBUMS: *They Call Me Piano Man* (1989) ★★★.

VANCE, DICK
b. Richard Thomas Vance, 28 November 1915, Mayfield, Kentucky, USA, d. 31 July 1985, New York City, New York, USA. Vance took up the trumpet after first playing the violin. He played professionally with various bands in Cleveland, where he was raised, and in the north-east. His first name-band engagement came in 1934 when he joined Lillian Armstrong, and he then played with Willie Bryant and others before joining Fletcher Henderson in 1936. In 1939 he joined Chick Webb shortly before the leader's death and stayed on with the band under Ella Fitzgerald. By this time Vance was writing arrangements extensively and during the 40s this activity took precedence over his playing. His arrangements, meanwhile, were being performed by bands led by Cab Calloway, Redman, Harry James and Earl 'Fatha' Hines. In the early 50s he played in and wrote arrangements for Duke Ellington's orchestra. In the mid-50s he formed his own band, occasionally sharing leadership with Taft Jordan, with which he played several residencies, including one at the Savoy Ballroom in Harlem. He also played on numerous recording sessions with many leaders. A competent player, Vance's most important contribution to jazz and, in particular, to big band jazz, was his talent for arranging.
● ALBUMS: with Fletcher Henderson *Sextet* (Alamac 1950) ★★★★, as arranger *Ellington '55* (Capitol 1953) ★★★★, with the Henderson All Stars *The Big Reunion* (Jazztone 1957) ★★★.

VANGUARD RECORDS
Formed in 1950 in New York City, Vanguard Records became one of the most important US folk and blues labels of the 50s and 60s. Brothers Maynard and Seymour Solomon founded the company and signed primarily classical and international/ethnic artists until 1954, when they began signing jazz acts. Among the jazz artists who recorded for the label were Louis Armstrong,

Larry Coryell, Count Basie, Stéphane Grappelli, Ruby Braff, Buck Clayton, Sadao Watanabe and Stomu Yamash'ta. In 1957 they recruited the Weavers, the most important folk group of its era. In 1959 they signed folk singer Joan Baez, who became their biggest selling artist. During the early 60s Vanguard hit its peak with a roster that included blues performers Mississippi John Hurt, Buddy Guy, Big Mama Thornton, Junior Wells, James Cotton, Skip James, Jimmy Rushing, Otis Spann, Pee Wee Crayton, Otis Rush, John Hammond, Johnny Shines and J.B. Hutto. In addition to Baez, the company's folk artists included Ian And Sylvia, Buffy Sainte-Marie, Eric Andersen, Mimi and Richard Farina, Odetta, Doc and Merle Watson, Paul Robeson and Tom Paxton. Vanguard also released country and bluegrass records, including performers Jerry Jeff Walker, the Clancy Brothers, Kinky Friedman and the Country Gentlemen.
Their catalogue also featured instrumentalists whose meditative music prefigured new age, such as John Fahey, Sandy Bull and Oregon. In the mid-60s Vanguard signed political protest-rockers Country Joe And The Fish, who became one of the label's most popular acts. Their 60s roster also included the Siegel-Schwall Blues Band and the Jim Kweskin Jug Band. In the early 70s the label ceased signing new acts, and briefly shifted direction at the end of that decade. During the 80s dance artists such as Alisha, who had a strong regional disco hit in the New York clubs with her 'Baby Talk', joined the organization. In 1986, the Solomon brothers sold Vanguard to the Welk Group, a company run by the son of bandleader Lawrence Welk, who did not take an active part in the running of the company. Vanguard has since reissued most of its original album catalogue on compact disc and began signing new artists again in 1990.
● COMPILATIONS: *The Best Of The Chicago Blues Volume One* (1988) ★★, *Greatest Folksingers Of The Sixties* (1988) ★★.

VAUGHAN, FRANKIE
b. Frank Abelson, 3 February 1928, Liverpool, England, d. 17 September 1999, High Wycombe, Buckingham-shire, England. While studying at Leeds College Of Art, Vaughan's vocal performance at a college revue earned him a week's trial at the Kingston Empire music hall. Warmly received, he went on to play the UK variety circuit, developing a stylish act with trademarks that included a top hat and cane, a particularly athletic side kick, and his theme song 'Give Me The Moonlight, Give Me The Girl' (Albert Von Tilzer-Lew Brown). His Russian-born maternal grandmother inspired his stage name by always referring to him as her 'Number Vorn' grandchild. After registering strongly in pre-chart days with 'That Old Piano Roll Blues', 'Daddy's Little Girl', 'Look At That Girl', and 'Hey, Joe', during the mid-to-late 50s Vaughan was consistently in the UK Top 30 with hits such as 'Istanbul (Not Constantinople)', 'Happy Days And Lonely Nights', 'Tweedle Dee', 'Seventeen', 'My

Boy-Flat Top', 'Green Door', 'Garden Of Eden' (number 1), 'Man On Fire'/'Wanderin' Eyes', 'Gotta Have Something In The Bank Frank' (with the Kaye Sisters), 'Kisses Sweeter Than Wine', 'Can't Get Along Without You'/'We Are Not Alone', 'Kewpie Doll', 'Wonderful Things', 'Am I Wasting My Time On You', 'That's My Doll', 'Come Softly To Me' (with the Kaye Sisters), 'The Heart Of A Man' and 'Walkin' Tall'.

In spite of the burgeoning beat boom, he continued to flourish in the 60s with hits including 'What More Do You Want', 'Kookie Little Paradise', 'Milord', 'Tower Of Strength' (number 1), 'Don't Stop Twist', 'Loop De Loop', 'Hey Mama', 'Hello Dolly', 'There Must Be A Way', 'So Tired' and 'Nevertheless' (1968). With his matinée idol looks he seemed a natural for films, and made his debut in 1956 in the Arthur Askey comedy, *Ramsbottom Rides Again*. This was followed by a highly acclaimed straight role in *These Dangerous Years*, and a musical frolic with the normally staid Anna Neagle in *The Lady Is A Square*. Other screen appearances included *The Heart Of A Man* with Anne Heywood, Tony Britton and Anthony Newley, and *It's All Over Town*, a pop extravaganza in which he was joined by then-current favourites such as Acker Bilk, the Bachelors, the Springfields, and the Hollies. In the early 60s, Vaughan began to experience real success in America, in nightclubs and on television. He was playing his second season in Las Vegas when he was chosen to star with Marilyn Monroe and Yves Montand in the 20th Century-Fox picture *Let's Make Love*. Although he gave a creditable performance, especially when he duetted with Monroe on Sammy Cahn and Jimmy Van Heusen's 'Incurably Romantic', his disaffection with Hollywood ensured that a US movie career was not pursued. At home, however, he had become an extremely well-established performer, headlining at the London Palladium and enjoying lucrative summer season work, appealing consistently to mainly family audiences. In 1985, he was an unexpected choice to replace James Laurenson as the belligerent Broadway producer Julian Marsh in the West End hit musical, *42nd Street*. A one-year run in the show ended with ill health and some acrimony. His career-long efforts for the benefit of young people, partly through the assignment of record royalties to bodies such as the National Association of Boys' Clubs, was recognized by an OBE in 1965 and a CBE in 1996. He was also honoured in 1993 when the Queen appointed him Deputy Lord Lieutenant of Buckinghamshire. In the preceding year he had undergone a life-saving operation to replace a ruptured main artery in his heart. However, in cabaret at London's Café Royal in 1994, the legendary side kick was still (gingerly) in evidence. He was awarded the CBE in 1997, and a year later BBC Radio 2 celebrated his 70th birthday with a documentary entitled *Mr. Moonlight*. In 1999 he experienced further health problems, leading to his death in September.

● ALBUMS: *Happy Go Lucky* (Philips 1957) ★★★, *Showcase* (Philips 1958) ★★★, *At The London Palladium* (Philips 1959) ★★★, *Let Me Sing And I'm Happy* (Philips 1961) ★★★, *Warm Feeling* (Philips 1961) ★★★, *Songbook* (1967) ★★★, *There Must Be A Way* (Columbia 1967) ★★★, *Double Exposure* (Columbia 1971) ★★★, *Frankie* (Columbia 1973) ★★★, *Frankie Vaughan's Sing Song* (One Up 1973) ★★★, *Sincerely Yours, Frankie Vaughan* (Pye 1975) ★★★, *Sings* (Columbia 1975) ★★★, *Someone Who Cares* (Pye 1976) ★★, *Seasons For Lovers* (Pye 1977) ★★★, *Moonlight And Love Songs* (SRT 1979) ★★, *Time After Time* (Hour Of Pleasure 1986) ★★★.

● COMPILATIONS: *The Very Best Of Frankie Vaughan* (EMI 1975) ★★★, *Spotlight On Frankie Vaughan* (Philips 1975) ★★★, *100 Golden Greats* (Ronco 1977) ★★★, *Golden Hour Presents* (Golden Hour 1978) ★★★, *Greatest Hits* (Spot 1983) ★★★, *Love Hits And High Kicks* (Creole 1985) ★★★, *Music Maestro Please* (PRT 1986) ★★★, *The Best Of The EMI Years* (EMI 1990) ★★★, *The Essential Recordings 1955-65* (1993) ★★★.

● FILMS: *Ramsbottom Rides Again* (1956), *Escape In The Sun* (1956), *These Dangerous Years* aka *Dangerous Youth* (1957), *The Lady Is A Square* (1959), *The Heart Of A Man* (1959), *Let's Make Love* (1960), *It's All Over Town* (1964).

VAUGHAN, MALCOLM

b. Abercynon, Mid Glamorgan, Wales. A popular ballad singer with a strong tenor voice, Vaughan first made an impression in the early 50s as the 'singing straight man' in a double act with comedian Kenny Earle. They were touring the UK variety circuit when Vaughan was spotted by EMI Records' recording manager Wally Ridley. In 1955, Vaughan had his first Top 10 hit on the HMV label with 'Every Day Of My Life', which stayed in the chart for four months. Several other hits followed through to 1959, including 'With Your Love', 'St. Therese Of The Roses', 'The World Is Mine', 'Chapel Of The Roses', 'My Special Angel', 'To Be Loved', 'More Than Ever (Come Prima)' and 'Wait For Me'. His UK television appearances included *Sunday Night At The London Palladium*, *Startime*, *Saturday Spectacular*, *Music Shop*, *Melody Dances* and *The Jack Jackson Show*. After surviving the initial onslaught of rock 'n' roll, Vaughan's recording career suffered, along with so many others of his style, in the face of the 60s beat boom. In the early part of the decade he still retained an association with Earle, although with variety on the wane, clubs and cabaret were the main showplaces. In 1990, *Malcolm Vaughan: The EMI Years* provided a reminder that he was still a popular nightclub attraction in the north of England.

● ALBUMS: *Hello, Malcolm Vaughan* (HMV 1959) ★★★.

● COMPILATIONS: *The Best Of Malcolm Vaughan* (One Up 1974) ★★★, *The Very Best Of Malcolm Vaughan – 16 Favourites Of The 50s* (MFP 1984) ★★★, *Malcolm Vaughan: The EMI Years* (EMI 1990) ★★★.

VAUGHAN, SARAH

b. Sarah Lois Vaughan, 27 March 1924, Newark, New Jersey, USA, d. 3 April 1990, Los Angeles, California, USA. Although she was not born into an especially musical home environment (her father was a carpenter and her mother worked in a laundry), the young Sarah Vaughan had plenty of contact with music-making. As well as taking piano lessons for nearly 10 years, she sang in her church choir and became the organist at the age of 12. Her obvious talent for singing won her an amateur contest at Harlem's Apollo theatre in 1942, and opportunities for a musical career quickly appeared. Spotted by Billy Eckstine, who was at the time singing in Earl 'Fatha' Hines' big band, she was invited to join Hines' band as a female vocalist and second pianist in 1943. Eckstine had been sufficiently impressed by Vaughan to give her a place in his own band, formed a year later.

It was here that she met fellow band members and pioneers of modern jazz Charlie Parker and Dizzy Gillespie. Recording with Eckstine's band in 1945, full as it was of modern stylists, gave her a fundamental understanding of the new music that characterized her entire career. After leaving Eckstine, she spent a very short time with John Kirby's band, and then decided to perform under her own name. In 1947 she married trumpeter George Treadwell, whom she had met at the Cafe Society. Recognizing his wife's huge potential, Treadwell became her manager, as she began a decade of prolific recording and worldwide tours. She began by recording with Miles Davis in 1950, and then produced a torrent of albums in either a popular vein for Mercury Records, or more jazz-orientated material for their subsidiary label EmArcy. On the EmArcy recordings she appeared with Clifford Brown, Cannonball Adderley and members of the Count Basie band; these remain some of her most satisfying work.

By the 60s, as Vaughan rose to stardom, her jazz activity decreased slightly, and the emphasis remained on commercial, orchestra-backed recordings. It was not until the 70s that she began to perform and record with jazz musicians again on a regular basis. Vaughan performed at the 1974 Monterey Jazz Festival and made an album in 1978 with a quartet consisting of Oscar Peterson, Joe Pass, Ray Brown, and Louie Bellson. The following year she recorded the *Duke Ellington Song Book*, on which a large number of top jazz players appeared, including Zoot Sims, Frank Foster, Frank Wess, J.J. Johnson, and Pass. In 1980 she appeared in a much-heralded concert at Carnegie Hall, and returned to the Apollo to sing with Eckstine in a show recorded and broadcast by NBC-TV. She recorded an album of Latin tunes in 1987, and around this time appeared in another televised concert, billed as *Sass And Brass*. With a rhythm section featuring Herbie Hancock, Ron Carter, and Billy Higgins, as well as a collection of trumpeters including Dizzy Gillespie, Don Cherry, Maynard Ferguson, and Chuck Mangione, she proved herself still a musical force to be reckoned with. Tragically, she died of lung cancer in April 1990.

Sarah Vaughan won the *Esquire* New Star poll in 1945, the *Down Beat* poll (1947-52) and the *Metronome* poll (1948-52). She also sang at the White House as early as 1965; Vaughan's name was synonymous with jazz singing for two generations. Gifted with an extraordinary range and perfect intonation, she would also subtly control the quality of her voice to aid the interpretation of a song, juxtaposing phrases sung in a soft and warm tone with others in a harsh, nasal vibrato or throaty growl. Her knowledge of bebop, gained during her time with Eckstine's band, enabled her to incorporate modern passing tones into her sung lines, advancing the harmonic side of her work beyond that of her contemporaries. Her recordings will continue to influence vocalists for many years to come. Vaughan probably ranks as a close second only to Ella Fitzgerald in terms of influence, vocal range and sheer, consistent brilliance.

● ALBUMS: *Sarah Vaughan* reissued as *Sarah Vaughan In Hi Fi* (Columbia 1950) ★★★★, *Sarah Vaughan Sings* 10-inch album (MGM 1951) ★★★, *Tenderly* 10-inch album (MGM 1952) ★★★, *Hot Jazz* 1944 recordings (Remington 1953) ★★★, *Early Sarah* 10-inch album (Allegro 1953) ★★★, *Images* reissued as *Swingin' Easy* (EmArcy 1954) ★★★★, *Sarah Vaughan* (Allegro 1955) ★★★, *My Kinda Love* (MGM 1955) ★★★, *After Hours With Sarah Vaughan* (Columbia 1955) ★★★★, *Sarah Vaughan Sings With John Kirby* 10-inch album (Riverside 1955) ★★★, *Divine Sarah* 10-inch album (Mercury 1955) ★★★, *Sarah Vaughan In The Land Of Hi-Fi* (EmArcy 1956) ★★★★, *Sarah Vaughan At The Blue Note* (Mercury 1956) ★★★, *Linger Awhile* (Columbia 1956) ★★★★, *Sassy* (EmArcy 1956) ★★★★, *Great Songs From Hit Shows* (Mercury 1957) ★★★★, *Sarah Vaughan Sings George Gershwin* (Mercury 1957) ★★★★, *Wonderful Sarah* (Mercury 1957) ★★★★, *In A Romantic Mood* (Mercury 1957) ★★★★, *Sarah Vaughan Concert* (Concord 1957) ★★★, *Close To You* (Mercury 1957) ★★★, *Sarah Vaughan And Billy Eckstine Sing The Best Of Irving Berlin* (Mercury 1958) ★★★★★, *Vaughan And Violins* (Mercury 1958) ★★★, *After Hours At The London House* (Mercury 1958) ★★★, *Tenderly* (Lion 1958) ★★, *Sarah Vaughan And Her Trio At Mr Kelly's* (Mercury 1958) ★★★, *No 'Count Sarah* (Mercury 1959) ★★★, with Eckstine *Billy And Sarah* (Lion 1959) ★★★, *The Magic Of Sarah Vaughan* (Mercury 1959) ★★★★, *Misty* (EmArcy 1959) ★★★★, *Dreamy* (Roulette 1960) ★★★★, *The Divine Sarah Vaughan* (Mercury 1960) ★★★★, with Count Basie *Count Basie/Sarah Vaughan* (Roulette 1960) ★★★★, *Divine One* (Roulette 1960) ★★★, *My Heart Sings* (Mercury 1961) ★★★, *After Hours* (Roulette 1961) ★★★★, *You're Mine, You* (Roulette 1962) ★★★, *Snowbound* (Roulette 1962) ★★★, *The Explosive Side Of Sarah* (Roulette 1962) ★★★, *Star Eyes* (Roulette 1963) ★★★, *The Lonely Hours* (Roulette 1963) ★★★★, *Sarah Sings Soulfully* (Roulette 1963) ★★★★, *Sassy Swings The Tivoli* (Mercury 1963) ★★★, *Vaughan With Voices* (Mercury 1964) ★★★, *Viva! Vaughan* (Mercury 1964) ★★★, with Dinah Washington, Joe Williams *We Three* (Roulette 1964) ★★★, *The World Of Sarah Vaughan* (Roulette 1964) ★★★, *Sweet 'N' Sassy* (Roulette 1964) ★★★, *Sarah Plus Two* (Roulette 1965) ★★★, *Sarah Vaughan Sings The*

Mancini Songbook (Mercury 1965) ★★★★, *The Pop Artistry Of Sarah Vaughan* (Mercury 1966) ★★★, *The New Scene* (Mercury 1966) ★★★, *Sassy Swings Again* (Mercury 1967) ★★★, *I'm Through With Love* (Xtra 1970) ★★★, *A Time In My Life* (Mainstream 1972) ★★★, with Michel Legrand *Sarah Vaughan/Michel Legrand* (Mainstream 1972) ★★★★, *Feelin' Good* (Mainstream 1973) ★★★, *The Summer Knows* (Mainstream 1973) ★★★, *Live In Japan* (Mainstream 1974) ★★★, *Sarah Vaughan And The Jimmy Rowles Quintet* (Mainstream 1975) ★★★, *More Sarah Vaughan – Live In Japan* (Mainstream 1976) ★★★, *I Love Brazil* (Pablo 1977) ★★★, with Louie Bellson, Ray Brown, Joe Pass, Oscar Peterson *How Long Has This Been Going On?* (Pablo 1978) ★★★, *Live At Ronnie Scott's* (Pye/Ronnie Scott's 1978) ★★★, *Duke Ellington Song Book One* (Pablo 1980) ★★★★, *Duke Ellington Song Book Two* (Pablo 1981) ★★★, *Songs Of The Beatles* (Atlantic 1981) ★★★, with Joe Comfort, Barney Kessel *The Two Sounds Of Sarah* (Vogue 1981) ★★★, *Send In The Clowns* (Pablo 1981) ★★★, *Crazy And Mixed Up* (Pablo 1982) ★★★★, *O, Some Brasileiro De* (RCA 1984) ★★★, *Jazz Fest Masters* 1969 recording (Jazz Masters 1992) ★★★★, *One Night Stand: Town Hall Concert 1947* (Blue Note 1997) ★★★★.

● COMPILATIONS: *Sarah Vaughan's Golden Hits!!!* (Mercury 1961) ★★★★, *Recorded Live* (EmArcy 1977) ★★★★, with Billy Eckstine (coupled with a Dinah Washington and Brook Benton collection) *Passing Strangers* (Mercury 1978) ★★★, shared with Ella Fitzgerald, Billie Holiday, Lena Horne *Billie, Ella, Lena, Sarah!* (Columbia 1980) ★★★★, *The Divine Sarah* 1946, 1947 recordings (Musicraft 1980) ★★★★, *Spotlight On Sarah Vaughan* (PRT 1984) ★★★, *The Sarah Vaughan Collection* (Deja Vu 1985) ★★★, *The Rodgers And Hart Songbook* (Pablo 1985) ★★★★, *The Best Of Sarah Vaughan – Walkman Series* (Verve 1987) ★★★★, *The Complete Sarah Vaughan On Mercury, Vol. 1 (1954-1956)* 6-CD box set (Mercury 1988) ★★★★★, *The Complete Sarah Vaughan On Mercury, Vol. 2: Sings Great American Songs (1956-1957)* 5-CD box set (Mercury 1988) ★★★★, *The Complete Sarah Vaughan On Mercury, Vol. 3: Great Show On Stage (1954-1956)* 6-CD box set (Mercury 1988) ★★★★★, *The Complete Sarah Vaughan On Mercury, Vol. 4 (1963-1967)* 6-CD box set (Mercury 1988) ★★★★★, *I'll Be Seeing You* 1949-62 recordings (Vintage Jazz Classics 1990) ★★★★, *The Singles Sessions* (Capitol/Blue Note 1991) ★★★★, *The Roulette Years* 1960-64 recordings (Roulette 1991) ★★★★, *The Columbia Years* 1949-53 recordings (Columbia 1991) ★★★★, *The Best Of Sarah Vaughan* 1978-81 recordings (Pablo 1992) ★★★★, *The Essential Sarah Vaughan: The Great Songs* (Verve 1992) ★★★★, *16 Most Requested Songs* 1949-53 recordings (Columbia 1993) ★★★★, *The Essence Of Sarah Vaughan* (Columbia 1994) ★★★★, *Verve Jazz Masters 18: Sarah Vaughan* (Verve 1994) ★★★, *Verve Jazz Masters, Vol. 42* (Verve/PolyGram 1995) ★★★, *Everything I Have Is Yours* 1945-47 recordings (Drive Archive 1997) ★★★, *Ultimate Sarah Vaughan* (Verve 1997) ★★★★, *Sarah Vaughan 1944-1946* (Collectables 1997) ★★★, *Sarah Vaughan 1946-1947* (Collectables 1998) ★★★, *Very Best Of Sarah Vaughan: 'Round Midnight* (Collectables 1998) ★★★, *Gold Collection* (Fine Tune 1998) ★★, *Jazz Profile* (Blue Note 1998) ★★★, *Time After Time* 1944-47 recordings (Drive Archive 1998) ★★★, *The Man I Love* 1945-48 recordings (Musica Jazz 1998) ★★★★, *Sarah Vaughan 1944-54* recordings (Musica Jazz 1999) ★★★★, *Compact Jazz: Sarah Vaughan Live* 1957-63 recordings (Verve 1999) ★★★, *Finest Hour* 1949-64 recordings (Verve 2000) ★★★, *Linger Awhile* 1957, 1981 recordings (Pablo 2000) ★★★, *The Mystery Of Man* 1984 recording (Kokopelli 2000) ★★★, *In The City Of Lights* 1985 recording (Justin Time 2000) ★★★, *Brazilian Romance* 1987 recording (Columbia 2000) ★★★, *Ken Burns Jazz, The Definitive Sarah Vaughan* (Columbia/Legacy 2001) ★★★★.

● VIDEOS: *Sass And Brass* (Excalibur 1990), *The Divine One* (1993).

● FURTHER READING: *Sassy – The Life Of Sarah Vaughan*, Leslie Gourse.

VAUGHN, BILLY

b. Richard Vaughn, 12 April 1931, Glasgow, Kentucky, USA, d. 26 September 1991, Escondido, California, USA. An extremely successful orchestra leader, arranger and musical director during the 50s and early 60s. In 1952, singing baritone and playing piano, he formed the Hilltoppers vocal quartet, with Jimmy Sacca, Seymour Speigelman and Don McGuire. They had a string of US hits through to 1957, commencing in August 1952 with Vaughn's composition 'Trying', and in the following year with the million-selling 'P.S. I Love You'. When Vaughn left the group in 1955 to become musical director for Dot Records, the other three members continued together until the early 60s, when they too accepted jobs with Dot.

Throughout the 50s, Vaughn contributed significantly to Dot's chart success, particularly with his arrangements for the somewhat antiseptic 'cover-versions' of rock 'n' roll and R&B hits, especially those by black artists, who were unacceptable to some sections of the US audience. Most of the Fontane Sisters' hits, which were backed by Vaughn's Orchestra, were cover versions, including their million-seller, 'Hearts Of Stone', which was first released by the R&B group Otis Williams And The Charms. Others such examples included Gale Storm's cover version of Smiley Lewis' 'I Hear You Knocking', written by Dave Bartholomew and Pearl King, and several Pat Boone hits, including another Bartholomew number, 'Ain't That A Shame', originally released by the co-writer of the song, Fats Domino. Several of Vaughn's own instrumental hits were in the same vein; his first, 'Melody Of Love' (1954), was also successful for Frank Sinatra and Ray Anthony, the Four Aces and David Carroll. 'Shifting, Whispering Sands (Parts 1 & 2)' (with narration by Ken Nordine) was a hit for country singer Rusty Draper, and the classic 'Raunchy' was a million-seller for Sun Records' musical director, Bill Justis. Vaughn's other US Top 20 chart entries included 'When The Lilacs Bloom Again', 'Look For A Star' and German-born orchestra leader Bert Kaempfert's 'A Swingin' Safari'. Vaughn was very popular in Germany; his versions of 'Wheels', 'La Paloma', and a revival of the 1937 song 'Sail Along Silv'ry Moon', reputedly sold a million copies in that country alone. From 1958-70 Vaughn was ever-present in the US album charts with 36 titles entering the Top 200, including the 1960 number 1, *Theme From A Summer Place*. Having been one of the most successful orchestra leaders during the rock 'n' roll era, Vaughn seemed unable to recreate that level of success in the face of the 60s beat boom. Ironically, his last single of any significance, in 1966, was a cover version of the Beatles' 'Michelle'.

● ALBUMS: *Sail Along Silv'ry Moon* (Dot 1958) ★★★, *Billy Vaughn Plays The Million Sellers* (Dot 1958) ★★★, *Christmas Carols* (Dot 1958) ★★, *Billy Vaughn Plays* (Dot 1959) ★★, *Blue Hawaii* (Dot 1959) ★★★, *Golden Saxophones* (Dot 1959) ★★★, *Theme From A Summer Place* (Dot 1960) ★★★★, *Look For A Star* (Dot 1960) ★★★, *Theme From The Sundowners* (Dot 1960) ★★★★, *Orange Blossom Special And Wheels* (Dot 1961) ★★, *Golden Waltzes* (Dot 1961) ★★★, *Berlin Melody* (Dot 1961) ★★★, *Greatest String Band Hits* (Dot 1962) ★★★, *Chapel By The Sea* (Dot 1962) ★★, *A Swingin' Safari* (Dot 1962) ★★★★, *1962's Greatest Hits* (Dot 1963) ★★★, *Sukiyaki And 11 Hawaiian Hits* (Dot 1963) ★★, *Number 1 Hits, Volume 1* (Dot 1963) ★★★, *Blue Velvet And 1963's Great Hits* (Dot 1963) ★★★, *Forever* (Dot 1964) ★★★, *Another Hit Album!* (Dot 1964) ★★★, *Pearly Shells* (Dot 1964) ★★, *Mexican Pearls* (Dot 1965) ★★★, *Moon Over Naples* (Dot 1965) ★★★, *Michelle* (Dot 1966) ★★★, *Great Country Hits* (Dot 1966) ★★, *Alfie* (Dot 1966) ★★★★, *Sweet Maria* (Dot 1967) ★★★, *That's Life And Pineapple Market* (Dot 1967) ★★★, *Josephine* (Dot 1967) ★★★, *I Love You* (Dot 1967) ★★★, *Ode To Billy Joe* (Dot 1967) ★★, *A Current Set Of Standards* (Dot 1968) ★★★, *As Requested* (Dot 1968) ★★★, *Quietly Wild* (Dot 1969) ★★, *The Windmills Of Your Mind* (Dot 1969) ★★★, *True Grit* (Dot 1970) ★★★, *Winter World Of Love* (Dot 1970) ★★★.

● COMPILATIONS: *Golden Hits/The Best Of Billy Vaughn* (Dot 1967) ★★★, *The Best Of Billy Vaughn* (MFP 1974) ★★★, *Moonlight Serenade* (Lotus 1979) ★★★, *Melody Of Love* (Varèse Sarabande 1994) ★★★.

VEE JAY RECORDS
Founded in 1953 by Vivian 'Vee' Carter and James 'Jay' C. Bracken, this US independent record label rose from regional obscurity to a position as one of black music's leading outlets. Their initial signings included the Spaniels, who provided the company's first major success when their haunting doo-wop ballad, 'Goodnite Sweetheart, Goodnite', was a hit in the R&B and pop chart. The couple, now married, established their offices in Chicago's East 47th Street. Vivian's brother, Calvin Carter, also joined the company; this intuitive individual was responsible for attracting several important acts, including vocal groups the El Dorados and the Dells, as well as gospel artists the Staple Singers and the Swan Silvertones. Vee Jay's staff was considerably bolstered by the addition of Ewart Abner, whose business acumen did much to facilitate the label's meteoric rise. By the early 60s the Vee Jay roster included the Jerry Butler, Dee Clark and Gene Chandler, each of whom enjoyed popular success, while influential blues performers Jimmy Reed and John Lee Hooker recorded their best-known material for the outlet. However, by 1963 the label was encountering financial difficulties. Vee Jay had diversified into white pop by securing the Four Seasons, and had won the rights to the Beatles' early releases when Capitol Records declined their option. When the former act scored several hits, the label was unable to meet royalty payments and a protracted law suit ensued. Capitol then rescinded their Beatles' agreement; although Vee Jay latterly retained material already licensed, the rights to all future recordings were lost. This controversial period also saw Abner's departure, while the label moved its operations to Los Angeles. However, by 1965 Vee Jay was back in Chicago, with Abner reinstated to his former position. Such upheavals proved fatal. Unsettled artists moved to other outlets, and when interim manager Randy Wood sued for breach of contract, Vee Jay filed for bankruptcy. In May 1966, the company closed its offices and released its remaining employees. Arguably capable of rivalling Tamla/Motown if they had overcome their internal problems, Vee Jay nonetheless holds an important place in the development of black music. Abner eventually rose to become president of Motown, while James Bracken died in 1972 owning a record shop. Calvin Carter died in 1986, while Vivian Carter ran a radio station in her home-town of Gary, Indiana. She later died in 1989.

● COMPILATIONS: *Chicago Blues: The Vee Jay Era* (Charly 1997) ★★★★.

VELOURS
From New York, USA, the Velours – featuring the wonderfully expressive lead of Jerome Ramos, whose halting and vibrato-laden vocal style was one of the most intriguing in doo-wop – were one of the most impressive groups of the doo-wop era. Other members included Charles Moffett, John Pearson, Don Haywoode, John Cheatdom and pianist Calvin Hayes. The group first recorded for Baton, although nothing was released, but in 1957 they joined Onyx and success followed. Among their songs, 'Can I Come Over Tonight?', 'This Could Be The Night' and 'Romeo' were particularly impressive. After some unsuccessful singles for Studio and Gone, the Velours broke up in the early 60s. In 1965 four members of the group – Don Haywoode, Jerome Ramos, John Cheatdom and Richie Pitts – regrouped. In 1967 they toured the UK and were informed when they arrived that they would be appearing as the 'Fabulous Temptations'. However, the following year, with new member Richie Pitts, they began recording as the Fantastics, and gained far greater success than they had ever achieved as the Velours.

VERDON, GWEN

b. Gwyneth Evelyn Verdon, 13 January 1925, Culver City, Los Angeles, California, USA, d. 18 October 2000, Woodstock, Vermont, USA. A vivacious, red-headed dancer, actress and singer, Verdon could be funny or tender, sassy or seductive, depending on the music and the mood. She studied dancing with Ernest Belcher from an early age, but initially followed her first husband into journalism, reviewing films and nightclub acts. After assisting the notable choreographer Jack Cole on *Magdalena* (1948), Verdon made her first appearance on Broadway two years later in *Alive And Kicking*. However, it was Cole Porter's *Can-Can* that made her a star in 1953. Her thrilling performance as the (very) high-kicking Claudine gained her a Tony Award, and she won another two years later for her portrayal of the bewitching Lola in *Damn Yankees* ('Two Lost Souls', 'Whatever Lola Wants', 'Who's Got The Pain?'), a show that was brilliantly choreographed by her future husband, Bob Fosse. He restaged his innovative dance sequences for the 1958 film version, for which, instead of casting an already established star, Verdon was invited to reprise her Broadway role. From then on, Fosse choreographed and/or directed all Verdon's shows. In 1957 she played Anna Christie in *New Girl In Town* ('Ven I Valse', 'On The Farm', 'It's Good To Be Alive', 'If That Was Love'), a musical adaptation of Eugene O'Neill's 1921 play, and on this occasion she shared the Tony with fellow cast member Thelma Ritter – the first time there had been a Tony-tie. In 1959, Verdon won outright when she starred with Richard Kiley in *Redhead*. After that, Broadway audiences had to wait another seven years before they saw Verdon on the musical stage, but the wait was more than worthwhile. In *Sweet Charity* (1966) she played a dancehall hostess with a heart of gold who yearns for marriage and roses round the door. Cy Coleman and Dorothy Fields provided her with some lovely songs, including 'If My Friends Could See Me Now' and 'There's Gotta Be Something Better Than This'. Verdon's final Broadway musical was *Chicago* (1975), a razzle-dazzle affair set in the roaring 20s, full of hoods and Chita Rivera. She then turned once more to films. She had appeared in several during the 50s, including *David And Bathsheba*, *On The Riviera*, *Meet Me After The Show*, *The Merry Widow*, *The I Don't Care Girl*, *The Farmer Takes A Wife*, as well as *Damn Yankees*. In 1983, she played a choreographer in the television movie *Legs*, and had several other good roles in big-screen features such as *The Cotton Club*, *Cocoon*, *Nadine*, *Cocoon: The Return* and *Alice*. In 1992 she donated a substantial amount of material documenting her own career and that of her late husband, Bob Fosse (he died in 1987), to the Library of Congress. A year later, Gwen Verdon received the 1993 New Dramatists Lifetime Achievement Award at a ceremony in which fellow Broadway legends such as Richard Adler, Chita Rivera, Cy Coleman, John Kander, and Fred Ebb, gathered to pay tribute. She continued to be honoured throughout the 90s,

with the Broadway Theatre Institute's award for Lifetime Achievement in the Theatre, the Actors' Fund of America's Julie Harris Lifetime Achievement Award, and the National Medal of Arts, which she received from the US President in November 1998. During that year Verdon had been serving as Artistic Director on a tribute to her late husband entitled *Fosse: A Celebration In Dance And Song* which opened on Broadway in January 1999.

● FILMS: *David And Bathsheba* (1951), *On The Riviera* (1951), *Meet Me After The Show* (1951), *The Merry Widow* (1952), *Dreamboat* (1952), *The Mississippi Gambler* (1953), *The I Don't Care Girl* (1953), *The Farmer Takes A Wife* (1953), *Gentlemen Marry Brunettes* (1955), *Damn Yankees* aka *What Lola Wants* (1958), *The Cotton Club* (1984), *Cocoon* (1985), *Nadine* (1987), *Cocoon: The Return* (1988), *Alice* (1990), *Marvin's Room* (1996), *Bruno* (2000), *Walking Across Egypt* (2000).

VERRELL, RONNIE

b. 21 February 1926, Rochester, Kent, England. While playing in a boy's club band Verrell heard a professional drummer and immediately decided this was what he wanted to do. Seeing and hearing Gene Krupa in a film confirmed his ambition. In 1939 he took one lesson from Max Abrams, the noted British drummer and teacher, but was too impatient to take further lessons. Thereafter, he taught himself and was given his first chance to play in public in Wales, where he had been evacuated when the bombing of London began. On his return to Kent he joined the Claude Giddings band in Gillingham. The outfit was well known for the quality of its young musicians, who included Tommy Whittle and pianist Arthur Greenslade, who later worked with Vic Lewis and Shirley Bassey. Verrell also played with Carl Barriteau and the Londonaires band which was briefly popular in Germany. In 1948 Verrell auditioned for the Ted Heath band when Jack Parnell was considering moving on.

He failed the audition but was hired instead by Cyril Stapleton. Three years later Parnell finally left Heath, and was replaced briefly by Basil Kirchin before Verrell took over the drum chair. This was the time when the Heath band reached its peak and as cracks appeared in the UK Musicians Union ban on visiting Americans, Heath was one of the first to tour the USA (on a reciprocal arrangement that brought Stan Kenton to the UK). The Heath band was part of a package that included June Christy, the Four Freshmen and Nat 'King' Cole and it culminated in a concert at Carnegie Hall. The band was a huge success and many of the individual musicians, Verrell among them, attracted favourable attention from critics and fans alike. Apart from the US tour, Verrell was with the Heath band on its Australasian tour. During his stint with the band Verrell was partly responsible for at least two of their chart successes in the UK. His solo feature on 'Skin Deep' helped the record to reach number 9 in 1954, and his lithely swinging backing assisted 'Swingin' Shepherd Blues' to its number 3 spot in 1958.

The band also had a Top 20 album success in 1962 with *Big Band Percussion*. After leaving Heath, Verrell worked extensively in television studio bands, among them the house band at ATV which was directed by Parnell. Subsequently, Verrell played in the Syd Lawrence band but continued to be active on television where he gained a kind of anonymous fame as 'Animal', the drummer on *The Muppet Show*. In the late 80s Verrell began playing occasionally with the Pizza Express All Stars in London and made infrequent appearances backing visiting American jazzmen, including Buddy Tate and Clark Terry. He also played in the recreated Ted Heath band led by Don Lusher. In the 90s he continued to divide his time between studio and jazz work. A solid danceband drummer and excellent timekeeper, Verrell was also explosive when it mattered and his work with the Heath band remains a high spot in the story of big band drumming in the UK.
● ALBUMS: with Ted Heath *Ted Heath At Carnegie Hall* (London 1957) ★★★, with Heath *Big Band Percussion* (Decca 1962) ★★★.

VINCENT, GENE
b. Vincent Eugene Craddock, 11 February 1935, Norfolk, Virginia, USA, d. 12 October 1971, Newhall, California, USA. One of the original bad boys of rock 'n' roll, the self-destructive Vincent was involved in a motorcycle crash in July 1955 and his left leg was permanently damaged. Discharged from the US Navy, he began appearing on country music radio and came under the wing of disc jockey 'Sheriff' Tex Davis, who supervised his recording of a demo of 'Be-Bop A-Lula'. In May 1956, the track was re-recorded at Capitol Records' Nashville studio, with backing by the Blue Caps. The original line-up comprised Cliff Gallup (lead guitar), Jack Neal (upright bass), Willie Williams (b. 1936, d. 28 August 1999; acoustic guitar) and Dickie Harrell (drums).
Weeks later, 'Be-Bop-A-Lula' stormed the charts, temporarily providing Capitol with their own version of Elvis Presley. The strength of the single lay in Vincent's engaging vocal and the loping guitar runs of the influential Gallup. Vincent's image was brooding, inarticulate and menacing and with such rock 'n' roll authenticity he was not easily marketable in the USA. His second single, 'Race With The Devil', failed to chart in his homeland, but proved successful in the UK, where he attracted a devoted following. Dogged by bad advice and often unsuitable material, Vincent rapidly lost the impetus that had thrust him to the centre stage as a rock 'n' roll icon. Even an appearance in the movie *The Girl Can't Help It* failed to arrest his commercial decline. A respite was offered by the million-selling 'Lotta Love', but line-up changes in the Blue Caps and a multitude of personal problems were conspiring against him. His damaged leg perpetually threatened to end his singing career and renewed injuries resulted in the limb being supported by a metal brace. Vincent's alcoholism and buccaneering road life made him a liability to promoters and by the late 50s, his career seemed in ruins.

He relocated to England, where Jack Good exacerbated his rebel image by dressing him in black leather and encouraging the star to accentuate his limp. Although he failed to retrieve past glories on record, he toured frequently and survived the car crash that killed his friend Eddie Cochran. Thereafter, he appeared regularly in the UK and France, having come under the wing of the notoriously proprietorial manager Don Arden. Increasingly redundant during the beat group era, his lifestyle grew more erratic and alcoholism made him a bloated and pathetic figure. A comeback album of sorts, *I'm Back And I'm Proud*, lacked sufficient punch to revitalize his career and he continued playing with pick-up groups, churning out his old repertoire. He often railed against old friends and grew increasingly disillusioned about the state of his career. Still regarded as a legend of rock 'n' roll and a true original, he seemed frustratingly stuck in a time warp and lacked any sense of a career pattern. The often intolerable pain he suffered due to his festering leg merely exacerbated his alcoholism, which in turn devastated his health. On 12 October 1971, his abused body finally succumbed to a bleeding ulcer and rock 'n' roll lost one of its genuinely great rebellious spirits.
● ALBUMS: *Bluejean Bop!* (Capitol 1956) ★★★★, *Gene Vincent And The Blue Caps* (Capitol 1957) ★★★, *Gene Vincent Rocks! And The Bluecaps Roll* (Capitol 1958) ★★★, *A Gene Vincent Record Date* (Capitol 1958) ★★★, *Sounds Like Gene Vincent* (Capitol 1959) ★★★, *Crazy Times!* (Capitol 1960) ★★★, *The Crazy Beat Of Gene Vincent* (Capitol 1963) ★★★, *Shakin' Up A Storm* (Columbia 1964) ★★★, *Bird Doggin'* reissued as *Ain't That Too Much* (London 1967) ★★★, *Gene Vincent* (London 1967) ★★, *I'm Back And I'm Proud* reissued as *The Bop They Couldn't Stop* (Dandelion 1970) ★★, *If Only You Could See Me Today* (UK) *The Day The World Turned Blue* (US) (Karma Sutra 1971) ★★.
● COMPILATIONS: *The Best Of Gene Vincent* (Capitol 1967) ★★★, *The Best Of Gene Vincent Volume 2* (Capitol 1968) ★★★, *Gene Vincent's Greatest* (Capitol 1969) ★★★, *Pioneers Of Rock Volume One* (Regal Starline 1972) ★★★, *The King Of Fools* (Regal Starline 1974) ★★★, *The Bop That Just Won't Stop* (Capitol 1974) ★★★, *Greatest Hits* (Capitol 1977) ★★★, *Greatest Hits Volume 2* (Capitol 1979) ★★★, *Rock On With Gene Vincent* (MFP 1980) ★★★, *The Gene Vincent Singles Album* (Capitol 1981) ★★★, *Dressed In Black* (Magnum Force 1982) ★★★, *Gene Vincent's Greatest Hits* (Fame 1982) ★★★, *From LA To 'Frisco* (Magnum Force 1983) ★★★, *For Collectors Only* (Magnum Force 1984) ★★★, *Forever Gene Vincent* (Rollin' Rock 1984) ★★★, *Born To Be A Rolling Stone* (Topline 1985) ★★★, *Gene Vincent: The Capitol Years* 10-LP box set (Charly 1987) ★★★★, *Into The Seventies* (See For Miles 1988) ★★★, *The EP Collection* (See For Miles 1989) ★★★, *The Gene Vincent Box Set* 6-CD box set (EMI 1990) ★★★★, *His 30 Original Hits* (Entertainers 1992) ★★★, *Rebel Heart Volume 1* (Magnum 1992) ★★★, *Be-Bop-A-Lula* (Charly 1993) ★★★, *Ain't That Too Much: The Complete Challenge Sessions*

(Hollowbody/Sundazed 1994) ★★★, *Rebel Heart Volume 2* (Magnum 1995) ★★, *Rebel Heart Volume 3* (Magnum 1996) ★★, *500 Miles* (Camden 1998) ★★★, *The EP Collection Volume 2* (See For Miles 1998) ★★★.

● FURTHER READING: *Wild Cat: A Tribute To Gene Vincent*, Eddie Muir. *Gene Vincent & The Blue Caps*, Rob Finnis and Bob Dunham. *I Remember Gene Vincent*, Alan Vince. *Gene Vincent: The Screaming End*, Alan Clark. *The Day The World Turned Blue*, Britt Hagerty. *Gene Vincent: A Discography*, Derek Henderson. *Race With The Devil: Gene Vincent's Life In The Fast Lane*, Susan Vanhecke.

● FILMS: *The Girl Can't Help It* (1956), *Hot Rod Gang* aka *Fury Unleashed* (1958), *It's Trad, Dad!* aka *Ring-A-Ding Rhythm* (1961).

VINCENT, JOHNNY

b. John Vincent Imbragulio, 3 October 1925, Laurel, Mississippi, USA, d. 4 February 2000, USA. Johnny Vincent earned his place in music history running Ace Records out of his hometown of Jackson, Mississippi. He gained experience of the record industry working as a travelling salesman during the late 40s for the William B. Allen Supply Company. His first label was Champion, which issued the obscure 'My Baby Boogies All The Time' by Arthur 'Big Boy' Crudup under the pseudonym Arthur Blues Crump (Crudup was already licensed to RCA-Victor Records). A three year spell as promoter, talent scout, A& R man and unofficial producer with Specialty Records followed. In 1955 Vincent set up Ace Records, which over the next two decades was responsible for releasing a large number of excellent blues, R&B and rock 'n' roll sides by artists such as Frankie Lee Sims, Charles Brown, Amos Milburn, Sammy Myers, Earl King, Huey 'Piano' Smith, and Joe Tex.

In addition to launching the auxiliary label Pink, Ace picked up distribution rights for labels such as KRC and Rex and by the early 60s could boast a wide roster of artists including Frankie Ford, Jimmy Clanton, Narvel Felts, and Mickey Gilley. A disastrous promotion and distribution deal with Vee Jay Records in 1962 hastened the demise of Ace, although the label had already lost many of its original blues artists by unwisely concentrating on the fickle pop market. Ace went bankrupt in 1970, and Vincent relocated to run the Memphis Record Company. Two years later he resurrected Ace, but was unable to steer the label back to its former heights. In 1997 Vincent concluded the sale of the masters to Castle Communications for reissue under their Sequel Records label, but was still struggling to revive the glory days when he died in February 2000.

VINCENT, MONROE

b. 9 December 1919, Woodville, Mississippi, USA, d. April 1982, Oakland, California, USA. Also known throughout his career as Vince Monroe, Polka Dot Slim and Mr. Calhoun, Vincent was 40 years old and living in Baton Rouge, Louisiana, before he made his first records, although he had been playing harmonica and singing blues since his youth in Mississippi. Having developed a style that mixed elements of Sonny Boy 'Rice Miller' Williamson and Louisiana R&B, he seems to have been something of an all-purpose performer at J.D. 'Jay' Miller's Crowley studio in the late 50s, recording in slightly different styles and using two different names, with the resulting records appearing on two different labels. He was resident in New Orleans for many years, playing in local bars and clubs, and making more records, under yet another pseudonym, in the early 60s. Later in his life, he moved to the west coast.

● COMPILATIONS: *Gonna Head For Home* (1976) ★★★.

VINNEGAR, LEROY

b. 13 July 1928, Indianapolis, Indiana, USA, d. 2 August 1999, Portland, Oregon, USA. After teaching himself to play bass, Vinnegar worked in clubs in the Chicago area (including the Beehive), accompanying jazz musicians such as Charlie Parker, before moving to the west coast in 1954. He immediately made an impact on the local music scene, then in the middle of the 'cool jazz' boom. He played and recorded with just about everyone; a short list might include Jack Sheldon, Stan Levey, Shorty Rogers, Dexter Gordon, Cy Touff, Russ Freeman, Elmo Hope, Stan Getz, Harold Land, Carl Perkins (with whom he had gone to school), Art Pepper and Teddy Edwards. He was also a member of the Shelly Manne trio (the third man being André Previn) which recorded the 1956 hit album *My Fair Lady*. Vinnegar continued to work with a variety of bands, sometimes as leader, at home in large and small groups. He sometimes appeared in non-jazz contexts and his eclecticism allowed him to play comfortably alongside musicians as diverse as Howard McGhee and Les McCann, or Serge Chaloff and film actor George Segal's Dixieland jazz group, Panama Hats. He played on McCann's and Eddie Harris' million-selling *Sweet Movement*. After several years of ill health which resulted in a move to Portland, Oregon, Vinnegar returned to recording with a 1992 session for Contemporary Records. An outstanding exponent of the 'walking bass' technique, Vinnegar always played with a wonderful plangency, bringing a zestful swing to any performance.

● ALBUMS: *Leroy Walks!* (Contemporary 1957) ★★★★, *Leroy Walks Again!!* (Contemporary 1962) ★★★★, *Jazz's Great Walker* (Vee Jay 1965) ★★★, *Walkin' The Basses* (Contemporary 1992) ★★★, *Integrity: The Walker Live At Lairmont* (Jazz Focus 1995) ★★★.

VINSON, MOSE

b. 7 August 1917, Holly Springs, Mississippi, USA. Vinson's piano playing was a time capsule of blues and boogie techniques learned in the 30s and 40s. As a five-year-old, he sat on his mother's lap to play piano in church. At 15, influenced by meeting Sunnyland Slim, he decided to move to Memphis, where he worked barrelhouses and bars, broadening his repertoire to play for white audiences, where the real money was. In the late

40s he played at the Parlor Club, accompanying the young B.B. King. Working as a plumber and janitor by day, in 1953 Vinson took a job as caretaker at Sam Phillips' Sun Records studio. Between sessions, he would sit at the piano and run through various pieces. Phillips decided to record him and cut two versions of '44 Blues', one retitled 'Worry You Off My Mind', and 'My Love Has Gone', also known as 'Come See Me', later featured on both Charly and Bear Family compilations. Musicians on the two sessions included Walter Horton, Joe Hill Louis and Joe Willie Wilkins. The following year, Vinson played on James Cotton's *Cotton Crop Blues*. When his style of music fell out of fashion, he continued to play in church and at home until he was taken up by the Center for Southern Folklore. Under their auspices, he played for schoolchildren and at various cultural functions. His contributions to *Memphis Piano Today* were recorded at his home in 1990, by which time his playing had suffered from the ravages of old age.

● ALBUMS: with Booker T. Laury *Memphis Piano Today* (Wolf 1991) ★★★, with Joe Hill Louis *The Be-Bop Boy* (Bear Family 1992) ★★★.
● COMPILATIONS: *Sun Records – The Blues Years* (Charly 1985) ★★★.

VIPERS SKIFFLE GROUP
Formed in 1956, the group consisted of various members, including Wally Whyton (b. 23 September 1929, London, England, d. 23 January 1997, London, England), Tommy Steele, Hank Marvin, Jet Harris and Bruce Welch. It grew out of the 'frothy coffee' scene, centred at the 2I's coffee bar in London's Soho district in the late 50s. Whyton was the musical brains, and with Bill Varley, wrote the group's first hit, 'Don't You Rock Me Daddy-O', which was even more successful for the 'King Of Skiffle', Lonnie Donegan. After having their 'cleaned up' version of 'Maggie May' banned by the BBC, the Vipers had two other UK chart entries in 1957 – 'Cumberland Gap' and 'Streamline Train'. However, the whole skiffle craze was short-lived, and before long Steele had become an 'all-round entertainer', Marvin, Harris and Welch had formed the Shadows, via the Drifters, and Whyton had carved out a career as a singer and broadcaster on radio programmes such as *Country Meets Folk* and *Country Club*, having previously hosted a number of UK children's television shows, one of which featured the glove-puppet Pussy Cat Willum. In 1960, the Vipers sang 11 songs in the musical play *Mr. Burke M.P.* at London's Mermaid Theatre. Whyton also played the part of 'The Commentator'.

● ALBUMS: *Coffee Bar Session* (Parlophone 1957) ★★.
● COMPILATIONS: *Coffee Bar Sessions* (Rollercoaster 1986) ★★, with Wally Whyton *10,000 Years Ago* 3-CD box set (Bear Family 1997) ★★★.

VIRTUES
This rock 'n' roll instrumental combo came from Philadelphia, Pennsylvania, USA. The band was formed by guitarist Frank 'Virtuoso' Virtue, which

also included Ralph Frederico (piano), Sonny Ferns (saxophone), Jimmy Bruno (rhythm guitar), and Barry Smith aka Joe Gillespie (drums). Their 'Guitar Boogie Shuffle', which went to number 5 in the US charts during 1959, was recorded in Virtue's basement studio the previous year. Having led a society band, the Virtuoso Trio, since World War II, Frank Virtue did not enhance the band's appeal to a teenage audience with their rocking guitar sound. The Virtues had no further hits, but the group was able to ride the twist dance craze in 1962 with 'Guitar Boogie Shuffle Twist' with modest success (number 96, US pop chart). Virtue established a recording studio in 1962, which, in the 70s became the centre of the Philadelphia Sound of Gamble And Huff.

● ALBUMS: *Guitar Boogie Shuffle* (1960) ★★.

VOCALEERS
The original members of this vocal group from Harlem, New York, USA, were Joe Duncan (lead), Herman Curtis (first tenor), William Walker (second tenor), Melvin Walton (baritone) and Teddy Williams (bass). One of the pioneering groups of the R&B era, the Vocaleers' great hit, 'Is It A Dream?' (number 4 R&B, 1953), became a part of the repertoires of a myriad of street-corner groups across the country. The group was formed in 1951 and the following year signed with Bobby Robinson's Red Robin label. Their first release was the ballad 'Be True', which established the group's sound of Duncan's plaintive lead answered by Curtis' falsetto, and earned the group local notices. Williams left the unit at this time and was replaced with Lamar Cooper. The Vocaleers made their last record in 1954, after Herman Curtis was replaced with Joe Powell; Curtis joined the Solitaires. The Vocaleers, with slightly different personnel, reunited in the late 50s, but after a few uninteresting records they disbanded for good in 1961.

● COMPILATIONS: *Is It A Dream?* (Relic 1992) ★★★.

VOXPOPPERS
Little is known about this group who had one US chart single, 'Wishing For Your Love', in 1958 before returning to obscurity. The group was a quintet (including saxophone, accordion, guitar, bass and drums) from New York City, and had earlier recorded both instrumentals and vocal ballads for such labels as Poplar and Amp-3. They cut 'Wishing For Your Love', written by Sampson Horton, for the latter label and when it received airplay, the larger Mercury Records picked up distribution and the single reached the US Top 20. They continued to record for Mercury and Warwick Records but disappeared from the scene before long.

WALDRON, MAL
b. Malcolm Earl Waldron, 16 August 1926, New York City, New York, USA. After studying piano and composition formally, Waldron began playing professionally with a succession of R&B bands. He also recorded with Ike Quebec and from 1954 was a regular associate of Charles Mingus. Waldron's own mid-50s band enjoyed a measure of success in live performances and on record, and he also led the house band for the Prestige label, playing and arranging on sessions for artists such as John Coltrane and Art Farmer. Late in the decade Waldron became Billie Holiday's regular accompanist, remaining with her for nearly two and a half years. After Holiday's death in 1959 he accompanied Abbey Lincoln, but was mainly active in studio work. In the early 60s he played with leading jazz musicians such as Eric Dolphy, Booker Little and Max Roach, but suffered a serious illness that set back his career. From the late 60s Waldron was resident in Europe, finally settling in Munich, where he helped to launch both the ECM Records and Enja labels by recording their debut releases. Although originally a bop pianist in the mould of Thelonious Monk, Waldron has proved adept at free jazz, most notably in various group sessions that feature soprano saxophonist Steve Lacy, with whom he has also recorded an outstanding series of duos. He has written for films, is the composer of a number of pieces for the ballet and for many years enjoyed the distinction of being the best-selling jazz album artist in Japan, where he has recorded with many local musicians. In 1998 he recorded Soul Eyes, an all-star celebration of his career featuring Joe Henderson, Steve Coleman and Abbey Lincoln.
● ALBUMS: Mal-1 (Prestige 1957) ★★★★, Mal-2 (Prestige 1957) ★★★★, Mal 3: Sounds (New Jazz 1958) ★★★, Mal 4: Trio (New Jazz 1959) ★★★, Impressions (New Jazz 1959) ★★★★, Left Alone (Bethlehem 1960) ★★★, with Eric Dolphy The Quest (New Jazz 1961) ★★★★, Les Nuits De La Negritude (1964) ★★★, All Alone (1966) ★★★, Trio (1966) ★★★, Sweet Love, Bitter (1967) ★★★, Ursula (1969) ★★★, Free At Last (ECM 1970) ★★★, Tokyo Reverie (1970) ★★★, Tokyo Bound (1970) ★★★, Blood And Guts (1970) ★★★, Spanish Bitch (1971) ★★, Number Nineteen (1971), The Opening (1971) ★★★, The Call (Japo 1971) ★★★, Live: 4 To 1 (1971) ★★★, First Encounter (Catalyst 1971) ★★★, Plays The Blues (Enja 1971) ★★★, Black Glory (Enja 1971) ★★★, Signals (Freedom 1971) ★★★, with Steve Lacy Journey Without End (Victor 1971) ★★★, Blues For Lady Day (Freedom 1972) ★★★★, A Little Bit Of Miles (1972) ★★, with Lacy Mal Waldron With The Steve Lacy Quintet (America 1972) ★★★, Mal Waldron On Steinway (1972) ★★★, Up Popped The Devil (Enja 1974) ★★★, Hard Talk (Enja 1975) ★★★, with Jackie McLean Like Old Times (1976) ★★★, One-Upmanship (Enja 1977) ★★★, Moods (Enja 1978) ★★★, Mingus Lives (1979) ★★★, Mal 81 (1981) ★★★, What It Is (1981) ★★★, One Entrance, Many Exits (Palo Alto 1982) ★★★★, with Lacy Snake Out (hatART 1982) ★★★, In Retrospect (1982) ★★★, Breaking New Ground (1983) ★★★, with Lacy Herbe De L'Oubli 1981 recording (hatART 1983) ★★★, Plays Erik Satie (1984) ★★★★, You And The Night And The Music (1984) ★★★, with David Friesen Encounters (Mue 1985) ★★★, with Marion Brown Songs Of Love And Regret (Freelance 1985) ★★★, with Friesen Dedication (Soul Note 1986) ★★★, Update (Soul Note 1986) ★★★★, with Sumiko Yoseyama Duo (1986) ★★★★, Space (Vent Du Sud 1986) ★★★★, with Lacy Let's Call This 1981 recordings (hatART 1986) ★★★, with Lacy Sempre Amore (Soul Note 1987) ★★★★, Eric Dolphy And Booker Little Remembered (1987) ★★★, with McLean Left Alone '86 (Evidence 1987) ★★★★, The Git Go: Live At The Village Vanguard (Soul Note 1987) ★★★★, with Lacy Live At Sweet Basil (King 1987) ★★★, No More Tears (For Lady Day) (Timeless 1988) ★★★, with Jim Pepper Art Of The Duo (Tutu 1988) ★★★, Seagulls Of Kristiansund (Soul Note 1988) ★★★, Both Sides Now (1988) ★★★★, Our Collines's A Tresure (Soul Note 1988) ★★★, with Brown Much More! (Freelance 1988) ★★★, Mal, Dance And Soul (Tutu 1988) ★★★, Quadrologue At Utopia, Volume 1 (Tutu, 1990) ★★★, The Git-Go At Utopia Volume 2 (Tutu 1990) ★★★★, with Lacy Hot House (Novus 1991) ★★★★, Crowd Scene 1989 recording (Soul Note 1992) ★★★★, Where Are You 1989 recording (Soul Note 1992) ★★★★, with Chico Freeman Up And Down 1989 recording (Black Saint 1992) ★★★, with Lacy Lets Call This ... Esteem (Slam 1993) ★★★, with George Haslam Waldron-Haslam (Slam 1994) ★★★★, Two New (Slam 1995) ★★★★, with Lacy Live At The Dreher, Paris 1981: Round Midnight Vol. 1 (hatART 1996) ★★★★, with Lacy I Remember Thelonious 1992 recording (Nel Jazz 1996) ★★★, Travelin' In Soul Time (BV Haast 1996) ★★★, with Lacy Communiqué 1994 recordings (Soul Note 1997) ★★★, with Lacy Live At The Dreher, Paris 1981: The Peak Vol. 2 (hatART 1997) ★★★★, Soul Eyes (RCA Victor 1998) ★★★.

WALKER, CHARLES
b. 26 July 1922, Macon, Georgia, USA, d. 24 June 1975, New York City, New York, USA. Walker's career as a blues singer and guitarist began in Newark, New Jersey, in 1955, and he recorded for a number of small labels in the late 50s and early 60s. Changing audience tastes and marriage prompted him to retire from music in 1962, but after his wife's death in 1968 he began to perform and record again, and was just beginning to be promoted to white audiences at the time of his death.
● ALBUMS: Blues From The Apple (1974) ★★★,

New York Rhythm 'N' Blues (1974) ★★★, *Blow By Blow* (1980) ★★★.

WALKER, CINDY

b. Texas, USA. Often described as the greatest living songwriter of country music, Walker's achievements were finally honoured when she was inducted into the Country Music Hall Of Fame in September 1997. The writer of many classic country hits from the 40s onwards, her successes have included 'Dream Baby' (Roy Orbison), 'Distant Drums' (Jim Reeves), 'Bubbles In My Beer' (Bob Wills), 'I Don't Care' (Webb Pierce, Ricky Skaggs), 'Blue Canadian Rockies' (Gene Autry) and 'You Don't Know Me' (Eddy Arnold, Ray Charles).

Walker was brought up in a musical family. Her mother Oree was a gifted piano player who accompanied her daughter up until her death in 1991, and her grandfather, F.L. Eiland, was renowned as a composer of hymns. Walker performed in local shows and achieved her first taste of success when a tune she composed for the Texas Centennial, 'Casa De Manana', was later adopted by the Paul Whiteman Orchestra. Later, on a family trip to Los Angeles, Walker visited the Crosby Building on Sunset Boulevard. By the time she came out she had convinced Larry Crosby that Bing Crosby should record her 'Lone Star Trail', and the song became Walker's first songwriting hit. She also recorded for Decca Records as a solo artist until 1947, reaching number 5 in the country charts in 1944 with her cover version of the standard 'When My Blue Moon Turns To Gold Again'. She also appeared as a cowgirl in several films. Country legend Bob Wills was an early champion of Walker's songwriting, recording five of her songs ('Dusty Skies', 'Cherokee Maiden', 'Blue Bonnet Lane', 'It's All Your Fault' and 'Don't Count Your Chickens') in 1941, and then commissioning her to write 39 more for the eight movies he was contracted to make in 1942.

Their partnership produced three hit singles in 'You're From Texas', 'Sugar Moon' and 'Bubbles In My Beer', while Walker penned other hits for Autry ('Silver Spurs'), Ernest Tubb ('Red Wine'), George Morgan ('I Love Everything About You'), Johnny Bond ('Oklahoma Waltz') and Eddy Arnold ('Take Me In Your Arms And Hold Me'). Despite moving back to Texas in 1954, she continued to pour out hits, including two country classics, 'I Don't Care' and 'You Don't Know Me', the latter proving most successful when Ray Charles included it on his ground-breaking 1962 album *Modern Sounds In Country And Western Music*. A number of other artists have covered the track successfully, including Mickey Gilley, Elvis Presley and Roy Orbison. Further hits during the 60s included 'Heaven Says Hello' (Sonny James), 'You Are My Treasure' (Jack Greene) and Jim Reeves' posthumous number 1 in 1966 with 'Distant Drums'. The run of hits has slowed down since then, although Merle Haggard successfully revived 'Cherokee Maiden' in 1976, and Ricky Skaggs topped the charts with his cover version of 'I Don't Care' in 1981. Her Hall Of Fame induction proved to be a fitting tribute to her reputation in country music.
● ALBUMS: *The Swingin' Cowgirl From Texas* (Bronco Buster 2000) ★★★★.

WALKER, T-BONE

b. Aaron Thibeaux Walker, 28 May 1910, Linden, Texas, USA, d. 16 March 1975, Los Angeles, California, USA. Walker, whose T-Bone acronym is a corruption of his middle name, was raised in Dallas where his parents operated an 'open house' to all the touring blues musicians. During his childhood, Walker was brought into contact with artists such as Blind Lemon Jefferson, and in fact he became Jefferson's 'eyes' around the streets of Dallas whenever the blind musician was in town. Inspired by the more sophisticated blues and singing style of pianist Leroy Carr, Walker took up the guitar, and began performing himself. During the mid-20s he toured Texas as a musician/comedian/dancer with Dr. Breeding's Big B Tonic Show, before joining a travelling revue led by singer Ida Cox. By 1929 he had made a solitary country blues record for Columbia Records as 'Oak Cliff T-Bone'. His recording career may very well have started and finished there, had he not travelled to Oklahoma City and met Chuck Richardson, the man who was teaching young Charlie Christian (a boyhood friend of Walker's) to play single string solos on the new electrified instrument – 'T-Bone' began his instruction alongside Christian that same day. Developing his act as a singer and dancer in the style of Cab Calloway (with whose band he toured for a week in 1930 as first prize in a talent contest), Walker was introduced to the slick world of jazz and big band swing. He moved to Los Angeles in 1934 and obtained a job with 'Big' Jim Wynn's band in Little Harlem.

Walker's popularity steadily grew throughout the late 30s and in 1940 he took a job with Les Hite's Orchestra. His amplified guitar, still a novelty, brought a distinctive touch to the ensemble's overall sound while an undoubted showmanship increased the attention lavished upon the artist. Upon arriving in New York with Hite, Varsity Records recorded the orchestra, and Walker's feature, 'T-Bone Blues', became a great success – although Frank Pasley and not 'T-Bone' played the electric guitar accompaniment. Leaving Hite, upon his return to California, Walker co-led a band with 'Big' Jim Wynn at the top Los Angeles nightspots, honing his provocative act which included playing the guitar behind his head while doing the splits – a sense of showmanship that would later influence Chuck Berry and Jimi Hendrix.

From 1942-44 Walker recorded for Capitol Records with Freddie Slack's band. Slack repaid the compliment by supporting Walker on the first release under the guitarist's name. The two tracks 'Mean Old World' and 'I Got A Break Baby', rapidly became standards for the next generation of electric blues guitarists. During 1945/6 Walker was in Chicago, starring at the Rhumboogie Club with Milt Larkins' or Marl Young's Orchestras

(Young's band accompanied Walker on the recordings he made in Chicago for the club's own Rhumboogie label and for disc jockey Al Benson's Swingmaster Records). Upon his return to the west coast, Walker was in great demand, both in concert and with his new records released on the Black & White label and its jazz subsidiary Comet (1946-47 – later purchased and released by Capitol Records). These included classics such as 'I'm Gonna Find My Baby', 'T-Bone Shuffle' and 'Call It Stormy Monday'. The latter melancholic ballad, also known as 'Stormy Monday' and 'Stormy Monday Blues', has since been the subject of numerous interpretations by artists as disparate as Chris Farlowe, Bobby Bland and the Allman Brothers.

In the late 40s the second musician's union ban and a heavy touring schedule with his old partner Big Jim Wynn prevented Walker from recording, but in 1950 he secured a four-year contract with Imperial Records where he demonstrated a harder, funkier style of blues, with sessions utilizing T.J. Fowler's band in Detroit and Dave Bartholomew's band in New Orleans, as well as his own working unit from Los Angeles. These experiments continued after moving to Atlantic Records from 1955-59, where he teamed up with blues harmonica player Junior Wells in Chicago and modern jazz guitarist Barney Kessel in Los Angeles. Although nominally versed in blues, Walker often sought the accompaniment of jazz musicians who allowed free rein for the guitarist's fluid style. He continued to record prolifically throughout the early 50s, but gradually eased such strictures in favour of regular concert appearances. He visited Europe on several occasions and performed successfully at many large-scale jazz and blues festivals. Later albums, including The Truth and Funky Town, showcased a virtually undiminished talent, still capable of incisive playing. However, by the early 70s his powers were diminished through ill health, and at personal appearances he often played piano instead of his guitar. In 1974 he suffered a severe stroke from which he never made a recovery. T-Bone Walker died of bronchial pneumonia on 16 March 1975, his reputation as a giant of blues music assured. The continuing reissue of compilations confirms his stature.

● ALBUMS: Classics In Jazz 10-inch album (Capitol 1953) ★★★, Sings The Blues (Imperial 1959) ★★★★, T-Bone Blues (Atlantic 1960) ★★★★, Singing The Blues (Imperial 1960) ★★★★, I Get So Weary (Imperial 1961) ★★★★, The Great Blues, Vocals And Guitar (Capitol 1963) ★★★★, I Want A Little Girl (Delmark 1967) ★★★, Stormy Monday Blues (Wet Soul 1967) ★★★★, The Truth (Brunswick 1968) ★★★, Blue Rocks (Charly 1968) ★★★, Funky Town (Bluesway 1968) ★★★, Feeling The Blues (B&B 1969) ★★★, Very Rare (Reprise 1973) ★★★, Dirty Mistreater (Bluesway 1973) ★★★, Good Feelin' 1968 recording (Polydor 1982) ★★★, Hot Leftovers (Pathé Marconi 1985) ★★★, Low Down Blues (Charly 1986) ★★★★, with 'Big' Joe Turner Bosses Of The Blues (Bluebird 1989) ★★★, Back On The Scene: Texas 1966 (Indigo 2001) ★★★.

● COMPILATIONS: The Blues Of T-Bone Walker (1965) ★★★★, Classics Of Modern Blues (Blue Note 1975) ★★★★, Stormy Monday Blues (Charly 1978) ★★★★, T-Bone Jumps Again (Charly 1980) ★★★, Plain Ole Blues (Charly 1982) ★★★, The Natural Blues (Charly 1983) ★★★, Collection – T-Bone Walker (Déjà Vu 1985) ★★★, I Don't Be Jivin' (Bear Family 1987) ★★★, The Inventor Of The Electric Guitar Blues (Blues Boy 1983) ★★★★, The Bluesway Sessions (Charly 1988) ★★★★, The Talkin' Guitar (Blues Encore 1990) ★★★, The Hustle Is On: Imperial Sessions, Volume 1 (Sequel 1990) ★★★★, The Complete 1940–1954 Recordings Of T-Bone Walker (Mosaic 1990) ★★★, The Complete Imperial Recordings, 1950-54 (EMI 1991) ★★★★, T-Bone Blues recorded 1955-57 (Sequel 1994) ★★★★, The Complete Capitol Black And White Recordings 3-CD set (Capitol 1995) ★★★★, T-Bone Standard Time: The Crazy Cajun Recordings (Edsel 1999) ★★★, The Essential Recordings Of T-Bone Walker 1942-47 recordings (Indigo 2000) ★★★★, The Very Best Of T-Bone Walker (Rhino 2000) ★★★★.

● FURTHER READING: Stormy Monday, Helen Oakly Dance.

WALLACE, ACE

b. Herman Wallace, 18 June 1925, St. Louis, Missouri, USA, d. 28 February 1996, St. Louis, Missouri, USA. One of the unregarded mainstays of the St. Louis blues scene, Wallace spent the 50s and 60s as a member of influential local bands led by trumpeter and disc jockey Gabriel and 'Big' George Brock And The Houserockers. Although born in St. Louis, when he was three, Wallace's parents relocated to Indiana where his father worked in the steel mills. Eight years later the family returned to St. Louis, at which time Herman and his brother Calvin began to learn the mandolin and harmonica. However, following the divorce of his parents, Wallace dropped out of school and enlisted in the army. On his return from service in the Philippines, where he was inspired by a local guitar player, he took up the latter instrument via lessons at a GI 'jazz school'. His progress was halted when, at the age of 25, he developed an eye condition and lost his sight. In the early 50s he came to the attention of Yank Rachell, who used Wallace as his back-up guitarist. When Rachell departed from St. Louis, Wallace took the name Ace (formed from the initials of his sister Anita and brothers Calvin and Edward) and formed his own band. Ace Wallace And The Trumps played regularly at James' Jump Palace on 16th Street, St. Louis, where they were immediately popular. However, marital problems drove Wallace away from the city to Detroit, where he played with John Lee Hooker and Earl Hooker. Inevitably, he returned to St. Louis once again, this time to take up a more permanent role in 'Big' George Brock And The Houserockers. He also appeared on several releases by the aforementioned Gabriel, including the latter's first effort, 'I'm Gabriel'. Ill health saw Wallace domiciled to a nursing home for much of his later life, although he still recorded compositions with a drum machine and taught several aspiring child guitarists.

WALLINGTON, GEORGE

b. Giacinto Figlia, 27 October 1924, Palermo, Sicily, Italy, d. 15 February 1993, New York City, New York, USA. His family emigrated in 1925 and so Wallington was brought up in the USA. In the 40s he worked with Dizzy Gillespie on Manhattan's 42nd Street and went on to play piano for many other leaders. Although the flowing lines of his playing were reminiscent of Bud Powell, his style was developed independently and as well as being an accomplished pianist he was an interesting composer. He wrote 'Lemon Drop', which was a bestseller for Gene Krupa and 'Godchild' which was recorded by the Miles Davis Nonet. In 1953 he travelled to Europe with Lionel Hampton and then led a series of groups of his own including musicians such as Jackie McLean, Phil Woods and Donald Byrd. Wallington withdrew from the music business in 1960, but made something of a comeback in the 80s when he played at the Kool Festival (1985) and recorded several albums prior to his death in 1993.

● ALBUMS: *The George Wallington Trio* 10-inch album (Progressive 1952) ★★★, *The George Wallington Trio* 10-inch album (Prestige 1952) ★★★★, *The George Wallington Trio, Volume 2* 10-inch album (Prestige 1953) ★★★★, *George Wallington And His All Star Band* 10-inch album (Blue Note 1954) ★★★★, *The Workshop Of The George Wallington Trio* 10-inch album (Norgran 1954) ★★★, *George Wallington With Strings* (Norgran 1954) ★★★, *George Wallington Quintet At The Bohemia* (Progressive 1955) ★★★★, *Variations* (Verve 1956) ★★★, *Jazz For The Carriage Trade* (Prestige 1956) ★★★★, *Jazz At Hotchkiss* (Savoy 1957) ★★★★, *Leonard Feather Presents* (VSOP 1957), *Giants Of Jazz* 3-LP box set (Time-Life) ★★★★, *Knight Music* (Atlantic 1958) ★★★, *The New York Scene* (New Jazz 1958) ★★★★, with Jimmy Raney *Swingin' In Sweden* (EmArcy 1958) ★★★, *The Prestidigitator* (East West 1964) ★★★, *Virtuoso* (Interface 1984) ★★★, *The Pleasure Of A Jazz Inspiration* (VSOP 1986) ★★★, *The Symphony Of A Jazz Piano* (Denon 1988) ★★★, with Jimmy Jones *Trios* (Vogue 1993) ★★★.

WALLIS, BOB

b. 3 June 1934, Bridlington, Yorkshire, England, d. 10 January 1991. Wallis started his first band in Bridlington in 1950, which lasted right through to 1957. Later he joined Papa Bue's Viking Jazz Band (1956), Diz Disley's Jazz Band (1957) and, briefly, Acker Bilk's Band (1958). From 1958 he had his own Storyville Jazzmen who were very popular throughout the 'trad' boom of the late 50s. His own trumpet playing and singing forcefully reflected the influence of Henry 'Red' Allen. He had two minor UK hits with 'I'm Shy Mary Ellen I'm Shy' (1961, number 44) and 'Come Along Please' (1962, number 33). Change in popular taste brought the demise of the Storyville Jazzmen but Wallis played with a variety of bands including Monty Sunshine's. He then moved to Switzerland, where he played throughout the 80s.

● ALBUMS: *Everybody Loves Saturday Night* (Top Rank 1960) ★★★★, *Bob Wallis's Storyville Jazzmen* (Storyville 1973) ★★★★, *Live* (Storyville 1975) ★★, *Jazz Doctor* (Storyville 1975) ★★★, *Doctor Jazz* (Storyville 1988) ★★★.

WALTON, WADE

b. 10 October 1923, Lombardy, Mississippi, USA, d. 10 January 2000, St. Louis, Missouri, USA. Walton was best known as a musical barber, entertaining visitors to his shop in Clarksdale, Mississippi, but he started in music in his youth, and toured with minstrel shows in his teens. A strong guitarist and harp player, he formed the Kings Of Rhythm with Clarksdale's most famous R&B artist, Ike Turner, but preferred to stay with his steady work when Turner moved on to a career as a professional musician. Paul Oliver recorded Walton in his shop, singing and playing or stropping his razor in rhythm, and he made an album for the Bluesville label in 1958. From the mid-60s he made a number of recordings, and appeared in short films, and often acted as unofficial host for blues fans visiting the town. He also performed regularly at the Sunflower River Blues and Gospel Festival.

● ALBUMS: *Shake 'Em On Down: The Blues Of Wade Walton* (Bluesville 1958) ★★★.

WANDERERS

A pop and jazz vocal group, the Wanderers were formed in 1952 in Harlem, New York, USA, by Alfonso Brown (lead), Robert Yarborough (baritone), Frank Joyner (second tenor) and Shephard Grant (d. 1970; bass). They had already worked under two previous names, the Larks and the Singing Wanderers. Under the latter name they won an amateur talent contest at the Apollo Theatre, before Brown was ejected in favour of Ray Pollard on lead. The group released its first single, 'We Could Find Happiness', in late 1953 on Savoy Records. Two more sides intended for Savoy were not released, though they were allocated catalogue numbers. By the following year they had moved on to Decca Records where two further singles were issued, 'Say Hey, Willie Mays' and 'The Wrong Party Again'. Presumably due to contractual obligations, these were both credited to their former name, the Singing Wanderers. They did shows with Eartha Kitt and others, and made numerous appearances on television's *The Ed Sullivan Show*. By 1957 the group had signed with Onyx Records for 'Single Of You', but a more permanent association was found with Curb Records (when MGM Records took over Onyx and transferred the group). However, it was not until 1961 that the group first made the charts, with a revision of 'For Your Love', and even this only reached number 93 in the *Billboard* charts. Later singles included one notable ballad in 'Somebody Else's Sweetheart' – the first Hal David and Burt Bacharach composition to be recorded. Despite being an interesting footnote in their career, it also flopped. The Wanderers made one final chart appearance in 1962 with 'There Is No Greater Love', which peaked at number 88 in the US charts. This was their first release after transferring to parent label MGM Records, but its success did not prevent the group from being dropped shortly thereafter. Nevertheless, the Wanderers continued out of contract as a potent live act, until calling a halt to their performances in 1970 when Shephard Grant died.

WARD, BILLY, AND THE DOMINOES

This group was sometimes billed as the Dominoes, or Billy Ward And His Dominoes. Ward (b. 19 September 1921, Los Angeles, California, USA), a songwriter, arranger, singer and pianist, studied music as a child in Los Angeles, and at the age of 14 won a nationwide contest with his composition 'Dejection'. During a spell in the US Army in the early 40s he took up boxing, and continued with the sport when he was released. After working as a sports columnist for the *Transradio Express*, and spending some time with a New York advertising agency, Ward became a vocal coach in his own studio at Carnegie Hall, and founded the Dominoes in 1950. The vocal quintet originally consisted of Clyde McPhatter (b. Clyde Lensley McPhatter, 15 November 1932, Durham, North Carolina, USA, d. 13 June 1972, New York City, New York, USA; second tenor), Charlie White (b. 1930, Washington, DC, USA; second tenor), Joe Lamont (baritone), Bill Brown (bass) and Ward on piano. Ward rarely sang, but over the years, was the only constant member of the group.

Important changes in personnel came in 1952 when White was replaced by James Van Loan, and Bill Brown by David McNeil; and in 1953, when Jackie Wilson (b. 9 June 1934, Detroit, Michigan, USA, d. 21 January 1984, New Jersey, USA) took over from McPhatter, who went on to found his own group, the Drifters. Ward originally formed the group as a gospel unit, and as such, they appeared on the *Arthur Godfrey Talent Show*. However, they began singing more blues numbers, and in the early 50s, made the R&B charts with 'Do Something For Me', 'Sixty Minute Man' (written by Ward and regarded by many as the prototype rock 'n' roll record, featuring a scorching lead vocal from McPhatter), 'I Am With You', 'Have Mercy Baby', 'I'd Be Satisfied', 'One Mint Julep', 'That's What You're Doing To Me', 'The Bells', 'Rags To Riches' and 'These Foolish Things'. By 1956, when *Billy Ward And The Dominoes* was released, the group's personnel consisted of Gene Mumford, Milton Merle, Milton Grayson, Cliff Owens and Ward. In the late 50s they had US Top 20 hits with 'St. Therese Of The Roses', 'Deep Purple' and 'Star Dust', which sold over a million copies. Afterwards, the recorded hits dried up, but the Dominoes, regarded as one of the important, pioneering R&B vocal groups of the 50s, continued to be a popular US concert attraction throughout the 60s.

● ALBUMS: *Billy Ward And His Dominoes* (Federal 1955) ★★★★, *Clyde McPhatter With Billy Ward* (Federal 1956) ★★★, *24 Songs* (King 1956) ★★★, *Sea Of Glass* (Liberty 1957) ★★★, *Yours Forever* (Liberty 1958) ★★★, *Pagan Love Song* (Liberty 1959) ★★★.

● COMPILATIONS: *Billy Ward And His Dominoes*

With Clyde McPhatter (King 1958) ★★★★, *Billy Ward & His Dominoes Featuring Clyde McPhatter And Jackie Wilson* (King 1961) ★★★★, *The Dominoes Featuring Jackie Wilson* (1977) ★★★★, *Have Mercy Baby* (1985) ★★★★, *14 Original Hits* (King 1988) ★★★★, *21 Original Greatest Hits* (King 1988) ★★★★, *Feat* (Sing 1988) ★★★, *Sixty Minute Man* (Charly 1991) ★★★★.

WARD, CLARA

b. *c.*1922, Pennsylvania, USA, d. 16 January 1973. Like so many of her contemporaries, Ward gained her first musical experience singing in church. As gospel music began to reach a wider audience, she formed a group, the Clara Ward Singers, that became enormously popular. Featuring such outstanding individuals as Marion Williams, the Ward Singers were a superb act and appealed to audiences both sacred and secular. In the 50s the group was at the height of its power, appearing at the 1957 Newport Jazz Festival and other prestigious venues. Under Ward's direction the group later broadened its appeal and became very showbiz-orientated. Eventually, as bookings continued to flood in, she formed several groups to sing under the Clara Ward banner. The Singers toured extensively, appearing in the Middle and Far East. In the early 60s, by which time Williams had moved on to form the Stars Of Faith, Ward accepted engagements at the Village Vanguard in New York and in a Las Vegas casino, the latter kind of establishment usually being shunned by gospel singers, for obvious religious reasons. In these unlikely surroundings, Ward was a huge success and her contract was regularly extended.

● ALBUMS: *Gospel Concert* (Vogue 1988) ★★★.

WARE, WILBUR

b. Wilbur Bernard Ware, 8 September 1923, Chicago, Illinois, USA, d. 9 September 1979, Philadelphia, Pennsylvania, USA. When Ware's multi-instrumentalist foster-father organized church music Wilbur became interested, and learned to play the banjo and double bass. He then performed in amateur string groups in Chicago. In the 40s he was playing with Stuff Smith (violin), Roy Eldridge (trumpet) and Sonny Stitt (alto saxophone) in the mid-west. He started leading his own groups in 1953 at the Bee Hive Club and the Flame Lounge in Chicago, and also gigged with Thelonious Monk and Johnny Griffin. Between 1954 and 1955 he toured with the bebop-altoist-cum-R&B-singer Eddie 'Cleanhead' Vinson and with the Jazz Messengers in the summer of 1956. He and Art Blakey formed the rhythm section of the renowned Monk group that included both Coleman Hawkins and John Coltrane (1957). He also played with Buddy De Franco that year and recorded with Sonny Rollins. In 1959 he returned to Chicago and was inactive for a while. In the late 60s he went back to New York, playing with Monk (1970) and recording with longtime associate, tenor saxophonist Clifford Jordan in 1969 and 1976. Wilbur Ware participated in some of the crucial music of his time – well documented by Riverside Records –

and developed the bass as a force both in solo and ensemble work.

● ALBUMS: *Chicago Sounds* reissued as *The Chicago Cookers* (Riverside 1957) ★★★★.

WARREN, DALE

b. Dale Henry Warren, 1 June 1925, Summerville, Kentucky, USA. A member of the Sons Of The Pioneers. It was not unexpected that Warren should pursue a career in entertainment; his father, Henry Green Warren, was the 'Uncle Henry' of Uncle Henry's Kentucky Mountaineers (later the Original Kentucky Mountaineers) and his piano-playing mother, Wava, performed with the group as Sally the Mountain Gal. In the early 30s, the group played various stations, before becoming popular with their *Early Morning Jamboree* on WHAS Louisville. It was here, as young Jimmy Dale, that Warren made his debut with his father, singing the occasional solo and standing on a box to play bass fiddle. They moved to WJJD Chicago's *Supper Time Frolics* in 1936 and stayed until the group disbanded in June 1947. During World War II, Warren served with the US Air Force but returned to the group on discharge. Late in 1947, Henry, Wava and Dale, with backing musicians, recorded for Capitol Records, after which Henry retired. Dale and Wava toured the Midwest being joined by Margie DeVere (Fiddling Kate), whom Dale later married. He formed the Jimmy Dale Quartet, but in 1949, he and Margie moved to California. He first played on the *Hometown Jamboree* with Cliffie Stone before spending a year with Foy Willing's Riders Of The Purple Sage, with whom he recorded and made film appearances. When the Sons Of The Pioneers were seeking a replacement for Ken Curtis, Warren was recommended and joined the group in December 1952, although Curtis remained a part of the radio trio for a further six weeks. Dale Warren, Lloyd Perryman and Tommy Doss made trio recordings for Decca Records in 1954 and from 1958-67, they appeared on their recordings for RCA Records. When Perryman died in 1977, Warren became the leader of the group. He introduced changes into the group's activities by cutting down on touring and having the group perform a more nostalgic kind of show at large major venues.

WARREN, EARLE

b. Earl Ronald Warren, 1 July 1914, Springfield, Ohio, USA, d. 4 June 1994, Springfield, Ohio, USA. As a child Warren played a number of instruments in a family band, but by his teens had settled on the alto saxophone. From 1930 he played in numerous territory bands until, in 1937, he joined Count Basie. Playing lead alto and nicknamed 'Smiley', he stayed with Basie until 1945 and thereafter returned several times in between leading his own band for short engagements. Throughout the 50s he played in various all-star bands, often teamed with other former Basie musicians, among them Buck Clayton, Jimmy Rushing and Dicky Wells. He only left Basie's side for good when his wife became ill, and went on to join vocal group the Platters (on baritone sax). He also managed Johnny Otis' show band. In the 70s and on through the 80s Warren continued to perform, sometimes as a soloist, sometimes in packages featuring other swing era veterans. A striking player with a rich tone, Warren's many years as section leader with Basie have sometimes obscured his importance. Although he was often subordinated in this setting to the solo voices of artists such as Lester Young and Buddy Tate, his solos were always worthy of attention and displayed both an inventive mind and great musical skill. After living in Switzerland for nearly a decade he returned to his home town of Springfield in 1992 for the last two years of his life.

● ALBUMS: *Earle Warren And The Anglo-American All Stars* (1974) ★★★, *Earle Warren* (1974) ★★★, *Earle Warren & The Counts Men* (Muse 1985) ★★★.

● FILMS: *Born To Swing* (1970).

WARREN, GUY

b. Kofi Ghanaba, 1923, Accra, Ghana. Warren was a visionary musician so far ahead of his time that he was for most of his career obliged to scrape a living on the margins of the jazz and African music scenes. As early as the 40s Warren was playing the sort of tough-edged African-jazz fusion which only really took off in the 70s and 80s. In 1938, already well on his way to becoming a master of traditional West African percussion and Afro-American kit drums, he joined the Accra Rhythmic Orchestra, with whom he stayed (after his first visit to the USA in 1939) until 1945. In 1947, he spent a few months with E.T. Mensah's Tempos, but found their mixture of highlife and dance band music insufficiently adventurous for his tastes, and made his way to London, where he soon became a member of Kenny Graham's innovative Afro-Cubists. He returned to Accra in 1949, briefly rejoining the Tempos and also working for Kwame Nkrumah's emergent nationalist organization, the Convention People's Party.

After a three-year sojourn in Nigeria and Liberia (where he worked as a radio disc jockey), he returned to the USA in 1953, settling in Chicago, and forming a variety of line-ups, all of which aimed to fuse traditional West African rhythms and songs with jazz sensibilities. He recorded a number of albums, none of which, tragically, remain available. In 1965, he returned once more to Ghana, but his style was by now so far ahead of anyone else in the country that he was unable to find either regular performing opportunities or a sympathetic record label.

He mounted the occasional concert in Accra, and in 1971 performed at the historic Soul To Soul concert featuring black American and African musicians, but spent more and more of his time as a near recluse at his home in Achimota – practising Buddhist meditation and teaching a small number of younger, similarly adventurous Ghanaian musicians, together with visiting overseas jazz musicians keen to learn the profundities of African rhythm. Warren's musical vision has now been taken up and developed by his master-drummer son, Glen.

● ALBUMS: *Africa Speaks America Answers* (1957) ★★★, *Theme For African Drums* (1959) ★★★, *African Sounds* (1961) ★★★, *Third Phase* (1963) ★★, *Afro-Jazz* (1963) ★★★.

WARREN, PAUL

b. Dorris Paul Warren, 17 May 1918, Lyles, Hickman County, Tennessee, USA, d. 12 January 1978. He acquired his interest in the fiddle from his father, who also played banjo, and drew his main inspiration from Fiddlin' Arthur Smith, whom he heard on the *Grand Ole Opry* broadcasts. In 1938, after playing at local dances, he became fiddle player with Johnnie Wright on WSIX Nashville, playing with the Tennessee Mountain Boys at various venues, until he was drafted in September 1942. While serving in the US Army in North Africa, he was captured and spent over two years in a German prisoner-of-war camp. He eventually returned to play with Johnnie And Jack on the *Louisiana Hayride* at Shreveport and on the *Opry*. He played not only on all their recordings made between 1947 and 1953, but also on all those made by Kitty Wells, including her hit 'It Wasn't God Who Made Honky Tonk Angels'. In February 1954, for some reason, he and fiddler Benny Martin exchanged bands and Warren began to play with Flatt And Scruggs. When the duo split in 1969, he continued to play with Flatt in the Nashville Grass until 1977. During those years, he played on hundreds of recordings, appeared on countless radio shows and made many personal appearances. Ill health caused his retirement and he died in 1978. Although he was undoubtedly one of country and bluegrass music's best fiddlers, he never made any solo studio recordings. This was partly due to the fact that Flatt was never inclined to allow any members of his band to record as solo artists. However, examples of Warren's fiddle playing, taken from live appearances or from radio shows, were later released on a tribute album.

● ALBUMS: *America's Greatest Breakdown Fiddle Player* (CMH 1979) ★★★.

WASHBOARD DOC

b. Joseph Doctor, 8 September 1911, Charleston, South Carolina, USA, d. 16 September 1988, New York City, New York, USA. A street musician from his arrival in New York in 1935, Washboard Doc was on the fringes of black musical life thereafter, claiming to have recorded alongside Ralph Willis and Sonny Terry. He certainly provided backing for Alec Seward, and played, with varying degrees of appropriateness, on many Victoria Spivey albums. Full albums by his trio led to a European visit in 1980.

● ALBUMS: *Washboard Doc And His Hep 3* (1978) ★★★, *Early Morning Blues* (L&R 1979) ★★★.

WASHBOARD WILLIE

b. William Paden Hensley, 24 July 1909, Phoenix City, Alabama, USA. Raised in Georgia, where he began drumming at the age of six, Washboard Willie moved to Detroit in 1945, and soon became a fixture on the city's blues scene, playing the bars with his Super Suds Of Rhythm, and making occasional records for independent record producer Joe Von Battle. These are of limited interest, as Von Battle could only fund minimal accompaniment (guitar, piano and bass guitar), rather than the horn section that Willie's jump-blues needed. His back-up work on 'Brother Will' Hairston's 'Alabama Bus', about the Montgomery bus boycott in the Civil Rights movement of the early 60s, is a demonstration of what the washboard and its associated kitchen implements can achieve. In 1973 he appeared in Europe, confirming in person that he was a lively and extrovert entertainer.

● ALBUMS: *Detroit Blues – The Early 1950s* (1966) ★★★, *Whuppin' That Board* (1969) ★★★, *American Blues Legends '73* (1973) ★★★, *Motor Town Boogie* (JSP 1982) ★★★.

WASHINGTON, DINAH

b. Ruth Lee Jones, 29 August 1924, Tuscaloosa, Alabama, USA, d. 14 December 1963, Detroit, Michigan, USA. Raised in Chicago, Dinah Washington first sang in church choirs for which she also played piano. She then worked in local clubs, where she was heard by Lionel Hampton, who promptly hired her. She was with Hampton from 1943-46, recording hits with 'Evil Gal Blues', written by Leonard Feather, and 'Salty Papa Blues'. After leaving Hampton she sang R&B, again achieving record success, this time with 'Blow Top Blues' and 'I Told You Yes I Do'. In the following years Washington continued with R&B, but also sang jazz, blues, popular songs of the day, standards, and was a major voice of the burgeoning, but as yet untitled, soul movement. However, her erratic lifestyle caught up with her and she died suddenly at the age of 39. Almost from the start of her career, Washington successfully blended the sacred music of her childhood with the sometimes earthly salacious secularity of the blues. This combination was a potent brew and audiences idolized her, thus helping her towards riches rarely achieved by black artists of her generation. She thoroughly enjoyed her success, spending money indiscriminately on jewellery, cars, furs, drink, drugs and men. She married many times and had countless liaisons. Physically, she appeared to thrive on her excesses, as can be seen from her performance in the film of the 1958 Newport Jazz Festival, *Jazz On A Summer's Day*. She was settling down happily with her seventh husband when she took a lethal combination of pills, probably by accident, after having too much to drink.

Washington's voice was rich and she filled everything she sang with heartfelt emotion. Even when the material was not of the highest quality, she could make the most trite of lyrics appear deeply moving. Amongst her popular successes were 'What A Diff'rence A Day Makes', her biggest solo hit, which reached number 8 in the USA in May 1959, and 'September In The Rain', which made number 35 in the UK in November 1961. Washington usually sang alone but in the late 50s she recorded some duets with her then husband, Eddie Chamblee. These records enjoyed a measure of success and were followed in 1960 with songs with Brook Benton, notably 'Baby (You've Got What It Takes)' and 'A Rockin' Good Way (To Mess Around And Fall In Love)', both of which proved to be enormously popular, reaching numbers 5 and 7, respectively, in the US charts. Washington left a wealth of recorded material, ranging from *The Jazz Sides*, which feature Clark Terry, Jimmy Cleveland, Blue Mitchell and others, to albums of songs by or associated with Fats Waller and Bessie Smith. On these albums, as on almost everything she recorded, Washington lays claim to being one of the major jazz voices, and probably the most versatile of all the singers to have worked in jazz.

● ALBUMS: *Dinah Washington Songs* 10-inch album (Mercury 1950) ★★★★, *Dynamic Dinah* 10-inch album (Mercury 1952) ★★★, *Blazing Ballads* 10-inch album (Mercury 1952) ★★★, *After Hours With Miss D* 10-inch album (EmArcy 1954) ★★★★★, *Dinah Jams* (EmArcy 1955) ★★★★★, *For Those In Love* (EmArcy 1955) ★★★, *Dinah* (EmArcy 1956) ★★★, *In The Land Of Hi-Fi* (EmArcy 1956) ★★★★, *The Swingin' Miss "D"* (EmArcy 1956) ★★★★, *The Fats Waller Songbook* reissued as *Dinah Washington Sings Fats Waller* (EmArcy 1957) ★★★★, *Music For A First Love* (Mercury 1957) ★★★, *Music For Late Hours* (Mercury 1957) ★★★★, *The Best In Blues* (Mercury 1958) ★★★, *Dinah Washington Sings Bessie Smith* (EmArcy 1958) ★★★, *Newport '58* (Mercury 1958) ★★★★, *The Queen!* (Mercury 1959) ★★★★, *What A Difference A Day Makes!* (Mercury 1959) ★★★, *Unforgettable* (Mercury 1960) ★★★, with Brook Benton *The Two Of Us* (Mercury 1960) ★★★★, *I Concentrate On You* (Mercury 1961) ★★, *For Lonely Lovers* (Mercury 1961) ★★★, *September In The Rain* (Mercury 1961) ★★★, *Tears & Laughter* (Mercury 1962) ★★★, *Dinah '62* (Roulette 1962) ★★★, *In Love* (Roulette 1962) ★★, *Drinking Again* (Roulette 1962) ★★★, *I Wanna Be Loved* (Mercury 1962) ★★★, *Back To The Blues* (Roulette 1963) ★★★, *Dinah '63* (Roulette 1963) ★★, *The Jazz Sides* (EmArcy 1976) ★★★★, *Mellow Mama* 1945 recording (Delmark 1992) ★★★★, *Live At Birdland 1962* (Baldwin Street Music 1997) ★.

● COMPILATIONS: with the Quincy Jones Orchestra *This Is My Story, Volume One* (Mercury 1963) ★★★★, *This Is My Story, Volume Two* (Mercury 1963) ★★★★, *Dinah Washington's Golden Hits, Volume 1* (Mercury 1963) ★★★★, *Dinah Washington's Golden Hits, Volume 2* (Mercury 1963) ★★★★, *In Tribute* (Roulette 1963) ★★★, *The Good Old Days* (Mercury 1963) ★★★, *Stranger On Earth* (Roulette 1964) ★★★, *The Best Of Dinah Washington* (Roulette 1965) ★★★, *The Queen And Quincy* (Mercury 1965)

★★★, *The Original Queen Of Soul* (Mercury 1969) ★★★, *Spotlight On Dinah Washington* (Philips 1977) ★★★★, *A Slick Chick: R&B Years* 1943-54 recordings (EmArcy 1983) ★★★★, *The Best Of Dinah Washington* (Mercury 1987) ★★★★, *The Complete Dinah Washington On Mercury, Vol. 1* 1946-49 recordings (Mercury 1990) ★★★★★, *The Complete Dinah Washington On Mercury, Vol. 2* 1950-52 recordings (Mercury 1990) ★★★★, *The Complete Dinah Washington On Mercury, Vol. 3* 1952-54 recordings (Mercury 1990) ★★★★, *The Complete Dinah Washington On Mercury, Vol. 4* 1954-56 recordings (Mercury 1990) ★★★★, *The Complete Dinah Washington On Mercury, Vol. 5* 1956-58 recordings (Mercury 1990) ★★★★, *The Complete Dinah Washington On Mercury, Vol. 6* 1958-60 recordings (Mercury 1990) ★★★, *The Complete Dinah Washington On Mercury, Vol. 7* 1961 recordings (Mercury 1990) ★★★, *Best Of Dinah Washington* (Roulette 1992) ★★★★, *The Dinah Washington Story* (Mercury 1993) ★★★★, *First Issue: The Dinah Washington Story, The Original Recordings* 1943-61 recordings (Mercury 1993) ★★★★, *Blue Gardenia* (EmArcy/Verve 1995) ★★★, *Ultimate Dinah Washington* (Verve 1997) ★★★, *Jazz Profile, Vol. 5* 1962-63 recordings (Blue Note 1997) ★★★★, *Smoke Gets In Your Eyes: The Best Of Dinah Washington* (Recall 1999) ★★★, *Diva: The Essential Collection* (MCI 2000) ★★★, *Verve Jazz Masters 19: Dinah Washington* 1946-59 recordings (Verve 2000) ★★★★, *Finest Hour* 1943-61 recordings (Verve 2001) ★★★.

● FURTHER READING: *Queen Of The Blues: A Biography Of Dinah Washington*, James Haskins.

WATKINS, DOUG

b. Douglas Watkins, 2 March 1934, Detroit, Michigan, USA, d. 5 February 1962, Holbrook, Arizona, USA. Watkins has the rare distinction of having played bass on Charles Mingus' 1961 record, *Mingus Oh Yeah*, on which the volatile leader switched to piano. Watkins never achieved the same critical status as his brother-in-law Paul Chambers, although he too was a very fine player, contributing a solid foundation for one of the most important modern jazz albums, Sonny Rollins' *Saxophone Colossus*. He left Detroit to tour with James Moody in 1953, then, after moving to New York, worked with Kenny Dorham and participated in the Horace Silver recording date, which led to the formation of Art Blakey's Jazz Messengers. He rejoined Silver from 1956-57 and then worked with Kenny Dorham again, and with Rollins, Jackie McLean, Lee Morgan, Donald Byrd, and Hank Mobley. He was relocating to San Francisco when he was killed in a car crash.

● ALBUMS: with Jackie McLean *4, 5 And 6* (Prestige/OJC 1956) ★★★, *Watkins At Large* (Transition 1956) ★★★, with Gene Ammons *Funky* (Prestige/OJC 1957) ★★★, with the Prestige All Stars *Two Guitars* (Prestige 1957) ★★★, with Donald Byrd *Two Trumpets* (Prestige 1957) ★★★★, with Byrd *Fuego* (Blue Note 1959) ★★★, *Soulnik* (OJC 1961) ★★★.

WAYNE, THOMAS

b. Thomas Wayne Perkins, 22 July 1940, Battsville, Mississippi, USA, d. 15 August 1971, Tennessee, USA. Wayne was a classic one-hit artist, the younger brother of Luther Perkins, the guitarist who developed and first played the trademark two-string guitar style behind Johnny Cash. Wayne attended Humes High School in Memphis, where a few years earlier the young Elvis Presley had come and gone with little fanfare. There Wayne formed a group called the De-Lons, which was recorded by Scotty Moore, guitarist for Presley, for the Fernwood Records label, which Moore co-owned. That first single did nothing, but Wayne's second single for Fernwood, a weepy ballad titled 'Tragedy', made it to number 5 in the US national chart. The song had renewed life in 1961 as a hit for the Fleetwoods. Wayne recorded for other labels but was unable to follow that hit, although Presley recorded a song he had written, 'The Girl Next Door Went A Walking', in 1960. Wayne eventually moved into production work, but his life was tragically cut short when he was killed in a car collision near Memphis in 1971.

WAYNE, WEE WILLIE

b. New Orleans, USA. Wayne was a blues singer and drummer who was discovered by Stan Lewis. As James Waynes, he recorded for Bob Shad's Sittin In With label in Houston in 1950. Among the titles released by Shad were 'Junco Partner' and 'Tend To Your Business', a big R&B hit in 1951. Wayne next joined Imperial, recording with Lee Allen's studio band in New Orleans from 1951-52. These tracks, including 'When Night Falls' and 'Two Faced Woman', were issued under the name Wee Willie Wayne. After a 1954 session in Los Angeles for Aladdin where he sang 'Crying In Vain', Wayne recorded 'Travelin' Mood' (Imperial 1955), which became popular in the New Orleans area. He continued to perform locally and in 1961 made a new version of 'Tend To Your Business' for Imperial, who issued an album of his work the following year. Wayne subsequently left the music business and in the late 60s was reported to be hospitalized, suffering from a mental illness.
● ALBUMS: *Travelin' Mood* (Imperial 1962) ★★★, *Travelin' From New Orleans* (Sundown 1982) ★★★.

WEAVERS

This US folk group was formed in 1949 by artists with a background of traditional music, and comprised Lee Hays (b. 1914, Little Rock, Arkansas, USA, d. 26 August 1981; vocals, guitar), Fred Hellerman (b. 13 May 1927, New York, USA; vocals, guitar), Ronnie Gilbert (b. vocals) and Pete Seeger (b. 3 May 1919, New York City, New York, USA; vocals, guitar, banjo). Previously, Seeger and Hays had been members of the Almanac Singers with Woody Guthrie. Unlike many similar groups of the time, the Weavers were able to attain commercial acceptance and success, without having to compromise their folk heritage. Virtually all their record releases charted, a precedent for a folk group. They have at times been credited with creating the climate for the post-war folk revival. Many songs became 'standards' as a result of the popularity achieved by the group, in particular, 'Goodnight Irene', which sold one million copies in 1950. Other successful songs were 'Kisses Sweeter Than Wine' and 'On Top Of Old Smoky', the latter remaining at number 1 for three months. Despite Seeger being blacklisted in 1952, and brought before the House of Un-American Activities Committee, the group still sold over four million records during that period. The Weavers disbanded the same year because of personal reasons as well as the pressures brought about by the McCarthy era. The group had lost bookings after being added to the blacklist of left-wing, or even suspected left-wing, sympathizers at the time.

In 1955, their manager Harold Leventhal, persuaded them to reunite for a Christmas concert at Carnegie Hall. Such was the success of the event that they continued to tour internationally for a few more years, while still recording for the Vanguard Records label. At this point, Seeger was still able to combine his role in the group with a successful solo career, but by 1958, he had left the group. He was replaced in fairly quick succession by Erik Darling (b. 25 September 1933, Baltimore, Maryland, USA) then Frank Hamilton and finally Bernie Krause. The Weavers disbanded at the end of 1963, after 15 years together, and capped the event with an anniversary concert at Carnegie Hall. Travelling and personal ambitions were cited as the reasons for the split. After the group left the music scene, there were many who tried to fill their space but none had the same combination of enthusiasm and commitment that had made the Weavers such a popular act. Lee Hays, in his latter years confined to a wheelchair, died after many years of poor health in August 1981. In compliance with Hay's wishes, his ashes were mixed with his garden compost pile! Nine months earlier, the original line-up had joined together to film the documentary *Wasn't That A Time?*, recalling the group's earlier successes.
● ALBUMS: *Folk Songs Of America And Other Lands* 10-inch album (Decca 1951) ★★★★, *We Wish You A Merry Christmas* 10-inch album (Decca 1952) ★★, *The Weavers At Carnegie Hall* (Vanguard 1957) ★★★, *The Weavers On Tour* (Vanguard 1957) ★★★, *The Weavers At Home* (Vanguard 1958) ★★, *Travelling On With The Weavers* (Vanguard 1959) ★★★, *Folk Songs From Around The World* (Decca 1959) ★★★, *The Weavers At Carnegie Hall, Volume Two* (Vanguard 1961) ★★★, *Almanac* (Vanguard 1963) ★★★, *Reunion At Carnegie Hall, 1963* (Vanguard 1964) ★★★, *The Weavers' Reunion, Part Two* (Vanguard 1964) ★★★, *The Weavers Song Bag* (Vanguard 1967) ★★★, *Together Again* (Loom 1984) ★★★.
● COMPILATIONS: *Greatest Hits* (Vanguard 1957) ★★★, *The Best Of The Weavers* (Decca 1959) ★★★, *Best Of The Weavers* (Decca 1965) ★★★, *The Weavers' Greatest Hits* (Vanguard 1971) ★★★★, *Weavers Classics* (Vanguard 1987) ★★★★, *Wasn't That A Time?* 4-CD box set (Vanguard 1994)

★★★, *Goodnight Irene: 1949-1953* 4-CD/1 DVD set (Bear Family 2000) ★★★, *Best Of The Vanguard Years* (Vanguard 2001) ★★★★.

WEBB, 'BOOGIE' BILL

b. 1924, Jackson, Mississippi, USA, d. 23 August 1990, New Orleans, Louisiana, USA. Among Webb's first guitar teachers was Roosevelt Holts, and he later played with Tommy Johnson and Ishmon Bracey. He retained the ability to play in the south Mississippi blues style throughout his life, but in the 40s he extended his musical points of reference when he teamed up with a young Chuck Berry, and later in New Orleans, when he played with Fats Domino's band. In 1952, he recorded four tracks, of which only two were issued, and he did not record again until the 60s. In the meantime, he lived for a period in Chicago, where he played with some of the big names of the time, including Muddy Waters. In 1966, he made the first of a number of recordings aimed at the blues revival, although his album was not released until 1989.
● ALBUMS: *Drinkin' And Stinkin'* (1989) ★★★.

WEBB, LIZBETH

b. 30 January 1926, Caversham, Oxfordshire, England. A much-admired ingénue in West End musicals during the late 40s and early 50s, Lizbeth Webb began her career as a singer with dance bands. Following a recommendation from an eminent leader of one of those popular ensembles, Geraldo, Charles B. Cochran chose her to understudy Carol Lynne in the Vivian Ellis/A.P. Herbert musical, *Big Ben* (1946). After Lynne, in Ellis' own words, 'retired from the cast to open her nursery', Webb took over the role of Grace Green in fine style, and was rewarded less than a year later, when Cochran, Ellis, and Herbert created *Bless The Bride* especially for her. As the young English girl, Lucy Veracity Willow, Webb captivated audiences with her delightful performance of one of Ellis' most exquisite ballads, 'The Silent Heart', and also shared two outstanding duets with Georges Guétary, 'I Was Never Kissed Before' and 'This Is My Lovely Day'. In the 50s she continued to shine in shows such as *Gay's The Word* ('On Such A Night As This', 'Sweet Thames'), in 1951, and *Guys And Dolls* (as Miss Sarah Brown, 1953). She also appeared in the 1953 *Royal Variety Performance*, and toured the UK provinces in *Jubilee Girl* (1956). In 1959, she appeared in the BBC Television adaptation of Eric Maschwitz and Hans May's 1948 hit musical, *Carissima*, before retiring from the stage in order to marry and become Lady Campbell. However, she was seen again in the West End some 10 years later in a brief revival of *The Merry Widow* at the Cambridge Theatre. Sadly, an injury prevented her from singing hit numbers from *Bless The Bride* in *Spread A Little Happiness*, a joyful celebration of the life of Vivian Ellis, following the composer's death in June 1996.

WEBER, JOAN

b. 1936, Paulsboro, New Jersey, USA, d. 13 May 1981. Joan Weber had a number 1 hit in the USA in January 1955, but was unable to follow up that success. The record was 'Let Me Go Lover', released on Columbia Records. Weber was 18 when she met manager Eddie Joy, who brought her to Charles Randolph Grean (a 'one-hit-wonder' himself in the late 60s), who worked in A&R at the famed Brill Building in New York. Grean gave Weber's demo tape of a song called 'Marionette' to Mitch Miller at Columbia, who signed her to the label. Miller took a song titled 'Let Me Go, Devil' and had it rewritten as 'Let Me Go Lover', which Weber recorded. Performed on the television programme *Studio One*, the song became an immediate success, selling half a million copies and reaching the top of the chart in the USA and peaking at number 16 in the UK. Weber had given birth around the time her record was most successful and was unable to spend time promoting her career. Subsequently, she was dropped from Columbia's roster and never had another hit.

WEBSTER, PAUL FRANCIS

b. 20 December 1907, New York City, New York, USA, d. 18 March 1984, Beverly Hills, California, USA. An important lyricist for movie songs from the 40s through to the 60s, Webster was educated at Cornell and New York Universities, but dropped out without graduating, to take a job first as a seaman, and then as a dancing instructor. He developed an interest in lyric writing, and in 1932 had a hit with 'Masquerade' (music by John Jacob Loeb). Among his other songs in the early 30s were 'My Moonlight Madonna' (music by William Scotti), 'Two Cigarettes In The Dark' (with Lew Pollack), and 'Got The Jitters' (Loeb). In 1934, Webster and Pollack were hired to write for films, and it was while he was in Hollywood that Webster collaborated with composer Duke Ellington on *Jump For Joy* ('I Got It Bad And That Ain't Good', 'Jump For Joy'), an all-black musical that opened in Los Angeles in 1941. He also had hits in the 40s with 'Lily Of Laguna' (music by Ted Fio Rito), and a succession of songs composed by Hoagy Carmichael, among them, 'Baltimore Oriole', 'The Lamplighter's Serenade', 'Doctor, Lawyer, Indian Chief' and 'Memphis In June'. Several of those numbers were introduced in minor films, but in the 50s and 60s Webster wrote the lyrics for numerous songs and themes that featured in some of the highest-grossing movies of the times. These included *The Great Caruso* (1951, 'The Loveliest Night Of The Year', with Irving Aaronson and Juventino Rosas), *Calamity Jane* (1953, 'Secret Love' (Oscar-winner), 'The Deadwood Stage', 'The Black Hills Of Dakota', with Sammy Fain), *Lucky Me* (1954, 'I Speak To The Stars', with Fain), *Battle Cry* (1955, 'Honey Babe', with Max Steiner), *Marjorie Morningstar* (1958, 'A Very Precious Love', with Fain), *The Alamo* (1960, 'The Green Leaves Of Summer', with Dimitri Tiomkin), *55 Days At Peking* (1963, 'So Little Time', with Tiomkin), *The Sandpiper* (1965, 'The Shadow Of Your Smile' (Oscar-winner), with Johnny Mandel) and *Doctor Zhivago* (1965, 'Somewhere My Love', with Maurice Jarre). In addition, Webster collaborated on the immensely popular title themes for several other films, including 'Love Is A Many-Splendored Thing' (1955, (Oscar-winner) with Fain), 'Friendly Persuasion (Thee I Love)' (1956, with Tiomkin), 'Anastasia' (1956, with Alfred Newman), 'Giant' (1956, with Tiomkin), 'April Love' (1957, with Fain), 'A Certain Smile' (1958, with Fain), 'Rio Bravo' (1950, with Tiomkin), 'The Guns Of Navarone' (1961, with Tiomkin), 'El Cid' (love theme, 1961, with Miklos Rozsa), and 'Tender Is The Night' (1962, with Fain). He also wrote the lyrics for 'Like Young' (music by André Previn), 'Black Coffee' (with Sonny Burke), which received a memorable rendering from Peggy Lee, and 'The Twelfth Of Never' (Jerry Livingston), a US Top 10 entry for both Johnny Mathis and Donny Osmond. His other collaborators included Henry Mancini, Frank Churchill, Walter Jurrman, and Louis Alter. Apart from his three Academy Awards, Webster was nominated on more than 10 other occasions. Among his honours were ASCAP, Dramatist's Guild, *Photoplay*, Limelight Film Critics, and Grammy Awards. He was elected to the Songwriters Hall of Fame in 1972.

WEDDING BELLS
(see *Royal Wedding*)

WEEDON, BERT
b. 10 May 1920, East Ham, London, England. Weedon may be one of the most omnipotent of British electric guitarists, given that fretboard heroes including Jeff Beck and George Harrison, began by positioning as yet uncalloused fingers on taut strings while poring over exercises prescribed in Weedon's best-selling *Play In A Day* and *Play Every Day* manuals. This self-taught guitarist started learning flamenco guitar at the age of 12 before playing in London dance bands. During World War II, he strummed chords in the touring groups of Django Reinhardt and Stéphane Grappelli. With such prestigious experience, he became the featured soloist with Mantovani, Ted Heath and, by the early 50s, Cyril Stapleton's BBC Show Band. By 1956, he was leading his own quartet and had released a debut single, 'Stranger Than Fiction', but only his theme to television's *$64,000 Question* sold even moderately before 1959. That year, his cover version of the Virtues' 'Guitar Boogie Shuffle' made the UK Top 10. Subsequent hit parade entries, however, proved less lucrative than countless record dates for bigger stars. Although he accompanied visiting Americans such as Frank Sinatra, Rosemary Clooney and Nat 'King' Cole – later the subject of a Weedon tribute album – his bread-and-butter was sessions for domestic artists from Dickie Valentine and Alma Cogan to the new breed of Elvis Presley-inspired teen-idols – Tommy Steele, Cliff Richard, Billy Fury, *et al*. Steele won music press popularity polls as Best Guitarist, but the accolade belonged morally to his middle-aged hireling.

In the early 60s, Weedon's singles hovered around the lower middle of the Top 40. The most notable of these was 1960's 'Apache' which was eclipsed by the Shadows' version. Although the group was dismissive of his 'Apache', they acknowledged an artistic debt to Weedon by penning 'Mr. Guitar', his last singles chart entry to date. Nevertheless, he remained in the public eye through a residency on the ITV children's series *Five O' Clock Club* – as well as a remarkable 1964 spot on *Sunday Night At The London Palladium*, on which he showed that he could rock out on his Hofner 'cutaway' as well as anyone. Indeed, it was as a rock 'n' roller that Weedon succeeded seven years later – with *Rockin' At The Roundhouse*, a budget-price album much at odds with the easy listening efforts that sustained him during the 70s. A renewal of interest in guitar instrumentals suddenly placed him at the top of the album chart in 1976 with *22 Golden Guitar Greats*. Nothing since has been as successful – and 1977's *Blue Echoes* was criticized severely in the journal *Guitar*, but – hit or miss – Bert Weedon, ever the professional, continued to record production-line albums throughout subsequent decades. In 1991, Weedon made history by becoming the first instrumentalist to be elected King Rat, the top post in the best-known showbusiness charity organization, the Grand Order of Water Rats. Ten years later he received an OBE in the Queen's Birthday Honours.

● ALBUMS: *King Size Guitar* (Top Rank 1960) ★★★, *Honky Tonk Guitar* (Top Rank 1961) ★★★, *The Romantic Guitar Of Bert Weedon* (Fontana 1970) ★★★, *Rocking At The Roundhouse* (Fontana 1971) ★★★, *Sweet Sounds Of Bert Weedon's Guitar* (Contour 1971) ★★★, *Bert Weedon Remembers Jim Reeves* (Contour 1973) ★★, *The Gentle Guitar Of Bert Weedon* (Contour 1975) ★★, *Bert Weedon Remembers Nat 'King' Cole* (Contour 1975) ★★, *22 Golden Guitar Greats* (Warwick 1976) ★★★, *Let The Good Times Roll* (Warwick 1977) ★★★, *Blue Echoes* (Polydor 1977) ★★, *Honky Tonk "Guitar" Party* (EMI 1977) ★★★, *16 Country Guitar Greats* (Polydor 1978) ★★★, *40 Guitar Greats* (Pickwick 1979) ★★★, *Heart Strings* (Celebrity 1980) ★★★, *Bert Weedon And His Dancing Guitars* (Dansan 1982) ★★★, *Love Letters* (Everest 1983) ★★★, *Mr. Guitar* (MFP 1984) ★★★, *An Hour Of Bert Weedon* (EMI 1987) ★★★, *Once More With Feeling* (Pickwick 1988) ★★★.

● COMPILATIONS: *Guitar Gold – 20 Greatest Hits* (Pickwick 1978) ★★★, *The Best Of The EMI Years* (HMV 2000) ★★★, *Bert Weedon Collection* (HMV 2000) ★★★.

WEIN, GEORGE
b. George Theodore Wein, 3 October 1925, Boston, Massachusetts, USA. After studying formally, Wein began playing piano professionally in his early teenage years. He led his own band in and around his home town for a period, frequently accompanying visiting jazz musicians. In 1950 he opened his own club in Boston, the Storyville, formed his own record label (which had the same name) and was thus launched on his second career as a jazz impresario. In 1954 he was invited to organize the first Newport Jazz Festival and subsequently played an important part in establishing other major international festivals,

including the annual Grande Parade du Jazz at Nice in the south of France, launching Festival Productions in 1960. In addition to his work on festivals around the world, he has also actively promoted such organizations as the New York Jazz Repertory Orchestra, and taught jazz in Boston. Although his work in promotion has been enormously time-consuming, Wein has never lost his desire to play piano and regularly appears with all-star bands on festival programmes and record dates. While his career as a pianist might perhaps be overlooked, his importance to jazz through his non-playing activities has been of great significance. Together with Norman Granz, he has been a major force in maintaining the highest standards of presentation and performance, and in ensuring that his artists are given the respect that is their due.

● ALBUMS: *Wein, Women And Song* (Atlantic 1955) ★★★, *The Magic Horn Of George Wein* (RCA Victor 1956) ★★★★, *George Wein & The Storyville Sextet – Jazz At The Modern* (Bethlehem 1960) ★★★, *George Wein & The Newport All-Stars* (Impulse! 1963) ★★★★, *George Wein Is Alive And Well In Mexico* (Columbia 1967) ★★★, *George Wein's Newport All-Stars* (Atlantic 1969) ★★★, *Tribute To Duke* (MPS 1969) ★★★, *The Newport Jazz Festival All-Stars* (Concord Jazz 1984), *European Tour* (Concord Jazz 1987) ★★★, *Swing That Music* (Columbia 1993) ★★★.

WEISS BROTHERS

Sam and Hy Weiss formed their Old Town Records label in 1952 on 125th Street, New York City – later moving to Broadway – with Sam as a 'sleeping partner'. He worked full-time for the Old Town Stationery Company, although he had formerly been a sales representative for the Apollo and Jubilee labels, as well as east coast distributor for Exclusive and Modern during the 40s. Hy was the main driving-force, producing records and hunting down such untapped talent as Robert And Johnny, the Harptones, Billy Bland and the Solitaires after the company took off in the mid-50s. Sam left in the late 50s to become a full-time record distributor, but the label carried on in his absence, going from strength to strength with acts such as the Fiestas, Arthur Prysock and Ella Johnson. Hy Weiss sold Old Town to MGM Records in the late 60s, but later repossessed the successful Prysock masters and has since produced several reissues by this, his biggest-selling artist.

WELK, LAWRENCE

b. 11 March 1903, Strasburg, North Dakota, USA, d. 17 May 1992, Santa Monica, California, USA. After achieving a measure of competence on the piano-accordion, Welk formed a dance band in the mid-20s, and soon became immensely popular, with engagements at leading hotels and endless one-night stands on the country's dancehall circuit. The band was widely criticized in the musical press for its lack of imagination and simplistic arrangements, coupled with occasionally elementary playing. Nevertheless, Welk's star continued to rise and his became one of the most successful broadcasting bands in the history of American popular music. Welk called his style 'champagne music' and he made no concessions to changing tastes, firmly believing that he knew exactly what middle-Americans wanted to hear. He must have been right, because he retained his popularity throughout the 30s and 40s, and in 1951 his regular radio shows transferred smoothly to television. For the next four years he had a weekly show from the Aragon Ballroom at Pacific Ocean Park, and in 1955 switched to ABC with even greater success. In 1961, two of his albums spent the entire year in the charts, with *Calcutta* holding the number 1 spot for 11 weeks. During his unprecedented chart run between 1956 and 1972, no less than 42 albums made the lists.

During the early 60s there was always a Welk album in the bestsellers. Also in 1961 he signed a lifetime contract with the Hollywood Palladium and a decade later was still on television, by now syndicated across the North American continent. The band's musical policy, which stood it in such good stead for so many years, had a central core of European music, including waltzes, seasoned with numerous ballads. Although the band's book occasionally hinted that Welk was aware of other forms of music, even jazz, the bland arrangements he used watered down the original so much that it sounded barely any different from the wallpaper music he usually played. The astonishing longevity of the band's popular appeal suggests that, however cynical musicians and critics might have been about him, Welk clearly had his finger much closer to the silent majority's pulse than almost any other bandleader in history. He died of pneumonia at his home in 1992.

● ALBUMS: *Lawrence Welk And His Sparkling Strings* (Coral 1955) ★★★, *TV Favourites* (Coral 1956) ★★★, *Shamrocks And Champagne* (Coral 1956) ★★★, *Bubbles In The Wine* (Coral 1956) ★★★, *Say It With Music* (Coral 1956) ★★★, *Champagne Pops Parade* (Coral 1956) ★★★, *Moments To Remember* (Coral 1956) ★★★, *Merry Christmas* (Coral 1956) ★★★, *Pick-A-Polka!* (Coral 1957) ★★★, *Waltz With Lawrence Welk* (Coral 1957) ★★★, *Lawrence Welk Plays Dixieland* (Coral 1957) ★★★, *Jingle Bells* (Coral 1957) ★★★, *Last Date* (Dot 1960) ★★★, *Calcutta!* (Dot 1961) ★★★, *Yellow Bird* (Dot 1961) ★★★, *Moon River* (Dot 1961) ★★★, *Silent Night And 13 Other Best Loved Christmas Songs* (Dot 1961) ★★★, *Young World* (Dot 1962) ★★★, *Baby Elephant Walk And Theme From The Brothers Grimm* (Dot 1962) ★★★, *Waltz Time* (Dot 1963) ★★★, *1963's Early Hits* (Dot 1963) ★★★, *Scarlett O'Hara* (Dot 1963) ★★★, *Wonderful! Wonderful!* (Dot 1963) ★★★, *Early Hits Of 1964* (Dot 1964) ★★★, *A Tribute To The All-Time Greats* (Dot 1964) ★★★, *The Lawrence Welk Television Show 10th Anniversary* (Dot 1964) ★★★, *The Golden Millions* (Dot 1964) ★★★, *My First Of 1965* (Dot 1965) ★★★, *Apples And Bananas* (Dot 1965) ★★★, *Johnny Hodges With Lawrence Welk's Orchestra* (Dot 1965) ★★★, *Today's Great Hits* (Dot 1966) ★★★, *Champagne On Broadway* (Dot 1966) ★★★, *Winchester Cathedral* (Dot 1966) ★★★, *Lawrence Welk's 'Hits Of Our Time'* (Dot 1967)

★★★, *Love Is Blue* (Ranwood 1968) ★★★, *Memories* (Ranwood 1969) ★★★, *Galveston* (Ranwood 1969) ★★★, *Lawrence Welk Plays 'I Love You Truly' And Other Songs Of Love* (Ranwood 1969) ★★★, *Jean* (Ranwood 1969) ★★★, *Candida* (Ranwood 1970) ★★★.

● COMPILATIONS: *Golden Hits/The Best Of Lawrence Welk* (Dot 1967) ★★★, *Reminiscing* (Ranwood 1972) ★★★, *22 All-Time Big Band Favourites* (Ranwood 1989) ★★★, *22 All-Time Favourite Waltzes* (Ranwood 1989) ★★★, *22 Great Songs For Dancing* (Ranwood 1989) ★★★, *22 Of The Greatest Waltzes* (Ranwood 1989) ★★★, *Dance To The Big Band Sounds* (Ranwood 1989) ★★★, *The Best Of Lawrence Welk* (Ranwood 1989) ★★★.

● FURTHER READING: *Wunnerful, Wunnerful*, Lawrence Welk. *Ah-One, Ah-Two: Life With My Musical Family*, Lawrence Welk.

WELLS, DICKY

b. Williams Wells, 10 June 1907, Centerville, Tennessee, USA, d. 12 November 1985, New York City, New York, USA. After starting out on other instruments, Wells took up the trombone in his mid-teens and a year later was playing in New York City with the band led by brothers Lloyd and Cecil Scott. He later worked with the bands of Elmer Snowden, Benny Carter, Charlie 'Fess' Johnson, Fletcher Henderson and Chick Webb, then toured Europe with Teddy Hill before joining Count Basie in the summer of 1938. He remained with Basie until 1950, taking some months off to play with Sy Oliver's ill-fated big band in 1946/7. During the 50s Wells worked with several bands, often in Europe, and usually in good company: Jimmy Rushing, Earl Hines, Buck Clayton and Bill Coleman. In the early 60s he spent long spells with Ray Charles and Reuben Phillips, but by the middle of the decade was back on the road again, touring extensively and continuing to record. Unfortunately, this period also saw the onset of personal problems as a result of alcoholism which prompted his premature retirement from music. In 1973, however, his autobiography, *The Night People* (co-written with Stanley Dance), was published and this revealing, warm and witty book helped to encourage him back onto the scene. His reappearance was well-received and, although he suffered ill health and was mugged twice (one attack putting him into a coma for several weeks), he continued to perform into the early 80s. In his playing, Wells chose to adopt a seemingly casual approach, liberally peppering his inventive solos with musical witticisms and deliberately jokey effects. In lesser hands, his style could have mirrored the comic excesses of an earlier generation of trombone players in jazz and popular music. Fortunately, his stylishness and wit, coupled with exemplary technique, allowed him to establish a reputation as one of the finest and most distinctive trombone soloists in jazz.

● ALBUMS: with Rex Stewart *Chatter Jazz* (RCA Victor 1959) ★★★, *Lonesome Road* (Uptown 1982) ★★★, *Trombone Four-In-Hand (1958-59)* (Affinity 1986) ★★★★, *Bones For The King (1958)* (Affinity 1986) ★★★.

● COMPILATIONS: *Dicky Wells In Paris, 1932* (Affinity 1992) ★★★, *1927-1943* (Classics 1992) ★★★, *Swingin' In Paris* 30s recordings (Le Jazz 1993) ★★★.

● FURTHER READING: *The Night People*, Dicky Wells with Stanley Dance.

WELLS, KITTY

b. Muriel Ellen Deason, 30 August 1919, Nashville, Tennessee, USA. The family relocated to Humphries County but returned to Nashville in 1928, where Deason's father, who played guitar and sang for local dances, worked as a brakeman for the Tennessee Central Railroad. She grew up singing in the church choir, learned to play guitar and in 1934, she dropped out of school to work in a local shirt factory. The following year, she teamed with her sisters Mabel and Willie Mae and their cousin, Bessie Choate, to form the singing Deason Sisters. In 1936, they appeared on WSIX Nashville singing 'Jealous Hearted Me', and were cut off in mid-song by the station, who for some reason believed the song to be too risqué for their listeners. The audience disagreed and the girls were given a regular early-morning programme. In 1937, Muriel met aspiring country singer Johnnie Wright and on 30 October that year, the two were married. Soon afterwards, the newlyweds and Wright's sister Louise began appearing on radio station WSIX as Johnnie Wright And The Harmony Girls. In 1939, Wright and Muriel teamed up with Jack Anglin (their future brother-in-law), first appearing as Johnnie Wright And The Happy Roving Cowboys with Jack Anglin, later becoming Johnnie And Jack And The Tennessee Hillbillies, then the Tennessee Mountain Boys. In 1943, Muriel first became known as Kitty Wells. Wright chose the name from an old song popularized on the *Grand Ole Opry* by the Pickard Family and the Vagabonds. Over these years, Wells did not always sing on a regular basis with Wright, due to the fact that, by this time, she had two children, Ruby Wright and Bobby Wright, to look after; a second daughter, Carol Sue Wright, followed. Wells made her first solo recordings for RCA-Victor Records in 1949, one song being 'Gathering Flowers For The Master's Bouquet', now generally rated to be the first recording, on a major label, of a song that has become a country gospel standard. A further session the next year failed to produce a hit and she left the label. In December 1951, she moved back to Nashville and with Johnnie And Jack becoming members of the *Grand Ole Opry* in January 1952, she decided to retire. However, for the session fee, she had been persuaded by Wright and Paul Cohen of Decca Records to record a demo of a female answer song to Hank Thompson's then current US country number 1, 'The Wild Side Of Life'. On 3 May 1952, under the production of Owen Bradley, she recorded 'It Wasn't God Who Made Honky Tonk Angels'. Two months later, unaware that it had been released, Kitty Wells found she had recorded a future million-seller. By 8 August, it was beginning a six-week stay at number 1 in the country charts and had become a Top 30 pop hit. The publishers of 'The Wild Side Of Life' sued on the grounds that their song's melody had been used. Since both songs had used the tune of the old song 'I'm Thinking Tonight Of My Blue Eyes' and 'The Great Speckled Bird', the case was thrown out of court. The song was the first woman's song in country music and the recording made Kitty Wells country music's first female singing star in her own right, giving her the distinction of becoming the first female country singer to have a number 1 record (initially *The Grand Ole Opry* management felt the lyrics were unsuitable, but an intervention by the influential Roy Acuff saw them relent). Inevitably, Kitty Wells' retirement was shelved and by the end of the 50s, she had registered 35 successive Top 20 country hits, 24 making the Top 10. There were further answer songs in 'Paying For That Back Street Affair', 'Hey Joe' and 'I'll Always Be Your Fraulein', and a less successful one called 'My Cold Cold Heart Is Melted Now'. During this time, as one of several duet hits with Red Foley, 'One By One' became a country number 1 in 1954. She also had Top 10 duets with Webb Pierce, including 'Oh, So Many Years' and 'Finally'.

She also recorded with Roy Acuff. In 1959, Decca took the unusual step of signing her to a lifetime contract. During the 60s, her list of chart hits extended to almost 70 and although only 'Heartbreak USA' (1961) made number 1, there were 11 more that made the Top 10. These included 'Left To Right' and 'Unloved Unwanted'. The hits slowed down during the 70s, the last two coming in 1979 and taking her total to 81 in all. From the 50s through to the end of the 70s, she toured extensively, making personal appearances not only in the USA and Canada but all over the world. After Jack Anglin's death in 1963, Johnny Wright toured with his wife and family as the Kitty Wells And Johnny Wright Family Show. In 1969, they hosted a syndicated television show that ran for many years. In the early 70s, she severed her connections with Decca (by then MCA Records) and signed with Capricorn where, backed by some of the Allman Brothers Band, she recorded *Forever Young* (the title track was a Bob Dylan song – a daring move for a traditional country singer at the time). She made her first appearance in Britain at the 1974 Wembley Festival. She also continued to record for several minor labels, including in 1989, two albums for Step One with Owen Bradley, the man who had produced her million-seller at Decca 37 years previously. Ten years later, Wells and Wright performed their final concert on New Year's Eve 2000 at the Nashville Nightlife Theater. Over the years Wells has won many awards, including being voted *Billboard*'s Female Country Artiste from 1953-65, but her greatest award came in 1976, when she was elected to the Country Music Hall Of Fame in Nashville. The plaque noted: 'In true country tradition her sincere vocal stylings convey the real feeling of the songs, be they happy or sad'. Many of her hits were country weepies such as 'Mommy For A Day', 'I Gave My Wedding Dress Away', 'This White Circle On My Finger' and 'I Hope My Divorce Is Never Granted'. There is little doubt that her successes opened the way for many subsequent female country music singers. In 1952, Kitty Wells was named the Queen Of Country Music by Fred Rose and in the opinions of country traditionalists, she still holds her title with dignity and sincerity. She has, as country historian Bill C. Malone noted, 'preserved an image of wholesomeness and domesticity that was far removed from the world she often sang about'. She retired at the end of 2000.

● ALBUMS: *Country Hit Parade* (Decca 1956) ★★★, *Winner Of Your Heart* (Decca 1956) ★★★★, *Dust On The Bible* (Decca 1959) ★★★, *After Dark* (Decca 1959) ★★★, *Kitty's Choice* (Decca 1960) ★★★★, *Kitty Wells & Red Foley's Greatest Hits* (Decca 1961) ★★★, *Heartbreak USA* (Decca 1961) ★★★★, *Queen Of Country Music* (Decca 1962) ★★★, *Singing On Sunday* (Decca 1962) ★★★, *Christmas With Kitty Wells* (Decca 1962) ★★, *Especially For You* (Decca 1964) ★★★★, *Country Music Time* (Decca 1964) ★★★, *Burning Memories* (Decca 1965) ★★★, *Lonesome, Sad & Blue* (Decca 1965) ★★★★, *Kitty Wells Family Gospel Sing* (Decca 1965) ★★, *Lonely Street* (Decca 1966) ★★★★, *Songs Made Famous By Jim Reeves* (Decca 1966) ★★★, *Country All The Way* (Decca 1966) ★★★, *The Kitty Wells' Show* (Decca 1966) ★★, *Kitty Wells* (Vocalion 1966) ★★★, *Love Makes The World Go Round* (Decca 1967) ★★★★, with Red Foley *Together Again* (Decca 1967) ★★★, *Queen Of Honky Tonk Street* (Decca 1967) ★★★, *Kitty Wells' Showcase* (Decca 1968) ★★★, with Johnnie Wright *We'll Stick Together* (Decca 1968) ★★★, *Country Heart* (Vocalion 1969) ★★★★, *Singing 'Em Country* (Decca 1970) ★★★, *Your Love Is The Way* (Decca 1970) ★★★, *Pledging My Love* (Decca 1971) ★★★, *They're Stepping All Over My Heart* (Decca 1971) ★★★, *I've Got Yesterday* (Decca 1972) ★★★, *Sincerely* (Decca 1972) ★★★, with Wright *Heartwarming Gospel Songs* (Decca 1972) ★★★, *Yours Truly* (Capricorn 1973) ★★★, *Forever Young* (Capricorn 1974) ★★★, with Jean Stafford *Queens Of Country Music* (Massive 1998) ★★.

● COMPILATIONS: *Kitty Wells' Golden Favourites* (Decca 1961) ★★★, *The Kitty Wells Story* (Decca 1963) ★★★, *Cream Of Country Hits* (Decca 1968) ★★★★, *Bouquet Of Country Hits* (Decca 1969) ★★★★, *Hall Of Fame, Volume 1* (Decca 1979) ★★★, *Early Classics* (Decca 1981) ★★★, *The Kitty Wells Story* (MCA 1986) ★★★, *The Golden Years 1949-1957* 5-album box set (Bear Family 1987) ★★★★, *Greatest Hits Volume 1* (Step One 1989) ★★★★, *Greatest Hits Volume 2* (Step One 1989) ★★★★, *Country Music Hall Of Fame Series* (MCA 1991) ★★★★, *The Queen Of Country Music* 4-CD box set (Bear Family 1993) ★★★★, *Kitty Wells Duets* (Pair 1996) ★★★, *God's Honky Tonk Angel (The First Queen Of Country Music)* (Edsel 2000) ★★★★.

● FURTHER READING: *Queen Of Country Music: The Life Story Of Kitty Wells*, A.C. Dunkleburger. *Kitty Wells: The Golden Years*, Pinson, Weize And Wolfe. *The Honky Tonk Angels: A Dual Biography*, Walt Trott.

WELSH, ALEX

b. 9 July 1929, Edinburgh, Scotland, d. 25 June 1982, London, England. Welsh began his musical career in Scotland playing cornet, and later trumpet, in trad jazz bands. In the early 50s he moved to London and formed a band that quickly became one of the most proficient of its kind. With every chair filled by musicians of great skill and enthusiasm, the Welsh band was a major force in the British trad jazz movement. Eschewing the fancy dress eccentricities and pop music escapades of many of his rivals (although 'Tansy' did reach the UK Top 50 in 1961), Welsh concentrated on creating exciting music that echoed the vitality of the best of Chicago-style dixieland jazz. Among Welsh's sidemen over the years were Archie Semple, Fred Hunt, Roy Crimmins, Roy Williams, John Barnes, Lennie Hastings and Al Gay. During the 60s and early 70s Welsh toured the UK and Europe, building up a rapturous following, and also made occasional successful sorties to the USA. In common with Chris Barber, Welsh saw the need to maintain a wide repertoire, drawing (as jazz always has) from the best of popular music and thus creating a band that effectively swam in the mainstream. By the mid-70s Welsh's health was poor, but he continued to play for as long as he could. Throughout his career Welsh blew with great exuberance, sometimes sang too and always encouraged his sidemen by his example. Not only popular with audiences, he was also respected and admired by his fellow musicians.

● ALBUMS: *Music Of The Mauve Decade* (Lake 1957) ★★★, *The Melrose Folio* (1958) ★★★, *Alex Welsh In Concert* (Columbia 1961) ★★, *Echoes Of Chicago* (1962) ★★★, *Strike One* (1966) ★★★, *At Home With Alex Welsh* (Dormouse 1967) ★★★, *Vintage '69* (1969) ★★, *Classic Concert* (Black Lion 1971) ★★★★, *An Evening With Alex Welsh, Part 1* (Polydor 1974) ★★★, *Dixieland Party* (Black Lion 1975) ★★, *If I Had A Talking Picture Of You* (Black Lion 1975) ★★★, *The Alex Welsh Showcase, Volume 1* (Black Lion 1976) ★★★, *The Alex Welsh Showcase, Volume 2* (Black Lion 1976) ★★★, *Alex Welsh In Concert* (Black Lion 1977) ★★★, *In A Party Mood* (One-Up 1977) ★★★, with Humphrey Lyttelton, Bruce Turner, George Chisholm *Salute To Satchmo* (Black Lion 1979) ★★★, *Dixieland To Duke* (Dormouse 1986) ★★★★, *Live At The Royal Festival Hall (1954-55)* (Lake 1988) ★★★, *Doggin' Around* 1973 recordings (Black Lion 1993) ★★★, *It Has To Be* 1955 recording (Lake 2001) ★★★.

WESS, FRANK

b. Frank Wellington Wess, 4 January 1922, Kansas City, Missouri, USA. Wess started out on alto saxophone, playing in bands in and around Washington, DC, where he was raised. Later, he switched to tenor saxophone and worked briefly in the band led by Blanche Calloway. He developed his musical abilities while on military service and, following his discharge at the end of World War II, he played in the bands of artists such as Billy Eckstine and Lucky Millinder. During this period he began to play the flute. In 1953 he joined the Count Basie band, mostly playing tenor and flute, and becoming a featured attraction with the band both as soloist and as duettist with fellow sideman Frank Foster. In the late 50s Wess reverted to alto saxophone but continued to feature his flute playing, becoming the first major jazz soloist to popularize this instrument and proving in the process that it could be used in a gimmick-free fashion. He left Basie in 1964, thereafter working in studios, leading his own small groups, making records and working in groups such as the New York Jazz Quartet and Dameronia, the band led by Philly Joe Jones. Wess also wrote numerous arrangements, for his own groups and for other bands. In the mid-80s he was briefly with Woody Herman and also continued to lead his own small group and to co-lead a quintet with Foster. In the late 80s and early 90s he was leading a splendid Basie-style big band, which included in its ranks Harry 'Sweets' Edison, Joe Newman, Snooky Young, Al Grey, Benny Powell, Marshal Royal and Billy Mitchell, and which made highly successful appearances in Japan. Albums by this band, *Dear Mr Basie* and *Entre Nous*, showed that Wess had ably assumed the role of big band leader and arranger in the Basie tradition. As a soloist (whichever instrument he uses), Wess plays with uncluttered swing, fashioning his phrases with care. His playing satisfactorily updates the stylistic traditions of the swing era and is always polished and highly sophisticated.

● ALBUMS: *Frank Wess Quintet* 10-inch album (Commodore 1952) ★★★, *Frank Wess* 10-inch album (Commodore 1952) ★★★, *Wess Of The Moon* (Commodore 1954) ★★★, *Flutes And Reeds* (Savoy 1955) ★★★, *North, South, East...Wess* (Savoy 1956) ★★, with Dorothy Ashby *In A Minor Groove* (New Jazz 1958) ★★★, *I Hear Ya Talkin'* (Savoy 1959) ★★★, *Frank Wess Quartet* (Moodsville 1960) ★★, *Southern Comfort* (Prestige 1962) ★★★, with Kenny Burrell *Steamin'* (Prestige 1963) ★★★, *Yo Ho! Poor You, Little Me* (Prestige 1963) ★★★, with Thad Jones *Touche* (Status 1965) ★★★, with Coleman Hawkins *Commodore Years* (Atlantic 1973) ★★★, *Flute Juice* (Progressive 1981) ★★★, with Johnny Coles *Two At The Top* (Uptown 1983) ★★★★, with Frank Foster *Two For The Blues* (Pablo Jazz 1983) ★★★, with Foster *Frankly Speaking* (Pablo Jazz 1984) ★★★, *Dear Mr Basie* (Concord Jazz 1989) ★★, *Entre Nous* (Concord Jazz 1990) ★★★, *Live At The 1990 Concord Jazz Festival: Second Set* (Concord Jazz 1991) ★★★, *Trombones And Flute* (1992) ★★★, *Jazz For Playboys* 1956-57 recordings (Savoy 1992) ★★★, *Tryin' To Make My Blues Turn Green* (Concord Jazz 1993) ★★★, *Going Wess* (Town Crier 1993) ★★★, with Clark Terry *Big Band Basie* (Reference 1996) ★★★, with Gene Harris *It's The Real Soul* (Concord Jazz 1996) ★★, *Surprise Surprise* (Chiaroscuro 1998) ★★★★, with Frank Vignola *Without A Doubt* (Koch 2000) ★★★.

WEST SIDE STORY

In 1949, when Jerome Robbins first shared his idea of updating William Shakespeare's love story *Romeo And Juliet* with Arthur Laurents and

Leonard Bernstein, the trio agreed that it should be set in New York City's Lower East Side, and concentrate on a feud between Jews and Catholics. Six years later, however, when they eventually got around to developing the concept, the then-current well-publicised conflict between native New Yorkers and Mexican immigrants caused them to set this musical around the gang fights involving Puerto Ricans on the Upper West Side. When it opened on 26 September 1957 at Broadway's Winter Garden Theatre, audiences were initially stunned by the powerful blend of dynamic choreography and thrilling music – with its Latin, jazz, and rock influences – which complemented perfectly the contemporary theme of brooding urban discord and violence. It was like nothing that had gone before, Laurents' story of two gangs, the American Sharks and Puerto Rican Jets, during those last days of summer. Persuaded to attend a school dance by his friend Riff (Mickey Calin), the Jets leader, Tony (Larry Kert) meets and falls in love with Maria (Carol Lawrence), sister of Sharks boss Bernardo (Kenneth LeRoy). This means there is big trouble ahead, and in a knife fight – a rumble – the following day, Riff is killed by Bernardo. Incensed by the death of his friend, Tony slays Bernardo, and is then told (wrongly) that Maria is dead. While grieving and wandering aimlessly around, he sees her, but as they run joyfully towards each other, Bernardo's friend Chino (Jamie Sanchez) shoots Tony dead. As the curtain falls, the conscience-stricken Jets and Sharks come together to carry his body away. Advancing and enhancing this harrowing tale at every stage, was a magnificent score composed by Leonard Bernstein and lyricist Stephen Sondheim. The finger-clicking 'Prologue' and 'Jet Song', prefaced tender ballads such as 'Something's Coming' and 'Maria' (Tony), 'Tonight' and 'One Hand, One Heart' (Tony and Maria), and 'Somewhere', as well as the electrifying 'America', in which Bernardo's girl Anita (Chita Rivera) and some of the Shark girls, mock the Puerto Rican obsession with the USA, and cynically contrast the immigrants' expectations, with the reality of their new homeland. Even the innocent Maria's 'I Feel Pretty' is tempered by the jokey warning remarks of her friends, while the Jets lampoon their own anti-social behaviour – as well as various shrinks and social workers – in the hilarious 'Gee, Officer Krupke!'. 'A Boy Like That', Anita's bitter question of Maria after she protects Tony, even though he murdered Bernardo, is answered simply with the poignant 'I Have A Love'. By the time lyricist Stephen Sondheim came on board, Bernstein had already written the words to some of those songs, but during the subsequent creative process, his lyrical contribution gradually became so minor that he gave Sondheim full credit. *West Side Story* received almost 100% favourable reviews, and ran for 732 performances on Broadway, before touring, and returning to New York in 1960 for a further 249 performances. The costumes for Broadway were by Irene Sharaff, and there were Tony Awards for director/choreographer Jerome Robbins, and Oliver Smith's now-famous fire escape sets. Robbins' co-choreographer was Peter Gennaro. Robbins was in charge again when *West Side Story* made its London debut on 12 December 1958 at Her Majesty's Theatre. Chita Rivera and Ken LeRoy reprised their roles, along with Marlys Watters (Maria), Don McKay (Tony), and George Chakiris (Riff). There were major New York revivals in 1968 at the State (89 performances, with Kurt Peterson as Tony, Victoria Mallory as Maria, and Barbara Luna as Anita), and 1980, 333 performances, Ken Marshall, Jossie de Guzman, Debbie Allen). West End audiences saw the show again in 1974 (Lionel Morton, Petra Siniawski, Christina Matthews, Roger Finch, Paul Hart), 1984 (Richard A. Pettyfer (Riff), Steven Pacey (Tony), Sam Williams (Bernardo), Jan Hartley (Maria), Lee Robinson (Anita), and 1998 (David Habbin (Tony), Katie Knight-Adams (Maria), Anna-Jane Casey (Anita), Edward Baker-Duly (Riff), and Graham MacDuff (Bernardo). The latter production was supervised by Arthur Laurents, Jerome Robbins having died some three months before it opened. Leonard Bernstein conducted the original full-length score for the first time in 1984 in a recording with opera stars Kiri Te Kanawa and José Carreras. The event, which was filmed and televised, ensured the album's substantial sales. Numerous other cast albums have been issued, and in 1996 RCA Victor released *The Songs Of West Side Story*, which was inspired by a 1992 AIDS Project Los Angeles benefit concert. Produced by David Pack, leader of the rock group Ambrosia, it featured many pop and country recording artists such as Kenny Loggins, Wynonna, Trisha Yearwood, Aretha Franklin, Phil Collins, Natalie Cole, Selena, and Patti LaBelle. The show has also spawned many hit singles in radically different interpretations from artists such as P.J. Proby ('Somewhere' and 'Maria') and the Nice ('America'). In 1997 it became the first Western musical to be licensed to China.

WESTON, PAUL

b. Paul Wetstein, 12 March 1912, Springfield, Massachusetts, USA, d. 20 September 1996, Santa Monica, California, USA. A leading arranger and conductor, who recorded numerous albums of mood music, and was particularly successful working with female singers such as Lee Wiley, Ella Fitzgerald, Doris Day, Dinah Shore, Kate Smith, Sarah Vaughan, Margaret Whiting, Connee Boswell, Rosemary Clooney, Judy Garland, and Diahann Carroll. Weston first attracted attention arranging for Rudy Vallee in the mid-30s, and made his name during a lengthy spell as one of Tommy Dorsey's staff arrangers after Dorsey had taken over the Joe Haymes band. Among Weston's most notable charts for Dorsey were those featuring Jo Stafford, whom he married in 1952. When Capitol Records were formed in 1943, Weston joined as conductor-arranger, and later became A&R director. Throughout the 40s he served as musical director on various radio shows, and late in the decade began recording mood music, an activity that was boosted by the development of the long-playing record. In 1951, he moved over to Columbia Records, but by the end of the 50s was back at Capitol. The extent of Weston's musicianship is also displayed on a series of records he and Stafford made under the names Jonathan And Darlene Edwards. Stafford's deliberately off-key singing to Weston's out-of-tempo playing is brilliantly executed and the results number among the most hilarious comedy albums ever made. One of them, *Jonathan And Darlene Edwards In Paris*, was awarded a Grammy in 1960.

In the 60s and 70s Weston conducted on several top-rated television programmes, starring Danny Kaye and Jonathan Winters. A gifted composer, Weston collaborated on several popular songs, including 'I Should Care' (with Axel Stordahl-Sammy Cahn), 'Day By Day' (Stordahl-Cahn), one of Stafford's biggest hits 'Shrimp Boats' (Paul Mason Howard), 'Autumn In Rome' (Cahn), 'Hey, Mr. Postman' (Don Raye), 'Indiscretion' (Cahn), 'The Gandy Dancers' Ball' (Howard), 'Congratulations' (Sid Robin) and 'No Other Love' (Bob Russell). He also wrote serious works such as 'Mass For Three Voices' and 'Crescent City Suite'. In 1971 Weston received the Trustees Award from the National Academy Of Recording Arts And Science (NARAS) for his 'inspiring and tireless dedication to the Academy's development'. During the 90s, he operated the Corinthian Records label in Beverly Hills, California, formed by himself and Stafford, which released the couple's new recordings and reissued their leased back catalogue.

● ALBUMS: as Paul Weston And His Orchestra *Crescent City – A Musical Portrait Of New Orleans* (Columbia 1954) ★★★★, *Mood For 12* (Columbia 1955) ★★★★, *Easy Jazz* (Columbia 1955) ★★★, *Solo Mood* (Columbia 1956) ★★★★, *Cinema Cameos* (Columbia 1956) ★★★, *Reflections Of An Indian Boy* (Columbia 1957) ★★, *Music For A Rainy Night* (Columbia 1957) ★★★, *Moonlight Becomes You* (Columbia 1958) ★★★, *The Music Of Jerome Kern* (Columbia 1958) ★★★, *Columbia Album Of Romberg* (Columbia 1958) ★★★, *Hollywood* (Columbia 1958) ★★★, *Carefree* (Capitol 1959) ★★★, *Memories That Linger On* (Decca 1959) ★★★, *Floatin' Like A Feather* (Capitol 1959) ★★★, *Music For Memories* (Capitol 1959) ★★★, *Music For Romancing* (Capitol 1959) ★★★, *Music For The Fireside* (Capitol 1959) ★★★, *Music For Dreaming* (Capitol 1959) ★★★, *The Sweet And Swingin'* (Capitol 1960) ★★★, *Music For My Love* (Capitol 1961) ★★★.

As Jonathan And Darlene Edwards *Sing Along With Jonathan And Darlene Edwards – Only The Chorus Is For Real* (Columbia 1959) ★★★, *Jonathan And Darlene's Original Masterpiece* (Columbia 1960) ★★★, *Jonathan And Darlene Edwards In Paris* (Columbia 1960) ★★★, *Songs For Sheiks And Flappers* (Corinthian 1988) ★★, *Darlene Remembers Duke, Jonathan Plays Fats* (Corinthian 1988) ★★★.

● COMPILATIONS: with Jo Stafford *Jo And Broadway* (Columbia 1960) ★★★, with Stafford *As You Desire Me* (Columbia 1960) ★★★, with Stafford *Swingin' Down Broadway* (Columbia 1960) ★★★★, *Paul Weston – The Original* (1985) ★★★★.

As Jonathan And Darlene Edwards *Jonathan And Darlene's Greatest Hits* (Corinthian 1987) ★★★.

WHEELER, GOLDEN

b. 16 December 1929, Baconton, Georgia, USA. Wheeler became interested in the blues during the 30s and learned to play harmonica from Buster Brown in the early 50s. Wheeler moved to Chicago in 1954 and began to play seriously the following year, inspired by Junior Wells and Little Walter. He formed his first band, but after a few years of low pay and problems with other musicians, he performed less and less, and did not resume an active musical career until 1987. Wheeler is a solid Chicago blues singer and player, and has recorded for the Mr. Blues label in 1976 (issued by Rooster in 1988) and for Wolf Records under his own name and as accompanist to Eddie King and Artie 'Blues Boy' White.

● COMPILATIONS: *Low Blows: An Anthology Of Chicago Harmonica Blues* two tracks by Wheeler (1988) ★★, *Chicago Blues Session, Volume 14* four tracks by Wheeler (1989) ★★.

WHEELER, ONIE

b. Onie Daniel Wheeler, 10 November 1921, Senath, Missouri, USA, d. 26 May 1984. Wheeler was a country singer whose career lasted for nearly 40 years, although only one single charted in the USA. Wheeler won a talent contest while serving in the armed forces during World War II and, upon leaving the service in 1945, he chose to pursue a singing career. He performed on a number of southern radio stations in Missouri, Arkansas and Kentucky, and moved to Michigan in 1948, where he made his first recordings for the tiny Agana label. Wheeler and his singing partner and wife Betty Jean went back to Missouri in 1952 and performed a stint on radio station KSIM in addition to performing in clubs. Continuing to move from one location to another, Wheeler was finally signed to OKeh Records in 1953 and released numerous singles for that label and then its parent, Columbia Records, fusing honky-tonk country and gospel styles. Although he did not quite perform in the rockabilly style, his up-tempo bop found him sharing billings with artists such as Elvis Presley and Jerry Lee Lewis. At the end of his Columbia contract in 1957, Wheeler recorded a number of tracks at the Sun Records studios in Memphis, which were not released for another two years. Further moves saw him relocate to California and back to St. Louis, Missouri, where he recorded for small labels into the early 60s. A 1962 session for Epic Records featured a duet between Wheeler and his daughter Karen. Working as a member of George Jones's roadshow, Wheeler recorded for United Artists Records and Musicor Records in 1964-65, after which he left Jones to join Roy Acuff's show. Wheeler gained his only placement on the country charts, 'John's Been Shucking My Corn', in 1971, on Royal American Records. After that, the recordings dwindled and Wheeler repaired

guitars at home, although he continued to tour sporadically in Europe and Asia. He underwent an operation on an aneurysm in January 1984 and died onstage at the *Grand Ole Opry* in May 1984.
● ALBUMS: *John's Been Shucking My Corn* (Onie 1971) ★★★, *Something New And Something Old* (1975) ★★.
● COMPILATIONS: *Onie's Bop* (Bear Family 1991) ★★★.

WHISKEY, NANCY

b. Glasgow, Scotland. Whiskey started her career playing and singing traditional songs but later, during the skiffle music boom in the 50s, she moved south, with her repertoire of Scottish traditional songs. She was given the surname Whiskey having become associated with the song 'The Calton Weaver', whose chorus includes the line 'Whiskey, Whiskey, Nancy Whiskey'. An EP recorded for Topic Records, *Nancy Whiskey Sings*, included the Irish rebel song 'The Bold Fenian Men' on the track listing, but this track did not appear on the record, having been substituted. Her major claim to fame came in 1957, when the Chas McDevitt Skiffle Group, featuring Nancy Whiskey, made the UK Top 5 with 'Freight Train'. They had a degree of success with a subsequent single, 'Greenback Dollar', which made the UK Top 30 the same year. In 1958, Nancy left the group to be replaced by Shirley Douglas, since which time she has occasionally performed as a folk artist; she appeared performing with McDevitt on UK television as recently as 1991.
● ALBUMS: with Chas McDevitt *Chas And Nancy* (Oriole 1957) ★★★.
● FILMS: *The Golden Disc* (1958).

WHITE CHRISTMAS

With this title, the score for this musical just had to be written by Irving Berlin, and a good score it was too. The problem with this film, which was released by Paramount in 1954, lay with the screenplay. It required three men, Norman Krasna, Norman Panama and Melvin Frank, to devise the story about Bob (Captain) Wallace (Bing Crosby) and Phil (Private First Class) Davis (Danny Kaye), who leave the US Army at the end of World War II and form a successful song-and-dance act, which eventually leads to them producing their own shows. After meeting with the Haynes Sisters singing duo (Rosemary Clooney and Vera-Ellen), the quartet end up at a Vermont holiday resort run by the ex-GIs' former (and much-respected) commanding officer (Dean Jagger). Business is bad owing to the lack of snow, but everything turns out fine when Wallace and Davis organize a benefit show, which – surprise, surprise – ends with the much-needed flakes drifting down while everyone sings 'White Christmas', and Crosby and Kaye are melting into the arms of Clooney and Vera-Ellen, respectively. Irving Berlin 'borrowed' the song from the 1942 Crosby-Fred Astaire film *Holiday Inn*, which was similar in many ways to *White Christmas*. The rest of the songs were a mixture of old and new. One of the most appealing was 'Sisters', in which Crosby and Kaye, waving feather boas and with their trousers rolled up to the knees, parody a typical Haynes Sisters routine. The remainder included 'The Best Things Happen While You're Dancing', 'The Old Man', 'Gee, I Wish I Was Back In The Army', 'Count Your Blessings Instead Of Sheep', 'Love, You Didn't Do Right By Me', 'Blue Skies', 'Choreography', 'Snow', 'What Can You Do With A General', 'I'd Rather See A Minstrel Show' and 'Mandy'. Also in the cast were Mary Wickes, John Brascia, Anne Whitfield, Grady Sutton, Sig Ruman, and the 21-year-old dancer George Chakiris. The dances and musical numbers were staged by Robert Alton and the film was nicely photographed in Technicolor and VistaVision by Loyal Griggs. The director was Michael Curtiz. *White Christmas* proved to be a tremendous box-office success, becoming one of the Top 20 films of the 50s in the USA, and the fifth highest-grossing musical.

WHITE, 'SCHOOLBOY' CLEVE

b. 10 June 1928, Baton Rouge, Louisiana, USA. White taught himself to play harmonica as a youngster and received his stage-name because of his youthful appearance. In the mid-50s he recorded with Lightnin' Slim and in his own right for J.D. 'Jay' Miller's Feature label, and in 1957 for Ace Records. In 1960 he moved to Los Angeles, California, and retired from music, although in 1970 he relocated to San Francisco and began to perform again. He has since recorded for Blues Connoisseur and his own Cherrie label, whose roster also includes J.J. Malone.

WHITE, EDWARD

b. 21 August 1910, London, England, d. 1994, Majorca, Spain. Prolific writer of light orchestral music, whose 'Puffin' Billy' is instantly recognisable in Britain and the USA through its use as a signature tune – in the UK for the BBC's *Children's Favourites*, and in the USA for *Captain Kangaroo*. The tune's association with these popular children's programmes has ensured that it remains in demand by television advertisers today. White was a natural musician, largely self-taught, whose early career (as Teddy White) found him variously on violin, alto saxophone and clarinet with leading London dance bands, especially Lou Preager. As a composer he achieved early success with 'Desert Star' thanks to a Jack Harris 1939 record for HMV Records. When RAF duties permitted, he continued broadcasting during World War II. By the end of the 40s his career as an orchestra leader and composer was firmly established, with regular work for the BBC and publishers' mood music libraries. Charles Williams recorded his 'Runaway Rocking Horse' in 1946, and other successes quickly followed, such as 'Caprice For Strings', 'Clockwork Clown', 'Effervescence', Cabana', 'Fairy On The Fiddles', 'Idle Jack', 'White Wedding', 'Yodelling Strings', 'Leading Lady', 'Paris Interlude' and 'The Roundabout'. In 1961 the very first stereo 45 single released in Britain featured *The Sound Of Ed White* playing his compositions 'Coral Reef' and 'Tropical

Blue' (Pye 7NSR 15320). White's best-known piece 'Puffin' Billy' (1954) was simply one of a number of short works he composed for London publishers Chappells. It was inspired by a trip to the Isle of Wight, off the south coast of England, where he saw some antiquated steam engines, one of which had 'Puffin' Billy' on the front. 'Puffin' Billy' was most recently used as the opening theme to the Comic Strips' two parodies of Enid Blyton's *Famous Five* adventures. He was married to singer Janie Marden, who predeceased him.

WHITFIELD, DAVID

b. 2 February 1925, Hull, Yorkshire, England, d. 15 January 1980, Sydney, Australia. A popular ballad singer in the UK during the 50s, with a tenor voice that proved to be suitable for light opera. After working as a labourer, and singing in local clubs, Whitfield spent some time in the merchant navy before signing to Decca Records and having hits in 1953 with 'Bridge Of Sighs', 'Answer Me' (number 1) and 'Rags To Riches'. He toured the variety circuit, and in 1954 appeared in the *Royal Command Performance* with other pop stars such as Guy Mitchell, Dickie Valentine, and Frankie Laine. Throughout the 50s, he defied the onslaught of rock 'n' roll, and registered strongly in the UK Top 30 with 'The Book', 'Santo Natale', 'Beyond The Stars', 'Mama', 'Ev'rywhere', 'When You Lose The One You Love', 'My September Love', 'My Son John', 'My Unfinished Symphony', 'Adoration Waltz', 'I'll Find You', 'Cry My Heart', 'On The Street Where You Live' and 'The Right To Love'. The extraordinary 'Cara Mia', on which Whitfield was accompanied by Mantovani And His Orchestra, dominated the UK number 1 position for a staggering 10 weeks, and sold over three and a half million copies.

The song also reached the US Top 10, a rare feat for a British singer at the time. He also had some success in the USA with 'Smile', originally written for the Charles Chaplin movie *Modern Times* (1936). By the turn of the 60s, singers of Whitfield's style had begun to go out of fashion, and in 1961 he indicated his future direction by releasing *My Heart And I*, a selection of operetta favourites that included 'I Kiss Your Hand, Madame' and 'You Are My Heart's Delight'. Subsequently, he toured abroad, and had sung aboard a Chinese passenger liner on a cruise in the South Pacific Islands, shortly after concluding his tenth tour of Australia, when he died in Sydney. His ashes were later scattered at sea, near to where he was born.

● ALBUMS: *Yours From The Heart* (Decca 1954) ★★★, *Whitfield Favourites* (Decca 1958) ★★★, *From David With Love* (Decca 1958) ★★★, *My Heart And I* (Decca 1960) ★★★, *Alone* (Decca 1961) ★★★, *Great Songs For Young Lovers* (Decca 1966) ★★★, *Hey There, It's David Whitfield* (Philips 1975) ★★★.
● COMPILATIONS: *The World Of David Whitfield* (Decca 1969) ★★★, *World Of David Whitfied Volume 2* (Decca 1975) ★★★, *Focus On David Whitfield* (Decca 1978) ★★★, *Greatest Hits* (Decca

1983) ★★★, *The Magic Of David Whitfield* (Decca 1986) ★★★, *Sings Stage And Screen Favourites* (Pickwick 1989) ★★★.
● FURTHER READING: *Cara Mia – The David Whitfield Story*, Alan Britton.

WHITMAN, SLIM

b. Otis Dewey Whitman Jnr., 20 January 1924, Tampa, Florida, USA. As a child, Whitman's stutter was ridiculed by other children and consequently, he left school as soon as he could. Even though his stutter is now cured, he has never cared for public speaking and says little during his stage act. Several members of his family were musical and he became interested in Jimmie Rodgers' recordings when he discovered that he too could yodel. After leaving school, he worked in a meat-packing plant where he lost part of a finger, which, several years later, led to him turning a guitar tutor upside down and learning to play left-handed. He later remarked, 'Paul McCartney saw me in Liverpool and realized that he too could play the guitar left-handed.' Whitman sang at his family's local church, the Church of the Brethren, and it was here, in 1938, that he met the new minister's daughter, Geraldine Crisp. After borrowing $10 from his mother for the license, he married her in 1941. Whitman regards his long-standing marriage as a major ingredient in his success, and he wrote and dedicated a song to her, 'Jerry'. During World War II, he worked as a fitter in a shipyard and then saw action in the US Navy. While on board, he soon realized his talents for entertaining his fellow crew members, but in his first concert, he tempted fate by singing 'When I'm Gone You'll Soon Forget Me'. However, his singing became so popular that the captain blocked his transfer to another ship – fortunately for Whitman, as the other ship was sunk with all hands lost.

After his discharge, he had some success in baseball, but he preferred singing, choosing the name Slim Whitman as a tribute to Wilf Carter (Montana Slim), and often working on radio. He first recorded for RCA-Victor Records at the suggestion of Tom Parker, in 1949. After moderate successes with 'I'm Casting My Lasso Towards The Sky' and 'Birmingham Jail', he moved to Shreveport, Louisiana, so that he could appear each week on the radio show *Louisiana Hayride*. His wife embroidered black shirts for Whitman and the band, which has led him to claim he was the original 'Man In Black'. His steel player, Hoot Rains, developed an identifiable sound, but it came about by accident: when Rains overshot a note on 'Love Song Of The Waterfall', Whitman decided to retain it as a trademark. Whitman maintained a level-headed attitude towards his career and was working as a postman while his first single for Imperial Records, 'Love Song Of The Waterfall', was selling half a million copies. 'You don't quit on one record,' he says, 'then I had 'Indian Love Call' and I decided to go. I was told that if I ever wanted my job back, I could have it'. 'Indian Love Call' came from Rudolph Friml's operetta *Rose Marie*, and in 1955, the song gave Slim Whitman 11 consecutive weeks at the top of the UK charts. 'All I did was throw in a few yodels for good measure,' says Slim, 'and the folks seemed to go for it.' The b-side of 'Indian Love Call', 'China Doll', was a UK hit in its own right, and his other chart records include 'Cattle Call', 'Tumbling Tumbleweeds', 'Serenade' and 'I'll Take You Home Again Kathleen', although, astonishingly, he has never topped the US country charts. He says, 'A lot of people think of me as a cowboy because I've sung 'Cattle Call' and one or two others. The truth is, I've never been on a horse in my life.'

In 1955, Whitman moved back to Florida, which restricted his appearances on the *Grand Ole Opry* because he found the trips too time-consuming. In 1956 Whitman became the first country star to top the bill at the London Palladium. Despite being a light-voiced country balladeer, he was featured in the 1957 rock 'n' roll movie *Disc Jockey Jamboree*. He has always taken a moral stance on what he records, refusing, for example, to record 'Almost Persuaded'. He says, 'I'm not a saint. It's just that I've no interest in singing songs about cheating or the boozer'. His popularity in Britain was such that his *25th Anniversary Concert* album was recorded at the Empire Theatre, Liverpool, in March 1973. He had a UK hit in 1974 with 'Happy Anniversary', but United Artists executive Alan Warner decided that his US country albums were unsuitable for the UK market, and that he should record albums of pop standards that could be marketed on television. His 1976 album, *The Very Best Of Slim Whitman*, entered the UK album charts at number 1, and was followed by *Red River Valley* (number 1) and *Home On The Range* (number 2). Whitman then repeated his role as a purveyor of love songs for the middle-aged in the USA. Since 1977, Whitman has toured with his son Byron (b. 1957), who, he says, is matching him 'yodel for yodel', and they have pioneered the double yodel. Of his continued success, constantly playing to full houses, he says, 'I don't know the secret. I guess it's the songs I sing and my friendly attitude. When I say hello, I mean it'. In 1996, Whitman's name was made known to younger audiences in the movie *Mars Attacks!* – after failing to destroy the evil, marauding Martian invaders with nuclear strikes, it is discovered that their brains explode upon hearing any Slim Whitman recording.

● ALBUMS: *Slim Whitman Sings And Yodels* 10-inch album (RCA Victor 1954) ★★★, *America's Favorite Folk Artist* 10-inch album (Imperial 1954) ★★★, *Slim Whitman Favorites* (Imperial 1956) ★★★, *Slim Whitman Sings* (Imperial 1957) ★★★★, *Slim Whitman Sings* (Imperial 1958) ★★★, *Slim Whitman Sings* (Imperial 1959) ★★★★, *Slim Whitman Sings Annie Laurie* (Imperial 1959) ★★★, *I'll Walk With God* (Imperial 1960) ★★, *First Visit To Britain* (Imperial 1960) ★★, *Just Call Me Lonesome* (Imperial 1961) ★★★, *Once In A Lifetime* (Imperial 1961) ★★★, *Heart Songs And Love Songs* (Imperial 1961) ★★★, *I'm A Lonely Wanderer* (Imperial 1962) ★★★, *Yodeling* (Imperial 1963)

★★★, *Irish Songs – The Slim Whitman Way* (Imperial 1963) ★★, *Love Song Of The Waterfall* (Imperial 1964) ★★★★, *Reminiscing* (Imperial 1964) ★★★, *More Than Yesterday* (Imperial 1965) ★★★, *Forever* (Imperial 1966) ★★★, *God's Hand In Mine* (Imperial 1966) ★★, *A Travellin' Man* (Imperial 1966) ★★★, *A Time For Love* (Imperial 1966) ★★★, *A Lonesome Heart* (Sunset 1967) ★★★, *Country Memories* (Imperial 1967) ★★★, *In Love, The Whitman Way* (Imperial 1968) ★★★★, *Unchain Your Heart* (Sunset 1968) ★★★, *Happy Street* (Imperial 1968) ★★★, *Slim!* (Imperial 1969) ★★★, *The Slim Whitman Christmas Album* (Imperial 1969) ★★, *Ramblin' Rose* (1970) ★★★, *Tomorrow Never Comes* (United Artists 1970) ★★★, *Guess Who* aka *Snowbird* (United Artists 1971) ★★★, *It's A Sin To Tell A Lie* (United Artists 1971) ★★★, *I'll See You When* (United Artists 1973) ★★★, *25th Anniversary Concert* (United Artists 1973) ★★★, *Happy Anniversary* (United Artists 1974) ★★★, *Everything Leads Back To You* (United Artists 1975) ★★★, *Home On The Range* (United Artists 1977) ★★★, *Red River Valley* (United Artists 1977) ★★★, *Ghost Riders In The Sky* (United Artists 1978) ★★★, *Till We Meet Again* (United Artists 1980) ★★★, *Just For You* (Suffolk 1980) ★★★, *Songs I Love To Sing* (Cleveland International 1980) ★★★, *Christmas With Slim Whitman* (Cleveland International 1980) ★★, *Mr. Songman* (Liberty 1981) ★★★, *I'll Be Home For Christmas* (1981) ★★, *Angeline* (Epic 1984) ★★★, *A Dream Come True – The Rarities Album* (1987) ★★★, with Byron Whitman *Magic Moments* (1990) ★★★.

● COMPILATIONS: *Country Hits Volume 1* (Imperial 1960) ★★★, *All Time Favourites* (Imperial 1964) ★★★, *Country Songs, City Hits* (1965) ★★★, *Birmingham Jail* (RCA Camden 1966) ★★★, *Fifteenth Anniversary* (Imperial 1967) ★★★, *The Very Best Of Slim Whitman* (United Artists 1976) ★★★, *All My Best* (Suffolk 1979) ★★★, *Slim Whitman's 20 Greatest Love Songs* (MFP 1981) ★★★, *Slim Whitman: The Collection* (Liberty 1989) ★★★, *The Best Of Slim Whitman (1952-1972)* (Rhino 1990) ★★★★, *20 Golden Greats* (1992) ★★★, *EMI Country Masters: 50 Original Tracks* (EMI 1993) ★★★, *Love Songs* (MFP 1994) ★★★, *Rose Marie: Slim Whitman 1949-1959* 6-CD box set (Bear Family 1996) ★★★, *50th Anniversary Collection* (EMI 1997) ★★★.

● FURTHER READING: *Mr. Songman – The Slim Whitman Story*, Kenneth L. Gibble.

● FILMS: *Jamboree* aka *Disc Jockey Jamboree* (1957).

WHYTON, WALLY

b. 23 September 1929, London, England, d. 22 January 1997, London, England. Broadcaster and singer Wally Whyton enjoyed a fascinating and varied professional career after initially training as a commercial artist. However, after socializing with Lionel Bart and his first exposure to the jazz records of Louis Armstrong and Bessie Smith, Whyton soon developed ambitions to become a singer. He subsequently formed a skiffle band, the Vipers, with himself on vocals and fellow members Johnny Martyn, Jean Van den Bosch, Tony Tolhurst and John Pilgrim. They established a residency at the 2I's Coffee Bar in New Compton Street, Soho, in 1956. A record contract with Parlophone Records ensued, and the group's second single, 'Don't You Rock Me Daddy-O', entered the UK Top 10 later that year. Their other chart successes were 'Cumberland Gap' and 'Streamline Train' (a version of 'Maggie May' was banned by the BBC), but the skiffle boom quickly faded, although the Vipers remained active until the end of the 50s. During that period several musicians passed through the group's ranks, including future Shadows Hank Marvin, Jet Harris and Tony Meehan. Hoping to concentrate on a career as a folk-singer, Whyton was then diverted into television entertainment when a one-off appearance on a Rolf Harris show led to a permanent spot. Eventually, he hosted his own children's series, The Five O'Clock Show, for Rediffusion. Here he introduced the hugely popular glove puppet Pussycat Willum, followed by other creations including Ollie Beak, Joe Crow and Spike McPike. Whyton recorded a series of successful children's albums, but also remained active on the folk scene. Recording for Argo and Phillips Records, he became a regular on BBC Radio, presenting Folk Room, Strings 'n' Things and Junior Choice. He was then approached to host Country Meet Folk, a series where the two complementary musical styles were to be combined. It ran for over six years after originally being devised as a six-week series. He was a natural choice as host when the BBC launched The Country Club show in the mid-70s. With his regular visits to Nashville and reports on the Silk Cut Country Music Festival at Wembley, Whyton effectively became 'the voice of country music' in Britain throughout the 70s and 80s. He was still presenting a show for the BBC World Service until a month before his death in January 1997.

● ALBUMS: Leave Them With A Flower/It's Me Mum (Bear Family 1998) ★★★.
● COMPILATIONS: with the Vipers Skiffle Group 10,000 Years Ago 3-CD box set (Bear Family 1997) ★★★.

WICKMAN, PUTTE

b. Hans-Olof Wickman, 10 September 1924, Falun, Sweden. He played clarinet from childhood, emerging in the years after World War II as a distinguished player in the swing era style of Benny Goodman. Soon, however, he began to adapt to the new sounds of bop, and was thus one of very few clarinettists to make the move. By the early 50s he was sufficiently well regarded to be on regular call to support visiting American jazz musicians and he also played with fellow-countryman Lars Gullin. In the 60s he moved into more commercial music, forming a dance band that became successful. In the 70s he returned to jazz, playing with increasing technical mastery as the years passed. His recordings of the 90s demonstrate a sometimes clinical accuracy, although Wickman never fails

to swing.
● ALBUMS: The Sound Of Surprise (Dragon 1969) ★★★, Happy New Year! (Odeon 1973) ★★★, Putte Wickman Quartet Live In Stockholm (Out 1977) ★★, Mr Clarinet (Four Leaf Clover 1985) ★★★, Bewitched (Four Leaf 1985) ★★★, The Very Thought Of You (Dragon 1988) ★★★, Some O' This And Some O' That 1989 recording (Dragon 1992) ★★★★, In Trombones (Phontastic 1992) ★★★, In Silhouette (Phontastic 1994) ★★★.
COMPILATIONS: Young, Searching And Swinging 1945-55 recordings (Phontastic 1990)★★★.

WIGGINS, GERRY

b. 12 May 1922, New York City, New York, USA. One of Wiggins' first professional jobs was playing piano for the club act of film actor-comedian Stepin Fetchit (Lincoln Perry). After hearing Art Tatum he turned to jazz and, following a spell with Les Hite, worked with Louis Armstrong and Benny Carter. In the mid-40s Wiggins settled in Los Angeles and established a reputation as a reliable accompanist for singers. During the 50s and 60s he worked for Lena Horne, Kay Starr, Nat 'King' Cole, Lou Rawls and Eartha Kitt. Also in the 60s he was active in film and television soundtrack work but he played with several jazz groups too, including Gerald Wilson's big band. In the mid-70s he toured Europe with Helen Humes, then in the 80s worked with Red Callender and also appeared on the international festival circuit. He continued to serve singers well, playing with Linda Hopkins. He also regularly returned to work with Wilson and occasionally led his own small groups. A solid, dependable pianist with eclectic tastes, Wiggins remains relatively unknown despite his many qualities.
● ALBUMS: Gerald Wiggins Trio 10-inch album (Discovery 1953) ★★★, Gerald Wiggins Trio (Dig 1956) ★★★, Around The World In 80 Days (OJC 1956) ★★★, Reminiscin' With Wig (Motif 1956) ★★★★, The King And I (Challenge 1957) ★★★, The Loveliness Of You (Tampa 1957) ★★★, Gerald Wiggins Trio (Tampa 1957) ★★★, Relax And Enjoy It (Contemporary 1961) ★★★, Wiggin' Out (Hifijazz 1961) ★★★, Wig Is Here (Black And Blue 1975) ★★★, with Red Callender Night Mist Blues (Hemisphere 1983) ★★★, Live At The Maybeck Recital Hall Vol. 8 (Concord Jazz 1990) ★★★★, Soulidarity (Concord Jazz 1996) ★★★.

WIGGS, JOHNNY

b. John Wigginton Hyman, 25 July 1899, New Orleans, Louisiana, USA, d. 9 October 1977, New Orleans, Louisiana, USA. Although he played violin for some years, Wiggs was concurrently developing a reputation as a cornet player. After playing briefly in New York in the mid-20s he settled in his home town, concentrating now on cornet. Active as a teacher throughout the 30s and early 40s, Wiggs resumed full-time playing in the late 40s. He led his own bands, made some records and worked with Eddie Miller and others but by the 60s was again playing part time. He continue to work into the 70s, recording with

Maxine Sullivan. A strong and effective player, the nature of Wiggs' career kept him in largely unwarranted shadows.

● ALBUMS: with Raymond Burke *New Orleans Jazz Chamber Music Session* 10-inch album (Paramount 1954) ★★★, with Burke *Chamber Jazz* 10-inch album (S/D 1955) ★★★.

WILBER, BOB

b. Robert Sage Wilber, 15 March 1928, New York City, New York, USA. After studying clarinet as a child, Wilber began leading his own band and while still a teenager became a student of Sidney Bechet. He recorded with Bechet, grew adept on the soprano saxophone, and was clearly at home in a traditional jazz setting. Nevertheless, Wilber's avid desire to expand his knowledge and expertise led him to further studies under Lennie Tristano. A mid-50s band Wilber led blended traditional with modern concepts in jazz and, perhaps predictably, fell between the two audiences for such music. During the late 50s and on through the 60s, Wilber played and recorded with distinguished leaders, such as Bobby Hackett, Benny Goodman, Bechet, Jack Teagarden and Eddie Condon. At the close of the 60s (at this time also playing alto saxophone), he became one of the original members of the World's Greatest Jazz Band. In the early 70s, he teamed up with Kenny Davern to form Soprano Summit, a band which brought him to the attention of new audiences around the world. This group stayed in existence until 1979 and soon afterwards he formed the Bechet Legacy band, recording extensively, often on his own record label, Bodeswell.

Active in jazz education, Wilber has also been musical director of the Smithsonian Jazz Repertory Ensemble, the house band for some of the Duke Ellington conventions, and has written for films, most notably the recreation of Ellington's music for *The Cotton Club* (1984). He continued leading his Bechet Legacy band throughout the 80s, making records (including a fine set which set out to recapture the essence of the King Oliver band), and accompanying his wife, singer Joanne 'Pug' Horton. He also recreated a Benny Goodman band for anniversary performances of the 1938 Carnegie Hall concert and published his autobiography, *Music Was Not Enough* (in collaboration with Derek Webster). In the early 90s Wilber was reunited with Davern for concert appearances and was still keenly exploring new ways of presenting older musical styles to a contemporary audience.

● ALBUMS: *Bob Wilber Jazz Band* 10-inch album, 1949 recording (Circle/Jazzology 1951) ★★★, *Young Men With Horns* 10-inch album (Riverside 1952) ★★★, *Spreadin' Joy* (Classic Jazz 1957) ★★★★, *Bob Wilber And His All Star Band* i (Music Minus One 1959) ★★★, *Bob Wilber And His All Star Band* ii (Music Minus One 1959) ★★★, *New Clarinet In Town* (Classic Jazz 1960) ★★★, *Evolution Of The Blues* (1960) ★★★★, *Blowin' The Blues Away* (1960) ★★★, *The Music Of Hoagy Carmichael* (Monmouth 1969) ★★★★, with Soprano Summit *Soprano Summit* (World Jazz 1973) ★★★★, with Soprano Summit *Soprano Summit II* (World Jazz 1974) ★★★★, with Soprano Summit *Chalumeau Blue* (Chiaroscuro 1976) ★★★, with Soprano Summit *Soprano Summit At The Big Horn Jazzfest* (Concord Jazz 1976) ★★★★, with Soprano Summit *Soprano Summit In Concert* (Concord Jazz 1976) ★★★★, with Scott Hamilton *Bob Wilber And The Scott Hamilton Quartet* (Chiaroscuro 1977) ★★★★, *At Thatchers* (J&M 1977) ★★, with Soprano Summit *Soprano Summit Live At Concord* (Concord Jazz 1977) ★★★★, *Rapturous Reeds* (Phontastic 1978) ★★★, with Joanne 'Pug' Horton *The Many Faces Of Bob Wilber And Pug Horton* (1978) ★★★, *Groovin' At The Grunewald* (Phontastic 1978) ★★★, *Original Wilber* (1978) ★★, *In The Mood For Swing* (Phontastic 1979) ★★★★, *The Music Of Fats Waller And James P. Johnson* (1979) ★★★, *Dizzy Fingers* (Bodeswell 1980) ★★★, with Bechet Legacy *Bob Wilber And The Bechet Legacy* (Bodeswell 1981) ★★★, *The Music Of King Oliver's Creole Jazz Band* (GHB 1981) ★★★, with Bechet Legacy *On The Road* (Bodeswell 1981) ★★★, with Horton *Don't Go Away* (1981) ★★★, with Bechet Legacy *Ode To Bechet* (Bodeswell 1982) ★★★★, *Reflections* (Bodeswell 1983) ★★★, with Dick Wellstood *The Bob Wilber-Dick Wellstood Duet* (Progressive 1984) ★★★★, *The Cotton Club* film soundtrack (1984) ★★★★, with Soprano Summit *Summit Reunion* (Chiaroscuro 1990) ★★★, *Dancing On A Rainbow* (Circle 1990) ★★, with Soprano Summit *Summit Reunion 1992* (Chiaroscuro 1992) ★★★, *Moments Like This* (Phontastic 1992) ★★, *Horns A-Plenty* (Arbors 1994) ★★★, with Soprano Summit *Jazz Im Amerika Haus, Vol. 5* (Nagel-Heyer 1995) ★★★, with Bechet Legacy *Bob Wilber & Bechet Legacy* 1984 recording (Challenge 1995) ★★★, *A Man And His Music* (Progressive 1995) ★★★, with Soprano Summit *Yellow Dog Blues* (Chiaroscuro 1995) ★★★★, with Bechet Legacy *The Hamburg Concert – Tribute To A Legend* (Nagel-Heyer 1996) ★★★, with Soprano Summit *Soprano Summit: Live At The Illiana Jazz Club* 1976 recording (Storyville 1996) ★★★, *Bean: Tribute To Coleman Hawkins* (Arbors 1996) ★★★★, *Bufadora Blow-Up: At The March Of Jazz '96* (Arbors 1997) ★★★, *Nostalgia* (Arbors 1997) ★★★, with Dick Hyman *A Perfect Match* (Arbors 1998) ★★★★, with Kenny Davern *Reunion At Arbors* (Arbors 1998) ★★★, *What Swing Is All About* (Nagel-Heyer 1998) ★★★, *The Wolverines At Bern At 35* (Arbors Jazz 1999) ★★★, with Davern *Summit Reunion* (Nagel-Heyer 1999) ★★, *Everywhere You Go There's Jazz* (Arbors 1999) ★★★, *Fletcher Henderson's Unrecorded Arrangements For Benny Goodman* (Arbors 2000) ★★★★.

● COMPILATIONS: *Bob Wilber's Wildcats* 1947 recordings (Riverside 2000) ★★★.

● FURTHER READING: *Music Was Not Enough*, Bob Wilber with Derek Webster.

WILD PARTY, THE

Football players, drop-outs, petty criminals and jazz musicians team up in an unlikely Hollywood farrago made in 1956 and directed by Harry Horner and starring Anthony Quinn and Nehemiah Persoff. Jazz, on-screen and off, is provided by a host of talented studio-cum-jazz musicians. Amongst them are Georgie Auld, Teddy Buckner, Pete Candoli, Bob Cooper, Buddy De Franco, Maynard Ferguson, Frank Rosolino, Bud Shank and Alvin Stoller. Persoff's on-screen piano playing was dubbed by Pete Jolly.

WILDE, MARTY

b. Reginald Leonard Smith, 15 April 1936, London, England. After playing briefly in a skiffle group, this UK rock 'n' roll singer secured a residency at London's Condor Club under the name Reg Patterson. He was spotted by songwriter Lionel Bart, who subsequently informed entrepreneur Larry Parnes. The starmaker was keen to sign the singer and rapidly took over his career. Reg Smith henceforth became Marty Wilde. His Christian name was coined from the sentimental film Marty, while the surname was meant to emphasize the wilder side of Smith's nature. Parnes next arranged a recording contract with Philips Records, but Wilde's initial singles, including a reading of Jimmie Rodgers' 'Honeycomb', failed to chart. Nevertheless, Wilde was promoted vigorously and appeared frequently on BBC Television's pop music programme 6.5 Special. Extensive media coverage culminated with a hit recording of Jody Reynolds' alluringly morbid 'Endless Sleep' in 1957.

Soon afterwards, Parnes persuaded the influential producer Jack Good to make Wilde the resident star of his new television programme Oh Boy!. The arrangement worked well for Wilde until Good objected to his single 'Misery's Child' and vetoed the song. Worse followed when Good effectively replaced Wilde with a new singing star, Cliff Richard. Before long, Richard had taken Wilde's mantle as the UK's premier teen-idol and was enjoying consistent hits. Wilde, meanwhile, was gradually changing his image. After considerable success with such songs as 'Donna', 'Teenager In Love', 'Sea Of Love' and his own composition 'Bad Boy', he veered away from rock 'n' roll. His marriage to Joyce Baker of the Vernons Girls was considered a bad career move at the time, and partly contributed to Wilde's announcement that he would henceforth be specializing in classy, Frank Sinatra-style ballads. For several months he hosted a new pop show, Boy Meets Girls, and later starred in the West End production of Bye Bye Birdie. Although Parnes was intent on promoting Wilde as an actor, the star was resistant to such a move. His last major success was with a lacklustre version of Bobby Vee's 'Rubber Ball' in 1961.

Later in the decade he recorded for several labels, including a stint as the Wilde Three with his wife Joyce, and future Moody Blues vocalist Justin Hayward. Wilde enjoyed considerable radio play and was unfortunate not to enjoy a belated hit

with the catchy 'Abergavenny' in 1969. He also found some success as the writer of hits such as Status Quo's 'Ice In The Sun'. By the 70s, Wilde was managing his son Ricky, who was briefly promoted as Britain's answer to Little Jimmy Osmond. Ricky later achieved success as a songwriter for his sister, Kim Wilde. In 1994, Marty Wilde appeared at London's Royal Albert Hall with Brenda Lee, Joe Brown, Eden Kane and John Leyton in the nostalgic Solid Gold Rock 'N' Roll Show. In the following year he presented Coffee Bar Kids, a BBC Radio 2 documentary programme that examined the origins of rock 'n' roll in the UK.

● ALBUMS: Wilde About Marty (Philips 1959) ★★★, Bad Boy (Epic 1960) ★★★, Showcase (Philips 1960) ★★★, The Versatile Mr. Wilde (Philips 1960) ★★★, Diversions (Philips 1969) ★★, Rock 'N' Roll (Philips 1970) ★★, Good Rocking – Then And Now (Philips 1974) ★★★.
● COMPILATIONS: Wild Cat Rocker (Jan 1981) ★★★, The Hits Of Marty Wilde (Philips 1984) ★★★.

WILDER, ALEC

b. Alexander LaFayette Chew Wilder, 16 February 1907, Rochester, New York, USA, d. 23 December 1980, Gainesville, Florida, USA. A composer of popular ballads, illustrative works, jazz and classical pieces, Wilder attended Collegiate School, New York, and studied privately at the Eastman School of Music. He became an active composer in 1930 when his first popular song, 'All The King's Horses', was interpolated into the Arthur Schwartz and Howard Dietz revue Three's A Crowd. Thereafter, he is reputed to have written several hundred popular songs, including 'Stop That Dancin' Up There', 'It's So Peaceful In The Country', 'J.P. Dooley III' (a jazz piece recorded by Harry James), 'Who Can I Turn To?', 'Soft As Spring', 'Moon And Sand', 'At The Swing Shift Ball', 'While We're Young', 'I'll Be Around', 'The Long Night', 'One More Road', 'All The Cats Join In' (featured by Benny Goodman And His Orchestra in the 1946 Walt Disney cartoon Make Mine Music), 'Kalamazoo To Timbuktu', 'Goodbye John', 'Crazy In The Heart', 'Winter Of My Discontent', 'You're Free', 'Is It Always Like This?', 'Summer Is A-Comin' In', and 'April Age'. Artists who have recorded from his popular catalogue include Frank Sinatra, Mabel Mercer, Bing Crosby, Mildred Bailey, Marlene Dietrich, Peggy Lee, Nat 'King' Cole, Jeri Southern, and Anita O'Day.

UK singer Elaine Delmar devoted a complete album, Elaine Sings Wilder, to him. Among his serious works were sonatas for flute, tuba and bassoon, a concerto for saxophone and chamber orchestra, quintets and trios for various musical instruments, piano works, four operas, the Juke Box ballet, and several unorthodox pieces, such as 'A Debutante's Diary', 'Sea Fugue Mama', 'She'll Be Seven In May', 'Neurotic Goldfish', 'Dance Man Buys A Farm', 'Concerning Etchings', 'Walking Home In The Spring', 'Amorous Poltergeist' and 'The Children Met The Train'. For over 50 years of

his life he lived in the Algonquin Hotel, Manhattan, and the Sheraton in Rochester, New York City. His memoir of the period he spent at the Algonquin was unpublished at the time of his death from lung cancer in 1980. Two of his books that did emerge are *Letters I Never Mailed* (1975), a collection of imaginary letters to real people, and *American Popular Song: The Great Innovators 1900-1950* (with James T. Maher) (1972). He hosted a weekly series based on the latter book for the National Public Radio.
● ALBUMS: *Alec Wilder And His Octet* 10-inch album (Mercury 1949) ★★★, *Alec Wilder Octet* 10-inch album (Columbia 1951) ★★★, *The Music Of Alec Wilder Conducted By Alec Wilder* (Columbia 1974) ★★★.
● FURTHER READING: *Alec Wilder And His Friends*, Whitney Balliett.

WILKINS, ERNIE

b. 20 July 1922, St. Louis, Missouri, USA, d. 5 June 1999, Copenhagen, Denmark. Wilkins studied formally at Wilberforce University, learning piano and violin before taking up the saxophone. He played locally before military service and in the post-war years played in the Jeter-Pillars Orchestra and that led by Earl 'Fatha' Hines. He then freelanced as player, composer and arranger until in 1952 he joined Count Basie, playing alto and tenor saxophones and, more importantly, becoming one of the bandleader's most respected composers and arrangers. He wrote 'Every Day I Have The Blues' for Basie's singer Joe Williams; the song went on to become one of the bestselling jazz records of all-time. He returned to freelancing in the 1955, concentrating on writing arrangements for many bands, including those of Basie, Tommy Dorsey, Dizzy Gillespie and Harry James. Wilkins' charts for the James band were outstanding and helped to create one of the best bands the trumpeter led. In many respects these arrangements, loosely swinging and with tight section work, closely resembled similar work that Wilkins did for Basie and which was partly responsible for boosting the Basie band into its second period of greatness. Whether James or Basie was the first to play in this manner remains a matter of some contention. In the 60s Wilkins' career stalled due to addiction problems but he still wrote for several big bands, including that led by Clark Terry. In the early 70s he was A&R director for Mainstream Records and later in the decade worked again with Terry, before settling in Copenhagen, Denmark. In the 80s he formed his own Almost Big Band. As a big band arranger, Wilkins belonged firmly in the post-Sy Oliver tradition and consistently adhered to the characteristics of a style which concentrated upon presenting an uncluttered ensemble sound that effectively framed the soloists.
● ALBUMS: with Kenny Clarke *Plenty For Kenny* (Savoy 1955) ★★★, *Here Comes The Swingin' Mr. Wilkins* (Everest 1959) ★★★, *The Big New Band Of The '60s* (Everest 1960) ★★★, *A Time For The Blues* (1973) ★★★, *Ernie Wilkins And The Almost*

Big Band (Storyville 1980) ★★★, *Montreux* (Steeple Chase 1983) ★★★, *On The Roll* (Steeple Chase 1983) ★★★, *K.a.l.e.i.d.o.d.u.k.e.* (Birdology 1991) ★★★.

WILLIAMS, ANDRE

b. 1 November 1936, Bessemer, Alabama, but raised in Chicago, Illinois, USA. Williams has made his lasting mark in the R&B industry as a recording artist, songwriter, and producer of the first doo-wop vocal groups and then soul acts. He is noted for his sly streetwise songs in which he basically talks (with a rhythmic feel) the lyrics rather than sings them, earning him the unofficial title 'The Father Of Rap'. Like many African-American artists, Williams began his career in the church, singing in the Cobbs Baptist Church choir in the 40s. He began singing in vocal groups in the early 50s, forming the Cavaliers. He later moved to Detroit and recorded several singles with the Don Juans for the Fortune Records label. Williams soon disengaged himself to establish a solo career on Fortune, making his biggest impact with two jokey records, 'Jail Bait' and 'Bacon Fat' (number 9 R&B) in 1957. He also concurrently sang with the Five Dollars who released several singles on Fortune. By the early 60s Williams was back in Chicago working as a producer and songwriter for various labels, including several spells with Berry Gordy's Motown Records where he worked with Mary Wells, Stevie Wonder and Eddie Holland. He produced Joyce Kennedy for Blue Rock, JoAnn Garrett for Checker Records and Duo, and co-wrote and produced two perennial dance classics, 'Shake A Tail Feather' for the Five Duotones and 'Twine Time' for Alvin Cash. Meanwhile, he recorded some solo tracks for Checker, obtaining a modest chart entry with 'Cadillac Jack' (number 46 R&B) in 1968. He also recorded some singles for Avin in Detroit and worked with Ike Turner. In the early 70s Williams went down to Texas to produce for Duke Records, but after the label was sold to ABC Records in 1974 he returned to Chicago. Williams continued to work as an artist manager and independent producer although personal problems and addictions sidelined him for a long spell. In a burst of productivity he released several albums in the late 90s which revealed that his salacious wit was still in perfect working order. These albums also included contributions from several contemporary garage rock bands, including the Jon Spencer Blues Explosion, who professed their admiration for the raw sexuality of Williams' songs.
● ALBUMS: *Directly From The Streets* (Ichiban 1990) ★★★, *Mr. Rhythm Is Back* (Revolvo 1994) ★★★, *Fat Back And Corn Liquor* (St. George 1996) ★★★, *Silky* (In The Red 1998) ★★★, with the Sadies *Red Dirt* (Bloodshot/Sonic Rendezvous 1999) ★★★, *Is The Black Godfather* (In The Red 2000) ★★★, *Bait And Switch* (Norton 2001) ★★★.
● COMPILATIONS: *Jail Bait* (Fortune 1984) ★★★★.

WILLIAMS, BIG JOE

b. Joe Lee Williams, 16 October 1903, Crawford, Mississippi, USA, d. 17 December 1982, Macon, Mississippi, USA. Big Joe Williams was one of the most important blues singers to have recorded and also one whose life conforms almost exactly to the stereotyped pattern of how a 'country' blues singer should live. He was of partial Red Indian stock, his father being 'Red Bone' Williams, a part-Cherokee. 'Big Joe' took his musical influences from his mother's family, the Logans. He made the obligatory 'cigar box' instruments as a child and took to the road when his stepfather threw him out around 1918. He later immortalized this antagonist in a song that he was still performing at the end of his long career. Williams' life was one of constant movement as he worked his way around the lumber camps, turpentine farms and juke joints of the south, playing with the Birmingham Jug Band in 1929. Around 1930 he married and settled in St. Louis, Missouri, but still took long sweeps through the country as the rambling habit never left him. This rural audience supported him through the worst of the Depression when he appeared under the name 'Poor Joe'. His known recordings began in 1935 when he laid down six tracks for Bluebird Records in Chicago.

From then on he recorded at every opportunity, including his durable blues classic 'Baby Please Don't Go'. He stayed with Bluebird until 1945 before moving to Columbia Records. He formed a loose partnership on many sessions with John Lee 'Sonny Boy' Williamson that has been likened to that of Muddy Waters and Little Walter. In 1952, he worked for Trumpet in Jackson, Mississippi, then went back to Chicago for a session with Vee Jay Records. Other recordings made for smaller companies are still being discovered. During 1951/2, he also made recordings of other singers at his St. Louis base. Williams found a wider audience when blues came into vogue with young whites in the 60s. He continued to record and tour, adding Europe and Japan to his itinerary. He still used cheap, expendable guitars fixed up by himself with an electrical pick-up and usually festooned with extra machine heads to accommodate nine strings. With his gruff, shouting voice and ringing guitar – not to mention his sometimes uncertain temper – he became a great favourite on the club and concert circuit. He had come full circle and was living in a caravan in Crawford, Mississippi, when he died. The sheer volume of easily accessible albums recorded during his last years tended to obscure just how big a blues talent Williams really was.

● ALBUMS: *Tough Times* (Fontana 1960) ★★★, *Mississippi's Big Joe Williams And His Nine-String Guitar* (Folkways 1962) ★★★★, *Piney Woods Blues* (Delmark 1962) ★★★★, *Blues On Highway 49* (Delmark 1962) ★★★, *Blues For 9 Strings* (Bluesville 1962) ★★★★, *Big Joe Williams At Folk City* (Bluesville 1963) ★★★, *Studio Blues* (Bluesville 1964) ★★★, *Starvin' Chain Blues* (Delmark 1966) ★★★, *Classic Delta Blues* 1964 recording (Milestone 1966) ★★★★, *Back To The Country* (Bounty 1966) ★★★, *Hell Bound And Heaven Sent* (Folkways 1967) ★★★, *Don't You Leave Me Here* (Storyville 1969) ★★★, *Big Joe Williams* (Xtra 1969) ★★★, *Hand Me Down My Old Walking Stick* (Liberty 1969) ★★★, *Crawlin' King Snake* (RCA 1970) ★★★, *Legacy Of The Blues, Volume 6* (Sonet 1972) ★★★, *Guitar Blues* (Storyville 1973) ★★★, *Malvina My Sweet Woman* (Old Blues 1974) ★★★, *Ramblin' Wanderin' Blues* (Storyville 1974) ★★★, *Tough Times* (Arhoolie 1981) ★★★, *Thinking Of What They Did* (Arhoolie 1981) ★★★, *Big Joe Williams 1974* (Arhoolie 1982) ★★★, *Going Back To Crawford* (Arhoolie 1999) ★★★, *These Are My Blues* 1965 live recording (Testament 1998) ★★, *No More Whiskey* (Evidence 1998) ★★.

● COMPILATIONS: *Field Recordings 1973-1980* (L&R 1988) ★★★, *Complete Recorded Works In Chronological Order Volumes 1 & 2* (Blues Document 1991) ★★★, *The Final Years* (Verve 1995) ★★★.

WILLIAMS, BILLY

b. 28 December 1910, Waco, Texas, USA, d. 17 October 1972. Williams formed the very successful gospel group the Charioteers in the early 30s while studying theology at Wilberforce College, Ohio. The group had regular radio spots in Cincinnati and New York and worked with Bing Crosby on the west coast. In the 40s they had seven hits of their own and also charted with Frank Sinatra. In 1949 Williams left and formed the Billy Williams Quartet with Eugene Dixon (bass), Claude Riddick (baritone) and John Ball (tenor). The group were often seen on television including over 160 appearances on Sid Caesar's *Your Show Of Shows*. They recorded with little impact for Mercury Records and MGM Records before joining Coral Records in 1954 and after a few unsuccessful covers of R&B hits the group collected nine US chart entries. The biggest of these was a revival of Fats Waller's 'I'm Gonna Sit Right Down And Right Myself A Letter': a US Top 3 and UK Top 30 hit in 1957. The jazzy R&B artist sadly lost his voice, due to diabetes, in the early 60s. He moved to Chicago where he became a social worker, employed on a model cities project and helping alcoholics until his death in 1972.

WILLIAMS, DOC

b. Andrew J. Smik Jnr., 26 June 1914, Cleveland, Ohio, USA. A noted traditionalist who, except for short spells at Memphis (1939) and Frederick (1945), was associated with the *Wheeling Jamboree* at WWVA Wheeling, West Virginia, for over 40 years, after first appearing with his band the Border Riders in 1937. He married Chickie (b. Jessie Wanda Crupe, 13 February 1919, Bethany, West Virginia, USA) in 1939 and she sang regularly with the band (in later years they were sometimes joined by their three daughters, Barbara, Madeline and Karen). Their family show also featured brother Cy Williams (fiddle) and Marion Martin (chordovox). Williams regularly played hundreds of shows a year in the USA and Canada. He has also made several trips to Britain, where he proved immensely popular around the country clubs. He has made many recordings for his own Wheeling label and though he never achieved any chart entries, he is associated with such songs as 'Wheeling Back To Wheeling', 'My Old Brown Coat And Me' and the tear-jerkers 'Daddy's Little Angel' and 'He Said He Had A Friend'. It has also been claimed that Chickie recorded the original version of 'Beyond The Sunset'.

● ALBUMS: *Sings Country & Western* (Wheeling 50s-70s), *25th Anniversary Album* (Wheeling 50s-70s), *Wheeling Back To Wheeling* (Wheeling 50s-70s), *Williams Family Sacred Album* (Wheeling 50s-70s), *Doc Williams Show* (Wheeling 50s-70s), *Collector's Series Volumes 1 & 2* (Wheeling 50s-70s), *Daddy's Little Angel* (Wheeling 50s-70s), *From Out Of The Beautiful Hills Of West Virginia* (Wheeling 50s-70s), *Doc & Chickie Together* (Wheeling 50s-70s), *Favorites Old And New* (Wheeling 50s-70s), *Reminiscing* (Wheeling 50s-70s), with Karen Williams *The Three Of Us* (Wheeling 50s-70s), *We've Come A Long Way Together* (Wheeling 50s-70s).

WILLIAMS, GENE

b. USA. Gene Williams first entered the entertainment industry as vocalist with the Claude Thornhill Orchestra, before forming his own dance band in 1950 in New York City, New York, USA. The musical sidemen enrolled included Harry Wegbreit, Jack Mootz, Don Josephs, Harry Di Vito, Dick Hoch, Sam Marowitz, Charlie O'Cain, Mickey Folus, Joe Reisman, Teddy Napoleon, Russ Saunders and Mel Zelnick. While Gene Williams himself and Adele Castle were the featured vocalists, Gil Evans, Hubie Wheeler, Chico O'Farrill and Joe Reisman served as the band's arrangers.

Their initial contracts came from college dates, before the membership elected to put the group on a more permanent footing. Mixing bebop instrumentals with the smooth style inherited from Williams' time with Thornhill, by 1952 they had secured engagements at venues such as the Glen Island Casino. Thereafter, however, they struggled to make any headway, hamstrung by the reduced air time available to dance bands with the advent of rock 'n' roll.

WILLIAMS, JODY

b. Joseph Leon Williams, 3 February 1935, Mobile, Alabama, USA. This legendary Chess studio guitarist was the leader of one of Howlin' Wolf's early bands. More people are familiar with Jody Williams' guitarwork than they are with his name. Anyone with Bo Diddley's 'Who Do You Love' or Billy Boy Arnold's 'I Wish You Would' (Williams wrote 'I Was Fooled', the b-side of the original Vee Jay single) or Billy Stewart's 'Billy's Blues' (the trial run for 'Love Is Strange'), has a sample of his ringing, nervy guitarwork. Though making only a handful of singles, few of them under his own name, he was an extremely busy session and house musician throughout the 50s. He arrived in Chicago in 1941, first taking up the harmonica before learning guitar with Ellas McDaniel (Bo

Diddley), but to greater effect than the future star. By 1951, they and tub bass player Roosevelt Jackson, had formed a band. Williams quickly became a proficient and in-demand musician, touring the USA in Charles Brown's band before he was 20. That year (1955), he played on Diddley's 'Diddy Wah Diddy', Arnold's 'I Wish You Would' and soloed alongside B.B. King on Otis Spann's 'Five Spot'. Inevitably, his own career was incidental to his other work. Singles appeared on Blue Lake, Argo and Herald as Little Papa Joe or Little Joe Lee or Sugar Boy Williams, since Joe Williams already sang with Count Basie's band. In the mid-60s, he abandoned music to study electronics, and later, computer maintenance. He has made sporadic appearances since then but has not been tempted back to performing.

WILLIAMS, JOSEPH 'JO JO'

b. 1920, Coahoma, Mississippi, USA. One of a legion of musicians whose name and record follow one another with Pavlovian accuracy, Williams played in bands whose members sometimes worked with better-known artists. Raised in north-west Mississippi and on the outskirts of Memphis, his first steps in music were with baling wire strung on the wall. During the 30s he witnessed Son House and Willie Brown playing for country suppers. He developed his guitar-playing in Memphis in the early 40s before moving on to Chicago. In 1953 he played his first professional gig, with pianist Lazy Bill Lucas. Two years later, Williams formed his own group with Lucas, drummer Johnny Swanns and Lucas' niece, 'Miss Hi Fi', singing. He then teamed up with harmonica player Mojo Buford in a band with Dave Members and Cadillac Sam Burton. With Buford, he became a member of Muddy Waters' Junior Band, playing Smitty's Corner when Waters was out of town. In 1959, he made two records, the first unnumbered, for the Atomic-H label. 'All Pretty Wimmens' epitomizes raucous, impromptu blues at its best, all the better for being obscure, as was the follow-up, 'Afro Shake Dance'. In 1962, he moved, with Lucas and Buford, to Minneapolis, playing bass in a group that recorded as Mojo And The Chi Fours, the material released on Folk Art and Vernon. Two years later, the band had two singles released on Adell. Williams recorded with Lazy Bill for Lucas' own label in 1970, and retired from music some time in the 70s.

● ALBUMS: *Lazy Bill And His Friends* (1970) ★★★.

WILLIAMS, L.C.

b. 12 March 1930, Crockett, Texas, USA, d. 18 October 1960, Houston, Texas, USA. Another artist whose given names are initials, Williams grew up in Mullican, Texas, before moving to Houston around 1945. There he worked in dancehalls and bars as both singer and dancer. He also learned to play drums. Having made the acquaintance of Lightnin' Hopkins, he recorded for Bill Quinn's Gold Star label, nicknamed 'Lightnin' Jr.', with Hopkins backing him on guitar and piano on three singles, and pianists Leroy Carter and Elmore Nixon on one side each of a fourth, all subsequently reissued. He also recorded for Freedom, another Houston label owned by Solomon Kahal, making six records, one combining 'My Darkest Hour' and 'I Want My Baby Back' reissued on Imperial Records, mostly with Conrad Johnson's Conney's Combo. In 1951 he recorded at least four titles, including 'Baby Child' and 'Fannie Mae', for Sittin In With, owned by New Yorker Bob Shad. Shad probably produced Williams' final commercial session, made the same year for Mercury Records with backing by saxophonist Henry Hayes And His Rhythm Kings. Williams, addicted to cheap wine, also suffered from tuberculosis. Just prior to his death, he recorded one title with Hopkins and harmonica player Luke 'Long Gone' Miles. When asked the significance of his initials, Williams' reply was 'love crazy'. Ironic, then, that his death was from lung collapse.

● ALBUMS: *Texas Blues – The Gold Star Sessions* (1992) ★★★, *The Big Three* (1992) ★★★.

WILLIAMS, LARRY

b. 10 May 1935, New Orleans, Louisiana, USA, d. 2 January 1980, Los Angeles, California, USA. Williams recorded a handful of raucous rock 'n' roll songs for Specialty Records that later influenced, among others, John Lennon. Williams learned to play the piano while in New Orleans, and moved to Oakland, California, with his family while in his teens. There he joined a group called the Lemon Drops. In 1954, while visiting his old hometown of New Orleans, he met and was hired as a pianist by Lloyd Price, who recorded for Specialty. Price introduced Williams to producer Robert 'Bumps' Blackwell. At that time Specialty head Art Rupe signed Williams. His first record was a cover version of Price's 'Just Because', which reached number 11 on the R&B chart for Williams and number 3 for Price. Backed by fellow Specialty artist Little Richard's band, Williams recorded his own 'Short Fat Fannie', which reached number 1 in the R&B chart and number 5 in the pop chart during 1957. To follow up his song about a fat girl, Williams next recorded one about a skinny girl, 'Bony Moronie', which was almost as big a hit. Williams had one final chart single for Specialty the following year, 'Dizzy, Miss Lizzy', which reached number 69 (it was later covered by the Beatles, with Lennon singing – they also covered 'Slow Down' and 'Bad Boy', while Lennon later recorded 'Bony Moronie' and 'Just Because', providing Williams with a steady royalties income until his death).

A number of singles and an album were issued by Specialty up to 1959, none of which were hits. In that year, he was arrested for selling drugs and sent to jail, causing Specialty to drop him and his career to fade. He recorded later for Chess Records, Mercury Records and for Island Records and Decca Records in the mid-60s, by which time he was working with Johnny 'Guitar' Watson. In 1966 Williams became a producer for OKeh Records and recorded an album with Watson for that label. He was virtually inactive between 1967

and 1979, at which point he recorded a funk album for Fantasy Records. In January 1980, Williams was found in his Los Angeles home with a gunshot wound in the head, judged to be self-inflicted, although it was rumoured that Williams was murdered owing to his involvement with drugs and, reportedly, prostitution.

● ALBUMS: *Here's Larry Williams* (Specialty 1959) ★★★★, *Larry Williams* (Chess 1961) ★★★, *Live* (Sue 1965) ★★★, *The Larry Williams Show* (Decca 1965) ★★★, with Johnny 'Guitar' Watson *Two For The Price Of One* (OKeh 1967) ★★★★, *That Larry Williams* (Fantasy 1979) ★★.

● COMPILATIONS: *Greatest Hits* (OKeh 1967) ★★★★, *Dizzy Miss Lizzy* (Ace 1985) ★★★, *Unreleased Larry Williams* (Specialty 1986) ★★★, *Hocus Pocus* (Specialty 1986) ★★★, *Alacazam* (Ace 1987) ★★★, *Slow Down* (Specialty 1987) ★★★, *The Best Of Larry Williams* (Ace 1988) ★★★★, *Bad Boy Of Rock 'n' Roll* (Specialty 1989) ★★★★, *Fabulous Larry Williams* (Ace 1991) ★★★.

WILLIAMS, LESTER

b. 24 June 1920, Groveton, Texas, USA, d. 13 November 1990, Houston, Texas, USA. Raised in Houston on the records of Blind Lemon Jefferson and Lonnie Johnson, Williams was inspired to take up the electric guitar after hearing fellow Texan 'T-Bone' Walker. His debut recording on the small local Macy's Records – 'Wintertime Blues' – was his biggest hit. In a poll held in 1952, the Pittsburgh Courier newspaper Williams beat all comers including Billy Eckstine and Nat 'King' Cole, it was alleged that the poll was fixed, but quite why, nobody knows. His last records were made for Imperial Records in 1956, although he continued to perform locally, and was rediscovered in 1986 for a tour of Europe, although he died four years later. An interesting an underrated rhythm and blues wailer, deserving of wider attention.

● ALBUMS: *Dowling Street Hop* (Krazy Kat 1982) ★★★, *Texas Troubador* (Ace 1987) ★★★, *I Can't Lose With The Stuff I Use* (Ace/Specialty 1993) ★★★.

WILLIAMS, ROBERT PETE

b. 14 March 1914, Zachary, Louisiana, USA, d. 31 December 1980, Rosedale, Louisiana, USA. Although he had been playing and singing blues since he was a young man, Williams first came to wider notice when he was recorded in 1958 by folklorist Harry Oster. At the time, Williams was serving a sentence for murder at the penitentiary at Angola. His sombre vocals and gentle, understated guitar accompaniments were impressive in themselves, but more significant was his unique ability to sing long, partially extemporized songs, sometimes based around a traditional formula, sometimes remarkably original and intensely personal. This exposure led to his being taken up by a younger audience, and on his release from prison he made many appearances at concerts and festivals in the USA and overseas. He also made many more records, most of which testify to his great creative imagination and artistry.

● ALBUMS: *Angola Prisoners Blues* (1958) ★★★, *Free Again* (Bluesville 1961) ★★★★, *Blues From Bottoms* (1973) ★★★, *Those Prison Blues* (Arhoolie 1981) ★★★, *Live* (Wolf 1988) ★★★, *With Big Joe Williams* (Storyville 1988) ★★★, *Robert Pete Williams And Roosevelt Sykes* (77 Records 1988) ★★★.

● COMPILATIONS: *Legacy Of The Blues Volume Nine* (Sonet 1973) ★★★, *Vol. 1 – I'm Blue As A Man Can Be* (Arhoolie 1994) ★★★★, *Vol. 2 – When A Man Takes The Blues* (Arhoolie 1994) ★★★★.

WILLIAMSON, CLAUDE

b. Claude Berkeley Williamson, 18 November 1926, Brattleboro, Vermont, USA. After studying piano formally at the New England Conservatory in Boston, Massachusetts, Williamson turned to playing jazz in the late 40s. He first worked with Charlie Barnet, where he was featured on 'Claude Reigns', then with Red Norvo and also briefly led his own small group. In the early 50s he toured with Bud Shank before settling in Los Angeles, where he led a trio for many years. He played too with Tal Farlow, appeared in the second edition of the Lighthouse All-Stars with Shank, Rolf Ericson, Bob Cooper and Max Roach, and recorded with Art Pepper. Amongst Williamson's better-known compositions is 'Aquarium', recorded by the All-Stars in 1954. His trio work kept him busy but musically static for several years. However, in the late 70s and early 80s he toured Japan and the records he made there spurred his career. Although he began as mainstream player, Williamson later adapted to bop and most of his subsequent work reflects this interest. Although little known on the international scene, Japan apart, his work bears much closer attention than it has usually enjoyed. His brother Stu Williamson was a jazz trumpeter.

● ALBUMS: *The Lighthouse All Stars Vol. 3* (1953) ★★★, *Kenton Presents Jazz: Claude Williamson* (Capitol 1954) ★★★, *The Lighthouse All Stars Vol. 4: Flute And Oboe* (1954) ★★★, with Art Pepper *Discoveries* (1954) ★★★, *Salute To Bud* (Affinity 1954) ★★★★, *Keys West* (Affinity 1955) ★★★★, *The Claude Williamson Trio* (Bethlehem 1956) ★★★★, *'Round Midnight* (Bethlehem 1957) ★★★★, *Claude Williamson In Italy* (1958) ★★, *The Claude Williamson Quintet* i (1958) ★★★, *The Claude Williamson Quintet* ii (1961) ★★★, *New Departure* (1978) ★★★, *Holography* (Interplay 1979) ★★★, *La Fiesta* (Interplay 1979) ★★★, *Tribute To Bud* (1981) ★★★★, *Theatre Party* (Fresh Sound 1988) ★★★, *Mulls The Mulligan Scene* (Fresh Sound 1988) ★★★, *Hallucinations* (VSOP 1995) ★★★, *Live! At The Jazz Bakery* 1995 recording (Fresh Sound 2001) ★★★.

WILLIAMSON, SONNY BOY 'RICE MILLER'

b. Aleck/Alex Ford, 5 December 1899, Glendora, Mississippi, USA. d. 25 May 1965, Helena, Arkansas, USA. Being a man who would never compromise a good story by affording undue attention to veracity, and mischievous to boot,

Sonny Boy's own various accounts of his life were never to be trusted and led to much confusion. Often referred to as 'Sonny Boy Williamson II' he was, in fact, older than John Lee 'Sonny Boy' Williamson, whose name, and associated glory, he appropriated some time in the late 30s or early 40s. Why he felt the need to do so is odd in light of the fact that he owed John Lee Williamson nothing in terms of style or ability, and alongside the latter and Little Walter Jacobs, was one of the most innovatory and influential exponents of the blues harmonica. He was the illegitimate child of Millie Ford, but he took to using his stepfather's name and by common association became 'Rice Miller'. He mastered his chosen instrument (he could also play guitar and drums) early in his life and seems to have taken to the road as soon as he was able, relying on his skill for a livelihood. His wanderings throughout the south brought him into contact with many blues artists.

The list includes Robert Johnson, Robert Lockwood, Elmore James and Howlin' Wolf, whose half sister, Mary, he married in the 30s. During this period Williamson used many names, working as 'Little Boy Blue', Willie Williamson, Willie Williams and Willie Miller (after his brother) and known to his friends as 'Foots' because of his habit of razoring his shoes, no matter how new they might be, to make them comfortable. He was cashing in on the popularity of John Lee Williamson (safely out of the way in Chicago) when he secured a job broadcasting over KFFA radio out of Helena on the *King Biscuit Show* in 1941. The show was heard all over the south and made Williamson famous. He continued to travel but now sought radio stations to advertise his activities. In the early 50s he recorded for Lillian McMurray's Trumpet label in Jackson, Mississippi, along with friends Willie Love and Elmore James. His work on this label includes many outstanding performances, with 'Mighty Long Time' being perhaps the greatest of all. On the strength of his increased popularity he extended his area of work and began to appear in the bars of Detroit, where he worked with Baby Boy Warren, and in Chicago (John Lee Williamson was dead by this time).

He began his career with Chess Records of Chicago in 1955 with his hit 'Don't Start Me Talkin'' and became a mainstay of the label almost until his death. In 1963, he took Europe by storm as a result of his appearances with the AFBF. His impressive appearance – tall and stooped in his famous grey/blue suit (quartered like a jester's doublet) and sporting a bowler hat and umbrella, along with his hooded eyes and goatee beard – hypnotized audiences as he wove back and forth, snapping his fingers and clicking his tongue in a display of perfect rhythmic control. His skill on the harmonica was augmented by many tricks of showmanship such as playing two instruments at once (one with his large and plastic nose) or holding the harp end in his mouth and manoeuvring it with his tongue. If Europe took to him, Williamson seems to have enjoyed Europe: he stayed after the tour had ended and played his way around the burgeoning blues clubs, travelling as far as Poland. He recorded for the Storyville label in Denmark and with Chris Barber in Britain, then returned to mainland Europe, often stating his intention to take up permanent residence.

He never lived to see the days when Chess tried to convert their roster of blues singers into pop stars by uniting them with the most unlikely material and musical support, but in earlier days he had been quite happy to follow a similar route, by recording with such groups as the Yardbirds and the Animals, and a jazz band led by Brian Auger. Some of these efforts stand up better than others but Williamson did not care – as long as he was paid. Despite moving around extensively, he still maintained a home in the USA with his second wife Mattie Lee Gordon. He was back in Helena, appearing on the *King Biscuit Show* once more, when he died in his sleep in 1965.

Apart from his skill as a harmonica player and singer Sonny Boy Williamson was also a 'character' and anecdotes about him are legendary, both among the blues fraternity and his fans in Europe. If he was difficult, contentious, and unreliable, he was also a charming man who played upon his reputation as an evil, dangerous, hard-living blues troubadour. His music reveals that he was also capable of being both sensitive and humorous. He will always remain something of a conundrum, but as an artist his stature is recognized and his fame deserved.

● ALBUMS: *Down And Out Blues* (Checker 1959) ★★★★, *Portraits In Blues Volume 4* (Storyville 1964) ★★★★, *The Real Folk Blues* (Checker 1965) ★★★★, *In Memoriam* (Chess 1965) ★★★, *More Real Folk Blues* (Checker 1966) ★★★, *Sonny Boy Williamson And The Yardbirds* (Mercury 1966) ★★, with Brian Auger Trinity *Don't Send Me No Flowers* (Marmalade 1968) ★★★, *Bummer Road* (Chess 1969) ★★★, *One Way Out* (MCA 1976) ★★★, *The Animals With Sonny Boy Williamson* 1963 recording (Charly 1982) ★★★, *King Biscuit Time* (Arhoolie 1989) ★★★, *Goin' In Your Direction* (Trumpet 1992) ★★★, *The EP Collection* (See For Miles 1994) ★★★★.

WILLIS, CHUCK

b. 31 January 1928, Atlanta, Georgia, USA, d. 10 April 1958. R&B singer Willis made his recording debut in 1951. The following year he reached number 2 in the black music charts with 'My Story', the first of several hits the artist enjoyed while signed to the renowned OKeh Records label. In 1956 Willis had his first hit for Atlantic Records when 'It's Too Late' reached the US R&B Top 3, and the following year he topped the same chart with the compulsive 'C.C. Rider'. In April 1958, the singer succumbed to peritonitis, in the wake of which his posthumous single, 'What Am I Living For', sold in excess of one million copies. The ironically titled b-side, 'I'm Gonna Hang Up My Rock 'N' Roll Shoes', also reached the R&B Top 10, and despite his brief life and career, Willis remained an influential stylist in the development of R&B. He composed many of his best-known recordings, and cover versions by acts as disparate as Derek And The Dominos, the Animals, Buddy Holly, Jerry Lee Lewis, the Band, Ted Taylor and Otis Redding are a tribute to their longevity.

● ALBUMS: *Chuck Willis Wails The Blues* (Epic 1958) ★★★, *The King Of The Stroll* (Atlantic 1958) ★★★.

● COMPILATIONS: *Tribute To Chuck Willis* (Epic 1960) ★★★, *I Remember Chuck Willis* (Atlantic 1963) ★★★, *His Greatest Recordings* (Atlantic 1971) ★★★, *Chuck Willis – My Story* (Official 1980) ★★★, *Keep A Drivin'* (Charly 1984) ★★★, *Be Good Or Be Gone* (Edsel 1986) ★★★.

WILLOWS

A New York doo-wop group formed in 1953 as the Five Willows, this quintet is best remembered for the up-tempo rocker 'Church Bells May Ring', a song that still enjoys airplay on US nostalgia-orientated radio stations. The group consisted of Tony Middleton, brothers Ralph and Joe Martin, Richie Davis and John Steele. Relying on bass singer Steele's vocal acrobatics to give them an identity, they were signed to small labels Allen and Pee-Dee before recording one single for Herald, and finally, their hit for Melba. The shuffle 'Church Bells May Ring' (originally called 'Church Bells Are Ringing') was released in early 1956 and the chimes on the track were played by a then unknown Neil Sedaka. The Willows continued to record for such labels as Club, Eldorado, Gone and Heidi, and the group finally retired in 1965. They recorded no albums, but their one hit, which peaked at number 62 pop and number 11 on the R&B charts, is featured on numerous anthologies.

WILLS, BILLY JACK

b. 1926, on a farm near Memphis, Hall County, Texas, USA. Billy Jack was the youngest brother of Bob Wills and the ninth of the Wills family's children. He naturally grew up influenced by his brother Bob's music and joined the Texas Playboys in 1945. He initially played bass but, after 1949, he usually played drums and also took some vocals. He added the lyrics to the old fiddle tune called 'Faded Love' that had been written by Bob and his father John Wills. He shared the vocal when it was first recorded in 1950 and the song reached number 8 in the US country charts. It went on to become a country standard and was later a hit for Patsy Cline (1963), Leon McAuliffe (1963), Tompall And The Glaser Brothers (1971) and Willie Nelson and Ray Price (1980). In the mid-50s, he formed his own band and recorded for Four Star.

● COMPILATIONS: *Billy Jack Wills & His Western Swing Band* (Western 1983) ★★★, *Crazy Man Crazy* (Western 1985) ★★★.

WILLSON, MEREDITH

b. Robert Meredith Reiniger, 18 May 1902, Mason City, Iowa, USA, d. 15 June 1984, Santa Monica, California, USA. An instrumentalist and musical director – then a composer-lyricist-librettist –

Willson was 55-years-old when he made his Broadway debut in 1957 with the hit musical *The Music Man*. Educated at the Damrosch Institute of Musical Art in New York, Willson was a flute and piccolo soloist with John Philip Sousa's concert band from 1921-23, and with the New York Philharmonic from 1924-29, playing under Arturo Toscanini. During the 30s and early 40s he worked extensively on radio as musical director on shows such as *Ship Of Joy*, *Carefree Carnival*, *Good News Of 1938*, *Maxwell House Coffee Time*, *Fanny Brice* and *John Nesbitt*. When he was in his late 30s, he composed a symphony, 'The Missions', and scored movies such as Charles Chaplin's *The Great Dictator* (1940) and Lillian Hellman's *The Little Foxes* (1941). He had composed the incidental music for Hellman's stage play of the same name, two years earlier. During World War II, Willson was a major in the Armed Forces Radio Service, and when he was released he had his own radio show from 1946 into the early 50s, and also hosted *The Big Show* with actress Tallulah Bankhead, and composed its closing theme, 'May The Good Lord Bless And Keep You'.

In December 1957, *The Music Man*, for which Willson wrote the book, music and lyrics, opened on Broadway to unanimously favourable reviews. It was set in Willson's home state of Iowa, c.1912, and starred Robert Preston, who was making his first appearance in a Broadway – in fact, any – musical. Preston triumphed in the role of the likeable conman, Professor Harold Hill, and Barbara Cook was splendid as librarian Marion Paroo. A wonderful set of songs, set in a variety of musical styles, included 'Rock Island', 'Goodnight My Someone', 'The Sadder-But-Wiser Girl', 'Marion The Librarian', 'My White Knight', 'Wells Fargo Wagon', 'Shi-poopi', 'Lida Rose', 'Will I Ever Tell You?', 'Gary, Indiana', 'Till There Was You', and the classics, 'Seventy-Six Trombones' and 'Trouble' ('Right here in River City/With a capital "T"/That rhymes with "P"/That stands for pool!'). Willson won Tony and Drama Critics Circle Awards, and the show ran in New York for 1,375 performances. It was filmed in 1962 with Preston, and Shirley Jones who replaced Cook. Apart from the original cast and film soundtrack records, Willson and his wife Rini performed the score on an album, complete with their own individual comments.

Willson's next musical, *The Unsinkable Molly Brown* (1960), had Tammy Grimes in the title role, and ran for over a year. The appealing score included 'I Ain't Down Yet', 'Belly Up To The Bar Boys', 'Keep A-Hoppin'' and 'Are You Sure?'. Debbie Reynolds replaced Grimes in the 1964 film version. Willson's final Broadway score (he also wrote the book) was for *Here's Love* (1963). Adapted from George Seaton's 1947 comedy-fantasy movie about a department store's Santa Claus, it starred Janis Paige and Craig Stevens, and ran for 334 performances. The songs included 'The Big Clown Balloons', 'Arm In Arm', 'You Don't Know' and 'Pine Cones And Holly Berries'. Broadway legend Chita Rivera was in the cast of Willson's stage musical swansong, *1491*, which closed out of town in 1969.

● FURTHER READING: *And There I Stood With My Piccolo*, Meredith Willson. *But He Doesn't Know The Territory*, Meredith Willson.

WILSON, HARDING 'HOP'

b. 27 April 1921, Grapeland, Texas, USA, d. 27 August 1975, Houston, Texas, USA. Although his nickname is a corruption of 'Harp', reflecting his early prowess on the harmonica, it is as a slide guitarist that Wilson will be remembered. As well as playing conventional guitar, he played steel guitar placed horizontally on a stand, a style usually associated with C&W musicians. He played and sang with great skill and expression, encompassing a range of rhythms and moods from rocking R&B to tormented slow blues. Working in east Texas and Louisiana, he made singles for the Goldband company in 1958, and the small Ivory label (owned by drummer 'Ivory' Lee Semien) in 1960 and 1961. These, plus a handful of tracks unissued at the time but released on an album after his death, account for his entire recorded legacy; however, they are sufficient to establish Wilson as one of the most original blues artists of his time.

● ALBUMS: *Steel Guitar Flash* (Ace 1988) ★★★, *Houston Ghetto Blues* (Bullseye 1995) ★★★★.

WILSON, JIMMY

b. 1921, Louisiana, USA, d. 1965, Dallas, Texas, USA. Wilson was singing in California with a gospel quartet when his distinctive, bluesy lead was noticed by impresario Bob Geddins, who recorded Wilson as the blues singer with his band, Bob Geddins' Cavaliers, and in his own right, for his Cava Tone label, often in the company of legendary Bay Area guitarist Lafayette Thomas. Some of these tracks created enough of a stir for Aladdin Records to take an interest and purchase some of Wilson's masters from Geddins, and later during 1952, Wilson began recording for Aladdin and its small subsidiary 7-11. In 1953 Wilson again signed with Geddins to record for his new Big Town label, and the first release, 'Tin Pan Alley', although not a Wilson original, was a tremendous success and has since become synonymous with his name. Most of Wilson's mid-50s output was issued on Big Town, although occasional releases appeared on Irma and Elko (the latter under guitarist Jimmy Nolan's name), and four tracks were issued on the Chart label. Later recordings did not match up to the doomy Bay Area sound of his Geddins tracks, despite a couple of attempts at the 'Tin Pan Alley' sound and a good local seller, 'Please Accept My Love' on Goldband, which was covered successfully by B.B. King. Wilson died in 1965 of drink-related problems, virtually forgotten by the record-buying public.

● COMPILATIONS: *Trouble In My House* (Diving Duck 1985) ★★, *Jimmy Wilson – San Francisco 1952-53* (1985) ★★★.

WILSON, JULIE

b. Julia May Wilson, 21 October 1924, Omaha, Nebraska, USA. An actress and singer, Wilson is acknowledged as one of the greatest interpreters of standard popular songs in the world of cabaret. Her sophisticated image, with a figure-hugging gown, and a gardenia tucked into her swept-back gleaming black hair, is a reminder of a bygone era. She started young, being voted 'Miss Nebraska' when she was only 17. A year later, she joined the chorus of a touring edition of the *Earl Carroll's Vanities* which was passing through Omaha, and ended up in New York. From there, she moved to a Miami nightclub, doing a solo act five shows a night. It was in Miami that she believes she learnt how to control an audience with the occasional aggressive 'drop-dead bitchy' remark. Next stop was Los Angeles where she won a contest on Mickey Rooney's radio show. The prize was a two-week engagement at Hollywood's top nightclub, the Mocambo. Soon afterwards she was offered the part of Lois Lane in the touring version of the musical *Kiss Me, Kate*, and in 1951 recreated the role at the London Coliseum. She stayed in London for nearly four years, appearing in various shows, including *Bet Your Life* (1952), and undergoing voice training at RADA.

Back in the USA, during the remainder of the 50s and throughout most of the 60s, Wilson took over roles on Broadway in *The Pajama Game* and *Kismet*, played in various regional productions, returned to London for *Bells Are Ringing*, and did some television work, including the soap opera *The Secret Storm*. In the 1969/70 Broadway season she appeared in two flop musicals, and subsequently played several cabaret engagements at New York's Brothers and Sisters club, as well as continuing to tour. In the mid-70s she went into semi-retirement in order to look after her ailing parents in Omaha. She returned to the New York cabaret scene with an evening of Cole Porter songs at Michael's Pub in 1984. Since then, she has attracted excellent reviews in two otherwise unsuccessful New York musicals, *Legs Diamond* (1988) and *Hannah ... 1939* (1990), recorded several superb albums, as well as, in critic Clive Barnes' words, 'putting over a torch song with the sultry heat of a flame thrower' in cabaret. There was great rejoicing at nightspots around the world, including London's Pizza On The Park, when in 1993, along with her long-time accompanist William Roy, she celebrated her 50 years in showbusiness.

● ALBUMS: *Love* (Dolphin 1956) ★★★, *This Could Be The Night* film soundtrack (MGM 1957) ★★, *My Old Flame* (Vik 1957) ★★★, *Julie Wilson At The St. Regis* (Vik 1957) ★★★, *Meet Julie Wilson* (Cameo 1960) ★★★, with Kay Stevens, Connie Russell, Cara Williams *Playgirls* (Warners 1964) ★★★, *Jimmy* Broadway Cast (RCA Victor 1969) ★★, *Julie Wilson At Brothers And Sisters* (Arden 1974) ★★★, *Bet Your Life* London Cast reissue (Blue Pear *c*.80s) ★★★, *Sings The Kurt Weill Songbook* (DRG 1987) ★★★★, *Sings The Stephen Sondheim Songbook* (DRG 1987) ★★★★, *Legs Diamond* Broadway Cast (RCA Victor 1988) ★★★, *Sings The Cole Porter Songbook* (DRG 1989) ★★★★, *Sings The Harold Arlen Songbook* (DRG 1990) ★★★★, *Live From The Russian Tea Room* (Cabaret Records 1993) ★★★, *The Cy Coleman Songbook* (DRG 1999) ★★★, and Ben Bagley recordings.

● FILMS: *The Strange One* (1957), *This Could Be The Night* (1957).

WILSON, SANDY

b. Alexander Galbraith Wilson, 19 May 1924, Sale, Cheshire, England. A composer, lyricist and author, Wilson studied at Harrow and Oxford University, where he wrote and appeared in many undergraduate productions. He began to make his mark in the West End by contributing songs to revues such as *Slings And Arrows* (1948) and *Oranges And Lemons* (1949). In 1950 he provided the lyrics for a provincial production of Michael Pertwee's musical play *Caprice*, and then was the author and composer of *See You Later* (1951) and *See You Again* (1952). His big break came in 1953 when he was asked to write the book, music and lyrics for *The Boy Friend*, a light-hearted spoof of the musical comedies of the 20s. The delightful score included 'I Could Be Happy With You', 'A Room In Bloomsbury', 'Won't You Charleston With Me?', 'It's Never Too Late To Fall In Love', 'Fancy Forgetting', and the lively title song. After starting its life as an hour-long entertainment at the tiny Player's Theatre, in London, *The Boy Friend* moved first to the Embassy Theatre, where it was expanded, before finally transferring to Wyndhams' Theatre in the West End on 14 January 1954. It ran for over five years, and Julie Andrews made her New York stage debut in the Broadway production, which lasted for over a year. The show has subsequently been produced in many countries throughout the world, and enjoyed revivals in New York (1958) and London (1967 and 1993). The 1971 film version was directed by Ken Russell, and starred Twiggy, Christopher Gable, Moyra Fraser and Tommy Tune. As well as *The Boy Friend*, Sandy Wilson has been the composer and/or author and lyricist of some of the most civilized and enjoyable shows (British or otherwise) ever to play the West End. They included *The Buccaneer* (1955), *Valmouth* (1958), *Pieces Of Eight* (1959), *Call It Love* (1960), *Divorce Me, Darling!* (1965), *As Dorothy Parker Once Said* (1966), *Sandy Wilson Thanks The Ladies* (in which he also appeared, 1971), *His Monkey Wife* (1971), *The Clapham Wonder* (1978) and *Aladdin* (1979).

● FURTHER READING: all by Sandy Wilson *This Is Sylvia. The Boy Friend. I Could Be Happy: His Autobiography. Ivor* (a biography of Ivor Novello). *The Roaring Twenties.*

WISDOM, NORMAN

b. 4 February 1915, Paddington, London, England. A slapstick comedian, singer and straight actor, Wisdom has been a much-loved entertainer for four decades in the UK, not to mention other such unlikely places as Russia, China, and – more recently – Albania. He broke into films in 1953 with *Trouble In Store*, and during the remainder of the 50s, had a string of box-office smashes with *One Good Turn*, *Man Of The Moment*, *Up In The World*, *Just My Luck*, *The Square Peg* and *Follow A Star*. Dressed in his famous tight-fitting Gump suit, he was usually accompanied by straight man Jerry Desmonde, and, more often than not, portrayed the little man battling against the odds, eventually overcoming prejudice and snobbery, to win justice and his inevitably pretty sweetheart. He nearly always sang in his films, and his theme song, 'Don't Laugh At Me', which he co-wrote with June Tremayne, was a number 3 hit in 1954 on Columbia Records. He also made the Top 20 in 1957 with a version of the Five Keys' 'Wisdom Of A Fool'. In 1958, Wisdom appeared in the London production of *Where's Charley?*, a musical based on Brandon Thomas' classic farce, *Charley's Aunt*. Frank Loesser's score included 'Once In Love With Amy' and 'My Darling, My Darling', and the show ran for 18 months.

In 1965, he played the lead in Leslie Bricusse and Anthony Newley's musical *The Roar Of The Greasepaint – The Smell Of The Crowd*, which toured UK provincial theatres. He was not considered sufficiently well-known in the USA to play the part on Broadway, but did make his New York debut in the following year, when he starred in *Walking Happy*, a musical version of *Hobson's Choice* with a score by Sammy Cahn and Jimmy Van Heusen. Wisdom also appeared on US television in the role of Androcles, with Noël Coward as Julius Caesar, in Richard Rodgers' musical adaptation of Bernard Shaw's *Androcles And The Lion*. His feature films during the 60s included *On the Beat*, *A Stitch In Time*, and *The Night They Raided Minsky's* with Jason Robards and Britt Ekland. Thanks to television re-runs of his films he is regarded with warm affection by many sections of the British public, and can still pack theatres, although, like many showbusiness veterans, he is not called on to appear much on television. In his heyday, he made two celebrated 'live' one-hour appearances on *Sunday Night At The London Palladium* in the company of Bruce Forsyth, which are considered to be classics of their kind.

In 1992, with the UK rapidly running out of traditional funny men (Benny Hill and Frankie Howerd both died in that year), Wisdom experienced something of a renaissance when he played the role of a gangster in the movie *Double X*, starred in a radio series, *Robbing Hood*, released the album *A World Of Wisdom*, completed a sell-out tour of the UK, and published his autobiography. In the following year he celebrated 50 years in showbusiness, and was still performing regularly. In 1995, he was awarded the OBE, and toured Albania as a guest of the Minister of Culture. Apparently, whereas the country's state censors banned most American and British films with their 'Marxist messages', Wisdom, in his customary role as 'the plucky proletarian', was considered politically and morally inoffensive. He was given the freedom of the capital, Tirana, met

President Sali Berisha, attended several rallies in his honour, and gave a 90-minute television performance.

In 1997, a plaque was unveiled in his honour at Pinewood Studios where he made some of his most successful films from 1953-56 (12 of them were released on video in 1994), and in the following year his long and successful career was celebrated on BBC Radio 2 with the documentary programme *Don't Laugh At Me: Norman Wisdom's 50 Years Of Laughter*, and in a weekend retrospective of his films at the Barbican Centre. To cap it all, in the year 2000 Wisdom received a knighthood for his services to entertainment.

● ALBUMS: *I Would Like To Put On Record* (Wing 1956) ★★★, *Where's Charley?* stage production (Columbia 1958) ★★, *Walking Happy* Broadway Cast (Capitol 1966) ★★★, *Androcles And The Lion* television soundtrack (RCA Victor 1967) ★★, *The Night They Raided Minsky's* (United Artists 1969) ★★★, with Des O'Connor, Beryl Reid, Mike Sammes Singers *One Man's Music: A Tribute To Noel Gay* (Columbia 1969) ★★★, *Jingle Jangle* (Class Original Cast, 1982) ★★★.

● COMPILATIONS: *A World Of Wisdom* (Decca 1992) ★★★, *The Wisdom Of A Fool* (See For Miles 1997) ★★★.

● VIDEOS: *Live On Stage* (1992).

● FURTHER READING: *Trouble In Store*, Richard Dacre. *Don't Laugh At Me*, Norman Wisdom. *'Cos I'm A Fool*, Norman Wisdom with Bernard Bale.

● FILMS: *A Date With A Dream* as a 'shadow boxer' (1948), *Trouble In Store* (1953), *One Good Turn* (1954), *Man Of The Moment* (1955), *As Long as They're Happy* (1955), *Up In The World* (1956), *Just My Luck* (1957), *The Square Peg* (1958), *Follow A Star* (1959), *The Bulldog Breed* (1960), *There Was A Crooked Man* (1960), *On The Beat* (1962), *The Girl On The Boat* (1962), *A Stitch In Time* (1963), *The Early Bird* (1965), *The Sandwich Man* (1966), *Press For Time* (1966), *The Night They Raided Minsky's* (1968), *What's Good For The Goose* (1969), *Double X* (1992).

WISE, CHUBBY

b. Robert Russell Wise, 2 October 1915, Lake City, Florida, USA, d. 6 January 1996. His father was an old-time fiddler but Robert first played banjo and guitar, before changing to fiddle at the age of 12, greatly influenced by Curly Fox and Clayton McMichen. In 1936, Wise drove taxis in Jacksonville and played fiddle in bars in his spare time, but in 1938, he became a full-time musician. After playing for a time with the Jubilee Hillbillies, he joined Bill Monroe on the *Grand Ole Opry* in 1942. He remained with Monroe until 1948, in a line-up that included Flatt And Scruggs and played on most of the band's best-known recordings. In 1947, he co-wrote 'Shenandoah Waltz' with Clyde Moody and it has also been suggested that, in 1938, he may well have worked with Ervin Rouse on the writing of the fiddle classic 'Orange Blossom Special'. He returned to Monroe briefly and in the early 50s, he played with several acts including Flatt And Scruggs until 1954, when he became a member of Hank Snow's

Rainbow Ranch Boys. Except for a spell in 1964, he played on the *Opry*, toured extensively and recorded with Snow until March 1970. He played with Snow's band when, in 1955, they dubbed on new instrumentation to several of Jimmie Rodgers' classic recordings (Snow devotes almost a chapter of his autobiography to memories of the days when Wise played with him). During that time, he also recorded with Mac Wiseman, Hylo Brown and Red Allen. He cut a solo album for Starday in 1961 and in 1969, he began to record for Stoneway. He relocated to Livingstone, Texas, where throughout the 70s into the early 80s, he recorded a series of albums for the label, made personal appearances and also recorded as a session musician or guest with various artists and bluegrass groups, including Charlie Moore, Mac Wiseman, Frank Wakefield and the Boys From Indiana and cut twin fiddle albums with Howdy Forrester. In 1984, he moved to Florida and although he cut down his workload drastically, he still made numerous festival appearances and recorded with the Bass Mountain Boys. He continued to remain active into the 90s, recorded a twin fiddle album with Raymond Fairchild and late in 1995, he recorded what turned out to be his final album for Pinecastle. In December 1995, he and his wife were visiting relatives in Maryland for Christmas, when he was hospitalized with pneumonia. Soon after being released from hospital, he suffered a fatal heart seizure and died in Washington DC on 6 January 1996. Wise was one of country music's greatest fiddlers and also noted for his humour. Once asked why he took up playing the fiddle, he replied, 'The fiddle bow fit my hand a lot better than them plough handles did'.

● ALBUMS: *Chubby Wise & The Rainbow Ranch Boys* (Starday 1961) ★★★, *Chubby Wise & His Fiddle* (Stoneway 1969) ★★★, *Chubby Fiddles Around* (Stoneway 1970) ★★★, *Chubby Plays Uptown* (Stoneway 1970) ★★★, *Chubby Plays, W.C. Averitt Sings Bluegrass* (Stoneway 1970) ★★★, *Hoedown* (Stoneway 1970) ★★★, *Chubby Wise Plays Bob Wills* (Stoneway 1970) ★★★★, *Precious Memories* (Stoneway 1971) ★★★, *Thru The Years With Chubby Wise* (Stoneway 1971) ★★★, *Chubby Plays Polkas* (Stoneway 1971) ★★★, *Waltzes* (Stoneway 1972) ★★★, *At His Best* (Stoneway 1972) ★★★, *Hoedown #2* (Stoneway 1973) ★★★, *Page 13* (Stoneway 1973) ★★★, with Howdy Forrester *Sincerely Yours* (Stoneway 1974) ★★★, with Forrester *Fiddle Favorites* (Stoneway 1975) ★★★, *Grassy Fiddle* (Stoneway 1975) ★★★, *The Golden Rocket* (Stoneway 1975) ★★★, *The Million Dollar Fiddle* (Stoneway 1976) ★★★★, *Sweet Milk And Peaches* (Stoneway 1977) ★★★, *Chubby Wise Plays Hank Williams* (Stoneway 1977) ★★★, *Moody Fiddle Sound* (Stoneway 1978) ★★★, with Mac Wiseman *Give Me My Smokies & The Tennessee Waltz* (Gilley's 1982) ★★★, *The Nashville Sound* (Guest Star 80s) ★★★, with Boys From Indiana *Live At Gilley's* (Gilley's 1988) ★★, with Raymond Fairchild *Cherokee Tunes & Seminole Swing* (Rebel 1990) ★★★, *In Nashville* (1993) ★★★, *An American Original* (Pinecastle 1993) ★★★.

WISEMAN, MAC

b. Malcolm B. Wiseman, 23 May 1925, Crimora, Virginia, USA. Wiseman attended the Conservatory of Music at Dayton, Virginia, and developed a great knowledge of the folk music of his native Shenandoah Valley. He first worked as a disc jockey on WSVA Harrisburg but was soon playing such shows as the *Tennessee Barn Dance* on WLOX Knoxville, where he also worked with Molly O'Day. During the 40s, his talent with bluegrass music saw him play and record with the bands of Bill Monroe and Flatt And Scruggs. He made his first solo recordings for Dot Records in 1951 and from 1957-61, he was the label's A&R man. After recording for Capitol Records, he returned to Dot but in the early 70s, he later recorded with Lester Flatt for RCA Records. Over the years Wiseman has worked on a variety of radio stations, played all the major US country venues and travelled extensively, including several tours to Britain, where he is always a popular artist. A prolific recording artist on various labels, his most popular recordings include such songs as 'Tis Sweet To Be Remembered'. His few actual chart hits include Top 10 successes with 'The Ballad Of Davy Crockett' and 'Jimmy Brown The Newsboy', and a minor hit with his humorous 'Johnny's Cash And Charley's Pride'. In 1979, he even charted with 'My Blue Heaven' as Mac Wiseman & Friend (the friend being Woody Herman). In 1993 he was inducted into the Bluegrass Hall Of Fame.

● ALBUMS: *I Hear You Knocking* (1955) ★★★, *Songs From The Hills* (1956) ★★★★, *Tis Sweet To Be Remembered* (Dot 1958) ★★★, *Beside The Still Waters* (Dot 1959) ★★★★, *Great Folk Ballads* (Dot 1959) ★★★★, *Mac Wiseman Sings 12 Great Hits* (Dot 1960) ★★★, *Keep On The Sunny Side* (Dot 1960) ★★★, *Fireball Mail* (Dot 1961) ★★★★, *Best Loved Gospel Hymns* (1961) ★★★, *Bluegrass Favorites* (Capitol 1962) ★★★, *Sincerely* (Hamilton 1964) ★★★, *A Master At Work* (Dot 1966) ★★★, *This Is Mac Wiseman* (Dot 1966) ★★★, *Songs Of The Dear Old Days* (Hamilton 1966) ★★★, *20 Old Time Country Favorites* (1966) ★★★, *Mac Wiseman i* (1967) ★★★, *Sings Johnny's Cash & Charley's Pride* (1970) ★★★, with Lester Flatt *Lester 'N' Mac* (RCA Victor 1971) ★★★, with Flatt *On The Southbound* (RCA Victor 1972) ★★★, with Flatt *Over The Hills To The Poorhouse* (RCA Victor 1973) ★★★, *Concert Favorites* (1973) ★★★, *Country Music Memories* (CMH 1976) ★★★, with Shenandoah Cut-Ups *New Traditions Volume 1* (Vetco 1976) ★★★, with Shenandoah Cut-Ups *New Traditions Volume 2* (Vetco 1977) ★★★, *Sings Gordon Lightfoot* (CMH 1977) ★★★, *Mac Wiseman ii* (1977) ★★★, with Osborne Brothers *Essential Bluegrass Album* (CMH 1979) ★★★★, *Songs That Made The Jukebox Play* (CMH 1980) ★★★, with Chubby Wise *Give Me My Smokies & The Tennessee Waltz* (Gilley's 1982) ★★★, with Merle Travis *The Clayton McMichen Story* (CHM 1982) ★★★, *Bluegrass Gold* (1982) ★★★, *Live In Concert* (1982) ★★, *If Teardrops Were Pennies* (1984) ★★★, *Mac Wiseman iii* (1986) ★★★, *Grassroots To Bluegrass* (CMH 1990) ★★★★, *Teenage Hangout* (1993) ★★★.

● COMPILATIONS: *Golden Hits Of Mac Wiseman* (Dot 1968) ★★★, *16 Great Performances* (1974) ★★★, *The Mac Wiseman Story* (CMH 1976) ★★★★, *Golden Classics* (Gusto 1979), *Early Dot Recordings Volume 1* (County 1985) ★★★★, *Early Dot Recordings Volume 2* (County 1985) ★★★★, *Greatest Bluegrass Hits* (CMH 1989) ★★★★, *Early Dot Recordings Volume 3* (County 1992) ★★★, *Rare Singles And Radio Transcriptions* (Cowgirlboy 1992) ★★★.

WISH YOU WERE HERE

In the early 50s, when Broadway audiences were enjoying such lavish musicals as *Call Me Madam*, *The King And I*, *Can-Can* and *Kismet*, *Wish You Were Here* went one better than all of them, and splashed out on a real swimming pool that was built into the stage. Perhaps the show's director, producer, choreographer, and co-librettist Joshua Logan still had fond watery memories of his association with the enormously successful *South Pacific* a few years earlier. In any event, the pool attracted a good deal of early publicity, as did a record of the title song by Eddie Fisher which soared to the top of the US chart just three weeks after the show opened at the Imperial Theatre on 25 June 1952. The story, which was adapted by Joshua Logan and Arthur Kober from Kober's 1937 play, *Having A Wonderful Time*, is set in Camp Karefree, a Jewish adult summer vacation resort in the Catskill Mountains. Teddy Stern (Patricia Marand) loses interest in her mature boyfriend, Herbert Fabricant (Harry Clark), when the young, suave and slinky waiter-cum-dancer Chick Miller (Jack Cassidy) sweeps her off her feet. It is all perfectly legal because, back home in New York, Chick is actually a law student. As well as the title number, which also became a hit for Jane Froman and Guy Lombardo, Harold Rome's amusing and tuneful score contained another appealing ballad, 'Where Did The Night Go', along with 'Tripping The Light Fantastic', 'Could Be', 'Ballad Of A Social Director', 'Mix And Mingle', 'Camp Kare-Free', 'Summer Afternoon', 'Shopping Around', 'Don José Of Far Rockaway' and 'Flattery'. *Wish You Were Here* was a warm and friendly show, so it was not surprising that it ran for nearly a year and a half, a total of 598 performances. The 1953 London production, with Bruce Trent, Shani Wallis, Elizabeth Larner and Dickie Henderson, stayed at the Casino Theatre (complete with swimming pool) for eight months. (The 1987 British film of the same name that starred Emily Lloyd and Tom Bell, is in no way related to this musical production.)

WITH A SONG IN MY HEART

Susan Hayward gave an outstanding performance in this 1952 20th Century-Fox film which was based on the life of the popular singer Jane Froman. There was hardly a dry eye in the house as producer Lamar Trotti's screenplay traced Froman's brave fight back to the top following a terrible air crash during World War II that left her confined to a wheelchair. David Wayne was fine as her mentor and husband, and so was Thelma Ritter, who played her hard-bitten nurse and companion. The 22-year-old Robert Wagner had a small but effective role as a shell-shocked young airman, and also in the strong supporting cast were Rory Calhoun, Richard Allan, Una Merkel, Helen Wescott, Leif Erikson, Max Showalter and Lyle Talbot. It was Jane Froman's own voice that was heard on the soundtrack singing a marvellous selection of songs, many of which were particularly associated with her. There were especially endearing versions of 'With A Song In My Heart' (Richard Rodgers-Lorenz Hart), 'I'll Walk Alone' (Jule Styne-Sammy Cahn), 'I'm Through With Love' (Gus Kahn-Matty Malneck-Fud Livingstone) and 'They're Either Too Young Or Too Old' (Frank Loesser), along with excellent readings of 'Embraceable You' (George and Ira Gershwin), 'It's A Good Day' (Peggy Lee-Dave Barbour), 'Indiana' (James Hanley-Ballard MacDonald), 'Blue Moon' (Rodgers-Hart), 'Deep In The Heart Of Texas' (Don Swander-June Hershey), 'Tea For Two' (Vincent Youmans-Irving Caesar), 'That Old Feeling' (Lew Brown-Sammy Fain), and several more. Musical director Alfred Newman won an Oscar for his scoring. Billy Daniels staged the dance numbers and the impressive Technicolor photography was by Leon Shamroy. Walter Lang directed what was certainly one of the best films of its kind.

WITHERSPOON, JIMMY

b. James Witherspoon, 8 August 1923, Gurdon, Arkansas, USA, d. 18 September 1997, Los Angeles, California, USA. Witherspoon crossed over into rock, jazz and R&B territory, but his deep and mellow voice placed him ultimately as a fine blues singer. He sang in his local Baptist church from the age of seven. From 1941-43 he was in the Merchant Marines and, during stopovers in Calcutta, he found himself singing the blues with a band led by Teddy Weatherford. In 1944, he replaced Walter Brown in the Jay McShann band at Vallejo, California, and toured with it for the next four years. In 1949 he had his first hit, 'Ain't Nobody's Business (Parts 1 & 2)', which stayed on the *Billboard* chart for 34 weeks. Other recordings at the time with bands led by Jimmy 'Maxwell Street' Davis are fine examples of rollicking west coast R&B (collected as *Who's Been Jivin' You*). Witherspoon's popularity as an R&B singer faded during the course of the 50s, but he made a great impression on jazz listeners at the Monterey Jazz Festival in October 1959, performing with a group that included Ben Webster. Other collaborations with jazz artists included *Some Of My Best Friends Are The Blues*, with horns and strings arranged and conducted by Benny Golson, and a guest performance on Jon Hendricks' *Evolution Of The Blues Song*. He won the *Down Beat* critics' poll as a 'new star' in 1961. Frequent tours of Europe followed, beginning in 1961 with a Buck Clayton group and later with Coleman Hawkins, Roy Eldridge, Earl Hines and Woody Herman. He also did community work, including singing in prisons.

In the early 70s he gave up touring for a sedentary job as a blues disc jockey on the radio station KMET in Los Angeles, but resumed active music thanks to the encouragement of Eric Burdon. During his touring with Burdon he introduced a young Robben Ford as his guitarist and toured Japan and the Far East. In 1974 his 'Love Is A Five Letter Word' was a hit, though some fans regretted his neglect of the blues. A record with the Savoy Sultans in 1980 was a spirited attempt to recall a bygone era. Despite suffering from throat cancer since the early 80s, Witherspoon continued to perform live and record the occasional studio set. *The Blues, The Whole Blues And Nothin' But The Blues*, released in 1992, was the first album on Mike Vernon's new label Indigo. Witherspoon, who died in 1997, was revered by generations during different eras and his name was often cited as a major influence during the 60s beat boom; his work is destined to endure.

● ALBUMS: *Goin' To Kansas City Blues* (RCA Victor 1957) ★★★★, with Eddie Vinson *Battle Of The Blues, Volume 3* (King 1959) ★★★, *At The Monterey Jazz Festival* (Hi Fi 1959) ★★★★, *Jimmy Witherspoon* (Crown 1959) ★★★, *Feelin' The Spirit* (Hi Fi 1959) ★★★★, *Jimmy Witherspoon At The Renaissance* (Hi Fi 1959) ★★★, *Singin' The Blues* reissued as *There's Good Rockin' Tonight* (World Pacific 1959) ★★★★, *Jimmy Witherspoon Sings The Blues* (Crown 1960) ★★★, *Olympia Concert* (Inner City 1961) ★★★, *Spoon* (Reprise 1961) ★★★, *Hey, Mrs. Jones* (Reprise 1962) ★★★, *Roots* (Reprise 1962) ★★★, *Baby, Baby, Baby* (Prestige 1963) ★★★★, *Evenin' Blues* (Prestige 1964) ★★★, *Goin' To Chicago Blues* (Prestige 1964) ★★★, *Blues Around The Clock* (Prestige 1964) ★★, *Blue Spoon* (Prestige 1964) ★★★, *Some Of My Best Friends Are The Blues* (Prestige 1964) ★★★, *Take This Hammer* (Constellation 1964) ★★★, *Blues For Spoon And Groove* (Surrey 1965) ★★★, *Spoon In London* (Prestige 1965) ★★★, *Blues Point Of View* (Verve 1967) ★★★, with Jack McDuff *The Blues Is Now* (Verve 1967) ★★★, *Blues For Easy Livers* (Prestige 1967) ★★★, *A Spoonful Of Soul* (Verve 1968) ★★★, *The Blues Singer* (Stateside 1969) ★★★, *Back Door Blues* (Polydor 1969) ★★★, *Hunh!* (Bluesway 1969) ★★★, *Handbags & Gladrags* (Probe 1970) ★★★, *Blues Singer* (Stateside 1970) ★★★, with Eric Burdon *Guilty!* (United Artists 1971) ★★★, *Ain't Nobody's Business* (Polydor 1974) ★★★, *Love Is A Five Letter Word* (Capitol 1975) ★★★, *Live* (MCA 1976) ★★★, *Jimmy Witherspoon And Ben Webster (That's Jazz)* (Warners 1977) ★★★, with New Savoy Sultans *Sings The Blues* (Muse 1980) ★★★, with Buck Clayton *Live In Paris, Big Blues* (Vogue 1981) ★★★, with Joe Turner *Patch, Patcha, All Night Long* (Pablo 1985) ★★★, *Midnight Lady Called The Blues* (Muse 1986) ★★★, *Rockin' L.A.* (Fantasy 1988) ★★★, *Call Me Baby* (Night Train 1991) ★★★, *The Blues, The Whole Blues And Nothin' But The Blues* (Indigo 1992) ★★★, with Robben Ford *Live At The Notodden Blues Festival* (Blue Rockit 1993) ★★★★, *Spoon's Blues* (Stony Plain 1995) ★★★, with Howard Scott *American Blues* (Avenue/Rhino 1995) ★★★, with Ford *Ain't*

Nothin' New But The Blues 1977 recording (AIM 1996) ★★★★, with Ford *Live At The Mint* (On The Spot 1996) ★★★, *Spoonful* (ARG Jazz 1997) ★★★, with Hal Singer *Big Blues* (JSP 1998) ★★, *Jimmy Witherspoon With The Duke Robillard Band* 1995 recording (Stony Plain 2000) ★★★★.

● COMPILATIONS: *The Best Of Jimmy Witherspoon* (Prestige 1969) ★★★★, *Never Knew This Kind Of Hurt Before: The Bluesway Sessions 1969-71* recordings (Charly 1988) ★★★, *Spoon So Easy: The Chess Years 1954-56* recordings (MCA/Chess 1990) ★★★, *Blowin' In From Kansas* (Ace 1991) ★★★★, *Jimmy Witherspoon & Jay McShann* 40s recordings (Black Lion 1992), *Jazz Me Blues: The Best Of Jimmy Witherspoon* (Prestige 1998) ★★★★.

WONDERFUL TOWN

Given that the score for this show was the work of the *On The Town* team of Leonard Bernstein (music) and Betty Comden and Adolph Green (lyrics), it does not take a great deal of imagination to realise that the wonderful, friendly, and generally too-good-to-be-true city in question is New York. This musical advertisement for the 'Big Apple' opened at the Winter Garden in New York on 25 February 1953. It had a book by Joseph Fields and Jerome Chodorov, based on their play *My Sister Eileen*, which was adapted from stories by Ruth McKinney. It concerns two young ladies, Ruth Sherwood (Rosalind Russell) and, of course, her sister, Eileen (Edie Adams), who have travelled from Ohio to the big city in an effort to find fame and fortune. Ruth is a writer who cannot seem to get a man, while Eileen the actress has difficulty holding them off. During their subsequent hilarious adventures, Eileen goes to jail for assaulting a policeman, and the editor of the classy *Manhattan* magazine, Robert Baker (George Gaynes), makes it clear that he hates Ruth's stories, but then falls in love with their writer. No big hits emerged from the effervescent, tuneful, and amusing score, which included 'Christopher Street', 'Ohio', 'One Hundred Easy Ways', 'What A Waste', 'A Little Bit In Love', 'Conga!', 'Swing!', 'It's Love', and 'Wrong Note Rag', although the lovely 'A Quiet Girl' is inclined to linger in the memory. Rosalind Russell, who had starred in the non-musical 1942 film of *My Sister Eileen*, was outstanding in this rare Broadway appearance. *Wonderful Town* ran for 559 performances in New York, and a further 207 in London with Pat Kirkwood and Shani Wallis. Over 30 years later, in 1986, a major West End revival starred one of Britain's favourite comedy actresses, Maureen Lipman, and in 1994 the New York City Opera offered another, with Kay McClelland and Crista Moore. The 1955 musical film, with Betty Garrett, Janet Leigh, and Jack Lemmon, reverted to the original title of the play, *My Sister Eileen*.

WOOD, DEL

b. Adelaide Hazlewood, 22 February 1920, Nashville, Tennessee, USA, d. 3 October 1989. Wood's parents gave her a piano for her fifth birthday with the hope that she would become a classical pianist. She had different ideas and aimed for a career at the *Grand Ole Opry*. She developed a thumping ragtime style that, in 1951, saw her record her version of 'Down Yonder', a tune that had proved a million-seller for the Skillet Lickers in 1934. Wood's version on the Tennessee label reached number 5 in the US country charts and also became a million-seller. After guesting on the *Opry* in 1952 and refusing the chance of playing with Bob Crosby, she joined the roster in 1953. Her playing proved so popular that she toured with *Opry* shows, even to Japan. She recorded for several labels, making popular versions of such numbers as 'Johnson Rag' and 'Piano Roll Blues'. She had no more chart entries, but she won herself the nickname of 'Queen Of The Ragtime Pianists'. She remained a member of the *Opry* until her death in the Baptist Hospital, Nashville, on 3 October 1989, following a stroke on 22 September, the day she was scheduled to appear on the *Legendary Ladies Of Country Music Show*.

● ALBUMS: *Down Yonder* (RCA Victor 1955) ★★★, *Hot Happy & Honky* (1957) ★★★, *Mississippi Showboat* (1959) ★★★, *Buggies, Bustles & Barrelhouse* (1960) ★★★, *Flivvers, Flappers & Fox Trots* (1960) ★★★, *Ragtime Goes International* (1961) ★★★, *Ragtime Goes South Of The Border* (1962) ★★★, *Honky Tonk Piano* (1962) ★★★, *Piano Roll Blues* (1963) ★★★, *It's Honky Tonk Time* (1964) ★★★, *Roll Out The Piano* (1964) ★★★, *Uptight, Lowdown & Honky Tonk* (1966) ★★★, *There's A Tavern In The Town* (60s) ★★, *Del Wood Favorites*, *Encore-Del Wood*, *Ragtime Favorites*, *Plays Berlin & Cohen Volumes*, *Ragtime Glory Special* (all 70s).

WOODE, JIMMY

b. James Bryant Woode, 23 September 1928, Philadelphia, Pennsylvania, USA. After extensive studies on both piano and bass, Woode settled on the latter instrument. Military service delayed the start of his professional career, but in 1946 he formed his own band which worked in the Boston area. Among his early musical associates were Nat Pierce, Joe 'Flip' Phillips and Zoot Sims, and he was also accompanist to Ella Fitzgerald and Sarah Vaughan. In the early 50s he was a member of the house band at George Wein's Storyville Club in Boston, where he played with numerous visiting jazz stars. By 1955 his reputation was such that he was invited to join Duke Ellington, a job he held for five years. After leaving Ellington he settled in Europe, becoming a member of the Clarke-Boland Big Band throughout most of its existence. The 60s and 70s were busy years for Woode; in addition to playing with various bands on a regular basis, he gigged with visiting Americans, including Don Byas and Johnny Griffin, ran his own music publishing company, and worked in radio, television and recording studios. This pattern continued throughout the 80s, with appearances in the Paris Reunion Band, led by Nathan Davis, and at Ellington reunions, including Ellington '88 at Oldham, England, where he was reunited with former Ellington rhythm-section partner Sam Woodyard. A solid section player, Woode continues to draw the respect of his fellow musicians.

● ALBUMS: with Duke Ellington *Such Sweet Thunder* (Columbia 1957) ★★★★, *The Colorful Strings Of Jimmy Woode* (Argo 1957) ★★★.

WOODMAN, BRITT

b. 4 June 1920, Los Angeles, California, USA, d. 13 October 2000, Hawthorne, California, USA. Following in the footsteps of his trombone-playing father, Woodman took up the instrument in childhood to play in his father's band. In the late 30s he worked mostly on the west coast, usually in lesser-known bands, although he ended the decade with Les Hite. After military service in World War II he played in Boyd Raeburn's musically adventurous band and was then with Lionel Hampton. At the end of the 40s he formalized his musical education, studying at Westlake College in Los Angeles, and then joined the Duke Ellington orchestra as lead trombonist. In the mid-50s he found time for record dates with Charles Mingus, a friend from childhood, and Miles Davis. His tenure with Ellington ended in 1960 and thereafter he worked in studio and theatre bands in Los Angeles and New York City. He continued with his film and television work, but appeared on record leading his own small band and with small groups led by Bill Berry and Benny Carter. He also played in the big bands of Berry, Toshiko Akiyoshi and the Capp-Pierce Juggernaut. Woodman's playing style reflected his career-long immersion in big band music, but was shot through with intriguing glimpses of his interest in bop.

● ALBUMS: *Britt Woodman In LA* (Falcon 1977) ★★★, with Joe Wilder, John LaPorta *Playing For Keeps* (GM 1996) ★★★★.

WOOLEY, SHEB

b. Shelby F. Wooley, 10 April 1921, near Erick, Oklahoma, USA. Wooley, who is part Cherokee Indian, grew up on the family farm, learned to ride as a child and rode in rodeos as a teenager. His father traded a shotgun for Sheb's first guitar and while still at high school, he formed a country band that played at dances and on local radio. After leaving school, he found work on an oilfield as a welder, but soon tired of this work and moved to Nashville. He appeared on the WLAC and WSM radio stations and recorded for the Bullet label. In 1946, he relocated to Fort Worth, where until 1949, he became the frontman for a major show on WBAP, sponsored by Calumet Baking Powder. He then moved to Los Angeles, where he signed with MGM Records and with thoughts of a film career, he also attended the Jack Koslyn School of Acting. In 1950, he had his first screen role (as a heavy) in the Errol Flynn film *Rocky Mountain*. In 1952, he made a memorable appearance as Ben Miller, the killer plotting to gun down Gary Cooper in the classic western *High Noon*. During the 50s, he appeared in several other films including *Distant Drums* and *Little Big Horn* (both

1951), *Man Without A Star* (1955) and *Giant* (1956). He is also well remembered for his performances as Pete Nolan in the television series *Rawhide*, which ran from 1958-65 (he also wrote some scripts for the series). During his career he has appeared in over 30 films.

Other artists began to record songs Wooley had written and in 1953, Hank Snow had a big hit with 'When Mexican Joe Met Jole Blon' – a parody of two hit songs. In 1958, his novelty number, 'The Purple People Eater', became a million-seller and even reached number 12 in the UK pop charts. He based the song on a schoolboy joke that he had heard from Don Robertson's son and initially, MGM did not consider it to be worth releasing. Further US pop successes included 'Sweet Chile'. He first appeared in the US country charts in 1962, when another novelty number, 'That's My Pa', became a number 1. It was intended that Wooley should record 'Don't Go Near The Indians' but due to film commitments Rex Allen's version was released before he could record it. Wooley jokingly told MGM that he would write a sequel and came up with the comedy parody 'Don't Go Near The Eskimos'. He developed an alter-ego drunken character, whom he called Ben Colder, and in this guise, he recorded and charted it and other humorous parodies of pop/country hits, including 'Almost Persuaded No. 2', 'Harper Valley PTA (Later That Same Day)' and 'Fifteen Beers (Years) Ago'. (The name Ben Colder was the selection made by MGM from the three alternatives that Wooley offered. The other two were Ben Freezin and Klon Dyke.) He had some further minor hits with serious recordings, including 'Blue Guitar' and 'Tie A Tiger Down'.

In 1969 Wooley joined the CBS network *Hee Haw* country show, remaining with it for several years, and also wrote the theme music. Throughout the 60s and 70s, he maintained a busy touring schedule, appearing all over the USA and overseas. In 1968, Ben Colder was voted Comedian of the Year by the Country Music Association. Wooley cut back his work during the 80s and although he has remained a popular entertainer, he has had no chart entries since 1971. Over the years, the parodies by the drunken Ben Colder have proved more popular than his serious recordings and have certainly accounted for the majority of his record sales.

● ALBUMS: *Blue Guitar* (MGM 1956) ★★★, *Songs For The Days Of Rawhide* (MGM 1961) ★★★, *That's My Pa & That's My Ma (And Other Selections)* (MGM 1962) ★★★★, *Tales Of How The West Was Won* (MGM 1963) ★★★★, *It's A Big Land* (MGM 1965) ★★★, *Warm & Wooley* (MGM 1969) ★★★.
As Ben Colder *Spoofing The Big Ones* (MGM 1963) ★★★, *Ben Colder As Played By Sheb Wooley* (MGM 1963) ★★★, *Big Ben Strikes Again* (MGM 1966) ★★★★, *Wine, Women & Song* (MGM 1967) ★★★, *Have One On Ben* (MGM 1969) ★★, *Wild Again* (MGM 1970) ★★★, *Live And Loaded (At The Sam Houston Coliseum)* (MGM 1971) ★★★, *Warming Up To Colder* (MGM 1972) ★★★, *The Wacky World Of Ben Colder* (MGM 1973) ★★★.
● COMPILATIONS: as Sheb Wooley *The Very Best Of Sheb Wooley* (MGM 1965) ★★★★, *Blue Guitar* (Bear Family 1985) ★★★, *Wild And Wooley, Big Unruly Me* (Bear Family 1997) ★★★★.
As Ben Colder *The Best Of Ben Colder* (MGM 1968) ★★★, *Golden Archive Series* (MGM 1970) ★★★, as Ben Colder *Golden Hits* (Gusto 1979) ★★★.
● FILMS: *Rocky Mountain Way* (1950), *Inside The Walls Of Folsom Prison* (1951), *Distant Drums* (1951), *Little Big Horn* aka *The Fighting Seventh* (1951), *Apache Drums* (1951), *High Noon* (1952), *The Toughest Man In Arizona* (1952), *Bugles In The Afternoon* (1952), *Sky Full Of Moon* (1952), *The Lusty Men* (1952), *Hellgate* (1952), *Cattle Down* (1952), *Texas Bad Man* (1953), *Johnny Guitar* (1954), *Seven Brides For Seven Brothers* (1954), *Rose Marie* (1954), *The Boy From Oklahoma* (1954), *Trial* (1955), *The Second Greatest Sex* (1955), *Man Without A Star* (1955), *Giant* (1956), *The Black Whip* aka *The Man With A Whip* (1956), *The Oklahoman* (1957), *Trooper Hook* (1957), *Ride A Violent Mile* (1957), *Terror In A Texas Town* (1958), *Hootenanny Hoot* (1963), *Country Boy* (1966), *The War Wagon* (1967), *The Outlaw Josey Wales* (1976), *Silverado* (1985), *Hoosiers* aka *Best Shot* (1986), *Uphill All The Way* (1986), *Purple People Eater* (1988).

WRAY, LINK
b. Frederick Lincoln Wray, 2 May 1929, Dunn, North Carolina, USA. Guitarist Wray formed his first group in 1942, but his musical ambitions were thwarted by his induction into the US Army. He first recorded for Starday in 1955 as a member of the country outfit Lucky Wray And The Palomino Ranch Hands. He subsequently formed the Raymen with Shorty Horton (bass) and Doug Wray (drums), and enjoyed a million-seller in 1958 with 'Rumble', a pioneering instrumental on which the artist's frenzied style and distorted tone invoked a gang-fight. The single incurred bans both on technical grounds and on account of its subject matter, but is now recognized as one of pop's most innovative releases, and includes the Who's Pete Townshend as a vociferous proponent. Wray achieved another gold disc for 'Rawhide' (1959), but ensuing releases, including 'Jack The Ripper' (1960), 'The Sweeper' (1963) and 'Batman Theme' (1965), failed to match this success. He continued to record, using a homemade three-track studio built in a converted chicken shack, and a 1971 album, *Link Wray*, was the subject of critical acclaim. It drew heavily on the artist's country roots – he is part-Shawnee Indian – yet was still imbued with the primitive atmosphere of his early work. Renewed interest in Wray resulted in several archive releases, while contemporary recordings, although of interest, failed to match the promise of his initial 'rediscovery' collection.
In the late 70s the guitarist forged a fruitful partnership with new-wave rockabilly singer Robert Gordon, before resurrecting a solo career the following decade. Wray's primeval sound is echoed in the work of the Cramps and many other more contemporary groups. He is particularly respected in the UK where his influence on 'trash' guitar groups, notably the Stingrays and

Milkshakes, has been considerable. In 1997 he made a new album with UK's prime R&B/Rock 'n' Roll reissue label Ace Records, having been previously associated with their Chiswick Records label. 'Rumble On The Docks' is vintage Link Wray and worth the price of the CD alone.

● ALBUMS: *Link Wray And The Raymen* (Epic 1959) ★★★★, *Jack The Ripper* (Swan 1963) ★★★★, *Great Guitar Hits* (Vermillion 1963) ★★★, *Sings And Plays Guitar* (Vermillion 1964) ★★★, *Yesterday And Today* (Record Factory 1969) ★★★, *Link Wray* (Polydor 1971) ★★★, *Be What You Want To Be* (Polydor 1972) ★★★, *Beans And Fatback* (Virgin 1973) ★★★, *The Link Wray Rumble* (Polydor 1974) ★★★, *Interstate 10* (Virgin 1975) ★★★, *Stuck In Gear* (Virgin 1976) ★★★, with Robert Gordon *Robert Gordon With Link Wray* (Private Stock 1977) ★★★, with Robert Gordon *Fresh Fish Special* (Private Stock 1978) ★★★, *Bullshot* (Charisma 1979) ★★★, *Live At The Paradiso* (Magnum Force 1980) ★★★, *Live In '85* (Big Beat 1986) ★★★, *Indian Child* (Creation 1993) ★★★, *Shadowman* (Ace/Hip-O 1997) ★★★, *Walking Down A Street Called Love: The Rumble Man Live In London And Manchester* (Cleopatra 1997) ★★★, *Barbed Wire* (Ace 2000) ★★★.

● COMPILATIONS: *There's Good Rockin' Tonight* (Union Pacific 1971) ★★★, *Rockin' And Handclappin'* (Epic 1973) ★★★, *Rock 'N' Roll Rumble* (Charly 1974) ★★★★, *Early Recordings* (Ace 1979) ★★★★, *Good Rocking' Tonight* (Chiswick 1983) ★★★★, *Link Wray And The Wraymen* (Edsel 1985) ★★★★, *Growlin' Guitar* (Ace 1987) ★★★, *Hillbilly Wolf: Missing Links Volume 1* (Norton 1990) ★★★, *Big City After Dark: Missing Links Volume 2* (Norton 1990) ★★★, *Some Kinda Nut: Missing Links Volume 3* (Norton 1990) ★★★, *Rumble! The Best Of Link Wray* (Rhino 1993) ★★★★, *Mr. Guitar: Original Swan Recordings* (Norton 1995) ★★★★, *Guitar Preacher: The Polydor Years* (Polydor 1995) ★★★, *Streets Of Chicago: Missing Links Volume 4* (Norton 1997) ★★★.

● VIDEOS: *Link Wray: The Rumble Man* (Visionary/Cleopatra 1996).

WRIGHT, BILLY

b. 21 May 1932, Atlanta, Georgia, USA, d. 28 October 1991, Atlanta, Georgia, USA. A promising gospel singer as a child, he would often sneak into Atlanta's famous 81 Theater to watch the secular shows and eventually turned to performing the blues. His soulful voice came to the attention of Savoy Records, who secured a US R&B Top 5 hit with his debut record 'Blues For My Baby' in 1949. Other less successful releases followed, but Wright's strength was in his live performances, earning him the nickname – Prince Of The Blues. After his Savoy tenure, Wright recorded for Peacock in 1955 and then passed on the baton to his devoted admirers Little Richard, James Brown and Otis Redding. In the late 50s he made his final recordings for Bobby Robinson's Fire Records and tiny local labels, Carrollton and Chris, before settling down in Atlanta, where he continued to perform and

introduces acts as a compere until his death in 1991.

● COMPILATIONS: *Stacked Deck* (Savoy 1980) ★★★, *Goin' Down Slow* (Savoy 1984) ★★★.

WRIGHT, CAROL SUE

b. Nashville, Tennessee, USA. The youngest of the three children of Kitty Wells and Johnnie Wright, she began to sing with her parents from an early age. In December 1955, standing on a chair to reach the microphone, Wright duetted with her mother when she recorded their well-known version of 'How Far Is Heaven?'. In the late 50s, she sang with her sister, Ruby Wright, as the Wright Sisters, recording under the production of Chet Atkins for the Cadence label, who saw them as the female version of the label's popular Everly Brothers. She toured for a time with the family show but eventually, with no desire to pursue a singing career, she restricted her appearances and devoted her time to raising her own family. In the 80s, she and sister Ruby ran the family Museum and Tourist attraction in Nashville.

WRIGHT, DALE

b. Harlan Dale Riffe, 4 February 1939, Middletown, Ohio, USA. As a teenager Wright was a disc jockey on WING in Dayton, Ohio. He was spotted by Harry Carlson of Fraternity Records when singing 'Walk With Me', with his group the Rock-Its, on a polio charity telethon. This song became his first single but it was his second release, the rocker 'She's Neat', that gave him his sole US Top 40 hit in early 1958. With the Rock-Its departing shortly after, Wright recorded his next single in Nashville with the Owen Bradley Quintet, subsequently forming the Wright Guys. Their first record together 'Please Don't Do It' (which also featured backing vocal duo the Dons) charted in 1958. Wright's sixth release the rocking novelty 'That's Show Biz' was his last record to create any real interest and even received airplay in the UK. In the 60s he recorded without success on the Alcar, Stardust, Boone and Revere labels, and in 1967 on Queen B on which he was backed by the label owner's son Bo Donaldson and his group the Heywoods.

● COMPILATIONS: *She's Neat: The Fraternity Sides* (Ace 1992) ★★★.

WRIGHT, ROBERT

b. 25 September 1914, Daytona Beach, Florida, USA. Together with George Forrest (b. George Forrest Chichester Jnr., 31 July 1915, Brooklyn, New York, USA, d. 10 October 1999, Miami, Florida, USA), Wright formed one of the longest partnerships in the American musical theatre. They first met in their teens at Miami High School (Forrest's family had moved to the west coast during the 20s), where they collaborated on the show *Hail To Miami High!* After writing numerous jazzy songs together in the early 30s, the team were hired to provide some fresh material – based on non-copyright music – for the film of Sigmund Romberg's stage operetta

Maytime. So successful were they, that, during the remainder of their stay in Hollywood, the two men worked as co-lyricists for previously written stage and/or screen songs by Rudolph Friml, Victor Herbert, Richard Rodgers, George Posford, Edward Ward, and Herbert Stothart, amongst others. Two of their most popular film songs were 'The Donkey Serenade' (music: Friml-Stothart), which was introduced in *The Firefly* by Allan Jones; and the title number for one of the best of the Nelson Eddy and Jeanette MacDonald vehicles, *Sweethearts*. They also contributed to films such as *Sinner Take All*, *Saratoga*, *Mannequin* ('Always And Always'), *Three Comrades*, *Balalaika* ('At The Balalaika', 'The Volga Boatman', 'Ride, Cossak, Ride'), *The Women*, *Music In My Heart* ('It's A Blue World', 'Ho! Punchinello'), and *Flying With Music* ('Pennies For Peppino') (1942).

In the early 40s Wright and Forrest turned to Broadway and began adapting the romantic music of classical and operetta composers – with new lyrics – for lavish stage musicals. One of their first efforts, 1944's *Song Of Norway*, was based on the life of Edvard Grieg, and proved an enormous hit. It was followed by *Gypsy Lady* (Victor Herbert, 1946), *Magdalena* (Heitor Villa-Lobos, 1948), and 1953's *Kismet*. The latter, based on themes by Alexander Borodin, contained several of their most memorable songs, including 'Stranger In Paradise', 'And This Is My Beloved', and 'Baubles, Bangles And Beads'. In 1961 Wright and Forrest wrote their first original Broadway score for *Kean* (they had written the words and music for a London production of *The Love Doctor* two years earlier), which, despite the presence of Alfred Drake and pleasant songs such as 'Elena' and 'Sweet Danger', folded after only three months. Four years later, *Anya*, an adaptation of Guy Bolton and Marcelle Maurette's play *Anastasia*, signalled a return to their previous policy – this time using the music of Sergei Rachmaninov – but the critically acclaimed production lasted for only two weeks. *Anya* was later drastically revised and re-titled *The Anastasia Affaire*. The songwriters' last stage musical together was *Grand Hotel*, which opened on Broadway in 1989, and ran for almost three years. The score was mostly their own work, with some additional numbers by Maury Yeston. Throughout their long careers, Wright and Forrest contributed material to some 16 produced stage musicals, 18 stage revues, 58 motion pictures, and numerous cabaret acts. In 1994 – the year Wright celebrated his 80th birthday – they were reported to be working on three projects for the stage. In the same year they travelled from their Miami base to London, and were present at a BBC Radio 2 concert production of their best-known work, *Kismet*, which they had written over 40 years ago. The following year they received the ASCAP/Richard Rodgers Award for their contribution to the American musical theatre. The duo were working on a P.G. Wodehouse musical at the time of Forrest's death in 1999.

YANA
b. Pamela Guard, 16 February 1932, Romford, Essex, England, d. 21 November 1989, London, England. A popular singer in the UK during the 50s and 60s, Guard became a model while still in her teens, before being 'discovered' when singing at a private party at London's Astor club. This led to engagements at several top nightspots, and a contract with Columbia Records. In the 50s her single releases included sultry renderings of 'Small Talk', 'Something Happened To My Heart', 'Climb Up The Wall', 'If You Don't Love Me', 'I Miss You, Mama', 'I Need You Now' and 'Mr Wonderful'. Her glamorous image made her a natural for television, and she was given her own BBC series in 1956. Later, following the advent of ITV, she appeared regularly on *Sunday Night At The London Palladium*. In 1958, Yana starred in Richard Rodgers and Oscar Hammerstein II's *Cinderella* at the London Coliseum: her solo numbers in the show and on the Original Cast album were 'In My Own Little Corner' and 'A Lovely Night', and she duetted with Tommy Steele ('When You're Driving In The Moonlight'), Betty Marsden ('Impossible') and Bruce Trent ('Do I Love You?' and 'Ten Minutes Ago'). Two years later she was back in the West End with Norman Wisdom in the London Palladium's longest-running pantomime, *Turn Again Whittington*. She was something of a pantomime 'specialist', and throughout the 60s and into the 70s, was one of Britain's leading principal boys. It is probably not a coincidence that the second of her three marriages was to the actor Alan Curtis, who is renowned for his performances of the 'Demon King' and other 'nasty' pantomime characters, although he is probably better known for his PA work at important cricket matches. In her heyday Yana toured abroad, including the Middle East, and she appeared on several US variety shows hosted by Bob Hope and Ed Sullivan. She also played small roles in the British films *Zarak*, with Victor Mature and Michael Wilding, and *The Cockleshell Heroes*, an early Anthony Newley feature. Her last performance is said to have been as the 'Good Fairy' in *The Wizard Of Oz* at an English provincial theatre in 1983. She died of throat cancer six years later.
● FILMS: *The Cockleshell Heroes* aka *Operation Cockleshell* (1955), *Zarak* (1956), *Interpol* aka *Pickup Alley* (1957).

YORK BROTHERS
A popular harmony duo comprising George York (b. 17 February 1910, Louisa, Lawrence County, Kentucky, USA, d. July 1974; guitar, harmonica, vocals) and Leslie York (b. 23 August 1917, Louisa,

Lawrence County, Kentucky, USA, d. 21 February 1984; guitar, vocals). George first worked in the coalmines before moving to Denver, where he played on local radio. In the late 30s, somewhat influenced by the Delmores, the brothers began their career in Portsmouth, Ohio, and made their first recordings for the Universal label in 1939. Their version of 'Little White Washed Chimney' (recorded as 'Going Home') sold well enough to gain them a contract with Decca Records. After recording for that label in 1941, and at a time when their popularity was spreading nationally, America's involvement in World War II saw both brothers drafted for service with the US Navy. After their discharge, they settled in Nashville where, until 1950, they played the *Grand Ole Opry*. They then relocated to Detroit until 1953, when they moved to Dallas, becoming regulars on the *Big D Jamboree* and the *Saturday Night Shindig*. Between 1947 and 1956, they recorded for King Records, and later for their own label. In the latter half of their career, their music changed from the old-time style of the usual brother harmony acts to anticipate the popular mix of nostalgia and sentimental ballads later popularized by such artists as Red Foley, even introducing a piano to add a honky tonk effect on some numbers. Leslie sang solo on some of their later recordings, due to the fact that George at times suffered throat problems. They eventually retired from the music but remained in Dallas where George owned a nightclub.

● ALBUMS: *The York Brothers Volume 1* (King 1958) ★★★, *The York Brothers Volume 2* (King 1958) ★★★, *16 Great Country Songs* (King 1963) ★★★★.

● COMPILATIONS: *Early Favorites* (Old Homestead 1987) ★★★, *Detroit In The 40's And 50's, Vol. 1* (Collector 2000) ★★★.

YORKE, PETER

b. 4 December 1902, London, England, d. 2 February 1966, England. A highly respected composer, conductor and arranger, Yorke was well known in Britain through his hundreds of broadcasts, and his themes have been widely used on television and radio. In the 30s he was one of the finest dance band orchestrators in England, working with Percival Mackey, Jack Hylton, Louis Levy and many others. After World War II he established himself as a light music composer and conductor through BBC radio shows such as *Sweet Serenade, Our Kind Of Music* and *The Peter Yorke Melody Hours*. From the late 40s onwards he made numerous 78s for Columbia Records, including some legendary titles with saxophonist Freddy Gardner (1911-50), which are regarded as models of their genre: 'I'm In The Mood For Love', 'I Only Have Eyes For You', 'Roses Of Picardy', 'These Foolish Things', 'Body And Soul' and 'Valse Vanite'. Yorke also recorded an early composition, 'Sapphires And Sables', which he used as his theme music, and his other notable pieces included 'Melody Of The Stars', 'Dawn Fantasy', 'Quiet Countryside', 'Caravan Romance', 'Carminetta', 'Faded Lilac', 'Fireflies',

'Flyaway Fiddles', 'Golden Melody', 'Oriental Bazaar', 'In My Garden' – suite, 'Midnight In Mexico', 'Parade Of The Matadors', 'Royal Mile', 'Highdays And Holidays', 'Brandy Snaps', 'Miss In Mink', 'Lazy Piano', and 'Ladies Night'. From 1957-67 'Silks And Satins' was used to close the popular British television soap *Emergency Ward 10*. Most of Yorke's original works were written for various London mood music libraries especially Chappells, Francis Day & Hunter, Bosworth, Harmonic, Conroy, Paxton, Southern and Josef Weinberger. He also conducted several albums of popular songs, mainly for the American market.

● ALBUMS: *Music For Sweethearts – Romantic Compositions Of Victor Herbert* (Brunswick 1956) ★★★, *Sapphires And Sables – Music In The Peter Yorke Manner* (Delyse-Envoy 1959) ★★★, *Mood For Love* (EMI-World Records 1979) ★★★★.

YOUNG AT HEART

Adapted by Julius J. Epstein and Lenore Coffee from Fannie Hurst's novel *Sister Act*, and the 1938 Claude Rains-John Garfield movie *The Four Daughters*, this 1954 Warner Brothers release provided a glimpse of the American suburban family viewed through the proverbial rose-coloured spectacles. The story concerns three sisters (one was dropped from the original), played by Doris Day, Dorothy Malone and Elizabeth Fraser, who live with their music teacher father (Robert Keith) and crusty aunt (Ethel Barrymore). Day is engaged to budding songwriter Gig Young, but one day, old chip-on-the-shoulder Frank Sinatra turns up on the doorstep and ruins the whole arrangement. Day marries Sinatra, but his career prospects remain at zero (the people 'upstairs' never give him a break), and one dark, snowy night he attempts to 'take the easy way out'. His will to live is rekindled when his wife tells him they are about to become a threesome. Perhaps because of the film's sentimental character, the Sinatra-Day combination failed to work as well as might have been expected, although, individually, they had some satisfying moments. At the time, both were probably at the peak of their vocal powers, and a collection of engaging songs gave them ample chance to shine – Day with such as 'Hold Me In Your Arms' (Ray Heindorf-Charles Henderson-Don Pippin) and the more upbeat 'Ready, Willing And Able' (Floyd Huddleston-Al Rinker-Dick Gleason), and Sinatra on 'Someone To Watch Over Me' (George and Ira Gershwin), 'Just One Of Those Things' (Cole Porter) and 'One For My Baby' (Harold Arlen-Johnny Mercer). Sinatra sings a number of these while working in a local 'joint' for what he calls 'tips on a plate'. Other numbers included 'You, My Love' (Mack Gordon-Jimmy Van Heusen), 'There's A Rising Moon (For Every Falling Star)' (Paul Francis Webster-Sammy Fain) and 'Young At Heart' (Carolyn Leigh-Johnny Richards). Photographed in Warnercolor and directed by Gordon Douglas, this was the kind of film that – at the time – made audiences feel warm all over.

YOUNG JESSIE

b. Obediah Donnell Jessie, 28 December 1936, Lincoln Manor, Dallas, Texas, USA. Young Jessie is one of the great unheralded singers of the Los Angeles R&B scene. He is best known for recording the original version of 'Mary Lou' (1955), which, although not a national hit, became a huge hit in California and Texas. The song was subsequently recorded with great success by rock 'n' roller Ronnie Hawkins in 1959 for Roulette and by rocker Bob Seger on his 1976 recording *Night Moves*. At Los Angeles' Jefferson High, Young Jessie studied piano and saxophone alongside Johnny 'Guitar' Watson. His first recordings came about as a member of a doo-wop vocal group, the Hollywood Blue Jays (the other members were Richard Berry, Beverley Thompson, Thomas Pete Fox and Cornelius Gunther), recording for the Dolphin label a Young Jessie-penned record, 'I Had A Love'. The group then went to Modern Records and recorded the same song as the Flairs on the label's new Flair subsidiary. After several more singles, Young Jessie embarked on a solo career on the Modern label. His only success was with 'Mary Lou', and he left Modern in 1957. After recording with no success at Atlantic Records and then Capitol Records, Young Jessie left the music business in 1959. He returned to recording in 1961, but subsequent soul-style records on Mercury Records, Vanessa, Bit, Combo and Ro-Mark failed to find an audience.
● ALBUMS: *I'm Gone* (Ace 1995) ★★★★.

YOUNG MAN WITH A HORN

Directed by Michael Curtiz, this film made in 1950 follows broadly upon Dorothy Baker's novel which was in its turn very loosely based on the life of Bix Beiderbecke. Any chance of reality went out the window with the casting of Kirk Douglas and the choice of Harry James to dub the character's trumpet playing. Hoagy Carmichael appears as a pianist but despite the fact that he actually did play piano with Bix he was ghosted by Buddy Cole. Amongst other musicians involved, mostly off-screen, are Babe Russin, Nick Fatool, Jack Jenney, Willie Smith, Stan Wrightsman and Jimmy Zito. Doris Day plays Douglas' long-suffering girlfriend and has a chance to sing between the melodramatics. (Alternative title: *Young Man Of Music*).

YOUNG, ERNIE

b. Ernest Lafayette Young, 2 December 1892, Giles County, Tennessee, USA, d. 8 June 1977, Nashville, Tennessee, USA, Young was a jukebox operator, record retailer and disc jockey. A move into production was therefore logical, given his access to retail outlets. Nashboro was founded in 1951 to record gospel, and Excello Records in 1952. Using the band led by Skippy Brooks for backing, Excello recorded many local blues artists, while Nashboro acquired a distinguished roster, including Edna Gallmon Cooke, Morgan Babb, the Consolers and the Swanee Quintet. Although there was occasional national chart success, Excello's predominant market was in the south. In 1955, Young finalized an agreement with Jay Miller whereby Miller recorded blues in his Crowley studio for Excello. A steady stream of classics was released, Excello's greatest chart success being Slim Harpo. In 1966, owing to his age and ill health, Young sold the label and retired.

YOUNG, FARON

b. 25 February 1932, Shreveport, Louisiana, USA, d. 10 December 1996, Nashville, Tennessee, USA. Young was raised on the farm his father bought just outside Shreveport and learned to play the guitar and sing country songs as a boy. Greatly influenced by Hank Williams (in his early days he was something of a soundalike) and while still at school, he formed a country band and began to establish a local reputation as an entertainer. In 1950, he gave up his college studies to accept an offer of a professional career and joined radio station KWKH, where he soon became a member of the prestigious *The Louisiana Hayride* show and found other work in the nightclubs and honky tonks. He became friends with Webb Pierce and for a time toured with him as a vocalist with Pierce's band. In 1951, he made his first recordings for the Gotham label with Tillman Franks and his band, and achieved minor success with 'Have I Waited Too Long' and 'Tattle Tale Eyes' before he joined Capitol Records. In the summer of 1952, Faron was dating a girl called Billie Jean Jones, when she attracted the attention of Hank Williams. He persuaded Young to arrange a double date, which resulted in Williams threatening him with a pistol and claiming Jones for himself. Young backed off and Billie Jean became the second Mrs. Hank Williams.

In 1953, Young formed his own band, moved to Nashville, where he became a member of the *Grand Ole Opry* and gained his first US country chart hit with a self-penned song called 'Goin' Steady'. His career was interrupted when, because of the Korean War, he was drafted into the army. Although interrupted by this, his career certainly benefited from the exposure he received after winning an army talent competition. This led to him touring the world entertaining US forces, as well as appearing on recruiting shows that were networked to hundreds of radio stations. Young returned to Nashville in November 1954 and resumed his career, gaining his first US country number 1 the following year with 'Live Fast, Love Hard, Die Young'. This established him beyond any doubt as a major recording star, and between 1955 and 1969 he amassed a total of 63 US country chart hits, of which 46 made the Top 20. He developed the knack of picking the best material by other writers and had a number 2 hit with Don Gibson's 'Sweet Dreams' and further number 1s with Roy Drusky's songs 'Alone With You' and 'Country Girl'. In 1961, he recorded 'Hello Walls', thereby making the song one of the first Willie Nelson compositions to be recorded by a major artist. It reached number 1 in the US country charts, also became a Top 20 US pop hit and was

Young's first million-seller.

In 1956, his popularity as a singer earned him a role in the movie *Hidden Guns*. This led to his own nickname of The Young Sheriff and his band being called the Country Deputies (at one time Roger Miller was a member of the band). In later years he became the Singing Sheriff before, as he once suggested, someone queried his age and started asking 'What's he trying to prove?' After the initial success with this easily forgettable B-movie western, he made further film appearances over the years including *Daniel Boone, Trail Blazer, Raiders Of Old California, Country Music Holiday, The Road To Nashville* and *That's Country*. He left Capitol for Mercury Records in 1962, immediately charting with 'The Yellow Bandanna', 'You'll Drive Me Back' and a fine duet recording with Margie Creath Singleton of 'Keeping Up With The Joneses'. In 1965, he had a US country Top 10 hit with 'Walk Tall', a song that had been a UK pop hit for Val Doonican the previous year. Young quit the *Grand Ole Opry* in the mid-60s, finding, like several other artists, that it was not only difficult keeping up the expected number of Saturday night appearances but also that he lost many other lucrative bookings. After the success of 'Hello Walls', he perhaps unintentionally tended to look for further pop chart hits, and in consequence, his recordings, at times, became less countrified in their arrangements. He soon returned to his country roots, usually choosing his favourite twin fiddle backings.

Young easily maintained his popularity throughout the 60s and 70s and toured extensively in the USA and made several visits to Europe, where he performed in the UK, France and Germany. He appeared on all the major network television shows but seemed to have little interest in having his own regular series. At times he has not endeared himself to some of his fellow performers with his imitations of their acts. In the 70s he was still a major star, with a series of Top 10 US country hits including 'Step Aside', 'Leavin' And Saying Goodbye', 'This Little Girl Of Mine' and 'Just What I Had In Mind'. 'It's Four In The Morning', another country number 1, had crossover success and also gave him a second million-seller. It also became his only UK pop chart success, peaking at number 3 during a 23-week chart run. He left Mercury in 1979 and briefly joined MCA Records. In 1988, he joined Step One Records and 'Stop And Take The Time', a minor hit, became country chart entry number 85.

Over the years, he became involved in several business interests and, with the exception of heavy losses in the 60s (in respect of investments to convert an old baseball stadium into a stock-car racing track in Nashville), he was very successful. Young became involved in publishing companies, a recording studio, and a booking agency, plus co-ownership of *Music City News* newspaper. He was always noted for very plain speaking and has incurred the wrath of the establishment on several occasions for his outspoken views. A suggested association with Patsy Cline led to various stories of his dalliances and whether correct or not, it may well be that he revelled in the publicity they caused. In September 1972, he gained unwanted publicity by his reaction to an incident at a show. At a time when 'This Little Girl Of Mine' was a hit for him, he invited six-year-old Nora Jo Catlett to join him on stage in Clarksville, West Virginia. She refused, whereupon Young swore at the audience, stormed off stage, grabbed the child and spanked her repeatedly (the child collected autographs and had been told by her mother not to approach the stage but to wait near the front until Young finished his act). The child's father swore out a warrant for his arrest and after pleading guilty to a charge of assault, he was fined $35. The following year a civil action claiming $200,000 was filed. In his defence, Young claimed the child spat in his face. Eventually, almost two years later, the Catlett family was awarded only $3400. He was involved in various actions, once stating, 'I am not an alcoholic, I'm a drunk', and on one occasion, he shot out the light fittings of a Nashville bar. He was reputed to have had affairs with many women while supposedly remaining happily married. In 1987, after 34 years of marriage, his wife finally obtained a divorce on the grounds of physical abuse. She claimed that he had also threatened her and their 16-year-old daughter with a gun and often shot holes in the kitchen ceiling. A fair and concise summary was offered in 1980 by Bob Allen, who parodied Young's hit song in his article entitled 'Live Fast, Love Hard And Keep On Cussin'.

During the 90s Young was stricken with emphysema and, in a fit of depression, shot himself in December 1996. Until his death he was semi-retired but still made concert performances as well as guest appearances on the *Grand Ole Opry*. Faron Young was one of country music's greatest legends, but went to his grave relatively unknown to many outside the genre. Paddy McAloon of English pop band Prefab Sprout paid tribute to him when he wrote the beautiful 'Faron Young' on the band's 1985 album *Steve McQueen*.

● ALBUMS: *Sweethearts Or Strangers* (Capitol 1957) ★★★, *The Object Of My Affection* (Capitol 1958) ★★★, *My Garden Of Prayer* (Capitol 1959) ★★, *This Is Faron Young* (Capitol 1959) ★★★★, *Talk About Hits* (Capitol 1959) ★★★, *Sings The Best Of Faron Young* (Capitol 1960) ★★★, *Hello Walls* (Capitol 1961) ★★★, *The Young Approach* (Capitol 1961) ★★★, *This Is Faron* (Mercury 1963) ★★★★, *Faron Young Aims At The West* (Mercury 1963) ★★★, *Country Dance Favorites* (Mercury 1964) ★★★★, *Story Songs For Country Folks* (Mercury 1964) ★★★★, *Story Songs Of Mountains And Valleys* (Mercury 1964) ★★★★, *Memory Lane* (Capitol 1965) ★★★, *Falling In Love* (Capitol 1965) ★★★, *Pen And Paper* (Mercury 1965) ★★★, *Faron Young* (Hilltop 1966) ★★★, *Faron Young Sings The Best Of Jim Reeves* (Mercury 1966) ★★★, *If You Ain't Lovin', You Ain't Livin'* (Capitol 1966) ★★★, *It's A Great Life* (Tower 1966) ★★★, *Unmitigated Gall* (Mercury 1967) ★★★, *Here's Faron Young* (Mercury 1968) ★★★, *I'll Be Yours* (Hilltop 1968) ★★★★, *This Is Faron Young* (Mercury 1968) ★★★,

Just Out Of Reach (Mercury 1968) ★★★, *The World Of Faron Young* (Mercury 1968) ★★★★, *I've Got Precious Memories* (Mercury 1969) ★★★, *Wine Me Up* (Mercury 1969) ★★★★, *20 Hits Over The Years* (Mercury 1969) ★★★★, *Occasional Wife/If I Ever Fall In Love With A Honky Tonk Girl* (Mercury 1970) ★★★, *Leavin' And Sayin' Goodbye* (Mercury 1971) ★★★, *Step Aside* (Mercury 1971) ★★★, *It's Four In The Morning* (Mercury 1972) ★★★, *This Little Girl Of Mine* (Mercury 1972) ★★★, *This Time The Hurtin's On Me* (Mercury 1973) ★★★, *Just What I Had In Mind* (Mercury 1973) ★★★, *Some Kind Of Woman* (Mercury 1974) ★★★, *A Man And His Music* (Mercury 1975) ★★★★, *I'd Just Be Fool Enough* (Mercury 1976) ★★★, *That Young Feelin'* (Mercury 1977) ★★★, *Chapter Two* (MCA 1979) ★★★, *Free And Easy* (MCA 1980) ★★★, *The Sheriff* (Allegiance 1984) ★★, with Jerry Lee Lewis, Webb Pierce, Mel Tillis *Four Legends* (1985) ★★★, *Here's To You* (Step One 1988) ★★★, *Country Christmas* (Step One 1990) ★★, with Ray Price *Memories That Last* (Step One 1992) ★★★.

● COMPILATIONS: *All-Time Great Hits* (Capitol 1963) ★★★★, *Capitol Country Classics* (Capitol 1980) ★★★, *The Young Sheriff (1955-1956 Radio Broadcasts)* (Castle 1981) ★★★★, *Greatest Hits Volumes 1, 2 & 3* (Step One 1988) ★★★★, *All Time Greatest Hits* (Curb 1990) ★★★, *The Capitol Years 1952 – 1962* 5-CD box set (Bear Family 1992) ★★★★, *Live Fast, Love Hard: Original Capitol Recordings, 1952-1962* (CMF 1995) ★★★★, *All American Country* (Spectrum 1997) ★★★★, *Faron Young & The Circle A Wranglers* (Bronco Buster 1998) ★★★★, *The Complete Capitol Hits Of Faron Young* (Collectors Choice 2000) ★★★★, *The Best Of Faron Young: The Millennium Collection* (Mercury 2001) ★★★★.

● FILMS: *Hidden Guns* (1956), *Daniel Boone, Trail Blazer* (1956), *Raiders Of Old California* (1957), *Country Music Holiday* (1958), *Second Fiddle To A Steel Guitar* (1965), *Nashville Rebel* (1966), *What Am I Bid?* (1967), *The Road To Nashville* (1967), *That's Country* (1977).

YOUNG, JIMMY

b. Leslie Ronald Young, 21 September 1921, Cinderford, Gloucestershire, England. A popular ballad singer in the UK during the 50s, Young carved out a new career for himself in broadcasting when rock 'n' roll took over in the latter part of the decade. The son of a miner, he was an excellent boxer and rugby player, but turned down an offer of a professional career with top rugby league club Wigan. Always keen on music, he was taught to play the piano by his mother, and received professional voice training. He worked as a baker and an electrician before joining the Royal Air Force in 1939. After demobilization he intended to train as a teacher, but was spotted, singing at a sports club, by BBC producer George Innes. He made his first broadcast two weeks later, and subsequently toured the UK variety circuit. From 1951 he had several successful records on the small Polygon label, including 'My Love And Devotion', 'Because Of You' and 'Too Young'. In January 1953, two months after the first UK singles chart appeared in the *New Musical Express*, Young had a hit with 'Faith Can Move Mountains' for his new label, Decca Records, and followed that with 'Eternally (Terry's Theme)', from the Charles Chaplin movie *Limelight*.

In 1955, Young became the first UK artist to top the *NME* chart with successive releases. The first, 'Unchained Melody', made the top spot in spite of intense competition from Al Hibbler, Les Baxter and Liberace. The second, the title song from the movie *The Man From Laramie*, and another 1955 hit, 'Someone On My Mind', clinched Young's position as the UK's second biggest-selling artist of the year – after Ruby Murray. Following further 50s hits, including 'Chain Gang', 'The Wayward Wind', 'Rich Man, Poor Man', 'More' and 'Round And Round', Young switched to EMI Records' Columbia label in the early 60s, and had some success with a recording of Charles and Henry Tobias' 1929 song 'Miss You', and a re-recording of 'Unchained Melody'.

In 1960, he introduced BBC Radio's popular record request programme, *Housewives' Choice*, for two weeks. It was the start of a new career that has lasted more than 40 years, initially as a conventional disc jockey and compere, and then, from 1967, as host of his own daily BBC morning radio show. This mixes records with consumer information, discussions on current affairs, and talks with figures in the public eye. He has interviewed every Chancellor and Prime Minister since 1963. For his radio work on the programme, he was awarded the OBE, and later, the CBE. In 1992, for *The Jimmy Young Story*, a silver anniversary celebration of his radio show, Young was interviewed by another distinguished broadcaster, David Frost. Young received the ultimate accolade in 2002 when he was knighted in the New Year's Honours List.

● ALBUMS: *T.T.T.J.Y.S.* (Polydor 1974) ★★★, *Too Young* (PRT 1981) ★★★.

● COMPILATIONS: *The World Of Jimmy Young* (Decca 1969) ★★★★, *This Is Jimmy Young* (EMI 1980) ★★★, *What A Wonderful World* (Flashback 1985) ★★★.

● FURTHER READING: *J.Y.: The Autobiography Of Jimmy Young*, Jimmy. Young.

ZACHERLE, JOHN

b. 26 September 1918, Philadelphia, Pennsylvania, USA. Zacherle was a television personality on the US east coast for many years. Zacherle – who used only his surname (pronounced zack-er-ley) on the air – also found his way to the pop charts in 1958 with a novelty song, 'Dinner With Drac (Part 1)'. Originally appearing as an undertaker in the live western serial, *Action In The Afternoon*, Zacherle moved over to Philadelphia television station WCAU to present *Shock Theater*. Debuting in September 1957, Zacherle's ghoulish character Roland presented late night showings of popular horror films. So successful was the character that Zacherle became an in-demand celebrity nicknamed the 'Cool Ghoul' by Dick Clark.

Cameo Records approached Zacherle in 1958. The result was 'Dinner With Drac (Part 1)', in which Zacherle imitated Dracula. The single reached US number 6 in March, but subsequent recordings failed to chart. Zacherle changed the name of his character to Zacherley for his television debut on Manhattan's rival WABC station in September. He has continued performing his role on radio into the new millennium, but other than one album, *Monster Mash*, has never reached the charts again.

● ALBUMS: *Spook Along With Zacherley* (Elektra 1960) ★★, *Monster Mash* (Parkway 1962) ★★★, *Scary Tales* (Parkway 1963) ★.

● VIDEOS: *Horrible Horrors* (Goodtime Video 1986).

● FURTHER READING: *Zacherley's Midnight Snacks*, various authors. *Zacherley's Vulture Stew*, various authors. *Zacherley: The Story Of Television's First Ghoul*, Louis D. Antonicello.

● FILMS: *Geek Maggot Bingo* (1983), *Brain Damage* voice only (1988), *Frankenhooker* (1990), *I Am Legend* (1994), *Niagaravation* (1995).

ZENTNER, SI

b. Simon H. Zentner, 13 June 1917, New York City, New York, USA, d. 31 January 2000, Las Vegas, Nevada, USA. After learning to play the trombone as a child, Zentner played in and around New York before joining Les Brown in 1940. During the 40s he played in a number of bands, including those led by Harry James and Jimmy Dorsey, and at the end of the decade entered a long period of studio work. From 1957 onwards, he periodically formed a big band for studio sessions and gained a substantial following among the record-buying public, including a Top 50 pop hit in 1961 with his reading of 'Up A Lazy River'. For these bands he employed studio musicians, many with strong leanings to jazz; among them were Don Fagerquist, Don Lodice, Joe and Ray Triscari, Alvin Stoller, Lanny Morgan, Frank Capp and

Gene Goe. Perhaps the most important among the regular members of the bands Zentner formed was pianist Bob Florence, whose arrangements were influential in establishing Zentner's reputation among big band fans. Zentner continued his series of recordings until 1968, and thereafter continued to form big bands to accompany leading singers and also for appearances at important venues in Los Angeles and Las Vegas. Leading by example, Zentner consistently showed that there was a substantial and enthusiastic audience for big band music, and that such music need not be repetitious or confined to recreations of old favourites.

● ALBUMS: *Introducing Si Zentner And His Dance Band/Si Zentner, His Trombone And Orchestra i* (Liberty 1957) ★★★★, *Si Zentner And His Orchestra* (Liberty 1957) ★★★, *Swing Fever/Si Zentner, His Trombone And Orchestra ii* (Liberty 1957) ★★★★, *Sleepy Lagoon: Si Zentner With Russell Garcia* (Liberty 1957) ★★, *A Thinking Man's Band* (Liberty 1959) ★★★, *Suddenly It's Swing* (Liberty 1960) ★★★★, with the Johnny Mann Singers *Great Band With Great Voices Vols 1 & 2* (Liberty 1961) ★★★★, *The Si Zentner Big Band Plays The Big Hits* (Liberty 1961) ★★, *Up A Lazy River (Big Band Plays The Big Hits: Vol. 2)* (Liberty 1962) ★★★, *The Stripper And Other Big Band Hits* (Liberty 1962) ★★, *Waltz In Jazz Time* (Liberty 1962) ★★★, *Rhythm And Blues* (Liberty 1962) ★★, *Exotica Suite* (Liberty 1962) ★★, *Desafinado* (Liberty 1963) ★★★, *In Full Swing* (Liberty 1963) ★★★, *From Russia With Love* (Liberty 1963) ★★★, *Si Zentner Plays The Big Big-Band Hits* (Liberty 1964) ★★★, *It's Nice To Go Trav'ling* (Liberty 1965) ★★★, *Put Your Hand On My Shoulder* (Liberty 1965) ★★★, *Swingin' Country* (Liberty 1966) ★★, *Warning Shot* (Liberty 1967) ★★★, *Right Here* (Liberty 1969) ★★★.

INDEX

Z